HELPING CHILDREN LEARN MATHEMATICS

SEVENTH EDITION

HELPING CHILDREN LEARN MATHEMATICS

Robert E. Reys
University of Missouri

Mary M. Lindquist
Columbus State University

Diana V. Lambdin
Indiana University

Nancy L. Smith
Emporia State University

Marilyn N. Suydam
The Ohio State University

Revised with the assistance of

Margaret Niess
Dianne Erickson
Karen Higgins
Oregon State University

John Wiley & Sons, Inc.

ACQUISITIONS EDITOR	*Brad Hanson*
DEVELOPMENTAL EDITOR	*Johnna Barto*
PRODUCTION EDITOR	*Sandra Dumas*
SENIOR MARKETING MANAGERS	*Kevin Molloy/Ilse Wolfe*
NEW MEDIA EDITOR	*Lisa Schnettler*
SENIOR DESIGNER	*Dawn Stanley*
ILLUSTRATION EDITOR	*Sandra Rigby*
PHOTO EDITOR	*Sara Wright*
PRODUCTION MANAGEMENT SERVICES	*mb editorial services*
COVER CREDIT	*Quilt: "Jazz City" © 1995 Elizabeth Barton/www.arches.uga.edu/~ebarton*

Photo Credits: All chapter openers and p. 339, Quilt: "Jazz City"© 1995 Elizabeth Barton/www.arches.uga.edu/~ebarton. Page 377, MicroWorld Pro and its logo are trademarks of LCSI.

This book was typeset in 10/12 New Caledonia by Progressive Information Technologies and printed and bound by Von Hoffmann Corporation. The cover was printed by Von Hoffmann Corporation.

The paper in this book was manufactured by a mill whose forest management programs include sustained yield harvesting of its timberlands. Sustained yield harvesting principles ensure that the number of trees cut each year does not exceed the amount of new growth.

This book is printed on acid-free paper. ∞

Helping Children Learn Mathematics, 7th Edition
ISBN 0-471-15163-7

Printed in the United States of America

10 9 8 7 6 5 4 3 2 1

About the Authors

ROBERT E. REYS is Curators' Professor of Mathematics Education at the University of Missouri-Columbia. He is a former mathematics teacher and district mathematics coordinator. His research interests are in the areas of calculators, mental computation, estimation, and number sense. He has authored more than 150 articles in professional journals, and was general editor for five yearbooks of the National Council of Teachers of Mathematics.

MARY M. LINDQUIST is the Fuller E. Callaway Professor of Mathematics Education, Emeritus at Columbus State University (Georgia). She works with undergraduate and graduate students in early childhood, middle grades, and secondary mathematics education. Mary was president of the National Council of Teachers of Mathematics and chair of the Commission on the Future of the Standards, the oversight committee for *Principles and Standards for School Mathematics* (NCTM 2000). She has served on many national and international committees, including those involved with the National Assessment of Education Progress (NAEP) and the Third International Mathematics and Science Study (TIMSS). Mary was awarded the prestigious Lifetime Achievement Award for her service, leadership, and research by the Mathematics Education Trust.

DIANA V. LAMBDIN is an Associate Professor of Mathematics Education at Indiana University in Bloomington, where she teaches undergraduate courses for prospective elementary teachers, supervises students' field experience, and works with masters and doctoral students in mathematics education. Prior to entering the field of teacher education, she was a mathematics teacher in Massachusetts, Michigan, and Iowa. Diana has been active as an author, editor, project evaluator, and workshop leader, and was a member of the writing team for *Principles and Standards for School Mathematics* (NCTM 2000).

NANCY L. SMITH has been an educator for over twenty years. She taught elementary school and middle school mathematics for ten years in Richmond, Missouri. She is currently an Associate Professor in the Division of Early Childhood/Elementary Teacher Education at Emporia State University in Emporia, Kansas. At ESU she teaches elementary mathematics education courses for preservice and inservice teachers, teaches general elementary education courses, and supervises student teachers.

MARILYN N. SUYDAM is Professor Emeritus at Ohio State University. She was an elementary school teacher prior to becoming a faculty member at Penn State University and later at Ohio State University. Marilyn made significant contributions in her pioneering efforts to review, analyze, synthesize, and interpret research in mathematics education for elementary school teachers and administrators. In recognition of her many contributions to mathematics education, Marilyn received the prestigious Lifetime Achievement Award from the National Council of Teachers of Mathematics.

About the Cover

The colorful cover of this edition of *Helping Children Learn Mathematics* is a patchwork quilt, with each chapter featuring a different square from that quilt. One reason we chose the quilt motif was that we often think of this book, metaphorically, as a patchwork quilt. Each chapter contributes a very different piece of an overall vision of how good teaching helps children learn mathematics.

Another reason for choosing a quilt motif for our cover is that patchwork quilts offer numerous opportunities for connections to the world of mathematics. Activities such as sorting, classifying, measuring, and exploring patterns can all begin with examining or creating patchwork designs. By experimenting with putting various shapes together, students can learn about angles, fractions, symmetry, and area. Many books and web-based resources are available to help teachers use quilts in their teaching.

Lastly, quilting is an activity that cuts across many disciplines. Often when students read historical and fictional stories about quilts, they engage in hands-on experiments with the colors, shapes, and patterns of patchwork (either cloth or paper). Quilts then offer new pathways and opportunities for exciting interdisciplinary studies involving social studies, literature, art, and mathematics.

Brief Contents

Contents

Preface

This edition of *Helping Children Learn Mathematics* coincides with one of the most exciting times in the history of mathematics education. Change is everywhere, and it continues to impact K–12 teaching, school mathematics curricula, standardized tests, and teacher education. A landmark document that captures the nature of these changes is the *Principles and Standards for School Mathematics* (NCTM, 2000) prepared by the National Council of Teachers of Mathematics. As a teacher of mathematics in elementary school, you not only experience these changes but, more important, you also have an opportunity to help lead the way.

This new edition of *Helping Children Learn Mathematics* is built around three main themes:

- helping children make sense of mathematics
- incorporating field experiences and
- emphasizing major ideas detailed in the *Principles and Standards for School Mathematics* (NCTM, 2000).

This book is intended for those of you who are or who will be teachers of mathematics in elementary school. It is designed to help you help children learn mathematical concepts and skills, as well as important problem-solving techniques. In the process, it will challenge your thinking and further stimulate your interest in mathematics.

Helping Children Learn Mathematics is divided into two main parts. The first part (Chapters 1–6) provides a base for understanding the changing mathematics curriculum and how children learn mathematics. It offers some guidelines for planning and evaluating instruction. Attention is directed to problem solving and assessment, both of which have profound implications for mathematics teaching at all levels. Their importance is reflected throughout the book as they are integrated into various chapters.

The second part (Chapters 7–17) discusses teaching strategies, techniques, and learning activities related to specific mathematical topics. Emphasis is on using models and materials to develop concepts and understanding so that mathematics learning is indeed meaningful. We believe that meaning is most effectively established by helping students discuss mathematics as they move from concrete materials and examples to generalizations and abstractions.

Helping Children Learn Mathematics is a unique resource. Following are fourteen (a baker's dozen plus one) features designed to make this book particularly useful.

Features of this Text

1. **Standards and Expectations.** We have highlighted excerpts of the Standards and Expectations in boxes throughout this book, and Appendix A provides a complete copy of the Standards and Expectations for grades pre–K through 8 from the *Principles and Standards for School Mathematics.* These Standards and Expectations provide a valuable resource for use with *Helping Children Learn Mathematics* as well as in your teaching career.

2. **Mathematical Processes.** The five mathematical processes, problem solving, communication, connections, representations, and reasoning and proof, identified by the *NCTM Standards* are addressed in a separate chapter (Chapter 5). The development of student competence with these processes must be a goal of every school mathematics program. These processes and the links among them are often established in rich problem-solving activities. A separate chapter is devoted to problem solving. Chapter 6 discusses various problem-solving strategies and also presents a wide variety of problems with which the strategies are useful. You will also find a problem-solving spirit reflected in the In the Classroom activities, as well as in many of the discussions throughout the book.
3. **Snapshots of a Lesson.** Snapshots of a Lesson provide a brief look into a variety of mathematical lessons at different grade levels. All chapters open with one of these Snapshots to remind you of the realities of teaching. The Snapshots both demonstrate many effective classroom practices and illustrate the vital role that you play as the teacher in leading and promoting students to talk and learn about mathematics.
4. **Focus Questions.** Focus questions guide the study of each of the chapters. Think about these questions in advance and use your readings and the activities in the chapter to help you form a response to each question.
5. **Lesson Ideas and In the Classroom activities.** Lesson Ideas and In the Classroom activities are used to highlight a wide variety of instructional topics. Lesson Ideas provide a skeletal outline for a lesson. In the Classroom activities focus on helping children learn specific mathematical topics. In every case, an objective and suggested grade level accompanies the activity. The In the Classroom activities are designed to be used with children. Some activities shown in *Helping Children Learn Mathematics* are enlarged and duplicated in *Teaching Elementary Mathematics: A Resource for Field Experiences.* The larger format enables teachers and children to work effectively with each exercise. Samples of an In the Classroom and a Lesson Idea from Chapter 9 are shown at right and on the next page.
6. **Research Base.** A research base has been threaded throughout. As a teacher, you are often called on to provide a rationale for curricular or instructional decisions, and we think you will find this integration of relevant research, along with its implications, useful.

In the Classroom 9-5

MULTIG

OBJECTIVE: **Using a game to practice basic multiplication facts.**

GRADE LEVEL: **3–4**

▼ Use the playing board here or make a larger one on heavy construction paper. Each player needs some buttons, macaroni, or chips for markers.

Don't forget the spinner. You can't play this game without it.

9 4 8 6 7 5

1. Take turns. Spin twice. Multiply the 2 numbers. Find the answer on the board. Put a marker on it.

56 25 40
36 49 20 81
30 64 35 48 32
56 42 63 28 54 45
32 48 54 72 24 16 35
16 24 28 36 40 30 25 20
63 45 81 56 49 42 64
20 25 72 45 24 36
40 49 32 28 54
30 16 72 48
42 35 63

2. Score 1 point for each covered ◇ that touches a side or corner of the ◇ you cover.
3. If you can't find an uncovered ◇ to cover, you lose your turn.
4. Opponents may challenge any time before the next player spins.
5. The winner is the player with the most points at the end of 10 rounds.

7. **Integrating Technology.** Technology as varied as calculators and the Internet is widely available to everyone—including young students. Calculators are powerful tools, and we have included calculator activities throughout the book. We have made a conscious effort to integrate a wide variety of other tools, such as spreadsheets, simulation packages, and the Internet, to enhance mathematics learning. A new section titled *Things to Do With Technology Resources* appears at the end of each chapter to provide ways to learn from and utilize technology. Math Links are also included in the chapters to highlight additional technology resources. The Wiley web site (www.wiley.com/college/reys) connects to

Lesson Idea 9-2

LOTS OF LINKS

Objective: Children model division with remainders using links to make equal-sized groups.

Grade Level: 3–4

Materials: 20 links (or other counters) for each child; an overhead projector

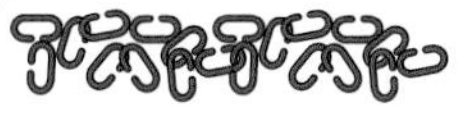

Activity: Discuss with children different ways to separate the links into equal-sized groups.

- Scatter 12 links on an overhead projector.
  - How can we place these links into equal-sized groups? (6 groups of 2, 4 groups of 3, 1 group of 12, etc.)
  - How many different ways can we do it?
- Scatter 15 links on the projector.
  - How many different ways can these links be split into equal-sized groups?
  - What happens if we try dividing 13 links into groups of 5?

    CCCCC CCCCC CCC — 2 groups and 3 leftovers
- Focus on numbers that can be divided into equal-sized groups without "leftovers":
  - Which of these numbers can be divided into groups of 3 without having leftovers?

    8 4 7 3 18

    Try each one.
  - Name a number that will have no leftovers if we divide it into groups of 5. How many numbers like this can you name?
  - Name a number that will have 1 leftover if we divide it into groups of 5. Can you name 3 numbers like this?

web resources, including electronic manipulatives, video clips, lesson plans, and the Instructor's Manual.

8. **Computational Alternatives.** Computational alternatives—mental computation, estimation, written techniques, as well as calculators—are explicitly discussed in Chapter 10. Technology has increased the importance of students' making wise choices among the computational alternatives, and we have dedicated a chapter to providing a balanced discussion of them.
9. **Encouraging Children to Construct Meaning.** As written techniques are developed, attention has been given to the value of encouraging young students to create, invent, construct, or use written methods that are meaningful for them. Much learning and understanding can be gained from exploring alternative algorithms, including some of the traditional algorithms that are part of our culture. However, tedious computational algorithms, such as long division, are de-emphasized. We believe that meaningful operations with numbers must be established, but our development focuses on the understanding of and facility with computational alternatives and pays less attention to the painfully laborious task of crunching large numbers.
10. **Cultural and Gender Equity.** Equity—treating students of different sexes as well as different ethnic and cultural backgrounds similarly, with equal expectations—is an important issue in mathematics classes. We have reflected equity and provisions for individual differences in many ways—from the wide range of student abilities portrayed in the Snapshots of a Lesson to In the Classroom activities. Our use of technology and our integration and discussion of research findings provide further insight into equity issues as well as other individual differences. We think such discussions will be helpful in implementing a mathematical environment that is positive and productive for everyone.
11. **Using Children's Literature.** Literature is a powerful ally in learning and one that has often been underused in mathematics classes. We have made direct efforts to identify books that might be used effectively to complement and supplement mathematics learning. In some cases, we have cited and discussed specific books within the text. We have identified and annotated a number of books to use with children in the Book Nook for Children sections at the end of each chapter.
12. **Things to Do.** Things to Do are found near the end of each chapter. These sections have been divided into two parts. One section relates directly to this book and is subtitled "From What You've Read." The "Going Beyond This Book" section has been expanded to include In the Field, In Your Journal, With Additional Resources, and With Technology, often including explorations into other resources and references as well as some microteaching with children. Some of these activities are linked to *Teaching Elementary Mathematics: A Resource for Field Experiences.* All of the Things to Do

embody our active learning and teaching approach to mathematics. These experiences are designed to engage you in inquiring and thinking about mathematics—investigations that will provide the greater understanding and insight that is needed to be a successful teacher.

13. **References.** Annotations to selected books and articles are provided. Many other helpful references (some new, some old, but all relevant) are listed at the end of each chapter to document research, as well as further illustrate ideas and other points made within the chapter. Some of these works discuss ideas that have been mentioned, but space did not allow us to develop them to the extent we would like. Others elaborate and extend ideas that will promote greater insight and understanding.
14. **Masters.** In our teaching, we have found certain materials to be frequently useful in a variety of ways. A number of these materials, some in color, are included as masters in Appendix B. These pages can be easily detached from the book and used as masters to make multiple copies for your students or to make a transparency for an overhead projector. As you teach and use these materials, we welcome feedback from you about other masters you would like to see in future editions.

New in this Edition

Chapter 1, Teaching Mathematics in a Changing World. This chapter is an introduction to the profession and the current issues important to today's teachers. To begin your study about helping children learn mathematics, the Snapshot of a Lesson highlights actual responses from fourth-grade students as they think about what mathematics is and what it means to learn mathematics.

Chapter 2, Learning Mathematics with Understanding. This chapter highlights the NCTM's Learning Principle. The beginning Snapshot of a Lesson highlights children learning a valuable lesson when using calculators. Ideas from both the behaviorist and constructivist theories on learning lead to some practical recommendations in support of helping children construct mathematical knowledge that is meaningful to them.

Chapter 3, Teaching: Your Role. This chapter highlights NCTM's Teaching Principle and has been rearranged into three major sections: developing a positive classroom climate, skills of an effective elementary mathematics teacher, and the importance of planning. A new In the Classroom activity demonstrates how to nest skill development within a problem solving experience. Current web site addresses have been provided to help you find lesson ideas and full lesson plans that integrate technology such as spreadsheets, dynamic geometry software, computer microworlds, and graphing calculators.

Chapter 4, Assessment: Enhanced Learning and Teaching. A new Snapshot of a teacher's use of journals begins this chapter to introduce NCTM's Assessment Principle. Many great examples of various forms and ways for assessing student understanding show the Assessment Principle in action. Math Links help to locate additional assessment strategies that enhance teaching and learning.

Chapter 5, Processes of Doing Mathematics. This chapter has been redesigned to shift the focus from problem solving to the five processes of doing mathematics: problem solving, reasoning and proof, communications, connections, and representations. In addition, the chapter focuses on ways to engage children in these processes.

Chapter 6, Helping Children with Problem Solving. Since problem solving is one of the most important skills to learn in mathematics, a separate chapter now extends this process standard. Much of the material in the sixth edition has been incorporated and highlighted through the use of color to more clearly represent the activities. A new Snapshot has been provided as well as problems based on processes and heuristics.

Chapter 7, Beginning Number Sense: Counting and Early Benchmarks. This chapter retains its strong development of different aspects of early number sense. Updates of the activities include a new In the Classroom idea focused on using calendars to count forward and backward.

Chapter 8, Extending Number Sense: Place Value. The structure of this chapter remains the same, but the focus questions help to highlight the important aspects of the Number and Operations Standard. The new colorful format provides a clearer representation of the materials and ideas in the figures and activities.

Chapter 9, Operations: Meanings and Basic Facts. No new additions have been made to this chapter; rather, the activities have been freshened using multiple colors to highlight important features of the Number and Operations Standard.

Chapter 10, Computational Tools: Calculators, Mental Computation, and Estimation. This chapter is connected with the computation expectation in the Number and Operations Standard. The activities have been clarified and freshened to better represent the use of various computational tools—mental computation, estimation, written computation, and technological tools. Specific activities emphasize how children can use calculators as learning tools.

Chapter 11, Standard and Alternative Computational Algorithms. The emphasis in this chapter is placed on having students make sense of computational algorithms. A new In the Classroom activity demonstrates how practice with algorithms can be embedded in higher order thinking processes.

Chapter 12, Fractions and Decimals: Meanings and Operations. This chapter retains the conceptual development of fractions and decimals, but a new In the Classroom has been provided that uses fraction bars. A new Lesson Idea was added for multiplying decimals using decimal paper and the area model.

Chapter 13, Ratio, Proportion, and Percent: Meanings and Applications. The structure of this chapter remains the same but new activities were added to proportional reasoning in making comparisons. The Snapshot demonstrates the use of spreadsheets as children learn about percents. The Golden Ratio is highlighted in a new In the Classroom activity.

Chapter 14, Patterns, Relationships, and Algebraic Thinking. This chapter has been significantly revised around important expectations in NCTM's Algebra Standard, and it focuses on encouraging the exploration of patterns and relationships in the early elementary mathematics curriculum as a way to support children's development of algebraic concepts. A new Snapshot and many new classroom activities highlight three important aspects of algebraic thinking—change, generalization, and equality. Things to Do activities highlight NCTM's Illuminations web site, providing many web resources to use in teaching algebra with technology.

Chapter 15, Geometry. The van Hiele levels provide a framework for the development of geometric experiences for elementary children. Activities and examples have been added to demonstrate the expectations in NCTM's Geometry Standard along with the use of computer tools, such as computer microworlds and dynamic geometry software, to help children visualize, make sense of, and develop conjectures about geometric ideas.

Chapter 16. Measurement. Measurement is one of the five NCTM Content Standards, and this chapter exemplifies how the five Process Standards, especially problem solving, communications, and reasoning, are central to learning and using measurement skills. New pictures have been added to illuminate measurement points in the early part of the chapter. A new In the Classroom was added to explore the magic ratio in every circle.

Chapter 17, Data Analysis, Statistics, and Probability. The Data Analysis and Probability Standard guided the development of this chapter centered on engaging children in the data analysis process. Children are encouraged to develop questions, collect data to answer those questions, analyze the data in a variety of ways, and use their results to answer their questions. A new In the Classroom provides activities on determining the likelihood of an event. Explorations with spreadsheets, graphing software, or graphing calculators to display and analyze data are provided in the Things to Do.

Supplements

The seventh edition of *Helping Children Learn Mathematics* is accompanied by the following instructor and student supplements.

Instructor's Manual and Test Bank

The Instructor's Manual is a useful resource for both veteran and new elementary methods instructors. It is available on the Wiley web site at www.wiley.com/college/reys. Each chapter includes:

- Chapter overview, student objectives, and key vocabulary;
- Supplemental lecture ideas, textbook extension ideas, and class and field activity suggestions;
- Extensive resource list (both print and media);
- Extensive transparency masters highlighting key textbook ideas, NCTM Standards 2000 summaries, and children's work samples (available in Microsoft Word and PowerPoint formats);
- A test bank of over 500 items featuring both objective and open-ended questions, classified by Bloom's taxonomy.

Teaching Elementary Mathematics: A Resource for Field Experiences, 2nd edition

This accompanying student resource is designed to be used by students when they participate in field experiences such as practica, observations, and professional development school (PDS) experiences in K–8 classrooms. This resource is aligned with and designed to support *Helping Children*

Learn Mathematics but may also be used as a stand-alone resource. Activities engage preservice elementary teachers in collecting information about the school and school resources, observing and interviewing teachers and children, and doing mathematics with children in the form of games, technology activities, and mini-lessons. Students not only learn more about elementary schools and teaching elementary mathematics but are also encouraged to reflect on their experiences.

Helping Children Learn Mathematics is an idea book. We believe that you will learn much from reading and talking about what you have read. The *NCTM Standards* highlighted communication as an important part of mathematics learning, and this book is designed to encourage and facilitate communication.

It is not possible—or desirable—to establish exact steps to follow in teaching mathematics. Too much depends on what is being taught, to whom, and at what levels. In your classroom, it is you who will ultimately decide what to teach, to whom to teach it, how to teach it, and the amount of time to spend. This book will not answer all of these questions for you, but we think you will find it very helpful in making wise decisions as you guide elementary school students in their learning of mathematics. We believe this book will be a valuable teaching resource that can be used again and again in your classroom long after the course has been completed.

Acknowledgments

We thank Margaret (Maggie) Niess (Oregon State University), Dianne Erickson (Oregon State University), and Karen Higgins (Oregon State University) for their major contributions to this edition. We also wish to acknowledge the many colleagues, friends, and students who have contributed in various ways to the development of this book over the years. In particular, we thank Barbara Reys, University of Missouri; Frank Lester, Indiana University; and Douglas Grouws, University of Iowa.

We acknowledge the help of specific reviewers for this seventh edition, including:

Peter Appelbaum, *Arcadia University*

Jennifer Bay-Williams, *Kansas State University*

Martha Boedecker, *Northwestern Oklahoma State University*

Carol Bonilla Bowman, *Ramapo College*

Rick Callan, *Franklin College*

Richard Caulfield, *Indiana University*

Astrida Cirulis, *National-Louis University*

Gerald R. Fast, *University of Wisconsin, Oshkosh*

K. Gaddis, *Lewis & Clark College*

Lowell Gadberry, *Southwestern Oklahoma State University*

Enrique Galindo, *Indiana University*

Madeleine Gregg, *University of Alabama*

Kim Harris, *University of North Carolina*

Kim Hartweg, *Western Illinois University*

Gae Johnson, *Northern Arizona University*

Henry S. Kepner, *University of Wisconsin–Milwaukee*

Diane H. Klein, Indiana University of Pennsylvania

Margie Mason, *College of William and Mary*

Sueanne McKinney, *Old Dominion University*

Alice Mills, *Quincy University*

Jean Mitchell, *California State University, Monterey Bay*

Don Ploger, *Florida Atlantic University*

Sara Powell, *University of Charleston (SC)*

Frank Powers, *University of Idaho*

Gay Ragan, *Southwest Missouri State University*

Denise M. Reboli, *King's College (PA)*

Candice L. Ridlon, *Towson University*

Linda Sheeran, *Oklahoma State University*

Marian Smith, *Florida A&M University*

Marilyn Soucie, *University of Missouri*

Gertrude R. Toher, *Hofstra University*

Frederick L. Uy, *California State University, Los Angeles*

Kay Wall, *University of Central Oklahoma*

Pat Wall, *Northern Arizona University*

Judy Wells, *Indiana State University*

We also wish to recognize the help of reviewers for previous editions, including Roda Amaria, Salem State College; Tom Bassarear, Keene State College; Daniel Brahier, Bowling Green State University; Christine Browning, Western Michigan University; Grace Burton, University of North Carolina, Wilmington; Bob Drake, University of Cincinnati; Marvel Froemming, Moorhead State University; Elsa L. Geskus, Kutztown University; Bob Glasgow, Southwest Baptist University; Claire Graham, Framingham State College; Janet Handler, Mount Mercy College; Kim Harris, University of North Carolina Charlotte; Ruth M.

Heaton, University of Nebraska, Lincoln; Ellen Hines, Northern Illinois University; Robert Jackson, University of Minnesota; Susan Johnson, Northwestern College; Todd Johnson, Eastern Washington University; Mary Kabiri, Lincoln University; Rick Kruschinsky, University of St. Thomas; Vena Long, University of Tennessee; Robert Matulis, Millersville University; William Merrill, Central Michigan University; Eula Ewing Monroe, Brigham Young University; Jamar Pickreign, Rhode Island College; Don Ploger, Florida Atlantic University; Jacelyn Marie Rees, McNeese State University; Tom Romberg, University of Wisconsin; Thomas E. Rowan, University of Maryland, College Park; Mary Ellen Schmidt, Ohio State University-Mansfield; Frances Stern, New York University; David L. Stout, University of West Florida; Juan Vazquez, Missouri Southern State College; Dorothy Y. White, University of Georgia; Margaret Wyckoff, University of Maine-Farmington; and Bernard Yvon, University of Maine.

R.E.R.

M.M.L.

D.V.L.

N.L.S.

M.N.S.

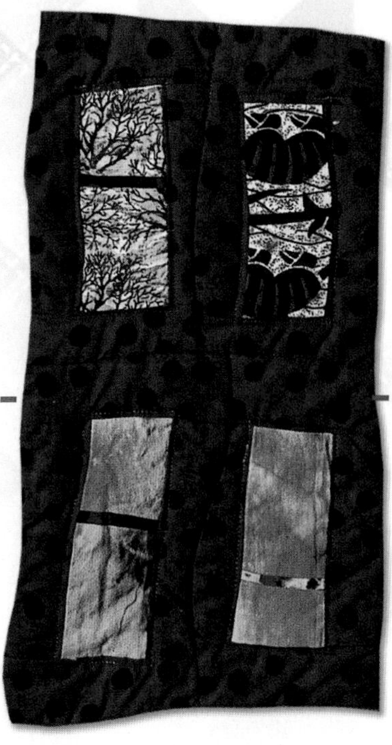

CHAPTER 1

Teaching Mathematics in a Changing World

Snapshot of a Lesson

Mrs. Freudenthal decided to integrate writing with the math lesson with her fourth-grade class at the beginning of the second school quarter. She asked the children to practice their writing by responding to at least three of the questions on the board, in any order they chose.

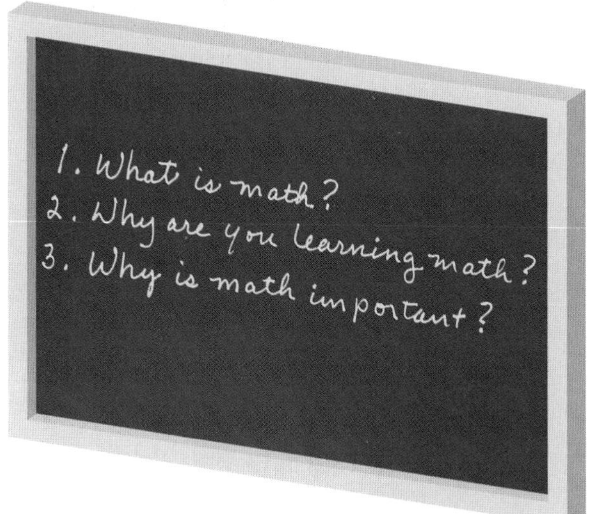

1. What is math?
2. Why are you learning math?
3. Why is math important?

The children busily worked on answering the questions. Here are some of their responses:

What is math?

JANICE: Math is a subject that uses numbers.

NICK: I think math is understanding the way numbers work when you add, subtract, multiply, or divide.

WILL: Math is a lot of numbers being added, subtracted, multiplied, and divided, also being graphed.

CHANTAL: I think math is the use of numbers in an interesting way.

ELIZABETH: Math is many numbers, but it can be pictures, too.

MAC: Math is numbers that go on infinitely that you can group, regroup, put together, take away, or cut in half to equal a certain number with whole numbers, fractions, or decimals.

COLE: Math is the use of numbers to get an answer to a problem.

BEN: Math is numbers and all kinds of weird symbols. I think that I will know all about numbers when I'm older but not now.

Why are you learning math?

BEN: I'm learning math so I won't get stuck on a real-life problem.

CHANTAL: I am learning math because it helps me in almost everything I do. Like in science, when I compare the average temperature change of January and August, I use math. In cooking I would need to measure how much water to pour in.

MAC: We are learning math because if you don't learn math, you're not going to do well in life. You won't have a job because even flipping hamburgers you need to know how many inches or feet you need to flip them, or digging a ditch, you need to know the diameter or how wide the hole should be, or if you work in a pharmacy, you work with decimals to find what the right prescription is. The more you think about it, the more you realize math is everywhere in your daily life.

Why is math important?

NICK: I think math is important because we need math to do our job. I don't think there is any job that doesn't use math.

REBECCA: Math is important because if you grow up and you want to be a cashier, you won't know how much money to give back to the person and how much money they gave you.

KYRA: Math is important because if no one knew how to do math, everyone would be on the streets.

While the children were working, Mrs. Freudenthal noticed that Thomas seemed to be struggling. He shifted around in his chair. He wrote something and erased it. Then he wrote something on the paper again and erased that.

Mrs. Freudenthal went to his desk and quietly asked, "Thomas, are you having problems with what to write?" Thomas nodded and said, "I just can't think of a good answer to the question."

MRS. FREUDENTHAL: Well, Thomas, let's talk about the questions. What is math to you?

THOMAS: Thinking!

MRS. FREUDENTHAL: Good idea, Thomas. Write that on your paper.

Thomas smiled and returned to completing the assignment.

Introduction

Soon you will be in your own classroom, responsible for helping children learn mathematics. What is mathematics to you? Clearly, for the children in Mrs. Freudenthal's class, concepts and operations with numbers are central to their understanding of mathematics. Does that mean mathematics in the elementary grades is only computation? Certainly not! See how the National Council of Teachers of Mathematics (NCTM), the largest professional organization of prekindergarten through high school teachers of mathematics in the world, envisions distribution of relevant content throughout the grades (Figure 1-1). While number concepts are an important part of this vision, algebra, geometry, measurement, and data analysis and probability are also important. The concepts of number are emphasized early and receive less instructional attention as algebra increases in importance. All five of these areas are closely interwoven; development of each area enhances children's understanding and use of mathematics as well as prepares them for future study of these areas. Does this vision match your experiences with the elementary curriculum?

The children in Mrs. Freudenthal's class clearly see the importance of arithmetic, but do you find any evidence for their recognition of the importance of these other areas of mathematics? Chantal's comment shows that she sees a need for measurement in cooking. Mac recognizes the use of diameter in digging holes. Teachers need to help children understand the relevance of all these areas of mathematics.

What mathematics will you be teaching? How will you help children learn mathematics? Three major *themes* of this book are designed to help you develop a clearer understanding of teaching mathematics in the elementary grades and to answer these two important questions. Specifically,

- The philosophy and recommendations of the *Principles and Standards for School Mathematics* (NCTM, 2000) are interwoven with an emphasis of helping children learn mathematics. The NCTM's content and process standards provide the link between what math means to teachers and what math means to students.
- Mathematics must make sense to children, and there are many ways teachers can help children make that sense. Research has shown that if children make sense of the mathematics they are learning, they can build on this understanding to learn more mathematics and use it to solve problems.

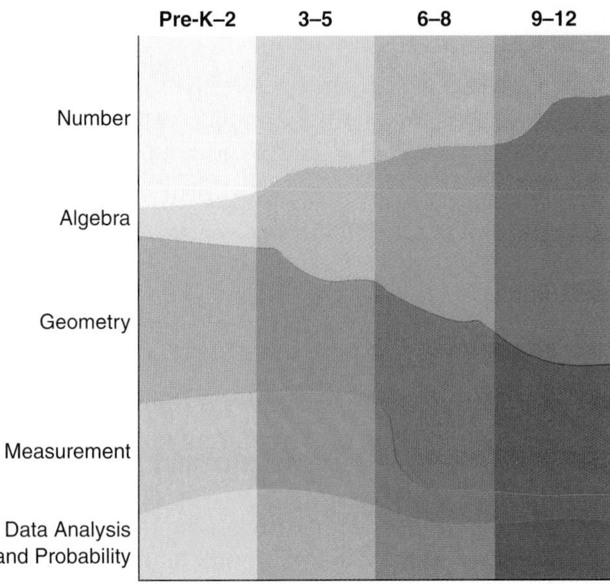

FIGURE 1-1 Vision of the mathematics content distribution through the grade levels.

(Source: *Principles and Standards for School Mathematics*, p. 30, copyright 2000 by the National Council of Teachers of Mathematics. All rights reserved.)

- Learning to teach mathematics requires practical experience. The snapshots, the activities used as illustrations, and the resources assist in developing the notion of helping elementary children learn mathematics. Working with children with these mathematical notions, carefully listening to their developing understanding, and reflecting on their learning in real classrooms are essential experiences in linking what mathematics means to teachers with what mathematics means to children.

You will also be asking other questions, as all teachers do, including these:

- What mathematical knowledge and understanding does each student bring to the class?
- What mathematics do students need to learn?
- How can each child, different in many ways from the others, be taught so that he or she will learn?
- How important is my own attitude toward mathematics?

The answers to such questions provide the framework for the elementary school mathematics program; your own answers will influence what you do when you are teaching.

No matter what age children you teach, you will probably have several general *goals*:

- To help children make sense of specific mathematical content, including both procedures and concepts.
- To help children learn how to apply mathematical ideas to solve problems.
- To foster positive dispositions, such as persistence, flexibility, willingness to learn, and valuing mathematics.

Developing ways to help children learn a range of mathematical content is considered in later chapters of this book. This first chapter focuses on an overall look at the mathematics program that has evolved (and will continue to change) as the world changes. Begin thinking about your own perceptions of mathematics and the role mathematics plays in elementary and middle schools. What influences the curriculum? How do your beliefs influence what you teach?

You are entering the teaching field at a particularly exciting time. The curriculum in mathematics, as well as in many other subject areas, is being adapted to the changing needs of our society, to the changing knowledge about how children learn, and to the changing viewpoints of mathematics. Before looking at the changes, think about the subject itself. What is mathematics to you?

FOCUS QUESTIONS

1. What is mathematics?
2. What determines the mathematics currently taught?
3. What are the NCTM's six principles for school mathematics?
4. What resources are available to help you continue developing your knowledge of mathematics and the learning and teaching of mathematics?

What Is Mathematics?

Over time, many people have described how mathematics fits within the area of human knowledge. Which of the following five views of mathematics is closest to your perception of mathematics? How will your view of mathematics affect how you help children learn?

1. *Mathematics is a study of patterns and relationships.* Children need to become aware of recurring ideas and of relationships between mathematical ideas. These relationships and ideas provide a unifying thread throughout the curriculum. Children should come to see how one idea is like or unlike others already learned. For instance, children in

first grade can consider how one basic fact (say, $3 + 2 = 5$) is related to another basic fact (say, $5 - 3 = 2$). Or children in later grades can consider the effect that changing the perimeter of a figure has on its area.

2. *Mathematics is a way of thinking.* It provides people with strategies for organizing, analyzing, and synthesizing information. People who are comfortable with mathematics use it to solve everyday problems. For example, some people write an equation, where as others form tables to record information.

3. *Mathematics is an art, characterized by order and internal consistency.* Many children think of mathematics as a confusing set of discrete facts and skills that must be memorized. Because teachers tend to focus on developing the skills required to "do" mathematics, they may forget that children need to be guided to recognize and appreciate the underlying orderliness and consistency as they construct their own understanding of mathematics.

4. *Mathematics is a language that uses carefully defined terms and symbols.* These terms and symbols enhance the ability to communicate about science, real-life situations, and mathematics itself.

5. *Mathematics is a tool.* It is what mathematicians use, but everyone in the course of daily life also uses it. Thus, children can come to appreciate why they are learning mathematical facts, skills, and concepts. They, too, can use mathematics to solve both abstract and practical problems, just as mathematicians do. Mathematics has become an essential part of the technological world, both in everyday life and in the workplace. People must be able to read, understand, and interpret technical material with embedded charts and diagrams. Energy bills provide information about usage to guide consumers in making decisions about energy consumption. Loan payment statements provide information about interest and payoff amounts. Businesses provide profit and loss information to guide future expenditures.

What Determines the Mathematics Being Taught?

Mathematics plays a prominent role in the elementary school program. It is second only to reading in the amount of time devoted to it and in the amount of money spent for curricular materials. Its importance is reflected in the degree of concern intermittently voiced by parents and other members of society.

Math Links 1.1

*I*n order to better understand the NCTM's vision for your own teaching, you should learn as much as you can about the NCTM's standards. You can find out more about the NCTM's *Principles and Standards for School Mathematics* by reading answers to Frequently Asked Questions on the NCTM web site, which you can access from this book's web site.

The federal government has not specified a national curriculum for school mathematics, as is the practice in most other countries. Instead, the NCTM has developed standards for curriculum, teaching, and assessment (NCTM, 1989, 1991, 1995). Because states and localities in the United States hold the rights to determine school policies, these standards documents are not prescriptive, but they have provided vision and direction for school mathematics.

In 2000, the NCTM published an update of the standards in a document titled *Principles and Standards for School Mathematics* (*NCTM Standards*). In this document, the principles and standards, shown in Figure 1-2, outline the important features of a high-quality mathematics education. The standards describe the mathematical content and processes that students should learn. Combined, the principles and standards present a vision for mathematics education programs in a changing world.

As you begin to think about your mathematics program, three general factors deserve careful attention: the needs of the subject, the needs of the child, and the needs of society. The evolution of these factors highlights the importance of the NCTM's principles. Each of the principles aids teachers in making decisions about the mathematics program they design and implement. The interaction of the principles with the needs of the subject, the students, and society can help shape a curriculum that produces mathematically literate citizens.

Needs of the Subject

The nature of mathematics helps determine what is taught and when it is taught in elementary grades. For example, whole numbers are the basis for many mathematical ideas; moreover, experiences with them arise long before children come to school. Thus lower grades emphasize whole-number work

Principles	
• ***Equity*** Excellence in mathematics education requires equity—high expectations and strong support for all students.	• ***Learning*** Students must learn mathematics with understanding, actively building new knowledge from experience and prior knowledge.
• ***Curriculum*** A curriculum is more than a collection of activities: it must be coherent, focused on important mathematics, and well articulated across the grades.	• ***Assessment*** Assessment should support the learning of important mathematics and furnish useful information to both teachers and students.
• ***Teaching*** Effective mathematics teaching requires understanding what students know and need to learn and then challenging and supporting them to learn it well.	• ***Technology*** Technology is essential in teaching and learning mathematics; it influences the mathematics that is taught and enhances students' learning.
Content Standards	**Process Standards**
• ***Number and Operations***	• ***Problem Solving***
• ***Algebra***	• ***Reasoning and Proof***
• ***Geometry***	• ***Communication***
• ***Measurement***	• ***Connections***
• ***Data Analysis and Probability***	• ***Representations***

FIGURE 1-2 *Principles and Standards for School Mathematics.*
(Source: NCTM, 2000, pp. 12, 14, 16, 20, 22, 24, Appendix.)

first, building on children's experiences. Work with rational numbers logically follows work with whole numbers. Such seemingly natural sequences are the result of long years of curricular evolution. This process has involved much analysis of what constitutes a progression from easy to difficult, based in part on what is deemed necessary at one level for the development of ideas at later levels. Once a curriculum is in place for a long time, however, people tend to consider it the only proper sequence. Thus omitting a topic or changing the sequence of topics often involves a struggle for acceptance.

Sometimes the process of change is aided by an event, such as when the Soviet Union sent the first Sputnik into orbit. The shock of this evidence of another country's technological superiority sped curriculum change in the United States. The "new math" of the 1950s and 1960s was the result, and millions of dollars were channeled into mathematics and science education to strengthen school programs. Mathematicians became integrally involved in planning mathematics education, and because of their interests and the perceived weaknesses of previous curricula, they developed curricula based on the needs of the subject. The emphasis shifted from social usefulness to such unifying themes as the structure of mathematics, operations and their inverses, systems of notation, properties of numbers, and set language.

New content was added at the elementary school level, and other topics were introduced at earlier grade levels.

Mathematics continues to change; new mathematics is created and new uses of mathematics are discovered. As part of this change, technology has made some mathematics obsolete and has opened the door for other mathematics.

THE TECHNOLOGY PRINCIPLE. You will teach at a time in which technology dominates activities both in and out of school. The Technology Principle (see Figure 1-2) acknowledges the impact of technology in teaching and learning mathematics as long as it enhances what is being learned and how it is being taught. As you teach your classes, you should keep asking three questions:

How can I help children use technology appropriately?

What mathematics do children need to use technology wisely?

What mathematics is no longer necessary?

Some parents continue to be concerned about the use of calculators in learning mathematics in elementary schools. An examination of the research on calculator use (Hembree & Dessart, 1992) strongly suggests that using calculators does not harm students; yet the concern has persisted. Children need to learn to use this tool appropriately, as they do any other tool. What is appropriate use? Later in this text, we consider more carefully what is meant by *appropriate*. At this point, begin to think about the appropriate use of technology.

THE CURRICULUM PRINCIPLE. No one knows exactly what mathematics will be needed for the twenty-first century, but it is clear that students will need to know how to reason mathematically and how to apply mathematical thinking to a wide range of situations. How you view mathematics will determine how you view teaching mathematics. If you view mathematics as a series of facts to learn and practice, then you will teach your students in that way. If you view mathematics as a logical body of knowledge of which you can make sense, you will design a curriculum that focuses on guiding children in making sense of mathematics.

Children need to be afforded the opportunity to experience a curriculum that is more than a collection of isolated skills or fun activities. They need to have a curriculum that focuses on the important mathematics topics and ideas at each grade (focused), that fits together in a meaningful way (coherent), and that grows across the grades (well-articulated). Throughout the remaining chapters of this text, you will investigate various topics and strategies to be incorporated into the mathematics curriculum for your students. The 10 content and process standards (see Standards in Figure 1-2) can guide you in judging whether your curriculum is coherent, focused, and well-articulated across the grades.

Needs of the Child

The mathematics curriculum has been influenced by beliefs about how children learn and, ultimately, about how they should be taught. Before the early years of the twentieth century, mathematics was taught to train "mental faculties" or provide "mental discipline." Struggling with mathematical procedures was thought to exercise the mind (as with any muscle), helping children's brains work more effectively. Around the turn of the twentieth century, mental discipline was replaced by *connectionism*. The predominant belief was that learning was the establishment of bonds, or connections, between a stimulus and response. Teachers resorted to endless drills in order to establish important mathematical connections.

By the 1920s, the Progressive Movement advocated *incidental learning*. It was believed that children would learn as much arithmetic as they needed and would learn it better if it was not systematically taught. The teacher was to use situations as they occurred and to create situations in which arithmetic would arise.

During the late 1920s, a committee of school superintendents and principals from midwestern cities surveyed pupils to find out when topics were mastered (Washburne, 1931). They then suggested the mental age at which each topic should be taught. Subtraction facts under 10 were to be taught to children with a mental age of 6 years 7 months, and facts over 10 at 7 years 8 months; subtraction with borrowing or carrying was to be taught at 8 years 9 months. The Committee of Seven had a strong impact on the sequencing of the curriculum for years to come.

Another change in thinking occurred in the mid-1930s, as *field,* or *Gestalt, theory* was advanced. Greater emphasis was placed on a planned program to encourage the development of insight and the understanding of relationships, structure, patterns, interpretations, and principles. This idea contributed to an increased concern for *meaning and understanding,* with William Brownell as a prominent spokesperson. Learning was seen as a meaningful process. The value of drill was noted, but it was placed after understanding; drill was no longer the major means of sequencing the curriculum and providing instruction.

The relative importance of drill and understanding is still debated today. Drill is necessary to build speed and accuracy and to make skills more automatic. Think about whether you would get through the day if you did not do some things automatically, but also think about whether you still need the same skills that your grandparents needed. People often juxtapose understanding and skill learning, but it is not an either-or situation. You need to know *why* as well as *how*. Both must be developed, and they can be developed together.

Changes in psychology have continued to evolve and affect education. During the second half of the twentieth century, educators believed that the developmental level of the child is a factor in determining the sequence of the curriculum. Topics cannot be taught until a child is developmentally ready to learn them. Or, from another point of view, topics must be taught in such a way that children at a given developmental level are ready to learn them.

Increasingly, educators' attention is drawn to the evidence that children *construct* their own knowledge; to help children learn mathematics, teachers must be aware of how children have constructed mathematics from their experiences both in and out of school. Such ideas and inferences have been taken into consideration as the mathematics curriculum has evolved.

THE TEACHING PRINCIPLE. To teach mathematics effectively, teachers must know more than just mathematics. They need to know their students as learners and adjust their pedagogical strategies to meet the varying experiences of their students. Teachers must design their lessons to reveal students' prior knowledge, to reveal students' misunderstandings, and to guide students in the construction of more complex understandings of mathematics. Effective teachers structure challenging and supportive classroom learning environments that are conducive to helping children make sense of mathematics. Effective teachers also encourage students to think, question, solve problems, and discuss their ideas. As with Thomas (in the *Snapshot of a Lesson*), teachers must support and encourage students without actually doing their thinking for them. In the *NCTM Standards* (2000), the Teaching Principle encourages that "Effective mathematics teaching requires understanding what students know and need to learn and then challenging and supporting them to learn it well" (p. 16). Teachers can help children make sense of mathematics in many ways. In fact, that is a theme of this book. Chapter 3 initiates the discussion of teaching; in succeeding chapters we focus on ways to teach and activities that illustrate those ways.

THE LEARNING PRINCIPLE. What it means to learn mathematics has certainly changed over the past century. In the twenty-first century, however, the phrase *mathematical proficiency* (proposed by the National Research Council, 2001, in *Adding It Up: Helping Children Learn Mathematics*) describes what it means for anyone to learn mathematics successfully. Figure 1-3 provides their description of the five strands. Their overriding recommendation is that "throughout the grades from pre-K through 8 *all students can and should be mathematically proficient*" (p. 10). Their warning, however, is that these strands must be interwoven and interdependent if students are to actually meet this goal.

In order to meet this goal of mathematical proficiency in a changing world, learning mathematics with understanding is essential. As stated in the NCTM's Learning Principle, students must actively build knowledge of mathematics from their personal experiences and prior knowledge. Research has shown that if children are able to make sense of the mathematics they are learning, they can build on this understanding to learn more mathematics and use that mathematics to solve problems in order to become mathematically proficient.

The ideas about developing mathematical proficiency are considered in more depth in Chapter 2, but the Teaching Principle and the Learning Principle (see Figure 1-2) should trigger some beginning questions for you: What does it mean to learn mathematics with understanding? How did you learn mathematics? How do you learn to understand what children know? Where do you turn to find what elements of mathematics children need to learn and how to challenge and support them to learn it?

Needs of Society

The practicality and usefulness of mathematics in everyday situations and in many vocations has also affected what is taught and when it is taught. Early in American history, mathematics was considered necessary primarily for clerks and bookkeepers. The curriculum was limited to counting, the simpler procedures for addition, subtraction, and multiplication, and some knowledge of measures and fractions. By the late nineteenth century, business and commerce had advanced to the point that mathematics was considered important for everyone. The arithmetic curriculum expanded to include such topics as percentage, ratio and proportion, powers, roots, and series.

Mathematical Proficiency	
• *Conceptual Understanding*	Comprehension of mathematical concepts, operations, and relations
• *Procedural Fluency*	Skill in carrying out procedures flexibly, accurately, efficiently, and appropriately
• *Strategic Competence*	Ability to formulate, represent, and solve mathematical problems
• *Adaptive Reasoning*	Capacity for logical thought, reflection, explanation, and justification
• *Productive Disposition*	Habitual inclination to see mathematics as sensible, useful, and worthwhile, coupled with a belief in diligence and one's own efficacy

FIGURE 1-3 Mathematical proficiency in a changing world. (Source: National Research Council, 2001, p. 5.)

The emphasis on teaching what was needed for use in occupations continued into the twentieth century. One of the most vocal advocates of *social utility* was Guy Wilson. He and his students conducted numerous surveys to determine what arithmetic was actually used by carpenters, shopkeepers, and other workers. He believed that the "dominating" aim of the school mathematics program should be to teach those skills and *only* those skills.

The outburst of public concern in the 1950s over the "space race" resulted in a wave of curriculum development and research in mathematics. Much of this effort was focused on the mathematically talented student. In the mid-1960s, however, concern was also expressed for the disadvantaged student as U.S. society renewed its search for equality of opportunity. With these changes—in fact, with *each* change—more and better mathematical achievement was promised.

In the 1970s, when it became apparent that once again the promise had not fully materialized, another swing occurred in curriculum development. Renewed emphasis was placed on skills needed for survival in the real world. The minimal-competency movement stressed the basics. As embodied in sets of objectives and in tests, the basics were considered to be primarily addition, subtraction, multiplication, and division with whole numbers and fractions. Thus the skills needed by children in colonial times were again considered by many to be the sole necessities, even though children were now living in a world with calculators and computers.

By the 1980s, it was acknowledged that no one knew exactly what skills were needed for the future but that everyone needed to be able to solve problems. The emphasis on problem solving matured through the last 20 years of the century to the point where problem solving was not seen as a separate topic but as a way to learn and to use mathematics.

With the 1990s the focus shifted to an emphasis on *accountability*. The first International Assessment of Educational Progress in 1991 revealed that the achievement levels of U.S. students were often below those of students from other countries. In 1995, one of the most widely discussed assessments, the Third International Study in Science and Mathematics (TIMSS), involving more than 40 countries, examined the curriculum, instruction, and achievement at grades 3–4, 7–8, and end of schooling. Although U.S. students ranked above the international average for fourth-grade students, eighth-grade students were below and twelfth-grade students ranked significantly below the average. What was the problem with the mathematics curriculum and instruction in the United States that led to this result? This question led to a more careful look at the results, with an attempt to explain them. Among the difficulties with the cross-international studies of educational achievement, the analysis highlighted the recognition that these tests did not take into account the United States' commitment to educating *all* students and the difference in students' opportunity to learn the content in the tests.

THE EQUITY PRINCIPLE. With the emergence into the twenty-first century, dramatic changes in the needs of society were recognized. No longer is it sufficient for only a few children to be mathematically literate—*all* children need the opportunity to make sense of mathematics. The United States has a commitment to all students succeeding and closing the gap between diverse groups. The Equity Principle (Figure 1-2) states clearly that to have excellence in mathematics education, mathematics can and must be learned by all students. This vision can be accomplished only if each person involved in education believes that all children can learn mathematics and provides each child with the opportunity to learn worthwhile mathematics. This challenge means designing instructional programs to meet different interests, strengths, needs, cultures, and mathematical backgrounds of your students. Plenty of evidence supports the statement that students can learn mathematics. What they need is access to high-quality instructional programs in which teachers and school personnel are prepared and have the ability to meet the variety of individual strengths and needs in their classes.

THE ASSESSMENT PRINCIPLE. Helping all students learn mathematics requires that assessment be an integral part of the instructional program. Rather than viewing assessments as being "done to students," the program must include assessments that are "done for students" to guide and enhance their learning (NCTM, 2001). In order to develop a program that provides for the strengths and needs of individual students, teachers must continue to gather information about their students' progress. Useful and effective assessment is more than a test at the end of the unit. Asking students questions during a lesson not only helps them describe their thinking and understanding; their responses also help direct the decisions the teacher must make to meet the students' needs. Observing students as they solve problems or build ideas provides a different look at student understanding. Ultimately, as the Assessment Principle directs, "Assessment should become a routine part of the ongoing classroom activity rather than an interruption" (NCTM, 2000, p. 23).

Meeting the guidelines in the Assessment Principle is considered in more detail in Chapter 4 to help you as you begin to integrate assessment with instruction. Meanwhile, there are important issues for you to ponder as you begin to think about assessment. Today's society seems focused on assessments that compare students' performance among various schools, states, and nations. If these tests are not aligned with school and community goals for mathematics education, will your students be able to demonstrate what they know and are able to do in mathematics? Will these tests provide information about the mathematical proficiency of your students? Society needs a citizenry and a workforce that can solve problems, reason mathematically, process and interpret data, and communicate in a technological world. Will performance tests measure these processes and skills? Will American schools be able to focus on improving mathematics programs in order to prepare students for life in today's society if these tests are not aligned with school and community goals and with the notions of mathematical proficiency?

Where Can You Turn?

There are many places you can turn for help with the curriculum, with helping students learn, and to continue developing your knowledge of mathematics and of mathematics learning and teaching. There are many resources available to support you. Here are a few suggestions that introduce some of the resources that are used throughout this book.

National Guidelines for School Mathematics

The latest update of the NCTM standards, *Principles and Standards for School Mathematics* (NCTM, 2000), is referred to throughout this book. The five content standards are specified in more detail at the various grade bands (pre-K–2, 3–5, 6–8, and 9–12). For your reference, Appendix A provides a complete version of these expectations for pre-K through grade 8, which can help you determine what children at different ages are expected to learn. The five process standards can also be found in Appendix A.

State Guidelines

Almost every state has standards, guidelines, or frameworks for school mathematics. Most are more

Math Links 1.2

The entire *NCTM Standards* document is available, both in print and electronically, from NCTM, which you can access from this book's web site. The electronic version also provides interactive activities to help you better understand the intent of each standard.

specific than the national standards and specify content grade by grade. Many states are in the process of aligning their state assessments with their standards. You should check to see what is available for your state and what emphasis is placed on these guidelines.

Research

The body of research in mathematics education, both about children's learning and about teaching, is substantial. The recommendations made by the NCTM (NCTM, 2000) have a strong research base. Research references are provided throughout the book to illustrate information about children's learning. Several references are used with which you should become familiar.

The first is the National Assessment of Educational Progress, better known as NAEP (pronounced "nape"). This assessment is the nation's measure of students' achievement and trends in achievement in the academic subjects. The mathematics assessments began in 1973 and now are given every four years to fourth-, eighth-, and twelfth-grade students.

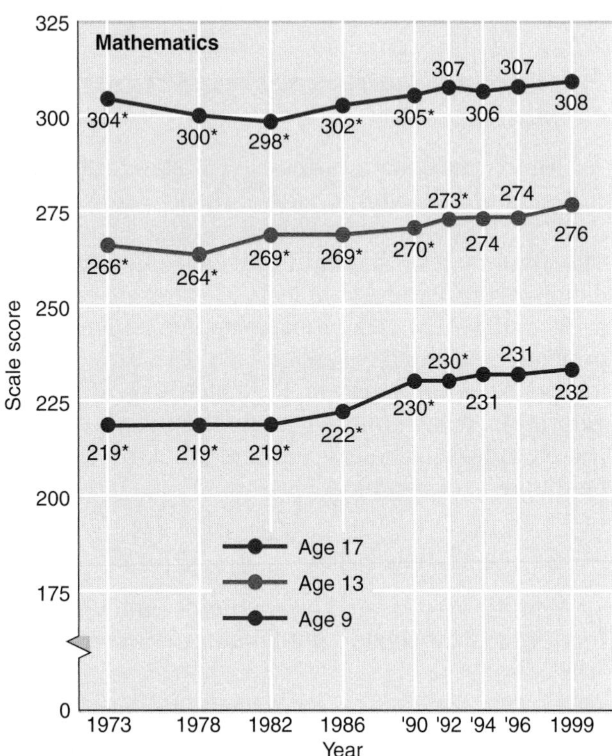

FIGURE 1-4 Trends in student performance: NAEP.
(Source: U.S. Department of Education, NCES. National Assessment of Education Progress, 1999, Long-Term Trend Assessment, and NAEP 1999 Trends in Academic Progress. Three Decades of Student Performance, 2000).

The assessments are updated to reflect the trends you have read about. A set of secured items from the 1973 battery is given periodically with a score of from 0 to 500; the results are shown in Figure 1-4. People often say, "students cannot do math like they used to do"; this graph paints a different picture of student performance on basic-skill items. In all three age groups, the average scores were identified by NAEP as significantly (statistically) higher in 1999 than in 1973.

Although students' performance is not declining, a comparison from around the world clearly shows that U.S. students could do better. Building on the results from the 1995 TIMSS study identifying U.S. students as inferior to some nations, a videotape study compared teaching in the eighth grades in the United States, Germany, and Japan. Ultimately, this study suggested that Japanese teaching more closely resembled the recommendations of the U.S. reform movement than American teaching (U.S. Department of Education, 1996). These results suggest that educators can learn much from knowing how other countries teach mathematics.

There are reports of research in many journals. Articles from the *Journal for Research in Mathematics Education* (JRME) are often used to guide the recommendations in this book. These articles often lead directly to the classroom ideas and recommendations found in NCTM journals, such as *Teaching Children Mathematics*.

History

If you want an enjoyable exploration, find some textbooks from the 1800s and early 1900s. Did you realize that before 1900, arithmetic was a college and then high school subject? Read the prefaces of the books, examine the size, look at the exercises, and find some activities that students completed during those times. Are these activities relevant for today's children in learning mathematics? If you are a student of history, you may want to examine the trends in mathematics education over the decades. How has the emphasis changed and how has it remained the same? Did students spend more time on learning procedures or problem solving? Were students provided with manipulatives to help them grasp the ideas?

Textbooks and Other Materials

Most teachers use a textbook when teaching elementary and middle school mathematics. Today's textbooks provide supplementary materials such as assessment, problems to solve, and extra practice.

Teachers' manuals also provide a wealth of materials and teaching suggestions.

There are many different types of textbooks. Some provide a great amount of drill and practice but offer little help in developing understanding and using mathematics. Others may provide more help in developing understanding but are short on practice of necessary skills. As you become experienced, you will be better able to judge the quality of a textbook. If you have not had much experience, you may want to follow the textbook until you become more comfortable with teaching. Keep questioning why you need to teach a given lesson. Does it help children develop the mathematics they need? Does it achieve this goal in a way that makes sense to children? Does it help children make sense of the mathematics?

Electronic Materials

The opportunity to have materials at your fingertips is increasing every day. The web provides immediate access to lesson plans, help with the mathematics itself, assessment items, and information that can be used in teaching mathematics. Because of the rapid change in web sites and addresses, multiple sites are not listed here.

A simple search of mathematics for elementary or middle school students and teachers will lead you to many other places. Again, a caution: Availability does not always mean quality. Just recently, a prospective teacher brought to class an activity that she had found on the web. It involved young children finding the capacity of their mouths by filling them with marshmallows. Not only was the mathematics questionable, because the unit of measurement was not firm, but it was also dangerous for children. Teaching involves making good judgments on many fronts.

Testing

The Assessment Principle (Figure 1-2) highlights the importance of assessment. You will learn more about assessment in Chapter 4, especially about assessment that will help you plan instruction and monitor children's progress.

All teachers need to be responsible for helping children learn, and the public demands accountability measures. Many states and localities require a plethora of tests. These tests are often standardized, norm-referenced, or criterion-referenced. The results of these tests are often published in papers for the community to see.

You can use these tests to help you in your quest to provide a sound mathematics education for your students. If the test is reasonable and aligned with your guidelines, then you can see how your students are doing in comparison to a standard or to other students, as well as which topics are presenting difficulty; however, do not be driven foolishly by a test that does not measure what is important. If you teach children to "do test items" but do not allow them to develop understanding, then any gains are likely only for the short term.

Math Links 1.3

To see an example of a helpful site for teachers, visit the Math Forum web site, which you can access from this book's web site. Some of the features at this site include an Internet mathematics library, a discussion board for teachers, lesson plans and activities created and submitted by teachers, Problems of the Week for students, and answers to math problems from Ask Dr. Math.

Professional Organizations

Being a part of a profession opens many opportunities and responsibilities. Your teaching career will be enhanced by the professional association you have with others and the support you can find from being a part of a professional organization. Journals, conferences, and other materials of a professional organization are often available to schools or to nonmembers.

For example, the NCTM offers many publications as well as a journal for elementary teachers of mathematics (*Teaching Children Mathematics*, formerly the *Arithmetic Teacher*) and one for middle school teachers (*Teaching Mathematics in Middle Grades*). You will find many references in this book to these journals. The NCTM also sponsors conferences, workshops, and other support activities. There are also more than 260 affiliated groups, both state and local, that offer many programs.

Math Links 1.4

You can visit the NCTM's online Teacher's Corner, which you can access from this book's web site. This site offers professional development opportunities, web resources, teaching resources, and activities for your classroom.

Professional Development

Begin to take advantage of the professional development opportunities that are available. Some of these are formal, such as workshops, college courses, and conferences; others are informal study groups. Your school, district, or state will provide some for you. Others will be commercially sponsored or sponsored by a professional organization. An increasing number of opportunities on the Web are designed so you can participate as your schedule permits.

Your school or district often has funds set aside for professional development that are available on request. Other districts have teachers design their own professional development plans and support you in carrying out that plan.

Other Teachers

Teachers learn from each other. You will learn from your school experiences, but do not let it stop there. Look for a school where sharing ideas about helping students learn mathematics and sharing teaching tips and materials is the norm. Look for teachers in other schools near you or far away but connected electronically who are willing to discuss and to share.

What Is Your Role Now?

As you prepare for teaching mathematics, be sure to think about the broader context of your work. Carefully consider these three challenges as you prepare to teach mathematics:

- *Examine your own disposition toward mathematics and who can learn it.* Be ready to question your beliefs, to evaluate proposed changes, and to make a difference in helping children learn mathematics.
- *As you begin working with children, stop and listen to them, individually and collectively.* Reflect on what you are hearing and learn with the children.
- *Realize that doing mathematics and teaching mathematics are different.* Teaching mathematics requires a depth of understanding about mathematics, about students, about schools, about curriculum, and about pedagogy. If you come to this realization and actively seek knowledge and experiences that integrate these areas, you are well on your way to becoming a teacher.

A Glance at Where We've Been

Teaching mathematics in a changing world means that the curriculum must change to reflect the needs of the subject, the child, and society. In this chapter you have seen a glimpse of the changing curriculum, as well as recommendations for teaching mathematics in the twenty-first century. In addition, resources have been identified to support your study through the rest of this book and, more important, as you teach. The challenge is to keep an open mind and continue your own learning about teaching children mathematics. Prepare to help your students make sense of mathematics.

Things to Do: From What You've Read

1. What are the three general goals mentioned in the introduction? Which do you think is the most important? Explain why.
2. Give an illustration (in addition to those in this chapter) of how mathematics is a study of patterns and relationships, a way of thinking, an art, and a language.
3. Which of the resources discussed in this chapter have you already used? Which ones do you think will be most helpful to you?
4. Explain in your own words the six principles that underpin the standards presented in *Principles and Standards for School Mathematics.*
5. Mathematical proficiency is described through five strands. Describe the five strands using specific examples from your personal experience and background. Explain how these strands are interwoven and interdependent.

Things to Do: Going Beyond This Book

IN THE FIELD

1. *As you observe in a school, look for signs of the role that mathematics plays in that school. Does it differ from class to class?

*Additional activities, suggestions, or questions are provided in *Teaching Elementary Mathematics: A Resource for Field Experiences* (Wiley, 2004).

2. Interview several students using the questions that Mrs. Freudenthal used in the *Snapshot of a Lesson*. How do your results compare with the children's responses in the *Snapshot of a Lesson*?
3. *Interview teachers (or some students) about their belief that all children can learn mathematics and what it would take to make this happen.
4. *Examine a copy of your state or district curriculum guide. How does the scope and sequence of topics align with the expectations for pre-K–2, grades 3–5, and grades 6–8 in the *Principles and Standards for School Mathematics* (see Appendix A)?

IN YOUR JOURNAL

5. Several educators have noted that the curriculum is in a continuous process of change in order to maintain balance as the needs of the subject, the child, and society pull it first one way and then another. Discuss this comment.
6. React to the three challenges presented in the close of the chapter.

WITH ADDITIONAL RESOURCES

7. Read Chapter 2 of *Principles and Standards for School Mathematics*. Choose the principle that you think is the most important; critique the discussion of that principle.
8. Read the Executive Summary of *Adding It Up: Helping Children Learn Mathematics*. Describe the five strands of mathematical proficiency and how they are intertwined and interdependent. What recommendations are provided for policies and practices needed if all children are to become mathematically proficient?
9. Examine the role of drill and practice for learning mathematics over the past century. Begin by reading one of the articles or books listed in the resources or by examining old textbooks. How is drill and practice viewed today in helping students learn mathematics? Has it changed over the past century?
10. Find a recent issue of *Teaching Children Mathematics* or *Teaching Mathematics in Middle Grades*. Select an article that describes a classroom application. Describe the principle(s) and/or the standard(s) that are considered in the recommendations for this classroom application.

WITH TECHNOLOGY

11. The Technology Principle recommends that technology does support effective mathematics teaching. Write a statement of your experience using calculators and describe your philosophy regarding calculators in learning elementary mathematics.
12. Conduct a web search for the National Assessment of Educational Progress (NAEP), The Nation's Report Card web site. Select the subject of Mathematics. Three achievement levels (Basic, Proficient, and Advanced) are described in detail for 1990–2000. What are the results for grade 4 and grade 8 across the decade?
13. NCTM has created a web site that "Illuminates the new Principles and Standards." Your task is to visit the site (illuminations.nctm.org) and select the button called "i-math investigations." You need to select a particular grade level,

Book Nook for Children

Butrick, Lyn McClure. *Logic for Space Age Kids.* Athens, Ohio: University Classic, 1984.

Engage students in thinking logically in the future! Zeno, from the planet of Zircon, ponders problems involving logical deduction. A problem is posed: "If all grandfathers are men, and if some astronauts are not men, then . . ." How should this sentence be finished? In this case a female astronaut completes the sentence with, "some astronauts are not grandfathers." Help children think about what is meant by the words *some, all,* and *no* by solving the problems presented in the story.

Hopkins, Lee B., and Barbour, Karen. *Marvelous Math: A Book of Poems.* New York: Aladdin, 1998.

Sixteen poems cover topics including division, multiplication, fractions, counting, and measurement—all relating math to the everyday world. The poems present mathematics as useful (it helps prove your brother will always be three years younger than you) and as scary (poor Sammy has a long division problem stuck in his brain). Use this book to engage students in the marvels of mathematics.

Phillips, Louis. *263 Brain Busters: Just How Smart Are You, Anyway?* New York: Penguin Books, 1985.

How many squares are on a checkerboard? How much hole is there in a hole six feet deep? Insert two punctuation marks so that 560 = 600. These problems are among the 263 Brain Busters that require logical thinking or involve humorous twists. A final chapter is titled "The Answers! (Honest!)".

pre-K–2, 3–5, 6–8 or 9–12. Select one of the elementary levels. Explore at least one of the ready-to-use, online, interactive, multimedia math investigations that illuminate the standards. Think about how you might use one of these investigations when you teach.

14. Conduct a web search for the "Ask Dr. Math" web site. Review the questions that elementary teachers and students send for Dr. Math to answer. Find a question and answer that you feel is particularly useful and explain why it is useful for you as you prepare to teach mathematics in the elementary level. Create a question to send to Dr. Math. Send it. How long is it before your question is answered? Was the answer helpful?

Resources

ANNOTATED BOOKS

Burns, Marilyn. *About Teaching Mathematics: A K-8 Resource.* (2nd ed.) Sausalito, Calif.: Math Solutions Publications, 2000.
Consider how to replace traditional math teaching with strategies that focus on students' thinking and reasoning. This book examines tough issues that teachers face in teaching mathematics and proposes teaching mathematics through problem solving.

Kilpatrick, Jeremy; Swafford, Jane; and Findell, Bradford. (eds.). *Adding It Up: Helping Children Learn Mathematics.* Washington, D.C.: National Academy Press, 2001.
What does research indicate about teaching and learning mathematics? The conclusions and recommendations drawn from research provide targets for improving the nation's teaching and learning of mathematics. After identifying what children know about numbers by the time they arrive in school, this book explores how students learn mathematics in elementary and middle grades.

Ma, Liping. *Knowing and Teaching Elementary Mathematics: Teachers' Understanding of Fundamental Mathematics in China and the United States.* Mahwah, N.J.: Lawrence Erlbaum Associates, 1999.
This book describes the nature and development of the "profound understanding of fundamental mathematics" elementary teachers need to become accomplished mathematics teachers; the book suggests why such teaching knowledge is much more common in China than in the United States, despite the fact that Chinese teachers have less formal education than their U.S. counterparts.

Mokros, Jan; Mokros, Janice R.; Economopoulos, Karen; and Russell, Susan J. *Beyond Arithmetic: Changing Mathematics in the Elementary Classroom (Investigations in Number, Data, & Space).* White Plains, N.Y.: Dale Seymour Publications, 1995.
Do you want help in implementing the NCTM's standards? Are you looking for new ways to help students be more successful in math? This book gives suggestions for teaching and assessing mathematics in ways that involve numbers, data, and space investigations.

National Council of Teachers of Mathematics. *Principles and Standards for School Mathematics.* Reston, Va.: NCTM, 2000.
A resource and guide for all who make decisions that affect the mathematics education of students in prekindergarten through grade 12. The recommendations are grounded in the belief that all students should learn important mathematical concepts and processes with understanding.

Teppo, A. R. (ed.). *Reflecting on Practice in Elementary School Mathematics: Readings from NCTM's School-based Journals and Other Publications.* Reston, VA: NCTM, 1999.
More than 60 articles provide an easy-to-read resource to give you great ideas that meet the calls for reform in teaching mathematics.

ANNOTATED ARTICLES

Bishop, Alan J. "What Values Do You Teach When You Teach Mathematics?" *Teaching Children Mathematics* 7(6) (February 2001), pp. 346–370.
This article uses educational research to support a connection between mathematics and culture and focuses on the values that teachers convey when teaching mathematics.

Flores, Alfinio. "Learning and Teaching Mathematics with Technology." *Teaching Children Mathematics* 8(6) (February 2002), pp. 308–310.
What is the impact of technology on learning and teaching mathematics in elementary education? What about student access to computers? What is the role of calculators in teaching and learning mathematics? Is the web useful and effective for children learning mathematics in the elementary grades?

Sellers, Patricia A., and Ahern, Kathryn A. "The TIMSS Report: Implications for Teachers in a New Millennium." *International Journal of Educational Reform* 9(4) (October 2000), pp. 321–327.
The TIMSS mixed results are difficult for most U.S. students and teachers to believe. Should teachers change their beliefs about how children learn mathematics and how these subjects should be taught? This article suggests that agreement about what constitutes effective teaching is needed.

ADDITIONAL REFERENCES

Hembree, Ray, and Dessart, Donald J. "Research on Calculators in Mathematics Education." In *Calculators in Mathematics Education,* 1992 Yearbook of the National Council of Teachers of Mathematics, edited by James T. Fey, pp. 23–32. Reston, Va.: NCTM, 1992.

National Council of Teachers of Mathematics. *Curriculum and Evaluation Standards for School Mathematics.* Reston, Va.: NCTM, 1989.

National Council of Teachers of Mathematics. *Professional Standards for Teaching Mathematics.* Reston, Va.: NCTM, 1991.

National Council of Teachers of Mathematics. *Assessment Standards for School Mathematics.* Reston, Va.: NCTM, 1995.

National Research Council. *Adding It Up: Helping Children Learn Mathematics.* Washington, D.C.: National Academy Press, 2001.

Washburne, Carleton. "Mental Age and the Arithmetic Curriculum: A Summary of the Committee of Seven Grade Placement Investigation to Date." *Journal of Educational Research,* 23 (March 1931), pp. 210–231.

U.S. Department of Education. *Pursuing Excellence: A Study of U.S. Eighth-Grade Mathematics and Science Teaching, Learning, Curriculum, and Achievement in International Context.* Washington, D.C.: U.S. Government Printing Office, 1996.

CHAPTER 2

Learning Mathematics with Understanding

Snapshot of a Lesson

As the fifth-grade mathematics class began, the students were asked to complete the Review Exercises, that Ms. Markle had put on the board.

John raised his hand and asked, "Can we use the calculators?" Ms. Markle responded, "Yes, if you think you need it for these problems."

While the students worked, Ms. Markle moved around the class, observing their progress. She noticed that several students had started by calculating the mean, completing the calculation longhand, adding the eight numbers and dividing by 8.

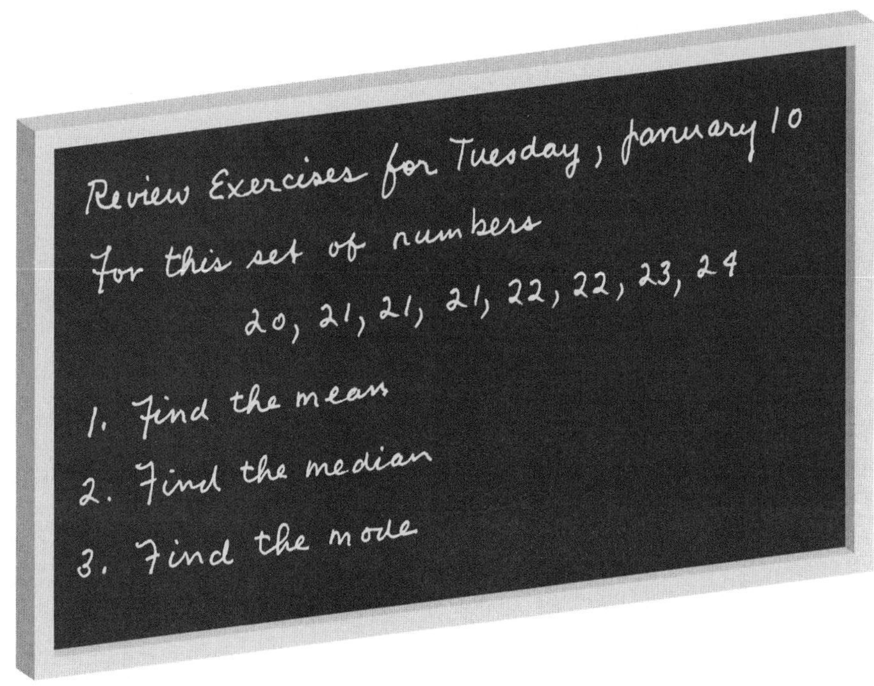

Review Exercises for Tuesday, January 10
For this set of numbers
20, 21, 21, 21, 22, 22, 23, 24
1. Find the mean
2. Find the median
3. Find the mode

```
  1            21
 20         8)174
 21           16
 21           14
 21            8
 22            6
 22
 23
 24
---
174
```

Some students wrote Mean = $21\frac{6}{8}$; others wrote Mean = $21\frac{3}{4}$. She also saw that a few of the students had mistakenly added the numbers to 164 and found the mean to be $20\frac{1}{2}$ or 20.5. One student completed the division incorrectly and found the mean to be $29\frac{1}{2}$.

As she walked around, Ms. Markle noted that some students used their calculators to find the mean. Several of these students wrote 21.75 as their response. A couple of students wrote the mean as 153.

After the students had completed their responses, Ms. Markle suggested that they discuss their answers and tell how they got them.

MS. MARKLE: First let's discuss these three words. When you find the mean, what are you finding? Terry?

TERRY: It's the average of the numbers.

MS. MARKLE: Yes, but what does that mean? Karen?

KAREN: You add up the numbers and then divide by how many numbers you added.

MS. MARKLE: Right, that is how you find the **number**. But, what is the **mean**? Alice?

ALICE: Well, suppose these numbers were weights in pounds for two-year-olds. For this group of children, the average weight would be $21\frac{3}{4}$ pounds.

At this point, Chris looked puzzled and raised his hand.

CHRIS: But wait, I got 153 for the mean.

MS. MARKLE: Thanks Chris. Now we have two different answers, and I have seen several other answers. Before you explain how you got your answer, let's talk more about the mean. When you find the mean, what value would you estimate it to be, given the numbers are all in the twenties? Harold?

HAROLD: All of these terms—mean, median and mode—that you asked us to find should be in the twenties because they tell us something about the numbers. Like Alice said, if the values were weights of little kids, you would not expect the average weight of two-year-olds to be 153. So 153 has to be wrong.

CHRIS: Wait. I found that value with my calculator doing exactly what you told me to do yesterday to find the mean. I just used my calculator! It must be right.

MS. MARKLE: Chris, why don't you share with us how you used your calculator so we can understand what you did.

CHRIS: Okay, I entered

$20 + 21 + 21 + 21 + 22 + 22 + 23 + \frac{24}{8} =$

MS. MARKLE: Has everyone done this with your calculator?

CLASS: Yes, and we get 153 too!

MS. MARKLE: Does that mean that the mean (or average) is 153 then? (Waiting for someone to volunteer . . . Several students raise their hands and the teacher calls on Karen because she was the one who had indicated the procedure for finding the mean.)

KAREN: (concerned) I guess it does because he did just what we said had to be done.

ALICE: But that doesn't make sense. I don't understand how the mean could be 153.

MS. MARKLE: Let's double-check what Chris did with the calculators. Why don't all of you follow along with your calculators as I write on the board what we are doing. First, let's do what Chris did.

(Writes on the board)

$20 + 21 + 21 + 21 + 22 + 22 + 23 + \frac{24}{8} =$

What does the calculator display?

CLASS: 153 (Ms. Markle writes 153 on the board.)

MS. MARKLE: Okay, now clear your calculators and follow along this time.

(Ms. Markle writes on the board)

$20 + 21 + 21 + 21 + 22 + 22 + 23 + 24 =$

Okay, what does the calculator display this time?

CLASS: 176 (Ms. Markle writes 176 on the board.)

MS. MARKLE: Now, we need to divide by 8.

(Ms. Markle writes these calculations on the board:)

$20 + 21 + 21 + 21 + 22 + 22 + 23 + 24 = 176$

$\frac{176}{8} =$

MS. MARKLE: What does the calculator display now?

CLASS: 21.75

(Ms. Markle completes the work on the board.)

$\frac{176}{8} = 21.75$

ALICE: I know what happened. You have to be careful how you use the calculator because of the order of operations. When Chris didn't enter the equal sign, the calculator used the correct order of operations to do the division first and the addition afterwards. That isn't the way to find the mean. To find the mean, the values need to be added first. Then you divide the sum by 8 to get the mean.

CHRIS: I get it! The calculator does not consider the calculations *until* the equal sign is entered and then it uses the order of operations that we use—multiply and divide first, then add and subtract. So the mean is 21.75. I guess we need to pay attention to order of operations when we use the calculator.

MS. MARKLE: Yes, and one way to help you when you are using the calculator is to first **estimate** what the result might be. When I asked you to think about what the mean was, you questioned your result because the mean should be a number in the twenties. Clearly, the number you get for the mean must make sense to you, regardless of what the calculator comes up with. Now I think it would be a good idea if we practice these ideas a bit more.

Introduction

How do children learn mathematics? This important question has no simple answer. Teachers provide their answers through classroom practices. In fact, every instructional activity within the classroom expresses the teacher's view of learning. Ms. Markle felt that it was important to have the students investigate the error in finding the mean, rather than simply telling the students the correct answer. She used the opportunity to teach the students more about how the calculator works while also having them consider their own understanding of the mean. The way in which you plan lessons, present topics, and handle questions reflects how you perceive learning and influences what happens in the classroom.

Consider this exchange about the amount of homework needed:

STUDENT: Do we have to do all thirty exercises on this page?

TEACHER: Yes, do every one of them. Why do you think they are there if you are not supposed to do them?

A common pitfall in assignments is too much practice too soon. Ms. Markle had taught the students about the mean, median, and mode on the previous day, but before having them do lots of problems, she determined that they still needed to talk about how they understood the concepts. Ms. Markle had her students work on some more practice exercises, allowing them to work in small groups so they could discuss their ideas. She also planned to have the whole class discuss the ideas in the next lesson. Research confirms that students rarely need all the practice provided in a textbook. Far more important than the quantity of exercises done is the developmental instruction that precedes them and the distribution of practice that follows (Koehler and Grouws, 1992).

Because teachers' beliefs about the learning process make such a difference in the classroom, a thoughtful study and understanding of how mathematics is learned should have high priority for every elementary teacher. The purpose of this chapter is to build on your previous knowledge from educational psychology and stimulate your thinking about how children learn mathematics.

FOCUS QUESTIONS

1. What does the NCTM's Learning Principle recommend for how students need to learn mathematics?
2. What tenets are important in a behaviorist approach to learning?
3. What tenets are important in a constructivist approach to learning?

4. What is procedural knowledge and how is it different from conceptual knowledge?
5. What are some practical recommendations implied by what is known about how children learn mathematics?

How Do Children Learn Mathematics?

The vision for mathematics education promoted by the National Council of Teachers of Mathematics (NCTM, 2000) is for all children to learn mathematics with understanding. This vision is highlighted in the Learning Principle.

The Learning Principle

Students must learn mathematics with understanding, actively building new knowledge from experience and prior knowledge.

NCTM, 2000, p. 20

In the presentation of the Learning Principle of the *Principles and Standards for School Mathematics (NCTM Standards)*, the NCTM states that "Learning with understanding is essential to enable students to solve the new kinds of problems they will inevitably face in the future" (NCTM, 2000, p. 21). The National Research Council recommendation concurs: "All young Americans must learn to think mathematically, and they must think mathematically to learn" (2001, p. 16).

The premise for mathematical learning is based on research that has been accumulating for many years and reflects advances in mathematics education, psychology, and medicine. At the elementary level, teachers are constantly faced with the mutual dependency of children's mathematics ability on their reading ability; however, once children have mastered the basic principles and skills of reading, enhancement in their reading is gained through continued practice and applying the skills to learn mathematics, history, and other subjects. On the other hand, mathematics builds on itself, becoming more abstract as the ideas build (e.g., from arithmetic to algebra). Evidence from medicine suggests that learning changes the physical structure of the brain, and different parts of the brain may be ready to learn at different times (National Research Council, 1999). Ultimately, to learn more abstract mathematical concepts, children need to have developed both physically and psychologically enough to handle the abstraction.

Early in the twentieth century, John Dewey asserted that learning comes from experience and active involvement by the learner. Much has been discovered since then about how children learn mathematics, but the importance of meaningful experience remains unchallenged. More recently, Jean Piaget argued that learners actively construct their own knowledge. This view of learning, known as *constructivism*, suggests that rather than simply accepting new information, students interpret what they see, hear, or do in relation to what they already know. As the Learning Principle indicates, students learn mathematics with understanding by actively building new knowledge from their personal experiences and prior knowledge.

Chris (in the *Snapshot of a Lesson*) translated the rule "add up the values and divide by the number of values in the group of numbers" literally as he used his calculator to find the mean. The student who concludes that 0.285 is greater than 0.4 because "0.285 has more digits" is building on what he or she already knows about whole numbers and interprets the information about decimals in light of this previous knowledge. These students have constructed knowledge, but they extended that knowledge to new situations incorrectly. Teaching mathematics includes guiding students as they extend the knowledge to new applications.

Teachers base their lessons on how they believe children learn. There are currently two distinct theories of learning. *Behaviorism* is associated with external, observable behaviors and actions. If the teacher demonstrates specific skills, the student will be able to duplicate these skills. For example, if a teacher instructs students in finding the mean of a set of numbers (the stimulus), the students are able to find the mean of a second set of numbers (the response). Behaviorism focuses on observable behaviors rather than thought processes students may use to demonstrate observable results.

Constructivism focuses on different actions—what happens between the stimulus and the response. From this consideration, the focus is on the thinking students do as they consider the stimulus. The learning outcome depends not only on the learning environment (what the teacher does) but also on the learner (how the learners merge these new ideas with what they already have experienced and understood). Each view holds implications for learning and teaching mathematics. Elements of the two major theories of how children think and learn are key to a further understanding of how children learn mathematics.

Building Behavior

Behaviorism focuses on external and observable behaviors—a stimulus and a response. This theory asserts that behavior can be shaped through rewards and punishments. Over the years, it has marshaled several distinguished advocates, including Edward L. Thorndike, B. F. Skinner, and Robert Gagné; however, few learning theorists today argue for an exclusively behaviorist approach to mathematics learning. Behaviorism has had a significant impact on mathematics programs, but strict adherence to a behaviorist approach to mathematics learning in elementary school is inappropriate because of its lack of consideration of how the child thinks about the stimulus in developing a response.

One of the major tenets of behaviorism is reinforcement, which is practice promoting the desired behavior. The value and power of meaningful practice are well documented; however, research has reported negative effects associated with excessive practice, premature practice, or practice without understanding (Koehler and Grouws, 1992). Such practice often leads to a fear or dislike of mathematics and an attitude that mathematics does not need to make sense when, in fact, making sense of mathematics is a major goal of mathematics learning. Because of its impact on mathematics education over the twentieth century, behaviorist psychology must be considered by teachers but used wisely. Keeping this point in mind, examine behaviorism a bit more closely.

The hierarchical nature of mathematics makes it a popular candidate for a behaviorist approach. Many behaviorists think of mathematics as being sequenced in a linear fashion, where one idea builds on another. More directly, behaviorism promotes learning a fixed set of skills in a fixed order. For example, the concept of multiplication as repeated addition suggests that students need to master addition before moving to the concept of multiplication.

The first consideration in planning a lesson from a behaviorist perspective is to state precisely the objectives, or goals, of instruction. These statements give the teacher direction in planning instruction and give the students clear expectations—both valuable outcomes that are consistently supported by research. Once an objective has been clearly stated, behaviorists recommend that the prerequisites for achieving that goal be identified and used as building blocks in planning instruction.

Consider the following example.

Objective: Correctly use the formula $A = \frac{1}{2}ba$ to find the area of a triangle.

Some prerequisite questions are:

What is area?

What is a triangle?

What is a triangle's base?

What is a triangle's altitude?

Clear answers to these prerequisite questions are necessary in order to reach the objective; however, this particular task analysis could be extended to include these questions:

How do you multiply by a fraction?

How do you multiply two whole numbers?

Thus it is hard to imagine constructing a complete task analysis for any objective, no matter how simple it may seem. Prerequisite knowledge must be considered in preparing lessons, but teachers must be guided by common sense, not by zeal to construct the definitive task analysis.

From a behavioral perspective, clarifying the objectives or goals for instruction focuses the instruction on desired learning outcomes. What behavior do you want the students to exhibit at the end of instruction? That outcome provides the focus of the lesson. Although forming behaviorally oriented objectives may be useful, focusing the lesson only on students demonstrating that behavior may result in a lesson that does not lead to an understanding of those actions. If the objective of the lesson is to use the formula correctly to find the area of a triangle, the lesson may focus on lower-level cognitive outcomes, where the students are only expected to correctly identify and use the base and altitude of the triangle to calculate the area. If, on the other hand, the objective of the lesson is to explain how the area of the triangle is half the area of a specific rectangle, the students are directed toward a higher cognitive level of understanding of the area of the triangle (see Figure 2-1). The prerequisite questions of the lesson must include the question of understanding the area of a rectangle. Also, the lesson must then focus the students in identifying the rectangle that is formed by the base and altitude of the triangle (Rectangle BEFC).

An emphasis on the expected outcomes for a lesson often results in lower-level cognitive understandings. An examination of many mathematics programs discloses a heavy influence of more easily measured outcomes that lead to programs where students are "shown" algorithms and mathematical relationships are "illustrated" on the textbook pages.

The behaviorist approach does have some attractive features: it provides instructional guidelines, allows for short-term progress, and lends

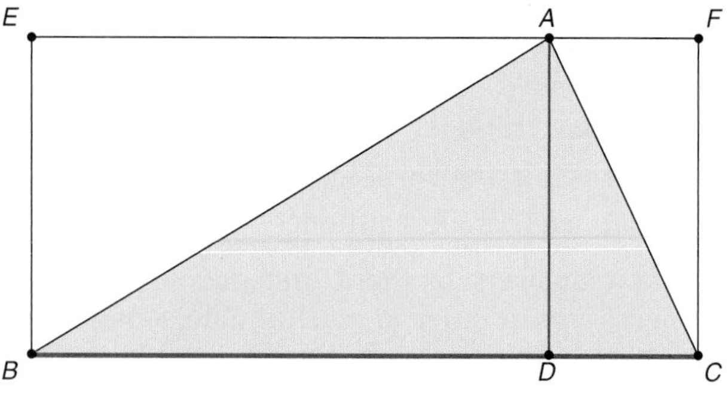

FIGURE 2-1 Triangle ABC has an area that is half the area of rectangle BEFC, a rectangle with length and width equal to the base and altitude of the triangle.

itself well to accountability pressures. Knowing what outcomes are to be assessed in standardized tests gives teachers specific directions for designing their lessons; however, a real and constant danger in using a behaviorist approach is to focus on simple, short-term objectives that are easily measured. These simple objectives focus more on mastery of specific ideas, rather than on higher-level understandings that develop connections making the knowledge meaningful and useful. The emphasis on short-term objectives often results in a deemphasis on long-term goals and higher-level cognitive processes such as problem solving.

It is possible for a behaviorist approach to have a positive effect on mathematics learning, providing more learner involvement and promoting higher-level thinking in mathematics. This possibility is illustrated by the use of many behaviorally oriented verbs, such as *explore, justify, represent, solve, construct, discuss, use, investigate, describe, develop,* and *predict*. An example is the objective guiding the lesson for having students explain how the area of the triangle is half the area of a rectangle. Each of these verbs encourages critical thinking and requires an active role for children in doing and eventually learning mathematics.

The behaviorist approach does lead to some useful ideas in teaching mathematics:

- Clear statements of objectives help teachers in designing a lesson directed at specific learning outcomes
- Clear statements of objectives and learning outcomes help students understand the expectations
- Reinforcement through drill and practice promotes desired outcomes, although this can be overdone
- Specific skills need to be learned in a fixed order.

Although identifying specific outcomes is an important guide to mathematics instructions, the constructivist perspective helps focus more directly on student understanding and students making sense of mathematics.

Constructing Understanding

The notion of meaningful learning advanced by William Brownell during the first half of the twentieth century was a forerunner of constructivism. Brownell conceived of mathematics as a closely knit system of ideas, principles, and processes—a structure that should be the cornerstone for learning mathematics. Connections among concepts should be established so that "arithmetic is less a challenge to the pupil's memory and more a challenge to his [or her] intelligence" (Brownell, 1935, p. 32).

In recent years, research has consistently confirmed that isolated "learnings" are not retained (Hiebert and Carpenter, 1992). Mathematics can and should make sense. If it does, it has meaning and is understood as a discipline with order, structure, and numerous relationships—and it is likely to be called on in a variety of problem-solving situations. Meaningful learning provides the basis for mathematical connections and is an integral part of constructivism.

In addition to Brownell, Jean Piaget, Jerome Bruner, and Zoltan Dienes have each contributed to the growth of constructivism. Many of the major recommendations for teaching mathematics advocated by the *Professional Standards for Teaching Mathematics* (NCTM, 1991) and more recently in the *NCTM Standards* (2000) are based on how children learn mathematics. Both documents provide strong support for change from the traditional behaviorist approach to constructivism. In fact, "educational research offers compelling evidence that students learn mathematics well only when they *construct* their own mathematical understanding" (National Research Council, 1989, p. 58).

What does it mean for students to construct their mathematical knowledge? It means different things to different people, and some of the myths associated with constructivism, such as "constructivist learners work alone" or "cooperative learning is constructivist," continue to linger (Clements, 1997). Although definitions vary, three basic tenets on which constructivism rests provide an answer to this question:

1. *Knowledge is not passively received; rather, knowledge is actively created or invented (con-*

structed) by students. Piaget (1972) suggested that mathematics understanding is made (constructed) by children, not found like a rock nor received from others as a gift.

2. *Students create (construct) new mathematical knowledge by reflecting on their physical and mental actions.* They observe relationships, recognize patterns, and make generalizations and abstractions as they integrate new knowledge into their existing mental structure (Dienes, 1960).

3. *Learning reflects a social process in which children engage in dialogue and discussion with themselves as well as with others (including teachers) as they develop intellectually* (Bruner, 1986). This tenet suggests that students are involved not only in manipulating materials, discovering patterns, inventing their own algorithms, and generating different solutions, but also in sharing their observations, describing their relationships, explaining their procedures, and defending the processes they followed.

These tenets have significant implications for learning and teaching mathematics. Can you identify evidence of these tenets in how Ms. Markle directed the lesson on mean, median, and mode? The tenets also suggest that constructivism is a process that takes time and reflects several developmental stages.

Research has documented that children's level of mathematical development provides a window of opportunity for a range of learning activities. At each stage of development, the lower limit of this window of opportunity rests on previous concepts and skills that have been established. The upper limit is determined by tasks that can be successfully completed only with step-by-step instruction. Learning activities and experiences that fall within this range have been identified by the Russian psychologist Lev Vygotsky as being within a child's "zone of proximal development" (Steele, 1999).

Research suggests that learning activities that fall within a child's zone of proximal development have a high probability of success, whereas engaging in activities outside the zone have much less likelihood of success. For instance, in the *Snapshot of a Lesson,* Ms. Markle's strategy was to guide the students in a step-by-step consideration of two different possibilities for using the calculator to obtain the mean. By connecting the operations with what the children would do manually, she was able to help Chris rethink his response for calculating the mean and recognize the importance of order of operations in calculator use. She had to have some idea about Chris's zone of proximal development, which she might have gained by observing Chris work on the problem. She had to have some idea of how to use what she knew about Chris to help him reconstruct how he thought about using calculators with multiple operations. The challenge provided by Vygotsky is to know your students well and to have a reasonably good understanding of these zones.

Theories of learning suggest that learning is a natural process. For children to learn mathematics, they need to make sense of it. Learning is active and internally monitored; it is a process of acquiring, discovering, and constructing meaning from experience. In this context, teaching math with the use of models and making connections with the children's experiences helps them make sense of mathematics. The process results in learning that is filtered through the student's unique knowledge base, thoughts, perceptions, and feelings.

Although Piaget, Bruner, and Dienes characterize the levels of development differently, as outlined in Figure 2-2, the frameworks proposed by each are remarkably similar. A careful examination of these frameworks reveals that:

- Children are actively involved in the learning process, and opportunities for talking about or otherwise communicating their ideas are essential.
- Several characteristic and identifiable stages of thinking exist, and children progress through these as they grow and mature.
- Learning proceeds from the concrete to the abstract. Here it is important to keep in mind that *concrete* is a relative term. To one child, joining two blocks and four blocks is concrete, but $2 + 4$ is not; another child may view $2 + 4$ as concrete and $x + y$ as abstract.
- Symbols and formal representation of mathematical ideas follow naturally from the concrete level, but only after conceptualization and meaningful understanding have been established. Without such understanding, children do not feel comfortable working with mathematical symbols, and the mathematics does not make sense to them.

Taken collectively, theories about how children learn help considerably in planning instruction and developing curricula. They provide a strong argument for using appropriate models and concrete materials to illustrate mathematical concepts and for actively involving students in the learning process. A major instructional implication is that teachers should explain new information in terms of knowledge students already possess. This idea raises a critical question: What mathematics do students need to know and be able to use?

Levels of Thinking by Elementary School Children as Characterized by Piaget	Levels of Developmental Learning as Characterized by Bruner	Levels of Mathematical Learning as Characterized by Dienes
Formal Operational: Considers the possible rather than being restricted to concrete reality. Capable of logical thinking that allows children to reflect on their own thought processes.	**Symbolic:** Manipulation of symbols. Child manipulates and/or uses symbols irrespective of their enactive or iconic counterparts.	**Formalization:** Provides an ordering of the mathematics. Fundamental rules and properties are recognized as structure of the system evolves.
		Symbolization: Describes the representation in language and/or mathematical symbols.
	Iconic: Representational thinking based on pictures, images, or other representations. Child is involved with pictorial and/or verbal information based on the real world.	**Representation:** Provides a peg on which to hang what has been abstracted. Images and pictures are used to provide a representation.
Concrete Operational: Thinking may be logical but is perceptually oriented and limited to physical reality.		**Generalization:** Patterns, regularities, and commonalities are observed and abstracted across different models. These structural relationships are independent of the embodiments.
Preoperational: Represents action through thought and language but is prelogical in development.	**Enactive:** Firsthand manipulating, constructing, or arranging or real-world objects. Child is interacting directly with the physical world.	**Free Play:** Interacts directly with physical materials within environment. Different embodiments provide exposure to the same basic concepts, but at this stage few commonalities are observed.

Early → Advanced

Introductory → Abstractions

FIGURE 2-2 Frameworks of the learning process.

What Mathematical Knowledge Should Be Learned?

The overriding goal for mathematics education is that students become mathematically proficient. According to the National Research Council (2001), mathematical proficiency incorporates five important strands: conceptual understanding, procedural fluency, strategic competence, adaptive reasoning, and productive disposition. The importance of teaching students skills (procedural fluency or knowledge) versus concepts (conceptual understanding or knowledge) in mathematics education has long been debated. Such debates create a false dichotomy that plays one against the other. The truth is that both skills and concepts are necessary for expertise in mathematics. Teachers need to understand what constitutes procedural and conceptual knowledge and the importance of helping students make connections and establish meaningful relationships between them.

Procedural knowledge is based on a sequence of actions, often involving rules and algorithms. For example, a student who has procedural knowledge of division knows how to complete the steps to the long-division algorithm. *Conceptual knowledge,* on the other hand, is based on connected networks that link relationships and discrete pieces of information (Hiebert and Carpenter, 1992). A student who has conceptual knowledge of division knows that division forms equal groups. Computation provides the setting for much procedural knowledge because algorithms can be acquired through a prescribed, step-by-step sequence of procedures. These procedures can be acquired with understanding or can be learned by rote. For example, to compute $23 + 49$, you might use a series of regroupings to apply a written algorithm and produce a sum of 72; or you might add 20 and 40 to get 60 and then add 12 more to get 72; or you could use the related mental computation of $23 + 50 = 73$, and then subtract 1 to get 72. Each of these algorithms illustrates procedural knowledge, and each can be developed with meaning and understanding.

It is also possible to learn the same algorithms as a series of steps devoid of meaning. For example, 23 + 49 could be memorized as "add the 3 and the 9 to get 12. Bring down the 2 and carry the 1. . . ." Such rote learning has no place in school mathematics, yet it highlights one of the ever-present dangers associated with algorithms. Research suggests that students with highly developed rules for manipulating symbols are reluctant to connect these rules to other representations that might give them meaning (Hiebert et al., 1997). Other research reports that once elementary students learn procedures to do written computation, they are more likely to use the written rather than mental procedures (Reys and Barger, 1994). These studies highlight the idea that once particular procedures are established and practiced, they become fixed, and the process makes later acquisition of understanding using the procedures less likely.

Although procedural knowledge may provide a rule or definition to answer a specific question, the resulting knowledge might be limited or devoid of important connections. For example, in response to the question "What is a square?" a student might respond correctly: "A square has four congruent sides and four right angles." Without further probing, however, you would not know if the student has an understanding of other relationships, such as a square is a rectangle, a parallelogram, a regular polygon, and an equilateral quadrilateral. On the other hand, In the Classroom 2-1 requires that students demonstrate a more in-depth understanding of the four-sided figures. Awareness of these relationships requires conceptual knowledge that may not be evident from the initial response.

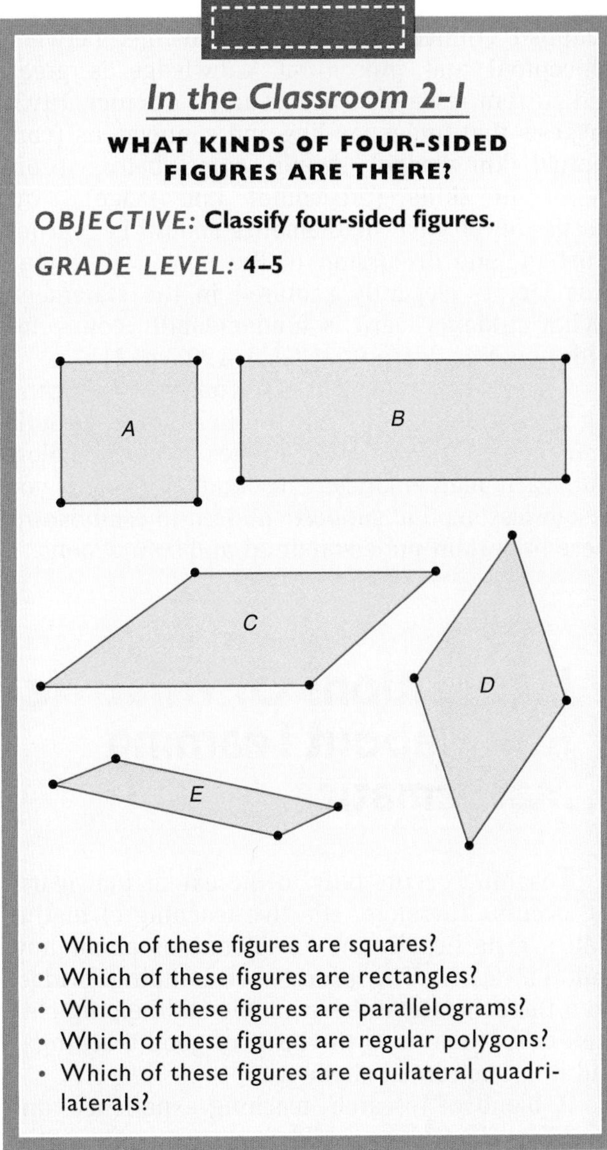

In the Classroom 2-1

WHAT KINDS OF FOUR-SIDED FIGURES ARE THERE?

OBJECTIVE: **Classify four-sided figures.**

GRADE LEVEL: **4–5**

- Which of these figures are squares?
- Which of these figures are rectangles?
- Which of these figures are parallelograms?
- Which of these figures are regular polygons?
- Which of these figures are equilateral quadrilaterals?

Both conceptual and procedural knowledge need to be developed with meaning and understanding. Although the nature of conceptual knowledge requires the establishment of meaningful relationships and connections, it is possible to develop procedural knowledge without regard for meaning. For example, the instruction "invert the divisor and multiply" produces a correct result for the quotient of two fractions. A student may be able to apply this procedure but have no way to explain why it works. If only the answer is important, then the student has no desire to learn why the algorithm works.

Conceptual knowledge requires that the learner actively think about relationships and make connections, along with adjustments to fit the new learning with previous mental structures. On the other hand, procedural knowledge can be acquired in a more passive mode, as when a student is required only to imitate a technique that is demonstrated or illustrated. Later, teachers can observe the consequence of such rote learning as the student grasps for a set of steps, a rule, or a formula to apply in some algorithmic manner. The student's ability to use procedural knowledge properly relies completely on memory, which may be inadequate to make the necessary recall because of a lack of connections and networks between conceptual and procedural knowledge. When this happens, errors occur. Students possessing only procedural knowledge have limited means of detecting and correcting errors and unreasonable answers.

Teachers need to acknowledge the importance of procedural and conceptual knowledge in mathematics learning. The need to help students establish connections and relationships between conceptual and procedural knowledge is great, and current research (Hiebert and Carpenter, 1992) suggests that understanding and connections (conceptual knowledge) should come before proficiency in skills (procedural knowledge). Any discussion of what mathematics should be learned must include discussion of the way it is taught. This fact is elegantly captured in the statement, "What students learn is fundamentally connected with how they learn it" (NCTM, 1991, p. 21).

The challenge for you is to construct the learning environment. How can you help students build connections and learning bridges as they explore and learn mathematics? This book will help you design lessons that support children in establishing these important understandings and connections.

Implications Of What We Know about Learning Mathematics

Teaching occurs only to the extent that learning occurs. Therefore, effective teaching of mathematics rests heavily on considerations about how children learn. The process of building bridges from the concrete to the symbolic and helping children cross them is at the heart of good teaching—and it is a continual challenge.

A blend of research, teaching experience, and thinking about how children learn mathematics leads to practical recommendations for teaching mathematics in a manner consistent with the NCTM's Learning Principle—the principle that emphasizes the importance of personal experiences and prior knowledge in actively building new mathematical knowledge. What follows are some recommendations for teaching mathematics that are extended and applied throughout this book. No priority of importance is suggested by the order in which they are listed.

Recommendation 1: Actively Involve Students

This recommendation is based on the conviction that active involvement encourages students to make sense out of what they are doing and thereby develop greater understanding of mathematics. Recall the ancient Chinese proverb

I hear and I forget;
I see and I remember;
I do and I understand.

This proverb reflects the importance of active involvement for students as they construct their own mathematical meaning. Active involvement may require physical activity but always demands mental activity. It takes many forms, including interaction of children and teachers, hands-on experience with manipulatives, and use of learning materials such as textbooks or technology. One of the daily challenges of teaching is to provide experiences that encourage, promote, and reward active involvement.

Suppose, for example, you were developing a lesson on volume. One approach might be to provide a formula for finding the volume of a right prism: $V = bhl$. You could show students drawings of various right prisms and then ask them to use the formula to compute the volume for each.

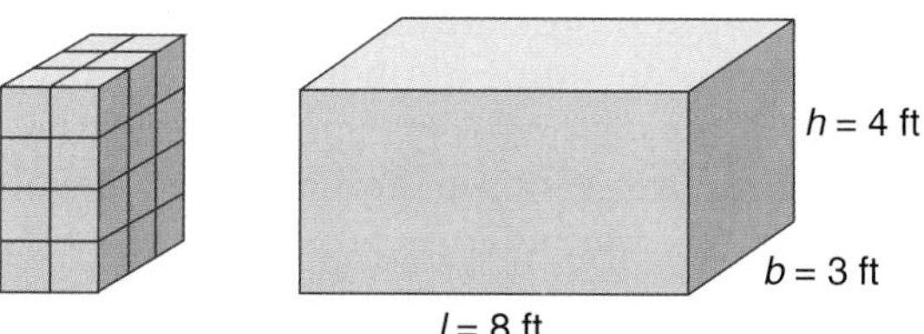

A more active, developmental approach to building an understanding of volume is developed though In the Classroom 2-2. Here children are provided with some blocks and asked to build different boxes (right prisms). As they build the boxes, they begin to relate the dimensions of the boxes to their volumes. Finding the volume of boxes is a primary objective for this activity; however, as students find the volumes of the boxes in the activity, they also learn that different boxes may have the same volume. Furthermore, the need to multiply the dimensions becomes clear, so the formula for the volume of a box evolves naturally from this active involvement.

Children are involved in using models, making decisions, and thinking about mathematics, rather than methodically applying a formula. They are also experiencing important mathematical properties. For example, with the 16-block arrangements they build a box that is $4 \times (2 \times 2)$ and they build a different box that is $(4 \times 2) \times 2$; because both boxes have 16 blocks, they are demonstrating that $(4 \times 2) \times 2 = 4 \times (2 \times 2)$. Similarly, as they continue to rearrange the boxes with a volume of 16 blocks, they construct models that show $(2 \times 2) \times 4 = (2 \times 8 \times 1)$ and, more important, they practice arithmetic and develop algebraic thinking.

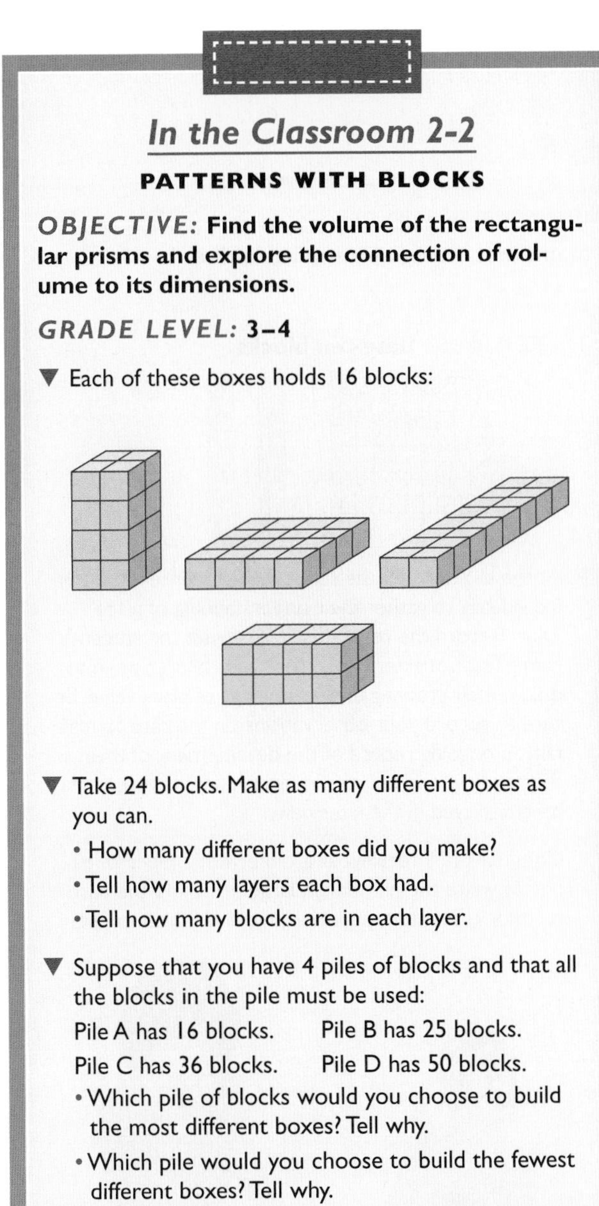

In the Classroom 2-2

PATTERNS WITH BLOCKS

OBJECTIVE: **Find the volume of the rectangular prisms and explore the connection of volume to its dimensions.**

GRADE LEVEL: **3–4**

▼ Each of these boxes holds 16 blocks:

▼ Take 24 blocks. Make as many different boxes as you can.

- How many different boxes did you make?
- Tell how many layers each box had.
- Tell how many blocks are in each layer.

▼ Suppose that you have 4 piles of blocks and that all the blocks in the pile must be used:

Pile A has 16 blocks. Pile B has 25 blocks.
Pile C has 36 blocks. Pile D has 50 blocks.

- Which pile of blocks would you choose to build the most different boxes? Tell why.
- Which pile would you choose to build the fewest different boxes? Tell why.

Recommendation 2: Teach to the Developmental Needs of Students

Effective and efficient learning of mathematics doesn't just happen. Children learn best when mathematical topics are appropriate for their developmental level and are presented in an enjoyable and interesting way that challenges their intellectual development.

It takes time to extract mathematics from real-life experiences and concrete materials. It takes time to search for patterns, observe relationships, and make connections, as errors naturally occur along the way. Yet this time is well spent because it helps develop a lasting facility not only to think about mathematics but also to think mathematically.

Students vary greatly in their development and readiness for learning. Thus some first graders will understand addition and develop fluency with basic facts before some third graders. Likewise, some middle-grade students may have difficulty visualizing the blocks shown In the Classroom 2-2, and they may need to "build" these boxes before the task becomes meaningful.

Teachers play a critical role in judging the developmental stage and subsequently determining zones of proximal development. The decisions reached allow teachers to establish rich environments for students to explore mathematics at an appropriate developmental level. Teachers must provide not only a rich classroom environment for learning mathematics but also the necessary direction to help children recognize relationships, make connections, and talk about mathematics.

Recommendation 3: Build on Previous Learning

Mathematics must be organized so that it is appropriate and understandable to students. Because mathematics includes both conceptual and procedural knowledge, the challenge is not only to develop these types of knowledge but also to understand relations between them. In no other discipline is previous knowledge and learning more critical. For example, it is fruitless to try to estimate a distance in kilometers if you don't have some sense of the length of a kilometer.

Quality mathematics programs are organized both to provide continuous development and to help students understand the basic structure of mathematics. Scope-and-sequence charts provide an overview of how a particular program is arranged. A careful examination of such a chart reveals how a sequence of activities is organized in a spiral approach.

Ideally, the *spiral approach* provides many opportunities over time to develop and broaden concepts. More specifically, it incorporates and builds on earlier learning to help guide the child through continued but increasingly more intricate study of related topics. Angle measurement, for example, is informally introduced in primary grades and returned to many times. When the concept of "angle" reappears in later grades, greater levels of sophistication are required. The diagram in Figure 2-3 shows how previous experience is used to develop the concept.

You should recognize, however, a danger associated with the spiral approach to curriculum. Although in theory the spiral mathematics curriculum provides for continuous growth and development, in reality many topics are revisited each year

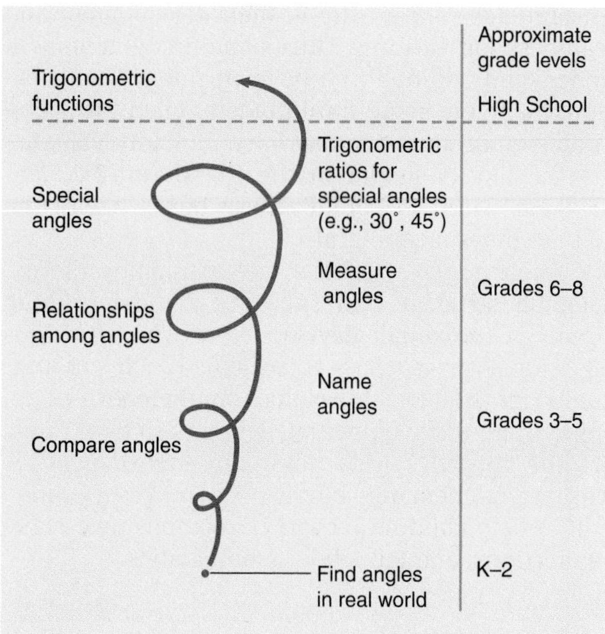

FIGURE 2-3 Spiral approach toward developing angles.

without appreciable change in the intellectual level of treatment. Consequently, much valuable time is spent each year treading water, merely reviewing topics rather than continuing an exploration that builds on prior learning or introduces new topics. For example, the Third International Mathematics and Science Study (TIMSS) reported that mathematics programs in the United States reflect more review of topics from year to year than other countries, such as Germany and Japan (TIMSS, 1996). Such repetition is detrimental because it turns students off. It robs both teachers and students of the excitement inherent in exploring fresh and new mathematics. It also diverts large amounts of instructional time from new learning to reviewing familiar concepts, which means that fewer new ideas can be experienced each year.

The spiral approach holds profound implications for learning and teaching. For example, instructional planning must consider the prerequisites for success on the current lesson, and the teacher must check to see if students have them. It is not unusual to find students who have skipped, never learned, forgotten, or incorrectly learned prerequisite topics. Detecting these weaknesses early and quickly allows the inclusion of review, so that later lesson development is not hampered by students' lack of prerequisites. The activity described In the Classroom 2-3 describes a strategy for

In the Classroom 2-3

PLACE VALUE

OBJECTIVE: **Identify students' growing levels of understanding about place value.**

GRADE LEVEL: **4**

MATERIALS: **Base-ten blocks**

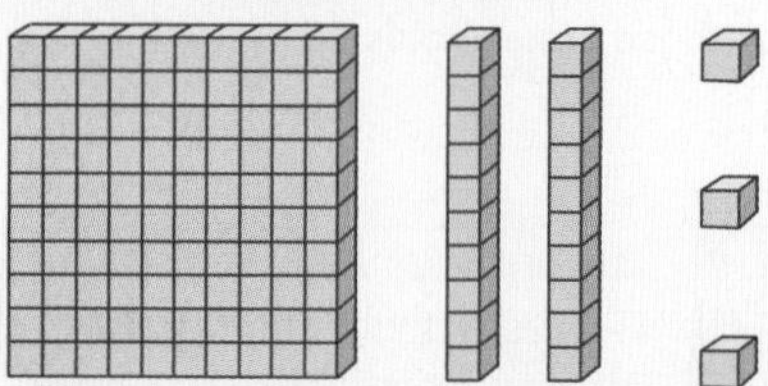

- At the beginning of the school year, interview children individually to gather their understanding of place value. Record the results on a card with the student's name. Then, quarterly, interview the children again to obtain their growing understandings of place value. Be sure to record your observations on the card to maintain an ongoing record of the development of their understandings and any misunderstandings that they may have displayed in the interview.
- Conduct the interview at a table with a piece of paper to write the number in large print and the base-ten blocks in a tub available for the children to use.

- Question students individually:
  1. Write a number on the paper, such as 137. Ask the student to read the number to you.
  2. Point to an individual digit in the number and ask the student to explain what it means. For example, point at the 3 and ask "What does this three mean?" Follow this questioning for each digit.
  3. Ask the student to use the base-ten blocks to describe the number; ask the student to explain why the block representation describes the number.
- Begin with two-digit numbers (such as 48), extending to three-digit numbers (such as 137), and, perhaps to four-digit numbers.

gathering information about students' growth in understanding of place value. Early in the second grade, students may be able to read the number, but as the year progresses, you will see that their understanding of place value is developing as they gain an ability to explain the digits by representing them with base-ten blocks. Maintaining a record of their growth is important in order to identify gaps or misunderstandings.

Besides knowing what students learned in earlier grades, teachers must look ahead to what will be expected of their students tomorrow, next month, and next year. Third-grade teachers must know what has happened in kindergarten, first grade, and second grade, as well as what will be expected of their students in later years. This broad perspective helps teachers better understand and appreciate the importance of their role. It also demands that teachers guard against gaps in learning mathematics and, whenever they are detected, fill them as best as possible.

Be aware that the gap for one student may not be a gap for another. Constantly reviewing with the whole class to ensure that *all* students understand is not appropriate. As a teacher, you will need to make many instructional decisions directed at continuing to challenge *all* your students, extending their experiences and their levels of understandings (as described in the spiral approach in Figure 2-3) rather than simply repeating them. If you maintain a record as In the Classroom 2-3, you will be able to provide the teachers in the following grade with important information about individual students so they can continue to extend the instruction for individual students.

Recommendation 4: Use Communication to Encourage Understanding

Models, manipulatives, and real-world examples provide many opportunities for thinking, talking, and listening. The importance of communication in mathematics learning is demonstrated by the fact that communication is one of the key process standards in the *NCTM Standards* (2000). Opportunities to explain, talk about mathematics, make conjectures, and defend one's thinking orally, as well as in writing, stimulate deeper understanding. Talking and writing about mathematics are essential parts of learning mathematics.

Although precision is valued in mathematics, precision in mathematical language is a product of learning; it is not necessarily a tool for learning mathematics. Teachers must be careful about pushing for too much precision in language too soon. Students at all levels should talk about mathematics before they are expected to communicate mathematics symbolically. Just as speaking precedes writing for children, so should the oral language of mathematics precede symbolization. Both student-to-student communication and student-to-teacher communication are important in the learning process.

In talking about mathematics, students are likely to provide valuable insights into their thinking and understanding. This talk may take different forms. For example, consider two second graders responding to the following question:

> Today is February 9. How many days are left in the month?

STUDENT-TO-STUDENT COMMUNICATION

WILLIAM: The answer is 21.

WHITNEY: I got 19.

WILLIAM: How did you get that?

WHITNEY: I said 9 plus 10 is 19 and 10 more is 29. That is one too many days, so it is 19. How did you get 21?

WILLIAM: I subtracted . . . [he proceeds to write

$$\begin{array}{r} 28 \\ -9 \\ \hline \end{array}$$

and then says] I messed up. I subtracted 8 from 9 instead of 9 from 28. You're right, it is 19.

This kind of talking between students is natural and provides many opportunities for explanations, justifications, and sharing of methods. Teachers may often be unaware of such conversations, but they should do all they can to stimulate and encourage student-to-student communication.

Consider now the following student–teacher interaction as a fourth-grade class is exploring primes and composite numbers by building rectangles with tiles.

STUDENT-TO-TEACHER COMMUNICATION

BOB: So every even number is composite.

TEACHER: Every even number? What about two?

This question stimulates additional thinking and encourages Bob to justify this overgeneralization.

Raising questions and challenging answers that have been proposed by students are excellent ways to stimulate thinking and talking about mathematics and create a classroom that encourages students to engage in communication. Such interaction allows students opportunities to talk about their ideas, get feedback for their thinking, and hear other points of view. Thus students learn from one another as well as from teachers.

In writing about mathematics, students provide insight into what they are thinking and what they understand. It may be helpful to write prompts to help students get started. For example,

I think the answer is . . . because . . .

Another way to do it is . . .

The thing I liked best was . . . because . . .

I still don't understand . . .

Children can and will tell you much about what they know and don't know. In the process, they are developing some important communication skills. Talking and writing about mathematics makes it more alive and more personal, thus heightening student interest. Reading and listening carefully to what is being said, as well as noticing what is *not* being said, allow you to better tailor your teaching.

Recommendation 5: Use Good Questions to Facilitate Learning

Questions are a vital element of the learning process. Students can and should ask questions of each other. Students can and should ask questions of teachers, and teachers can and should ask questions of students. Teachers need to know when to ask a question and what kinds of questions to ask. Teachers also need to know when to answer a question and when to ask another question that will facilitate answering the original question.

In theory, there are no bad questions. Some that are raised may be unnecessary because they have just been answered, but the person asking was not paying attention. Some questions may be stated poorly and may be misunderstood. Some questions may be more appropriate at another time. There may be times, for example, when low-level questions with a unique answer are appropriate (e.g., "What is seven times six?"). At other times, more open-ended questions are most effective ("About how many tennis balls will fit in our room?"). The attention here (and in further discussion of questions in Chapter 3) is to focus on the need for good questions that stimulate thinking and learning.

What are good questions? Good questions take a variety of different forms but are generally characterized by their potential to encourage critical thinking, establish relationships, and promote meaningful connections. Here are some examples of several different types of good generic questions that need to be an integral part of mathematics learning:

What would be a reasonable estimate for the answer?

How did you solve that problem?

Can you solve that a different way?

What is different about these solutions?

What pattern do you see?

Can you explain that a different way?

Explain how . . .

Explain why . . .

What are some possible solutions for . . . ?

What is another example of . . . ?

Are there other patterns . . . ?

What do you think would happen if . . . ?

What do you still not understand about . . . ?

How would you help someone else understand?

How is . . . related to . . . ?

How is this . . . related to . . . that we studied earlier?

How would you use this . . . to . . . ?

How does . . . affect . . . ?

How are . . . and . . . similar?

How are . . . and . . . different?

All of these questions are appropriate for either students or teachers to ask. It is important that teachers be sensitive to the need to raise good questions and encourage their students to do so as well.

Recommendation 6: Use Manipulatives to Aid Learning

Manipulative materials and models have a critical role throughout elementary school in helping students learn mathematics. By their very nature, mathematical thoughts are abstract, so any model that embodies them is imperfect and has limitations. Even though the model is not the mathematics, the model provides a context for the mathematical concept under consideration. Research shows that learning occurs best when students have a meaningful context for the mathematical knowledge and understand fundamental relationships associated with the knowledge (National Research Council, 1999). Helping children link, connect, or establish meaningful bridges from the model (context) to the mathematics is a challenge, but it is a rewarding struggle.

Suppose you were developing the concept of a circle. A plate could be used to illustrate this concept, but it would also illustrate many other mathematical concepts: area, boundary, circumference, and diameter, to name but a few. When a concept is being formed, the learner has no way of knowing which attributes characterize it. Thus irrelevant variables (e.g., design on the plate, its attractive finish, a chip or crack) may be the only things "seen." It may not be clear exactly what characterizes a circle.

Other models, such as coins or jar lids, could be introduced, but the focus might still be on the interior rather than the boundary of these models. Additional models, such as a wheel rim, a bike tire, a ring, and the core from a roll of paper towels, would reinforce the roundness associated with a circle but would also make it clear that a circle is associated with the outer edge or boundary of the models (see Figure 2-4). Research has shown that mildly attracting attention to the important attributes enhances learning, so the teacher might take a piece of chalk or a water-soluble pen and mark around the outer part of the coin or plate to highlight the circle.

The use of perceptually different models, such as those shown in Figure 2-4, is called multiple embodiment, or *multi-embodiment*. Research has shown that transfer across contexts is difficult when the concept appears in only a single context rather than in multiple contexts (National Research Council, 1999). The more different the models or contexts, the more likely the students are to extract only the common characteristics and make abstractions. It is foolhardy to make abstractions from a single model in mathematics. Multi-embodiment encourages students to abstract but to do so with

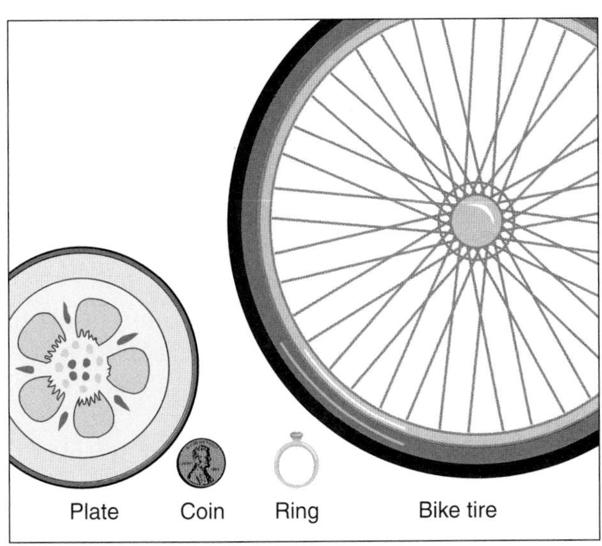

FIGURE 2-4 Some models of a circle.

discretion. It also decreases the likelihood of a mathematical concept being uniquely associated with a particular model. Such associative learning can occur whenever a single model is used to illustrate a mathematical concept.

Although research has documented the value of providing multi-embodiments, important questions remain. For example, how long should a model be used? The length of time that a model is used depends on both the student and the content. It is safe to say that, in general, too little time is spent with a model. That is, students are rushed (or dragged) too quickly through firsthand experiences with models and then confronted with symbolic representations. Students need to feel comfortable with a model and both observe and talk about the key mathematical features it embodies. Even at this stage, leaving a model doesn't mean that it will never be used again. In fact, the same model may be used at various levels throughout elementary school to develop new and/or more sophisticated concepts.

Mathematical learning depends heavily on abstraction and generalization. The multi-embodiment principle rests on the value of experiencing a mathematical concept in a variety of different physical settings. Within each embodiment, many attributes or characteristics appear. The use of *mathematical variability* ensures that, within a given embodiment, various mathematical features are allowed to change. Many different examples and nonexamples are needed before children can make generalizations.

Reconsider one of the embodiments of a circle—the plate shown in Figure 2-4—to develop the concept of a circle. In order to dispel the attention given to physical features, such as size, design, or chips, several different kinds of plates could be used. This experience with variability would attempt to refocus attention on the plate's roundness. The model is unchanged, but examples within it are varied. These changes within a given model enhance the prospects of the learners focusing on only the significant mathematical attributes.

Similarly, if rings are used, different designs, styles, and materials provide a reminder that the rings model a circle. It is also advisable to point out that some rings don't model a circle. For example, consider this "adjustable ring":

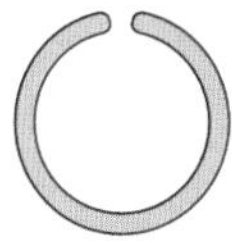

Although it is a ring, it does not model a circle because it is not a closed figure. Such *nonexamples* play an important role in concept formulation. An oval serving platter could be used with the plates to provide a nonexample within that multi-embodiment.

Research confirms that students learn more when presented with a combination of examples and nonexamples of a mathematical concept than with examples alone (Hiebert and Carpenter, 1992). Implementation of mathematical variability provides opportunities to vary examples and include nonexamples.

Recommendation 7: Encourage Students' Use of Metacognition

Metacognition refers to what one knows or believes about oneself as a learner and how one controls and adjusts one's behavior. Students need to become aware of their strengths, weaknesses, and typical behaviors and of the repertoire of procedures and strategies they use to learn and do mathematics and, more specifically, solve problems.

Metacognition is a form of looking over your own shoulder—observing yourself as you work and think about what you are thinking. Students who monitor their mathematical thinking search for understanding and strive to make sense of the mathematics being learned. Competent problem solvers are efficient at keeping track of what they know and of how well or poorly their attempt to solve a problem is proceeding. They continuously ask:

What am I doing?

Why am I doing it?

How will it help me?

A growing research base suggests that what students know or believe about themselves as mathematics learners not only greatly affects their performance but also influences their behavior as they do mathematics (Renga and Dalla, 1993).

Examples of metacognitive knowledge range from knowing that practice improves task performance and that drawing a picture often helps in understanding a problem to knowing that "I get scared when I see a word problem." Metacognitive knowledge often helps students control and adjust behavior. Thus if Sheena knows that she has frequently made keystroking errors with her calculator, she is more likely to work slowly and to check on the reasonableness of her calculator's answers.

The development of metacognition requires that children observe what they know and what they do and reflect on what they observe. Encouraging students to "think about their thinking" is an important ingredient of mathematics learning. Teachers can do several things to help students develop this metacognitive awareness:

- Be explicit about how students work when solving problems. Teachers often present complete polished solutions to students, which may hide many critical decisions made while planning the lesson. For example, consider the following questions:

  Why did you do that?

  How did you know not to use that information?

  Why did you decide to estimate?

- Teachers routinely address such questions when preparing lessons, but students are often not aware of this background. There is value in sharing some of the behind-the-scenes decision making with students.
- Point out to students various aspects of problem solving, such as:

  Some problems take a long time to solve.

  There may be more than one right answer to a problem.

  Some problems can be solved in several different ways.

  You don't have to solve problems the way the teacher does.

- Students should also be encouraged to become more aware of metacognition and the need to think about their mathematical thinking. For example, teachers might ask students to discuss the following questions:

  What mathematics problems do you like best? Tell why.

  What mathematics problems are most difficult?

  What can you do to improve as a solver of these problems?

  What do you do when you find a mathematics problem that you don't know how to do?

  What errors do you make most often in mathematics? Why do you think you make them?

Recommendation 8: Show Positive Attitudes Toward Mathematics

Students' attitudes toward mathematics are a by-product of learning and are linked to both motivation and success in mathematics. Students' values, including attitudes, are greatly influenced by teachers. Teachers who enjoy teaching mathematics and share their interest and enthusiasm for the subject tend to produce students who like mathematics (Fennema et al., 1990).

Thus if teachers' words or actions suggest that, for example, boys or students of Asian background are likely to excel in mathematics, that sends a message of diminished expectation to girls or to students who are from a different ethnic background. If it is made clear that mathematics exists in every culture and that high achievement is expected of all students regardless of race or gender, however, then a different message is sent. The power of this message of "mathematics is for everyone" is documented by research consistently confirming that teacher expectations greatly affect student performance (Koehler and Grouws, 1992).

Similarly, if the mathematics instruction places heavy emphasis on computational skills, students will view computation as important; however, if teachers reward creative solutions or approaches to problems, students will develop respect for divergent thinking. Furthermore, if teachers make it clear that critical thinking and problem solving are valued and respected, critical thinking and problem solving will be viewed as important by students. Establishing what is important and valued within each mathematics classroom not only greatly influences what is learned and how it is learned but affects students' attitudes toward mathematics as well.

Recommendation 9: Avoid Negative Experiences that Increase Anxiety

Mathematics anxiety, or "mathophobia," is a fear of mathematics or an intense negative feeling about mathematics. Some classic symptoms of mathematics anxiety (such as poor performance, misunderstandings, and dislike of mathematics) are shown in Figure 2-5. Insecurity—as well as fears of failure, punishment, ridicule, or stigmatizing labels—may reflect other negative emotions. In some students, mathematics anxiety may be reflected as a negative attitude or as a negative emotional reaction to mathematics.

Mathematics anxiety is often associated with experiences while trying to learn mathematics. Research suggests that primary-grade children are generally positive about mathematics, yet the likelihood of mathematics anxiety increases as children move into middle school and junior high school (Renga and Dalla, 1993). Students who experience mathematics anxiety tend to take less mathematics during secondary school, thereby blocking their access to many careers.

What can be done about mathematics anxiety? The following suggestions address ways to help students cope with the problem of mathematics anxiety:

- Emphasize meaning and understanding rather than memorization. Students' brains do not

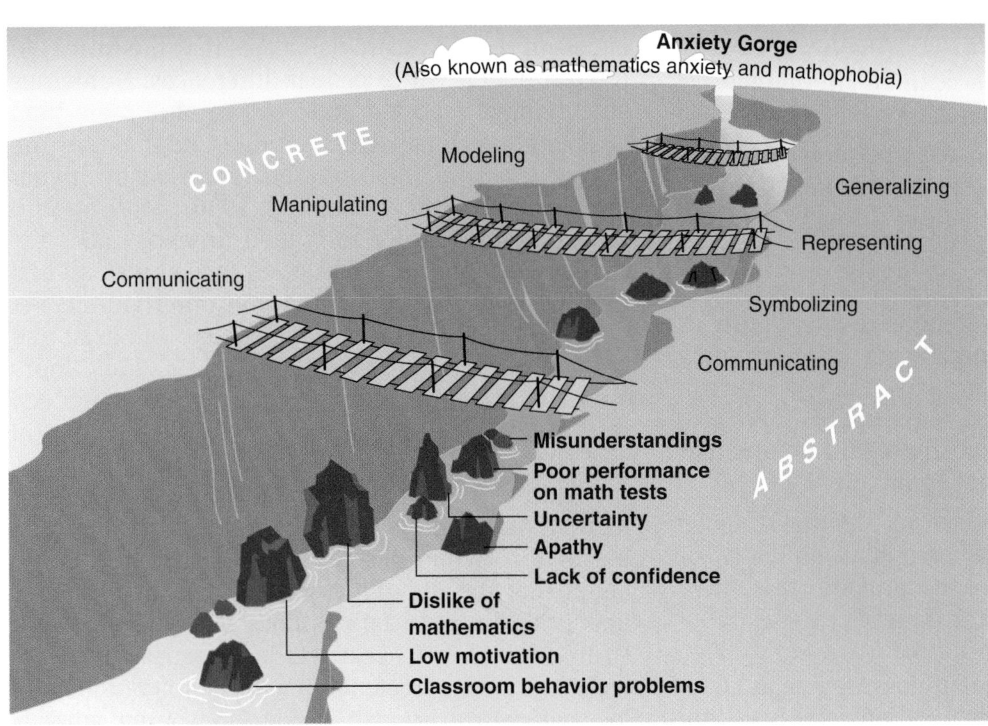

FIGURE 2-5 Bridges linking meaning to mathematics.

easily learn isolated facts, things that are not logical or that have no meaning (Caine and Caine, 1995). Mathematics learning must be characterized by sense making (i.e., the mathematics learned must make sense to the learner). Children attempting to memorize mathematics without understanding are likely to fall into the "anxiety gorge" in Figure 2-5. Helping students make connections between concrete models and either conceptual or procedural knowledge facilitates understanding and promotes greater learning success.

- Model problem-solving strategies rather than present a finished solution. Encourage students to offer suggestions and try their ideas, and see what happens. Help students realize that incorrect strategies and steps are a natural part of problem solving. Remind students that in the long run the problem-solving journey is more important than the resulting answer. This focus on the process rather than the answer helps reduce anxiety associated with "wrong" answers.
- Provide mathematical experiences that are interesting and challenging but that allow children to be successful. Self-confidence results from successful experiences in learning mathematics.
- Help all students appreciate the power, usefulness, and importance of mathematics. Make it clear that success in mathematics is for everybody, and avoid any suggestion that different mathematics expectations are associated with race or gender.
- Show an enjoyment for mathematics.
- Maintain and project a positive attitude toward mathematics and students.
- Encourage students to tell you how they feel about mathematics. What do they like? Why do they like it? This self-reflective (or metacognitive) diagnosis can help you detect symptoms of mathematics anxiety.
- Be careful not to overemphasize speed tests or drills in your classroom. Some children enjoy the challenge of competition. Others are uncomfortable with timed pressure; for these students, timed races breed apprehension and fear of mathematics.
- Use diagnostic techniques to identify students who are experiencing particular difficulty or need special help, and provide this help quickly to get them back on track.

Research indicates that unless action is taken or help provided, the level of anxiety does not lessen on its own (Hart and Walker, 1993). The best strategy is prevention, and the second best is early detection followed by some of the specific actions highlighted previously.

Recommendation 10: Treat Gender Aptitudes as Equal

A complex assortment of social forces produces or influences gender inequities related to mathematics. For example, parents of young children may express different expectations in mathematics classes for their sons than for their daughters. School counselors may subtly discourage girls from pursuing mathematical careers. Such factors may contribute to fewer girls taking advanced mathematics courses, which may prematurely foreclose, or at least delay, options for careers in mathematics, science, and technical fields.

Research suggests that teachers may actually treat boys differently from girls in the classroom. For example, teachers may call on boys more often in mathematics classes than girls, and teachers may be less likely to praise girls for correct responses and be less willing to prompt girls who give wrong answers (Ansel and Doerr, 2000). Teachers also are more likely to attribute boys' failure to a lack of motivation than they are for girls' failure. Girls may take such criticism to heart and think this is a true indicator of their talent in mathematics.

Risk taking, or the willingness of students to take a chance in answering a question of which they are not certain, may influence gender differences on tests. Research suggests that the format of the test may produce gender differences. Numerous studies have reported that boys gamble more than girls in choosing answers to questions that they are not sure of, and this may be rewarded by higher scores (Ramos and Lambating, 1996). More specifically, multiple-choice tests tend to favor males because these objective tests often focus on small bits of knowledge, require a choice of one right answer with no chance to explain the choice, and exist in a competitive environment that girls find more stressful. On the other hand, more open-ended tests favor girls because such tests are less stressful and allow for more creative, complex answers.

Although both boys and girls experience *learned helplessness*, girls are particularly susceptible to this syndrome. Learned helplessness is the belief that the individual cannot control outcomes and is destined to fail without the existence of a strong safety net. Learned helplessness includes feelings of incompetence, lack of motivation, and low self-esteem. It usually develops from what is perceived as failure or lack of success in learning, and it is often associated with mathematics. Students feel there is little sense in trying because the opportunity for success is beyond their control.

Strong efforts to confront and eliminate gender biases are reflected in the Equity Principle of the *NCTM Standards* (see Figure 1-2). Among successful actions taken by teachers to address gender inequities are the following:

- Dispelling myths (such as "mathematicians work in complete isolation" or "only white males do mathematics") that discourage women and some minorities from pursuing careers in mathematics (Henrion, 1998)
- Having equally high expectations for both boys and girls, and clearly communicating these expectations to both students and their parents
- Engaging both boys and girls in answering difficult problems, raising questions and communicating their mathematical thinking, and making sure boys don't dominate the class discussion or the teacher's time
- Calling attention to female role models in mathematics and science, as well as helping students become increasingly aware of the career opportunities for people with strong mathematics backgrounds. Some useful books are included in the Resources section to support you in finding biographies and stories about women mathematicians and scientists.
- Communicating to parents the importance of encouraging and supporting their daughters to aspire to and persist in nontraditional fields, such as mathematics
- Discussing learned helplessness with people having problems, and developing ways to prevent or help remedy the situation (Renga and Dalla, 1993)
- Providing a variety of ways (e.g., different testing formats, interviews, and portfolios) to assess student performance

Recommendation 11: Work to Improve Student Retention

An important aspect of learning is *retention*. For example, if students can read a clock in class but not when they get home, their retention of this skill is so limited that it is virtually useless. Retention reflects the amount of knowledge kept, skill maintained, or problem-solving behaviors consistently exhibited.

Forgetting is a problem in all disciplines, but the cumulative nature of mathematics increases its importance. Forgetting occurs over a summer, a spring vacation, a weekend, a day, or even shorter periods. Skills and specific knowledge can be subject to dramatic changes, often decreasing from their peak during instruction. Answers to the following questions are quickly forgotten when they are not used regularly:

What is a prime number?

State the transitive property.

Skills, such as how to do the following exercises, are also quickly lost without regular maintenance:

What is the quotient of $\frac{2}{3}$ and $\frac{1}{5}$?

Use the formula for the area of a trapezoid.

Thus classroom and achievement tests often report volatile levels of performance on mathematical skills and knowledge.

Problem solving, on the other hand, is less susceptible to big declines, and performance is more stable over time. One reason is that problem solving is a complex behavior requiring several higher-level thinking processes. Such processes take time to develop, but once established, they are retained longer than other skills and often improve as time goes by.

Retention is an important goal in mathematics education. Instructional efforts must recognize the importance of retention and try to maximize it. Research suggests several ways of improving retention:

- *Meaningful learning is the best way to shore up retention.* All phases of mathematics (knowledge, skills, and problem solving) that have been developed with meaning and learned with understanding are retained longer.
- *The context in which a concept is learned provides useful links to long-term retention* (National Research Council, 1999). For example, measuring the diameter and perimeter of many different circles can facilitate exploring the perimeter or circumference of a circle. Physically measuring them and recording and observing patterns provides a link to remembering that the ratio of the circumference and diameter is constant.
- *Establishing connections in the spirit of the NCTM Standards aids long-term retention.* Connections help children see how mathematical ideas are related to each other and to the real world. Mathematical topics must not be taught in isolation as discrete topics, but rather they must be developed in conjunction

with problem solving and applications in meaningful contexts. For example, in the previous discussion of the perimeter (circumference) of a circle, alerting students that the word *rim* is contained within the word *perimeter* and then connecting *rim* to a bicycle tire can help them retain the notion of perimeter. Research documents the value of establishing connections to not only gain better understanding but also to promote greater retention and recall.

- *Periodic reviews of key ideas help anchor knowledge and can contribute substantially to the retention of mathematical knowledge of children at any age.* Such maintenance is provided in the spiral development of high-quality mathematics programs. These reviews may be overt or subtle. In either case, they help remove rustiness, provide important reinforcement and refreshers that improve immediate performance, and contribute to higher levels of learning and improve retention.

A Glance at Where We've Been

Mathematics learning can and must have meaning. This statement is the cornerstone of all instructional planning and teaching.

Conceptual and procedural knowledge are essential elements of mathematics learning, but decades of research have revealed no single best path to their development. There is, however, a strong and growing research base from learning theories to guide the learning process. These theories recognize the importance of the concrete level and offer effective ways to help children learn mathematics with meaning and understanding.

Research and experience suggest that there is significant value in children constructing their own knowledge and that the teacher plays an important role in facilitating such construction. In addition to hands-on experiences, children learn from telling, explaining, clarifying, making conjectures, and reflecting on what they have done. They also learn from watching, listening, reading, following directions, imitating, and practicing. All of these experiences contribute to learning mathematics; teachers have the responsibility of deciding the proper balance of these experiences.

Mathematics learning is influenced by factors specific to the individual, such as previous experience, environmental influences, maturation, ability, and motivation. Consequently, no single comprehensive learning theory can be unequivocally applied to all students at all levels for all mathematical knowledge. Mathematics learning is a slow process that requires years of development. Many individual differences exist, and the rate of learning varies greatly among children. Given these variables, the essential role of teachers is to help children construct mathematical knowledge that is meaningful to them. In performing this role, teachers must make countless decisions to plan appropriate learning activities, establish an inviting classroom environment, and organize the classroom to ensure that all children are actively participating in experiencing, learning, abstracting, and constructing mathematics that is meaningful to them.

Things to Do: From What You've Read

1. Give an example of meaningful learning in mathematics. Then give an example of non-meaningful learning. State in your own words what distinguishes them.
2. Examine and label the examples of procedural and conceptual knowledge found on Master 2-3 in the *Helping Children Learn Mathematics Instructor's Manual* (available at the Wiley Book Companion web site, www.wiley.com/college/reys). Provide some other examples of your own to help distinguish between procedural and conceptual knowledge in mathematics.
3. Defend the statement in Figure 2-1 that triangle ABC has an area that is half the area of rectangle BEFC using the different regions in the diagram.
4. Examine the learning frameworks in Figure 2-2. Tell how the models proposed by Piaget, Bruner, and Dienes are alike. How are they different?
5. Identify the three tenets on which constructivism is based. From the *Snapshot of a Lesson*, identify evidence of these tenets in how Ms. Markle directed the lesson on mean, median, and mode.
6. State in your own words what the zone of proximal development is. Do you think it is important? Tell why.
7. What is metacognition? Examine the activity described In the Classroom 2-1. Describe how

metacognition might be used to think about your thinking during that activity.

8. List some characteristics of mathematics anxiety. Discuss how the use of learning bridges can save victims from the "anxiety gorge."
9. What are some specific actions an elementary teacher can take to better ensure gender equity?
10. Describe some specific steps that teachers can take to improve retention of mathematics learning.
11. Do you think the learning recommendations identified in this chapter are equally appropriate for elementary and middle school students? Tell why or why not.

Things to Do: Going Beyond This Book

IN THE FIELD

1. *Use In the Classroom 2-1 with a child. Did the child realize that two of the pictured boxes are the same box, just in a different position? Would it make sense to try this activity with children if blocks were not available? Why?
2. Interview several second and third graders using the directions from In the Classroom 2-3. Were all the children able to use the base-ten blocks to explain the place values? Describe the different levels of understanding that you found. Did you find that any of the children had misunderstandings about place value? Compare your results with others in your class to compile a summary of the different understandings.
3. **Classroom Manipulatives*. Identify models and manipulatives that are available to use in a mathematics classroom that you visit. Did you see them being used? If so, what models and manipulatives were being used and how?
4. **Equity in Whole-Class Lessons*. Observe a mathematics class and be sensitive to the verbal and physical clues that suggest boys are treated differently from girls. If you see evidence that boys are treated differently from girls, discuss some examples.
5. **Student Attitudes*. Ask a child some questions to learn about their attitudes and perceptions about mathematics. For example:

   If I say, "Let's do some mathematics," what would you do?

   What school subject do you like most? Are you good at it?

   Do you think knowing mathematics will help you when you grow up? Tell why.

   Do you think your teacher liked to teach mathematics? Tell why.

   Summarize what you learned about this child's feelings about mathematics.

IN YOUR JOURNAL

6. Reflect on your own experiences learning mathematics. Describe how you learned mathematics.
7. Consider the two learning theories, behaviorism and constructivism. Describe personal experiences that suggest the influence of these theories on your learning of mathematics.
8. Select one of the 11 learning recommendations in this chapter that connects with some of your own personal experiences in learning mathematics. Discuss how your experiences influenced your learning of mathematics.

WITH ADDITIONAL RESOURCES

9. Examine an article discussing gender/race/culture as related to learning mathematics, such as Renga and Dalla (1993), Ramos and Lambating (1996), Sumrall (1995), or McLean (2002). Describe significant issues raised and implications for you as a teacher.
10. Examine one of the vignettes from the *Professional Standards for Teaching Mathematics* (NCTM, 1991). Present this vignette to your classmates, and discuss its value in helping you help children learn mathematics.
11. Obtain a publication from the Math/Science Network (Lawrence Hall of Science, University of California, Berkeley, Calif. 94720), such as *Math for Girls and Other Problem Solvers* or *Use Equals To Promote the Participation of Women in Mathematics*. Review one of their publications and share your reactions.
12. Examine the Learning Principle in the *Principles and Standards for School Mathematics* (NCTM, 2000). Describe some specific ideas

*Additional activities, suggestions, or questions are provided in *Teaching Elementary Mathematics: A Resource for Field Experiences* (Wiley, 2004).

that would be useful in planning instruction and helping children learn mathematics.

13. Examine the book *Gender Equity: Sources and Resources for Education* by Sanders, Koch, and Urso, 1997. Describe some things you can do in your teaching to help encourage girls to study mathematics.
14. Examine the NCTM Yearbook *Multicultural and Gender Equity in the Mathematics Classroom* (Trentacosta and Kenney, 1997). Read one of the articles, and then identify and discuss several specific implications for mathematics teaching.
15. Examine the book by Reimer and Reimer in *Book Nook for Children* and report how you might use this resource. Do you think this personalization helps promote more interest in learning mathematics? Do you think helping children learn more about women's contributions in mathematics is an important instructional goal? Tell why.

WITH TECHNOLOGY

16. With some classmates or children, complete the activity, The Staircase Problem, on Master 2-5 in the *Helping Children Learn Mathematics Instructor's Manual* (available at the Wiley Book Companion web site, www.wiley.com/college/reys).
17. Check the Women's Educational Equity Act (WEEA) at the Equity Resource Center web site, www.edu.org/womensequity/ for a history of Title IX, a list of publications, current articles, and other web site links. Report on something related to equity and mathematics that you find at this site.
18. Conduct a web search for the Ask Dr. Math web site. Review the questions that elementary teachers and students send for Dr. Math to answer. Do you find any evidence of mathematics anxiety in the questions that you see? Do you see a difference in the questions submitted by girls and boys?

Book Nook for Children

Hutchins, Pat. *The Doorbell Rang*. New York: Greenwillow Books, 1986.

Sharing cookies among friends introduces beginning division concepts. Victoria and Sam begin to share 12 cookies. Before they can place six cookies on each plate, the doorbell rings, and they are joined by two friends. As the doorbell continues to ring, the children must divide the cookies among 6 friends and then 12 friends. The surprise guest at the end of the book is Grandma with more cookies to be shared.

Reimer, Luetta, and Reimer, Wilbert. *Mathematicians Are People, Too: Stories from the Lives of Great Mathematicians*. (2 volumes) New York: Pearson, 1997.

Share moments of mathematical discovery experienced by famous mathematicians with your students. Use these stories to demonstrate that both males and females are mathematicians, that mathematicians come from a variety of cultures, and that the work of mathematicians is applied to many diverse fields. Use this book with children in grades 3–7 to experience the stories of great mathematics, including Pythagoras, Galileo, Pascal, Albert Einstein, and Ada Lovelace.

Resources

ANNOTATED BOOKS

Ginsburg, Herbert P., and Baron, Joyce. "Cognition: Young Children's Construction of Mathematics." In *Research Ideas for the Classroom: Early Childhood Mathematics*. (ed. Robert J. Jensen). Reston, Va.: NCTM, and New York: Macmillan, 1993, pp. 3–21.
Explore issues of how children learn and how to implement effective arithmetic instruction in the primary grades. Research on children's cognitive development, as well as studies on the formation of early numerical concepts, is examined. Ideas for establishing learning environments that are conducive to the development of a conceptual understanding of mathematics are explored.

Hiebert, James; Carpenter, Thomas P.; and Fennema, Elizabeth. *Making Sense: Teaching and Learning Mathematics With Understanding*. Portsmouth, N.H.: Heinemann, 1997.
Consider elements necessary in a classroom in order for children to learn mathematics with understanding. Explore examples of different and diverse classrooms that help clarify ways of teaching for understanding.

Koehler, Mary S., and Grouws, Douglas A. "Mathematics Teaching Practices and Their Effects." In *Handbook of Research on Mathematics Teaching and Learning*. (ed. Douglas Grouws). New York: Macmillan, 1992, pp. 115–126.
Review of research (mostly in elementary and middle-level grades) on teaching of mathematics. Discusses

critical dimensions of quality of instruction and meaningful learning.

National Council of Teachers of Mathematics. *Learning Mathematics for a New Century: 2000 Yearbook.* Reston, Va: NCTM, 2000.
This yearbook provides a variety of articles responding to important questions as we enter the twenty-first century: Where have we been? Why is mathematics education important in the twenty-first century? What is the role of technology? Where shall we go?

National Research Council. *Adding It Up: Helping Children Learn Mathematics.* Washington, D.C.: National Academy Press, 2001.
What does research indicate about teaching and learning mathematics? The conclusions and recommendations drawn from research provide targets for improving the nation's teaching and learning of mathematics. After identifying what children know about numbers by the time they arrive in school, this book explores how students learn mathematics in the elementary and middle grades.

Stigler, James W., and Hiebert, James. *The Teaching Gap: Best Ideas from the World's Teachers for Improving Education in the Classroom.* New York: Free Press, 1999. Authors describe the teaching practices of three countries (Japan, Germany, and the United States) gathered through the TIMSS video study and make recommendations to improve American classroom education.

ANNOTATED ARTICLES

Boling, Ann Neaves. "They Don't Like Math? Well, Let's Do Something." *Arithmetic Teacher,* 38 (March 1991), pp. 17–19.
Students in grade 4 say math is their favorite subject. Then what happens in grades 6 and beyond that causes students to be more likely to say that math is their least favorite subject? This article contains current ideas about the causes and what can be done to overcome the problems.

Clements, Douglas H. "(Mis?)Constructing Constructivism." *Teaching Children Mathematics,* (December 1997), pp. 198–200.
A good article that explores the meaning and myths of constructivism in teaching mathematics.

Harrington, Aidan. "Understanding Then Doing: Doing Then Understanding." *Mathematics Teaching,* 177, (December 2001), pp. 10–12.
Consider the tension between doing and understanding through the discussion of the author's problems with teaching mathematics to a group of students who are objecting to not being shown how to do the problems.

Kazemi, Elham, and Stipek, Deborah. "Promoting Conceptual Thinking in Four Upper-Elementary Mathematics Classrooms." *Elementary School Journal* 102(1), (September 2001), pp. 59–80.
Investigate classroom practices that promote conceptual mathematical thinking and how teachers can promote student participation in a classroom community where conceptual understandings are valued and developed.

Steele, Diana. "Learning Mathematical Language in the Zone of Proximal Development." *Teaching Children Mathematics,* 4 (September 1999), pp. 38–42.
Use this classroom vignette to consider how children learn mathematical language; see how Vygotsky's ideas can be put into action in the mathematics classroom.

ADDITIONAL REFERENCES

Ansel, Ellen, and Doerr, Helen. "NAEP Findings Regarding Gender: Achievement, Affect, and Instructional Experiences." In *Results from the Seventh Mathematics Assessment of the National Assessment of Educational Progress* (eds. E. A. Silver and P. A. Kenney). Reston, Va.: NCTM, 2000.

Brownell, William A. "Psychological Considerations in the Learning and the Teaching of Arithmetic." In *The Teaching of Arithmetic,* Tenth Yearbook (ed. W. D. Reeves). Reston, Va.: NCTM, 1935, pp. 1–31.

Bruner, Jerome. *Actual Minds, Possible Worlds.* Cambridge, Mass.: Harvard University Press, 1986.

Caine, Renate, and Caine, Geoffrey. "Reinventing Schools through Brain-Based Learning." *Educational Leadership,* (April 1995), pp. 43–47.

Dienes, Zoltan P. *Building Up Mathematics.* London: Hutchinson Education, 1960.

Fennema, Elizabeth; Peterson, Penelope L.; Carpenter, Thomas P.; and Lubinski, Cheryl. "Teacher Attributions and Beliefs about Girls, Boys and Mathematics." *Educational Studies in Mathematics,* 21 (February 1990), pp. 55–69.

Hart, Laurie E., and Walker, Jamie. "The Role of Affect in Teaching and Learning Mathematics." In *Research Ideas for the Classroom: Middle Grades Mathematics* (ed. Douglas T. Owens). Reston, Va.: NCTM, and New York: Macmillan, 1993, pp. 22–38.

Henrion, Claudia. *Women in Mathematics: The Addition of Difference.* Bloomington, Ind.: Indiana University Press, 1998.

Hiebert, James, and Carpenter, Thomas P. "Learning and Teaching with Understanding." In *Handbook of Research on Mathematics Teaching and Learning* (ed. Douglas Grouws). New York: Macmillan, 1992, pp. 65–97.

Hiebert, James; Carpenter, Thomas; Fuson, Karen; Murray, A.; Oliver, P. Human; and Wearne, Diane. *Designing Classrooms for Learning Mathematics with Understanding.* Portsmouth, N.H.: Heinemann Educational Books, 1997.

McLean, Deborah L. "Honoring Traditions: Making Connections with Mathematics Through Culture." *Teaching Children Mathematics,* (November 2002), pp. 184–188.

National Council of Teachers of Mathematics. *Principles and Standards for School Mathematics.* Reston, Va.: NCTM, 2000.

National Council of Teachers of Mathematics. *Professional Standards for Teaching Mathematics.* Reston, Va.: NCTM, 1991.

National Research Council. *Everybody Counts: A Report to the Nation on the Future of Mathematics Education.* Washington, D.C.: National Academy Press, 1989.

National Research Council. *How People Learn: Brain, Mind, Experience, and School.* Washington, D.C.: National Academy Press, 1999.

Piaget, Jean. *To Understand Is to Invent.* New York: Grossman, 1972.

Ramos, Ismael, and Lambating, Julia. "Risk Taking: Gender Differences and Educational Opportunity." *School Science and Mathematics,* 96(2) (February 1996), pp. 94–98.

Renga, Sherry, and Dalla, Lidwins. "Affect: A Critical Component of Mathematical Learning in Early Childhood." In *Research Ideas for the Classroom: Early*

Childhood Mathematics (ed. Robert J. Jensen). Reston, Va.: NCTM, and New York: Macmillan, 1993, pp. 22–39.

Reys, Barbara J., and Barger, Rita. "Mental Computation: Issues from the United States Perspective." In *Computational Alternatives for the 21st Century: Cross Cultural Perspectives from Japan and the United States* (eds. Robert E. Reys and Nobuhiko Nohda). Reston, Va.: NCTM, 1994, pp. 31–47.

Sanders, Jo; Koch, Janice; and Urso, Josephine. *Gender Equity Sources and Resources for Education Students.* Mahwah, N.J.: Lawrence Erlbaum, 1997.

Sumrall, William J. "Reasons for the Perceived Images of Scientists by Race and Gender of Students in Grades 1–7." *School Science and Mathematics,* 95(2) (February 1995), pp. 83–90.

Third International Mathematics and Science Study (TIMSS). *U.S. National Research Center Report No. 7.* East Lansing, Mich.: TIMSS U.S. National Research Center, Michigan State University, December 1996. http://ustimss.msu.edu/

Trentacosta, Janet, and Kenney, Margaret J. (eds.). *Multicultural and Gender Equity in the Mathematics Classroom.* 1997 Yearbook. Reston, Va.: NCTM, 1997.

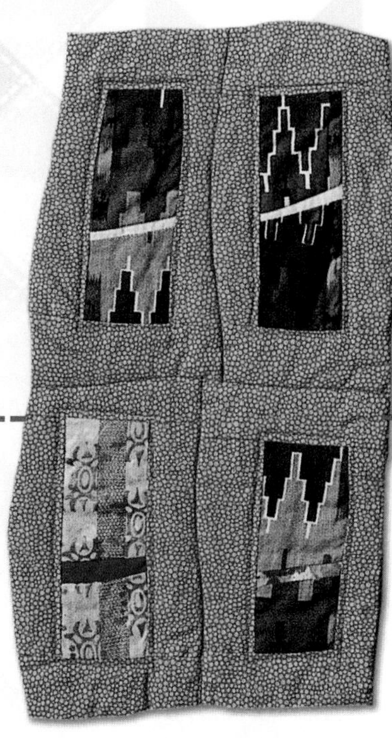

CHAPTER 3

Teaching: Your Role

Snapshot of a Lesson Plan

A typical lesson plan for a lower-grade class is framed around a children's book—*Frog and Toad are Friends: A Lost Button.*

Grade Level

pre-K to 2

Topic

Classification

Objective

Students will classify and describe objects by their attributes and determine relationships among them.

Rationale

NCTM's Pre-K–2 *Standards:* Algebra and Problem Solving—sort, classify, and order objects by size and number; Geometry and Reasoning—recognize, name, and compare two- or three-dimensional shapes and develop mathematical arguments about relationships; Communication—organize their mathematical thinking.

Theme

Book: *Frog and Toad Are Friends: A Lost Button*

Materials

Frog and Toad Are Friends: buttons of various colors, shapes, and sizes (or paper buttons or attribute blocks)

Launch

Ask children to tell about some times when they lost something. Discuss how they find things they have lost. Tell children to listen to a story about how Toad knew which button was his. Read *A Lost Button.*

Investigate

WHOLE-CLASS DISCUSSION

Initiate discussion about the story. How did Toad identify his button? Bring out the fact that attributes (characteristics) of objects help us describe something. Examples: a person—tall/short, brown/blond/black hair, male/female; a book—blue cover, paperback/hardback, small/large. Ask students to contribute similar ideas.

Talk about the buttons children are wearing on their clothing. Have them describe those buttons using four attributes: size (e.g., large, small), color, shape (e.g., round, square), and number of holes.

MODELING

Place a handful of buttons (or attribute blocks) in a pile on the overhead. Tell students to pretend Toad wants to sort the buttons into piles by their attributes. Hold up some buttons from the piles and discuss how we would describe them using the four attributes. Then show how the buttons can be sorted by size, color, shape, or number of holes. Regroup the buttons and ask students how they could be sorted another way using other attributes.

SMALL-GROUP WORK

1. A sorting game (collaborative small-group work). Divide the class into groups of four. Give each group a collection of buttons (in a cup). Two members of the group should pretend to be Frog and sort the buttons. The other two members will pretend to be Toad and guess what attribute was used to sort. Then allow the pairs to change roles.

   Circulate while the children work and check for understanding by telling students Toad is looking for a particular button (e.g., large, round, white, with two holes). Have students find buttons fitting various descriptions in their piles.
2. A hiding game (independent practice). Tell students they are going to play a Frog and Toad guessing game. Model how to play the game before they begin in their groups. One person in the group is Toad and removes a button from the pile. The other group members may ask yes/no questions to try to find what kind of button was hidden (e.g., Is it big? round? red?) Group members should take turns hiding buttons and guessing.

Summarize

Conduct a brief whole-class discussion where children share examples of what happened during their small-group work.

Gearing Down

If the sorting task seems too difficult for some students, reduce the number of attributes to three or even just two. (For example, take away all the buttons that are not round, so that shape is no longer a distinguishing attribute.)

Gearing Up

If the sorting task seems too simple for some students, place two intersecting circles of yarn on the desk (forming a Venn diagram). Have students collaborate to sort the buttons so everything in one circle has a certain attribute (e.g., large) and everything in the other circle has another attribute (e.g., red) and buttons with both attributes (large and red) are placed in the intersection of the two circles. Buttons that do not belong in either circle should be left off to the side (e.g., small, nonred circles or large blue circles). Once sorting by two intersecting sets is understood, the students can go back to taking turns having one pair sort and the other pair identify how the buttons have been sorted (what each circle represents).

Assessment

While students are playing both games, walk around and observe their participation. Note those students who can successfully identify buttons by their attributes and students who have difficulties.

References

Balka, D. *Attribute Logic Block Activities.* Oak Lawn, Ill.: Ideal School Supply Co., 1985.

Baratta-Lorton, M. *Mathematics Their Way.* Menlo Park, Calif.: Addison-Wesley, 1995.

Lobel, A. *Frog and Toad Are Friends.* New York: Harper Collins Publishers, 1970.

Introduction

Teachers play many different roles in the classroom. Think about how the work of a teacher may be compared to the work done by a counselor, gardener, police officer, parent, actor, architect, friend, guide, or cheerleader. Can you think of other metaphors to describe some of the roles that teachers play?

You may find yourself playing several of these different roles as a teacher. The roles you play depend on your personality, your school, and many other factors, including the students in your class. Consider some of the roles that the teacher writing the *Snapshot of a Lesson* played: first deciding on the focus of the lesson (objective), next choosing the task from a book the children were reading, then planning the lesson. During the lesson the teacher plans to pose the task at the overhead (see Figure 3-1), give directions, ask questions; then listen to, observe, and help students; assess understanding; and finally, assign grades (perhaps) and reflect on the success of the lesson.

This chapter focuses on the roles that all teachers must assume in the classroom: planning, teaching, assessing, and reflecting. Each of these teacher roles will be elaborated on and more fully described in subsequent chapters when you read about how to help children learn specific mathematics concepts and skills. Thus, this chapter serves as an organizer for much of what you will learn throughout the rest of this text.

Chapter 2 described research on how children learn mathematics. Growing acceptance that children actively construct their own understandings as they build new ideas on what they already know has significantly influenced how mathematics is taught in many contemporary schools. The NCTM's Teaching Principle affirms the importance of designing instruction to build on students' prior knowledge:

The Teaching Principle

Effective mathematics teaching requires understanding what students know and need to learn and then challenging and supporting them to learn it well.

NCTM, 2000, p. 16

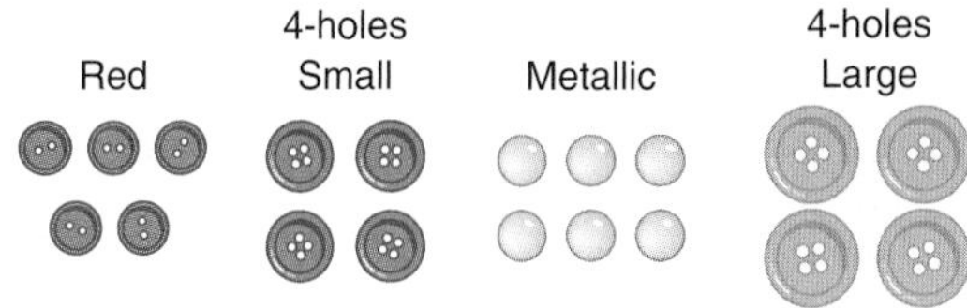

FIGURE 3-1 Buttons and their attributes.

In this chapter we make general recommendations for mathematics teaching in today's technological and global society and provide concrete suggestions for how you, as a teacher, may approach the challenges of teaching mathematics.

FOCUS QUESTIONS

1. How can you meet the needs of children through high expectations, positive environment, and equitable instruction?
2. What are the skills of an effective mathematics teacher?
3. Why does an effective elementary teacher plan mathematics lessons so carefully? What decisions must the teacher make when planning lessons?
4. What are four key strategies used to teach mathematics classes?
5. Why is the role of reflection so important for teachers?

Developing a Positive Classroom Climate

The recommendations in this chapter are based on understanding what children know, how children learn, and how teachers can support children in their mathematics learning. The following recommendations focus on developing a positive classroom climate by setting reasonable teacher expectations, developing the learning environment, and meeting the needs of all students.

Establishing Clear Expectations

Clear expectations for student behavior and achievement are necessary in a well-run elementary classroom. Students tend to do what they think the teacher means rather than what the teacher says. To provide these clear expectations, "teachers must think through what they really expect from their students and then ensure that their own behavior is consistent with those expectations" (Good and Brophy, 2000, p. 127).

Some examples of ways to establish clear expectations include the following.

- Respect and value student ideas and ways of thinking; also, expect your students to respect and value each other.
- Establish a mathematics class motto for your students: "Do only what makes sense to you." This motto encourages students to question, reflect, and seek explanations that make sense to them. It also paves the way for constructing knowledge that students find meaningful and that they understand.
- Another class motto might be: "Maybe one answer—certainly many paths." Focusing on answers places the priority on the end result. As teachers, help your students realize that processes are just as important. Probe behind the scenes to learn the paths (i.e., seek students' explanations of the thinking that led to their answers). This focus on process requires communication, which may be oral justification or notes in journals.
- Encourage children to reflect on their learning. Metacognition is an important part of the learning process. Individual reflection or interaction with others (both teachers and peers) encourages students to communicate and explain their thinking.
- Maintain high expectations for every child regardless of gender or cultural background. Make it clear that you expect all children to be successful in mathematics, and be careful to involve both boys and girls in all aspects of mathematics learning.

Setting a Positive Learning Environment

Setting a positive learning environment is concerned with the physical setting and more: "If we want students to learn to make conjectures, experiment with alternative approaches to solving problems, and construct and respond to others' mathematical arguments, then creating an environment that fosters these kinds of activities is essential" (NCTM, 1991, p. 56). The teacher is largely responsible for ensuring that an appropriate environment is established.

The following activities can help establish an appropriate environment.

- Provide a safe and intellectually stimulating environment for learning mathematics. Incorrect answers and conceptual errors are natural as children construct their mathematical knowledge. Children who are uninhibited with concerns about intuitive responses and faulty answers are more likely to observe patterns, make conjectures, engage in discussions, and take risks when doing mathematics.
- Accept the fact that confusion, partial understanding, and some frustration are a natural part of the process of learning mathematics. Not all students will learn the same things at the same time, nor will they all demonstrate the same level of proficiency. Learning mathematics is a long-term process. Sometimes progress is slow; at other times, it is reflected in moments of insight such as "I've got it!" or "Now I understand."
- Project a positive attitude toward mathematics. Children are influenced by their teachers. If a teacher has mathematics anxiety, this feeling is likely to influence students' feelings. Make it clear that you value mathematics, and help children become aware of the importance of mathematics.
- Use classroom organizations that facilitate learning. Researchers have demonstrated that whole-class instruction and cooperative small-group work are both effective ways to promote mathematics learning. The challenge for teachers is to know when and how to use these techniques effectively.

Recommendations for shifts in the classroom environment to reflect a constructivist view of how children learn mathematics are listed in Table 3-1.

Meeting the Needs of All Students

Equity of educational opportunity is one of the NCTM's fundamental principles. The NCTM's Equity Principle states that "excellence in mathematics education requires equity—high expectations and strong support for all students" (NCTM, 2000, p. 12). Similarly, the *Professional Standards for Teaching Mathematics* call for every child to have equal opportunities to learn mathematics, and state (NCTM, 1991, p. 4): "Every child" means

- Students who have been denied access in any way to educational opportunities as well as those who have not.
- Students who are African American, Hispanic, Native American, and other minorities as well as those who are considered to be a part of the majority.

Table 3-1 • Five Shifts in Classroom Environment

Mathematics Instruction Should Shift: Toward	Away From
Classrooms as mathematics communities	Classrooms as simply a collection of individuals
Logic and mathematical evidence as verification	The teacher as the sole authority for right answers
Mathematical reasoning	Mere memorizing procedures
Conjecturing, inventing, and problem solving	An emphasis on the mechanistic finding of answers
Connecting mathematics, its ideas, and its applications	Treating mathematics as a body of isolated concepts and procedures

Adapted from *Professional Standards for Teaching Mathematics* (NCTM, 1991).

- Students who are female as well as those who are male.
- Students who have not been successful in school and in mathematics as well as those who have been successful.

Throughout this book you will investigate strategies that promote this goal of equity; several references can support you (e.g., see Cuevas and Driscoll, 1993, and Koontz, 1997).

It is important to note that providing equal opportunities to learn does not necessarily mean providing exactly the same instruction. The key to equity is fairness and justice, adapting instruction appropriately for the needs of students. In an equitable mathematics classroom, the teacher (Koontz, 1997):

- Fosters a climate of openness
- Encourages student interaction and cooperation
- Demonstrates an attitude of acceptance
- Encourages students to gather and organize information
- Provides visual cues to develop cognitive strategies
- Makes connections to past concepts and applications
- Elicits the verbalization of students' reasoning
- Promotes silent reflection
- Encourages equity

As the United States becomes more culturally diverse, teachers face increased challenges and opportunities in making mathematics relevant for all students. It is important to plan lessons and activities that take into account the realities of students' daily lives, as well as to ensure that students' cultural backgrounds are reflected in the mathematics curriculum. Some useful resources for planning mathematics lessons that celebrate cultural diversity include *The Multicultural Math Classroom: Bringing in the World* (Zaslavsky, 1996) and *Multicultural Mathematics Materials* (Krause, 1983). Some interesting articles by teachers telling how they addressed issues of cultural diversity or gender equity in their classrooms include De La Cruz (1999), Karp et al. (1998), Smith et al. (1999), Tevebaugh (1998), and Zanger (1998).

If students in your classroom are at different academic levels or if they have identified learning problems or disabilities, providing equitable treatment may mean adapting instruction to meet their particular needs. To meet the needs of individual children who are learning mathematics, you must first determine what their strengths and weaknesses are, using one or more of the procedures mentioned here or using a specific diagnostic test. The results of such evaluations are used to select instructional materials, group students for instruction, adapt materials, or decide what needs to be taught or retaught to individuals and to the class (see Gearing Up and Gearing Down in the Snapshot at the beginning of this chapter). Guidelines for diagnosis in mathematics include (Driscoll, 1981):

1. Make sure that a child's apparent mathematical deficiency is really a deficiency.
2. Remember that each child progresses through several stages of development before reaching an adult conceptual level.
3. Strengthen your diagnosis with the liberal use of manipulative materials.
4. Don't lose sight of the emotional side of students in your diagnosis.
5. Be flexible and patient in piecing together an accurate picture of a child's thinking.
6. Maintain a climate of acceptance.
7. Distinguish between errors that are random (careless) and those that occur more systematically (misconceptions).

Both observations and interviews are highly effective in revealing behaviors that are not noticeable from paper-and-pencil tests; however, tests are also useful tools in diagnosis, especially when you

Nine Types of Adaptation

Size
Adapt the number of items that the learner is expected to learn or complete.

For example:
Reduce the number of social studies terms a learner must learn at any one time.

Time
Adapt the time allotted and allowed for learning, task completion, or testing.

For example:
Individualize a timeline for completing a task; pace learning differently (increase or decrease) for some learners.

Level of Support
Increase the amount of personal assistance with a specific learner.

For example:
Assign peer buddies, teaching assistants, peer tutors, or cross-age tutors.

Input
Adapt the way instruction is delivered to the learner.

For example:
Use different visual aids; plan more concrete examples; provide hands-on activities; place students in cooperative groups.

Difficulty
Adapt the skill level, problem type, or the rules on how the learner may approach the work.

For example:
Allow the use of a calculator to figure math problems; simplify task directions; change rules to accommodate learner needs.

Output
Adapt how the learner can respond to instruction.

For example:
Instead of answering questions in writing, allow a verbal response; use a journal for some students; allow students to show knowledge with hands-on materials.

Participation
Adapt the extent to which a learner is actively involved in the task.

For example:
In geography, have a student hold the globe, while others point out locations.

Alternate Goals
Adapt the goals or outcome expectations while using the same materials.

For example:
In social studies, expect one student to be able to locate just the states while others learn to locate capitals as well.

Substitute Curriculum
Provide different instruction and materials to meet a learner's individual goals.

For example:
During a language test one student is learning computer skills in the computer lab.

FIGURE 3-2 Nine types of curriculum and instruction adaptations.

(Source: Reproduced with permission from Ebeling, D., Deschenes, C., and Sprague, J. (1994). *Adapting curriculum and instruction in inclusive classrooms: Staff development kit.* Bloomington, Ind.: Institute for the Study of Developmental Disabilities, 1994.)

analyze how children reached their answers, not merely their final scores.

Effective remediation begins with effective diagnosis. Once you have a clear picture of a child's needs, you can plan activities to provide the missing prerequisites that are at the source of a difficulty, develop the understanding that has been missed, provide the practice that is needed, and give the encouragement that is so vital in effective remediation.

At times you may be able to group pupils who need help on a particular point; sometimes you may decide to adapt regular classroom instruction for the special needs of individuals; at other times you may need to work with individuals in small groups or one-on-one.

Ebeling et al. (1994) identify nine ways (see Figure 3-2) that curriculum and instruction can be adapted for students who have special needs. These students may include, for example, those who are gifted, those who have a learning disability, or those who need accommodation because of a physical handicap. Deciding which type(s) of adaptation is appropriate for a given student is a matter of the teacher's familiarity with three things: (1) the individual student and his or her special needs, (2) the activity and its subject-content demands (what is required to successfully complete the assignment), and (3) options available for adaptations, modifications, or accommodations.

Skills of the Effective Elementary Mathematics Teacher

Maintaining a Focus on Mathematics

It is extremely important when planning mathematics lessons to maintain a focus on important mathematics. Lessons can certainly be considerably enhanced by using children's literature as a springboard, by involving students in hands-on explorations or by setting problems in real-world contexts; however, the primary question when planning a lesson should be "What mathematics will the children learn from this?" rather than "Will they have fun?" It is not appropriate to use manipulative materials just as toys, to engage students in talking and writing only about their feelings (and never about the mathematics itself), or to do lessons that are just fun for fun's sake. Mathematics lessons should involve students in tasks that are mathematically rich. When children are genuinely engaged in solving mathematical problems that make sense to them, the learning they take away from that experience is likely to be deep and lasting. The *Snapshot of a Lesson Plan* provides an example of important mathematics activities focused around the *Principles and Standards for School Mathematics* (2000).

Selecting Appropriate Tasks

Appropriate tasks are "projects, questions, problems, constructions, applications, and exercises in which students engage" (NCTM, 1991, p. 20). These tasks must encourage students "to reason about mathematical ideas, to make connections, and to formulate, grapple with, and solve problems" (p. 32).

Lappan (1993) states:

> No other decision that teachers make has a greater impact on students' opportunity to learn and on their perceptions about what mathematics is than the selection or creation of the tasks with which the teacher engages the students in studying mathematics. Here the teacher is the architect, the designer of the curriculum (p. 524).

Expanding on this idea, Reys and Long (1995) suggest that good tasks:

- Are often authentic in that they come from the students' environment;
- Are challenging yet within students' reach;
- Pique the students' curiosity;
- Encourage students to make sense of mathematical ideas;
- Encourage multiple perspectives and interrelated mathematical ideas;
- Nest skill development in the context of problem solving.

In the Classroom 3-1 presents examples of two tasks. The first task can be used in an introductory lesson on adding fractions, while the second task can be used as an application for circle graphs of data.

Not only must the teacher choose appropriate tasks, but the task must be based on understanding how children learn. Elementary teachers must meet the following goals:

- Provide rich learning situations that motivate students. Interesting problems are more stimulating and effective in promoting mathematics. These situations are often driven by real-world applications that involve, connect, integrate, and use many different mathematical concepts and skills. Select a balance of problem situations to

In the Classroom 3-1

MATH TASKS!

OBJECTIVE: **Use classroom tasks to test skill development in the context of problem solving**

GRADE LEVEL: **3–4**

TASK 1: **Egg Carton Math**

▼ Egg Carton 1 has $\frac{1}{2}$ of a carton of eggs. Show how many of the egg carton cups are filled.

Egg Carton 1

▼ Egg Carton 2 has $\frac{1}{6}$ of a carton of eggs. Show how many of the egg carton cups are filled.

Egg Carton 2

▼ Combine the eggs into egg carton 3. What fraction of a whole carton of eggs is filled?

Egg Carton 3

TASK 2: **Circle graphs**

▼ Collect data on how many hours you spend doing these activities in a day. Remember there are 24 hours in a day, so the total of hours is 24.

Activity	Time spent in hours
Working in your classes at school	
Eating	
Playing with friends	
Talking to your family	
Playing sports	
Sleeping	
Other	
Total	24 hours

▼ Use the data that you collected to create a circle graph that shows how you spend your day.

appeal to different groups and involve your students in choosing the contexts. Task 2 in In the Classroom 3-1 connects to students' lives in a context that is familiar to all of them.

- Make reading and writing an integral part of mathematics. As the *Snapshot of a Lesson Plan* shows, many children's books offer starting points for mathematical thinking and rich mathematics lessons. Such books help make interdisciplinary connections that stimulate student interest and provide reminders of the power and usefulness of mathematics. These books also provide a context for a variety of rich mathematical experiences. The Book Nook for Children at the end of each chapter will help you develop a repertoire of children's books that can be used for this purpose. Writing is a natural extension of reading and of talking. Writing provides valuable insight into, as well as development of, students' thinking and communication skills.
- Establish and practice expected classroom routines, so students know how to accomplish complex mathematical tasks.
- Expect students to make sense of the tasks, to use reasoning and problem-solving techniques to explore solution strategies for the task, and to communicate effectively both solution paths and solutions to the task. In Task 1 of In the Classroom 3-1, it is important for the teacher to provide opportunities for students to work individually and in pairs, so that students can help each other make sense of the task, as well as see a variety of ways that problems may be solved.

Talking in the Mathematics Classroom

The purpose of effective classroom talk or discourse is to make certain that the classroom discussion helps students make sense of mathematics. The role of the teacher obviously involves orchestrating mathematical discourse and much, much more. The teacher is the organizer, cheerleader, and conductor of the entire process, making appropriate tools available and finding ways to help children assume major responsibility for their own learning. A flow of ideas, with interactions not only from teacher to student but also from student to teacher and student to student, using a variety of modes, is expected in order to help every child learn more mathematics (NCTM, 1991).

The following tasks can help create effective classroom talk.

- Pose questions and tasks to encourage children to talk about their mathematical thinking as well as to listen and respond to other students' ideas. Interaction among children provides them with opportunities to talk about their ideas, obtain feedback, and learn other points of view. Students can learn from one another as well as from the teacher. What key questions could you ask as part of a lesson based on Task 1 of In the Classroom 3-1?
- Expect students to communicate their thinking, to you and to other students. In addition, model and expect that your students will question and be questioned by their peers. Students must explain and justify their thinking. Explain how you would encourage students to explain and justify their thinking in accomplishing the button sort in the *Snapshot*.
- Make your mathematics class a safe place to conjecture and make mistakes. Students often learn a great deal by listening to others and analyzing mistakes. Be certain to give students the opportunity to change their minds about conjectures and possible solutions. What possible mistakes might students make in doing Task 2? How should you handle these situations?

Questioning as a Critical Part of Classroom Talk

We discussed in Chapter 2 the importance of good questions to facilitate learning. Questions can be aimed at checking children's knowledge of a fact or their ability to perform a skill. These types of questions are relatively low level. At a higher level are questions that require the analysis or synthesis of information—as when we ask a child to explain why a procedure works. In mathematics lessons, teachers often use questions of the first type and only infrequently those of the second type (Evertson et al., 1980). Although the ability to answer fact-checking, lower-level questions may be correlated with the ability of children to score high on some achievement tests, such questions give the child an erroneous picture of mathematics as involving only short answers, with one correct answer per question. Encourage children to do more talking about mathematics: why a procedure works, what would happen if something were changed in the problem, how the mathematics could be applied in a real-life situation.

As you plan a lesson, consider the types of questions you want to ask. Try to include a range of them, with more questions requiring children to think rather than merely supply a fact from memory or perform a learned procedure. (See the list of questions included in Recommendation 5 in Chapter 2.) Encourage students to make conjectures, examine the validity of their thoughts, and consider how they would convince someone else that they are right (Burns, 1985). Ask such questions as:

Who has a different solution?

Can you find another way to explain that?

Why do you think that's true?

Why doesn't Becca's answer make sense to you?

Vacc (1993) proposes three types of questions: factual, reasoning, and open questions with a wide range of acceptable answers. Her aim is in accord with the NCTM *Professional Standards* (NCTM, 1991, pp. 3–4), which look at five categories of questions that teachers should ask. For example, develop a set of questions to ask in the lesson using Task 1 of In the Classroom 3-1, based on these five categories:

1. Questions that help students work together to make sense of mathematics: "What do others think about what Janine said?" and "Can you convince the rest of us that that makes sense?"
2. Questions that help students rely more on themselves to determine whether something is mathematically correct: "Why is that true?" and "How did you reach that conclusion?"
3. Questions that seek to help students learn to reason mathematically: "How could you prove that?" and "What assumptions are you making?"
4. Questions that help students learn to conjecture, invent, and solve problems: "What would happen if . . . ?" and "Do you see a pattern?"
5. Questions that relate to helping students connect mathematics, its ideas, and its applications: "How does this relate to . . . ?" and "Have we ever solved a problem like this one before?"

Choosing Appropriate Grouping for Instruction

There are three basic patterns of grouping for mathematical instruction:

- Whole class, with teacher guidance
- Small group, either with teacher guidance or with pupil leaders
- Individuals working independently

Whole-class instruction is used extensively by many teachers, yet small-group work can mean that children work on content that is focused on their particular needs and at the same time learn to work together to solve problems. Most effective teachers use some combination of whole-class, direct instruction with small-group cooperative learning, and other student-centered modes of instruction.

Here are some guidelines to aid you in determining which grouping pattern to use.

1. Use large-group instruction:
   - If the topic can be presented to all pupils at approximately the same point in time (i.e., if all pupils have the prerequisites for understanding the initial presentation).
   - If pupils need continuous guidance from the teacher to attain the knowledge, skill, or understanding.
2. Use small-group instruction:
   - If pupils can profit from pupil-to-pupil interaction with less teacher guidance.
   - If exploration and communication about mathematics are being encouraged.
   - If cooperative learning skills and effects are being fostered.
3. Use individual instruction:
   - If pupils can follow a sequence or conduct an activity on their own.
   - If the focus is individual practice for mastery.

The kind of teaching envisioned by the *NCTM Standards* (NCTM, 1991, 2000) is probably very different from the kind of teaching you experienced. The emphasis is shifting from a teacher-directed classroom to one in which students are actively involved in learning. The teacher is, of course, still in control, but he or she involves the students through discussions and activities, usually by incorporating much small-group work. Presentations and discussions with the whole class have not disappeared, but children learn much more effectively when they work with materials to solve problems and talk about their results with each other.

Farivar and Webb (1994) point out that "Simply putting students in small groups will not guarantee that they will interact in ways that are beneficial to learning" (p. 521). They draw on extensive research to outline how students learn how to "use one another" as resources for doing mathematics by developing skills in communication, team building, small-group socialization, and helping.

Math Links 3.1

*I*f you would like to see this kind of small group work in action, you can view the video clips, "Learning about Area, Perimeter, and Fractions with and from Peers," at the NCTM Illuminations web site, which you can access from this book's web site.

Sometimes instruction should be teacher directed. This approach has been found to be particularly effective in teaching basic skills to young students and those who are slow learning or otherwise "educationally at risk" (Thornton and Wilson, 1993). These learners succeed better with structured activities, close supervision, and active, teacher-led instruction. Even so, most effective teachers use a combination of grouping patterns. For example, a teacher might develop new material with the whole class and allow children to break up for individual or small-group work during part of the period for one or more activities. The class is then brought together for a teacher-mediated discussion so that children can hear ideas from students in other groups. The teacher ends the discussion by providing closure on the lesson for the day. This method of integrating whole- and small-group work has proved more effective than direct instruction alone for developing higher-level thinking skills (Thornton and Wilson, 1993, p. 275). The *Snapshot of a Lesson Plan* shows how the teacher might mix various organizational styles in a lesson on identifying and classifying objects.

Guidelines from research that can help teachers to merge active student learning with active mathematics teaching include the following:

- Be proactive by constructing detailed long- and short-range plans and by checking prerequisite concepts or skills.
- Make students aware of the major objective(s) of the lesson.
- Spend at least half of the period developing material in a way that *actively* engages all students and emphasizes understanding.
- Involve students in important problem solving, estimation, mental math, and mathematical extensions related to the lesson.
- Communicate the expectation that, if students pay attention, they will be able to master the material.
- Be clear. Provide relevant examples and counterexamples.
- Ask many "why," "how," and other high-level questions.
- Be organized; maintain a brisk pace to foster time-on-task.
- Allow time for guided work before independent seatwork.
- Regularly assign a small amount of homework (or seatwork) to develop fluency with knowledge or skills previously mastered, to stimulate

thinking about the next day's lesson, or to provide open-ended challenges (Thornton and Wilson, 1993, p. 274).

Research has indicated the effectiveness of such student-centered learning modes as cooperative learning and peer teaching or tutoring (Thornton and Wilson, 1993). Cooperative learning involves setting a group goal and having students collaborate in groups to help each other. Those who have experienced it find that it brings a sense of relief that the burden for coming up with an answer is not solely on the individual. A student can learn *from* the group as well as contributing *to* the group, and both actions result in more positive attitudes.

The lesson might begin with the teacher meeting with the whole class to provide an overall perspective, present new material, pose problems or questions for investigation, and clarify directions for the group activity. The class then divides into small groups, usually with four members each. Students work together cooperatively in each group, discussing the problem or question, making and testing conjectures, verifying that each student is satisfied that the group answer is reasonable. For example, think about children making sense out of the button-sorting task in the *Snapshot of a Lesson Plan* at the beginning of this chapter. Some groups may want button manipulatives, whereas others may be satisfied with a picture. Students may have different ideas about which attributes are most important and need to listen to each other to decide on a mutually agreed-upon solution path. This communication of ideas with one another is especially valuable in the learning process because the students help each other learn mathematical ideas. The teacher moves from group to group, providing assistance by asking thought-provoking questions as needed (Davidson, 1990).

Despite the additional planning and class time needed for cooperative learning, it seems easy to justify the time spent when one considers the positive factors: increase in mathematical communication, the social support for learning mathematics, an opportunity for all students to experience success in mathematics, the possibility that several approaches to solving a problem might arise, and the opportunity to deal with mathematics through a discussion of meaningful problems (Fitzgerald and Bouck, 1993, pp. 251–252)

Cooperative learning may evolve to two children working together to teach each other in a peer-teaching situation. The process of teaching—of deciding how to help someone else learn—promotes the learning of both children.

Whatever the structure of the lesson—whether it is more teacher-directed or more student-centered—the teacher orchestrates the classroom discourse by "deciding when to provide information, when to clarify an issue, when to model, when to lead, and when to let students struggle with a difficulty" (NCTM, 1991, p. 35). You learn to make these decisions through planning and through experience. Research indicates that no one mode of instruction can be considered best. Teachers should learn many instructional modes and use them when appropriate. The *NCTM Standards* (2000) urge teachers to consider the goal, the task, and the students (i.e., to ask what will best help them learn).

Choosing and Using Manipulative Materials, Models, and Technological Tools

Effective teachers use models, manipulatives, and technology when appropriate to explore problems and provide experiences that help children make sense of mathematics and build their mathematical thinking. They provide a variety of different models (through multiple representations). Next, they allow children ample time to become familiar with the materials and help them construct knowledge as they make connections between the models and materials.

All through this book, we stress the importance of having children use manipulative materials to model mathematical ideas. Commonly used materials in the elementary school include chips or tiles, interlocking cubes, pattern blocks, attribute blocks, tangrams, base-ten blocks, fraction models, geoboards, measuring instruments, spinners and dice, and play money. Research indicates that lessons using manipulative materials have a higher probability of producing greater mathematical achievement than do lessons without such materials (Sowell, 1989). Handling the materials appears to help children construct mathematical ideas and retain them. Thompson (1994) points out that some discrepant findings in research stem from the fact that "concrete materials do not automatically carry meaning for students" (p. 557). Like many others, he suggests that the focus must continually be on *understanding*. Clements and McMillen (1996) are also concerned with what *concrete* means and report evidence on the value of computer manipulatives as concrete. Furthermore, research indicates that student learning is enhanced when the children connect real-world situations, manipulatives, pictures, and spoken and written symbols. Clearly, it is helpful when students are

Math Links 3.2

To try out a variety of electronic manipulatives that could be used with children, go to the National Library of Virtual Manipulatives for Interactive Mathematics web site, which you can access from this book's web site. This site includes several common manipulatives, such as base-ten blocks and fraction pies as well as graph tools, puzzles, and games.

able to "see" concepts as the result of experiencing them through the use of models.

When planning a lesson involving manipulatives, Ross and Kurtz (1993, p. 256) suggest the teacher should be certain that:

- Manipulatives have been chosen that support the lesson's objectives.
- Significant plans have been made to orient students to the manipulatives and corresponding classroom procedures.
- The lesson involves the active participation of each student.
- The lesson plan includes procedures for evaluation that reflect an emphasis on the development of reasoning skills.

One of the practical challenges a teacher faces is how to store materials so that they can be found and used easily (Suydam, 1990). Shelves and small plastic boxes (or dishpans) help to make these materials manageable. Children should be able to reach and remove things easily themselves without assistance from the teacher. It is also helpful to:

- Color code or label the materials and put a matching code or label on the storage space.
- Prepackage manipulatives into sets for one student, two students, or a small group.
- Put extra pieces into a spare parts container.
- Package sets of materials in durable individual containers, such as heavy plastic bags or transparent containers.
- Store individual sets of materials in trays, such as box lids, shallow pans, or stackable bins.

To help children who are disorganized, you might use materials with built-in organization (such as bead frames or an abacus) or materials that fit together (such as Unifix cubes), rather than separate objects such as lima beans or blocks. Or you can use containers that keep counters separated, such as egg cartons, muffin tins, or mats with clearly delineated spaces.

There is one more thing to consider: have the children pass out and collect the materials as much as possible. You don't have to do it all!

Recent increases in the availability of technology in today's homes and classrooms are having a profound effect on teaching and learning. In the fall of 1999, 95 percent of public schools were connected to the Internet (as compared with only 35 percent just five years before; National Center for Education Statistics [NCES]). Computers have become an essential tool in our society. Between 1984 and 1996, the percentage of students that reported using computers in school increased substantially, with 72 percent of the fourth graders using a computer at school at least once a week (*The Condition of Education, NCES* 1998). The NCTM has affirmed the importance of this trend with its Technology Principle: "Technology is essential in teaching and learning mathematics; it influences the mathematics that is taught and enhances students' learning" (NCTM, 2000, p. 24).

A wide variety of electronic technology can be useful in various ways in the classroom. Students use each type of computer software in a slightly different way, and the different types of software also offer different benefits to children.

Drill-and-practice software provides practice for a skill that has been previously taught. The computer presents a problem to the student, waits for an answer, and indicates whether the student is right or wrong. Some drill-and-practice programs keep records or provide a score, or they may even adjust the difficulty level of problems presented as a result of the types of responses (and errors) that the student makes.

Tutorial software actually provides instruction on new skills. It may introduce information, present examples, and provide practice. If the student either grasps the concept easily or has difficulty, the program may branch to a more difficult lesson or provide additional instruction.

Simulation software allows students to experience events or to explore environments that might otherwise be too expensive, messy, dangerous, or time-consuming to experience in the classroom.

Math Links 3.3

In addition to locating resources for students on the Web, teachers can also find resources to support their teaching. An example of this type of teacher site is MarcoPolo. This site, which you can access from this book's web site, provides standards-based Internet materials for K–12 teachers.

www.mathforum.org	Example 1: A geometry lesson and sketchpad Example 2: Link to a Java Applet in Traffic Jam
www.pbs.org/teachersource	Example 1: Use Tesselmania in a geometry lesson Example 2: Use a spreadsheet in a car wash problem
www.thegateway.org	Department of Education site with many links to lessons and units
www.enc.org/resources	Description of many resources available for the teacher
www.education.ti.com	Resources for calculator lessons

FIGURE 3-3 Web sites for teacher resources.

For example, through computer simulation, students may run a business, go on an expedition, or conduct a probability experiment (such as flipping coins or drawing randomly from a collection) with many more trials than would be feasible to conduct by hand.

Educational games engage students in fun activities that address specific educational objectives or aid in the development of logical thinking or problem-solving skills. Games usually include randomized events, offer an opportunity to "win," and present some obstacles to winning that the child must overcome.

Problem-solving programs are designed to aid in the development of higher-order problem-solving strategies. Although similar to a simulation, where students are placed in a situation in which they can manipulate variables and receive feedback, problem-solving programs do not necessarily model real-life situations. One type of problem-solving software involves programming. Students may write programs in computer languages such as Logo to instruct the computer to operate in a particular way; in the process, the students may develop logical thinking and problem-solving skills.

Finally, technology may be used as a *tool* to enhance both teaching and learning. Technology efficiently and effortlessly provides assistance with graphing, visualizing, and computing. Useful classroom technological tools include word processors, databases, spreadsheets, hypermedia, dynamic geometry software, computer microworlds, and graphing calculators. The World Wide Web offers teachers and students access to data and resources that were never before so accessible.

Figure 3-3 provides a list of web sites that offer potential resources for you to explore.

The Importance of Planning

At the heart of good teaching lies planning. Children learn best from lessons that are interesting and carefully organized, directed by thoughtful questions, and enriched by activities and materials that give them the opportunity to develop ideas about mathematics. Careful development of ideas, with clear explanations, careful questioning, and manipulative and technological materials, is particularly important in helping children learn mathematics.

Teachers plan mathematics lessons in a variety of ways. Some teachers just list the objectives they want children to attain or at least take a step toward attaining. Some jot down key questions they want to ask. Some teachers lay out the materials for children to use or run off a worksheet for the children to use. Others read the comments in the teacher's guide to the textbook. All of these approaches require teachers to think through what they plan to do.

Few teachers have the time to write out a complete, detailed plan for every mathematics lesson they teach. Some do it occasionally, when they know the idea they want to teach must be developed especially carefully. Experienced teachers often have detailed mental plans, although they may not write more than a page of sketchy notes. They may have taught a similar lesson many times before and therefore have a good sense of appropriate sequencing, timing, questioning, and potential pitfalls. For beginning teachers, however, writing detailed lesson plans is particularly important because they are not likely to have rich mental memories from teaching the lesson before. Careful planning helps make initial teaching experiences good ones, for both the children and the teacher.

Lesson plans give you the security of knowing what you will do and say, of having interesting activities and materials ready for the children's use, and of anticipating what the children might do. A detailed lesson plan also gives you a way to judge how well the lesson went. Even though you might not have been able to follow your plan precisely, it helps you evaluate your behavior and assess the actions and responses of the children. A written lesson plan also makes your plans and ideas accessible for sharing with other teachers, who can provide helpful comments and suggestions. Moreover, through writing detailed plans you learn how to plan in your head.

Planning for mathematics instruction is important for several reasons:

1. *Planning establishes definite goals and helps to ensure that all essential content is included, whether you are considering the year's work, a unit's work, or a day's work.* The purposes of each lesson are delineated clearly to help you avoid omissions and mistakes.

2. *Planning permits scheduling work in feasible units of time and in a sensible sequence.* The amount of time allotted to teaching a particular topic is determined on the basis of relative importance and relative difficulty. The sequence of topics is determined on the basis of the specific mathematics content and the developmental level of the children. Mathematics appears to be more highly sequenced than some other bodies of knowledge. For example, it is difficult to teach how to multiply with fractions before children know how to multiply with whole numbers.

On the other hand, sometimes a particular sequencing is not as crucial as it seems. For instance, for many years, it was considered mandatory to delay instruction on decimals until after instruction on whole numbers was well under way (i.e., until the intermediate grades). As children use calculators, however, they encounter decimals much earlier. With these experiences, they are able to learn decimal ideas before the intermediate grades.

Developmental level must also be considered, however. For example, a child at the concrete operations level, where ideas must be rooted in concrete illustrations and it is difficult to manipulate abstract relationships, would find it difficult (if not impossible) to learn with understanding how to find the volume of a cube from a two-dimensional drawing or picture.

3. *Planning helps to ensure that a lesson begins interestingly and involves each child, throughout the lesson.* Time is relatively flexible in most elementary schools, with no ringing of bells to signify that students are to move on to the next class. Nevertheless, there are constraints such as lunch time or another subject that must be taught. Often, however, you will be able to allow more time than you'd originally planned for a lesson in which the children are totally involved or in which they need more help in grasping an idea. Sometimes you will be able to end a lesson sooner than you'd thought because they have learned the content quickly or have had difficulty so that you need to reconsider how to teach them.

4. *Planning aids in holding the children's interest and attention, whether they are working as a total class, in small groups, or individually.* Research supports that time on task is associated with achievement gains. That is, the more time a student spends actively engaged in tasks related to the topic, the more he or she achieves on a test of that content. Thus the teacher's goal is to have the children actually working on content for as much as possible of the time available for mathematics instruction. Moreover, children who are actively involved are less likely to create discipline problems.

5. *Planning helps avoid unnecessary repetition while ensuring necessary repetition for review and practice.* In most schools, with most textbooks, you will be using a spiral approach (as described in Chapter 2), in which mathematical ideas and skills are taught at several points in a year or over a several-year period. At each encounter, a topic should be approached in more depth. As you plan, you will need to consider the extent to which your pupils are ready for another look at a topic they have previously encountered. Sometimes you may want to delay instruction on a particular topic, but be wary of scheduling all the instruction on a given topic for a single period of time. Children may need the time between to assimilate it.

Some schools take a mastery learning approach, in which children are to master each topic or skill before they go on to the next. This approach has decided advantages, not the least of which may be achievement. But mastery learning also has some disadvantages, in that children who have not yet learned a skill may be stuck at that point in the curriculum, unable to go on to new mathematical ideas with which they might be more successful. Frequently, a later topic will provide practice related to the earlier idea, and then the child learns it. Also, some educators argue against the mastery approach by observing that the level of achievement a student demonstrates one day—right after practicing a skill—may be quite different from what he or she can do a couple of days later. Thus, even if students seem to have mastered an idea or skill, it is important for them to continue to work with it in subsequent lessons. The advantage of requiring all children to master prerequisite topics before they go on to new material must be carefully weighed against the disadvantages, and efforts must be made to compensate for those disadvantages.

6. *Planning creates a feeling of confidence for you.* You know what you want to do, and your class will recognize that you are prepared. If you think about the good teachers you have had, you will

probably recognize that they were well prepared for teaching.

As Rathmell (1994) indicates:

> Planning for instruction that promotes the development of children's thinking and reasoning about mathematics not only helps them make sense of the content they are studying but also helps them learn ways of thinking that later will enable them to make sense of *new* content. (p. 290)

Levels of Planning

You must plan more than each day's mathematics lesson. At the beginning of the school year, you need to consider what you want to have the children in your class accomplish during the year. These goals are not something you must develop on your own. Most schools prepare scope-and-sequence charts or guides, or they rely on those provided with the textbook series they use. Your district or state may provide a curriculum framework for your grade level, and the NCTM's *Principles and Standards for School Mathematics* (NCTM, 2000) indicates, in broad terms, the mathematical content and processes appropriate for students at each of the grade bands (pre-K–2, 3–5, 6–8, and 9–12). (See Appendix A for these content expectations.)

You should be familiar with the *NCTM Standards,* your state education requirements, and your school's scope-and-sequence guide or chart before you do any planning. Such materials are designed to ensure that children are taught the desired range of content across grade levels. It would also be wise to check with your principal and other teachers to determine whether any changes have been made to meet the needs of children in your school and to learn how much flexibility you have in making changes for your class.

After ascertaining the goals of mathematics instruction and the order in which topics are taught, you need to consider the approximate amounts of time you want to spend on each phase of the curriculum in terms of its relative importance. This allotment helps you fit in all the mathematics content you want to include.

The goals for the year can be considered by textbook units or chapters and the specific objectives to be taught about each topic. The *NCTM Standards,* your state education requirements, and your school's curriculum guide or the textbook's planning chart can help you here and with the decision about how much time to assign to teaching each topic, which is also important. Most mathematics textbooks contain 130 to 150 lessons. Given the typical 180-day school year, you may have some opportunity to spend extra time on some topics or to teach others that are not included in the textbook.

In planning for a unit or chapter, begin by outlining, in sequence, what topics are to be taught and how much time you will spend on each. Next, outline what you want to accomplish each week, and then you are ready to develop daily lesson plans. Some schools require teachers to maintain a lesson plan book in which they note the objectives (and sometimes other details as well) for each day's lessons for a week. Even if this practice is not required, it is a good idea. It keeps you aware of progress toward the goals for the year, and it gives you a guide to follow each day. You cannot expect to follow it exactly, but it may serve as a guide, and as you plan each week, you can review the progress of the children in your class and then vary or pace the content to be taught to meet their individual needs. Or you can plan to teach different content to small groups or individuals.

Components of a Lesson Plan

The most important consideration in planning a lesson is deciding what sort of tasks the students will be doing. Students learn best when tasks are motivating and challenging, but not out of reach, and when tasks involve them in actually *thinking* about the mathematics at hand. The *Professional Standards for Teaching Mathematics* (NCTM, 1991, p. 25) suggests:

> Teachers should choose and develop tasks that are likely to promote the development of students' understanding of concepts and procedures in a way that also fosters their ability to solve problems and to reason and communicate mathematically. Good tasks are ones that do not separate mathematical thinking from mathematical concepts or skills, that capture students' curiosity, and that invite them to speculate and to pursue their hunches.

Remember to keep the importance of appropriate tasks in mind. If you do, then the following guidelines may be useful as you develop lesson plans for a particular mathematical topic:

- *State clearly the objective or objectives.* What mathematical skill or idea are you trying to teach? What do you want the children to learn? Is the purpose to introduce a new topic, develop understanding, apply concepts in a new setting, or provide review? What do the children already know? Do they have the necessary prerequisites?

- *Decide how the class is to be organized.* Should the lesson involve the total class, small groups, individual work, or some combination of these?
- *Determine the procedures to be followed.* What teaching strategy will be most effective? What type of motivation will capture the children's interest and attention? What must be reviewed to relate this lesson to previous work? What will you do and what will the children do? What questions will you ask? How will you and the children interact? What varied activities will be incorporated? What materials will you and the children use? How will the materials and activities be tailored to meet individual needs? Should practice be assigned, and if so, will it be from the textbook, from worksheets, or from a follow-up activity? Will there also be homework? What and how much? (The assignment of homework depends on school policy. You will need to find out what role homework has in your school.)
- *Decide how much time to spend on each part of the lesson.* What is the lesson's relative importance in terms of the time available, as well as the difficulty it might present to the children?
- *Decide how you will assess or evaluate—both as the lesson proceeds and after it is completed.* What should you look for during the lesson? How will you and the children know what they have learned? Will writing be involved? Will each child meet with some success during the lesson?
- *Write the plan for the lesson.* Putting your plan into writing will help you clarify many of your ideas and give you a record that can be used in evaluating the lesson and in planning subsequent lessons. Moreover, if you diverge from the plan, you will be able to pinpoint the point of divergence and return later to pick up where you left off.

Planning Different Types of Lessons

Three different structures provide variety for lessons: investigative, direct instruction, and review-teach-practice. You will probably choose to use different types of lessons on different days, depending on your goals and your students' previous experiences with the content at hand. It is important to keep in mind that within each of these lesson structures you should maintain the overarching goals of ensuring student understanding and maintaining active student involvement. It is likely that you will design many lessons that incorporate aspects of more than one of these lesson formats at the same time. A direct instruction lesson might also involve some review and practice, or an investigative lesson might also include some direct instruction. In other words, the four lesson structures should not be seen as entirely distinct. Nevertheless, it is useful to outline the general characteristics of each form.

INVESTIGATIVE LESSONS Investigative lessons are most appropriate for developing problem-solving skills, learning new concepts, or applying and deepening understanding of previously learned ideas. An investigative lesson involves students in pursuing a problem or exploration on their own. The task at hand may have been identified by the teacher or by some of the students, but the lesson itself revolves around ideas that the students generate through their own investigations of the task. Obviously, the teacher is responsible for guiding the lesson, but the students are expected to identify their own approaches, strategies, and solutions. An investigative lesson generally involves three phases: (1) launch, (2) explore or investigate, and (3) summarize (Lappan et al., 1996). The lesson plan outline in Figure 3-4 gives more information about how to organize the lesson and the *Snapshot* lesson is a variation on this type of lesson.

The *launch phase* provides motivation for the lesson and explains the problem at hand. The launch might come from a student presenting a problem that he or she has been struggling with and asking classmates to work on, too. Or the teacher might provide motivation for a task, situation, or problem by reading a children's story, sharing a newspaper clipping, playing a game, presenting a puzzle, or using any of many other motivators.

Once all the students understand the challenge, the *investigative phase* of the lesson involves students in working on it, either independently or with others. This phase of the lesson might involve learning stations, individual work, paired problem solving, or cooperative groups. Students might be using models, manipulatives, computers, calculators, or other tools. Note that in an investigative lesson, the challenge should be a true problem for the students, so it is important that you do not explain up front how to address the challenge. The students should not be simply mimicking strategies or skills that you have just shown them. Instead, they should be deciding how to get started and what to try. Your role as teacher is to let them go. You should circulate around the room, listening in on conversations, observing what individuals or groups are doing, and occasionally interjecting

Investigative/Problem-Based Lesson Plan Outline

Grade Level ______

Topic ______

Title of the lesson ______

Objective Determine the main learning outcomes you expect from your students. Decide on the context you will use (real-life examples, manipulatives, problems or puzzles, etc.)

Rationale Why are these ideas important?

Prerequisites What background do the students need prior to participating in this lesson?

Materials List all materials needed:

a. math manipulatives (and how many of each)
b. books, including page numbers (and how many of each)
c. other supplies (scissors, markers, posters, etc., and how many of each)
d. handouts—attach a copy of each

Lesson Outline (include approximate times for each segment of your lesson)

LAUNCH: Setting the Stage for the Lesson
Describe briefly how you will launch the lesson. Your aim is to motivate students to get involved in the activities to follow and to ensure that everyone understands what they are to do.

INVESTIGATE: Lesson Development
This part of the lesson may involve one continuous activity (whole class, small group, or individual), or it may be divided into several lesson segments that involve different activities. For each segment, give a step-by-step description of what you (the teacher) will be doing and what the students will be doing. In particular, provide examples of the types of questions you may ask and of any products that the students will produce. If your lesson is segmented, include approximate times for each segment and describe your plans for transitions from one segment to the next.

SUMMARIZE: Closure
Describe how you will bring the lesson development to a close. Include questions you may ask yourself and/or your students to help you know if the lesson was a success.

Gearing Down What will you do if your lesson, as planned, turns out to be too advanced for some or all students? How can the lesson be modified (on the spot) for slower students?

Gearing Up What will you do if your lesson, as planned, turns out to be too easy for some or all students? How can the lesson be modified (on the spot) for faster students?

Assessment Identify what types of data you will collect to help determine how well individual children understood the goals of your lesson and where they had trouble. Assessment data may come from a variety of sources: for example, classroom observations, written classwork (either individual or group), homework, etc. Your dual goals in planning for assessment are to be able to make appropriate follow-up instructional decisions and to be able to report on the progress of students (e.g., assign grades or write a narrative report).

References Include titles and pages of books or other references consulted in planning the lesson.

FIGURE 3-4 Investigative/Problem-Based lesson plan format.

questions or comments to help students recognize where they may be going wrong or to suggest a different approach.

During the *summarize phase* of the lesson, the class comes back together to talk about its findings. Using information you gathered from observing while the children were working independently, you orchestrate a discussion in which various groups or individuals report what they tried and what they discovered. It is important to be neither too judgmental nor too affirming about student ideas and responses. Encourage students to challenge each other's ideas. They need practice in learning how to judge when mathematical ideas are valid and when they are not. It is also important to avoid finalizing the solution to the problem prematurely. Students learn a lot from listening to each other and from hearing about alternative approaches. Your job is to encourage the students to share their ideas while maintaining control of the discussion and trying to guide it in ways that advance your curricular agenda. During the final portion of the summarize phase, it may be important to help students be explicit in stating what they have learned from the investigation. This is the appropriate point for identifying generalities or stating rules that have been formulated.

One of the most important mathematics outcomes for children is to develop their problem-solving skills. Problem solving is more thoroughly discussed in Chapters 5 and 6. Problem solving can help build a foundation for all your mathematics teaching if you consider it as you design your lessons. Problem-based lessons are a type of investigative lessons, and the general lesson plan can be applied.

DIRECT INSTRUCTION LESSONS The main difference between investigative problem-based lessons and direct instruction lessons is the central role of the teacher in directing the instruction. For example, direct instruction lessons are appropriate

Direct Instruction Lesson Plan Format

Grade Level ______

Topic ______

Title of the lesson ______

Objective Determine the main learning outcomes you expect from your students. Decide on the context you will use (real-life examples, manipulatives, problems or puzzles, etc.)

Rationale Why are these ideas important?

Prerequisites What background do students need prior to participating in this lesson?

Lesson Outline (include approximate times for each segment of your lesson)

LAUNCH: Setting the Stage for the Lesson
Describe how you will begin the lesson.
How is this lesson connected to previous lessons?

INSTRUCT: Development of the lesson

Whole-Class Teacher Instruction What concepts, definitions, formulas, algorithms, etc. will you use in your instruction?

List all examples that you will use, and order them appropriately.

Provide a list of directions for the class/individual activities to follow.

Class/Individual Activities This part of the lesson may be individual or small group. Students work on problems or exercises that follow rather closely from what they learned during your whole-class instruction.

You circulate, assisting students, answering questions, and providing extension tasks to students who finish early.

Include a copy of the task, assignment, or worksheet that students will work on.

Make a list of the questions you will be asking as you circulate.

Include several simpler problems that you may use in helping students who have trouble.

Include several more challenging problems that you may pose to early finishers.

SUMMARIZE: Closure

How will you decide whether students have learned what you wanted them to?

What sort of grades, if any, will you be able to record as a result of this lesson?

Provide an answer key for any worksheets or problem sets.

Provide a plan for documenting student progress on the objectives of the lesson.

Gearing Down What will you do if your lesson, as planned, turns out to be too advanced for some or all students? How can the lesson be modified (on the spot) for slower students?

Gearing Up What will you do if your lesson, as planned, turns out to be too easy for some or all students? How can the lesson be modified (on the spot) for faster results?

Assessment Identify what types of data you will collect to help determine how well individual children understood the goals of your lesson and where they had trouble. Assessment data may come from a variety of sources: for example, classroom observations, written classwork (either individual or group), homework, etc. Your dual goals in planning for assessment are to be able to make appropriate follow-up instructional decisions and to be able to report on the progress of students (e.g., assign grades or write a narrative report).

References Include titles and pages of books or other references consulted in planning the lesson.

FIGURE 3-5 Direct instruction lesson plan format.

when the teacher wants to communicate specific knowledge, to introduce new vocabulary, or to teach certain procedures. In a direct instruction lesson, the teacher exercises more control than in an investigative/problem-based lesson, and the lesson generally has a tighter focus.

A lesson plan for a direct instruction lesson usually consists of three major parts—launch, instruct, and summarize—each of which may be subdivided into smaller segments of various types, depending on the content of the lesson. In the first part of the lesson, the teacher introduces the students to a problem or task and the class talks together, led by the teacher, about how it might approach the problem and what previously learned concepts and skills may be brought to bear. In the second part, the teacher should not merely *show* the students how to proceed but should elicit ideas from the students while helping them move toward the concepts or skills that are the goal of the lesson. Guided practice is included during the lesson presentation phase. Afterward, the students have a chance to work with the ideas presented earlier in the lesson and to make them their own. The task during this phase should be closely related to the original task but not so similar that the students are simply copying what the teacher has just shown them. Finally, the teacher summarizes. Figure 3-5 provides a template for a direct instruction lesson plan.

REVIEW-TEACH-PRACTICE LESSONS The most familiar form of mathematics lesson, review-teach-practice, may also be one of the least effective, especially if mainly used as a means to introduce different content from that of the previous work. Most Americans are familiar with this lesson format, where the teacher begins by reviewing homework or problems worked during a previous lesson; proceeds to explaining a new concept or showing how to perform a new skill, with demonstration on sample problems; and then assigns exercises (of the same type just demonstrated) for student practice. The remainder of the lesson usually involves students practicing solving similar problems on their own while the teacher assists individual students.

The Third International Mathematics and Science Study (TIMSS) indicated that this sort of mathematics lesson is common in the United States and Germany (*Pursuing Excellence*, 1996). Unfortunately, neither Germany nor the United States performed particularly well on tests of student achievement. Many educators attribute much of this poor performance to the ineffective nature of the review-teach-practice lesson format.

By contrast, the structure of typical lessons in Japan (whose students were top TIMSS scorers) is similar to the investigative lesson: the teacher poses a thought-provoking problem and then students struggle with it and present ideas or solutions to the class, which discusses these solution methods. Then the teacher uses the discussion to highlight the key mathematical concepts before students practice similar problems.

Review-teach-practice lessons in the United States and Germany concentrate on skill acquisition, or teaching students to do something, while in Japan the typical lesson focus is on understanding mathematical concepts. U.S. and German classrooms spend more than twice as much time practicing routine procedures (although many Japanese students practice skills in paid tutoring sessions after school). Japanese students spend most of their class time inventing new solutions and being engaged in conceptual thinking about mathematics.

Analysis of TIMSS data suggests that what occurs in lessons is critical to students' learning. The specific topics taught and how these topics are presented and developed shapes what students learn and are able to do. Rather than the focused coherence seen in other countries, U.S. lessons often consist of episodic encounters between students and curricular content. Topics and concepts are presented in a fragmented and disjointed manner in which underlying themes or principles are either not identified or merely stated but not developed; however, drill-and-practice lessons are necessary for students to gain expertise and fluency.

Clearly, students need drill-and-practice in order to be able to perform a desired behavior or procedure with fluency. Just as we practice learning to walk or driving a car, we practice basic addition facts or how to multiply fractions. The choice is not if, but when. Research has long indicated that drill and practice should follow, not precede, the development of meaning (Brownell and Chazal, 1935). Research also indicates that drill-and-practice activities should not consume as much time as developmental work that helps children to understand a mathematical idea or procedure (Suydam and Weaver, 1981). Finally, children should be able to apply their knowledge in new settings.

Workbooks published to accompany textbook series provide practice on the content presented in the textbook, lesson by lesson. Whether to assign this practice material (in addition to all the practice that students get incidentally in the course of problem solving, or in addition to practice already presented in the textbook itself) is a decision you must make in terms of children's needs. Keep in mind that they must understand an idea or procedure before they are asked to practice it. On the other hand, practicing a skill that has already been mastered is boring and thus can be harmful. Therefore, it is advisable to include practice on previously learned topics as a small but regular component of each practice session.

Many games can also be used to provide practice. They offer a motivating format and a competitive aspect that many children love. An example of such a game is Bingo. By changing the rules slightly and perhaps producing specialized math bingo cards, you can make it into a game that provides practice on place value ("the number has 3 tens and 2 ones"), one of the operations ("the number is the sum of 50 and 24"), or geometric ideas ("the number of sides in a hexagon").

Other Considerations in Planning

Using the Strategic Moment

Despite careful lesson planning, teachers must make many minute-to-minute decisions. It would be sad if you did not take advantage of a situation because you had not planned for it (see Figure 3-6). Making use of teachable or strategic moments and events is imperative.

To some extent, you can encourage strategic moments by how you arrange the environment (e.g., by bringing in something new and therefore exciting). You must know what concepts you want

Several first-grade children come into the room all excited by the parade they saw yesterday, with "hundreds" and "thousands" of marchers. You've planned a lesson on measurement for that day. What do you do?

All the traffic lights in town are off. Why? The computer has failed. You've planned a lesson on multiplication with two-digit numbers. Do you discuss the computer's role in society instead?

You are teaching a lesson on estimation. You have the class use calculators to find 3762.5 × 795.6 quickly. A child asks, "Why is there no zero after the decimal point in the answer?" How do you continue the lesson on estimation?

FIGURE 3-6 Some examples of strategic moments.

to teach and how these develop for the children in your class, and then recognize the strategic moment when it arises.

Experience will also help you make the many on-the-spot decisions that are a part of teaching. You will learn what works and what doesn't. Try to define for yourself the goals you want to attain and how to attain them, and then try to work within that framework. Consider how children develop and learn. Observe the children in your class as individuals, and watch for their errors and their successes. These observations will help you diagnose their needs and plan their instruction. The better you know your children, the more ready you will be to see and grasp strategic moments and make valid decisions.

Adapting Textbook-Based Lessons

Beginning teachers often wonder how much to depend on a textbook for lesson planning. To what extent can textbook lessons be used "as is"? How and why should they be adapted for individual use? Obviously, answers to these questions depend on the textbook and how closely its goals and methods align with your own. Schmalz (1990, 1994) offers suggestions for planning with a textbook, yet maintaining the spirit of the teaching suggestions made in the *Standards.* She suggests, for instance, that the first topic to be taught need not be Chapter One of the text but instead a topic of which most of the students are unsure. Avoiding the obvious review, which seems boring to many students, is only one of her reasons. It certainly does not make sense to try to develop your own original lesson plans if you have a textbook that provides a general outline for each lesson. If you determine that the lessons are developmentally appropriate for your students and that they engage the students in genuine problem solving and conceptual development, there is no reason not to use the lessons or adapt them as seems necessary. Teachers' guides to textbooks provide a variety of ideas for teaching a lesson incorporating the textbook page. Suggestions are often given for follow-up activities, such as written work and games. Many guides also provide suggestions for remediation, enrichment, and variation for children with learning disabilities and other special needs.

In some cases, embedding textbook lessons in a motivating theme or context can considerably enhance them. The context provides an organizing framework for teaching and learning the lesson and helps tie the lesson (or several lessons) together. Contexts for lessons may be taken from real-life situations found in current events or on the calendar or developed from integrative themes tied to other subjects such as science, social studies, or children's literature. Table 3-2 shows some examples of how contexts or themes can enhance mathematics lessons.

Using Children's Literature to Motivate Mathematics Lessons

Teachers often use children's trade books to enhance lessons in language arts, social studies, science, music, art, dance, and drama, but it is also easy, effective, and appropriate to use children's literature in mathematics lessons. Notice how the *Snapshot of a Lesson Plan* that opens this chapter uses *Frog and Toad Are Friends,* a Caldecott Award–winning "I Can Read" book, as a springboard for a

Table 3-2 • Using Contexts or Themes for Planning Lessons

This Is a Context or Theme	This Is Not a Context or Theme
Sorting M&Ms for party favors gives a reason for using this manipulative.	M&Ms (alone) are a manipulative, not a context.
Planning a schedule for a class field trip involves telling time.	Time is a math topic, not a context.
Ordering carpet for classrooms in the school is a context. We need to know the area of the room to find out how much to order.	Area of rectangles is a math concept, not a context.
Measuring classroom objects to decide how to fit them into storage containers gives purpose to a lesson.	Measuring length of classroom objects doesn't give a reason for doing so.

lesson on sorting and classifying. Fiction and nonfiction books can provide "rich, authentic explorations of time and place and human experiences that make the concepts children are exploring vivid, relevant, and involving" (Whitin and Wilde, 1992, p. xi). Stories can provide children with a common starting point from which to share and discuss mathematical ideas. Mathematics and language skills develop hand-in-hand as children talk about problems and read and write about mathematical ideas.

Use of children's literature in mathematics lessons can enhance learning in many ways. Children's literature:

- Integrates mathematics into other curriculum areas.
- Provides a meaningful context for mathematics.
- Supports the art of problem posing.
- Demonstrates that mathematics develops out of human experience.
- Fosters the development of number sense.
- Addresses humanistic, affective elements of mathematics.
- Celebrates mathematics as a language.
- Restores an aesthetic dimension to mathematical learning (Whitin and Wilde, 1992).

If you want to integrate use of children's literature with a lesson on a particular mathematics topic, many teacher reference books are available

Math Links 3.4

You can also find many annotated children's book lists on the Internet. For example, go to the Eisenhower National Clearinghouse site, which you can access from this book's web site, to learn more about using children's literature in math and science and to view a list of suggested books.

to help you identify stories that work well. These books include *Math and Literature* (Grades 4–6) (Bresser, 1995); *Math and Literature* (K–3) (Burns, 1992); *Story Stretchers for the Primary Grades: Activities to Expand Children's Favorite Books* (Raines and Canady, 1992); *The Wonderful World of Mathematics: A Critically Annotated List of Children's Books in Mathematics* (Thiessen and Matthias, 1998); *How to Use Children's Literature to Teach Mathematics* (Welchman-Tischler, 1992); *Read Any Good Math Lately?* (Whitin and Wilde, 1992); and *It's the Story That Counts* (Whitin and Wilde, 1995). Suggestions for literature that may be used for particular mathematics topics are included in the Book Nook for Children at the end of each chapter in this book.

Integrating Assessment and Instruction

Assessment should be an integral aspect of mathematics instruction. Teachers need to ascertain whether they have taught what they think they have taught and whether each child has learned what they think he or she has learned. As you will read in Chapter 4, which is devoted entirely to the topic of assessment, teachers assess for several purposes (NCTM, 1995):

- To monitor student progress
- To make instructional decisions
- To evaluate students' achievement
- To evaluate their mathematics program

In the final analysis, all the assessment information teachers collect is useful as they plan lessons. They know more about the achievement and progress of each child, as well as what his or her individual needs are.

In addition, many teachers have found it helpful to keep an evaluative record of the effectiveness of their lessons. They jot down notes in their plan books or their teachers' guides about the things that went well and the things that didn't during each lesson (see Figure 3-7). They keep records of

FIGURE 3-7 A sampling of stick-on notes from a fifth-grade teacher's textbook.

activities tried, articles read, ideas they want to try, and other anecdotal records. These notes help them to plan the following year. You may think you will remember what happened, but without such notes you will probably forget.

Finally, the *Professional Teaching Standards* (1991) considers *analysis:* "the systematic reflection in which teachers engage. It entails the ongoing monitoring of classroom life—how well the tasks, discourse, and environment foster the development of every student's mathematical literacy and power" (p. 20). Such analyses are a primary source of information for planning and improving instruction during the course of a lesson and as lessons build during the year.

A Glance at Where We've Been

Among the many roles that teachers play, some of the most important involve choosing tasks; planning lessons; asking questions; listening to, observing, and helping students; assessing understanding; and assigning grades. In addition, teachers must work at identifying expectations, setting a positive learning environment, and meeting the needs of all students in order to achieve the goals of having students make sense of mathematics and be able to use appropriate mathematics in their lives outside the classroom. In order to accomplish these goals, teachers must work at developing the skills of an effective elementary mathematics teacher. Some of these skills include maintaining a focus on important mathematics, choosing appropriate tasks, managing classroom discourse, choosing appropriate grouping for instruction, and using learning tools effectively.

Planning lies at the heart of good teaching. Planning helps ensure that all essential content is included, permits scheduling the work in feasible periods of time and in a sensible sequence, helps control the pace of a lesson, aids in holding children's attention, helps avoid unnecessary repetition while ensuring necessary review and practice, and creates a feeling of confidence for you. Planning must be done for the year, the unit, and the day. Lesson plans should include clearly stated objectives, procedures, and evaluation. There are certain guidelines to aid in determining when and how to use various types of lessons (investigative/problem-based, direct instruction, and review-teach-practice) and which grouping pattern to use (large-group, small-group, or individual instruction). Knowing how to take advantage of strategic moments is also important. Finally, assessment and reflection are other integral parts of mathematics instruction.

Things to Do: From What You've Read

1. According to the NCTM's *Professional Teaching Standards,* there are five ways that mathematics instruction and classroom environments have been changing in recent years. Consider the *Snapshot of a Lesson Plan* that opens this chapter, and point out instances where planning for each of these shifts in classroom environment is evident or where they could be made more prominent.
2. Discuss the importance of high expectations for students in elementary mathematics classes. How can you set a positive learning environment in your mathematics class?
3. How can lessons be adapted for students with specific sorts of special needs?
4. Why is lesson planning important? Examine the examples of year and unit planning on Master 3-9 in the *Helping Children Learn Mathematics Instructor's Manual* (available at the Wiley Book Companion web site, www.wiley.com/college/reys). Why is it important to plan for the year and unit in addition to making daily lesson plans?
5. What must be considered as you plan a lesson? What should be included in a daily lesson plan?
6. Briefly describe the most important differences among the three different types of lessons described in this chapter. When and why would you choose to use each type?
7. Describe the five varieties of questions that teachers should be prepared to incorporate into their daily teaching activities.
8. Write a lesson plan for a lesson that you might teach.
9. Plan a follow-up activity to assess learning resulting from the lesson *Snapshot of a Lesson Plan* at the beginning of this chapter.

Things to Do: Going Beyond This Book

IN THE FIELD

1. **Analyzing Classroom Discourse.* Observe in a classroom, recording the way teacher and pupils interact. What proportion of time does the teacher talk? What types of questions are asked? What evidence is there that children have learned some mathematics? How many of the children have an opportunity to talk? Make a list of what they say (either to the class or to each other). In your opinion, is the classroom discourse about significant mathematics? Why?
2. **Grouping in the Classroom.* Consider the suggestions for planning and grouping offered by Larson (1983). Talk over these suggestions with a classroom teacher, and write a summary of the ideas you want to try in your classroom.
3. **The Learning Environment.* Read the NCTM standard on the learning environment in the *Professional Standards* (NCTM, 1991, pp. 57–61). Compare the kind of teaching portrayed there with what you recall from your elementary school experiences or what you have observed in a school recently.

IN YOUR JOURNAL

4. Reflect on your former mathematics teachers. What did they do that supported and encouraged you in learning mathematics? How did the skills of your effective teachers relate to the ideas presented in this chapter about skills of effective mathematics teachers?
5. Select and describe a lesson you think lends itself to working with children in cooperative learning groups. How do cooperative learning groups support children in this lesson?

*Additional activities, suggestions, or questions are provided in *Teaching Elementary Mathematics: A Resource for Field Experiences* (Wiley, 2004).

WITH ADDITIONAL RESOURCES

6. Compare two different scope-and-sequence charts from textbooks for a particular grade level. How does the scope of the content included differ? What proportion is the same? How does the sequence differ?
7. Select a content topic. Compare the way it is taught in two different textbooks.
8. Select a content topic. Follow its development through three grade levels in a textbook series. Trace what is review and what is new development of mathematical content.
9. Examine a textbook and the supplemental materials that accompany it to see what assistance is provided for adapting instruction for various levels of students. Are suggestions for modifying lessons included? Are there extra challenge worksheets or review sheets for students who need extra practice? How would you use these materials if your class included students with widely varying levels of understanding and skill?
10. Read one of the following articles: De La Cruz (1999), Karp et al. (1998), Smith et al. (1999), Tevebaugh (1998), or Zanger (1998). Prepare to describe to others what you learned about specific classroom-tested ways of addressing issues of diversity in the classroom.
11. Select a topic and plan a week's work for it for a particular grade level. What strategies would you use in teaching this topic and why?
12. The *Snapshot of a Lesson Plan* built a lesson around the book *Frog and Toad Are Friends.* The Book Nook For Children provides annotations of many different children's books. These annotations suggest that children's literature has a powerful role to play in teaching and learning mathematics. Use the ideas for one of the children's books to develop a lesson plan for teaching a specific topic in elementary mathematics.
13. With some classmates or children, complete the activity, Can You Find a Pattern? on Master 3-13 in the *Helping Children Learn Mathematics Instructor's Manual* (available at the Wiley Book Companion web site, www.wiley.com/college/reys.)

WITH TECHNOLOGY

14. Explore NCTM's Electronic Examples at http://standards.nctm.org/document/eexamples/. Select one of the examples and develop a lesson plan that integrates the example in the children's activities. Describe any special preparation needed in order for the lesson to be effective.
15. Collect five resources for incorporating different technologies in teaching mathematics in the elementary grades. For each, describe the technology. Select one of the ideas to write a lesson plan that describes how you will incorporate the idea in a particular class.
16. Figure 3-3 contains relatively stable web site addresses that provide examples of lesson plans for teaching elementary mathematics. Find a lesson plan that you could use with your grade level of interest. Modify the lesson plan to fit a specific classroom situation with which you have had experience.

Book Nook for Children

Bresser, Rusty. *Math and Literature (Grades 4–6).* White Plains, N.Y.: Cuisenaire, 1995.
This resource gives intermediate-grade teachers 20 lessons based on popular children's books, including *Counting on Frank, The Giraffe That Walked to Paris,* and *Jumanji.*

Crawford, Sheryl A.; Sanders, Nancy; and Girouard, Patrick. *15 Easy & Irresistible Math Mini Books,* New York: Scholastic, 2002.
Easy-to-read stories and activities that invite kids to add, subtract, measure, tell time, and practice other important early math skills.

Simmons, Karen and Guinn, Cindy. *Math, Manipulatives & Magic Wands: Manipulatives, Literature Ideas, and Hands-On Math Activities for the K-5 Classroom.* Gainesville, Fla.: Maupin House, 2001.
Students learn national math standard skills as part of literature-based hands-on projects. Projects, ideas, literature links, and blackline masters make this a good resource that enriches the language-arts block and helps you teach the language of math to all your students.

Thiessen, Diane, and Matthais, Margaret. *The Wonderful World of Mathematics: A Critically Annotated List of Children's Books in Mathematics.* Reston, Va.: NCTM, 1998.
This book reviews approximately 500 books in mathematics for preschool through grade 6. The reviews describe each book's content and accuracy and discuss whether activities for the reader are included. Each book is rated in terms of its usefulness in teaching mathematics. The

grade level of each book is included in the bibliographical entry.

Welchman-Tischler, Rosamond. *How to Use Children's Literature to Teach Mathematics.* Reston, Va.: NCTM, 1992.
This book promotes the connection between mathematics and children's literature. The first seven chapters present activities organized according to the following themes: (1) providing a context; (2) introducing manipulatives; (3) modeling a creative experience; (4) posing an interesting problem; (5) preparing for a concept or skill; (6) developing a concept or skill; and (7) providing a context for review. The eighth chapter provides a discussion of how mathematical thinking can be applied using children's literature. Twenty books for teachers and 81 books for children are listed.

Whitin, David, and Wilde, Sandra. *Read Any Good Math Lately?* Portsmouth, N.H.: Heinemann, 1992.
Stories are good ways for learners to explore the mathematics of their own lives and the lives of others. Each chapter of the book explores books on a given mathematics topic. The book ends by giving a series of mini-essays on the best of the new mathematical books for young readers and includes a "Top Twenty-Five."

Resources

ANNOTATED BOOKS

Artzt, Alice F., and Newman, Claire M. *How to Use Cooperative Learning in the Mathematics Class.* Reston, Va.: NCTM, 1990.
This book introduces new ideas and updates older methods on how to incorporate a cooperative learning approach into the K–12 mathematics classroom. Information on cooperative learning is provided with research results and strategies for using cooperative learning groups effectively in the mathematics classroom. Sample mathematics activities using cooperative groups are presented.

Davidson, Neil. *Cooperative Learning in Mathematics: A Handbook for Teachers.* Reading, Mass.: Addison-Wesley, 1990.
Small-group cooperative learning provides an alternative to both traditional whole-class expository instruction and individual instruction systems. Consider some of these realistic, practical strategies for using small groups in mathematics teaching, curriculum levels, and mathematical topic areas.

Hiebert, James; Carpenter, Thomas P.; and Fennema, Elizabeth. *Making Sense: Teaching and Learning Mathematics With Understanding.* Portsmouth, N.H.: Heinemann, 1997.
What elements are necessary to teach for understanding in mathematics? This book describes successful diverse classrooms and ideas that make sense.

Jones, Sonia, and Tanner, Howard. *Becoming a Successful Teacher of Mathematics.* New York: Routledge Falmer, 2001.
Based on research conducted with teachers in the UK, the authors encompass teaching of mathematical thinking, dealing with children's misconceptions in mathematics, using information and communication technology to enhance the teaching of mathematics, and managing and controlling the class.

Koontz, T. *Multicultural and Gender Equity in the Mathematics Classroom: The Gift of Diversity.* Reston, Va.: NCTM, 1997.
A multicultural vision of research and practice can reinforce diversity and gender equity to ensure a powerful mathematics program for all students. A variety of perspectives and diverse voices are addressed and suggest possible classroom models.

Krause, Marina C. *Multicultural Mathematics Materials.* Reston, Va.: NCTM, 1983.
Activities and games with roots in different parts of the world that can enhance your mathematics curriculum with the vitality of ethnic and cultural diversity. The materials are classified by geographic region: Africa, Asia, Oceania, Europe, the Mid-East, South America, Middle America, and North America.

Lampert, Magdalene. *Teaching Problems and the Problems of Teaching.* New Haven, Conn.: Yale University Press, 2001.
An experienced classroom teacher and noted researcher on teaching describes her fifth-grade math class through the course of a year, showing how classroom dynamics—the complex relationship of teacher, student, and content—are critical in the process of bringing each student to a deeper understanding of mathematics, or any other subject.

National Council of Teachers of Mathematics. *Professional Standards for Teaching Mathematics.* Reston, Va.: NCTM, 1991.
A dynamic vision of teaching mathematics in the early childhood grades. The approach is oriented toward fostering students' abilities to construct their own mathematics.

Raines, Shirley C., and Canady, Robert J. *Story Stretchers for the Primary Grades: Activities to Expand Children's Favorite Books.* Mt. Rainier, Md.: Gryphon House, 1992.
This book is organized around thematic units for a literature-inspired curriculum for grades 1–3. The book extends children's enthusiasm for stories and connects children's books and teaching ideas with other areas of the curriculum.

Seymour, Dale, and Beardslee, Ed, (eds.), *Critical Thinking Activities for Grades K-3.* Palo Alto, Calif.: Dale Seymour Publications, 1997.
These activities are designed around three important elements of critical thinking in mathematics: recognizing patterns, using visual imagery, and logical reasoning.

Thornton, Carol A., and Wilson, Sandra J. "Classroom Organization and Models of Instruction." In *Research Ideas for the Classroom: Early Childhood Mathematics* (ed. Robert J. Jensen). Reston, Va.: NCTM, and New York: Macmillan, 1993, pp. 269–293.
Early childhood mathematics classrooms should be places where interesting problems are explored. They should introduce children to important mathematical ideas. Read about the research that is related to the effective implementation of various instruction and

models for teaching and learning of mathematics at the primary level.

ANNOTATED ARTICLES

Bright, George W. "Understanding Children's Reasoning." *Teaching Children Mathematics,* 3 (September 1996), pp. 18–22.
Think about ways to gain information about children's thinking in a mathematics lesson. A distinction is made between probing and harassing; solution strategies of children; planning instruction on the basis of children's thinking.

Burns, Marilyn. "What I Learned from Teaching Second Grade." *Teaching Children Mathematics,* 3 (November 1996), pp. 127–134.
A second-grade mathematics teacher discusses how she created a structure for classroom learning; use of homework as a medium to inform parents about their children's mathematics learning; tactics that support learning.

De La Cruz, Yolanda. "Reversing the Trend: Latino Families in Real Partnerships with Schools." *Teaching Children Mathematics,* 5(5) (January 1999), pp. 296–300.
Parental participation in the mathematics education of Hispanic American children under the Children's MathWorlds Family Connection (CMWFC) program is discussed. Obstacles to mathematics learning are resolved by parental involvement.

Holzbert, Carol. "The Best of the Web for Teachers." *Instructor,* 10 (2), (September 2001), pp. 84–86, 88–90.
A list of web sites that can help teachers with research assignments, curriculum boosters, and class activities. The sites include gateways to learning, mathematics references, social studies references, language arts references, and science references. Each listing includes the name, the Web address, and a brief description.

Kelly, Margaret. "A Script for a Mathematics Lesson." *Arithmetic Teacher,* 38 (December 1990), pp. 36–39.
A format for sequencing instructional activities during the typical elementary mathematics class to elicit better teaching and more learning is provided as well as illustrating each component by presenting a lesson on fractions appropriate for fourth or fifth grade.

Lindquist, Mary Montgomery. "Assessing through Questioning." *Arithmetic Teacher,* 35 (January 1988), pp. 16–18.
Four different techniques for questioning are given to assess students' understanding: silent questions, oral questions, written questions, and students' questions.

Scheibelhut, Carolyn. "I Do and I Understand, I Reflect and I Improve." *Teaching Children Mathematics,* 1 (December 1994), pp. 242–246.
Integration of writing in the study and teaching of mathematics in elementary school is discussed along with the importance of reflection about and the advantages of using writing in the teaching of mathematics.

Vacc, Nancy Nesbitt. "Planning for Instruction: Barriers to Mathematics Discussion." *Arithmetic Teacher,* 41 (February 1994), pp. 339–341.
Students can communicate mathematically if given the opportunity. Read about the barriers and how you can overcome them as you plan for instruction that includes discussion.

ADDITIONAL REFERENCES

Brownell, William A., and Chazal, Charlotte B. "The Effects of Premature Drill in Third-Grade Arithmetic." *Journal of Educational Research,* 29 (September 1935), pp. 17–28.

Burns, Marilyn. "The Role of Questioning." *Arithmetic Teacher,* 32 (February 1985), pp. 14–16.

Burns, Marilyn. *Math and Literature (K–3).* White Plains, N.Y.: Cuisenaire, 1992.

Clements, Douglas H., and McMillen, Sue. "Rethinking 'Concrete' Manipulatives." *Teaching Children Mathematics,* 2 (January 1996), pp. 270–279.

Driscoll, Mark J. "Diagnosis: Taking the Mathematical Pulse." In *Research within Research: Elementary School Mathematics.* Reston, Va.: NCTM, 1981.

Evertson, C.; Emmer, E., and Brophy, J. "Predictors of effective teaching in junior high mathematics classrooms." *Journal for Research in Mathematics Education,* 11 (May 1980), pp. 167–178.

Farivar, Sydney, and Webb, Noreen M. "Helping and Getting Help—Essential Skills for Effective Group Problem Solving." *Arithmetic Teacher,* 41 (May 1994), pp. 521–525.

Fitzgerald, William M., and Bouck, Mary Kay. "Models of Instruction." In *Research Ideas for the Classroom: Middle Grades Mathematics* (ed. Douglas T. Owens). Reston, Va.: NCTM, and New York: Macmillan, 1993, pp. 244–258.

Franke, Megan, and Carey, Deborah. "Young Children's Perceptions of Mathematics in Problem-Solving Environments." *Journal of Research in Mathematics Education,* 28(1), (January, 1997), pp. 8–25.

Good, Thomas L. and Brophy, Jere E. *Looking in Classrooms,* New York: Longman, 2003 (4th ed.).

Karp, Karen; Allen, Candy; Allen, Linda G.; and Brown, Elizabeth Todd. "Feisty Females: Using Children's Literature with Strong Female Characters." *Teaching Children Mathematics,* 5(2) (October 1998), pp. 88–94.

Koehler, Mary Schatz, and Prior, Millie. "Classroom Interactions: The Heartbeat of the Teaching/Learning Process." In *Research Ideas for the Classroom: Middle Grades Mathematics* (ed. Douglas T. Owens). Reston, Va.: NCTM, and New York: Macmillan, 1993, pp. 280–298.

Lappan, Glenda. "What Do We Have and Where Do We Go from Here?" *Arithmetic Teacher,* 40 (May 1993), pp. 524–526.

Lappan, Glenda; Fey, James; Fitzgerald, William; Friel, Susan; and Phillips, Elizabeth. *Getting to Know Connected Mathematics: A Guide to the Connected Mathematics Curriculum.* White Plains, N.Y.: Dale Seymour Publications, 1996.

Larson, Carol Novillis. "Organizing for Mathematics Instruction." *Arithmetic Teacher,* 31 (September 1983), pp. 16–20.

Lobel, A. *Frog and Toad Are Friends.* New York: Harper Collins Publishers, 1970.

National Center for Education Statistics, 1996.
National Council of Teachers of Mathematics. *Principles and Standards for School Mathematics.* Reston, Va.: NCTM, 2000.

Pursuing Excellence: A Study of U.S. Eighth-Grade Mathematics and Science Teaching, Learning, Curriculum, and Achievement in International Context. Washington, D.C.:

Rathmell, Edward C. "Planning for Instruction Involves Focusing on Children's Thinking." *Arithmetic Teacher,* 41 (February 1994), pp. 290–291.

Reys, Barbara J., and Long, Vena M. "Teacher as Architect of Mathematical Tasks." *Teaching Children Mathematics,* 1 (January 1995), pp. 296–299.

Ross, Rita, and Kurtz, Ray. "Making Manipulatives Work: A Strategy for Success." *Arithmetic Teacher,* 40 (January 1993), pp. 254–257.

Sawada, Daiyo. "Mathematics as Problem Solving: A Japanese Way." *Teaching Children Mathematics,* 6 (September 1999), pp. 54–59.

Schmalz, Rosemary. "The Mathematics Textbook: How Can It Serve the Standards?" *Arithmetic Teacher,* 38 (September 1990), pp. 14–16. Reprinted in *Arithmetic Teacher,* 41 (February 1994), pp. 330–332.

Smith, Nancy L.; Babione, Carolyn; and Vick, Beverly Johns. "Dumpling Soup: Exploring Kitchens, Cultures, and Mathematics." *Teaching Children Mathematics,* 6(3) (November 1999), 148–152.

Sowell, Evelyn J. "Effects of Manipulative Materials in Mathematics Instruction." *Journal for Research in Mathematics Education,* 20 (November 1989), pp. 498–505.

Suydam, Marilyn. "Planning for Mathematics Instruction." In *Mathematics for the Young Child* (ed. Joseph N. Payne). Reston, Va.: NCTM, 1990.

Suydam, Marilyn N., and Weaver, J. Fred. *Using Research: A Key to Elementary School Mathematics.* Columbus, Ohio: ERIC Clearinghouse for Science, Mathematics and Environmental Education, 1981.

Tevebaugh, Tara N. "Mathematics Is *Not* a Universal Language." *Teaching Children Mathematics,* 5(4) (December 1998), pp. 214–216.

Third International Mathematics and Science Study (TIMSS). *U.S. National Research Center Report No. 7,* East Lansing, Mich.: TIMSS U.S. National Research Center, Michigan State University, December 1996. http://ustimss.msu.edu/

Thompson, Patrick W. "Research into Practice: Concrete Materials and Teaching for Mathematical Understanding." *Arithmetic Teacher,* 41 (May 1994), pp. 556–558.

US Department of Education. *Condition of Education.* Washington D.C.: US Dept. of Education, Office of Educational Research and Improvement, National Center for Education Statistics, 1998.

Vacc, Nancy Nesbitt. "Questioning in the Mathematics Classroom." *Arithmetic Teacher,* 41 (October 1993), pp. 88–91.

Whitin, David, and Wilde, Sandra. *It's the Story That Counts.* Portsmouth, N.H.: Heinemann, 1995.

Wood, Terry L.; Nelson, Barbra S.; and Warfield, Janet. *Beyond Classical Pedagogy: Teaching Elementary School Mathematics* (Studies in Mathematical Thinking and Learning Series). Mahwah, N.J.: Lawrence Erlbaum Associates, 2001.

Wood, Terry, and Sellers, Patricia. "Assessment of a Problem-Centered Mathematics Program: Third Grade." *Journal of Research in Mathematics in Education.* (May, 1996), 27(3), pp. 337–354.

Zanger, Virginia Vogel. "Math Storybooks." *Teaching Children Mathematics,* 5(2) (October 1998), pp. 98–102.

Zaslavsky, Claudia. *The Multicultural Math Classroom: Bringing in the World.* Portsmouth, N.H.: Heinemann, 1996.

CHAPTER 4

Assessment: Enhanced Learning and Teaching

Snapshot of a Teacher's Use of Journals

Mr. Johnston decided to use journals with his fourth-grade mathematics class. He was convinced that journals were an excellent way to assess students' thinking about and attitudes toward mathematics. He also believed there was a strong connection between students' attitudes and abilities in mathematics. He thought that a good way to get at this relationship would be to give his students a journal entry that would shed light on their dispositions toward mathematics.

During the first day of their mathematics class, Mr. Johnston made journals for his students, consisting of two pieces of construction paper with 10 pages of blank paper stapled inside. He explained that these pages were to be the students' journals. Mr. Johnston passed out the journals and asked students to decorate the covers in any way they wished. On the second day, he gave his students their first journal entry. They were to answer the questions: "What color is mathematics?" and "What is mathematics?" Students looked at him a bit perplexed, but soon began writing, and did so over the next 15 minutes.

Mr. Johnston took the journals home with him that evening to read what students had written. He was shocked at the emotions his students displayed in their writings. Here are some of their responses:

NEAL: Math is dull grays because it is boring at this point. Math is like science because science and math have a lot of writing. Math is fun and it is boring, too.

LAURA: I think math should be the color yellow if you had to pick a color because I dislike yellow and I really dislike math. When I think about math I think I HATE this and I wish I didn't have to do this because it is hard and it gives me a headache.

MARCI: The color I would give math is black because it's not interesting. It is boring. Mathematics is a lot of paperwork. It is math problems. I think math is very boring. It is not really interesting. I hate math. It means to learn something new.

ANNE: Math is the color of white and blue, which is shining and bright. And mathematics is that you have to be bright and smart. Math is something everyone should know. I think math is fun, especially geometry. Math teaches you a lot. Everything is made out of math, and it is a fun thing to do.

KATIE: I think math seems to be the color yellow because I'm bright in math. Mathematics is working with numbers. I think math is very important for when I go shopping or something like that. It means to add, subtract, divide, and multiplication. Math means that you have to memorize a lot.

JARED: Math is BLACK. Math is something that no one likes. Math is incredibly unfun.

SUMMER: The color of math to me is brown! I don't like it! Math gives me headaches for some reason and headaches make me sick and I hate it!

ALLAN: The color I give math is yellow because math is cheerful. Math is +, −, ×, ÷, $, lots of things. Math is fun and relaxing. I can do math very well and math comes easy to me.

MARY: I think the color of math is blue because sometimes it's fun and sometimes not and blue is sort of fun and sort of a boring color. Mathematics is addition, subtraction, multiplication, and division. I think about, oh great, what another boring subject. It means to learn how to get along in this world.

As Mr. Johnston read these journal entries, he knew he had his work cut out for him in this mathematics class. He decided that one of his goals for the year would be for all of his students to leave his mathematics class at the end with a positive attitude toward the subject. The journal entries helped him target the students who would be his greatest challenge!

Introduction

In previous chapters we discussed what mathematics children are expected to know and to be able to use, as well as the ways in which they learn it and how to assess their progress. Clearly, methods of assessing students need to change as a result of other changes in your methods of instruction. Alternative assessments provide teachers with opportunities to evaluate a wide range of goals and objectives in the mathematics classroom that go beyond procedural skills. Mr. Johnston's use of journals is an excellent example of how the information teachers gather through alternative forms of assessment helps them make important decisions that guide their teaching.

Many people tend to equate assessment with testing, but it is important to think more broadly. The *NCTM Standards* assert in the Assessment Principle that assessment is an integral part of mathematics instruction that contributes to all students' mathematics learning.

> **The Assessment Principle**
>
> Assessment should support the learning of important mathematics and provide useful information to teachers and students.
>
> (NCTM, 2000, p. 22)

According to the NCTM's *Assessment Standards for School Mathematics* (NCTM, 1995), assessment is "the process of gathering evidence about a student's knowledge of, ability to use, and disposition toward, mathematics and of making inferences from that evidence for a variety of purposes" (p. 3). As a teacher, you will need to plan assessments, gather evidence in many ways—such as those discussed in this chapter—interpret the evidence you collect, and use the results for a variety of purposes. Many books have been written on the subject of assessment, so what is presented in this chapter is only a brief overview of the information available. For more in-depth coverage on any of the topics surveyed here, refer to some of the references provided at the end of the chapter. Two useful books on assessment are Webb (1993) and Lambdin et al. (1996).

The NCTM's six *Assessment Standards* (1995) are short but powerful statements against which you can judge your assessment practices. The first standard focuses on the *mathematics*. You should always ask yourself if you are assessing mathematics that is important for students to learn. Although this may sound like a rhetorical question, it is not. The easiest aspects of mathematics to assess are often the most trivial. It makes no sense to assess a mathematical skill or concept just because it is easy to assess. You need to plan assessments that tap into important mathematics in ways that are meaningful to children.

The second standard asks if your assessments enhance students' opportunities for *learning* mathematics. Have you thought of tests as a way to help in the learning or as a hurdle to jump? The best assessments are integral to the learning process, not something separate. Children infer what is valued in mathematics by what is important enough to assess. For example, if problem solving is important and yet never or rarely assessed, students soon conclude that it is not an important part of their learning. The result is that they do not become problem solvers. Similarly, if cooperative learning is valued, teachers need to assess this important process so that students grow in their ability to work with each other.

There are many questions that you could ask yourself about the third standard, the *equity* standard. As you strive to help all children learn mathematics, look carefully at your assessment procedures and ask questions such as these:

- What opportunities has each student had to learn the mathematics being assessed?
- How does the assessment help students demonstrate their best work?
- How have the effects of bias been minimized throughout the assessment? (NCTM, 1995, p. 16)

These three standards and the other three (*openness, inferences, and coherence*) can be used to judge the appropriateness of a wide variety of forms of educational assessment.

Math Links 4.1

You can read more about these ideas in a full text view of the NCTM's Assessment Standards on the NCTM web site, which you can access from this book's web site.

www.wiley.com/college/reys

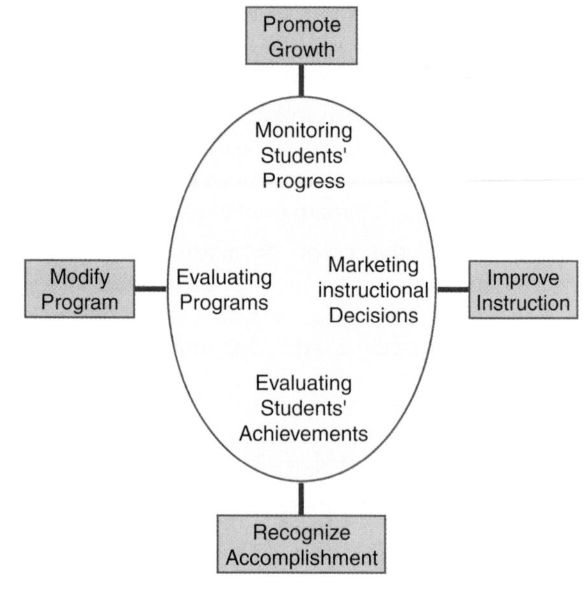

FIGURE 4-1 Four purposes of assessment and their results.

(Source: Reprinted with permission from "Assessment Standards for School Mathematics," p. 25, copyright 1995 by the National Council of Teachers of Mathematics.)

FOCUS QUESTIONS

1. What are some ways we can assess what students know and can do?
2. How do your assessments enhance and guide students' learning?
3. How do your assessments help you make instructional decisions?
4. Do your assessments provide opportunities for students to share their thinking?
5. What do your assessments communicate to students about what you value in teaching and learning mathematics?
6. How do you use multiple forms of assessment to make judgments about students?
7. How do you keep assessment records and communicate the results of assessments?

Purposes and Phases of Assessment

The NCTM's *Assessment Standards* identify four purposes of assessment and discuss the results of each different purpose (see Figure 4-1). The first three purposes of assessment (making instructional decisions, monitoring students' progress, and evaluating students' achievement) are the focus in this chapter because they are the aspects you are most likely to be involved in within the classroom.

Making Instructional Decisions

As a teacher, you will be making many instructional decisions. As with any decision, the better informed you are, the wiser are the choices you usually make. The NCTM *Assessment Standards* suggest ways that you may use assessment information differently in making instructional decisions than teachers did years ago (see Table 4-1).

One shift in assessment practices is a move toward gathering assessment data continuously rather than periodically or at the end of a chapter, when it is too late to modify your instruction. Another trend is toward using a wide variety of sources of information (rather than tests primarily). The third change is related to keeping the needs and progress of students in mind when making long-range teaching plans (rather than following a set plan of study regardless of how well students are doing).

Monitoring Student Progress

Several shifts in monitoring student progress are also called for by the NCTM *Assessment Standards* (Table 4-1). These include assessing a

Table 4-1 • Major Shifts in Assessment Practices

Toward	Away From
Shifts in Assessing to Make Instructional Decisions	
Integrating assessment with instruction	Depending on scheduled testing
Using evidence from a variety of assessment formats and contexts	Relying on any one source of information
Using evidence of every students' progress toward long-range planning goals	Planning primarily for content coverage
Shifts in Assessing to Monitor Students' Progress	
Assessing progress toward mathematical power	Assessing knowledge of specific facts and isolated skills
Communicating with students about performance in a continuous, comprehensive manner	Simply indicating right or wrong answers
Using multiple and complex assessment tools	Primary reliance on answers to brief questions on quizzes and tests
Students learning to assess their own progress	Teachers and external agencies as the sole judges of progress
Shifts in Assessing to Evaluate Students' Achievement	
Comparing students' performance with performance criteria	Comparing student with student
Assessing progress toward mathematical power	Assessing knowledge of specific facts and isolated skills
Certification based on balanced, multiple sources of information	Relying on only a few, narrowly conceived sources of evidence
Profiles of achievement based on public criteria	Single letter grades based on variable or nonpublic criteria

Adapted with permission from *Assessment Standards for School Mathematics*,

wide range of student abilities rather than focusing on testing students' factual knowledge and skills; providing more extensive and elaborated feedback to students on their progress; using a wider variety of methods for gathering information (rather than relying primarily on tests and quizzes); and involving students more in the assessment process.

Evaluating Student Achievement

Teachers today are also doing several things differently in terms of grading and certifying students' achievement (Table 4-1). One change is a move toward judging students' performance against stated criteria rather than by comparing students with one another. The second and third shifts were mentioned earlier: assessing a broad range of components of mathematical power rather than isolated skills and knowledge, and using a variety of sources for gathering assessment information. Finally, there are trends toward making achievement criteria more open and public.

The number of shifts listed in this opening section is an indication of the need for change in many of our assessment practices. This change will come through time and open minds. This chapter is an opportunity for you to begin asking yourself questions about how you will assess students in order to make decisions, monitor progress, and evaluate achievement.

Phases of Assessment

The assessment process has four phases: (1) deciding what to assess and what kind of assessment tool to use, (2) gathering evidence, (3) interpreting the evidence, and (4) using the results. In the boxes around the edge of Figure 4-1, you see how the results of an assessment may be used differently, depending on the reason for undertaking the assessment. If the purpose of your assessment is to make an instructional decision (e.g., whether to continue working on a particular concept with your students or to move on to a new topic), you are using the results of your assessment to improve instruction. By contrast, assessments undertaken to monitor students' progress generally result in actions to promote individual student growth (e.g., you might determine that a particular student could benefit from more hands-on work with fractions).

When you are planning an assessment, it is important to think about the purpose of the assessment, the methods you will use to collect data, how you will interpret the evidence you collect (e.g., how you will award points for students' written problem-solving work), and how you will summarize and use your findings. Will the outcome of your assessment be to change your lesson plans for the next week? Or will you use the information when explaining to parents what their children's strengths and weaknesses are? How you answer these questions may affect the sorts of data you decide to collect.

When you are gathering evidence, think about the variety of tasks or activities you might use and try to choose appropriately. For example, if you want to find out what your students understand about decimals, you could have them complete some worksheets on addition and subtraction of decimals. But that task might not provide you with as much information as having them show you how they could use base-ten blocks to represent an addition or subtraction problem with decimals or having them write about using base-ten blocks and draw pictures to accompany their writing.

When you are interpreting evidence, it is important to think ahead of time about the criteria you will use to judge the adequacy of responses. You should think about how you *hope* your students respond to a task or question and what sorts of difficulties or misconceptions they *might* have. What sorts of responses will you consider exemplary, adequate, or flawed? What will you consider adequate evidence of understanding?

Finally, when using results from assessments, think about how you will communicate your judgments and how they will affect future instructional decisions. For example, how well will a numeric or letter grade help your students understand where they went wrong and what they need to do differently? Can you supplement the grade with written comments? Can you find time for brief individual conferences with some of your students? How will you use what you've learned about your class, as a whole, in planning for future instruction?

Math Links 4.2

As you can see, there is much to consider when you assess your students. There are many helpful web sites that can assist you, such as the Eisenhower National Clearinghouse site, which you can access from this book's web site. This site provides strategies, resources, and articles with audio and video clips.

Ways to Assess Students' Abilities and Dispositions

There are many different ways to gather information about the abilities, dispositions, and interests of students. What type of information to collect and how to obtain it depend on the purpose for which it will be used. You first need to ask yourself what mathematics learning you want to assess.

For example, if you want to assess the principle discussed in Chapter 2—that mathematics learning should be meaningful to students—then you want to observe students and ask them questions that elicit their level of understanding, to find out whether they have attached meaning to what they are doing. If you want your students to be persistent and willing to approach problems in a variety of ways, then you need to assess these characteristics through problems of a challenging nature. If you want your students to be able to communicate well and to work well with others, as discussed in Chapter 2, then you should make those characteristics part of your assessment.

Once you have engaged your students in activities likely to elicit the behaviors that you want to judge, you need some sort of guidelines or framework to use in looking at the data you collect. For example, if you want to see how well your students can communicate about the notions of area and perimeter, you might ask them to write a letter to a younger child comparing and contrasting these two ideas and providing an example of a real-world problem using each measure. But how will you judge which student letters are better than others? You may choose to use a rubric or scoring guide.

A *rubric* or *scoring guide* is a rating scale that can be designed or adapted for use with a certain class of students or a particular task. Generally, a scoring guide is used to assign anywhere from 0 to 10 points to student work to provide a generalized rating of performance. This determination is different from awarding points when grading a quiz or test, where you generally count the number of correct answers to arrive at a score. Instead, with a rubric you look at overall performance on the task and rate that performance along a continuum.

Criteria for scoring guides are either holistic or analytic. Holistic criteria assign a single score based on the overall quality or to one aspect of the student's product or process. Holistic scoring guides are often considered to reveal general impression scores. The simplest type of holistic scoring guide

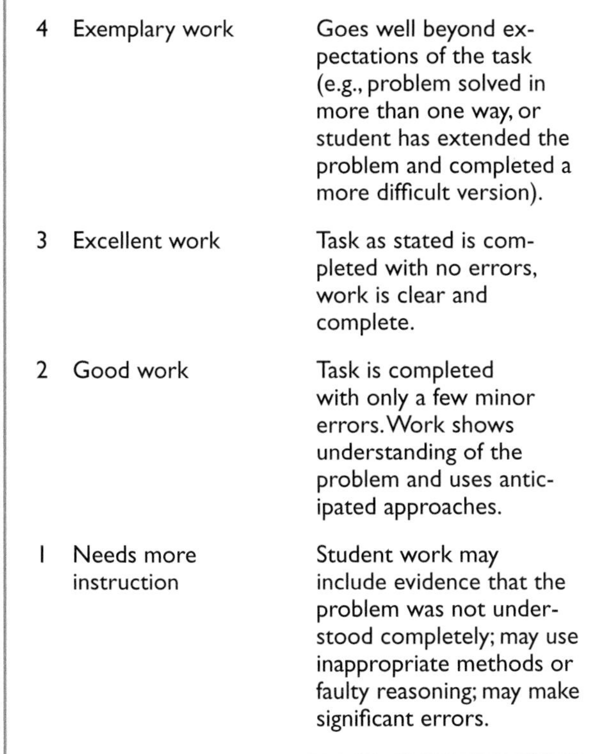

4	Exemplary work	Goes well beyond expectations of the task (e.g., problem solved in more than one way, or student has extended the problem and completed a more difficult version).
3	Excellent work	Task as stated is completed with no errors, work is clear and complete.
2	Good work	Task is completed with only a few minor errors. Work shows understanding of the problem and uses anticipated approaches.
1	Needs more instruction	Student work may include evidence that the problem was not understood completely; may use inappropriate methods or faulty reasoning; may make significant errors.

FIGURE 4-2 General holistic scoring guide for math problem solving.

may have three or four points and general descriptors of the achievement necessary to attain them. For example, you might award points for a student's problem-solving work as shown in the scoring guide in Figure 4-2. On the other hand, when analytic criteria are used in scoring guides, various dimensions or traits are scored separately. (See Figure 4-10 later in the chapter for an example of an analytic scoring guide for assessing open-ended questions.)

Another way of constructing a scoring guide is to think about sorting students' work into three piles: (1) students who do not understand the outcome (the concept or process), (2) students who are developing the outcome (but are not quite there), and (3) students who have attained the outcome and can apply it and communicate it. For any specific task, you can develop *performance indicators* to help you judge which student work to put in which categories. Ultimately, these performance indicators provide descriptions of how well the students are making sense of the mathematics.

For example, you might design a task for students to show what they know about the meaning of decimals by using base-ten blocks to build specified decimal numbers (e.g., 3 tenths or 1 and 5 hundredths) and to demonstrate decimal relationships (e.g., build 2 tenths and build 22 hundredths and explain which one is larger). Each flat block could represent a whole number, each rod a tenth, and each little cube a hundredth. In this example the student has displayed 2.46.

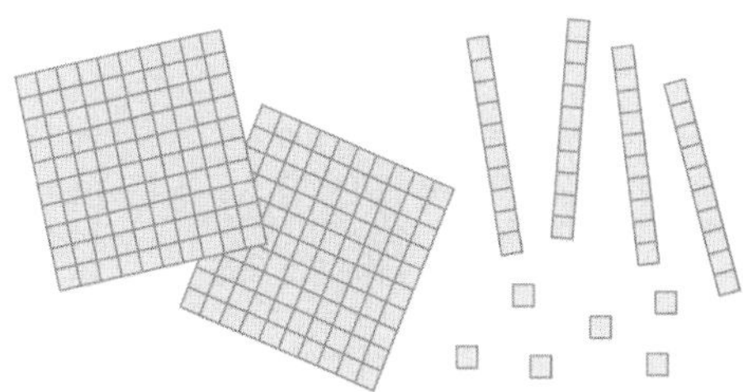

Figure 4-3 shows a three-category rubric or scoring guide with performance indicators for this task. This type of scoring guide is often called an annotated holistic rubric.

Think about a broad range of different techniques for obtaining information to assess students' learning and their dispositions according to the NCTM's vision. Scoring rubrics such as these can be adapted for use with many of these data collection techniques. As you proceed with this chapter, consider combinations of assessment methods (e.g., giving a written test and then asking individual children to explain how they arrived at the solution). What advantage might there be for using combinations of assessments? Are tests alone the most accurate method of assessing how students are making sense of mathematics?

Observation

Observing students as they work and making judgments about their performance from observation is probably one of the most commonly used assessment methods in the classroom. Yet many teachers never go one important step further: to make notes about their observations or think carefully about what they want to look for and why. Watching and listening may seem easy and commonplace, but it takes practice and planning to hone your observation skills. For example, it is helpful to plan what you will observe on a given day. Suppose you are teaching first grade and your students are solving problems involving addition facts. You may want to observe and record which students are using physical materials, which are doing most of the problems mentally, which are

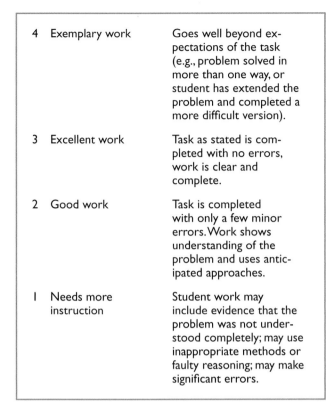

Sample Performance Indicators for a Student Who:

Does not understand	Is developing understanding	Understands
• When told to use one flat to represent a whole, cannot use blocks to show how many tenths would be equivalent to that one whole • When told to use one flat to represent a whole, cannot use blocks to show how many hundredths would be equivalent to that one whole • Has difficulty understanding that the same blocks can be used to represent different powers of 10 in different problems (may think a flat must represent 100 if earlier experiences assigned a value of 1 to each small cube)	• When told to use one flat to represent a whole, can state which block would represent one tenth (rod) and which block would represent one hundredth (little cube) • Can use blocks to show why 10 tenths and 100 hundredths are each equivalent to one whole • May interchange value of blocks when building decimals • May have difficulty building decimals with blocks, especially when the decimal includes zeros (e.g., 3.04). • May have difficulty stating what number is represented by a given collection of blocks (e.g., 5 flats, 2 rods, and 3 little cubes)	• Understands that the same blocks can be used to represent different powers of 10 in different problems • When told which block represents one, can state what number is represented by any collection of blocks • Can build, order, and compare decimal using blocks to illustrate • Can build alternative models for the same decimal (e.g., can represent 3.45 either with 3 flats, 4 rods, and 5 little cubes or with 3 flats and 45 little cubes)

FIGURE 4-3 Scoring guide with performance indicators for base-ten block task on decimals.

using thinking strategies to determine basic facts (which will be discussed in Chapter 9), and which are relying on memorized facts. At times, you may plan to observe only one student in a cooperative group setting:

> Does José jump right in or wait for others to begin?
>
> Is he willing to listen?
>
> Does he know his doubles facts? Does he know the facts that make ten?
>
> Is he able to use known facts to figure out unknown facts? If so, what strategies does he use?
>
> What sense does he make of the mathematics? Does the mathematics fit with his understanding? Is he confused by the mathematics?
>
> Does he accept or challenge the ideas of others?
>
> Is he willing to play different roles within the group?
>
> Is he persistent? Does the problem interest him?

From such observations, you can gain insight into a student's attitude and disposition toward mathematics. This knowledge, in turn, can help you plan ways to encourage strengths and work on weaknesses.

Sometimes, you may want to scan all of your students while they are engaged in tasks:

> What does the frown on Rhonda's face mean?
>
> Why is the cluster of students at the back table off the task?
>
> How is Roger attempting to arrive at an answer?
>
> Which students in the class do not appear to be grasping the new concept?

Your notes about what you have observed will certainly be useful for anecdotal records that you can use for individual assessment, for future planning, and for reporting to parents. Your observations can also help you decide what to do immediately in the classroom, while you are leading a discussion or presenting a new concept.

Some practical tips are helpful in organizing yourself for classroom observations (Beyer, 1993). Some teachers find it helpful to set aside a page in a notebook for each student or to use individual notecards in a file. But it can be clumsy to have to page through the notebook or fumble through the cards when you are walking around the room. To make observation notes easier to handle, some teachers like to tape an index card for each student in the class on a single page of heavy cardboard, with the cards overlapping as shown in Figure 4-4. When you want to write notes about a particular individual, you just flip to his or her card. When a card is full, you can file it away in that student's file and

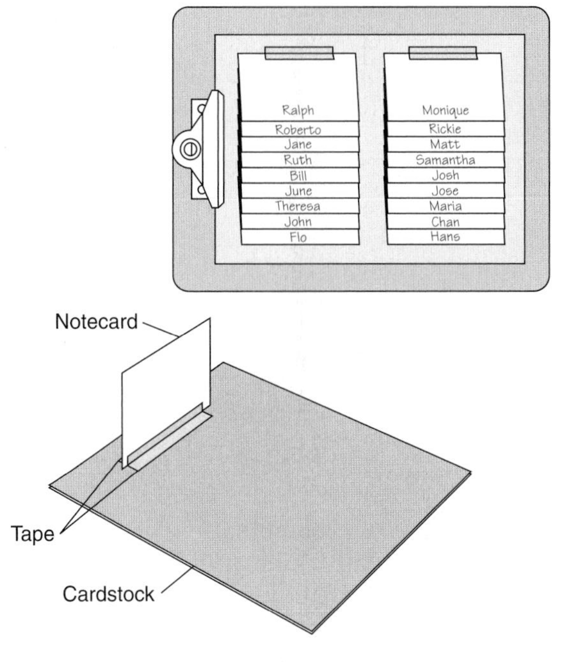

FIGURE 4-4 Flip cards for recording classroom observations. Cards can be arranged alphabetically or by classroom seat assignments, whatever will help you find the right card quickly.

replace it with a fresh card. Another handy idea is to carry a page of computer labels on your clipboard as you circulate around the class. Post-its also work well for recording insights about your students. Make notes about individual students on the labels (putting name and date on each). Later you can paste the labels into the individual students' folders or pages in your observation notebook. If you want to remember to collect data on certain students on a given day, you can write their names on labels in advance as a reminder. Whichever form or process you use, it is extremely important to remember to date your observations.

Some interesting articles about classroom observation include Beyer (1993), Chambers (1995), Cross and Hynes (1994), Ross and Kurtz (1993), and Sgroi et al. (1995).

Questioning

We discussed in Chapters 2 and 3 the value of asking questions of students to help direct their mathematical thinking. Good questioning techniques can also complement and enlighten your assessment observations. For example, suppose Rhonda was frowning during a fifth-grade class in which students were using calculators to investigate the decimal representations of fractions. The calculator has shown these results:

$$1/9 = 0.1111111$$
$$2/9 = 0.2222222$$
$$3/9 = 0.3333333$$

You know that Rhonda is a confident and capable mathematics student, so what might be the cause of the frown? In this case, a direct question to Rhonda about what is puzzling her may be appropriate. (Maybe Rhonda recognizes that the calculator is limited in how many decimal places it can represent. She may already understand that the ones and twos will repeat indefinitely in the decimal expansions for $\frac{1}{9}$ and $\frac{2}{9}$, respectively. In fact, she may already be thinking about the implications of the pattern she has observed and be bothered by extrapolating to $\frac{9}{9} = 0.9999999\ldots$, since she knows that $\frac{9}{9} = 1$ and finds it hard to believe that 1 and .9 repeating indefinitely are equal.) In other cases, asking a direct question such as "What don't you understand?" may not help because a less-confident or less-capable student may not know how to talk about what's confusing. You may need to ask a series of questions to probe for the cause.

For example, suppose Raymond thinks that $\frac{1}{9}$ is exactly equal to 0.1111111 because the calculator shows it that way. To help Raymond understand that this result is only an approximation, you may need to ask Raymond the following questions:

> What does $\frac{1}{9}$ mean? Can you show what it means by drawing a picture or performing a computation?

If Raymond responds that it means one of nine equal parts of a whole, you could proceed in this manner:

> Can you draw a sketch and label the parts with both notations (fractional and decimal)?
>
> If each part is equal to $\frac{1}{9}$, what is the total of all nine parts? Can you explain why so that your little brother could understand?
>
> If each part is equal to 0.1111111, what is the total of all nine parts? Can you explain why?
>
> Is this total exactly equal to one?
>
> Is it near to one?
>
> What do you think now about $\frac{1}{9}$ and 0.1111111? Do they represent exactly the same amount?

Alternatively, instead of responding that $\frac{1}{9}$ means one of nine parts, Raymond might respond that $\frac{1}{9}$ means one divided by nine. In that case, your questions to him should be a bit different. You might ask him to divide 1 by 9 using paper and pencil to see what happens. After working on this computation he is likely to observe that there is always a remainder no matter how many places you carry out the division. So $\frac{1}{9}$ must be represented by a decimal with ones repeating indefinitely after the decimal point.

Asking good questions is an art that needs to be developed and practiced. When you teach through questioning, you actively involve students and know more about what they are thinking. In planning your lessons, you should think of questions that will help you gauge whether students are making sense of the mathematics, whether they are approaching a problem in different ways, whether they can generalize, or whether they can explain their thinking. Limit the number of questions that can be answered yes or no or with one-word responses. For example, instead of asking "Should we add, subtract, multiply, or divide to solve this problem?" ask "What could we do to understand this problem better?" or "What sort of picture can we draw to help decide what operation to use?" As a teacher, you should also work to develop more high-level and open-response questioning, asking students to explain or defend their answers or to describe another way to solve the problem.

For example, look at the *Snapshot of a Lesson* that opens Chapter 13 and examine the questions that Mr. Flores asked. The questions about which students took the most and the least shots are low-level questions that do not give you much information. The questions about who is the best shot, however, elicit a great deal of information about students' thinking and their understanding of the mathematics. Remember that students need time to think about their answers to such questions. Practice waiting silently.

Finally, recognize that you can involve many more of your students in thinking deeply about mathematics if you think of ways to get everyone involved in asking and answering questions. For example, you can pose a question to the class and ask everyone to "think-pair-share." The students should first think about their own answers, then pair up with a partner to talk about their ideas, and finally be ready to offer suggestions to the entire class. (For even more opportunities for small group discussion, you can have the pairs join up for discussion in groups of four or six before you bring the whole class together to talk about the question.) With this questioning model, everyone is encouraged to think and talk about the question. The conversation in the classroom is no longer "ping-pong" from teacher to individual student and back.

Some useful references on questioning include Burns (1985), Mumme and Shepherd (1990), Spangler (1992), Sullivan and Clarke (1991), and Vaac (1993).

Math Links 4.3

If you would like to see effective questioning in action, view the video clips, Gathering Evidence, at the NCTM Illuminations web site, which you can access from this book's web site.

Interviewing

Interviewing is a combination of questioning and observing, usually done with one student in a quiet place. It is a powerful way to learn about a student's thinking and to give her or him some special attention. Key factors in a successful interview are establishing rapport with the child, accepting responses without judging, and encouraging the child to talk and explain.

At the beginning of the school year, Ms. Morihara decided to conduct short interviews with her new fourth graders to assess their understanding of odd and even numbers. Here is what Tonya said during that interview:

MS. MORIHARA: Tonya, is 9 an odd or even number?

TONYA: It's odd . . . unless you go by 3s, then it's even.

MS. MORIHARA: Oh, that's interesting. Can you show me what you mean with tiles?

Ms. Morihara gave Tonya 9 tiles to explain her thinking. Tonya stacked the tiles into four groups of two and showed her the one that was left over.

TONYA: See, if we divide evenly by twos, there is one left over so it is odd.

Tonya then divided the 9 tiles into three groups of 3.

TONYA: But, if we divide it into groups of 3, there aren't any left over, so it is even. That is why 9 is both odd and even.

MS. MORIHARA: Thank you very much, Tonya, for explaining your thinking to me.

This interview with Tonya shows how just a short interview can provide a wealth of information regarding a student's understanding of mathematics. If you were to probe Tonya's thinking even further, what questions would you ask her? How would you attempt to change her misconceptions?

Although you will certainly not have time to interview all of your students each day or even every week, choose a few to interview each week until you have had a chance to talk with each one individually. Teachers are often surprised at how students value private time with them and how much they learn in a short time about the individual student. You may be able to squeeze in an interview or two each day during whole-class silent reading time, work-station time (when other students are circulating from station to station), or seatwork time.

Before interviewing a student, you need a basic plan of what you want to investigate, what materials you will need, what questions you will ask, and when and how you will record the information. You may want to have alternative paths to take if the interview proceeds in different ways.

The interview itself generally has three parts: initiation, questioning/hypothesis formulation, and questioning/hypothesis testing (Long and Ben-Hur, 1991). During the initiation phase, the interviewer puts the student at ease by chatting informally, asking nonthreatening personal interest questions, showing the child the materials that will be used and ensuring that he or she is familiar with them, and explaining the purpose of the interview. Next, the interviewer begins posing tasks, always making certain to rephrase questions in the student's own language when necessary and to encourage the student to explain, elaborate, and show what he or she knows. Students often understand more than it appears at first glance.

It is the interviewer's responsibility to ask questions in a variety of ways in order to formulate hypotheses about how the child is thinking about the task and what the child does and does not understand. It is critical that the interviewer remain nonjudgmental about student responses, even though students often look for subtle clues about the correctness of their answers. Some noncommittal phrases that are helpful in prompting children to explain their thinking further (without indicating whether previous responses have been right or wrong) include the following:

- I am interested in knowing more about your thinking. Talk to me about it.
- Pretend you are the teacher and I am your student. Please help me understand.
- Can you explain that in a different way?
- I like it when you take the time to explain your thinking.
- I think I understand now, but what if . . . ?

As the second phase of the interview is proceeding, the interviewer begins to formulate hypotheses about what the child knows and where the child has trouble.

The third phase of the interview is the time to ask questions specifically designed to test those hypotheses, to see if the difficulties really are what they seem to be. A big temptation for many teachers is to slide into teaching during an interview. It is important to resist the temptation to fix errors or misconceptions on the spot. Think about the most effective ways to help your children grow in their mathematical understandings and take the time to follow the process of sound instruction. If there is lots of time, teaching may be appropriate, but reteaching or tutoring is often better reserved for another time or another day. The focus of a classroom interview should be to figure out what a student knows, not to help him or her on the spot. In the Classroom 4-1 is a plan for interviewing third-grade students about their understanding of place value.

A useful chapter about classroom interviews is "Listening to Children: The Interview Method" (Labinowicz, 1985). Additional sources of information on interviews include Cross and Hynes (1994), Kamii and Lewis (1991), Labinowicz (1987), Long and Ben-Hur (1991), Peck et al. (1989), and Weaver (1955).

Math Links 4.4

It is interesting to see the kind of insight into a child's thinking a teacher can gain from an interview. You can see this in the video clips, Understanding a Child's Development of Number Sense, at the NCTM Illuminations web site, accessible from this book's web site.

Performance Tasks

In a class that is alive with problem solving and investigations, many valuable opportunities arise to observe students working on performance tasks. In fact, the only way to assess some skills is through performance tasks. For example, if one objective is for children to know how to measure with a ruler, then they need to be assessed doing such measuring. Questions on written tests that line up a picture of a ruler with an object do not reveal much about the actual skill of measuring.

Performance tasks often mirror the real world, are open-ended, and require time for grappling with a problem. It is often helpful to pair children

In the Classroom 4-1

PRIMARY INTERVIEW ON PLACE VALUE

OBJECTIVE: **To determine students' understanding of place value.**

GRADE LEVEL: **3**

MATERIALS: **Unifix cubes, paper and pencil, base-ten blocks**

TASKS:

1. Can you show me 24 Unifix cubes? Observe if child counts accurately (says numbers in proper order, uses one-to-one correspondence, has a method for keeping track of which cubes have been counted).
2. Now let's suppose we want 34 cubes. Can you show me that? Does child count out 10 more or count over from beginning?
3. Can you write the number 34 here?
4. Let's put the 34 cubes into groups of ten. How many tens do you think we can make? Do you think you'll have any cubes left over? Shall we count out the 34 cubes into piles to make sure?
5. Let's look at 34, the number you wrote. Can you show me with the cubes what the 3 means? Can you show me what the 4 means?
6. Now let's make four piles of 10 cubes each. And let's have five leftover. Do you know how many cubes we have here altogether? How can you tell? (Does student know to count the piles by 10 and add the leftovers? Or does he or she count all?)
7. a. If the child has trouble with the questions above, check further by asking him or her again to count out several different numbers of cubes (e.g., 17, 26, or 30) and to predict how many tens and how many left over. Ask the reverse question. For example, if we have 2 tens and 7 left over, how many cubes would that be?
   b. If the child has no trouble with the questions above, probe for understanding of place value of larger numbers such as 123 or 347 using base-ten blocks and asking how many piles of 100 could be made and how many piles of 10 and how many ones. Also ask the reverse question: if we have three flats and six sticks and two units, how many cubes would that be altogether? Extension: Check to see how many different ways the child can show 136.

INTERVIEW REMINDERS:

Listen and watch carefully! Let them do it! Don't teach!

Be flexible. Ask for more examples, if needed.

Ask: How would you show a friend? How would you explain it to a little kid?

when observing performance of such tasks, so that you can hear their conversation as they work. In planning, you should list some of the areas you want to observe as the pairs work on appropriate tasks.

As an example of a performance task, look back at In the Classroom 2-2 (Chapter 2). In that activity, children are asked to build different boxes (right prisms) with some blocks. As they build boxes of various dimensions and various volumes, the formula for the volume of a box evolves naturally. The children are involved in using models, making decisions, and thinking mathematically, rather than just applying a formula. Figure 4-5 lists three areas you might plan to observe and examples of the notes you might make while observing the performance task from In the Classroom 2-2.

As indicated in Chapter 3, the *Professional Standards for Teaching Mathematics* (NCTM, 1991) emphasize worthwhile mathematical tasks as a core dimension. You may want to begin with simple tasks and then build up to longer, more complicated ones. Often, you will be surprised at the tenacity of very young children on a task that is engaging them; you should not rule out richer tasks for this age. Badger (1992), Moon (1993), and Sanford (1993) provide additional interesting reading about performance assessment in the elementary math classroom.

	Jason	Amy	Lawanda	Tyler	Zaria	Kristin	Becca	Drew
Strategy								
Used trial and error								
Organized by length (or height or width)								
Found and used patterns								
Made other comparisons								
Used a combination of strategies								
Result								
Found few or all combinations								
Found the connection to factors of the number								
Found/did not find the formula								
Able/unable to describe the procedure								
Attitude								
Worked well with others								
Curious, explored other shapes, other numbers								
Enthusiastic								
Remained engaged								

FIGURE 4-5 Observation guide for block-building activity.

Self-Assessment and Peer Assessment

Self-assessment is an activity that engages many people. For example, actors, athletes, and musicians often study videotapes of their performances in order to figure out how to improve. In a similar way, when math students engage in activities that promote self-awareness and self-evaluation, they can eliminate weaknesses and become better problem solvers. Students are often the best assessors of their own work and feelings. When students evaluate their own work, the responsibility for learning is theirs.

You can begin the self-assessment process by having students validate their own thinking or their answers to selected exercises. For example, in a nonthreatening way, you could ask Dwayne to show you how he arrived at the answer in the following case:

```
  28
X 46
 168
 112
 280
```

You may also want to ask him to explain how he obtained the answer to this problem:

```
  24
X 39
 216
 72
 936
```

It is important to ask about correct answers as well as incorrect ones, and standard approaches as well as nonstandard, so that children do not think they are questioned only when something is wrong. Asking only about incorrect answers does not help build their self-esteem or establish the feeling that they have control of the mathematics.

It is helpful for students to learn to ask themselves a variety of mental self-assessment questions while they are engaged in problem solving. You can help students develop the habit of self-assessment by prompting them with questions such as "What are you doing now?" "Why are you doing that?" "How will it help you find the solution?" (Kenney and Silver, 1993). Eventually, these questions will become second nature to the students, and you will no longer need to prompt them. Being able to think about one's own thinking and to monitor one's own problem-solving efforts (*metacognition*) is one of the goals of problem-solving instruction.

Engaging students in self-assessment of their problem-solving efforts after they have finished solving problems is another useful way to improve their monitoring abilities. For example, you might ask students to write a sentence or two in response to prompts like those in Figure 4-6 after they have finished a problem-solving activity.

Students can also analyze each others' strategies for solving problems. As they listen to and discuss how another student or group of students solved a problem, they begin to see different ways to proceed and to make judgments about which way makes the most sense to them, which seems easier or different, and which leads to stumbling blocks. Not only will they learn from such discussions and self-assessments, but you will also learn a lot about the students.

Sometimes knowing about students' attitudes, beliefs, and feelings about mathematics and mathematical tasks helps you, as a teacher, know how to design lessons more effectively. No one is better at assessing how a student feels about a given task than the student who is doing it. You may want to give a simple attitude inventory (see Figure 4-7). How would you plan a lesson that involves problem solving if you find from the survey that most of your students have a negative attitude toward problem solving? How could this information help you in grouping students in the lesson?

You might assign students to write math journals or letters to themselves or to others. One teacher had her students write letters to themselves about their strengths and weaknesses at the beginning of each grading period. Months later, they read back over their letters to see if they had made progress in any of the areas they had previously self-identified as weaknesses (see Figure 4-8). This information can be shared with parents during conference time.

FIGURE 4-6 Self-assessment questions for problem solving.

Think about the problem you just worked on. Then answer these questions by circling what you think:

1. How sure are you that your answer is right?

ABSOLUTELY SURE	PRETTY SURE	SORT OF SURE	NOT SO SURE	I KNOW I GOT IT WRONG

Why are you sure (or not sure) about your answer?

2. How hard was this problem for you?

VERY, VERY HARD	PRETTY HARD	SORT OF HARD	NOT SO HARD	REALLY EASY

Why was this problem at this difficulty level for you?

3. Have you ever solved a problem like this one before?

YES, MANY TIMES	YES, ONCE OR TWICE	NOT SURE	DON'T THINK SO	NO, DEFINITELY NOT

If so, describe the other problems and tell why they were like this one. If not, what was different about this problem from the others you've seen?

Attitude Inventory Items

Pretend your class has been given some math story problems to solve. Mark true or false depending on how the statement describes you. There are no right or wrong answers for this part.

_______ 1. I will put down any answer just to finish a problem.
_______ 2. It is no fun to try to solve problems.
_______ 3. I will try almost any problem.
_______ 4. When I do not get the right answer right away I give up.
_______ 5. I like to try hard problems.
_______ 6. My ideas about how to solve problems are not as good as other students' ideas.
_______ 7. I can only do problems everyone else can do.
_______ 8. I will not stop working on a problem until I get an answer.
_______ 9. I am sure I can solve most problems.
_______ 10. I will work a long time on a problem.
_______ 11. I am better than many students at solving problems.
_______ 12. I need someone to help me work on problems.
_______ 13. I can solve most hard problems.
_______ 14. There are some problems I will just not try.
_______ 15. I do not like to try problems that are hard to understand.
_______ 16. I will keep working on a problem until I get it right.
_______ 17. I like to try to solve problems.
_______ 18. I give up on problems right away.
_______ 19. Most problems are too hard for me to solve.
_______ 20. I am a good problem solver.

FIGURE 4-7 A problem-solving attitude survey for elementary students.
(Source: Reprinted with permission from "How to Evaluate Progress in Problem Solving," copyright 1987 by the National Council of Teachers of Mathematics. All rights reserved.)

Math

6-3

Letter to Myself Writing #7 9-3-99

Dear Self,

I'm going to start off blunt. My weeknesses in Math are word problems I can get 'em, but for me, it's tough My strenths are problems, especially in division. My perdiction about my performance is that I will hopefully get better on word problems. One peice of advice is to not ruch through anything.

Sincerly,
Self

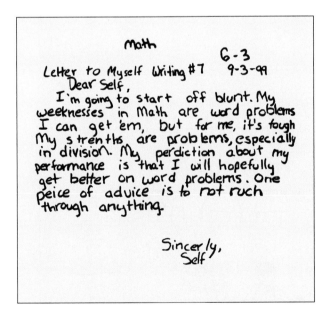

FIGURE 4-8 Sample student self-assessment "letter to myself" written at the beginning of the year. Students can compare this letter with a letter written at the end of the year to show their growth over the school year.

You may learn more from young children by asking them to answer questions or complete tasks such as the following:

> What are you really good at in math? What things do you need to improve on?
>
> Draw a picture of what mathematics looks (feels) like to you.
>
> If you were telling a friend about the favorite thing you do in mathematics class, what would you tell him or her? What other things about math class might you tell your friend? Why?

You can learn much about older children's view of mathematics through discussions. Several questions suggested by Spangler (1992) include the following:

> If you and a friend got different answers to the same problem, what would you do?
>
> If you were playing Password (one-word clues) and you wanted a friend to guess the word *mathematics,* what clues would you give?
>
> How do you know when you have solved a problem correctly?

Student self-assessment instruments for mathematics can be found in a variety of sources (e.g., Charles et al., 1987; Stenmark, 1991). Other useful resources on self- and peer-assessment include

Clarke (1992), Collinson (1992), Garafalo and Bryant (1992), and Kenney and Silver (1993).

Work Samples

Work samples can include written assignments, projects, and other student work that you collect and evaluate. Figure 4-9 reproduces the work of four children on the following problem:

> A carpenter makes only 3-legged and 4-legged tables. At the end of one day, he had used 31 legs. How many stools and tables did he make?

Figure 4-10 provides a typical analytic scoring scale for assessing children's work in problem solving on three measures (understanding the problem, planning a solution, and getting an answer).

Table 4-2 shows one teacher's scores for each of the four children on the three measures in Figure 4-10. There are, in fact, many different schemes for scoring problem solving, and each involves judgment. For example, try scoring the papers in Figure 4-9 using the same analytic scoring scale to see whether you agree with the scorer in

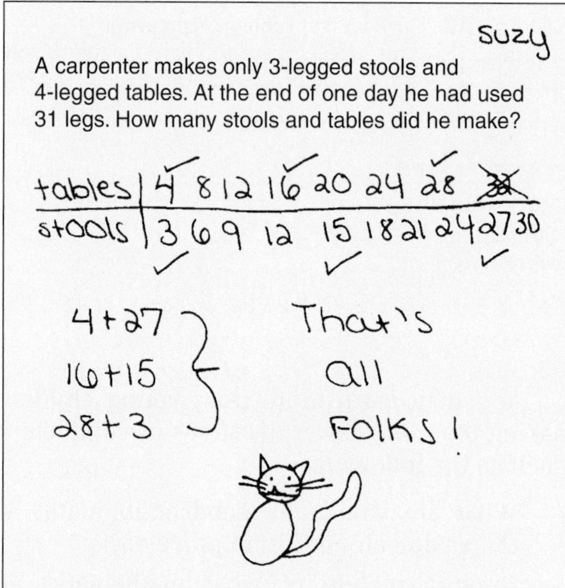

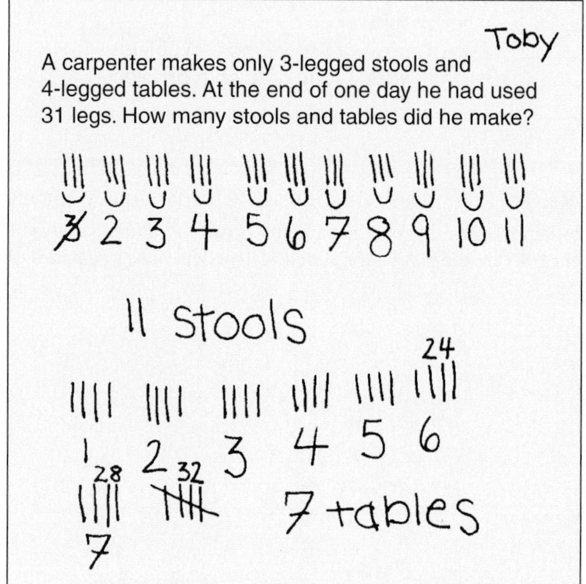

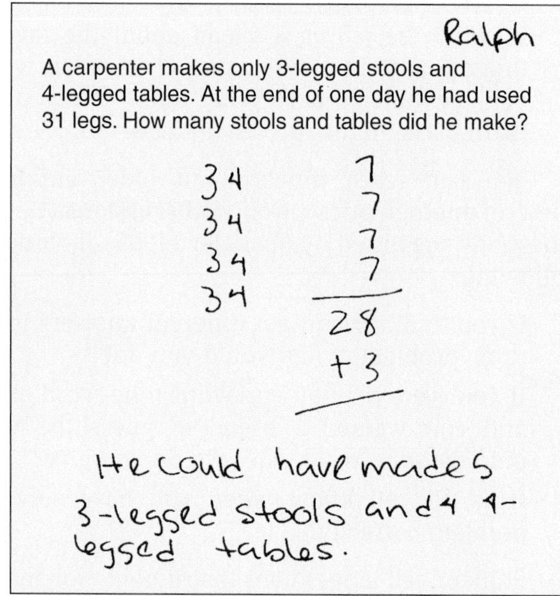

FIGURE 4-9 Samples of children's problem-solving work.

Analytic Scoring Scale

Understanding the Problem
0: Complete misunderstanding of the problem
1: Part of the problem misunderstood or misinterpreted
2: Complete understanding of the problem

Planning a Solution
0: No attempt or totally inappropriate plan
1: Partially correct plan based on part of the problem being interpreted correctly
2: Plan could have led to a correct solution if implemented properly

Getting an Answer
0: No answer, or wrong answer based on an inappropriate plan
1: Copying error, computational error, partial answer for a problem with multiple answers
2: Correct answer and correct label for the answer

FIGURE 4-10 A scale for scoring problem solving.
(Source: Reprinted with permission from "How to Evaluate Progress in Problem Solving," copyright 1987 by the National Council of Teachers of Mathematics. All rights reserved.)

Table 4-2. (You may well disagree, but you should be able to justify your position.)

Perhaps more important than scoring children's work is analyzing it to see what you can learn about the students. Looking again at the work of the four students in Figure 4-9, for example, you might conclude that only Suzy searched for more than one answer to the problem.

Portfolios

Portfolios have long been used to evaluate works of art, but only recently has this technique been emphasized in mathematics. A portfolio is a "purposeful collection of student work that exhibits the student's efforts, progress, and achievement in one or more areas. The collection must include student participation in selecting the contents, the criteria for selection, and criteria for judging merit, and evidence of student self-reflection" (Paulson et al., 1991, p. 60). A student's mathematics portfolio might include such things as special problem-solving tasks, writings, investigations, projects, and reports. These samples could be presented through a variety of media, including paper and pencil, audio or videotapes, and computer disks. Some teachers keep both classroom working portfolios, in which students keep the majority of their work, and assessment portfolios, which contain selected samples of their work for purposes of making judgments about students' attitudes, abilities, and dispositions in mathematics.

If you have your students keep portfolios, you will need to answer the following questions:

What is the purpose of the portfolio? Who will be the audience? (The students themselves? You as teacher? parents?)

What will be included and who selects? (Problem-solving work? Tests and quizzes? Writing about math? Only best efforts or a collection of representative work?) See Figure 4-11 for a list of the items one teacher chose to require.

Where will the portfolios be kept? (In notebooks? In folders? In the classroom? In student desks or lockers or at home?)

Will you grade the portfolios? (If so, on what basis? Will the portfolio include already graded items, and if so, is a student graded twice on the same material? Is the portfolio graded on the basis of completeness, comprehensiveness, insight, etc.? Can a well-compiled portfolio that contains many poor papers receive a high grade? Can a messy, incomplete portfolio belonging to an excellent math student—and containing all A papers—receive a low grade?)

How often will you give feedback? (Monthly, quarterly, at the end of each grading period?)

These are only representative questions; there are many more to be considered. Once you have decided these things for yourself, portfolios can be a rich source of information for you and your students.

Table 4-2 • Scoring for Children's Work in Figure 4-9 Using the Scale in Figure 4-10

	Understanding the Problem	Planning a Solution	Getting an Answer	Total
Suzy	2	2	1	5
Toby	1	1	0	2
Katie	2	2	1	5
Ralph	2	2	1	5

Minimum requirements for inclusion in your portfolio at the end of each grading period:

1. 3 homework assignments
2. 3 writing samples
3. 2 quizzes
4. 2 examples of class notes
5. 1 example of special project work
6. 1 example of cooperative group work

Your portfolio is not limited to the above. At the end of each grading period, you will choose five pieces of work to remain in your portfolio to represent the grading period's work.

FIGURE 4-11 One teacher's specifications for portfolio contents.

A particular benefit of portfolios is their value as a self-assessment tool for students. It is important for students to date the entries so that they (and others) can see their growth over time. It is also helpful if they describe each task and reflect on it. Figure 4-12 provides some advice for getting started with math learning portfolios.

Getting Started with Portfolios

Start small and simple.
- Especially if you have many students, portfolios are a lot of work.

Developing a rationale is important.
- Why do you want your students to keep portfolios?
- What will you say to students and parents about your goals?

Portfolios need to be accessible.
- Establish a central place in your classroom for keeping portfolios.

Class time allocated for portfolio work is time well spent.
- Students need guidance in labeling and choosing.
- Sharing samples of student work in class is important.
- Students need guidance in being reflective.

A table of contents is essential.

The criteria you identify for judging students' portfolios reflect your goals and values.
- What categories of mathematical tasks will you require be included?
- Will you require examples of both draft and revised work?
- Will you require written reflections?
- Will you put grades on the portfolios? If so, how?

FIGURE 4-12 Tips for getting started with portfolios.

Some useful references on the subject include Clarke (1992), Kuhs (1997), Lambdin and Walker (1994), and Mumme (1990).

Writings

The *NCTM Standards* call for more emphasis on communication in mathematics. As stated in Figure 4-13, numeracy and literacy go hand in hand. Student writings as a form of communication can provide another source for assessment. You may want students to keep a journal or to add writing to other assignments.

A simple way to begin is to ask students to write about what they did or did not understand for one assignment, how they felt about an activity, what they learned today in class, or what they like about mathematics. Your creativity in providing suggestions will help spark theirs. For example, you might ask them to write a letter to a

Words and numbers are of equal value,
for, in the cloak of knowledge,
one is wrap and the other woof.
It is no more important to count the sands
Then it is to name the stars.

FIGURE 4-13 An idea to engage students in writing about numbers.

(Source: From The *Phantom Tollbooth* by Norton Juster. Text copyright © 1961 by Norton Juster. Text copyright renewed 1989 by Norton Juster. Reprinted by permission of Random House Children's Books, a division of Random House, Inc.)

Describe an activity our class might do to help us understand how big one million really is.

Let's play teacher! You want to teach some first graders how to subtract two-digit numbers. Give examples of the problems and materials you will use. Tell what you will say and what you will have the children do.

Audrey claims that her teacher could improve the average test score in the class by 10 points if she just added 10 points to everyone's score. Kelly doesn't believe that would work. What do you think? Explain your thinking.

Which decimal is closer to one-half, 0.307 or 0.32? How do you know? Explain how you could show or prove it.

What connections are there between fractions and decimals? Explain and use examples in your explanation.

FIGURE 4-14 Sample writing prompts for having children explain their understanding of mathematical concepts.

friend about math class or to write a poem about triangles. The snapshot at the beginning of this chapter illustrates how Mr. Johnston's use of a creative journal entry provided him a wealth of information about his students' disposition toward mathematics. As writing becomes a part of math class, you can use it to assess children's knowledge of and attitudes toward mathematics. Figure 4-14 provides some sample ideas for writing prompts.

Teacher-Designed Written Tests

Tests can inform and guide your instruction, rather than simply determine grades. Students learn from tests, but too often the lessons they learn may not be those intended. When too much emphasis is placed on written tests, students can learn that they do not have to know why some procedure works, to explain how they solved a problem, or to be able to solve word problems because a passing grade may be obtained without ever doing these things.

Carefully constructed and correctly analyzed tests can tell us a lot about students. For example, the children's papers in Figure 4-15 are for a simple test on subtraction of two-digit numbers, but they reveal a lot about the students. Notice how many of them missed the problems with zeros. If the first or seventh item had not been on the test, the teacher might not have realized that Jim regroups—and then ignores—even when regrouping is not necessary. (Try analyzing the kinds of errors the other students made and what characterizes each student.)

Most paper-and-pencil tests do not give you the opportunity to learn how a student arrived at an answer. One way to gain more insight is to ask the students to explain in writing what they did. If children are accustomed to explaining orally in class, then this task will be easier for them, and you will receive more meaningful explanations. Ask for explanations on a few items, and accept them in the children's language. Otherwise, they will soon learn to parrot explanations that are meaningless to them.

There is no reason why paper-and-pencil tests cannot include estimation items and require manipulatives and calculators. Tests can also permit the use of textbooks or notebooks, ask thought provoking questions, and require students to connect new learnings to previous ones. They need not be races against time in which the students regurgitate all they remember from the week or about the procedure last taught.

Thoughtful, well-constructed tests are one way—often a very efficient way—to gather information. Alone, they do not give a complete assessment of students' knowledge, but they can add one more piece to the puzzle.

Achievement Tests

At some point you will undoubtedly be asked to administer standardized or statewide tests. The results of these tests may often be reported back too late to be applied to instruction that year, but they can be used to take a look at your students' achievements in general. For example, if you see that your students did poorly in measurement, then you need to rethink what you are doing in that area. If student test results come back late in the year at your school, you might ask to see the results from the previous year for students in your class. Sometimes this information can provide valuable insight into what areas of study need extra work this year.

Remember that norm-referenced tests are designed to spread children across the whole normal distribution. There will always be 50 percent of the students below average and 50 percent above average. Thus some items on such tests are not intended for everyone at a grade level to answer correctly. The fact that an item on multiplying fractions appears on a fourth-grade test does not mean that this is a recommended skill for all students at this level. Refer to your school, district, or state curriculum framework for expectations for your grade level.

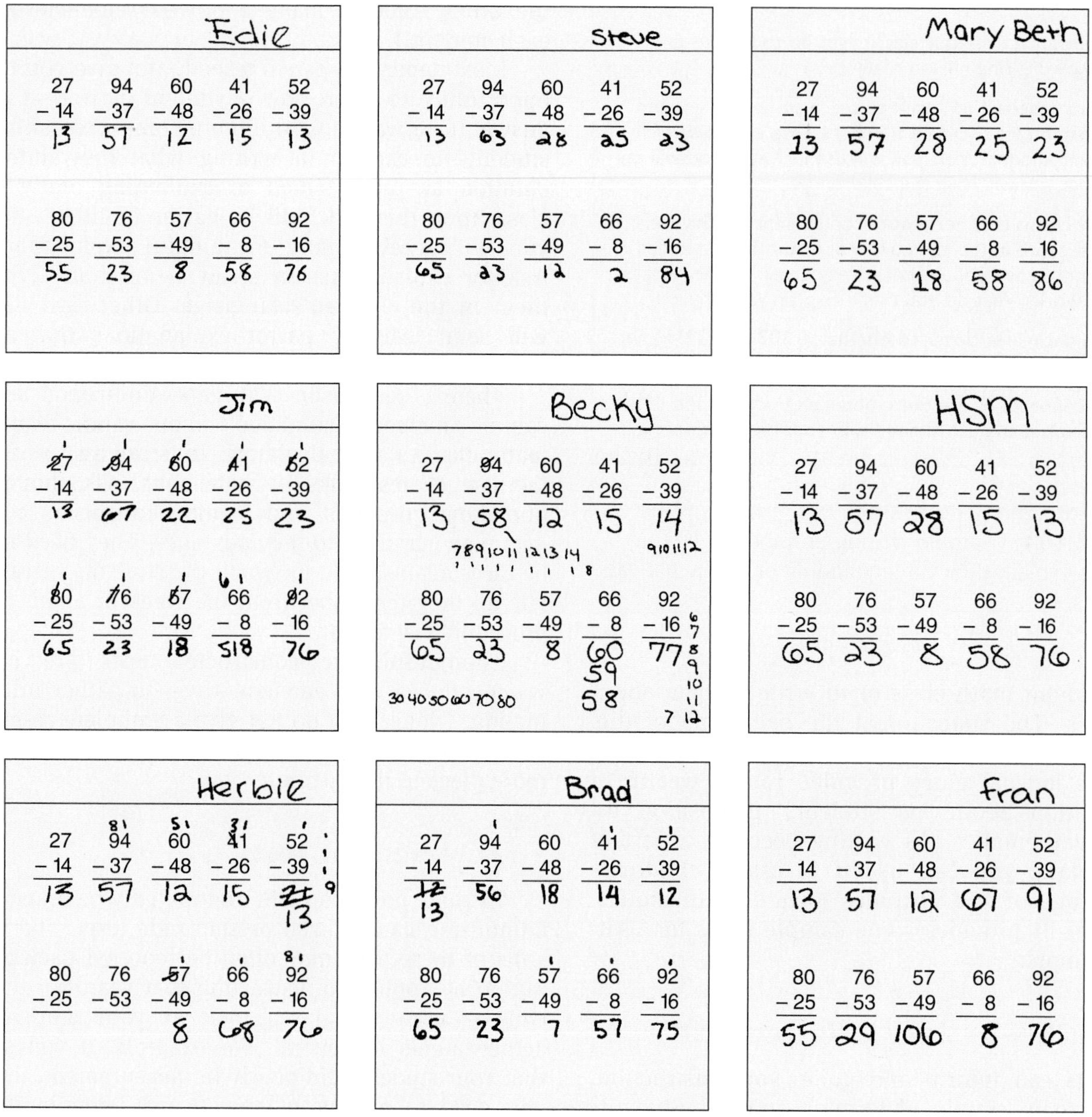

FIGURE 4-15 Samples of children's papers for a written test of subtraction.

Achievement tests are changing. Some allow the use of calculators; some ask questions in an open format rather than multiple-choice format; some ask for explanations; and some include problem-solving situations.

If you help your students learn in a way that is meaningful to them and help build their confidence and the attitude that they can do mathematics, then you will not have to worry about the results of achievement tests.

Keeping Records and Communicating about Assessments

It is important to keep both informal and formal records of students' learning and their disposition toward mathematics. Certain types of recordkeeping may be required by your school system, but you can always keep additional records of your own.

A word of caution: Do not become burdened with a multitude of records, but keep enough that you can reflect on your students' progress and can justify any major decisions about them or what to teach. The type of records you keep also will depend on the ways you report information to students, parents, and the school administration.

Recording the Information

Teachers are aware of many things about their students and keep many informal records about them. For example, you may know from daily interactions that Treena is always willing to answer in math class, that Joshua does not work well with Katrina, that Yong knows how to compute but seems to lack understanding about when and why certain operations are used, and that Cary is often absent on math test days. But maybe you need to jog your memory about Rachel before her parents come for the next parent conference. Or maybe you are thinking about changing the composition of cooperative groups and wondering if Jerry and Richard worked well together in the past.

Because of the volume of information about students that may be useful, it is often helpful as well as necessary to record some of it. Several techniques for recording information are described here. You may find others or modify these to suit your needs.

CHECKLISTS Checklists may be used in a variety of ways to record individualized information about students' understandings, attitudes, or content achievement. They may be simply lists that are marked in different ways, rating scales, or annotated checklists (see Figures 4-16 through 4-21).

MATH CLASS PARTICIPATION									
	Center A	Center B	Center C	Group Leader	Group Recorder	Group Reporter	Bulletin Board	Materials	Other
NAME	DATE: March								
Atkins, Willie	2	4	6	5	13	10	✓	✓	MCounts
Bero, Chuck	9	10	11	10	5			March	
Connel, Brenda	2	3	5			10		✓	
Coroi, Troy	11	10	9	5		13	✓	March	MCounts
Cosby, Kim			2		5		✓	✓	
Foster, Greg	12		2		10	5		✓	
Hale, Carol	2	4	6	13	5		✓	✓	
Jones, Tempie		12	13				March		
Jones, Zelda	10	9	6			5		March	
McGee, Leslie	6	4		5	13		March	✓	
Mory, Kelly	11		12	13	10		✓		
Navarro, Sarita		10	4	10			✓	March	
Nelson, Clara	5	6	2			5	March	✓	
Odom, Ruby		2		5		13		✓	
Pak, Yong	12	11	10	13				March	
Porter, Jessie		5		10	5		March		
Roy, Lulu	10		12			10			
Stewart, Scott		2				5	✓		
Tucker, Enoka	11		3	5	13		March		MCounts
Watt, Mary Lee	10	2	3		5	10		March	
Weaver, J. T.	12	2	5	10			✓		
White, Emma	3		5	13	10		✓		MCounts
Wortaszek, Sam	4	10	3		10	5	March		
Yi, Sik			11	10					
Zuber, Albert		11			10				

FIGURE 4-16 This checklist of student participation in math class activities is useful for tracking which children need to be encouraged to participate and which need to be supported in their involvement. For example, as Brenda's teacher, you would see that she has worked at the math centers and has been responsible for materials, and you could use this information as a reminder to support her interest by making her a group leader.

CLASS OBSERVATION
Class 5th period Week Feb. 6-10/13-17

NAMES	COMMENTS	ACTION NEEDED	ACTION TAKEN
Atkins, Willie			
Bero, Chuck	Needs a challenge	*	Yes
Connel, Brenda			
Coroi, Troy			
Cosby, Kim	No homework for 3 days	*	Called
Foster, Greg			
Hale, Carol	Doing much better with fractions – fraction bars helped		
Jones, Tempie			
Jones, Zelda	What a difference in geometry – good spatial sense		
McGee, Leslie			
Mory, Kelly			
Navarro, Sarita			
Nelson, Clara	Wants to be on math team next year – mother says yes	*	Called mother
Odom, Ruby			
Pak, Yong			
Porter, Jessie	Spend some time with Jessie – he can do this		
Roy, Lulu			
Stewart, Scott	Is beginning to work well in a group		
Tucker, Enoka			
Watt, Mary Lee			
Weaver, J. T.			
White, Emma			
Wortaszek, Sam			
Yi, Sik	Loves group work – helps with language		
Zuber, Albert			

FIGURE 4-17 This annotated checklist is useful for recording classroom observations as well as actions the teacher took when necessary. Such checklists are also useful for providing reminders of points to discuss when communicating with parents and students.

The beauty of checklists is that they can be adapted to your situation and, in fact, may help you think about your goals and the needs of each child you are teaching.

You cannot spend all your time keeping records, so select a few significant aspects of students' learning and attitudes and target a few children each day. For example, you may want to observe and keep records about children working in cooperative groups one week and the next week focus on individual children's understanding of a new topic.

If you use a checklist, you will want to keep it handy so that you can make quick entries as children are engaged in tasks. If you wait until the end of the day, you may forget some of the day's gems or be too preoccupied with other tasks to jot them down.

If you are recording information that is meant only for you, keep the checklist away from the eyes of your students. Be especially sensitive to children's feelings. A public checklist that shows the progress of each class member's skill attainment may be a great boost for those at the top but detrimental to those at the bottom, who often need the most encouragement.

STUDENT FILES Many teachers keep a record of students' learning in the form of a file of work samples from each child. If children are keeping their own portfolios, those may suffice, and you will not need to keep additional samples of their work in your own student files. In either case, you may want to keep a summary profile for each child, like the one shown in Figure 4-20. Sometimes the school's format for reporting to parents requires that you keep such a record.

CLASS RECORDS Often, the only class record is the grade book. Although it may be necessary to

GROUP OBSERVATION	DATE	TASK	COMMENTS	DATE	TASK	COMMENTS
GROUP A	1/18	Problem:	Group worked well			
John		Quarter	together – would not			
Caryl		Change	stop until they had all			
Luther			the possibilities			
Jara						
GROUP B						
Todd						Need to observe!
Kate						
David						
Cathy						
GROUP C	1/18	Problem:		1/22	Data	
Tamia		Quarter	Need to watch, that			Brandi made a real effort
Larry		Change	Brandi doesn't take			to obtain the ideas from
Maude			over – talk with her –			others – they arrived at
Brandi			give some questions to ask			a neat different question
GROUP D		Data:				
Otis		What's	Chose TV programs –			
Sandra		My	finally focused on			
Gloria		Favorite?	G-4 – were on task			
Chon ho						
GROUP E	1/22	Data:		1/24	Same	
Renea		Favorite	Could not agree on			
Lisa			topic – all wanted			
Tamio			their own			
Gary						

FIGURE 4-18 This annotated checklist is used to record the teacher's observations of group work. Notes such as these can help the teacher in assessing group interactions and making decisions on how to group students for future work.

STUDENT DISPOSITIONS CLASS: 3rd Grade Math MONTH: October	Helen	Art	Whit	Beverly	Anita	Jim
Confidence						
Is sure of answer	✓			✓		
Knows how to proceed	✓			✓		
Flexibility					✓	
Will change direction	✓ If prodded		✓			
Tries several ways			✓			
Perseverance						
Stays with task	✓					
Enjoys involved problems		✓		✓		
Curiosity						
Wants to find out why		✓				✓
Challenges			✓	✓		
Sharing						
Works well with others		✓				✓
Shows leadership				✓		

FIGURE 4-19 This checklist of student dispositions is helpful in determining which students might need special activities or encouragement to help boost their confidence or perseverance in problem solving, for example. It can also be used for support in parent conferences or in discussions with students.

Student Profile in Mathematics K–4

Date Feb.

Student Jeremy Gelder Teacher Matt Bell Grade 2

Content Areas	
Number Sense & Numeration	Still sees numbers as ones - needs to develop place value
Estimation	Good feel for numbers – size of quantities
Concepts of Operations	Good problem solver
Computation	
Geometry & Spatial Sense	Geometry he loves
Measurement	
Statistics & Probability	
Fractions & Decimals	
Patterns & Relationships	Better at spatial patterns
Math Power	
Problem Solving	Likes to think in creative ways
Reasoning	
Communication	Explains well
Connections	
Concepts	Developing
Procedures	Doesn't like to follow procedures – invents his own
Dispositions	
Confidence	Growing
Flexibility	
Perseverance	On many tasks
Curiosity	Great
Reflection	
Other Comments	

FIGURE 4-20
Sample student profile.

keep such a record, you must realize the limitations of a grade book. Alternatively, you could modify it with shorthand entries of your choosing to tell you more than attendance; grades on assignments, quizzes, and tests; and cumulative grades.

You could also supplement the grade book with a cumulative checklist made from your daily or weekly checklists. You can determine which items to include by reviewing the usefulness and frequency of your entries in these earlier checklists. The cumulative checklist will then give you a picture of the class as a whole and help you plan.

Communicating the Information

Most teachers have three main audiences to whom the information they have gathered will be communicated: students, parents or guardians, and administration. Each group will receive different amounts of information in different ways.

TO STUDENTS Much of your communication of information to students will be done orally or through actions, but also you will be writing comments on work samples, portfolios, tests, journals, or other forms of assessment materials. You may give a letter or number grade. All of these communications influence children's feelings about the value of different aspects of mathematics, their expectations of what they can accomplish, and their sense of their own worth.

Be positive and fair. Use information from your checklists or from student portfolios when letting each student know whether he or she is meeting expectations, and look for ways to demonstrate to each that he or she can do what is expected. Finally, remember that it is important that children grow in their ability to self-assess. One of your goals should be to help children become independent learners. If they always have to rely on you to validate their work and their thinking, they will not reach this goal.

I can draw these shapes ☐ yes ☐ not yet	I recognize patterns ☐ yes ☐ not yet	I can sort ☐ yes ☐ not yet	I can count ___ objects ☐ yes ☐ not yet
I can count by 1's (to 127) ☐ yes ☐ not yet	I can count by 2's (to 106) ☐ yes ☐ not yet	I can count by 5's (to 125) ☐ yes ☐ not yet	I can count by 10's (to 120) ☐ yes ☐ not yet
I can read a graph ☐ yes ☐ not yet	I can match sets ☐ yes ☐ not yet	I can make a pattern ☐ yes ☐ not yet	I can make a graph ☐ yes ☐ not yet
I can do addition to 10 ☐ yes ☐ not yet	I can do subtraction from 10 ☐ yes ☐ not yet	I can give number sentences ☐ yes ☐ not yet	I can recognize and count money ☐ yes ☐ not yet
I can read and use the calendar ☐ yes ☐ not yet	I can tell time ☐ yes ☐ not yet	I can write number sentences ☐ yes ☐ not yet	I can recognize numbers 0-20 ☐ yes ☐ not yet
I can build a double digit number ☐ yes ☐ not yet	I can build a triple digit number ☐ yes ☐ not yet	I know and use > and < signs ☐ yes ☐ not yet	I can recognize random 2 digit numbers ☐ yes ☐ not yet

FIGURE 4-21 Primary development checklist.

(Source: Reprinted with permission of the McGraw-Hill Companies from *The Whole Language Catalog: Forms of Authentic Assessment*, p. 3, by Lois Bridges Bird, Kenneth S. Goodman, and Yetta M. Goodman, copyright 1994 by SRA. All rights reserved.)

Dear Parents,

Your child will be developing a "portfolio" in math class this year. One of the primary purposes of this project is to allow students the opportunity to reflect on their work, including exemplary work, work that is considered a "personal best," or work that they feel is in some way memorable. Through this project, students can begin to develop critical self-evaluative tools that will be extremely valuable in the years ahead.

A second purpose of the portfolio project is to allow students to share some of their work with you. Please take some time this week to discuss your child's portfolio with him or her. Your child has been given written guidelines for the portfolio project. Please review the guidelines together.

Please help your child this week as he or she finalizes selections for the portfolio. There is no set number of pieces required, but a selection of 5 or 6 pieces is suggested. Help your child select pieces that best meet the guidelines and that are *most* representative of the major math content areas that we have covered during this grading period. The attached "News Bulletin" from this grading period may provide you with a better idea of the topics your child has studied and the activities he or she has participated in. Students have been asked to provide written accounts about *why* they chose particular pieces for their portfolios, so be sure to talk with your child about why he or she is choosing each piece for inclusion in the portfolio. (If you wish, you too may include some written comments about the pieces selected or the selection process.)

After you have read the "News Bulletin" and have helped your child with his or her portfolio selections, please sign and detach the form below. Your child is to return the signed form, along with his or her portfolio, by Friday, November 15.

Thank you for helping to make your child's mathematical experience a memorable one!

Sincerely,

I have read and discussed the "News Bulletin" with my child and have helped him or her select choice pieces for his or her portfolio. ______________

FIGURE 4-22 Letter to parents about math portfolios.

TO PARENTS OR GUARDIANS You will be reporting to parents or guardians both in written form and orally. The format of these reports is often determined by the school system, but you are responsible for the quality. You will grow in your ability to communicate with parents, but it is important from the beginning that you keep records and use them to illustrate or justify your oral and written comments. Phone calls can be useful for immediate feedback to parents not only when there is a problem, but also to applaud good behavior or outstanding achievement. Parents and children are often surprised and gratified when a teacher calls home to report something good. Some teachers try to make good calls home to all students early in the year. This practice can set up good relationships with parents and establish the expectation that a teacher phone call need not necessarily mean bad news. Some teachers use regular newsletters to keep parents informed about classroom activities and goals or letters to parents to tell them about special events or request their help. With today's broad access to e-mail, many teachers use that form of communication to maintain contact with parents. (Figure 4-22 shows a letter one teacher sent to parents to enlist their assistance in developing and maintaining their children's math portfolios.)

At parent conferences, you have an opportunity to explain goals for your instruction and to enlist parents' aid in helping their child meet those goals. It is helpful if you have collected a wide variety of samples of student work to share with the parents as you talk about their child's progress. Parent conferences are also times for gathering information. Parents often provide insights about their children that may not be evident to you in the classroom. The information you glean from them should be included in notes in your student files.

TO THE SCHOOL ADMINISTRATION When you begin teaching, you will need to find out what types of records and grades are required in your school and how they are used:

- What sort of report card format is used? A/B/C letter grades? S/I/N (satisfactory, improving, needs improvement) progress indicators? Numeric grades? Narrative reports?

- Does the administration expect written reports on each child?
- Is there an official checklist?
- Is the class grade record sufficient?
- Is information on students passed to the next teacher, kept in a permanent file, or used to make tracking decisions?
- Is the information used in teacher evaluations?

The type and use of records vary from school to school, so it is necessary to find out about your own situation. When you know how the records are to be used, you will be better able to provide information that is suitable for particular uses.

A Glance at Where We've Been

Assessment is an integral part of teaching. This chapter looks at student assessment to help you make informed decisions about providing instruction, monitoring student progress, and evaluating student achievement. There are many ways to gather, analyze, and present the information from assessments.

The different ways to gather information range from informal observations to formal achievement tests. Collecting information about students' learning is only one goal; the other is to collect information regarding their dispositions toward mathematics. Information needs to be recorded in some way so you can analyze it. There are numerous techniques for recording and communicating information. Portfolios, in particular, can provide a broad and useful picture of student progress and show growth over time.

Assessment can make a difference in how you help your students learn mathematics. You can use it in a positive way to encourage the children to become independent learners, to modify your instruction, and to communicate with parents.

Things to Do: From What You've Read

1. Make a list of as many assessment-related concepts and terms as you can think of (e.g., *achievement, portfolio, observation, conference, test*). Draw a concept map to show how these ideas are related to one another in your mind.
2. Describe the four different purposes of assessment and their results.
3. What recommendations for shifts in assessment (Table 4-1) are most closely connected to the classroom? How are they connected?
4. A narrow view is that assessment in mathematics focuses on how well students can carry out procedures in a limited amount of time. Describe a broader view of mathematics assessment.
5. Identify an error pattern in the work of at least four of the students in Figure 4-9.
6. Write a "letter to self" similar to that shown in Figure 4-8. In your letter you should reflect on your current strengths and weaknesses, as well as your future goals as a teacher of elementary school mathematics.
7. What records could you keep to assist with a parent–teacher conference? What other ways can you communicate with parents about their children's progress?
8. List three ideas for keeping records of your observations of students as they work during class.

Things to Do: Going Beyond This Book

IN THE FIELD

1. **Scoring Problem Solving.* Collect a set of problem-solving papers from students. Analyze and score them using the analytic scale in Figure 4-10. You may choose to use the children's work samples on Masters 4-6 to 4-10 in the *Helping Children Learn Mathematics Instructor's Manual.* (Available at the Wiley Book Companion web site, www.wiley.com/college/reys.)
2. **Observing Students in Class.* Observe one or two students during a mathematics class. Describe what you observed. If you were to work with these students in mathematics, what course of action would you take?
3. **Trying a Performance Task.* Try a performance task with a couple of students. Make a list of observations and use it as the basis for your description of the children's performance. You may find samples in *Measuring Up:*

*Additional activities, suggestions, or questions are provided in *Teaching Elementary Mathematics: A Resource for Field Experiences* (Wiley, 2004).

Prototypes for Mathematics Assessment (Mathematical Sciences Education Board, 1993).

4. **How Teachers Grade.* Talk to one or more classroom teachers about how they grade their students in math. Ask what sorts of tasks are figured into the grade and how they are weighted. Ask to see the teacher's gradebook so you can understand what sorts of records it includes. Find out what other records the teacher keeps (e.g., folders, portfolios, notes).

IN YOUR JOURNAL

5. Defend your position on this statement: Students' work on tests provides the most accurate assessment of their mathematical understanding.
6. Will student use of calculators interfere with assessing their understanding of mathematics? Explain your decision on this issue.
7. Which assessment practices do you think provide the best evidence of children's understanding of mathematics? Explain why you like these particular practices.

WITH ADDITIONAL RESOURCES

8. Watch the videotape *A Look at Children's Thinking* (Richardson, 1990) or a similar video on interviewing students. Describe what you learned from the students and the interviewer.
9. Read one of the articles on interviewing listed in the Resources section. Design an interview and use it with three students. Describe what you learned about each student.
10. Develop a test that involves the use of manipulatives.
11. Analyze a test in an elementary mathematics textbook. Would it make a difference if the students used calculators? What items would you need to change?
12. Analyze a test in an elementary mathematics textbook to determine whether it requires writing about mathematics. If not, what changes could you make so that it would do so? What other changes could you make to the test so that it would be more authentic?
13. Examine a standardized test. Does it allow use of calculators? Identify examples of good and poor questions, and explain your opinions.
14. Many teachers use cooperative learning methods during instruction but face the problem of aligning assessment techniques with that instruction. Read the article by Kroll et al. (1992), which describes methods to include cooperative problem solving in assessment and offers suggestions for choosing appropriate problems and incorporating aspects of both individual and group grading. Identify a math problem that you think would be useful as a group problem-solving assessment and design a scoring guide for assessing student work on it, adapting Kroll et al.'s suggestions.

WITH TECHNOLOGY

15. Design an assessment that you could give to students to assess their understanding regarding order of operations using a calculator.
16. Create problems that you might ask on a test where the capabilities of the calculator do not simply give the students the answer.
17. Many state departments of education post sample items from their statewide assessments on their web sites. Check the web site for your state and obtain an example of an open-ended item. Then examine and discuss the rubric that is provided.

Book Nook for Children

Zaccaro, Edward. *Challenge Math for the Elementary and Middle School Student.* Bellevue, Iowa: Hickory Grove Press, 2000.

Challenge children in grades 4–8 using some of more than 1,000 problems (presented with three levels of difficulty) in areas such as algebra, astronomy, trigonometry, probability, and more.

Resources

ANNOTATED BOOKS

Hatfield, Mary M.; Morrow, Jean; and Edwards, Nancy T. *Mathematics Methods* for *Elementary and Middle School Teachers.* New York: John Wiley & Sons, 2000.
An activity-based approach to teaching with an emphasis on using manipulatives to build conceptual understanding. Practical teaching ideas, updated assessment techniques, and the NCTM *Assessment Standards* give teachers the background to introduce elementary and middle school students to the wonders of mathematics.

Kallick, Bena, and Brewer, Ross. *How to Assess Problem-Solving Skills in Math (Grades K–2).* New York: Scholastic Trade, 1999.

Assess students' problem-solving skills with these classroom-tested strategies. The tips include creating a comfortable assessment environment, developing interesting problems that will capture students' attention, and scoring students' work. Includes original math problems designed for grades K–2. Filled with creative ideas for scoring and reporting.

Krulik, Stephen, and Rudnick, Jesse A. *Assessing Reasoning and Problem Solving. A Sourcebook for Elementary School Teachers.* Boston, Mass: Allyn & Bacon, 1998.
Assess what elementary students know about math, and how they arrive at their answers using math problems that children can relate to and enjoy solving—individually or in small groups—in the classroom. Teacher's notes and both traditional and alternative assessment ideas are included to assess what students know about math and how they reason, solve problems, and communicate about it.

Moon, Jean, and Schulman, Linda. *Finding the Connections: Linking Assessment, Instruction, and Curriculum in Elementary Mathematics.* Portsmouth, N.H.: Heinemann, 1995.
Classroom practices in grades K–6 provide a model for integrating assessment with instruction; ideas for communicating with parents, students, and administrators; and guided opportunities to practice and reflect on the assessment process.

Romberg, Thomas A. (ed.). *Mathematics Assessment and Evaluation: Imperatives for Mathematics Educators* (SUNY Series, Reform in Mathematics Education). Albany, N.Y.: State University of New York, 1992.
This book considers issues that surround mathematics tests, such as the need for valid performance data, the implications of mathematics standards in test development, the procedures used to construct a sample of state assessment tests, gender differences in test taking, and methods of reporting student achievement.

ANNOTATED ARTICLES

Cooney, Thomas J.; Sanchez, Wendy B., and Ice, Nicole F. "Interpreting Teacher's Movement toward Reform in Mathematics Assessment." *Mathematics Educator,* 11(1), (Winter 2001), pp. 10–14.
Discusses calls for change in educational reform in mathematics education. Describes one approach to systemic assessment reform in a large suburban county. Presents teacher reactions toward the projects.

Long, Madeleine J., and Ben-Hur, Meir. "Informing Learning through the Clinical Interview." *Arithmetic Teacher,* 38 (February 1991), pp. 44–46.
Consider the clinical interview for teaching and assessing student progress. Contains helpful phrases to use in obtaining useful information about student understanding.

Richardson, Kathy. "Assessing Understanding." *Arithmetic Teacher,* 35 (February 1988), pp. 39–41.
Describes interviews with four primary-age children and shifting from the assessment of performance to the assessment of understanding.

Sullivan, Peter, and Clarke, David. "Catering to All Abilities through 'Good Questions.'" *Arithmetic Teacher,* 39 (October 1991), pp. 14–18.
"Good" questions are particularly useful with the range of abilities found in most classrooms, particularly with mixed-ability classes. Think about how you might use these questions.

Warren, Elizabeth, and Nisbet, Steven. "How Grade 1–7 Teachers Assess Mathematics and How They Use the Assessment Data." *School Science & Mathematics,* 101(7), (November 2001), pp. 348–356.
Explore mathematics assessment methods employed by teachers in Australia, in particular the use of the relationships between grade level, assessment data, and assessment techniques.

ADDITIONAL REFERENCES

Badger, Elizabeth. "More than Testing." *Arithmetic Teacher,* 39 (May 1992), pp. 7–11.

Beyer, Ann. "Assessing Students' Performance: Using Observations, Reflections, and Other Methods." In *Assessment in the Mathematics Classroom,* 1993 Yearbook (ed. Norman Webb). Reston, Va.: NCTM, 1993.

Bird, Lois Bridges; Goodman, Kenneth S.; and Goodman, Yetta M. *The Whole Language Catalog: Forms for Authentic Assessment.* New York: SRA, 1994.

Burns, Marilyn. "The Role of Questioning." *Arithmetic Teacher,* 32 (February 1985), pp. 14–16.

Chambers, Donald L. "Improving Instruction by Listening to Children." *Teaching Children Mathematics,* 1 (February 1995), pp. 378–380.

Charles, Randall; Lester, Frank; and O'Daffer, Phares. *How to Evaluate Progress in Problem Solving.* Reston, Va.: NCTM, 1987.

Clarke, David J. "Activating Assessment Alternatives in Mathematics." *Arithmetic Teacher,* 39 (February 1992), pp. 24–29.

Collinson, Judith. "Using Performance Assessment to Determine Mathematical Dispositions." *Arithmetic Teacher,* 39 (February 1992), pp. 40–47.

Cross, Lee, and Hynes, Michael C. "Assessing Mathematics Learning for Students with Learning Differences." *Arithmetic Teacher,* 41 (March 1994), pp. 371–377.

Garafalo, Joe, and Bryant, Jerry. "Assessing Reasonableness: Some Observations and Suggestions." *Arithmetic Teacher,* 40 (December 1992), pp. 210–212.

Juster, Norton. *The Phantom Tollbooth.* New York: Random House, 1993.

Kamii, Constance, and Lewis, Barbara Ann. "Achievement Tests in Primary Mathematics: Perpetuating Lower-Order Thinking." *Arithmetic Teacher,* 38 (May 1991), pp. 4–9.

Kenney, Patricia Ann, and Silver, Edward A. "Student Self-Assessment in Mathematics." In *Assessment in the Mathematics Classroom,* 1993 Yearbook (ed. Norman Webb) Reston, Va.: NCTM, 1993.

Kroll, Diana L.; Masingila, Joanna O.; and Mau, Sue Tinsley. "Cooperative Problem Solving: But What about Grading?" *Arithmetic Teacher,* 39 (February 1992), pp. 17–23.

Kuhs, Therese M. *Measure for Measure: Using Portfolios in K–8 Mathematics.* Portsmouth, N.H.: Heinemann, 1997.

Labinowicz, Ed. *Learning from Children: New Beginnings for Teaching Numerical Thinking.* Menlo Park, Calif.: Addison-Wesley, 1985.

Labinowicz, Ed. "Assessing for Learning: The Interview Method." *Arithmetic Teacher,* 35 (November 1987), pp. 22–25.

Lambdin, Diana V., and Walker, Vicki L. "Planning for Classroom Portfolio Assessment." *Arithmetic Teacher,* 41 (February 1994), pp. 318–324.

Lambdin, Diana V.; Kehle, Paul E.; and Preston, Ronald V. *Emphasis on Assessment: Readings from NCTM's School-Based Journals.* Reston, Va: NCTM, 1996.

Mathematical Sciences Education Board. *Measuring Up: Prototypes for Mathematics Assessment.* Washington, D.C.: National Academy Press, 1993.

Moon, C. Jean. "Connecting Learning and Teaching through Assessment." *Arithmetic Teacher,* 41 (September 1993), pp. 13–15.

Mumme, Judy. *Portfolio Assessment in Mathematics.* Santa Barbara, Calif.: Regents of the University of California, 1990.

Mumme, Judith, and Shepherd, Nancy. "Implementing the Standards: Communication in Mathematics." *Arithmetic Teacher,* 38 (September 1990), pp. 18–22.

National Council of Teachers of Mathematics. *Curriculum and Evaluation Standards for School Mathematics.* Reston, Va: NCTM, 1989.

National Council of Teachers of Mathematics. *Professional Standards for Teachers of Mathematics.* Reston, Va: NCTM, 1991.

National Council of Teachers of Mathematics. *Assessment Standards for School Mathematics.* Reston, Va.: NCTM, 1995.

National Council of Teachers of Mathematics. *Principles and Standards for School Mathematics.* Reston, Va.: NCTM, 2000.

Paulson, F. Leon; Paulson, Pearl R.; and Meyer, Carol A. "What Makes a Portfolio a Portfolio?" *Educational Leadership,* 48 (February 1991), pp. 60–63.

Peck, Donald M.; Jencks, Stanley M.; and Connell, Michael L. "Improving Instruction through Brief Interviews." *Arithmetic Teacher,* 37 (November 1989), pp. 15–17.

Richardson, Kathy. *A Look at Children's Thinking.* Assessment Videos for K–2 Mathematics. Norman, Okla.: Educational Enrichment, 1990.

Ross, Rita, and Kurtz, Ray. "Making Manipulatives Work: A Strategy for Success." *Arithmetic Teacher,* 40 (January 1993), pp. 254–258.

Sanford, Susan. "Assessing Measurement in the Primary Classroom." In *Assessment in the Mathematics Classroom,* 1993 Yearbook (ed. Norman Webb). Reston, Va.: NCTM, 1993.

Sgroi, Laura A.; Gropper, Nancy; Kilker, Mary Tom; Rambusch, Nancy M.; and Semonite, Barbara. "Assessing Young Children's Mathematical Understandings." *Teaching Children Mathematics,* 1 (January 1995), pp. 275–277.

Spangler, Denise A. "Assessing Students' Beliefs about Mathematics." *Arithmetic Teacher,* 40 (November 1992), pp. 148–152.

Stenmark, Jean K. (ed.). *Mathematics Assessment: Myths, Models, Good Questions, and Practical Suggestions.* Reston, Va.: NCTM, 1991.

Vaac, Nancy Nesbitt. "Implement the Professional Standards for Teaching Mathematics: Questioning in the Mathematics Classroom." *Arithmetic Teacher,* 41 (October 1993), pp. 88–91.

Weaver, J. Fred. "Big Dividends from Small Interviews." *Arithmetic Teacher,* 2 (April 1955), pp. 40–47.

Webb, Norman. (ed.). *Assessment in the Mathematics Classroom,* 1993 Yearbook. Reston, Va.: NCTM, 1993.

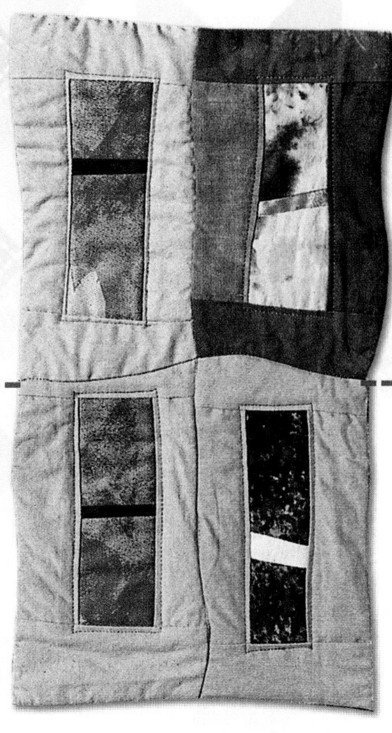

CHAPTER 5

Processes of Doing Mathematics

Snapshot of a Classroom Investigation

Janelle is a second grader in a colorful, lively, classroom. The desks are arranged in groups of four, although the children typically spend a good portion of each day working at various learning centers around the classroom—an art center, a pet center, and a reading corner with a cozy rug and comfy pillows. A significant amount of time is also spent on mathematical problem solving. Janelle and her classmates are often actively engaged in interactive, investigative activities, many of which grow out of questions they bring up themselves.

One day Janelle was proudly showing her new size-2 sport shoes to everyone. When she was chatting with Elizabeth, she noticed that they were approximately the same height. "You're just about the same size as me," she observed, "What size shoe do you wear?" "Two," Elizabeth responded. "So do I!" said Janelle, "I wonder if people who are the same size always have the same shoe size?"

Janelle and Elizabeth shared this thought with their teacher, Mrs. Lester. They were familiar with posing questions and figuring out how to investigate them. They were eager to poll their classmates to see whether their idea about shoes and heights was right. Janelle designed a recording sheet by borrowing a class list from the teacher and copying everyone's name onto the page. She drew two boxes next to each name—one for height and the other for shoe size.

Elizabeth and Janelle recruited Alex to help them go around the classroom asking people about their shoe sizes and their heights. Janelle was the recorder. It wasn't hard to figure out shoe sizes because if their classmates didn't know, they just took off their shoe and looked inside. But very few of the children knew how tall they were, so most of the boxes for height had to be left blank.

Janelle, Elizabeth, and Alex sat on the floor by the reading corner and looked at their data. "Hey, you know what? I just thought of something," said Alex. "I was thinking about who is big and who is small in our class, even if we don't really know exactly how big they are. Some of the biggest kids in the class have shoe sizes that are smaller than some of the smaller kids. Something doesn't make sense here!"

"Who do you mean?" asked Elizabeth.

"Well, Mac is one of the biggest kids, but he only wears size $3\frac{1}{2}$. Chantal wears size 12, but she's smaller than Mac," said Alex.

"Maybe boys' and girls' shoes come in different sizes," Janelle suggested.

Even Mrs. Lester didn't know for sure if that was true, but this idea led Janelle, Elizabeth, and Alex to try comparing the heights and shoe sizes of girls and boys separately.

Elizabeth made a new recording sheet (Figure 5-1). She wrote boys' names on the left and girls' names on the right and put shoe sizes next to the

(This Snapshot of a Lesson is adapted from a true story in *Mathematics in the Making* by Heidi Mills, Timothy O'Keefe, and David Whitin, 1996. Photo: David Young-Wolff/Photo Edit.)

names. She and Janelle looked on the list for two girls or two boys with the same shoe sizes. She planned to ask them to stand back to back to see whether they were the same height. The students had decided that they didn't have to bother with finding a way to measure heights because they could just compare people directly. (Note that they were now investigating a new statement: If you have the same shoe size, then you are the same height—rather than the converse—if you're the same height, you have the same shoe size, which they had started out with.)

James and Nicky had the same shoe size on the chart, so Janelle drew a line to connect those two names. But when James and Nicky stood back to back, they were not the same size. Janelle decided to note this by scribbling over the arrow connecting their names. Janelle also connected Cole's and Nick's names with a scribbly line because they were different heights, even though they wore the same size shoes. She used smooth lines to mark pairs of students who matched both in shoe size and in height.

Janelle, Elizabeth, and Alex were *doing mathematics*. They were involved in observing apparent patterns and regularities, formulating conjectures, gathering data, talking with their peers and with their teacher about their ideas, and inventing ways to represent their findings. Their work involved the fundamental mathematical processes that this chapter is all about: problem solving, reasoning and proof, communication, connections, and representations.

FIGURE 5-1
Elizabeth's recording sheet for shoe sizes and heights.

Boys			Girls		
Name	Shoe Size	Height	Name	Shoe Size	Height
Nick	2		Jamie	12	
Thomas	3		Emma	2	
Alex	3		Janelle	2	
Nicholas	4		Chantal	12	
Brian	2		Elizabeth	2	
James	3 1/2		Natasha	4	
Mac	3 1/2		Tiffany	2	
Nicky	3 1/2		Melinda	2 1/2	
Neema	4 1/2		Michaela	3	
Cole	2		Christy	2	
Ashton	12		Vandana	2	
Ben	3		Katie	3	
			Eloise	12	
			Rebecca	4 1/2	

Introduction

As we have seen in earlier chapters, school mathematics is moving in new directions. Now, in many mathematics classrooms, it is rare for a lesson to be taught to rows of children studiously bent over worksheets, practicing computations, rules, and formulas. Instead, it is more common to observe children first working in small groups while talking and using tiles or blocks to model a problem, then moving to their desks to write individually about what they have discovered, and finally engaging in a whole-class discussion about what has been learned. Students are encouraged to share their ideas, observations, and problem-solving processes. They listen carefully to each other, and they challenge and question each other.

In doing mathematics, students are actively involved in a wide variety of physical and mental actions—actions that can be described by verbs such as *exploring, investigating, patterning, experimenting, modeling, conjecturing,* and *verifying.* Doing mathematics is learning mathematics.

The *Principles and Standards for School Mathematics* (NCTM, 2000) highlight this active vision of learning and doing mathematics by identifying the five process standards listed in Table 5-1 (i.e., problem solving, reasoning and proof, communication, connections, and representations). These process standards share equal billing with the five content standards (i.e., number, algebra, geometry, measurement, and data). The *NCTM Standards* make it clear that doing mathematics means engaging in these fundamental processes.

This chapter provides a brief introduction to these five important processes for doing and making sense of matheamtics. In Chapter 6, we give special attention to problem solving as a foundation on which the entire mathematics curriculum can be organized.

FOCUS QUESTIONS

1. What are some advantages of learning mathematics through problem solving?
2. For young children, what does mathematical reasoning involve and how does it help them make sense of mathematical knowledge and relationships?
3. How can elementary children be encouraged to communicate their mathematical thinking?
4. What connections are important to aid elementary children in learning mathematics?
5. What are three major goals for representation as a process in elementary school mathematics?

Math Links 5.1

You can read more about the process standards on the NCTM web site, which you can access from this book's web site. Once you have found the index, you can click on each individual process standard to read more about it.

Math Links 5.2

A variety of web resources for each process standard, which may be used by both teachers and children, may be found at NCTM's Illuminations web site, which you can access from this book's web site.

Problem Solving

What comes to mind when you think of problem solving? Some people think of challenging situations they may have encountered in real life, such as when their car got stuck in a snow bank, and they were unable to get it out until they put floor mats under the wheels to provide greater traction. Similarly, when you think of problem solving in the mathematics classroom, you may think of challenging situations involving numbers or shapes or patterns. For example, a state official may need to figure out how many distinct license plates can be produced if each must be printed with a unique identifier consisting of exactly six characters. Perhaps the characters may be chosen only from among the 10 numeric digits (0–9) and 25 of the 26 letters of the alphabet (with the letter *O* excluded because it can be confused with the numeral zero). How many different license plates are possible? That's a problem!

Alternately, when you think of mathematical problem solving you may remember the story problems or word problems that often came at the end of each chapter of the mathematics text when you were in elementary school. After you had learned to perform certain computations (say, multiplication of fractions), your text may have provided problems in context that used those same skills. In many cases, these may not have been genuine problems because the techniques to use had been clearly outlined in the preceding pages.

Problem solving, as envisioned by the *NCTM Standards,* is much more than just finding answers to lists of exercises. Problem solving is a "major means of developing mathematical knowledge"

Table 5-1 • Process Standards for School Mathematics

Problem Solving	Instructional programs from pre-K through grade 12 should enable all students to: • Build new mathematical knowledge through problem solving. • Solve problems that arise in mathematics and in other contexts. • Apply and adapt a variety of appropriate strategies to solve problems. • Monitor and reflect on the process of mathematical problem solving.
Reasoning and Proof	Instructional programs from pre-K through grade 12 should enable all students to: • Recognize reasoning and proof as fundamental aspects of mathematics. • Make and investigate mathematical conjectures. • Develop and evaluate mathematical arguments and proofs. • Select and use various types of reasoning and methods of proof.
Communication	Instructional programs from pre-K through grade 12 should enable all students to: • Organize and consolidate their mathematical thinking through communication. • Communicate their mathematical thinking coherently and clearly to peers, teachers, and others. • Analyze and evaluate the mathematical thinking and strategies of others. • Use the language of mathematics to express mathematical ideas precisely.
Connections	Instructional programs from pre-K through grade 12 should enable all students to: • Recognize and use connections among mathematical ideas. • Understand how mathematical ideas interconnect and build on one another to produce a coherent whole. • Recognize and apply mathematics in contexts outside of mathematics.
Representation	Instructional programs from pre-K through grade 12 should enable all students to: • Create and use representation to organize, record, and communicate mathematical ideas. • Select, apply, and translate among mathematical representations to solve problems. • Use representations to model and interpret physical, social, and mathematical phenomena.

(NCTM, 2000, p. 116). By general agreement, a problem is a situation in which a person wants something and does not know immediately what to do to get it. Problem solving is the foundation of all mathematical activity. As such, problem solving should play a prominent role in the elementary school mathematics curriculum. The children in the *Snapshot of a Classroom Investigation* identified a problem in which they were interested—whether children who are the same height wear the same shoe size. As they collected data, they were confronted with a conflict in their original problem statement: Chantal with a shoe size of 12 was shorter than Mac, a taller boy with a shoe size of $3\frac{1}{2}$. Typical of young children, they exhibited flexibility with their problem statement, shifting their problem to whether children with the same shoe size were the same height. This new problem caused them to adapt their data collection strategy for solving the problem. The children were not computing answers, but they were working with numbers and doing mathematics.

Consider a different type of problem, actually a game that can be played by children in upper elementary grades. To investigate this particular problem, you will need to play the game with one or more opponents. You'll need two dice, 12 small chips or tiles or markers each, and a piece of paper on which to make a game board for each person (see In the Classroom 5-1).

Place your chips on the game board, putting as many or as few as you like on each of the 12 numbered spaces. (For example, you might choose to put all your chips on your favorite number, 4, or one chip on each space, or two chips on each of the even spaces and leave all the odd spaces empty. It's your decision.) Roll the dice. Say you get 3 and 5. Find the sum $(3 + 5 = 8)$. If you have any chips on the 8 space, you may remove one of them. When anyone rolls, everyone plays, so your opponents also should be removing a chip from the 8 space on their boards, if they can. Roll the dice again, sum the results, and remove another chip. The goal of the game is to be the first person to remove all your chips from your board. Try the game a couple of times before reading on.

Here's the problem: Find a good strategy for placing your chips at the start of this game, so that you are more likely to be able to clear your board quickly. Which squares are good to avoid? Are there certain sums that rarely (or never) came up when you rolled the pair of dice? Why? Which squares are good to put chips on? Are there certain sums that came up rather often? Why? Can you explain why some sums are more likely than others? A fourth-grade class played this game several times, worked on the problem of finding a useful game strategy, talked about what they discovered,

In the Classroom 5-1

ROLLING THE DICE

OBJECTIVE: **Using a dice game to investigate experimental and theoretical probabilities and to develop analytical reasoning skills.**

GRADE LEVEL: **3–4**

MATERIALS: **Twelve counters or chips for each player, one pair of dice for each four players.**

RULES OF THE GAME

Up to four players can play together with one pair of dice. Each player has his/her own game board. You begin by placing all 12 of your counters on your game board. The game board has 12 spaces numbered 1–12. You may place as many counters as you choose (from 0 to 12) on each space. You may leave spaces blank, and you may put one or more than one counter on any space.

Players take turns rolling the dice. The first player rolls the two dice and finds their sum. (For example, if 2 and 3 are rolled, the sum is 5.) Each player may remove one counter from his or her 5 space. Even if there is more than one counter on that space, only one may be removed. If there are no counters on that space, no counters may be removed from any space. The next player rolls the two dice and finds their sum (e.g., $4 + 4 = 8$). Each player now removes one counter from his/her 8 space, and so on. The goal of the game is to empty your board. The first player with no counters left on his/her board is the winner.

ANALYZING THE GAME

When you have played several times, talk with each other about these questions:

- Which sums were rolled most often?
- Which sums were never rolled, or not rolled very often?
- Why do you think some sums came up more often than others?
- Can you prove which sums are most likely to occur?
- What do you think is a good strategy for placing your counters on the game board? Why?

WRITING ABOUT THE GAME

Write advice to a friend who is new to the game. Tell him or her your favorite strategy for placing counters on the game board, and explain why you believe this strategy is a good one.

ROLLING THE DICE GAME BOARD

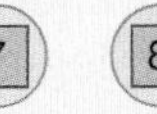

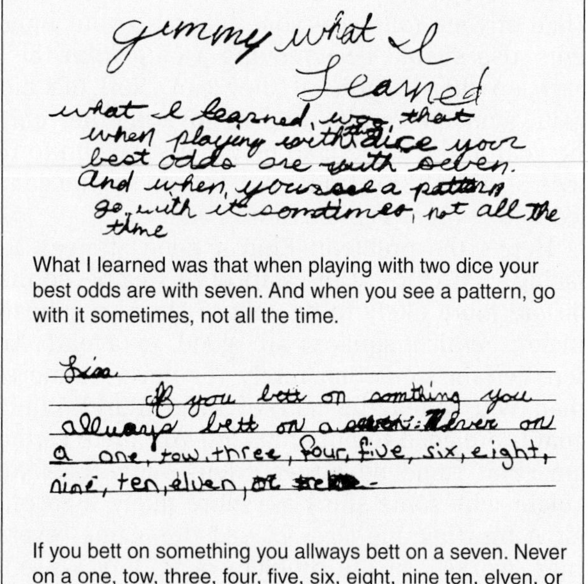

What I learned was that when playing with two dice your best odds are with seven. And when you see a pattern, go with it sometimes, not all the time.

If you bett on something you allways bett on a seven. Never on a one, tow, three, four, five, six, eight, nine ten, elven, or trelv.

T.J.

That number seven is the best number to beat on not to [two] or twelve if you go to a cuceno [casino] you should no [know] that.

FIGURE 5-2 Fourth-grade students' writing about playing the dice game.

and then wrote about their findings. See Figure 5-2 for what some of the children wrote.

In a classroom where mathematics is taught through problem solving, students given the challenge of the dice game might already have had previous experiences with making organized lists or making tables. Nevertheless, their teacher would *not* have provided them with advice about exactly how to solve the problem if he or she wanted this to be a true problem-solving challenge. A reasonable approach is to begin experimenting by playing a few games. It is helpful to keep a list of the sums obtained when the dice are rolled. If you don't keep a list, it may be hard to be sure which sums come up more often than others. Haphazard experimentation is not likely to produce a good, well-justified solution. Solving this problem requires students to think logically and to make some important decisions, particularly about how to keep track in a systematic way of the sums that come up. (Perhaps even better is keeping track of the pairs of dice that lead to those sums; writing down $5 + 2 = 7$ is more informative than just writing 7, since 7 could be obtained in several different ways.) A skill such as making an organized list or a table can be useful in a wide variety of problem situations.

When you roll two dice, you are much more likely to roll a sum of 7 than a sum of 3, since there are only two ways to get 3 ($1 + 2$ and $2 + 1$), but there are many more ways to get 7. As this problem helps develop general problem-solving expertise, it also deepens students' understanding of probability (helping them to recognize that we can compare the likelihood of rolling various sums by seeing how many ways those sums can be formed). The probability of rolling a 7 is actually $\frac{6}{36}$, whereas the probability of rolling a 3 is only $\frac{2}{36}$ (refer to Figure 5-3 to see two ways of representing the 36 different possible sums: $1 + 1$, $1 + 2$, . . . , all the way up to $6 + 6$). Students who work on this problem are learning about probability *through* problem solving. They are also developing and using a strategy for playing a game that can be used to solve other problems in mathematics, as well as in other contexts.

What kinds of problems are appropriate for elementary school students? In the early grades, most school mathematics problems are related in some way to the children's own experiences, as in the *Snapshot of a Classroom Investigation*, because their world is relatively circumscribed and children relate best to concrete situations. By upper elementary, however, the universe of problem contexts should diversify. Increasingly, problems can grow out of situations in the world at large or from the investigation of mathematical ideas. Mathematics instruction in the upper grades can take advantage of the increasing sophistication of students and their growing knowledge of such topics as probability, statistics, and geometry.

Upper elementary students can deal with messier and more complex problems than primary children can, not only because they are more capable and confident in working with mathematical ideas than younger children, but also because they can use technology to alleviate much of the drudgery that—until recently—often constrained school mathematics to considering problems with "nice numbers." Computers, calculators, and electronic data-gathering devices such as calculator-based laboratories (CBLs) and calculator-based rangers (CBRs) provide simpler methods for gathering and analyzing data that in years past might have been considered too much trouble. Similarly, classroom Internet connections make it possible for students

						6+1					
					5+1	5+2	6+2				
				4+1	4+2	4+3	5+3	6+3			
			3+1	3+2	3+3	3+4	4+4	5+4	6+4		
		2+1	2+2	2+3	2+4	2+5	3+5	4+5	5+5	6+5	
	1+1	1+2	1+3	1+4	1+5	1+6	2+6	3+6	4+6	5+6	6+6
Sums	**2**	**3**	**4**	**5**	**6**	**7**	**8**	**9**	**10**	**11**	**12**

+	1	2	3	4	5	6
1	1	1	1	1	1	1
2	2	2	2	2	2	2
3	3	3	3	3	3	3
4	4	4	4	4	4	4
5	5	5	5	5	5	5
6	6	6	6	6	6	6

FIGURE 5-3
Two tables showing possible outcomes for rolling two dice.

to look up facts and figures quickly and easily for use in posing and solving a wide variety of real-world problems. Graphing calculators and easy-to-use computer software enable students to move effortlessly between different representations of problem data. They can also compute with large quantities of data and with "messy" numbers, both large and small, with relative ease. As a result, problems in the elementary school can and should be responsive to student questions and interests. (*Note:* With the importance of problem solving to the development of mathematical knowledge, in Chapter 6 we consider issues of how to teach mathematics through problem solving and how to assess students' through problem-solving work.)

Reasoning and Proof

From their earliest experiences with mathematical challenges and problems, children should understand that they are expected to supply reasons for their arguments. The question "Why do you think so?" should be commonplace in the classroom. Teachers should not be the only ones asking, "Why?" Asking why comes naturally to small children. They should be encouraged to sustain their natural curiosity for justification as they share their mathematical ideas with each other. When children observe a pattern (e.g., whenever you add two odd numbers, the answer is even), they should be encouraged to ask why. One second grader used square tiles to represent and sort various numbers (see Figure 5-4) and then explained his reasoning as follows: "All the even numbers are just rectangles. But all the odd numbers are rectangles with 'chimneys.' If you put two groups with chimneys together, the new one doesn't have a chimney. So two odds makes an

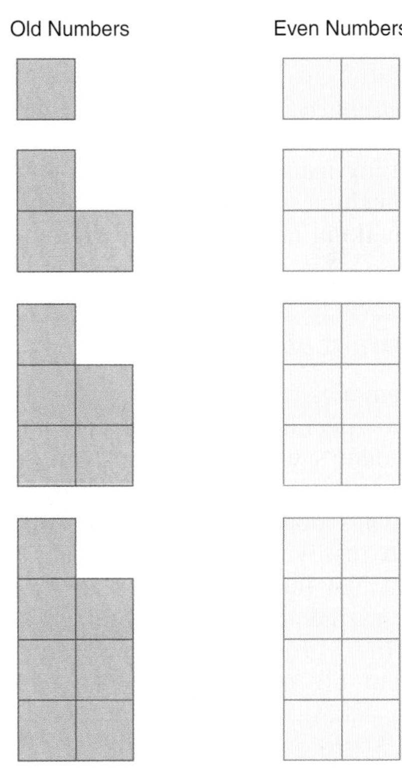

FIGURE 5-4 Pictures of odds and evens can help students justify why the sum of two odd numbers is always even.

even." If students are consistently expected to explore, question, conjecture, and justify their ideas, they learn that mathematics should make sense, rather than believing that mathematics is a set of arbitrary rules and formulas. This notion underlies NCTM's reasoning and proof process standard.

Being able to reason mathematically is essential to making sense of mathematics and, ultimately, to justifying mathematical conjectures. Proof is often interpreted as a formal process, reserved for students in advanced mathematics. On the contrary, in the elementary classroom, clear articulation of the reasoning is sufficient and thus equivalent to proof. Reasoning and proof cannot be taught in a single unit or lesson; they must be consistent expectations throughout all units and lessons in all grades. "By developing ideas, exploring phenomena, justifying results, and using mathematical conjectures in all content areas and—with different expectations of sophistication—at all grade levels, students should see and expect that mathematics makes sense" (NCTM, 2000, p. 56).

But what must elementary teachers consider in order to promote an environment where children are nurtured and encouraged to make sense of mathematical ideas and thus develop their abilities to reason mathematically, providing proofs of mathematical conjectures? Russell (1999) identifies four important points about active mathematical reasoning in elementary school classrooms: (1) reasoning is about making generalizations, (2) reasoning leads to a web of generalizations, (3) reasoning leads to mathematical memory built on relationships, (4) learning through reasoning requires making mistakes and learning from them.

Reasoning Is About Making Generalizations

Mathematics is much more than just finding answers to specific problems or computations. Indeed, in today's world, machines can do much of the computational drudgery. Reasoning mathematically involves observing patterns, thinking about them, and justifying why they should be true in more than just individual instances. A simple example of mathematical reasoning occurs when a kindergartner, proud of his new-found ability to think about big numbers, eagerly challenges his mother by asking, "Do you know how much 2 trillion plus 3 trillion is? It's 5 trillion!" There is no doubt that this boy has never seen a trillion of anything, nor is he able to write numbers in the trillions. But he is familiar with the pattern in smaller cases (2 apples + 3 apples = 5 apples; 2 hundred + 3 hundred = 5 hundred), so he is able to generalize to adding trillions.

Russell (1999) offers another example of making generalizations in the story of Katie, a third grader who was working with a partner to find factor pairs for 120. The students believed at first that 3×42 might be such a factor pair (a result obtained by incorrectly counting squares on a rectangular array on graph paper); however, Katie reasoned that answer must be incorrect because she remembered that 6×20 was a valid factor pair for 120, and from previous experience in finding factor pairs, she had figured out that if you halved one factor, you should double the other factor to keep the product the same. This is a powerful and useful generalization. Using this line of reasoning, Katie reported that the correct factor pair must be 3×40, not 3×42. When children go beyond specific instances of mathematical ideas to consider general cases, they are reasoning mathematically.

Reasoning Leads to a Web of Generalizations

A second point about mathematical reasoning is that it "leads to an interconnected web of mathematical knowledge within a mathematical domain" (Russell, 1999, p. 1). Students should expect newly encountered mathematical ideas to fit with ideas they have already learned. Students have much more mathematical power if they have many ways to think about a number or fact or assertion. Students might understand in the first grade that "three quarters" is between "one half dollar" and "one dollar"; however, they have a much more extensive understanding of the fact that three quarters is between one half and one when they also understand this relationship in terms of fractions ($\frac{1}{2}$, $\frac{3}{4}$, 1), in terms of equivalent fractions ($\frac{2}{4}$, $\frac{3}{4}$, $\frac{4}{4}$), in terms of decimals (0.5, 0.75, and 1.00), and by visualizing pieces of a pie or portions of a collection of trading cards. When students incorrectly claim that 0.25 must be larger than 0.5 because 25 is more than 5, they probably have not developed a robust web of connections for such ideas. They are unable to reason about the other meanings they may know for these two numbers, and are thereby unable to recognize the contradiction in their thinking.

Reasoning Leads to Mathematical Memory Built on Relationships

A third point about mathematical reasoning is that the development of a web of mathematical understandings is the foundation of what Russell calls *mathematical memory* (or mathematical sense), a capability that provides the basis for insight into mathematical problems. For example, consider the problem of finding the sum of the first 100 counting

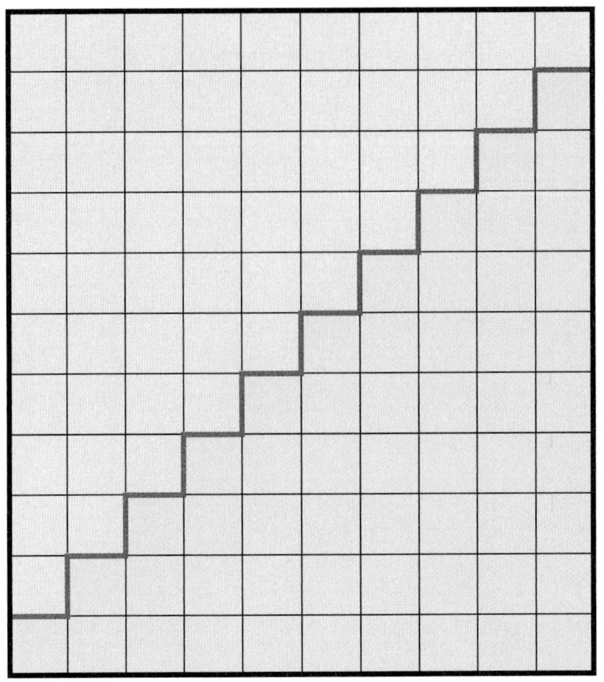

FIGURE 5-5 A 10-by-11 rectangle built with two staircases from 1 to 10 can help you remember the formula for the sum of a series of numbers.

numbers: $1 + 2 + 3 + . . . + 100$. Some time in your years of studying mathematics, you probably encountered a formula that would allow you to calculate the sum of any arithmetic series (a list of numbers where the difference between consecutive numbers is always the same—here, the difference is always just one). If you are like most people, you have long since forgotten that formula because it is not something that you use every day. On the other hand, if you have ever seen a geometric illustration of that formula, your web of mathematical understanding may be strong enough to help you reconstruct the formula with little trouble.

Picture the sum from 1 to 100 as a set of stairs. Picture another identical set of stairs. Turn the second set of stairs upside down on the first, and you have a rectangle (100 wide, 101 high). (See Figure 5-5 for a picture of a related, simpler problem: a 10-by-11 rectangle built from two staircases from 1 to 10.) It's easy to find the area of the 100-by-101 rectangle ($100 \times 101 = 10{,}100$). The sum you want is half of this (100×101 divided by 2, or 5,050) because the rectangle is made of two staircases instead of just the one original staircase.

Using the same idea, you can figure out how to find the sum, S, from 1 to any number, n. It's just $S = \frac{n(n+1)}{2}$. A similar line of reasoning can be used to find the sums for various other arithmetic series (such as $1 + 3 + 5 + . . . + 175$ or $12 + 15 + 18 + . . . + 639$). In other words, if you can connect the idea of summing numbers in a series with the geometric illustration of the dual staircases, you'll never again need to worry about forgetting the formula for the sum of an arithmetic series.

Learning through Reasoning Requires Making Mistakes and Learning from Them

A final, important point about mathematical reasoning and proof is that one of the best ways to develop stronger reasoning and proof abilities is to study flawed or incorrect reasoning. There will be many times when your students think they've figured something out, but their reasoning just isn't quite right. That's just human nature. For example, a student might observe that you can make the problem $29 + 95$ easier to do mentally by adding 29 and 100, then subtracting 5 (obtaining the correct sum, 124). Can this same shortcut be used to make the problem 29×95 easier to do mentally (i.e., can you multiply 29 times 100, and then subtract 5)? It turns out that just isn't correct! Why? Rather than just tell your students that this doesn't work, it would be much better to help them investigate why the shortcut works for addition and why it does not work for multiplication. Some possible approaches would be to try adding and multiplying a wide variety of examples to try to figure out what is going on. Or it might help to represent the problems geometrically (using a 29-by-95 array to represent the multiplication and comparing it with a 29-by-100 array may offer some insights; see Figure 5-6).

Your role as a teacher is to encourage students constantly to examine their own thinking and the thinking of others, and to help them uncover and understand flawed reasoning when it occurs.

Communication

Because language is a powerful tool for organizing thinking about mathematical ideas, it is extremely important for students to have many experiences with talking and writing about mathematics, describing and explaining their ideas. Conversely, it is also important that students often be on the receiving end of communications: hearing about, reading about, and listening to the descriptions and explanations of others. Two-way communication about mathematical ideas helps students identify, clarify, organize, articulate, and extend their thinking. Have you ever noticed how

9
10
10

10 10 10 10 10 10 10 10 10 5

29 × 95

9
10
10

10 10 10 10 10 10 10 10

29 × 100

FIGURE 5-6 Visualizing 29 × 95 and 29 × 100 helps students identify the flaw in their reasoning.

struggling to explain an idea helped you figure out what you were really thinking? Reflection and communication are intertwined. Sharing your ideas with others through talking or writing forces you to think more deeply about those ideas. Also, in thinking about your ideas, you often deepen your understanding and, consequently, are able to communicate even more clearly. Communication is obviously a process rather than an end in itself.

Students should be encouraged to communicate their mathematical thinking in a variety of modes: through pictures, gestures, graphs, charts, and symbols, as well as through words (both spoken and written). Figures 5-4, 5-5, and 5-6 clearly illustrate the power of visuals in communicating about mathematics. Such nonverbal communication is often useful in promoting learning.

Especially at first, students' efforts at verbal communication about mathematical ideas may be idiosyncratic (they may use symbols and expressions that they have made up on their own). Over time, with more experience and practice, students learn to use conventional and more precise language to express their ideas. Indeed, mathematics as a language has a vocabulary, syntax, and symbolism all its own. Sometimes words or phrases used in everyday conversation may be used in mathematics with different, more precise, meanings. The symbolism of mathematics (particularly equations and graphs) often helps clarify concepts and promote understanding. Throughout their elementary school years, students should have daily opportunities for communicating about

Math Links 5.3

If you would like the opportunity to see a teacher facilitating children's communication, view the video clips, Teaching, Learning, and Communicating about Fractions, at the NCTM Illuminations web site, which you can access from this book's web site.

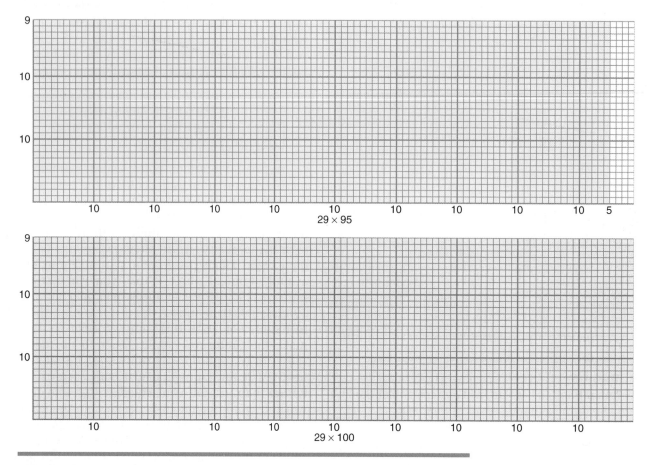

mathematical ideas. Gradually, they should be expected to incorporate more precise mathematical terms in their explanations.

Making writing a regular part of the mathematics curriculum provides students with opportunities to review, reiterate, and consolidate their thinking about mathematical ideas. One of the simplest yet most effective modes of writing about mathematics is open-ended writing as follow-up to a lesson. In response to the prompt "What did you learn today?" even young children can describe their activities and their understanding in a variety of ways. Wilde (1991) shares writing about a fraction lesson by Vilavanh, a fifth grader who needed extra help in math:

> When you do fractions you have to think what number is higher or lower than can equal a whole pizza. When you are splitting a pizza you have to think how many pieces will each person get. When you have a number like this—$\frac{1}{2}$, $\frac{1}{8}$—the number that is higher has to give eight pieces to a person. You'll only have a little piece. The person who gets $\frac{1}{2}$ gets a bigger piece, gets a lot, because $\frac{1}{2}$ is bigger than $\frac{1}{8}$.

Vilavanh apparently is beginning to understand that a fraction with a larger denominator represents division into more pieces, and thus the pieces are smaller. Teachers can use students' writing diagnostically. When the writings of many students in a group or class reveal similar confusions or misconceptions, the teacher can more appropriately plan future lessons.

Mathematics journals can be used to prompt students to write about mathematics. The regularity of writing in a journal can help students monitor their own understanding of mathematical concepts. Students can be encouraged to write about such questions as "What am I puzzled about?" and "What mistakes do I make and why?" When teachers take time to respond to student journals on a regular basis, however briefly, the journals can become a regular chain of communication between student and teacher.

Other forms of writing in math class include having students write their own word problems, having them describe their solutions to problem-solving activities, having them describe a procedure or process, and writing about connections between and among ideas. Young children can be encouraged to use their own invented spelling, and all students can benefit by accompanying words with pictures and symbols so they can express themselves as fully and completely as possible.

Some useful references on writing and communication in mathematics classes include Azzolino (1990), Ciochine and Polivka (1997), Countryman (1992), Ford (1990), Van Zoest and Enyart (1998), and Wilde (1991).

Connections

Although mathematics is often represented as a list of topics or a collection of skills, this is a shallow view. Mathematics is actually a well-integrated domain of study. The ideas of school mathematics are richly connected. It is important for the elementary school curriculum to provide children with ongoing opportunities to experience and appreciate the connectedness of the subject.

At least three types of connections are important in learning mathematics. First, ideas within mathematics itself are richly connected with one another. Students who learn about fractions, decimals, and percentages in isolation from one another miss an important opportunity to see the connections among these ideas. For example, in Figure 5-7, we can see why $\frac{1}{4}$, .25, and 2 tenths + 5 hundredths are actually all names for the same quantity.

A second important type of connection is between the symbols and procedures of mathematics and the conceptual ideas that the symbolism represents. For example, why do we refer to 3^2 as "3 squared"? 3^2 is 3×3, or 9. A drawing of 9 dots, arranged in a 3-by-3 array, forms a square. Similarly, any array of x-by-x dots would form a square; thus students can recognize why x^2 is read as "x squared." The area of any geometric figure is generally reported in square units (e.g., square feet, square centimeters, square miles). Why? Because measuring area is actually just measuring how many "squares" it would take to cover a surface. If the squares are one inch on each side, then you are measuring in square inches. In fact, you can write "in.^{2}" instead of "square inches" for the same reason. So here you can see connections between number theory (the "square numbers" 4, 9, 16, etc., as shown in Figure 5-8), algebraic language (x squared), and measurement (square inches).

A third type of connection is between mathematics and the real world (or mathematics and other school subjects). Classroom instruction should provide many opportunities for children to experience how mathematics is used in domains

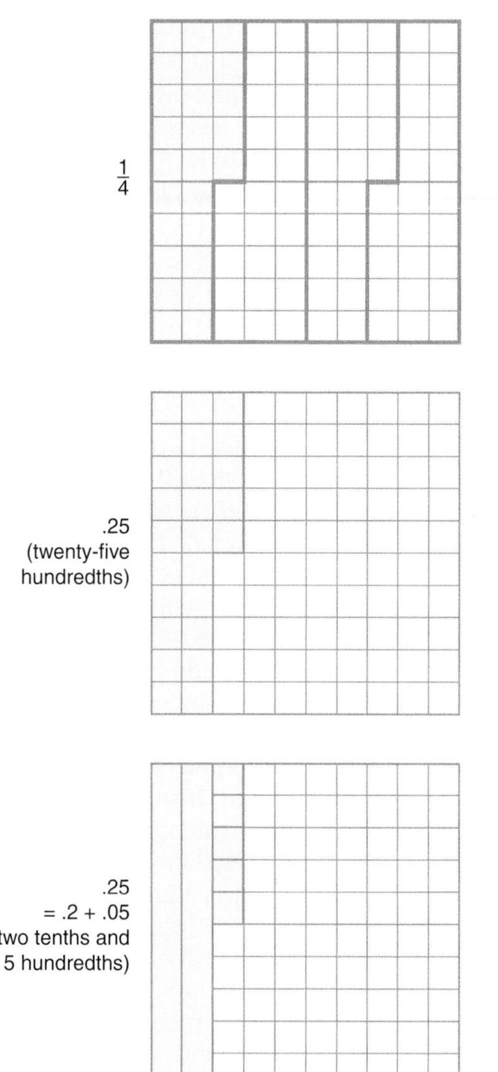

FIGURE 5-7 Representations for $\frac{1}{4}$, 25 hundredths (.25), and 2 tenths plus 5 hundredths (.25 = .2 + .05) show that they are equivalent.

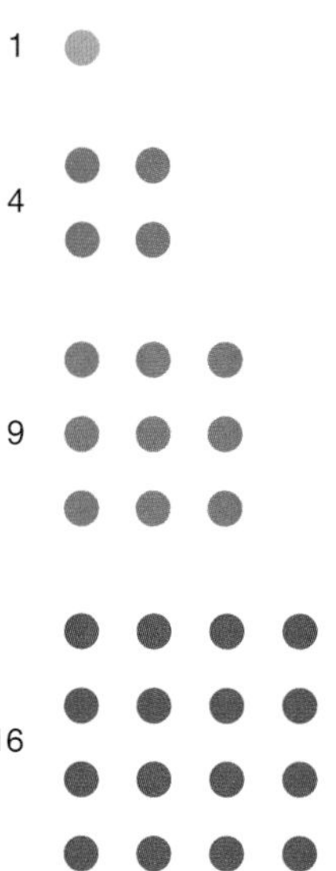

FIGURE 5-8 Arranging dots in square patterns connects the numbers 1, 4, 9, and 16 to their reference as square numbers.

such as science, business, home economics, social studies, and art. Applications of mathematics can be highlighted through integrated or thematic curricula, through mathematics lessons motivated by problem situations or by situations in children's literature, and through consistently engaging students in real-world problems as they occur in the classroom. (For example, this class has 24 students. Today 4 desks are empty. Everyone who is here today wants to buy the school lunch. How many orders for lunch should be sent to the office?) As they encounter problems from real-world contexts where mathematics is a significant part of the solution, students come to recognize and value the utility and relevance of the subject.

Math Links 5.4

If you would like to learn more about connections between mathematics and other school subjects, visit the Eisenhower National Clearinghouse site, which you can access from this book's web site. This site provides strategies, resources, and articles with audio and video clips.

Representations

When most people think of mathematics, they may think of numbers such as 2, 29, or 5280 or of numeric or symbolic expressions such as 5×2, $(a + b)(a - b)$, or $5798 \div 13$ or equations such as $x^2 + y^2 = r^2$ or $2x + 7 = 13$. Alternatively, they may think of tables of numbers or graphs or geometric figures. All are commonly used representations for mathematical ideas. Interestingly, it often is possible to use a variety of these different representations to illustrate the same mathematical ideas. Different representations for an idea can lead us to different ways of understanding and using that idea. This is the power of representation.

The school mathematics curriculum has traditionally involved children in learning about a wide variety of representations for mathematical ideas; however, different representations were often learned in isolation from one another. For example, students might have learned about fractions in one chapter and decimals in another, but not have been provided with enough opportunities to connect these two different representations for the same numbers. It is important to challenge and encourage students to connect and to compare and contrast the utility and power of different representations.

The *NCTM Standards* discusses three major goals for representation as a process in school mathematics: (1) creating and using representations to organize, record, and communicate mathematical ideas; (2) selecting, applying, and translating among representations to solve problems; and (3) using representations to model and interpret physical, social, and mathematical phenomena.

Creating and Using Representations

In the *Snapshot* that opened this chapter, children are developing their own individual representations for organizing, recording, and communicating data about the heights and shoe sizes of their classmates. When they discovered that their initial recording sheet wasn't helpful in showing how heights and shoe sizes were related (or not related) and didn't help with sorting out boy-girl differences, they devised a new representation. It is important for young children to have repeated opportunities both to invent their own ways of recording and communicating mathematical ideas and to work with conventional representations. The mathematical symbols and representations that are used every day (e.g., base-ten notation, equations, coordinate graphs) have been polished and refined over many centuries. When students come to understand them in deep ways, they have a set of tools that expands their capacity to think mathematically.

Selecting, Applying, and Translating Among Representations

As mentioned earlier, mathematical ideas can often be represented in different ways. Each of these representations may be appropriate for different purposes. For example, a student who can think flexibly about numbers is probably able to think about the number 24 in many different ways: 2 tens and 4 ones, 1 ten and 14 ones, a little less than 25, double 12, the perimeter of a square with side 6, the area of rectangles with sides 2×12 or 4×6, and so on. Depending on the problem at hand, some of these representations may be more useful than others. Technology now offers students many opportunities for experiences with translating among representations. Data analysis software can help students easily compare and contrast various graphical representations. It is important that students consider the kinds of data and questions for which the graphical representation is appropriate.

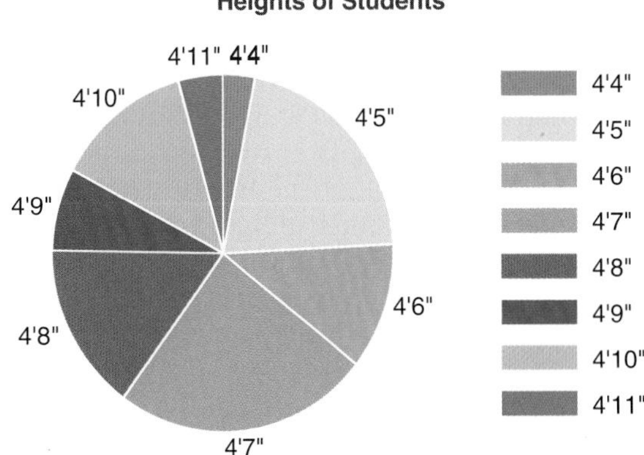

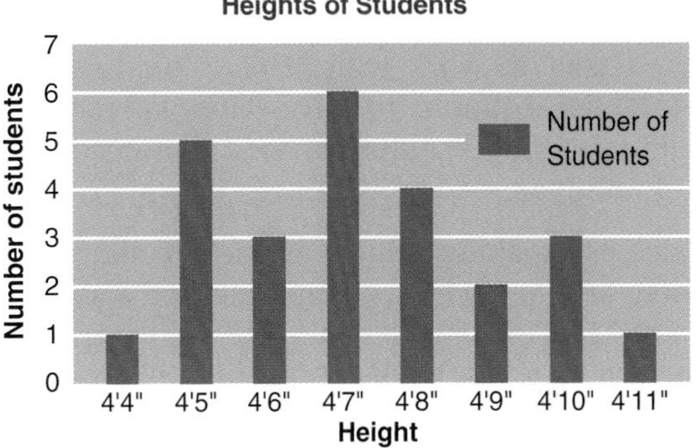

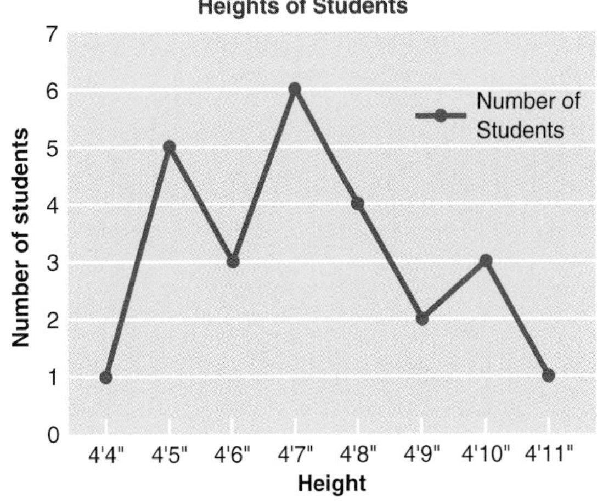

FIGURE 5-9 Which graph best represents the heights of students in the class?

For example, Figure 5-9 shows the results when a class was asked to describe the heights of the students in the class. They recorded their heights in the appropriate rows in a spreadsheet and prepared three graphs: a bar graph, a circle graph, and a line graph. Which graph best represents the data collected? Children are used to being lined up by height. However, the pie graph does not order the heights as clearly as either the bar or line graph. The line graph incorrectly gives the impression that there are children of heights between the measurement points. On the other hand, the bar graph shows that the most common height of the children is 4 feet 7 inches and that the second most common height is 4 feet 5 inches.

Using Representations to Model and Interpret Phenomena

Much of mathematics involves simplifying problems—stripping away context and excess information to reduce them to symbols or representations that are easier to work with. This is mathematical modeling. For example, to solve the following word problem, you might reduce it to a picture or to a table of numbers:

> Alice is stacking soup cans for display on a shelf at the end of a supermarket aisle. She wants the display to look like a pyramid. On the top row she wants to put just one can, on the next-to-top row 3 cans, on the next row down 5 cans, and so on. Alice decides the display can be 6 rows high. How many cans should she start with on the bottom row?

Once you've made a picture or a table of numbers, the fact that the problem is about stacking soup cans is no longer really important. You've modeled the problem and used the power of mathematics to solve it. Similarly, when students ask, when solving word problems, "Do I add or do I subtract?" they are asking for advice about modeling the situation at hand. It is important to encourage students not to move too quickly and unthinkingly from real-world situations to abstract models. The best answer to the question about adding or subtracting is to ask, "What's going on in the problem?" or "Can you draw a picture or can you act it out to help you decide which operation to use?"

It is also important to check back at the end of solving a problem to ensure that the solution obtained from the mathematical model fits the original situation. A classic example is a problem where students are asked to determine how many buses are needed to take a school of children on a field trip. The problem tells how many students need to be transported and how many can fit in each bus. Many students correctly pick out the numbers in the problem and divide, but then offer nonsensical answers such as $3\frac{1}{4}$ or 3.25. They have forgotten to check back with the context of the problem, to see that a more sensible answer would be 4 buses or perhaps 3 buses and a van.

In sum, representations are ways of thinking about ideas. Individuals develop their own idiosyncratic ways of thinking, but mathematics offers a broad repertoire of conventional representations that are helpful in problem solving and in communicating about mathematical ideas. One of the most important goals of mathematics instruction should be to help students build bridges from their own ways of thinking to the conventional, so that they come to understand, value, and use these powerful mathematical tools.

Math Links 5.5

Acting out the problem is another way children often model and solve problems. For example, use the electronic manipulative available from this book's web site to solve the Tower of Hanoi problem. How did the manipulative facilitate solving the problem?

Teaching Mathematics Through Problem Solving

The previous discussion about problem solving as one of the five fundamental processes for school mathematics described the general nature of problem solving and briefly considered the types of problems that may be appropriate for elementary school students; however, the important aspect is that problem solving can serve as a foundation for all your mathematics teaching because it involves students in work with all the fundamental processes of doing mathematics (reasoning, communicating, connecting, and representing).

Problem solving is a way of teaching. This means it involves more than the presentation of word problems; it involves the way you encourage children to approach mathematical learning. A situation is posed, as in a word problem, and then there is a search for a resolution, often using some of the same processes or procedures as are used in solving a word problem. But the situation that is posed often has a mathematical basis beyond the application of some procedures. Students or the teacher may pose the problem. In either case, using problems as a jumping-off point for mathematics instruction involves the teacher in posing questions that provoke student thought and also in encouraging students to pose their own questions. Using problem solving as a foundation for mathematics instruction requires students to engage in a search for a reasonable solution or solutions.

One group of researchers proposes that

> students should be allowed to make the subject problematic . . . allowing students to wonder why things are, to inquire, to search for solutions, and to resolve incongruities. It means that both curriculum and instruction should begin with problems, dilemmas, and questions for students. (Hiebert et al., 1996)

Franke and Carey (1997) are among those who have begun the process of documenting the changes in children's perceptions about mathematics when they are taught in an environment reflecting the spirit of the *NCTM Standards*. They write about students who have been involved in the Cognitively Guided Instruction (CGI) program. In the CGI model of instruction, the teacher poses a rich mathematical task. Students take time to work individually or in small groups to solve the problem and then share their approaches with each other. Students are encouraged to listen carefully to each other and to question each other about processes and strategies. The teacher's role is to choose appropriate tasks and to orchestrate the classroom discourse, using what he or she knows about the students' developmental level. A key aspect of CGI is the teacher's ability to analyze the children's thinking and to guide classroom problem solving accordingly. The CGI first graders studied by Franke and Carey (1997) "perceived of mathematics as a problem-solving endeavor in which many different strategies are considered viable and communicating mathematical thinking is an integral part of the task" (p. 8). In a study of another problem-centered mathematics program, after two years in the program third graders scored significantly higher on standardized measures of computational proficiency and conceptual understanding and held stronger beliefs about the importance of finding their own or different ways to solve problems than those in "textbook classes" (Wood and Sellers, 1996).

It seems to be generally accepted that Japanese students do quite well on conceptual mathematics questions and problem-solving items in international assessments. Therefore, it is interesting to learn what sorts of problem solving are typical in Japanese elementary classrooms. Sawada (1999) describes a typical fifth-grade Japanese lesson in which the teacher poses a single contextualized problem that the students spend more than 35 minutes working. Although the teacher functions as a guide with a definite agenda, student contributions to the follow-up class discussion are used to structure both the content of the lesson and its flow. Similarly, in the United States today, problem solving as a way of teaching is merging with problem solving as only a curriculum component. Problem solving has been the focus of numerous books, collections of materials, and research studies, but many questions continue to be raised about the nature and scope of problem solving:

- What is a problem and what does problem solving mean?
- How can problem solving be taught effectively?
- What problem-solving strategies should be taught?
- How can problem solving be evaluated?

In Chapter 6 we focus on helping you answer these questions and discuss more about teaching problem solving.

A Glance at Where We've Been

Learning and doing mathematics involves engaging in five key processes: problem solving, reasoning and proof, communication, connections, and representations.

Problem solving requires that students be engaged in questions where the solution is not known, nor is easily identified. Good problems give students an opportunity to extend what they know, building their understanding of mathematical ideas. An important role for teachers is to select challenging problems, mathematics tasks, or opportunities that engage their students in the process of problem solving. Careful attention to establishing this environment will support students in enhancing their mathematical understanding.

Being able to reason mathematically is essential in order to make sense of mathematics and, ultimately, to justify or prove mathematical conjectures. To meet this challenge, children must be expected to supply reasons for their arguments from their earliest experiences with challenges and problems.

Communication provides a way for children to share their ideas with others. Their knowledge deepens as they help others understand their mathematical ideas and conjectures. Listening to the explanations of other children is equally important in the communication process. Two-way communication about mathematical ideas helps children identify, clarify, organize, articulate, and extend their thinking. Children need to be encouraged to present their ideas in a variety of modes (e.g., pictures, gestures, graphs, charts, and symbols) in addition to spoken and written words.

Connecting mathematical ideas helps children expand their understanding. At least three types of connections are important in learning mathematics: mathematics connected with other mathematical ideas; symbols connected to mathematical procedures; and mathematics extended and connected to contexts outside of mathematics. Teachers need to emphasize mathematical connections to encourage their students in building a disposition for making connections.

A variety of representations can be used to express the same mathematical idea. The different representations lead to different ways of understanding and using that idea. Children need to be encouraged to (1) create and use a variety of representations; (2) select, apply, and translate among representations to solve problems; and (3) use representations to model and interpret physical, social, and mathematical phenomena.

These five key mathematical processes are inextricably linked with each other and to the mathematics content that students learn (number, algebra, geometry, data, and measurement). Through these processes, students engage actively in making sense of the mathematics they are learning.

Things to Do: From What You've Read

1. What are the five key mathematical processes described in this chapter? For each process, briefly describe how the classroom snapshot that opens this chapter shows children engaging in that process.
2. a. Solve this problem: A programmer designed a new program that required the user to enter a three-character password in order to be recognized as a legal user. The first character must be a W or K. The second character must be a number: 1, 2, 3, 4, 5. The third character must be a symbol selected from $, %, *. How many possible passwords can be created for this program? What is the probability of guessing the password on the first try?

   b. Describe your work on this problem considering each of the five mathematical processes:

   - Problem Solving: Do you consider this task a problem? Why or why not?
   - Reasoning and Proof: Did your solution provide proof that your solution is correct?
   - Communication: How did you communicate your solution? Did you use multiple ways to explain your solution? Listen or read another student's solution to the problem. Was it communicated in the manner you communicated your solution?
   - Connections: Connect this problem with another mathematical idea. Connect this problem with another problem outside of mathematics.
   - Representations: Show a solution to the problem in more than one way. Describe how you used different representations in these ways.
3. Make a list of as many different representations for the number 75 as you can think of. Compare your list with the lists of others. You might use equivalent expressions, models, words, pictures, and so on. It is a sign of flexibility in thinking to be able to represent numbers and other mathematical ideas in many different ways.
4. What are the three distinct types of connections that are important in school mathematics? Give two examples of each type of connection.

Things to Do: Going Beyond This Book

IN THE FIELD

1. **Mathematical Processes in the Classroom.* Observe an elementary school classroom while children are engaged in a math lesson or investigation. You may choose to use the Pentomino Problem on Master 5-9 in the *Helping Children Learn Mathematics Instructor's Manual.* (Available at the Wiley Book Companion web site, www.wiley.com/college/reys.) Make a list of instances in which the children show evidence of using one or more of the five mathematical processes. Tell what the children were doing or saying and what tasks were involved. What role did the teacher play?
2. Plan a bulletin board focused on describing the five mathematical processes.
3. Check a textbook for evidence that students are encouraged to make connections.

*Additional activities, suggestions, or questions are provided in *Teaching Elementary Mathematics: A Resource for Field Experiences* (Wiley, 2004).

4. **What Is "Doing Math"?* Talk to one or more elementary teachers about their vision of what it means to "do mathematics." Ask whether they connect math to other areas of their curriculum and, if so, how. Write a reflection about how teachers' views of mathematics fit (or do not fit) with a view involving the five mathematical processes discussed in this chapter.

IN YOUR JOURNAL

5. Select a problem from a mathematics problem-solving text. Solve the problem. As you solve the problem, keep track of what you are doing in your journal. After you have finished solving the problem and recording your activities, summarize your actions in solving the problem.
6. Explain in your journal how you would plan to engage students in the five mathematical processes as you planned a unit.

WITH ADDITIONAL READINGS

7. Read one of the suggested readings on writing and communication in mathematics classes. Summarize the main ideas for supporting communication in the classroom.
8. Begin a resource folder for yourself that contains sections for each of the five mathematical processes. Collect and review recent articles in journals, such as *Teaching Children Mathematics*, to locate ideas that support the five mathematical processes.

WITH TECHNOLOGY RESOURCES

9. Obtain catalogs from software companies; select promising software to promote the five mathematical processes.
10. Write a review of a current mathematics software program that is used by children in a local elementary school. Explain how children are encouraged to incorporate the mathematical processes.
11. NCTM has created a web site that "illuminates the new principles and standards." Your task is to visit the site (illuminations.nctm.org) and select the button called "i-math investigations." You need to select a particular grade level, pre-K–2, 3–5, 6–8, or 9–12. Select one of the elementary levels. Explore at least one of the ready-to-use, online, interactive, multimedia math investigations that illuminate the standards. Explain how they support children to engage in the five mathematical processes.
12. Collect some numerical data about children (e.g., height, arm span, hand span). Record the data in a spreadsheet and create at least three different charts. Describe which chart best represents the data.

Book Nook for Children

Hamm, Diane Johnston. *How Many Feet in the Bed?* New York: Simon and Schuster, 1991.

A fun counting book that begins with "How many feet are in the bed?" Two—until more family members jump into the bed. Keep counting as you join the happy life of one family.

Sciedzka, Jon. *Math Curse.* New York: Viking, 1995.

Mrs. Fibonacci has told her class, "You know, you can think of almost everything as a math problem." The Math Curse has begun. Suddenly the book's hero cannot look anywhere without thinking of math problem after math problem—in the closet, at the dinner table, on the bus. He is agitated until he realizes he can solve all the problems he sees. Encourage your students to solve the problems and then challenge them to find more math problems in their world.

Resources

ANNOTATED BOOKS

Miller, Elizabeth D., and Hayes, Jeri. (eds.). *Read It! Draw It! Solve It!–Grade 1: Problem Solving with Animal Themes.* Parsippany, N.J.: Pearson Learning, 1999.
Integrate reading and mathematics while encouraging young students to think and express themselves creatively. With enough reproducible activities for each day of the school year, Resource Books for grades 1–5 give students ample opportunity to visually solve field-tested word problems by drawing a picture. This Resource Book is based on animal themes. Several problems have multiple solutions, which helps promote divergent thinking. Lots of new field-tested word problems to help young students boost reasoning and creative problem solving—one picture at a time.

ANNOTATED ARTICLES

Ciochine, John G., and Polivka, Grace. "The Missing Link? Writing in Mathematics Class!" *Mathematics Teaching in the Middle School*, 2 (March–April 1997), pp. 316–320.

Develop reasoning and communication skills through writing activities in your mathematics class. Children learn mathematics best by arguing about strategies and expressing opinions in a carefully written form. The forms of the writing include formal essays about mathematical problems, writing to prompts, or focused journal writing. Students learn to clarify, refine, and consolidate thinking.

Ducolon, Colin K. "Quality Literature as a Springboard to Problem Solving." *Teaching Children Mathematics*, 6(7), (March 2000), pp. 442–447.
How can literature boost the processing skills and knowledge of elementary students? The book considers the importance of problem-solving skills in understanding mathematics, the creation of different levels of mathematical problem-solving questions by students, and the use of literature in the development of integrated curriculum in mathematics.

Ford, Margaret I. "The Writing Process: A Strategy for Problem Solvers." *Arithmetic Teacher*, 38 (November 1990), pp. 35–38.
A strategy that includes various communication ideas helps students write stories to help in the process of solving problems. The strategy is a five-step process that includes prewriting, writing, conference, revising and editing, and publication.

O'Brien, Thomas C., and Moss, Ann C. "On the Keeping of Several Things in Mind." *Teaching Children Mathematics*, 6 (October 1999), pp. 118–122.
A problem-solving activity is aimed at finding out how fifth-grade students would approach a nontraditional problem in which several conditions must be met. The authors challenge teachers to incorporate student observations in their teaching.

Sawada, Daiyo. "Mathematics as Problem Solving: A Japanese Way." *Teaching Children Mathematics*, 6 (September 1999), pp. 54–58.
A typical fifth-grade mathematics lesson as taught in a Japanese elementary school is followed by a reflective commentary focused on problem solving, using manipulative aids, and multiple solutions.

Van Zoest, Laura E., and Enyart, Ann. "Discourse of Course: Encouraging Genuine Mathematical Conversations." *Mathematics Teaching in the Middle School*, 4(3), (1998), pp. 150–157.
Analyze the discourse in your classroom and make progress toward the goal of dynamic and productive mathematical discourse.

Weinberg, Susan. "Going Beyond Ten Black Dots." *Teaching Children Mathematics*, 2 (March 1996), pp. 432–435.
Second graders' responses to finding the sum of the numbers from 1 through 10 after reading the book, *Ten Black Dots*. Includes student work that demonstrates their problem solving.

Wilde, Sandra. "Learning to Write About Mathematics." *Arithmetic Teacher*, 38 (February 1991), pp. 38–43.
Think about making writing a regular part of the mathematics curriculum. Writing skills can be used in creating word problems, in bilingual classrooms, as process problems, in mathematics journals, and as a diagnostic tool. Includes examples of students' math work and written explanations.

ADDITIONAL REFERENCES

Azzolino, Aggie. "Writing as a Tool for Teaching Mathematics: The Silent Revolution." In *Teaching and Learning Mathematics in the 1990s*, 1990 Yearbook(eds. Thomas J. Cooney and Christian R. Hirsch). Reston, Va.: NCTM, pp. 92–100.

Courtryman, Joan. *Writing to Learn Mathematics: Strategies that Work*. Portsmouth, N.H.: Heinemann, 1992.

Franke, Megan Loef, and Carey, Deborah A. "Young Children's Perceptions of Mathematics in Problem-Solving Environments." *Journal for Research in Mathematics Education*, 28 (January 1997), pp. 8–25.

Hiebert, James; Carpenter, Thomas P.; Fennema, Elizabeth; Fuson, Karen; Human, Piet; Murray, Hanlie; Olivier, Alwyn; and Wearne, Diana. "Problem Solving as a Basis for Reform in Curriculum and Instruction: The Case of Mathematics," *Educational Researcher*, 25 (May 1996), pp. 12–21.

Mills, Heidi; O'Keefe, Timothy; and Whitin, David. *Mathematics in the Making: Authoring Ideas in Primary Classrooms*. Portsmouth, N.H.: Heinemann, 1996.

National Council of Teachers of Mathematics. *Principles and Standards for School Mathematics*. Reston, Va.: NCTM, 2000.

Russell, Susan Jo. "Mathematical Reasoning in the Elementary Grades." In *Developing Mathematical Reasoning in Grades K–12* (ed. Lee V. Stiff). Reston, Va.: NCTM, 1999, p. 1–12.

Wood, Terry, and Sellers, Patricia. "Assessment of a Problem-Centered Mathematics Program: Third Grade." *Journal for Research in Mathematics Education*, 27 (May 1996), pp. 337–353.

CHAPTER 6

Helping Children with Problem Solving

Snapshot of an Investigative/Problem-Based Lesson

This problem-based lesson uses square tiles to develop student understanding of prime numbers and factors. Prime numbers are numbers that are divisible only by one and themselves. Factors are numbers that evenly divide a given number.

GRADE LEVEL: 4

TOPIC: DESCRIBING CHARACTERISTICS OF PRIMES AND FACTORS

Objectives

1. Students build new mathematical knowledge through problem solving. By building rectangular models for multiplication and sorting and classifying the models, they learn to recognize characteristics of prime numbers and of factors of numbers (*NCTM Standards*, Grades 3–5: Problem-Solving).
2. Students recognize, describe, and label prime numbers, factors and multiples (*NCTM Standards*, Grades 3–5: Numbers and Operations).

MATERIALS: 30 SQUARE TILES FOR EACH PAIR OF STUDENTS

Launch

Ms. Gaea introduces the lesson by showing the students the small tiles they had worked with on other projects: "Today we will explore the shapes and sizes of lots of different rectangles that you can build with these tiles. The problem is to figure out how many different rectangles can be made with each number of tiles and then to think about classifying the different numbers according to how many rectangles you can make."

Ms. Gaea places 6 tiles on the overhead:

"One way to make a rectangle using six tiles is like this: 1×6 tiles. Are there any other ways?"

Students suggest 2×3, 3×2, and 6×1 as Ms. Gaea models the rectangles on the overhead with the tiles. When students are certain they have described them all, Ms. Gaea leads a discussion of whether they would count a 1×6 as different from a 6×1. Students decide not to count them separately. Seri suggests that these representations are just another example of the commutative property, which they explored at some length earlier.

Investigation

Ms. Gaea shows the students a table on the blackboard. It includes the numbers 1 to 30 in a list. She fills in 2 through 5 by writing 2×1 for 2 and 3×1 for 3 and drawing a sketch. Then the students help her identify the sketches for 4 and direct her to describe each sketch as 2×2 and 1×4.

PRIME AND FACTOR TABLE

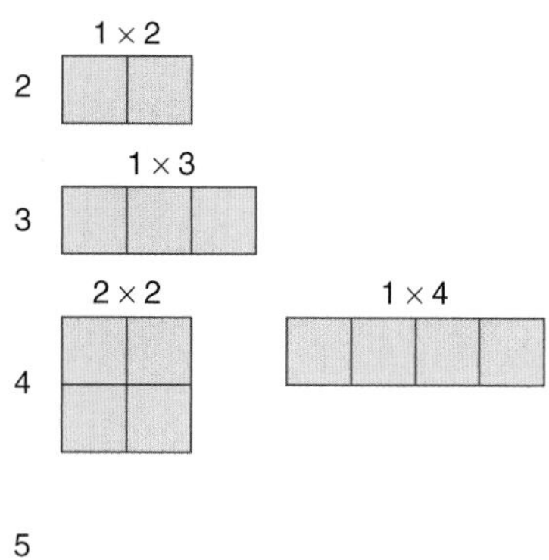

Given the student responses, Ms. Gaea believes they are ready to continue completing the table to 20. She assigns three or four problems to each pair of students, to sketch and determine the number of possible rectangles that can be constructed with the tiles and sketched on their papers.

Students in pairs take turns as rectangle-maker and recorder for the 3 or 4 numbers between 1 and 20 that they are given. One student from each group places the sketches and results in the table on the board. Ms. Gaea observes the students' work and checks each pair's answer.

Summarize

Ms. Gaea now asks the children to turn their attention to the table on the board. "What do you notice about the numbers in this table, and the rectangles you were able to make for each number?" The children eagerly volunteer some of their observations. They notice that some numbers have lots of different rectangles, but others have few, or only 1. Ms. Gaea asks students to provide examples as they make these observations. One group of students also observes that you can build squares with certain numbers of tiles, but that most numbers can make only non-square rectangles.

Ms. Gaea calls on a variety of students to help her make a list on the board of all the numbers that have only one rectangle and another list of all the numbers that have squares (1, 4, 9, 16, 25). She tells the students that the numbers that make squares can be called "square numbers." After some discussion, the class agrees that the next several square numbers would be 36, 49, and 64.

Ms. Gaea indicates that the numbers where you can only make one rectangle are prime numbers. Under the word *PRIME* written on the board Ms. Gaea asks if 17 is a prime (yes) and if 15 is a prime (no) and asks students for other examples of numbers that are prime or are not prime. She also asks several children to explain why the numbers chosen are prime or not.

Next, she refers to the word *FACTOR* and talks about the factors of various numbers by referring to the rectangles on the board. She indicates that the number 4 has three factors (1, 2, 4) and the number 6 has four factors (1, 2, 3, 6).

Now it is the students' turn to identify the factors for the other numbers in the table. To help them begin, Ms. Gaea asks them to find the factors of 15. After the students identify 1, 3, 5, 15, she asks if 15 is prime. Maria responds that 15 is not prime because it has more than just the two factors of 1 and 15, "It has factors of 3 and 5."

"What about the number 23?" Prompting the students, she asks, "How many rectangles can be made with 23 tiles?" The students conclude that since they can create only one rectangle with 23 tiles, 23 must be a prime. Karyn clarifies their understanding: "1 and 23 are the only factors. Since 23 has only 2 factors, it must be a prime."

Independent Practice

Ms. Gaea continues asking the students about the numbers from 1 to 30, discussing how many rectangles can be made, what the factors are, and whether the number is prime. After she is convinced they are comfortable with the ideas, she provides them with an opportunity for some independent practice. With a list of the numbers 25 to 35, she asks them to:

- make the possible rectangles for the numbers;
- list the factors for each number;
- determine which numbers are primes; and
- write an explanation for their decision.

Assessment

As they are working, she circulates in the classroom and asks individual students to explain one of their answers. This interaction gives her an opportunity to determine who understands prime numbers and factors and who needs further explanation.

Introduction

Problem solving in mathematics is a skill people need throughout their lives. Students in school encounter problems when they attempt to understand concepts, discover new relationships, and make sense of mathematical connections to other subjects in their world. Adults also have problems in their daily lives—as individuals, consumers, citizens, and workers. In fact, solving problems that arise in day-to-day living—such as moving the couch to the basement, making decisions about getting a second mortgage, preserving the environment, coping with international economics problems, or being successful in a choice of many careers—are all reasons for gaining competence in mathematics problem solving. Because problems are so central to living, teachers need to be concerned about the gains students make in tackling and persisting in their search for solutions to mathematics problems that arise in a variety of settings.

The *Principles and Standards for School Mathematics* (NCTM, 2000) recommend that instructional "programs from prekindergarten through grade 12 should enable all students to

- build new mathematical knowledge through problem solving;
- solve problems that arise in mathematics and in other contexts;
- apply and adapt a variety of appropriate strategies to solve problems;
- monitor and reflect on the process of mathematical problem solving."

This chapter provides a description of how elementary school teachers can plan to support positive progress toward expertise in children's problem-solving skills in each of these four areas. For example, new concepts may be introduced through problems in contexts with which elementary school children are familiar, such as number of children in the room or pattern blocks. Problem solving can also be used to gain fluency with specific skills, such as working with money or thinking about large numbers. Students can also pose their own problems to solve. Different problem-solving strategies are also important for young children to add to their "toolbox." Children who are effective problem solvers frequently plan, ask themselves if what they are doing makes sense, and adjust solution strategies when necessary.

FOCUS QUESTIONS

1. What is the difference between solving problems and practicing exercises?
2. How can problem-solving opportunities be provided effectively for elementary students?
3. Where in a sequence of mathematics lessons can problem-solving situations be posed?
4. What types of problems should you plan for use in your mathematics sequence? What characteristics should your problems include?
5. What strategies for solving problems should elementary students develop for their mathematics "toolbox"?
6. What questions should students learn to ask themselves when they are solving problems and reflecting on their solutions?

What Is a Problem and What Is Problem Solving?

A *problem* involves a situation in which a person wants something and does not know immediately what to do to get it. That means that some creative effort and higher-level thinking is needed to find a solution. If a problem is so easy that children know how to obtain the answer or know the answer immediately, there is really no problem at all.

To gain skill in solving problems, one must have many experiences in doing so. Research indicates that children who are given many problems to solve score higher on problem-solving tests than children who are given few. This finding has led many textbooks and teachers to offer a problem-solving program that simply presents problems—and nothing more.

Unfortunately, children have often been expected to learn how to solve word problems merely by solving them, with virtually no guidance or discussion of how to do it. Thus a typical page in a children's textbook (after they have been taught how to add large numbers) might begin with exercises such as

```
  3194      5479      6754
  5346      3477      8968
+ 8877    + 6399    + 7629
```

Next would appear story problems such as

(A) 7809 people watched television on Monday. 9060 people watched on Tuesday.

9924 people watched on Wednesday

How many people watched in the three days?

Whether story problems such as these really are problems for most children is debatable.

In effect, these problems are exercises with words around them. The biggest difficulty lies in doing the computation. The choice of what computation to perform is obvious. Do what you have been doing most recently. If the past week's work has been on addition, solve the problems by adding; if the topic has been division, then find two numbers in the word problem and divide. The problems generally provide practice on content just taught, with the mathematics placed in a more-or-less real-world setting. It is little wonder that children taught in this way flounder on tests, where problems are not conveniently grouped by operation.

Consider, as an alternative, the following problem—and try it yourself:

(B) Begin with the digits

1 2 3 4 5 6 7 8 9

Use each of them at least once, and form three 4-digit numbers with the sum of 9636.

To obtain a solution (or solutions), the children will have the desired practice in addition, but they will have to try many possibilities. They will be aided in reaching a solution if they apply some mathematical ideas. For instance, knowing that the sum of three odd numbers is odd will lead them to avoid placing 1, 3, and 5 all in the ones place. The children have the prerequisites for solving the problem, but the solution is not immediately apparent. They may have to guess and check several possibilities.

The decision to add the three numbers in problem (A) presents little if any challenge to most children in terms of determining what to do. The problem is merely a computational exercise that provides practice with addition. The children know what to do because the pattern has been set by the previous examples. With problem (B), however, they probably have to try several alternatives. Interest in obtaining a solution or solutions and acceptance of the challenge of trying to do something you have not done before (but believe you can do) are key aspects of problem solving.

Whether a problem is truly a problem or merely an exercise depends on the person faced with it. For example, tying a shoelace is no longer a problem for you, but it is for a three-year-old. What is a problem for Ann now may not be a problem for her in three weeks, or it may not be a problem now for Armando. Problems that you select for children must truly be seen as problems.

Math Links 6.1

*A*nother good source of problems is the Internet. Take a look at the Ole Miss Problem of the Week site, which you can access from this book's web site.

Many teachers are prone to select only problems that can be solved immediately, which often means the problems are too easy. Children form the idea that problems should be solved readily, so a problem where the route to solution is not immediately apparent is viewed as impossible. Finding the right level of challenge for students is not easy, but you can do it by trying out a range of problems, providing time, and then encouraging students to explore many ways around the obstacles initially posed. Don't underestimate their abilities. Weinberg (1996) comments on her fear that a problem was too difficult for her second-grade class and how amazed she was by their strategies for solving it.

A distinction is sometimes made between routine and nonroutine problems. *Routine problems* can be solved by application of a mathematical procedure in much the same way as it was learned. Many textbook word problems are routine problems. *Nonroutine problems* often require more thought because the choice of mathematical procedures to solve them is not as obvious.

Results from national assessments have shown that most students have difficulty with problems that require some analysis or thinking. Students are generally successful in solving routine one-step problems like those found in most textbooks. They have great difficulty, however, in solving multistep or nonroutine problems, particularly those that involve application of more than one single arithmetic operation. The 1992 National Assessment of Educational Progress (NAEP) included some non–multiple-choice items where students had to construct their own answers and provide a rationale for their responses. Students at all grades tended to have difficulties with these problem-solving items (Kouba et al., 1997). The 1996 NAEP tests provided similar results (Silver and Kenney, 2000).

Results from the 1992 assessment indicate that students at all three grade levels (4, 8, and 12) performed well on addition and subtraction word problems set in familiar contexts and involving only one step or calculation (Kenney and Silver, 1997). Eighth- (and twelfth-) grade students did well on multiplication and division problems involving one step as long as one of the factors was a whole number. Difficulties arose when fourth-grade students applied an incorrect strategy of "when in doubt, add," and when some students at all three grade levels—but especially grade four—attempted to solve multistep problems as though they involved a single step. Similar findings follow in the 1996 assessment (Silver and Kenney, 2000) and the 2000 NAEP findings indicate an increase in the percentage of students performing at the proficient level in fourth and eighth grade over the 10-year period from 1990–2000. Fourth-grade students who perform at the proficient level are expected to consistently apply integrated procedural knowledge and conceptual understanding to problem solving in the five NAEP content strands. (See the web site nces.ed.gov/nationsreportcard/mathematics/achieveall.asp for more information.)

Unfortunately, in many mathematics programs, problem solving has been limited to finding the answers to word problems in textbooks. Mathematical problem solving involves more. Whenever children are faced with providing a solution to a task they have not mastered, they are solving a problem.

A strong problem-solving program builds on the natural, informal methods that the child has when entering school. Many of the best problem-solving situations come from everyday happenings. "How many more chairs will we need if we're having five visitors and two children are absent?" or "How many cookies will we need if everyone is to have two?" may be of concern to a group of first graders. "Who has the higher batting average, Benny or Marianne?" or "What's the probability of our class winning the race?" may be urgent questions for a group of fifth graders.

A problem-solving approach should pervade the mathematics curriculum. Teachers need to use problem situations to introduce new topics, as a continuing thread throughout instruction, and as a culmination to ascertain whether children can apply what they have learned to a new situation (Midgett and Trafton, 2001). See the *Snapshot* where children learn about primes and factors in a problem-solving environment.

How Can Problem Solving Be Taught Effectively?

Because problem solving is difficult to teach and to learn, researchers have devoted much attention to it over the years. Their work has focused on characteristics of those children who are successful or unsuccessful at solving problems, on characteristics of problems, and on teaching strategies and classroom conditions that may help children be more successful at problem solving. On the basis of this research, some broad generalizations can be made (Hembree and Marsh, 1993; Kroll and Miller, 1993; McClain and Cobb, 2001):

- Young children enter school able to solve many problems. Instruction should build on what children already know.
- Students can begin solving problems in the earliest grades. Engaging students in problem solving should *not* be postponed until after they have mastered computational skills.
- Problem-solving strategies can be specifically taught, and when they are, not only are they used more but students also achieve correct solutions more frequently.
- No *one* strategy is optimal for solving all problems. Some strategies are used more often than others, with various strategies being used at different stages of the problem-solving process.
- Teaching a variety of strategies (in addition to providing an overall plan for how to go about problem solving) provides children with a repertoire from which they can draw as they meet a wide variety of problems. They should be encouraged to solve different problems with the same strategy and to discuss why some strategies are appropriate for certain problems.
- Students need to be faced with problems whose method of solution is not apparent, and they need to be encouraged to test many alternative approaches.
- Not only can students learn to apply a variety of problem-solving strategies, but they can also be encouraged to adapt strategies to suit new situations.
- Children's problem-solving achievements are related to their developmental level. Thus they need problems at appropriate levels of difficulty.
- Children can begin development of mathematical autonomy early in elementary school.

Factors for Success in Problem Solving

Major factors that contribute to students' difficulties with problem solving in the middle grades are knowledge, beliefs and affects, control, and sociocultural factors (Kroll and Miller, 1993). At all levels, teachers should be aware of the importance of each of these areas in problem-solving instruction.

KNOWLEDGE Students need experiences throughout their school years that encourage them to connect their thinking about problems at hand to problems they have solved in the past. Students must learn to recognize problems that are structurally similar and to choose appropriately among approaches for solving them, rather than to rely on surface problem features in deciding how to attack problems. For example, the use of key words in problem solving instruction (e.g., *in all* means to add, *how many left* means to subtract) is counterproductive because it relies on a problem's surface features only. Students should choose a solution approach based on a clear understanding of a problem.

BELIEFS AND AFFECTS Students' success in solving problems is often strongly linked to their attitudes, confidence, and beliefs about themselves as problem solvers. It is important for teachers to show students that they believe *all* students can be good problem solvers. It is also important for teachers to encourage students to develop their own strategies for and approaches to problem solving. Teachers who believe there is only one way to solve a problem prevent students from truly experiencing what it means to be a problem solver and to do mathematics.

CONTROL It is extremely important for students to learn to monitor their own thinking about problem solving. Research indicates that good problem solvers often spend a considerable amount of time up front, making sure they understand a problem, and at the end, looking back to see what they did, how their solution might be modified or improved, and thinking about how this problem is similar and different from other problems they have seen. By contrast, weaker problem solvers tend to be impulsive, jumping right into trying to solve (often crunching numbers with little regard for what they mean), without stopping to think about what approach might be most productive. Teachers can help students monitor their thinking and develop better control mechanisms by structuring opportunities where students are encouraged to monitor and reflect on their own thinking processes.

SOCIOCULTURAL FACTORS The atmosphere of the classroom should encourage students to use and further develop problem-solving strategies created naturally through experiences outside the classroom. Furthermore, the classroom climate itself (with its opportunities for discussion, collaboration, sharing, and encouragement among students) plays an important role in helping students develop as problem solvers. To teach problem solving effectively, teachers need to consider the time involved, planning aids, needed resources, the role of technology, and how to manage the class.

Time

Effective teaching of problem solving requires time. Attention must focus on the relationships in the problem and on the thinking processes involved in reaching a solution. Thus students must have time to digest, or mull over, a problem thoroughly—time to understand the task, time to explore methods of solution, time to think about the solution. Moreover, teachers need to encourage students to extend the amount of time they are willing to work on a problem before giving up. It takes more time to tackle a problem that you do not know how to solve than to complete an exercise where you know how to proceed. (Consider problems (A) and (B) in this chapter. How long did it take you to solve each?)

Some time for problem solving is already included as part of the mathematics program. Additional time can be gained by organizing instructional activities so that some of the time allotted for practicing computational and other skills is directed toward problem solving. This approach is logical because students will be using and practicing such skills as they solve many problems.

Planning

Instructional activities and time must be planned and coordinated so that students have the chance to tackle numerous problems, to learn a variety of problem-solving strategies, and to analyze, write about, and discuss their methods of attack. You will probably use a textbook when you teach mathematics; you need to consider how to use it most effectively to help you teach problem solving. For instance, you might identify your objectives for using problem-solving materials in the textbook, examine the entire book for problems to use, regroup textbook materials to suit your objectives, use the textbook to develop questions to ask about problem solving, extend textbook problems with materials you develop yourself, and use "challenge problems" (found in many textbooks) with all children.

As you plan, consider including problems with the following characteristics:

- Problems that contain superfluous or insufficient information:

  (C) A bag contains 2 dozen cookies for 99¢. Becca bought 3 bags. How many cookies did she get?

  (D) Andy would like to be as tall as his uncle, who is 6 feet 4 inches. How much more must Andy grow?

- Problems that involve estimation:

  (E) Anita has 75¢. Does she have enough money to buy a candy bar costing 35¢ and a notebook costing 49¢?

- Problems that require students to make choices about the degree of accuracy required:

  (F) Kurt is helping his father build a pen for his rabbit. He finds three pieces of lumber in the garage that they can use for the frame. One piece is 8 feet long; the other two are each 7 feet long. What is the largest size rectangular pen that they can build?

- Problems that involve practical applications of mathematics to consumer or business situations:

  (G) Which is the better buy, a 6-ounce jar of jelly for $1.79 or a 9-ounce jar for $2.79?

- Problems that require students to conceptualize very large or very small numbers:

  (H) Have you lived one million hours?

  (I) How thick is your fingernail?

- Problems that are based on students' interests or events in their environment or that can be personalized by adding their names:

  (J) Some of you play soccer every Tuesday. If today were Wednesday, January 21st, on what date would you play next?

- Problems that involve logic, reasoning, testing of conjectures, and reasonableness of information:

  (K) Three children guessed how many jelly beans were in a jar. Their guesses were 80, 75, and 76. One child missed by 1. Another missed by 4. The other child guessed right. How many jelly beans were in the jar?

Math Links 6.2

*U*se the electronic manipulative (Musser e-manipulative) available from this book's web site to solve the Counterfeit Coin problem.

- Problems that are multistep or require the use of more than one strategy to attain a solution:

  (L) Ellie has $10.00 in her pocket. A ticket to the movie is $5.50. The theater offers a popcorn and drink special for $3.79. If Ellie buys the popcorn and drink, does she have enough money for a $1.45 candy bar, too?

- Problems that require decision making as a result of the outcome (perhaps there are many answers—or no answers):

  (M) Is a traffic light needed in front of the school?

In addition, you should sometimes choose to pose problems that are open ended. Such problems have no one correct answer, but rather an answer that depends on the approach taken. Each solution is, however, expected to be reasonable. Such problems are especially appropriate for cooperative group work and should be followed with a class discussion in which the mathematical ideas and planning skills are explored and students get a chance to clarify their thinking and validate their decisions. Consider the following open-ended problems:

(N) Design a pentagonal tree house with two rooms. Make a 3-D model of your tree house, including furniture. Estimate the cost for building the tree house. Make a purchasing plan for furnishing the tree house if your parents give you a budget of $100 to spend.

(O) Your group has decided to plan a track-and-field competition. What events would be fun? What equipment will you need? Where and when should different events be held so that they will not interfere with each other? Develop a map and time schedule for the competition. How will you collect and display data from the events to determine winners?

It is important to recognize that open-ended problems such as (N) and (O) are much more effective when reasonable constraints are specified to ensure that the level of mathematics in the problems remains high. For example, you could improve problem (N) considerably by specifying that students must state the number of friends who will be sharing the treehouse and by requiring them to list furnishing costs for that group of friends from their choice of catalogs or used furniture ads that you provide. You might also offer a choice of prefab tree houses, rather than giving a cost per square foot to build a typical tree house. If you do not include constraints such as these in an open-ended problem such as (N), students are likely to spend most of their time simply debating what to buy, with very little time spent estimating or computing how to spend their $100. The unfortunate result can be a fun activity with little mathematics involved. By contrast, providing reasonable and interesting constraints can turn an open-ended problem into a much more realistic challenge.

Math Links 6.3

For another realistic, open-ended problem examine the internet plan, Data Does It: Planning a Trip, found at the NCTM Illuminations web site, which you can access from this book's web site.

Problems (P) and (Q) are a different sort of open-ended problem. The numeric answer is not at all difficult to determine in these problems (and everyone should get the same answer). The challenge is to see how many different and interesting ways there are to find that answer.

(P) Using graph paper and scissors, how many pentominos can you make? Notice that as described in (a.) of Figure 6-1 the pentominos must have sides adjoining, not vertices alone. How many of these pentominos will fold into an open box? For example, the first figure in (b.) in Figure 6-1 will fold into a box, but the second figure will not.

(Q) How many marbles are in (Figure 6-2)? Find the answer in as many different ways as you can.

Resources

Although many textbooks include a range of problems, if your textbook does not provide sufficient challenges you may find it helpful to acquire additional problems to stimulate and challenge your students. Fortunately, there are many sources of problems. The list of references at the end of this chapter includes several such sources. In addition, you can try the following ideas:

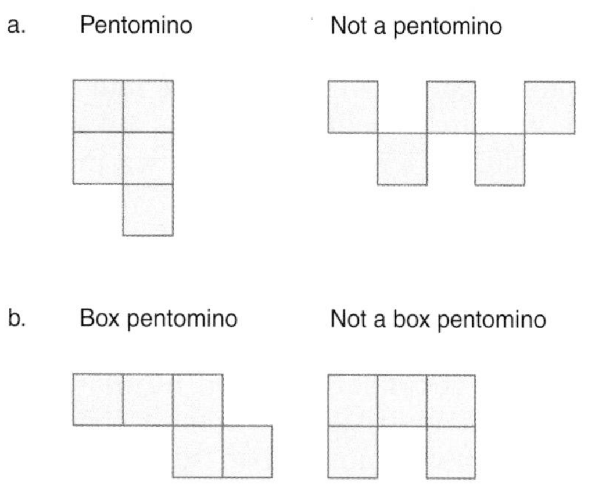

FIGURE 6-1 How many box pentominos can you make using five tiles?

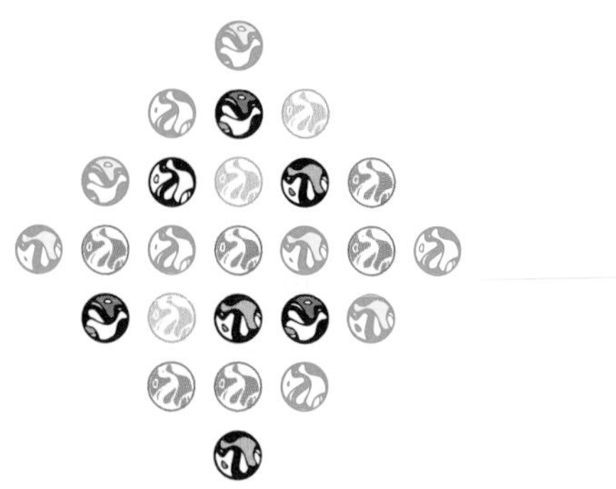

FIGURE 6-2 How many different ways can you find the number of marbles in the picture?

- Write problems yourself (possibly using ideas from newspapers or from events in your community). For example, see Silbey (1999) for a description of a broad assortment of problems drawn from a single newspaper circular describing activities related to Washington, D.C.'s annual cherry-blossom festival.
- Use situations that arise spontaneously, particularly questions children raise. ("If a bank robber stole a million dollars, how heavy and bulky would it be? Could he run down the street with it in his pocket? In a shopping bag?")
- Attend problem-solving sessions at professional meetings.
- Share problems with other teachers.
- Have children write problems to share with each other (Kliman and Richard, 1992; Silverman et al., 1992).
- Collect or make videotapes to bring real-life problem situations into the classroom (Kelly

Math Links 6.4

Collect problems from professional journals such as *Teaching Children Mathematics*, newspapers, magazines, resource books such as the *Addenda* and *Navigations Series* from the National Council of Teachers of Mathematics, and web sites such as Figure This! found on the NCTM web site, which you can access from this book's web site.

and Wiebe, 1993; Cognition and Technology Group, 1993).

- Use literature as a context for solving mathematical problems embedded in or related to the text in the story (Ameis, 2002; Strutchens, 2002).

It is never too soon to start a problem file, with problems grouped or categorized so you can locate them readily. File them by mathematical content, by strategies, or by how you are going to use the idea. Laminating the cards permits them to be used repeatedly by students for individual or small-group problem solving.

Technology

The calculator's potential for increasing problem-solving proficiency has been recognized since the 1970s. Many problems can now deal with more realistic numbers rather than merely with numbers that come out even. Calculators also help us shift attention from computation to problem solving; however, research has indicated that use of calculators does not necessarily improve problem-solving achievement. Students must still be able to determine *how* to solve a problem before they can use calculators to attain the solution. Examples of problems where calculators would be helpful would be problems (H), (L), or (N) in the preceding section.

An example of a game that provides practice in developing good number sense with problem-solving skills is to provide a starting number, an operation, and an answer such as:

$$2.5 \times \text{some number} = 8.50$$

Two students play this game by trading a calculator back and forth until they "get as close to" 8.50 as they can. A sample game might proceed as follows:

Round 1:

Player 1: $2.5 \times 4 = 10$

Player 2: $2.5 \times 3.5 = 8.75$

Round 2:

Player 1: $2.5 \times 3.3 = 8.25$

Player 2: $2.5 \times 3.4 = 8.50$

Research also indicates that children tend to use more and different strategies when they use calculators (Wheatley, 1980). The main reason is that the time once spent on performing calculations can be spent on extending the use of problem-solving strategies. More problems also can be considered when calculations are no longer as burdensome. Consider using calculators whenever they:

- Extend a child's ability to solve problems.
- Eliminate tedious computations and decrease anxiety about inability to do computations correctly.
- Allow time for devoting extended attention to a problem or considering more problems.
- Allow consideration of more complex problems or of problems with realistic data.
- Provide motivation and confidence that a problem can be solved.

A computer can also be an important problem-solving tool. As with calculators, computers allow for processing problems with realistic data. But computers can also be used to present problems of different types (e.g., problems involving graphics and graphing). For example, students can collect data from classmates on their favorite types of bicycles. The data can be entered into a spreadsheet, then circle graphs or histograms can be generated. Students can also try to determine whether boys and girls choose the same bikes by separating the data by gender and drawing a histogram where boys' choices are compared with girls' choices.

Many fine software programs provide a variety of problem-solving experiences. Some, such as Numbers Undercover, involve computation. Others, such as The Factory Deluxe, address spatial visualization. Still others, such as Math Shop, provide direct experiences with problem solving. The Cruncher teaches spreadsheet skills for solving such real-life problems as how many weeks of allowance equal a new CD player.

Logo and BASIC, still available to students in some schools, can also provide rich problem-solving experiences. These languages encourage students to think about what will happen, try it and see what actually occurs, and then try something else. Other tools, such as the Geometer's Sketchpad, provide opportunities to create geometric figures, make conjectures, and explore relationships. For example, students can explore the sum of angles of triangles, quadrilaterals, and other polygons and try to make predictions for 10-sided polygons.

In recent years, the World Wide Web has become an extremely rich resource for mathematics education. On the Web, teachers and students can

Math Links 6.5

Some examples of sites to consider are listed on this book's web site.

find a wealth of challenging and interesting mathematics problems, search for data for real-world problem-solving investigations, and seek answers to mathematical queries and conundrums.

Class Management

When you teach problem solving, you will find it useful at times to teach the whole class, to divide the class into small groups, or to have children work individually or with one other child. Large-group activities are effective for presenting and developing a new problem-solving strategy and for examining a variety of strategies for solving the same problem. You can focus children's attention on a problem's components, pose questions to help them use one strategy or find one solution, lead them to use other strategies or find other solutions, and encourage them to generalize from the problem to other problems. Individuals may suffer, however, because the faster students tend to come up with answers before others have had a chance to consider the problem carefully. Moreover, what may be a problem to some students may appear trivial or impossibly difficult to others. Discussions about problem solving are feasible with large groups, but the process of solving problems should be practiced in small groups as well as individually.

Small-group instruction makes it possible to group students by problem-solving ability and interests. They have the opportunity to work cooperatively at an appropriate level of difficulty in this type of group. Children's anxiety level is lowered as they all work together, discussing problems, sharing ideas, debating alternatives, and verifying solutions. In small groups, students can generally solve more problems than when working alone, although the groups may take longer on each problem. Research indicates that when groups discuss problem meanings and solution paths, they achieve better results than when they are told how to solve the problem (Suydam and Weaver, 1981). Groups are clearly a means of promoting communication about mathematics.

When pairing children to work together, you may want to pair children of comparable abilities or of slightly different abilities so that one child can help the other. Both children can end up learning from a peer-teaching situation.

Some problem solving should be done individually so that children can progress at their own pace and use the strategies with which they are comfortable. You will also want to have in the classroom sources of problems to which individual children can turn in their free time: a bulletin board, a problem corner, or a file of problems.

Posing Problems

Another way to help students with problem solving is to encourage them to write, share, and solve their own problems. Through problem-posing experiences, students become better aware of the structure of problems, develop critical-thinking and reasoning abilities, and learn to express their ideas clearly.

It is often helpful to begin problem posing by having students modify familiar problems. For example, third-grade students may have read the story *The Doorbell Rang* (Hutchins, 1986) and considered problems such as "If Mama baked 12 cookies, how many cookies can each child have if there are 2 children (or 4 or 6 or 12 children)?"

The problem can be rewritten in various ways. One simple modification is to change the numbers. Some changes in number leave the difficulty level of the problem essentially unchanged (18 cookies, 6 children). Other changes may make an important difference in the problem solution (12 cookies shared by 8 children or 12 cookies shared by 5 children). Another interesting way to reformulate a problem is to exchange the known and unknown information. For example, "Mama baked a lot of cookies, and each child got 3. How many cookies did Mama bake, if there were two children (or 4 or 6 or 12 children)?" Alternatively, consider a more open-ended problem: "If we want to be able to share 18 cookies fairly with different groups of children, without breaking any cookies, what different sizes can the groups be?"

Moses et al. (1990) suggest four principles for helping students as they learn to pose problems:

1. Focus students' attention on the various kinds of information in problems: the information a problem may give them (the *known*), the information they are supposed to find (the *unknown*), and the *restrictions* that are placed on the answer. Encourage students to ask "what if" questions. For example, what if you make the known information different? What if you switch what is known in the problem and what is unknown? What if you change the restrictions?
2. Begin with mathematical topics or concepts that are familiar.
3. Encourage students to use *ambiguity* (what they are not sure about or what they want to know) as they work toward composing new questions and problems.

4. Teach students about the idea of *domain* (the numbers they are allowed to use in a particular problem). Extending or restricting the domain of a problem is an interesting way to change it. For example, the problem "name three numbers whose product is 24" is very different depending upon whether you consider a domain of all whole numbers, only even whole numbers, all integers (both positive and negative), or perhaps even fractions and decimals.

The teacher plays a key role in establishing a classroom environment where thinking deeply about problems and how the problems can be changed or rewritten is encouraged. The teacher can model an inquiring mind by frequently asking "What if?" when discussing problems and by encouraging conjecturing and problem reformulation.

Another useful problem-posing activity is having students write their own problems (rather than modify problems already at hand). This is generally best done after students have had considerable experience with posing problems that are modifications of familiar problems. When asking students to compose problems on their own, it is often important for the teacher to specify certain goals or constraints for the task. Otherwise, the assignment may become nothing more than an exercise in creativity. (Students may write fantastic stories with no discernible mathematics content or pose problems that are so convoluted or complicated that no solution is possible.) For example, students might be assigned to write a word problem that matches a given mathematical number sentence or figure:

- Write a word problem for 250 ÷ 5 = 50.
- Write a comparison word problem for 12 − 8 = 4.
- Write a multiplication word problem for the tree diagram (e.g., two kinds of ice cream and three possible toppings for each gives six different types of sundaes).

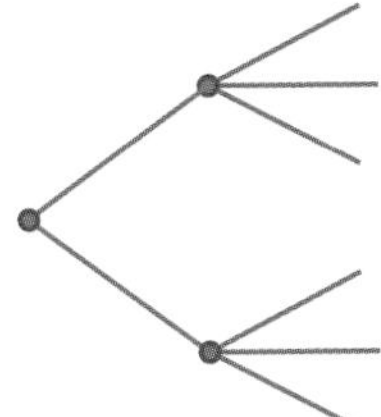

Situations or data offered in magazine advertisements, newspaper articles, world records, sales flyers, and so on can also provide effective problem-posing prompts. A sixth-grade teacher challenged her students to write and illustrate problems that involved multiplication or division and that included extraneous information. Students responded with creative problems such as this:

> At midnight, the wind over Jamaica started to increase as Hurricane Lucas came closer. Every 10 minutes from then on, the wind doubled, and five trees were pulled from the ground. At 12:30, the wind speed was 120 miles per hour. At what speed was the wind blowing at 12:00 midnight?

Students need help with learning to write problems. Lessons of this sort can easily be integrated with language arts instruction. A writing workshop approach may be used, consisting of stages such as brainstorming and prewriting, writing, several rounds of peer critique followed by rewriting, and, finally, editing and publication. Student problems may be published on bulletin boards, on cards (to be made available for other students to solve), or in a class book of problems. The sixth-grade teacher mentioned earlier obtained a small classroom grant to produce enough copies of her class's illustrated book of problems to distribute one to each sixth-grade class in the school district. Her students proudly went on a field trip, which took them from school to school delivering their books to sixth-grade classrooms, where they shared problem-solving experiences with other students their own age. A third-grade teacher in another state engaged her students in taking "the mathematician's chair" as they challenged their peers with mathematics problem-solving situations they had authored themselves (Hildebrand et al., 1999). She assessed their written work using a 4-point rubric that considered three aspects of each problem they authored: problem attributes, problem structure, and use of language conventions.

What Problem-Solving Strategies Should Be Taught?

You cannot consider problem solving in mathematics education without finding numerous references to the contribution of George Polya (1973). He proposed a four-stage model of problem solving:

1. *Understand* the problem.
2. *Devise* a plan for solving it.

3. *Carry out* your plan.
4. *Look back* to examine the solution obtained.

This model forms the basis for the problem-solving approach used in most elementary school mathematics textbooks. Such an approach, which focuses on teaching students to see, plan, do, and check, can help them see problem solving as a process consisting of several interrelated actions. Students have a guide to help them attack a problem, suggesting actions that will lead them to the goal.

However, Polya's model can be misleading if taken at face value. Except for simple problems, it is rarely possible to take the steps in sequence. Students who believe they can proceed one step at a time may find themselves as confused as if they had no model. Moreover, the steps are not discrete, nor is it always necessary to take each step. As students try to understand a problem, they may move unnoticed into the planning stage. Or, once they understand the problem, they may see a route to a solution without any planning. The stages do not always aid in finding a solution. Many children become trapped in an endless process of read, think, reread—and reread and reread—until they give up.

Specific strategies are needed to help children move through the model. Polya himself delineates many of these strategies. Many textbooks provide lists of the strategies presented at various grade levels. These strategies are tools for solving problems, whereas the four-stage model provides a guideline for how a problem solver may move through the process of solving a problem.

This section describes and provides examples of several problem-solving strategies (see Table 6-1). Although not exhaustive, this set of strategies can be applied in a wide variety of problem settings.

A teacher needs a plan for introducing these strategies; it is not feasible to focus on them all in a given year. Children need time to gain confidence in applying each strategy. A plan also ensures that students are exposed to the range of strategies you want them to learn and that they have the opportunity to practice them at an appropriate level. Thus you may decide to introduce "act it out" and "make a drawing" in grade 1, "look for a pattern" and "solve a simpler or similar problem" in grade 2, and so on. No one sequence is best. In successive grade levels, children will practice and use the strategies they have already learned. Of course, students should not be limited to using the strategies that you have already discussed with the class. They should always be encouraged to use their own ideas in approaching new situations. If you see a student successfully using a strategy that you haven't yet talked about in class, you might encourage her to share her ideas with the rest of the class. You might also help the children identify a label for that new strategy so it can be referenced again in future class discussions. You could place the strategy on your bulletin board class strategy list by the label the child suggests. For example, Jessica might discover that solving a simpler, parallel problem is a good way to get started on problems that involve large numbers or numbers that seem hard to think about. In a follow-up whole-class discussion, you might suggest naming this "Jessica's simpler strategy," and you might begin future problem-solving discussions by asking whether Jessica's simpler strategy might be useful in attacking the problem at hand.

Textbooks also outline the scope and sequence for any strategies included in the series. Use this outline to compare the scope of your textbook's program with what you want to implement. Then you can devise a plan, if necessary, for extending children's learning beyond what the textbook covers.

The discussion that follows includes several illustrative problems, covering a range of mathematical topics and grade levels that could be used to develop each problem-solving strategy. Usually a problem can also be solved with another strategy; it is rare that a problem can be solved with only one strategy. For this reason, a repertoire of strategies is useful. (On the other hand, not all strategies can be used effectively to solve a given problem.) Often, more than one strategy must be used to solve a problem. For example, students may begin to use the identify-all-possibilities strategy but find there are so many possibilities that they also need to use the make-a-table strategy to keep track of them. By becoming familiar with possible strategies, students acquire a repertoire that can be drawn on to attack a problem, and making a start is often the most difficult point. Moreover, when one strategy fails, the children have others to turn to, thus enhancing their confidence that they can find a path to a solution.

As you read, do stop and try to solve the problems!

Table 6-1 • A List of Useful Problem-Solving Strategies

Act it out	Guess and check
Make a drawing or diagram	Work backward
Look for a pattern	Write an open sentence
Construct a table	Solve a simpler or similar problem
Identify all possibilities	Change your point of view

Act It Out

This strategy helps children visualize what is involved in the problem. They actually go through the actions, either themselves or by manipulating objects. This physical action makes the relationships among problem components clearer in their minds.

When teaching children how to use the act-it-out strategy, it is important to stress that other objects may be used in place of the real thing. Obviously, real money is not needed when a problem involves coins—only something labeled "25¢" or whatever. Because children are adept at pretending, they probably will suggest substitute objects themselves. Make sure they focus their attention on the actions rather than on the objects per se.

Many simple real-life problems can be posed as you develop the act-it-out strategy in the early grades:

> (1) Six children are standing at the teacher's desk. Five children join them. How many children are then at the teacher's desk?

The value of acting it out becomes clearer, however, when the problems are more challenging:

> (2) Twelve people met at a public park for a nature walk. Before they set off to look for birds, they all introduced themselves and each person shook hands with each of the other people. How many handshakes were exchanged?
>
> (3) A man buys a horse for \$60, sells it for \$70, buys it back for \$80, and sells it for \$90. How much does the man make or lose in the horse-trading business?
>
> (4) Gum balls cost 5¢ each. There are gum balls of 5 different colors in the machine. You can't see them because it's dark. What would be the least number of nickels you'd have to spend to be sure of getting at least 3 gum balls of the same color?
>
> (5) LeRoy had $\frac{3}{4}$ of a bag of marbles, Violet had 70% of a bag of marbles, Dwayne had 0.8 of a bag of marbles, Jodi had 9% of a bag of marbles, while Phil had $\frac{3}{8}$ of a bag of marbles. Line up the partial bags of marbles from largest to smallest. If you were to combine all of the marbles together, estimate how many full bags you could fill.

Make a Drawing or Diagram

Probably within the past week or so you have used the drawing strategy to help solve a real-life problem. Perhaps you had to find someone's house from a complicated set of directions, so you drew a sketch of the route. Or maybe you were rearranging a room and drew a diagram of how the furniture was to be placed. This strategy provides a way of depicting the information in a problem to make the relationships apparent (Kelly, 1999).

When teaching this strategy, stress to the children that there is no need to draw detailed pictures. Encourage them to draw only what is essential to tell about the problem. For example, the appearance of the bus, the pattern of the upholstery, the presence of racks above the seats, and similar details are irrelevant in drawing a picture that will help solve the bus problem:

> (6) A bus has 10 rows of seats. There are 4 seats in each row. How many seats are there on the bus?
>
> (7) You enter an elevator on the main floor. You go up 6 floors, down 3 floors, up 9 floors, down 7 floors, up 8 floors, down 2 floors, down 5 more floors. Then you get off the elevator. On what floor are you?
>
> (8) How much carpet is needed to cover our classroom floor?
>
> (9) A snail is at the bottom of a jar that is 15 cm high. Each day the snail can crawl up 5 cm, but each night he slides back down 3 cm. How many days will it take the snail to reach the top of the jar?
>
> (10) It takes 3 minutes to saw through a log. How long will it take to saw the log into 4 pieces?
>
> (11) A patch of lily pads doubles its size each day after it starts growing in a pond. If a pond was completely covered just today, what part of it was covered in lily pads five days ago?

At times you can reverse this strategy by presenting a picture for which the children have to make up a problem:

> (12)

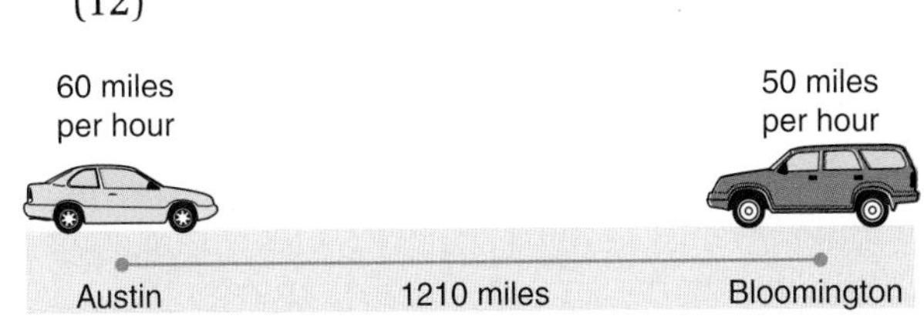

Look for a Pattern

In many early learning activities, children are asked to identify a pattern in pictures or numbers. When pattern recognition is used to solve problems, it involves a more active search. Students often construct a table, then use it to look for a pattern.

(13) Triangle dot numbers are so named because that number of dots can be used to form a triangle with an equal number of dots on each side:

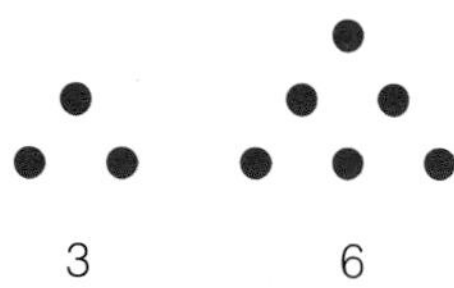

What triangle dot number has 7 dots on a side? Ten dots on a side? What about 195 dots on a side? Is 57 a triangle dot number?

(14) How long would it take to spread a rumor in a town of 90,000 people if each person who heard the rumor told it to 3 new people every 15 minutes?

(15) Little Island has a population of 1,000 people. The population doubles every 30 years. What will the population be in 30 years? 60 years? 300 years? When will the population be over a million? Over a billion?

(16) An explorer found some strange markings on a cave wall. Can you find and complete the pattern between the numbers in the first row and the numbers in the second row?

5	6	1	3	0	8	16
11			7		17	

Construct a Table

Organizing data into a table helps children discover a pattern and identify information that is missing. It is an efficient way to classify and order large amounts of information or data, and it provides a record so that children need not retrace nonproductive paths nor do computations repeatedly to answer new questions.

(17) Can you make change for a quarter using only 9 coins? only 17? only 8? How many ways can you make change for a quarter?

(18) About how many direct ancestors have you had in the last 400 years?

(19) A carpenter makes only 3-legged stools and 4-legged tables. At the end of one day he had used 31 legs. How many stools and how many tables did he make?

(20) Ann, Jan, and Nan all like pizza. One likes her pizza plain. One likes pizza with mushrooms. One likes pizza with anchovies. Which kind of pizza does each girl like? Here are three clues:

1. Ann doesn't know the girl who likes her pizza plain.
2. Jan's favorite kind of pizza is cheaper than pizza with mushrooms.
3. The one who likes mushrooms is Ann's cousin.

(21) Your teacher agrees to let you have 1 minute of recess on the first day of school, 2 minutes on the second day, 4 minutes on the third day, and so on. How long will your recess be at the end of 2 weeks?

Notice that the mathematical idea involved in problem (21) can be stated in terms of other situations. Such reformulation can alter the difficulty level of the problem. It can also give children practice in recognizing similarities in problem structure—an ability that appears to be closely allied to good problem-solving skills. Here is one alternative to that problem:

(22) Suppose someone offers you a job for 15 days. They offer you your choice of how you will be paid. You can start for 1¢ a day and double the new amount every day. Or you can start for $1 and add $1 to the new amount every day. Which would you choose? Why?

Problems such as (21) and (22) would lend themselves well to making a table (see Table 6-2) in a spreadsheet.

Textbooks frequently teach part of the table-construction strategy. They have students read a table or complete a table that is already structured. It is important for students to learn to read a table, and thus problems such as this one are presented:

Table 6-2 • A Spreadsheet Beginning to Solve Problem 22

	A	B	C	D
1	Day Number	Double	Add $1	Difference
2	1	.01	1.00	−.99
3	2	.02	2.00	−1.98
4	3	.04	3.00	−2.96
5	4			

(23) Here is a bus schedule. What time does the bus from New York arrive? (Ask other questions about arrival, departure, and traveling times.)

It is also vital that children learn how to construct a table. They need to determine for themselves what its form should be (e.g., how many columns are needed), what the columns or rows should be labeled, and so on. For this purpose, you can present problems that require children to collect information and then organize it into a table in order to report it. A spreadsheet can be helpful with this task.

(24) Make a table that shows how many cars pass through the traffic lights at each intersection by the school.

Identify All Possibilities

This strategy is sometimes used with *look for a pattern* and *construct a table*. Children don't always have to actually examine all possibilities; rather, they have to account for all information in some systematic way. They may be able to organize the possibilities into categories and then dismiss some classes of possibilities before beginning a systematic search of the remaining ones. Sometimes, however, they do need to actually check all possibilities.

(25) In how many different ways can a bus driver get from Albany to Bakersville? The driver always moves toward Bakersville.

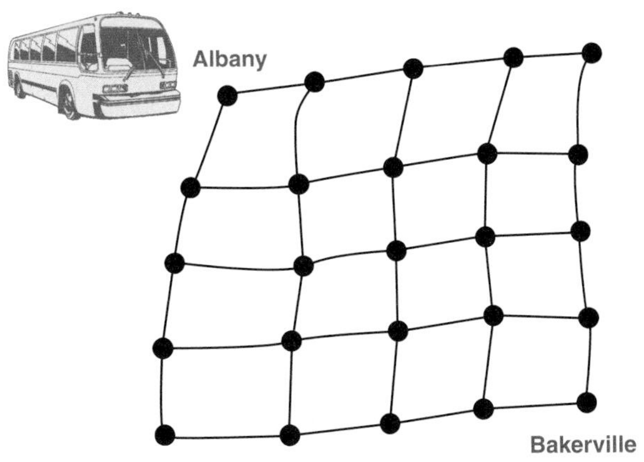

(26) In how many ways can you add 8 odd numbers to get a sum of 20? (You may use a number more than once.)

(27) Ask a friend to think of a number between 1 and 10. Find out what number it is by asking him or her no more than five questions that can be answered only by yes or no. How many questions would you need to ask to find any number between 1 and 20? Between 1 and 100?

(28) If each letter is a code for a digit, what is the following addition problem? Use 1, 2, 3, 6, 7, 9, and 0.

$$\begin{array}{r} \text{SUN} \\ +\ \text{FUN} \\ \hline \text{SWIM} \end{array}$$

(29) You need 17 lb. of fertilizer. How many bags of each size do you buy to obtain at least 17 lb. at the lowest cost?

Guess and Check

For years, children have been discouraged from guessing. They have been told, "You're only guessing," in a derisive tone. But guessing is a viable strategy when students are encouraged to incorporate what they know into their guesses, rather than making blind or wild guesses.

An educated guess is based on careful attention to pertinent aspects of the problem, plus knowledge from previous related experiences. There is some reason to expect to be in the ballpark. Then the child must check to be sure. It is also important to recognize that the guess-and-check strategy involves making repeated guesses, and *using what has been learned from earlier guesses to make each subsequent guess better and better*. Too often, children just check a guess and, upon finding that it is wrong, make another guess that may be even more off the mark. It is essential to help children learn how to refine their guesses efficiently. Consider the following problem:

(30) Suppose it costs 23¢ to mail a postcard and 37¢ for a letter. Bill wrote to 12 friends and spent $3.46 for postage. How many letters and how many postcards did he send?

You might begin by making a guess of 6 letters and 6 postcards. On checking, you find that results in postage of $3.60. It is important not to just make another guess randomly. $3.60 is too much postage (because Bill spent $3.46), so you need to *guess fewer letters*. Maybe you guess 4 letters and 8 postcards. That produces postage of $3.32—a bit too little. When you try 5 letters and 7 postcards, you discover the solution.

(31) If two whole numbers have a sum of 18 and a product of 45, what are the numbers?

(32) Place the numbers 1 through 9 in the cells so that the sum in each direction is 15.

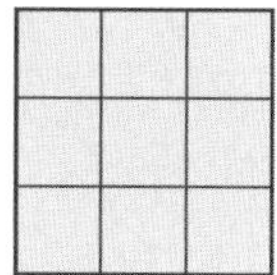

(33) Maggie hit the dartboard with 4 darts. Each dart hit a different number. Her total score was 25. Which numbers might she have hit to make that score?

(34) Use the numbers 1 through 6 to fill the 6 circles. You may use each number only once. Each side of the triangle must add up to 9.

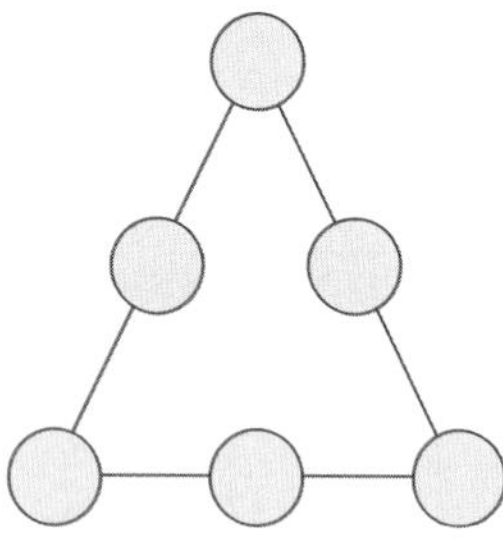

Work Backward

Some problems are posed in such a way that children are given the final conditions of an action and are asked about something that occurred earlier. In other problems, children may be able to determine the endpoint and work backward (many mazes are like that).

(35) Complete the following addition table:

1			3			
	12		11	15		
6		6			7	
2			5	9		
						13
5						14

(36) Sue baked some cookies. She put half of them away for the next day. Then she divided the remaining cookies evenly among her three sisters so each got 4 cookies. How many cookies did she bake?

Write an Open Sentence

The open-sentence (or equation) strategy is often taught in textbooks; in some, in fact, it is the only strategy taught. Research indicates that it is useful (Suydam and Weaver, 1981) but not so useful that it should be taught exclusively. True, once you can write an open sentence, you can probably solve the problem, but writing the sentence in the first place may be difficult. Thus some problems cannot be solved easily with this strategy, and sometimes other problem-solving strategies may be needed first to clarify the problem. In particular, children must be able to perceive a relationship between given and sought information in order to write the sentence. Also, children need to learn that more than one sentence may be formed to solve some problems.

(37) An ant travels 33 cm in walking completely around the edge of a rectangle. If the rectangle is twice as long as it is wide, how long is each side?

(38) Two thirds of a number is 24 and one half of the number is 18. What is the number?

Solve a Simpler or Similar Problem

Some problems are made difficult by large numbers or complicated patterns, so the way to solve them is unclear. For such a problem, making an analogous but simpler problem may aid in ascertaining how to solve it. Thus, for the following problem, you might have second or third graders first consider what they would do if Cassie had 3¢ and Kai had 5¢:

(39) Cassie saved \$3.56. Kai saved \$5.27. How much more money has Kai saved?

(40) We get 32.7 miles per gallon of gas in our van. If our van's tank holds 14 gallons and we fill it up, how far can we go without filling up again?

(41) Tickets to the college football game cost \$15.95 for bleacher seats in the end zone and \$25.95 for seats on the home sidelines. Last week 2,340 people sat in the end-zone bleachers and 6,020 people sat on the home sidelines. How much money was collected from the sale of end-zone bleacher seat tickets?

You may need to encourage students to break some problems down into manageable parts. When problems require a series of actions, children often fail to recognize the need to answer one question before another can be answered. They need help in identifying the questions that must be answered.

Many kinds of problems are interrelated. Knowing how to solve one problem usually means that children can solve another problem that is somewhat similar. The insight and understanding that permit them to solve more complicated problems are built through solving easier problems, where relationships are easier to see and possibilities for solving can be readily considered. Momentarily, children can set aside the original problem to work on a simpler one; if that problem can be solved, then the procedure used can be applied to the more complicated problem.

(42) Place the numbers 1 to 19 into the 19 circles so that any three numbers in a row give the same sum.

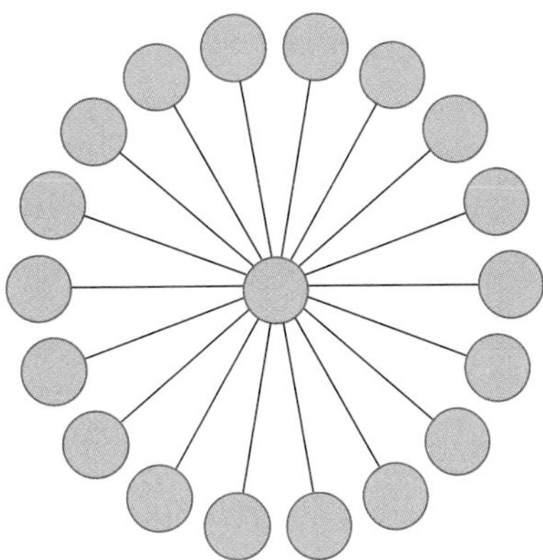

Students might tackle this problem by first trying simpler problems such as placing the numbers 1 to 5 or 1 to 7 or 1 to 9 in a similar pattern of circles.

Children often need to restate a problem, expressing it in their own words. Sometimes this repetition indicates points at which they do not understand the problem, and you can then help them clarify it. At other times, rephrasing helps them ascertain what the problem means or requires, so that they see a possible path to a solution. Rephrasing can be a way of eliminating unimportant words or of changing to words that are more easily understood. Try rewording each of the following problems so that children will understand the terms.

(43) Find three different integers such that the sum of their reciprocals is an integer.

(44) I bought some items at the store. All were the same price. I bought as many items as the number of cents in the cost of each item. My bill was \$2.25. How many items did I buy?

Change Your Point of View

This strategy often is used after several others have been tried without success. When children begin to work on most problems, they tend to adopt a particular point of view or make certain assumptions. They quickly form a plan of attack and implement it to determine whether it produces a plausible solution. If the plan is unsuccessful, they tend to return to the problem with the same point of view to ascertain a new plan of attack, but some faulty logic may have led them to adopt that point of view. They need to try to redefine the problem in a completely different way. Encourage them to ask themselves such questions as: "What precisely does the problem say and not say? What am I assuming that may or may not be implied?"

Problem (20), the pizza problem, is one version of a set of logic problems that are useful in presenting this strategy. Following are some other problems that most students will rather quickly attack in a particular way. Only when it is apparent that an incorrect answer has been obtained (or no answer) will they see the value of looking at the problem from another point of view.

(45) How many squares are there on a checkerboard? (Note: The answer is more than 64.)

(46) Without lifting your pencil from the paper, draw four straight line segments through the 9 dots.

(The key to solving this problem is recognizing that the lines you draw are allowed to extend beyond the edges of the rectangle formed by the dots.)

(47) A state with 750 schools is about to begin a "single elimination" basketball tournament—one loss and you're out. How many games must be played to determine a champion? (Note: Here it may be helpful to think about how many games each individual team plays in the tournament, rather than to focus on counting games played by pairs of teams.)

The Importance of Looking Back

Some of the best learning about problem solving may occur after the solution has been attained. It is important to think about how a problem was solved. In fact, research indicates that time spent discussing and reconsidering children's thinking may be more important than any other strategy in helping them become better problem solvers (Kroll and Miller, 1993; Suydam and Weaver, 1981). Thus, this step, which should be included regularly in instructional planning, may focus on one or more helpful strategies.

Generalize

The generalization strategy is used to extend solutions to broader and more far-reaching situations. Analyzing the structural features of a problem rather than focusing only on details often results in insights more significant than the answer to the specific situation posed in the problem. This sort of thinking about generalizations is important in developing students' mathematical reasoning abilities.

According to research (Suydam, 1987), being able to see similarities across problems is one of the characteristics of good problem solvers.

(48) First solve: A boy selling fruit has only three weights and a double-pan balance. But with them he can weigh any whole number of pounds from 1 to 13 pounds. What weights does he have? Then consider: Should he buy a fourth weight? How many additional weighings could be made with four weights?

(49) When five consecutive numbers are added together their sum is 155. Find the numbers. How can this problem be expressed in symbols so that other totals could be considered?

Getting children to focus on the relationships involved in a problem and then generalizing can sometimes be accomplished by giving children problems without numbers:

(50) A store sells Ping-Pong balls by the box. For the amount of money Maria has, she can buy a certain number of boxes. What price does she pay per ball?

Check the Solution

Checking has long been advocated as a way to help children pinpoint their errors, provided they do not simply make the solution and the check agree. One way of checking is going through the procedures again; another is verifying the reasonableness of the answer. Is it a plausible answer to the question posed in the problem? Estimating the answer before obtaining the solution can aid in this verification process.

Find Another Way to Solve It

Most problems can be solved with many different strategies. Use of each strategy adds to an understanding of the problem. You may have felt uncomfortable with the classification of some of the problems in this chapter under one or another strategy. But even for the problems where you felt the classification was satisfactory, there is probably another way each could be solved. (Try it and see!)

Find Another Solution

Too often, children are given problems for which there seems to be one and only one correct solution. Many textbook problems are like that. In real-life situations, however, two or more answers may be acceptable (depending, sometimes, on the circumstances or the assumptions), or only one answer may be obtained via very different approaches. You probably noticed that some of the problems given here have several solutions. For many others, such as the following problem, each person tackling the problem will have a different answer:

(51) Find out how many days (or minutes) old you are.

Study the Solution Process

This strategy aims to help the child put the problem into perspective: the thinking used at each stage, the facts that were uncovered, the strategies that were employed, and the actions that were productive and nonproductive. Again, giving a problem without numbers helps children focus on the process they follow, as well as the relationships in the problem, as they describe how they would go about finding the answer. Different students can also be asked to share with the group the varying ways in which they proceeded to reach the same solution. Having children write about how they solved a problem also adds to their understanding of the problem-solving process. In addition, you could teach students to evaluate their solution process for both successes and failures.

Learning Metacognitive Strategies

People who are good problem solvers can think about their own thinking. They can monitor the skills they have and the things they already know, how they can use these skills to solve new problems, and make judgments about what they are doing. Older children are better at these skills than younger children, but experience and teaching are helpful for many children in the development of these monitoring and regulatory skills around their problem-solving performance.

Teachers can suggest strategies for students to use. In fact, developing a set of questions such as the following that students can use in the process of solving a problem can be helpful:

1. Questions that inform the student about what they already know and support them in making plans:
   - Do I understand what I just read?
   - What do I know about the problem?
   - What information helps me in understanding the problem?
   - What am I trying to find out?
   - Do I know any strategies that could help me?
   - What information do I have about this topic?
   - Have I done anything like it before?
   - How will I use the strategies I know?
2. Questions that help students monitor their thinking:
   - Can I predict or estimate the outcome of the task?
   - How much time will this take?
   - In what order will I try to complete these tasks?
   - How am I doing?
3. Questions that make judgments about what they are doing:
   - Does what I'm doing make sense?
   - Am I done?
   - How could I spot an error?
   - Do I need to revise?
   - Do I have to try something else?
   - Do I need to try this later?

Using Problem-Solving Opportunities

In this chapter, we presented a wide variety of problems. Many of the problems involve students in mathematical reasoning and communication. Nonverbal problems, embodied in different representations such as pictures or materials, also need to be used. Real-world problems arise in a variety of modes, offering many opportunities for making connections. Make use of problems posed spontaneously by children or by situations in which you find yourself. Bring in games that present good problem-solving situations, games that present children with the opportunity to use many different strategies. Have children work cooperatively in small groups. Be aware that personalizing problems (e.g., by substituting the names of children in your class) can help many children accept problems that otherwise would seem remote or uninteresting.

Throughout your instruction, you need to encourage enjoyment in solving problems. You have helped children achieve this sense of enjoyment in part when they begin to believe that they *can* solve a problem. They need an atmosphere in which they feel both free and secure. Your positive attitude toward problem solving will stimulate a similar attitude on the part of the children.

Some ideas that may help students get started on a difficult problem are to read the problem aloud to the student or have another student explain the problem. Also consider asking a simpler problem to get the student started, or have hint cards prepared ahead of time for students to consult if they wish. The main thing for you to consider is how to make the level of the task appropriate for the child.

How Can You Assess Problem Solving?

It is more difficult to assess children's problem-solving skills than many other skills in the mathematics curriculum. Teachers are interested in knowing whether students can:

- Formulate problems.
- Apply a variety of strategies to solve problems.
- Solve problems.
- Develop a set of questions that allow them to monitor their own thinking.
- Verify and interpret results.
- Generalize solutions.

To assess problem solving, you must go beyond the open-ended or multiple-choice format of a paper-and-pencil test. Chapter 4 describes the assessment process, and many of the points to follow are also discussed in Chapter 4. We briefly review them here as well, because it is so important that assessment be considered a vital component of teaching children to be problem solvers.

It takes a long time to develop problem-solving skills. Therefore, assessment is a long-term process that cannot be accomplished solely with short-term measures. It needs to be continuous over the entire school mathematics program (Charles et al., 1987).

Assessment of problem solving should be based on your goals, using techniques consistent with those goals. If the mathematics program encompasses the ability to solve both routine and nonroutine problems, then assessment measures must include both types of problems. If the program includes emphasis on the process of problem solving, then assessment measures must incorporate ways of evaluating children's use of the process.

As you plan each lesson, consider how you will determine whether its objectives have been attained. Paper-and-pencil measures have a place in this type of evaluation, but also consider procedures such as the following:

- Presenting students with a problem-solving situation and observing how they meet it;
- Interviewing students;
- Having students describe to a group how they solved a problem;
- Having one student teach another how to solve a problem.

You need to assess as you go along in order to ascertain children's understanding and difficulties with understanding, for guidance in developing the next lesson. Remember that problem solving cannot be learned in any one lesson. The process must develop and thus be assessed over time.

Observations

As children work individually or in small groups, you can move about the room, observing them as they work, listening as they talk among themselves, making notes, questioning, and offering suggestions. Focus on how each student goes about the task of solving a problem. You might want to consider the following points:

- Is there evidence of careful reading of the problem?
- Do individual children seem to have some means of beginning to attack a problem?
- Do they apply an appropriate strategy, or do they simply try to use the last procedure you taught?
- Do they have another strategy to try if the first one fails?
- How consistent and persistent are they in applying a strategy?
- Are careless errors being made, and if so, when and why?
- How long are they willing to keep trying to solve a problem?
- How well are they concentrating on the task?

- How quickly do they ask for help?
- What strategies does each child use most frequently?
- Do they use manipulative materials? How?
- What do their behaviors and the expressions on their faces indicate about their interest and involvement?

Then make a brief note—an anecdotal record—that describes the situation and the behaviors you have observed.

Interviews

An interview can help overcome the limitations of writing—your own limitations in developing a written test item and the child's in developing a written answer. An interview lets you delve further into how a student goes about solving a problem. You can follow the child's thought patterns as he or she describes what is done and why.

Basically, you need to present the student with a problem; let the student find a solution and describe what he or she is doing; and question the student, eliciting specific details on what he or she is doing and why. Make notes as the student works and talks. Sometimes it is helpful to have an exact record of the replies.

You may want to have a student use a tape recorder when working alone. Or have a group of students discuss various ways of solving a problem. You can play the tape back later and analyze students' thinking more carefully and from a different perspective than if you are involved in the interview.

Inventories and Checklists

An inventory can be used to check on what a student knows about problem-solving strategies. You might give students one or several problems and ask them to solve each problem with a specified strategy or even two or three specified strategies. Your aim is to find out whether the student can apply each strategy—not what the answer to the problem is. You can also record your observations on a checklist, which then serves as an inventory.

Paper-and-Pencil Tests

You will also want to use written tests to assess children's ability to solve problems. Make sure that those you develop follow the guidelines of your problem-solving program (i.e., select good problems that are interesting and challenging, allow sufficient time for the process, and so on). Of particular interest are paper-and-pencil tests that assess the stages of problem solving (see Schoen and Oehmke, 1980; Charles et al., 1987).

Evaluation should be an ongoing component of the problem-solving program. Use it not just to assess where students are, but also to help you plan what to do next. If children do not use a strategy you have taught, you need to consider why, and then try again. If they try to use a strategy, you have evidence on how well they use it and whether they need more practice. Do not let evaluation become just a recording process. It is a way of helping you solve the problem of how to teach problem solving more effectively!

A Glance at Where We've Been

Problem solving is one of the most important skills in mathematics because it provides the opportunity for students to become independent learners. Therefore, problem solving should pervade the mathematics curriculum. Children need many experiences with problems that they do not immediately know how to solve. These problems can be investigations to start new topics, problems that arise in class or in children's lives, and applications. Children should be taught to use a variety of problem-solving strategies, providing them with a repertoire from which they can draw. You will need to provide not only a large resource of good problems but also enough time for problem solving, as well as tactics for making progress on a difficult problem. Your instruction must coordinate textbook materials with the use of calculators and other technology, as well as large-group, small-group, and individual work.

An overall strategy for approaching problems is desirable (understand, plan, carry out, look back). In addition, children need specific strategies that give them ways to begin to approach a problem, plus thoughtful questions that help students assess their own thinking process. This chapter has described such strategies, provided sample problems, and discussed the assessment of problem solving by means of observations, interviews, inventories, and tests.

Things to Do: From What You've Read

1. Provide a mathematics example of each of the *NCTM Standards* (2000) problem-solving standards listed in the introduction to this chapter.

2. When choosing problems for classroom work, what characteristics distinguish practice exercises from problem-solving tasks?
3. What are some questions you will teach students to use to help them solve problems? What other tactics will you use to help students who are stuck while solving a problem?
4. Describe why Polya's four-step plan is inadequate for helping students become good problem solvers. Why is it useful?
5. First solve, then identify levels (such as primary or intermediate) for problems presented in the chapter.
6. Identify problems in the chapter for which calculators or spreadsheets would be useful. Are there problems for which having a calculator or a spreadsheet available would take away all of the challenge? (These are important considerations when you are choosing problems for your class and deciding when students may and may not use calculators in their problem-solving efforts.) Solutions for the problems presented in this chapter may be found in the *Helping Children Learn Mathematics Instructor's Manual* (available at the Wiley Book Companion web site, www.wiley.com/college/reys).
7. Solve problems (5), (11), and (38) using two different strategies for each. Choose one other problem from the chapter for which you can use three different strategies to solve.
8. Why isn't finding the answer the final step in solving a problem?
9. Choose a content topic for a particular grade level (e.g., number, geometry, data). Make up at least one interesting problem for that topic that can be solved by each of these strategies: Look for a pattern, make a drawing or diagram, and construct a table.

Things to Do: Going Beyond This Book

IN THE FIELD

1. Start a file with problems from this chapter and add other problems, especially nonroutine ones. Many math education web sites offer long lists of interesting problems. Solve the problems and identify strategies that were useful in your solution. Categorize the problems in the way you find most useful.
2. **Assessing problem-solving strategies*: Choose a problem from this chapter and pose it to two children. You may choose to use the children's work samples on Masters 6–9 to 6–15 in the *Helping Children Learn Mathematics Instructor's Manual* (available at the Wiley Book Companion web site, www.wiley.com/college/reys). Identify the strategies each child uses. Use the analytic scoring scale in Figure 4-10 to score their work and write an evaluation of their efforts.
3. **Mathematical processes in the classroom*: Observe an elementary school classroom while children are engaged in a math lesson or investigation. Make a list of instances in which the children show evidence of using problem-solving strategies. Tell what the children were doing or saying and what tasks were involved. What role did the teacher play?
4. Search textbooks for a particular grade level. Find at least one problem that could be solved by using the following strategies: make a drawing or diagram, act it out, and solve a simpler or similar problem.
5. Plan an interactive bulletin board focused on problem solving.
6. Check a textbook for a list of the problem-solving strategies taught. Write an evaluation of it using the list of strategies in this text, categories for problem solving, and the *NCTM Standards* list of outcomes.

IN YOUR JOURNAL

7. Discuss in your journal: We don't teach textbook word problems anymore because no one has to solve that kind of problem.
8. Answer true or false, then defend your answer: Before solving a problem, pupils should be required to draw a picture of it.

WITH ADDITIONAL READINGS

9. Read *Counting on Frank* (Clement, 1991). Write a lesson plan where this book would be read aloud to grade 4–6 students as a motivator for some sort of problem-solving lesson.
10. Read O'Brien and Moss (1999). Choose your own context and problems similar to those used by these authors with fifth graders (problems with consistent data and with inconsistent data). If possible, try these problems with

* Additional activities, suggestions, or questions are provided in *Teaching Elementary Mathematics: A Resource for Field Experiences* (Wiley, 2004).

students of a similar age and analyze how they approach them.

WITH TECHNOLOGY RESOURCES

11. Obtain catalogs from software companies; select promising software to promote problem solving.
12. Make up problems using newspaper or magazine articles or data from reference books (e.g., *Guiness Book of World Records*) or web sites. Add the problems to your file.

Book Nook for Children

Anno, Mitsumasa. *Anno's Counting House*. New York: Philomel Books, 1982.
Ten children move one-by-one from their current home to the house next door. Window cutouts in the divider pages give readers a glimpse of some of the children in the four levels of the house, but the readers cannot verify the number of children in the house until they turn the page. An interesting approach to the partitions of 10 is provided.

Chwast, Seymour. *The Twelve Circus Rings*. San Diego, Calif.: Gulliver Books, Harcourt Brace Jovanovich, 1993.
What happens in circus rings? Lots of performers are performing if there are 12 circus rings. The performers accumulate with "six acrobats, five dogs a-barking . . . " reminiscent of the *Twelve Days of Christmas*. At the end of the book, students are asked to reason through and find totals such as "How many monkeys are playing?" in all 12 rings.

Clement, Rod. *Counting on Frank*. Milwaukee, Wis.: Gareth Stevens, 1991.
This story for younger children is about a boy who likes to ask questions. The best and biggest question is of course "What if?" "What if I drew with this ballpoint pen until it ran out, how long would the line be?"

Nozaki, Akihiro. *Anno's Hat Tricks*. Illustrated by Mitsumasa Anno. New York: Philomel Books, 1985.
Tom, Hannah, and Shadowchild interact with children and invite them to help figure out the color of their hats. The questions become more difficult as the book progresses. The text and illustrations invite children to explore some intriguing problems.

13. *Spreadsheet*. Use a spreadsheet to help solve problems (21) and (22) of this chapter.
14. *Calculator*. Show how the calculator can be used to solve problems (I), (L), and (N) in this chapter.
15. *Logo*. Use *Logo* programming to create a procedure that can be used to draw any regular polygon depending on the values input to the procedure.
16. *Geometer's Sketchpad*. Use the *Sketchpad* to establish a conjecture about the sum of the angles for regular polygons.
17. Make a file of ideas that use computer software and/or calculators in solving the problems. Be sure to find problems for different grade levels.

Resources

ANNOTATED BOOKS

Andrews, Angela, and Trafton, Paul R. *Little Kids—Powerful Problem Solvers: Math Stories from a Kindergarten Classroom*. Portsmouth N.H.: Heinemann, 2002.
Kindergarteners can do great math, especially if they are engaged and challenged from the start. This collection of stories from Angela's classroom is arranged by month of the school year. Each story will provide you with inspiration for a classroom lesson. Making sense of math is the focus of the teaching; respecting children's thinking makes it possible. The collections shows how children can make sense of experience and observations; how they can estimate, predict, hypothesize, analyze, and apply mathematical concepts in practical and visible ways; how they can help, and occasionally hinder, but ultimately challenge each other; and the ability of even very young children to persist until they have resolved problems.

Burns, Marilyn. *50 Problem-Solving Lessons: Grade 1–6*. Sausalito, Calif.: Marilyn Burns Education Associates; New York, NY: White Plains, 1996.
For many years, Marilyn Burns has produced a newsletter for teachers. Each newsletter contains classroom-tested activities from teachers across the country that are featured in this compilation of newsletters. The lessons span the strands of the math curriculum and are illustrated with children's work.

Charles, Randall, and Lester, Frank (and others). *Problem-Solving Experiences in Math*. Parsippany, N.J.: Pearson Learning, 1994.
This series of supplementary problem-solving books has a volume for each grade, K–8. More than one way to solve a problem is shown in this valuable resource. Students find the solutions using multiple strategies and a systematic approach that works! Designed to supplement any math textbook, the Teacher Sourcebooks and the black line masters for each grade level provide skill-building activities that include one-step, multiple-step, and process math problems.

Illingworth, Mark. *Real-Life Math Problem Solving* (Grades 4–8). New York: Scholastic Trade, 1999.
Investigate many classroom-tested problems with solutions that are motivating and require multiple steps. These problems will get student's thinking flexibly, creatively, and analytically. Understanding how math is used in the real world will boost students' interest in math and increase their confidence. Includes ideas for setting up a problem-solving classroom and assessment strategies. All activities and strategies are geared to the NCTM standards.

ANNOTATED ARTICLES

Desoete, Annemie; Roeyers, Herbert; and Buysse, Ann. "Metacognition and Mathematical Problem Solving in Grade 3." *Journal of Learning Disabilities*, 34(5), (September–October 2001), pp. 435–439.
This overview of two studies examines the relationship between metacognition and mathematical problem solving in 165 children with average intelligence in grade 3 in order to help teachers and therapists gain a better understanding of contributors to successful mathematical performance. The analysis reveals three metacognitive components connected with mathematical problem solving.

Jitendra, Asha. "Teaching Students Math Problem-Solving Through Graphic Representations." *Teaching Exceptional Children*, 34(4), (March–April 2002), pp. 34–39.
This study examines the usefulness of graphic representations in teaching students with learning disabilities for problem solving in mathematics. Cases of students with phobia for mathematics are examined. Assessment on the performance of students in problem-solving activities is provided. The use of schematic diagrams in teaching is explained.

Levin, Barbara; Berger, Dina; and Cave, Linda. "Where Did You Go This Summer?" *Teaching Children Mathematics*, 8(1), (September 2001), pp. 18–20.
This article focuses on a mathematics problem-solving lesson given to elementary students. The problems involve calculating the distance that students traveled during their summer vacation. The article describes how students learn about place value and the concepts greater than, less than, and between. Opportunities for students to learn about one another through their summer travels are also described.

ADDITIONAL REFERENCES

Ameis, Jerry A. "Stories Invite Children to Solve Mathematical Problems." *Teaching Children Mathematics*, 8(5), (January 2002), p. 260.

Chancellor, Dinah, and Porter, Jeanna. "Calendar Mathematics." *Arithmetic Teacher*, 41 (February 1994), pp. 304–305.

Charles, Randall; Lester, Frank; and O'Daffer, Phares. *How to Evaluate Progress in Problem Solving*. Reston, Va.: NCTM, 1987.

Cognition and Technology Group at Vanderbilt University. "The Jasper Experiment: Using Video to Furnish Real-World Problem-Solving Contexts." *Arithmetic Teacher*, 40 (April 1993), pp. 474–478.

Hembree, Ray, and Marsh, Harold. "Problem Solving in Early Childhood: Building Foundations." In *Research Ideas for the Classroom: Early Childhood Mathematics* (ed. Robert J. Jensen). Reston, Va.: NCTM; and New York: Macmillan, 1993, pp. 151–170.

Hildebrand, Charlene; Ludeman, Clinton. J.; and Mullin, Joan. "Integrating Mathematics with Problem Solving Using the Mathematician's Chair." *Teaching Children Mathematics*, 5 (March 1999), pp. 434–441.

Hutchins, Pat. *The Doorbell Rang*. New York: Green Willow Books, 1986.

Kelly, Janet. "Improving Problem Solving Through Drawings." *Teaching Children Mathematics*, 6 (September 1999), pp. 48–51.

Kelly, M. G., and Wiebe, James H. "Using the Video Camera in Mathematical Problem Solving." *Arithmetic Teacher*, 41 (September 1993), pp. 41–43.

Kenney, Patricia Ann, and Silver, Edward A. (eds.). *Results from the Sixth Mathematics Assessment of the National Assessment of Educational Progress*. Reston, Va.: NCTM, 1997.

Kliman, Marlene, and Richards, Judith. "Writing, Sharing and Discussing Mathematics Stories," *Arithmetic Teacher* (November 1992) Vol. 40 Issue 3, pp. 138–142.

Kouba, Vicky L.; Zawojewski, Judith S.; and Strutchens, Marilyn E. "What Do Students Know about Numbers and Operations?" In *Results from the Sixth Mathematics Assessment of the National Assessment of Educational Progress* (eds. Patricia Ann Kenney and Edward A. Silver). Reston, Va.: NCTM, 1997.

Kroll, Diana Lambdin, and Miller, Tammy. "Insights from Research on Mathematical Problem Solving in the Middle Grades." In *Research Ideas for the Classroom: Middle Grades Mathematics* (ed. Douglas T. Owens). Reston, Va.: NCTM; and New York: Macmillan, 1993, pp. 58–77.

McClain, Kay, and Cobb, Paul. "An Analysis of Development of Sociomathematical Norms in One First-Grade Classroom." *Journal for Research in Mathematics Education*, 32 (May 2001), pp. 236–266.

Midgett, Carol, and Trafton, Paul R. "Learning through Problems: A Powerful Approach to Teaching Mathematics." *Teaching Children Mathematics*, 7 (May 2001), p. 532.

O'Brien, Thomas C., and Ann C. Moss. "On the Keeping of Several Things in Mind." *Teaching Children Mathematics*, 6 (October 1999), pp. 118–122.

Polya, George. *How to Solve It*. Princeton, N.J.: Princeton University Press, 1973 (1945, 1957). Worth, Ill.: Creative Publications.

Schoen, Harold L., and Oehmke, Theresa. "A New Approach to the Measurement of Problem-Solving Skills." In *Problem Solving in School Mathematics, 1980* (eds. Stephen Krulik and Robert E. Reys). Reston, Va.: NCTM, 1980, pp. 216–227.

Silbey, Robyn. "What Is in the Daily News? Problem-Solving Opportunities." *Teaching Children Mathematics*, 5 (March 1999), pp. 390–394.

Silver, Edward A. and Kenney, Patricia Ann. *Results from the Seventh Mathematics Assessment*. Reston, Va.: NCTM, 2000.

Suydam, Marilyn N. "Indications from Research on Problem Solving." In *Teaching and Learning: A Problem-Solving Focus* (ed. Frances R. Curcio). Reston, Va.: NCTM, 1987, pp. 99–114.

Suydam, Marilyn N., and Weaver, J. Fred. *Using Research: A Key to Elementary School Mathematics*. Columbus, Ohio: ERIC Clearinghouse for Science, Mathematics and Environmental Education, 1981.

Weinberg, Susan. "Going Beyond Ten Black Dots." *Teaching Children Mathematics*, 2 (March 1996), pp. 432–435.

Wheatley, Charlotte L. "Calculator Use and Problem-Solving Performance." *Journal for Research in Mathematics Education*, 11 (November 1980), pp. 323–334.

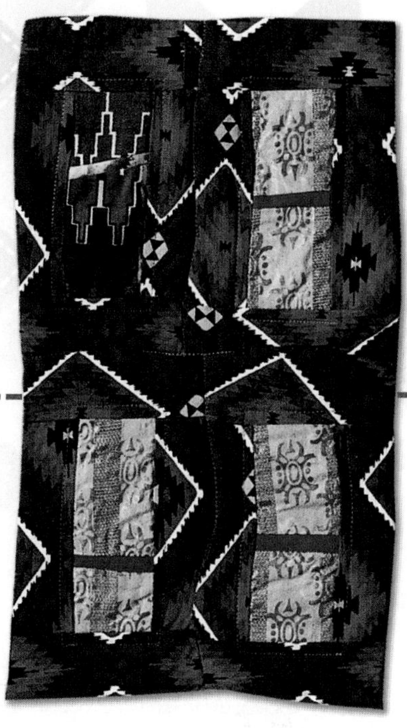

CHAPTER 7

Beginning Number Sense: Counting and Early Benchmarks

Snapshot of a Lesson

Key Ideas for an Early Lesson on Numbers

1. Maintain and/or improve skill in recognizing the number of objects in small groups.
2. Increase awareness of number patterns.
3. Develop counting skills.

Necessary Materials

Overhead projector and about 20 counters or beans.

Miss Chen

Orientation

The kindergarten children are learning to recognize by sight the number of objects in small groups. The teacher, Miss Chen, spends a few minutes each day on this activity. She has just placed four beans on the face of the overhead. She turns on the overhead for two seconds, then turns it off.

MISS CHEN: How many beans did you see?

Less than half the children raise their hands, so Miss Chen decides to do it again. This time nearly all the children raise their hands.

MISS CHEN: How many beans? Barry?

BARRY: Four.

One child, Susan, is in obvious disagreement, so Miss Chen calls on her.

SUSAN: Five.

MISS CHEN: Okay, let's check. I will turn on the overhead and Susan can count the beans for us.

Susan counts the images.

SUSAN: There are only four. When I saw the pattern, I thought there was one in the middle.

MISS CHEN: I am glad Susan is looking for patterns. That is the key to recognizing groups of things. Let's try another one, and be sure to look for patterns.

Miss Chen places five beans on the overhead, turns it on for two seconds, and then turns it off.

MISS CHEN: How many beans?

All the children have a hand up; Miss Chen points to one of them, who says five. The others agree.

MISS CHEN: We will try one more.

Miss Chen places five beans on the overhead in a different arrangement. She then turns it on for two seconds.

MISS CHEN: How many beans did you see? Bonny?

BONNY: Five, but it looks different than the other five.

SUSAN: It is different because there are six. It fits the pattern for six.

MISS CHEN: Let's check it.

Miss Chen turns the projector on, and Bonny confirms there are five. Susan and many other children are looking for patterns, but their recognition skills need sharpening. They see part of a pattern but are not sensitive to small differences. That's why this activity is used for a couple of minutes each day.

MISS CHEN: Thanks, Bonny, there are only five. We really have to watch those patterns carefully. That's enough for today.

Many children groan and plead for more. They really enjoy this activity, but Miss Chen realizes the value of not overdoing a good thing. Therefore, she is careful not to "burn them out" with too much at one time. Even though the children don't realize it, this activity reviews counting and increases their readiness for addition and subtraction.

Introduction

This chapter begins the second part of *Helping Children Learn Mathematics,* in that it discusses teaching strategies, techniques, and learning activities related to specific mathematical topics—in this case, beginning number sense. Number sense, like common sense, is difficult to define or express simply. It refers to an intuitive feel for numbers and their various uses and interpretations.

Number sense also includes the ability to compute accurately and efficiently, to detect errors, and to recognize results as reasonable. People with number sense are able to understand numbers and use them effectively in everyday living (McIntosh et al., 1997). Good number sense also includes recognizing the relative magnitudes of numbers and establishing referents, or benchmarks, for measures of common objects and situations in their environments.

Math Links 7.1

A variety of recommended Web resources for Number, which may be used by teachers and children, may be found at the NCTM's Illuminations web site, which you can access from this book's web site.

Instructional programs from prekindergarten through grade 2 should enable all students to:	Pre-K–2 Expectations: All students should
Understand numbers, ways of representing numbers, relationships among numbers, and number systems.	• count with understanding and recognize "how many" in sets of objects; • develop understanding of the relative position and magnitude of whole numbers and of ordinal and cardinal numbers and their connections; • connect number words and numerals to the quantities they represent, using various physical models and representations.

FIGURE 7-1 Number and Operation Standard for Grades Pre-K–2.

These ideas regarding number sense are reminiscent of Brownell's ideas about meaningful learning (see Chapter 2). Students need to develop concepts meaningfully so that numbers are used effectively both in and out of school. Helping students to develop such number sense requires appropriate modeling, posing process questions, encouraging thinking about numbers, and in general creating a classroom environment that nurtures number sense.

The Number and Operation Standard of the *Principles and Standards for School Mathematics* (NCTM, 2000) includes several concepts and skills related to beginning number sense. Figure 7-1 presents part of the standard for prekindergarten through grade 2. (See Appendix A for a full description.)

Suppose we explore several examples of number sense in action. What does the number 5 mean to young children? It can mean many things. It might be their current age or their age next year. It might be how old they were when they started kindergarten. Figure 7-2 illustrates a few uses and interpretations of the number 5 suggested by young children. Other children would provide different examples. In fact, the examples in Figure 7-2 might be different for the same children tomorrow because children's concepts of numbers continuously grow and change. A few examples illustrating the multidimensional nature of number sense for older children are shown in Figure 7-3.

Number sense is not a finite entity that a student either has or does not have. Its development is a lifelong process. In an effort to facilitate the development of number sense in elementary school, the NCTM has published several books on number sense (Burton et al., 1993; Reys et al., 1991).

Children begin to develop some sense about numbers long before they begin to count. For example, young children can answer these kinds of questions:

How old are you? [two]

What channel should we watch? [thirteen]

On what floor is your doctor's office? [four]

How many sisters do you have? [one]

Math Links 7.2

The full-text electronic version of the Number and Operation Standard, with electronic examples (interactive activities), is available at the NCTM's web site, which you can access from this book's web site. After reading the Chapter 3 introduction, click on pre-K–2, 3–5, or 6–8 to read about the Number and Operation Standard at those levels.

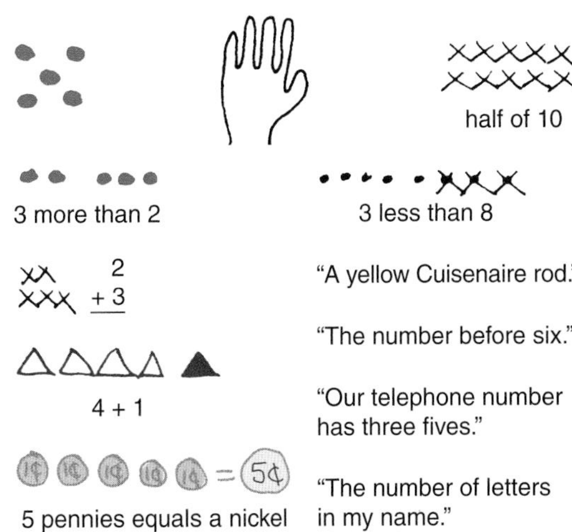

FIGURE 7-2 The meanings of the number five suggested by young children.

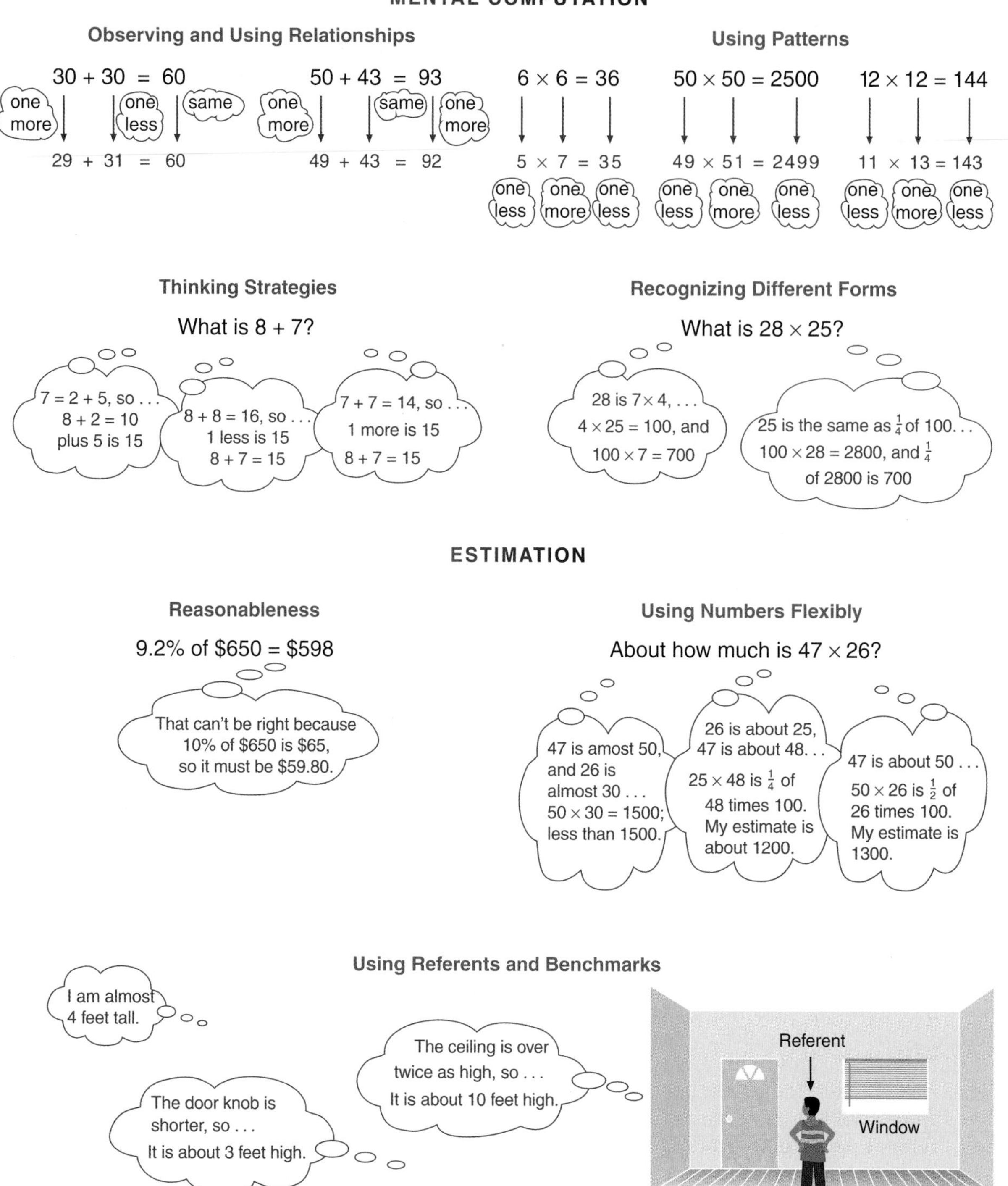

FIGURE 7-3 Some examples of number sense in action.

Such early experiences introduce the number names as well as their symbols—13 on the channel indicator or 4 on the elevator. These names and symbols are memorized through sound and sight recognition and provide an important beginning, but a child's knowledge of these concepts alone does not indicate the child's grasp of number.

For one thing, these experiences underscore a very important characteristic of number. It is an abstraction. It can't be adequately illustrated in just one situation. The multiple meanings of 5 illustrated in Figure 7-2 demonstrate how quickly the concept of *five* becomes associated with different situations. Research into how children develop number sense makes it clear that the more varied and different their experiences, the more likely it is that they will abstract number concepts from their experiences (Payne and Huinker, 1993). Helping children further their development of number and number sense has a high instructional priority. The goal of this chapter is to stimulate your thinking about number sense and its development during the early years before children are comfortable with numbers and counting.

FOCUS QUESTIONS

1. How does children's number sense develop?
2. How can technology help children develop number sense?
3. What characteristics are associated with the different counting stages?
4. How can teachers use questions to promote students' thinking about numbers?

Prenumber Concepts

Numbers are everywhere, and thus even young children have a vast amount of early number experience, as shown in Figure 7-2. Many of these experiences do not rely on numbers per se but provide the basis for building early number concepts and the foundation for later skills. Such experiences are called *prenumber experiences.* As a teacher, you will need to help children take advantage of them. Different steps are involved in developing prenumber concepts that lead eventually to meaningful counting skills and number sense. Although the learning paths that children take are bound to differ greatly, they all begin with classifying whatever is to be counted.

Classification

Classification is fundamental to learning about the real world, and it can be done with or without numbers. For example, children can be separated into groups of boys and girls (which is classification) without considering number. Yet classification skills are prerequisite to any meaningful number work. If children want to know how many girls are in the class, they must be able to recognize (i.e., classify) the girls. Thus, before children can count, they must know what to count, and classification helps identify what is to be counted.

Young children learn to distinguish between dogs and cats, reptiles and mammals, toys they enjoy and those they never use. These distinctions are examples of classification in action. Classification not only helps children make some sense of things around them, but also helps them become flexible thinkers. Classifying objects in different ways fosters the development of thinking skills.

As children classify, or sort, materials, such as buttons (see *Snapshot of a Lesson Plan* in Chapter 3), they must decide whether each object has the given characteristic. If children disagree on how an object should be classified, it forces them to defend their answers and clarify how the classification process was done. This type of argumentation is the beginning of helping children see the need for explaining their thoughts in mathematics, one of the goals of the *NCTM Standards*. At this point, there may be no counting as materials are classified, although words such as *more, few, many, most,* and *none* will likely be used in describing the resulting collections.

Classification allows people to reach general agreement on what is to be counted. For example, consider a pile of buttons and the following question: How many plastic buttons have two holes? The answer is a number that tells *how many.* When a number is used in this way, it is called a *cardinal number.* Before finding the specific cardinal number, however, you must first decide which buttons are plastic and how many of them have exactly two holes. Once this classification is done, the members to be counted are well defined, and the results should be the same.

Stories provide opportunities for classification. Books such as *Where's Waldo?* by Martin Handford challenge students to find objects in a vast and often complex picture containing many different items. Such search-and-find challenges provide practice in visual discrimination as well as in classification.

Attribute blocks, sometimes called *logic blocks,* provide an excellent model for classification activities and help develop logical thinking. These blocks can be made from cardboard (see Appendix

Math Links 7.3

A collection of sorting and classifying lessons and activities for grades K–2 may be found at the NCTM's Illuminations web site, which you can access from this book's web site.

B for an attribute block master), but they are also commercially available in wood or plastic. They differ in several attributes, including color, shape, and size. Consider, for example, the 24 pieces shown in Appendix B and In the Classroom 7-1. These pieces illustrate three attributes:

Size:	Large, Small (L, S)
Color:	Blue, Yellow, Green (B, Y, G)
Shape:	Square, Triangle, Pentagon, Circle (S, T, P, C)

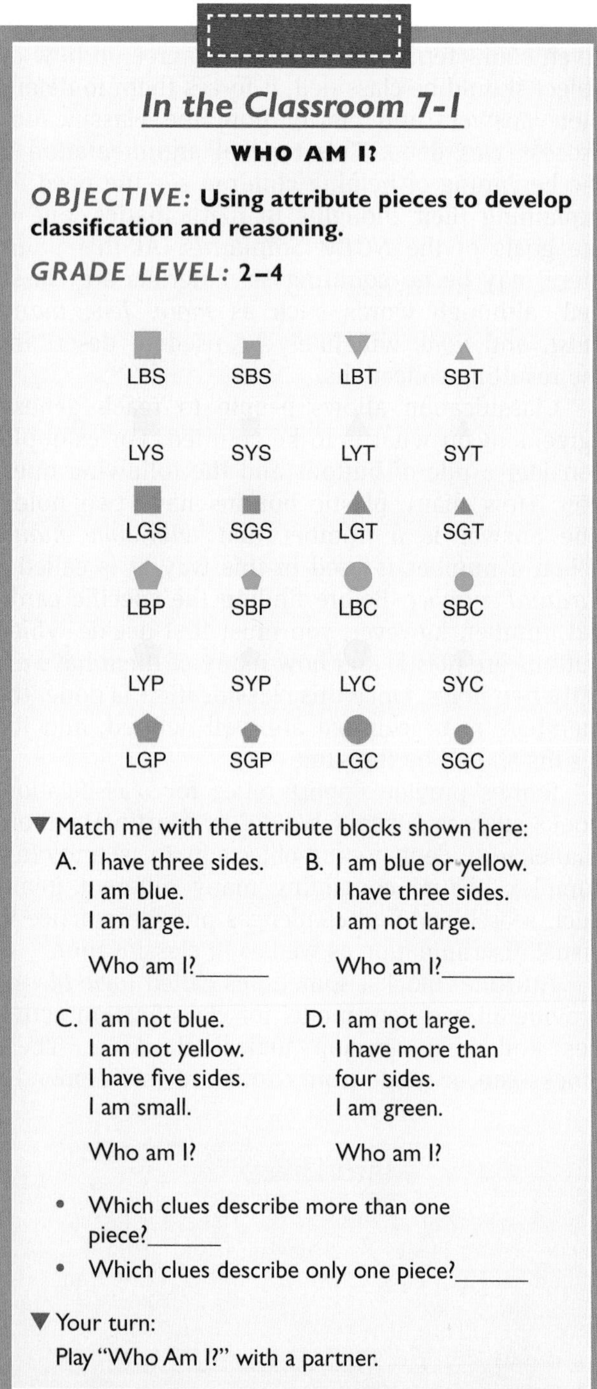

In the Classroom 7-1

WHO AM I?

OBJECTIVE: **Using attribute pieces to develop classification and reasoning.**

GRADE LEVEL: **2–4**

LBS	SBS	LBT	SBT
LYS	SYS	LYT	SYT
LGS	SGS	LGT	SGT
LBP	SBP	LBC	SBC
LYP	SYP	LYC	SYC
LGP	SGP	LGC	SGC

▼ Match me with the attribute blocks shown here:

A. I have three sides.
I am blue.
I am large.

Who am I?______

B. I am blue or yellow.
I have three sides.
I am not large.

Who am I?______

C. I am not blue.
I am not yellow.
I have five sides.
I am small.

Who am I?

D. I am not large.
I have more than four sides.
I am green.

Who am I?

- Which clues describe more than one piece?______
- Which clues describe only one piece?______

▼ Your turn:

Play "Who Am I?" with a partner.

The first block can be described in words as the "Large Blue Square." Later in primary and elementary school, symbols, such as LBS, can be meaningfully attached to the attribute pieces, but at this stage a clear verbal description of the pieces by young children is the goal. As children manipulate the blocks and describe them, they begin to make natural connections between the concrete model and different ways of representation. Many of the 24 pieces are alike in some attributes, but no two pieces are alike in all attributes, which provides opportunities for "Who am I?" games, as presented in In the Classroom 7-1. Such activities encourage children to think logically and develop communication skills. In the process, children informally explore fundamental notions, including matching, comparison, shape, sets, subsets, and disjoint sets as well as set operations.

Communication and language can be further developed as the set operations of union and intersection are encountered. The combining, or union, of *disjoint sets* (sets with no members in common) is a natural model for addition. The logical connection *or* can be used to develop the union of two or more sets. For example, as Figure 7-4 shows, the union of triangles and squares produces a set that contains all attribute blocks that are either triangles *or* squares.

The intersection of sets can be used to explore the logical connective *and.* Using the attribute blocks, you could examine the pieces that are pentagons *and* blue. Children might place these in yarn loops as shown in Figure 7-5. This arrangement also allows children to identify other subsets,

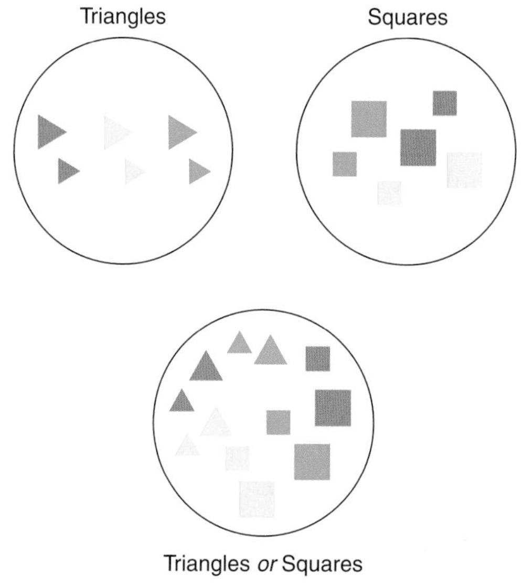

FIGURE 7-4 The union of two sets illustrates the mathematical meaning of "or."

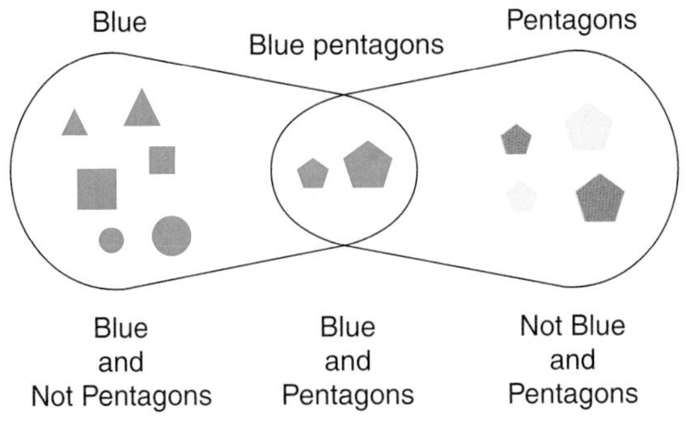

FIGURE 7-5 The intersection of two sets illustrates the mathematical meaning of "and."

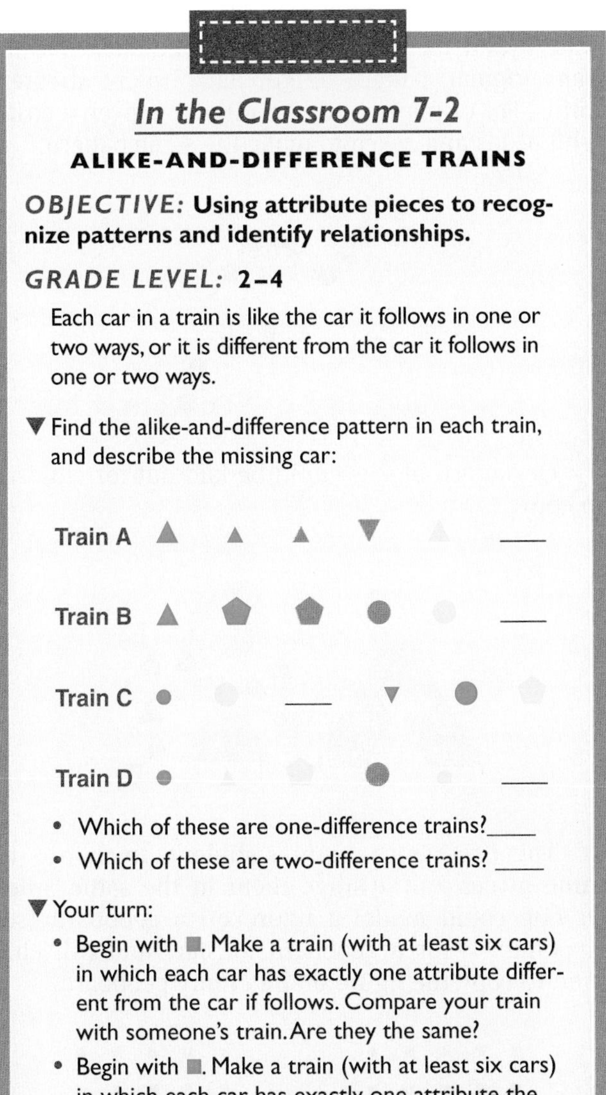

In the Classroom 7-2

ALIKE-AND-DIFFERENCE TRAINS

OBJECTIVE: **Using attribute pieces to recognize patterns and identify relationships.**

GRADE LEVEL: **2–4**

Each car in a train is like the car it follows in one or two ways, or it is different from the car it follows in one or two ways.

▼ Find the alike-and-difference pattern in each train, and describe the missing car:

Train A ▲ ▲ ▲ ▼ ▲ ___

Train B ▲ ⬟ ⬟ ● ● ___

Train C ● ● ___ ▼ ● ⬟

Train D ● ▲ ⬟ ● ● ___

- Which of these are one-difference trains?____
- Which of these are two-difference trains? ____

▼ Your turn:

- Begin with ■. Make a train (with at least six cars) in which each car has exactly one attribute different from the car if follows. Compare your train with someone's train. Are they the same?
- Begin with ■. Make a train (with at least six cars) in which each car has exactly one attribute the same as the car it follows. Compare your train with a classmate's train. Tell how they are alike.

such as pieces that are blue and not pentagons. Using *not* to describe a relationship is an important step in development.

The logical connectives *and, or,* and *not* can be used to help children classify pieces according to their attributes. For example, the "alike and difference trains" shown In the Classroom 7-2 provide opportunities for students to use attribute blocks to classify and to search for patterns and use logical thinking as well. Children at all grade levels can benefit from structured activities with these materials.

Attribute blocks almost guarantee student involvement, but they also require teachers to assume an active role. When children are engaged in activities with attribute blocks, directed questions and probes can provide clues about their thinking processes. Observing children's actions reveals much about their maturity. For example, when asked to choose a piece that is blue and a triangle, one child might choose a blue piece but not a triangle. Another might select a triangle that is not blue. These responses may only reflect poor listening skills; however, additional questioning may show that the two children don't understand what the word *and* means or are unable to keep two different attributes in mind simultaneously. Carefully observing and questioning children as they are using these materials will help you better understand what they are thinking, which in turn will help you design more appropriate learning activities.

Many different experiences are needed to sharpen children's observation skills and provide them with the basis on which to build the notion of numbers. Consider another example, in which children are asked to count money:

How much money is this?

Three, if coins are counted

Seven, if cents are counted

This example provides a reminder that a number name alone, such as three or seven, is rarely reported. In this case, "three coins" describes both *cardinality* (i.e., how many) and what was actually counted. This example also provides another reminder that what is to be counted must be well defined or clearly understood. If there is any confusion about what is being counted, then counting discrepancies are certain to happen.

Such discrepancies occur in many different forms but are particularly troublesome with a number line. Two children standing on a number line that has been made from a roll of adding machine tape and fastened to the floor provide an example:

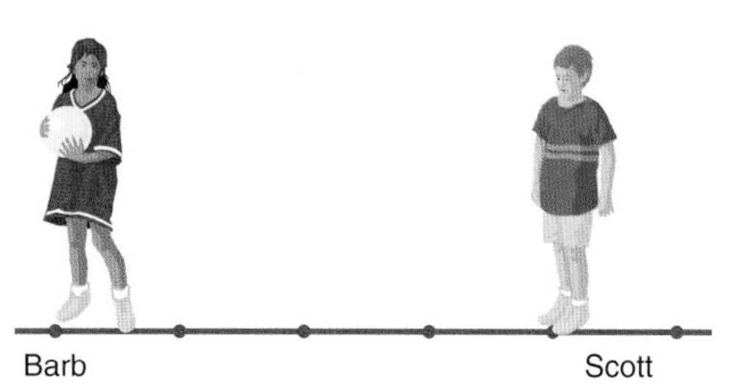

You can ask,

How far is it from Barb to Scott?

Is it 4? or 3? or 5?

The solution depends on what is to be counted:

Should the intervals between the dots be counted?

Should the dots be counted?

All of the dots?

Research confirms that confusion between dots and intervals often contributes to later misunderstanding with a number line (Sowder, 1992). Confusion over what should be counted is a classification problem that must be solved before counting can be meaningful. Thus classification is a very important step in developing number sense and early counting skills.

Patterns

Mathematics is the study of patterns. Creating, constructing, and describing patterns require problem-solving skills and constitute an important part of mathematics learning. Patterns can be based on geometric attributes (shape, symmetry), relational attributes (sequence, function), physical attributes (color, length, number), or affective attributes (like, happiness). Sometimes patterns combine several attributes. For example, a child's list of favorite colors provides a pattern involving physical attributes (color) and affective attributes (like).

Paper, cubes, attribute blocks, pattern blocks, and other manipulatives (objects) provide opportunities for children to stack, arrange, and order objects in various ways. Number sense and mathematical exploration grow from such patterning. In the early grades, patterns help children develop number sense, ordering, counting, and sequencing (Coburn et al., 1992). Later, patterns are helpful in developing thinking strategies for basic facts, discussed in Chapter 9, and in developing algebraic thinking, considered in Chapter 14. In addition, as children grow older, their experiences with patterns accelerate as they explore graphing, number theory, and geometry. Patterns, as with puzzles, are usually intellectually inviting and stimulating for people of all ages.

Exploring patterns requires active mental involvement and often physical involvement. The opportunities to do patterning are limitless, but there are several different types of pattern activities that children should encounter regularly. Let's consider four different ways that patterns might be used in developing mathematical ideas.

COPYING A PATTERN Children are shown a pattern and then asked to make one "just like it." The original pattern might take many different forms. For example, children might be given a string with beads and asked to make the same pattern:

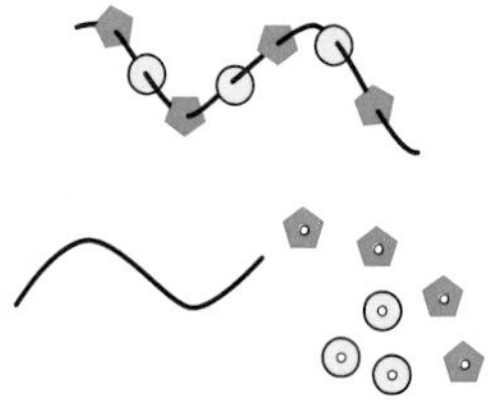

Or pattern blocks could be laid out for children to copy:

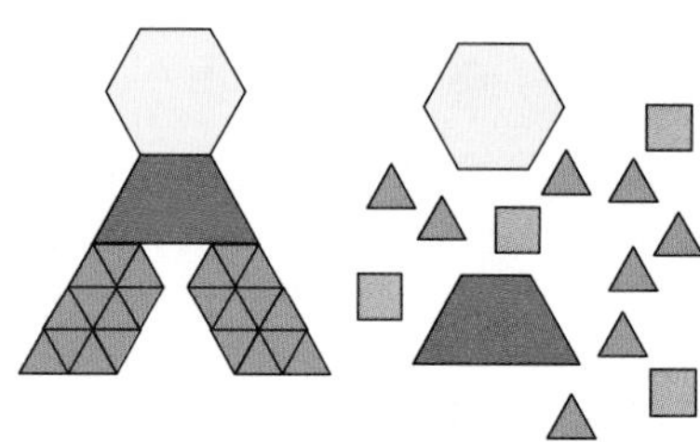

This experience requires students to choose the same pieces and arrange them in the same order. Or one could model a figure on a geoboard (see Appendix B for a geoboard master) and ask children to copy the figure on an empty geoboard.

FINDING THE NEXT ONE The trains In the Classroom 7-2 illustrate problems where children "find the next one." In that case, "the next one" is the next car in the train. Consider a somewhat easier pattern suggested by "stairs" of Cuisenaire rods:

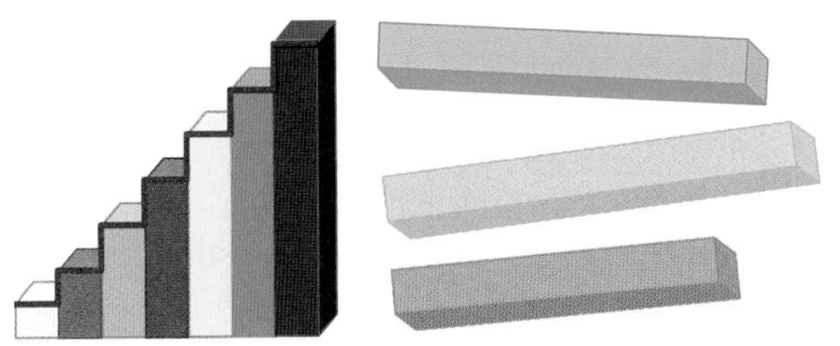

Children might be asked to find the next rod for the staircase. This find-the-next activity naturally leads to continuing or extending the pattern.

EXTENDING A PATTERN Children are shown a pattern and asked to continue it. For example, an initial pattern can be made with blocks, and children can be asked to continue the pattern:

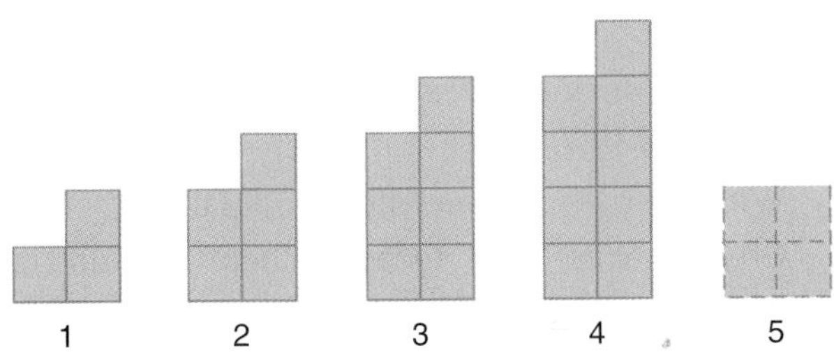

Notice how this visual pattern might serve as the foundation for exploring several important mathematical ideas. It could lead to classifying odd numbers. It could be used to observe something common about the representations—that they are all a rectangle plus one. This latter observation might lead to the algebraic generalization $2N + 1$ to describe odd numbers.

Math Links 7.4

An electronic manipulative, called Color Patterns, that gives children practice extending patterns is available from the National Library of Virtual Manipulatives for Interactive Mathematics, which you can access from this book's web site. This activity could be used for practice or assessment.

MAKING THEIR OWN PATTERNS Children need opportunities to create their own patterns and are eager to do so. Sometimes the patterns they make are highly creative and reveal insight into their mathematical thinking.

Language and communication are important elements of patterning activities. Children should be encouraged to "think out loud" as they search for patterns. Ask them to explain why they selected a certain piece or why they did what they did. Sometimes children "see" different patterns than you anticipate. As teachers, you must try to learn and understand children's patterns and encourage them to share their thinking.

Comparisons

Comparison of quantities is another important part of learning to count and is also essential in developing number awareness. Comparisons are plentiful in classrooms as children use materials. Teacher-led activities frequently provide opportunities for comparisons, with questions such as:

Does everyone have a piece of paper?

Are there more pencils or desks?

These questions either directly or indirectly involve comparisons that may lead to the important and powerful mathematical notion of one-to-one correspondence.

Look at Figure 7-6A and consider this question: Are there more hearts or gingerbread cookies? Counting would provide a solution, particularly with the cookies scattered on a plate; however, if the cookies are arranged in an orderly fashion (Figure 7-6B), you can make direct comparisons and answer the question without counting. Sometimes placing connectors (laying string or yarn; drawing lines or arrows) provides a visual reminder of the one-to-one correspondence that underlies many comparisons, as in Figure 7-6C.

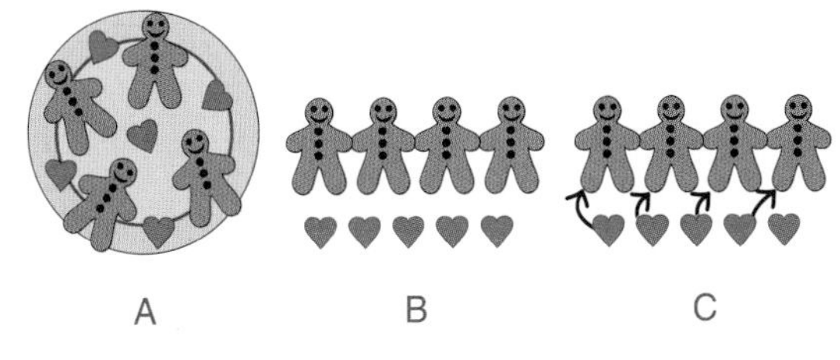

FIGURE 7-6 Models for making comparisons by (A) counting; (B) physically comparing without counting; and (C) one-to-one correspondence.

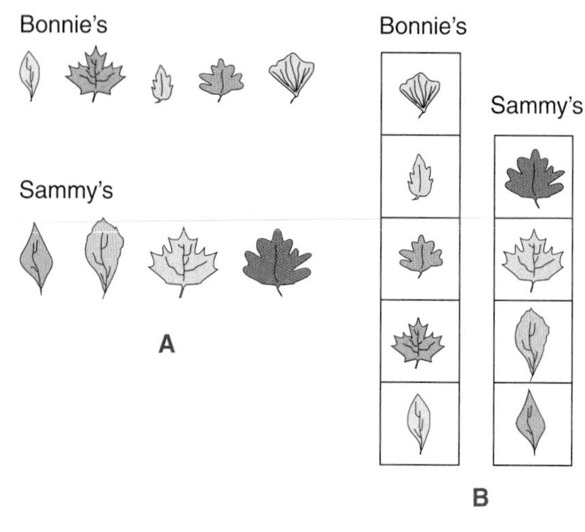

FIGURE 7-7 A framework for comparison that eliminates irrelevant attributes.

When making comparisons, students must be able to discriminate between important and irrelevant attributes. In Figure 7-7A, for example, who has more leaves—Bonnie or Sammy? The leaves are very different; their sizes, shapes, and colors vary. Still, the procedure for setting up a correspondence is the same.

To ensure that members of two sets are arranged in an orderly fashion for comparison, a method that is sometimes helpful involves using pieces of square paper or index cards. In this case, placing each leaf on a card and then stacking the cards on a common base, as in Figure 7-7B, provides a helpful framework. This method provides a graphical representation of the information, allowing quick and accurate visual comparisons.

Several different but equally valid verbal descriptions may be used for the example given in Figure 7-7:

Bonnie has more leaves than Sammy.

Sammy has fewer leaves than Bonnie.

Children need to become familiar with descriptions of relationships such as *more than, less (fewer) than,* and *as many as.* A grasp of these terms can be followed by more explicit characterization:

Bonnie has one more leaf than Sammy.

Sammy has one less leaf than Bonnie.

In these cases, the notion of order and succession are being developed. Children must come to realize that 4 is the number between 5 and 3 as well as one more than 3 and one less than 5. Understanding of such relationships can evolve naturally as comparisons are made and discussed.

When comparisons are made among several different things, ordering is involved. For example, children can print their first names on some grid paper:

Then they can physically compare their names with others' names to answer questions such as these:

Who has the longest name?

Who has the shortest name?

Can you find someone with a name the same length as yours?

Can you find someone whose name has one more (less) letter than your name?

Ordering often requires several comparisons, and a graph might help organize the information. The graph in Figure 7-8 was constructed by classifying children's names according to length. It summarizes much information and presents it in an organized form. The graph could be used to answer the previous questions and additional questions such as these:

Which length name is most popular?

Greg wasn't here today. Where should his name go on our graph?

Can you think of anyone you know who has a shorter name than Tim?

FIGURE 7-8 Classification of children's names on a graph for comparison.

As more things are ordered, the ordering process becomes more complicated, and most children need some guidance to be able to order things efficiently. That's why organizational techniques, such as graphing (see Chapter 17), are particularly helpful and will contribute to the early development of numbers.

Conservation

The phenomenon of *conservation of number*—that a given number does not vary—reflects how children think. You need to be aware of the symptoms of the lack of conservation of number in children and its implications for early number development and counting. This idea occurs in different forms, but let's look at an example involving counting and numbers.

Two rows of blocks are arranged side by side, and a teacher and a five- or six-year-old child look at them together:

The teacher, asking the child to make a comparison to decide whether there are more orange blocks or more purple blocks, initiates the following dialogue:

T: How many purple blocks?

S: (Counting them) Six.

T: How many orange blocks?

S: (Counting again) Six.

T: Are there more purple blocks or orange blocks?

S: They are the same.

Now the teacher spreads out the orange blocks as follows:

T: How many purple blocks now?

S: Six.

T: How many orange blocks now?

S: Six.

T: Are there more purple blocks or orange blocks?

S: More orange blocks.

T: I thought you said there were six purple and six orange.

S: I did, but this six (pointing to row of orange blocks) is bigger.

This example illustrates a typical case where a young child thinks a number varies and depends on arrangement or configuration. Here the child believes that stretching out the row makes it longer; the fact that the number remains the same creates no conflict. Look at the following grouping of marbles.

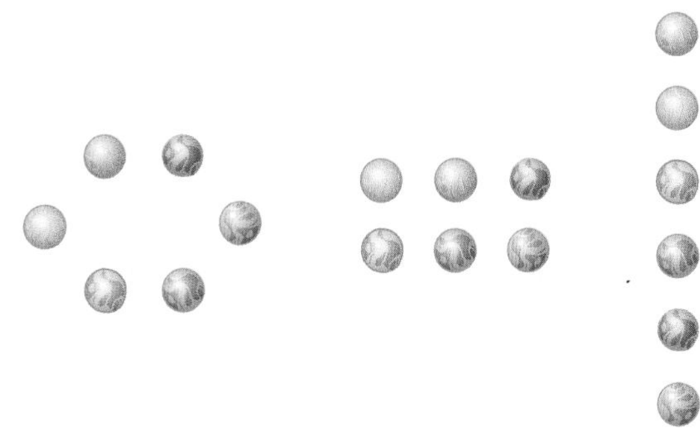

Some children count six marbles in each of these groups but report one group has more. For adults it seems inconceivable that "this six" could be more than "that six," but as this and other examples in this book show, children's logic and adults' logic can be very different.

Conservation was described by Jean Piaget and has been the subject of much research. Rarely do children conserve number before five or six years of age. Children up to this age don't realize that moving the objects in a set has no effect on the number of the objects. Thus many children in kindergarten and some in first and second grade are nonconservers. A child can be adept at counting and remain naive about conservation. Whenever this happens, instructional activities (such as the different configurations of five objects on the overhead in the opening *Snapshot Lesson*) should be used to increase the child's awareness of the invariance of number.

Group Recognition

The patterns encountered in classifying and making comparisons provide many number-sense experiences. In fact, before actually counting, children are aware of small numbers of things: one nose, two hands, three wheels on a tricycle. Research shows that most children entering school can identify quantities of three things or less by inspection alone without the use of counting techniques (Clements, 1999).

The skill to "instantly see how many" in a group is called *subitizing,* from a Latin word meaning "suddenly." It is an important skill to develop. In fact, one instructional goal for first-grade students is to develop immediate recognition of groups of up to five or six. Sight recognition of quantities up to five or six is important for several reasons:

1. *It saves time.* Recognizing the number in a small group is much faster than counting each individual member of that group.
2. *It is the forerunner of some powerful number ideas.* Children who can name small groups give evidence of knowing early order relations, such as 3 is more than 2 and 1 is less than 4. Some may also realize that 3 contains a group of 2 and a group of 1.
3. *It helps develop more sophisticated counting skills.* Children who recognize the number in a small group will more quickly begin counting from that point.
4. *It accelerates the development of addition and subtraction.* Early work with these operations involves manipulation with objects. Being able to recognize the quantity in a small group frees children of the burden of counting small quantities to be joined or removed and allows them to concentrate on the action of the operation.

In the opening *Snapshot of a Lesson,* the teacher used beans and the overhead projector to develop sight recognition. The overhead projector allowed careful control of time so that the children could not count individual beans. The teacher placed the beans in different arrangements to encourage children to identify different patterns—and to do so quickly. Several different approaches were demonstrated as the children counted. Sight recognition is also evidenced by children's skills in reading the number of dots on the face of a die or on a domino. In fact, both of these materials provide natural as well as interesting models for developing and practicing this skill.

As children grow older, their ability to recognize quantities continues to improve, but it is still limited. Certain arrangements are more easily recognized or subitized. For example, look at these arrangements:

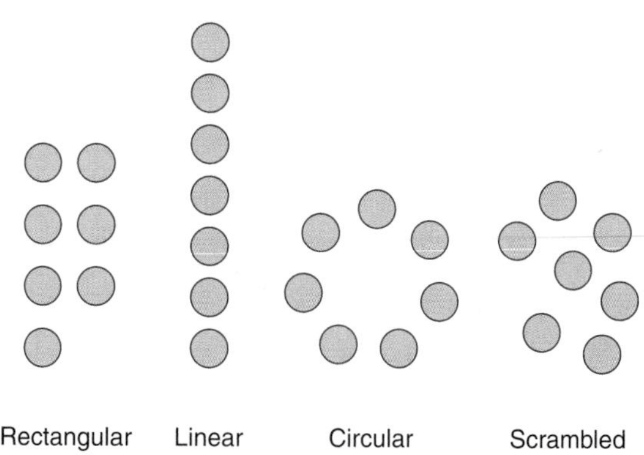

Children usually find rectangular arrangements easiest, followed by linear, and then circular, whereas scrambled arrangements are usually the most difficult. If the arrangement does not lend itself to some grouping, people of any age have more difficulty with larger quantities. Few adults can recognize by inspection groups of more than 6 or 8, and even these groups must be in common patterns such, as those found on playing cards or dominoes. For example, look at these pictures of birds:

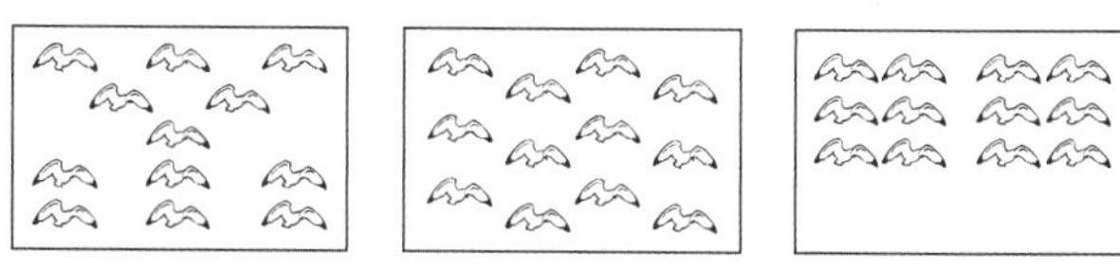

How many birds do you see? Each picture shows 12 birds, but you probably used different processes to count them. The picture at the left provides no clear groups, so you could either count every bird or perhaps immediately identify the numbers in some subset of the birds and then count the rest. In the other two pictures, some natural groupings are suggested: four groups of 3 and two groups of 6. It is even more difficult to recognize larger groupings without counting or forming some subsets of numbers. Nevertheless, small-group recognition is a powerful ally in counting larger groups.

Counting

Patterns facilitate the counting process; however, there are no sound patterns within the first 12 number names. Children learn these number names by imitating adults and older children. As young children practice counting, they often say nonconventional sequences of number names. It is not unusual to hear a young child count "one, two, five, eight, fifteen, twenty, six, hundred." This counting may sound strange, but it is perfectly natural. It reflects the child's struggle to remember both the number names and their order, both of which are necessary in order to count.

Eventually children may count apples, blocks, cards, rocks, stones, twigs, even petals on a flower. Try counting the petals on the flowers shown in Figure 7-9. They provide a very interesting setting for practicing counting and remind you that numbers are everywhere in nature.

Items such as blocks or petals are *discrete objects* (i.e., materials that lend themselves well to handling and counting). *Continuous quantities,* such as the amount of water in a glass or the weight of a person, are measured rather than counted.

What is counting? It is a surprisingly intricate process by which children call number values by name. A close look at the counting process shows that finding how many objects are present involves two distinct actions. A child must say the number-name series, beginning with one, and point to a different object as each number name is spoken. Children exhibit several different but distinct stages of counting, which we discuss as follows.

FIGURE 7-9 Models from nature for counting practice.
(Top photo: PhotoDisc/Getty Images; bottom photo: Digital Vision/Getty Images)

Counting Principles

How do children count? Look at an actual counting situation. Suppose seven shells are to be counted. A child who is what is called a "rational counter" says each number name as the shells are counted, as indicated in Figure 7-10. The last number named, "seven," reports the total.

As adults, you probably cannot recall your own struggle with counting. Yet observing young children can remind you how counting strategies vary

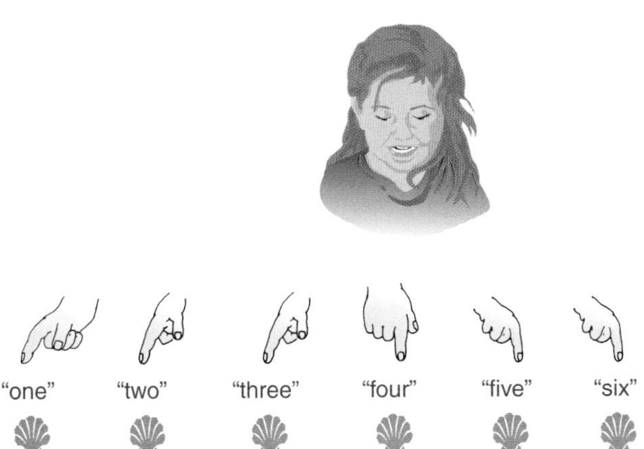

FIGURE 7-10 Rational counting: Correct sequence, with correct correspondence.

Math Links 7.5

Some examples of children counting may be viewed at the University of Melbourne web site, which you can access from this book's web site. These examples show difficulties young children may have due to their level of development and maturity.

www.wiley.com/college/reys

and are developed sequentially over a period of years (Fuson, 1988). Here are four important principles on which the counting process rests:

1. *Each object to be counted must be assigned one and only one number name.* As shown in Figure 7-10, a *one-to-one* correspondence between each shell and the number name was established.

2. *The number-name list must be used in a fixed order every time a group of objects is counted.* The child in the figure started with "one" and counted "two, three, . . ., seven," in a specific order. This is known as the *stable order rule.*

3. *The order in which the objects are counted doesn't matter* (this is known as the *order irrelevance rule*). Thus the child can start with any object and count them in any order.

4. *The last number name used gives the number of objects.* This principle is a statement of the *cardinality rule,* which connects counting with *how many.* Regardless of which block is counted first or the order in which they are counted, the last block named always tells the number.

These principles help you recognize the levels of children's counting skills. Careful observation of children, coupled with a good understanding of these principles, can pinpoint counting errors. Once the trouble is diagnosed, instruction can focus on the specific problem.

Counting Stages

There are several identifiable counting stages, and each reflects one or more of the counting principles. For example, some children may count the objects correctly and still not know how many objects have been counted. In response to the question "How many shells are on the table?" a child might correctly count "one, two, three, four, five, six, seven," as shown in Figure 7-10, and yet be unable to answer the question. This child does not realize that the last number named tells how many.

ROTE COUNTING A child using rote counting knows some number names, but not necessarily the proper sequence, as shown in Figure 7-11A. In this case, the child provides number names, but these names are not in correct counting sequence.

FIGURE 7-11 Rote counting errors.

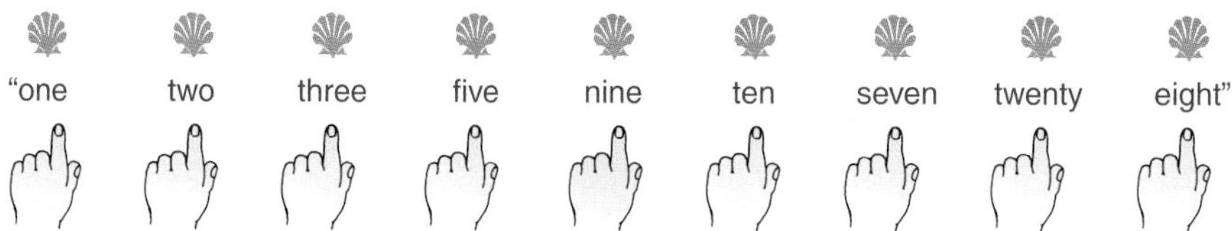
"one two three five nine ten seven twenty eight"

A. Incorrect sequence, correct correspondence

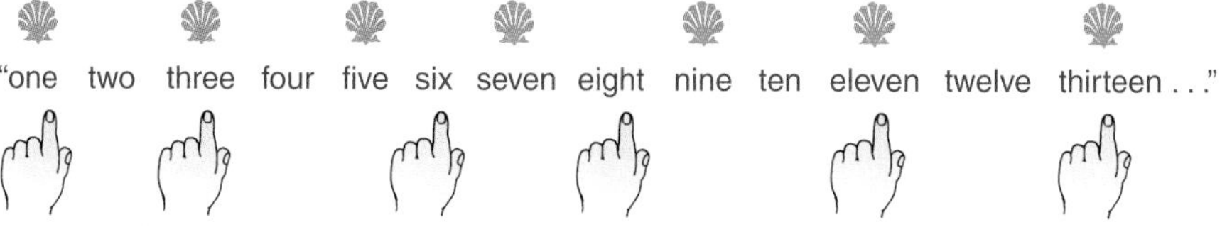
"one two three four five six seven eight nine ten eleven twelve thirteen . . ."

B. Correct sequence, incorrect correspondence (counts too fast)

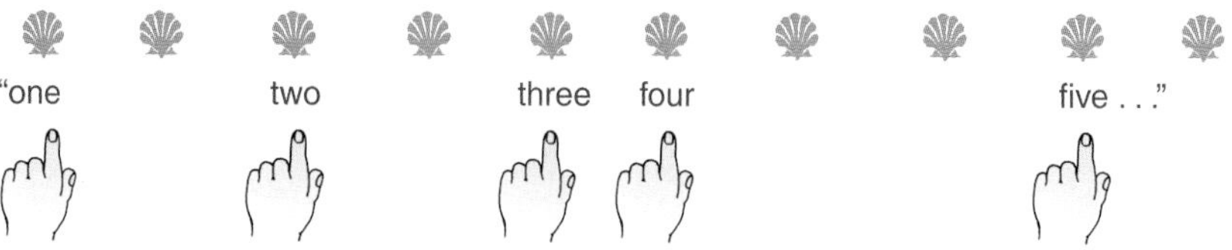
"one two three four five . . ."

C. Correct sequence, incorrect correspondence (points too fast)

Research shows that such children may "count" the same objects several times and use a different counting sequence each time (Fuson, 1988). Children who exhibit this error need to spend more time on the *stable order rule* as described in the second counting principle.

Rote counters may know the proper counting sequence, but they may not always be able to maintain a correct correspondence between the objects being counted and the number names. Figure 7-11B shows an example in which the rote counter is saying the number names faster than pointing, so that number names are not coordinated with the shells being counted. Rote counters may say the number names until they perceive all the objects as being counted. It is also possible that the rote counter points faster than saying the words, as illustrated in Figure 7-11C. This rote counter is pointing to the objects but is not providing a name for each of them. Asking children to slow down their counting and stressing the importance of one-to-one correspondence helps children with these types of rote counting errors.

It is important that children understand all four counting principles. Without this understanding, rote counters may not have their number names in the proper sequence, or they may not consistently provide a number name for each object being counted. A one-to-one correspondence may not be shown, which is a critical distinction between rote and rational counting. Using a one-to-one correspondence in counting represents significant progress and establishes one of the prerequisites to rational counting.

RATIONAL COUNTING In rational counting, the child gives a correct number name as objects are counted in succession; however, in rational counting the child not only uses one-to-one correspondence but also is able to answer the question about the number of objects being counted. In fact, rational counters exhibit all four counting principles.

Rational counting is an important skill for every primary-grade child. Children notice their own progress in developing this skill and become proud of their accomplishments. Early in first grade, some children will count to 10, others to 20, some to 50, and a few to over 100 (Fuson, 1988). No upper limit should be imposed, although a goal of 100 is clearly reasonable for most children by the end of first grade. Instruction should provide regular practice and encourage each child to count as far as he or she can.

Counting Strategies

Once mastery of rational counting to 10 or 20 has been reached, more efficient and sophisticated counting strategies should be encouraged.

COUNTING ON In counting on, the child gives correct number names as counting proceeds and can start at any number and begin counting. For example, the child can begin with 8 pennies and count "nine, ten, eleven"; or begin with 78 pennies and count "seventy-nine, eighty, eighty-one"; or begin with 98 pennies and count "ninety-nine, one hundred, one hundred one." Counting-on practice leads children to the discovery of many valuable patterns. Counting on is also an essential strategy for developing addition.

COUNTING BACK When children count back, they give correct number names as they count backward from a particular point. For example, to count back to solve the problem, "Bobbie had 22 rabbits and 3 were lost," a child might count "twenty-one, twenty, nineteen" and conclude there were 19 left. At an early stage, counting back can be related to rockets blasting off (counting down—five, four, three, two, one, blast off); later, it becomes helpful in developing subtraction.

Many children find it difficult to count backward, just as many adults find it difficult to recite the alphabet backward. The calculator provides a valuable instructional tool to help children improve their ability to count backward. Many children are surprised to learn that it is as easy to count backward on a calculator as it is to count forward.

Instruction in counting should include practice counting backward as well as forward. Counting backward, "Five, four, three, two, one," helps children establish sequences and relate each number to another in a different way. In the Classroom 7-3 provides an activity that uses a calendar to practice counting forward and backward. In the Classroom 7-4 provides an activity that integrates such practice with pattern recognition.

SKIP COUNTING In skip counting, the child gives correct names, but instead of counting by ones, counts by twos, fives, tens, or other values. The starting point and direction are optional. In addition to providing many patterns, skip counting provides readiness for multiplication and division.

Skip counting, coupled with counting on and counting back, provides excellent preparation for counting change in a monetary transaction. Thus, given the coins shown, children would be encouraged to choose the largest-valued coin and then begin counting on—"twenty-five, thirty, thirty-five, forty."

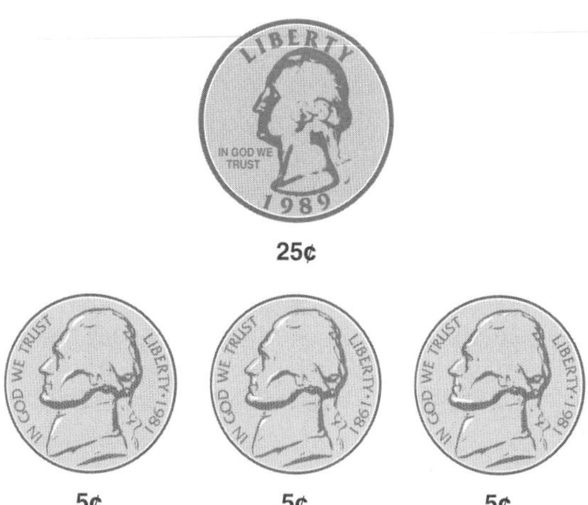

Counting change is a very important skill whose usefulness children recognize. It holds great appeal for them. It should be introduced and extended as far as possible in the primary grades. Interestingly enough, most of the difficulties associated with counting change can be traced to weaknesses in counting. This finding suggests that teachers should take advantage of every opportunity to encourage accurate and rapid counting.

In the Classroom 7-3

NUMBERS ON A CALENDAR

OBJECTIVE: **Using a calendar to count forward and backward.**

GRADE LEVEL: **2–3**

▼ Look at the calendar pictured below.

SUNDAY	MONDAY	TUESDAY	WEDNESDAY	THURSDAY	FRIDAY	SATURDAY
		1	2	3	4	5
6	7	8	9	10	11	12
13	14	15	16	17	18	19
20	21	22	23	24	25	26
27	28	29	30	31		

1. A calendar has many patterns. Tell a pattern you see.
2. What day and date is 7 days after the 7th?
3. What day and date is one week after the 5th?
4. If you start on Monday and count on 7 days, what is the day?
5. If you start on Sunday and count back 4 days, what is the day?
6. What day and date is 5 days before the 30th?
7. What day and date is 5 days after the 21st?
8. Count on 7 days after the 11th. What is the date? The day?
9. Count back 7 days from the 27th. What is the date? The day?
10. Make up some counting problems on your own that use the calendar. Give them to a friend to solve.

Counting Practice

Counting practice should include counting on and counting back by ones. Situations that encourage thoughtful counting often present problems embedded in real-world models. These situations may provide practice in counting either forward or backward. For example:

If the six numbers on the cube are each different and are consecutive whole numbers (i.e., whole numbers in order):

Name some possible numbers that could be on the six faces of this cube.

What is the smallest possible number on the cube?

What is the largest possible number on the cube?

This problem requires counting, but it also encourages higher-level thinking and logical reasoning. For example, questions such as, "Is there more than one correct answer?" should be raised and discussed. The problem also illustrates that unique answers

In the Classroom 7-4

HUNTING FOR NUMBERS

***OBJECTIVE:* Using a hundred chart to identify patterns and develop number sense.**

GRADE LEVEL: **2–3**

▼ Look at this chart:

1	2	3	4	5	6	7	8	9	10
11	12	13	14	15	16	17	18	19	20
21	22	23	24	25	26	27	28	29	30
31	32	33	34	35	36	37	38	39	40
41	42	■	44	45	46	47	48	49	50
51	52	53	54	55	56	57	58	59	60
61	62	63	64	65	66	67	68	69	70
71	72	73	74	75	76	77	78	79	80
81	82	83	84	85	86	87	88	89	90
91	92	93	94	95	96	97	98	99	100

- What is hidden by the ■?
- What number is after ■?
- What number is before the ■?

▼ Put a ● on any number.

- Begin at ● : Count forward five.
- Begin at ● again: Count backward five.

▼ Put a ▲ on a different number.

- Begin at ▲ : Count forward five.
- Begin at ▲ again: Count backward five.

▼ Tell about any patterns you see.

don't always exist. These experiences may even encourage children to formulate similar problems.

Books such as *Anno's Counting Book* and *Anno's Counting House* by Mitsumasa Anno, *Bears on Wheels* by Berenstain and Berenstain, and *I Can Count the Petals of a Flower* by John and Stacy Wahl provide a variety of rich and stimulating contexts for counting. These books engage children in counting and provide insight into how children count. Other books, such as *How Many Snails? A Counting Book* by Paul Giganti and *Count on Your Fingers African Style* by Claudia Zaslavsky, focus on numerical relationships. These and many other books are included in *The Wonderful World of Mathematics: A Critically Annotated List of Children's Books in Mathematics* (Thiessen & Matthias, 1998). Such books are useful for counting-based discussions between children and adults. For example, *Anno's Counting Book* provides a sequence of pictures of different scenes of the house where little people move from one house to another. Initially the teacher or parent can ask questions such as:

> How many children are in the house?
> How many are boys?
> How many are girls?
> How many are wearing hats?
> How many are on the second floor?

Starter questions are provided to encourage active participation and maintain a high level of interest. After students start counting, not only are many new things to count identified, but children also experience important aspects of early number sense.

Practice in skip counting from 1 and other start numbers, including 0, contributes to developing good counting skills and greater number sense. The hundred chart is an ideal model for practicing skip counting, as In the Classroom 7-5. Here, finding patterns and problem solving are integrated with the counting practice.

Research has shown some predictable trouble spots for children when counting. For example, children often slow down, hesitate, or stop when they reach certain numbers, such as 29; however, as soon as they establish the next number as 30, their counting pace quickens, until they are ready to enter the next decade (set of ten numbers). Bridging the next century (set of one hundred numbers) poses a similar challenge. As children count "... one hundred ninety-eight, one hundred ninety-nine," they may pause and be uncertain how to name the next number. Bridging to the next ten or hundred are among the common transitional points of counting difficulty identified by Labinowicz (1985):

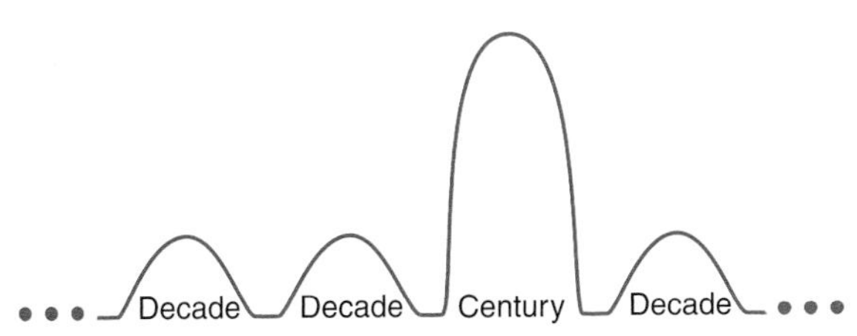

Bumps in the road for successful counters

Not only is the calculator a valuable instructional tool that helps improve children's ability to count, but it is also a powerful counting tool that

they love to explore. Early counting with the calculator should emphasize the physical link between pressing the keys and watching the display. Because the display changes constantly, the students begin to recognize patterns. Calculator counting involves a physical activity (pressing a key each time a number is counted), through which students can relate the size of a number to the amount of time needed to count it.

In the Classroom 7-6
COUNTING ON . . . AND ON . . . AND ON . . .
OBJECTIVE: Using calculators to count and develop number sense.
GRADE LEVEL: 1–3
Start here Count by 3's.
Circle every number that you have counted.
I can use my [calculator] to count. It's easy
How?
I want to count by ones. So I'll enter 1 + 1.
I now press =.
It's counting
Enter 1 + 1
Press = = = = = = =
Time yourself Press 1, +, 1, =.
Keep pressing =. Stop at 100.
• How long did it take to count from 1 to 100? ________
• Guess how long it will take to count from 1 to 1000. ________
• Count from 1 to 1000. How long did it take? ________

Children are usually surprised to find that it is as easy to count by any number on the calculator as to count by ones. A calculator can start at zero and count by ones (In the Classroom 7-6) or begin at any starting point and skip count by any number

▼ Start at 5 every time:

(In the Classroom 7-7). Calculators can also easily count backward (In the Classroom 7-8).

Estimation is a natural part of counting, and In the Classroom 7-6 encourages students to estimate the time it takes to count by ones to 100 and 1,000 with the calculator. By expanding this activity, students will come to realize that it takes about the same amount of time to count to 1,000 by ones as to count to 1,000,000 by 1,000 or to 100 by 0.1. Such counting experiences develop important place-value concepts and contribute to number sense.

In the Classroom 7-8
COUNTING BACKWARD
OBJECTIVE: Using calculators to skip count backward
SKIPPING AROUND
GRADE LEVEL: 1–3
Can you start at 7 and count by 5's?
Yes, but you decide which of these does it on your
Sure. See if this makes your count backward
10 − 1 = = =
Can you make your count like this
10, 9, 8, 7, 6 . . .
▼ Try these:
15 − 1 : 14, 13
20 − 2 : 18
35 − 3 :

Counting from a particular number or by a certain number leads students to see many patterns. For example, using the hundred chart from In the Classroom 7-4 helps students recognize that adding 49 to a number is the same as adding 50 and subtracting 1, which is a powerful pattern often used in mental computation. Calculator counting opens exciting mathematical explorations and promotes both critical thinking and problem solving. According to Huinkier (2002), "using calculators as learning tools can empower young children with the capacity to investigate number ideas in ways that were previously inaccessible to them" (p. 316).

Early Number Development

Comparing and counting experiences help children develop early foundations for number sense. Today's children also have had many experiences, primarily while watching television (*Sesame Street,* for example), that develop counting skills. Classroom instruction for early number development should be designed to build on these experiences.

Developing Number Benchmarks

Number benchmarks are perceptual anchors that become internalized from many concrete experiences, often accumulated over many years. For example, the numbers 5 and 10 (the number of fingers on one and two hands) provide two early number benchmarks. Children recognize four fingers as being one less than five and eight as being three more than five or two less than ten:

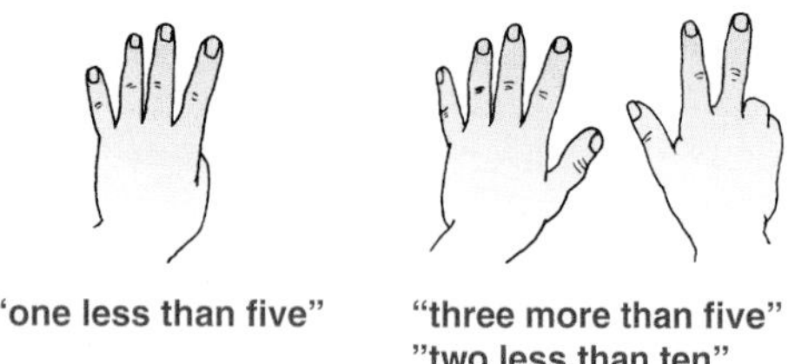

The five-frame (5×1 array) and the ten-frame (5×2 array) (Appendix B) use these early benchmarks:

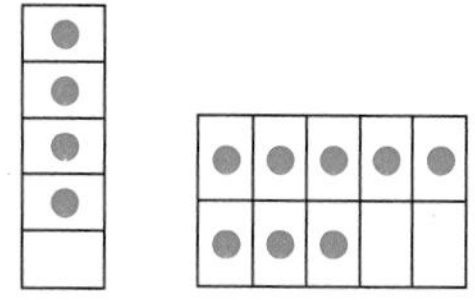

In Japan, the early benchmarks of 5 and 10 are later used with the ten-frame and the Japanese *soroban* (which is similar to an abacus) to promote counting, quick recognition of quantities, and mental computation (Shigematsu et al., 1994).

In the Classroom 7-9 illustrates an activity that encourages the development of benchmark numbers. Because the goal is to develop an intuitive sense of the anchor number (not laborious counting), these early activities show numbers of dots that are significantly different from the anchor.

Of course, many different anchors can be drawn from children's experiences. You might show a bowl of peanuts and ask, "About how many can you hold in one hand?" Change the contents of the bowl to other things, such as erasers, centimeter cubes, marbles, or balls. As children grow older, they should be comfortable and skilled with more and more benchmark numbers.

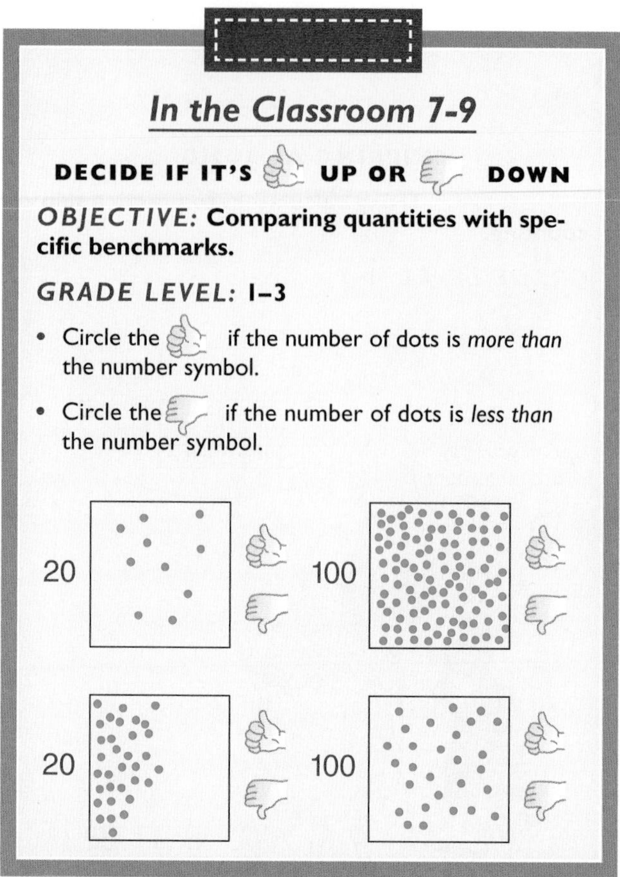

Making Connections

Development of the numbers 1 through 5 is principally done through sight recognition of patterns, coupled with immediate association with the oral name and then the written symbol. For example, as Figure 7-12 illustrates, a picture of a tricycle and the question, "How many wheels?" can be used to develop the number 3. It is important that the number of wheels be linked to both oral name and written symbol. It is also important to provide different configurations of dots, blocks, and other objects, as well as different forms of the numerals, such as **3** and 3, to broaden their experiences.

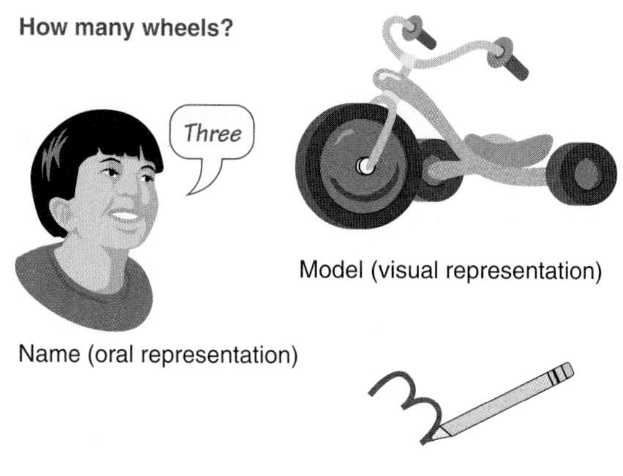

FIGURE 7-12 A number development model linking visual, oral, and written representations.

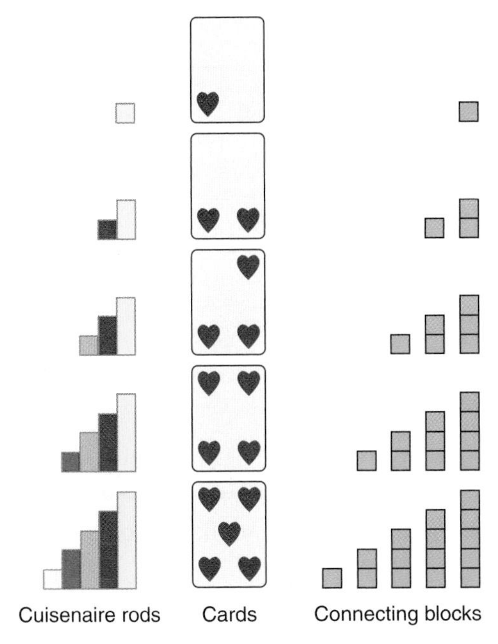

FIGURE 7-13 Three models for *one more* or *one less.*

Many valuable relationships are established as the numbers 1 through 5 are developed, but none are more useful than the notions of *one more* and *one less.* These connections are fundamental in early counting and also in learning place value with larger numbers. The notions *one more* and *one less* evolve from many different real-world experiences, such as these:

David has one less cookie than Jean-Paul.

Mira has one more apple than Beth.

They have one less player on their team.

Their group has one more girl than our group.

The concepts of *one more* and *one less* can be modeled in different ways. Figure 7-13 shows three such models. These arrangements provide a basis for developing the concept of 5 as well as discussing *one more* or *one less.* Using these models for discussion can help children establish important connections that link numbers such as 4 and 5. For example, children might say:

The yellow rod is one step longer than the purple rod.

The five card is just like the four card except it has an extra heart in the middle.

Having many experiences with such models and patterns helps children abstract numbers and establish useful connections between them.

The hearts on the cards and the trains of blocks in Figure 7-13 provide clear reminders of the numbers represented and the notion of *one more* or *one less.* Both the staircase of rods and the trains of blocks vividly illustrate not only these concepts but also an important, yet subtle, difference between the models. The staircase of rods illustrates the concept of *more,* but it is not absolutely clear how much more until the length of the rods has been made clear. If you used a single rod without identifying a unit rod, it would not be possible to associate the rod with a unique number. Thus the rods are a different model for developing numbers than the cards or trains of blocks.

Some models illustrate zero more clearly than others. For example, a rod of length zero is more difficult to grasp than a card with zero hearts. Care should be taken to introduce zero as soon as it becomes natural to do so, using models appropriate for the purpose. Help children distinguish between zero and nothing by encouraging the use of zero to report the absence of something. For example, when reporting the score of a game, it is better to say "Cardinals three, Bears zero" than to say "three to nothing."

As the numbers through 10 are developed, it is important that various patterns among them be discovered, recognized, used, and discussed. Many patterns suggesting many different relationships are shown in this number chart:

0	1	2	3	4	5	6	7	8	9	10

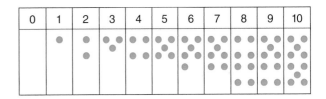

For example, the number 7 is shown by 5 dots and 2 more dots. The number 10 is composed of two groups of 5 dots. It is also useful to explore other patterns.

On the number chart, 6 is shown as 5 dots and 1 dot, but other representations are possible, as shown in Figure 7-14, and they should be explored and discussed with students. Part (B) of Figure 7-14, for example, shows that 6 can be represented as one group of 3, one group of 2, and one group of 1. It can also be shown as two groups of 3, as in parts (A) and (D), or three groups of 2, as in part (C). No mention is made of addition or multiplication in this context, but such observations provide helpful connections when these operations are developed.

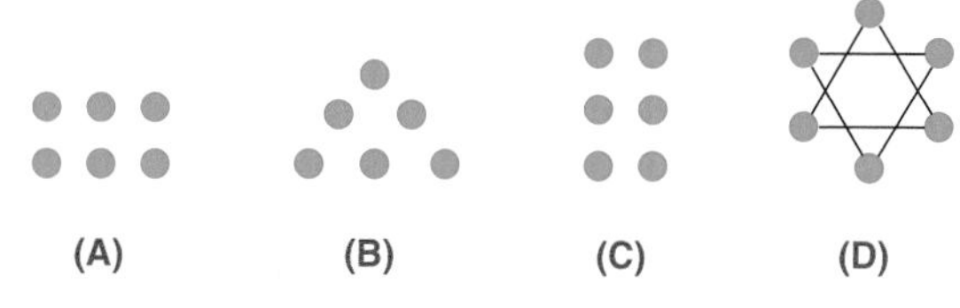

FIGURE 7-14 Some representations of 6.

Similar illustrations and applications of the numbers 7 through 10 should be presented. For example, 7 days in a week may suggest a natural grouping; 8 vertices (corners) of a cube suggest two groups of 4; and the number of boxes in a tic-tac-toe grid suggest three groups of 3.

Most children realize very early that 10 is a special number. At the early stage of number development, the most unusual thing about 10 is that it is the first number represented by two digits, 1 and 0. In addition to having 10 fingers and toes, children encounter the number 10 in many situations, such as in playing games and changing money. These experiences can be extended to include discussion about different representations of 10:

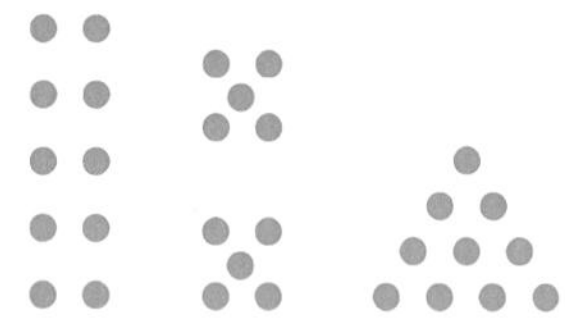

Can you find two groups of 5?

Can you find five groups of 2?

Does the group of 4, 3, 2, and 1 remind you of bowling?

The number 10 provides the cornerstone for our number system, and its significance is developed further in Chapter 8.

A ten-frame is certainly one of the most effective models for facilitating patterns, developing group recognition of numbers, and building an understanding of place value. The ten-frame can be made from an egg carton shortened to contain 10 boxes, or it may simply be outlined on paper or tagboard (see ten-frame in Appendix B). This frame is a powerful organizer and helps provide the base for many thinking strategies and mental computations. Initially, children might use counters to make different representations of the same number in the ten-frame, as illustrated in Figure 7-15. Encountering a variety of groupings on the ten-frame should stimulate discussion about different patterns.

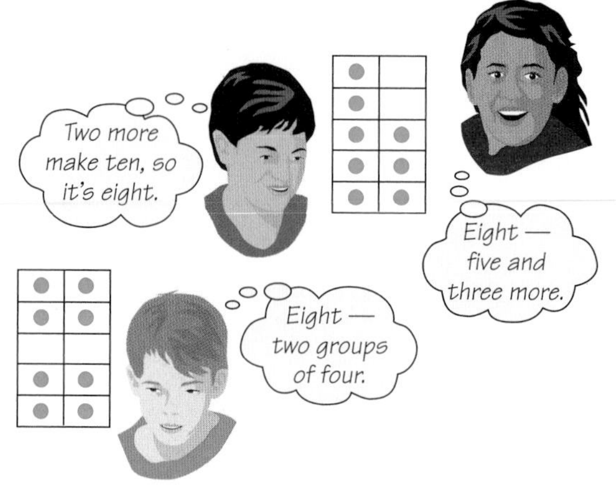

FIGURE 7-15 Representations of 8 on a ten-frame.

Figure 7-16 shows some of the connections that might be constructed as children examine different representations on the ten-frame. These relationships encourage children to think flexibly about numbers, thereby promoting greater number sense. Experiences with the ten-frame also facilitate the development of addition, subtraction, multiplication, and division, as well as place value.

Cardinal, Ordinal, and Nominal Numbers

By this point we have discussed some important considerations in number development. The emphasis has been on finding a correct number name for a given group. This aspect of number provides a *cardinal number,* which answers the question "How many?" Another important aspect of number emphasizes arranging things in an order and is known as *ordinal number;* it answers the question "Which one?"

An emphasis on ordering or arranging things in a given sequence leads to ordinal numbers. The order may be based on any criterion, such as size, time of day, age, or position in a race. Once an order is established, however, the counting process not only produces a set of number names but also names each object according to its position. Thus, in counting the rungs on the ladder in Figure 7-17, number 1 is first, 2 is second, 3 is third, and so on.

Many children know some ordinal numbers such as first, second, and third before they begin school. Encounters with statements such as the

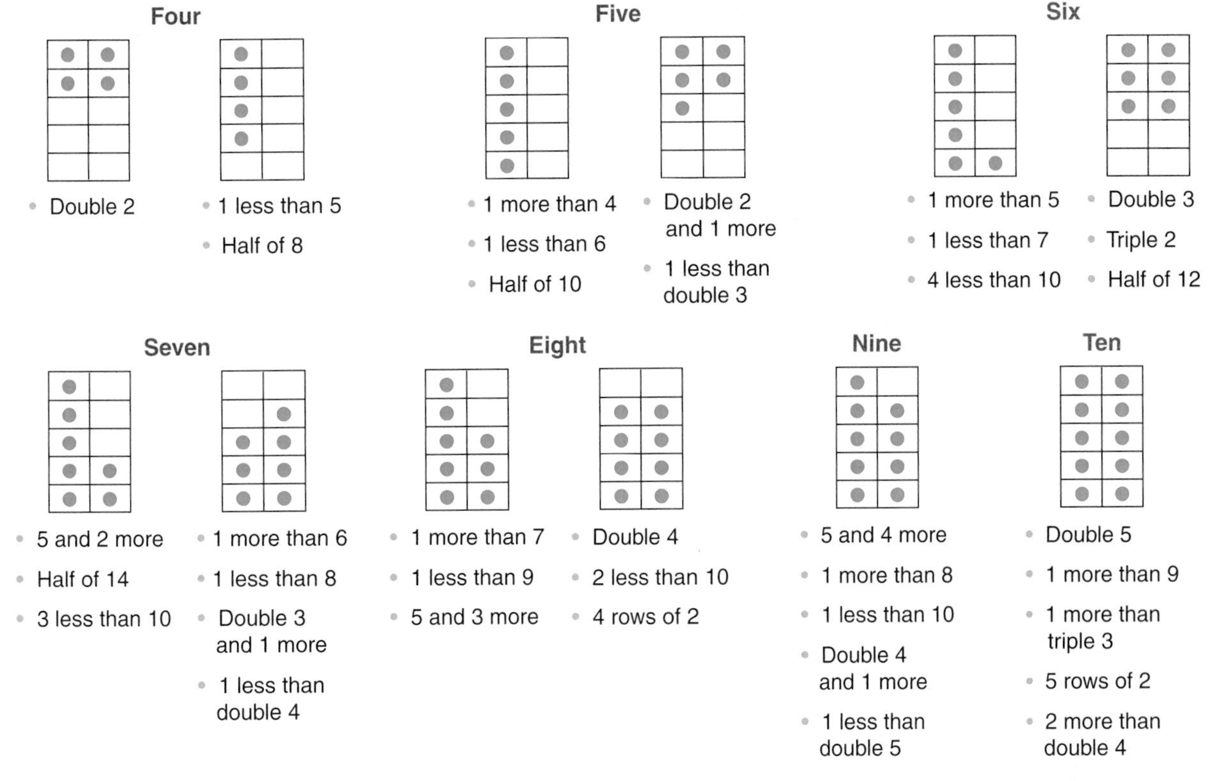

FIGURE 7-16 Connections from representations on the ten-frame.

following provide early and valuable experience with ordinal numbers:

The first letter of the alphabet is A.

Bob is second in line.

Cary was third in the race.

It is important that the development of early number concepts provides children with opportunities to learn both ordinal and cardinal numbers. Don't worry about which to teach first; just be sure both are given attention.

It is possible for a child to recognize a pattern of 4 beans but not be able to count to 4 correctly. Such a child could give the cardinal number 4 to answer the question "How many beans do you see?"

For this child, the notion of cardinal number is limited. Recognizing patterns of 5 is another common example of this occurrence. Although such instances are rare, when they do occur, they are usually limited to small numbers.

A knowledge of ordinal relationships, along with logical thinking, leads to more challenging experiences, such as those suggested in Figure 7-18. These questions are guaranteed to generate much discussion as they help children further clarify notions of ordinal numbers.

Another aspect of number provides a label or classification and is known as *nominal.* Examples are the number on a player's uniform, the license plate of a car, a postal zip code, and a telephone number. The nominal numbers provide essential information for identification but do not necessarily use the ordinal or cardinal aspects of the number.

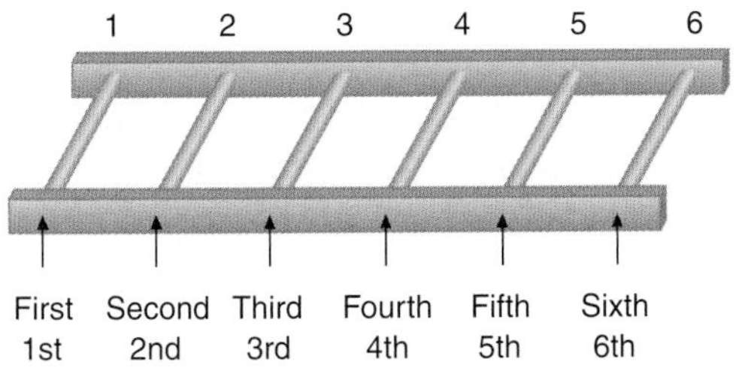

FIGURE 7-17 A counting model for ordinal numbers.

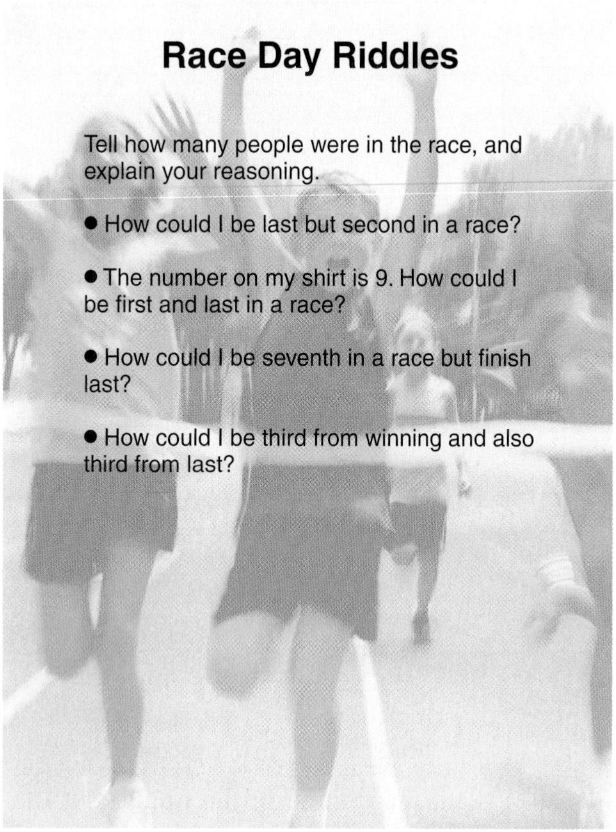

Race Day Riddles

Tell how many people were in the race, and explain your reasoning.

- How could I be last but second in a race?
- The number on my shirt is 9. How could I be first and last in a race?
- How could I be seventh in a race but finish last?
- How could I be third from winning and also third from last?

FIGURE 7-18 Thinking about ordinal relationships. (Julia Fishkin/The Image Bank/Getty Images)

When using cardinal, ordinal, and nominal numbers, children do not need to distinguish between the terms. Distinctions can be made informally by asking questions within problem situations such as:

How many pieces are on the chess board?

Which pawn is third?

Where is the queen?

These questions not only help children think about numbers but also illustrate that numbers have different uses.

Writing Numerals

Young children should focus their attention on number development and relationships among numbers. Because young children typically have difficulty writing numerals as well as letters, they should spend less time writing numerals. The lack of development of the small muscles needed to write presents one problem, and the limited eye-hand coordination of many young children constitutes another difficulty. Both of these make it difficult or impossible for young children to write numerals. If children are pressured into premature symbolization, it can create unnecessary frustrations and anxieties.

First graders can usually recognize a number symbol and say it correctly long before they write it. Many young children initiate early writing of numerals on their own, and they get a feeling of great accomplishment from it; however, research shows that children learn these writing skills much more quickly as second graders than as kindergartners.

Children should begin by tracing the digits:

0 1 2 3 4 5 6 7 8 9

Textbooks provide guidance to children in different forms. Usually a starting point is indicated as well as the direction:

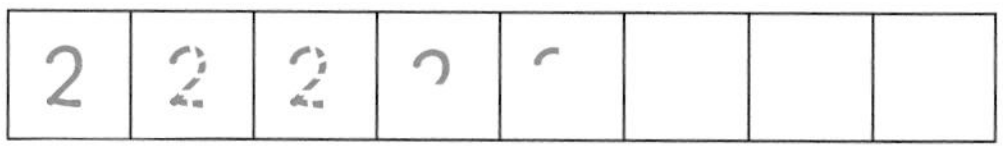

2	2	2	?	ˊ			

Encourage children to draw the appropriate number of objects beside the numeral being written to help them connect the number concept with its symbolic representation. When children are learning to write numerals, have them work on this writing skill aside from "mathematics." Thus children can master this skill and use it freely before applying it in written computational situations; otherwise, the writing task consumes all their concentration, and they forget about the mathematics being done.

Many children develop the necessary writing skills on their own. Even then, these youngsters need monitoring and maybe some occasional guidance. Others, however, need systematic step-by-step procedures to help them. Although there is no one best way to form a numeral, some patterns may help. Guiding a child's hand until the child takes the initiative in writing helps him or her get started. Later, outlines of numerals for children to trace are helpful. Here are some additional suggestions; these will not be necessary in all cases, but some children will profit from them:

1. *Cut out shapes of numerals.* Use the overhead projector to project a numeral on the chalkboard or wall and have a child trace the numeral's silhouette.

2. *As one child is tracing the projected numeral, have class members trace it in the air.* As the tracing is being done, describe it verbally such as "go to the right and then down." This activity can be extended to using only dots to form the outline or pattern for the children to follow.

3. *Have a child who can make numerals stand behind someone who cannot.* Ask the skilled child to use a finger and gently "write" a numeral on the other child's back. The child in front should identify the numeral and write it on the chalkboard, trace it on the wall, or write it in the air. This approach calls on the tactile sense and helps some children better develop their writing skills.

4. *Use numerals that have been cut from sandpaper and pasted to cards, or take some cord and glue it in the shape of numerals.* Place a mark on each numeral to show the child where to begin tracing it with his or her finger. This approach is particularly helpful with children who persist in reversing numerals.

5. *Cover numerals to be traced with a transparency.* Then give the child a water-soluble pen and have him or her practice tracing the numerals.

6. *For children having difficulty writing numerals, a calculator is helpful.* The calculator display provides a visual reminder of a number's symbol and removes the burden of writing complicated numerals.

The fact that numerals take different forms also should be mentioned but not belabored.

Some familiarity with these forms will help avoid confusion when a 4 appears as a printed number or as a digital display on a clock or calculator. The wide use of digital numbers in everyday living demands planned instruction to make children familiar with them.

A Glance at Where We've Been

Good number sense is a prerequisite for all later computational development. Young children need to recognize small groups of objects (up to 5 or 6) by sight and name them properly. Activities involving sight recognition of the numbers of objects in small groups provide many opportunities to introduce and use key terms such as *more, less, after, before, one more,* and *one less.* To foster a better number sense, instruction on the numbers through 5 should focus on patterns and develop recognition skills. Models such as the ten-frame provide a powerful tool for helping children explore and construct relationships for numbers to 10 and beyond.

Counting skills usually start before children begin school but must be developed by careful and systematic instruction before written work is appropriate. Counting processes reflect various levels of sophistication, beginning with rote counting and eventually leading to rapid skip counting forward and backward. Although the four counting principles are established in the primary grades, counting skills are extended in the intermediate grades and often are further refined throughout our lives.

Competence with and understanding of the numbers 0 through 10 are essential for meaningful later development of larger numbers. The relationship of the sets of objects, the number names, the written symbols, and the order between numbers must be well understood. This knowledge is the basis for the successful study of elementary mathematics, and it prepares children for the necessary understanding of large numbers and place value.

Things to Do: From What You've Read

1. Why is number sense difficult to define?
2. Provide two activities to illustrate each expectation related to number sense from the *NCTM's Standard:* Numbers and Operations.
3. Suppose you send a note home to parents encouraging them to help their children improve sight-recognition skills. One parent responds, "Why should my child learn to recognize a group of 5? After all, you can just count them." How would you respond?
4. Four fundamental principles of counting were identified in this chapter. Describe in your own words what each means and why it is necessary. Examine the children's work samples on Masters 6-7 to 6-13 in the *Helping Children Learn Mathematics Instructor's Manual* (available from this book's web site, www.wiley.com/college/reys). These samples display a wide range of numeral writing skills from several kindergarten students. After viewing the samples, make observations about what the children know about writing numerals.
5. Distinguish between rote and rational counting. Examine the children's interview excerpts on Master 6-5 in the *Helping Children Learn Mathematics Instructor's Manual* (available from this book's web site, www.wiley.com/college/reys). Use the information from this chapter to determine which counting principles are understood and used by the children.
6. What is meant by conservation of number? Why is its development an important part of number sense? Examine the children's interview excerpts on Master 6-4 in the *Helping Children Learn Mathematics Instructor's Manual* (available from this book's web site, www.wiley.com/college/reys). Use the segments to determine if these children are able to conserve number.
7. Describe how the following activity could help older children sharpen their understanding of ordinal and cardinal numbers.

   How many ordinal numbers are in this sentence? "The 500 residents of Centerville celebrated the 100th anniversary of the town's founding by setting off a $200 fireworks display at the corner of Fifth and Broadway on January 1st."
8. Describe how counting could be used to answer these questions:
   a. How many floors are between the seventh and fifteenth floors?
   b. If Alfinio has read to the bottom of page 16, how many pages must he read to reach the top of page 21?
9. Describe how the ten-frame serves as a useful model for early number development.
10. What is subitizing? Tell why it is an important skill to help children develop.

Things to Do: Going Beyond This Book

IN THE FIELD

1. **Observing Counting.* Observe a young child counting in your classroom. Identify any counting errors and where they took place, such as bridging to the next decade. Also identify any counting principles that were exhibited.
2. **Counting Resources.* Find the instructor's guidebook or teacher's edition being used in a K–2 mathematics classroom in your school. Examine it to learn how resources, such as calculators and children's books, are used to support counting.
3. **Using Attribute Pieces.* In the Classroom 7-1 and 7-2 provide several patterning and logical reasoning activities using attribute pieces with children. Explore these trains with several children. How many different correct solutions did children find for Train A? Did your children find one-difference trains to be the same difficulty as two-difference trains? Did students feel comfortable knowing that more than one correct answer exists?

IN YOUR JOURNAL

4. Observe children counting on the playground. How do children demonstrate their counting abilities? In your journal, describe their counting activities and the strategies they appear to use.
5. There are controversies related to teaching counting in the classroom. In your journal,

---

*Additional activities, suggestions, or questions are provided in *Teaching Elementary Mathematics: A Resource for Field Experiences* (Wiley, 2004).

respond to this statement: "Counting is an immature habit that teachers need to help students break."

WITH ADDITIONAL RESOURCES

6. Examine *Number Sense and Operations* (Burton et al., 1993), *Developing Number Sense in Middle Grades* (Reys et al., 1991), or the *SENSE* series (McIntosh et al., 1997). How do these books characterize number sense? Report on several instructional activities designed to foster number sense.
7. Select a patterning activity from *Patterns* (Coburn et al., 1992) that would be appropriate for primary grades. Describe how you would prepare for, use, and extend this activity.
8. Examine the chapter "Concepts of Number" by Van de Walle (1990) in *Mathematics for the Young Child.* Describe three different instructional activities for promoting early number sense.
9. Read "Bring on the Buttons" (Whitin, 1989) and describe some ways in which buttons could be used to develop classification skills.
10. Compare two current textbook series:
    a. Find how far each series expects children to be able to count when they begin first grade and when they complete first grade.
    b. Find examples of activities designed to develop number sense. Describe the activities and identify the grade level. Do you think these activities would be effective? Tell why.
    c. Find an example of a visual pattern that connects numbers to geometry.
11. Review *The Wonderful World of Mathematics: A Critically Annotated List of Children's Books in Mathematics* (Thiessen and Matthias, 1998). Find three multicultural books related to counting that are highly recommended.
12. Read one of the vignettes in the *Professional Standards for Teaching Mathematics* (NCTM, 1991) that involves early development of number. Describe the role of the teacher.
13. Read the book *How Many Snails: A Counting Book* (Giganti, 1988). Then read the article by Whitin, Mills, and O'Keefe (1994) to see how this book was used to explore mathematical problem solving. Discuss how the project was done and how the examples of children's work provides insight into their development of number sense.
14. View a segment from the videotape series *Number Sense Now!* (Fennell, 1992). Discuss ways in which this tape might help students become more sensitive to the importance and power of number sense.

    With some classmates or children, complete the activity, Construct a Pattern, on Master 6-6 in the *Helping Children Learn Mathematics Instructor's Manual* (available from this book's web site, www.wiley.com/college/reys). What role does patterning play in the mathematical development of learners?

WITH TECHNOLOGY

15. *Counting with Calculators.* In the Classroom 7-6, 7-7, and 7-8 provide structured calculator counting activities. Try one or more of them with some children in a classroom that has calculators available. Were the children experienced at using the calculators or were they viewed as a novelty? Were the childen comfortable making estimates for the counts? Describe some patterns that emerged.
16. *Virtual Calculators.* Investigate the NCTM Illuminations web site for ideas for learning about number relationships and properties of numbers using calculators and hundreds boards, which you can access from this book's web site, www.wiley.com/college/reys. Illuminations provides a virtual calculator and hundreds board that displays the patterns and relationships among numbers. Explore this resource by entering 5 + and then repeatedly enter the = symbol on the calculator. How does the hundreds board change? Describe how this virtual tool can be used as an instructional tool. Identify advantages of using this tool over the handheld calculator and the paper hundreds board.

Resources

ANNOTATED BOOKS

Baratta-Lorton, Mary. *Mathematics Their Way.* Palo Alto, CA: Addison-Wesley, 1976.
This is an activity-centered mathematics program for early childhood education. The goal of the activities in the book is to develop understanding and insight of the patterns of mathematics through the use of concrete materials. Relationships and interconnections in mathematics are stressed, so young children can deal flexibly with mathematical ideas and concepts.

Burton, Grace; Mills, Ann; Lennon, Carolyn; and Parker, Cynthia. *Number Sense and Operations.* Reston, VA: NCTM, 1993.

Book Nook for Children

Anno, Mitsumasa. *Anno's Counting Book.* New York: Thomas Y. Crowell, 1977.
How would you describe a picture that refers to zero? This book begins with a barren winter landscape—a hazy, blue sky above a hazy, white hill. On the next page the scene brightens: one tree, one bird, one house. Turn the page again and the snow has started to melt and you find two buildings, two trucks, two trees, two children, two dogs, and two adults. Suddenly there is almost more than you can count on each page! And the numbers continue to increase.

Carter, David A. *How Many Bugs in a Box?* New York: Simon & Schuster, 1988.
All kinds of boxes full of bugs to count from one to ten. Children can lift open the boxes and find colorful, comical bugs that pop out, run, eat—and even swim!

Carle, Eric. *The Very Hungry Caterpillar.* New York: Putnam, 1990.
"In the light of the moon a little egg lay on a leaf." So begins this modern classic tale of science and gluttony that teaches counting and the days of the week. Follow this hungry caterpillar's path as he eats his way through one apple (and the pages of the book itself) on Monday, two pears on Tuesday, three plums on Wednesday, and so on, through cherry pie and sausage—until he is really fat and has a stomachache. Can you guess what happens next?

Dee, Rudy. *Two Ways to Count to Ten: A Liberian Folktale.* New York: Henry Holt, 1988.
Long ago, when all the animals lived together in peace, the mighty leopard was king of the jungle, and all the animals respected their king. But it came time to name a successor and all the animals vied for the position. Join the laughter as you count the number of beasts that fail the test.

Demi. *Demi's Count the Animals 1-2-3.* New York: Grossett & Dunlap, 1986.
Meet new animals in the journey of counting from one to twenty. Each rhyme is preceded by the bold-faced numeral and number word that is being featured.

Feelings, Muriel. *Moja Means One: Swahili Counting Book.* New York: Dial Books for Young Readers, 1971.
Count from 1–10 in Swahili and experience an introduction to the culture, sights, and sounds of East Africa. The book introduction explains the languages spoken and some informative details about the area. The book also provides you with the pronunciation codes for the words.

Giganti, Paul. *How Many Snails? A Counting Book.* New York: Scott Foresman (Pearson K–12), 1994.
Use these many opportunities to help children practice their counting. A series of simple questions directs them to determine the differences between seemingly similar objects, encouraging them to develop powers of observation, discrimination, and visual analysis.

Hanford, Martin. *Where's Waldo?* Boston: Little, Brown, 1987.
This search-and-find book challenges students to find objects in pictures containing many different items.

Nozaki, Akirhiro, and Anno, Mitsumasa. *Anno's Hat Tricks.* New York: Philomel Books, 1985.
Use this book to write a lesson plan in elementary school mathematics. The hat "tricks" develop critical thinking skills and integrate subjects while teaching children the process of elimination. Students feel a sense of accomplishment as they begin to understand the concepts behind the hatter's tricks.

Wahl, John, and Wahl, Stacy. *I Can Count the Petals of a Flower.* Reston, VA: NCTM, 1976.
This book provides a variety of rich and stimulating context teaching children to count using the petals of a flower.

Zaslavsky, Claudia. *Count on Your Fingers African Style.* New York: Crowell Publishers, 1980.
Focus on numerical relationships in the African marketplace where people buy and trade using many different languages, including various methods of finger counting. This book explores the practicality of math within the context of African culture and helps children see that math can be fun and creative.

This book is part of the *Curriculum and Evaluation Standards for School Mathematics* Addenda Series, Grades K–6. This series was designed to illustrate the Standards and to help teachers translate them into classroom practice. Both traditional and new topics are explored in this book. Familiar activities have been redesigned and infused with an investigative flavor.

Coburn, Terrence G.; Bushey, Barbara J.; Holton, Liana C.; Latozas, Debra; Mortimer, Debbie; and Shotwell, Deborah. *Patterns.* Reston, VA: NCTM, 1992.
This book is part of the *Curriculum and Evaluation Standards for School Mathematics* Addenda Series, Grades K–6. This series was designed to illustrate the Standards and to help teachers translate them into classroom practice. Both traditional and new topics are explored in this book. Familiar activities have been redesigned and infused with an investigative flavor.

Labinowicz, Ed. *Learning from Children: New Beginnings for Teaching Numerical Thinking.* Menlo Park, CA: Addison-Wesley, 1985.
Although research on children's mathematical thinking has much to say to teachers, little attempt has been made by researchers to communicate it directly to teachers. The author of this book attempts to build a bridge between theory, research, and classroom practice with the aim of supporting informed change in the schools. Clinical interviews of children and observation of the teaching-learning process with small groups of children are the focus of the research described in this book.

Reys, Robert; Gideon, Joan (Editor); McIntosh, A.; Hope, J.; and Reys, Barbara J. *Number Sense: Simple Effective Number Sense Experiences Grade 1–2.* Palo Alto, CA: Dale Seymour Publications, 1997.
These 10-minute activities help students develop a sense of what numbers represent and how to use them by exploring relationships and patterns, encouraging mental computation, recognizing equivalent representations of a number, establishing benchmarks, improving estimation skills, and exploring the idea of reasonableness. Includes activity masters, teacher's notes, and ideas for extending the activity.

ANNOTATED ARTICLES

Doverborg, Elisabet; and Samuelsson, Ingrid P. "To Develop Young Children's Conception of Numbers." 162 (June 2000), *Early Child Development and Care,* p. 81–107.
These authors evaluated an instructional procedure that focused on reflective problem solving and used young children's fascination with stars as a starting point to develop their concept of numbers. They found that test group performance on mathematics problem-solving tasks indicated developing understanding of the concept of numbers 1 through 5, compared to that of a reference group.

Sowder, Judith T. "Estimation and number sense." In *Handbook of Research on Mathematics Teaching and Learning* (ed. D. A. Grouws). New York: Macmillan, 1992, pp. 371–389.
This chapter focuses on topics in estimation and related areas that have proved to be interesting to researchers. Computational estimation, number sense, and measurement estimation are discussed as well as assessment issues related to estimation. Considerations for continuing research on estimation and related topics are shared by the author.

Wickett, Maryann S. "Serving Up Number Sense and Problem Solving: Dinner at the Panda Palace." *Teaching Children Mathematics,* 3(9), (May 1997), pp. 476–480.
This article provides strategies for using literature to teach number sense and problem solving that help you develop class discussions that reflect students' thinking, give students opportunities to share their approaches and understandings, and give the teacher additional insights into students' thinking.

Zaslavsky, Claudia. "Developing Number Sense: What Can Other Cultures Tell Us?" *Teaching Children Mathematics,* 7(6), (February 2001), pp. 312–319.
This article presents ways to introduce number systems from finger counting to number words, to concrete materials, to the numerals invented by various societies to enhance students' number sense by learning about the systems of other cultures.

ADDITIONAL REFERENCES

Clements, Douglas G. "Subitizing: What is it? Why teach it?" *Teaching Children Mathematics* (March 1999), pp. 400–405.

Fennell, Francis. *Number Sense Now!* (videotape and guidebook). Reston, VA: NCTM, 1992.

Fuson, Karen C. *Children's Counting and Concepts of Number.* New York: Springer-Verlag, 1988.

Huinker, DeAnn. "Calculators as Learning Tools for Young Children's Explorations of Numbers." *Teaching Children Mathematics,* 8(6), (February 2002), pp. 316–321.

McIntosh, Alistair; Reys, Barbara; and Reys, Robert. *Number SENSE, Simple Effective Number Sense Experiences: Grades 1–2 & 3–4.* Palo Alto, CA: Dale Seymour Publications, 1997.

National Council of Teachers of Mathematics. *Professional Standards for Teaching Mathematics.* Reston, VA: NCTM, 1991.

Payne, Joseph N., and Huinker, DeAnn M. "Early Number and Numeration." In *Research Ideas for the Classroom: Early Childhood Mathematics* (ed. Robert J. Jensen). Reston, VA: NCTM; and New York: Macmillan 1993, pp. 43–70.

Reys, Barbara J.; Barger, Rita; Bruckheimer, Maxim; Dougherty, Barbara; Hope, Jack; Lembke, Linda; Markovitz, Zvia; Parnas, Andy; Reehm, Sue; Sturdevant, Ruthi; and Weber, Marianne. *Developing Number Sense in the Middle Grades.* Reston, VA: NCTM, 1991.

Shigematsu, K.; Iwasaki, H.; and Koyama, M. "Mental Computation: Evaluation, Curriculum and Instructional Issues from the Japanese Perspective." In *Computational Alternatives for the 21st Century: Cross Cultural Perspectives from Japan and the United States* (eds. Robert E. Reys and Nobubiko Nohda). Reston, VA: NCTM, 1994.

Thiessen, Diane, and Matthias, Margaret (eds.). *The Wonderful World of Mathematics: A Critically Annotated List of Children's Books in Mathematics.* Reston, VA: NCTM, 1998.

Van de Walle, John. "Concepts of Number." In *Mathematics for the Young Child* (ed. Joseph N. Payne). Reston, VA: NCTM, 1990, pp. 62–87.

Whitin, David J. "Bring on the Buttons." *Arithmetic Teacher,* 36 (January 1989), pp. 4–6.

Whitin, David J.; Mills, Heidi; and O'Keefe, Timothy. "Exploring Subject Areas with a Counting Book." *Teaching Children Mathematics,* 1(3), (November 1994), pp. 170–177.

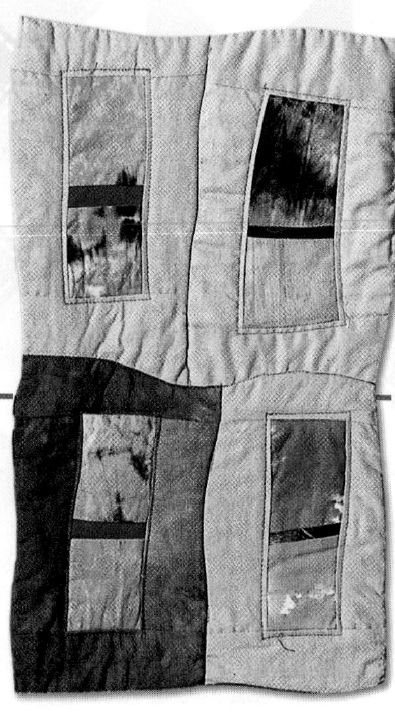

CHAPTER 8

Extending Number Sense: Place Value

Snapshot of a Lesson

Key Ideas for a Primary-Grade Lesson on Place Value

1. Develop number sense by using tens (bean sticks) for a quick benchmark estimate.
2. Illustrate the place-value concept with two different models.
3. Provide concrete representations of two-digit numbers and their corresponding symbolization.

Necessary Materials

- *Bean Sticks:* Each child should have a set of 10 bean sticks and a small pile of loose beans. (A bean stick is a tongue depressor or popsicle stick on which 10 beans have been glued. Children should each make their own bean sticks, thereby convincing themselves that there are indeed 10 beans on a stick. Gluing on the beans will also instill pride in ownership of the sticks.) The teacher also needs some loose beans and a set of bean sticks.

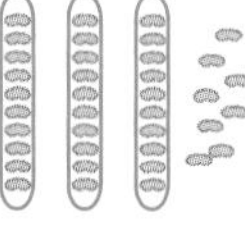

- *Place-Value Mat:* Each child should have a place-value mat and a water-soluble pen. (A place-value mat is a piece of heavy construction paper that has been laminated so children can write on it. It has two columns—for tens and ones.) The teacher needs a transparency of a place-value mat for use on the overhead projector.

Tens	Ones

Orientation

In previous lessons, these second graders have been counting by ones and tens, as well as counting on (by ones). This lesson continues to develop number sense and place value, as the children count the sticks and beans in several different ways. (For example, they count the sticks first and then the separate beans or count the beans first and then the sticks, which is more difficult for the children but an important skill to develop.) To encourage students to decide about how many beans there are without counting, Mrs. Golden places the bean sticks and four beans on the overhead, turns it on for only a couple of seconds, and then turns it off.

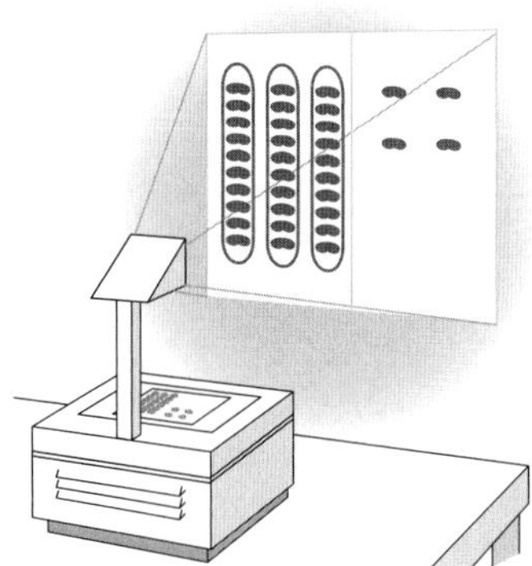

MRS. GOLDEN: Did you see more than 30?

Tranh raises his hand immediately.

TRANH: Yes.

MRS. GOLDEN: Tell us how you knew that so quickly. Did you count them?

TRANH: No, I didn't need to count. There are 3 sticks—that makes 30. There are also some other beans, so I know there are more than 30.

MRS. GOLDEN: Are there more than 40?

SANDRA: No. You have 30, but there are not 10 more beans to make 40, so I know there are not more than 40.

MRS. GOLDEN: Good. Now let's count them together.

Ten, twenty, thirty, thirty-one
thirty-two, thirty-three, thirty-four

Mrs. Golden points to appropriate pieces as the children count.

MRS. GOLDEN: Now, let's start with the beans instead of the sticks and count them a different way.

One, two, three, four, fourteen,
twenty-four, thirty-four

Mrs. Golden again points to appropriate pieces as the children count.

MRS. GOLDEN: Does it matter how you count the beans?

DERREK: No, you get the same answer. But it's easier for me to start with the sticks first.

MRS. GOLDEN: That's fine, Derrek. We will learn to count in different ways, but you should use what is easiest for you. Now everyone try modeling the number with beans and then writing this number on our number mats.

Tens	Ones
3	4

Before continuing, Mrs. Golden checks for any difficulties in modeling the number or writing the correct numerals. Writing the numerals on the place-value mat helps children naturally associate the symbol with the model and understand the significance of place value in a concrete way.

MRS. GOLDEN: Here are some practice numbers for you to pair and share:

25 52 forty-one 89

I want you to take turns and show each of them on your mat to your partner one at a time. Be sure to model the number with your beans and sticks first and then write the number on your mat. When you finish, ask your partner to check the number before you clear the mat. Then your partner does the next one and you check it.

Introduction

Children must make sense of numbers and the ways in which numbers are used in and out of school. This sense making of numbers is a hallmark of NCTM *Standards* (2000), which include several concepts and skills related to extending number sense to place value. Place value is critical to this understanding or sense making and is one of the cornerstones of our Hindu-Arabic number system. Figure 8-1 presents this emphasis in the standards for prekindergarten through grade 2 and grades 3–5.

Math Links 8.1

The full-text electronic version of the Number and Operation Standard, with electronic examples (interactive activities), is available at the NCTM's web site, which you can access from this book's web site. After reading the Chapter 3 introduction, click on pre-K–2, 3–5, or 6–8 to read about place value in the Number and Operation Standard at those levels.

Math Links 8.2

A variety of web resources for place value, that may be used by teachers and children, may be found at the NCTM's Illuminations web site, under the Number and Operation Standard; you can access the site from this book's web site.

www.wiley.com/college/reys

FOCUS QUESTIONS

1. What instructional experiences can help develop children's understanding of our number system?
2. How can you help children bridge the gap between the concrete and symbolic representations of numbers?
3. How can calculators help children develop place-value concepts?
4. How does understanding place value help children develop skills in reading and writing numbers?
5. What is the role of estimation in developing number sense and place-value concepts?
6. What kinds of tasks help teachers engage students in mathematical thinking and reasoning so that students build understanding of numbers and relationships among numbers?

Instructional programs from prekindergarten through grade 2 should enable all students to:	Pre-K–2 Expectations All students should	Grades 3–5 Expectations All students should
Understand numbers, ways of representing numbers, and number systems.	• Use multiple models to develop initial understandings of place value and the base-ten number system; • Develop a sense of whole numbers and represent and use them in flexible ways, including relating, composing, and decomposing numbers; • Connect number words and numerals to the quantities they represent, using various physical models and representations.	• Understand the place-value structure of the base-ten number system and be able to represent and compare whole numbers and decimals; • Recognize equivalent representations for the same number and generate them by decomposing and composing numbers.

FIGURE 8-1 Number and Operation Standard for grades Pre-K–2 and 3–5.

Our Numeration System

Although we say "our" numeration system, it is multicultural, and it is "ours" only to the extent that it is a part of our cultural heritage. History tells us that "our numeration system" is really the result of continuous development and refinement over many centuries. The number system we use, called the Hindu-Arabic system, was probably invented in India by the Hindus and transmitted to Europe by the Arabs, but many different countries and cultures contributed to its development.

The Hindu-Arabic numeration system has four important characteristics:

1. *Place value:* The position of a digit represents its value; for example, the 2 in $23 names "twenty" and has a different mathematical meaning from the 2 in $32, which names "two."
2. *Base of ten:* The term *base* simply means a collection. Thus, in our system, 10 is the value that determines a new collection, and the system has 10 digits, 0 through 9.
3. *Use of zero:* A symbol for zero exists and allows us to represent symbolically the absence of something. For example, 309 shows the absence of tens in a number containing hundreds and ones.
4. *Additive property:* Numbers can be summed with respect to place value. For example, 123 names the number that is the sum of 100 + 20 + 3.

These properties make the system efficient and contribute to the development of number sense. That is, once children understand these characteristics, the formation and interpretation of numbers—either large or small—is a natural development.

Perhaps you are familiar with Roman numerals, which are still in use today in our society. They are different from the Hindu-Arabic system in that they lack place value, have no symbol for zero, and no base. The Roman numeral system is repetitive and additive, and it includes a subtractive element that decreases the number of digits in the numeral. Computation with Roman numerals is a difficult and cumbersome process.

Thinking Place Value

Place value is an essential feature of the Hindu-Arabic number system. In fact, place value, together with base ten, allows you to manipulate, read, and symbolize both large and small numbers. The power of place value can and should be developed early. For example, each of the piles shown has the same number of buttons. Decide how many buttons are in each pile.

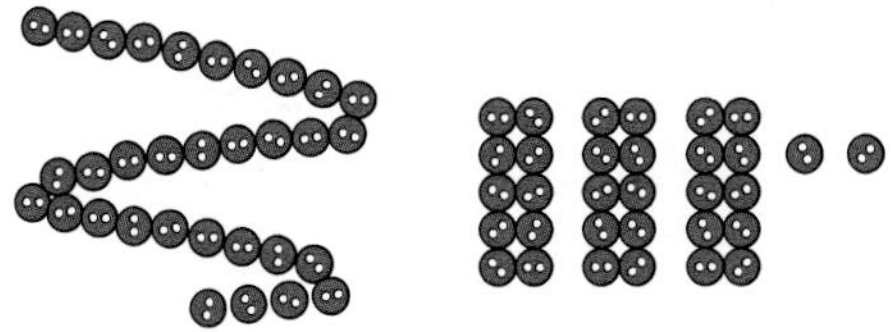

Which pile would you use to decide how many? Explaining which pile and telling why that pile was chosen leads to a discussion of how grouping by tens facilitates counting and organizing larger quantities.

The ten-frame (Appendix B) provides a convenient model for counting, grouping, and eventually representing two-digit numbers. It is a natural model for place value and often provides valuable mental imagery for children in naming and distinguishing between two numbers. For example, Mrs. Golden asked the children to illustrate 25 and 52:

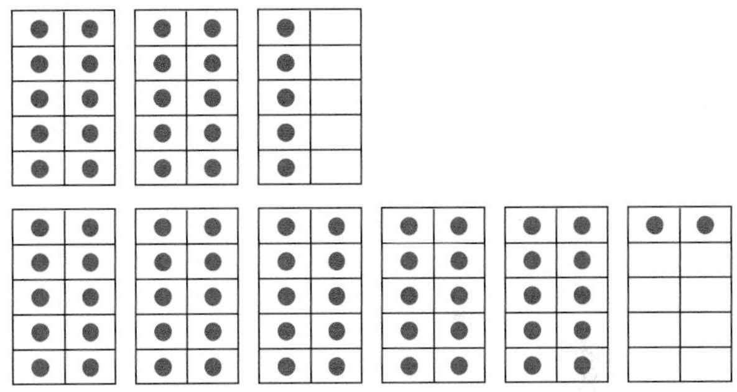

This exercise alerts students to the physical differences between these values, which are formed with the same digits but are different because of place value.

Grouping or Trading

Children in the first three grades need experience in counting piles of objects; trading for grouped tens, hundreds, and thousands; and talking about the results. The fourth national mathematics assessment reported that fourth-grade students had not mastered grouping and place value (Kouba et al., 1989). The *Snapshot of a Lesson* at the beginning of this chapter demonstrates how students might count and model different numbers. The bean sticks and ten-frame thus provide two early models for counting and grouping.

Lesson Idea 8-1

Getting Started

Objective: Practice in grouping by tens

Grade Level: 1 – 2

▼ Provide a pile of beans or counters.

▼ Ask children to group by ten.

▼ Some questions to ask:
- How many beans in each group?
- How many groups of ten?
- How many beans left over?
- Which pile is easier to count?

▼ Provide a pile of interlocking cubes.

▼ Ask children to build trains with ten cubes in a train.

- How many cubes in each train?
- How many trains of ten?
- How many cubes left over?
- Which group is easier to count?

Developing Representation

▼ Some questions to ask:
- How many groups (trains) do you have? ________
- How many beans (cubes) are left over? ________

As children work with these models, they need piles of materials (e.g., beans, buttons, cubes, or other counters) to practice counting and grouping.

Lesson Idea 8-1 provides some early guided practice in grouping by tens. These models (beans and interlocking cubes) are different, but each shows how grouping by ten helps determine the number in the group more quickly. The interlocking cubes in the train stay together and provide a natural step toward the base-ten blocks shown later in Figures 8-3 and 8-5.

Trading and grouping by tens provide problem-solving activities that contribute to number sense and provide opportunities for developing mental computation. Lesson Idea 8-2 illustrates another grouping experience that further facilitates counting and trading. Although it may be easy to decide which group has more or less when the values differ greatly (as between B and the others), it may be difficult when the values differ only slightly (as between A and C). Furthermore, as the numbers in the groups increase, it often becomes more difficult (and sometimes impossible) to decide without counting and grouping. The activities highlighted in Lesson Ideas 8-1 and 8-2 provide opportunities for students to tell what they are doing and establish a firm foundation for the later development of written computation.

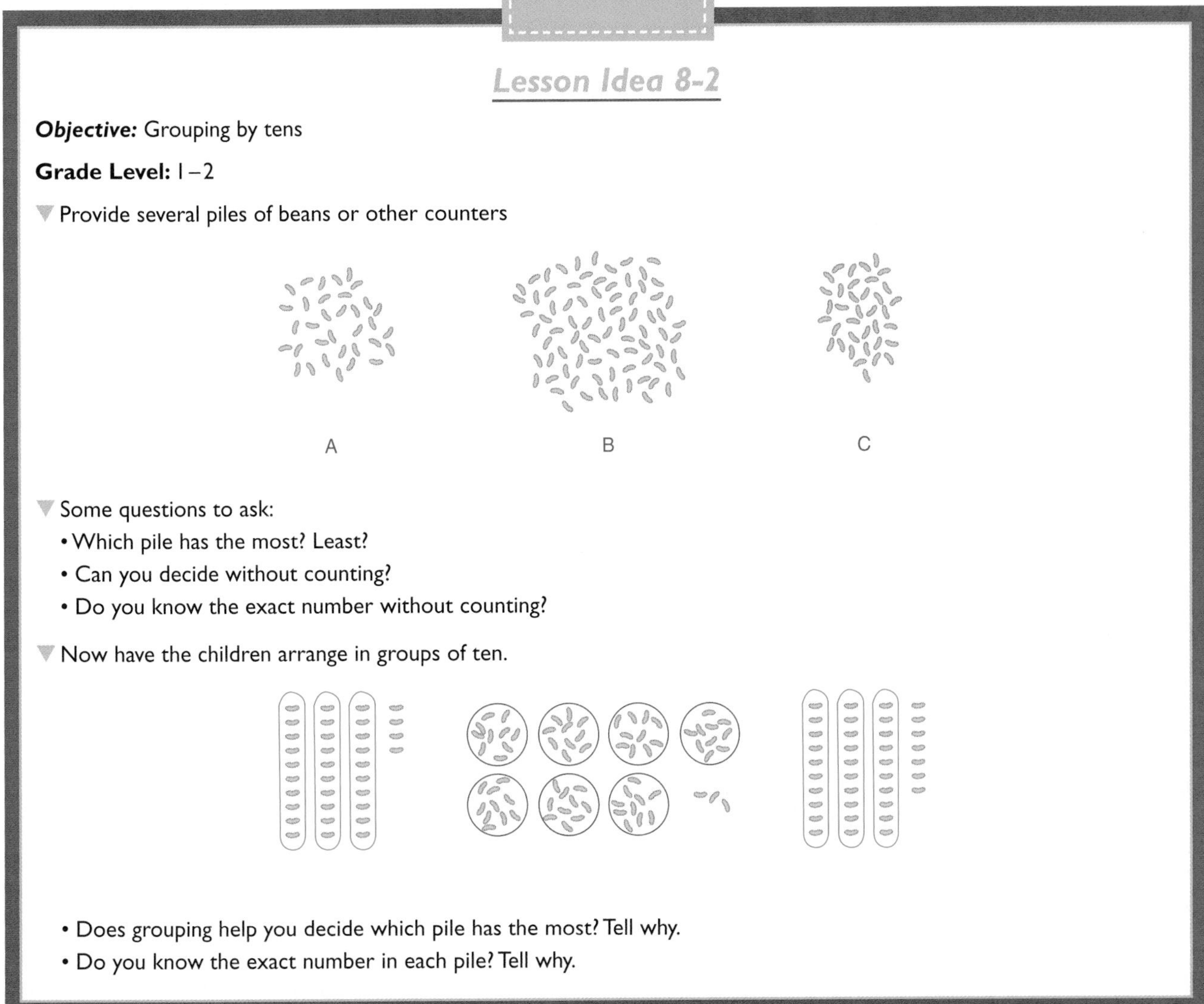

Lesson Idea 8-2

Objective: Grouping by tens

Grade Level: 1–2

- Provide several piles of beans or other counters

A B C

- Some questions to ask:
  - Which pile has the most? Least?
  - Can you decide without counting?
  - Do you know the exact number without counting?
- Now have the children arrange in groups of ten.
  - Does grouping help you decide which pile has the most? Tell why.
  - Do you know the exact number in each pile? Tell why.

Asking children to group by tens as they count the larger piles serves several valuable purposes. First, if a child loses count, correction is often easier if these smaller groups have been formed. It is also easier to check for errors by inspecting groups of 10 than to recount the entire pile. The most important purpose of this practice, however, is that it shows children how an unknown quantity can be organized into a form that can be interpreted by inspection. This process of grouping by tens is the framework for place value.

Nature of Place Value

A thorough understanding of place value is necessary if computational algorithms for addition, subtraction, multiplication, and division are to be learned and used in a meaningful way; however, place value develops from many various experiences, such as counting and mental computation (e.g., $1 plus $0.25 to get $1.25). Development of place value promotes number sense, which facilitates estimation and sharpens a sense of reasonableness about computational results. Place value rests on two key ideas:

1. *Explicit grouping or trading rules are defined and consistently followed.* These ideas are implicit in the bulletin board display shown in Figure 8-2. Such a display provides a constant reminder of the importance of grouping by tens to place value. Our base-ten system is characterized by trading 10 ones for 1 ten (or 1 ten for 10 ones), 10 tens for 1 hundred, 10 hundreds for 1 thousand, and so on. The two-way direction of these trades (e.g., 10 tens for 1 hundred or 1 hundred for 10 tens) should be stressed because there are times when each type of trade must be used. It also should be noted that similar trades are followed with numbers less than one—decimals. Thus, 1 can be traded for 10 tenths (or 10 tenths for 1), 10 hundredths for 1 tenth (or 1 tenth for 10 hundredths), and so on.

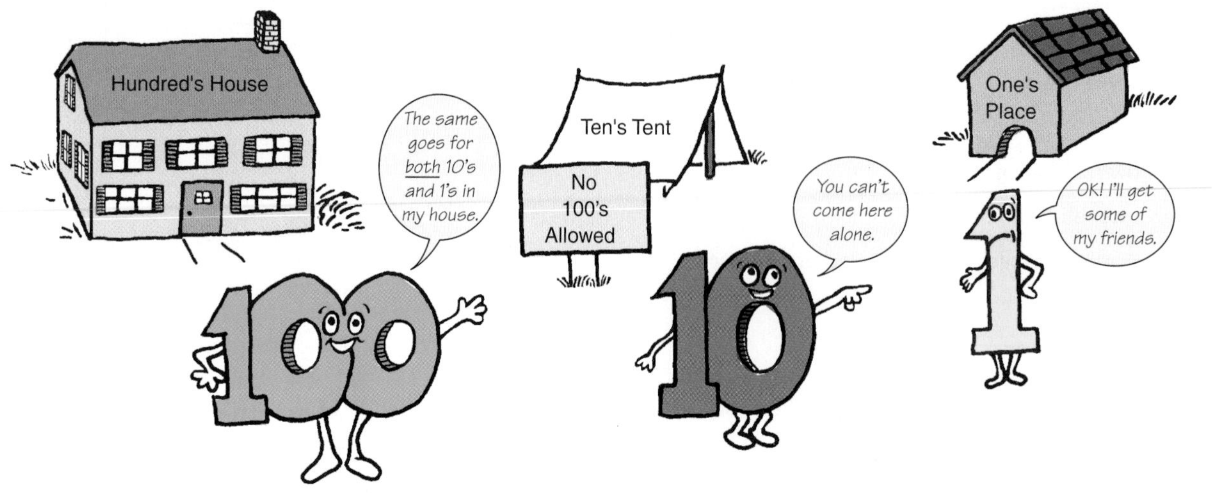

FIGURE 8-2 A bulletin board display for place value.

2. *The position of a digit determines the number being represented.* For example, the 2 in 3042 and the 2 in 2403 represent completely different quantities: 2 ones in 3042 and 2 thousands in 2403. Furthermore, the zero plays a similar yet different role in each of these numbers. It has positional value in each case, but it reports the lack of a quantity for that place. Although the notion of zero will continue to be expanded and developed throughout elementary school mathematics, children should experience the role of zero in place value early and often.

In the Hindu-Arabic number system, place value means that any number can be represented using only 10 digits (0–9). Think about the problems of representing numbers without place value! Each number would require a separate and unique symbol. Your memory storage would quickly be exceeded, and you would probably have to use only the few numbers with symbols you could remember. Nevertheless, place value is difficult for some children to grasp. Oral counting or rote recitation of numbers by young children is often interpreted as understanding place value. Yet many children who can count correctly have absolutely no concept of place value. In most cases, the confusion or misunderstanding can be traced to a lack of counting and trading experiences with appropriate materials and the subsequent recording of these results. Early and frequent hands-on counting activities, similar to those described in Chapter 7, are essential to establishing this concept.

Place-value concepts are encountered before starting school. For example, many children distinguish between the one- and two-digit numbers on a channel indicator of a television, a timer for a microwave oven, and house or apartment numbers. Children learn early that apartment numbers 201 and 102 are different.

Modeling

Hands-on experience with manipulatives is essential in establishing and developing the concept of place value. Research suggests that instruction should focus on concrete models that are connected to oral descriptions and symbolic representations of the models (Thompson, 1990; Wearne and Hiebert, 1994). Bean sticks and the ten-frame provide two effective models for developing place value.

Figure 8-3 illustrates some additional physical models that are effective in helping students understand not only place value but larger numbers as well. All of the models shown in Figure 8-3 represent the same three-digit number, 123. The value of using different embodiments is that a child is less likely to associate place value with a particular model. In fact, a key instructional goal is to develop concepts to a level that does not depend on any one physical model, instead providing for abstraction of the commonality among all models.

Models may be either proportional or nonproportional, but all are based on groups of 10. In proportional models for base ten, such as popsicle sticks, the material for 10 is ten times the size of the material for 1; 100 is ten times the size of 10, and so on. Measurement provides another proportional model. For example, a meter stick, decimeter rods, and centimeter cubes can be used to model any three-digit number.

Proportional Models

Flats Longs Units

Base-10 Blocks

Bundles Sticks Beans

Bean Sticks

Sacks Bands Depressors

Tongue Depressors

Nonproportional Models

Abacus

Dollars Dimes Pennies

Money

Counters

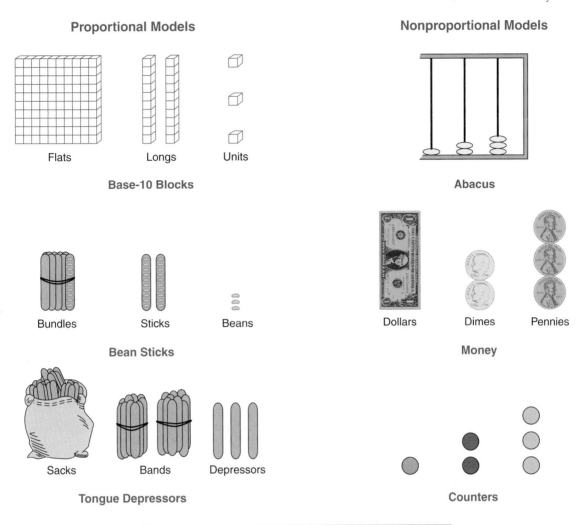

FIGURE 8-3 Place-value models: Proportional models and Nonproportional models.

Nonproportional models, such as money, do not maintain any size relationships. Ten pennies are bigger than a dime but are a fair trade in our monetary system. Ten dimes are the same as a dollar, but they are not proportional in size. These ideas introduce children to a level of abstraction based entirely on trading rules. Young students often focus on size proportionality, which is why they are often willing to trade a dime for one or two pennies, or why they prefer to have a few dimes rather than a dollar bill.

Although both types of embodiments are important and should be represented, proportional models are more concrete, and children need to use and clearly understand them before moving on to nonproportional models.

Of the nonproportional models shown in Figure 8-3, the abacus and the counters are similar. In each model, different-colored beads or counters provide the basis for trading. For example, 10 orange beads (or counters) might be traded for 1 red, 10 red for 1 blue, and so on. Use of a trading mat can help keep the counters in order. The beads on an abacus are arranged in a fixed order. The color distinction is important for the early establishment of proper trades, but it should be dropped as soon as possible so that attention shifts from color of the beads or counters to their position. Only the position of the bead counter has long-range significance.

Math Links 8.3

You can try an electronic manipulative, called Chip Abacus, that gives children practice trading with colored chips. The model is nonproportional because 10 chips are traded for one chip of another color. To access the manipulative, go to this book's web site.

Developing Place Value

A Place to Start

In developing place value and establishing number names, it is far better to skip beyond the teens and start with the larger numbers. The names for the numbers 11–19 are not consistent with the names for other numbers, even though the symbolization or visual pattern is wholly consistent. The numbers 11–19 do not exhibit the place-value characteristic in their names that other numbers do. To do so, they would have to be renamed onety-one (1 ten and 1 one), onety-two, . . . , onety-nine, which would make them consistent with larger numbers, such as forty-one, forty-two, . . . , forty-nine. In many other countries, such as Japan, the naming pattern for the numbers 11–19 is consistent with the naming of larger numbers. This feature reinforces place value early and helps Japanese children name the teen numbers (Yoshikawa, 1994).

What does a number such as 25 mean? It is important that children have the capability of thinking of numbers in various ways. With such number sense, 25 might be thought of several different ways. When multiplying, a square array of 5×5 may come to mind. When thinking of money, several combinations of coins—such as 25 pennies, 2 dimes and 5 pennies, 5 nickels, or 1 quarter—may be imagined. With certain items, such as eggs, one more than 2 dozen and 4 six-packs plus one are two different representations of the quantity 25. With metric measures, 25 centimeters might be thought of as 2 decimeters and 5 centimeters; however, it could also be thought of as 0.25 or $\frac{1}{4}$ meter. Children with good number sense know when a particular form is useful.

Of course, if place value is to be called on, the tens and ones model is needed. It might use money (2 dimes and 5 pennies) or another model, such as bean sticks. With the bean sticks, 25 could be represented several different ways:

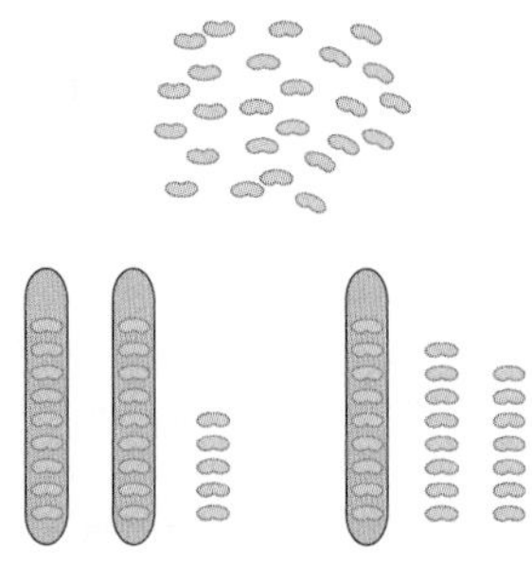

Which way is better? It depends on what is to be done with the 25 beans because there are times when each form may be useful. The grouping at the top, for example, would be easier to divide among several people. Either of the groupings on the bottom would be easier to count.

The notion of representing a quantity with the least number of pieces for a particular model is critical in place value. Establishing its importance at an early stage can eliminate some later errors such as:

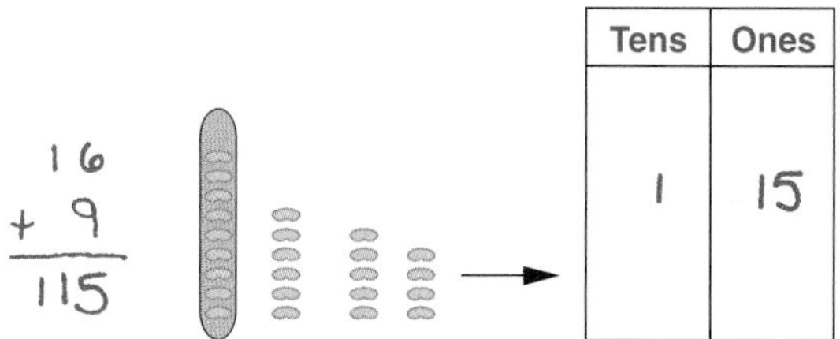

Because 10 or more of something (namely, ones) exist on the place-value mat, a trade must be made. Making the ten-for-one trade results in the least number of pieces and thus 25 becomes the only representation that is meaningful:

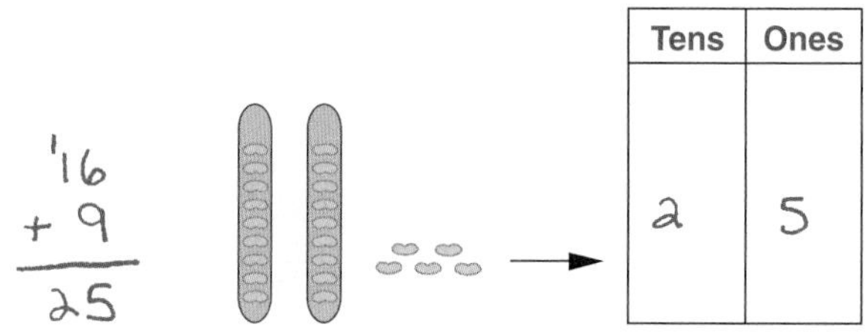

Figure 8-4 highlights the advancement from a concrete model to a symbolic representation. The bridges from the physical models to the symbolic representation must be crossed back and forth many times if meaningful learning is to occur.

Careful attention must be given to linking modeling with the language. As children become fluent in talking about their models, it will become natural to them to describe 25 in different ways.

Many children reverse the digits of numbers. Although this error is generally caused by carelessness, it may be symptomatic of a disability known as *dyslexia*. In either case, it is important that children understand the consequences of such reversals. That's why Mrs. Golden included the first two practice numbers, 25 and 52, at the end of the *Snapshot of a Lesson* at the beginning of this chapter.

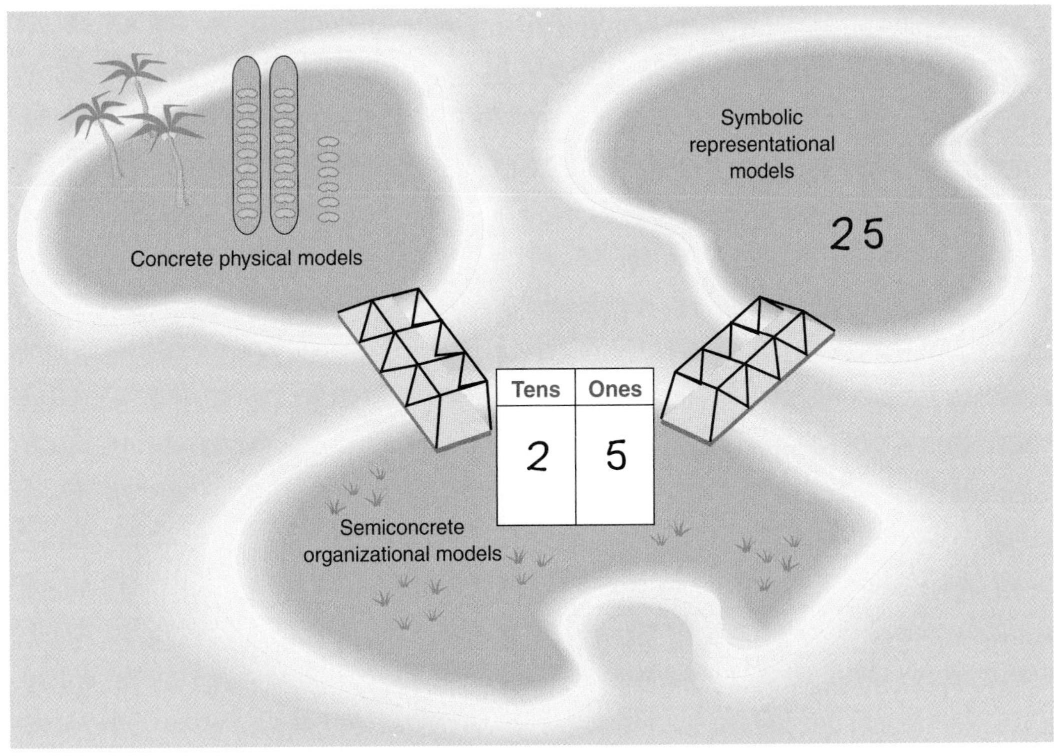

FIGURE 8-4 The idea of place value can help children cross from concrete models of numbers to their symbolic representations.

Although the same digits are used, the resulting numbers—25 and 52—are different. Children should compare the modeled numbers and talk about them in an effort to better appreciate the magnitude of the differences.

The base-ten blocks, together with the place-value mat, as shown in Figure 8-5, can be used to model the additive property and illustrate expanded notation. A variety of strips, such as those in Figure 8-5, which connect the base-ten blocks to number symbols in an expanded form, can be used effectively to review key ideas.

Lesson Idea 8-3 shows two slightly different hundred charts. One chart goes from 1 to 100, the other from 0 to 99. One advantage of the latter chart is that the tens digit in each row is constant, whereas in the 1-to-100 chart the tens digit always changes in the last column. Either hundred chart can be used to explore place value, patterns, mental computation, and algebraic thinking. For example, 43 + 30 can be determined by counting mentally 43, 53, 63, 73 and is a natural by-product of counting by tens on the hundred chart.

Furthermore, 43 + 29 can be found by counting 43, 53, 63, 73 and then dropping back one to 72. Counting by tens and then dropping back or bumping up illustrate how to adjust numbers and be flexible when using and thinking about numbers.

Consider the following diagram and how patterns and generalizations lead to algebraic thinking:

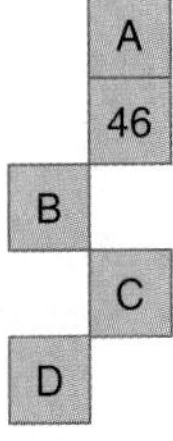

Patterns from the hundred chart suggest these solutions directly from the hundred chart:

$$A = 46 - 10$$
$$B = 46 + 10 - 1$$
$$C = 46 + 20$$
$$D = 46 + 30 - 1$$

If the diagram is shifted on the hundred chart, then 46 changes to some number N. Although the

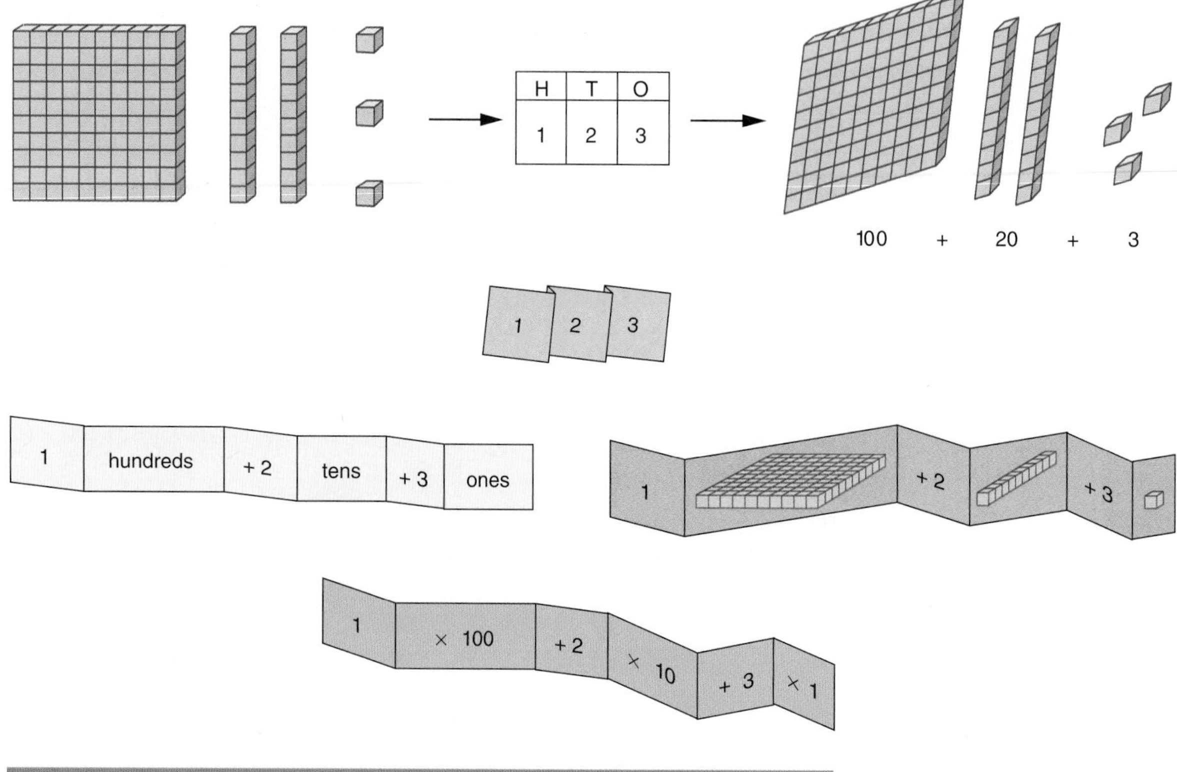

FIGURE 8-5 Connecting models and symbols that reinforce place value.

starting number N has changed, the solutions are similar, as

$$A = N - 10$$
$$B = N + 10 - 1$$
$$C = N + 20$$
$$D = N + 30 - 1$$

Such activities illustrate a variable and the power of patterns in promoting algebraic thinking.

Lesson Idea 8-4 highlights an activity that extends the modeling to three-digit numbers and provides some opportunities to order numbers according to place value. Modeling three-digit numbers establishes the importance of position for each digit more clearly. It provides an early reward for looking at the "front-end" (lead) digits of a number. For example, when students are asked to show the number closest to 400 in Lesson Idea 8-4, they can concentrate on the values with 4 hundreds. Furthermore, when asked to show a number that is at least 100 more than 314, students can focus on hundreds and ignore the other digits. This ability to focus on certain digits in numbers is an important part of number sense.

In the Classroom 8-1 reinforces place value and provides practice in important mental computational skills. Scores are found by counting the darts in each circle, which provides practice counting by ones, tens, and hundreds, and then computing the totals.

A calculator provides many opportunities to practice and develop important place-value concepts. Wipe Out is a place-value game that involves either addition or subtraction using a calculator. The goal is to change (wipe out) a predetermined digit by subtracting or adding a number. This activity can be made into a competitive game for two people. The players take turns entering a number and naming a specific digit the other player must change to 0.

For example, Kelly enters 431, naming the 3 to be wiped out:

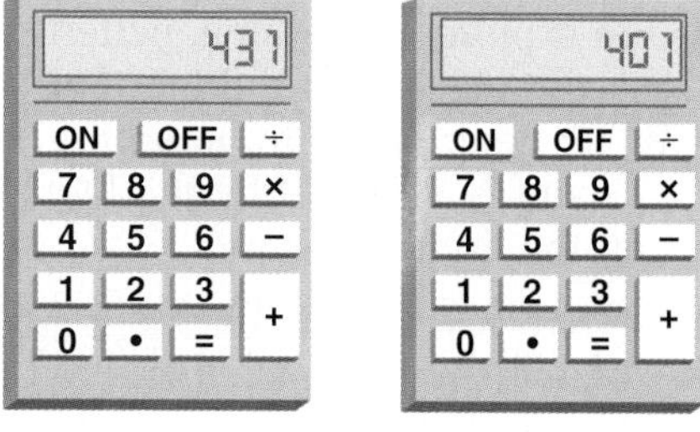

Lesson Idea 8-3

Objective: Using a hundred chart to explore place value and pattern

Grade Level: 3

▼ Provide a hundred chart for each student to use.

1	2	3	4	5	6	7	8	9	10
11	12	13	14	15	16	17	18	19	20
21	22	23	24	25	26	27	28	29	30
31	32	33	34	35	36	37	38	39	40
41	42	43	44	45	46	47	48	49	50
51	52	53	54	55	56	57	58	59	60
61	62	63	64	65	66	67	68	69	70
71	72	73	74	75	76	77	78	79	80
81	82	83	84	85	86	87	88	89	90
91	92	93	94	95	96	97	98	99	100

↑ Fifth column

0	1	2	3	4	5	6	7	8	9
10	11	12	13	14	15	16	17	18	19
20	21	22	23	24	25	26	27	28	29
30	31	32	33	34	35	36	37	38	39
40	41	42	43	44	45	46	47	48	49
50	51	52	53	54	55	56	57	58	59
60	61	62	63	64	65	66	67	68	69
70	71	72	73	74	75	76	77	78	79
80	81	82	83	84	85	86	87	88	89
90	91	92	93	94	95	96	97	98	99

▼ Some questions to ask:

- What is alike for all the numbers in the fifth column?
- How are the numbers in the fourth and sixth columns alike? Different?
- Tell where you stop, if you start on any square in the first three rows and count forward ten more squares.
- Start on a different square in the first three rows and count forward ten more squares. Where did you stop?
- After you have done this several times, tell about a pattern that you found.

▼ Cut out a piece like this  and lay it on the chart.

- What numbers are covered? Tell how you found them.
- Move the piece to a different place, and tell what numbers are covered.
- Do it again with different shapes like  and

▼ Here is only a part of a hundred chart:

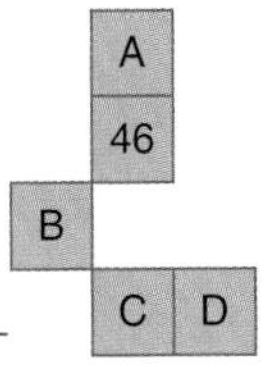

A
46
B
C D

- Use what you know about a hundred chart to
- Find A_____ B_____ C_____ D_____
- Tell two different ways to find C.
- Suppose 46 is replaced by N.
- Find A_____ B_____ C_____ D_____

Tanya wipes out the 3 by subtracting 30, which also leaves the other digits unchanged:

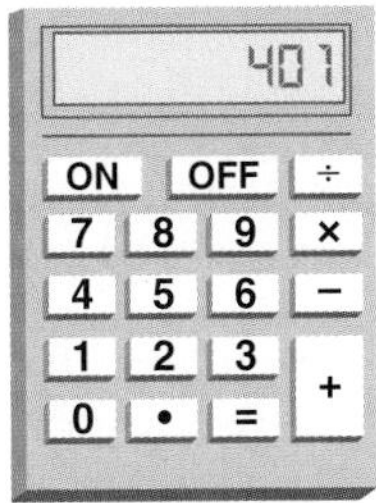

A player scores a point for changing the digit to 0 on the first try. A record of the game in table form reinforces the identification of the correct place value:

WIPE OUT RECORD Name: Tanya

Entered	Wiped Out	Keys Pressed	Display	Score
431	3	-30	401	1
24	4	+6	30	1
849	8	-800	49	1
206	2	-200	6	1

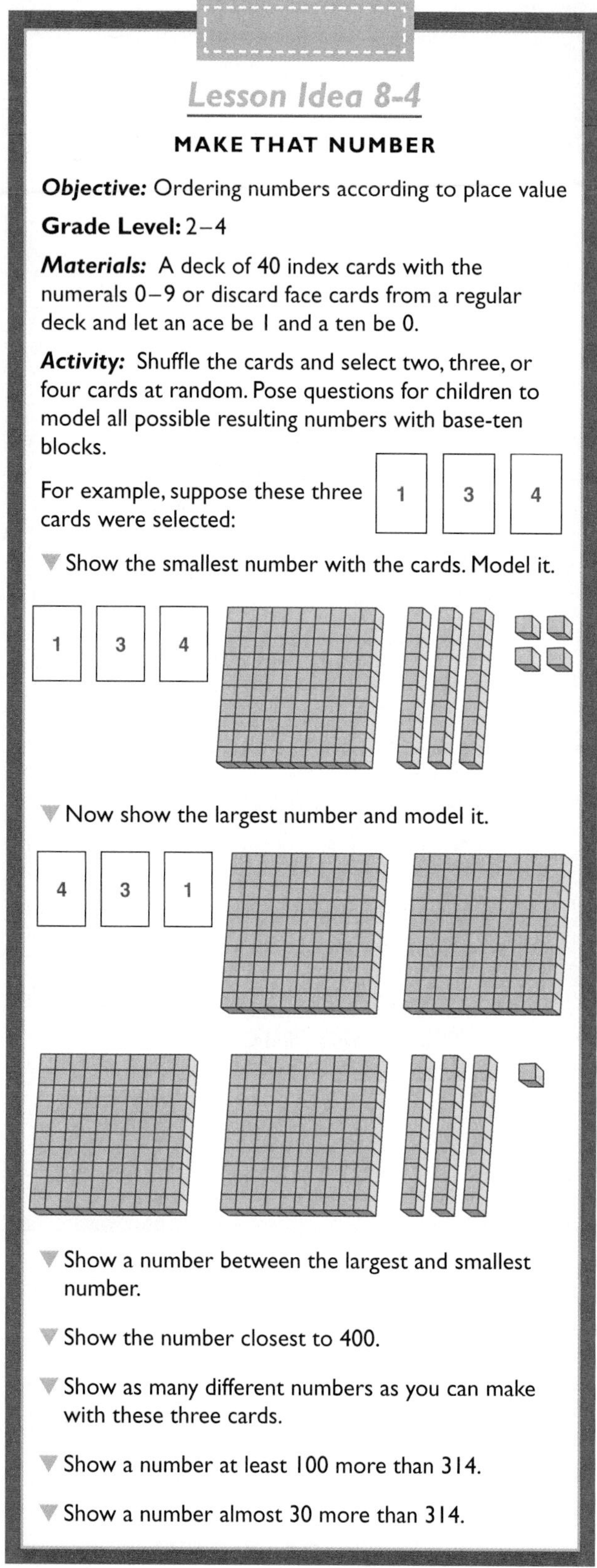

Lesson Idea 8-4

MAKE THAT NUMBER

Objective: Ordering numbers according to place value

Grade Level: 2–4

Materials: A deck of 40 index cards with the numerals 0–9 or discard face cards from a regular deck and let an ace be 1 and a ten be 0.

Activity: Shuffle the cards and select two, three, or four cards at random. Pose questions for children to model all possible resulting numbers with base-ten blocks.

For example, suppose these three cards were selected: 1 3 4

- Show the smallest number with the cards. Model it.

- Now show the largest number and model it.

- Show a number between the largest and smallest number.
- Show the number closest to 400.
- Show as many different numbers as you can make with these three cards.
- Show a number at least 100 more than 314.
- Show a number almost 30 more than 314.

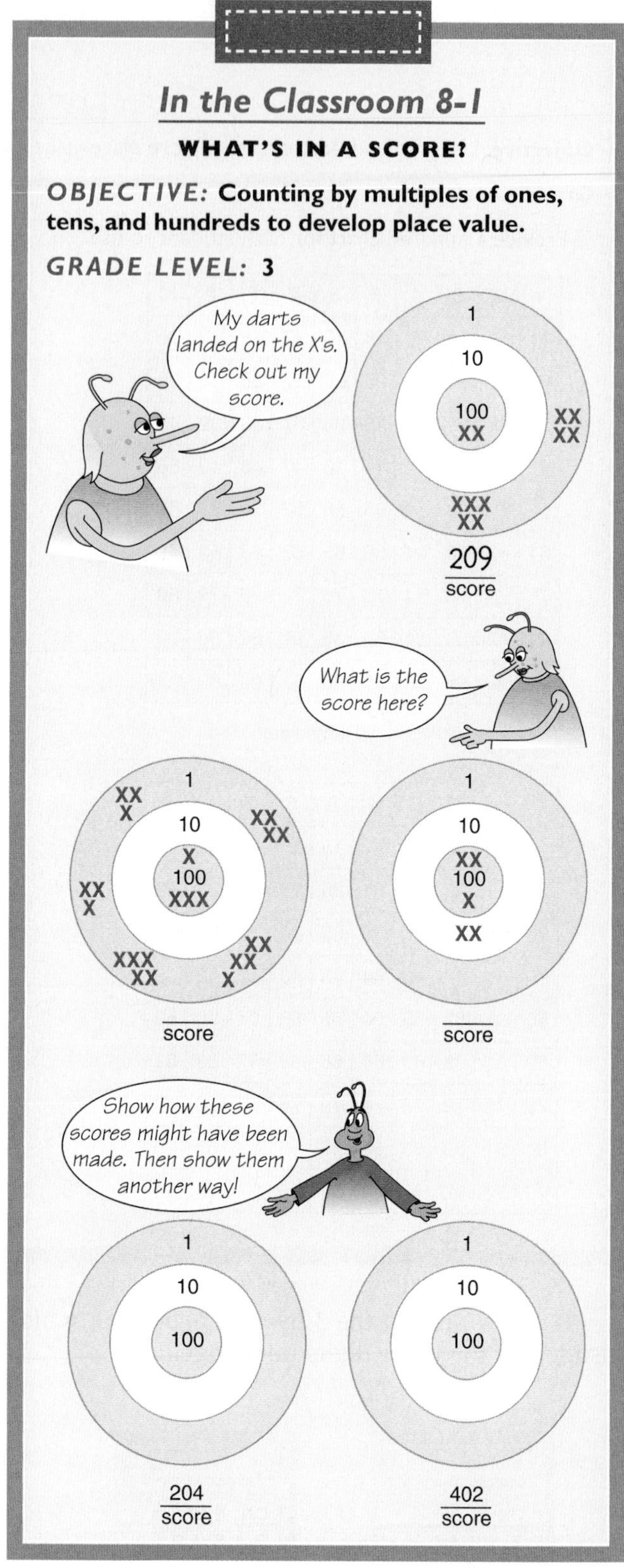

In the Classroom 8-1

WHAT'S IN A SCORE?

OBJECTIVE: **Counting by multiples of ones, tens, and hundreds to develop place value.**

GRADE LEVEL: 3

A variation of Wipe Out focuses more attention on the place value of the digits (Hopkins, 1992). In this variation, which can be played with or without a calculator, the teacher chooses a multidigit number with no two digits the same, such as 5849. The teacher identifies a digit (e.g., the 5 in 5849) to be wiped out, and students must try to change only that digit to 0 by using one operation. Students are called on until the correct answer is given, and points are awarded according to their responses.

Response	Scoring
Student names operation and digit to be wiped out: "Subtract five."	Teacher scores 2 points.
Student names operation and digits entered: "Subtract five, zero, zero, zero."	Teacher scores 1 point.
Student names operation and number: "Subtract five thousand."	Class scores 2 points.

Although Wipe Out or a variation of it can be played without a calculator, it is much more exciting with one. Children don't get bogged down with computation. The focus remains on place value. Furthermore, they are often surprised by what happens when they make a place-value error, which increases their place-value understanding.

The challenge of wipe out–type activities is illustrated by a question included on a recent national assessment, shown in Figure 8-6. The figure shows this open-ended question along with examples of satisfactory responses. Although calculators were available, the decision about whether to use a calculator was made by each student; however, more than 60 percent of the fourth graders made no response or provided an incorrect response. This performance level indicates the value of wipe out–type activities and reminds us that connections need to be established between such activities and mental computations.

Question: Laura wanted to enter the number 8375 into her calculator. By mistake, she entered the number 8275. Without clearing the calculator, how could she correct her mistake?

Satisfactory Responses:

1. 8275 + 100 = 8375
2. She could add 100 more.
3. If she subtracted 100 she could add 200.

FIGURE 8-6 An example from a national assessment test that reinforces the connection between wipe out–type calculator game and mental computation skills.

Research reports that many children lack an understanding of the relative sizes of numbers greater than 100 (Payne and Huinker, 1993). This results from many factors, one of which may be the lack of opportunities to model, which helps children develop a visual awareness of the relative sizes of numbers. For large numbers, children can use variations of the models shown in Figure 8-1. For the base-ten blocks, lay another place-value mat to the left of the mat holding hundreds, tens, and ones. This thousands mat holds thousands, ten-thousands, and hundred-thousands. Figure 8-7 provides another demonstration of how two numbers can have the same digits but be different. How are 2130 and 1032 alike and different? As children engage in discussion to answer this question, their knowledge of place value and their sense of numbers will grow. Using the same digits to represent different numbers helps children appreciate the importance of representing the place values accurately. Although the numbers 2130 and 1032 use the same digits, the models that represent these numbers are dramatically different. This type of experience helps develop number sense and alerts children to the importance of the front-end, or lead, digits, which in this case denote thousands.

As the number of digits increases, children should be encouraged to focus on the front-end digits. The front-end digits are used when comparing and ordering numbers, as well as when computing mentally and estimating:

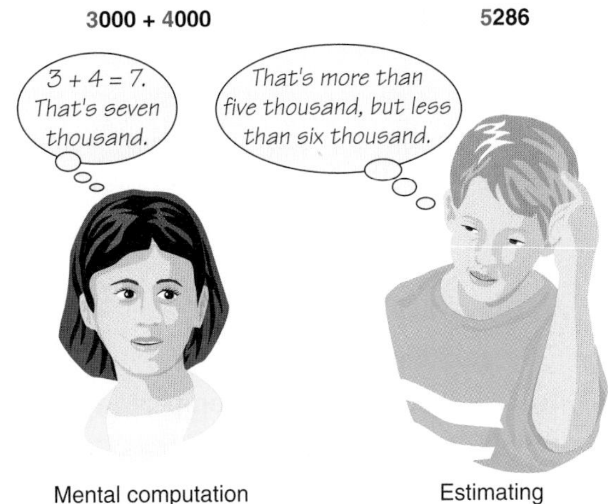

The front-end approach can be naturally extended and applied to larger numbers. For example, students could be asked to decide which number is larger when the front-end digits are the same:

Thousands

H	T	O	H	T	O
		2	1	3	0

How many thousands? [2]
How many hundreds? [1]
How many tens? [3]
How many ones? [0]
Can you say the number?
[two thousand one hundred thirty]

Thousands

H	T	O	H	T	O
		1	0	3	2

How many thousands? [1]
How many hundreds? [0]
How many tens? [3]
How many ones? [2]
Can you say the number?
[one thousand thirty-two]

FIGURE 8-7 Using a thousands mat to demonstrate how two numbers can have the same digits but be different.

And then asked the same question when the back-end digits are the same:

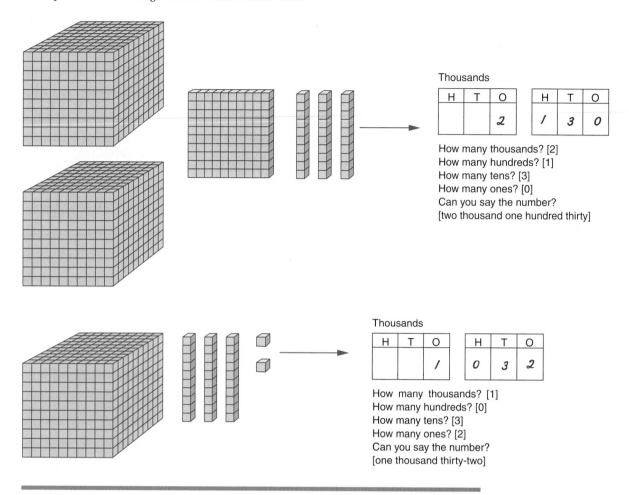

2	4	5	6
1	4	5	6

This task helps students compare and order larger numbers.

Try this problem:

Norway has an area of 125181 square miles.

New Mexico has an area of 121400 square miles.

Greece has an area of 50944 square miles.

Why is it easy to tell which has the least area?

Can you tell which is the greatest area by comparing the first front-end digit? the first two front-end digits? the first three front-end digits?

Which has the greatest area?

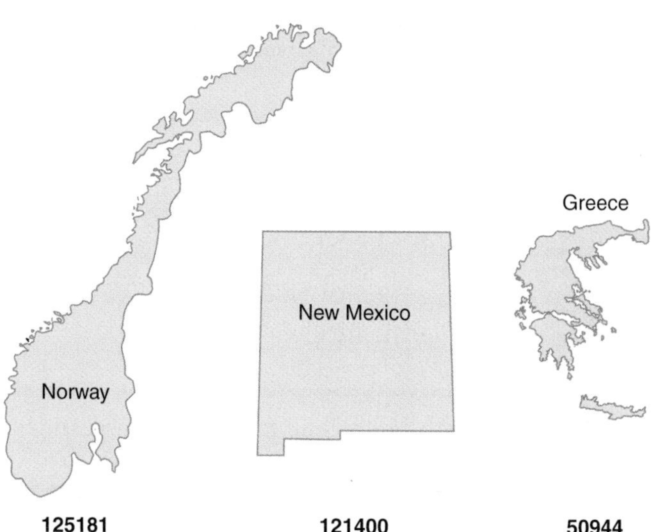

This problem reminds students of the importance of place value when comparing numbers. For example, the front-end approach is used only when the numbers have the same number of digits. It is not needed to compare 125181 square miles with 50944 square miles because the numbers of digits are different.

Counting and Patterns

As noted in Chapter 7, calculators are useful in counting and pattern recognition. Seeing each value displayed on the calculator helps students develop important insight into what digits are changing and when. In the Classroom 7-6 provides a calculator counting activity. When children are counting by ones, they observe that the digit on the right (ones place) changes every time they "count," while the next digit (tens place) changes less frequently, and it takes much counting to change the third digit (hundreds place). On the other hand, Figure 8-8 develops an additional understanding of place value by displaying results of counting by ones, tens, and hundreds.

Calculator counting provides many opportunities to discuss patterns related to place value. Such counting can also contribute to a better grasp of large numbers, thereby helping to develop students' number sense. For example, in Chapter 7, In the Classroom 7-6 asked pupils to record how long it took to count from 1 to 1000 by ones. Students might also be asked to find how long it takes to count from 1 to 1000000 by thousands. Many pupils are surprised to learn that it takes about the same time. One fourth grader said, "That means there are as many thousands in one million as ones in one thousand." This is a profound observation—of the type that leads to a better understanding of both place value and large numbers, and it also reflects a growing sense of numbers.

As Figure 8-8 shows, counting on by tens or by hundreds never changes the ones place; however, when counting by tens, the tens place changes on each count and the next digit (hundreds) changes every 10 counts. Observing these patterns in counting larger and larger numbers helps students recognize place-value properties. In the Classroom 8-2 uses calculators and patterns to help students add multiples of 100. Similar exercises should be provided with other powers of 10.

As you have seen, the hundred chart provides a useful model for counting and pattern recognition related to place value. Activities involving counting with multiples of 10 were illustrated in Lesson Idea 8-3. In the Classroom 8-3 shows how similar ideas can be extended to a thousand chart. For example, consider this diagram and the thousand chart In the Classroom 8-3:

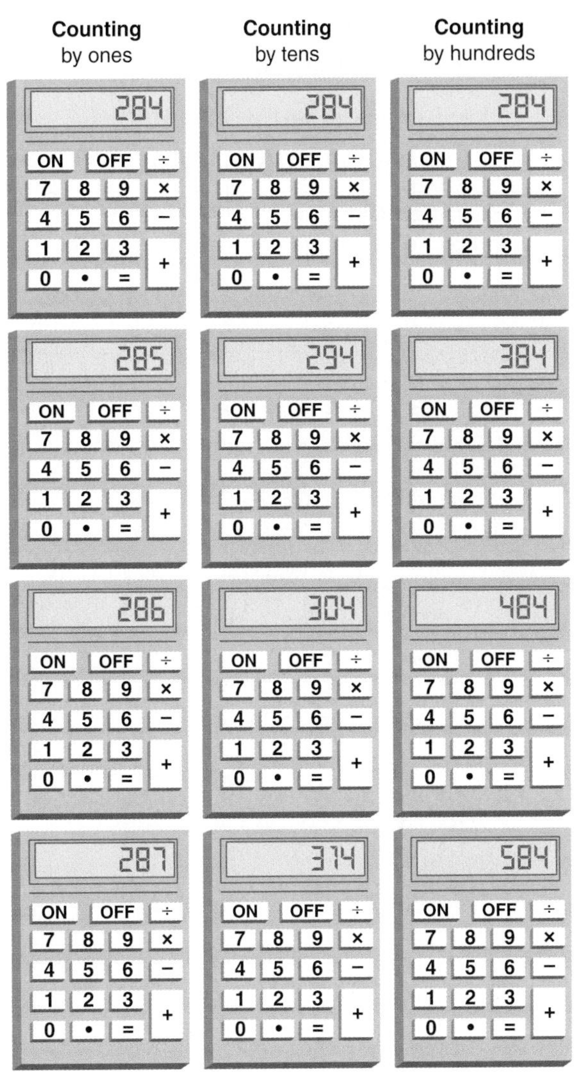

FIGURE 8-8 Calculator counting to illustrate place-value patterns.

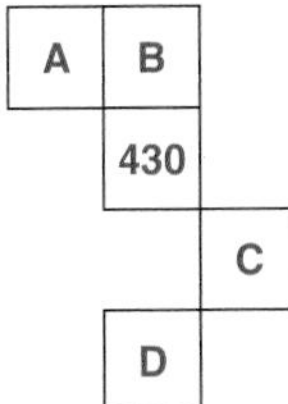

A solution for this diagram requires the use of patterns:

$$A = 430 - 100 - 10$$
$$B = 430 - 100$$
$$C = 430 + 100 + 10$$
$$D = 430 + 200$$

In the Classroom 8-2
HITTING HUNDREDS
OBJECTIVE: Counting by hundreds to develop place value and pattern recognition.
GRADE LEVEL: 2–3
Which target can you hit?
2 5 + 1 0 0 = =
Start 25
Rule +100
I hit 225.
225
250
▼ Which target will you hit?
Write what your shows.
Start Rule Which target? Guess Check
20 +100 200 220
35 +100 335 500
41 +100 410 441
86 +100 586 580
97 +100 897 970
169 +100 469 696
123 +100 321 323

This activity also leads to algebraic thinking when 430 is replaced by any number N. Then

$$A = N - 100 - 10$$
$$B = N - 100$$
$$C = N + 100 + 10$$
$$D = N + 200$$

This activity further develops students' number sense and provides practice in important mental computation skills. (See Appendix B for copies of several master charts.)

In the Classroom 8-3

THE POWER OF 10 ON THE THOUSAND CHART

OBJECTIVE: Using a thousand chart to identify patterns and skip count by tens and hundreds.

GRADE LEVEL: 2–3

10	20	30	40	50	60	70	80	90	100
110	120	130	140	150	160	170	180	190	200
210	220	230	240	250	260	270	280	290	300
310	320	330	340	350	360	370	380	390	400
410	420	430	440	450	460	470	480	490	500
510	520	530	540	550	560	570	580	590	600
610	620	630	640	650	660	670	680	690	700
710	720	730	740	750	760	770	780	790	800
810	820	830	840	850	860	870	880	890	900
910	920	930	940	950	960	970	980	990	1000

▼ Count by 10:

- Start on any square in the first three rows.
- Count forward 10 squares, and tell where you stopped.
- Start at a different square, and count forward 10 squares.
- After you have done this several times, tell about a pattern that you found.
- Describe a quick way to count "a hundred more" on this thousand chart.

▼ Count by 100:

- Tell how you could use the thousand chart to add 300 to 240.
- Tell how you could use the thousand chart to add 290 to 240.

▼ Connect the charts:

- Tell how using the hundred chart helps you use the thousand chart.

Regrouping and Renaming

Counting suggests many patterns, but one of the most important for young children is observing what happens when we model the number after 9 (or 19, 29, etc.). Trading occurs in every case. The pattern involved in bridging from one decade to another should be recognized and clearly understood by children.

Regrouping and place value are intertwined in later development of computation. Regrouping happens whenever bridging occurs, as from one ten to

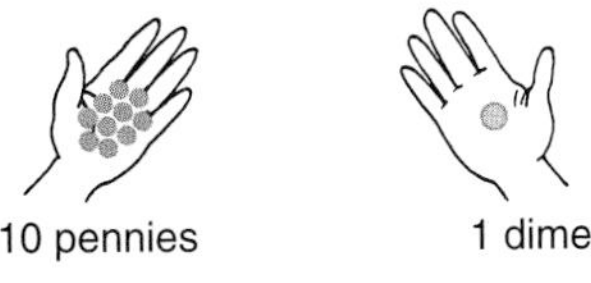

FIGURE 8-9 Nonproportional model illustrating relation between regrouping and place value.

another (such as 29 to 30) or from one hundred to another (such as 799 to 800). Regrouping also happens when 6 tens 7 ones are considered as 5 tens 17 ones, or 245 is thought of as 24 tens 5 ones, or 40 pennies are traded for 4 dimes. The importance of clearly understanding the regrouping process cannot be overemphasized. Understanding is most likely to develop when children experience this bridging with physical models and practice trading and regrouping.

Whenever trading occurs, there are accompanying changes in how we record the number. Understanding this changed notation requires many experiences with problems involving trading and the related recording process. Figure 8-9 shows how regrouping affects digits and place value.

Figure 8-10 further illustrates the regrouping process with two different models. Similar models with larger numbers should be used as soon as children have grasped the trading principles involving ones, tens, and hundreds. In fact, this extension process demonstrates the power of mathematical abstraction. Extending to thousands should be done with proportional models to illustrate the dramatic

FIGURE 8-10 Nonproportional and proportional models illustrating some relationships between regrouping and place value.

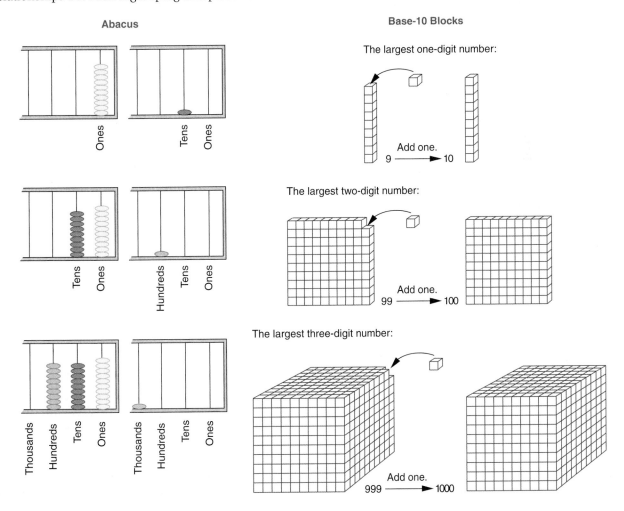

Math Links 8.4

An electronic manipulative that gives children experience representing numbers with an abacus, called Electronic Abacus, is available on the NCTM Illuminations web site, which you can access from this book's web site. Here children can represent numbers and regroup into fives and tens.

size increase that continues to occur as new places are used. Children soon recognize that it becomes cumbersome to model large numbers with proportional models (see Powers of Ten in Appendix B).

The calculator can be used with very large numbers. Minor variations of In the Classroom 7-6 (such as finding how long a calculator takes to count to one million or one billion) can help students develop a better grasp of large numbers.

Reading and Writing Numbers

Reading and writing numbers are symbolic activities and should follow much modeling and talking about numbers. The key word is *symbolic.* This recommendation is based on research with young children and alerts us to the danger of a premature focus on symbols (Payne and Huinker, 1993). A sustained development of number sense should precede reading and writing numbers. This approach ensures that the symbols the students are writing and reading are meaningful to them.

Consider some ways in which understanding place value helps develop reading and writing numbers. Take the example of the number 123. The places (hundreds, tens, ones) as well as the value of each (1, 2, 3) are easy to identify. The 1 means one hundred. The 23 is both 2 tens 3 ones and 23 ones, and 123 is 1 hundred 2 tens 3 ones; 12 tens 3 ones; and 123 ones.

These representations may be shown on the place-value mat:

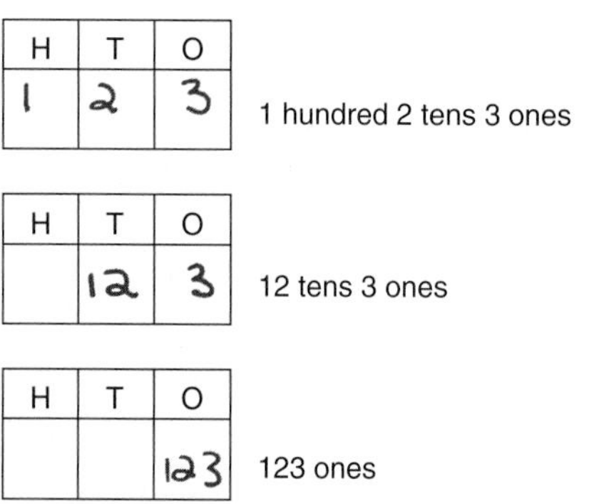

H
T
O
1
2
3
1 hundred 2 tens 3 ones
H
T
O
12
3
12 tens 3 ones
H
T
O
123
123 ones

The skill of reading numbers in different ways (and understanding of the grouping that allows these representations) can be useful in many operations with whole numbers. For example, rereading provides a nice stepping stone to mental computation; more specifically, it leads to multiplying a number by 10:

H	T	O
3	8	0

Reads: 3 hundreds 8 tens 0 ones.
Realizes there are no ones.
Rereads: 38 tens, which is 380.

Although it seems logical to write number words as they sound, this procedure can lead to difficulty. If this were done, sixty-one would be incorrectly written as 601 and one hundred twenty-three as 100203. The exercise in the *Snapshot of a Lesson* where children were asked to show forty-one was aimed at detecting this error. If a child made this mistake, the teacher could use the place-value mat as a model to demonstrate:

Modeling several numbers on the mat can help clarify this notion.

Similar problems exist in naming and representing larger numbers. Consider the following questions from a national assessment:

> The census showed that three hundred fifty-six thousand, ninety-seven people lived in Middletown. Written as a number, the population is
>
> 350697
>
> 356097
>
> 356907
>
> 356970
>
> What number is four hundred five and three tenths?
>
> 45.3
>
> 405.3
>
> 453
>
> 4005.3

About 70 percent of fourth graders and 90 percent of eighth graders correctly connected the place-value language and symbolic representation. Yet research shows that number sense development lags behind language (McIntosh et al., 1997). Children need to make sense of large numbers in order to read

How Big is BIG?

A million . . .

- dollars is ______ $100 bills.
- days is about ______ years.
- miles is about ______ times around the equator of the earth

A billion . . .

- dollars would by about ______ trail bikes.
- seconds in about ______ years.
- people live in ________ .

FIGURE 8-11 Questions to promote thinking about size of numbers.

FIGURE 8-12 Children constructing a cubic meter box.
(Photo by Gene Sutphen)

and write them. Calculator counting (In the Classroom 7-6) provides an effective way of contributing to their number sense. Open-ended questions such as those shown in Figure 8-11 encourage children to estimate and think about numbers. As they share their answers and talk about different ways of understanding millions and billions, their number sense grows. Reading books listed in the Book Nook for Children such as *If You Made a Million*(Schwartz, 1989) and *In One Day* (Parker, 1984), found in *The Wonderful World of Mathematics: A Critically Annotated List of Children's Books in Mathematics* (Thiessen and Matthias, 1998) gives children additional insight and appreciation of larger numbers.

It is helpful for students to link some of the models to larger numbers. For example, students might begin with a one-cubic-centimeter block. If they then make a cubic-meter box, that box will hold one million cubic-centimeter cubes, as illustrated in Figure 8-12.

Base-ten blocks also can be used to help students make the connection between the concrete model and the symbolic representation, as in Figure 8-13. This model helps students mentally "see" that ten thousand is a long piece made up of ten cubes, where each cube is one thousand. Although this model can be constructed with physical models, children quickly appreciate the power of constructing mental images to represent larger numbers.

When students begin to develop an intuitive grasp of larger numbers and begin to use millions and billions intelligently, they are ready to write and read these larger numbers. Place-value mats can be naturally expanded to represent larger numbers:

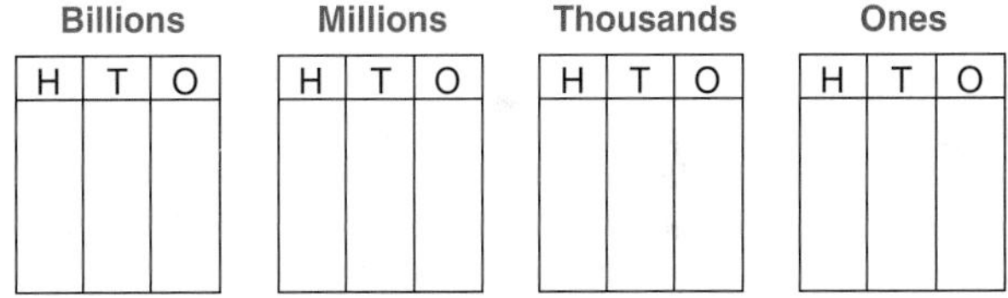

To develop facility in reading large numbers, children need careful instruction and practice in actually naming them aloud. For example, would you read 12,345,678 as "one ten-million two million three hundred-thousand four ten-thousand" and so on? Certainly not! You would use the

Math Links 8.5

An Internet-based lesson plan for middle school students, The Next Billion, may be found on the NCTM's Illuminations web site, which you can access from this book's web site. In this lesson, students access an online population counter to predict when the world population will reach 7 billion.

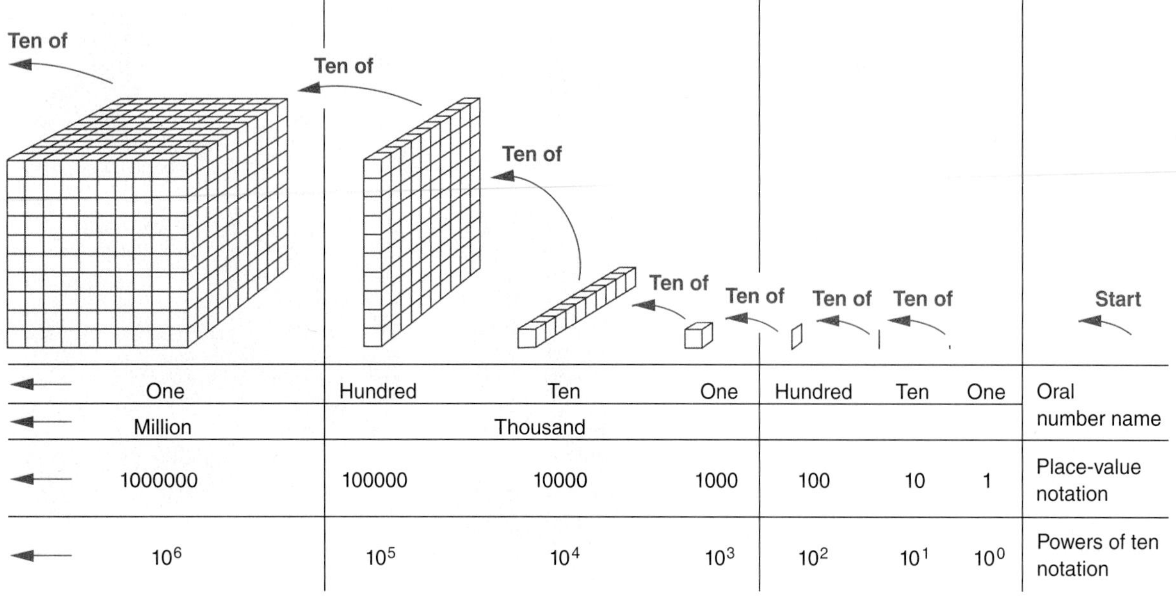

Ten of
Ten of
Ten of
Ten of
Ten of
Ten of
Ten of
Start
One
Hundred
Ten
One
Hundred
Ten
One
Oral number name
Million
Thousand
1000000
100000
10000
1000
100
10
1
Place-value notation
10^6
10^5
10^4
10^3
10^2
10^1
10^0
Powers of ten notation

FIGURE 8-13 Connecting the symbolic representation of one million with a concrete model. (Adapted from Labinowicz, 1989.)

period names and read it as "twelve million, three hundred forty-five thousand, six hundred seventy-eight." This example is a clear application of an organizing strategy: the digits within each period are read as hundreds, tens, and ones, as with "three hundred forty-five thousand." For this reason, children need to think of larger numbers (those of more than three digits) in blocks of three digits.

Recognition and understanding of the hundreds, tens, and ones pattern provide a powerful organizational strategy that can be called on in naming numbers. Only the key terms—ones, tens, and hundreds—along with recognition of the periods for thousands, millions, and billions are needed to name very large numbers.

In many countries, commas are not used to separate blocks of three digits. Instead, for example, the number 2346457 is written as 2 346 457. The blocks of digits remain visible but are separated by spaces rather than commas. Some newspapers, journals, and textbooks in the United States now print numbers this way. This change has instructional implications for both reading and writing numbers. In particular, children must become even more sensitive to the importance of writing numbers clearly and distinctly.

For practice in reading and writing, newspapers provide a rich context to explore numbers of all sizes. Examine a newspaper and highlight all of the numbers reported in headlines and related stories. You may be surprised at the high frequency with which numbers occur. This emphasizes the importance of developing notions of place value and number sense. In the Classroom 8-4 illustrates how newspapers provide a powerful source to help students become more sensitive to the frequent use of numbers.

Naming numbers is clearly an important skill. Yet with the widespread use of calculators, a more efficient way to read multidigit numbers is becoming common. For example, 32764 is read as "three two seven six four" and 4.3425 as "four point three four two five." Each of these readings is correct and much easier to say than the respective periods. There is the danger that children will say the digits without any realization of the value of the numbers involved, but such interpretations are not necessary at every stage of the problem-solving process. If it is only desired to copy a number displayed on a calculator, then a direct translation of digits is without a doubt the best way to read the number. Rather than requiring children to read numbers in a specific way, it is far better to recognize the value of each technique and encourage children to choose wisely—namely, to select the technique that is most appropriate for a given situation.

In the Classroom 8-4

MAKING MORE SENSE OF NUMBERS BY READING AND WRITING

OBJECTIVE: **Using the newspaper to explore numbers**

GRADE LEVEL: **4–5**

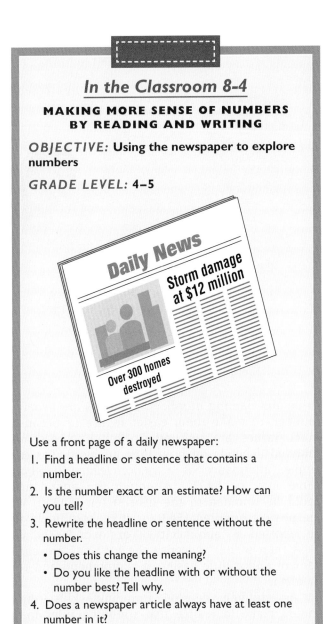

Use a front page of a daily newspaper:

1. Find a headline or sentence that contains a number.
2. Is the number exact or an estimate? How can you tell?
3. Rewrite the headline or sentence without the number.
   - Does this change the meaning?
   - Do you like the headline with or without the number best? Tell why.
4. Does a newspaper article always have at least one number in it?
5. How many articles on your front page can you find that do not include a number?

Estimation and Rounding

An important aspect of developing number sense is recognizing that some numbers are approximate (such as our national debt) and some are exact (such as the number of people killed in a fatal airplane crash). Approximate values are associated with estimation, often involving rounding, and are encountered regularly in our daily lives.

Estimation

Estimation provides a natural way to develop number sense and place-value concepts. Children love to estimate, and they enjoy many types of estimating situations that challenge their skills:

About how many balloons could fill this room?

About how many pennies tall are you?

About how many dollar bills can you lift?

These types of questions stimulate thinking and invite involvement.

This section focuses on estimating quantities. This experience provides an important foundation for number sense and place value, but practice situations must be well chosen. If the number of objects is small, it is natural to count and unnecessary to estimate. When the number becomes large and tedious or too time-consuming to count, however, then estimates are useful.

Experience in making comparisons of different quantities is important at every grade level. Research has demonstrated that children use several different techniques for estimating, and there is a wide range of performance at each grade level. Providing opportunities for children to share strategies is an effective way to help children develop competence and confidence in estimating (Sowder, 1992).

Figure 8-14 illustrates three different thinking processes students use in making an estimate. Students also should be encouraged to share their thinking strategies. Sharing may offer insight into not only the thinking processes used but also any misconceptions held by the students.

Benchmarks are an important and useful tool in estimating (see Figure 7-3). If you know your own height, for example, that information can help you estimate someone else's height. You can decide if the other person is taller or shorter than you are, and this decision helps you make an estimate. In this case, you have used your height as a benchmark for comparison.

Math Links 8.6

If you would like to see an estimation lesson developed to help fourth graders estimate quantities and develop number sense for a million, you can view the video clips and lesson plans for An Apple a Day from the PBS Mathline web site, which you can access from this book's web site.

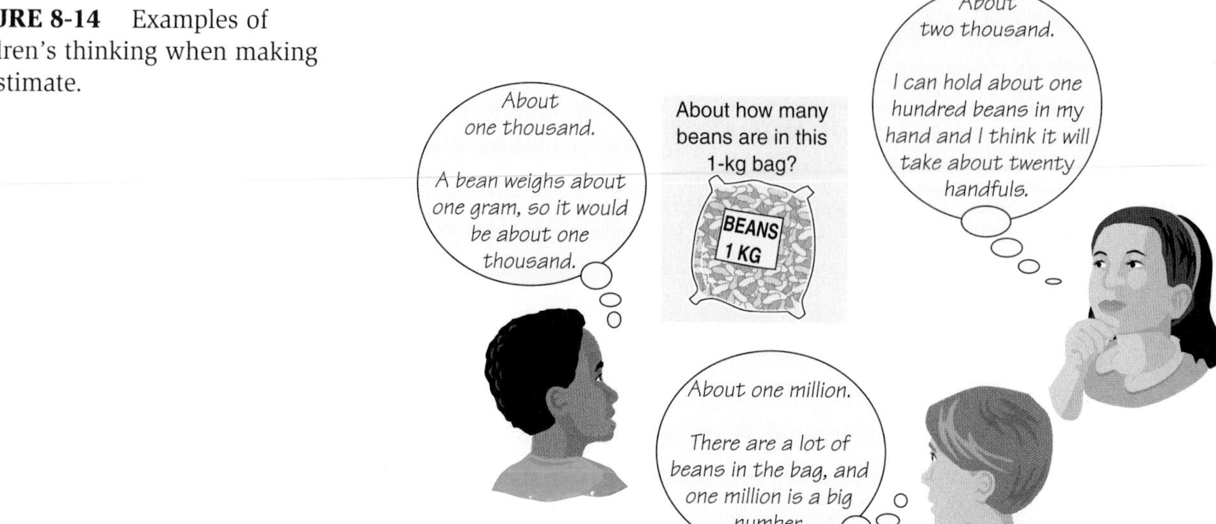

FIGURE 8-14 Examples of children's thinking when making an estimate.

Good estimation skills require the development of number sense; thus they evolve slowly over time. The foundation for estimation includes counting, models, and meaningful interpretations of real-life encounters with numbers of all sizes. For example, the bulletin board display shown in Figure 8-15 provides some benchmarks that can help children better grasp the relationships between small and large numbers when estimating length. Frequent practice with the lower portion of the display provides an enjoyable activity that helps develop both estimation skills and number sense.

The benchmark principle is used in many different ways. Figure 8-16 demonstrates how providing additional information (new benchmarks) can be helpful in producing closer estimates. It is important that students make initial estimates and then refine or adjust them in light of new information. For example, Figure 8-16 produces a "trail" of estimates, with each estimate reflecting changes resulting from new benchmarks. This trail encourages students to continue to think about numbers and provides teachers with insight into their thinking.

Rounding

As students estimate, they become more comfortable with numbers that are not exact. Thus early estimation of quantity and use of benchmarks provide some useful preparation for rounding numbers.

Rounding is an important skill that integrates understanding of approximate values with place value and naming numbers. Numbers are usually rounded to make them easier to use or because exact values are unknown. How numbers are rounded depends on how they are used. For example, attendance at a major league baseball game may be 54321. Although the attendance could be rounded to the nearest ten (54320) or the nearest hundred (54300), it is more likely to be reported as "about 54000" or "over 50000" or "less than 60000" because these values are convenient and a little easier to comprehend and remember.

As children develop rounding skills, they should come to realize that rounding rules may vary and are not universal. For example, here are two different rules from current textbooks for rounding a number ending in 5:

1. Change the 5 to a 0 and increase the previous digit by 1.
2. Change the 5 to a 0. If the digit preceding the 5 is even, leave it alone. If the digit preceding the 5 is odd, increase it to the next even digit.

In either case, 75 would round to 80; however, 85 would round to 90 using rule 1 and 80 using rule 2. Neither rule is right or best, but this variability across textbooks can confuse children. Checking to make sure students understand the specific rules of rounding that are to be used avoids some of the confusion.

Regardless of the rounding rule used, the precision of the rounded numbers reflects the problem context. For example, a meter stick could serve as a

About how long is . . .

1 cm?
About the length of a

10 cm?
About the length of a

100 cm or 1 m?
About the height of a

1m

3rd floor

2nd floor

1st floor

1000 cm or 10 m?
About the height of a

10000 cm or 100 m?
About the length of a

Your turn:

Name another "thing" that is about as long as

1 cm ________ 10 cm ________

100 cm or 1 m ________ 1000 cm or 10 m ________

10000 cm or 100 m ________

FIGURE 8-15 A bulletin board display to develop benchmarks of length.

number line. Consider this train of Cuisenaire rods, with 7 decimeter rods and 4 centimeter rods:

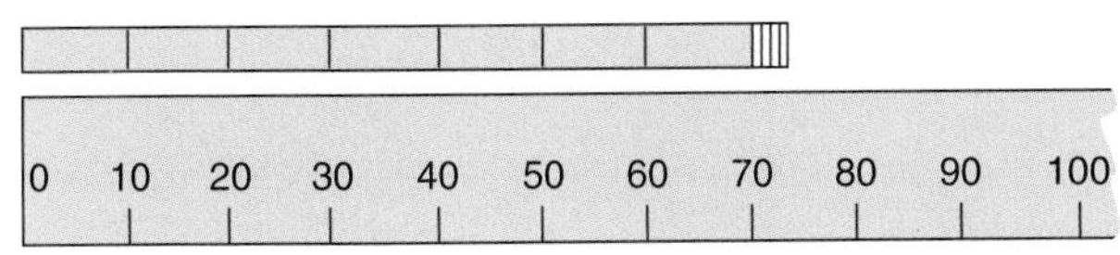

Is the train closer to 7 or 8 decimeters?

Is it closer to 0 or 1 meter?

If you round to the nearest decimeter, then the length is 7 decimeters. If you round to the nearest meter, the length is 1 meter. How numbers are rounded depends on how the values will be used. For example, if you were to cut a strip of cloth to cover this train, it would be foolish to round to the nearest decimeter and cut a length of 7 decimeters; however, a meter of cloth would provide plenty of material to cover the train. Children must think about numbers before rounding them and not just indiscriminately apply rounding rules.

Even in a given context, interpretation of rounded numbers is challenging, as illustrated by this national assessment question:

> The length of a dinosaur was reported to have been 80 feet (rounded to the nearest 10 feet). What length other than 80 feet could have been the actual length of the dinosaur?

Several different answers, such as 76 or 84 feet, were acceptable. Only 20 percent of the fourth graders and less than half of the eighth graders reported an acceptable answer. This performance shows that interpreting a rounded result needs to be addressed in elementary and middle grades.

How Many Beans?

This jar is full of beans.

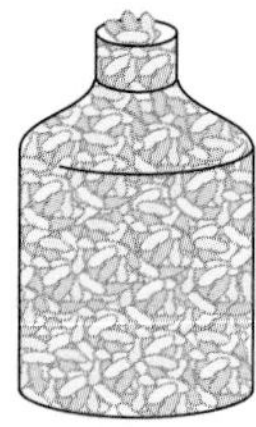

• Estimate about how many beans are in the jar. ____

This cup holds about 100 beans.

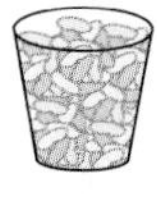

One cup of beans has been poured in the jar.

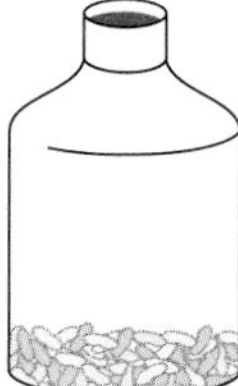

• Now estimate about how many beans are in the jar. ____

Four cups of beans have been poured into the jar.

• About how many beans do you think are in the jar now? ____

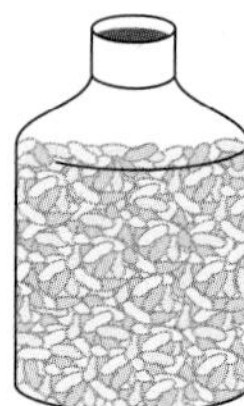

FIGURE 8-16 Using benchmarks to estimate.

Base-ten blocks provide a natural method for developing rounding skills with larger numbers. Questions such as these focus attention on the quantity and the idea of *closer to*, which is essential in rounding:

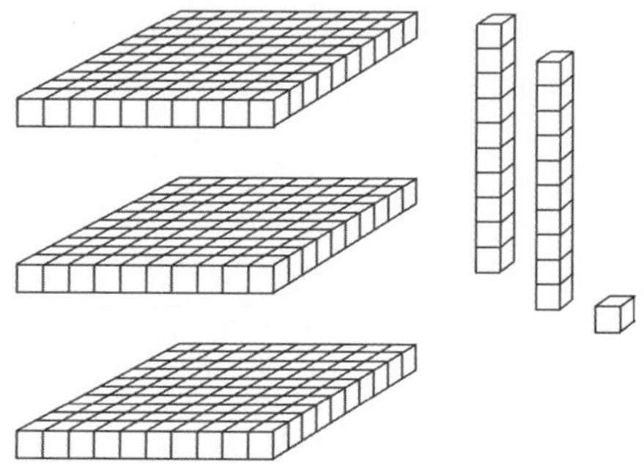

Is this more than three hundred? [yes]

Is this more than four hundred? [no]

Is this closer to three or four hundred? [closer to three hundred]

This model can also be extended to help children become more aware that 350 is halfway between 300 and 400.

A rollercoaster model could be used to develop rounding skills. If children understand the number line, the rollercoaster provides an effective tool for rounding.

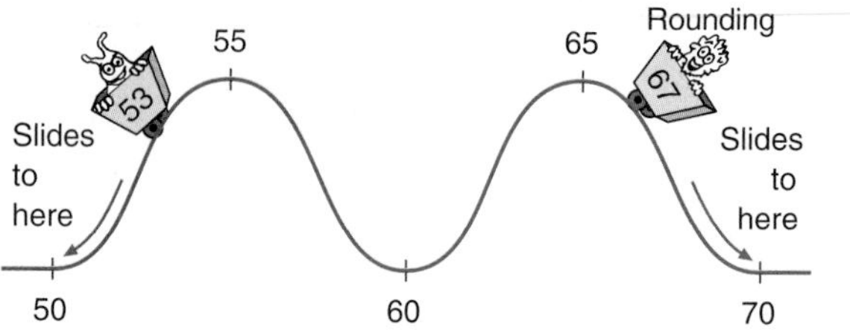

Children know what happens when the coaster stops at certain points. The model also suggests that something special happens at the top: The coaster could roll either way. This observation provides an opportunity to discuss a rule of rounding, such as "if the number ends in 5, you go over the hump to the next valley." In rounding, attention is given to the back-end digit or digits. Children should view rounding as something that not only makes numbers easier to handle but, more important, makes sense.

Perhaps the biggest difficulty related to rounding is knowing whether to round to the nearest ten, hundred, thousand, or whatever. Normally this decision depends on the purpose of rounding and the context of the problem. Consider, for example, the following well-known (to sports fans) situation:

> Carl Furillo (former Major League Baseball player for the Dodgers) had a lifetime batting average of .2994 in the major leagues, yet he is not considered a .300 hitter.

This suggests that Major League Baseball has a particular procedure for rounding batting averages.

Encourage students to explore different ways to round. For example, consider these prices:

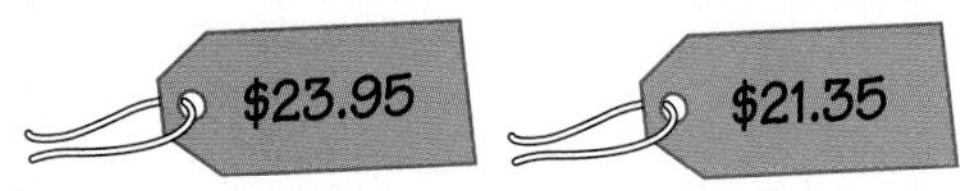

> How would you round these prices if you wanted to round them to the same number?
>
> What would you round these prices to, in deciding how much money is needed to make each purchase?

Such real-world situations encourage students to think about both the advantages and consequences of rounding numbers. Meaningful rounding (knowing how much precision is necessary and what to round to) will improve through practice in many different problem contexts.

A Glance at Where We've Been

Children must have a clear understanding of our number system if they are going to be mathematically literate. They must be able to distinguish the four characteristics of our number system: the role of zero, the additive property of numbers, a base of ten, and place value. Many counting and trading experiences (particularly grouping by tens) are necessary.

As children develop their skills with the aid of various models (such as bean sticks, base-ten blocks, and an abacus), they need to learn how to organize the results in some systematic fashion and record them. Place-value mats serve as a visual reminder of the quantities involved and provide a bridge toward the symbolic representation of larger numbers. Establishing these bridges from the concrete to the abstract is the heart of good teaching. It is particularly critical in developing place value, whose importance is second to none in all later development of number concepts.

Place-value concepts are developed over many years. The trading rules help plant the seeds early, but recognition of the power and importance of place value is developed, refined, extended, and expanded throughout the study of mathematics. Estimation provides a natural setting for students to experience larger numbers and develop place-value concepts via rounding.

Systematic study of place value over a long period is essential. For example, review of important place-value concepts must be provided as computation is being established. This type of study also provides an opportunity not only to maintain but also to extend many place-value concepts learned earlier. The point is that place value is not just taught for a couple of days in one or two grades; rather, systematic instruction on place value must be planned and integrated throughout the elementary school mathematics program.

Things to Do: From What You've Read

1. Identify four characteristics of our number system. Select one characteristic and make a visual representation of it.
2. Show how 201 and 120 would be represented with three different place-value models.
3. Distinguish between proportional and nonproportional models. Name an example of each.
4. Tell why trading activities are so important with respect to place value. Describe several materials that could be used for trading.
5. Estimation provides many opportunities to explore place value. Describe an estimation activity that would encourage students to think about 10, 100, 1000, and 10000 and distinguish among these values.
6. Describe some ways that benchmarks are used in estimating length and quantity.
7. Describe ways in which modeling, reading, and writing numbers can be used to get children actively involved in talking about mathematics and linking concrete materials with their symbolic representations.
8. It has been suggested that centuries, decades, and millenniums can be used to demonstrate some notions of place value. Describe how this could be done.
9. Examine Lesson Idea 8-4. Show the six different numbers that could be made with the three cards. Which is closest to 400? Which number less than 400 is next closest to 400?
10. Use your calculator. Enter the largest number possible in the display and name this number. How many digits does it have? Add one to this number and describe what your calculator does.

Things to Do: Going Beyond This Book

IN THE FIELD

1. **Early Number Sense.* Ask a child some questions, such as, What number comes before seventeen? thirty? two hundred? What number comes after thirty-nine? two-hundred nine? How many tens are in forty? forty-seven? Try to capture the words students use to describe how they determined their answers. Explain how their answers help you better understand their thinking and their level of number sense.

* Additional activities, suggestions, or questions are provided in *Teaching Elementary Mathematics: A Resource for Field Experiences* (Wiley, 2004).

2. **Checking Place-Value Concepts.* Give a second or third grader some of the following tasks: Write three hundred forty eight. Write a large number. Name that number. How many tens are in 250? How many hundreds are in one thousand? Explain how the answers to these questions helped you better understand the child's development of place value. [You can find more children's place value work samples on Masters 8-4 to 8-9 in the *Helping Children Learn Mathematics Instructor's Manual* (available at the Wiley web site, www.wiley.com/college/reys.) Use these samples to increase your understanding of children's place value development.]

3. **Patterns on a Thousand Chart.* In the Classroom 8-3 provides an extension of the hundred chart. (See Appendix B for other variations.) Show the chart to at least three children (grades 3–5) and say, "Please tell me about some patterns that you see." After each description, say, "Tell me about any other patterns you see." Be sure to allow them time to think and reflect; pattern recognition takes time. Make a list of the patterns for each child and compare their observations.

IN YOUR JOURNAL

4. *Working with Base 5.* Make bean sticks for base five. In your journal, describe how to demonstrate any number up to 24 with your bean sticks and loose beans. Alternatively, use pennies and nickels for base five, and describe how you would show all numbers up to 24.

5. *Ordering Numbers.* Describe the thinking a child needs to develop to be able to order the numbers 453 and 421.

6. *Rounding Down.* Describe two real-life situations in which you would round down.

WITH ADDITIONAL RESOURCES

7. *Models for Large Numbers.* Different models exist for helping children develop a concept of large numbers. Each of the articles (Bickerton-Ross, 1988; Harrison, 1985; Joslyn, 1990; Parker and Widmer, 1991; Thompson, 1990) shows and describes useful physical models. Examine one or more of these articles and describe the approach taken to help children better understand large numbers.

8. *Understanding Large Numbers.* Select either *Number Sense and Operations* (Burton et al., 1993), *Developing Number Sense in the Middle Grades* (Reys et al., 1991), or *Number SENSE* (McIntosh et al., 1997). Choose an activity that you think would be useful to help students develop a better understanding of large numbers and demonstrate how you would implement the activity.

9. *The Importance of Number Sense.* View a segment from the videotape series *Number Sense Now!* (Fennell, 1992). Discuss ways in which this tape might help students become more sensitive to the importance and power of number sense.

10. *Standards Exploration.* Check the Number and Operation Standard for pre-K–2 (www.standards-e.nctm.org) for additional explorations of groups of ten and place value. Discuss how the samples of student work influence your thinking of place value.

WITH TECHNOLOGY

11. *Counting with a Calculator.* In the Classroom 8-2 provides a structured counting activity that can be facilitated with a calculator. Use this activity as a guide and ask primary-grade students to count by hundreds and predict which results will occur. Ask them to count with the calculator and compare results. Describe any difficulties or discoveries that you observed.

ANNOTATED BOOKS

Burns, Marilyn. *Math by All Means: Place Value Grade 1–2.* Sausalita, CA: Math Solutions Publications,1994.
Students learn about place value through explorations with grouping, counting, measuring, and graphing. Includes activities from strands of statistics, geometry, and logical reasoning.

Dehaene, Stanislas. *The Number Sense: How the Mind Creates Mathematics*. New York: Getty Center for Education in the Arts, January 2000.
Dehaene makes the case for the human mind's innate grasp of mathematics—a number sense. The book is about mathematics, but even readers with the worst math anxiety will find the book an intriguing exploration of the world of numbers and the human mind.

McIntosh, A., Reys, B., Reys, R. and Hope, J. *Simple Effective Number Experiences* (SENSE), *Grades 4–6.* Palo Alto, CA: Dale Seymour Publications, 1997.
These 10-minute activities help students develop a sense of what numbers represent and how to use them by exploring relationships and patterns, encouraging mental computation, recognizing equivalent

Book Nook for Children

Berry, David. *The Rajah's Rice: A Mathematical Folktale from India.* New York: W.W. Freeman & Company, 1994.
When Chandra, an Indian village girl who bathes the raja's elephants, cures the beasts after they fall ill, the raja offers her jewels as a reward. She refuses, accepting only a measure of rice for the hungry villagers: two grains on the first square of a chessboard, four on the second, and so on, doubling the amount for each subsequent square. Although the amount seems insignificant at first, it grows at an alarming rate, since doubling has little effect on small numbers, but an increasingly enormous effect as the numbers grow larger. The raja's storehouse is soon empty, and he must admit that he cannot fill her seemingly modest request.

Butler, Christina M. *Too Many Eggs.* Boston, MA: David R. Godine Publisher, 1988.
Mrs. Bear is baking a cake for Mr. Bear's birthday but does not know how to count. The reader helps Mrs. Bear by taking punched-out eggs from the cupboard in the back of the book and placing them in Mrs. Bear's mixing bowls throughout the story. This book is a great way to extend children's counting activities to beginning addition.

Gerstein, Mordicai. *Roll Over!* New York. Crown Publishers, 1984.
This counting book uses foldout flaps to reveal the consequences of rolling over in a crowded bed with 10 inhabitants. Readers can soon predict the outcome of the small boy's command, "Roll over," but the uniqueness of each animal who falls out of bed still provides an element of surprise. This book depicts subtraction as counting back by showing one fewer in the bed!

Hawkins, Colin, and Hawkins, Jacqui. *How Many Are in This Old Car? A Counting Book.* New York: G. P. Putnam's Sons, 1988.
Bear goes for an outing in his touring car. He is joined progressively by a variety of animals, who climb aboard despite his concern about the capability of the old car to handle a crowd. As each animal appears, cartoon-style balloons containing humorous rhyming couplets express the amusing comments and concerns of the growing number of riders. This book is a good introduction for counting on.

Parker, Tom. *In One Day.* Boston, MA: Houghton Mifflin Co., 1984.
Three hundred sixty-five statistics describing things Americans do in one day are presented in this book. Some of the diverse topics included are data on health, spending habits, accidents, crime, and our environment. Pay attention to the time when the data were collected because some of the facts are obviously outdated, but you can share facts and talk about estimation and number sense. Across the border of each page is a running list of the organizations from whom the data were collected.

Schwartz, David M. *If You Made a Million.* New York: Lothrop, Lee & Shepherd Books, 1989.
Marvelosissimo the Mathematical Magician and his team of cheerful kids (and their multitude of animal friends) wield dusters, brooms, plungers, shovels, and cement as they take on feeding fish, dusting ducks, painting pots, transplanting trees, building bridges, and babysitting ogres. For each job, they'll be paid an appropriate amount of money. But soon the questions arise—what does that much money look like, and how can it be spent, saved, or used to pay off a loan? The fantasy cleverly introduces money from 1 penny to 1 million dollars. Photographs of coins and bills show relationships, and as the denominations get larger, comparisons are used. Marvelosissimo and his friends also become involved with writing checks and earning interest on money deposited in a bank.

representations of a number, establishing benchmarks, improving estimation skills, and exploring the idea of reasonableness. Includes activity masters, teacher's notes, and ideas for extending the activities. This series includes a similar book for grades 1–2.

ANNOTATED ARTICLES

Sowder, Judith. "Estimation and Number Sense." In *Handbook of Research on Mathematics Teaching and Learning* (ed. Douglas Grouws). New York: Macmillan, 1992, pp. 371–389.
This article focuses on estimation and distinguishing between estimation and approximation. It includes research on computational estimation, the relationship between number sense and its importance for estimation, and measurement estimation. A section on assessment issues related to estimation is also included as these issues provide unique challenges to educators.

Thompson, Ian. "Teaching Place Value in the UK: Time for a Reappraisal?" *Educational Review*, 51(3), (November 2000), pp. 291–299.
This article is a critical appraisal of what is traditionally considered to be one of the most important concepts in the teaching and learning of number in primary school: place value. A consideration of the concept from a variety of perspectives suggests that the concept is too sophisticated for many young children to grasp. The conclusion drawn is that there is a need for a reappraisal of the teaching of place value in primary school.

ADDITIONAL REFERENCES

Bickerton-Ross, Linda. "A Practical Experience in Problem Solving: A '10,000' Display." *Arithmetic Teacher*, 35 (December 1988), pp. 14–15.

Burton, Grace et al. *Number Sense and Operations.* Reston, VA: NCTM, 1993.

Fennell, Francis. *Number Sense Now!* (videotape and guidebook). Reston, VA: NCTM, 1992.

Harrison, William B. "How to Make a Million." *Arithmetic Teacher*, 32 (September 1985), pp. 46–47.

Hopkins, Martha H. "Wipe Out Refined." In *Calculators in Mathematics Education*, 1992 Yearbook (eds. James T. Fey and Christian R. Hirsch). Reston, VA: NCTM, 1992.

Joslyn, Ruth E. "Using Concrete Models to Teach Large Number Concepts." *Arithmetic Teacher*, 38 (November 1990), pp. 6–9.

Kouba, Vicky L.; Carpenter, Thomas P.; and Swafford, Jane O. "Number and Operations." In *Results from the Fourth Mathematics Assessment of the National Assessment of Educational Progress* (ed. M. Lindquist). Reston, VA: NCTM, 1989.

McIntosh, Alistair; Reys, Barbara; and Reys, Robert. *Number SENSE: Simple Effective Number Sense Experiences: Grades 3–4 & 4–6.* Palo Alto, CA: Dale Seymour Publications, 1997.

National Council of Teachers of Mathematics. *Principles and Standards for School Mathematics.* Reston, VA: NCTM, 2000.

Parker, Janet, and Widmer, Connie. "How Big Is a Million?" *Arithmetic Teacher*, 39 (September 1991), pp. 38–41.

Payne, Joseph N., and Huinker, DeAnn M. "Early Number and Numeration." In *Research Ideas for the Classroom: Early Childhood Mathematics* (ed. Robert J. Jensen). Reston, VA: NCTM; and New York: Macmillan, 1993, pp. 43–70.

Reys, Barbara J.; Barger, Rita; Bruckheimer, Maxim; Dougherty, Barbara; Hope, Jack; Lembke, Linda; Markovitz, Zvia; Parnas, Andy; Reehm, Sue; Sturdevant, Ruthi; and Weber, Marianne. *Developing Number Sense in the Middle Grades.* Reston, VA: NCTM, 1991.

Thiessen, Diane, and Matthias, Margaret (eds.). *The Wonderful World of Mathematics: A Critically Annotated List of Children's Books in Mathematics.* Reston, VA: NCTM, 1998.

Thompson, Charles S. "Place Value and Larger Numbers." In *Mathematics for the Young Child* (ed. Joseph N. Payne). Reston, VA: NCTM, 1990, pp. 89–108.

Wearne, Diane, and Hiebert, James. "Place Value and Addition and Subtraction." *Arithmetic Teacher*, 41(5), (January 1994), pp. 271–275.

Yoshikawa, Shigeo. "Computational Estimation: Curriculum and Instructional Issues from the Japanese Perspective." In *Computational Alternatives for the 21st Century: Cross Cultural Perspectives from Japan and the United States* (eds. Robert E. Reys and Nobubiko Nohda). Reston, VA: NCTM, 1994.

CHAPTER 9

Operations: Meanings and Basic Facts

Snapshot of a Lesson

Objective

Children develop multiplication ideas as repeated addition and division ideas as repeated subtraction using groups of candies.

Needed Materials

Flannelboard or magnetic board; flannel or magnetic "candies": 20 small yellow, 15 medium orange, and 12 large red; disks for each child: 25 yellow, 20 orange, and 15 red.

Procedures

Read this story to children, stopping to ask questions and model each situation on the board:

Once upon a time there was a little old lady who lived in a little old house in the middle of a little old town. She was such a nice little old lady that all the children who lived in the town liked to come and visit her. For a special treat, she would often give them candy. She had three kinds, each wrapped in a different color:

- small yellow ones
- medium orange ones
- large red ones

Put a sample of each on the board.

She let the children choose the kind of candy they wanted, but she realized there could be a problem—everyone might want the largest. So she made a rule: each child could have

- 4 yellow, or
- 3 orange, or
- 2 red

Put each grouping on the board.

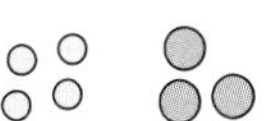

Present these situations and questions for consideration, using the board:

1. One day 3 children came to visit. They all took red candies. How many red candies could each child take? Who can show how many pieces the children took altogether?

   Expected response: $2 + 2 + 2 = 6$; possibly 3 groups of 2, 3 twos are 6, or $3 \times 2 = 6$. Have child show and count.
2. Another day, 2 children took red.

   (a) How many pieces altogether?

(b) How do you know?

(c) Is there any other way to know?

Ask questions (a), (b), and (c) for the next examples. After several examples with the whole group watching the board, have each child use disks.

3. 3 children took orange
4. 2 children took yellow
5. 4 children took orange
6. 3 children took yellow
7. If needed:
   2 children took orange
   4 children took yellow
8. 6 children—3 took yellow, 3 took red
9. 4 children—2 took red, 2 took orange
10. 5 children—2 took orange, 3 took yellow
11. If needed:
    5 children—all took yellow
    6 children—all took red
12. Suppose the old lady had 8 pieces of yellow candy. How many children could choose yellow? How do you know?

After several examples using the board, have each child solve the following problems with disks.

1. 15 orange candies (how many children?)
2. 10 red candies
3. 12 red candies
4. 12 yellow candies
5. 12 orange candies
6. 9 orange candies
7. 8 red candies

Practice

Worksheet paralleling lesson (use to evaluate):

3 children.
All took red.
Make a drawing.

Extension

1. If the old lady gave away 2 candies, how many children came? What color candies did she give? What if she gave 9 candies? 15?
2. If she gave away 6 candies, how many children might have come, and what color candies did they get? Can you find more than one answer to this question? Find some other numbers of candies that have more than one answer.
3. Pretend you see boots all lined up outside a classroom. How many children are in the room if there are 18 boots and each child left boots?
4. Ask children to make up similar problems.

Introduction

The *Snapshot of a Lesson* incorporates several essential components of a well-planned classroom activity involving computation. First and foremost, it involves the student actively in manipulating objects to answer questions. It provides problem-solving experiences that promote reasoning and discussion. "How do you know?" is an important question because it encourages students to think about "why" and not just "what." Also, computational ideas are posed in a potentially real situation.

These components are important in elementary school mathematics lessons, particularly as children develop understanding of the relevance and meaning of computational ideas. An understanding of addition, subtraction, multiplication, and division—and knowledge of the basic number facts for each of these operations—provides a foundation for all later work with computation. To be effective in this later work, children must develop broad concepts for these operations. This development is more likely to happen if you present each operation with multiple representations using various physical models. Such experiences help children recognize that an operation can be used in several different types of situations. Children also must understand the properties that apply to each operation and the relationships between operations.

Learning the basic number facts is one of the first steps children take as they refine their ideas about each operation. By using these facts, plus an understanding of place value and mathematical

Instructional programs from prekindergarten through grade 12 should enable all students to:	Pre-K–2 Expectations All students should:	Grades 3–5 Expectations All students should:
• Understand meanings of operations and how they relate to one another	• Understand various meanings of addition and subtraction of whole numbers and the relationship between the two operations • Understand the effects of adding and subtracting whole numbers • Understand situations that entail multiplication and division, such as equal groupings of objects and sharing equally	• Understand various meanings of multiplication and division • Understand the effects of multiplying and dividing whole numbers • Identify and use relationships between operations, such as division as the inverse of multiplication, to solve problems • Understand and use properties of operations, such as the distributivity of multiplication over division • Describe classes of numbers according to characteristics such as the nature of their factors
• Compute fluently and make reasonable estimates	• Develop and use strategies for whole-number computations, with a focus on addition and subtraction • Develop fluency and basic number combinations for addition and subtraction • Use a variety of methods and tools to compute, including objectives, mental computation, estimation, paper and pencil, and calculators	• Develop fluency with basic number combinations for multiplication and division and use these combinations to mentally compute related problems, such as 30×50 • Develop fluency in adding, subtracting, multiplying, and dividing whole numbers • Develop and use strategies to estimate the results of dividing whole numbers

FIGURE 9-1 Number and Operation Standard with expectations for children in grades prekindergarten–2 and 3–5.

properties, a child can perform any addition, subtraction, multiplication, or division with whole numbers. Understanding the operations and having immediate recall of number facts are essential in doing estimation, mental computation, and pencil-and-paper algorithms; but these skills are just as essential when using calculators and computers. Without such devices, the basic facts form the building blocks for performing more difficult, multidigit calculations. When calculators are readily available, the basic facts (along with operation sense and understanding of place value) provide a means for quickly checking the reasonableness of answers. Moreover, knowing the basic facts lets children perform calculations or estimate answers in many everyday situations where it would be slower to use a calculator. So no matter what type of computation a child is using—mental computation, estimation, paper-and-pencil, or a calculator—quick recall of the basic number facts for each operation is essential.

In addition to remembering basic number facts, students need to make gains in the ability to answer questions requiring computational accuracy and in situations where efficiency is useful. Figure 9-1 provides a partial listing of the expectations identified in *Principles and Standards for School Mathematics* (NCTM, 2000) description of the

Number and Operations Standard that we will focus on throughout this chapter.

FOCUS QUESTIONS

1. What different models can be used to represent each of the operations: addition, subtraction, multiplication, and division?
2. What word problems and other situations help develop meaning for each of the operations?
3. What mathematical properties pertain to each operation?
4. What is the three-phase process for helping children learn basic facts?
5. How should thinking strategies for the basic facts be taught?
6. How does number theory provide opportunities to discover mathematics in the elementary mathematics curriculum?

Math Links 9.1

The full-text electronic version of NCTM's Number and Operation Standard, with electronic examples (interactive activities), is available at the NCTM's web site, which you can access from this book's web site. Click on pre-K–2, 3–5, or 6–8 to read more about the Number and Operation Standard.

Math Links 9.2

A variety of Web resources for basic facts that may be used by teachers and children may be found at the NCTM's Illuminations web site (accessible from this book's web site) under the Number and Operation Standard.

www.wiley.com/college/reys

Helping Children Develop Number Sense and Computational Fluency

Ultimately, the instructional goal is that children not only know how to add, subtract, multiply, and divide, but, more important, know *when* to apply each operation in a problem-solving situation. Children also should be able to recall the basic facts quickly when needed.

How can teachers help children attain these skills and understandings? Begin by finding out what each child knows. Then capitalize on their knowledge while continuing to build on the number concepts they have already constructed (Kouba and Franklin, 1993). Most children entering school are ready in some ways and not ready in others for formal work on the operations. Four prerequisites for such work seem particularly important: (1) facility with counting, (2) experience with a variety of concrete situations, (3) familiarity with many problem-solving contexts, and (4) experience using language to communicate mathematical ideas.

Facility with Counting

Children use counting to solve problems involving addition, subtraction, multiplication, and division long before they come to school, as research has indicated (Baroody and Standifer, 1993). Any problem with whole numbers can be solved by counting, provided there is sufficient time. Because there is not always the time to solve problems by counting, children need to be able to use more efficient operations and procedures that help them cope with more difficult computation. Figure 9-2 illustrates this idea by comparing the counting method with the multiplication operation.

Counting nevertheless remains an integral aspect of children's beginning work with the operations. They need to know how to count forward, backward, and by twos, threes, and other groups

How many bottles?

We can count —
1, 2, 3, 4, 5, 6

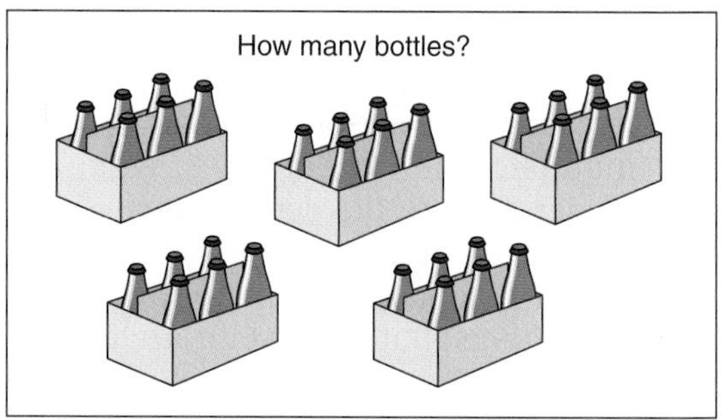
How many bottles?

We could count, but it's more efficient to use a combination of counting (6 bottles in a carton, 5 cartons) and multiplication — $5 \times 6 = 30$.

FIGURE 9-2 An example showing the efficiency of using operations.

(see Chapter 7). They need to count as they compare and analyze sets and arrays as they affirm their initial computational results, but they need more than counting to become proficient in computing.

Math Links 9.3

You can use electronic manipulatives, such as Number Line Arithmetic and Rectangle Multiplication (accessible from this book's website), to illustrate basic facts.

Experience with a Variety of Concrete Situations

Children need to have many experiences in real-life situations and in working with physical objects to develop understanding about mathematical operations. Research has indicated that work with actual physical objects promotes achievement for most children (Sowell, 1989). Understanding improves if they can relate mathematical symbols to some experience they have had or can visualize. A basic fact cannot be learned with meaning unless it has been experienced in a situation that gives it meaning.

Manipulative materials serve as a referent for later work with the operations, as well as for constructing the basic facts. They also provide a link to connect each operation to real-world problem-solving situations. Whenever a child wants to be sure that an answer is correct, materials can be used for confirmation.

Familiarity with Many Problem-Solving Contexts: Using Word Problems

Word problems are an essential part of learning to use mathematics effectively. Word problems are used in mathematics classes for developing conceptual understanding, teaching higher-level thinking and problem-solving skills, and applying a variety of mathematical ideas. Word problems require reading, comprehension, representation, and calculation. Children generally have little difficulty with single-step word problems but have more difficulty with multistep, complex problems.

As with other mathematical content, a variety of problem-solving contexts or situations should be used to familiarize students with the four basic operations, continuing all along the way until computational mastery is achieved. Children need to think of mathematics as problem solving—as a means by which they can resolve problems through applying what they know, constructing possible routes to reach solutions, and then verifying that the solutions make sense. Students must realize that mathematics is a tool that has real-life applications. Most children already know that computation is used in everyday life. Mathematics lessons need to be connected to those experiences, but students also need to realize that $6 \times 8 = \square$ or $9 + 2 = \square$ also may be problems—ones that they can solve. They need to have the attitude, "I don't know the answer, but I can work it out."

Experience in Using Language to Communicate Mathematical Ideas

Children need to talk and write about mathematics; experiences to develop meanings need to be put into words. Manipulative materials and problems can be vehicles for communicating about mathematics. Such discussion of mathematics is a critical part of meaningful learning. All early phases of instruction on the operations and basic facts should reflect the important role language plays in their acquisition. The *Principles and Standards for School Mathematics* (NCTM, 2000) discusses the roles of language in great depth in presenting the recommendations on communication, and thus provides a valuable source of additional information.

The move to symbols is often made too quickly and the use of materials dropped too soon. Instead, the use of materials should precede and then parallel the use of symbols. Children should be recording symbols as they manipulate materials. As illustrated in the lesson that opened this chapter, language should be used to describe what is happening in a given situation. Then and only then will children see the relation of symbols to manipulation of materials and problem setting (Carey, 1992).

The language that children learn as they communicate about what they are doing, and what they see happening as they use materials, helps them understand the symbolism related to operations. Thus the referent for each symbol is strengthened. Children should begin their work with operations after talking among themselves and with their teacher about a variety of experiences. They need to be encouraged to continue talking about the mathematical ideas they meet as they work with the operations. As soon as feasible, they need to put their ideas on paper—by drawings alone at first. As soon as they are able to write, children should also be encouraged to write number sentences and narrative explanations of their thinking.

Developing Meanings for the Operations

As we explained earlier, children encounter the four basic operations in natural ways when they work with many diverse problem situations. By representing these problem situations (e.g., acting them out, using physical models, or drawing pictures), they develop meanings for addition, subtraction, multiplication, and division. Mastery of basic facts and later computational work with multidigit examples must be based on a clear understanding of the operations.

Thus both computational proficiency and understanding of operations are desired outcomes of mathematics instruction. The following general sequence of activities is appropriate for helping children develop meaning for the four basic operations:

1. Concrete—modeling with materials: Use a variety of verbal problem settings and manipulative materials to act out and model the operation.
2. Semiconcrete—representing with pictures: Provide representations of objects in pictures, diagrams, and drawings to move a step away from the concrete toward symbolic representation.
3. Abstract—representing with symbols: Use symbols (especially numeric expressions and number sentences) to illustrate the operation.

In this way, children move through experiences from the concrete to the semiconcrete to the abstract, linking each to the others.

The four operations are clearly different, but there are important relationships among them that children will come to understand through modeling, pictorial, and symbolic experiences:

- Addition and subtraction are inverse operations; that is, one undoes the other:

$$5 + 8 = 13 \longleftrightarrow 13 - 5 = 8$$

- Multiplication and division are inverse operations:

$$4 \times 6 = 24 \longleftrightarrow 24 \div 4 = 6$$

- Multiplication can be viewed as repeated addition:

$$4 \times 6 \longleftrightarrow 6 + 6 + 6 + 6$$

- Division can be viewed as repeated subtraction:

$$24 \div 4 \longleftrightarrow 24 - 6 - 6 - 6 - 6$$

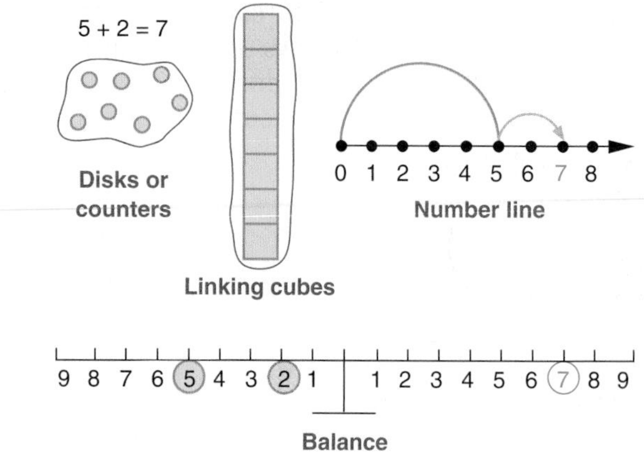

FIGURE 9-3 Some models for addition.

These relationships can be developed through careful instruction with a variety of different experiences.

Addition and Subtraction

Figure 9-3 illustrates a variety of models (including counters, linking cubes, balance scale, and number line) that can be used to represent addition. Each model depicts the idea that addition means "finding how many in all."

The models for addition can also be used for subtraction. Each model can be applied in the three following different situations that lead to subtraction.

1. *Separation,* or take away, involves having one quantity, removing a specified quantity from it, and noting what is left. Research indicates that this subtraction situation is the easiest for children to learn; however, persistent use of the words *take away* results in many children assuming that this is the *only* subtraction situation and leads to misunderstanding of the other two situations. This is why it is important to read a subtraction sentence such as $8 - 3 = 5$ as "8 minus 3 equals 5" rather than "8 take away 3 equals 5." Take away is just one of the three types of subtraction situations.

Peggy had 7 balloons. She gave 4 to other children. How many did she have left?

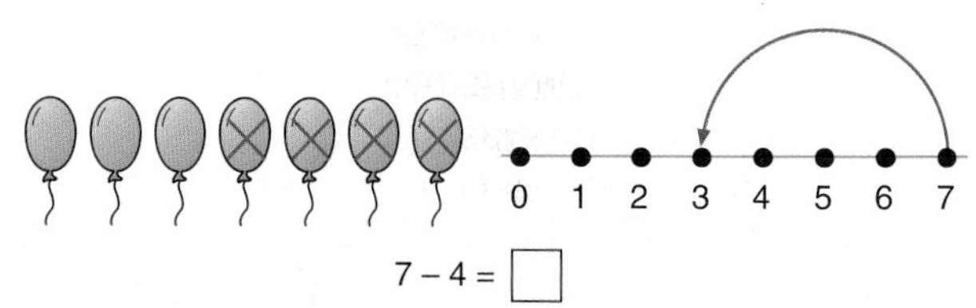

2. *Comparison*, or finding the difference, involves having two quantities, matching them one-to-one, and noting the quantity that is the difference between them. Problems of this type are also solved by subtraction, even though nothing is being taken away.

> Peggy had 7 balloons. Richard had 4 balloons. How many more balloons did Peggy have than Richard?

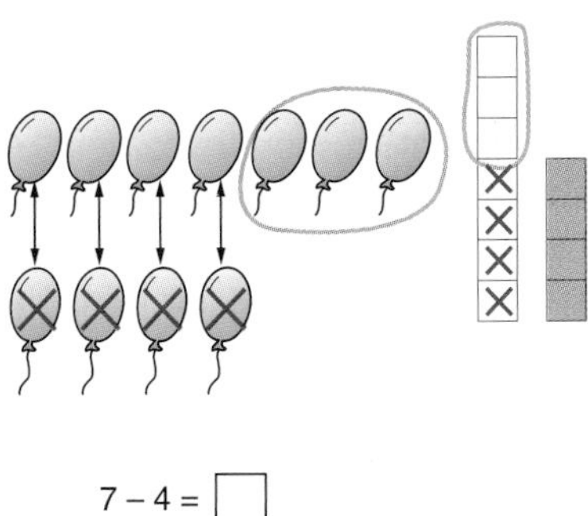

3. The final type of subtraction situation is known as *part-whole*. In this type of problem, a set of objects can logically be separated into two parts. You know how many are in the entire set and you know how many are in one of the parts. Find out how many must be in the remaining part.

> Peggy had 7 balloons. Four of them were red and the rest were blue. How many were blue?

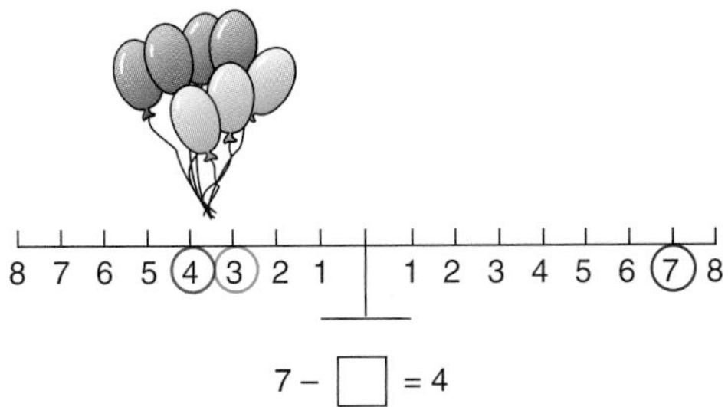

Some educators refer to this sort of subtraction situation as a "missing-addend" problem because it may be helpful to "think addition" to find the answer. For example, in the preceding problem, you could ask yourself: 4 plus what equals 7?

The importance of providing many varied experiences in which children use physical objects to model or act out examples of each operation cannot be overemphasized. The *Snapshot of a Lesson* at the beginning of this chapter provided one such experience. It illustrates a way to involve each child in forming equal-sized groups as a lead-in to learning about multiplication. Writing symbols for each action is not essential at this early stage. Moving, counting, and questioning are the important components.

Lesson Idea 9-1 illustrates a slightly more symbolic activity. The children solve problems in a variety of ways using the dot sticks, followed by individual practice. Similar activities can be done with counters, linking cubes, or other objects.

Initially, you should use symbols as a complement to the physical manipulation of objects. They are a way of showing the action with the materials and should always be introduced in conjunction with a concrete material or model. As the work progresses, the amount of symbolization you offer and encourage should increase.

The number line is used in some textbooks as a model for addition and subtraction, but it must be used with caution. Over the years, research has

Lesson Idea 9-1

DOT STICKS

Objective: Children model and solve addition problems using dot sticks.

Grade Level: 1

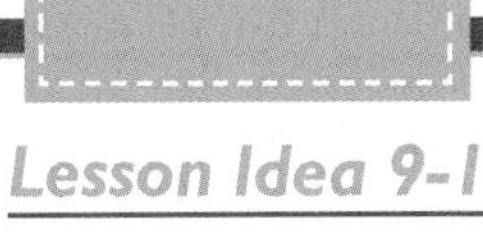

- Ask children to pick up 4 dots. (Most children will pick up the 4 stick.)
  - Is there another way to pick up 4 dots?

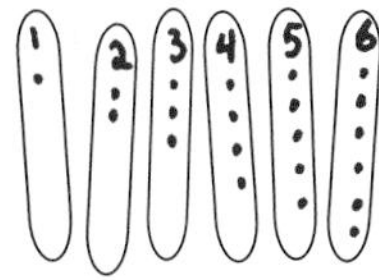

- Now ask them to pick up 6 dots.
  - How many ways can you do it?
  - Can you pick up 6 dots using 3 sticks?
- Ask for 11 dots.
  - Can you do it with 2 sticks?
  - 3 sticks?
  - 4 sticks?
- Ask for 8 dots using only 3 sticks.
- Ask how many different ways you can pick up 10 dots: List them on the chalkboard.
- Follow up with individual worksheets.

shown that children often find number lines difficult to use and interpret. Sometimes they are not sure whether they should count spaces between tic-marks or the tic-marks themselves when attempting to model a problem, or they may not be sure where on the number line to begin counting. (For example, to find 5 + 7 on a number line, they may put their finger on 5 as they begin counting from 1 up to seven, whereas they actually should begin counting when pointing at 6.) In other cases, children seem unsure how to relate the number line to a problem situation. For example, consider this number line:

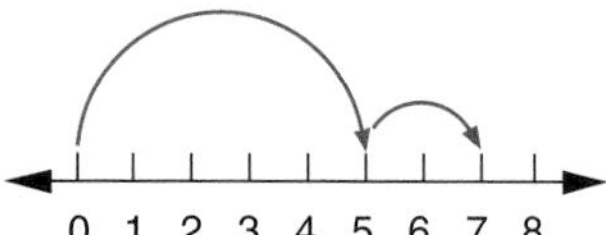

In the second national mathematics assessment, about twice as many nine-year-olds responded that "5 + 7" was pictured as did those responding with the correct answer, "5 + 2 = 7." The same error was made by 39 percent of the 13-year-olds. Carpenter et al. (1981, p. 19) suggested:

> Since the model does not seem to clearly suggest the operation, the meaning must be developed or misunderstandings may occur. The mathematics curriculum should be constructed to ensure that students have a meaningful development of the basic operations. Certainly, many types of models can help this development, but they must be carefully selected and meaningfully taught.

Multiplication and Division

The same sequence of experiences used for developing understanding of addition and subtraction—moving from concrete, to pictorial, to symbolic—should also be followed for multiplication and division; however, one important way that multiplication and division problems differ from addition and subtraction problems is that the numbers in the problems represent different sorts of things. For example, consider a problem such as "Andrew has two boxes of trading cards. Each box holds 24 cards. How many cards does he have altogether?" This problem may be written $2 \times 24 = 48$, where the *first factor* (2) tells us how many groups or sets of equal size are being considered, while the *second factor* (24) tells us the size of each set. The third number (48), known as the *product*, indicates the total of all the parts (here, the total number of cards). By contrast, the old saying "you can't add apples and oranges" points out the fact that in addition and subtraction problems, a common label must be attached to *all* the numbers involved. Apples and oranges can be added only if we relabel all the numbers in the problem with a common label (such as "fruit"). In the trading card problem, the labels for the numbers would be, respectively, boxes (2), cards per box (24), and cards (48).

Figure 9-4 illustrates some of the most commonly used models for illustrating multiplication situations: sets of objects, arrays, and the number line. Research indicates that children do best when they can use various representations for multiplication and division situations and can explain the relationships among those representations (Kouba and Franklin, 1995).

Researchers have identified four distinct sorts of multiplicative structures: equal groups, multiplicative comparisons, combinations, and areas/arrays (Greer, 1992). Problems involving the first two of these structures are most common in elementary school, although students should eventually become familiar with all four. The four multiplicative structures are described here to help you, as the teacher, understand and recognize their variety. You are not expected to teach these labels to children, but you should try to ensure that they

Math Links 9.4

If you would like to see a variety of lesson plans for developing addition and subtraction meaningfully, Do It with Dominoes and Links Away may be found at the NCTM's Illuminations web site, which you can access from this book's web site.

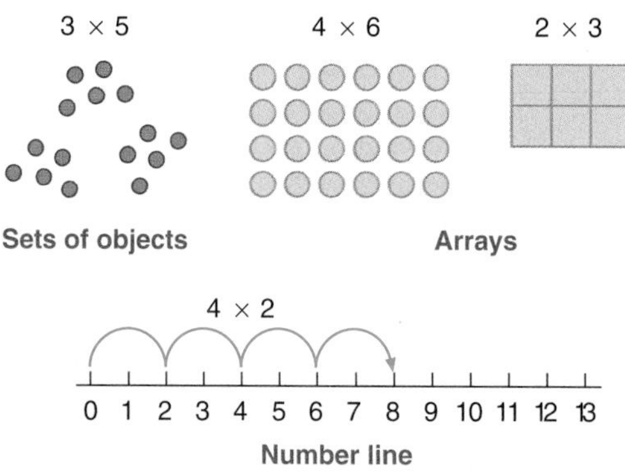

FIGURE 9-4 Commonly used models for multiplication.

encounter a broad range of problem situations involving multiplication and division.

1. *Equal-groups problems* involve the most common type of multiplicative structure. When both the number and size of the groups are known (but the total is unknown), the problem can be solved by multiplication. The problem given earlier, about Andrew's trading card collection, is an example of an equal-groups problem. When the total in an equal-groups problem is known, but either the number of groups or the size of the group is unknown, the problem can be solved by division. The two distinct types of division situations that can arise (depending on which part is unknown) are measurement or partition division (described later).

2. *Comparison problems* involve another common multiplicative structure. With comparison problems for subtraction, there were two different sets that needed to be matched one-to-one to decide how much larger one was than the other. In similar fashion, comparision problems with multiplicative structures involve two different sets, but the relationship is not one-to-one. Rather, in multiplicative situations, one set involves multiple copies of the other. An example of a multiplicative comparision situation might be: "Hilary spent \$35 on Christmas gifts for her family. Geoff spent 3 times as much. How much did Geoff spend?" In this case, Hilary's expenditures are being compared with Geoff's, and the problem is solved by multiplication. The question does not involve "How much more?" (as it would if the problem involved additive/subtractive comparision). Instead, the structure of the problem involves "How many times as much?" If the problem is changed slightly to include information about how much Geoff spent but to make either Hilary's expenditures unknown or the comparison multiplier unknown, then the problem could be solved by division. Examples of these problem structures are: (a) Hilary spent a certain amount on Christmas gifts for her family, and Geoff spent 3 times as much. If Geoff spent \$105, how much did Hilary spend? (b) Hilary spent \$35 on Christmas gifts for her family and Geoff spent \$105. How many times as much money as Hilary spent did Geoff spend?

3. *Combinations problems* involve still another sort of multiplicative structure. Here the two factors represent the sizes of two different sets and the product indicates how many different pairs of things can be formed, with one member of each pair taken from each of the two sets. Combination problems are also sometimes known as *Cartesian product problems* (Quintero, 1985). For example, consider the number of different sundaes possible with four different ice cream flavors and two toppings, if each sundae can have exactly one ice cream flavor and one topping:

Toppings	Ice cream flavors: Vanila	Cherry	Mint	Chocolate
Pineapple				
Butterscotch				

Other examples of combination problems are the number of choices for outfits given 5 T-shirts and 4 shorts or the number of different sandwiches possible with 3 choices of meat, 2 choices of cheese, and 2 kinds of bread.

4. Finally, *area and array problems* also are typical examples of multiplicative structure. The area of any rectangle (in square units) can be found either by covering the rectangle with unit squares and counting them all individually or by multiplying the width of the rectangle (number of rows of unit squares) by the length (number of unit squares in each row). Similarly, in a rectangular array—an arrangement of discrete, countable objects (such as chairs in an auditorium)—the total number of objects can be found by multiplying the number of rows by the number of objects in each row. The array model for multiplication can be especially effective in helping children visualize multiplication. It may serve as a natural extension of children's prior work in making and naming rectangles using tiles, geoboards, or graph paper:

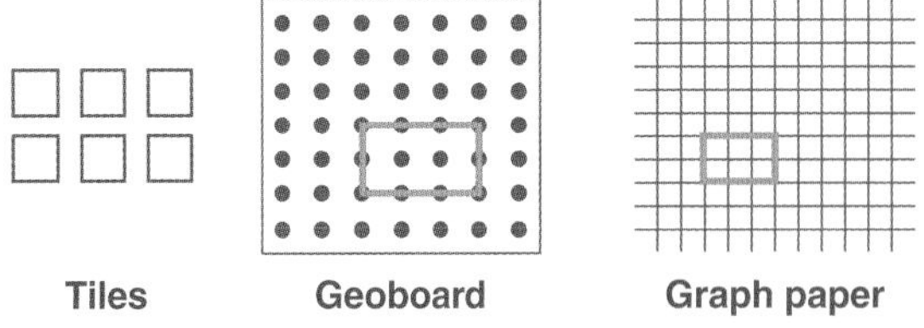

These illustrations show a 2-by-3 or 3-by-2 rectangle. Thus, each rectangle contains six small squares. Asking children to build and name numerous rectangles with various numbers is a good readiness experience for the concept of multiplication. In the Classroom 9-1 through 9-3 illustrate several experiences designed for this purpose.

Just as sets of objects, the number line, and arrays are useful in presenting multiplication, they can also be useful in presenting division, with the

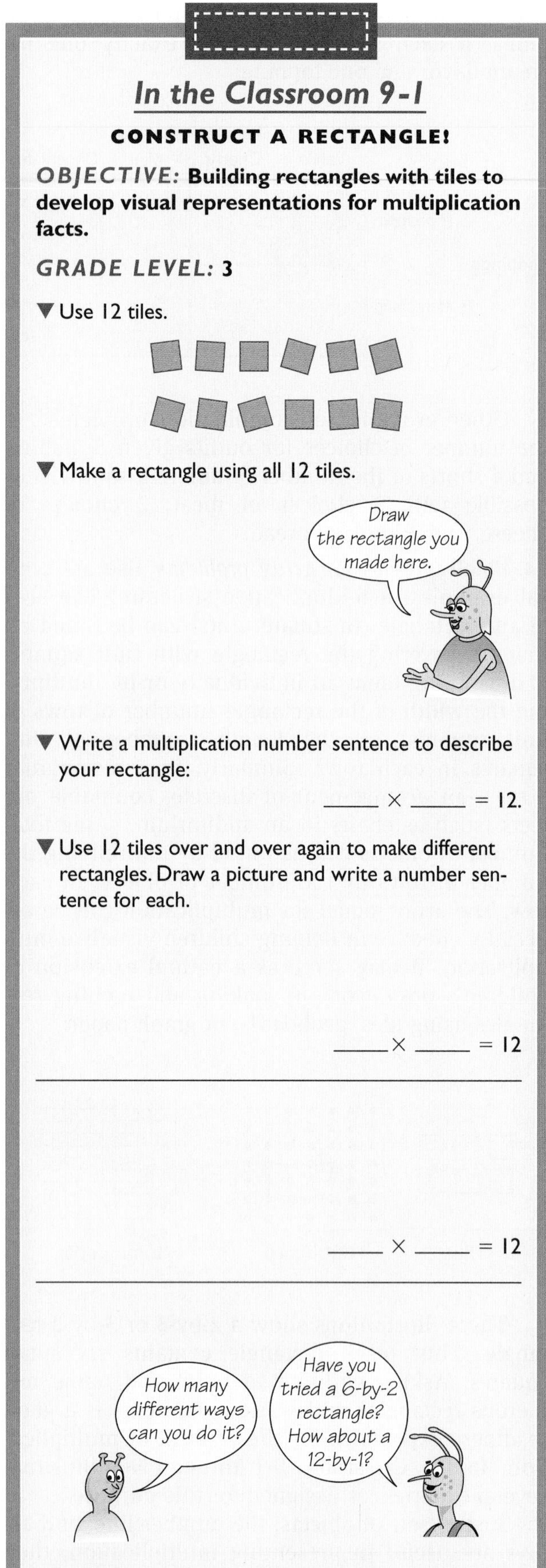

▼ Use 12 tiles over and over again to make different rectangles. Draw a picture and write a number sentence for each.

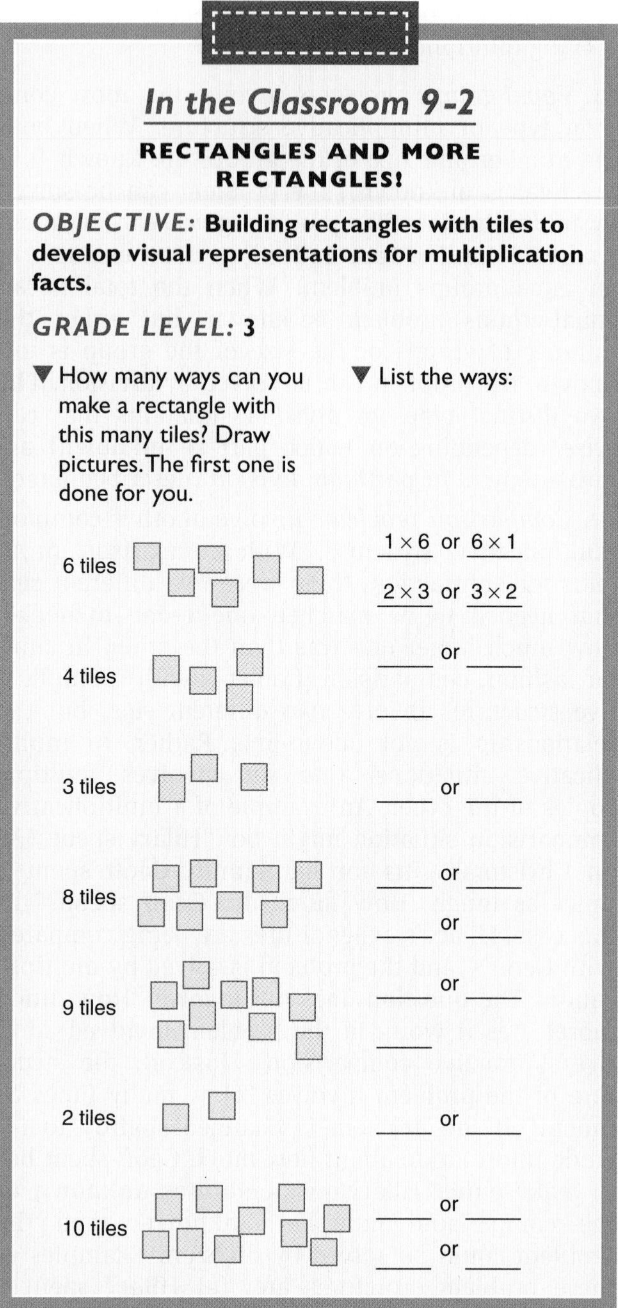

relationship to repeated subtraction frequently shown. For division, however, two different types of situations must be considered: *measurement* and *partition*.

Have you tried a 6-by-2 rectangle? How about a 12-by-1?

In the Classroom 9-2
RECTANGLES AND MORE RECTANGLES!
OBJECTIVE: Building rectangles with tiles to develop visual representations for multiplication facts.
GRADE LEVEL: 3
▼ Use 12 tiles.
▼ Write a multiplication number sentence to describe your rectangle:
▼ How many ways can you make a rectangle with this many tiles? Draw pictures. The first one is done for you.
▼ List the ways:
6 tiles
1 × 6 or 6 × 1
2 × 3 or 3 × 2
4 tiles
____ or ____
3 tiles
____ or ____
8 tiles
____ or ____
____ or ____
9 tiles
____ or ____
2 tiles
____ or ____
10 tiles
____ or ____
____ or ____

1. In *measurement* (or repeated subtraction) situations, you know how many objects are in each group and must determine the number of groups.

> Jenny had 12 candies. She gave 3 to each person. How many people got candies?

Here, you can imagine Jenny beginning with 12 candies and making piles of 3 repeatedly until all the candies are gone. She is measuring how

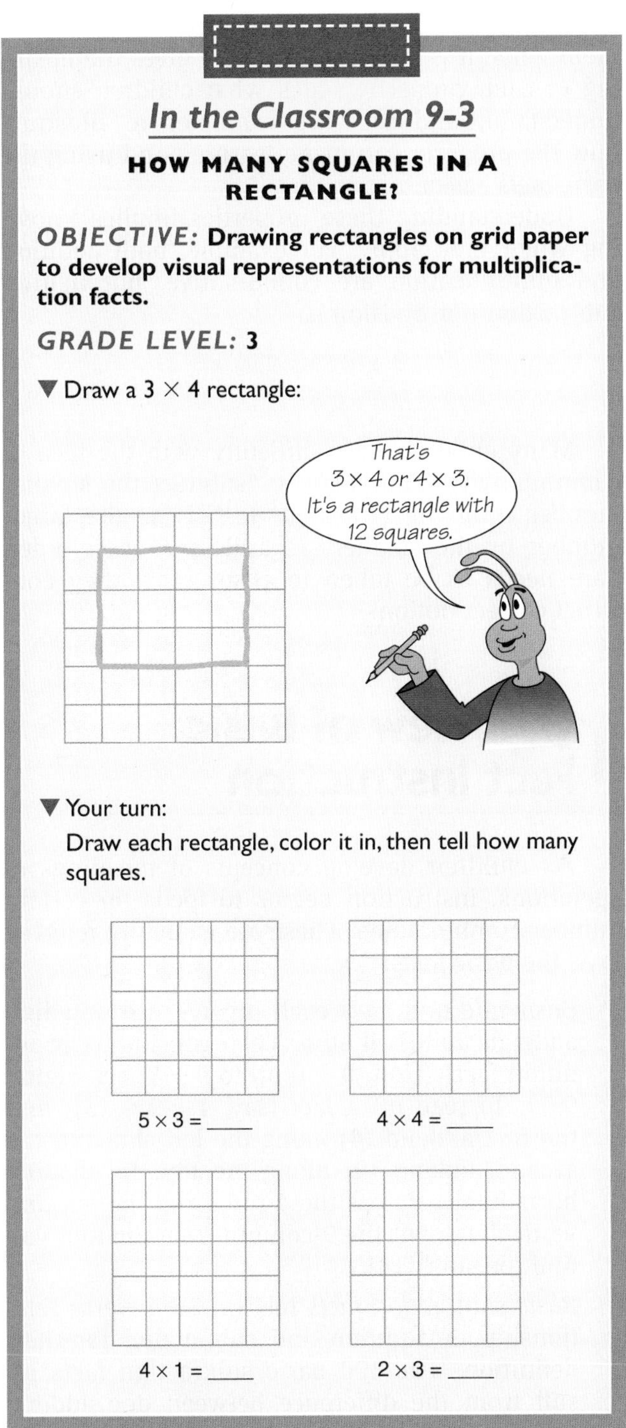

many groups of 3 she can make from the original pile of 12.

In the Classroom 9-3
HOW MANY SQUARES IN A RECTANGLE?
OBJECTIVE: Drawing rectangles on grid paper to develop visual representations for multiplication facts.
GRADE LEVEL: 3
▼ Draw a 3 × 4 rectangle:
That's 3 × 4 or 4 × 3. It's a rectangle with 12 squares.
▼ Your turn:
Draw each rectangle, color it in, then tell how many squares.
5 × 3 = ____
4 × 4 = ____
4 × 1 = ____
2 × 3 = ____

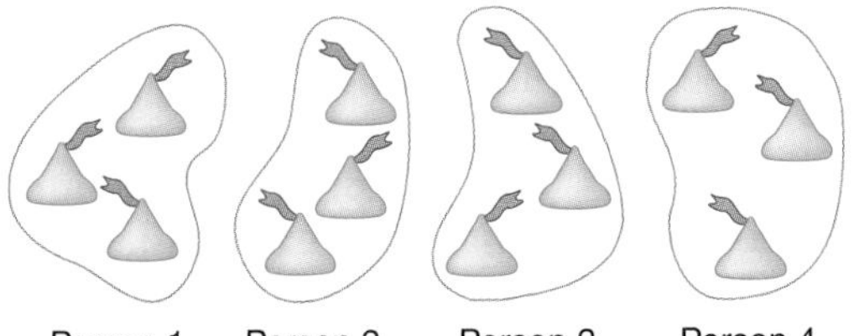

Another example might be measuring how many 2-foot hair ribbons can be made from a 10-foot roll of ribbon. Imagine repeatedly stretching out 2 feet and cutting it off, thus measuring how many hair ribbons you can make.

2. *Partition*, or sharing, situations are those in which a collection of objects is separated into a given number of equivalent groups and you seek the number in each group. By contrast with measurement situations, here you already know how many groups you want to make, but you don't know how many objects must be put in each group.

> Gil had 15 shells. If he wanted to share them equally among 5 friends, how many should he give to each?

Here imagine Gil passing out the shells to his five friends (one for you, one for you, one for you, then a second to each person, and so on) until they are all distributed, and then checking to see how many each person got.

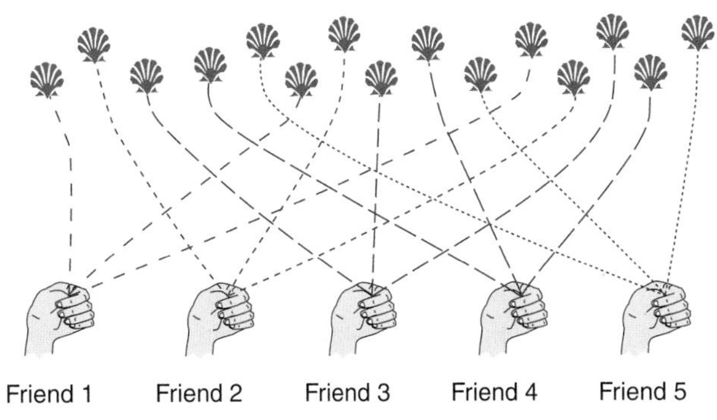

Partitioning (or sharing) is difficult to show in a diagram, but it is relatively easy to have children act out. Dealing cards for a game is another instance of a partition situation.

It is certainly not necessary for children to learn these terms or to name problems as measurement or partition situations, but it is important for you as a teacher to know about the two types of division situations so you can ensure that your students have opportunities to work with examples of each. It is vital that students be able to identify when a problem situation requires division, and that means being able to recognize both types of situations as involving division. Lesson Idea 9-2 illustrates an activity that can be used to introduce the idea of division to children in a meaningful way.

Lesson Idea 9-2

LOTS OF LINKS

Objective: Children model division with remainders using links to make equal-sized groups.

Grade Level: 3–4

Materials: 20 links (or other counters) for each child; an overhead projector

Activity: Discuss with children different ways to separate the links into equal-sized groups.

- Scatter 12 links on an overhead projector.
  - How can we place these links into equal-sized groups? (6 groups of 2, 4 groups of 3, 1 group of 12, etc.)
  - How many different ways can we do it?
- Scatter 15 links on the projector.
  - How many different ways can these links be split into equal-sized groups?
  - What happens if we try dividing 13 links into groups of 5?

  CCCCC CCCCC CCC 2 groups and 3 leftovers
- Focus on numbers that can be divided into equal-sized groups without "leftovers":
  - Which of these numbers can be divided into groups of 3 without having leftovers?

    8 4 7 3 18

    Try each one.
  - Name a number that will have no leftovers if we divide it into groups of 5. How many numbers like this can you name?
  - Name a number that will have 1 leftover if we divide it into groups of 5. Can you name 3 numbers like this?

Mathematical Properties

An understanding of the mathematical properties that pertain to each operation (Table 9-1) is vital to children's understanding of the operation and how to use it. This understanding is not a prerequisite to work with operations, but it must be developed as part of understanding operations.

In elementary school, children are not expected to state these properties precisely or identify them by name. Rather, the instructional goal is to help children understand the commutative, associative, distributive, and identity properties and to use them when it is efficient. Table 9-1 gives the meaning of each property, states what children should understand, and provides examples to illustrate how the property can make learning and using the basic facts easier.

Understanding these properties implies knowing when they apply. For example, both addition and multiplication are commutative, but neither subtraction nor division is:

$7 - 3$ is *not* equal to $3 - 7$

$28 \div 7$ is *not* equal to $7 \div 28$

Many children have difficulty with the idea of commutativity. They tend to "subtract the smaller number from the larger" or to "divide the larger number by the smaller" regardless of their order. Care needs to be taken to ensure that they construct correct notions.

Overview of Basic Fact Instruction

As children develop concepts of meanings of operations, instruction begins to focus on certain number combinations. These are generally referred to as the *basic facts:*

- *Basic addition facts* each involve two one-digit addends and their sum. There are 100 basic addition facts (from $0 + 0$ up to $9 + 9$; see Figure 9-5). To read off a fact (say, $4 + 9 = 13$), find the first addend (4) along the left side and the second addend (9) along the top. By reading horizontally across the 4-row from the left and vertically down the 9-column from the top, you find the sum (13).
- *Basic subtraction facts* rely on the inverse relationship of addition and subtraction for their definition. The 100 basic subtraction facts result from the difference between one addend and the sum for all one-digit addends. Thus the 100 subtraction facts are also pictured in Figure 9-5, the same table that pictures the 100 basic addition facts. You read off a basic subtraction fact (say, $13 - 4 = 9$) by finding the box in the 4-row that contains the sum 13, then reading up that column to find the difference (9) at the top of the table. Note that a sentence such as $13 - 2 = 11$ is neither represented in Figure 9-5 nor considered a basic subtraction fact because $2 + 11 = 13$ is not a basic addition fact (since 11 is not a one-digit addend).

Table 9-1 • Mathematical Properties for Elementary-School Children

Property	Mathematical Language	Child's Language	How It Helps
Commutative	For all numbers a and b: $a + b = b + a$ and $a \times b = b \times a$	If 4 + 7 = 11, then 7 + 4 must equal 11, too. If I know 4 × 7, I also know 7 × 4.	The number of addition or multiplication facts to be memorized is reduced from 100 to 55.
Associative	For all numbers a, b, and c: $(a + b) + c = a + (b + c)$ and $(ab)c = a(bc)$	When I'm adding (or multiplying) three or more numbers, it doesn't matter where I start.	When more than two numbers are being added (or multiplied), combinations that make the task easier can be chosen. For example, 37 × 5 × 2 can be done as 37 × (5 × 2) or 37 × 10 rather than (37 × 5) × 2.
Distributive	For all numbers a, b, and c: $a(b + c) = ab + ac$	8 × (5 + 2) is the same as (8 × 5) + (8 × 2).	Some of the more difficult basic facts can be split into smaller, easier-to-remember parts. For example, 8 × 7 is the same as (8 × 5) + (8 × 2) or 40 + 16.
Identity	For any whole number a: $a + 0 = a$ and $a \times 1 = a$	0 added to any number is easy; it's just that number. 1 times any number is just that number.	The 19 addition facts involving 0 and the 19 multiplication facts involving 1 can be easily remembered once this property is understood and established.

- *Basic multiplication facts* each involve two one-digit factors and their product. There are 100 basic multiplication facts (from 0 × 0 up to 9 × 9).
- *Basic division facts* rely on the inverse relationship of multiplication and division, but there are only 90 basic division facts. Because division by zero is not possible, there are no facts with zero as the divisor.

+	0	1	2	3	4	5	6	7	8	9
0	0	1	2	3	4	5	6	7	8	9
1	1	2	3	4	5	6	7	8	9	10
2	2	3	4	5	6	7	8	9	10	11
3	3	4	5	6	7	8	9	10	11	12
4	4	5	6	7	8	9	10	11	12	13
5	5	6	7	8	9	10	11	12	13	14
6	6	7	8	9	10	11	12	13	14	15
7	7	8	9	10	11	12	13	14	15	16
8	8	9	10	11	12	13	14	15	16	17
9	9	10	11	12	13	14	15	16	17	18

FIGURE 9-5 The 100 basic facts for addition.

Development and mastery of the addition and subtraction facts begins in kindergarten or first grade and continues as multiplication and division facts are developed and practiced in third and fourth grades. Some children, however, have not mastered the facts several years later. Sometimes the problem may be a learning disability that makes it virtually impossible for a child to memorize the facts. Use of a calculator may allow such a child to proceed with learning mathematics. Or, as research by Clark and Kamii (1996) indicates for multiplication, a child may have trouble with multiplication facts because he or she has not developed the ability to think multiplicatively.

More commonly, children's difficulties in mastering basic facts may stem from one (or both) of the following two causes, and in these cases teachers can definitely provide help. First, the underlying numerical understandings may not have been developed. Thus the process of remembering the facts quickly and accurately becomes no more than rote memorization or meaningless manipulation of symbols. As a result, the child has trouble remembering the facts. Second, the skill of fact retrieval itself may not be taught by teachers or understood by children, resulting in inefficient strategies. Teachers can do something about both of these problems by using a three-phase process for helping children learn basic facts:

- *Get ready*: Start from where the children are.
- *Get set*: Build understandings.
- *Go*: Focus on how to remember facts.

Get Ready: Starting Where Children Are

Many children come to school knowing some basic facts. For instance, the chances are great that they can say "one and one are two," "two and two are four," and maybe even "five and five are ten." They may know that 2 and 1 more is 3, and that 6 and "nothing more" is still 6. But they probably don't know that $6 + 7 = 13$, nor do they have a clear concept of the meanings of symbols such as + and =.

Similarly, they may know that if you have 3 and take away 2, you have only 1 left. But they probably won't know $3 - 2 = 1$ (or "three minus two equals one"). They may know that buying three pieces of gum at 5¢ each will cost 15¢, but they won't know that $3 \times 5 = 15$. They may know that eight cookies shared among four children means that each child gets two cookies, but they won't know that $8 \div 4 = 2$.

In other words, they can solve simple problems involving facts, but they are not likely to be able to either recognize or write the facts. Nor do many children understand *why* $5 + 5 = 10$ or realize that $4 + 2 = \square$ asks the same question as:

$$\begin{array}{r} 4 \\ +2 \\ \hline \end{array}$$

It is our task to help children organize what they know, construct more learning to fill in the gaps, and, in the process, develop meaning.

You need to begin by determining what each child knows, using responses from group discussions, observations of how each child works with materials and with paper-and-pencil activities, and individual interviews. Many teachers use an inventory at the beginning of the year, administered individually to younger children and in a questionnaire format in later grades. The purpose of such an inventory is to discover:

- Whether the children have the concept of an operation: "What does it mean to add?" "Why did you subtract?" "When can you multiply?"
- What basic facts they understand (demonstrated by drawing a picture to illustrate a written fact or, conversely, by writing the fact for a given illustration)
- What strategies they use to find the solution to combinations: "How did you know $7 + 9 = 16$?"
- What basic facts they know fluently (can answer within about 3 seconds, without stopping to figure them out)

Teachers use such information to plan instruction. Do some children need more work with manipulative materials to understand what multiplication means? Do some children need help in seeing the relationship of $17 - 8$ and $8 + 9$? Do some children need to be taught that counting on from a number is quicker than counting each number? Which children need regular practice in order to master the facts? You can group children to meet individual needs (as suggested in Chapter 3) and provide activities and direct instruction to fill in the missing links and strengthen understanding and competency. The calculator can be one of the tools. Research has indicated that the development of basic facts is enhanced through calculator use.

Get Set: Building Understanding of the Basic Facts

The emphasis in helping children learn the basic facts is on aiding them in organizing their thinking and seeing relationships among the facts. Children should learn to use strategies for remembering the facts before drill to develop fluency.

Generally, the facts with both addends or both factors greater than 5 are more difficult for most children, but that is relatively difficult to determine with accuracy. What is difficult for an individual child is really the important point. Although many textbooks, workbooks, and computer programs emphasize practice on the generally difficult facts, many also encourage the child to keep a record of those facts that are difficult for him or her and suggest extra practice on those. The teacher should suggest or reinforce this idea.

How can the basic facts for an operation be organized meaningfully? Many textbooks present facts in small groups (e.g., facts with sums to 6: $0 + 6 = 6$, $1 + 5 = 6$, $2 + 4 = 6$, and so forth). Other textbooks organize the facts in "families" (for example, facts in the "2–3–5 family" are $3 + 2 = 5$, $2 + 3 = 5$, $5 - 3 = 2$, and $5 - 2 = 3$). Still other textbooks organize the facts by "thinking strategies" (e.g., all facts where 1 is added, or containing "doubles" such as $7 + 7$). No one order for teaching the basic facts has been shown to be superior to any other order. Thus the teacher can use professional judgment about what each group of children needs and choose whether to use the sequence in a given textbook.

A variety of thinking strategies can be used to recall the answer to any given fact. Thinking strategies are efficient methods for determining answers on the basic facts. The more efficient the strategy, the more quickly the student will be able to construct the correct answer for the sum, difference, product, or quotient of two numbers and, eventually, develop fluency with the facts so he or she can quickly recall them.

Research has shown that certain thinking strategies help children learn the basic facts (Rathmell, 1978; Thornton and Smith, 1988). Understanding of the facts develops in a series of stages characterized by the thinking children use. Some of these thinking strategies involve using concrete materials or counting. Others are more mature in the sense that a known fact is used to figure out an unknown fact. Teachers want to help children develop these mature, efficient strategies to help them recall facts. The next section on thinking strategies for basic facts provides more detail on how these skills can be developed.

Many children rely heavily on counting—in particular, finger counting—and fail to develop more efficient ways of recalling basic facts. For example, a child might count 4 fingers and then 5 more to solve 4 + 5. This strategy is perfectly acceptable at first; however, this counting process should not be repeated every time 4 + 5 is encountered. Teachers want the child to move beyond counting on from 4 (which is relatively slow and inefficient), to thinking "4 + 4 = 8, so 4 + 5 is 9" or using some other more efficient strategy. Eventually, the child must be able to recall "4 + 5 = 9" quickly and effortlessly. Some children discover efficient fact strategies on their own, but many need explicit instruction. When the teacher is satisfied that the children are familiar with a particular strategy (able to model it with materials and beginning to use it mentally), it is time to practice the strategy.

Math Links 9.5

A variety of drill activities may be found on the web. For example you can try games such as Mathcar Racing, Soccer Shootout, Tic Tac Toe Squares, Line Jumper, and Power Football, all of which you can access from this book's web site.

Go: Mastering the Basic Facts

Consider this scene: Pairs of children are keying numbers on a calculator and passing it back and forth. Other pairs are seated at a table, some playing a card game and others playing board games. Several are busily typing numbers on computer keyboards. Still others are working individually with flashcards. What are they all doing? Probably they are practicing basic facts.

If children are to become skillful with the algorithms for addition, subtraction, multiplication, and division and proficient at estimation and mental computation, they must learn the basic facts to the level of immediate, or automatic, recall so that they gain computational fluency and efficiency in problem solution. When should this mastery level be attempted? As soon as children have a good understanding of the meanings of operations and symbols, the process of developing fluency with basic facts can begin. That is, as Ashlock and Washbon (1978) suggest, children should be able to:

- State or write related facts, given one basic fact.
- Explain how they got an answer, or prove that it is correct.
- Solve a fact in two or more ways.

Research has shown that drill increases speed and accuracy on tests of basic facts (Wilson, 1930). In the Classroom 9-4 contains several interesting individual activities that provide drill practice for basic facts; however, drill alone will not change a child's thinking strategies so that they become efficient. Drill, therefore, is most effective when the child's thinking is already efficient.

Some principles for drill have been proposed, based on research with primary-grade children (Davis, 1978):

- Children should attempt to memorize facts only after understanding is attained.
- Children should participate in drill with the intent to develop fluency. Remembering should be emphasized. This is not the time for explanations.
- Drill lessons should be short (5 to 10 minutes) and should be given almost every day. Children should work on only a few facts in a given lesson and should constantly review previously learned facts.
- Children should develop confidence in their ability to remember facts fluently and should be praised for good efforts. Records of their progress should be kept.

- Drill activities should be varied, interesting, challenging, and presented with enthusiasm.

Computer software provides a natural complement to more traditional materials and activities, such as flashcards, games, and audiotaped practice, for establishing the quick recall of basic facts. For example, children may try games found in the Math Links box on p. 209 to practice basic facts. Children must provide the correct answer to "equalize" the spaceship before the aliens invade.

Most programs keep track of the number of exercises attempted and the number answered correctly. Some display the time taken to give correct answers, thus encouraging students to compete against their own records for speed as well as mastery. Requiring short response time (within three or four seconds) is important because it promotes efficient strategies and encourages children to develop fluent recall.

Many children enjoy computer software that displays a cumulative record of their individual progress. This feature allows children to diagnose for themselves the basic facts they know and don't

In the Classroom 9-4

TEST YOUR FACTS!

OBJECTIVE: **Using a variety of activities and puzzles to practice multiplication and division facts.**

GRADE LEVEL: **3–4**

▼ Fill in the empty box:

5	7	*35*
4	*9*	36
5	8	
9		81
	6	48

▼ Complete these five-facts and match them with the clock minutes.

$7 \times 5 =$ *35*

$2 \times 5 =$ __

$6 \times 5 =$ __

$4 \times 5 =$ __

$5 \times 5 =$ __

▼ Fill in each empty box to make the next number correct:

12 → ÷2 → 6 → ×3 → 18 → □ → 3 → □ → 3 → □ → 24 → □ → 6 → □ → 3 → □ → 27 → □ → 3 → □ → 12 → □ → 2

▼ Multiply each number in the middle ring by the number in the center:

Center: 7; middle ring: 3, 7, 6, 2, 5, 8, 4, 9

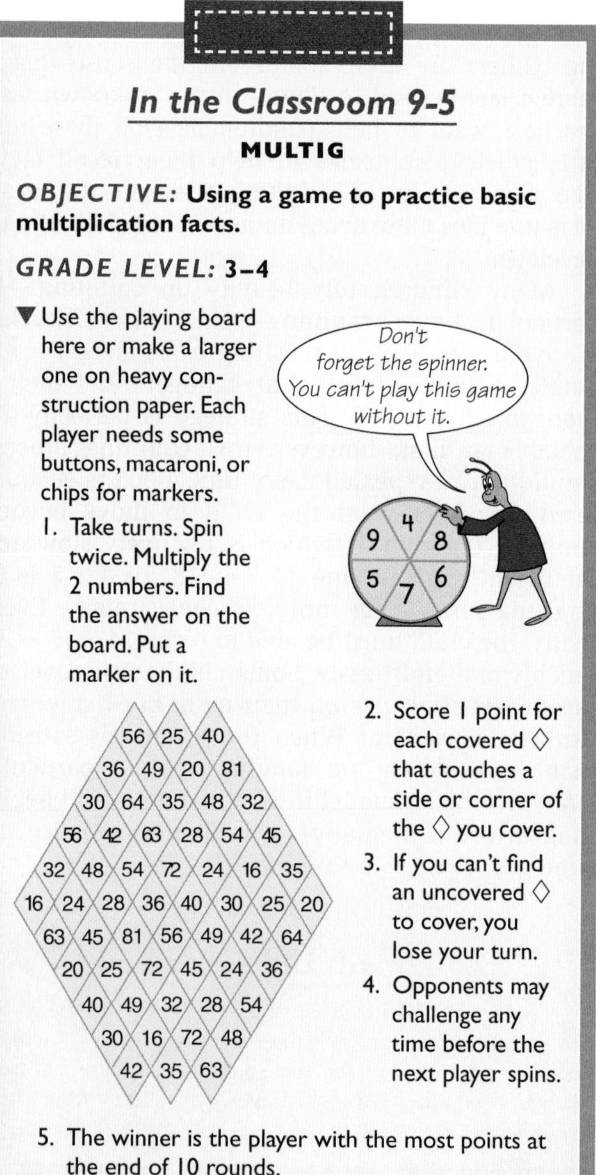
In the Classroom 9-5

MULTIG

OBJECTIVE: **Using a game to practice basic multiplication facts.**

GRADE LEVEL: **3–4**

▼ Use the playing board here or make a larger one on heavy construction paper. Each player needs some buttons, macaroni, or chips for markers.

1. Take turns. Spin twice. Multiply the 2 numbers. Find the answer on the board. Put a marker on it.
2. Score 1 point for each covered ◇ that touches a side or corner of the ◇ you cover.
3. If you can't find an uncovered ◇ to cover, you lose your turn.
4. Opponents may challenge any time before the next player spins.
5. The winner is the player with the most points at the end of 10 rounds.

know. It also provides a source of motivation because each student can compete against himself or herself, with the goal of complete mastery always in mind.

When using flashcards, the child should go through the entire set and separate the cards into a pack of those known and a pack of those unknown. Each time the child works with the cards, he or she should review those in each pack, moving newly learned facts to the known pack. This approach makes progress evident.

Another point from research also must be taken into account: the frequency with which basic addition and multiplication facts occur in elementary school textbooks is probably a source of the difficulty. Facts with numbers larger than 5 occurred up to half as frequently as those in the range of 2 to 5; 0 and 1 occurred relatively infrequently. Thus teachers need to ensure that more

In the Classroom 9-6

ADDITION BINGO!

OBJECTIVE: **Using a bingo game to practice basic addition facts.**

GRADE LEVEL: **1–2**

▼ Each player needs a different Bingo card and some buttons or macaroni for markers.

9	6	17	11	5
5	8	10	3	7
15	11	Free	13	14
7	9	2	1	12
2	13	11	18	17

The leader needs a pack of cards like these with all possible combinations (basic facts).

9 + 5   7 + 6   8 + 4

▼ It's easy to play:

- The leader draws a card and reads the addends on it.
- Each player covers the sum on his or her Bingo card.

Not all sums are given on each card.

Some sums are given more than once on a Bingo card, but a player may cover only one answer for each pair of addends.

The winner is the first person with 5 markers in a row!

In the Classroom 9-7

ZERO WINS!

OBJECTIVE: **Using a game to develop number sense and practice addition and subtraction facts.**

GRADE LEVEL: **2–3**

▼ Make two identical sets of 19 cards with a number from 0 to 18 on each!

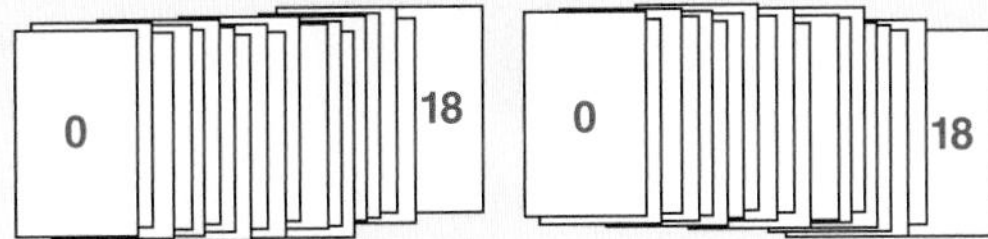

▼ Follow these rules:

- After shuffling, the leader deals 4 cards to each player and puts the remaining cards face down in the center of the table.
- Players must add or subtract the numbers on their 4 cards so they equal 0. For example, suppose you had these cards:

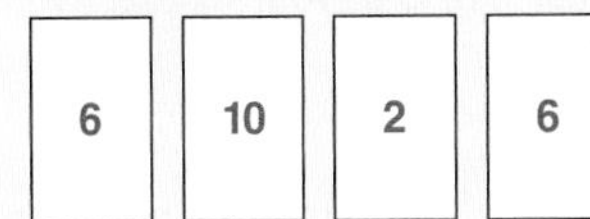

- With these cards you could write
  $10 - 6 + 2 - 6 = 0$
  or
  $6 + 6 - 10 - 2 = 0$
  or various other number sentences.
- On each round of play, the players may exchange one card if they wish, and each player takes a turn being first to exchange a card on a round. To make an exchange, the first player draws a card and discards a card, face up. Other players can draw from either the face-down pile or the face-up discard pile.

The first player to get 0 on a round wins the round!

practice is provided with facts involving 0, 1, and especially 6 through 9.

Several types of drill-and-practice procedures in the form of games are noted In the Classroom 9-5 through 9-8. Children in all age groups find such games an enjoyable way to practice what they know. These activities supplement the many other drill-and-practice procedures that you will find in textbooks, journals, computer software, and other sources.

Math Links 9.6

Some basic fact games and puzzles also involve using strategy and problem solving. Number Bounce, Number Puzzles, and The Product Game illustrate this type of activity, all of which you can access from this book's web site.

www.wiley.com/college/reys

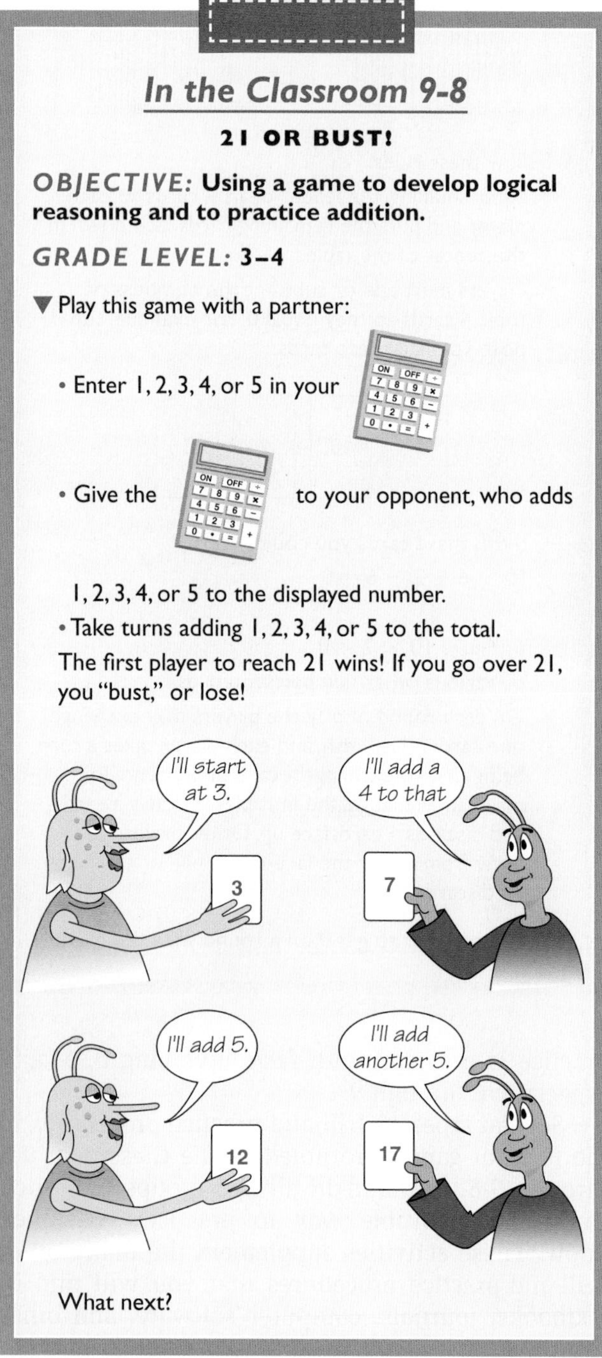

In the Classroom 9-8

21 OR BUST!

OBJECTIVE: **Using a game to develop logical reasoning and to practice addition.**

GRADE LEVEL: **3–4**

▼ Play this game with a partner:

- Enter 1, 2, 3, 4, or 5 in your calculator.
- Give the calculator to your opponent, who adds 1, 2, 3, 4, or 5 to the displayed number.
- Take turns adding 1, 2, 3, 4, or 5 to the total.

The first player to reach 21 wins! If you go over 21, you "bust," or lose!

I'll start at 3.
3
I'll add a 4 to that
7
I'll add 5.
12
I'll add another 5.
17

What next?

Thinking Strategies for Basic Facts

In the following four sections, we discuss thinking strategies for basic facts for addition, subtraction, multiplication, and division and illustrate ways to teach them.

Thinking Strategies for Addition Facts

The 100 basic facts for addition are shown in Figure 9-5. They are not presented to children in this completed form; rather, the children gradually and systematically learn the facts and may fill in or check them off on the chart.

Lesson Idea 9-3 presents questions that a teacher might use to help children see the orderliness of the basic addition facts. This overview can help children see their goal as they begin to work on fluency with facts.

The thinking strategies that can be used when teaching basic addition facts include commutativity; adding 0, 1, and doubles; counting on; and adding to 10 and beyond. For many facts, more than one strategy is appropriate.

1. *Commutativity.* The task of learning the basic addition facts is simplified because of the commutative property. Changing the order of the addends does not affect the sum. Children encounter this idea when they note that putting 2 blue objects and 3 yellow objects together gives the same quantity as putting 3 blue objects and 2 yellow objects together:

In work with the basic addition facts, children will see or write, for example:

$$\begin{array}{r} 2 \\ +5 \\ \hline \end{array} \quad \text{and} \quad \begin{array}{r} 5 \\ +2 \\ \hline \end{array}$$

or

$$2 + 5 = \square \quad \text{and} \quad 5 + 2 = \square$$

Students must realize that the same two numbers have the same sum, no matter which comes first. They need to be able to put this idea into their own words; they do not need to know the term *commutative property*. They need to use the idea as they work with basic facts, not merely parrot a term.

Lesson Idea 9-3

THE BIG PICTURE

Materials: Activity sheet for each child; a transparency of it for use on the overhead projector.

0 +0	1 +0	2 +0	3 +0	4 +0	5 +0	6 +0	7 +0	8 +0	9 +0
	1 +1	2 +1	3 +1	4 +1	5 +1	6 +1	7 +1	8 +1	9 +1
		2 +2	3 +2	4 +2	__	__	__	__	__
			3 +3	4 +3	__	__	__	__	__
				4 +4	5 +4	__	__	__	__
					5 +5	__	__	__	__
						6 +6	__	__	__
							7 +7	__	__
								8 +8	__
									9 +9

Objective: Children discover the patterns of the basic facts using an organized table.

Grade Level: 2

- Ask each child to study carefully examples on the activity sheet.
  - What is alike about the examples?
  - What patterns are apparent?
- Discuss the top row of examples—those involving 0. Have the children fill in each of the sums.
- Discuss the second row of examples.
  - Why isn't $\begin{array}{r}0\\ \underline{+1}\end{array}$ included? (This fact is in the top row.)
  - How can each sum be found quickly? (By counting on one.)
- Look at the diagonal containing these facts:

  $\begin{array}{r}0\\ \underline{+1}\end{array}$ $\begin{array}{r}1\\ \underline{+1}\end{array}$ $\begin{array}{r}2\\ \underline{+2}\end{array}$ $\begin{array}{r}3\\ \underline{+3}\end{array}$ $\begin{array}{r}4\\ \underline{+4}\end{array}$ $\begin{array}{r}5\\ \underline{+5}\end{array}$ $\begin{array}{r}6\\ \underline{+6}\end{array}$ $\begin{array}{r}7\\ \underline{+7}\end{array}$ $\begin{array}{r}8\\ \underline{+8}\end{array}$ $\begin{array}{r}9\\ \underline{+9}\end{array}$

  - Find the sums.
- On the overhead projector, quickly fill in the remaining sums. Then focus attention on the entire table.
  - What patterns are apparent?
  - What is the largest sum? What are its addends?
  - What is the smallest sum? What are its addends?
  - Ask children to circle all examples whose sum is 8.
  - Where are they?
  - What patterns do you see in the addends?
  - Why isn't $\begin{array}{r}5\\ \underline{+7}\end{array}$ in the chart?
- Continue discussing patterns as long as you feel your children are benefiting from the experience. Encourage the children to understand that all the basic facts to be memorized are included on this sheet.

Encourage the use of commutativity by using materials such as a chain of loops:

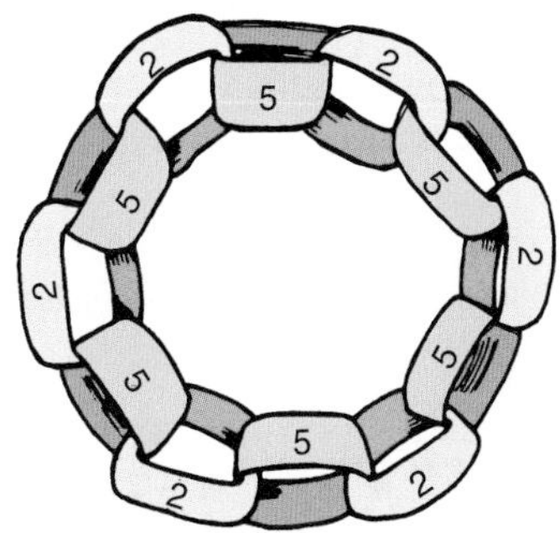

Have the children note that 5 is followed by 2 and 2 is followed by 5 all around the chain. The chain can be turned as they read and add:

$$5 + 2 = 7, \quad 2 + 5 = 7, \quad 5 + 2 = 7, \quad \ldots$$

The calculator can also help children verify that the order of the addends is irrelevant. Have them key into their calculators:

$$5 + 8 = \quad \text{and} \quad 8 + 5 =$$

Use a variety of combinations, so the idea that the order does not affect the outcome becomes evident. In the Classroom 9-9 presents another way of helping them develop and use the idea of commutativity.

The blank boxes in Figure 9-6 help you see that the commutative property reduces the number of facts to be learned by 45. Each blank box below the diagonal of the table can be matched with a box above the diagonal with the same addends and sum. (If there are 100 facts altogether, why are there 55 distinct facts to learn, rather than just 50?)

2. *Strategies for Adding One and Adding Zero. Adding one* to a number is easy for most children. In fact, most children learn this idea before they come to school, and they only have to practice the recognition and writing of it rather than develop initial understanding. To reinforce their initial concept, experiences with objects come first, followed by such paper-and-pencil activities as these:

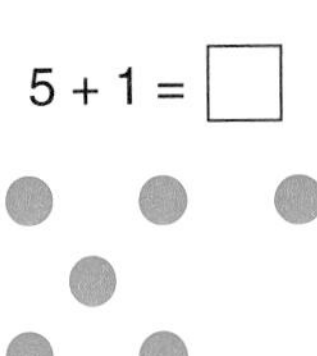

In the Classroom 9-9

ARRANGING AND REARRANGING

OBJECTIVE: **Developing number sense by using counters to illustrate different sums to 10.**

GRADE LEVEL: 2

▼ Use 10 counters and string for the rings to make this arrangement:

A B

- How many counters are in Ring A? ______
- How many counters are in Ring B? ______

▼ Rearrange your counters and rings to show the same numbers, and then move 1 counter from Ring A to Ring B.

- How many counters are now in Ring A? ______
- How many counters are in Ring B? ______

▼ See how many different ways you can put 10 counters in the two rings.

- Use your counters and rings, and list the ways here:

4 + 6 ______ ______ ______

______ ______ ______ ______

______ ______ ______

Recognition of the pattern is then encouraged:

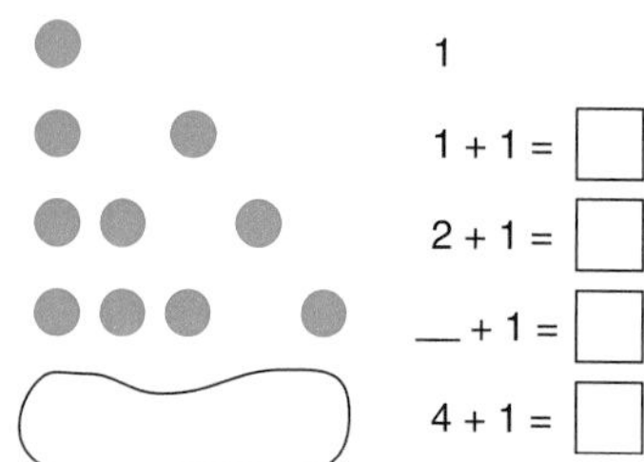

The strategy for *adding zero* applies to facts that have zero as one addend. These facts should be learned, through experience, as a generalization: *Zero added to any number does not change the number.* This idea follows from many concrete examples in which children see that any time they add "no more" (zero) they have the same amount. Activities then focus on this pattern:

+	0	1	2	3	4	5	6	7	8	9
0	0	1	2	3	4	5	6	7	8	9
1		2	3	4	5	6	7	8	9	10
2			4	5	6	7	8	9	10	11
3				6	7	8	9	10	11	12
4					8	9	10	11	12	13
5						10	11	12	13	14
6							12	13	14	15
7								14	15	16
8									16	17
9										18

FIGURE 9-6 Addition facts derived by the commutative thinking strategy.

○ 1 + 0 = □ 0 + 1 = □

○○ 2 + 0 = □ etc.

○○○ 3 + 0 = □

○○○○ 4 + 0 = □

Although adding zero may seem easy to adults, this is actually one of the hardest strategies for children to learn. Concrete modeling of the situation is tricky because it is difficult to picture adding nothing. Therefore, explicit work on facts involving zero should be postponed until children have mastered some of the other fact strategies.

3. *Strategies for Adding Doubles and Near Doubles. Doubles* are basic facts in which both addends are the same number, such as 4 + 4 or 9 + 9. Most children learn these facts quickly, often parroting them before they come to school. Connecting doubles facts to familiar situations often helps students remember them (e.g., two hands shows 5 + 5 = 10, an egg carton shows 6 + 6 = 12, two weeks on a calendar shows 7 + 7 = 14) Students can profit from work with objects followed by drawings:

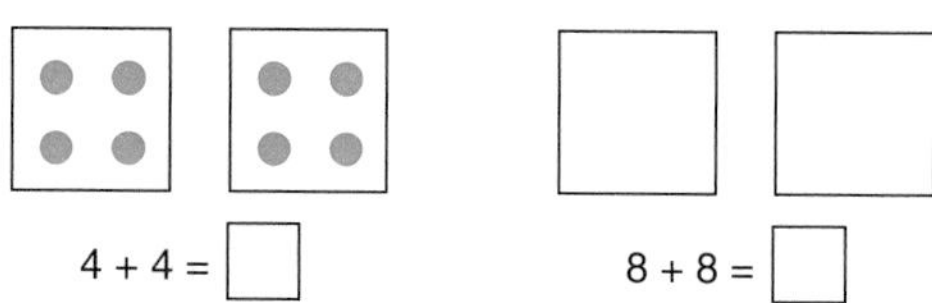

Another strategy, "near doubles," can be used for the facts that are one more or one less than the doubles:

Think

7 + 8 = □ 7 + 7 = 14
So 7 + 8 is one more.
7 + 8 = 15

Think

7 + 6 = □ 7 + 7 = 14
So 7 + 6 is one less.
7 + 6 = 13

Lesson Idea 9-4 shows one way of presenting this strategy.

Lesson Idea 9-4

NEARLY DOUBLE

Materials: Flannel board or magnetic board and disks for demonstration, 1 die, a pile of chips or tiles, and paper for each pair of children for seat work.

Objective: Children determine strategies for adding doubles and near doubles using plastic disks.

Grade Level: 1

- Put a group of 6 disks on the board and have children do the same at their seats.
- Have them add a second group of 6 (and do so for demonstration too).
  - Ask: How many in each group? How many in all?
- Write 6 + 6 = 12 on the board.
- Have children add one more disk to the second group:
  - Ask: How many in the first group?
    How many in the second group?
    How many in all?
- Write 6 + 7 = 13 on the board.
- Demonstrate how children can use their dice and chips to build more examples like this and to write the corresponding sentences on their papers. Each pair of children should repeatedly roll their die. After each roll they should model, say, and write a near doubles fact. For example, if they roll 5, they use chips to model, say, and write 5 + 6 = 11.

A Addition facts derived by the adding one and adding zero strategies

+	0	1	2	3	4	5	6	7	8	9
0	0	1	2	3	4	5	6	7	8	9
1	1	2	3	4	5	6	7	8	9	10
2	2	3								
3	3	4								
4	4	5								
5	5	6								
6	6	7								
7	7	8								
8	8	9								
9	9	10								

B Addition facts derived by the adding doubles and near-doubles strategies

+	0	1	2	3	4	5	6	7	8	9
0	0	1								
1	1	2	3							
2		3	4	5						
3			5	6	7					
4				7	8	9				
5					9	10	11			
6						11	12	13		
7							13	14	15	
8								15	16	17
9									17	18

FIGURE 9-7 Addition facts derived by four strategies.

The four thinking strategies in the preceding two sections can be used with the addition facts shown in Figure 9-7, parts A and B.

4. *Counting On.* The strategy of *counting on* can be used for any addition facts but is most easily used when one of the addends is 1, 2, or 3. To be efficient, it is important to count on from the larger addend. For example,

Think

2 + 6 = □ 6 . . . 7 . . . 8
2 + 6 = 8

Initially, children will probably count all objects in a group, as noted in Chapter 7.

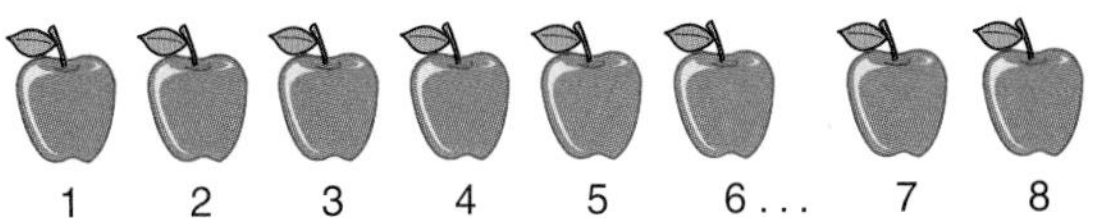

They need to learn to start from the larger addend, 6, and count on, 7, 8. (Notice that understanding of the commutative property is assumed.) Research indicates that young children will count on but not necessarily from the larger addend (Ginsberg, 1977). Thus the strategy must be taught to many children using activities such as this one:

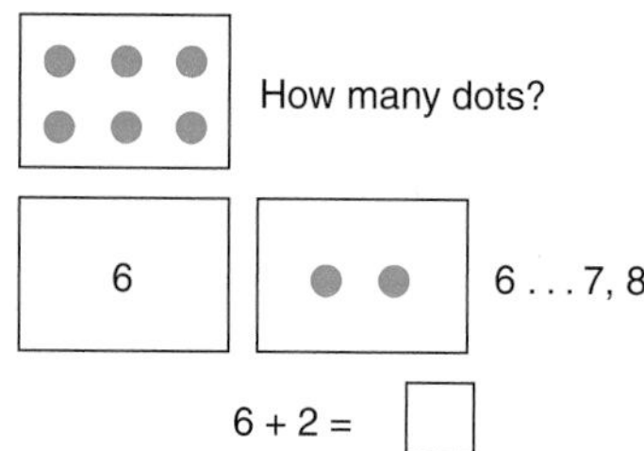

The counting-on strategy can be rather efficiently used with the addition facts noted in Figure 9-8 (where at least one addend is 1, 2, or 3); however, it is *not* efficient to use counting on when both addends are larger than 3 (e.g., for 6 + 8 = 14 or 5 + 8 = 13 or 9 + 8 = 17). Counting on for facts such as these is both slow and prone to error. Unfortunately, some children develop the habit of using counting on all the time and thereby fail to develop more efficient strategies, sometimes still relying on counting on even after they have graduated to middle school or high school. It is important to help students move beyond counting on because fluency (efficiency and accuracy) is extremely important for work with basic facts. When students are slowed down by inefficient strategies for basic fact retrieval, they are often hampered in doing more advanced work in mathematics.

+	0	1	2	3	4	5	6	7	8	9
0										
1		2	3	4	5	6	7	8	9	10
2		3	4	5	6	7	8	9	10	11
3		4	5	6	7	8	9	10	11	12
4		5	6	7						
5		6	7	8						
6		7	8	9						
7		8	9	10						
8		9	10	11						
9		10	11	12						

FIGURE 9-8 Addition facts derived by the counting-on strategy.

5. *Adding to 10 and Beyond.* With the strategy of *adding to 10 and beyond,* one addend is increased and the other decreased, to make one of the addends 10. This strategy is used most easily when one of the addends is 8 or 9, although some children also find it useful when adding 6 or 7. Here is an example:

Think

8 + 5 = □ 8 + 2 = 10 and 5 = 2 + 3
So 10 + 3 = 13, so
8 + 5 = 13

The child recognizes that 8 is close to 10, and then mentally breaks 5 apart into 2 + 3. The 2 is used with the 8 to "add to ten," and the 3 is used to go "beyond." A ten-frame can be helpful in teaching this strategy because it provides a visual image of adding to 10 and going beyond:

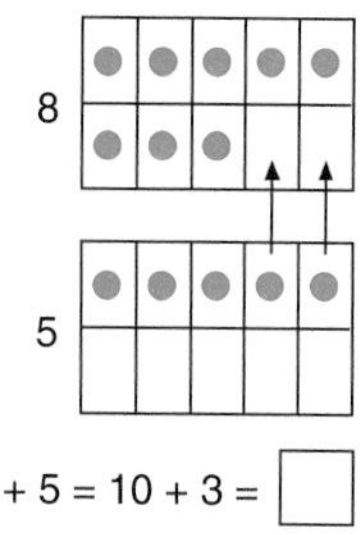

The research of Funkhouser (1995) indicates that working with five-frames as a base and then moving to ten-frames may be particularly helpful for children with learning disabilities.

Children must know the sums to 10 well in order to use the adding-to-ten-and-beyond strategy. Practice with regrouping to 10 is needed to help them become proficient. They also need to realize how easy it is to add any single digit to 10 to get a number in the teens, without having to think about counting on. Which is easier?

10 + 5 or 9 + 6
7 + 8 or 5 + 10

As another example, change this problem to an easier one:

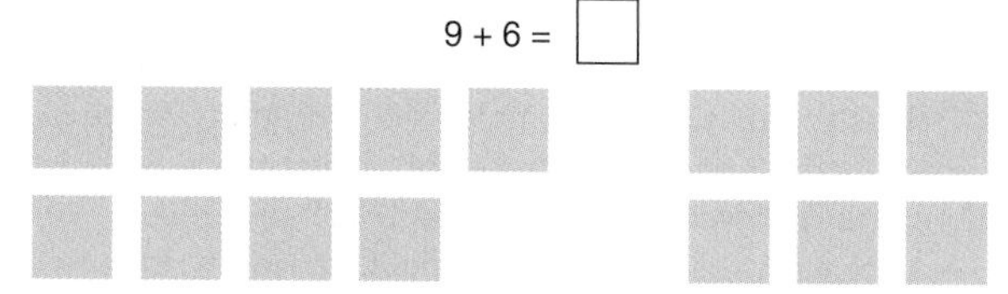

In all cases, talk the strategy through with drawings as well as objects:

+	0	1	2	3	4	5	6	7	8	9
0										
1										
2										11
3									11	12
4									12	13
5									13	14
6									14	15
7									15	16
8				11	12	13	14	15	16	17
9			11	12	13	14	15	16	17	18

FIGURE 9-9 Addition facts derived by the adding-to-10 strategy.

+	0	1	2	3	4	5	6	7	8	9
0	0	1	2	3	4	5	6	7	8	9
1	1	2	3	4	5	6	7	8	9	10
2	2	3	4	5	6	7	8	9	10	11
3	3	4	5	6	7	8	9	10	11	12
4	4	5	6	7	8	9			12	13
5	5	6	7	8	9	10	11		13	14
6	6	7	8	9		11	12	13	14	15
7	7	8	9	10			13	14	15	16
8	8	9	10	11	12	13	14	15	16	17
9	9	10	11	12	13	14	15	16	17	18

FIGURE 9-10 Addition facts derived by all thinking strategies for addition.

8 + 4 = □ 10 + 2 = □

The adding-to-10-and-beyond strategy can be used with the addition facts shown in Figure 9-9.

In many cases, more than one strategy can be used to aid in recalling a fact. This point should be made with the children. It encourages them to try different ways of recalling a fact, and it may strengthen their understanding of the relationships involved. Notice from Figure 9-10 that, when the strategies for adding one, adding zero, adding doubles and near doubles, counting on, and adding-to-10-and-beyond have been learned, only six basic facts remain. These missing facts can be derived using one of the strategies (and commutativity) or simply taught separately. Children should be encouraged to look for patterns and relationships because almost all of the 100 basic addition facts can be developed from a variety of relationships with other facts.

It also should be noted that children might invent strategies of their own, such as:

6 + 7 = □ **Think**
6 is 5 + 1
7 is 5 + 2
So 10 + 3
13

6 + 8 = □ **Think**
3 + 3 + 8
3 + 11
14

Encourage their ideas!

Thinking Strategies for Subtraction Facts

For each basic addition fact, there is a related subtraction fact. In some mathematics programs, the two operations are taught simultaneously. The relationship between them is then readily emphasized, and learning the basic facts for both operations proceeds as if they were in the same family. Even when they are not taught simultaneously, however, the idea of a fact family is frequently used (see Figure 9-11).

"Think addition" is the major thinking strategy for learning and recalling the subtraction facts. Encourage children to recognize, think about, and use the relationships between addition and subtraction facts. They can find the answers to subtraction facts by thinking about missing addends.

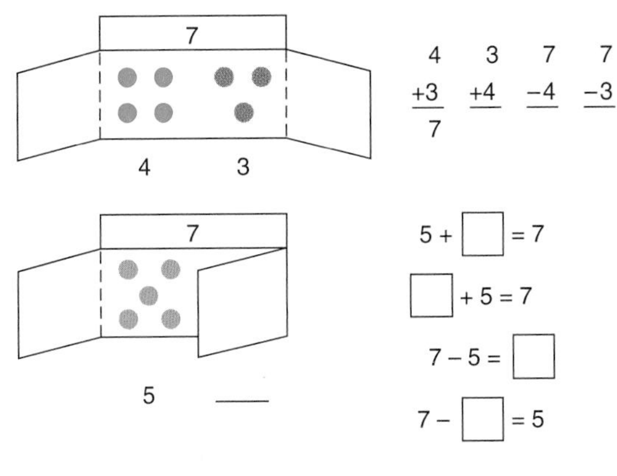

FIGURE 9-11 Examples of fact families.

For example,

$$15 + 7 = \square \qquad \begin{array}{l}\textbf{Think}\\ 7 + 8 = 15 \\ \text{So } 15 - 7 = 8\end{array}$$

Other strategies for finding subtraction facts also can be taught: using 0 and 1, doubles, counting back, and counting on.

1. *Using 0 and 1.* Once they have learned strategies for adding 0 and adding 1, most children find it rather easy to learn the related subtraction facts involving 0 and 1. They can profit from work with materials and from observing patterns similar to those used for addition facts.

2. *Doubles.* The strategy for doubles may need to be taught more explicitly for subtraction facts than for addition facts. It rests on the assumption that children know the doubles for addition. Here is an example:

$$16 - 8 = \square \qquad \begin{array}{l}\textbf{Think}\\ 8 + 8 = 16 \\ 16 - 8 = 8\end{array}$$

3. *Counting Back.* The strategy of counting back is related to counting on in addition, and therefore it is most effectively used when the number to be subtracted is 1, 2, or 3:

$$9 - 3 = \square \qquad \begin{array}{l}\textbf{Think}\\ 9 \ldots 8, 7, 6 \\ 9 - 3 = 6\end{array}$$

As for other strategies, use problems and a variety of manipulative materials to help children gain facility in counting back from given numbers. Focus especially on the numbers involved in subtraction facts, as in the following examples.

Write the numbers in order backward:

10	9						

Write the numbers you say when you count back.

Write the answer.

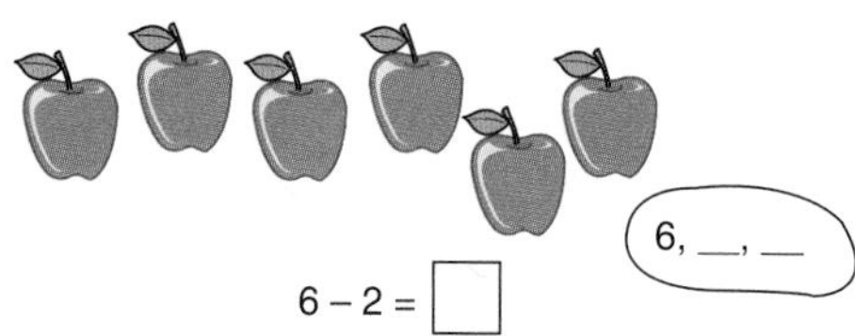

4. *Counting On.* The strategy of counting on is used most easily when the difference is 1, 2, or 3 (i.e., when it is easy to see that the two numbers involved in the subtraction are close together). "Think addition" by counting on:

$$8 - 6 = \square \qquad \begin{array}{l}\textbf{Think}\\ 6 \ldots 7, 8 \\ 8 - 6 = 2\end{array}$$

Activities for developing this strategy include the following:

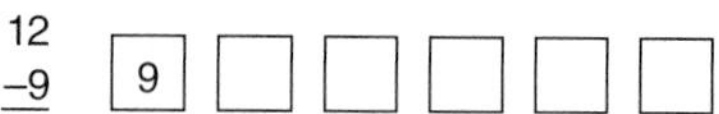

Begin with 9. Count on until you reach 12. How many?

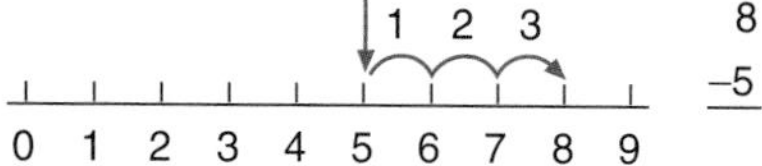

Begin with 5. Count on until you reach 8. How much?

The emphasis in using the counting-on strategy can also encompass adding on: "How much more would I need?" The child is encouraged to use known addition facts to reach the solution. This is particularly valuable with missing-addend situations, such as $6 + \square = 9$.

Thinking Strategies for Multiplication Facts

Multiplication is frequently viewed as a special case of addition in which all the addends are of equal size. The solution to multiplication problems can be attained by adding or counting, but multiplication is used because it is so much quicker.

Instruction on multiplication ideas begins in kindergarten as children develop ideas about groups, numbers, and addition. In grades 1 and 2, counting by twos, threes, fours, fives, tens, and possibly other numbers should be taught. Such expressions provide a basis for understanding the patterns that occur with the basic multiplication facts. Use of the calculator as described in Chapter 7 can aid teachers in developing ideas about these patterns of multiplication. Using the constant function on calculators, children realize that two sixes equal 12, three sixes equal 18, and so on.

The basic multiplication facts pair two one-digit factors with a product, as shown in Figure 9-12. The basic multiplication facts should not be given to children in the form of a table or chart of facts until they have been meaningfully introduced.

×	0	1	2	3	4	5	6	7	8	9
0	0	0	0	0	0	0	0	0	0	0
1	0	1	2	3	4	5	6	7	8	9
2	0	2	4	6	8	10	12	14	16	18
3	0	3	6	9	12	15	18	21	24	27
4	0	4	8	12	16	20	24	28	32	36
5	0	5	10	15	20	25	30	35	40	45
6	0	6	12	18	24	30	36	42	48	54
7	0	7	14	21	28	35	42	49	56	63
8	0	8	16	24	32	40	48	56	64	72
9	0	9	18	27	36	45	54	63	72	81

FIGURE 9-12 The 100 basic facts for multiplication.

×	0	1	2	3	4	5	6	7	8	9
0	0	0	0	0	0	0	0	0	0	0
1		1	2	3	4	5	6	7	8	9
2			4	6	8	10	12	14	16	18
3				9	12	15	18	21	24	27
4					16	20	24	28	32	36
5						25	30	35	40	45
6							36	42	48	54
7								49	56	63
8									64	72
9										81

FIGURE 9-13 Multiplication facts derived by the commutative thinking strategy.

Rather, the facts should be developed through problem situations, experiences with manipulative and other materials, and various thinking strategies. The table becomes the end result of this process of developing understanding of operations and facts.

The thinking strategies for multiplication facts provide an efficient way for a child to attain each fact. These strategies include commutativity, using 1 and 0, skip counting, repeated addition, splitting into known parts, and patterns.

1. *Commutativity.* Commutativity applies to multiplication just as it does to addition. It is, therefore, a primary strategy for helping students learn the multiplication facts. In the Classroom 9-2 through 9-4 (presented earlier) emphasize this property. The calculator is also useful in reinforcing the idea. Children can multiply 4 × 6, then 6 × 4, for example, and realize that the answer to both is 24.

Here are some other examples:

$$3 \times 6 = 18 \longrightarrow 6 \times \square = 18$$
$$7 \times 5 = 35 \longrightarrow \square \times 7 = 35$$

After they have tried many combinations, students should be able to verbalize that the order of the factors is irrelevant. Figure 9-13 (where each box in the upper right can be matched with an unshaded box in the lower left) shows that, as for addition, there really are only 55 multiplication facts to be learned if you recognize the power of commutativity.

2. *Skip Counting.* The strategy of skip counting works best for the multiples children know best, twos and fives, but it also may be applied to threes and fours (or other numbers) if children have learned to skip count by them.

Here is an example for 5:

Think

$4 \times 5 = \square$ 5, 10, 15, 20
$4 \times 5 = 20$

Skip counting around the clock face (as you do when counting minutes after the hour) is a good way to reinforce multiples of 5 by skip counting. The facts that can be established with the skip-counting strategy for twos and fives are noted in Figure 9-14.

3. *Repeated Addition.* The strategy of repeated addition can be used most efficiently when one of

×	0	1	2	3	4	5	6	7	8	9
0										
1										
2			4	6	8	10	12	14	16	18
3			6			15				
4			8			20				
5			10	15	20	25	30	35	40	45
6			12			30				
7			14			35				
8			16			40				
9			18			45				

FIGURE 9-14 Multiplication facts derived by the skip-counting strategy.

the factors is less than 5. The child changes the multiplication example to an addition example:

$$3 \times 6 = \square \qquad \begin{array}{l}\underline{\text{Think}}\\ 6 + 6 + 6 = 18\\ 3 \times 6 = 18\end{array}$$

Because this strategy is based on one interpretation of multiplication, children should have had many experiences with objects and materials. Drawings and the calculator can be used to provide additional experiences to help develop this strategy as well as the concept for the operation. Lesson Idea 9-5 illustrates these ideas. In Figure 9-15, note the facts that can be learned with this strategy.

4. *Splitting the Product into Known Parts.* As children gain assurance with some basic facts, they can use their known facts to derive others. The strategy known as *splitting the product* is based on the distributive property of multiplication. It can be approached in terms of "one more set," "twice as much as a known fact," or "known facts of 5."

- The idea of *one more set* can be used for almost all multiplication facts. If one multiple of a number is known, the next multiple can be determined by adding a single-digit number. For example, to find 3×5 if doubles are already known, you can think of 2×5 (10) and add one more 5 (to get 15). The computation is slightly more difficult when the addition requires renaming (as, for example, below, where

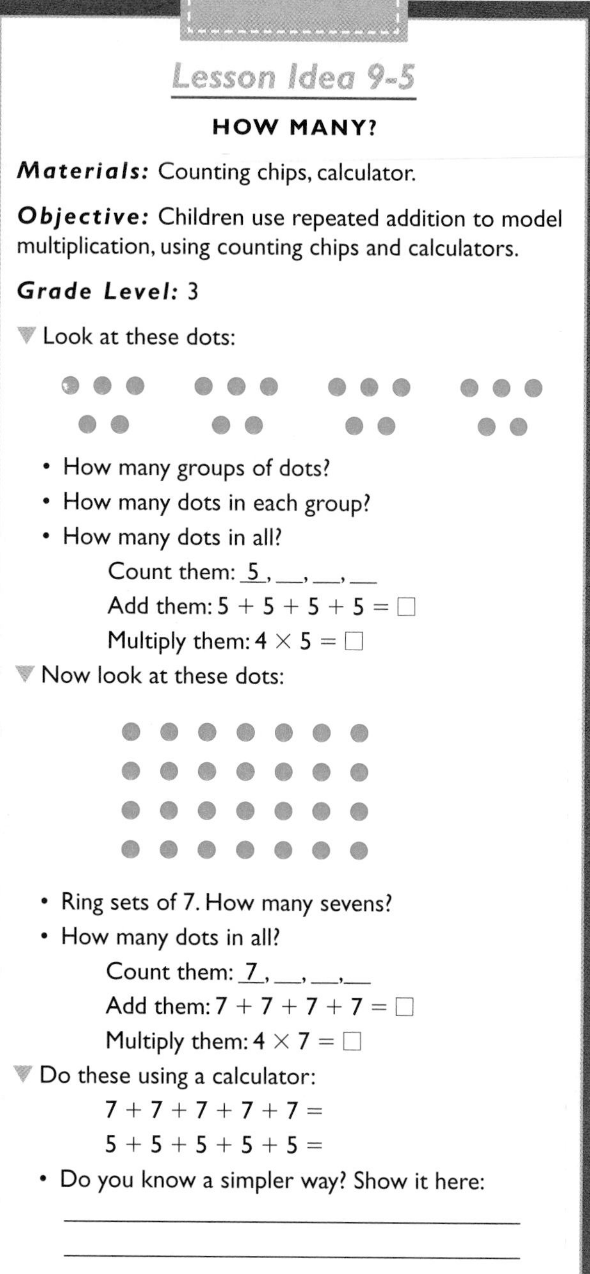

Lesson Idea 9-5

HOW MANY?

Materials: Counting chips, calculator.

Objective: Children use repeated addition to model multiplication, using counting chips and calculators.

Grade Level: 3

▼ Look at these dots:

- How many groups of dots?
- How many dots in each group?
- How many dots in all?

  Count them: <u>5</u>, __, __, __

  Add them: $5 + 5 + 5 + 5 = \square$

  Multiply them: $4 \times 5 = \square$

▼ Now look at these dots:

- Ring sets of 7. How many sevens?
- How many dots in all?

  Count them: <u>7</u>, __, __, __

  Add them: $7 + 7 + 7 + 7 = \square$

  Multiply them: $4 \times 7 = \square$

▼ Do these using a calculator:

$7 + 7 + 7 + 7 + 7 =$

$5 + 5 + 5 + 5 + 5 =$

- Do you know a simpler way? Show it here:

____

____

x	0	1	2	3	4	5	6	7	8	9
0										
1										
2			4	6	8	10	12	14	16	18
3			6	9	12	15	18	21	24	27
4			8	12	16	20	24	28	32	36
5			10	15	20					
6			12	18	24					
7			14	21	28					
8			16	24	32					
9			18	27	36					

FIGURE 9-15 Multiplication facts derived by the repeated addition strategy.

8×7 is found by adding one more set of 7 to the known fact $7 \times 7 = 49$):

$$8 \times 7 = \square \qquad \begin{array}{l}\underline{\text{Think}}\\ 7 \times 7 = 49\\ 8 \times 7 = 49 + 7\\ 8 \times 7 = 56\end{array}$$

Each fact can be used to help learn the next multiple of either factor. Illustrating this strategy using an array model can be helpful:

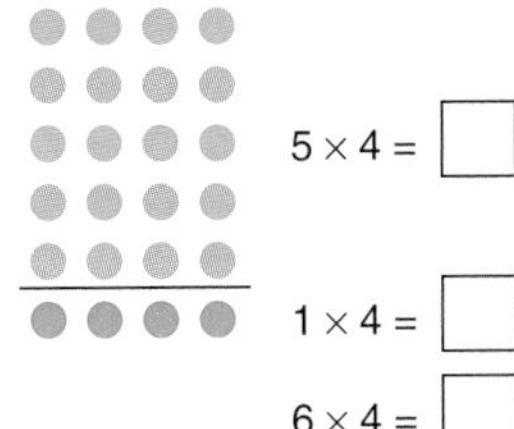

Ask children to name each part of the array and write the multiplication fact for the whole array.

- *Twice as much as a known fact* is a variation of the foregoing strategy. It can be applied to multiples of 4, 6, and 8 because an array with one of these numbers can be split in half. The product is twice as much as each half:

$6 \times 8 = \square$ **Think**
3 × 8 = 24
6 × 8 is twice as much, or 24 + 24
6 × 8 = 48

Note that a difficulty may arise when renaming is needed to do the doubling by addition.

Again, using models helps provide a visual image of this strategy:

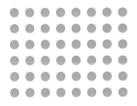

2 sevens is ____
2 sevens is ____
4 × 7 = □

In this case, children work with already divided arrays.

As they progress, children can divide an array, such as the following; write about each part; and write the multiplication fact for the whole array.

Some options for the array above (6 × 8) might be:

(5 × 8) = 40 and 1 × 8 = 8,
so 6 × 8 = 40 + 8 = 48
or 6 × 4 = 24 and 6 × 8 is twice as much,
so 6 × 8 = 24 + 24 = 48.

- *Working from known facts of 5* also will aid children. It can be helpful for any problem with large factors but is most useful for multiples of 6 and 8 because both 5 sixes and 5 eights are multiples of 10, so it is rather easy to add on the remaining part without renaming.

For example, to figure 7 × 6, recognize that 7 can be conveniently split into 5 + 2 because 5 × 6 (30) is easy to work with.

$7 \times 6 = \square$ **Think**
5 × 6 = 30
2 × 6 = 12
So 7 × 6 is 30 + 12, or 42

To illustrate this strategy, the array is divided so that 5 sixes or eights (or some other number) are separated from the remaining portion:

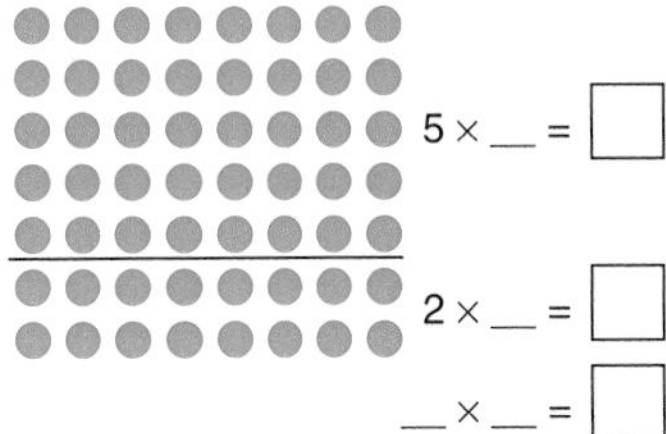

Call attention to how the array is divided. Have the children work with other arrays, determining when it seems reasonable to work with particular numbers. The facts that can be solved by splitting the product into known parts are shown in Figure 9-16.

5. *Using 0 and 1.* The facts with zero and one are generally learned from experience working with multiplication. Children need to be able to generalize that "multiplying with 1 does not change the other number" and that "multiplying by 0 results in a

x	0	1	2	3	4	5	6	7	8	9
0										
1										
2										
3										
4							24	28	32	36
5							30	35	40	45
6					24	30	36	42	48	54
7					28	35	42	49	56	63
8					32	40	48	56	64	72
9					36	45	54	63	72	81

FIGURE 9-16 Multiplication facts derived by the strategy of splitting the product into known parts.

×	0	1	2	3	4	5	6	7	8	9
0	0	0	0	0	0	0	0	0	0	0
1	0	1	2	3	4	5	6	7	8	9
2	0	2								
3	0	3								
4	0	4								
5	0	5								
6	0	6								
7	0	7								
8	0	8								
9	0	9								

FIGURE 9-17 Multiplication facts derived by the strategies for 0 and 1.

product of 0." Figure 9-17 indicates the facts that can be learned with these strategies.

The preceding strategies account for all the multiplication facts. However, one more strategy can provide help with some difficult facts.

6. *Patterns.* Finding patterns is helpful with several multiplication facts. One of the most useful and interesting patterns concerns nines. Look at the products of the facts involving nine. The digits of the products always sum to 9. Furthermore, the tens digit of each product is always one less than whatever factor was being multiplied times 9.

1 × 9 = 9	0 + 9 = 9
2 × 9 = 19	1 + 8 = 9
3 × 9 = 27	2 + 7 = 9
4 × 9 = 36	3 + 6 = 9
↑ The tens digit is 1 less than 4.	↑ The *sum* of the digits of 36 is 9.

So for 5 × 9,

The tens digit is one less than 5 ⟶ 4

The sum of the digits is 9, so 4 + □ = 9 ⟶ 5

Thus, 5 × 9 = 45

Now try 7 × 9 = ❒

Challenge children to find this and other interesting patterns in a table or chart such as the one in Figure 9-12. They should note, for instance, that the columns (and rows) for 2, 4, 6, and 8 contain all even numbers, and the columns for 1, 3, 5, 7, and 9 alternate even and odd numbers.

You will probably find that children also enjoy various forms of "finger multiplication" (see Figure 9-18), seemingly magical tricks for using finger manipulations to determine basic facts. Actually, though, finger multiplication works because of the patterns that are inherent in the basic fact table.

Thinking Strategies for Division Facts

Teaching division has traditionally taken a large portion of time in elementary school. Now, with the increased use of calculators, many educators advocate reducing the attention accorded to it. Nevertheless, children still need an understanding of the division process and division facts. The facts help them to respond quickly to simple division situations and to understand better the nature of division and its relationship to multiplication.

Just as "think addition" is an important strategy for subtraction, "think multiplication" is the primary thinking strategy to aid children in understanding and recalling the division facts. Division is the inverse of multiplication; that is, in a division problem you are seeking an unknown factor when the product and some other factor are known. The multiplication table illustrates all the division facts; simply read it differently. For the division fact 54 ÷ 9 = ❒, look in the 9-row of the multiplication table for the number 54, then read up that column to find the other factor, 6. Students generally do not learn division facts separately from multiplication facts. Instead, they learn division facts such as 48 ÷ 6 = 8 by remembering (and connecting with) multiplication facts such as 6 × 8 = 48.

It is important to realize that most division problems, in computations and in real-world problem situations, do not directly involve a multiplication fact that you have learned. For example, consider the computation 49 ÷ 6. There is no basic fact involving 49 and 6. So, what do you do? In this situation most people quickly and automatically mentally review the 6-facts that they know, looking for the facts that come closest to 49 (6 × 7 = 42—too small, 6 × 8 = 48—just a little too small, 6 × 9 = 54—too big). From this mental review, you can conclude that 49 ÷ 6 = 8, with 1 left over. Children need practice in thinking this way (mentally finding the answers to problems involving one-digit divisors and one-digit answers plus remainders).

Just as fact families can be developed for addition and subtraction, so can they be useful for multiplication and division:

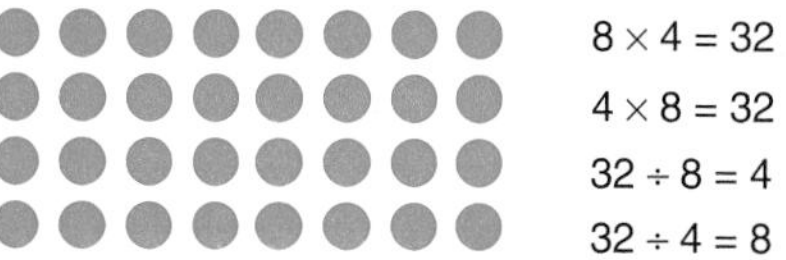

Because of its relationship to multiplication, division can be stated in terms of multiplication:

Finger Multiplication for 9-Times Facts Only

1. Hold both hands in front of you with palms facing away.
2. To do 3 × 9, bend down the third finger from the left.
3. The fingers to the left of the bent finger represent tens. The fingers to the right of the bent finger represent ones. Read off the answer: 2 tens and 7 ones, or 27.
4. To do 5 × 9, bend down the fifth finger from the left, etc. Try this method for any 9-facts: 1 × 9 through 10 × 9.

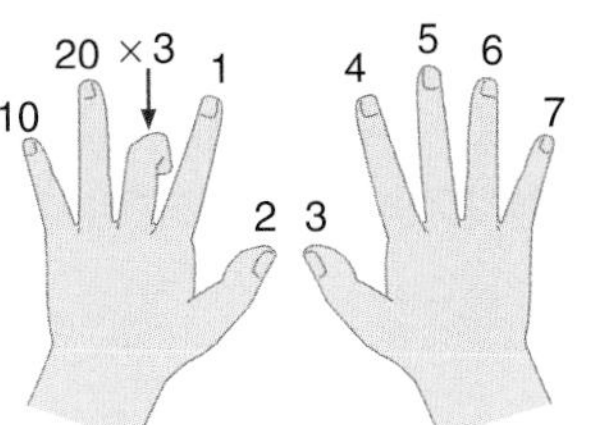

3 × 9 = 20 + 7 = 27

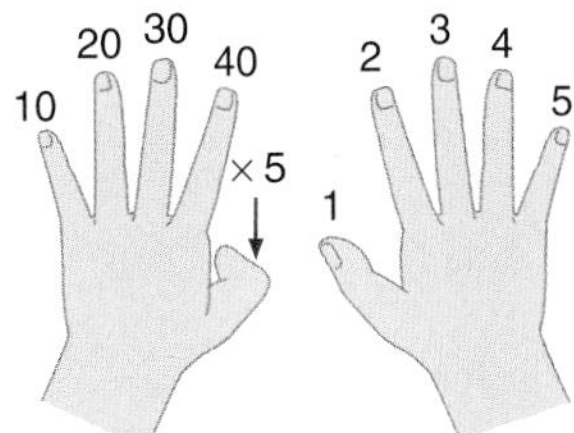

5 × 9 = 40 + 5 = 45

Finger Multiplication for Facts with Factors 6 and Higher Only

1. Hold both hands in front of you with palms facing you.
2. Think of a multiplication in which both factors are 6 or more (up to 10). For example, you can do anything from 6 × 6 up to 10 × 10.
3. For each factor, find the difference from 10.
   - Let's try the example 8 × 9.
   - For the factor 8, think 10 − 8 = 2, and bend down 2 fingers on the left hand.
   - For the factor 9, think 10 − 9 = 1 , and bend down 1 finger on the right hand.
4. Look at all fingers that are still up, and count by ten (10, 20, 30, 40, 50, 60, 70).
5. Look at the fingers that are bent down. Multiply the number of fingers bent down on the left hand by the number bent down on the right hand (2 × 1 = 2).
6. So 8 × 9 = 70 + 2 or 72.
7. Try this method for any multiplication facts from 6 × 6 up through 10 × 10.

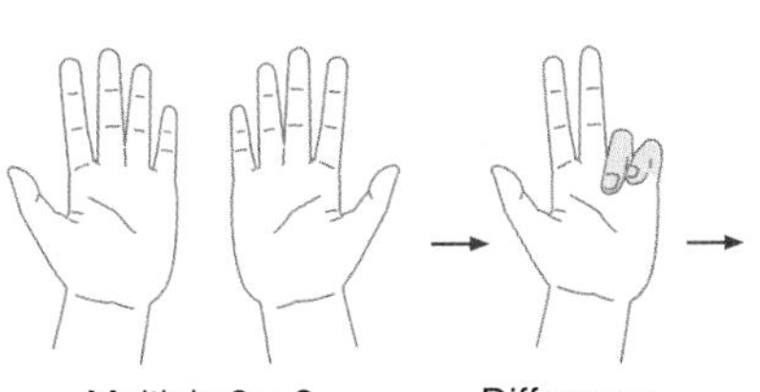

Multiply 8 × 9 | Difference between 8 and 10 is 2 (fold down 2 fingers) | Difference between 9 and 10 is 1 (fold down 1 fingers)

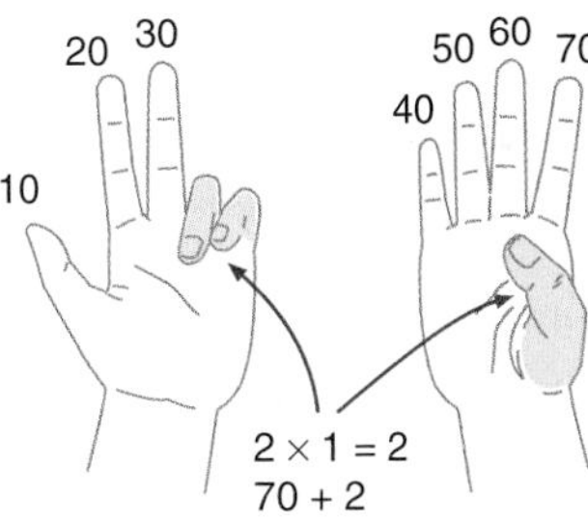

FIGURE 9-18 Two forms of finger multiplication.

$$42 \div 6 = \square \longrightarrow 6 \times \square = 42$$

Thus children must search for the missing factor in the multiplication problem. Because multiplication facts are usually encountered and learned first, children can use what they know to learn the more difficult division facts. Moreover, division is related to subtraction, and division problems can be solved by repeated subtraction:

$$12 \div 3 = 12 - 3 - 3 - 3 - 3$$

However, repeated subtraction and the related strategies of counting backward or skip counting are confusing for many children. You may discuss them as ideas children might like to try, particularly when these strategies occur spontaneously in the course of some students' work, but don't be surprised if only a few children actually use them.

$15 \div 3 = \square$

Think
15 . . . 12, 9, 6, 3, 0
That's 5 numbers
$15 \div 3 = 5$

$28 \div 7 = \square$

Think
$28 - 7$
$21 - 7$
$14 - 7$
$7 - 7$
0
(4 subtractions)
$28 \div 7 = 4$

Splitting the product into known parts relies heavily on knowledge of multiplication facts, as well as on the ability to keep in mind the component parts.

$35 \div 7 = \square$

Think
$2 \times 7 = 14$
$3 \times 7 = 21$
$14 + 21 = 35$
$2 + 3 = 5$
So $35 \div 7 = 5$

As with multiplication, work with arrays helps children relate the symbols to the action.

In general, children have little difficulty in dividing by one. They need to exercise caution when zero is involved, however. Division by zero and division of zero present two different situations. Divide 0 by 6 ($0 \div 6$); the result is 0. Check this by multiplying: $6 \times 0 = 0$. But division by zero is impossible.

For example, to solve $6 \div 0 = \square$ would require a solution so that $6 = \square \times 0$. However, there is no value for $\square$ that would make this sentence true. Therefore, $6 \div 0$ has no solution, and division by zero is undefined in mathematics. Just as you may have difficulty remembering which is possible, division *of* 0 or division *by* 0, so will children have difficulty in remembering and need to be given practice.

Thinking strategies for division are far more difficult for children to learn than are the strategies for the other operations. The child must remember more, and regrouping is often necessary. When skip counting, for instance, the child must keep track of the number of times a number is named even as the struggle to count backward proceeds. Therefore, the primary burden falls on the child's facility with the multiplication facts. Being able to recall those facts quickly will facilitate recall of the division facts.

A Glance at Where We've Been

Skill in computation with whole numbers is developed through concrete experiences. In this chapter, we considered the importance of experiences with counting, concrete experiences, problem-solving contexts, and language, and we described and modeled meanings for each operation. We also presented mathematical properties to be developed as part of the understanding of the operations.

The next part of the chapter focused on the basic facts for each operation. Starting from what children know, the facts are developed using experiences that range from concrete to pictorial to symbolic. Thinking strategies for the basic facts for each operation help children move from counting to more mature, efficient ways of developing the facts. Specific suggestions for providing practice and promoting mastery help children master the basic facts for quick recall.

Things to Do: From What You've Read

1. What prerequisites must children have before engaging in the lesson that opens this chapter?
2. Discuss each of these statements:
   (a) When you teach multiplication, you begin preparation for learning division.
   (b) Children should not be allowed to count on their fingers when they start addition.
   (c) With the wide use of calculators, there is little need for children to attain prompt recall of the basic facts.
3. What properties of addition and multiplication are especially helpful in teaching the basic facts?
4. Describe the thinking strategies a child might use with each of the following computations:

   $8 + 0 = \square$ $8 \times 5 = \square$ $7 + 8 = \square$
   $18 \div 3 = \square$ $16 - 7 = \square$

5. For each addition fact strategy (i.e., commutativity, adding one, doubles and near doubles, adding zero, counting on, adding to 10 and beyond), list three different facts that could use that strategy and explain what a child would think when using that strategy.
6. When is counting back an effective strategy for subtraction? Give an example.

7. How can Cuisenaire rods be used to show the commutative property of addition? Sketch several examples and describe an activity using Cuisenaire rods that would involve students in investigating this property.
8. Explain why division by zero is considered "undefined" by mathematicians.
9. There are two types of division that arise in real-world problems: measurement (or repeated subtraction) division and fair sharing (or partitive) division.
   (a) Write a partitive (or fair sharing) division word problem that would correspond to $24 \div 6$. Draw a picture to illustrate the solution to your problem and in simple language explain why your numerical answer makes sense.
   (b) Write a measurement (or repeated subtraction) division word problem that would correspond to $4\frac{1}{2} \div \frac{3}{4}$. Draw a picture to illustrate the solution to your problem and in simple language, explain why your numerical answer makes sense.
10. Choose a method for developing meanings and thinking strategies for teaching addition, subtraction, multiplication, or division and plan a lesson idea for teaching.

Things to Do: Going Beyond This Book

IN THE FIELD

1. Plan an interactive bulletin board to help children learn about one or more thinking strategies for subtraction.
2. Examine a recently published textbook for grades 2, 3, or 4. Analyze how basic facts for the four basic operations are presented in that text. How are the facts grouped? Are thinking strategies presented? If so, how do they compare with the strategies described in this chapter? How would you use this text in teaching basic facts? If you think you would probably want to supplement the text, explain what sorts of supplementary materials and experiences you would use and why.
3. **Building on children's literature.* Find a popular trade book (perhaps from the Book Nook for Children) that would be useful as a motivator for a problem-based lesson revolving around one of the four basic operations (addition, subtraction, multiplication, or division). Identify the operation that the story evokes and write a problem that you might challenge students to work on after hearing the story. If possible, read the story to some children, have them try solving your problem, and analyze their written work for evidence of understanding of the basic operation the story involves.
4. **Timed tests.* Observe children as they take a timed test on basic facts. What behaviors and emotions can you document? How are the results of the test used by the teacher? Talk to at least five children or adults about their memories of timed tests on basic facts. What do they say about their experiences?
5. **Student difficulties with basic facts.* Talk to a fifth- or sixth-grade teacher about what he or she does with students who are not fluent in basic facts. Do they receive special instruction in fact strategies? Do they use calculators routinely for classwork and homework? How many in the class have problems with basic facts? Which facts cause the most difficulties?
6. *Use the Basic Addition and Multiplication* Facts charts, found in Appendix B of your text or in *Teaching Elementary Mathematics: A Resource for Field Experiences,* to assess a child's fluency with the basic facts. Randomly say a fact for the child to answer orally. Use the chart to record his or her responses. You may want to develop some symbols to indicate correctness and quickness of response.

IN YOUR JOURNAL

7. Read the Number Standards for Grades pre-K–2 and 3–5 in the NCTM's *Principles and Standards for School Mathematics* (www.nctm.org). What recommendations are made concerning teaching basic facts? Write a position paper either agreeing with the NCTM's recommendations or taking an opposing position. Clearly explain and defend your position.

WITH ADDITIONAL RESOURCES

8. See the activity described in "Problem Solving with Combinations" (English, 1992). How is it related to ideas presented in this chapter?
9. Look at the book *Mental Math in the Primary Grades* by Jack Hope et al. (1987). How do the strategies described in that book compare to those described in this chapter? The book

*Additional activities, suggestions, or questions are provided in *Teaching Elementary Mathematics: A Resource for Field Experiences* (Wiley, 2004).

Book Nook for Children

Burningham, John. *Pigs Plus.* New York: Viking Press, 1983.
Mishaps occur when an old jalopy and its driver make an eventful trip. Simple addition concepts and sentences are used to describe these events. Each mishap is a separate little story told in three foldout pages. The first page shows the distressed riders and an appropriate numeral, the second page shows one pig to the rescue with a "+1," and the last page shows the pigs with the problem solved.

Charosh, Mannis. *Number Ideas through Pictures.* New York: Thomas Y. Crowell Publishers, 1974.
Colorful drawings and simple text gradually lead the child into activities and generalizations in an exploration of odd, even, square, and triangular numbers. An example of this visualized process is presented in the context of adding two odd numbers.

Endelee, Judith Ross, and Tessler, Stephanie Gordon. *Six Creepy Sheep.* Hornesdale, PA: Boyds Mills Press, 1992.
This counting book uses rhymes to depict how six sheep dressed as creepy ghosts are frightened off, one by one, by trick-or-treaters until only one creepy sheep is left to knock on the door of a lonely barn.

Hawkins, Colin. *Take Away Monsters.* New York: G. P. Putnam's Sons, 1984.
Monstrous characters, clever situations, and good rhymes support learning mathematics. Add paper mechanics that allow subtraction problems by using paper mechanics on each page to be solved as the illustration changes to accurately reflect the answer. For example, a verse states, "Five monsters living in jail. One escapes, and they all start to wail." The partial number sentence $5 - 1 =$ appears with the verse. When the reader pulls a tab, the humorous scene depicting five monsters is transformed.

Hulme, Joy N. *Counting by Kangaroos: A Multiplication Concept Book.* New York: Scientific American Books for Young Readers, 1995.
Multiplication is illustrated using animals from Australia. Groups of three squirrel gliders, four Koalas, five bandicoots, . . . ten wallaby joys all crowd a house.

includes black-line masters for instruction, activity sheets for individual seatwork, and suggestions for using manipulatives to help children develop basic fact strategies. How might you integrate use of materials from that book with regular textbook instruction on basic facts?

10. Pick a concept or skill from this chapter and compile a brief bibliography of recent articles with research or teaching ideas on the topic.
11. Find the Focus issue on The Magic of Number in the journal *Mathematics Teaching in Middle School.* Read one of the articles and give a written or oral report to your teaching peers.

WITH TECHNOLOGY

12. Find a calculator activity, software package, or game on the web that focuses on basic facts. Share the ideas you find.
13. Find a computer program that claims to help children learn basic facts and try it out. Many of these programs are on the market. Most focus on encouraging development of quick responses, but few encourage use of thinking strategies. Write a half-page review of the computer program (similar to those published in teacher journals). In your review you should identify the name and publisher of the program, the cost, and the type of hardware required to run it. Explain how the program works. Include answers to the following questions:
    - Does the program help children learn strategies for basic facts?
    - Does the program keep track of student progress?
    - Does it modify the facts presented to the student according to which ones he or she has gotten right or wrong in the past?
    - Do you think the program would be effective in promoting quick recall of facts? Why?
    - Do you think children would enjoy using this program? Why?
    - How would you use such a program if your classroom had only one or two computers?
    - Would you recommend this program to other teachers? Why?

Resources

ANNOTATED BOOKS

Fosnot, Catherine T., and Dolk, Maarten. *Young Mathematicians at Work: Constructing Number Sense, Addition, and Subtraction.* Portsmouth, NH: Heinemann, 2001.

In our efforts to reform mathematics education, we've learned a tremendous amount about young students' strategies and the ways they construct knowledge, without fully understanding how to support such development over time. In this book, the authors tell what they have learned after several years of intensive study in numerous urban classrooms. The first in a three-volume set, *Young Mathematicians at Work* focuses on young children ages four to eight as they construct a deep understanding of number and the operations of addition and subtraction. Drawing from previous work, they define mathematics as an activity of structuring, modeling, and interpreting one's "lived world" mathematically. They describe teachers who use rich problematic situations to promote inquiry, problem solving, and construction, and children who raise and pursue their own mathematical ideas. Sample mini-lessons on the use of the open number line model are provided to show you how to support the development of efficient computation.

Piccirilli, Richard. *Mental Math Kids Can't Resist! (Grades 2–4).* New York: Scholastic Professor Book Division, 2000.
Tips, shortcut strategies, and 60 practice pages that reinforce math skills. Students apply the strategies as they work on computation, problem solving, and estimation.

Trafton, Paul, and Thiessen, Diane. *Learning through Problems, Number Sense and Computational Strategies, A Resource for Primary Teachers.* Portsmouth, NH: Heinemann, 1999.
A good book for K–4 teachers who are looking for a better way using problem solving. Kids can come up with all sorts of ingenious solutions to problems, gaining confidence in working on new problems. The problems focus on simple, everyday situations.

ANNOTATED ARTICLES

Askew, Mike. "Mental mathematics." *Mathematics Teaching,* 160(6), (September 1997), pp. 3–6.
Focuses on the mental methods of computation that children use. Highlighting two aspects of mental mathematics used by children in the seven- to twelve-year-old age group; illustration of the process of computation; what children are expected to know at certain stages; how to manage mental mathematics programs.

Buckleitner, Warren. "Tech Notebook: Math Motivators." *Instructor,* 109 (April 2000), pp. 66–69.
A collection of computer programs for teaching elementary mathematics. At the primary level, students are taught skip counting, measurement, graphs, number patterns, place value, addition, and subtraction. An action game teaches mental math, addition, and multiplication, as well as other skills for upper elementary students.

Leutzinger, Larry P. "Developing Thinking Strategies for Addition Facts." *Teaching Children Mathematics,* 6 (September 1999), pp. 14–18.
Leutzinger demonstrates activities for primary-grade students to address basic facts like counting on, using doubles, and making ten with a focus on reasoning and communication. Probability, spatial sense, and money are also discussed.

Sowell, Evelyn J. "Multipurpose Mathematics Games From Discards." *Arithmetic Teacher,* 23 (October 1976), pp. 414–416.
Sowell gives suggestions for developing effective mathematics games and gives rules for two specific games.

"The Magic of Number," Focus Issue of *Mathematics Teaching in Middle School, 7* (April 2002).
This focus issue provides several suggestions for teaching numbers and operations according to the *Standards.*

ADDITIONAL REFERENCES

Ashlock, Robert B., and Washbon, Carolynn A. "Games: Practice Activities for the Basic Facts." In *Developing Computational Skills,* 1978 Yearbook (ed. Marilyn N. Suydam). Reston, VA: NCTM, 1978, pp. 39–50.

Baroody, Arthur J., and Standifer, Dorothy J. "Addition and Subtraction in the Primary Grades." In *Research Ideas for the Classroom: Early Childhood Mathematics* (ed. Robert J. Jensen). Reston, VA: NCTM, and New York: Macmillan, 1993, pp. 72–102.

Carpenter, Thomas P.; Corbitt, Mary Kay; Kepner, Henry S. Jr.; Lindquist, Mary Montgomery; and Reys, Robert E. *Results from the Second Mathematics Assessment of the National Assessment of Educational Progress.* Reston, VA: NCTM, 1981.

Clark, Faye B., and Kamii, Constance. "Identification of Multiplicative Thinking in Children in Grades 1–5." *Journal for Research in Mathematics Education,* 27 (January 1996), pp. 41–51.

Davis, Edward J. "Suggestions for Teaching the Basic Facts of Arithmetic." In *Developing Computational Skills,* 1978 Yearbook (ed. Marilyn N. Suydam). Reston, VA: NCTM, 1978, pp. 51–60.

English, Lyn. "Problem Solving with Combinations." *Arithmetic Teacher,* 40 (October 1992), pp. 72–77.

Funkhouser, Charles. "Developing Number Sense and Basic Computational Skills in Students with Special Needs." *School Science and Mathematics,* 95 (May 1995), pp. 236–239.

Ginsberg, Herbert. *Children's Arithmetic: The Learning Process.* New York: Van Nostrand Reinhold, 1977.

Greer, Brian. Multiplication and Division as Models of Situations. In *Handbook of Research on Mathematics Teaching and Learning* (ed. Douglas A. Grouws). New York: Macmillan, 1992, pp. 276–295.

Hope, Jack A.; Leutzinger, Larry; Reys, Barbara J.; and Reys, Robert E. *Mental Math in the Primary Grades.* Palo Alto, CA: Dale Seymour, 1987.

Kamii, Constance; Lewis, Barbara A.; and Booker, Bobby M. "Instead of Teaching Missing Addends." *Teaching Children Mathematics,* 4 (April 1998), pp. 458–461.

Kouba, Vicky L., and Franklin, Kathy. "Multiplication and Division: Sense Making and Meaning." In *Research Ideas for the Classroom: Early Childhood Mathematics* (ed. Robert J. Jensen). Reston, VA: NCTM, and New York: Macmillan, 1993, pp. 103–126.

Kouba, Vicky L., and Franklin, Kathy. "Research into Practice: Multiplication and Division: Sense Making and Meaning." *Teaching Children Mathematics,* 1 (May 1995), pp. 574–577.

Quintero, Ana Helvia. "Conceptual Understanding of Multiplication: Problems Involving Combination." *Arithmetic Teacher,* 33 (November 1985), pp. 36–39.

Rathmell, Edward C. "Using Thinking Strategies to Teach the Basic Facts." In *Developing Computational Skills,* 1978 Yearbook (ed. Marilyn N. Suydam). Reston, VA: NCTM, 1978, pp. 13–38.

Sowell, Evelyn J. "Effects of Manipulative Materials in Mathematics Instruction." *Journal for Research in Mathematics Education,* 20 (November 1989), pp. 498–505.

Thornton, Carol A., and Smith, Paula J. "Action Research: Strategies for Learning Subtraction Facts." *Arithmetic Teacher,* 35 (April 1988), pp. 8–12.

CHAPTER 10

Computational Tools: Calculators, Mental Computation, and Estimation

Snapshot of a Lesson

Third graders are working at tables in small groups. At each table, paper, pencils, and calculators are available. Mr. Diggs has placed four items at the front of the room (prices are also shown on the board) for all the children to see. The focus of the lesson is to provide opportunities to use different computational tools.

MR. DIGGS: Here are some things you can buy. Please choose any two of them. Decide how much money the items you chose would cost.

He waits until the children have decided. He also observes how the children are doing their computations.

MR. DIGGS: Make a list of the money spent in your group, and then have a reporter from your group write the totals on the board.

After a few minutes, this list is compiled:

Amounts spent:	$0.50	$0.75	$1.00	$1.98
Number of students:	8	6	9	4

MR. DIGGS: Many of you spent $1.00. Why do you think $1 was so popular?

WHITNEY: Because we like apples. I'm hungry and could eat two apples.

MR. DIGGS: I'm hungry, too, and wish that I had a couple of apples. Is there another reason? Justin, what do you think?

JUSTIN: Because it is easy to add 50 cents plus 50 cents.

WILLIAM: I think it's easy to add 25 cents plus 25 cents. That is why I got 50 cents.

SARAH: It is also easy to add 50 cents and 25 cents.

JUSTIN: Easiest for me is 50 cents plus 50 cents because it makes a dollar.

This discussion provides insight into which computations are easy for the children and confirms

Mr. Diggs' observation that the children did these computations mentally. He then moves the discussion to another sum that was reported.

MR. DIGGS: Four people spent $1.98. Would someone tell me what you bought and how you decided it was $1.98?

AARON: I bought two pens. Each cost $0.99, so that if it was one penny more, it would be a dollar. Two of them would make two dollars–minus 2 cents, that's $1.98.

KELLY: I did it a little differently. I knew that one more penny would make $0.99 a dollar. So I took one penny from the $0.99 and made it $0.98 and added one dollar to it to get $1.98.

ROBERT: I couldn't hold the numbers in my head, so I used paper and pencil.

MR. DIGGS: That sounds like another good way to get the answer.

BARBARA: I used a calculator. Is that okay?

MR. DIGGS: Barbara, you can use the calculator whenever you need it, but try to do it in your head first. If it is too hard to do in your head, then try doing it a different way, as Robert did.

Mr. Diggs wants to move this activity along to develop more number sense and include estimation. He asks, "Suppose I spent more than $3, what two items could I buy?"

WHITNEY: Four pens would be almost $4.

MR. DIGGS: That's right, Whitney, but I asked you to buy only two things.

LINDSAY: You could buy two toys.

MR. DIGGS: Lindsey, tell us more about how you decided on two toys.

LINDSEY: Well, I thought $1.67 is more than one and a half dollars. I know that one plus one is two, and two halves make another dollar, so that makes three dollars. So it must be more than three dollars but less than four.

MR. DIGGS: Good thinking. It often helps to decide what is the most and least that could be possible when we compute. Why do you think no one chose to buy two toys?

Mr. Diggs anticipates an answer that the prices of the toys are hard to compute but asks this question to refocus the discussion on how we decide which computational tools to use. He plans to ask for other possibilities, such as a pen and a toy, and observe the strategies the children use. These activities give him insight into how his students are thinking and the level of confidence, as well as skill, his students have with various computational tools.

Introduction

Computation has evolved from using counting and calculating devices, such as piles of stones in ancient times or using a *soroban* (a Japanese abacus), to using written computational algorithms. More recently, the calculator has become available, and no computational tool has had a greater impact on school mathematics.

Competence with a variety of computational tools is not merely useful; it is essential. The importance of computational tools is reflected in the NCTM's *Principles and Standards for School Mathematics,* in the Number and Operations Standard as described in Figure 10-1.

Historically, elementary school mathematics has emphasized written computation far more than other tools. This, together with the fact that learners are more likely to select tools with which they are familiar, means that students often tend to use written computation even though other more efficient computational options exist.

Teachers need to establish a better balance of instructional attention to these computational

Math Links 10.1

The full-text electronic version of the Number and Operation Standard, with electronic examples (interactive activities), is available at the NCTM's web site, which you can access from this book's web site. Click on pre-K–2, 3–5, or 6–8 to read more about this standard.

Math Links 10.2

A variety of Web resources for computational tools, which may be used by teachers and children, may be found at the NCTM's Illuminations web site (accessible from this book's web site) under the Number and Operation Standard.

Instructional programs should enable all students to:	Pre-K–2 Expectations All students should:	Grades 3–5 Expectations All students should:
Compute fluently and make reasonable estimates.	Use a variety of methods and tools to compute, including objects, mental computation, estimation, paper and pencil, and calculators.	Select appropriate methods and tools for computing the whole numbers from among mental computation, estimation, calculators, and paper and pencil according to the context and nature of the computation and use the selected method or tool.

FIGURE 10-1 Number and Operation Standard with expectations for children in grades prekindergarten–2 and 3–5 to develop operation sense.

tools so children can learn to make appropriate choices. To make this happen, teachers must recognize and teach that different options are available for doing computation. One insightful view of computation is shown in Figure 10-2. It illustrates that all computation begins with a problem situation involving calculation and then highlights the series of decision-making stages that must be completed when doing computation. Notice that regardless of the type of computation done, estimation is always used to check on the reasonableness of the result.

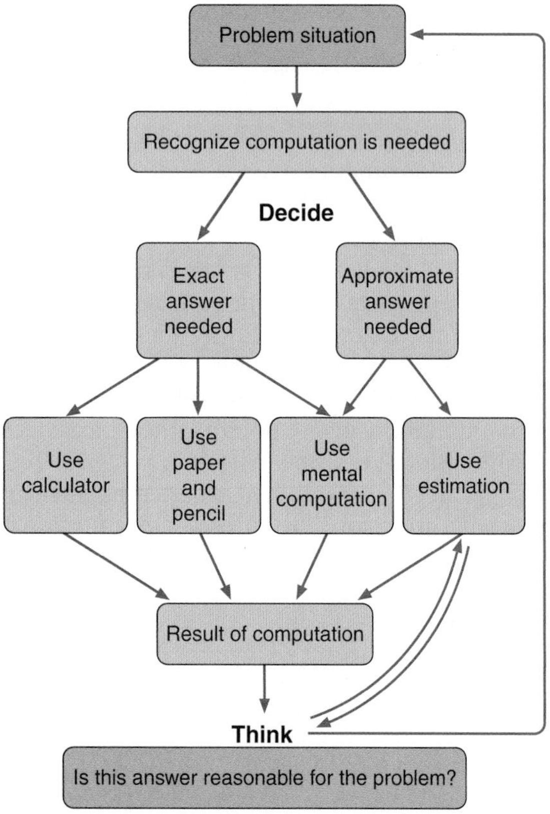

Problem situation
Recognize computation is needed
Decide
Exact answer needed
Approximate answer needed
Use calculator
Use paper and pencil
Use mental computation
Use estimation
Result of computation
Think
Is this answer reasonable for the problem?

FIGURE 10-2 Computational decisions and tools.

In every computational situation, two important decisions are essential: the type of result that is needed and how that result can best be produced. Is an estimate appropriate or is there a need for exactness in the result? Would a calculator be helpful in obtaining an estimate? Or do the numbers in the situation allow for a mental strategy? Thus important goals of mathematics learning related to computation are to help students:

- Develop competence with each of the computational tools.
- Make wise choices among the computational tools available.
- Choose tools that are consistent with the computation desired and ability to use that tool.
- Apply the chosen tool correctly.
- Use estimation to determine the reasonableness of an answer (result) for the particular problem being solved.

Helping students select and use these tools appropriately and effectively contributes to their number sense.

FOCUS QUESTIONS

1. What computational tools should students develop?
2. What are some myths about calculators?
3. How are computational estimation and mental computation different?

4. What are some different strategies for doing computational estimation?

Computational Choices

Developing competence with the four computational tools—mental computation, estimation, written computation, and technological tools such as calculators—is an important goal for elementary school mathematics. Mental computation, estimation, and calculators are discussed here; written computation is considered extensively in Chapter 11.

As teachers you need to think about which computations are needed and are important enough to learn in school and how you should direct instructional time. Research reports that more than 80 percent of all mathematical computations in daily life involve mental computation and estimation of numerical quantities rather than written computation. Ironically, research in the United States also shows that 70–90 percent of the instructional time in elementary school mathematics directed toward computation has focused on written computation procedures (Sowder, 1992).

Many proposals have been made regarding computation, ranging from prohibiting calculator use to eliminating the teaching of written algorithms. Thoughtful recommendations also have called for helping children learn to make appropriate computational tool choices. For example, a report by the National Research Council suggests:

> Children should use calculators throughout their school work, just as adults use calculators throughout their lives. More important, children must learn when to use them and when not to do so. They must learn from experience with calculators when to estimate and when to seek an exact answer; how to estimate answers to verify the plausibility of calculator results; and how to solve modest problems mentally when neither pencil nor calculator is convenient. (1989, p. 47)

Most people recognize the importance of each of the computational tools and suggest that a redistribution of instructional time is needed. Is there a better balance of instructional time for the computational alternatives than has historically occurred in elementary schools? The percentage of time to devote to each tool remains an unanswered question and certainly depends on the developmental levels of the students.

Changes in the time devoted to computational alternatives are needed, but the specific percentages are open to debate. In the spirit of stimulating debate and discussion, consider Figure 10-3; this presentation depicts an approximation of what has happened in the past, the current situation, and a proposal for a better balance.

Any future prediction is subject to error. Thus the percentage of time devoted to these tools is subject to question. Nevertheless, the decline in attention to standard written algorithms over the years and into the future is indisputable. Instructional time previously devoted to developing proficiency with tedious written algorithms can become available for other uses. Much of this time can be dedicated to developing increased number sense, together with greater attention to the other computational tools—calculators, mental computation, and estimation. Reflecting on your experience and thinking about the future needs of your students will challenge you to develop ways of providing a proper balance in your computation instruction.

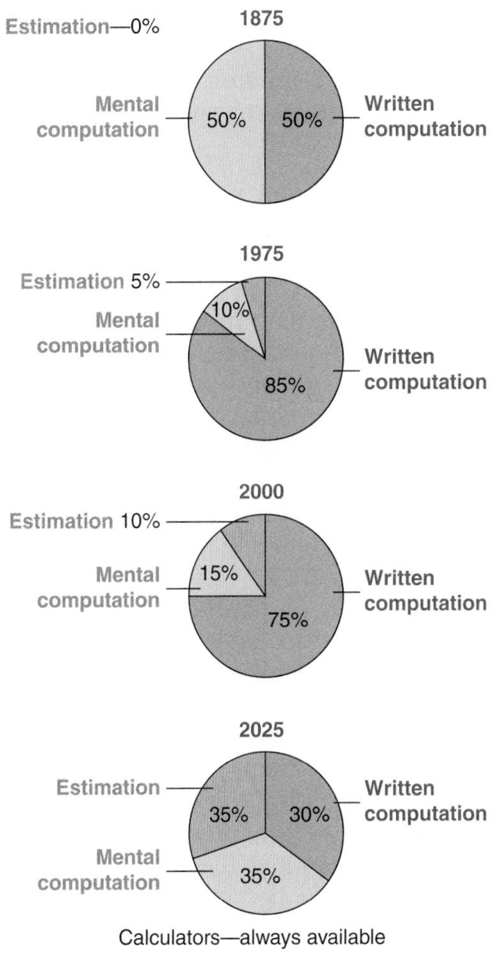

FIGURE 10-3 How time devoted to computation in elementary school has been spent in the past and might be spent in the future.

Calculators

The NCTM position statement on calculators has recommended that "appropriate calculators should be available to all students at all times." This statement suggests that as students' mathematical knowledge grows, their use of calculators changes. Children outgrow calculators just as they outgrow shoes. The calculator needs of students in primary grades are different from those of students in the intermediate grades and middle school. Electronics companies have anticipated these changing needs with the development of fraction calculators, scientific calculators, and graphing calculators.

Even though calculators have been in schools for more than 20 years, several myths continue to exist.

MYTH 1: CALCULATOR USE DOES NOT REQUIRE THINKING. Teachers must make it clear to parents that calculators don't think—they only follow instructions. Consider the following problem:

> A bus holds 32 children. If 1,000 children are being bused to a concert, how many buses are needed?

Suppose a calculator is available. Does the calculator decide which keys to press and in what order to press them? Does the calculator interpret the result? The answer to both questions is no!

Research shows that this problem is difficult to solve with or without a calculator. To use the calculator effectively, students must decide which buttons to use and the order in which to use them. Furthermore, a calculator result must be properly interpreted. For example, the calculator result of 31.25 requires students to decide if 31.25 makes sense for this problem situation or whether 31 or 32 buses are needed.

Children intent on producing an answer without reflecting on reasonableness are likely to get answers that don't make sense. Calculators don't discourage thinking! In fact, proper use of calculators encourages thinking because using a calculator frees students from tedious and laborious computation and allows them to dwell on the important problem-solving processes that generally precede, and often follow, the computation.

MYTH 2: USE OF CALCULATORS HARMS STUDENTS' MATHEMATICS ACHIEVEMENT. Research has addressed this issue and consistently reported that the use of "calculators in concert with traditional instruction . . . can improve the average student's basic skills with paper and pencil, both in basic operations and in problem solving" (Hembree and Dessart, 1992). Moreover, "students using calculators possess a better attitude toward mathematics and an especially better self-concept in mathematics." Many parents and some teachers worry that students will become so dependent on calculators that they won't learn to compute. Research shows this is not the case. Teachers must not only make effective use of calculators in their teaching but also help any skeptics put their fears to rest.

MYTH 3: COMPUTATIONS WITH CALCULATORS ARE ALWAYS FASTER. Calculators make tedious computations easy. For example, a calculator can compute 2345×67 or $34567 \div 89$ instantly, which shows the power of a calculator; however, it is much faster to do many simple calculations, such as 4×40, $99 + 99 + 99 + 99$, $\frac{1}{2} + \frac{1}{4}$, or 1000×23, mentally than to enter them into a calculator. In the Classroom 10-1 provides one way of helping children recognize the power of mental computations as well as the calculator.

MYTH 4: CALCULATORS ARE USEFUL ONLY FOR COMPUTATION. The most obvious use of calculators is to calculate, but in the process of calculating, many powerful mathematical ideas emerge. For example, calculator counting forward and backward, as was shown with In the Classroom 7-6, 7-7, and 7-8, provides patterns and practice in many important skills, such as basic multiplication and division facts. Using calculators to count by powers of ten (10, 100, 1000) and decimals (tenths, hundredths) suggests additional patterns for older children.

Computational skills must be learned, and the calculator provides a useful tool in this process. As a teacher, you need to carefully consider the value of using calculators for computation whenever computational skills are not the main focus of instruction. Clearly, the establishment of basic facts must remain an important goal of primary grades. Basic facts are natural stepping stones to mental computation and estimation, and to the long-term development of number sense. It is essential that rapid recall of basic facts (e.g., 4×7, $8 + 6$) be an instructional goal; however, as suggested previously, calculators can be used to facilitate basic fact learning in many meaningful ways that encourage students to think.

When is calculator use appropriate? Many teachers are unsure how to use calculators with their students. Some teachers resort to unproductive uses of the calculator, such as having students turn the calculator upside down to spell words or using the calculator to check written calculations. These activities may be somewhat motivational,

In the Classroom 10-1

CALCULATORS—
TO USE OR NOT TO USE

OBJECTIVE: **Encourage recognition of the power of mental computation and wise use of calculators.**

GRADE LEVEL: **3–5**

▼ Divide into two groups. One group must use calculators. The other group must NOT use calculators.

▼ Once groups are decided, the leader reads each computation out loud one at a time. Read the computation aloud, for example. "4 × 1000" → "four times one thousand."

▼ Decide who does the computation correctly the fastest. Then do the next computation.

	Must Use Calculators	Must NOT Use Calculators
1. 4×1000	______	______
2. $400 + 50 + 8$	______	______
3. $99 + 99 + 99 + 99$	______	______
4. $1000 - 200$	______	______
5. $50 + 50 + 50 + 50 + 50 + 50$	______	______
6. $\frac{1}{2} + \frac{3}{4}$	______	______
7. $6300 \div 7$	______	______
8. $10 \times 10 \times 10 \times 10$	______	______
9. $0.75 + 0.25 + .050$	______	______
10. \$1.00 − \$0.25	______	______

▼ Which group got the most correct answers the fastest?

▼ Make a list of 5 computations that you think children *using calculators* will do the fastest.

▼ Make a list of 5 computations that you think children *NOT using calculators* will do the fastest.

but their educational value is questionable. They may communicate the message that a calculator is only for playing games or, even worse, that using a calculator is cheating and should be done only after written computation. Research shows that the more teachers use calculators in their classroom, the more they develop creative and productive ways to use them (Fey, 1992). A calculator should be used as a *computational tool* when it:

1. Facilitates problem solving.
2. Relieves tedious computation.
3. Focuses attention on meaning.
4. Removes anxiety about computational failures.
5. Provides motivation and confidence.

In addition to making the calculator available as a computational tool, you can also use calculators productively as an instructional tool. Teachers' editions of most textbooks contain useful suggestions for using calculators as instructional tools. Several resources are listed at the end of this chapter (CAMP-LA, 1991). A calculator should be used as an *instructional tool* when it:

1. Facilitates a search for patterns.
2. Creates problematic situations.
3. Supports concept development.
4. Promotes number sense.
5. Encourages creativity and exploration.

Calculators also provide a safety net for students having particular difficulties in learning computational procedures. If students are learning disabled, making it difficult or impossible for them to successfully use traditional computational procedures, the calculator provides equity and allows them to engage in other problem solving.

When using calculators with students, teachers can provide experiences that will help them make appropriate use of this tool. As with any new tool, you need to provide time for students to explore with the calculator on their own and discuss rules for handling and caring for them. You can help dispel the calculator myths discussed earlier by demonstrating the following concepts:

1. Calculators do not think for themselves.
2. Not all problems can be solved with a calculator.
3. It is sometimes faster to compute mentally.

Math Links 10.3

To learn more about what the NCTM recommends concerning the use of technology, such as calculators and computers in classrooms, and to see how they are communicating it to parents, visit the Family Corner at NCTM's web site, which you can access from this book's web site. There you will find NCTM's position statement on technology.

Dear Parents:

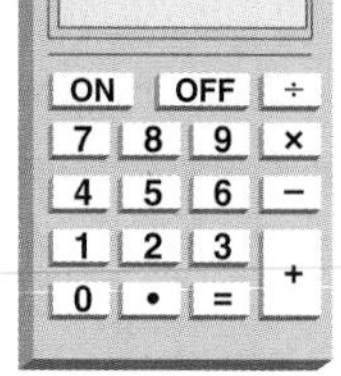

We are using calculators in our second-grade class this year in many different ways. Sometimes we use them to develop skills in counting and recognizing patterns; other times to explore new topics, such as decimals, and often when solving problems that require tedious computations. Research suggests that a variety of early experiences with calculators will help young children make wise use of calculators both in and out of school.

If you have questions about how we are using calculators, please ask your child to share some things he or she has been doing with this tool. If you have further questions, please let me know.

FIGURE 10-4 A sample note to parents about calculators in primary grades.

Communicate with parents so that they understand what is happening and why calculator use is important. Often, a simple note to parents is effective (see Figure 10-4). This note serves several useful purposes. It establishes communication between teacher and parents. It also lets parents know that calculators are used in their children's classroom and tells why they are being used. Learning how and when to use calculators as well as other computational tools is an important goal for every mathematics program.

Mental Computation

Mental computation is done without the aid of external tools. This sounds simple enough, and is certainly a natural way to do many computations. The naturalness of "doing it in your head" is demonstrated in the *Snapshot* at the beginning of this chapter as well as by the fact that many young children (before being able to write) have already developed ways of computing. In fact, research has documented a wide variety of creative mental computation techniques that children have constructed (Cobb and Merkel, 1989; Kamii et al., 1993).

Doing mental computation builds onto and naturally extends the thinking strategies used to develop the basic facts discussed in Chapter 9. Extending basic facts is an early step in developing more powerful mental computation strategies and skills. For example, the basic fact 4×6 could serve as a foundation or stepping stone for many mental computations, such as:

> 4×600 is 4×6 hundreds, which is 24 hundreds, or 2400.
>
> 4×6000 is 4×6 thousand, which is 24 thousands, or 24000.

These extended facts build on basic facts and place-value concepts, suggesting different patterns and relationships in the process. Mental computation together with calculators can be used to explore a range of patterns that suggest different relationships and may stimulate conjectures and discoveries. As patterns emerge, students can explore relationships between

4×6 and 4×60 and 4×600 and 4×6000

Students can tell how these results are alike and how they are different. A slightly different exploration can be generated by challenging students to "Tell why these are the same."

$4 \times 600 \quad 40 \times 60 \quad 400 \times 6 \quad 4000 \times 0.6$

Doing mental computation encourages flexible thinking and rewards thoughtful analysis that often uses very different techniques.

FIGURE 10-5 Different ways to mentally compute.

Notice the range of strategies used in Figure 10-5. Each strategy is meaningful to the student using it; however, that strategy may not be known by everyone and may even seem strange to others. Talking about ways different children compute mentally encourages freedom of thought and flexibility of strategies. Children often can learn new strategies by hearing their classmates' explanations. In fact, encouraging students to share and explain how they did the problem in their heads is an important part of instructional activities promoting mental computation (McIntosh et al., 1997).

As children develop their mental computation abilities, it is important that they encounter a range of activities that encourages and rewards the wide variety of skills used when doing mental computation. Rather than have everyone use the same strategy to solve a problem, the goal of mental computation instruction is to encourage individual students to use strategies that make sense to them. Here are some things children should be encouraged to do:

- Always try mental computation before written methods or calculator use.
- Use numbers that are easy to work with:

	One way to think
397 × 4 = ?	400 × 4 = 1600 3 × 4 = 12 1600 – 12 = 1588
$6.98 + $7.98 + $9.98 = ?	7 + 8 + 10 = 25 3 × 2 cents = 6 cents $25 – 6 cents = $24.94

- Look for an easy way:

2 × 3 × 7 × 5 = ?	2 × 3 = 6 6 × 5 = 30 30 × 7 = 210 or 2 × 5 = 10 3 × 7 = 21 10 × 21 = 210
6 × 8 × 19 × 0 = ?	0 is a factor, which means the product is zero.

- Use logical reasoning

15 × 120 = ?	That's halfway between 10 × 120 and 20 × 120 . . . halfway between 1200 and 2400 . . . that's 1800 or That's 10 × 120 plus half of 10 × 120 . . . 1200 + 600 that's 1800

- Use knowledge about the number system

56 – 24 = ?	50 – 20 = 30 6 – 4 = 2 30 + 2 = 32 or 54 – 24 = 30 so 56 – 24 = 32

Why emphasize mental computation? Here are several reasons for helping students develop mental computation:

- *Mental computation is very useful.* A majority (more than three-fourths) of all calculations by adults are done mentally. Encouraging, developing, and rewarding mental computation early is an important step toward developing this practical and lifelong skill.
- *Mental computation provides a direct and efficient way of doing many calculations.* For example, research has shown that the computation 200 – 5 is easier to do mentally than in a written form. Students are more likely to make sensible judgments about the results and less likely to report 205 (a common error for the written form). Likewise, in the middle grades, computations such as $\frac{3}{4} - \frac{1}{2}$ are easier to compute mentally than in a written form (McIntosh et al., 1995).
- *Mental computation is an excellent way to develop critical thinking and number sense and to reward creative problem solving.* Students must choose (invent) a strategy and use it. In this process, they become aware that there is more than one way to perform most calculations mentally and are encouraged to seek simple and economical methods that make sense to them (Cobb and Merkel, 1989).
- *Proficiency in mental computation contributes to increased skill in estimation.* Mental computation provides the cornerstone for all estimation processes, offering a variety of alternative algorithms and nonstandard techniques for finding answers.

Mental computation encourages flexible thinking, promotes number sense, and encourages creative work with numbers in an efficient manner. Thus, 165 + 99 might be solved in several different ways, such as:

> "I subtracted 1 from 165 and added it to 99. Then I added 164 + 100 to get 264."
>
> "I added 165 plus 100 and got 265, then I subtracted 1 and got 264."

Research has documented many insightful techniques; however, the dominant strategy among children above grade 2 was applying written algorithms mentally when doing the computation (McIntosh et al., 1997). Thus when asked to compute 165 + 99 mentally, the typical description was:

> "I added 5 plus 9 and got 14. I carried the ten, and 5 + 9 plus 1 is 15. I carried that 1 and got 2. It's two-six-four or 264."

Many students think of mental computation as applying written algorithms in their heads (Reys and Barger, 1994). This notion of mental computation is far different from the mental computation described here and is often difficult and impractical.

Research suggests that practice with written computational algorithms increases the likelihood of students trying to apply written methods mentally. This phenomenon is an international dilemma. Although the range of different mental computation strategies in Canada and the United States was far greater than in Japan, in each country a learned paper/pencil strategy was the dominant strategy reported by students. It appears that the application of written algorithms mentally most likely reflects the emphasis given to written algorithms in school and appears to inhibit the development of flexible and more efficient mental computation strategies (Reys et al., 1995; Reys and Yang, 1998; Shigematsu et al., 1994). Increasing emphasis on flexible, student-generated strategies enables students to compute mentally without relying on written algorithms to do so.

Many useful mental computation strategies have been documented and identified. Just as teachers can help children develop a repertoire of problem-solving strategies, they also can help children develop a collection of mental computation strategies. Figure 10-6 presents several common strategies for whole-number addition. As you examine these examples, see if you have ever used any of these strategies. Chances are, you have!

Among the guidelines you should follow when developing mental computation are these:

- *Encourage students to do computations mentally.* Make it clear that mental computation is not only acceptable but desired when possible. Students report that mental computation is not encouraged and often discouraged in school (Sowder, 1992). It has been suggested that when teachers say, "Show your work," students interpret this to mean that

Problem	Strategy	How I Did It
43 + 48	Adding from the left	40 plus 40 is 80, 3 plus 8 is 11, 80 plus 11 is 91
43 + 48	Counting on	I'll count by tens. 48 . . . 58 . . . 68 . . . 78 . . . 88 Then I'll count by ones. 89 . . . 90 . . . 91
43 + 48	Making tens	48 plus 2 is 50, 50 plus 40 is 90, 90 plus 1 more is 91
43 + 48	Doubling	48 plus 48 is 96. Since 43 is 5 less than 48, 96 minus 5 is 91.
43 + 48	Making compatibles	43 and 7 are compatible because they make 50, 50 plus 40 is 90, 90 plus 1 more is 91.
43 + 48	Bridging	I'll break up a number and add the parts. 43 plus 8 is 51, add 40 more is 91
Can you think of any other ways to solve this problem?		

FIGURE 10-6 Some examples of flexible mental computation strategies for whole-number addition.

mental computation is unacceptable. Thus instead of doing 1000×945 mentally, a student might write:

$$\begin{array}{r} 945 \\ \times\ 1000 \\ \hline 000 \\ 000 \\ 000 \\ 945 \\ \hline 945000 \end{array}$$

Applying this written algorithm is both unnecessary and inefficient, yet it is often preferred by students, presumably because they think it is required.

- *Learn which computations students prefer to do mentally.* Research suggests that, when given the choice, students from grade 4 and up prefer to use written computations rather than calculators or mental computation. For example, most fifth graders chose to do 1000×945 with either a calculator or paper/pencil. Although this is not a wise choice, research suggests that such choices typically reflect the student's lack of experience and confidence in doing computations mentally. In the Classroom 10-2 and 10-3 illustrate one way to explore the computational preferences of students with whole numbers and with fractions. These In the Classroom activities include a range of computations. Some look easy, such as $1 - \frac{1}{3}$, yet only about 15 percent of fifth graders could produce a correct result (Reys et al., 1993).
- *Find out if students are applying written algorithms mentally.* Ask students to tell how they did a computation in their heads. When students tell how it was done, the strategies and thinking used become clear.
- *Plan to include mental computation systematically and regularly as an integral part of your instruction.* Systematic attention and practice

In the Classroom 10-2

HOW WOULD YOU DO IT?

OBJECTIVE: **Encourage wise use of computational alternatives.**

GRADE LEVEL: **4–5**

	In your head	With a calculator	With paper/pencil
60×60	☐	☐	☐
945×1000	☐	☐	☐
450×45	☐	☐	☐
$24 \times 5 \times 2$	☐	☐	☐
$2000\overline{)16000}$	☐	☐	☐
$45\overline{)450}$	☐	☐	☐
4×15	☐	☐	☐
$50 \times 17 \times 2$	☐	☐	☐

Follow Up

▼ Write a computation YOU would solve with a calculator.

▼ Write a computation YOU would solve mentally.

▼ Write a computation YOU would solve with paper/pencil.

In the Classroom 10-3

HOW WOULD YOU DO IT?

OBJECTIVE: **Encourage wise use of computational alternatives.**

GRADE LEVEL: **4–5**

	In your head	With a calculator	With paper/pencil
$\frac{1}{2} + \frac{1}{4}$	☐	☐	☐
$1 - \frac{1}{3}$	☐	☐	☐
$\frac{3}{4} + \frac{3}{4}$	☐	☐	☐
$\frac{1}{5} + \frac{1}{6}$	☐	☐	☐
$\frac{1}{2} + \frac{5}{6}$	☐	☐	☐
$1\frac{1}{2} + 2\frac{3}{4}$	☐	☐	☐
$2 - \frac{3}{4}$	☐	☐	☐
$\frac{1}{2} - \frac{1}{3}$	☐	☐	☐

Follow Up

▼ Write a computation YOU would solve with a calculator.

▼ Write a computation YOU would solve mentally.

▼ Write a computation YOU would solve with paper/pencil.

will improve your students' mental computation performance. Experiences should focus on development of strategies and thinking patterns that make sense to students. These may be self-generated strategies as well as those learned from others.

- *Keep practice sessions short, perhaps 10 minutes at a time.* Many teachers use activities such as Follow Me while children are waiting in line: "3 + 7 + 10 − 4 + 20 . . ." or Today's Target, where the date serves as the target. For example, teachers post the date and ask students questions such as those shown in Figure 10-7A. Figure 10-7B depicts a variety of student ideas for meeting the Target Date.

Figure 10-7A can be varied by changing target numbers to something besides dates. For example, you might say, "Today's target is 100," and then ask students different ways to make 100. You might also change the questions and ask them to use "addition and subtraction."

- *Develop children's confidence.* Pick numbers that are easy to work with at first (such as 3 × 99 or $\frac{1}{2}$ of 84) then increase the difficulty (e.g., try 5 × 75 or $\frac{2}{3}$ of 96).

Experiences with compatible numbers (numbers that are easy to compute) such as those shown In the Classroom 10-4 help children develop confidence, number sense, and promote a valuable skill.

- *Encourage inventiveness.* There is no one right way to do any mental computation, but there may be certain ways that are more efficient and interesting. Asking students, "How did you do that?" can reveal highly ingenious mental computation strategies. For example, 60 × 15 was given to students in an interview (Hope et al., 1987). Among the strategies reported were:

  "10 times 60 is 600. 5 times 60 is 300. 600 plus 300 is 900."

  "60 times 10 is 600 and half of 600 is 300, so it is 600 plus 300 or 900."

  "60 is 4 times 15, so that is 4 times 15 times 15. 15 squared is 225 times 4 is 900."

Today's Target Date is May [24]
Try to make today's target by:
Adding three numbers
Finding the difference between two numbers
Multiplying two numbers
Using a fraction

FIGURE 10-7A Today's target and ways to hit the target.

Some solutions to the [24] target

Adding three numbers

8 + 8 + 8
20 + 12 + 2
10 + 10 + 4

Finding the difference between two numbers

30 − 6
25 − 1
100 − 16

Multiplying two numbers

4 × 6
8 × 3
24 × 1

Using a fraction

$23\frac{9}{10} + \frac{1}{10}$
$48 \times \frac{1}{2}$
$24\frac{1}{2} - \frac{1}{2}$

FIGURE 10-7B Some students' solutions to hit the target.

The latter strategy was reported by an eighth grader and is a reminder of the interesting techniques employed by students when doing mental computation. Many mental computational strategies are self-developed, and the power of self-learned out-of-school mental computation techniques has been documented (Sowder, 1992).

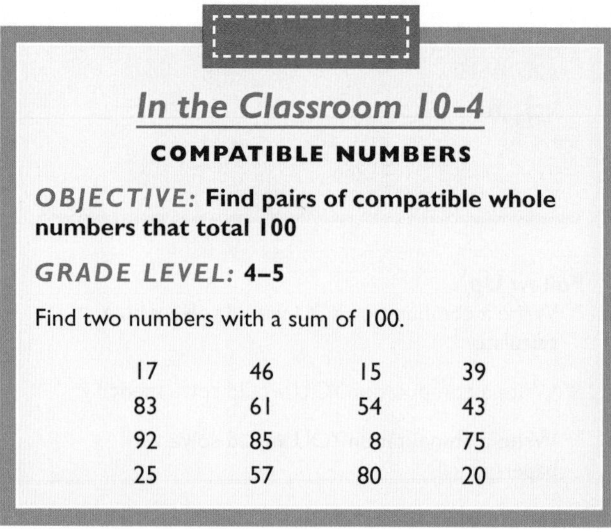

In the Classroom 10-4

COMPATIBLE NUMBERS

OBJECTIVE: **Find pairs of compatible whole numbers that total 100**

GRADE LEVEL: **4–5**

Find two numbers with a sum of 100.

17	46	15	39
83	61	54	43
92	85	8	75
25	57	80	20

- *Mental computation or estimation?* Make sure children are aware of the difference between estimation (in which answers are approximations) and mental computation (in which answers are exact).

Computational Estimation

Computational estimation is a process of producing answers that are close enough to allow for good decisions without making elaborate or exact computations. Real-world situations using estimation are diverse and plentiful. Computational estimation is typically done mentally, but there are circumstances that may require recording some results. Figure 10-8 illustrates how estimation serves as a monitoring function at three different places in the problem-solving process.

Estimation *before starting exact computation* helps build a general sense of what to expect. Estimation *while doing computation* provides an immediate or intermediate check to determine if the computation is moving in the right direction. *After the computation is completed,* estimation provides an opportunity to reflect on an answer and helps determine if the result makes sense. As children become aware of different uses of estimation, they develop a greater respect for its power and view it as an essential part of the total computational process.

FIGURE 10-8 Different times to estimate.

Math Links 10.4

An Internet-based lesson plan for middle school students, Five's a Crowd: A Game of Population Density, may be found on NCTM's Illuminations web site, which you can access from this book's web site. In this lesson, students collect area and population data from a web site, then estimate quotients to determine population density.

Students who are proficient at written computations are not necessarily good estimators. In fact, research with Taiwanese students documented their considerable skill at tedious written computations, yet these same students performed much lower when asked to estimate the identical computations (Reys and Yang, 1998). Several examples from that research are reported in Table 10-1. Notice that in each case, the numbers involved are tedious to compute, yet these same numbers lend themselves well to estimation. For example, 534.6×0.545 is rather complex with a written algorithm. Yet recognizing that 0.545 is about half suggests that the only reasonable estimate is about 290 (that is, one-half times a number between 500 and 600 is between 250 and 300, so 290 is the only reasonable answer of the three choices). Nevertheless, nearly 90 percent of the Taiwanese students selected 29.1357. This is an unreasonable answer, yet one that might result by applying a "counting the digits to the right of the decimal point" rule. The low performance on estimating the sum of two fractions ($\frac{12}{13} + \frac{7}{8}$) was similar to the results from the second national assessment of 13-year-olds in the United States. Because both fractions were slightly less than one, the sum should be less than two. Yet more than half of these students (United States and Taiwanese) selected either 19 or 21. This research provides a vivid reminder that teachers must look beneath correct answers to check on students' understanding and their ability to produce reasonable answers.

Research has also confirmed that good mental computation skills and number sense provide the foundation for the successful development of computational estimation techniques. Systematic

Table 10-1 • Percentage Correct by Sixth Graders in Taiwan (Reys and Yang, 1998)

Written Computation Items		Percentage Correct by Sixth Graders
$\frac{12}{13} + \frac{7}{8}$		61
$72 \div 0.025$		54
534.6×0.545		61
Estimation Items		
Without calculating an exact answer, circle the best estimate for $\frac{12}{13} + \frac{7}{8}$.	A. 1 *B. 2 C. 19 D. 21 E. I don't know	10 25 36 16 13
Without calculating an exact answer, circle the best estimate for $72 \div 0.025$.	A. A lot less than 72 B. A little less than 72 C. A little more than 72 *D. A lot more than 72	31 18 18 33
This multiplication has been carried out correctly except for placing the decimal point: $534.6 \times 0.545 = 291357$ Place the decimal point using estimation.	A. 29.1357 *B. 291.357 C. Other Answer	87 11 2

attention to computational estimation can significantly improve performance. Students must be given the opportunity to estimate. Although some dramatic improvements can occur quickly, the development of good computational estimation skills is a lengthy process that is accomplished only over a period of years (Sowder and Kelin, 1992).

Estimation provides the first mathematical encounter that is not exact, yet it is nonetheless a natural part of mathematics. As young children talk about mathematics, their language and vocabulary include words such as *about, almost, just over,* and *nearly.* As children grow older, additional vocabulary is added to describe mathematical answers, including *approximate, reasonable,* and *unreasonable,* as well as phrases such as *in the ballpark.* Developing comfort and confidence in using language to describe the inexactness found in the real world not only contributes to developing number sense but also prepares children for computational estimation.

Instruction should begin with making students aware of what estimation is about, so they develop a tolerance for error. Estimation involves a different mindset from that used to compute an exact answer. The "exact-answer mentality" must be changed before children develop specific estimation strategies. This change begins when students recognize that estimation is an essential and practical skill. That's why teachers must consistently emphasize computational estimation within different problem situations and along with computation procedures.

Immediate feedback to students on how well they have done in providing estimates is important. Be lenient in accepting responses initially. Ask students to explain how they obtained their estimates, because the discussion helps clarify procedures and may even suggest new approaches to estimating in a given problem. Beware of letting them confuse estimation, which produces an answer that is close, with mental computation, which produces an exact answer.

One of the keys to developing good estimation strategies is to help children be flexible when thinking about numbers. Suppose you wanted students to evaluate 418 + 349. One child might think, "400 + 300 is 700, and 49 + 18 is less than 100, so the sum is between 700 and 800." This approach uses the leading digits. Another child might think, "418 is about 400 and 349 is almost 350, so the sum is about 750." This child rounded to numbers that are easy to compute, and used number sense to make adjustments and produce an estimate.

As with mental computation, it is important that children develop different strategies. It is also critical that they think about the problem, the operations, and the numbers involved and not rely on a fixed set of rules to produce an estimate. When estimation is mentioned, many adults think of rounding; however, as in mental computation, several strategies can be developed with children so they possess a repertoire of strategies from which to choose.

Front-End Estimation

The front-end strategy for estimation is a basic yet powerful approach that can be used in a variety of situations. Two important things must be checked: (1) the leading, or front-end, digit in a number, and (2) the place value of those digits. To help students understand this strategy, Figure 10-9 shows a three-digit number hidden behind a sheet of paper on the board. Give students the opportunity to see one digit of their choosing. Some students choose the ones digit, but others choose the hundreds digit and find that this gives the most useful information. A few exercises such as this one help students begin to grasp the power of the leading, or front-end, digits.

Figure 10-10 shows how the front-end digits are used to obtain an initial estimate. The unique advantage of the front-end strategy is that all of the numbers to be operated on are visible in the original problem. Thus students can reach an estimate quickly and easily. The strategy also encourages students to use number sense as they think about the computations. In the Classroom 10-5 encourages students to use the front-end digits to make a quick estimate. A front-end estimate provides a lower bound, and this initial estimate can be adjusted as needed by using the remaining digits.

Adjusting or Compensating

Number sense has many dimensions, one of which is recognizing when something is a little more or a little less. As students use any estimation strategy, it becomes natural to begin refining their initial estimate by making adjustments or compensating. For example: About how much will 4 items at $0.78 each cost?

FIGURE 10-9 Illustrating the power of front-end estimation.

FIGURE 10-10 Front-end estimation in action.

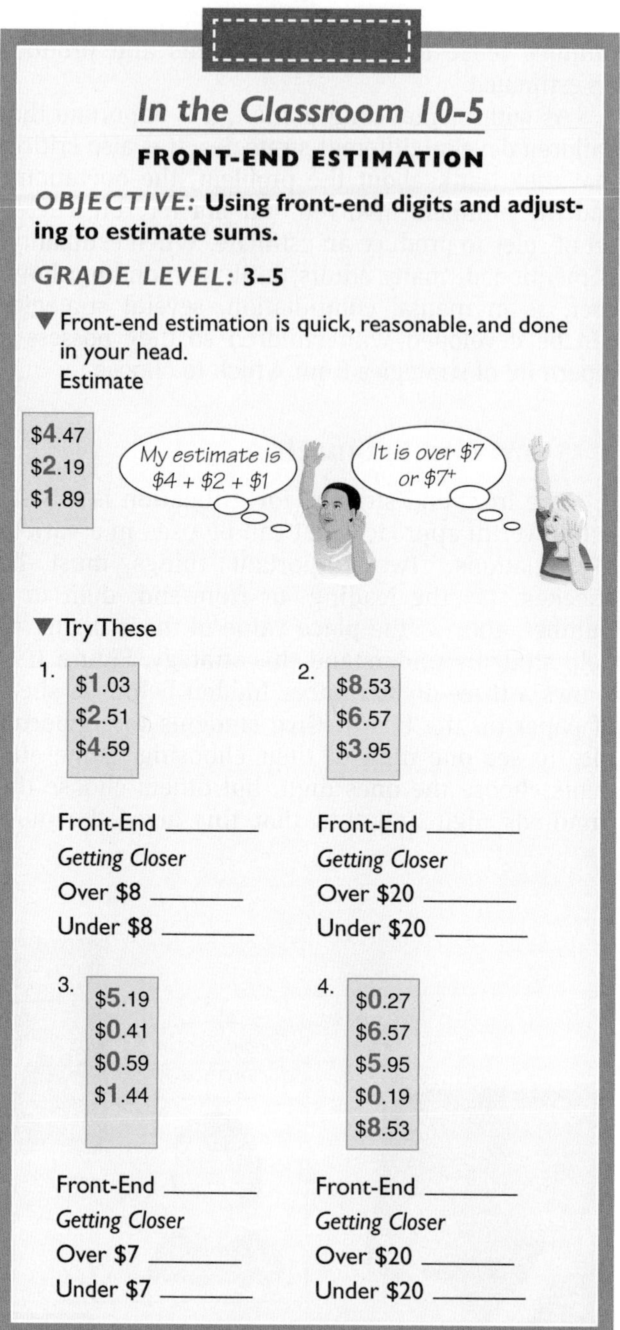

One person might think: 4 × $1 but less than $4. Another person might think: 4 × $0.75 is $3 but more than $3. In each case, the amount "less than $4" or "more than $3" reflects an adjustment or compensation that is made to the initial estimate.

Figure 10-11 illustrates how adjusting is accomplished. This process of adjustment or compensation cuts across all estimation strategies and all operations.

Compatible Numbers

Compatible numbers, or friendly numbers, are easy to compute mentally and seem to go together naturally. Work with the ten-frame helps children recognize that 6 and 4 are compatible with 10. This experience extends naturally to help them recognize that 60 and 40 are compatible with 100. These compatibles aid the development of other pairs, such as 65 and 35, that are also compatible with 100 and should be extended to other numbers. Figure 10-12 illustrates how compatible numbers can be used to make computations easier for a variety of different operations.

When the compatible numbers strategy is used, the numbers in the problem are rounded to numbers that are easier to work with. Notice in Figure 10-12 that 64 × 8 is not compatible for multiplication, but these same numbers are compatible for division. Similarly, 60 and 8 are not compatible for division but are compatible for multiplication. Thus any decision on compatibility must consider the operation as well as the numbers.

Figure 10-13 shows how the compatible numbers strategy works for division, with which it is particularly powerful. Given these problems, children need to be encouraged to think about why 7

FIGURE 10-11 Example of front-end estimation with adjustment.

and 2800 are compatible numbers for the problem. Asking them to pose possible "compatible numbers pairs" and to tell why encourages thoughtful ideas and provides insight into their number sense. Consider some possible compatible pairs for

$23\overline{)7029}$

$23\overline{)6900}$ 69 is divided evenly by 23, so 23 and 69 are compatible for division. Because both values are close to the original, the estimate of 300 is very close.

$20\overline{)10000}$ 10000 is divided evenly by 20. Although 20 and 10000 are compatible, 10000 is far removed from the original dividend, so the estimate of 500 will be very rough.

$25\overline{)7500}$ 75 is evenly divided by 25, so 75 and 25 are compatible. Both rounded values are close to the original values, so the estimate of 300 will be close.

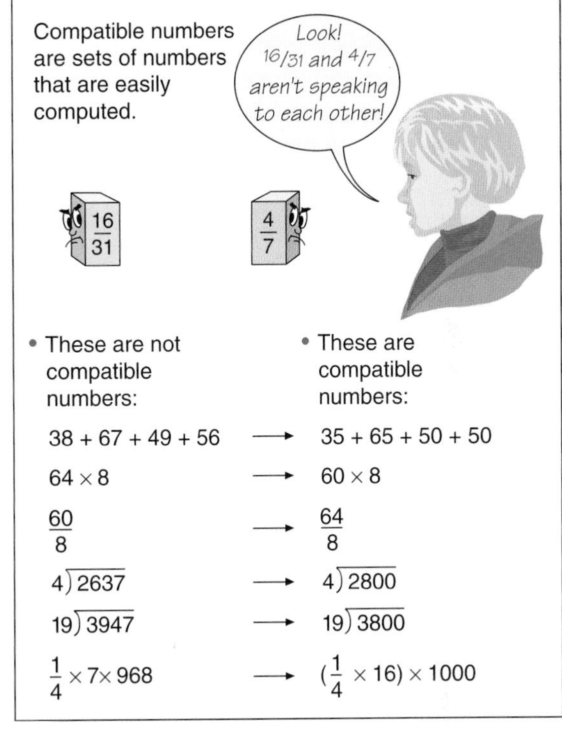

FIGURE 10-12 Examples of different compatible numbers.

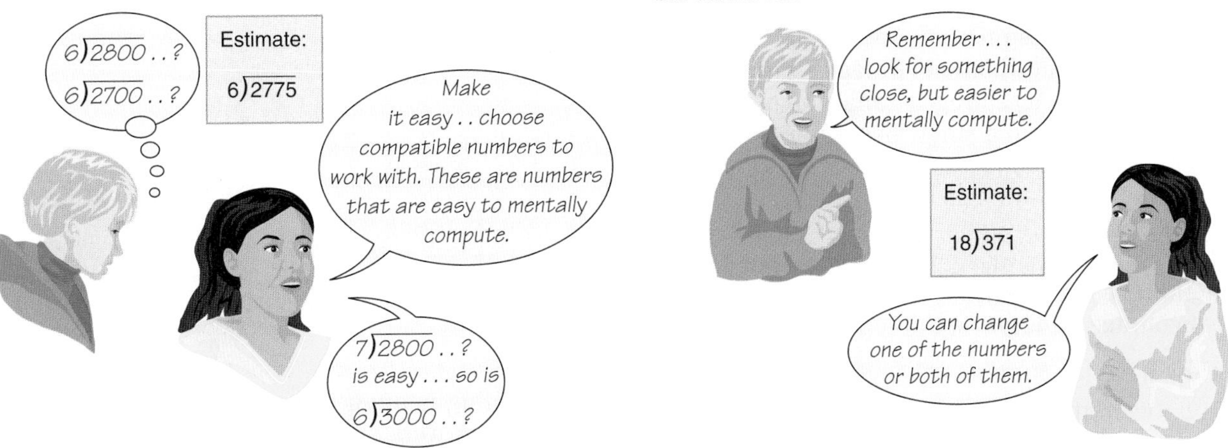

6)2800 . . ?
6)2700 . . ?
Estimate:
6)2775
Make it easy . . choose compatible numbers to work with. These are numbers that are easy to mentally compute.
7)2800 . . ? is easy . . . so is 6)3000 . . ?
Remember . . . look for something close, but easier to mentally compute.
Estimate:
18)371
You can change one of the numbers or both of them.

FIGURE 10-13 Examples of the compatible numbers strategy for division.

Compatible numbers can be applied to all types of computations, and they are often used in addition. In the following example, the student first used the front-end strategy and then compatible numbers to adjust the initial estimate:

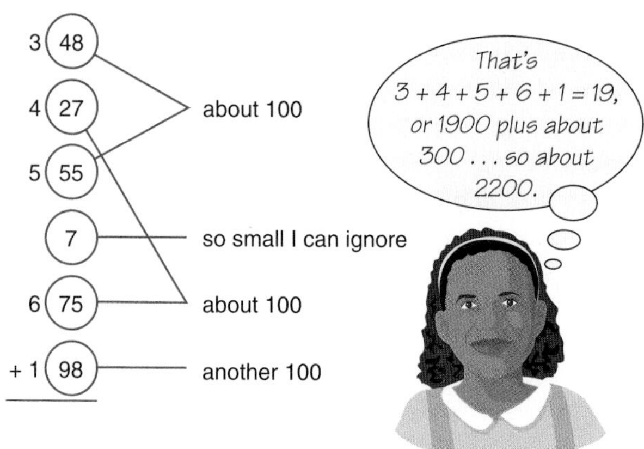

Flexible Rounding

Rounding to get easier numbers to work with was discussed in Chapter 8. Estimation also uses rounding to produce numbers that are easier to compute. Rounding in estimation is more sophisticated than front-end estimation because the numbers are changed or reformulated. Rather than applying rigid rounding rules, however, the general premise for flexible rounding is to round to any numbers that are close but also easy to compute. Flexible rounding is appropriate for all operations with all types of numbers, but it is particularly well-suited to multiplication. Children should be adept at the process of rounding to compatible numbers. Figure 10-14 shows how students started with the same problem but rounded differently. Notice that each approach produced a different result, but each is a reasonable estimate. It is important for students to know they have the freedom to choose different estimation strategies, but they need to realize that different strategies produce different estimates. Accepting a range of reasonable estimates, rather than a single best estimate, fosters number sense and encourages students to choose and use their own strategies.

Problems like the one shown in Figure 10-14 need to be accompanied by questions that go beyond those asking what the estimate is to those that encourage children to think about the process:

How have the numbers changed?

Why were these numbers changed?

The key to the effective use of rounding in estimation is to round to compatible numbers, which involves substituting numbers that are close to the original numbers but are more manageable to compute mentally. Children should be encouraged to think of possible substitutions and to reason about their choice from among them. The choices illustrated in the following example lead naturally to such questions as "Which pair would you choose to make the estimate?" and "Why?"

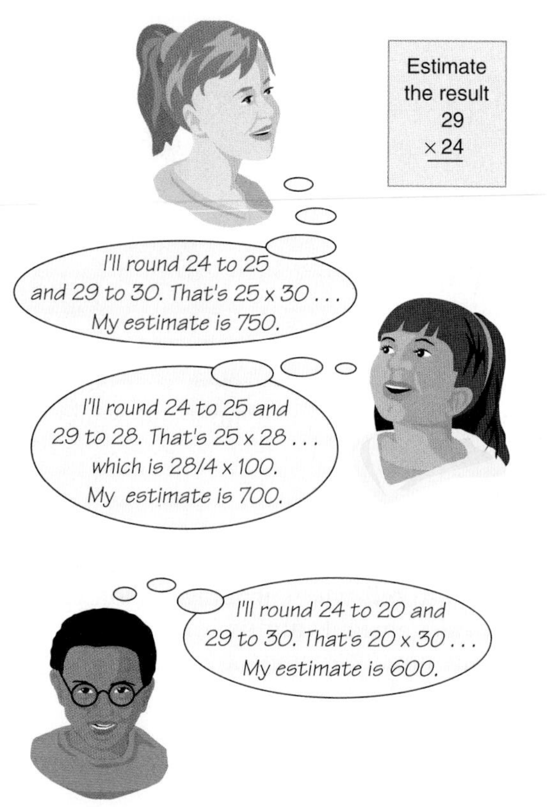

FIGURE 10-14 Examples of flexible rounding and different estimates that result.

Adjusting is often done to compensate for how the numbers were rounded, as in the following example in which an initial estimate is made by rounding:

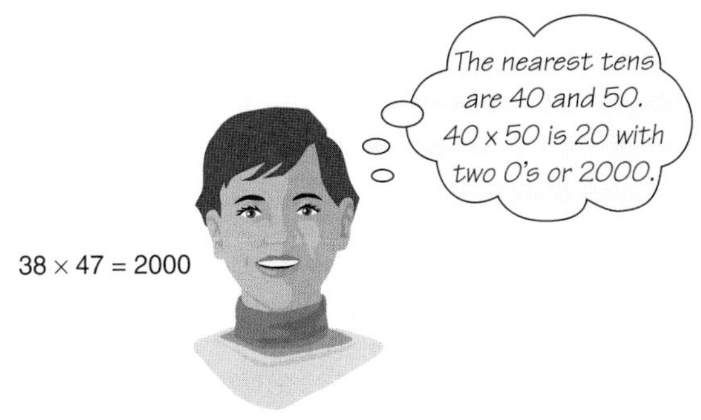

Next, the student makes an adjustment to refine the initial estimate:

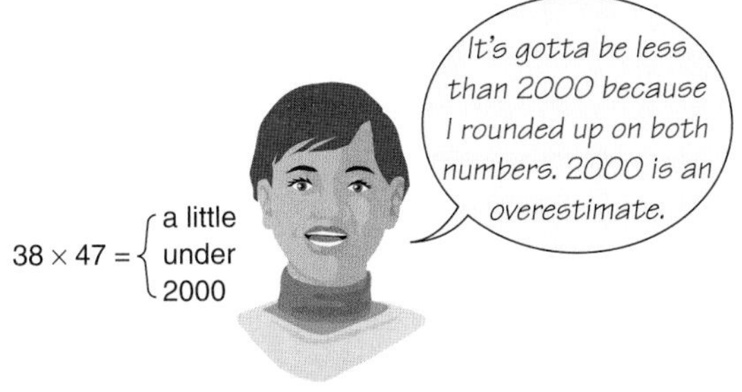

Here are some other examples:

Computation	Think	Results
42 × 61	40 × 60 = 2400	A little more than 2400
39 × 78	40 × 80 = 3200	A little less than 2400
27 × 32	30 × 30 = 900	About 900

For the first two examples, the rounding procedure makes clear whether the result is an underestimate or an overestimate, but in the last example, it is not so obvious. Students must think about the numbers used to produce their estimate.

As students' mental computation skills progress, the rounding procedures they use to produce estimates reflect more flexibility. When estimating, students should always round to numbers that are easy for them to compute mentally. This means that traditional rounding rules (such as if the digit is more than 5, round the preceding digit up) are not necessarily followed, and common sense is the hallmark. It also means that different people may round the same numbers in a problem differently, depending on what is easiest for them, as was shown in Figure 10-14.

Clustering

The *clustering,* or averaging, *strategy* uses a mean for an estimate. Whenever a group of numbers cluster around a common value, this two-step process is used:

1. Estimate the average value of the numbers.
2. Multiply by the number of values in the group.

Figure 10-15 gives a glimpse of this strategy in action. Questions such as the following can help give meaning to this strategy:

What number do all the values cluster around?

Why is the average estimated?

Why is the estimated average multiplied by 6 (or by 5)?

FIGURE 10-15 Examples of the clustering strategy for addition.

Asking what the estimated total is for these and a range of similar problems helps children become adept at using this strategy.

Clustering is a limited but useful strategy. It is appropriate for estimating sums of groups of numbers quickly. The strength of this strategy is that it eliminates the mental tabulation of a long list of front-end digits or rounded numbers.

Choosing Estimation Strategies

Estimation strategies take many different forms, often for the same problem. In fact, it is rare that a single strategy is used. Figure 10-16 illustrates how several different strategies might be applied to different situations. The choice of strategies depends on the situation, as well as on the numbers and operations involved. A challenge for you as the teacher is to help your students become aware of the wide array of estimation strategies that exist and to help your students develop confidence in their ability to engage in estimation.

Useful guidelines for developing computation estimation include the following:

- *Provide situations that encourage and reward computational estimation.* For example, 78 + 83 should be computed mentally to produce an exact answer, but 78342 + 83289 is more likely to promote estimation. Thus make sure the numbers are messy enough so that students want to estimate, rather than use a different alternative.
- *Check to learn if students are computing exact answers and then rounding to produce estimates.* Research has documented the popularity of this technique (Sowder, 1992), and unfortunately,

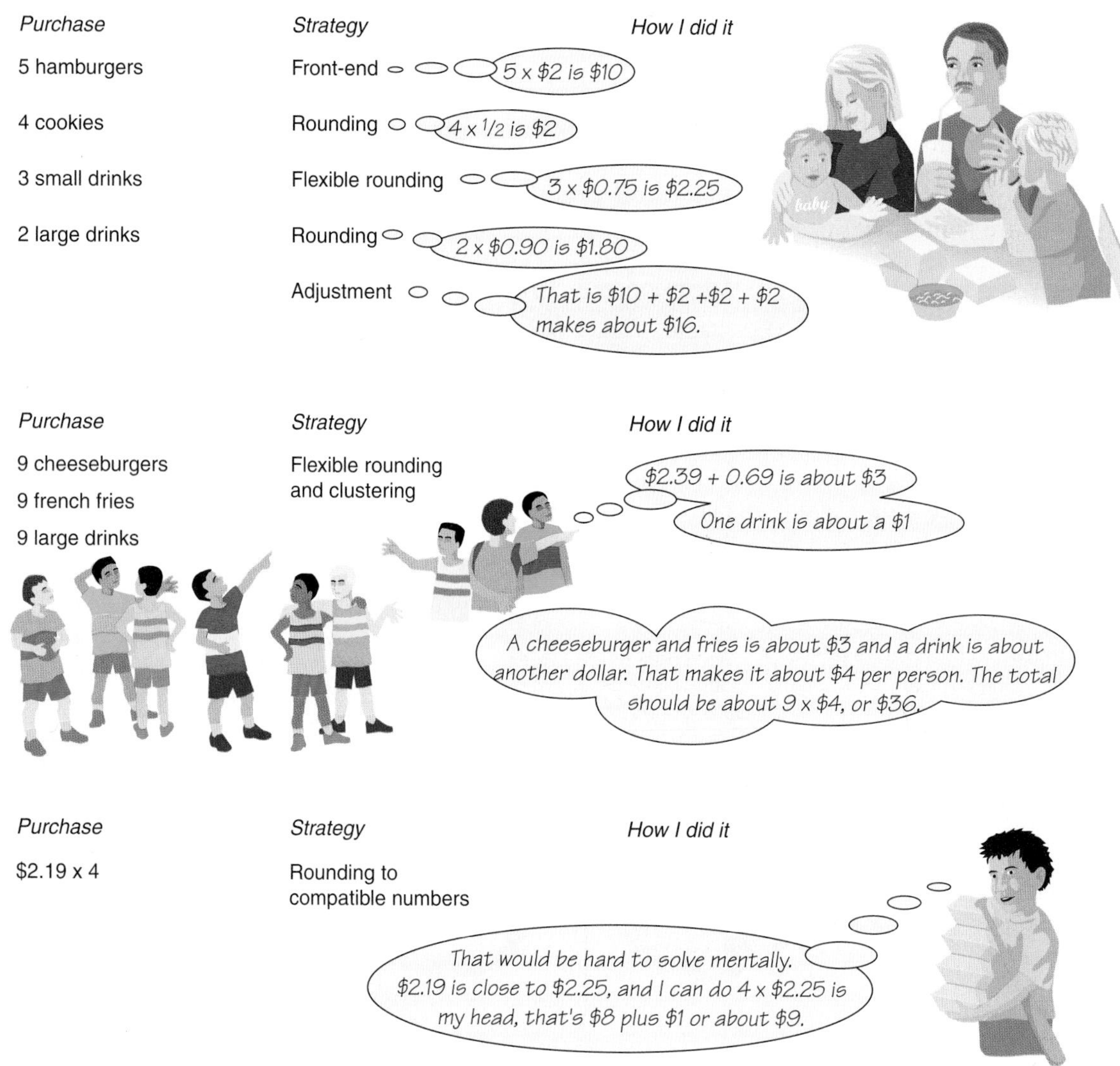

FIGURE 10-16 Integrating computational strategies.

these approaches often go undetected. Talking with students and observing their approaches to estimation provide checks to ensure that they are truly engaging in the process of estimating.

- *Ask students to tell how their estimates were made.* Research suggests that students often develop individual and unique approaches to computational estimation processes (Sowder, 1992). By sharing them, students develop an appreciation of different estimation processes.
- *Destroy the one-right-answer syndrome early.* Help students realize that several different yet acceptable estimates might be made for the same problem. One way to do this is to invite students to identify acceptable intervals for good estimates. Their discussion will generally reveal different strategies and help everyone learn about other strategies. Such experiences help students become more comfortable with the notion that several different but correct estimates exist.
- *Encourage students to think carefully about real-world applications that involve estimates.* Critical thinking skills can be sharpened in deciding when to overestimate and underestimate. Figure 10-17 illustrates several situations to encourage such thinking.

Over or Under

1. Your car usually gets about 25 miles per gallon on the highway. Your gas tank is about one-quarter full and it is 100 miles to the next gas station. Is this a good time to over- or underestimate your gas mileage?
2. You are talking with a car dealer about buying a car, and you ask about the gas mileage. Do you think the car dealer will over- or underestimate the gas mileage of the car?
3. You have $20 to spend on groceries for a group picnic. As you place each item in the grocery cart, is this a good time to over- or underestimate the cost of each item?
4. You are forecasting the lava speed of an active volcano. As the lava is moving down the mountainside toward a town, a decision needs to be made when to evacuate the town. Should you over- or underestimate the speed of the lava?
5. Your plane is scheduled to leave at 4:00 and it usually takes about one hour to get to the airport. Should you over- or underestimate the time needed to get to the airport when deciding what time to leave?

FIGURE 10-17 Examples of real-world situations in which under- or overestimations are needed.

A Glance at Where We've Been

Teachers must help students develop confidence and skill in using computational alternatives. This instruction should include ready access to and appropriate use of calculators. As basic facts are established, mental computation becomes an important tool for many computations. When the computations become too tedious to compute exact answers via mental computation, then estimation is a natural next step. "Is the answer more than . . ." and "Should it be less than . . ." are questions encouraging estimation and number sense. When exact answers are too tedious to obtain mentally, calculators and written algorithms are the appropriate tools; however, care needs to be taken to develop confidence and proficiency with mental computation and estimation before introducing and practicing formal written algorithms. Such a plan will challenge each of us to reflect on the worth of different computational tools and strive to provide the balance of the instructional time that each method deserves.

Things to Do: From What You've Read

1. What are some goals related to computation that involve computational tools such as calculators?
2. How would you respond to the following statement by a parent? "Calculators should not be used in school, because if students use them, they will never have to think."
3. Do you think the proposal in Figure 10-3 regarding percentage of instructional time devoted to developing computational alternatives applies to grades 2–6? If not, choose a grade level and decide how you think instructional time devoted to computation should be allocated. Be prepared to defend your proposal.
4. Distinguish between mental computation and estimation.
5. Several uses of the calculator as an instructional tool and a computational tool were discussed. Are these two approaches mutually exclusive? Explain and give an example to illustrate what you mean.
6. What do you think are the strongest reasons for encouraging and developing good mental computational skills?

7. A fifth-grader described this solution to 7×499 in her head: "I put the 499 on top and the 7 on bottom, then I get 3 and carry the 6 and 9 carry the 6 and 7 times 4 is 28 plus 6 is 34. . . ." Would you say this student was successfully doing mental computation? Explain why. Describe some other strategies that might be explored.
8. Discuss why it is important for students to develop a tolerance for an acceptable range of answers when doing computational estimation.
9. Explain why compensation and adjustment are an integral part of making estimates.
10. Figure 10-4 shows a possible letter to parents about calculator use in second grade. Prepare a letter to sixth-grade parents telling them that calculators will be used in your class and can be used on homework. Briefly explain why you are allowing and encouraging calculator use.
11. Here is an actual quote from a fourth grader telling what she thinks her teacher wants:

> I think she doesn't like us to use mental (computation) because she can't see the writing. And she doesn't like us to use the calculator a whole lot because then we'll get too used to it and we won't want to learn and stuff. . . . And she likes us to use written (computation) because she can see what we're doing, and if we're having problems she can see what we're doing wrong.

How would you respond to this student? Suppose you had an opportunity to talk with the student's teacher. What would you tell her teacher?

Things to Do: Going Beyond This Book

IN THE FIELD

1. *Do It Mentally. Ask at least two students to compute 99 + 165 mentally. Ask them how they did it. Describe the strategies that were used.
2. **About How Much?* Ask several people to estimate 29×24 and tell how they made their estimate. Describe their strategies and results. Did any of them use the strategies shown in Figure 10-14?
3. In the Classroom 10-1, 10-2, and 10-3 provide activities to check on student preferences for computing. Choose one of these activities to use with children in grades 2 to 5. Describe any surprises about how you thought students would do and how they actually did respond.
4. Check the NCTM web site, which you can access from this book's web site, for their position statement on calculators. Tell how this statement might be useful when talking with parents about calculator use in your classes.

IN YOUR JOURNAL

5. *Computational Tools.* Keep a log of the computational tools (mental computation, estimation, calculator, written computation) that you use for one day. Estimate what percentage of your computations made use of each tool. In your journal, summarize your results and describe a plan for improving your use of these different computational tools.
6. *Estimation.* In your journal, discuss why the following is not a good assignment: "I want you to estimate the answers to these problems, then compute the correct answers, and see how far off your estimate was from the correct answer."
7. *Calculators and Mathematics Achievement.* In your journal, describe ways that teachers can ensure that the use of calculators will not harm students' mathematics achievement.
8. *Assessing Mental Computation and Estimation.* Select a standardized achievement test. Review the test and determine the attention given to assessing mental computation and computational estimation. In your journal, discuss the strengths and weakness of test items that you found addressing mental computation or estimation.
9. Examine the potential test items on Master 10-4 in the *Helping Children Learn Mathematics Instructor's Manual.* Each item is designed to measure the mathematical understanding of your students. For each item, decide if students should use a calculator, should not use a calculator, or it doesn't matter if they use a calculator. Explain your thinking for each item. (Available at the Wiley Book Companion web site.)

WITH ADDITIONAL RESOURCES

10. Read the article "Computation in the Elementary Curriculum: Shifting the Emphasis" by Reys and Reys, 1998. Do you agree or disagree with their proposal for change? Tell why.

*Additional activities, suggestions, or questions are provided in *Teaching Elementary Mathematics: A Resource for Field Experiences* (Wiley, 2004).

11. Review one of the mental math books by Hope et al. (1987, 1988). Select a lesson and highlight the key ideas for your classmates.
12. Review the *Computation Estimation* book by Reys et al. (1987). Select a lesson and highlight the key ideas for your classmates.
13. Examine one of the CAMP-LA books. For the grade level of your choice, select an activity that illustrates a calculator activity you would like to use and tell why you chose the activity.
14. Read the article by Huinker (2002) titled "Calculators as Learning Tools for Young Children's Explorations of Number." Summarize this article and describe an activity that incorporates the calculator in expanding opportunities and possibilities for young children to explore number concepts.
15. Check the article by Harries and Dobson (1996) or McIntosh et al. (1997) for a summary of different ways students do computations orally and on paper. Do you agree with the summary? Tell why.

WITH TECHNOLOGY

16. *Calculator as an instructional tool.* Find or create a problem to use in a classroom where the calculator is used as an instructional tool. Explain how the calculator supports the instruction of the mathematics of the problem.
17. *Calculator as a computational tool.* Find or create a problem-solving task where the calculator is used as a computational tool. Explain how the calculator facilitates problem solving in this task.
18. *Calculators and order of operations.* Sometimes calculators use arithmetic logic in performing operations. For example, if you entered $3 + 5 \times 4$, the calculator would display the solution 32. Other calculators use algebraic logic, which evaluates expressions according to mathematical convention for order of operations. For $3 + 5 \times 4$, the result would be 23. Explain how you would solve these two problems using each type of calculator: (a) $(253 - 85) \div 4$; (b) $253 - 85 \div 4$.
19. Try each of the "Calculating Capers" in the "Math by the Month" section of *Teaching Children Mathematics*, February 2002 (Cloke et al.) Identify when and how you might use these acitivites in the classroom. Describe how the calculator use in these activities helps children learn mathematics.
20. Try the Three-Step Challenge found on Master 10-9 in the *Helping Children Learn Mathematics Instructor's Manual.* You will find that to solve this problem you will probably use estimation, mental computation, and a calculator. How did these tools help you solve this problem? (Available at the Wiley Book Companion web site.)

Book Nook for Children

Neuschwander, Cindy, and Woodruff, Liza. *Amanda Bean's Amazing Dream: A Mathematical Story*. New York: Scholastic Trade, 1998.
Known to her friends as Bean Counter, young Amanda Bean happily counts "anything and everything" by ones, twos, fives, and tens. Although her teacher tells her that learning multiplication is important, Amanda remains unconvinced until a strange dream presents her with arithmetic challenges that overwhelm her counting skills. She awakens (in both senses) and learns to multiply "anything and everything." The book ends with suggestions by Marilyn Burns for using the book in teaching multiplication.

McCourt, Lisa, and Tuckman, Brad. *The Candy Counting Book: Delicious Ways to Add and Subtract*. Mahwah, NJ: Troll, 1999.
Budding mathematicians are invited to take a bite out of some counting fun in this yummy book. Kids learn to add and subtract using delicious story problems and classic candies.

Murphy, S. D, and Schindler, S. D. *Betcha! Estimating (Mathstart, Level 3)*. New York: Scott Foresman (Pearson K-12), 1997.
What good is estimating? Two friends find that estimation skills are particularly helpful in a jellybean-counting contest. They practice their estimation skills versus counting of cars, toys, and people on their way to estimating the number of jelly beans in a jar.

Pinczes, Elinor J., and MacKain, Bonnie. *One Hundred Hungry Ants*. Boston, MA: Houghton Mifflin, 1993.
A great book for teaching multiplication, division, and grouping strategies begins with ants looking for a picnic, but they discover that spending too much time organizing can result in not getting the product! The ants march in one group of 100, two groups of 50, four groups of 25, and so on. Encourage the students to model the ants, draw new patterns, and write a happier ending for the story.

Resources

ANNOTATED BOOKS

Burns, Marilyn. *Math by all Means: Multiplication Grade 3.* New Rochelle, NY: Math Solutions Publications, 1991.
Students develop understanding of multiplication from a variety of problem-solving perspectives—geometrical, numerical, and practical situations. Includes activities from strands of probability, statistics, patterns and functions, and geometry.

Hope, J. A.; Leutizinger, L. P.; Reys, B. J.; and Reys, R. E. (1988). *Mental Math in the Primary Grades,* Palo Alto, CA: Dale Seymour Publications.
This book provides structure activities designed to encourage and promote the development of mental computation. A range of manipulatives and models are used to provide concrete models to facilitate different mental computation strategies.

McIntosh, A.; Reys, B. J.; Reys, R. E.; and Hope, J. *Number Sense: Simple Effective Number Sense Experiences: Grades 1-2, 3-4, 4-6. 6-8.* Palo Alto, CA: Dale Seymour Publications, 1997.
These 10-minute activities help students develop a sense of what numbers represent and how to use them by exploring relationships and patterns, encouraging mental computation, recognizing equivalent representations of a number, establishing benchmarks, improving estimation skills, and exploring the idea of reasonableness.

Ohanian, Susan, and Burns, Marilyn. *Math by all Means: Division Grades 3-4.* Sausalito, CA: Math Solutions Publications, 1995.
Students construct their own understanding of division through examining patterns, analyzing statistical data, and solving problems with money. They also investigate division from a geometric perspective and learn to use division in real-world contexts.

ANNOTATED ARTICLES

"Explorations of Number." *Teaching Children Mathematics,* 8(6), (February 2002), pp. 316–321.
Calculators expand opportunities and possibilities to help young children explore ways of representing numbers and number relationships. Young children can use calculators to investigate number ideas in ways that were previously inaccessible to them.

Markovitz, Zvia, and Sowder, Judith. "Developing Number Sense: An Intervention Study in Grade 7." *Journal for Research in Mathematics Education,* 25 (January 1994), pp. 4–29.
This study demonstrated that 12 male students were more likely to use strategies for mental computation and estimation after instructional intervention.

Reys, B. J.; Reys, R. E.; and Hope, J. A. "Mental Computation: A Snapshot of Second, Fifth, and Seventh Grade Student Performance." *School Science and Mathematics,* 93 (1993), pp. 306–315.
As a report of baseline data on mental computation abilities, this study addresses difficulties of different types of mental computation and student preferences on modes of computation.

Reys, R. E. "Computation versus Number Sense." *Mathematics Teaching in the Middle Grades,* 4(2), (October 1998), pp. 110–112.
Reys offers two different tests for teachers to research their own students' number sense. Test results from Taiwan are included.

Reys, R. E.; Reys, B. J.; McIntosh, A.; Emanuelsson, G.; Johansson, B.; and Yang, D. C. "Assessing Number Sense of Students in Australia, Sweden, Taiwan, and the United States." *School Science and Mathematics,* 99(2), (February 1999), pp. 61–70,
This report focuses on number sense proficiency of students age 8–14 and gives selected findings from a study along with discussion of number sense and its importance, assessment instruments, and implications for teaching.

Reys, R. E.; Reys, B. J.; Nohda, N.; and Emori, H. "Mental Computation Performance and Strategy Use of Japanese Students in Grades 2, 4, 6, and 8." *Journal for Research in Mathematics Education,* 26(4),(1995) pp. 304–326.
This article reports results of assessing attitude, computational preferences, and mental computation performance; it includes assessments.

Reys, R. E., and Yang, D. C. "Relationship Between Computational Performance and Number Sense among Sixth and Eighth Grade Students in Taiwan." *Journal for Research in Mathematics Education,* 29(2), (March 1998), pp. 225–237.
This study shows that student performance on written computation was significantly better than in similar situations that required number sense. The results support looking past the correct answer when testing computation.

ADDITIONAL REFERENCES

CAMP-LA: *Activities Enhanced by Calculator Use.* Book 1, Grades K–2; Book 2, Grades 3–4; Book 3, Grades 5–6. Orange, CA.: Cal State Fullerton Press, 1991.

Cloke, Gayle; Ewing, Nola; and Stevens, Dory. "Math by the Month: Calculating Capers." *Teaching Children Mathematics,* 8(6), (February 2002), pp. 344–346.

Harries, Tony, and Dobson, Alan. "Oral and Written Methods of Calculation." *Mathematics Teaching,* 154 (March 1996) pp. 32–35.

Hembree, Ray, and Dessart, Donald J. "Research on Calculators in Mathematics Education." In *Calculators in Mathematics Education,* 1992 Yearbook of the National Council of Teachers of Mathematics (ed. James Fey). Reston, VA: National Council of Teachers of Mathematics, 1992, pp. 23–32.

Hope, Jack A.; Leutzinger, Larry; Reys, Barbara J.; and Reys, Robert E. *Mental Math in the Primary Grades.* Palo Alto, CA.: Dale Seymour Publications, 1988.

Hope, Jack A.; Reys, Barbara J.; and Reys, Robert E. *Mental Math in the Middle Grades.* Palo Alto, CA.: Dale Seymour Publications, 1987.

Huinker, DeAnn. "Calculators as Learning Tools for Young Children's Explorations of Numbers." *Teaching Children Mathematics,* February 2002, Vol. 8 Issue 6, pp. 316–322.

Reys, B. J., and Reys, R. E. "Computation in the Elementary Curriculum: Shifting the Emphasis." *Teaching Children Mathematics,* 5(4), (December 1998), pp. 236–241.

Reys, R. E.; Trafton, P. R.; Reys, B. J.; and Zawojewski, J. S. (1987) *Computational Estimation (grades 6, 7, 8).* White Plains, N.Y.: Cuisenaire-Dale Seymour.

CHAPTER 11

Standard and Alternative Computational Algorithms

Snapshot of a Lesson

On the chalkboard, third-grade teacher Mrs. Garcia has drawn a problem:

MRS. GARCIA: I've put a problem on the board. Can your group solve it using the materials in front of you? [Each group has a different type of material.] After you've had a chance to try, we'll share the ways we attacked it.

We first thought about using 10 boxcars, which would hold 80 boxes. That still leaves 56 boxes. But 7 X 8 = 56. So with 7 more cars, we can load all the boxes. We needed 17 boxcars altogether.

After seven or eight minutes, all the groups are ready to tell how they solved the problem:

We changed 136 to 13 tens and 6 ones, because we couldn't work well with 1 hundred. We took 8 from each one of the tens in our minds, but that got too mixed up. So we said, 10 boxcars would hold 80 boxes — that's 8 tens. 5 tens left. 5 more boxcars would hold 40 boxes. There's 1 ten and 6 ones left. That's 2 more eights. So you'd need 10 + 5 + 2 boxcars

We laid out 136 cubes, and then separated them into groups of 8.

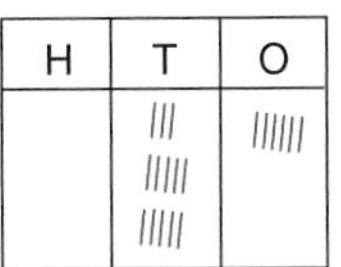

H
T
O

We keyed 8 on the calculator, then the division sign, then 136 — but the answer was less than 1! So we knew we'd used the wrong order. We had to key 136, then the division sign, then 8 — 136 divided by 8.

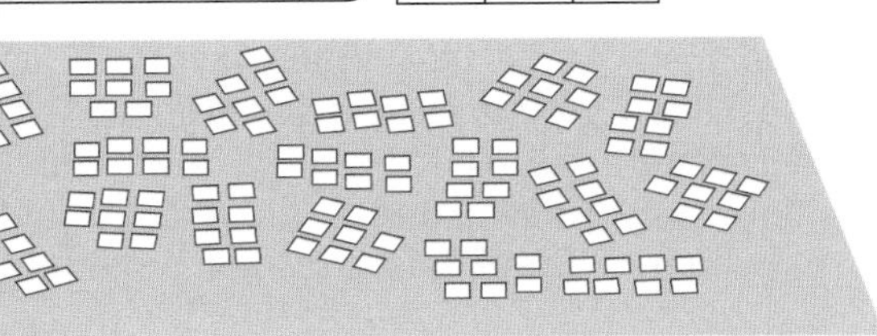

MRS. GARCIA: Good work everyone! You all found reasonable ways to figure out how many boxcars would be needed. Jenna's group recognized this as a division problem: 136 divided by 8. Now, how would you write that problem using math symbols?

Several children write each of these formats:

$$136 \div 8 \quad \frac{136}{8} \quad 8\overline{)136}$$

MRS. GARCIA: Yes, all show 136 divided by 8. We will use the third way when we work with paper and pencil. We know now that the answer is 17. Will you put the answer in place, Hamad?

Hamad writes:

$$\begin{array}{r} 17 \\ 8\overline{)136} \end{array}$$

Several other children say "No!" They are asked why.

CHILDREN: The answer has 1 ten and 7 ones, so it must be written in those places.

MRS. GARCIA: Good. Enrique, I noticed that you had a way of recording your thinking on your paper. Will you explain to us what you wrote?

We know there are at least 10 eights in 136, because 10 x 8 = 80. When I subtract, there are 56 left. 56 ÷ 8 is 7.

MRS. GARCIA: That's great! Does what Enrique wrote make sense to you, Sarah? Tell us why. What about you, Jacob? Can you use your own words to explain what Enrique wrote? Okay. Now let's try: 259 ÷ 6. See if you can find an answer and also write down your thinking so others can understand it.

Introduction

For hundreds of years, computational skill with paper-and-pencil procedures, called *algorithms,* has been viewed as an essential component of children's mathematical education. The teaching of computation has become more exciting in the past few years. Instead of teachers merely presenting a stream of algorithms, showing children just what to do, step by step by step, the focus has shifted to more attention on what children construct or develop for themselves. Computation has become a problem-solving process, one in which children are encouraged to reason their way to answers, rather than merely memorizing procedures that the teacher says are correct.

This change also means that children can explore alternative algorithms. The algorithms that teachers usually present have been refined over the centuries. They are highly efficient, but they do not necessarily reflect the way children think as they compute. Accuracy and efficiency are still important, but efficiency is of lesser importance. The focus is on reasoning and thinking as emphasized in NCTM's *Principles and Standards for School Mathematics* (2000), through the Reasoning and Proof Standard (see Appendix A).

Math Links 11.1

*T*he full-text electronic version of the Number and Operation Standard, with electronic examples (interactive activities), is available at NCTM's web site, which you can access from this book's web site. Click on pre-K–2, 3–5, or 6–8 to read more about this standard.

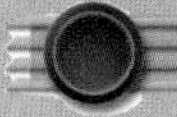
www.wiley.com/college/reys

Although calculators are readily available to relieve the burden of computation, the ability to use algorithms is still considered essential. The *NCTM Standards* stress the need for children to be able to choose computational techniques that are appropriate for problems at hand and also to determine whether the answers they obtain are reasonable. As described in the Number and Operations Standard (see Appendix A), students must have access to computational methods that are supported by an understanding of numbers and operations.

A balance between conceptual understanding and computational proficiency is essential for developing computational fluency. To develop such an enhanced ability, revisions in the teaching of computation include:

- Fostering a solid understanding of and proficiency with simple calculations
- Abandoning the teaching of tedious calculations using paper-and-pencil algorithms in favor of exploring more mathematics
- Fostering the use of a wide variety of computation and estimation techniques—ranging from quick mental calculation to those using computers—suited to different mathematical settings
- Developing the skills necessary to use appropriate technology and then translating computed results to the problem setting
- Providing students with ways to check the reasonableness of computations (number and algorithmic sense, estimation skills)

Many parents and some teachers have worried that students will become so dependent on calculators that they will forget how to compute. This concern is not supported by research. Hembree and Dessart (1986) reported from an analysis of many research studies that the use of "calculators in concert with traditional instruction . . . can improve the average student's basic skills with paper and pencil, both in basic operations and in problem solving" (p. 96).

Over the years, educators have developed several models for teaching the basic operational algorithms. Underlying the development of these models is the idea that children must be actively involved in constructing their own mathematical learning. Children may be more comfortable using a standard operational algorithm or an alternative variation; the choice is theirs. In this chapter, we emphasize the importance of teaching children to choose an appropriate calculation procedure, depending primarily on whether an exact or approximate answer is needed.

FOCUS QUESTIONS

1. Why are manipulative materials useful in helping children develop understanding of algorithms?
2. How can teachers help children develop the addition algorithm? Do all children need to use the same addition algorithm?
3. What are two standard subtraction algorithms and how did they develop?
4. How does the distributive property support the development of the multiplication algorithm?
5. What is the partial-products algorithm for multiplication, and how is it related to the traditional multiplication algorithm?
6. Why is the traditional division algorithm the most difficult for children to master?

Math Links 11.2

A variety of Web resources for whole-number computation, which may be used by teachers and children, may be found at NCTM's Illuminations web site (accessible from this book's web site) under the Number and Operation Standard.

Teaching Algorithms with Understanding

Computational fluency with addition, subtraction, multiplication, and division includes the ability to use various methods for computing and to

> **Math Links 11.3**
>
> You can use electronic manipulatives, such as Rectangle Multiplication and Rectangle Division (accessible from this book's web site), to illustrate whole-number computations larger than the basic facts.
>
> 
>

recognize the relationships among the various methods. This ability requires that children learn the procedures for particular algorithms; however, they must also gain a conceptual understanding that supports this procedural understanding. As teachers focus their instruction on algorithms, they need to support children in gaining "a balance and connection between computational proficiency and conceptual understanding" (NCTM, 2000, p. 35). Two instructional considerations are important in ensuring that children do not just learn algorithmic procedures by rote, but that they learn them with understanding.

Role of Materials in Learning Algorithms

The use of manipulative materials in developing understanding of the algorithms is essential. In the *Snapshot of a Lesson* that opened this chapter, the use of materials was the basis for working with symbols. Materials form a bridge between the real-life problem situation and the abstract algorithm, helping to forge the recognition that what is written down represents real objects and actions. Children must be given sufficient time to handle the materials and make the transition to pictures and symbols (Thompson, 1991). Unifix cubes, base-ten blocks, rods, Popsicle sticks, beansticks and loose beans, buttons, and myriad other materials, either derived from the problem setting or representative of that setting, help children construct an understanding of when and how an algorithm works.

Importance of Place-Value Ideas

Each of the algorithms for whole-number computation is based on place-value ideas, many of which were discussed in Chapter 8. Children need to have a firm understanding of these ideas before they can work effectively with the algorithms. Linking place-value ideas directly with renaming ideas is a necessary step as children explore and develop algorithms for each operation. Providing numerous trading activities is accompanied by renaming activities.

Regroup 138 ones into tens and ones using base-ten blocks:

138 is _____ tens _____ ones

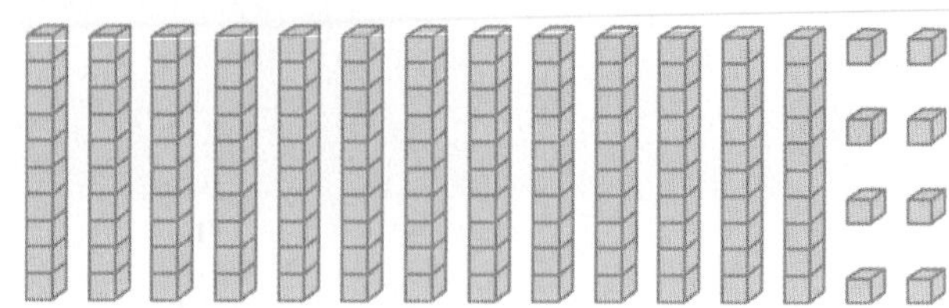

Show 46 with bundles of tens and ones, using Popsicle sticks and masking tape to bundle them:

46 is _____ tens _____ ones

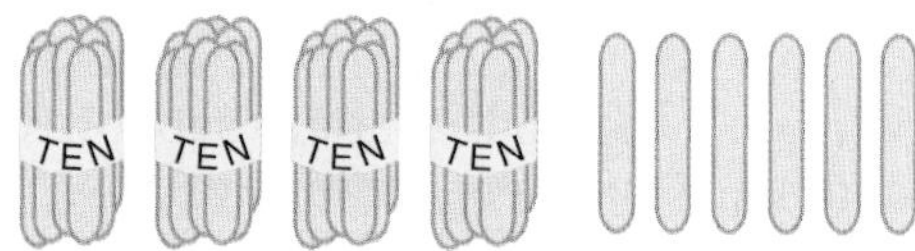

Rename:

- 7 tens 16 ones = 8 tens ________ ones

Tens	Ones
7	16

T	O
8	6
~~7~~	~~16~~

- 35 is 2 tens ________ ones

Tens	Ones
3	5

T	O
2	?
~~3~~	~~5~~

- 5 tens 3 ones to show more ones:

Tens	Ones
5	3

T	O
4	13
~~5~~	~~3~~

Write:

- 6 tens 5 ones in five different ways
- 37 in all the different ways you can

Don't be surprised at the many different ideas that arise in response to this last activity. Students frequently can handle challenges that you thought were beyond them.

Developing the algorithms that work with multidigit numbers has to evolve from students' understanding of place value, which

> . . . involves building connections between key ideas of place value—such as quantifying sets of objects by grouping by ten and treating the groups as units—and using the structure of the written notation to capture this information about groupings. (Wearne and Hiebert, 1994, p. 273)

Addition

Fluency with basic addition is a goal for the pre-K–2 grades, but gaining fluency depends on many diverse experiences in grouping and counting. As children work with multiple objects, they develop a concrete understanding of addition. They move objects together and use a counting strategy to identify a new total number of objects. Initially, they may begin by recounting all the objects; this strategy often yields to a more efficient strategy of counting on. A closer look at how children make sense of addition reveals a wide variety of estimation and computation strategies with addition.

Encouraging Children's Addition Strategies

You've just walked into a first-grade classroom. After a brief activity to review renaming (e.g., renaming 52 as 5 tens 2 ones and also as 4 tens and 12 ones, and so on), a problem is posed to the children:

> Jill and Jeff both collected baseball cards. Jill had 27 cards and Jeff had 35. How many did they have together?

To focus attention on the reasonableness of the answers they will find, you might begin with such questions as:

> Would they have more than 50 cards? Why do you think so?
>
> More than 100 cards? Why do you think so?

Then, actual cards or slips of paper to represent cards could be given to each group of four or five children, with the direction to figure out an answer, show it on paper, and be ready to tell why it is right. Instead of providing them with cards, you might simply encourage students to use whatever aids they are accustomed to using for math problem solving, such as tiles, base-ten blocks, an abacus, or drawing pictures. At other times, instead of working in groups, the children might be asked to solve the problem individually and to write an explanation of what they did. They need time and repeated opportunities to explore and invent strategies and to make connections between different ways of thinking about or doing the same process. After each group or individual has reached an answer, the whole class may meet to share the ways in which they solved the problem. The teacher may record on the board the essence of each explanation.

- Group 1 counted out 27 cards and counted out 35 cards, and then counted all the cards together, one by one:

$$27 + 35 = 62$$

- Group 2 made 2 piles of ten cards, with 7 extras and 3 piles of ten cards, with 5 extras:

$$\begin{array}{l} 2 \text{ tens} + 7 \\ \underline{3 \text{ tens} + 5} \\ 5 \text{ tens} + 12\text{, which is renamed as } 6 \text{ tens} + 2\text{, or } 62 \end{array}$$

- Group 3 recognized that 20 and 30 make 50, and 7 and 5 make 12:

$$\begin{array}{r} 20 + 7 \\ \underline{+\,30 + 5} \\ 50 + 12\text{, or } 62 \end{array}$$

- Group 4 relied on what Kim's older brother had shown her, first adding 5 + 7, to get 12, writing the 2 ones and "carrying 1" ten, then adding it to 2 tens and 3 tens to get 6 tens, or 62 altogether. The teacher showed another way to record this way of thinking about the problem.

$$\begin{array}{r} {}^{1} \\ 27 \\ \underline{+35} \\ 62 \end{array} \qquad \begin{array}{r} 27 \\ \underline{+35} \\ 12 \\ \underline{50} \\ 62 \end{array}$$

- Group 5 did almost the same thing, but because they thought about adding 20 + 30 before adding 7 and 5, the teacher proposed recording their work a little differently:

$$\begin{array}{r} 27 \\ \underline{+35} \\ 50 \\ \underline{12} \\ 62 \end{array}$$

- Group 6 decided to work with a multiple of ten that is easier to think about, and then compensated. They checked their answer by doing the problem a different way too!

$$\begin{array}{rr} 27 + 3 = 30 & 27 - 5 = 22 \\ \underline{+35 - 3 = 32} & \underline{+35 + 5 = 40} \\ 62 & 62 \end{array}$$

- Group 7 added 27 + 5 = 32, and then 32 + 30 = 62. Some of the students in the class pointed out that you could also think 27 + 30 = 57, and then 57 + 5 = 62.

Everyone was sure they were right and could tell why—and they were sure that the other groups were right, too! Is 62 correct just because it is the answer every group reached? "No," retorted a number of children! It is a reasonable answer because 27 is almost 30, and 35 more would make it 65, but 27 is 3 less than 30, so 62 is right. Note that some of the students worked from left to right, as research has indicated children frequently do when constructing their own algorithms (Kamii et al., 1993). Not all children used the manipulative materials, but those who did were able to describe or write an algorithm that modeled what they had done with the materials. Or they used procedures that they had invented outside of school.

STANDARD ADDITION ALGORITHM Perhaps it has occurred to you that some of the procedures the children used were as plausible for mental computation as for paper-and-pencil computation. Children need to recognize this, too, as well as that much addition involving one- and two-digit numbers can and should be done mentally. Lots of activities with renaming have given these children a good base from which to tackle addition algorithms. Note that only the group that relied on what Kim's brother had told them came up with the standard algorithm:

	Think
1	7 + 5 = 12
27	Write 2 in the ones column
+35	and 1 in the tens column.
62	2 + 3 + 1 = 6 tens

That most students did not use the standard algorithm should not surprise you. That algorithm is the result of centuries of refinement. It is commonly used because it is efficient (requires less writing than some other algorithms), but it is also less obvious. Someone probably needed to tell you about placing the one ten from 12 in the tens column. When students attempt to use the standard algorithm without understanding why it works, they may be more prone to errors than when they do addition in ways that intuitively make sense to them. For this reason it is important for the students to develop this idea from activities such as those in Figure 11-1. Here children experience the "creation and placement of the one" (or regrouping) by trading 10 units for 1 ten using the base-ten blocks.

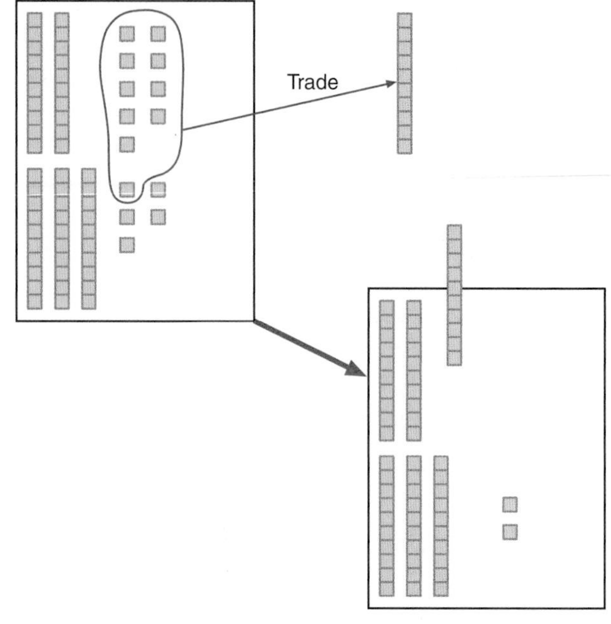

FIGURE 11-1 Base-ten blocks build the ideas of regrouping in the standard addition algorithm.

As groups share their different ways of working, children learn from each other. At some point, the teacher will probably want to share his or her way (the standard algorithm), noting that it is shorter than some of theirs and that this is probably the way that parents and other adults learned to add. Using chips and a place-value mat as in Figure 11-2 provides a natural progression in building the notion of regrouping before introducing the standard algorithm.

PARTIAL-SUM ADDITION ALGORITHM The algorithm used by group 5 is similar to the standard algorithm but less obscure because all the partial sums are shown separately, so there is less

Math Links 11.4

Practice using electronic base-ten blocks to add whole numbers. See if you can use them to illustrate some of the students' strategies.

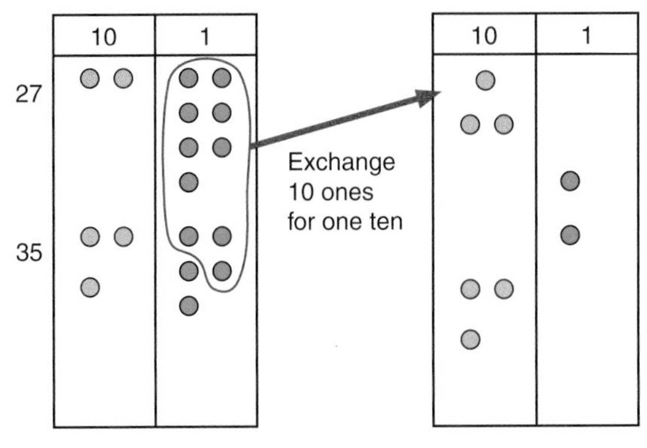

FIGURE 11-2 Use of chips and a place-value mat for modeling the standard addition algorithm.

chance for errors with regrouping. As group 5 used it, they added from left to right (tens first, then ones), which is more natural than working right to left. But this same partial-sum algorithm works equally well starting with ones, then tens, and so on (as the teacher showed, for group 4). The partial-sum algorithm can be used as an alternative algorithm for addition (an end-goal for students) or it can be useful as a transitional algorithm (intermediate step on the way to learning the standard algorithm). Ideally, however, children should be encouraged to work with the procedure they find easiest to understand. There is no reason why all children should end up using the same algorithm.

The next problem the teacher posed to the children involved the addition of 13 and 54. Until recently, teachers might have introduced this problem, which does not require regrouping, far earlier than the one involving 27 and 35, which does involve regrouping. Teachers have come to realize, however, that this type of artificial control of problem situations leads students to misconceptions about the operation and the algorithm. It is more realistic and better pedagogically for them to work, from the outset, on addition computations stemming from problems that involve both regrouping and no regrouping.

The addition of

$$\begin{array}{r}437\\+25\\\hline\end{array} \quad \text{or} \quad \begin{array}{r}437\\+521\\\hline\end{array} \quad \text{or} \quad \begin{array}{r}254\\+283\\\hline\end{array} \quad \text{or} \quad \begin{array}{r}672\\+188\\\hline\end{array}$$

is simply an extension of the regrouping procedure to the hundreds place. Children need enough experience with numbers with more than two digits so they realize that there are no hidden difficulties; if they had no calculators, they could do the computation. Most practice, however, focuses on two-digit numbers, with which they do need to become proficient.

Adding multiples of 10, 100, and so on is another simpler case. This is an important skill for students to develop, for use both in mental computation and estimation and as a building block in performing written computations:

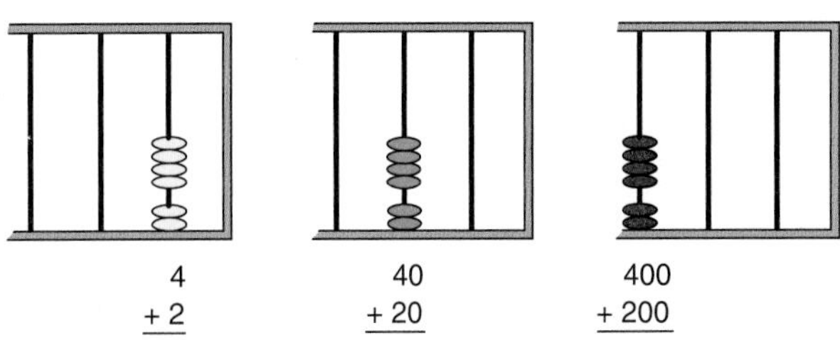

As children work with addition (and other operations), they must be encouraged to estimate in order to ascertain whether the answer they reach is approximately correct. Use of *compatible numbers*—numbers that are easy to compute mentally—is a powerful estimation strategy. Some problem-solving activities to practice mental computation and sharpen estimation skills, as well as deepen understanding of addition algorithms, are found In the Classroom 11-1.

Column Addition

Column addition with three or more one-digit addends is often introduced after some of the basic addition facts are learned, so it may be used to provide varied practice. One new skill is required—adding an unseen addend. In this example, the 4 resulting from the addition of 3 + 1 must be added mentally to 2:

	Think
3 }	3 + 1 = 4
1 }	
+2	4 + 2 = 6

As with other topics, column addition is introduced through a problem situation:

> Sasha bought a lollipop for 3¢, a jellybean for 1¢, and a gumdrop for 2¢. How much did he spend?

The children can model the situation using manipulative materials, flannel board objects, or drawings:

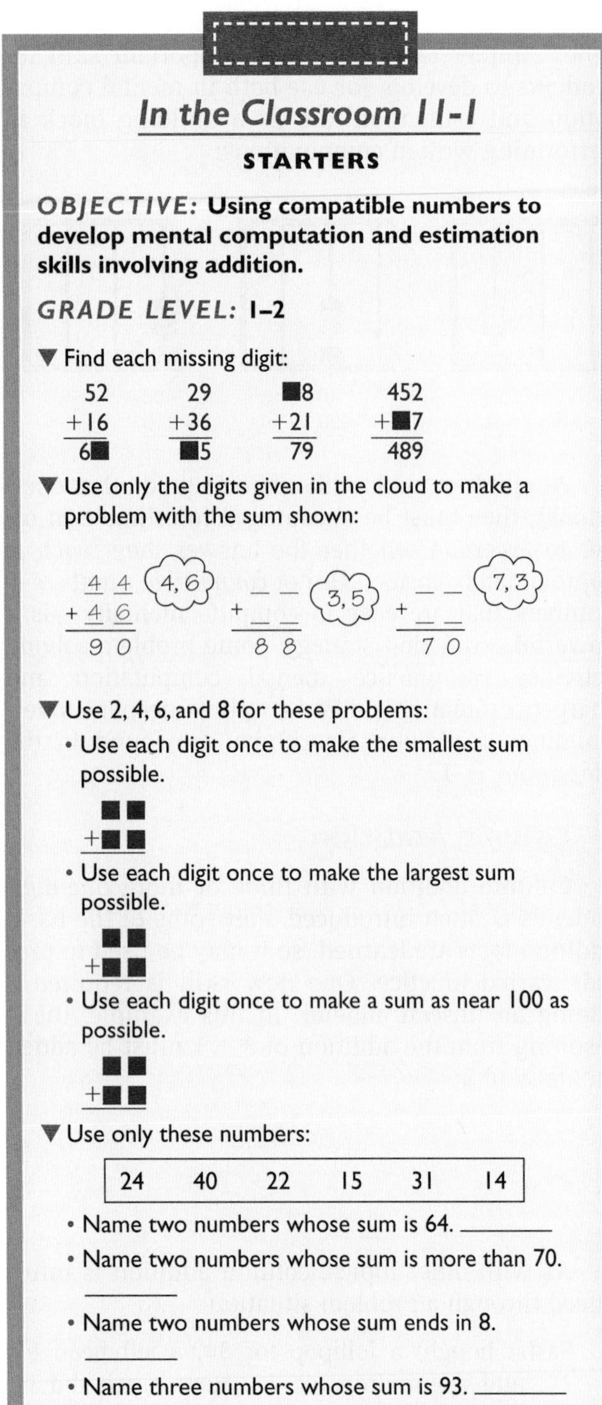

In the Classroom 11-1

STARTERS

OBJECTIVE: **Using compatible numbers to develop mental computation and estimation skills involving addition.**

GRADE LEVEL: **1–2**

▼ Find each missing digit:

```
  52      29     ■8     452
+16     +36    +21    +■7
  6■      ■5     79     489
```

▼ Use only the digits given in the cloud to make a problem with the sum shown:

```
  4 4  (4,6)     _ _  (3,5)     _ _  (7,3)
+ 4 6          + _ _          + _ _
  9 0            8 8            7 0
```

▼ Use 2, 4, 6, and 8 for these problems:

- Use each digit once to make the smallest sum possible.

```
  ■■
+■■
```

- Use each digit once to make the largest sum possible.

```
  ■■
+■■
```

- Use each digit once to make a sum as near 100 as possible.

```
  ■■
+■■
```

▼ Use only these numbers:

24	40	22	15	31	14

- Name two numbers whose sum is 64. ________
- Name two numbers whose sum is more than 70. ________
- Name two numbers whose sum ends in 8. ________
- Name three numbers whose sum is 93. ________

The materials or pictures help the children to bridge from the situation to the solution with symbols.

Is it better to teach children to add down, to add up, or to group numbers that add to 10 (using the associative property)? Research has indicated that adding either up or down (and using the opposite to check) is better than grouping (Wheatley and Wheatley, 1978). Fewer errors of omitting numbers or using a number more than once are likely to occur. "Be consistent" is the best rule.

Higher-Decade Addition

Combinations such as 17 + 4 or 47 + 8 or 3 + 28, called *higher-decade combinations*, are used in a strategy sometimes referred to as "adding by endings." Note that the two-digit number may come either before or after the one-digit number.

The need for higher-decade addition arises in many real-life problems; for instance, adding 6¢ tax to a purchase of 89¢. The skill is also necessary in column addition and in multiplication. The strategy of counting on will probably occur to some children, and it is clearly one way of solving this type of problem, but not necessarily the most efficient way. In the Classroom 11-2 focuses attention on the relationship of 9 + 5, 19 + 5, 29 + 5, and so on. As a result of this activity, children realize the following:

- In each example, the sum has a 4 in the ones place because 9 + 5 = 14, and the tens place has 1 more ten.
- The sum of 9 + 5 is more than 10, so the sum of 19 + 5 is more than 20 and the sum of 29 + 5 is more than 30.
- For 59 + 5, there is a 4 in the ones place and 6 (5 + 1) in the tens place.

Children need to learn to perform such additions automatically, without adding ones and then tens as they do with examples such as 27 + 32 and

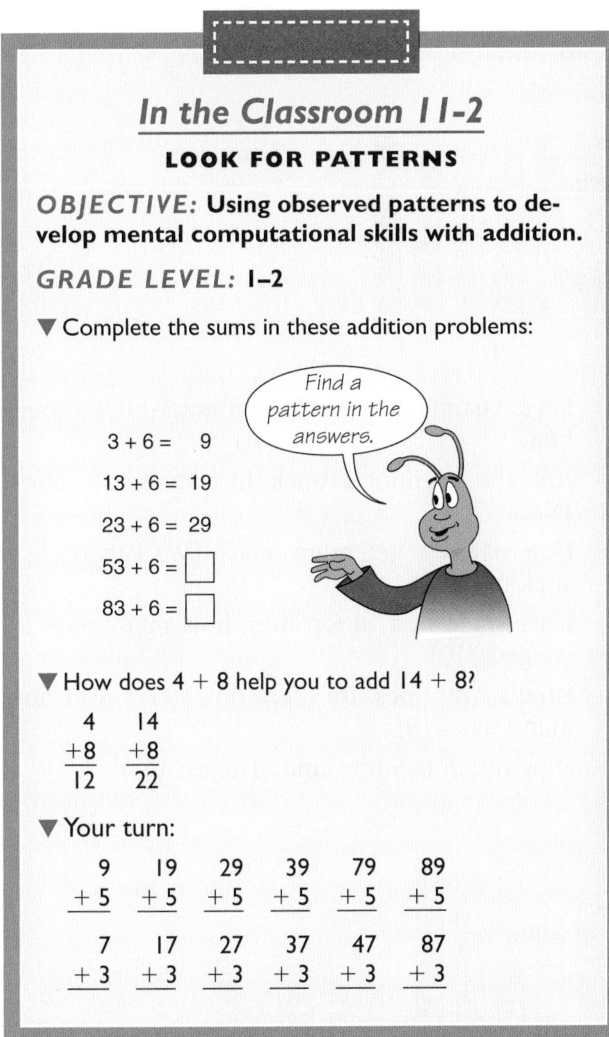

In the Classroom 11-2

LOOK FOR PATTERNS

OBJECTIVE: **Using observed patterns to develop mental computational skills with addition.**

GRADE LEVEL: **1–2**

▼ Complete the sums in these addition problems:

3 + 6 = 9
13 + 6 = 19
23 + 6 = 29
53 + 6 = ☐
83 + 6 = ☐

Find a pattern in the answers.

▼ How does 4 + 8 help you to add 14 + 8?

4	14
+8	+8
12	22

▼ Your turn:

9	19	29	39	79	89
+ 5	+ 5	+ 5	+ 5	+ 5	+ 5

7	17	27	37	47	87
+ 3	+ 3	+ 3	+ 3	+ 3	+ 3

without always counting on. Children who have already developed good number sense and facility with basic-fact addition strategies (such as those described in Chapter 9) should have little difficulty thinking through higher-decade addition problems.

Looking for patterns such as those In the Classroom 11-2, and explicitly discussing them with classmates and with the teacher, not only encourages mental computation but also greatly increases the skill of higher-decade addition.

Subtraction

Like addition, subtraction of multidigit numbers requires knowledge of basic facts and of place value.

Standard Subtraction Algorithms: Decomposition or Equal Additions

The standard subtraction algorithm taught in the United States for the past 50 or 60 years is the *decomposition algorithm.* It involves a logical process of decomposing or renaming the sum (the number you are subtracting from). In the following example, 9 tens and 1 one is renamed as 8 tens and 11 ones:

	Think
$\overset{8\ 1}{\not{9}1}$	11 − 4 = 7 ones
−24	8 tens − 2 tens = 6 tens
67	

Before the decomposition algorithm gained prominence in this country, the *equal-additions algorithm* was taught. The equal-additions algorithm is still taught and used in many other countries around the world (Ron, 1998). If you have children in your classroom whose parents were educated outside the United States, particularly in Europe or in South America, you may find that some confusion results when those parents attempt to help their children with computations. It helps if you, as the teacher, are well aware of the existence and validity of alternative algorithms. Asking students to explain their methods can help you uncover the reasons for errors that may arise if students confuse the steps from different algorithms.

In the equal-additions subtraction algorithm, both the sum and the known addend (the number you are subtracting) are renamed. In this example, ten is added to each number involved in the subtraction: here 10 ones have been added to the sum (91) and 1 ten has been added to the known addend (24):

	Think
9¹1	11 − 4 = 7 ones
−$\overset{3}{\not{2}}$4	9 tens − 3 tens = 6 tens
67	

This algorithm works because the difference between the numbers (91 and 24) remains the same after both have been increased by the same amount [that is, 91 − 24 = (91 + 10) − (24 + 10)]. It may help to picture a number line. The distance between 91 and 24 on the number line is what you are finding when you subtract. If you move both numbers up the number line the same amount (10), the distance between them remains the same. The reason for adding 10 to each number (but adding it in different forms) is to make the subtraction possible without any borrowing or regrouping.

Although this algorithm may seem strange to many Americans, people who have learned to subtract this way generally find it easy and natural to use. What is important is that individuals understand *what* they are doing and *why* when they learn an algorithm. Research has confirmed that both the decomposition algorithm and the equal-additions algorithm are effective in terms of speed and accuracy when taught meaningfully (Brownell, 1947), with a problem setting, manipulative materials, and clear rationale.

Children often naturally develop different algorithms for subtraction, just as they do for addition. They may try to work from left to right, and at this point some confusion may begin. But, if they think carefully about the numbers, they may construct alternatives such as the following:

$$\begin{array}{r} 74 \\ -58 \\ \hline 20 \\ -4 \\ \hline 16 \end{array}$$

or

$$\begin{array}{r} 70 + 4 \\ -50 - 8 \\ \hline 20 - 4 = 16 \end{array}$$

or

$$\begin{array}{r} 74 \\ -58 \\ \hline \end{array} \rightarrow \begin{array}{r} 58 \\ + \\ \hline 74 \end{array} \rightarrow \begin{array}{r} {}^{1} \\ 58 \\ +6 \\ \hline 74 \end{array} \rightarrow \begin{array}{r} {}^{1} \\ 58 \\ +16 \\ \hline 74 \end{array} \rightarrow \begin{array}{r} 74 \\ -58 \\ \hline 16 \end{array}$$

To learn to use algorithms with understanding, children need to connect the steps that are used to solve a problem with manipulatives to the steps in the symbolic solution of the algorithm. Questions that encourage children to focus on the connections between manipulatives and symbols are important. Consider the following example using a problem posed by Rathmell and Trafton (1990, p. 168):

> There were 61 children who did not sign up for hot lunch. Of these, 22 went home for lunch. The rest brought a cold lunch. How many brought a cold lunch?
>
> What are we trying to find? (How many brought cold lunch?)
>
> Do you think it will be more or less than 60? (Less, because there are 61 children who didn't have hot lunch, but some of those went home for lunch.)
>
> How many did not sign up for hot lunch? (61)
>
> How many went home? (22)
>
> How can we show this? (Use cubes to model 61, then separate out 22 cubes.)

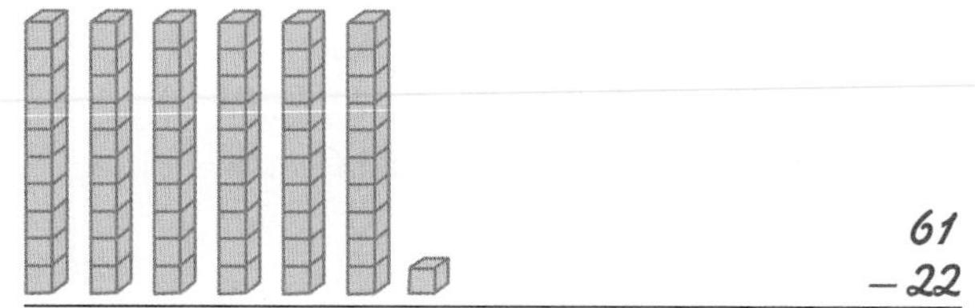

> Let's assume we want to subtract off the ones first.
>
> Are there enough ones to subtract 2 ones? (No.)
>
> How can we get more ones? (We can trade a stick of tens.)
>
> If we trade in a 10 for ones, how many ones do we get? (10)
>
> How many ones are there now? (11) And how many tens? (5)
>
> How much is 5 tens and 11 ones? (61)

> Now are there enough ones to subtract 2? (Yes, we have 11 ones. 11 is more than 2.)
>
> What is 11 −2? (9)

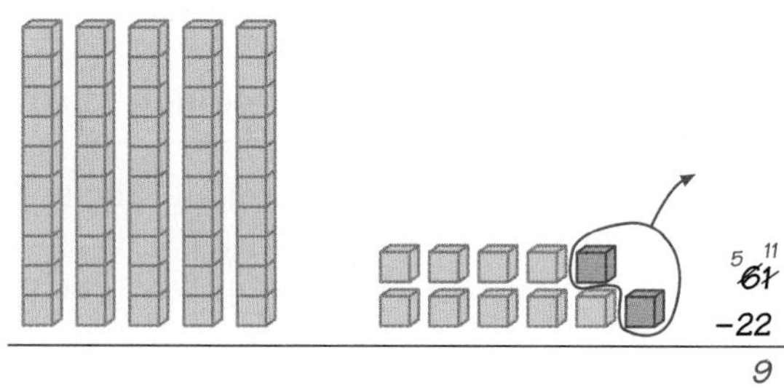

> Now what do we subtract? (the tens)
>
> What is 5 tens minus 2 tens? (3 tens)
>
> So, if we have 9 ones and 3 tens, how many children are eating a cold lunch? (39)
>
> Does this answer make sense? Why? (Yes, 39 makes sense because it is close to 40. There

were about 60 kids who didn't have hot lunch. There were about 20 kids who went home. 60 − 20 = 40. So there should be about 40 kids who brought cold lunch. Because 39 is close to 40, it makes sense.)

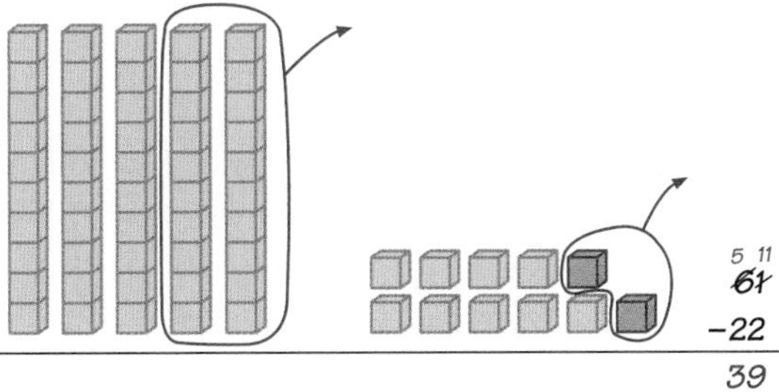

Experiences with regrouping from tens to hundreds or in both places are also helpful. Lesson Idea 11-1 (Race-to-a-Flat and Give-Away-a-Flat) describes two games played with base-ten blocks that can help develop students' understanding of regrouping for addition or subtraction.

*P*ractice using electronic base-ten blocks to subtract whole numbers. See if you can use them to illustrate the previous problem.

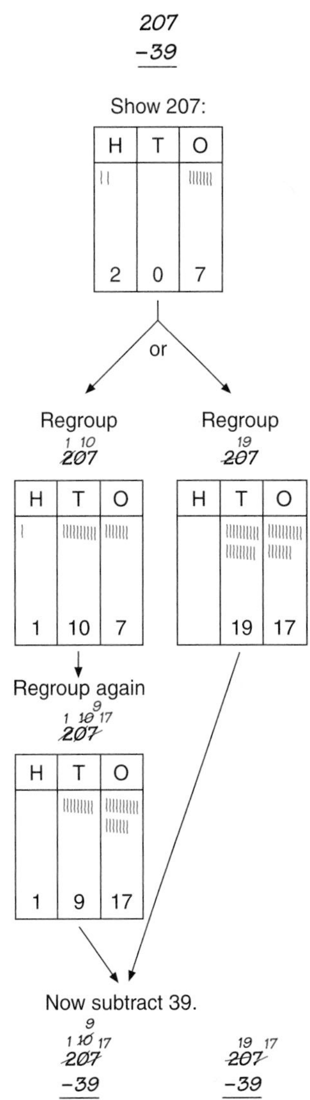

FIGURE 11-3 Place-value representations for the subtraction model.

Zeros in the Sum

The presence of zeros in the sum demands special attention. In this example with zero in the ones place only, 50 is renamed as 4 tens and 10 ones:

```
 4 10
 850
−287
```

Zero in the tens place is slightly more difficult, especially when regrouping in the ones place is also necessary. Two ways to approach the regrouping (using either one step or two steps) are shown in Figure 11-3.

A larger difficulty lies with numbers having more than one zero. One alternative is multiple renaming, renaming from hundreds to tens, then renaming again from tens to ones:

```
                         9 10     9 10
          4 10       4 10     4 10
 500      500        500      500
−257     −257       −257     −257
                               243
```

If students learn a procedure like this rotely, without understanding, it is likely that they may make errors but be unable to notice or correct them. Place-value experiences are important in preparing children to cope with these problems. They must clearly understand that 500 can be renamed as 4 hundreds and 10 tens, or as 4 hundreds, 9 tens, and 10 ones. They will then find it easier to recognize the need for multiple regrouping when they see multiple zeros and will be able to do all the renaming at once:

```
          4 9 1
 500      500     500 = 4 hundreds, 9 tens, 10 ones
−283     −283
```

Lesson Idea 11-1

RACING WITH BASE TEN BLOCKS

Objective: Develop students' understanding of regrouping for addition or subtraction using base-ten blocks.

Grade Level: 1–5

Number of Players: 2–5

Materials: Base-ten blocks, place-value mat (full-sized paper divided into three columns) for each player, and one pair of dice

Place-Value Mat

Flats	Longs	Units

RACE-TO-A-FLAT

Before the Game Begins: Choose one player to be the base-ten "banker."

How to Play: Players take turns rolling the dice, adding the numbers on the tops of the two dice, and then asking the banker for that number of units. For example, if you roll a 4 and a 5 as shown on the dice, ask for 9 units.

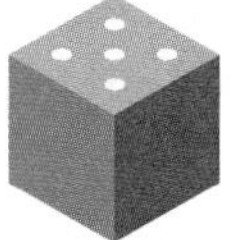
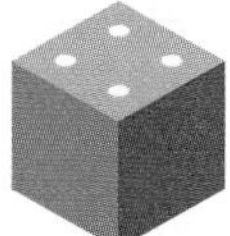

Place the pieces on your place-value mat. You may never have 10 or more pieces in any portion of your place-value mat. Whenever you can, you must trade units for a long (or longs for a flat). When all the trading is complete, it is the next player's turn to roll the dice, collect units, and trade pieces. The first player to trade up to a flat is the winner.

GIVE-AWAY-A-FLAT

Before the Game Begins: Choose one player to be the base ten "banker." Banker distributes one flat to each player who places it in the flats column on her or his place-value mat.

How to Play: Players take turns rolling the dice, finding the sum of the numbers on the tops of the two dice, and *giving away* that numbers of units to the banker. Clearly, trades will have to be made during each player's first turn and possibly again during subsequent turns. The first player to return all of her or his base-ten pieces to the banker is the winner.

Questions for Give-Away-a-Flat

1. Is it possible to give away one long with one roll of the dice?
2. Is it possible to give away two longs with one roll of the dice?
3. Can you win the game with one roll of the dice?
4. What is the fewest number of rolls required to give away all of the pieces?
5. What is the most number of rolls required to give away all of the pieces?

Variations: To challenge fifth and sixth graders, race to a cube (1000) or give away a cube. For games involving larger goals, students can multiply the two dice instead of adding.

Alternately, if they understand that 500 can be thought of as 50 tens, they can think of renaming it directly as 49 tens and 10 ones. In Figure 11-3, for the problem 207 − 39, 207 can be renamed as 19 tens and 17 ones in one step. The need to do this is not readily recognizable by all children, however; those who need to do the double renaming should be allowed to do so.

Multiplication

Before children tackle the multiplication algorithms, they must have a firm grasp of place value, expanded notation, and the distributive property, as well as the basic facts of multiplication. As with the other operations, it is wise to review each of these prerequisites before beginning work with the multiplication algorithms. It is also wise to develop situations or problems for which children compute mentally, without concern for the paper-and-pencil forms.

Multiplication with One-Digit Multipliers

Children should be encouraged to talk about their thinking, as the meaning of multiplication is reinforced with materials:

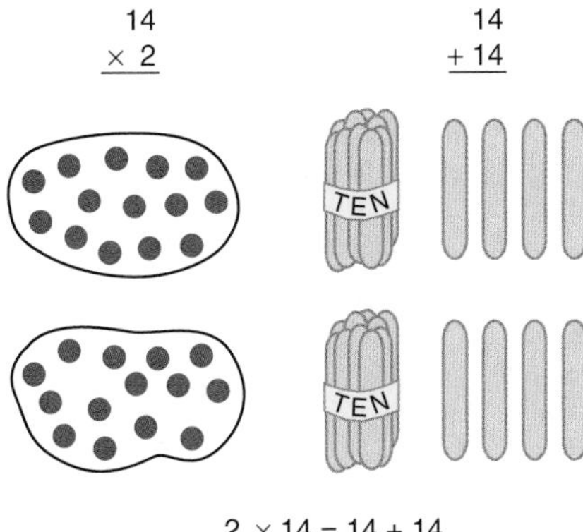

Looking at the previous models, you see not only that 14 can be represented by one bundle of tens and 4 ones, but also that 2 × 14 can be represented by *two* bundles of tens and *two* groups of 4 ones. This points out the use of the distributive property:

$$\begin{aligned} 2 \times 14 &= 2 \times (10 + 4) = (2 \times 10) + (2 \times 4) \\ &= 20 + 8 = 28 \end{aligned}$$

Arrays are also used to develop meaning and visual images of multiplication:

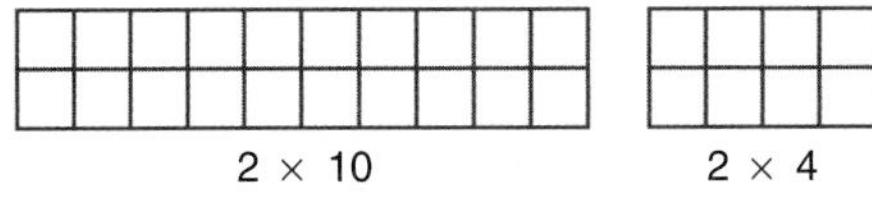

Place-value ideas are noted along with materials:

T	O
1	4
1	4
2	8

T	O
1	4
×	2
2	8

Expanded algorithms can be developed or constructed by the children easily:

$$\begin{array}{r} 14 \\ \times\ 2 \\ \hline \end{array}$$

$$\begin{array}{l} \text{1 ten 4 ones} \\ \times \quad\ \ 2 \\ \hline \text{2 tens 8 ones} \end{array} \qquad \begin{array}{r} 14 \\ \times\ 2 \\ \hline 8 \\ +\ 20 \\ \hline 28 \end{array} \qquad \begin{array}{r} 2 \times 10 = 20 \\ 2 \times \ 4 = \underline{\ 8} \\ 20 + \ 8 = 28 \end{array}$$

The partial-products algorithm for multiplication (Figure 11-4) is one form of the expanded algorithm, where all the individual products produced by the multiplication are recorded on separate lines, then summed. Just as the partial-sums algorithm is a useful alternative or transitional algorithm for addition, the partial-products algorithm can be useful for multiplication.

The traditional American multiplication algorithm is a streamlined version of the partial-products algorithm. In the traditional algorithm, some of the partial products are added mentally before writing down their sum. In some cases this traditional method is more efficient (because it requires less writing), but it is not as easy to understand step-by-step and it may be more susceptible to error (because steps are combined and done mentally).

The distributive property helps children understand the relationship between the partial-products algorithm and the traditional algorithm (see Figure 11-4). Lesson Idea 11-2 illustrates an activity that uses the distributive property in mental computation, a skill that is useful in estimation as well. The calculator also promotes a focus on estimation, while decreasing the amount of time spent on

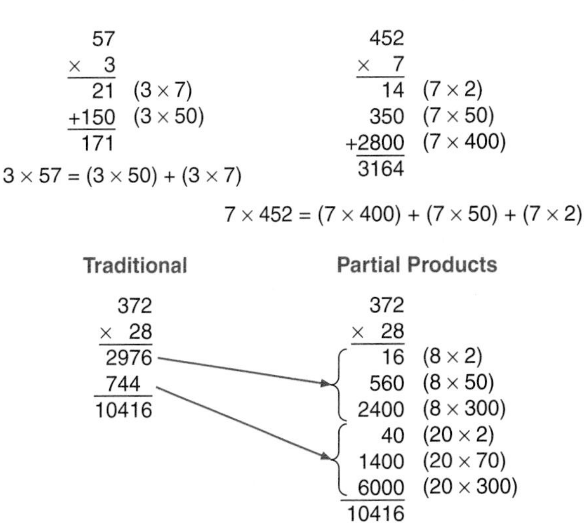

FIGURE 11-4 Multiplication comparing the traditional multiplication algorithm with the partial products algorithm.

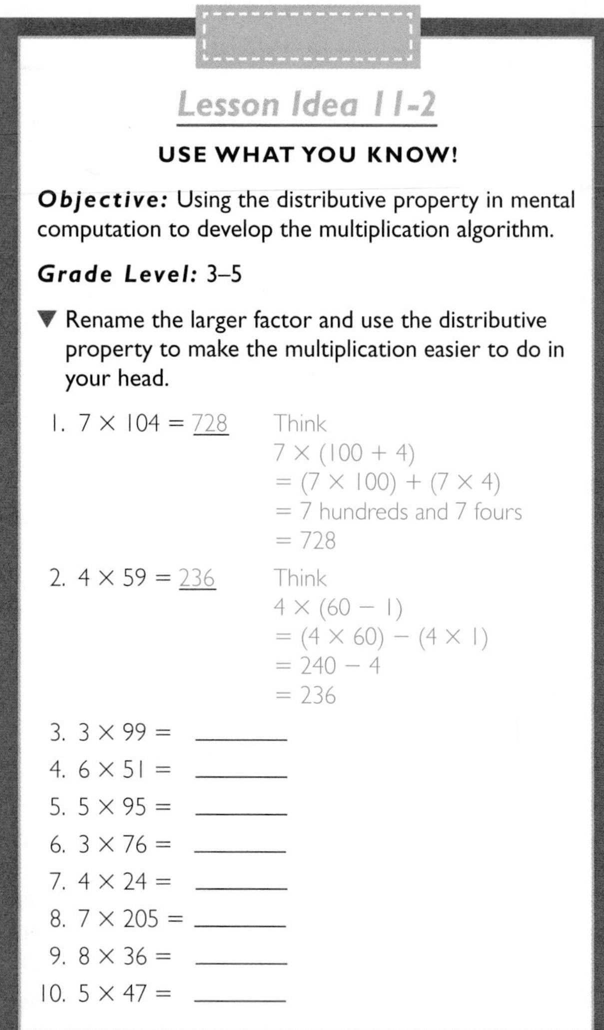

Lesson Idea 11-2

USE WHAT YOU KNOW!

Objective: Using the distributive property in mental computation to develop the multiplication algorithm.

Grade Level: 3–5

▼ Rename the larger factor and use the distributive property to make the multiplication easier to do in your head.

1. 7 × 104 = 728 Think
   7 × (100 + 4)
   = (7 × 100) + (7 × 4)
   = 7 hundreds and 7 fours
   = 728
2. 4 × 59 = 236 Think
   4 × (60 − 1)
   = (4 × 60) − (4 × 1)
   = 240 − 4
   = 236
3. 3 × 99 = ______
4. 6 × 51 = ______
5. 5 × 95 = ______
6. 3 × 76 = ______
7. 4 × 24 = ______
8. 7 × 205 = ______
9. 8 × 36 = ______
10. 5 × 47 = ______

written computations. Some activities with that focus are found In the Classroom 11-3.

Multiplication with Two-Digit Multipliers

As children work with two-digit multipliers, the use of manipulative materials becomes cumbersome. Arrays or grids provide one means of bridging the gap from concrete materials to symbols and illustrating, once again, which is why the partial-products algorithm makes sense. As shown in Figure 11-5, a grid can also provide entirely new ways of viewing and writing about a multiplication example. Some other materials are used to tie the work to previously learned procedures, but increasingly the emphasis shifts to working with symbols, as shown in Figure 11-6. This approach is possible because of the earlier base built on the use of materials and understanding of the distributive property.

It is always important for students to connect new ideas to earlier understandings, continually building on a foundation of previous knowledge.

In the Classroom 11-3

WHAT'S MISSING?

OBJECTIVE: **Using number puzzles to develop estimation skills with multiplication.**

GRADE LEVEL: **3–5**

▼ Guess the numbers that will go into the circles and boxes.
Write your number and then check it on a calculator.
Score 2 points if correct on the first try and 1 point if correct on the second try.

(4) (6) (7) (8) [32] [48] [68] [82]

○ × □ = 408 ○ × □ = 272

○ × □ = 476 ○ × □ = 336

○ × □ = 384 ○ × □ = 492

▼ Try these using only 2, 3, and 4. (You may use the same numeral more than once.)

□□ × □ = 4 6 □□ × □ = 6 6

□□ × □ = 8 4 □□ × □ = 1 2 6

▼ Now use only 4, 6, 8, and 9.

- Make the largest product. (Use each numeral only once.)

□□□ × □

- Make the smallest product: (Use each numeral only once.)

□□□ × □

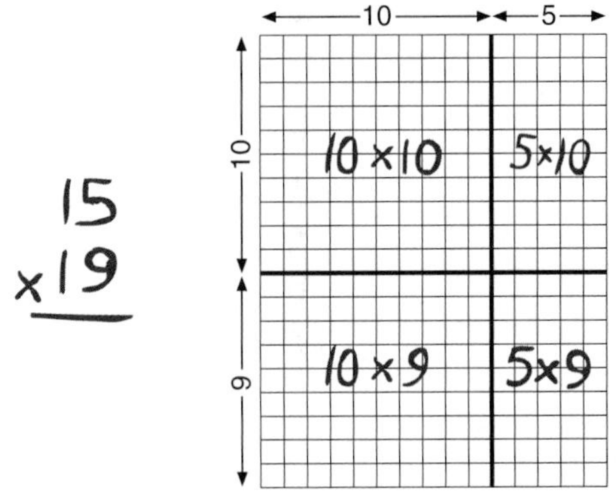

FIGURE 11-5 Use of a grid to solve multiplication with two-digit multiplier.

Children should see that the process of multiplying by a two- or three-digit number is just an extension of the procedure for multiplying by a one-digit number. Similarly, illustrating this process by using an array is essentially the same no matter what the multiplier. Moreover, in the middle grades, when students begin to learn about symbol manipulation in algebra, they should be able to connect the new idea of multiplying binomials to their prior understanding of multidigit multiplication. In Figure 11-7, the illustration of the "foil" method for multiplying two binomials should look familiar because it is the same as the illustration for multiplying two two-digit numbers together; the simple explanation is that the distributive property governs both of these parallel procedures.

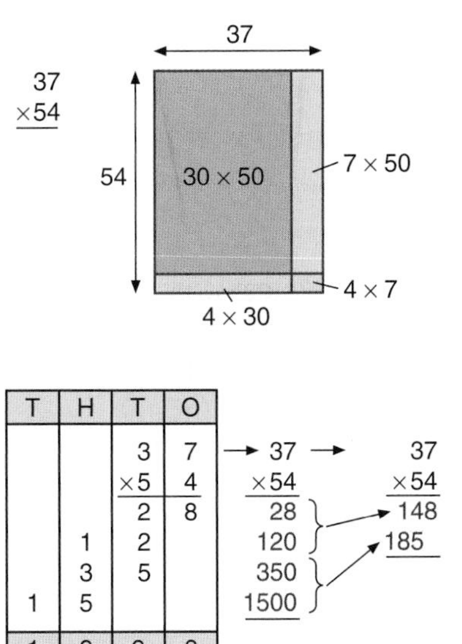

FIGURE 11-6 Multiplication with two-digit multiplier.

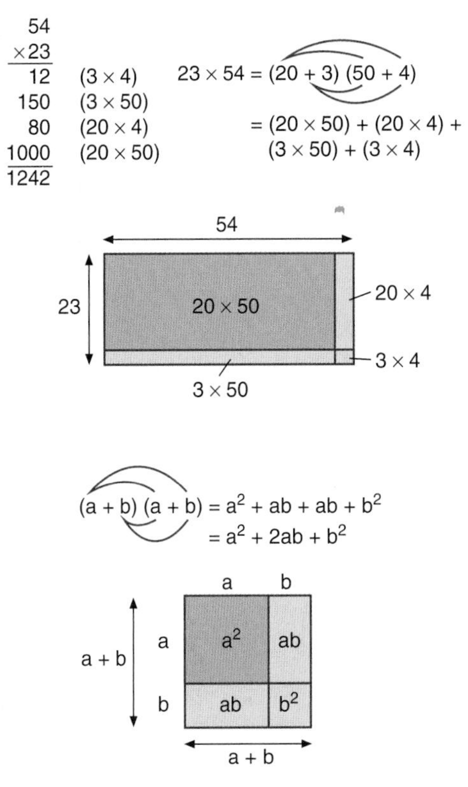

FIGURE 11-7 Extending multiplication ideas to algebra.

An activity for using calculators with multidigit multipliers can be found In the Classroom 11-4, which aids in strengthening the meaning of the algorithms and of multiplying by powers of ten.

Multiplication by 10 and Multiples of 10

As we have shown, the ability to work flexibly with powers of 10 is an important prerequisite to handling multiplication algorithms with understanding. Multiplying by 10 comes easily to most children, and it is readily extended to multiplying by 100 and 1000 as children gain an understanding of larger numbers. Children can be shown a series of examples, after which they are asked to discuss and generalize, noting that, when there is a zero in the ones place, each digit moves one place to the left in the product. In the Classroom 11-5 shows how a calculator can help children develop ideas about the effect of multiplying by powers of 10.

Multiplying by 20, 30, 200, 300, and so on is an extension of multiplying by 10 and 100. Emphasize what happens across examples and generalize from the pattern. For example, have children consider 3×50:

In the Classroom 11-4

ANALYZING MULTIPLICATION

OBJECTIVE: Analyzing multiplication to develop number sense and mental computation skills.

GRADE LEVEL: 3–5

▼ Use the partial product from the completed problems to help you find the missing numbers *mentally*.

```
   387
 ×264
  1548
 23220
 77400
102168

   264
 ×387
  1848
 21120
 79200
102168
```

$387 \times 60 =$ ____

$2640 \times 70 =$ ____

$200 \times 387 =$ ____

$2640 \times$ ____ $= 79200$

$264 \times 80 =$ ____

$264 \times 300 =$ ____

I know I can do these mentally!

▼ Check your mental answers with a calculator. Score one point for each correct answer.

$3 \times 5 = 15$

3×5 tens $= 15$ tens $= 150$

$3 \times 50 = 150$

Then have them consider 4×50:

$4 \times 5 = 20$

4×5 tens $=$ ______ tens $=$ ______

$4 \times 50 =$ ______

After several more examples, you can give them other examples for which they are to find the pattern:

```
 20    70    90  . . .   36    52
× 7   × 6   × 8         ×20   ×30
```

A similar sequence can be followed for examples with hundreds, such as 2×300:

$2 \times 3 = 6$

2×3 hundreds $=$ _____ hundreds $=$ _____

$2 \times 300 =$

Finally, examples such as these might be given:

```
 273    418
× 50   × 80
```

In the Classroom 11-5

ZEROS COUNT

OBJECTIVE: Using calculators to look for patterns and develop number sense involving multiplication by powers of ten.

GRADE LEVEL: 3–5

▼ Use your  to find the product:

$8 \times 10 =$ ____
- How many 0's in 10? ____
- How many 0's in the product? ____

$36 \times 100 =$ ____
- How many 0's in 100? ____
- How many 0's in the product? ____

$290 \times 1000 =$ ____
- How many 0's in 1000? ____
- How many 0's in the product? ____ Why?

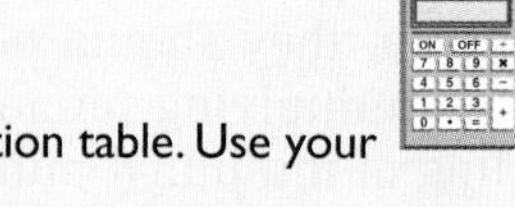

▼ Complete this multiplication table. Use your calculator to check your answers.

×	10	100	1000
7			
14		1400	
28			28000
240			
989			

In making estimates, it is tremendously helpful for children to be able to use multiplication by rounded numbers. Consider one child's thinking when asked to make an estimate:

```
       Think
       That's about 20 × 400.
 427   2 × 4 = 8.
× 19   2 × 400 = 800
       So 20 × 400 would be 8000
```

Another child's thinking will differ:

Think

```
 427    That's about 20 × 425.
× 19    2 × 425 = 850
        20 × 425 = 8500
        So 19 × 427 would be about 8500
```

Both 8000 and 8500 are good estimates. When making estimates, students should round to numbers that are easy for them to compute. Consequently, different estimates are not only to be expected but also encouraged. In conjunction with estimation, students also need to answer questions such as these:

- How do I know how many zeros will be in the product?
- How is the number of zeros in the estimate related to the factors?
- How many digits will be in the estimated product?

Multiplication with Zeros

When zeros appear in the factor being multiplied, particular attention needs to be given to the effect on the product or partial product. Many children are prone to ignore the zero. Thus, for 9 × 306, their answer may be

```
  5
 306
×  9
 324
```

When an estimate is made first, children have a way of determining whether their answer is in the ballpark. Writing each partial product separately, rather than attempting to add them mentally, can also help avoid place-value errors due to zeros. In the previous problem, a student might actually write the partial products 54 and 0 and 2700. Use of a place-value chart may also help students understand what the correct procedure must be, as will expanded notation:

Estimate

```
 306    9 × 3 = 27
×  9    9 × 300 = 2700
```

T	H	T	O
	3	0	6
			9
2	7	5	4

$$9 \times 306 = 9 \times (300 + 6) = (9 \times 300) + (9 \times 6) = 2750 + 54 = 2754$$

Multiplication with Large Numbers

How can we use a calculator to solve computations involving numbers that appear too big for the calculator? As children experiment with using a calculator for multiplication, there will come a time when they overload the calculator. Sometimes the number to be entered contains more digits than the display will show. At other times the product will be too big for the display. For instance, if this example is entered in a four-function calculator, an error message results:

```
  2345678
×    4003
```

When this happens, children should be encouraged to estimate an answer and then use the distributive property plus mental computation along with the calculator.

Estimate

$4000 \times 2000000 = 8000000000$
$4003 = 4000 + 3$
$= (4 \times 1000) + 3$

Calculate

$4 \times 2345678 = 9382712$ (with the calculator)
$9382712 \times 1000 = 9382712000$ (mentally)
$3 \times 2345678 = 7037034$

Add

```
    7037034
+9382712000
```

Such examples show how an understanding of multiplication, plus problem-solving skills, can be used with calculators to reach a solution. Use of the calculator, mental computation, and paper-and-pencil recording may be integrated to solve a single problem. This sort of approach reminds us that calculator algorithms differ from the currently used paper-and-pencil algorithms.

Division

The traditional division algorithm is without doubt the most difficult of the algorithms for children to master, for several reasons:

- Computation begins at the left, rather than at the right as for the other operations.
- The algorithm involves not only the basic division facts but also subtraction and multiplication.
- There are several interactions in the algorithm, but their pattern moves from one spot to another.
- Trial quotients, involving estimation, must be used and may not always be successful at the first attempt—or even the second.

Teachers struggle to teach division, and children struggle to learn division; it is little wonder that the use of calculators is posed as a means of resolving the dilemma of the division algorithm. As *An Agenda for Action* (NCTM, 1980, p. 6) indicates:

> For most students, much of a full year of instruction in mathematics is spent on the division of whole numbers—a massive investment with increasingly limited productive return. . . . For most complex problems, using the calculator for rapid and accurate computation makes a far greater contribution to functional competence in daily life.

On the national mathematics assessments, some exercises were given with and without the use of calculators. On the fourth assessment, third graders were given the problem $3\overline{)42}$. When calculators were not used, about 20 percent of the answers were correct; when calculators were used, about 50 percent were correct (Lindquist et al., 1988). On one item on the sixth assessment, students who reported using a calculator scored 82 percent correct, and those who reported they did not use a calculator scored only 35 percent (Kenney and Silver, 1997). Even more dramatic were results from the second assessment (Carpenter et al., 1981). One exercise was given only to 13- and 17-year-olds when calculators were not used because nine-year-olds had not yet been taught division with a two-digit divisor. Thirteen-year-olds scored 46 percent and 17-year-olds scored 50 percent without calculators. With calculators, the scores rose dramatically, to 82 percent and 91 percent, respectively. Fifty percent of the nine-year-olds obtained the correct answer when they used calculators. Considering that half of the 17-year-olds could not perform the division even after years of practice, is it not reasonable to let them use the tool with which they are successful—and which they will use anyway for the rest of their lives?

The *NCTM's Standards* stress that in today's technological society, teachers should rethink how computation is taught and how it is performed. Helping students understand *when* division is appropriate and *how to estimate* answers to division problems is extremely important. In terms of actually performing computations, division with one-digit divisors should be the focus of instruction, followed by some work with two-digit divisors so that students understand how such division is done. Performing more complex division—perhaps any that takes more than 30 seconds to do—with paper and pencil is a thing of the past for adults. Thus schools should not demand that children spend countless hours mastering an antiquated skill. Teachers can't afford the instructional time for this task. Instead, estimation skills should be used to define the bounds of the quotient, so that the reasonableness of calculator answers can be determined—just as such estimates should be used with division with one-digit divisors and, in fact, with all addition, subtraction, and multiplication.

Division with One-Digit Divisors

It is essential to begin division instruction with real-world problems. The most important thing is for students to develop an understanding of what division is all about. There is no reason for children not to encounter division problems with remainders from the outset of their work with division. Children should be encouraged to use blocks or counters to model division situations and to explain their thinking. The teacher should help students see how their thinking can be clearly and efficiently recorded on paper. Thus learning a paper-and-pencil algorithm will essentially turn into learning a way to record what is done concretely.

For example, Burns (1991) posed problems and had third-grade students explain their answers and the methods they used to reach them. One problem called for four children to divide 54 marbles equally. Group 1 counted out 54 cubes (to represent the marbles), divided them into four groups, and wrote:

> We think we get 13 each. We think this because we took the cubes and dealed out them one by one. We had two left. Bryce was sick so we gave the extra to him. (Burns, 1991, p. 16)

Other groups wrote:

> Group 2: We had 54. We gave each person 10 because we thout if there was 40 there would be 4 tens and 14 would be left. Each person gets 3, witch leves 2. Each person gets 13.
>
> Group 3: We drew 54 marbles and then I numbered them 1, 2, 3, 4, and then we counted the ones and then we knew that each child gets 13 marbles and we lost the other two.
>
> Group 4: I wrote down 54. I took away 12. I got 42. I took another 12 away. I got 30. I took another 12 away. I got 18. I took another 12 away. I got 6. Then I took away 4. I got 2. I chiped each of them into halfs that made 4 halfs. Each person got 13 and a half. (Burns, 1991, pp. 16–17)

Burns noted that, from listening to each others' methods, the children not only heard different approaches to solving division problems, but they

```
Group 1          Group 2          Group 3              Group 4

  54               54               (1)(2)(3)(4)       4)54
 - 4 (1)          - 40 (10)      (1)(2)(3)(4)(1)      - 12   3 × 4
  50               14            (2)(3)(4)(1)(2)        42
 - 4 (2)          - 12 (3)       (3)(4)(1)(2)(3)      - 12   3 × 4
  46                2            (4)(1)(2)(3)(4)        30
 - 4 (3)                         (1)(2)(3)(4)(1)      - 12   3 × 4
  42                             (2)(3)(4)(1)(2)        18
 - 4 (4)                         (3)(4)(1)(2)(3)      - 12   3 × 4
  38                             (4)(1)(2)(3)(4)         6
   .                             (1)(2)(3)(4)(1)         4   1 × 4
   .                             (2)(3)(4)(1)(2)         2
   .
  10                                                  Our answer is
 - 4 (12)                                                13 1/2
   6
 - 4 (13)
   2
```

FIGURE 11-8 Solutions of groups 1–4 (Marilyn Burns).

also learned that division can be done in a variety of ways. Their teacher might have helped the class see how each of their different explanations could be recorded symbolically in a slightly different way, but always with the same final result. Refer to Figure 11-8 to see how each group's work might be recorded.

DISTRIBUTIVE ALGORITHM Clearly, there are many ways to figure and record the answer to a division computation, and certain methods are much more efficient than others. Two algorithms have been used for division most frequently; both are effective. The *distributive algorithm* is most common and familiar and is considered the standard division algorithm by most Americans. Consider the problem of sharing $954 among 4 people (refer to Figure 11-9A).

When using the distributive algorithm for this problem, first share as many of the 9 hundreds as possible (8 hundreds can be shared, 2 to each of the 4 people). Record how many were given to each person above (2 hundreds). Record the total number shared below (8 hundreds). Be careful to preserve place value by writing these numbers in the proper columns. "Subtract and bring down" and note that you still have 1 hundred and 5 tens to be shared (or 15 tens). Begin the process again, sharing as many of the tens as possible, recording the number for each person above, recording the total shared below, and subtracting to see how much more still remains to be shared. Share 12 of the 15 tens, 3 to each of the 4 people, so write 3 above (in the tens place) and 12 below. Now, "subtract and bring down" again, noting now that you still have 3 tens and 4 ones to be shared (or 34 ones). Once again, share as many as possible, this time writing 8 above and 32 below, and then subtracting. You now have just 2 ones left. Starting with $954, you were able to give $238 to each of 4 people, with $2 left over.

SUBTRACTIVE ALGORITHM The *subtractive algorithm*, although not as familiar as the distributive algorithm, provides an intuitive and straightforward method for helping children learn to divide. This algorithm is easier than the standard algorithm for most children to learn because it is flexible enough to be made to correspond to a wide variety of approaches to thinking about division. Refer to Figure 11-9B for an example of how the subtractive algorithm might be used to solve this same division problem. You have $954 to share among four people. Perhaps begin by giving each person $50. Subtract and see that you still have $754 to share. Obviously, you didn't need to start with such a small share. Now choose to give each person $100. You still have $354 to share. You might give each person $50 again, leaving $154 still to share. You don't have enough to share $50 again, so maybe give each person $30. That leaves $34. Now give each person

```
A.
    2             23              238 r2
 4)954         4)954           4)954
   8             8               8
   15            15              15
                 12              12
                  34              34
                                  32
                                   2

B.                              C.
   238 r2                          238 r2
 4)954                           4)954
   200    50 × 4                   120    30 × 4
   754                             834
   400   100 × 4                   120    30 × 4
   354                             714
   200    50 × 4                   120    30 × 4
   154                             594
   120    30 × 4                   120    30 × 4
    34                             474
    32     8 × 4                   120    30 × 4
     2   238                       354
                                   120    30 × 4
D.                                 234
   238 r2                          120    30 × 4
 4)954                             114
   800   200 × 4                    80    20 × 4
   154                              34
   120    30 × 4                    32     8 × 4
    34                               2
    32     8 × 4
     2
```

FIGURE 11-9 Some different division algorithms.

\$8, leaving \$2 as remainder. The total each person received was \$50 + \$100 + \$50 + \$30 + \$8, or \$238, the same answer you obtained above with the standard algorithm. The choices made here in using the subtractive algorithm were arbitrary. You might instead have chosen to repeatedly distribute \$30, over and over, and in that case the problem would take a long time to complete (see Figure 11-9C). On the other hand, if you were efficient, the solution would look very much like the standard algorithm solution (see Figure 11-9D).

The thinking process used in the subtractive algorithm is also clearly illustrated by the work of groups 2 and 4 in the previous problem involving marbles. Both groups were computing 54 ÷ 4. Group 4 began by recognizing that 12 marbles could be shared fairly among four people (three to each). So they first shared just 12 marbles (leaving 42 still to be shared). Then they repeatedly shared 12 more each time (leaving 30, then 18, then 6 still to be shared). Finally, they shared four of those final six, leaving two marbles (which, amusingly, they cut in half to complete the sharing). Because each person was awarded three marbles four distinct times (for a total of 12 marbles), and also was awarded 1 more marble plus $\frac{1}{2}$ marble, the solution can be written $54 \div 4 = 13\frac{1}{2}$. By contrast, Group 2 initially thought about sharing 40 of the 54 marbles among the four people (10 to each). That left 14 still to be shared. Those 14 could be distributed three per person. Thus each person got 10 + 3 marbles (or 13), and two marbles were left over.

In using the subtractive algorithm, the child can choose to subtract off any multiple of the divisor at each step. Although the process may take more or less time, depending on how efficient the thinking is, the answer will be correct no matter how many steps are required. If children are extremely efficient, the subtractive algorithm can look almost exactly like the traditional division algorithm. Thus the subtractive algorithm can serve as a transitional algorithm (a stage on the way to learning to divide using the traditional method), or children may learn it as an alternative algorithm.

Although teachers can help children understand algorithms such as those described previously, they also need to let them explore. As with the other operations, children develop their own algorithms. Some are closely allied with manipulative materials, as shown in Figure 11-10. Others use number sense, reasoning in terms of the numbers involved, as the following examples indicate:

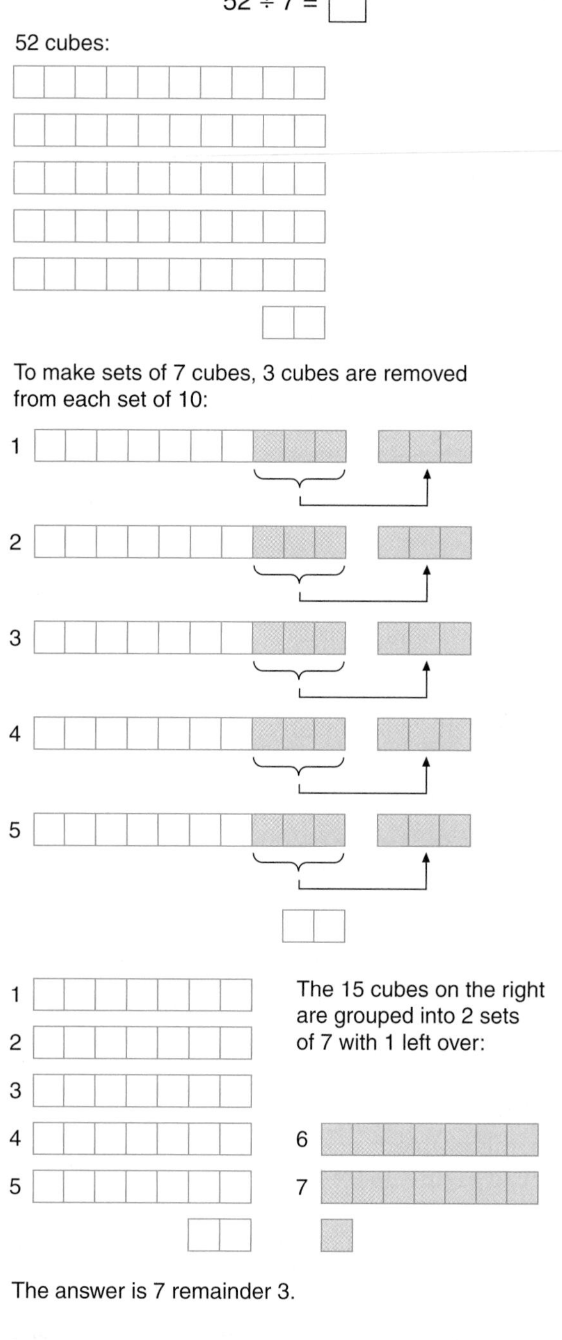

FIGURE 11-10 Alternative algorithm for division using manipulative materials.
(Adapted from Harel and Behr, 1991.)

52 ÷ 7 52 divided by 7 is close to 49 divided by 7, or 7. But there are 3 left over. So the answer is 7 remainder 3.

85 ÷ 5 20 divided by 5 is 4. There are four 20s in 80, so 4 × 4 = 16, and then there is one more 5. So the answer is 17.

69 ÷ 4 60 + 9. 60 divided by 4 is 15, and 9 divided by 4 is 2, with a remainder of 1. So the answer is 17 remainder 1.

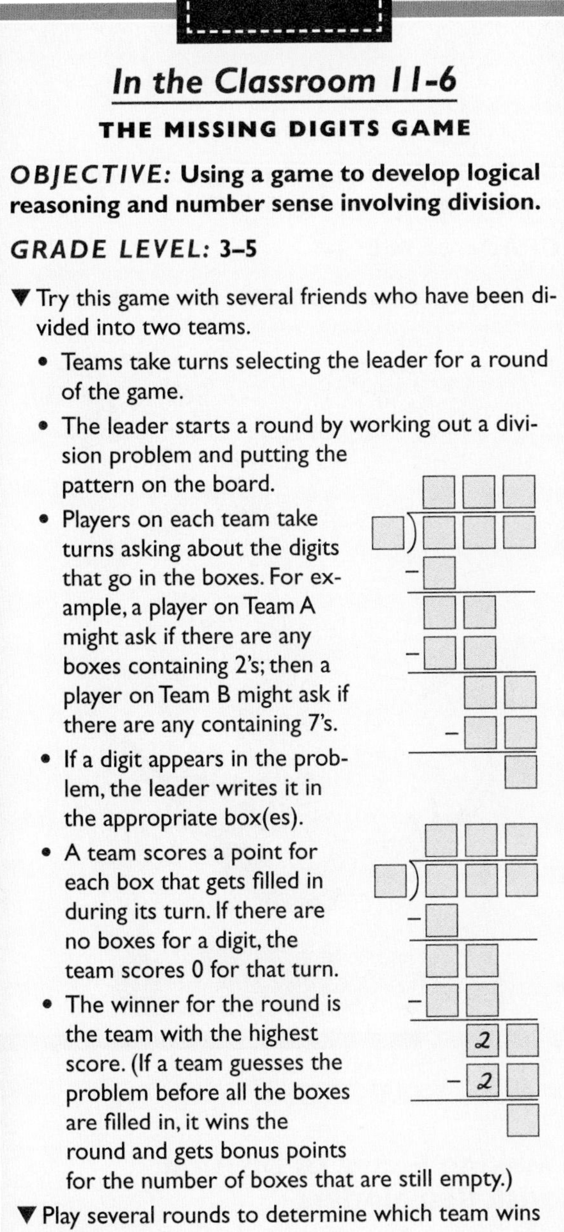

In the Classroom 11-6

THE MISSING DIGITS GAME

OBJECTIVE: **Using a game to develop logical reasoning and number sense involving division.**

GRADE LEVEL: **3–5**

▼ Try this game with several friends who have been divided into two teams.
- Teams take turns selecting the leader for a round of the game.
- The leader starts a round by working out a division problem and putting the pattern on the board.
- Players on each team take turns asking about the digits that go in the boxes. For example, a player on Team A might ask if there are any boxes containing 2's; then a player on Team B might ask if there are any containing 7's.
- If a digit appears in the problem, the leader writes it in the appropriate box(es).
- A team scores a point for each box that gets filled in during its turn. If there are no boxes for a digit, the team scores 0 for that turn.
- The winner for the round is the team with the highest score. (If a team guesses the problem before all the boxes are filled in, it wins the round and gets bonus points for the number of boxes that are still empty.)

▼ Play several rounds to determine which team wins the game!

Have you begun to believe that the possibilities for constructing ways to find an answer are myriad? Just when you think you've seen all the possible algorithms, another student will probably come up with a new one. Enjoy this process. Be an explorer right along with the children. But you also have another role. Just because all these algorithms are correct doesn't mean that children never come up with incorrect algorithms. They do.

You need to watch for this possibility—and you need to make children aware of the need to prove that a procedure really works across examples. You also need to be aware of consistent error patterns that crop up in children's work—error patterns that usually indicate some difficulty such as lack of knowledge about place value, or a lack of mastery of some basic facts, or some other misunderstanding. Fortunately, there are sources of information, such as Ashlock (1998), to which you can turn. This source not only helps you identify the patterns but also provides specific suggestions for how to help the child get onto the right track.

As with the other operations, it is important that children work with manipulative materials as well as place-value charts. They need to keep in mind the problem situation and not forget that it is the process of sharing that is of concern, not merely working their way through the algorithm. A variety of experiences, such as those In the Classroom 11-6 and 11-7, may help children gain facility with the division algorithm.

There is evidence from research that students also need to be encouraged to do more reasoning about their work. In particular, middle-school students were found to have a difficult time providing written explanations of their reasoning about division problems with remainders (Silver et al., 1993). They did not associate "sense-making" with the solution of school mathematics problems. Some students assess their results by spurious criteria, such as whether a number "divides evenly" (Garofalo and Bryant, 1992). Help students become aware of

In the Classroom 11-7

MAKING EXAMPLES

OBJECTIVE: **Using number puzzles to develop number sense involving division.**

GRADE LEVEL: **3–5**

▼ Make (and work out) a division example with
- A dividend of 47 and a divisor of 3
- A dividend of 81 and a divisor of 5

▼ Now make (and work out) a division example with
- A quotient of 6 r2
- A quotient of 10 r4
- A quotient of 23 r5

I know I can do this . .

▼ Try these:
- A divisor of 6 and a quotient of 15 r3
- A divisor of 3 and a quotient of 25 r2
- A dividend of 83 and a quotient of 11 r6

the real-world applications of the mathematics they are learning, but also help them become aware of how "reason-able" the solution is.

Determining a reasonable answer can be particularly difficult with the division algorithms, but questions can help students make sense of them. A necessary first step in determining a quotient is to estimate the number of places in the quotient:

$$6\overline{)839}$$

Are there as many as 10 sixes in 839? [Yes, 10 sixes are only 60.]

Are there as many as 100 sixes? [Yes, 100 sixes are 600.]

Are there as many as 200 sixes? [No, 200 sixes are 1200.]

So the quotient is between 100 and 200—and probably closer to 100.

An alternative to this is the following sequence:

$$3\overline{)187}$$

Are there enough hundreds to divide into three piles? [No.]

Are there enough tens? [Yes, 18 tens.]

So the quotient has two digits, and you decide that there are 6 tens.

So you know the answer is between 60 and 70.

Such procedures help develop an early recognition of the range for a quotient. They help students make sense of the algorithm while developing valuable estimation skills.

In the Classroom 11-8

EASY DOES IT!

OBJECTIVE: **Using calculators to develop number sense involving division.**

GRADE LEVEL: **3–5**

▼ Use your calculator to find the missing numbers:

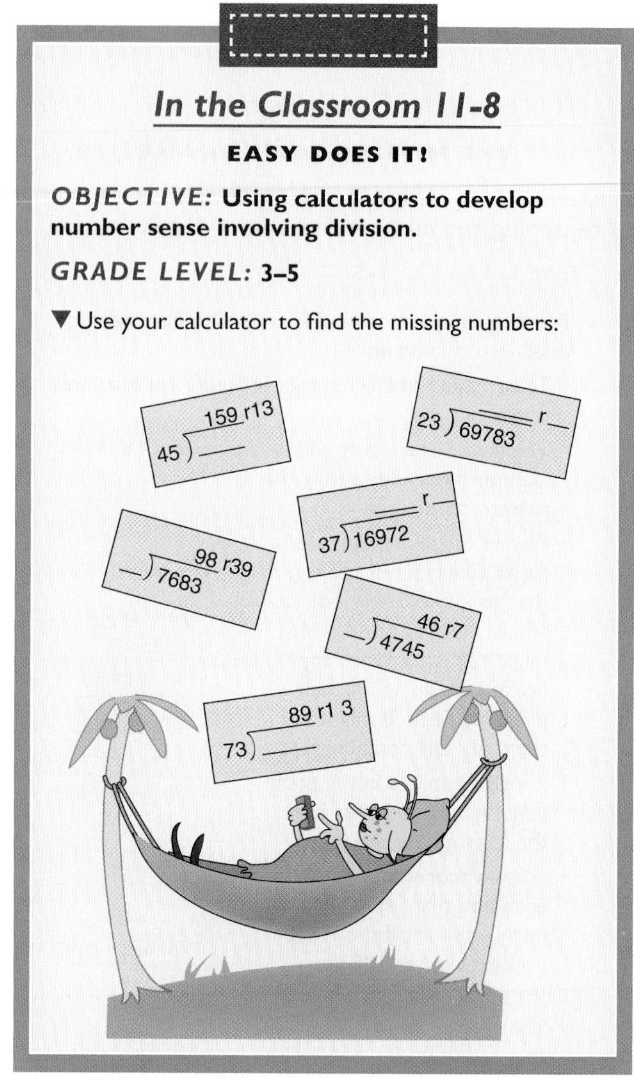

Division with Two-Digit Divisors

Work with two-digit divisors should aim toward helping children understand what the procedure involves but not toward mastery of an algorithm. The calculator does the job for most adults, and there is little reason to have children spend months or years mastering multidigit division. Other mathematics is of more importance for children to learn.

The development of division with two-digit divisors proceeds through stages from concrete to abstract, paralleling the work with one-digit divisors. Much practice may be needed with the symbolic form if proficiency is the goal. Use of the calculator is interwoven into the activities, as indicated In the Classroom 11-8, where the calculator is used to strengthen understanding of the relationships between numbers.

Making Sense of Division with Remainders

Children should encounter division problems involving remainders from the time they begin to work with division ideas (just as they should encounter addition involving regrouping right from the outset). It is artificial and counterproductive to begin teaching division with problems that always come out even, saving problems involving remainders for later. As long as problems remain on a concrete level, the concept of remainder is rather easy. Here are some examples of varied situations:

- Pass out 17 candies to 3 children. (Each child receives 5 candies with 2 candies left over. Or, if the candies can be cut into pieces, each child could have 5 candies plus $\frac{2}{3}$ of a candy.)
- To make each Valentine's card you need 3 pieces of lace. You have 17 pieces of lace. How

many cards can you make? (You can make 5. You'll probably have to discard the two extra pieces of lace.)

- If 17 children are going on the class trip and 3 children can ride in each car, how many cars are needed? (You will need 6 cars. With 5 cars you could seat only 15 children, with 2 children still waiting for a ride. With 6 cars, you can seat all 17 children, with 1 seat left over.)
- Separate a class of 17 children into 3 teams. (There can be 5 children on each team, and the 2 children left over can be the scorekeepers, or perhaps you could make two teams of 6 and 1 team of 5.)

Note that the remainder is handled differently in each of these real-world problems. In the candy problem, both the whole number (5) and the remainder $\left(\frac{2}{3}\right)$ are reported as parts of the answer. In the Valentine problem, the answer involves only the whole-number part (the remainder must be discarded or ignored). In the class trip problem, the quotient is rounded up because the remainder cannot be ignored (no matter how small). In the team problem, children need to find some other use for the remainder (or they may abandon the attempt to form equal-sized groups if they want everyone to be able to play).

Thus it is important for children to think about and be able to deal with remainders as they appear in real-world problems. With calculators, the results of inexact division are expressed in decimal form, and children need to learn how to interpret the remainder when it is not an integer (see Chapter 13).

Initially, children are taught to write the remainder in one of the following ways:

$$\begin{array}{r} 2 \\ 6\overline{)13} \\ \underline{12} \\ 1 \end{array} \quad \text{with 1 left over}$$

$$\begin{array}{r} 5 \\ 5\overline{)27} \\ \underline{25} \\ 2 \end{array} \quad \text{remainder 2 (later shortened to R2 or r2)}$$

It is important to emphasize the real-life situations from which examples arise and to decide whether a "remainder of 2" makes sense in that situation. Activities such as the game In the Classroom 11-9 provide practice in identifying the remainder.

Calculators can be used to solve problems with remainders, but the correct answer depends on the thinking a child does. Consider this problem:

A bus holds 36 children. If 460 children are being bused to a concert, how many buses do we need?

Research shows this problem to be difficult for children to solve with or without a calculator. An answer of 12 remainder 28 is often reported without a calculator, and 12.777 buses are reported with a calculator. The children seem more intent on producing an answer than on deciding if their answer makes sense. A sensible answer would be 13 buses (12 buses will be full and the last bus will have some empty seats).

In the Classroom 11-9

THE REMAINDER GAME (FOR 2 TO 4 PLAYERS)

OBJECTIVE: **Using a game to practice mental computation involving division.**

GRADE LEVEL: **3–5**

MATERIALS:

- A copy of this gameboard on heavy paper
- Four cards of each numeral 0 to 9
- A counter for each player

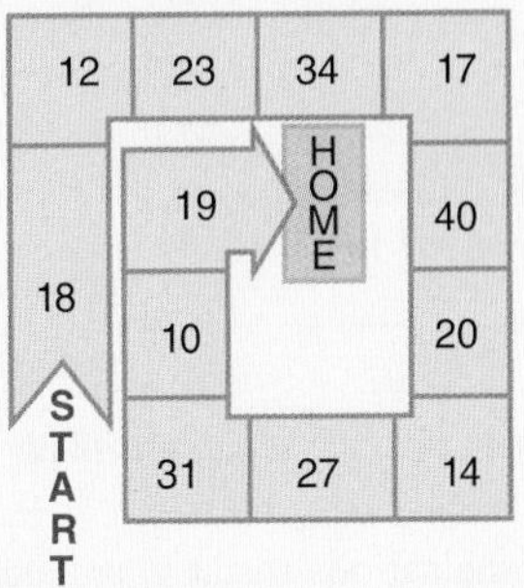

GAME RULES:

1. **Place the cards face down in a pile.**
2. **The first player draws a card.**
   - **For a player's first turn, divide the first number on the board by the number drawn.**
   - **For a player's additional turns, the dividend is the number on the space where his or her counter landed on the previous turn.**
3. **Move the counter forward by the number of spaces indicated by the remainder. If the remainder is 0, no move is made.**
4. **Each of the other players go in turn.**
5. **To get "home," a player must be able to move the exact number of spaces left. The first person home wins!**

*In the Classroom 11-10**

NUMBER NET

***OBJECTIVE:* Working with others to develop logical reasoning and number sense involving division.**

***GRADE LEVEL:* 3–5**

▼ Work with a partner or in a small group to determine the missing values:

Dividend	*Divisor*	*Quotient*	*Integral Remainder*
632	73	—	—
345	—	—	45
—	34	—	27
—	—	—	18
—	746	89	—
7439	—	274	—
—	—	56	73

▼ If the solutions are not unique, explain why not. If no solution is possible, explain why.

- Which combinations result in unique solutions?
- Given any two numbers in a row, can a solution always be found? Why or why not?
- Given only one number in a row, can a solution always be found? Why or why not?
- Which combinations make finding a solution easy? Difficult? Why?

*In the Classroom 11-10 is adapted from Usnick and Lamphere (1990).

Some activities have been developed for calculators with "integer division" capabilities so that any remainder is displayed as a whole number. These activities were designed to help students develop conceptual understanding of division and the relationships among the dividend, divisor, and remainder. They involve estimation skills, so students have a better chance of success if they are reasoning as they work. An example is given In the Classroom 11-10.

Checking

Just as it is important to estimate before computing, it is important to check after computing. Ordinarily, addition and subtraction are used to check each other, as are multiplication and division. Unfortunately, checking does not always achieve its purpose of ascertaining correctness. In fact, if you talk with children as they perform the check, you will find that they frequently force the check (i.e., make the results agree without actually performing the computation). Children need to understand the purpose of checking, as well as what they must do if the solution in the check does not agree with the original solution.

The calculator can serve many other functions, but its use in checking has not been overlooked by teachers. Nevertheless, the calculator should not be used primarily to check paper-and-pencil computation. It insults students to ask them to spend large amounts of time on a computation and then use a machine that does the computation instantly. Encourage estimation extensively, both as a means of identifying the ballpark for the answer *and* as a means of ascertaining the correctness of the calculator answer. The words "use your calculator to check" should generally be used only when the calculator is to perform the computation following an estimate.

Choosing Appropriate Methods

As the *NCTM Standards* and the discussion in Chapter 10 make very clear, children must learn to choose an appropriate means of calculating. Sometimes paper and pencil is better; sometimes mental computation is more efficient. Other times use of a calculator is better than either, and sometimes only an estimate is needed. In the Classroom 11-11 illustrates one way of getting students to think about which method of calculation is most appropriate.

Encouraging students to defend their answers often yields valuable insight into their thinking. Children need to discuss when each method or tool is appropriate, and they need practice in making the choice, followed by more discussion, so that a rationale for their choice is clear. They need to realize that this is a personal decision. A problem that one child chooses to do with a calculator may be done with mental computation by another.

Building Computational Proficiency

Computational fluency with addition, subtraction, multiplication, and division is an important part of mathematics education in the elementary grades; however, "developing fluency requires a balance and connection between conceptual understanding and computational proficiency" (NCTM,

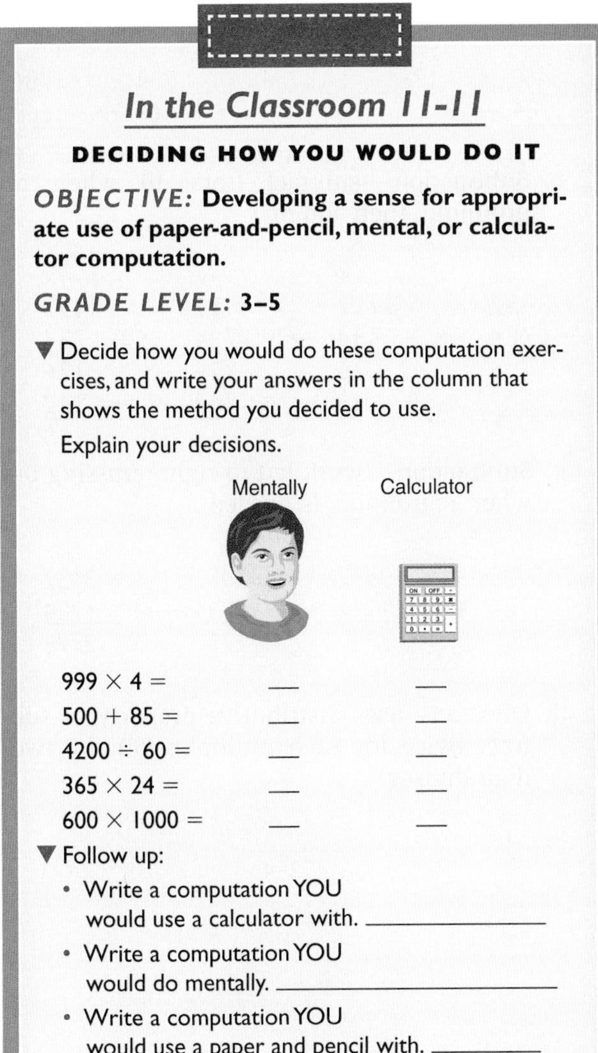

In the Classroom 11-11

DECIDING HOW YOU WOULD DO IT

OBJECTIVE: **Developing a sense for appropriate use of paper-and-pencil, mental, or calculator computation.**

GRADE LEVEL: **3–5**

▼ Decide how you would do these computation exercises, and write your answers in the column that shows the method you decided to use.
Explain your decisions.

	Mentally	Calculator
$999 \times 4 =$	___	___
$500 + 85 =$	___	___
$4200 \div 60 =$	___	___
$365 \times 24 =$	___	___
$600 \times 1000 =$	___	___

▼ Follow up:
- Write a computation YOU would use a calculator with. ___________
- Write a computation YOU would do mentally. ___________
- Write a computation YOU would use a paper and pencil with. ___________

2000, p. 35). Research has demonstrated that extensive practice without understanding is either forgotten or remembered incorrectly (Hiebert, 1999; Kamii and Dominick, 1998). On the other hand, practice is important to help students gain the computational fluency desired. Teachers must carefully provide practice opportunities intertwined with the development and maintenance of conceptual understanding. If students use reasoning, their practice is more likely to help them develop computational fluency.

Many kinds of computer software are available on the market. The challenge is to identify programs that require more than mindless practice with the algorithms. You will find that most programs are typically visually appealing, and they use a variety of characters in a story format; however, few programs involve problem solving or estimation. Some involve the use of games to motivate the child's participation. The question you should ask is whether the software offers advantages over the materials you already have available. Your search for useful computer software must be guided by the mathematics and not by the "bells and whistles" features.

Worksheet activities are available for motivating students to practice their skills with computation. Some worksheets feature a mystery for the students to solve using the answers obtained by completing the computations. In the Classroom 11-12 illustrates one example of this type of worksheet. In this example, the answers to some of the multiplication problems provide clues to identifying the mystery number. The student must organize these clues to help identify the mystery number. While these types of worksheets provide needed practice, overuse can lead to mindless practice rather than actually helping students gain computational fluency.

In the Classroom 11-12

WHAT NUMBER AM I?

OBJECTIVE: **Practice with multiplication to solve a mystery.**

GRADE LEVEL: **3–4**

▼ **Directions:** Solve each of the multiplication problems. Some of the solutions can help you identify the clues to help you find the mystery number. Circle the answers that are solutions to some of the problems; cross out the other clues. Use the clues to find the mystery number.

1.	15×9	**2.**	51×21	**3.**	63×24	**4.**	68×21
5.	77×21	**6.**	18×15	**7.**	22×14	**8.**	69×66
9.	18×9	**10.**	72×9	**11.**	88×18	**12.**	34×31

Answer	Clue
162	I am less than 100.
189	I am more than 100.
1502	I am an even number.
1071	I am an odd number.
1085	I am divisible by 3.
1308	I am divisible by 4.
280	I am divisible by 5.
647	I am a multiple of 3.
4554	I am a multiple of 5.
1607	I am a multiple of 10.
208	The sum of my digits is an even number.
1428	The sum of my digits is an odd number.

A Glance at Where We've Been

Although computational skill is viewed as an essential component of children's mathematical achievement, its role in the curriculum and the methods of teaching it are changing. The development of algorithms for each operation emphasizes the use of manipulative materials, place-value ideas, and estimation. In the chapter we provided suggestions for developing the standard algorithms and we presented many transitional and alternative algorithms. The use of calculators has been interwoven with many activities that use the algorithms, as well as activities using other materials.

Things to Do: From What You've Read

1. What prerequisites must a child have in order to succeed in the chapter's opening *Snapshot of a Lesson?*
2. Consider each example. Describe what a child would think as he or she worked. What questions might you ask to develop or explain the procedure? How could manipulative materials be used?

```
A.   1          C.    14        E.
    536            734            45
    279          - 2⁷69          x 3
  +  83              5           15
      8                         120

B.  2 14        D.  5           F.
    3̶4̶9             79              9
  - 184           x 6         38)291
      5               4
```

3. Explain why we do not recommend spending long periods of time drilling students on the long-division algorithm. What level of facility with division would you be satisfied with? How would you justify this position when parents question your teaching of computational algorithms?
4. Analyze each of the following student-invented algorithms. Do they work all the time? If so, explain why they work. If not, explain why not.

a. Subtraction — uses missing addend addition

```
                1          11          111          111
 3452         1784        1784        1784         1784
-1784  →  +      8  →  +    68  →  +   668  →  + 1668
              3452        3452        3452         3452
```

b. Subtraction — subtract from 10 when regrouping, then add on

```
                    10          1010          1010
   410           3 410        23 410        23 410
  3452            3452          3452          3452
 -1784   →       -1784   →     -1784   →     -1784
     6              26           326          1326
 +   2          +   42         + 342         + 342
                                              1668
```

c. Subtraction — work left to right, crossing out when regrouping is needed

```
                  1           11           111
  3452          3452         3452         3452
 -1784    →    -1784    →   -1784    →   -1784
  2             2̶7           2̶7̶7          2̶7̶7̶8
                1            16           166
```

d. Division—uses distributive property to subtract twice for each multiplication by two-digit divisor

```
      2058 r20
  23)47354
     40
      7
      6
      135
      100
       35
       15
       204
       160
        44
        24
        20
```

Use base-ten blocks to model the previous problems. Do they help you prove they work? For more practice with base-ten blocks, try the problems on Masters 11-1 and 11-2 found in the *Helping Children Learn Mathematics Instructor's Manual.* (Available at the Wiley Book Companion web site.)

5. Some people wonder why it makes sense to encourage students to invent their own computational algorithms, since students are unlikely to discover the standard algorithms on their own. The standard algorithms, which are generally quick and efficient, were refined through centuries of invention and modification. Why not

just teach these standard algorithms directly to students?

6. Sketch a diagram to show how 12 × 17 can be modeled with an array on grid paper. Relate the model to the transitional algorithm for 12 × 17, showing how each of the partial products in the array relates to the model.

7. Hands-on modeling of the traditional division algorithm: Consider a problem such as 798 ÷ 6. Model the dividend (798) with base-ten blocks. The divisor (6) tells how many equal-sized piles you want to make. Start by sharing the biggest blocks possible, and then make trades if necessary. Next, share the next-biggest blocks. Again, make trades if necessary and continue the process until all blocks possible have been shared. Try several other problems such as 458 ÷ 3, 597 ÷ 2, 4782 ÷ 4, and 7365 ÷ 5. After doing several of these problems using just the materials, do them over again and record your findings step by step.

   Questions to ask yourself (repeatedly), after sharing cubes or flats or longs or units:

   - How many did you put into each pile? (Write this number up top in the appropriate place.)
   - How many did you share altogether? (Write this number below.)
   - How many do you still have left to be distributed? (Write this number after subtracting.)

8. Consider problems involving subtraction with regrouping, such as 52−25, 91−79, and 47−18. How would you approach these problems if you were teaching second grade? What do you think children need to understand or be able to do before they can start learning subtraction with regrouping?

9. Assume you are a sixth-grade teacher. You notice that several of your students are making the same mistake when multiplying multidigit numbers. When computing 15 × 23 or 173 × 234, they seem to forget to "move over the numbers" on each line. They are writing:

```
   23             23                234              234
 × 15   in-     × 15              × 173   in-      ×173
  115   stead    115    and         702   stead     702
   23   of       23                1638   of      1638
  138            345                234            234
                                   2574          40482
```

What will you do to help these students? How will you help them correct their mistake?

10. For the problem 4578 ÷ 7, find the quotient by using the transitional division algorithm known as the subtractive algorithm. Then do the problem again, using at least three more steps or three fewer steps than you used the first time to illustrate the flexible nature of this algorithm.

11. Write two story problems involving 35 ÷ 6 where the answers appropriate for the real world would actually not be the exact answer to the computation ($5\frac{5}{6}$). For your first story problem involving 35 ÷ 6, the appropriate answer should be 5. For your second story problem involving 35 ÷ 6, the appropriate answer should be 6.

12. Examine the games in the Lesson Idea 11-1.

    Answer the following questions about Race-to-a-Flat:

    a. Can you win a long with one roll of the dice? Can you win two longs with one roll? three longs?
    b. Can you win a flat with one roll of the dice?
    c. What is the fewest number of rolls you would need to win a flat? the most rolls to win a flat?
    d. What is the fewest number of units a player will need to play this game?
    e. How many units, longs, and flats should you give each student, so that he or she is sure to have enough pieces to play the game no matter what rolls he or she gets?

    Answer the following questions about Give-Away-a-Flat:

    a. Is it possible to give away a long with one roll of the dice? two longs?
    b. Can you win the game with one roll of the dice?
    c. What is the fewest number of rolls required to give away all of the blocks?
    d. What is the most number of rolls required to give away all of the blocks?
    e. How many units, longs, and flats should you give each student, so he or she is sure to have enough pieces to play the game no matter what rolls he or she gets?

Things to Do: Going Beyond This Book

IN THE FIELD

1. **Computation in Textbooks and Classrooms.* Choose a textbook for the grade level of a classroom you can visit and analyze a lesson plan on computation in the teacher's guide. What stages from concrete to abstract are involved in the lesson? Talk to the teacher about how he or she teaches computation. Is the textbook approach supplemented? How? What manipulatives, if any, are used? How?
2. **Addition with Regrouping.* Develop three evaluation items that would assess students' understanding of adding two two-digit numbers with regrouping. Explain why you chose the examples that you did. Try your items with several children and analyze their responses.
3. **Transitional Algorithms.* Ask a classroom teacher if you can spend some time working with a student who is having trouble with paper-and-pencil computation (addition, subtraction, multiplication, or division, depending on age and grade level). See if you can figure out what the child's problem is. You might try helping him or her by suggesting the use of one of the transitional algorithms described in this chapter.

IN YOUR JOURNAL

4. You are a fourth-grade teacher. Following advice from the *Standards* (2000), you have decided to spend less time this year than in the past on multidigit multiplication and on long division. Instead, you will spend more time on mental computation, number sense, computations embedded in problem situations, and developing students' abilities to recognize and work with patterns and functions (early algebraic thinking). At the upcoming open house for parents, you want to explain to the parents how you have decided to modify your teaching approach and why. You decide that getting them involved with three or four problems as examples may be the best way to help them understand. Identify three problems to present at the open house. Write a brief narrative explaining why you chose each problem and how you would use it with the parents to convince them of the reasonableness of your new approach to teaching mathematics.
5. Solve the mystery of the number In the Classroom 11-12. Find or create a worksheet that would require that the students demonstrate more than computational skills. Describe in your journal how your worksheet motivates students to think about the mathematics they are practicing.

WITH ADDITIONAL RESOURCES

6. Choose a textbook for grade 3 or 4. Trace the development of multiplication algorithms. How are they introduced? What steps do children go through?
7. Choose a textbook series. Trace the development of division algorithms. What phases of development have been or should be modified because of the use of calculators?
8. The author's daughter Becca investigating a multiplication problem is the focus of the article by Whitin (1993). After you have read about her investigation, write an evaluation of her work.
9. Read the Number Standards for grade bands pre-K–2 and 3–5 in *Principles and Standards for School Mathematics* (NCTM, 2000). What recommendations are made concerning teaching computational algorithms? Write a position paper in which you either agree with the NCTM's recommendations or take an opposing position. In either case, clearly explain and defend your point of view.
10. Pick a concept or skill from this chapter and compile a brief bibliography of recent articles containing research or teaching ideas on this topic.

WITH TECHNOLOGY RESOURCES

11. *Drill and Practice Software.* Find a drill-and-practice software program that is available at a local school. Learn to use this program and identify how you might use this software when teaching algorithms such as those developed in this chapter.
12. *Calculators.* In division, the calculator provides a decimal remainder. For example, for $476 \div 23 = 20.69565217$. Describes two different ways you could find the fractional remainder using a simple calculator.

*Additional activities, suggestions, or questions are provided in *Teaching Elementary Mathematics: A Resource for Field Experiences* (Wiley, 2004).

Book Nook for Children

Anno, Mitsumasa. *Anno's Math Games.* New York: Philomel Books, 1987.
The task for the reader in the first section is to look at the pictures and figure out what is different and how it is different. For example, an animal may not belong to the set because it flies or is extinct. Folklore and inventions introduce the second section, "Putting Together and Taking Apart." Charts record all 25 examples of the possibilities of crossing five colors with five articles of clothing (Cartesian products). The reader can extend "Putting Together" by exploring how five puzzle pieces can fit into various shapes. Playing cards introduce sequences and cardinal and ordinal numbers in "Numbers in Order." These concepts are extended in examples involving sequences and locations such as grids, a theater, and apartment houses. The last section, "Who's the Tallest?," introduces attributes that can be measured, such as weight and time, and discusses concepts that can't be measured, such as scary or sad.

Anno, Mitsumasa. *Anno's Magic Seeds.* New York: Philomel Books, 1999.
Jack meets a wizard who gives him two magic seeds and instructs him to eat one, which will sustain him for a full year, and to plant the other. The following spring, the plant bears two seeds. Jack eats one and plants the other, as he does for several years until he determines to plant both seeds. The next year he has two plants each bearing two seeds, so he eats one seed and plants the other three. Six seeds! As the years go by, he marries, raises a family, plants many crops, endures a flood, and saves enough seeds to feed his family and start planting again.

Anno, Masaichiro, and Anno, Mitsumasa. *Anno's Mysterious Multiplying Jar.* New York: Philomel Books, 1983.
A mysterious jar contains rippling water that becomes a wide, deep sea with one island containing two countries. "Within each country there were 3 mountains . . . On each mountain there were 4 walled kingdoms." The pattern continues and accumulates until each of nine boxes contains 10 jars. How can you count the number of walled kingdoms? This multiplication pattern introduces factorials ($4! = 4 \times 3 \times 2 \times 1 = 24$ walled kingdoms on 4 walled kingdoms on each of the 3 mountains and there are 2 countries each containing those 3 mountains and one island). The authors introduce additional ideas to explore with this multiplication pattern.

Froman, Robert. *The Greatest Guessing Game: A Book about Dividing.* New York: Crowell, 1978.
Division concepts are introduced through guessing or estimating. A little girl and her friends try to estimate how much root beer is in each of three glasses and decide how many walnuts should be given to each person. Problems such as \$6.00 divided by 4 and \$8.27 divided by 5 are introduced in situations where the friends earn money by helping others and then share their wages equally. Throughout the book, readers are challenged to make an estimate and that estimate is considered as an initial guess—a guess on which to make the next guess in the progress toward a solution.

Trivett, John V. *Building Tables on Tables: A Book about Multiplication.* New York: Crowell, 1975.
Trivett transforms the subject of tables into a lively, challenging topic and invites the reader into a world of options where there are many names for the same number. Grouping 12 counters involves the reader in exploring the different possibilities: three groups of four (3×4 or $4 + 4 + 4$) or uneven regroups of $(3 + 4 + 5)$ or $(3 + 3 + 6)$ or $(2 \times 3 + 6)$. Where problems require more than one operation, he suggests the use of circles for grouping.

13. *Internet software.* A search of the Internet will identify many web sites teachers can use to create math worksheets. Find one of these sites and create a worksheet for practicing basic skills. Explain when or if you would recommend use of these worksheets.

ANNOTATED BOOKS

Fosnot, Catherine T., and Dolk, Maarten. *Young Mathematicians at Work: Constructing Number Sense,*

Addition, and Subtraction. Portsmouth, NH: Heinemann, 2001.
The first in a three-volume set, *Young Mathematicians at Work* focuses on young children between the ages of four and eight as they construct a deep understanding of number and the operations of addition and subtraction. From the work of the Dutch mathematician Hans Freudenthal, the authors define mathematics as "mathematizing"—the activity of structuring, modeling, and interpreting one's "lived world" mathematically. They describe teachers who use rich problematic situations to promote inquiry, problem solving, and construction, and children who raise and pursue their own mathematical ideas. The authors argue for number sense and the development of a repertoire of strategies. Sample lessons on the use of the open number line model show you how to support the development of efficient computation.

Morrow, Lorna J., and Kenney, Margaret J. (eds.). *The Teaching and Learning of Algorithms in School Mathematics* (1998 Yearbook). Reston, VA: NCTM, 1998.
This NCTM Yearbook addresses questions about teaching and learning algorithms at all school levels of mathematics. Consider potential curricular changes needed to reflect the broadening views about algorithms, especially the importance of algorithms in performance-based assessments. Capsule lessons with alternative algorithms suggest changes for the mathematics curriculum.

ANNOTATED ARTICLES

Burns, Marilyn. "Introducing Division through Problem-Solving Experiences." *Arithmetic Teacher*, 38 (April 1991), pp. 14–18.
Burns offers five ways to introduce division to third graders without resorting to an algorithm using a problem-solving focus.

Campbell, Patricia F. "Connecting Instructional Practice to Student Thinking." *Teaching Children Mathematics*, 4 (October 1997), pp. 106–110.
This article explores children's thinking and its interconnection with a teacher's instructional decisions. Students frequently devise problem-solving techniques that are different from an adult's technique.

Carpenter, Thomas P.; Franke, Megan L.; Jacobs, Victoria R.; Fennema, Elizabeth; and Empson, Susan B. "A Longitudinal Study of Invention and Understanding in Children's Multidigit Addition and Subtraction." *Journal for Research in Mathematics Education*, 29(1), (1998), pp. 3–20.
This three-year study focused on children's development of number concepts. It shows that children can invent addition and subtraction strategies and explores those strategies.

Carroll, William M., and Porter, Denise. "Invented Strategies Can Develop Meaningful Mathematics Procedures." *Teaching Children Mathematics* 3 (March 1997), pp. 370–374.
Carroll and Porter investigate children's invented algorithms for meaningful computation. They assert that most primary students are capable of developing their own solution processes.

Fennema, Elizabeth; Carpenter, Thomas P.; Franke, Megan L., Levi, Linda; Jacobs, Victoria R.; and Empson, Susan B. "A Longitudinal Study of Learning to Use Children's Thinking in Mathematics Instruction." *Journal for Research in Mathematics Education*, 27(4), (1996), pp. 403–434.
This study looked at how teacher beliefs changed as they learned about how student's mathematics thinking developed. It notes changes in their teaching over a four-year period.

Garofalo, Joe, and Bryant, Jerry. "Assessing Reasonableness: Some Observations and Suggestions." *Arithmetic Teacher*, 40 (December 1992), pp. 210–212.
Garofalo and Bryant present five ways teachers can help students learn to evaluate the reasonableness of their answers.

Graeber, Anna O. "Research into Practice: Misconceptions about Multiplication and Division." *Arithmetic Teacher*, 40 (March 1993), pp. 408–411.
In order to help students make sense of multiplying and dividing with fractions between zero and one, this article offers activities to help students move away from the misconception that multiplying makes things larger and dividing makes things smaller.

Harel, Guershon, and Behr, Merlyn. "Ed's Strategy for Solving Division Problems." *Arithmetic Teacher*, 39 (November 1991), pp. 38–40.
This article asserts that good teachers build on student's knowledge and honor creative solutions. An example of such a solution from a second grader is demonstrated.

Hiebert, James. "Relationships between Research and the NCTM Standards." *Journal for Research in Mathematics Education*, 30 (January 1999), pp. 3–19.
Distinguishing between values and research problems, Hiebert focuses on how research should help to shape the *Standards*. Relevant research findings are included.

Huinker, DeAnn M. "Multiplication and Division Word Problems: Improving Students' Understanding." *Arithmetic Teacher*, 37 (October 1989), pp. 8–12.
This article suggests how to teach students to solve word problems and understand the operations they will need to use. Samples of teaching approach and classroom test results are included.

Kamii, Constance; Lewis, Barbara A.; and Livingston, Sally Jones. "Primary Arithmetic: Children Inventing Their Own Procedures." *Arithmetic Teacher*, 41 (December 1993), pp. 200–203.
Kamii presents evidence supporting the idea that primary students can invent their own algorithms and offers suggestions of how to motivate them to do so.

Kouba, Vicky L., and Franklin, Kathy. "Multiplication and Division: Sense Making and Meaning." In *Research Ideas for the Classroom: Early Childhood Mathematics* (ed. Robert J. Jensen). Reston, VA.: NCTM; and New York: Macmillan, 1993, pp. 103–126.
Instead of having students memorize rules, this discussion of research shows that instruction should strengthen conceptual understanding of multiplication and division. Action research ideas are included.

Merseth, Katherine Klippert. "Using Materials and Activities in Teaching Addition and Subtraction Algorithms." In *Developing Computational Skills*, 1978 Yearbook (ed. Marilyn N. Suydam). Reston, VA: NCTM, 1978, pp. 61–77.
This article offers detailed activities that help teachers develop strong connections for students as they move from concrete understanding to algorithms.

Silver, Edward A.; Shapiro, Lora J.; and Deutsch, Adam. "Sense Making and the Solution of Division Problems Involving Remainders: An Examination of Middle School Students' Solution Processes and Their Interpretations of Solutions." *Journal for Research in Mathematics Education*, 24 (March 1993), pp. 117–135.
These researchers looked at how middle school students solved division story problems and considered models that helped explain students' difficulty.

Smith, Jacque. "Links to Literature: Assessing Children's Reasoning: It's an Age-old Problem." *Teaching Children Mathematics,* 2 (May 1996), pp. 524–528.
Using the song "Billy Boy," this teacher helped students communicate mathematically as they discussed the lyrics. She also assessed student problem solving through discussion.

Stanic, George M. A., and McKillip, William D. "Developmental Algorithms Have a Place in Elementary School Mathematics Instruction." *Arithmetic Teacher,* 36 (January 1989), pp. 14–16.
This article shows students moving from concrete materials to the standard algorithms. A description of using developmental algorithms to improve skills is included.

Thompson, Frances. "Two-Digit Addition and Subtraction: What Works?" *Arithmetic Teacher,* 38 (January 1991), pp. 10–13.
This article focuses on a study of three instructional strategies in second-grade classrooms. Findings of results with proportional materials, nonproportional materials, and nonproportional materials, with pictorial models are discussed. Recommendations for teaching are offered.

Trafton, Paul R., and Zawojewski, Judith S. "Implementing the Standards: Meanings of Operations." *Arithmetic Teacher,* 38 (November 1990), pp. 18–22.
Along with activities on concepts of operations, patterns, relationships, and understanding, this article discusses the concepts and importance of number sense, numeration, operations, and whole-number computations.

Van de Walle, John A. "Implementing the Standards: Redefining Computation." *Arithmetic Teacher,* 38 (January 1991), pp. 44–51.
Highlighting the teaching of computation and estimation as suggested by the *NCTM Standards,* the author discusses redefining computation. Specific activities for implementation in K–4 and 5–8 are included.

Van de Walle, John, and Thompson, Charles S. "Partitioning Sets for Number Concepts, Place Value, and Long Division." *Arithmetic Teacher,* 32 (January 1985), pp. 6–11.
This article offers ways to use manipulatives to teach counting, place value, and division with two-digit divisors. It asserts the value of using partitioning to develop these concepts.

Wearne, Diana, and Hiebert, James. "Place Value and Addition and Subtraction." *Arithmetic Teacher,* 41 (January 1994), pp. 272–274.
Wearne and Hiebert show development of the understanding of addition and subtraction as two students solve problems. One student has an understanding of place value as memorized rules; the other student has conceptual understanding of place value. The article discusses the importance of understanding place value.

Whitin, David J. "Becca's Investigation." *Arithmetic Teacher,* 41 (October 1993), pp. 78–81.
This is a detailed discussion of Whitin's daughter's self-initiated process as she investigated patterns in multiplication. The 11-year-old generated hypotheses, discovered patterns, developed questions, and rejected inappropriate procedures. The article goes on to encourage classroom environments that encourage questioning.

ADDITIONAL REFERENCES

Ashlock, Robert B. *Error Patterns in Computation,* 7th ed. New York: Merrill, 1998.

Brownell, William A. "An Experiment on 'Borrowing' in Third-Grade Arithmetic." *Journal of Educational Research,* 41 (November 1947), pp. 161–171.

Carpenter, Thomas P.; Corbitt, Mary Kay; Kepner, Henry S., Jr.; Lindquist, Mary Montgomery; and Reys, Robert E. *Results from the Second Mathematics Assessment of the National Assessment of Educational Progress.* Reston, VA: NCTM, 1981.

Carroll, William M., and Porter, Denise. "Alternative Algorithms for Whole-Number Operations." In *The Teaching and Learning of Algorithms in School Mathematics* (1998 Yearbook) (ed. Lorna J. Morrow and Margaret J. Kenney). Reston, VA: NCTM, 1998, pp. 106–114.

Hembree, Ray, and Dessart, Donald J. "Effects of Hand-Held Calculators in Precollege Mathematics Education: A Meta-Analysis." *Journal for Research in Mathematics Education,* 17 (March 1986), pp. 83–99.

Kamii, Constance, and Dominick, Ann. "The Harmful Effects of Algorithms in Grades 1–4." In *The Teaching and Learning of Algorithms in School Mathematics* (1998 Yearbook) (ed. Lorna J. Morrow and Margaret J. Kenney). Reston, VA: NCTM, 1998, pp. 130–140.

Kenney, Patricia Ann, and Silver, Edward A. (eds.). *Results from the Sixth Mathematics Assessment of the National Assessment of Educational Progress.* Reston, VA: NCTM, 1997.

Lindquist, Mary M.; Brown, Catherine A.; Carpenter, Thomas P.; Kouba, Vicky L.; Silver, Edward A.; and Swafford, Jane O. *Results from the Fourth Mathematics Assessment of the National Assessment of Educational Progress.* Reston, VA: NCTM, 1988.

Moyer, John C., and Moyer, Margaret Bannochie. "Computation: Implications for Learning Disabled Children." In *Developing Computational Skills,* 1978 Yearbook (ed. Marilyn N. Suydam). Reston, VA: NCTM, 1978, pp. 78–95.

National Council of Teachers of Mathematics. *An Agenda for Action.* Reston, VA: NCTM, 1980.

National Council of Teachers of Mathematics. *Principles and Standards for School Mathematics.* Reston, VA: NCTM, 2000.

Rathmell, Edward, and Trafton, Paul. "Whole Number Computation." In *Mathematics for the Young Child* (ed. Joseph N. Payne). Reston, VA: NCTM, 1990, pp. 153-172.

Ron, Pilar. "My Family Taught Me This Way." In *The Teaching and Learning of Algorithms in School Mathematics* (1998 Yearbook) (ed. Lorna J. Morrow and Margaret J. Kenney). Reston, VA: NCTM, 1998, pp. 115–119.

Usnick, Virginia E., and Lamphere, Patricia M. "Calculators and Division." *Arithmetic Teacher,* 38 (December 1990), pp. 40–43.

Wheatley, Grayson H., and Wheatley, Charlotte L. "How Shall We Teach Column Addition? Some Evidence." *Arithmetic Teacher,* 25 (January 1978), pp. 18–19.

CHAPTER 12

Fractions and Decimals: Meanings and Operations

Snapshot of a Lesson

Orientation

A fifth-grade class has reviewed ways to model fractions given a whole object or a set of objects. The teacher, Mrs. Benson, is introducing the lesson for today, in which she provides a fractional part and the students must construct the whole.

MRS. BENSON: Good, you know a lot about fractions. Today, we are really going to test our brains. You found that it is fairly easy to show a fractional part of a whole. What if I give you a fractional part and you have to show me the whole?

JUSTIN: I'm not sure what you mean.

MRS. BENSON: Well, if I told you that this picture represents three-fifths of a cake, could you draw the whole cake?

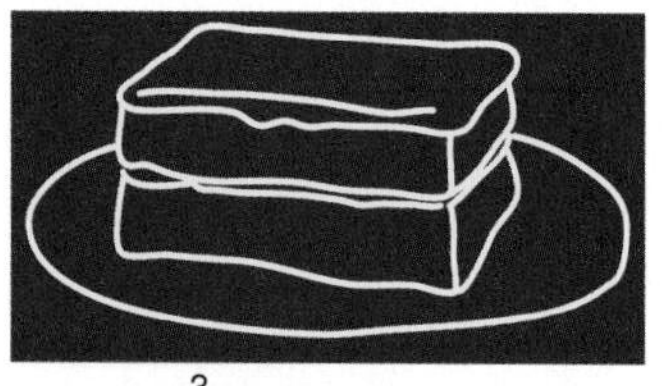

$\frac{3}{5}$ of the cake

ROSA LEE: It sure would be a skinny cake.

CAMILLE: That depends on how the two-fifths was cut off.

MRS. BENSON: You are both right; you won't be able to tell exactly what the shape of the cake was before it was cut unless I tell you where it was cut. Let's pretend you can see that it was cut here (pointing to the right side). What do you know?

GILBERT: You have three of the five equal pieces. If we divide this into three equal parts, we know how large one-fifth is.

MRS. BENSON: Let's do that. Who can tell me how to finish the problem?

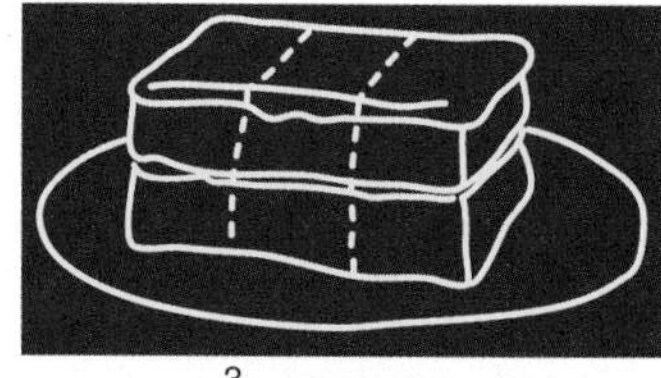

$\frac{3}{5}$ of the cake

OLAV: All you have to do now is add the missing two-fifths. Rosa Lee, you are right, it is a skinny cake. It would look like this. [Coming to the board, he draws two more parts.]

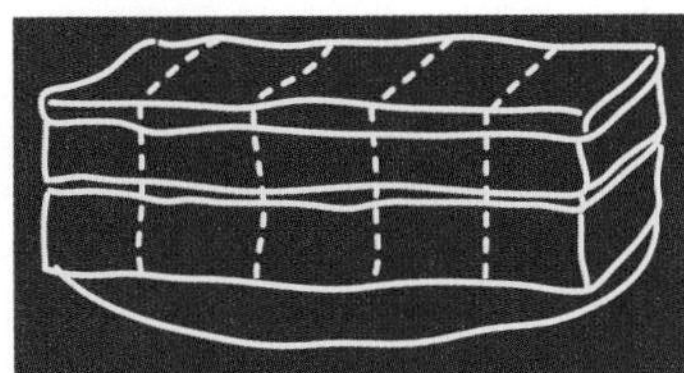

The whole cake

MRS. BENSON: How about another one? I have two-sevenths of a piece of licorice. How long was the licorice to begin with? Each of you draw a small line segment and label it two-sevenths.

JUSTIN: Does it matter how long it is?

MRS. BENSON: No, Justin, but we'll each be doing a slightly different problem. How long did you draw yours?

JUSTIN: About 5 centimeters.

MRS. BENSON: Do each one of you have a picture something like this?

$\frac{2}{7}$ of the licorice

What do you do next?

WINIFRED: That must be two of the seven parts, so one part would be about this long (holding up her fingers). Now, we need seven of those.

MRS. BENSON: Suppose I know that the twelve pieces of candy in a box are three-fifths of the original amount. How many pieces were in the box?

DENISE: I drew twelve pieces but then I don't know what to do.

MRS. BENSON: Let's think, what does this picture tell you?

$\frac{3}{5}$ of the candy

DENISE: I think it means that three of five parts are in the box; this is three equal parts. Oh, there are twelve pieces, so there must be four in each part.

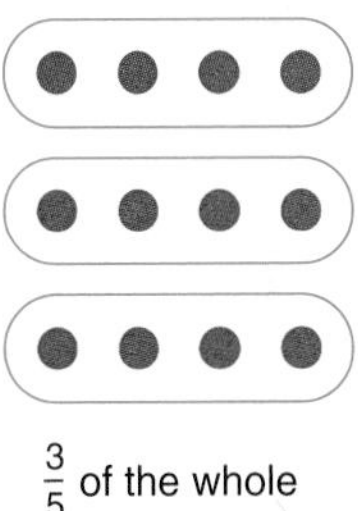

$\frac{3}{5}$ of the whole

MR. BENSON: Good, let's circle the three sets of four.

DENISE: You need two more sets of four. So there must have been twenty pieces to begin with.

MR. BENSON: Does that make sense? Is twelve three-fifths of twenty?

After a few more examples using improper fractions and mixed numbers, the students continue to explore the problems that Mrs. Benson had ready for them. She ended the lesson by having the children make up problems and having a partner solve them.

Introduction

Fractions and decimals have long been a stumbling block for many students. One reason may be that curricula tend to rush to symbolization and operations without developing strong conceptual understandings for numbers and operations with them. The *Snapshot of a Lesson* depends on children making sense of finding a whole when only part of the whole is described. Much of this chapter is devoted to concept development of fractions and decimals and the processes underlying operations with these numbers, using models and oral language. Developing fluency in the use of fractions and decimals for older children is recommended only after they have developed estimation skills and conceptual understanding, as discussed in *Principles and Standards for School Mathematics* (2000). Figure 12-1 provides the relevant expectations about fractions and decimals for prekindergarten through grade 5 as identified in the Number and Operations standard.

As you will see, the concepts associated with fractions and decimals are complex; however, two rather simple but powerful ideas—*partitioning* and *equivalence*—can help tie many of the ideas

Instructional programs from prekindergarten through grade 12 should enable all students to:	Pre-K–2 Expectations All students should:	Grades 3–5 Expectations All students should:
• Understand numbers, ways of representing numbers, relationships among numbers, and number systems.	• Connect number words and numerals to the quantities they represent, using various physical models and representations. • Understand and represent commonly used fractions, such as $\frac{1}{4}$, $\frac{1}{3}$, and $\frac{1}{2}$.	• Understand the place-value structure of the base-ten number system and be able to represent and compare whole numbers and decimals. • Develop an understanding of fractions as parts of unit wholes, as parts of a collection as locations on number lines, and as divisions of whole numbers • Use models, benchmarks, and equivalent forms to judge the size of fractions. • Recognize and generate equivalent forms of commonly used fractions, decimals, and percents.
• Understand meanings of operations and how they relate to one another. • Compute fluently and make reasonable estimates.	• Understand various meanings of addition and subtraction.	• Understand various meanings of multiplication and division. • Develop and use strategies to to estimate computations involving fractions and decimals in situations relevant to students' experience. • Use visual models, benchmarks, and equivalent forms to add and subtract commonly used fractions and decimals. • Use a variety of methods and tools to compute, including objects, mental computation, estimation, paper and pencil, and calculators.

FIGURE 12-1 Number and Operations Standard with expectations for children's learning of fractions and decimals in grades prekindergarten–2 and 3–5.

Math Links 12.1

The full-text electronic version of this standard, with electronic examples (interactive activities), is available at the NCTM's web site, which you can access from this book's web site. Click on pre-K-2, 3-5, or 6-8 to read more about the Number and Operation Standard.

together (Kieren, 1980). In reference to fractions and decimals, partitioning is the process of sharing equally (a cake shared equally among five people or six candy bars shared equally among four people). Equivalence focuses on different representations of the same amount (three-fourths of a cake is the same amount as six-eighths of that cake, so three-fourths is equivalent to six-eighths).

One idea related to equivalence that you should keep in mind is that decimal fractions are

Math Links 12.2

A variety of web resources for fractions and decimals, which may be used by teachers and children, may be found at the NCTM's Illuminations web site (accessible from this book's web site) under the Number and Operations Standard.

just another notation for common fractions. For example, 0.5 and $\frac{5}{10}$ are two different ways to represent the same fractional part. Each of these fractions is equivalent to one-half.

Both common fractions and decimal fractions can represent fractional parts; however, decimal fractions represent partitions of only tenths, hundredths, and powers of tenths; common fractions can represent any partitioning.

This initial concentration on common fractions (simply called *fractions* from here on) is not meant to imply that the entire study of fractions should not be integrated with the study of decimals. After a beginning foundation has been built with fractions, decimal notation can be introduced. In fact, many of the operations with decimals are easier than the corresponding operations with fractions and can be taught meaningfully before the entire study of operations with fractions is completed.

There is some controversy regarding the importance of the study of fractions, since technology uses decimals almost exclusively; however, since common fractions are important in daily life and necessary for further study in mathematics, current recommendations suggest that the development of computational fluency include more common fractions (National Research Council, 2001).

FOCUS QUESTIONS

1. What are models for the part-whole and quotient meanings of fractions?
2. How can you use concrete and pictorial models to develop children's understanding of equivalent fractions and ordering fractions?
3. Describe how children can use estimation strategies for adding and subtracting by rounding to whole numbers and benchmark numbers to determine reasonableness of answers to fraction and decimal problems.
4. How can linear and area models assist the development of children's conceptual understanding of adding, subtracting, multiplying, and dividing fractions or decimals?
5. What are some ways to assess children's understanding of multiplying and dividing fractions?

Conceptual Development of Fractions

The *Principles and Standards for School Mathematics* (NCTM, 2000) emphasize that students should be given the opportunity to develop concepts as well as number sense with fractions and decimals. One way to help children develop conceptual understanding is to use problems presented in familiar contexts (Irwin, 2001). A careful examination of the items on the seventh mathematics assessment of the National Assessment of Educational Progress (NAEP) reveals that concepts and models underlying fractions are not well developed by grade 4. Although older students can relate fractions to pictorial models, they do not realize that these models can be helpful in solving problems (Wearne and Kouba, 2000); however, a curriculum that emphasizes many physical models and representations—pictorial, manipulative, verbal, real-world, and symbolic—is more successful in aiding students' development of conceptual understanding than more traditional approaches that depend on repetition of rote procedures (Cramer, Post, & del Mas, 2002).

Many materials, such as Cuisenaire rods and pattern blocks, are available to assist you in helping children develop concepts about fractions. Some of the most effective materials, such as construction paper, white paper, and counters, are commonly found in the classroom.

Mathematics literature can also serve as an excellent basis for a conceptual development of fractions. For example, one book, *Ed Emberley's Picture Pie, A Circle Drawing Book* (Emberley, 1984), allows students to see and make colorful pictures and patterns from fractional parts of a circle. Another book, *The Doorbell Rang* (Hutchins, 1987), is an excellent source to use when introducing the concept of partitioning. Books can often help lay the groundwork for an understanding of mathematical concepts.

Math Links 12.3

A wide variety of electronic fraction manipulatives may be found at the National Library of Virtual Manipulatives for Interactive Mathematics web site, which you can access from this book's web site.

Three Meanings of Fractions

Three distinct meanings of fractions—part-whole, quotient, and ratio—are found in most elementary mathematics programs. Most fraction work is based on the part-whole meaning, often with little development of the other two meanings. Ignoring these other meanings may be one source of students' difficulty.

PART-WHOLE The part-whole interpretation of a fraction such as $\frac{3}{5}$ indicates that a whole has been partitioned into five equal parts and three of those parts are being considered. This fraction may be shown with a region model:

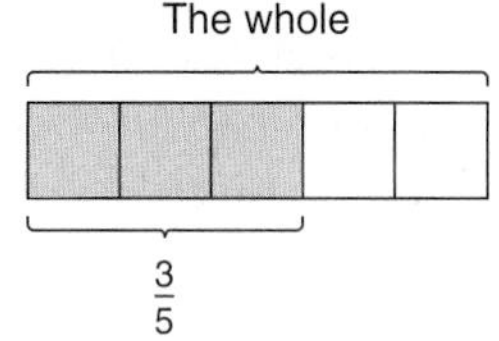

QUOTIENT The fraction $\frac{3}{5}$ may also be considered as a quotient, $3 \div 5$. This interpretation also arises from a partitioning situation. Suppose you had 20 big cookies to give to five people. You could give each person one cookie, then another, and so on until you had distributed the same amount to each. You could represent this process mathematically by $20 \div 5$; each person would get four cookies.

Now consider this problem:

> You have three big cookies and you want to give them to five people; that is, you want to divide the three cookies equally among five people, or $3 \div 5$.
>
> How much would each person get?
>
> Would anyone get a whole?

One way to solve the problem using pictures of the cookies is shown in Figure 12-2. This interpretation of fractions is used when a remainder in a division problem is expressed as a fraction. It is also the interpretation that is needed to change a fraction to decimal notation (i.e., $\frac{5}{8}$ is $5 \div 8$ or 0.625).

RATIO The fraction $\frac{3}{5}$ may also represent a ratio, as in examples where there are three boys for every five girls. Here is a model for this situation:

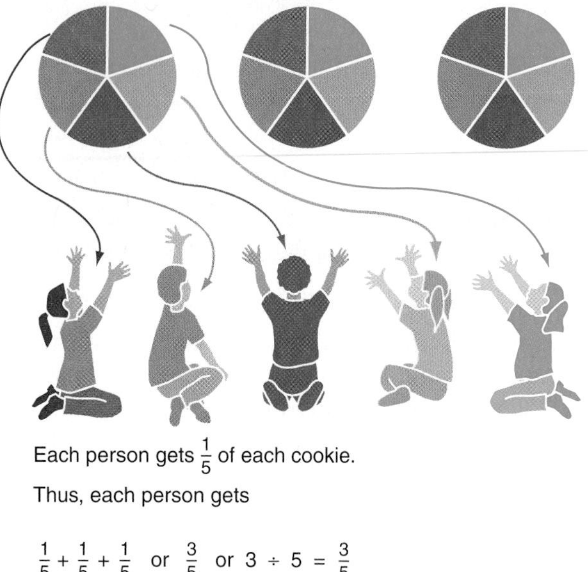

Begin with 3 cookies. Cut each into 5 parts
Each person gets $\frac{1}{5}$ of each cookie.
Thus, each person gets
$\frac{1}{5} + \frac{1}{5} + \frac{1}{5}$ or $\frac{3}{5}$ or $3 \div 5 = \frac{3}{5}$

FIGURE 12-2 An example of the quotient interpretation of a fraction.

You can see that this interpretation is conceptually different from the other interpretations of fractions. In this chapter, we discuss only part-whole and quotient interpretations. The ratio interpretation is discussed in Chapter 13.

Models of the Part-Whole Meaning

Four models concentrate on the part-whole meaning: region, length, set, and area. Any of these models may also be used for the quotient interpretation; however, the region model is most often used because it is the simplest. Other attributes, such as capacity, volume, or time, also can be used as models.

REGION The region model is the most concrete form and is most easily handled by children. The *region* is the whole (the unit), and the parts are *congruent* (same size and shape). The region may be any shape, such as circle, rectangle, square, or triangle. A variety of shapes should be used when presenting the region model, so that the children do not think that a fraction is always a "part of a pie."

As Figure 12-3 indicates, the rectangle is the easiest region model for children to draw and to partition. (Try partitioning each of the shapes shown into three equal parts to see which is easiest.) The circle does have one advantage; it is easy to see as a whole. Because the region is the most

Some Types of Regions

Circle: Easy to see it is a whole; difficult to partition.

Rectangle: Easy to partition; difficult to know if it's a whole.

Triangle: Difficult to partition; difficult to know if it's a whole.

FIGURE 12-3 Types of regions for concrete models.

common model, and the rectangle the easiest for children to draw, rectangles are used extensively throughout this chapter.

LENGTH Any unit of length can be partitioned into fractional parts, with each part being equal in length. Children can fold a long, thin strip of paper (*partition* it) into halves, fourths, and so on. Later this activity should lead to indicating fractions as points on a number line. That is, by partitioning a unit, or the distance between two points such as 4 and 5, into thirds, children can find one-third of the unit and will see that it is more than 4. If the children understand that each unit has been partitioned into thirds, they will realize that the point is $4 + , \frac{1}{3}$ or $4\frac{1}{3}$, as shown in Figure 12-4.

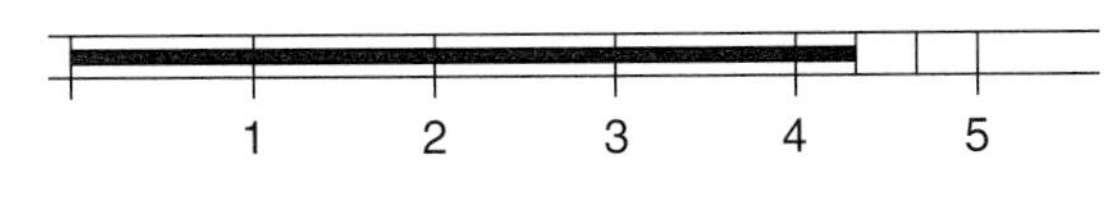

FIGURE 12-4 Length model of $4\frac{1}{3}$.

SET The set model uses a set of objects as a whole (the unit). This model sometimes causes difficulty, partly because students have not often considered a set of, say, 12 objects as a unit. About three-fourths of fourth-grade students chose a correct region model for a given fraction, whereas only about half chose the correct fraction that represents a set model (Wearne and Kouba, 2000). The more obvious reason for difficulty is that the students have not physically partitioned objects and considered this as sharing of a set. The set meaning is often presented only as a number out of the set, such as five red pencils in a set of twelve pencils is $\frac{5}{12}$. Using a combination set and area model, as in the *Snapshot of a Lesson* in Chapter 3, could bridge this gap.

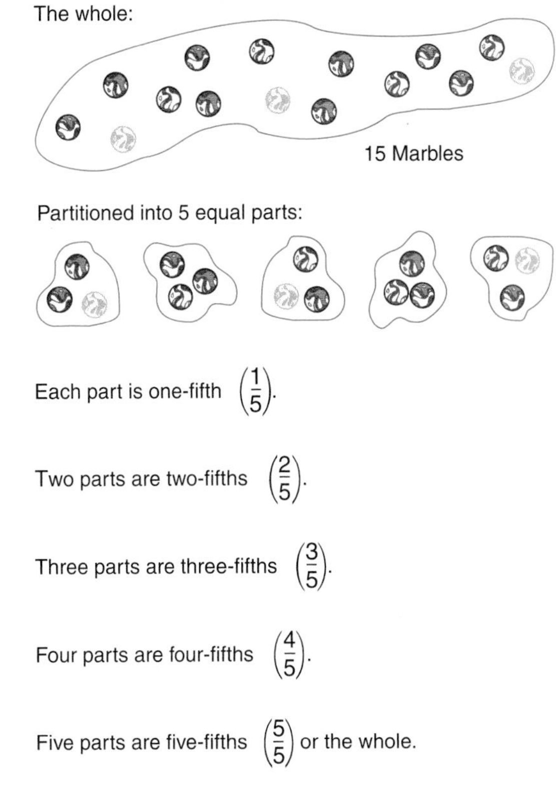

The whole:
15 Marbles
Partitioned into 5 equal parts:
Each part is one-fifth $\left(\frac{1}{5}\right)$.
Two parts are two-fifths $\left(\frac{2}{5}\right)$.
Three parts are three-fifths $\left(\frac{3}{5}\right)$.
Four parts are four-fifths $\left(\frac{4}{5}\right)$.
Five parts are five-fifths $\left(\frac{5}{5}\right)$ or the whole.

FIGURE 12-5 An example of a set model.

Without mentioning fractions, children should be given experiences partitioning sets, which provides a background for both division and fractions. For example, a student may be asked to give 12 toys to four children. Later, attention should focus on whether a given number of objects can be partitioned equally among a given number of people:

Can 15 toys be partitioned (shared) equally among 5 people? [yes]

4 people? [no]

3 people? [yes]

2 people? [no]

With this understanding, the set model can be related to fractions (e.g., finding fifths by partitioning the set into five equal parts). Figure 12-5 shows a set of 15 marbles that have been partitioned into five equal parts. Each part is one-fifth of the whole set. From this modeling, children develop the set meaning of fractions and can answer questions such as these:

What is one-fifth of 15? [3]

Two-fifths of 15? [6]

Three-fifths of 15? [9]

Experience of this type allows children to solve many practical problems and gives background for multiplication of fractions.

AREA The area model is a sophisticated one that is a special case of the region model. In the area model, the parts must be equal in area but not necessarily congruent (same size and shape). Before using this model, children must have some idea of when two different shapes have equal areas. Figure 12-6 shows eight squares partitioned into fourths in different ways. Can you see how the parts of each square are equal in area? This model is more appropriate for older children (about third and fourth grade) than for younger ones.

In the Classroom 12-1 gives examples and nonexamples of models of the fraction three-fourths. It is one way to assess children's understanding of the different models. Use it first as a self-assessment, and then try it with elementary students.

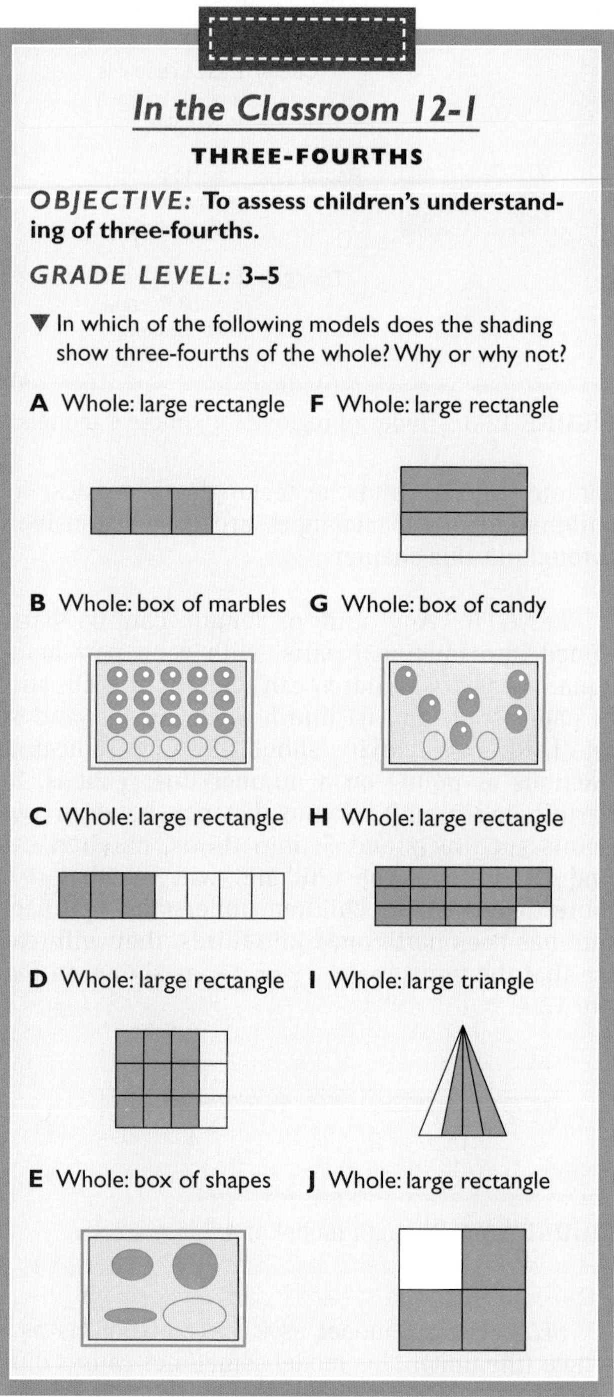

In the Classroom 12-1
THREE-FOURTHS
OBJECTIVE: To assess children's understanding of three-fourths.
GRADE LEVEL: 3–5
▼ In which of the following models does the shading show three-fourths of the whole? Why or why not?
A Whole: large rectangle
F Whole: large rectangle
B Whole: box of marbles
G Whole: box of candy
C Whole: large rectangle
H Whole: large rectangle
D Whole: large rectangle
I Whole: large triangle
E Whole: box of shapes
J Whole: large rectangle

Making Fractions Meaningful

Explaining, in order, all the meanings and models of fractions, as done so far in this chapter, is not the way to teach them. If you are beginning to build children's conceptual understanding of fractions, start with the simplest meaning and model—something that can be made meaningful for children. The part-whole meaning and the region model provide a good starting place. After introducing this model and the language and symbols associated with fractions, begin using other part-whole models (length, set, and area). Other meanings of fractions (quotient and ratio) can be

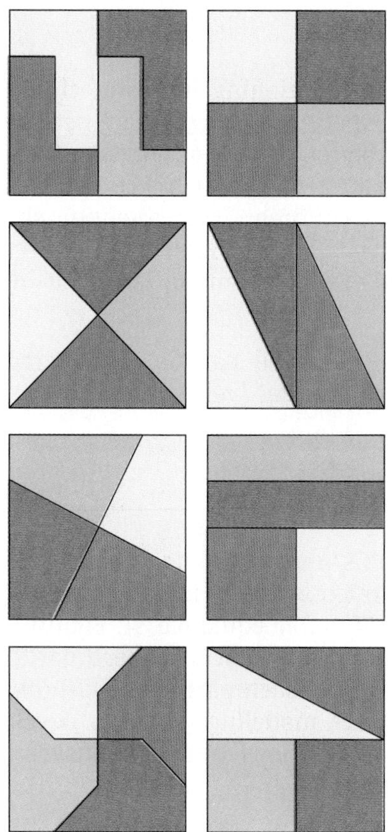

FIGURE 12-6 Ways to partition an area model.

introduced after children become more familiar with ordering and finding equivalent fractions and as they are introduced to improper fractions and mixed numbers.

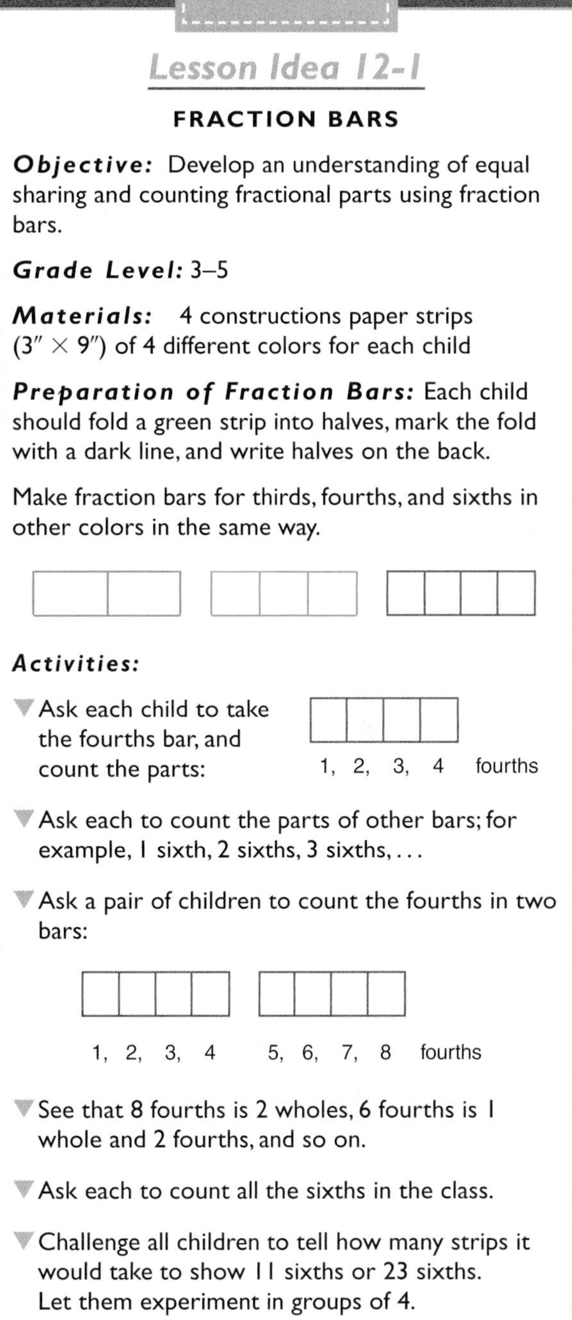

Lesson Idea 12-1

FRACTION BARS

Objective: Develop an understanding of equal sharing and counting fractional parts using fraction bars.

Grade Level: 3–5

Materials: 4 constructions paper strips (3″ × 9″) of 4 different colors for each child

Preparation of Fraction Bars: Each child should fold a green strip into halves, mark the fold with a dark line, and write halves on the back.

Make fraction bars for thirds, fourths, and sixths in other colors in the same way.

Activities:

- Ask each child to take the fourths bar, and count the parts: 1, 2, 3, 4 fourths
- Ask each to count the parts of other bars; for example, 1 sixth, 2 sixths, 3 sixths, . . .
- Ask a pair of children to count the fourths in two bars:

  1, 2, 3, 4 5, 6, 7, 8 fourths
- See that 8 fourths is 2 wholes, 6 fourths is 1 whole and 2 fourths, and so on.
- Ask each to count all the sixths in the class.
- Challenge all children to tell how many strips it would take to show 11 sixths or 23 sixths. Let them experiment in groups of 4.

PARTITIONING Underlying the idea of part-whole is the meaning of *part* and of *whole.* The whole is whatever is specified as the unit. At first, the whole should be obvious. Children must learn to partition the whole into equal parts and then to describe those parts with fractional names.

Let the children do the partitioning. For example, each child could be given a "candy bar" (a piece of paper the size of a large candy bar) to share with a friend. Have them fold the "candy bar" to show how they would share it. Talk about whether a fold like the one sketched here would be a "fair share" for two people.

Through other examples, develop sharing equally among 4, 3, 6, and 5 people. For some of the more difficult sharing problems, such as with 5 people, you may want to use a strip of paper that has already been marked. See Lesson Idea 12-1 for an example of a way to start this sharing. Have the children make the models of the fractional parts using construction paper and keep them for explorations about fractions. Doing a little work with fractions often makes them a natural part of the mathematics.

When children become familiar with the process of sharing regions and describing the parts with words and counting parts, move to the other models. Children especially like to share objects (set model), and tying it closely to sharing a "candy bar" will help extend their ideas about fractions. For example, share 12 marbles between two friends. Because you can share fairly, each friend gets half of the marbles. What about four friends?

WORDS As soon as you have developed the idea of equal parts, introduce the words *halves, thirds, fourths,* and so on. Be sure to ask such questions as, "How many equal parts in a whole would I have if each part was a fifth? An eighth? A twenty-fourth?" In response to an item on the NAEP mathematics assessment, only half of the fourth-grade students responded that 4 fourths made a whole (Wearne and Kouba, 2000).

COUNTING Once children are familiar with the fractional part words, begin counting parts.

Math Links 12.4

If you would like to see children partitioning, you can view video clips and lesson plans for "To Half or Half Not" from the PBS Mathline web site, which you can access from this book's web site.

This process should not be any more difficult than counting apples, but the children need to know what they are counting. A few ideas to practice counting fractional parts are given in Lesson Idea 12-1.

SYMBOLS Both symbols and written words should be used together or alternately until students understand the meaning of the symbol.

> Using the written fraction symbol is appropriate only after children can name, count, and compare using oral language with facility. . . . Written symbols are developed in the same way as oral language. The same kind of questioning can be used, but now the model and the oral language are connected with the symbol. (Payne et al., 1990, p. 185)
>
> Connections can be depicted as follows:

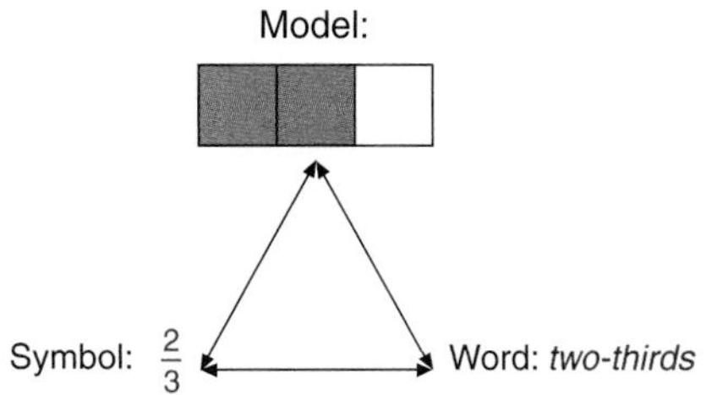

When children can match the words with the model, it is time to tell them that the $\frac{2}{3}$ symbol is the same as the word *two-thirds.* Then they need many opportunities to connect different representations:

1. Connect the model and the words.
2. Connect the model and the symbol.
3. Connect the words and the symbol.

Textbooks usually concentrate on tasks like number 2, so you will find plenty of examples of these. Task 3 requires oral work, so you need to provide opportunities to have children solve problems and describe the solutions.

DRAWING A MODEL In this developmental sequence, children have modeled fractions by folding paper or by choosing a picture. You also want them to be able to draw a picture. The rectangle is probably the easiest shape to use to show a good approximation to a fractional part. Encourage the children to be as accurate as possible, but do not worry if their drawings are not perfect. For example, which of these two drawings would you accept as a picture of two-thirds?

Bob's work

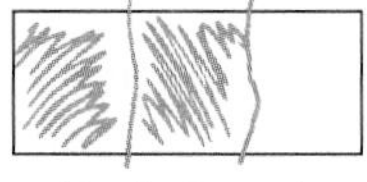
Marilyn's work

Bob's work is neater than Marilyn's, but he seems to have missed the point that the three parts must be equal. You might help Marilyn be a little neater, but she does seem to have the idea of two-thirds.

EXTENDING THE MODEL The results of a question on the second national mathematics assessment are listed in Table 12-1 (Carpenter et al., 1981). Little has changed in the over 30 years since this item was given; the performance level on a similar question on the 1996 assessment was almost identical for fourth-grade students. There is no doubt that this model showing more parts than indicated by the denominator is more complicated than those described in the previous section, but it is useful for introducing equivalent fractions and for ordering fractions.

You can also use paper folding to introduce the model in Table 12-1 and to introduce equivalent fractions. For example, give each child a sheet of plain paper. Have each child fold the paper into thirds and shade two-thirds. Now fold the paper in

Table 12-1 • Results of National Assessment Question Using the Region Model

What fractional part of the figure is shaded?

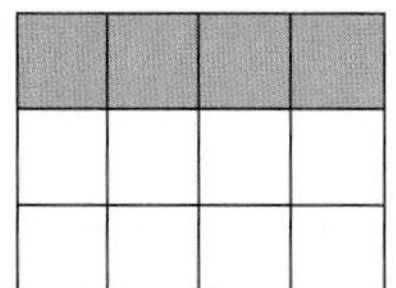

Responses	Percent Responding Age 9	Age 13
Acceptable responses $\frac{1}{3}, \frac{4}{12}, .33$	20	82
Unacceptable responses $\frac{1}{4}, .25$	5	4
Top 4, top part, $\frac{4}{8}$	36	6
Other	15	6
I don't know	17	1
No response	7	1

half the other way. Ask how many parts and what kind of parts [6, sixths]. Then, ask what part is shaded. Encourage both $\frac{2}{3}$ and $\frac{4}{6}$. Tell the children that $\frac{2}{3}$ and $\frac{4}{6}$ are called *equivalent fractions* because they represent the same amount.

After more examples and practice with folding paper, children should be ready to understand what happens with the paper folding through drawings.

- Begin by drawing a picture of the paper folded in thirds and shade $\frac{2}{3}$.

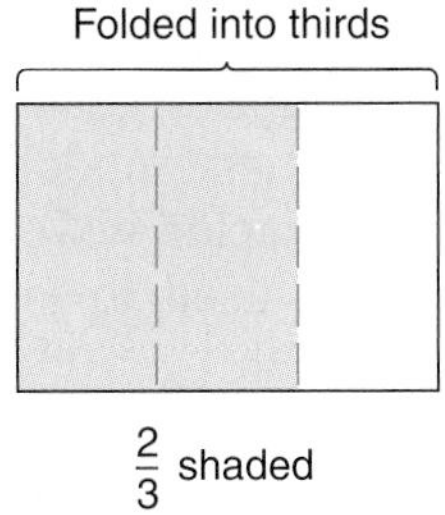

- Now draw the fold made when partitioning it into halves, making certain the children can identify the way the paper was folded in both directions.

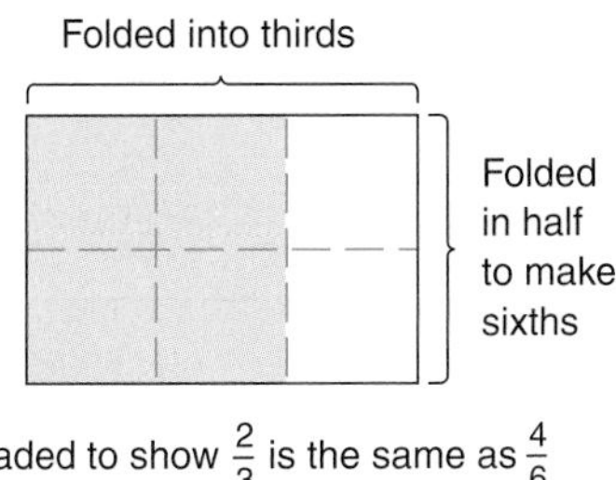

- Ask children to show $\frac{1}{3}$, $\frac{2}{3}$, $\frac{4}{6}$, and so on and to name an equivalent fraction for each.

Next, move to pictures showing only the folded paper, such as the following representation:

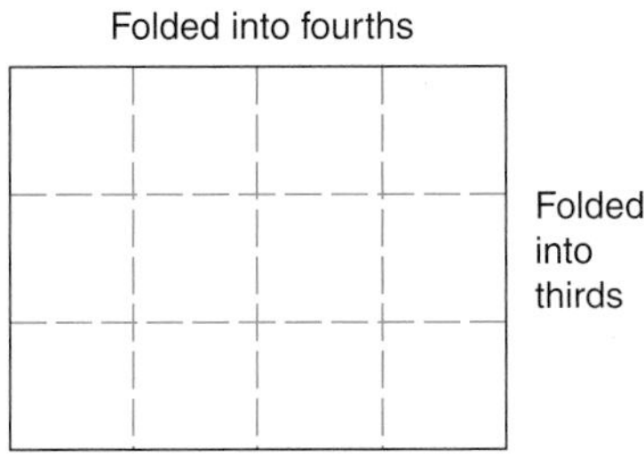

Make certain the students can identify the way the paper was folded in both directions. Have them show

$$\frac{1}{3}, \frac{2}{3}, \frac{1}{4}, \frac{3}{4},$$

and so on and give an equivalent fraction.

This sequence, which begins with partitioning and gradually introduces the words, symbols, and more complicated models and meanings, along with activities such as those in this chapter's *Snapshot of a Lesson*, provides a strong background for further development of fractions and operations with fractions. Before moving to operations with fractions, children need a firm understanding of equivalence. When children have worked with whole numbers, they most often have described the number of objects with only one number. That is, if they have counted eight objects, they will say eight and write 8. Fraction parts can be described in many ways, depending on the subunit (denominator) that is chosen. For example, we can represent one-half of a pie with $\frac{1}{2}$ or $\frac{3}{6}$ or $\frac{4}{8}$. Depending on the problem being solved, one name may be more appropriate than another.

Ordering Fractions and Equivalent Fractions

Part of understanding fractions is realizing that they are numbers and can be ordered, added, subtracted, multiplied, and divided. The goal is to have children order fractions and find equivalent fractions symbolically, but you can help children connect the concrete to the symbolic. Not only will this connection help children realize what they are doing when they are ordering and finding equivalent fractions, but it also will give another context in which to practice relating fractions and the models. Many problems involving ordering capture children's interest because they want to know which is more, which is shorter, which is larger, and so on. The problems about equivalent fractions are central to understanding fractions and being able to operate (add, subtract, multiply, and divide) with them.

CONCRETE MODELS If children have made concrete models, it is not difficult for them to order fractions and find equivalent fractions using various models. For example, children can make fraction bars, as described in Lesson Idea 12-2, and then use them to find out which is larger, $\frac{2}{3}$ or $\frac{3}{4}$. Folding the thirds strip so that it is $\frac{2}{3}$ long and the fourths strip so that it is $\frac{3}{4}$ long provides a concrete model for the comparison.

This model can also be used to show equivalent fractions. Children can readily see that $\frac{2}{3}$ is the same amount as $\frac{4}{6}$. The extended model with paper

Lesson Idea 12-2

COMPARING MODELS

Objective: Use concrete models to represent fractional parts of a whole.

Grade Level: 3–5

Materials needed: Pattern blocks

The four basic shapes of the pattern blocks that you will use are the hexagon, triangle, rhombus, and trapezoid. Each child or pair of children will need multiple copies of each shape.

Let children have a chance to explore by making designs and seeing how they could make the hexagon with the other pieces.

Idea One: Use the hexagon as the whole. What is the size of each of the other pieces? Use the pieces to show that

$$\frac{2}{6}=\frac{1}{3} \quad \frac{3}{3}=1 \quad \frac{3}{6}=\frac{1}{2} \quad \frac{2}{3}>\frac{1}{2} \quad 2\frac{2}{3}=\frac{8}{3}$$

Idea Two: Use the figure made from two hexagons as the whole.

Use [rhombus] to cover the yellow shape. How many does it take? What fractional part of the whole is the rhombus? What fractional part of the whole is the trapezoid?

Use the shape to show that $\frac{3}{4}$ is greater than $\frac{2}{3}$.

Idea Three: Give the shape of a fractional part and have children construct the whole as in the lesson snapshot

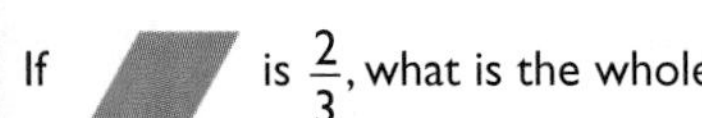

If [rhombus] is $\frac{2}{3}$, what is the whole?

If [trapezoid] is $\frac{3}{4}$, make the whole.

If [triangle] is $\frac{1}{5}$, make the whole.

If [triangle] is $\frac{2}{5}$, draw the whole.

folding, as described previously, can also be used to identify equivalent fractions.

For simplicity, we emphasize the rectangle and paper models. Children need to work with multiple representations, as suggested by Principle 6 in Chapter 2. The pattern blocks (see Appendix B) are another model accessible to young children. See Lesson Idea 12-2 for a mixture of ideas to begin your lesson planning using pattern blocks for ordering and finding equivalent fractions.

PICTORIAL MODELS Children are able to order fractions if given pictures of the models, such as the fraction strips in Figure 12-7. (A more complete set of fraction strips is given in Appendix B.) The accurate scale of these models allows children to compare lengths to decide which is larger, $\frac{3}{4}$ or $\frac{2}{3}$. This set can also be used to identify equivalent fractions. It is clear that $\frac{1}{2}$, $\frac{2}{4}$, and $\frac{3}{6}$ all represent the same amount.

Children can also construct or draw their own pictorial models to represent fractions. Lesson Idea 12-3 illustrates one way that children can make a model of two fractions and easily compare the fractions. This model does not depend on the accuracy of the size of the parts, as the model in Figure 12-7 does. It also leads to understanding a symbolic way of comparing fractions as well as to a way of adding and subtracting fractions.

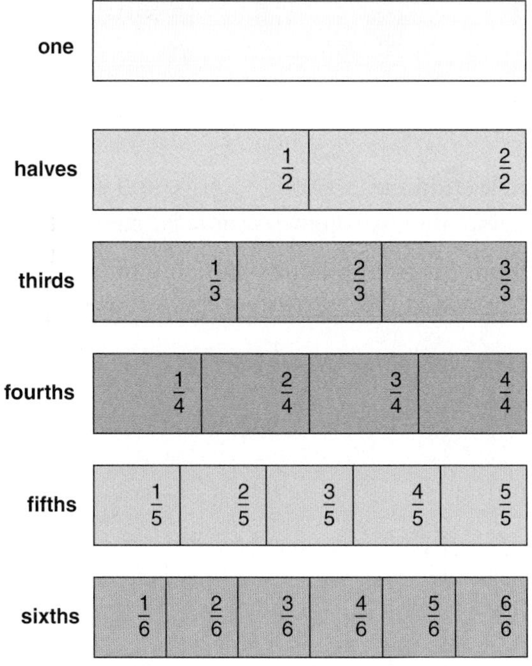

FIGURE 12-7 Pictorial model of fraction strips.

Lesson Idea 12-3

COMPARING FRACTIONS

Objective: Compare fractions by changing them to equivalent fractions using a paper folding model.

Grade level: 3–5

Problem: Jacqui ate $\frac{1}{3}$ of the cake. Tom ate $\frac{2}{7}$ of the cake. Who ate more?

One way to model: Draw the cake twice. Show $\frac{1}{3}$ on one picture and $\frac{2}{7}$ on the other. Can you tell who ate the most?

Show thirds

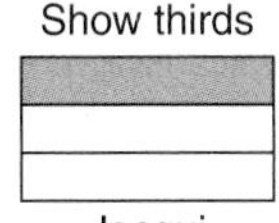

Jacqui

Show sevenths

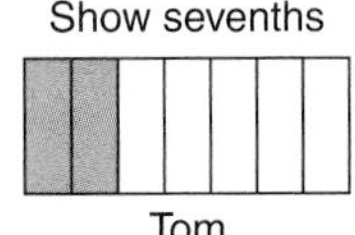

Tom

It is difficult to compare these pictures, so show both partitions on each of the pictures.

Show both thirds and sevenths

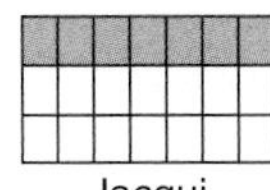

Jacqui

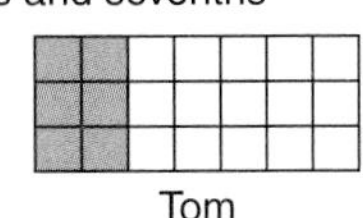

Tom

Now you can see that Jacqui ate seven pieces and Tom ate six pieces. So Jacqui ate more cake.

What size are these pieces? That is, what part of the cake is each piece? Can you describe the $\frac{1}{3}$ as an equivalent fraction? Can you express $\frac{2}{7}$ as an equivalent fraction?

SYMBOLIC REPRESENTATION It is easier to compare two measurements given in the same unit (78 meters and 20 meters) than two measurements given in different units (83 meters and 4318 centimeters). Similarly, it is easier to compare two fractions that are symbolically represented by the same subunit ($\frac{3}{5}$ and $\frac{2}{5}$) than two fractions that are represented by different subunits ($\frac{2}{3}$ and $\frac{5}{7}$). In mathematics, difficult situations are often changed into a simpler case (i.e., representing the things to be compared in the same unit). With fractions, simpler means expressing each fraction as an equivalent fraction in the same subunit or common denominator. The pictorial model shown in Lesson Idea 12-3 can be extended to develop this idea. Once the rectangle has been partitioned into both thirds and sevenths, it is partitioned into twenty-firsts so that $\frac{2}{3}$ is 14 of the 21 parts or $\frac{14}{21}$, and $\frac{5}{7}$ is 15 of the 21 parts or $\frac{15}{21}$.

Thus, 21 is the common denominator for comparing the fractions $\frac{2}{3}$ and $\frac{5}{7}$:

$$\frac{2}{3} = \frac{14}{21}$$

and

$$\frac{5}{7} = \frac{15}{21}$$

Therefore,

$$\frac{5}{7} > \frac{2}{3}$$

We have considered models that represent fractional parts such as $\frac{2}{3}$ or $\frac{3}{4}$ in more than one way. Students with this background are familiar with the concept of equivalent fractions, but they may not have developed many of the skills associated with finding equivalent fractions symbolically. Finding an equivalent fraction rests on the generalization that both the numerator and denominator may be multiplied (or divided) by the same number.

To develop the generalization for finding an equivalent fraction symbolically, begin with the paper-folding model and symbolically describe what is happening.

- Make a model of $\frac{3}{4}$ by folding a piece of paper in fourths (A); then fold it in half the other way (B).

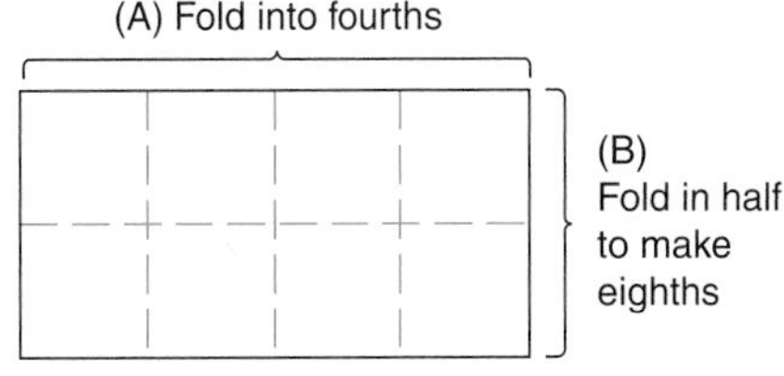

- Ask what happened to the fourths when the paper was folded in half.
- Use shading to confirm that you created twice as many equal parts (or 2×4) and twice as many shaded parts (or 2×3).

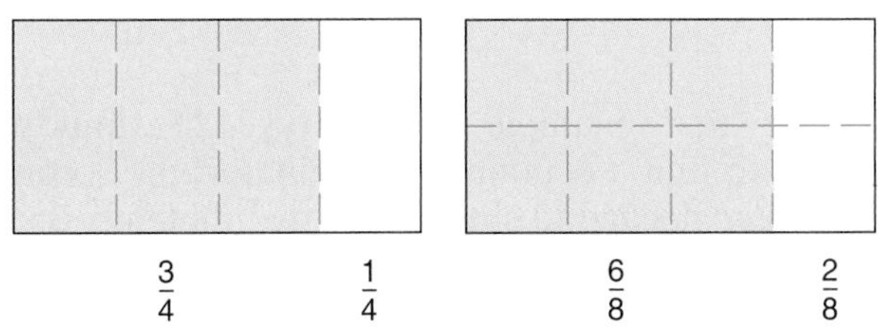

- Express the model symbolically:

$$\frac{2 \times 3}{2 \times 4}$$

or

$$\frac{3 \times 2}{4 \times 2} = \frac{6}{8}$$

After more examples such as these, children should be able to make the generalization that both numerator and denominator may be multiplied by the same number and the resulting fraction is equivalent.

Conversely, you could begin with the model of eight parts and describe how to get to four parts. In this case, you begin with the eight parts and group them by two, or 8 ÷ 2, which is 4. You also group the number of parts under consideration by two, or 6 ÷ 2. Thus,

$$\frac{6}{8} = \frac{6 \div 2}{8 \div 2} = \frac{3}{4}$$

Again, examples of this type should lead to the generalization that the numerator and denominator may be divided by the same number and the resulting fraction is equivalent.

After students have made the generalization, which should not rest on the one example shown here, that both the numerator and denominator may be multiplied or divided by the same number, then they are ready to move to exercises such as these:

$$\frac{2}{3} = \frac{\square}{12}$$

$$\frac{4}{6} = \frac{\square}{3}$$

In this example, students need to think "What is 3 multiplied by to get 12?" Once they have established it is 4, they should think and write:

$$\frac{2 \times 4}{3 \times 4} = \frac{8}{12}$$

In the second example, they should realize that 6 was divided by 2 to obtain 3, so 4 also has to be divided by 2:

$$\frac{4 \div 2}{6 \div 2} = \frac{2}{3}$$

The first example is the type of thinking needed to find a common denominator; the second is the type needed to simplify many problems. Both are ways to express fractions as equivalent fractions in order to solve some problem.

Children also should be helped to see that a common fraction cannot always be changed to an equivalent one with a certain specified denominator if the numerator must be a whole number. For example, $\frac{5}{12}$ cannot be changed to thirds even though you can divide 12 by 4 to get 3. When you

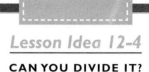

Lesson Idea 12-4

CAN YOU DIVIDE IT?

Objective: Use an area model to learn how to compare fractions.

Grade Level: 3–5

Here are a few ideas to start your discussion. After children understand these, have them investigate other fractional parts.

- All of these regions have been divided into parts with vertical (up and down) lines. Use horizontal (across) lines to see if you can change the model to the fraction given. The first one has been done.

  - To fourths:
  - To tenths:
  - To sixths:
  - To eighths:
  - To twelfths:
  - To tenths:
  - To ninths:
  - To sixths:

- Choose the fractional part fifths. Draw the picture to decide whether you can change fifths to sixths, sevenths, eighths, ninths, tenths, and so forth. What is your conjecture? Write why you think this is true.

divide 5 by 4, you do not get a whole number. Similarly, you cannot change $\frac{2}{3}$ to fifths:

$$\frac{2}{3} = \frac{\square}{5}$$

There is no whole number that you can multiply 3 by to get 5. Exercises such as those in Lesson Idea 12-4 focus on these skills.

In the past there has been much emphasis on finding the *least common denominator*. With some decreased emphasis on paper-and-pencil fraction computation (NCTM, 1989, p. 21), this skill is not as essential as it once was; however, to add or subtract fractions, you often need to find a common denominator.

The product of two denominators always gives a common denominator for two fractions. This idea has already been examined in Lesson Idea 12-3, where we ordered two fractions. We will revisit this idea with adding and subtracting fractions when a common denominator is needed.

At times, however, the product of the denominators is not the least common denominator. For example, a common denominator of $\frac{5}{6}$ and $\frac{3}{4}$ is 6×4, or 24, but the least common denominator is 12. The least common denominator is the smallest number that both 6 and 4 will divide. With small denominators, the least common denominator can often be found by inspection, which is probably a more beneficial approach than learning a routine.

When children can order fractions symbolically, they may enjoy the quick and easy game In the Classroom 12-2. If they have difficulty playing, they may need to return to a concrete or pictorial representation. If the game is too easy, choose a game board with 48 squares and fractions less than $\frac{1}{3}$ that may be expressed as an equivalent fraction with denominator of 48 (e.g., $\frac{1}{4}$ or $\frac{3}{16}$).

In the Classroom 12-2

WHOLE HOG

OBJECTIVE: **Practice in comparing fractions. Choose a partner, and each of you make your own gameboard by copying the H on the grid paper or drawing the 18 squares.**

GRADE LEVEL: **3–5**

▼ Cut ten squares of paper. Write one of these fractions on each square:

$$\frac{1}{2} \quad \frac{1}{3} \quad \frac{1}{6} \quad \frac{2}{6} \quad \frac{1}{9} \quad \frac{2}{9} \quad \frac{3}{9} \quad \frac{1}{18} \quad \frac{2}{18} \quad \frac{3}{18}$$

▼ Be sure each of you has a crayon.

Now you are ready to go Whole Hog!

GAME RULES

1. **Put the fraction cards in a pile face down.**
2. **Each of you take a card from the top of the pile.**
3. **Turn your cards over and decide who has the larger fraction.**
4. **The player with the larger fractions must color that fractional part of her or his H.**
5. **Put both cards at the bottom of the pile.**
6. **Keep choosing a card and play as before.**
7. **If a player with the larger fraction cannot color the fractional part shown on the card, both players must put their cards back and take the next cards on top.**
8. **Continue playing until one person colors the whole H. That person is the first to go Whole Hog and loses the game.**

▼ Make a new H and play again.

Benchmarks

Some fractions look intimidating, so children first need to develop facility with some friendly fractions such as halves, thirds, and fourths, and be able to relate other fractions to these. By building what are referred to as *benchmarks* in *Principles and Standards for School Mathematics* (NCTM, 2000), children will be able to reason with these more complicated fractions. For example, what fractions are near one-half? Consider the following fractions:

$$\frac{6}{11} \quad \frac{11}{23} \quad \frac{18}{35} \quad \frac{44}{90} \quad \frac{354}{700} \quad \frac{800}{1605} \quad \frac{100001}{200000}$$

How do you know each fraction is near $\frac{1}{2}$? Which are more than $\frac{1}{2}$? Which are less than $\frac{1}{2}$? Beginning with smaller numerators and denominators, children can build this same intuitive feel for fractions near the benchmark $\frac{1}{2}$.

Students should also be able to tell if a fraction is near 0 or near 1. Can you write a fraction that is near 0 (near 1)? How do you know? What would a model look like for any fraction near 0 (near 1)?

Consider the use of benchmarks to put in order a set of fractions: $\frac{13}{25}$, $\frac{2}{31}$, $\frac{5}{6}$, $\frac{4}{11}$, and $\frac{21}{21}$. This would be a time-consuming task if you tried to find a common denominator. If you use benchmarks as shown in the following number line, the task becomes rather easy: $\frac{13}{25}$ is a little more $\frac{1}{2}$, and $\frac{4}{11}$ is a little less than $\frac{1}{2}$, $\frac{2}{31}$ is near zero, $\frac{5}{6}$ is a little less than one, and $\frac{21}{20}$ is a little more than one.

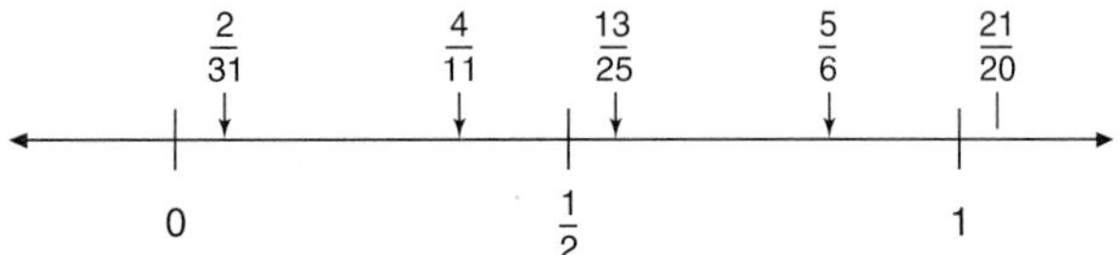

Children can also use their knowledge of benchmarks to check the reasonableness of computations with fractions or to estimate answers. For example, how do you know that $\frac{3}{5} + \frac{6}{7}$ is not $\frac{9}{12}$? If you know that $\frac{3}{5}$ is a little more than $\frac{1}{2}$ and $\frac{6}{7}$ is almost 1, then you know that the sum must be more than 1.

Mixed Numbers and Improper Fractions

Through models, you can lead naturally into mixed numbers and improper fractions, even as children are learning the initial concepts of fractions. For example, a natural representation of the following model is the mixed number $2\frac{1}{4}$.

Adding partitions in the model to show all the fourths leads to the initial counting of 9 fourths and to the representation by the improper fraction $\frac{9}{4}$.

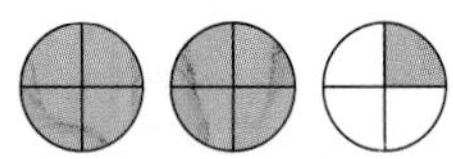

To help children gain experience with mixed numbers and improper fractions, use models as much as possible and ask them to write *both* types of numbers to represent the models. When children understand the process, they need practice in changing from one form to the other without the use of models. Do not rush to a routine, however, but encourage students to think problems through, as in the example that follows. The thinking depends on understanding the equivalence of a whole in terms of the fractional parts (e.g., 5 fifths or 6 sixths make a whole).

Example: Change $8\frac{2}{3}$ to an improper fraction.

See if you can follow Cerise's thinking:

I know that 1 is 3 thirds.

So, I need to figure how many thirds in 8 wholes. That is 8 groups of 3 thirds, which is 24 thirds.

Now, I have to add on the 2 thirds, so it is 26 thirds.

It is also important that students can think through changing an improper fraction to a mixed number. For example, $\frac{17}{6}$ is 17 sixths; since 6 sixths make a whole, 17 would make 2 wholes, and there would be 5 sixths more. So $\frac{17}{6}$ is $2\frac{5}{6}$.

Operations with Fractions

The key to a meaningful presentation of the operations with fractions is to establish a firm background in fractions, especially equivalent fractions. Problem situations that involve operations with fractions should be presented so that children use what they know about the situation to make sense of the operations. Whenever possible, the meanings given to operations with whole numbers should be extended to fractions. There are, however, meanings of operations that do not extend directly. For example, for the multiplication of two fractions, multiplication is not repeated addition. Other differences also must be kept in mind, such as when multiplying two whole numbers, the product is always larger than either factor; but in multiplying two proper fractions, the product is always less than either factor.

Children gain a better understanding of operations with fractions if they learn to estimate answers by using whole numbers and benchmarks such as one-half. For example, before computing the answer to $3\frac{2}{3} + 4\frac{5}{6}$, they should be able to realize that the answer is more than 7. In fact, since $\frac{2}{3}$ and $\frac{5}{6}$ are each more than $\frac{1}{2}$, the answer is more than 8. Developing this type of number and operation sense makes it easier to establish what are reasonable answers to problems. Many calculators can perform operations with fractions. It is important that the conceptual understanding be firmly established so that answers can be checked for reasonableness.

Addition and Subtraction

Instead of beginning addition and subtraction of fractions with a symbolic sentence such as $\frac{2}{3} + \frac{1}{4}$, begin with joining and separating situations. Problems involving these situations, together with pictorial models, can:

- Help children see that adding and subtracting fractions can solve problems similar to those with whole numbers
- Give children an idea of what a reasonable answer is
- Help children see why a common denominator is necessary when adding or subtracting.

Use children's knowledge of solving whole-number addition and subtraction word problems to begin examining how to add and subtract fractions. If children understand how to count fractional parts (e.g., 3 sevenths and 2 more sevenths is 5 sevenths) and how to compare two fractions with a pictorial model, they may find their own ways to solve joining and separating problems with fractions.

Look at the set of word problems in Figure 12-8.

Children should have no problem solving the first two of these word problems. Have them show how they solved each one, encouraging them to tell how the two problems are alike (e.g., by joining situations: in problem A, Cyrilla ate 2 apples, and in problem B she ate 2 fifths). Also, although quite simple, have children draw a picture to show the first two problems. Then let them try the next problem, discussing how problem C is like the other two and how it is different. Encourage children to draw a picture of the cake.

A

Cyrilla ate 2 apples, and Carey ate 1 apple. How many apples did they eat altogether?

B

Cyrilla ate $\frac{2}{5}$ of a pie, and Carey ate $\frac{1}{5}$ of a pie. How much pie did they eat altogether?

C

Cyrilla ate $\frac{2}{3}$ of a cake, and Carey ate $\frac{1}{4}$ of the cake. How much of the cake did they eat altogether?

FIGURE 12-8 Three joining problems.

Children may come up with many ways to approach the problem. If they have drawn pictures to compare fractions, they may draw a picture as shown here (like the model in Lesson Idea 12-3).

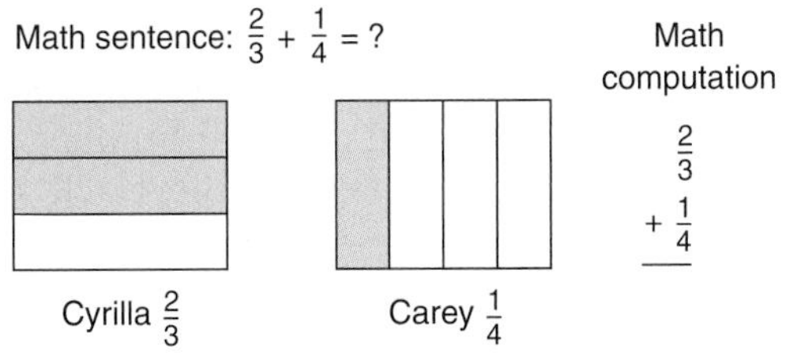

Show both portions on each cake:

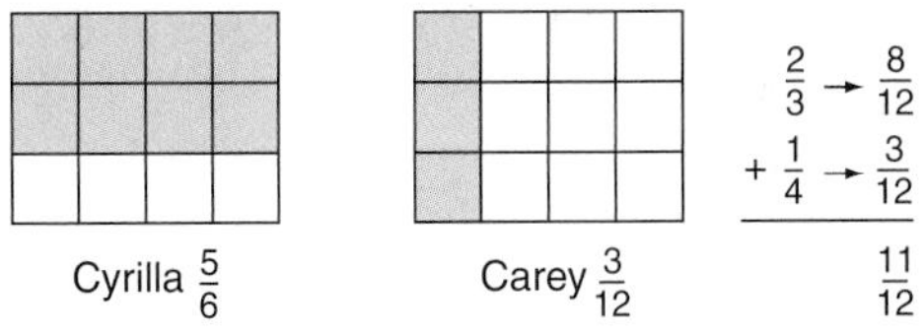

Notice how the picture would change if Carey had eaten $\frac{3}{4}$ of the cake. Carey would have eaten $\frac{9}{12}$. Together, they would have eaten $\frac{17}{12}$. Do you see how the picture could then be used to see they ate one whole cake and $\frac{5}{12}$ of another?

Note that in adding fractions, the whole (the unit) is assumed to be the same. If Cyrilla ate $\frac{2}{3}$ of a cake, and Carey ate $\frac{3}{4}$ of a cake, then there would have to be two cakes, and the cakes are assumed to be the same size. If Cyrilla eats $\frac{2}{3}$ of a very small cake and Carey eats $\frac{3}{4}$ of a very large cake, you would need more information about the size of each cake before determining how much they ate together.

Adding mixed numbers is no more difficult than the previous problem. Children who have made sense of adding proper fractions can put this together with their knowledge of adding whole numbers. You may want to watch to see how children handle a computation such as $5\frac{2}{3} + 3\frac{3}{4}$. Adding the whole numbers gives 8, and adding the fractions gives $\frac{17}{12}$ as shown previously, or $8\frac{17}{12}$. Children can then use their knowledge that $\frac{17}{12}$ is $1\frac{5}{12}$ so the total can be expressed as $9\frac{5}{12}$.

Often, children who have been taught a routine for this problem may say that the sum is $8\frac{7}{12}$. What error are they making?

You can approach subtracting two proper fractions in the same way that you approached adding. If you begin with subtraction problems that involve comparison, such as how much more cake did Cyrilla eat than Carey in Problem C (Figure 12-8), then you can use the same model. Note that the background of knowing which fraction is larger is important in real-life situations. In Problem C, it would not make sense to ask how much more cake Carey ate than Cyrilla.

Subtracting fractions greater than one or mixed numbers is often more difficult, partly because children have not changed a mixed number to another mixed number or because they lack understanding of regrouping.

Using a model such as fraction bars, as In the Classroom 12-3, can assist children in thinking about how fraction equivalents are useful when subtracting where regrouping is necessary.

In addition, the symbolic subtraction example in Figure 12-9 requires regrouping $6\frac{3}{7}$ to $5\frac{10}{7}$. Help children understand that

$$1 \text{ is } \tfrac{7}{7} \quad \text{and } 6 \text{ is } 5 + 1, \text{ or } 5 + \tfrac{7}{7}$$

Thus,

$$6\tfrac{3}{7} \text{ is } \quad 5 + \tfrac{7}{7} + \tfrac{3}{7}, \text{ or } 5\tfrac{10}{7}$$

$6\frac{3}{7}$	**Are the denominators the same?**
$-2\frac{4}{7}$	Yes. (If not, change them to like fractions.)
	Can I take $\frac{4}{7}$ from $\frac{3}{7}$?
$5\frac{10}{7}$	No, I must regroup $6\frac{3}{7}$.
$-2\frac{4}{7}$	$(1 = \frac{7}{7}$, so $\frac{3}{7} + \frac{7}{7} = \frac{10}{7}$.)
$3\frac{6}{7}$	Now subtract the fraction parts, then the whole parts.

FIGURE 12-9 Subtracting mixed numbers.

If children are having difficulty with regrouping fractions, the following model can help them see, for example, that $6\frac{3}{7} = 5\frac{10}{7}$.

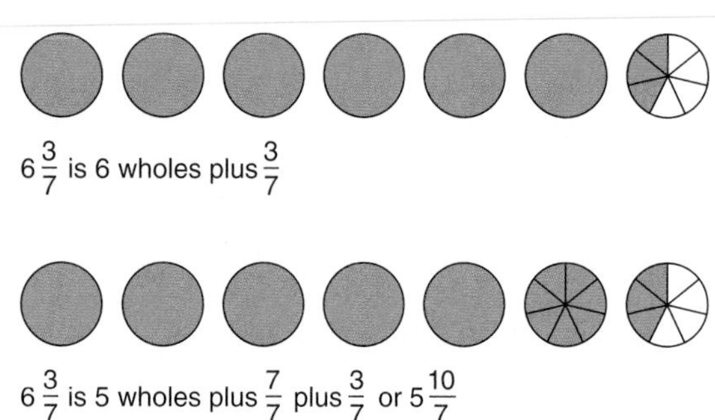

$6\frac{3}{7}$ is 6 wholes plus $\frac{3}{7}$
$6\frac{3}{7}$ is 5 wholes plus $\frac{7}{7}$ plus $\frac{3}{7}$ or $5\frac{10}{7}$

Multiplication

The algorithm for multiplication of fractions is one of the simplest. Multiply numerators to find the product numerator, and multiply denominators to find the product denominator.

This algorithm can be taught in minutes (and forgotten in seconds unless a great amount of practice is provided); however, simply teaching this algorithm does not provide insight into why it works or when to use it. A development is suggested that gives the underlying meanings of multiplication, an idea of the size of an answer, and the reason why the algorithm works before presenting the algorithm itself. Many children who have a good background with fractions will come up with their own methods (Warrington and Kamii, 1999).

We examine four different cases: a whole number times a fraction or mixed number, a fraction times a whole number, a fraction times a fraction, and a mixed number times a mixed number. In each case, we tie multiplication to a meaning of multiplication of whole numbers, using the knowledge that 3×4 means three groups of four and 3×4 is the area of a 3-by-4 rectangle.

WHOLE NUMBER TIMES A FRACTION Begin with a problem:

> You have 3 pans, each with $\frac{4}{5}$ of a pizza. How much pizza do you have?

How is this problem like having three bags, each with four marbles? See if this sketch helps you see the similarity between multiplying whole numbers and multiplying a whole number times a fraction:

In the Classroom 12-3

SUBTRACTING FRACTIONS WITH FRACTION BARS

OBJECTIVE: **Children use fraction bars to subtract fractions.**

GRADE LEVEL: **3–5**

MATERIALS: **Fraction bars (see Appendix B)**

PROBLEM: **Ivar has $3\frac{1}{4}$ candy bars. La Sharo has $1\frac{5}{6}$ candy bars. How much more candy does Ivar have than La Sharo?**

1. Have the children model the problem with fraction bars.

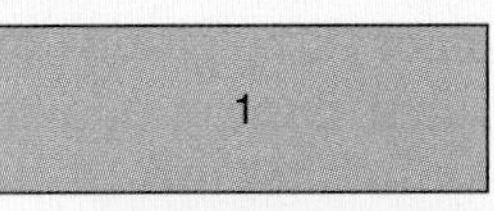

2. Have the children estimate the problem to the nearest whole number. (approximately $3 - 2 = 1$)

3. Trade the strips until the two sets of candy bars can be easily compared.

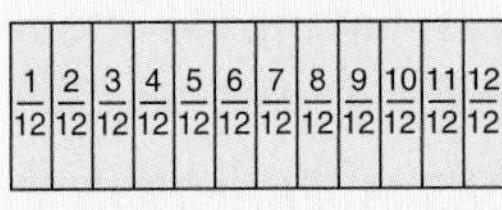

4. Compare La Sharo's $1\frac{10}{12}$ candy bars with Ivar's $3\frac{3}{12}$ candy bars.

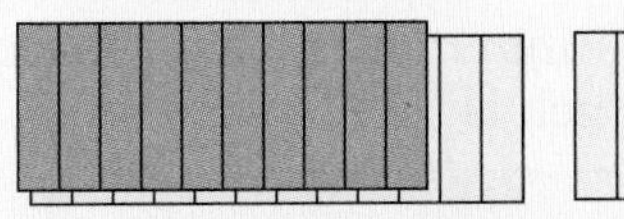

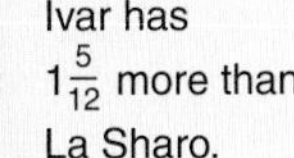

5. Show a symbolic representation.

$$\begin{array}{r} 3\frac{1}{4} \\ -1\frac{5}{6} \\ \hline \end{array} \rightarrow \begin{array}{r} 3\frac{3}{12} \\ -1\frac{10}{12} \\ \hline \end{array} \rightarrow \begin{array}{r} 2\frac{15}{12} \\ -1\frac{10}{12} \\ \hline 1\frac{5}{12} \end{array}$$

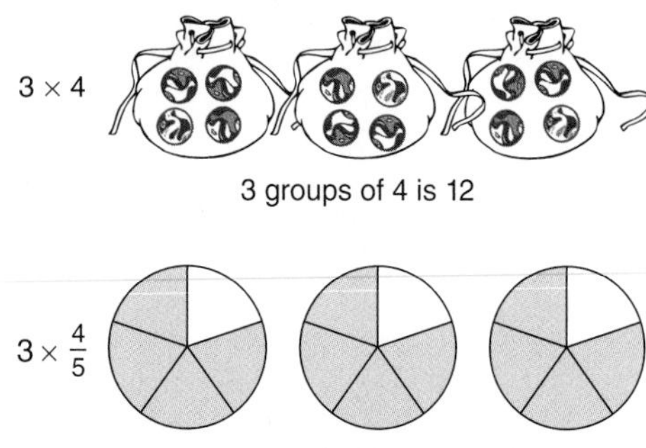

3 groups of 4 is 12

3 groups of 4 fifths is 12 fifths

Symbolize three groups of four as 3×4. It makes sense to consider three groups of $\frac{4}{5}$ to mean $3 \times \frac{4}{5}$. How did we find three groups of four? We might have put out three groups of four marbles and counted them. Similarly, to find three groups of $\frac{4}{5}$, put out three pans of pizza, each having $\frac{4}{5}$ of a pizza in it, and count the number of fifths. Or, to find 3×4, we can consider repeated addition:

$$4 + 4 + 4 = 12$$

Thus,

$$3 \times \frac{4}{5} \text{ is } \quad \frac{4}{5} + \frac{4}{5} + \frac{4}{5} = \frac{12}{5}$$

After the students have solved problems like this one with pictures, see if they can solve them without pictures or repeated addition. Be sure to place strong emphasis on the words. Have them listen carefully as you read:

$5 \times \frac{2}{3}$ is 5 groups of two-thirds, which is 5 *groups of* 2 or 10 (thirds), or $\frac{10}{3}$

FRACTION TIMES A WHOLE NUMBER Again, begin with a problem:

> You have $\frac{3}{4}$ of a case of 24 bottles. How many bottles do you have?

If children have worked with the set model for fractions, they have the background to solve this problem with physical objects. Now, children must move to solving fractions symbolically and tying it to multiplication.

First, look at why it makes sense to consider this problem as a multiplication problem. If you had 5 cases with 24 bottles in each, what would you do to find out how many? You would multiply 5×24. Similarly, 20 cases would be 20×24, 53 cases would be 53×24, and, thus, $\frac{3}{4}$ case would be $\frac{3}{4} \times 24$.

Next review how to find $\frac{3}{4}$ of 24. First partition (or divide) the set into four equal parts (each part would have 6), or, in other words, first find $\frac{1}{4}$ of 24. Thus, $\frac{3}{4}$ would be three times as many, or $3 \times 6 = 18$.

$\frac{3}{4} \times 24 = \square$

Think
$\frac{1}{4} \times 24 = 6$
$\frac{3}{4}$ is 3 times as many,
or $3 \times 6 = 18$

At first glance, this procedure looks slightly different from the algorithm for multiplying numerators and multiplying denominators. Physically, first divide the number in the set by 4 and then multiply that by 3. When you perform the standard algorithm, you multiply first and then divide:

$$\frac{3}{4} \times 24 = \frac{3}{4} \times \frac{24}{1} = \frac{3 \times 24}{4} = \frac{72}{4} = 18$$

One way to approach these problems is to use commutativity. Since $3 \times 4 = 4 \times 3$, you want

$$\frac{3}{4} \times 24 = 24 \times \frac{3}{4}$$

Then find $\frac{3}{4} \times 24$ by using the procedures discussed in multiplying a whole number by a fraction. Although this approach may be easier, the opportunity to present the "of" meaning of multiplication is lost. Children do not readily see that $\frac{3}{4}$ of a case of 24 is the same as having 24 groups of three-fourths.

FRACTION TIMES A FRACTION Consider another problem:

> If you own $\frac{3}{4}$ of an acre of land and $\frac{5}{6}$ of this is planted in trees, what part of the acre is planted in trees?

Why is this a multiplication problem? A picture may help you see how this is related to the area of a rectangle and thus to multiplicaton. Consider first the acre partitioned into fourths and shade the amount you own, which is $\frac{3}{4}$:

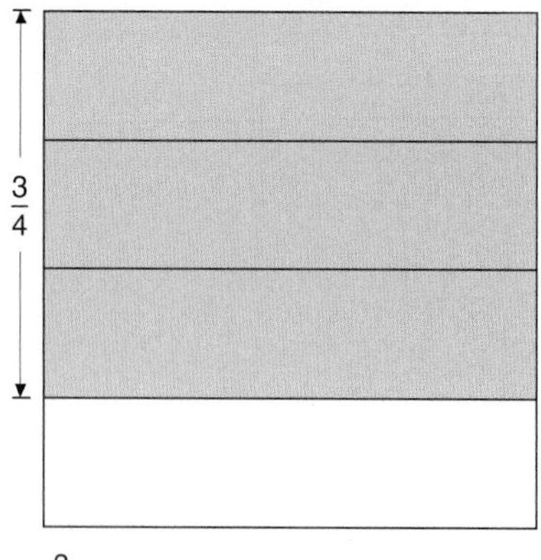

$\frac{3}{4}$ of an acre (the amount you own)

Since you know that $\frac{5}{6}$ of this land is planted, partition your property into sixths. To find what part of the whole acre is planted in trees, you need to identify the size of each of the small rectangles. Do you see that there would be 24 rectangles of this size? So each is one twenty-fourth of the acre, and you have planted 15 of them (or $\frac{15}{24}$ of the acre).

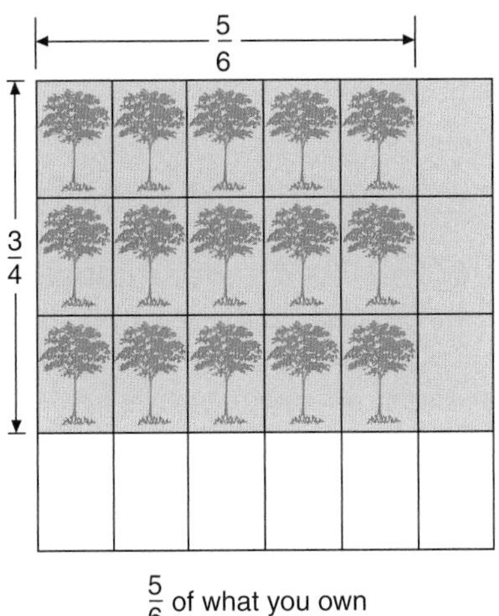

$\frac{5}{6}$ of what you own

What you have is a tree-planted rectangle that is $\frac{3}{4}$ by $\frac{5}{6}$, and its area is found by multiplying $\frac{3}{4} \times \frac{5}{6}$.

This model needs to be developed slowly and only after children have had experience with finding areas of rectangles. After children use a model for problems such as this, make a list of multiplication exercises and products (do not reduce the answers). See if the children notice a pattern for multiplying two fractions.

If children have had experience with finding area, this model can be used to see the procedure for multiplying fractions (multiply the numerators, multiply the denominators). You can refer to the diagrams to show why the procedure works. You have partitioned the acre into fourths one way and sixths the other way, thus creating 4×6, or 24, equal parts (the denominator). Trees were planted in three rows of five, or 15 of these parts, so 3×5 is the numerator. Symbolically, write

$$\frac{3}{4} \times \frac{5}{6} = \frac{3 \times 5}{4 \times 6} = \frac{15}{24}$$

At this point, return to earlier examples and let children know that this process also holds for those cases. A word of caution: Do not rush to canceling. Be sure that children can do multiplication this way, reducing answers only if necessary and applying multiplication to problems, before introducing canceling.

MIXED NUMBER TIMES A MIXED NUMBER Problems that involve multiplication of mixed numbers can also be solved with models. Consider the following problem:

You have a piece of cloth that is $2\frac{1}{4}$ yards by $1\frac{1}{2}$ yards. How many square yards do you have?

Part A in Figure 12-10 presents a model that shows how to change both mixed numbers in this problem to improper fractions. The model in part B shows how to multiply the mixed numbers without first changing them to improper fractions.

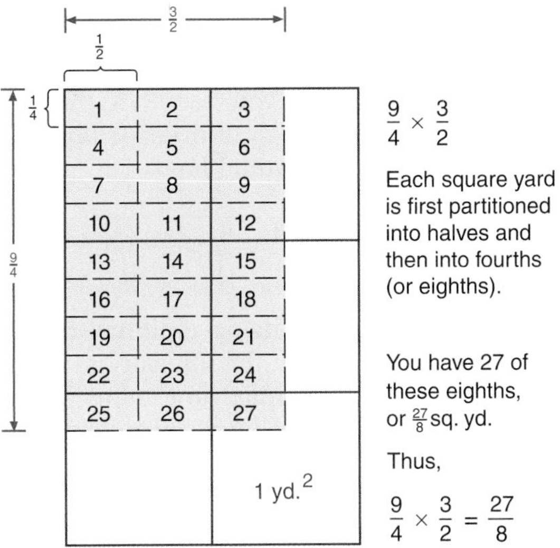

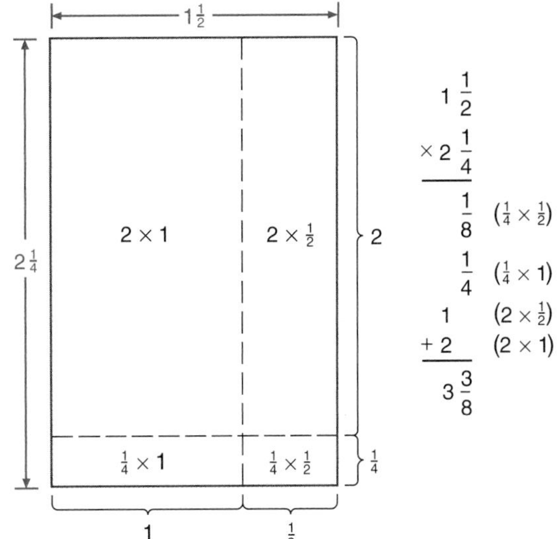

FIGURE 12-10 Multiplication models.

Division

The two meanings of division—partitioning and measurement—were explained in Chapter 9. In a partitioning situation with whole numbers, the whole is being shared equally among a given number of groups. In a measurement situation, a given number or amount is being put in each group. Begin looking at the division of fractions by using the measurement situation and the same problem that was presented in Chapter 9:

> How many 2-foot hair ribbons can be made from a 10-foot roll of ribbon?

Here, you are finding how many 2-foot pieces (the size of the group) are in the whole, or how many twos in ten. If you were drawing a picture of how you could do this in real life, the picture might look like the following:

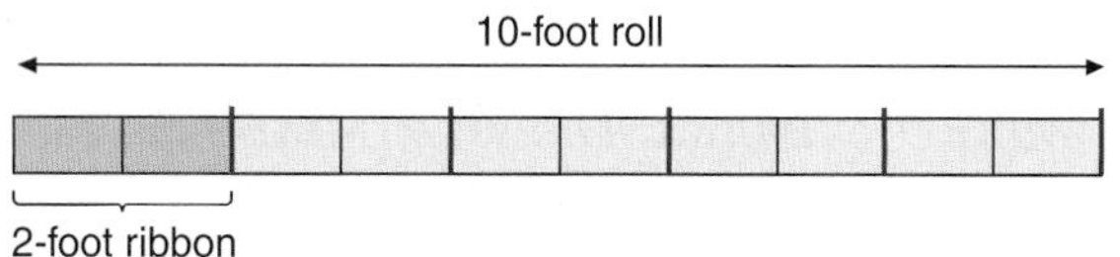

You can readily see that there would be five hair ribbons, each 2 feet long. Symbolize this by $10 \div 2 = \_\_$, or $10 \div 2 = 5$.

Following the same line of reasoning, draw a picture to show how to find the number of hair ribbons you could make from this roll if each ribbon were $\frac{1}{2}$ foot long? $\frac{1}{4}$ foot long? Although this is slightly tedious, do you see how the picture could be used? What is a symbolic shortcut for you?

See if your picture agrees with the one that Susie drew when she was finding the number of hair ribbons, each $\frac{1}{4}$ foot long, that she could make from a 3-foot long roll.

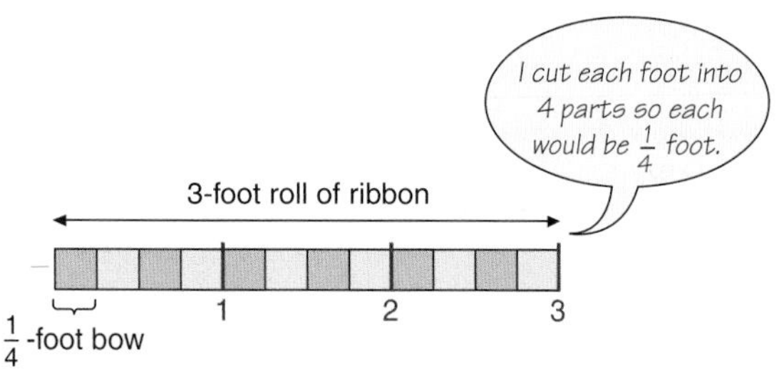

In this problem, we want to know how many one-fourths are in 3, or $3 \div \frac{1}{4} = \square$. There are 12, each $\frac{1}{4}$ foot long, in a 3-foot roll of ribbon. Do you notice that the picture also shows that you have 3 groups of 4 (or 3×4 hair ribbons)?

How would you draw a picture to help you find how many $\frac{3}{4}$-foot-long pieces there are in a 6-foot roll of ribbon? Again, mark off lengths that are $\frac{3}{4}$-foot long. See the following picture.

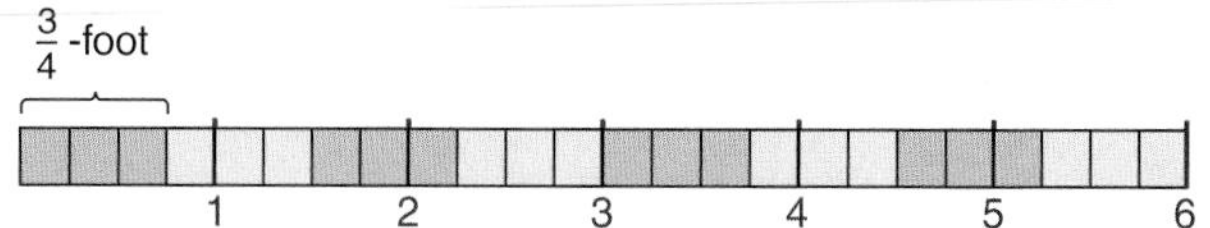

Note that fourths are first marked off and then grouped by threes to see how many $\frac{3}{4}$-foot pieces are in a 6-foot roll. That is, we multiplied by 4 and divided by 3. You probably learned this as inverting the divisor and then proceeding by multiplying. Look at the symbolic algorithm:

$$6 \div \frac{3}{4} = \frac{6}{1} \times \frac{4}{3} = \frac{6}{1} \times \frac{4}{1} \times \frac{1}{3} = \frac{24}{3}, \text{ or } 8.$$

One difficulty that students, including adults, often have is with ribbon being left after cutting as many $\frac{3}{4}$-foot pieces as possible. For example, suppose that you have only 2 feet of ribbon on the roll and you want to cut as many $\frac{3}{4}$-foot-long ribbons as you can. You know that you can cut at least two because you can get one from each foot of ribbon. Can you cut as many as three, each being $\frac{3}{4}$ foot long? Look at this picture.

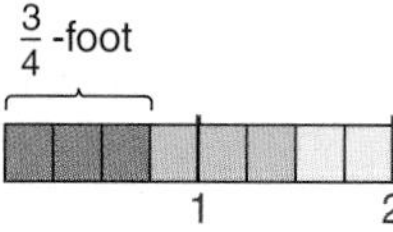

You can cut two full ribbons, as shown by the two shaded parts, but notice that you do not have enough for another full hair ribbon. What part of another can be made? Do you see that the unshaded part of the ribbon is $\frac{2}{3}$ of a hair ribbon? If you use the algorithm, you would have

$$2 \div \frac{3}{4} = \frac{2}{1} \times \frac{4}{3} = \frac{2}{1} \times \frac{4}{1} \times \frac{1}{3} = \frac{8}{3} = 2\frac{2}{3}.$$

This last example also helps children reason through problems in which the divisor is larger than the dividend. For example, how many bows, each $\frac{1}{2}$-foot long, could be cut from a strip of ribbon that is $\frac{1}{3}$-foot long, or $\frac{1}{3} \div \frac{1}{2}$? You know that since $\frac{1}{2}$ is larger than $\frac{1}{3}$, you could not get a hair bow. What part of one do you have? Draw a picture to convince yourself that you would have enough ribbon to make $\frac{2}{3}$ of a hair bow.

Development of Decimals

In introducing decimals, you should link them to other knowledge—in particular, to common fractions and to place value. Although you will need to weave both of these ideas into your teaching, we have separated them for ease of discussion.

Relationship to Common Fractions

Decimal fractions are just another notation for tenths, hundredths, and other powers-of-ten parts of a unit. Thus basic to decimals is an understanding of these fractional parts—an understanding that should be built when developing meaning for common fractions.

TENTHS Before introducing the decimal notation for tenths, review what students should know about tenths from their background with fractions. They should know that partitioning a unit into tenths results in 10 equal parts. They also should be able to make the connection between the model, the oral name, and the fraction. And they should know that 10 tenths make a whole, that 7 tenths is less than a whole, and that 27 tenths is more than a whole.

With this background, children should be ready to learn that 0.3 is a new symbol for $\frac{3}{10}$. At this point, you should link the place-value ideas to the new notation (see the discussion in Chapter 8 on place value). You also need to stress that 0.3 is read just like $\frac{3}{10}$. Also look at $\frac{27}{10}$ or $2\frac{7}{10}$. This amount is written 2.7 and read as "two and seven-tenths." Note that the word *and* is said for the decimal point. Reading decimals in this way helps connect ideas about decimals and fractions. A quick game to play that provides practice in writing decimal and fraction notation is described in In the Classroom 12-4. Before introducing hundredths, you should make certain that students have made all the connections in this triangle.

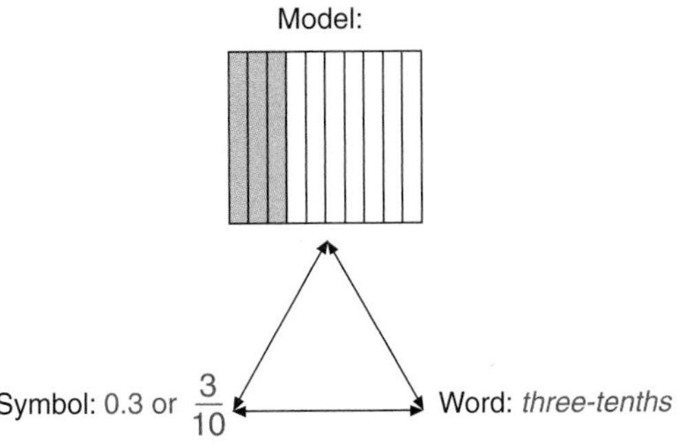

In the Classroom 12-4

CAN YOU BEAT THE TOSS?

OBJECTIVE: **Write numbers as fractions or decimals.**

GRADE LEVEL: **3–5**

MATERIALS: **Paper and pencil for children; a penny for the teacher**

Directions:

- The teacher reads a number.
- Each child writes the number in either decimal or fraction notation.
- Each child receives 1 point if he or she writes the number correctly.
- The teacher tosses a coin.
  - If it's *heads*, then those who wrote a *decimal* receive one more point.
  - If it's *tails*, then those who wrote a *fraction* receive one more point.

Suggested Numbers:

two-tenths	one and three-tenths
seven-tenths	twenty-two and five-tenths
five and seven-tenths	thirty-four and no-tenths
eleven and four-tenths	

Challenge Numbers:

sixteen-tenths	five and eleven-tenths

HUNDREDTHS To begin extending decimals to hundredths, provide each child with copies of the model of hundredths, shown in Figure 12-11 (Appendix B contains a sheet with multiple copies). Make certain that the children know that the unit (entire square or grid) is one, and that each part (small square) is one hundredth. Using the model, ask them to shade in $\frac{3}{100}$, $\frac{7}{100}$, $\frac{10}{100}$, and $\frac{21}{100}$.

Have the children color in the first and second columns on the hundredth model and three more small squares. Ask what part of the whole is covered. Elicit both responses, $\frac{2}{10} + \frac{3}{100}$ as well as $\frac{23}{100}$. Then write

$$\frac{23}{100} = \frac{2}{10} + \frac{3}{100}$$

Now connect the place-value interpretation and the decimal notation 0.23. You can also use the model to show that 0.2 = 0.20. Continue having children make the connections shown in the triangle (i.e., by connecting the model, the symbol, and the word).

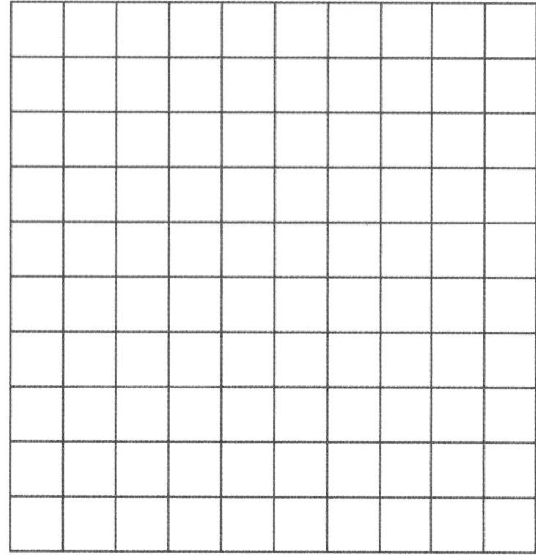

FIGURE 12-11 Model of hundredths.

THOUSANDTHS AND OTHER DECIMALS One national assessment reported that

> . . . although thirteen- and seventeen-year-olds appeared to have facility with tenths and hundredths, their competency was less developed for thousandths and smaller decimal numbers. (Carpenter et al., 1981, p. 39)

This deficiency occurs partly because there is less emphasis on these decimals but also because teachers often expect children to generalize after hundredths to all the other places. Most of the work with smaller decimals should be done primarily through the place-value interpretation because the fractions become unwieldy; however, thousandths should be developed as one-tenth of a hundredth, and the understanding that ten thousandths is $\frac{1}{100}$ of a hundredth should be developed through a model.

DECIMALS AND OTHER COMMON FRACTIONS Students need to develop the ability to relate fractions with decimals. If decimals have been introduced carefully, students should be able to write the fraction notation for a decimal and the decimal notation for any fraction expressed in tenths, hundredths, and so on.

The ability to relate fractions to decimals when the fractions are expressed in tenths, hundredths, and so on does not ensure that students can express other fractions as decimals. Table 12-2 shows two exercises from a national assessment, as well as the responses of 13-year-olds. In each case, less than 40 percent responded correctly. Analyze the errors made in both examples and consider what they indicate about students' grasp of fractions and decimals. Would you not hope that more students

Table 12-2 • Results of National Assessment Items on Equivalence of Decimals and Fractions

Exercise	Percent Responding Age 13
A. Which decimal is equal to 1/5?	
○ .15	12
• .2	38
○ .5	3
○ I don't know.	6
B. Which decimal is equal to 5/8?	
○ .6	7
• .625	27
○ $.\overline{714285}$	3
○ .85	30
○ I don't know.	30

would realize that $\frac{5}{8}$ is just a little more than one-half and thus could not equal 0.85, which is almost a whole?

When you have established that many fractions can be written as decimals, you can turn to the meaning of a fraction as division. Begin with an example that can be easily changed to a decimal, (e.g., $\frac{4}{5}$). Children should know that $\frac{4}{5} = \frac{8}{10} = 0.8$. Then proceed to the idea that $\frac{4}{5}$ means $4 \div 5$. To divide 4 by 5, a child needs to be able to divide decimals and to realize that 4 is also 4.0:

$$\frac{4}{5} = 4 \div 5, \quad 5\overline{)4.0} = 0.8$$

Therefore,

$$\frac{4}{5} = 0.8$$

Children can explore many interesting patterns that occur when converting fractions to decimals. Some can be investigated with a calculator. For example, look at the decimal equivalents for ninths:

$$\frac{1}{9} = 0.11111\ldots$$
$$\frac{2}{9} = 0.22222\ldots$$
$$\frac{3}{9} = 0.33333\ldots$$

You should do a few of these calculations by hand to show that the pattern continues forever. If you use only the calculator, students may think that $\frac{1}{9} = 0.11111111$ (or the number of places on their calculator screen).

Students can also be helped to see that $\frac{1}{3}$ does not equal 0.33, 0.333, or 0.3333 by looking at the meaning of $\frac{1}{3}$. If $\frac{1}{3} = 0.33$, then each of three equal parts of a whole would be 0.33. Thus the whole would be 0.33 + 0.33 + 0.33, or 0.99, which is not one. Similarly, $\frac{1}{3} \neq 0.3333$, even though this is a better approximation.

Relationship to Place Value

The place-value interpretation of decimals is most useful in understanding computation with decimals. Let's look now at a way to develop this interpretation and consider how to use it in ordering and rounding decimals.

INTERPRETATION Return to whole numbers and think about what children know about place value. Take, for example, the number 2463. By third grade, children can identify the places (ones, tens, hundreds, and thousands) as well as what number is in each (3, 6, 4, and 2). They know, for example, that the four means four hundreds. They also have learned how the places were formed: beginning with ones as a unit, grouping ten of these to form a new unit (tens), grouping ten of these to form a new unit (hundreds), and so forth.

In introducing place-value ideas with decimals, begin with ones as the unit. Instead of grouping by tens, take one-tenth of the one to form the new unit of tenths. To indicate this new unit in our place-value system, use a decimal point after the ones place. Children also should be helped to realize that 10 of the tenths make a one (just as 10 of any unit make the next larger unit). They also should be able to identify the tenths place in a number. This interpretation should be integrated with the interpretation of decimals as fractions.

Again, when introducing hundredths, you should give the place-value interpretation. Given a number such as 51.63, a child should be able to tell what number is in the tenths place and the hundredths place, as well as the relationships between the places (hundredths is $\frac{1}{10}$ of the tenths, or 10 hundredths is one tenth). After introducing thousandths in a similar way, the children should be able to generalize to any decimal place.

A place-value mat, or grid, can assist with decimals. When learning about decimals, it is most important that a decimal such as 24.09 be read as twenty-four *and* 9 hundredths-not "two, four, point, zero, nine." The words *tenths* and *hundredths* help students keep the tie between fractions and decimals. Consider 32.43, for example:

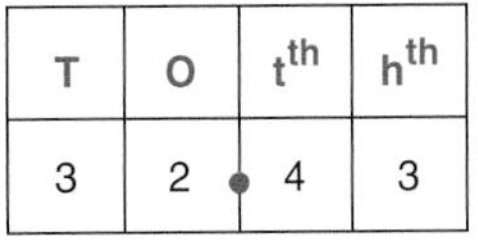

32 *and* 43 hundredths
32 *and* 4 tenths, 3 hundredths

Now use the grid for writing other decimals. (Remember to use models when first developing place value, as described in Chapter 8.)

Write 8 hundredths:

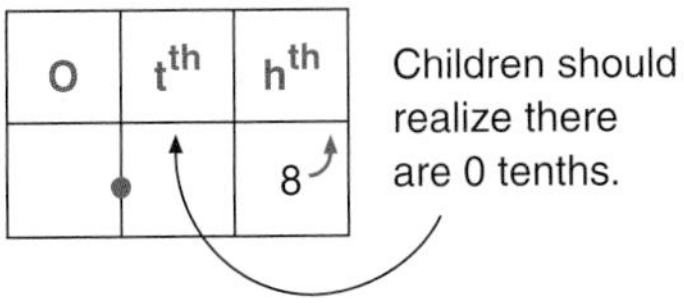

What is 29 hundredths?

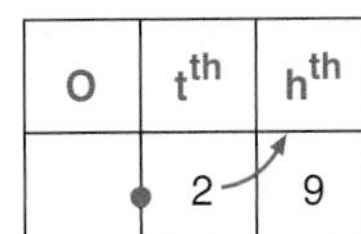

What is 29 tenths?

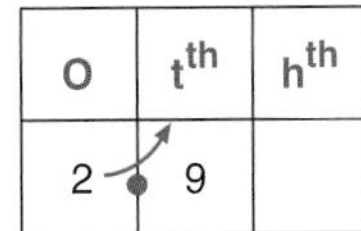

Now look at 4.3 on the grid:
How many tens? [0]

T	O	t th	h th
	4 •	3	

You could write a 0 in the tens place, but this is not customary. However, sometimes it is helpful to write a 0 in the hundredths place:

How many hundredths? [0]
What does that tell you?

T	O	t th	h th
	4 •	3	0

4.3 is equivalent to 4.30.

Children who are well acquainted with the models and the grid for place value should be able to handle decimals with ease.

Math Links 12.5

Practice using electronic base-ten blocks (accessible from this book's web site) to represent decimals. The process is similar to using base-ten blocks to represent whole numbers; however, the values the blocks represent will be different.

Ordering and Rounding Decimals

The ordering and rounding of decimals should follow directly from an understanding of decimals and the ability to order and round whole numbers. This understanding must include being able to interpret the decimals in terms of place value and being able to think of, for example, 0.2 as 0.20 or 0.200.

Here is an example of two children discussing which is larger—23.61 or 23.9?

CARTER: I think that 23.61 is larger because it has more places, just like 2361 is larger than 239.

BENNY: But we know that the 23 in each of them is the same, so all we have to do is compare the decimals.

CARTER: Okay, it's not like whole numbers.

BENNY: Well, sort of. We begin with the largest place—the tens are the same, the ones are the same, so we need to look at the tenths. The 9 is larger than the 6, so 23.9 is larger than 23.61.

CARTER: I follow you until that last part. Now you have a 9 and a 61, and 61 is larger.

BENNY: But the 9 is 9 tenths and the 61 is 61 hundredths. Want to look at a model?

CARTER: I get it, I remember the model. Nine tenths is 9 strips, or 90 little squares. It is 90 hundredths, so it is larger.

As you see from this conversation, if the children really understand the notation and the meaning of the decimals, they can figure out ways to compare decimals.

In rounding a decimal such as 24.78 to the nearest tenth, children need to ask themselves the same types of questions as with whole numbers. Children must also understand that 24.7 = 24.70.

Questions	Expected Responses
What "tenths" is 24.78?	It's between 24.7 and 24.8 (or 24.70 and 24.80).
Is it nearer 24.7 or 24.8?	Looking at 24.70 and 24.80, 24.78 is nearer 24.80.
How will you round it?	To 24.8.

Decimal Operations

One advantage of decimals over fractions is that computation is much easier and basically follows the same rules as for whole numbers. In teaching the algorithms for decimals, you should build on the place-value interpretations and the corresponding whole-number algorithms. Given the wide availability of calculators, it is important that you spend as much time seeing whether answers are reasonable as you spend on the algorithms. Thus estimation skills (described in Chapter 10) become crucial.

In the Classroom 12-5

WHAT'S YOUR ANSWER?

OBJECTIVE: **Use estimations about decimal quantities to answer questions.**

GRADE LEVEL: **4–5**

▼ Use the data in this table. These are data about the countries of the United Kingdom.

Country	*Area (Thousands of km²)*	*Population (Millions)*
England	50.363	46.221
N. Ireland	5.452	1.543
Scotland	30.415	5.131
Wales	8.019	2.750

▼ Answer these questions:

- About how much larger is England than Scotland? _______
- About how large is the United Kingdom? _______
- About what is the population of the United Kingdom? _______
- Do twice as many people live in Wales as live in N. Ireland? _______
- Is England more than six times larger than Wales? _______

In the Classroom 12-5 combines estimation skills and operations with decimals. To answer these questions, encourage students to use whole numbers that are compatible. They can be presented questions of this type before learning about decimal computation.

Addition and Subtraction

Children who have a good concept of decimals have little trouble extending the whole-number algorithms for addition and subtraction to decimals. They realize that they need to:

- Add or subtract like units (tens with tens, hundredths with hundredths, and so forth).

- Regroup in the decimal places as they did with whole numbers.

Difficulty with adding or subtracting decimals arises mainly when the values are given in horizontal format or in terms of a story problem and the decimals are expressed in different units (e.g., 51.23 + 0.4 + 347). To deal with this difficulty, it is wise to have children first focus on an approximate answer. Will it be more than 300? more than 500? more than 1000? Some children may need help in lining up the like units and so may benefit from using a grid:

H	T	O	t^{th}	h^{th}
	5	1 •	2	3
		0 •	4	0
3	4	7 •	0	0

Multiplication and Division

Before examining how to multiply or divide two decimals, consider multiplying and dividing a decimal by a whole number. These operations are conceptually easier to explain and allow for some development that will be helpful when multiplying or dividing two decimals. They also build the understandings needed for effective use of calculators.

Consider the following problem:

Six tables are lined up end to end. Each table is 2.3 meters long. How long is the line of tables?

Students should be able to solve this problem by adding decimals. From their previous work with multiplication, they should also realize it is a multiplication problem. Thus they should see that:

$$6 \times 2.3 = 2.3 + 2.3 + 2.3 + 2.3 + 2.3 + 2.3 = 13.8$$

However, just as children moved away from repeated addition to find the product of two whole numbers, they need to do so with this type of problem. In order to motivate the need for moving toward another way of thinking about decimal problems, have students use decimal paper to model a decimal multiplication using the area model (see Figure 12-10, for example). Lesson Idea 12-5 shows how children can estimate the product of two decimal numbers using decimal paper and the area model.

There is another way to think about it: multiplication depends on a firm foundation of the place-value interpretation of decimals.

Lesson Idea 12-5

MULTIPLYING DECIMALS USING DECIMAL PAPER AND THE AREA MODEL

Objective: Children use the area model to find the product of decimals.

Grade level: 4–5

Materials: Decimal paper

Problem: Find the area of a porch that is 3.2 meters by 1.9 meters.

1. **Estimate using rounding to the nearest whole number.**
2. **Use the area model to find 3.2 meters × 1.9 meters, as in the example:**

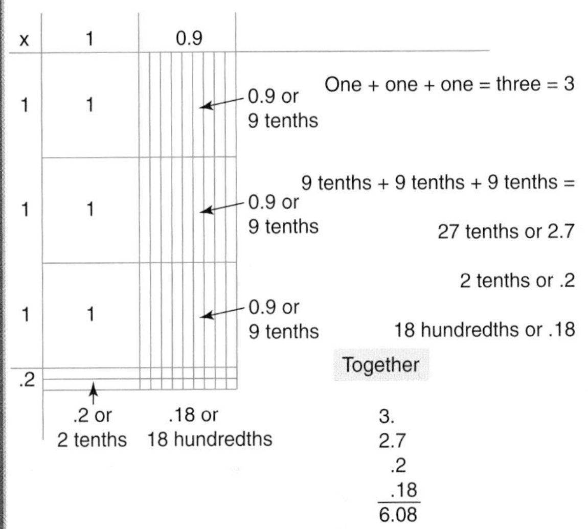

3. **Is the result reasonable? (Compare with original estimate: 6 m² is approximately 6.08 m².)**

	Think	
2.3	23	tenths
× 6	× 6	
	138	tenths, which is 13.8
2.37	237	hundredths
× 6	× 6	
	1422	hundredths, which is 14.22

Working with the grid can help students remember that 138 tenths is 13.8. In using this method, you should first have the students decide on a reasonable answer. For example, is 6 × 2.37

more than 12? as much as 18? They can also check by repeated addition.

The distributive algorithm that was used for dividing whole numbers may be used for dividing a decimal by a whole number. Consider this problem:

> A vinegar company distributed 123.2 million liters of vinegar equally to eight customers. How much vinegar did each customer receive?

First, ask for reasonable answers.

> Did each customer get more than 10 million liters? [Yes, that would be only 80 million liters.]
>
> Did each get more than 20 million liters? [No, that would be 160 million liters.]
>
> What is an estimate for the answer? [Between 10 and 20 million liters]

Talk through the division as follows:

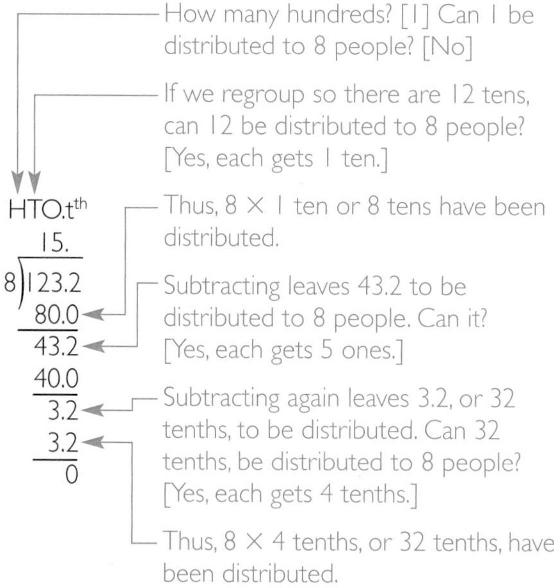

After this method is introduced, do some problems with remainders and then develop division to a specified number of places:

```
   15.4
8)123.8
   80.0
   43.8
   40.0
    3.8
    3.2
     .6    Remainder is .6
```

Note that keeping the decimal in the algorithm helps children see that the remainder is 0.6, not 6.

Now try the same problem, carrying out the division to two places (123.8 = 123.80):

```
   15.47
8)123.80    123.8 = 123.80
   80.0
   43.8
   40.0
    3.8
    3.2
     .60
     .56
     .04    Remainder is .04
```

There are several ways to teach multiplication of a decimal by a decimal. If all teachers do is give students a rule for counting off decimal places, students will not develop a sense of decimals. Children can discover the rule by using calculators and examining patterns. Another way is to change the decimals to fractions and develop the rule through multiplication of fractions. Another method is to use place value and the knowledge that tenths times tenths is hundredths, as shown here:

	Think	
3.2	32	tenths
× 1.6	× 16	tenths
	512	hundredths or 5.12

No matter which method you choose to teach multiplication of decimals, it is important that children be able to check to see that their answers are reasonable.

To divide a decimal by a decimal, children can essentially turn the problem into one they already know how to do. That is, they can make the divisor a whole number by multiplying the divisor by a power of ten, such as 10, 100, or 1000. In order not to change the problem, the dividend must also be multiplied by the same number:

```
.5)1.25  Change to  5)12.5
 ↑  ↑
Multiply
by 10
```

There is a shortcut for this procedure: Move the decimal point the number of places in the divisor needed to make it a whole number, and then do the same in the dividend.

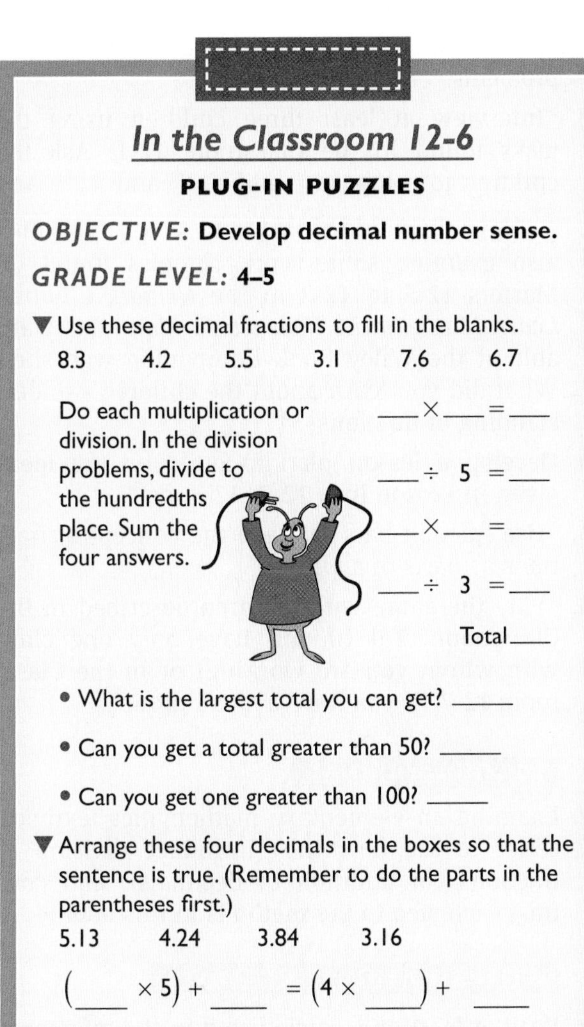

In the Classroom 12-6
PLUG-IN PUZZLES
OBJECTIVE: Develop decimal number sense.
GRADE LEVEL: 4–5
▼ Use these decimal fractions to fill in the blanks.
8.3 4.2 5.5 3.1 7.6 6.7
Do each multiplication or division. In the division problems, divide to the hundredths place. Sum the four answers.
___ × ___ = ___
___ ÷ 5 = ___
___ × ___ = ___
___ ÷ 3 = ___
Total___
• What is the largest total you can get? _____
• Can you get a total greater than 50? _____
• Can you get one greater than 100? _____
▼ Arrange these four decimals in the boxes so that the sentence is true. (Remember to do the parts in the parentheses first.)
5.13 4.24 3.84 3.16
(___ × 5) + ___ = (4 × ___) + ___
▼ Pick the two decimals from those listed that will make the sentence true.
21.21 42.42 36.36 63.63 27.27
(___ ÷ 7) × 8 = (___ ÷ 9) × 6

Although this rule can be learned quickly, there is still the question of why it works. Students can easily be told how to turn the problem into one they can already do and be convinced that it works (using the calculator or multiplying to check); however, what would you say to the inquisitive child who asks why it works? One way is to appeal to fractions. We know that:

$$1.25 \div .5 = \frac{1.25}{.5}$$

We also know that the numerator and denominator can be multiplied by the same number without changing the value of the fraction. Thus,

$$\frac{1.25}{.5} = \frac{1.25 \times 10}{.5 \times 10} = \frac{12.5}{5}$$

or

$$1.25 \div .5 = 12.5 \div 5$$

Students need more practice to develop fluency with multiplication and division of decimals than with addition and subtraction. The reason is partly because multiplication and division of whole numbers are not as firmly fixed as addition and subtraction; it is also because new rules are needed. You will find a great variation in skill level among children in your class. You might want to begin collecting some challenging activities such as the one In the Classroom 12-6 as well as games and other practice materials to develop computational fluency. Calculators can also be used as checking devices for children to check the accuracy of their work and the dependability of their developing understanding.

A Glance at Where We've Been

This chapter examined how to approach fractions and decimals in a meaningful way. This goal can be reached through thoughtful teaching that first develops an understanding of the fractions and decimals through models and appropriate language. It involves careful sequencing and a pace that does not rush to the symbols alone. The operations with these numbers can also be developed in a meaningful way, instead of through rules learned by rote. A firm foundation of fractions and decimals and the operations can assist students in using these numbers to solve problems. Eventually, children are expected to gain fluency in their ability to estimate and to use operations to find reasonable answers to fraction and decimal problems. Thus, throughout the development in this chapter, we have included applications to let students see how these numbers are used and to give meaning to the numbers and operations, so that students' learning can better match the vision of the *Principles and Standards for School Mathematics* (NCTM, 2000).

Ages or grade levels have not been given because older children often profit from some of the beginning concepts. It will be your job to realize which pieces of this topic your students are missing. This task is not as difficult as it sounds if you are familiar with the background and how the concepts and skills interweave.

Things to Do: From What You've Read

1. The part-whole meaning of a fraction can be developed with different attributes, such as length and numerosity (sets). Draw part-whole models for four different attributes to show $\frac{3}{4}$.
2. Illustrate three different meanings of $\frac{3}{4}$.
3. How can you develop the idea of equivalent fractions?
4. What is partitioning? How is this process related to division and to fractions?
5. Explain why the areas are equal in each square in Figure 12-6.
6. Illustrate how two fractions may be ordered using the method shown in the Lesson Idea 12-3 activity.
7. Show, with pictures, why $2\frac{3}{5}$ is equivalent to $\frac{13}{5}$; show why $2\frac{3}{5}$ is equivalent to $1\frac{8}{5}$.
8. What is a benchmark for fractions? How are benchmarks used? Propose a problem that could be solved using benchmarks for fractions.
9. How is multiplication of fractions different from multiplication of whole numbers?
10. Describe how decimal and common fractions are alike and different.
11. Describe how to explain, with meaning, that 2.8×3.7 is 10.36.
12. Develop and describe a pattern using the measurement concept by taking a 2-yard length of rope and dividing it first into 2-yard pieces, then 1-yard pieces, $\frac{1}{2}$-yard pieces, $\frac{1}{4}$-yard pieces, and $\frac{1}{8}$-yard pieces.

Things to Do: Going Beyond This Book

IN THE FIELD

1. Create five story problems that ask children to order and compare fractions.
2. Design a worksheet that would be a good follow-up to the *Snapshot of a Lesson* that opened this chapter. Include three models—region, length, and area—and a couple of challenging problems.
3. *Interview at least three children using the tasks found In the Classroom 12-1. Ask the children to compare $\frac{1}{3}$ and $\frac{1}{4}$; $\frac{2}{5}$ and $\frac{2}{7}$; $\frac{1}{2}$ and $\frac{3}{7}$. Have them add $\frac{3}{8} + \frac{2}{8}$ and $\frac{2}{3} + \frac{1}{4}$. You may also examine some work samples found on Masters 12-5 to 12-7 in the *Helping Children Learn Mathematics Instructor's Manual.* (Available at the Wiley Book Companion web site.) What did you learn about the children's understanding of fractions?
4. Develop a lesson plan to build on the ideas given in Lesson Idea 12-2, 12-3, or 12-4.
5. *Use fraction bars to teach the concept of fractions as parts of a whole.
6. *Play the game with children described In the Classroom 12-6 (if you have only one child with whom you are working) or In the Classroom 12-7 (if you have a small group).

IN YOUR JOURNAL

7. Examine an elementary mathematics textbook series to see how they introduce division of fractions (or addition of decimals), and contrast each step to the methods in this book.

WITH ADDITIONAL READINGS

8. Read at least one article listed in the references from *Arithmetic Teacher, Teaching Children Mathematics, or Mathematics Teaching in the Middle School.* Describe how it complements or contradicts the suggestions in this chapter.

WITH TECHNOLOGY RESOURCES

9. Experiment with a calculator that has a fraction key. What fraction skills and understanding would be important if such calculators were used?

*Additional activities, suggestions, or questions are provided in *Teaching Elementary Mathematics: A Resource for Field Experiences* (Wiley, 2004).

Resources

ANNOTATED BOOKS

Lamon, Susan J. *Teaching Fractions and Ratios for Understanding: Essential Content Knowledge and Instructional Strategies for Teachers.* New York: Lawrence Erlbaum, 1999.

This book provides an overview of proportional reasoning and instructional strategies for teaching these ideas.

National Council of Teachers of Mathematics. *Making Sense of Fractions, Ratios, and Proportions: 2002 Yearbook.* Bonnie Litwiller and George Bright (Eds.). Reston, VA: NCTM, 2002.

Book Nook for Children

Dennis, Richard. *Fractions Are Parts of Things.* New York: Crowell, 1973.
Halves, thirds, and fourths are introduced as parts of a unit and parts of a set. A shade pulled halfway down, a half glass of water, and six children who can be separated into two groups in different ways are a few of the examples used to illustrate the concept of fractions. A variety of geometric shapes are shaded to represent different fractions. This simple text and appropriate accompanying illustrations introduce fraction concepts; some of the shaded representations become quite challenging.

Emberley, Ed. *Ed Emberley's Picture Pie: A Circle Drawing Book.* Boston, MA: Little Brown & Co., 1984.
While not exactly a drawing book, this book shows how to assemble shapes into pictures from fractional parts of a circle. Older children can cut out their own shapes, though you'll probably still need to give them the starting circles (pies) until they're confident.

Hutchins, Pat. *The Doorbell Rang.* New York: Greenwillow, 1987.
This book is an excellent source to use when introducing the concept of partitioning.

Mathews, Louise. *Gator Pie.* New York: Dodd, Mead & Co., 1979.
Alvin, Alice, and other alligators inhabit this delightful book on beginning fraction concepts. Alvin and Alice decide to share a pie they find in the woods, but before they can cut it, other alligators arrive; so they need to consider cutting the pie in thirds, fourths, eighths, and finally, hundredths, when a whole army arrives. Each new situation in the well-written text includes graphic models; "Three gators," gulped Alice, "That means three pieces." "Cut three one-thirds," muttered Al, as a circular model of the pie is shown cut into three equal pieces. The detailed illustrations of the main characters and other woodland creatures humorously complement the story line.

Fractions and decimals are emphasized as pivotal concepts in the middle school. The understanding begins in elementary school, and fluency follows this understanding.

ANNOTATED ARTICLES

Bezuk, Nadine, and Cramer, Kathleen. "Multiplication of Fractions: Teaching for Understanding." *Arithmetic Teacher,* 39 (November 1991), pp. 34–37.
Five teaching activities demonstrate the Lesh Translation Model for developing conceptual understanding of multiplication of fractions. The model shows relationships between five representations.

Pothier, Yvonne, and Daiyo, Sawada. "Partitioning: An Approach to Fractions." *Arithmetic Teacher,* 38 (December 1990), pp. 12–16.
Included with sample activities, this article includes a discussion of how to use prepartitioned models to help students construct meaningful concepts of fractions.

Thompson, Charles S., and Walker, Vicki. "Connecting Decimals and Other Mathematical Content." *Teaching Children Mathematics,* 2 (April 1996), pp. 496–502.
Consider these common misconceptions regarding decimals. Activities focusing on reasoning, communication, and problem solving for developing and strengthening connections between decimals, fractions, place value, and physical models are offered.

Wentworth, Nancy M., and Monroe, Eula Ewing. "What Is the Whole?" *Mathematics Teaching in the Middle School,* 1 (April-May 1995), pp. 356–360.
Three examples of how to represent common fractions are given, along with illustrations of misconceptions regarding fractions. The article discusses effective ways to encourage students to construct meaningful representations. Also included is a discussion of constructivist mathematics education and an illustration of a teacher who misunderstands a unit on fractions.

ADDITIONAL REFERENCES

Carpenter, Thomas P.; Corbitt, Mary Kay; Kepner, Henry S., Jr.; Lindquist, Mary Montgomery; and Reys, Robert E. *Results from the Second Mathematics Assessment of the National Assessment of Educational Progress.* Reston, Va.: NCTM, 1981.

Cramer, Kathleen A.; Post, Thomas R.; and DelMas, Robert C. "Initial Fraction Learning by Fourth and Fifth Grade Students: A Comparison of the Effects of Using Commercial Curricula with the Effects of Using the Rational Number Project Curriculum." *Journal for Research in Mathematics Education,* 33 (March 2002), pp. 111–144.

Irwin, Kathryn C. "Using Everyday Knowledge of Decimals to Enhance Understanding." *Journal for Research in Mathematics Education,* 32 (July 2001), pp. 399–420.

Kieren, Thomas E. "Knowing Rational Numbers: Ideas and Symbols." In *Selected Issues in Mathematics Education* (ed. Mary Montgomery Lindquist). Berkeley, CA: McCutchan Publishing, 1980, pp. 69–81.

National Council of Teachers of Mathematics. *Curriculum and Evaluation Standards for School Mathematics.* Reston, Va.: NCTM, 1989.

Payne, Joseph N.; Towsley, Ann N.; and Huinker, DeAnn M. "Fractions and Decimals." In *Mathematics for the Young Child* (ed. Joseph N. Payne). Reston, VA: NCTM, 1990, pp. 175–200.

Warrington, Mary Ann, and Kamii, Constance. "Multiplication with Fractions: A Piagetian, Constructivist Approach." *Mathematics Teaching in the Middle School,* 3 (February 1998), pp. 339–343.

Wearne, Diana, and Kouba, Vicky L. "Rational Number Properties and Operations." In *Results from the Seventh Mathematics Assessment of the National Assessment of Educational Progress.* (eds. E. A. Silver and P. A. Kenney). Reston, Va.: NCTM, 2000.

CHAPTER 13

Ratio, Proportion, and Percent: Meanings and Applications

Snapshot of a Lesson

Orientation

Mr. Flores and his students have been working on percents, a very important and often misunderstood concept. He wants to help them appreciate the power of percents and recognize some of the difficulties in making interpretations and judgments based solely on percents. For today's lesson, Mr. Flores has collected the results from the first four basketball games for the sixth-grade team.

Mr. Flores has entered the following data into a spreadsheet and projected the data from the computer screen to an overhead projector.

	A	B	C	D
1				
2	Player's	Shots	Shots	Percent
3	Name	Made	Taken	
4				
5	Billy	12	25	48%
6	Doug	8	17	47%
7	Harlan	1	8	13%
8	Bryan	3	5	60%
9	Rustin	15	43	35%
10	Eric	1	1	100%
11	Whitney	0	2	0%
12	Nick	0	0	# DIV/0!

Mr. Flores begins by entering only the names and the middle column (shots taken) and asks:

Which students have taken the most shots?

Which students have taken the fewest shots?

Would this information help you decide who is the best shot? Tell why.

After some discussion, he also enters the first column of data (shots made) and asks:

If you wanted to find the best shooters, which students would you check? Why?

Is it easy to compare $\frac{15}{43}$ with $\frac{12}{25}$? Why? Why not?

Is it easy to compare $\frac{12}{25}$ with $\frac{3}{17}$? Why? Why not?

Before revealing Column D, Mr. Flores asks the students what they notice. Joe thinks Billy and Doug shot about the same because 12 is about half of 25 and 8 is about half of 17. He predicts both shooting percentages will be a little less than 50 percent. Susan notices that Rustin made about a third of his shots, so he wasn't as accurate as Billy and Doug. She predicts his shooting percentage will be close to 33 percent. After more discussion, Mr. Flores has the spreadsheet calculate Column D and asks:

How does the percent column help us compare shooters? Do these results support what we noticed earlier?

How can Nick and Whitney have the same shooting percentage?

What if you looked only at the shooting percentages? Of all the players, who would be the best shot? Do you agree that that person is the best shot?

The class also noticed how the spreadsheet handled Nick's data by placing #DIV/0! in the percent column. This provided Mr. Flores with an opportunity to introduce how dividing column B12 by C12 results in division by zero, which is undefined. They also talked about how in the real world 0 percent would be reported only for players who took shots; and that if a player didn't take a shot, no percent would be reported.

After discussing each of the next two questions, Mr. Flores reenters columns B and C, and the class examines the results.

What if each player took one more shot and missed it—which percents would change the most? The least? Tell why.

	A	B	C	D
1				
2	Player's	Shots	Shots	Percent
3	Name	Made	Taken	
4				
5	Billy	12	26	46%
6	Doug	8	18	44%
7	Harlan	1	9	11%
8	Bryan	3	6	50%
9	Rustin	15	44	34%
10	Eric	1	2	50%
11	Whitney	0	3	0%
12	Nick	0	1	0%

What if each player took one more shot and hit it—which percents would change the most? The least? Tell why.

	A	B	C	D
1				
2	Player's	Shots	Shots	Percent
3	Name	Made	Taken	
4				
5	Billy	13	26	50%
6	Doug	9	18	50%
7	Harlan	2	9	22%
8	Bryan	4	6	67%
9	Rustin	16	44	36%
10	Eric	2	2	100%
11	Whitney	1	3	33%
12	Nick	1	1	100%

The class continues to interpret the data, generate other "what if" questions, and use the spreadsheet to answer those questions. As the discussion continues, Mr. Flores also asks questions designed to help students gain a greater understanding of percents.

Introduction

"Family income this year increased by 10 percent."

"Ian did only half the work Angela did."

"Her salary is three times my salary."

"The cost of living tripled during the last eight years."

"Your chances of winning the lottery are less than one in a million."

"I can purchase a 12-ounce bottle of soda for \$1 or a 16-ounce bottle for \$1.50. Which bottle is the better buy?"

Frequently heard statements like these reflect the fact that much of quantitative thinking is relational. In such thinking, what is important is the equivalent relationship between numbers, rather

Math Links 13.1

The full-text electronic version of the following standard, with electronic examples (interactive activities) is available at the NCTM's web site, which you can access from this book's web site. Click on 3–5 or 6–8 to read more about ratio, proportions, and percents in the Number and Operation Standard.

Instructional programs from prekindergarten through grade 12 should enable all students to:	Grades 3–5 Expectations All students should:	Grades 6–8 Expectations All students should:
Understand relationships among numbers, compute fluently, and make reasonable estimates	Recognize and generate equivalent forms of commonly used fractions, decimals, and percents	Understand and use ratios and proportions to represent quantitative relationships

FIGURE 13-1 Number and Operations Standard with expectations for children in grades 3–5 and grades 6–8.

than the actual numbers themselves. A greater emphasis on relational equivalence leads to increased opportunities to use these relationships in real-world situations, which often require fluency in ratios, proportions, and percents, as well as fractions and decimals. Problems such as those provided in the *Snapshot of a Lesson* in Mr. Flores's class and the previous examples contribute familiar and interesting contexts for students to explore and learn to apply.

Students in elementary and middle school grades must be able to express appropriate relationships by using fractions, ratios, proportions, and percents. This goal is identified in the *Principles and Standards for School Mathematics* as shown as follows (NCTM, 2000) and is clarified in the standards represented in Figure 13-1.

Consider the prices of three carpets as you think about these expectations. Notice how the expectation in grades 3 through 5 provides the groundwork on which ratios and proportions are considered in grades 6–8.

CARPET SALE

A	B	C
$9.00 sq. yd.	$18.00 sq. yd.	$27.00 sq. yd.

The difference in price between these carpets (A and B or B and C) is $3 per square yard. The cost of carpet A is $\frac{1}{2}$ the cost of carpet B and $\frac{1}{3}$ the cost of carpet C. Yet B is twice as expensive as A, and C is 50 percent more expensive than B. In comparing relative cost, the ratio relationship of the prices rather than the prices themselves are important.

Math Links 13.2

A variety of Web resources for ratio, proportion, and percent, that may be used by teachers and children, may be found at the NCTM's Illuminations web site (accessible from this book's web site under the Number and Operations Standard).

FOCUS QUESTIONS

1. How is a ratio different from a proportion?
2. How can teachers use student intuition to develop students' thinking about proportions?
3. Why do students mistakenly use an additive method to solve proportions rather than the correct multiplicative method?
4. What different model or manipulative can you use to develop the idea of percents for elementary students?

Ratios

Ratios involve comparing things. Some of children's earliest experiences with comparisons involve rates. For example, if a child pays one dime for three stickers, the rate is three stickers for one dime.

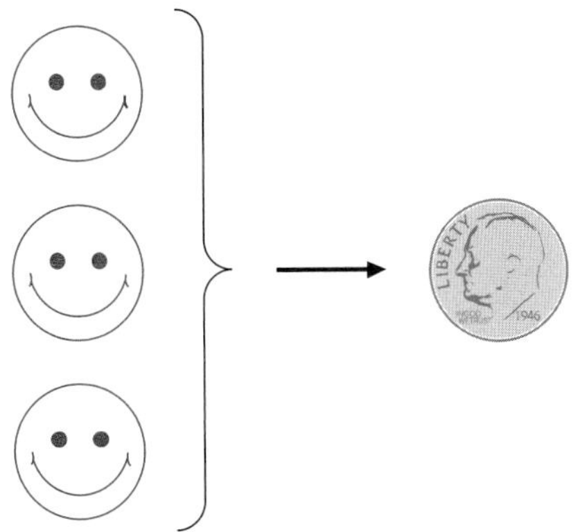

This ratio may be read as "three to one" and recorded as 3 to 1, 3:1, or $\frac{3}{1}$. Any of these forms is acceptable.

We can also form ratios to report the number of stickers to nickels as 3 to 2 or stickers to pennies as 3 to 10:

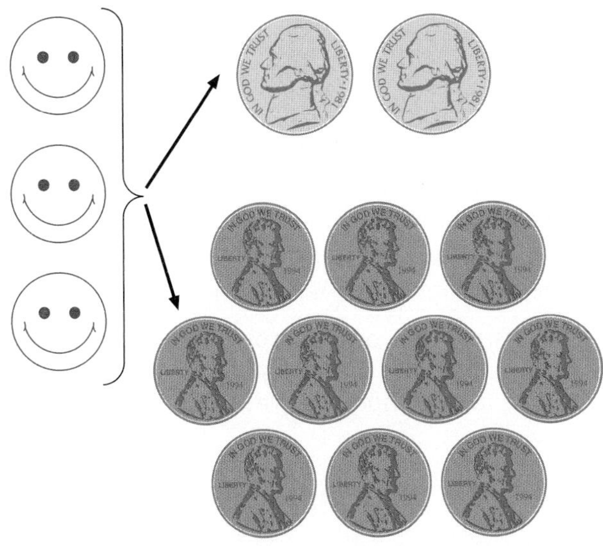

This ratio can also be expressed as ten pennies for every three stickers, which can be written as 10 to 3 or as the quotient 10 ÷ 3. The latter form provides a per-sticker cost of over three pennies and illustrates a powerful application of ratios.

Early experiences with ratios should stimulate children to think of two related numbers simultaneously. As children use manipulatives such as coins or draw pictures, they should be encouraged to think about ordered pairs of numbers, such as (3 stickers, 2 pennies). The models help link the operation of multiplication directly to ordered pairs and ratios.

Using facts about money (the number of pennies in a nickel, nickels in a quarter, and so on) provides natural and meaningful experiences with ratios. In the Classroom 13-1 shows how organizing such information not only visually displays many ratios, but also helps students realize that a ratio is a multiplicative comparison of two or more numbers in a given order. The activity also provides patterns that encourage students to explore relationships, generate formulas, and engage in algebraic thinking.

The money model also provides a natural extension of ratio to more than two numbers. For example, the ordered triple (2, 10, 50) relates 2 quarters, 10 nickels, and 50 pennies. Using a calculator to skip count by 5's or 25's or a spreadsheet to extend patterns are excellent uses of technology. The children's book *If You Made a Million* (Schwartz, 1989) also provides photographs and explanations of ratios using coins.

Children encounter ratios in many different forms: "three video games for a dollar," "twice as long," "half as much," and so on. Real-world examples of ratios help develop a greater awareness and understanding. For example, the values (8–12–20) on a sack of lawn fertilizer use a ratio to report the percents of phosphorus, nitrogen, and potash the fertilizer contains. Students frequently encounter prices such as two cans for 99¢, three pounds for $1.99, and 88¢ per dozen, which provide meaningful contexts for ratios.

This example is a reminder of the importance of the order of the entries and the need to understand what each entry represents. An ordered pair from In the Classroom 13-1, such as (5, 25), could represent 5 quarters and 25 nickels or 5 nickels and 25 pennies. Whether a ratio has two, three, or more entries, it has little meaning until the nature of the entries is known.

Suppose you are ready to extend some ideas on multiplication to develop the concept of ratio. After the students use models and complete and discuss In the Classroom 13-1, you might consider how some of those tasks lead directly to writing ratios, as shown in Figure 13-2.

Students are sometimes confused by the different symbols used to record ratios. Linking the symbols to appropriate models and promoting class

In the Classroom 13-1

KNOW YOUR COINS

OBJECTIVE: **Using value of coins to develop patterns and proportions and to examine algebraic relationships.**

GRADE LEVEL: **4–6**

▼ Use patterns to help complete this table:

Number of

Quarters	1	2		4	5	6	□
Nickels	5	10	15	20		30	△
Pennies	25	50	75	1	125	150	○

- Describe a pattern you found in each row.
- Write a ratio for the number of quarters to nickels. ______
- Write a ratio for the number of nickels to pennies. ______
- Write a ratio for the number of quarters to pennies. ______

▼ Try these:

- How many nickels will be needed for 8 quarters? ______
  Tell two different ways to decide.
- How many pennies will be needed for 10 quarters? ______
  Tell two different ways to decide.
- Give three numbers (not shown in the table) that could go
  in the △ row ______
  in the ○ row ______
- Give three numbers that could *not* go
  in the △ row ______
  in the ○ row ______
- How many quarters would you have when □ + △ + ○ first exceeds $30? ______

discussion can help minimize this confusion. Chips or cut-out wheels could be used to model these tasks before writing down ratios. A table might help organize the information. After the ratios are recorded, guided discussion centering on the information and the situation helps children talk about the mathematics.

Ratios, Ratios, Ratios, . . .

▼ Write a ratio to compare three bicycles with wheels.

- There are 3 bicycles and 6 wheels. $\frac{3}{6}$
- We can write this ratio as 3:6 or 6 or 3 to 6.

▼ Write a ratio to compare four bicycles with wheels.

- There are 4 bicycles and 8 wheels. $\frac{4}{8}$
- We can write this ratio as 4:8 or 8 or 4 to 8.

▼ Write a ratio to compare the number of wheels

- on a bicycle and a wagon 2 to 4
- on a tricycle and a wagon 3 to 4

FIGURE 13-2 Writing record for ratios.

For example, questions such as the following provide early practice in verbalizing and describing some of the mathematics surrounding the concept of ratio:

> If I have three bicycles and six wheels, is the ratio three to six or (3, 6)?
>
> If the ratio of bicycles to wheels is four to eight, how many bicycles do I have?
>
> If the ratio of bicycles to wheels is five to ten, how many wheels do I have?
>
> If I have six bicycles, how many wheels are there? What is the ratio of bicycles to wheels?

Ratios provide one interpretation for fractions, namely, where one integer is compared to another. In elementary school, however, the emphasis is

Math Links 13.3

You may view a lesson plan and video clips called *Mix It Up*, a PBS Mathline video, which you can access from this book's web site. In this lesson, children use the context of a fruit salad to express ratios.

typically on smaller numbers such as 1 to 2, 2 to 3, and 3 to 4. These ratios are the most frequently used, and they are much easier to model and conceptualize than 7 to 9 or 11 to 14. Several real-life examples may be examined in the counting book, *Each Orange Had 8 Slices: A Counting Book* (Giganti, 1992).

Far more important than how the ratio is expressed is the understanding of the relationship. Young children with a good understanding of numbers use "twice as much" just as often and as comfortably as "half as much." Instruction should take advantage of these different expressions to develop further reversible thinking.

Proportions

Proportions are two or more equal ratios and are frequently used in problem situations. Competence in proportional reasoning is one of the important mathematics outcomes that children must master. It has been called the "capstone of elementary arithmetic, number, and measurement concepts" (Lesh, Post, and Behr, 1988).

Consider the following problem:

> Suppose 10 horses need 4 acres of pasture to live comfortably. How many acres would 15 horses require to live comfortably?

In approaching such a problem, you want students to use their intuition or existing skills to try to figure out the problem, rather than teach them an algorithm. Consider the five student responses to the horse and pasture problem as described in Figure 13-3. Many students, like Karen, use manipulatives or draw pictures; others (as Tom did) may make a table or list; some may use their knowledge of equivalent fractions as Carrie did, while some may follow the method that Chia Lin used by finding a unit rate or density. Can you guess what led these students in Figure 13-3 to think of this problem in the particular ways they chose?

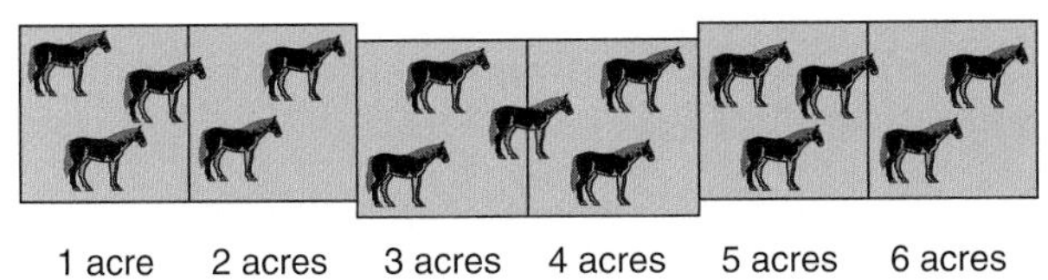

KAREN: *Using a picture or a diagram* I drew the picture and then counted the acres to be 6.

TOM: *Using patterns* I noticed:

- 10 horses need 4 acres of pasture . . . so
- 20 horses need 8 acres of pasture

Then I split the difference and got 15 horses need 6 acres of pasture.

CARRIE: *Using equivalent fractions* I did it this way:

$$\frac{10 \text{ horses}}{4 \text{ acres}} = \frac{5 \text{ horses}}{2 \text{ acres}} = \frac{15 \text{ horses}}{? \text{ acres}}$$

$\frac{5}{2} = \frac{15}{6}$

So, the 15 horses need 6 acres of land

CHIA LIN: *Using a unit rate or density* I thought, 4 divides into 10 two times with a remainder of $\frac{2}{4}$ or $\frac{1}{2}$

So there are $2\frac{1}{2}$ horses per acre. Then I saw how many acres it would take for 15 horses. I divided 15 by $2\frac{1}{2}$. Or $15 \div \frac{5}{2}$ which is the same as $15 \times \frac{2}{5}$. That means that it would be 6 acres.

BOB: *Using an incorrect addition/subtraction strategy* I figured there are six more horses than acres (10 − 4).

Horses	10	15
Acres	4	?

So I subtracted 6 from 15 and the number of acres is 9.

FIGURE 13-3 Methods children use to solve the horse and pasture problem.

Bob in Figure 13-3 reflects a common misconception that students bring to solving proportion problems: "when in doubt, add" (Miller and Fey, 2000). The concept of proportion is closely linked to multiplication, yet it is often difficult for students to make the necessary connections. Having students share their solutions—both correct and incorrect—on the board may help develop this important idea.

Let's look at a similar measurement example. When asked to find the length of the side *L*, students frequently report 9 rather than 15:

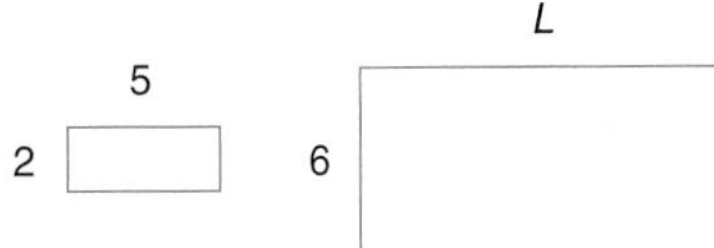

Such students tend to add an amount rather than multiply by a scale factor. Research shows that this error reflects students' misconception of ratio and proportion and is not simply the result of carelessness (Cramer et al., 1993).

There are several contexts where proportional reasoning is needed (NRC, 2001; Miller and Fey, 2000): (1) missing number problems, as in the horse/acre problem shown in Figure 13-3, (2) numerical comparison problems, as in the hot cross buns problem in Figure 13-4, and (3) scaling problems, as in the triangles measurement problem in Figure 13-5. Comparison problems ask children to determine which of two given ratios represents more or less.

In the hot cross buns problem of Figure 13-4, the students first need to determine what the problem is asking. A student might think: Is 3 buns for 51¢ the same as 4 buns for 64¢? Or compare 3:51 with 4:64. Next, the student needs to determine a method for approaching the problem. Reducing the fractions helps begin this thinking:

$$\frac{3}{51} = \frac{1}{17} \quad \text{or} \quad \frac{4}{64} = \frac{1}{18}$$

Which one is the better buy?

Students are more likely to reason that the first choice is better because you can get 1 hot cross bun for 17¢, while you have to pay 18¢ for each hot cross bun at the second place.

Another way to look at this problem is to compare fractions with common denominators:

$$\frac{1}{17} = \frac{18}{306} \quad \text{compared to} \quad \frac{1}{18} = \frac{17}{306}$$

making the first choice better.

Look for some patterns in the similar triangles in Figure 13-5. Triangle A is similar to triangle B because the extended ratios of the sides 1:2:2.5 and 2:4:5 are equal. Likewise, triangles B and C are similar. What about triangles D and E? If triangle D is similar to A, can you find the length of the longest side of D? If triangle E is also similar to A, can you find the lengths of its other two sides?

Once students have made sense of proportions by solving many problems in a variety of ways, a more algebraic method for solving missing number

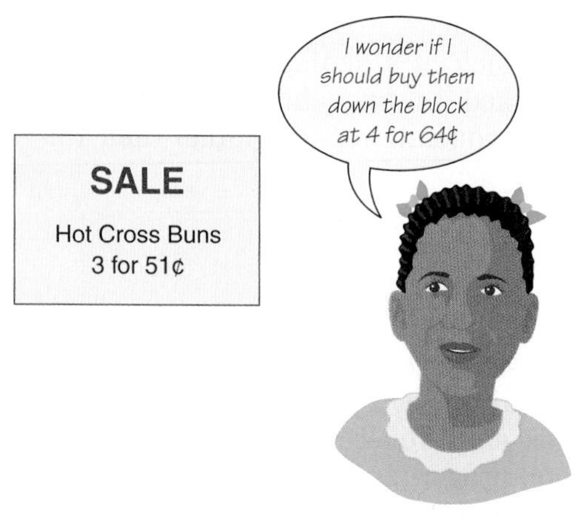

I wonder if I should buy them down the block at 4 for 64¢
SALE
Hot Cross Buns
3 for 51¢

FIGURE 13-4 Comparing prices of hot cross buns in two places.

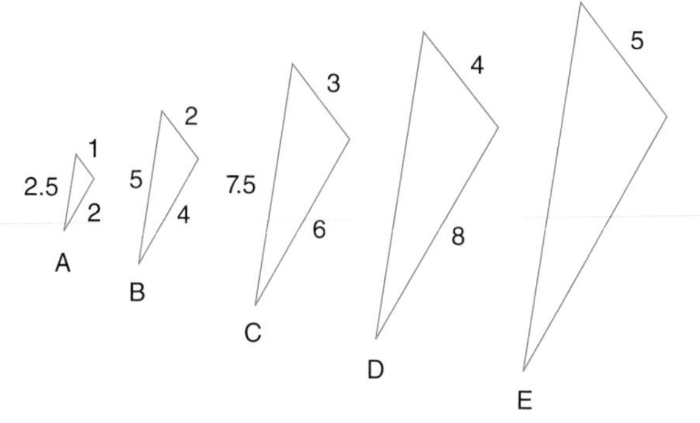

FIGURE 13-5 Some similar triangles.

problems can by addressed. For example, consider the following problem:

How much will a dozen balloons cost if 3 balloons cost 49¢?

Middle-grade students will be able to write an algebraic equation in a variety of ways:

$\frac{3}{49} = \frac{12}{\square}$ Thinking $\frac{3 \text{ balloons}}{49¢}$ as $\frac{12 \text{ balloons}}{\square¢}$ (where the symbol □ is the cost of the balloons)

$\frac{3}{12} = \frac{49}{\square}$ Thinking $\frac{3 \text{ balloons}}{12 \text{ balloons}}$ as 49¢ is to □¢

$\frac{49}{3} = \frac{\square}{12}$ What would students be thinking in this case?

$\frac{12}{3} = \frac{\square}{49}$ What would students be thinking in this case?

Although students should recognize the equivalence of these statements, they should feel free to use the form of their choice.

Next the students can solve the problem in a variety of ways:

If $\frac{49}{3} = \frac{\square}{12}$ rewrite the fractions with a common denominator of 12.

So, $\frac{196}{12} = \frac{\square}{12}$

Then □ = 196¢ or $1.96, meaning that a dozen balloons will cost $1.96

Alternately, students may use an alphabetic symbol (say C for cost) and multiply both sides of the problem by 12.

$$12 \times \frac{49}{3} = 12 \times \frac{C}{12} \quad \text{or} \quad 196 = C$$

Eventually, students should experience several of these different forms of algebraic expressions.

The pennies-nickels comparisons shown In the Classroom 13-1 contain many equivalent ratios

X	Y
1	5
2	10
3	15
4	20
5	25
6	30
7	35

FIGURE 13-6 Table comparing number of nickels (X) to number of pennies (Y).

(1:5 = 2:10, 2:10 = 3:15, and so on). The concept of equivalent ratios is important and can be anchored in different ways. For example, Figure 13-6 shows a table displaying the result of 5 pennies for 1 nickel as $y = 5x$. These tabular data provide opportunities to discover patterns, explore an algebraic relationship, and observe that the ratio of all of these proportions is constant.

Another skill that may help students make sense of proportions is to use estimation skills. Think about the following problem.

> A trout swam 5.8 meters in 3 seconds. At this rate, how far could it travel in 19 seconds?

Students could think:

> That's about 6 meters in 3 seconds or 2 meters per second. And 2 meters per second times about 20 seconds would give 40 meters.

Another student could say:

> 19 seconds is about 6 times the 3 seconds, so approximately 6 meters times six would be about 36 meters.

Although each of these estimates is different, each of them is reasonable. This type of estimation thinking is very productive. It should be both encouraged and rewarded. It uses estimation along with ratios to produce ballpark answers. Frequent experiences similar to this one will improve students' judgment, making them less likely to fall victim to unreasonable answers resulting from indiscriminate number crunching. Suppose the student mistakenly set up the proportion:

$$\frac{5.8}{3} = \frac{19}{\square}$$

And then found that $\square = 9.8$

What was the mistake the student made? How could he determine that he was making an error in his thinking? What would a correct proportion be? Using estimation to produce a ballpark result would help the student realize that 9.8 is an unreasonable answer and encourage the student to reflect on the procedures used.

In the Classroom 13-2 provides opportunities to use student intuition, skill with ratios, and knowledge of proportions to solve missing number

In the Classroom 13-2

COMPARING HORSES OF DIFFERENT SIZES

OBJECTIVE: **Using proportional reasoning to compare and then sketch horses of different sizes.**

GRADE LEVEL: **5–6**

MATERIALS: **Butcher paper and felt-tipped pens, a yardstick**

ACTIVITY: **Ask for students' questions, given that they will sketch the horses in actual size as described below and with the following information.**

A typical riding horse stands 15 hands (a measurement of a horse from the ground to a point between the neck and back called the withers) and weighs 1000 lbs. The smallest horse on record stood 5 hands and weighed 14 kg. The largest horse stood 18 hands and weighed 1,450 kg.

Some questions students might want to answer before beginning the drawing:

1. If a typical horse is 60 inches high, how high is a hand?
2. If a typical horse weighs 450 kg, how many kilograms are in a pound?
3. How tall in inches is the smallest horse on record? largest horse on record?
4. How many pounds did the smallest horse on record weigh? largest horse on record?
5. How does the pound per inch height for the smallest horse compare to the normal-sized horse? to the largest horse?

Once students have answered these questions, have them draw a sketch of one of the horses in groups of two or three.

Solve the following proportion. Deanna
Use whatever method is easiest for you.

A. 20 : 30 = 40 : 60
doors walls doors walls

20×2=40
30×2=60 so 20:30=40:60
if there are 20 doors in 30 walls double that there'd be 40 doors in 60 walls. The numbers are equal.

Solve the following proportion. Ned
Use whatever method is easiest for you.

B. 9 : 81 = 15 : ___
teams players teams players

If there are 9 & 81 (teams) (players) then that means there are 9 players on every team. So when 135 players there are 15 teams Then you have to take 15×9

Solve the following proportion. Trevor
Use whatever method is easiest for you.

A. 20 : 30 = 40 : 60
doors walls doors walls

For every 20 doors there are 30 walls. The ratio is 2:3 or 2/3
40 is $\frac{2}{3}$ of 60 so there are 60 walls for every 40 doors

Solve the following proportion. Hal
Use whatever method is easiest for you.

B. 9 : 81 = 15 : ___
teams players teams players

9:81 = 15:135
teams players teams

I 9 into 81 one and I got that their was 9 players on each team So I add 6 more teams times total was 135.

Solve the following proportion. Yang
Use whatever method is easiest for you.

A. 20 : 30 = 40 : 50 (+10 +10)
doors walls doors walls

20 + 10 = 30
40 + 10 = 50

Solve the following proportion. Carmen
Use whatever method is easiest for you.

B. 9 : 81 = 15 : 225
teams players teams players

9 teams 81 players
9 players per team
ratio is 9:81 or 1/9 in simplest form
15 teams 15 players per team 15×15=225

FIGURE 13-7 Samples of students' solutions to proportion problems.

problems, compare problems, and solve a scaling problem.

Figure 13-7 illustrates how some students solved the same two proportion problems. Notice that not all solutions are correct. Which ones are correct? Incorrect? Can you diagnose those student's difficulties? Notice that the students tried to make sense of the problem and approached it in a way that was meaningful to them.

Consider using other real-life applications with which children are familiar, such as recipes, photographs of different sizes, maps, and scale drawings or models. Figure 13-8 highlights a project where students use geometry scaling and measurement skills to do some practical problem solving.

Math Links 13.4

You can see fifth graders applying proportions in *Blazing the Trail*, a PBS Mathline video, which you can access from this book's web site. These students use map skills to complete an orienteering project.

www.wiley.com/college/reys

Draw Your Classroom

- First measure your classroom.
- Next decide on a scale to use.
- Now make a scale drawing of the room.
  - Show where doors, windows, tables, and desk are located
  - Be sure to put your scale on your drawing, such as 1 in.: 5 ft or 1 cm: 1 m

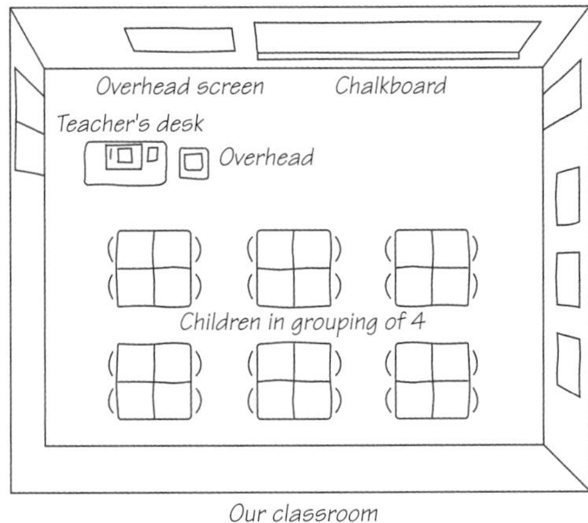

FIGURE 13-8 A scaling project.

The concepts of ratio and proportionality can be naturally connected to geometry problems. One natural, powerful connection to geometry uses similarity. Two figures are similar if their respective sides are in the same ratio (i.e., proportional). Thus all squares are similar, but all rectangles are not.

An interesting application of ratio and proportion appears in many architectural designs. The ratios of the sides of rectangles vary, but one ratio, (the *golden ratio*) has occurred in many architectural structures and works of art. In the Classroom 13-3 has an activity that uses this famous ratio.

Another famous ratio is π (pi). This ratio will be explored in Chapter 16 on Measurement.

Children's books, such as *Anno's Math Games* (Anno, 1987), provide different yet interesting contexts to explore ratios and proportions and connect them to percent. Other books, such as *In One Day* (Parker, 1984), encourage students to think about different ways of relating numbers. Also, look at Chapter 14 in the *2002 NCTM Yearbook* (Thompson, Austin, and Beckmann, 2002) for other ideas on using literature to explore proportional reasoning.

Percents

You only need to read a newspaper or watch television to be reminded that percent is one of the most widely used mathematical concepts:

Save 23 to 55%

MONEY MARKET CERTIFICATES 14.70% YIELDS 16.07%

City Asks For 40% Budget Increase

Serious crimes drop 5 percent

Wholesale Price Index Up 0.6 Pct.

38 Percent Plunge In Profits

Understanding of percent is taken for granted, although there is plenty of evidence to the contrary. Incorrect usage of percent is common among secondary students and adults. Flagrant errors abound, suggesting that often the most basic ideas are unclear (Gay and Aichele, 1997). For example, about one-third of the 17-year-olds and adults missed the following question on the first national assessment:

> If 5% of the students are absent today, then 5 out of how many are absent?

An error on such a fundamental idea suggests they did not know that 100 is the comparison base for percent. Low performance is found in other countries also, as only about half of the sixth graders tested in Japan correctly reported that 100% of 48 is 48 (Reys and Reys, 1993).

Misconceptions, distortions, and confusion surrounding percent are surprisingly easy to find. Here are some examples:

1. "Prices reduced 100%." If this advertisement were correct, the items would be free. Probably, the prices were reduced 50%. If an item that originally cost $400 was on sale for $200, then the ad based the 100% on the sale price, when it should have been based on the original price.
2. "Of all doctors interviewed, 75% recommended our product." This type of claim could be an effective advertisement for a company. If, however, the ad said "3 out of the 4 doctors we interviewed recommended our product," the consumer reaction might be different. Percents can often be used to disguise the number involved. Thus they can be misused. Percents allow for easy comparisons because of the common base of 100, but they may appear to represent a larger sample than actually exists.

In the Classroom 13-3

EXPLORING THE GOLDEN RATIO

OBJECTIVE: **Students will first estimate the golden ratio, then compare measurements of rectangles to see how close they are to the golden ratio.**

GRADE LEVEL: **5–6**

MATERIALS: **Playing cards, boxes, envelopes, boxes, posters, other rectangular objects**

ACTIVITY: **Describe the history of the golden ratio to students, then measure a variety of rectangles to see if they approximate the golden ratio.**

▼ The Pythagoreans studied the golden ratio 2500 years ago. This ratio, also called the divine proportion, has many interesting applications in geometry. This ratio can be approximated by finding relationships in the Fibonacci sequence.

1. **Find the first 15 terms in the Fibonacci sequence. (Hint: 1 + 1 = 2, 1 + 2 = 3, 3 + 5 = 8 . . .)**
   1, 1, 2, 3, 5, 8, ___, ___, ___, ___, ___, ___, ___, ___, ___
2. **Divide the 6th number by the 5th number $\frac{8}{5} = 1.6$**
   Divide the 8th number by the 7th number ___ = ___
   Divide the 12th number by the 11th number ___ = ___
   Divide 2 more numbers by their preceding numbers:

   How do your answers compare to the golden ratio, which is approximately 1 to 1.618?
3. **Measure the rectangle drawn around the Parthenon. Is this famous old building "golden"?**
4. **Measure other rectangles: cards, box faces, envelopes, books to see if any of these rectangles are "golden."**

Discussing the following questions and providing real-life examples can help students develop a number sense for percents:

- Can you eat 50% of a cake?
- Can you eat 100% of a cake?
- Can you eat 150% of a cake?
- Can a price increase 50%?
- Can a price increase 100%?
- Can a price increase 150%?
- Can a price decrease 50%?
- Can a price decrease 100%?
- Can a price decrease 150%?

Ironically, the understanding of percent requires no new skills or concepts beyond those used in mastering fractions, decimals, ratios, and proportions. In fact, percent is not really a mathematical topic, but rather the application of a particular type of notational system. The justification for teaching percent in school mathematics programs rests solely on its social utility. Consequently, percent should be taught and learned in application situations similar to the one given in the *Snapshot of a Lesson* at the beginning of this chapter. Because the primary objective is to solve problems involving percent, the use of calculators is appropriate and allows students to focus on the concepts of percents rather than get bogged down in the written algorithm for multiplication. Special function keys such as the percent key and the memory keys also could be introduced.

As is true with decimals and fractions, percents express a relationship between two numbers. Percents are special ratios based on 100 and without a doubt are the most widely used of all ratios. Percent is derived from the Latin words *per centum,* which mean "out of a hundred" or "for every hundred." Thus the origin of percent and its major uses are more closely associated with ratio and proportions than with either decimals or fractions.

When is percent understood? Students understand percent when they can use it in many different ways. For instance, if a child understands 25%, he or she can do the following tasks.

1. Find 25% in various contexts:

   Cover 25% of a floor with tiles.

   Determine 25% off the price of a given item.

   Survey 25% of the students in class.

   In many such situations, estimates of 25 percent are not only appropriate but essential.

2. Identify characteristics of 25%:

   25% of the milk in a glass is less than half.

   If 25% of the milk in a glass is spilled, then 75% remains.

3. Compare and contrast 25% with a range of other percents and numbers such as 5%, 50%, 100%, one-fourth, one-half, and 0.25.

   25% is half as much as 50%, one-fourth as much as 100%, five times as much as 5%, less than one-half, and the same as one-fourth and twenty-five hundredths.

Understanding Percents

Percents should be introduced only after students thoroughly understand fractions and decimals and have had experience with ratios and proportions. Percent is not studied extensively in elementary school, although it is typically introduced in fifth or sixth grade.

Initially, students need a variety of experiences with the fundamental concepts of percent, and these experiences should be connected to various concrete models and real-world contexts. Computation applying percent in problem-solving situations is generally reserved for later. Students who understand that percent means parts out of one hundred and have a good pictorial representation of percent are more successful in solving percent problems than those who do not. Lembke found that students naturally use benchmarks to make initial judgments about percent situations (Lembke and Reys, 1994). Helping students develop the concepts for common percent benchmarks and their fraction and decimal equivalents—such as 10 percent, 25 percent, 33 percent, 50 percent, and 75 percent—helps them apply their percent number sense to problem-solving situations.

Initial instruction should build on familiar models. A dollar is made up of 100 cents; therefore, it provides a natural connection among percents, fractions, and decimals. For example, 25 cents is $0.25, one-fourth of a dollar, and also 25 percent of a dollar.

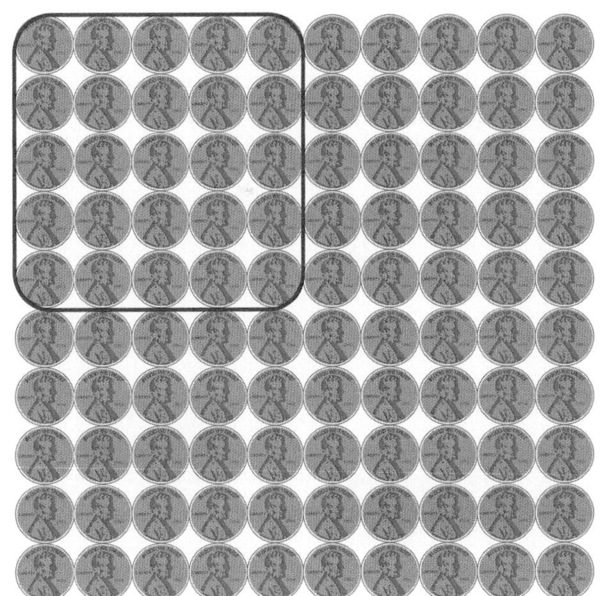

This model should be expanded to illustrate a wide range of percents, such as 50 percent, 90 percent, 5 percent, 100 percent, 99 percent, 1 percent, and 200 percent. These percents should be illustrated with a variety of different situations and models. For example, a meter stick provides an easily accessible and effective model. Cover part of the

Math Links 13.5

An electronic model, called *Fraction Pie,* helps demonstrate the connection among fractions, decimals, and percents using a number line and a circle, rectangle, or set model. You can access this site from this book's web site.

meter stick with blue paper and ask children to estimate the percent of the meter stick that is covered.

Students could be shown the meter stick face down (if the scale is on both sides, cover one side with masking tape) and then asked:

> Estimate what percent of the meter stick is blue.
>
> About what percent of the meter stick is not blue?
>
> How can you check your estimate? [Turn the stick over.]

This model allows many different situations (25%, 50%, 1%, and so forth) to be presented and discussed quickly. Patterns may also emerge as students realize that the sum of the covered and uncovered portions always totals 100 percent. Shaded fraction circles (Appendix B) can also be used to provide multiple representations and help students see connections between fractions and percents.

A related activity involving area could have students using a stack of 20 cards with the B-side down. On the A side, specific percents of the card are colored red (0%, 10%, 20%, . . . , 100%), with the remainder (100%, . . . , 0%) white.

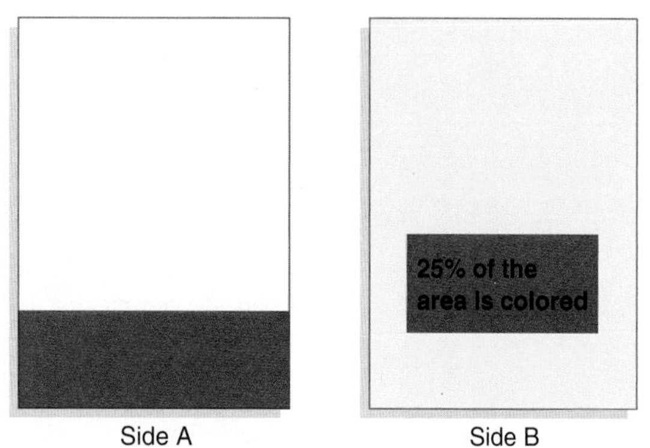

Ask students to take turns trying to win cards by looking only at side A and trying to predict the percents shown on side B.

Geoboards (Appendix B) also may be used to model percents. Lesson Idea 13-1 provides some additional tasks that use models to develop important concepts about percent. Each of these tasks provides ideas that can be used to relate percents and fractions.

These early experiences with percent should be followed by activities that center on direct translation experiences involving 100. The national assessment data revealed that only 31 percent of seventh graders could correctly write the decimals 0.42 and 0.9, respectively, as percents. These data are reminders of the fragile nature of students' understanding and the importance of connecting percents with decimals and fractions. Having students use base-ten blocks or share decimal paper (Appendix B) provides another concrete model for percents and helps students see the connections between decimals and percents.

Figure 13-9 illustrates how the same diagram can be represented symbolically by a fraction, a decimal, and a percent. It should be emphasized that each small square represents 1 percent and the large square represents 100 percent. Practice activities using this model to convert percents to fractions and decimals, and vice versa, should be plentiful. For example, Figure 13-9 provides a visual reminder that 17 percent can also be thought of as $17 \times \frac{1}{100}$, so the symbol % can be thought of as equivalent to the fraction $\frac{1}{100}$. Also, 17 percent can be thought of as $\frac{17}{100}$, so the concept of ratio is reinforced. This approach helps students feel comfortable with different interpretations of percent. Calculators that convert fractions, decimals, and percents are useful when students are discovering patterns and relationships.

The importance of establishing 100 as the base for percent cannot be overemphasized. Also, 50 percent should be recognized as the fraction $\frac{50}{100}$ or the product $50 \times \frac{1}{100}$. It is also important that students know that an infinite number of equivalent fractions ($\frac{1}{2}, \frac{2}{4}, \frac{3}{6}, \ldots, \frac{50}{100}, \ldots$) also represent 50%.

In the Classroom 13-4 provides a natural means of developing some important ideas in an informal and yet meaningfully structured way. Each of the four activities should further develop children's concept of percent. Activities B, C, and D require some collection and recording of data before reporting the percents. The use of three different base numbers (10 logs, 100 pennies, and 20 chips) helps strengthen the link between ratio and percent. Even though answers on each activity

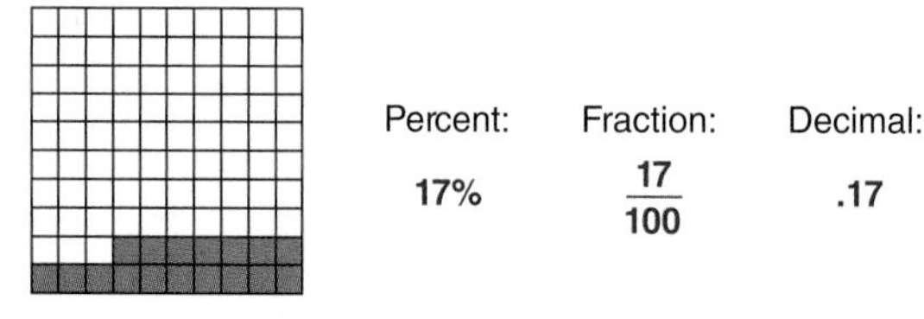

FIGURE 13-9 Models and symbolizations of 17%.

Lesson Idea 13-1

USING PERCENT MODELS

Objective: Students explore models that develop percent concepts.

Grade Level: 5–6

Materials: Several different models, each of which displays clearly the 100 parts in a whole.

Activity: Pose additional questions to accompany the following teacher-led discussions.

1. **Construct a model that has 100 parts but at the same time has the potential of displaying equivalent subsets of these 100 elements. Here are two models:**

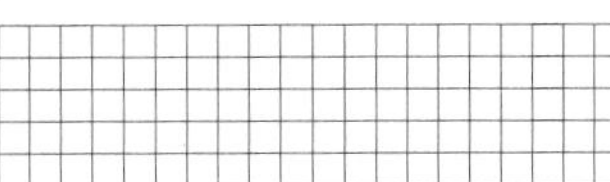

Rope with 100 discs arranged 10 pink, 10 purple, 10 pink, 10 purple, ...

Rectangle 5 × 20 with all small squares as shown.

2. **Find representations of various percents on each model. For example, when representing 50 percent, help students realize that any 50 of the parts could be chosen—for example, in either of the two ways shown here:**

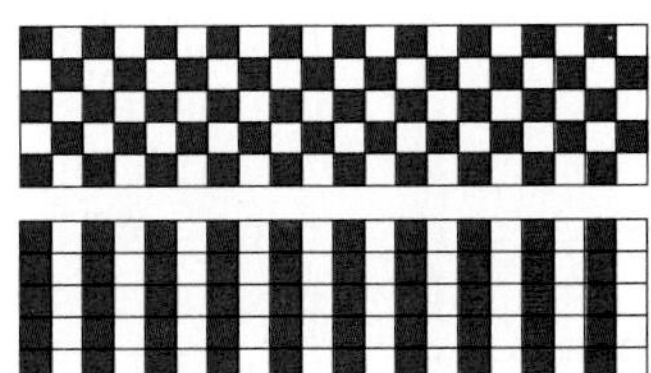

3. **Have students consider the model as a whole and ask for all the fractions that show the same amount as 50 percent. Write the results on the board:**

Fifty percent: 50%

$\frac{1}{2}$ $\frac{50}{100}$ $\frac{5}{10}$

4. **Repeat using 20 percent:**

Twenty percent: 20%

$\frac{2}{10}$ $\frac{1}{5}$ $\frac{20}{100}$

5. **Compare the representations for 50 percent and 20 percent on each model. Ask questions such as**
   - **Which is greater, 50 or 20 percent?**
   - **What fractional part is covered by 20 percent?**
   - **What fractional part remains uncovered?**
6. **Any multiple of 10 can be illustrated easily with these models. Continue to model different percents and their corresponding fractions until generalizations of these relationships are established.**

depend on the data recorded, some patterns will emerge. A few questions from the teacher should trigger some stimulating discussion. For example, do the percents in each item total 100 percent? Why does this happen? Can you think of a time when it would not?

One particularly troublesome aspect of percents involves small percents between 0 percent and 1

In the Classroom 13-4

USING PERCENTS

OBJECTIVE: **Using different models to relate quantities to percent.**

GRADE LEVEL: **4–5**

A. Color this circle:
- 25% red
- 50% blue

What percent is uncolored? ____

B. Use 3 colors:
- Blue
- Green
- Yellow

Color each log with only one color.
Color all logs.

	Number Colored	Percent Colored
Blue	____	____
Green	____	____
Yellow	____	____

C. Take 100 pennies, shake, and toss them in a box. Count the number of heads.

	Number	Percent
Heads	____	____
Tails	____	____

Did you need to count the tails? ____

D. Here are 20 poker chips. Count the number of each color.

	Number	Percent
Red	____	____
Blue	____	____
White	____	____

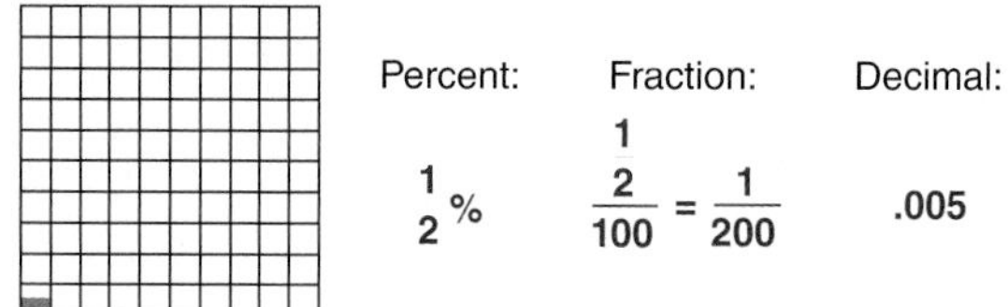

Percent:
Fraction:
Decimal:
$\frac{1}{2}$%
$\frac{\frac{1}{2}}{100} = \frac{1}{200}$
.005

FIGURE 13-10 Model and symbolizations of $\frac{1}{2}$%.

percent. For example, $\frac{1}{2}$ percent, as in "$\frac{1}{2}$ percent milk fat," is not well understood. A visual representation, as in Figure 13-10, can help show that $\frac{1}{2}$ percent is indeed less than 1 percent. Understanding rests on the earlier agreement that each small square represents 1 percent, which cannot be mentioned too often. As is true with all percents, this percent also can be shown symbolically as a fraction or a decimal. However, it is more important in elementary school to establish the intuitive notion of relative size of small percents than to devote extensive time to the algebraic gymnastics of showing the fraction and decimal equivalents.

Development of percents greater than 100 percent also is challenging and should be illustrated with models. Once the idea is established that a given region represents 100 percent, more than one such region can be used to represent percents greater than 100 percent. For example, 234 percent could be represented by two completely shaded large squares and a partially shaded one (see Figure 13-11). Using every opportunity to show equivalence of percents, fractions, and decimals helps establish and maintain these relationships.

Applying Percents

In elementary school, students should solve percent problems meaningfully and avoid rushing toward symbolic methods. Whenever possible, students should be asked to discuss how to solve percent problems mentally, using what they know about common percent benchmarks. Even when a formal method is required, using informal methods first to obtain an estimate will help students focus on the reasonableness of formal results.

Although percents are regularly encountered in many real-life problem-solving situations, only three basic types of problems involve percents. Several different formal methods can be used to solve percent problems; two methods typically found in elementary and middle school textbooks are equation and ratio, both of which utilize algebraic thinking. The effective use of these methods requires a firm understanding of the concepts of percent and ratio as well as the ability to solve simple equations and proportions. Such skills are developed over a period of several years and need not be rushed.

In the equation method, the following equation is used:

$$\text{percent} \times \text{total} = \text{part}$$

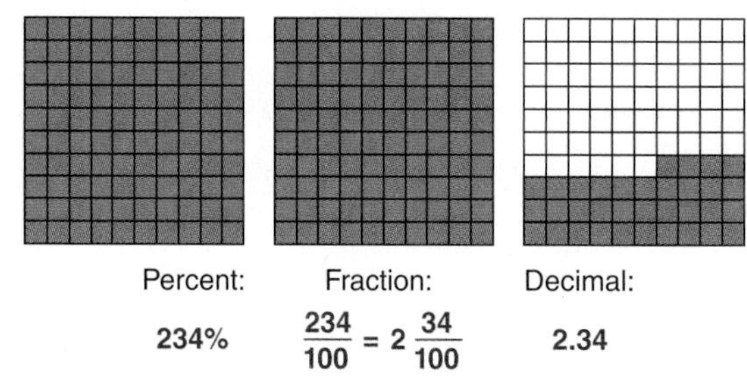

FIGURE 13-11 Model and symbolizations of 234%.

Math Links 13.6

An electronic manipulative, *Percent Gauge*, solves the three types of percent problems using the ratio method and displays shaded figures as a model. You can access this manipulative from this book's web site.

The two known values are placed in the equation and then students solve the equation for the third, unknown value.

In the ratio method, a (part) is b (percent) of c (total). The variables are set up as equal ratios or a proportion:

$$\frac{b\,(\text{percent})}{100} = \frac{a\,(\text{part})}{c\,(\text{total})}$$

Students place the three known values into the proportion and solve for the fourth, unknown value.

Now let's take a brief look at each of the three types of percent problems and how they may be solved using both informal and formal methods:

1. **Finding the percent of a given number.**

   Lucas receives $60 per month for a paper route. Next month he will get a 10 percent raise. How much will his raise be?

   The context of this problem suggests that the raise will be something considerably less than $60. The situation might be solved mentally or modeled as shown in Figure 13-12.

   This problem could also be solved in these ways:

   Ratio method: $\frac{10\%}{100\%} = \frac{R}{60}$ $\quad R = \$6$

   Equation method: $R = 10\%$ of $\$60$
   $R = .1 \times 160$
   $= \$6$

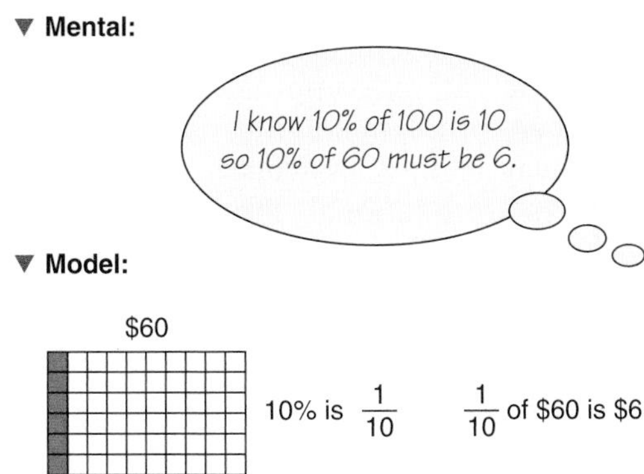

FIGURE 13-12 Use of mental strategy or model for finding a percent of a number.

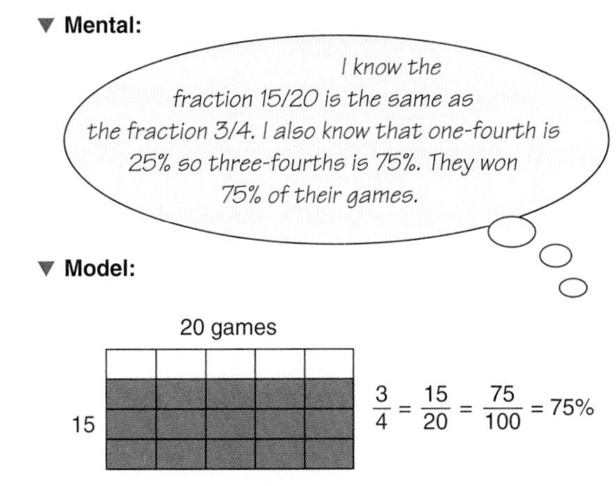

▼ Mental:
I know 10% of 100 is 10 so 10% of 60 must be 6.
I know the fraction 15/20 is the same as the fraction 3/4. I also know that one-fourth is 25% so three-fourths is 75%. They won 75% of their games.
▼ Model:
1/10 of $60 is $6
20 games
15
3/4 = 15/20 = 75/100 = 75%

FIGURE 13-13 Use of mental strategy or model for finding what percent one number is of another number.

The computation is simple and may disguise the level of difficulty this type of problem presents. Only about one-third of seventh graders were successful at solving this type of problem on the fourth national assessment.

2. **Find what percent one number is of another number.**

   The Cardinals won 15 of their 20 games. What percent did they win?

   Intuitively, it is clear that the Cardinals did not win all of their games, so the answer must be less than 100 percent. Similarly, they won more than half of their games, so it must be more than 50 percent. The situation could be solved mentally or modeled as shown in Figure 13-13.

   Here are two other ways to find the solution:

   Ratio method: $\frac{P\%}{100\%} = \frac{15}{20}$ $\quad P = 75\%$

   Equation method: $P \times 20 = 15$
   $P = \frac{15}{20} \times 5$
   $= \frac{75}{100} = 75\%$

Once again the computation is easy, but the national assessment provides a reminder of the difficulty students have with percent. For example, 43 percent of seventh graders correctly answered "30 is what percent of 60?" but only 20 percent correctly answered "9 is what percent of 225?"

3. **Find the total (100%) when only a percent is known.**

   The sale price on a coat was $40 and it was marked down 50%. What was its original price?

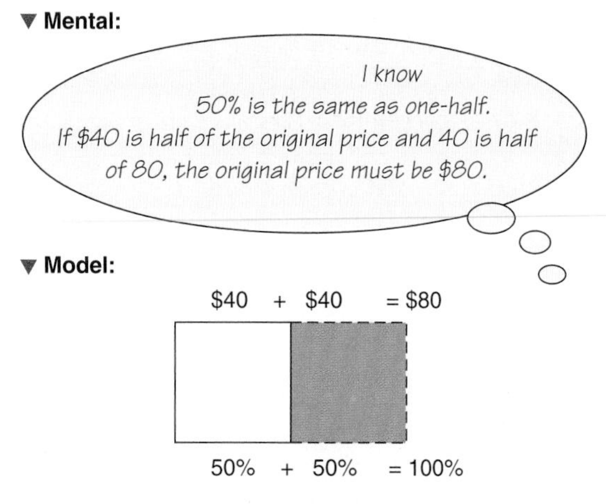

FIGURE 13-14 Use of mental strategy or model for finding the total when only a percent is known.

Common sense suggests that the original price should be more than \$40. Guess-and-test is often a very effective strategy in solving this type of problem. For example, if children guess an original price of \$60, then the sale price of \$30 is too low. Still, they are on the right track, and if they continue this approach, it will eventually lead to the correct price of \$80. The problem could be solved mentally or modeled as shown in Figure 13-14. The model provides a base for either of these solutions, where *OP* is the original price:

Ratio method: $$\frac{50\%}{100\%} = \frac{\$40}{OP} \qquad OP = \$80$$

Equation method: $$50\% \text{ of OP} = \$40$$
$$\text{OP} = \frac{\$40}{50} \times 2$$
$$= \frac{80}{100} = 80\%$$

This type of problem is typically more difficult to solve, as was confirmed by results from the fourth national mathematics assessment (Lindquist et al., 1988). Less than 22 percent of seventh graders correctly answered a question of this type.

The consistently poor performance on percent problems means that instruction must become more meaningful. If emphasis is placed on a particular method before the problem is thought through and well understood, the result will probably be confusion and poor performance. Instructional emphasis in elementary school must be on thinking aloud and talking about what should be done and what a reasonable answer would be. These teacher-led discussions should occur before any serious efforts are made to solve the problem with pencil and paper. Early emphasis on writing a solution to a percent problem forces many students to operate mechanically (without any conscious thinking) on the numbers to produce an answer.

Students should be encouraged to think quantitatively in solving problems involving percent. Research does not support the teaching of a single method (such as ratio or equation) to solve such problems. Instruction, therefore, should be flexible and not locked into a single method. Research also recommends that teachers present a variety of problems involving percent and then follow student leads flexibly toward solutions. More specifically, some verbalization of the solution should accompany the actual problem-solving process. This helps clarify what was done (right or wrong) and provides some closure to the process. It also promotes consideration of the reasonableness of an answer.

This less formal, intuitive approach lacks the structure and security of emphasizing a particular method, but it has several important advantages. In particular, it encourages students to understand the problem in their own minds along with possible solutions and decreases the likelihood of their applying a method blindly.

A Glance at Where We've Been

Ratios compare two or more numbers. They take different forms and have many applications; money (pennies for nickels), measurements (12 inches in a foot), consumer purchases (3 for 29¢), scale drawings, and blueprints are but a few. Together with proportion, ratios provide an opportunity to practice many computational skills as well as strengthen problem-solving skills. Proportions provide a way to find answers to problems where the numbers are relational. Proportional reasoning is an important skill for students to gain because it facilitates algebraic thinking. Ratios and proportions also provide a natural means of studying percent, which has a comparison base of 100. Because few mathematical topics have more practical usage than percents, it is essential that meaningful and systematic development of percent be provided. Instruction should include the use of concrete models that support the development of number sense.

Things to Do: From What You've Read

1. Give a real-life example of a ratio and a proportion. How could you help children distinguish between them?
2. Describe how estimating the number of heartbeats in an hour or in a lifetime uses ratios. How could you use a calculator or a spreadsheet to solve the problem?
3. Describe how proportions could be used to compare two products: If a 24-ounce can of pears sells for $1.90 and a second 32-ounce can of pears sells for $2.65, which one is the better buy?
4. Describe how you could use a meter stick, graduated in millimeters, to illustrate each of the following percents:
   a. 35 percent
   b. 3.5 percent
   c. 0.35 percent
5. Make up a story for each of these sentences:
   a. $\frac{5}{12} = \frac{x}{\$180}$
   b. 40% of 95 =
6. Rose was making $34,000 per year. She received a 10 percent raise. Later in the year, the company started losing money and reduced all salaries by 10 percent. Rose said, "I'm making less money than last year." Is her thinking correct? Tell why.
7. Here is a partially completed chart:

Decimal	Fraction	Percent
—	—	5%
.1	$\frac{1}{10}$	10%
—	$\frac{1}{4}$	—
.333 ...	—	—
.5	—	—
—	2/3	—
—	—	.75

   Explain why it would be helpful to have students learn these popular percents and their related fraction and decimal forms.
8. Describe how you would think through a solution to this problem: The population of a city increased from 200,000 to 220,000. What is the percent increase? Demonstrate two different ways to solve the problem.
9. Suppose you ask a student to enlarge the 1-by-2 rectangle shown here and a 2-by-4 rectangle is correctly produced. Then you ask the student to enlarge it again so the base is 6. The student draws a 4-by-6 rectangle and says, "If I doubled it, the base would have been 8, so I added 2 on and the other side is 4." Would you say this student is an "adder" or a "multiplier"? Describe some additional questions you might ask to gain more insight into this student's understanding of ratio.

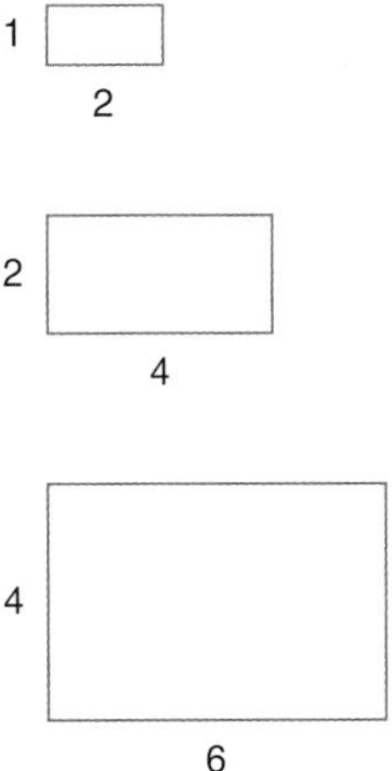

Things to Do: Going Beyond This Book

IN THE FIELD

1. **Finding Out about Proportions.* Ask several fifth or sixth graders this question: "A design is 2 cm wide and 2.4 cm long. If the picture is to be enlarged so that it is 5 cm wide, how long will it be?" Ask them to explain their reasoning and answer. Check to see if students tended to be "adders" (i.e., added 3 cm to the dimensions, thus getting 5 cm wide and 5.4 cm long). If they modeled the solution correctly and used multiplication, report the thinking they used.
2. **Know Your Coins.* In the Classroom 13-1 provides a structured activity for exploring patterns and connecting them to ratio. Use this activity as a guide to ask a fifth or sixth grader a series of questions. What patterns seemed to be the strongest? Explain how experiencing this activity would help develop the notion of ratio.

*Additional activities, suggestions, or questions are provided in *Teaching Elementary Mathematics: A Resource for Field Experiences* (Wiley, 2004).

3. **Finding Out about Percents.* Ask fifth or sixth graders some of these questions: What is 50% of $80? What is 100% of 50? What does the $\frac{1}{2}$% on a milk carton mean? Is it possible to get a raise of 200%? In each question, ask them to explain their thinking. Do you think they have a good understanding of percent? Tell why. You can find more percent work samples on Masters 13-5 to 13-8 in *Helping Children Learn Mathematics Instructor's* Manual (available at the Wiley web site). Use these samples to increase your understanding of students' percent development.

IN YOUR JOURNAL

4. Ratios may be used to determine the best buy. Use local newspaper advertisements to find information and set up ratios to compare prices for different sizes of the same product. Respond in your jounral to this question: Can you refute the claim "the larger the quantity, the lower the unit price"?

WITH ADDITIONAL READINGS

5. *Ratio and Proportion.* Review *The Wonderful World of Mathematics* (Thiessen and Matthias, 1998). Several books focus on multiplication and division and use these concepts to develop ratio or proportion. Choose one of the books to read with some children and describe how they reacted.
6. Read the article "Proportional Reasoning" by Miller and Fey (2000) or any article from the *2002 NCTM Yearbook.* Describe instructional suggestions they offer from research to help students better understand proportions.
7. Read the article, "Our Diets May Be Killing Us" by Shannon (1995), "Diet, Ratios, Proportions: A Healthy Mix" by Telese and Abete (2002), or "Integrating Mathematics and Literature in the Elementary Classroom" by Kliman (1993). Describe how you could use ideas like those to make a ratio or percent lesson.
8. Describe how the white, red, purple, and brown Cuisenaire rods (Appendix B) could be used to develop ratios. Describe several different equivalent ratios that could be made with these rods. See the article "Percentages and Cuisenaire Rods" by Erickson (1990) as an example of an activity.
9. Read the articles, "Toys 'R' Math" (Tracy and Hague, 1997) or "Children's Literature: Impetus for a Mathematical Adventure" (Gibbons, 1996). Discuss some ways these stories might be used to help students understand ratio and proportion.
10. Read the article, "Teaching Percentage: Ideas and Suggestions" (Glatzer, 1984). Try his shortcuts to solve some percent problems mentally. You can find a summary of these shortcuts on Master 13-3 in the *Helping Children Learn Mathematics Instructor's Manual* (available at the Wiley web site).

WITH TECHONOLOGY RESOURCES

11. Develop a spreadsheet similar to those in the article by Hoeffner et al. (1990) that allows children to solve some real-life ratio and percent problems.

Book Nook for Children

Anno, Mitsumasa. *Anno's Math Games.* New York: Philomel Books, 1987.
Uses proportion to compare the relative numbers of sugar cubes in different-sized containers. A wealth of ideas appear in this book that can be extended to a number of situations; for this reason, it may be desirable to explore one chapter at a time.

Clement, Rod. *Counting on Frank.* Milwaukee, WI: Gareth Stevens Children's Books, 1991.
Frank (a dog) and his young owner (who wears sunglasses just like his dog's) are the stars of this outstanding book that engages students in estimation. Each double-page spread with its hilarious illustrations shows the two companions investigating new and outlandish situations. The family, including the ever-present Frank, sits surrounded by green peas to illustrate the estimate, "If I had accidentally knocked fifteen peas off my plate every night for the last eight years, they would now be level with the table."

Giganti, Jr., Paul. *Each Orange Had 8 Slices: A Counting Book.* New York: Greenwillow Books, 1992.
If each orange has eight slices and each slice has two seeds, how many seeds are there in all? You can multiply, add, or count your way through the math puzzles hiding in the world all around you.

Parker, Tom. *In One Day.* Boston, MA: Houghton Mifflin, 1984.
Three hundred sixty-five statistics describe things Americans do in one day. Topics included are data on health, spending habits, accidents, crime, and our environment. Often the data are presented in a descriptive manner involving comparisons. Fact 312 states, "Americans need 115 million gallons of drinking water to quench their thirst. Imagine a tumbler of ice water 500 feet tall and 200 feet in diameter. Other illustrations use ratio dramatically to show data; the nation's daily consumption of 23 million gallons of soft drinks is depicted as a large soda bottle overshadowing the Statue of Liberty."

Schwartz, David M. *If You Made a Million.* New York: Lothrop, Lee & Shepherd Books, 1989.
Examples illustrated by Marvelosissimo, the Mathematical Magician, and his eight friends include tasks to earn a particular amount of money, such as feed the fish to earn one penny or bake a cake to earn \$5. Also, the examples include items to buy, such as a hippopotamus for \$1,000 or tickets to the moon for \$1,000,000. Photographs of coins and bills show relationships; one dollar bill equals 4 quarters, 10 dimes, 20 nickels, or 100 pennies. As the denominations get larger, comparisons are used; a fifty-foot stack of pennies would be \$100; a school bus filled with nickels would be \$1,000,000. Marvelosissimo and his friends also become involved with writing checks and earning interest on money deposited in a bank.

ANNOTATED BOOKS

Burns, Marilyn. *The I Hate Mathematics! Book.* Boston, MA: Little, Brown & Co., 1975.
"Street Math" and "Things to Do When You Have the Flu" are two of the chapters in this challenging book that sets out to show the reader how much fun mathematics can be. Each page presents one or more intriguing facts, questions, or experiments involving ratios, volume, estimation and measurement, spatial relationships, clock arithmetic, strategy games, and probability. The text is upbeat, and drawings add humor and clarity.

Curcio, Frances R., and Bezuk, Nadine S. *Understanding Rational Numbers and Proportions (Curriculum and Evaluation Standards for School Mathematics Addenda Series, Grades 5–8).* Reston, VA: National Council of Teachers of Mathematics, 1994.
The purpose of this document is to provide teachers with ideas and materials to support the implementation of the *NCTM Standards.* This book presents several topics and activities to exemplify the *NCTM Standards* and provides examples to help students make the transition from elementary to high school mathematics.

Laithwaite, Eric. *Size: The Measure of Things.* New York: Franklin Watts, 1988.
Interestingly written, clear and helpful pictures complement text and diagrams provide highly informative reading and reference. The author presents size in terms of relationships: scaling, size ranges, size and time, length and frequency, biggest and smallest, size in numbers, complexity, and so on, with attention in each instance both to natural contexts and to human creations. The numerous examples exploring the relative size of area, volume, speed, distances, and sets can help students develop references and comparisons for number.

National Council of Teachers of Mathematics. *Making Sense of Fractions, Ratios, and Proportions: 2002* Yearbook, Bonnie Litwiller and George Bright (Eds.). Reston, VA: NCTM, 2002.
Chapter 14 in this yearbook by Thompson, Austin, and Beckmann provides ideas on using literature to explore proportional reasoning. Other chapters in the book provide ideas for teaching fractions, ratios, and proportions. The book emphasizes that fractions, ratios, and proportion are pivotal concepts in the middle school but that their development and understanding begin in the elementary school and shows the importance of proportional reasoning as a foundation of many applications of mathematics to real life and as an essential element of more sophisticated mathematics.

Thiessen, Diane, and Matthias, Margaret. *The Wonderful World of Mathematics: A Critically Annotated List of Children's Books in Mathematics.* Reston, VA: NCTM, 1998.
The NCTM formed a committee to review childrens' books with an eye toward how they could be used in mathematics. This list is annotated by grade level, and each book is identified as fitting into one of four categories (early number concepts, number, measurement, and geometry).

ANNOTATED ARTICLES

Bennett, Albert B., and Nelson, Ted. "A Conceptual Model for Solving Percent Problems." *Mathematics Teaching in the Middle School,* 1 (April 1994), pp. 20–25.
This article demonstrates a way to use a 10-by-10 grid to solve percent problems and offers different methods to finding solutions.

Fujimura, Nobuyuki. "Facilitating Children's Proportional Reasoning: A Model of Reasoning Processes and Effects of Intervention on Strategy Change." *Journal of Educational Psychology,* 93 (2001), pp. 589–603.
This research project studied 140 fourth graders as they solved proportion problems in juice-mixing after an intervention of one of a number of models. The findings indicate that different approaches are particularly helpful, depending on where students are having difficulty.

Glatzer, David J. "Teaching Percentage: Ideas and Suggestions." *Arithmetic Teacher,* 31 (February 1984), pp. 24–26.
Glatzer presents teaching ideas for percentage, patterns in percentages, percentages as ratios, and fractional percentages.

Miller, Jane L., and Fey, James T. "Proportional Reasoning." *Mathematics Teaching in the Middle School,* 5 (5), (January 2000), pp. 310–314.
This article looks at strategies to develop proportional reasoning among students and discusses a study to compare proportional reasoning of students in a standards-based program with students in a control group.

ADDITIONAL REFERENCES

Cramer, Kathleen; Post, Thomas; and Currier, Sarah. "Learning and Teaching Ratio and Proportion: Research Implications." In *Research Ideas for the Classroom: Middle Grades Mathematics* (ed. Douglas T. Owens). Reston, VA: NCTM; and New York: Macmillan, 1993, pp. 159–178.

Erickson, Dianne. "Percentages and Cuisenaire Rods." *Mathematics Teacher,* 83, (November 1990), pp. 648–654.

Gay, Susan, and Aichele, Douglas B. "Middle School Students' Understanding of Number Sense Related to Percent." *School Science and Mathematics,* 97 (January 1997), pp. 27–36.

Gibbons, Estelle. "Children's Literature: Impetus for a Mathematical Adventure." *Teaching Children Mathematics,* 3 (November 1996), pp. 142–147.

Hoeffner, Karl; Kendall, Monica; Stellenwerf, Cheryl; Thames, Pixie; and Williams, Patricia. "Problem Solving with a Spreadsheet." *Arithmetic Teacher,* 38 (November 1990), pp. 52–56.

Kliman, Marlene. "Integrating Mathematics and Literature in the Elementary Classroom." *Arithmetic Teacher,* 40 (February 1993), pp. 318–321.

Lembke, Linda O., and Reys, Barbara J. "The Development of, and Interaction between, Intuitive and School-Taught Ideas about Percent." *Journal for Research in Mathematics Education,* 25 (May 1994), pp. 237–259.

Lesh, Richard.; Post, Thomas.; and Behr, Merlyn. (1998). "Proportional reasoning." In J. Hiebert and M. Behr (Eds.), *Number Concepts and Operations in the Middle Grades* (pp. 93–118). Reston, Va.: National Council of Teachers of Mathematics.

Lindquist, Mary M.; Brown, Catherine A.; Carpenter, Thomas P.; Kouba, Vicky L.; Silver, Edward A.; and Swafford, Jane O. *Results from the Fourth Mathematics Assessment of the National Assessment of Educational Progress.* Reston, VA.: NCTM, 1988.

National Research Council. *Adding it Up.* J. Kilpatrick, J. Swafford, and B. Findell (Eds). Mathematics Learning Study Committee, Center for Education, Division of Behavioral and Social Sciences and Education. Washington, DC: National Academy Press, 2001.

Shannon, Brenda K. "Our Diets May Be Killing Us." *Mathematics Teaching in the Middle School,* 1 (April–May 1995), pp. 376–382.

Telese, James A., and Abete, Jr. Jesse. "Diet, Ratios, Proportions: A Healthy Mix." *Mathematics Teaching in the Middle School,* 8 (September 2002), pp. 8–13.

Thompson, D.; Austin, R.; and Beckmann, C. "Using Literature as a Vehicle to Explore Proportional Reasoning." In *Making Sense of Fractions, Ratios, and Proportions (2002 Yearbook)* (eds. Bonnie Litwiller and George Bright). Reston, Va: NCTM, 2002, pp. 130–137.

Tracy, Dyanne M., and Hague, Mary S. "Toys 'R' Math." *Mathematics Teaching in the Middle School,* 2 (January 1997), pp. 141–145.

Wiebe, James H. "Manipulating Percentages." *Mathematics Teacher,* 79 (January 1986), pp. 23–26.

CHAPTER 14

Patterns, Relationships, and Algebraic Thinking

Snapshot of a Lesson

Mr. Trynka posed the following mathematics problem to his fifth graders:

> The Doggone-It Pet Shop wants to build pens for different kinds of puppies. The shop will build the pens according to the following diagram provided to the lumberyard. How many panels are needed to build 5 pens? How many panels are needed to build 7 pens?

1 pen with 4 sides

2 pens with 7 sides

3 pens with 10 sides

To help the students think about the problem, Mr. Trynka suggested that the students begin by thinking about the number of sides of the pens needed as more and more pens are built. He provided each student with a bag of toothpicks to build a model of the pens. The students were asked to make a conjecture about the number of sides needing construction as the number of pens increased.

After the children considered the problem, building different models to develop their conjecture, Mr. Trynka called on four students to demonstrate their thinking at the board.

Chia-Lin drew:

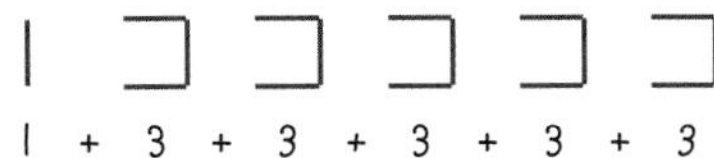

She explained that putting the pieces together would make 5 puppy pens. "So the number of toothpicks to build five pens would be 16."

Oscar drew a different diagram:

"I thought about the problem in a different way:

6 sides

5 tops

5 bottoms

That makes it 16 toothpicks."

Arlinda added to the discussion: "I made a pattern by imagining the pens: four toothpicks for the first pen. The next 4 pens each need 3 toothpicks. So $4 + 3 + 3 + 3 + 3 = 16$.

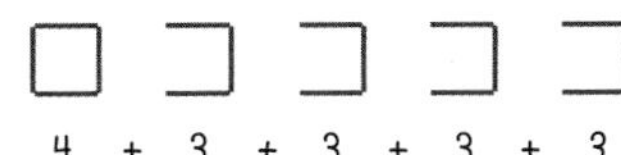

Juan said, "I thought about the problem differently. This is my diagram."

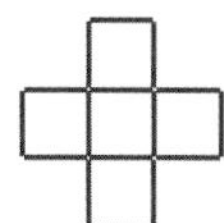

There are 4 toothpicks in the middle pen plus 3 toothpicks in each of the outside pens. That gives me $4 + 3 \times 4 = 16$ toothpicks and five pens.

Since each of the students provided a different way to think about this problem, Mr. Trynka asked the class to work in pairs to extend the different models for building seven pens.

Jason and Karina volunteered to show how to extend Chia-Lin's model. They demonstrated that with each new pen to be added, the amount of lumber would be increased by the amount needed to build three additional sides.

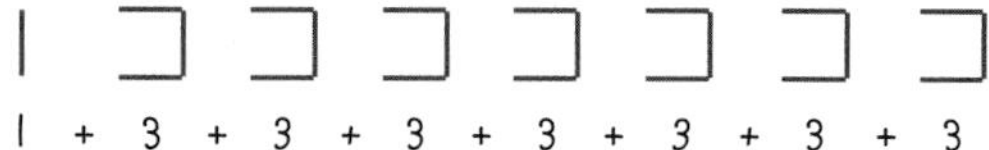

Matt and Marina extended Arlinda's model, showing its similarity to Chia-Lin's model. They showed that the only difference was in how the pattern began. The first pen consisted of four sides rather than thinking of 1 side and then three additional sides. Adding three sides created each additional pen.

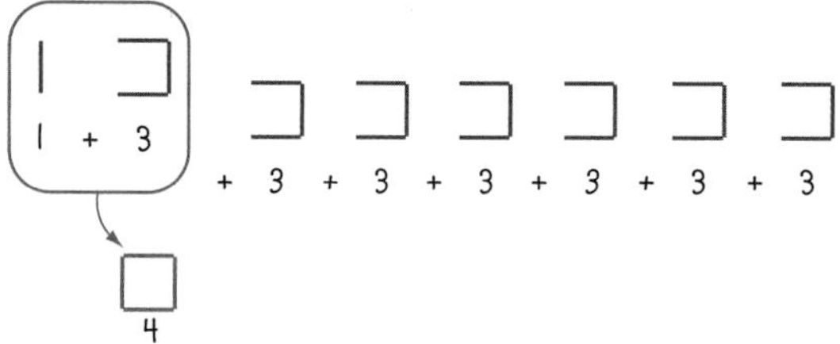

Sharon and Julie extended Oscar's model on the board, showing that to construct an additional pen, they would need one additional side, one additional top and one additional bottom.

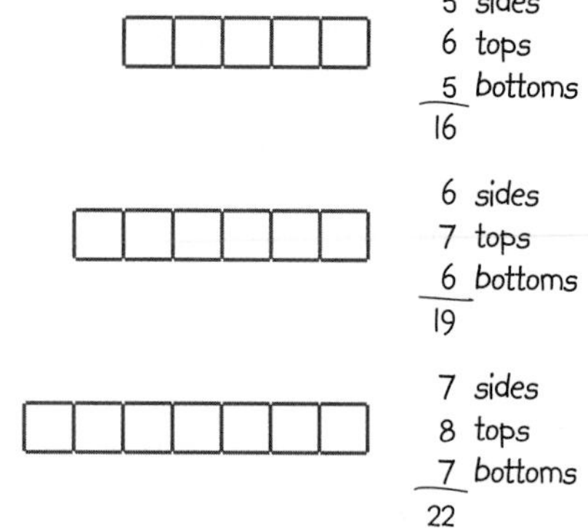

After these models were discussed, Mr. Trynka asked, "Are the models the same, since they had the same result?"

JASON: Yes, in each model, three additional sides are added for each pen. So these models are adding 3 sides with each pen. But, we can't figure out where to put the pens for Juan's model.

Jason's partner Tauni drew two different possibilities for the next pen on Juan's model on the board.

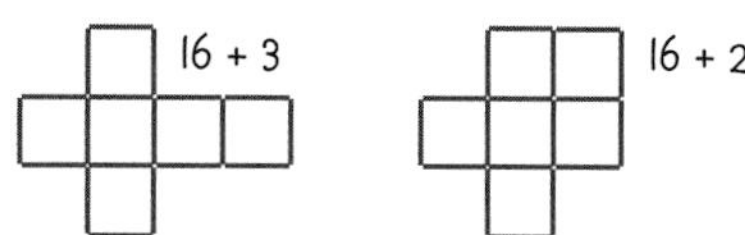

TAUNI: Unless we agree where the next pen goes, we don't know how to extend this model. We could make it work to be $4 + 3 \times 5$ for the first diagram. But, we aren't sure that is what we are supposed to do.

MR. TRYNKA: If you use your first idea would it be the same as the other models?

JASON: Well, yes, because we would be adding multiples of three just like they did. But, I think we have to agree on how the pens are to be added to know for sure.

Introduction

Students in the upper elementary grades often form early opinions about algebra, calling it "the math where you move symbols around," or "hard arithmetic," or sometimes "the math that uses symbols because you do not know what you are talking about." How do students get these ideas? If they already have these ideas, what is the rationale for suggesting a shift in the mathematics curriculum to designing algebra as a strand beginning early at pre-kindergarten and extending through grade 12?

Math Links 14.1

The full-text electronic version of the Algebra standard is available at the NCTM's web site. Click on pre-K–2, 3–5, or 6–8 to read more about this standard.

Historically, the study of algebra has been delayed to a time when students have demonstrated a solid foundation in arithmetic. In the 1990s, a shift in thinking about how students learn algebra began to emerge. The February 1997 Special Issues of *Teaching Children Mathematics, Mathematics Teaching in the Middle School,* and *Mathematics Teacher* focused on algebraic thinking and ways that children can be engaged in experiences and activities to foster the development of algebraic thought. With the *Principles and Standards for School Mathematics* (NCTM, 2000), a new direction for algebra is recommended in the Algebra standard (see Figure 14-1).

As described by the NCTM, "The Algebra Standard emphasizes relationships among quantities, including functions, ways of representing mathematical relationships, and the analysis of change" (2000, p. 37). The ideas in the standard are recommended for helping children build a solid foundation of understanding connected with other areas of mathematics, including geometry and data analysis. Also, algebraic thinking is preparation for more advanced work in mathematics in the

Instructional programs should enable all students to:	Pre-K–2 Expectations All students should:	Grades 3–5 Expectations All students should:
• Understand patterns, relations, and functions	• Sort, classify, and order objects by size, number, and other properties • Recognize, describe, and extend patterns such as sequences of sounds and shapes or simple numeric patterns and translate from one representation to another • Analyze how both repeat and growing patterns are generated	• Describe, extend, and make generalizations about geometric and numeric patterns • Represent and analyze patterns and functions, using words, tables, and graphs
• Represent and analyze mathematical situations and structures using algebraic symbols	• Illustrate general principles and properties of operations, such as commutativity, using specific numbers • Use concrete, pictorial, and verbal representations to develop an understanding of invented and conventional symbolic notations	• Identify such properties as commutativity, associativity, and distributivity and use them to compute with whole numbers • Represent the idea of a variable as an unknown quantity using a letter or a symbol • Express mathematical relationships using equations
• Use mathematical models to represent and understand quantitative relationship	• Model situations that involve the addition and subtraction of whole numbers, using objects, pictures, and symbols	• Model problem situations with objects and use representations such as graphs, tables, and equations to draw conclusions
• Analyze change in various contexts	• Describe qualitative change, such as a student's growing taller • Describe quantitative change, such as a student's growing two inches in one year	• Investigate how a change in one variable relates to a change in a second variable • Identify and describe situations with constant or varying rates of change and compare them

FIGURE 14-1 Algebra Standard with expectations for children in grades prekindergarten–2 and 3–5.

Math Links 14.2

A variety of Web resources for algebra that may be used by teachers and children may be found at NCTM's Illuminations web site under the Algebra Standard.

middle grades and high school. From the early grades, algebraic thinking evolves through directed experiences with patterns and the use of multiple representations. Rather than emphasizing symbolic representations of ideas, children use graphs, words, pictures, tables, and numbers to represent their understanding of mathematical ideas and relationships. As their ability to communicate about the relationships evolves, they create their own symbols to express the ideas. Their algebraic thinking or reasoning grows as they think about and make connections to describe repeating or growing patterns. As children solve problems in which they analyze patterns and relationships, using words, tables, equations, and graphs, their algebraic thinking skills emerge and expand. As they investigate mathematical models and analyze changes in various contexts, their algebraic thinking develops. As students communicate their thinking about specific relationships, their understanding of the language of algebra grows along with their algebraic thinking.

The development of algebraic thinking is an essential consideration in the Algebra Standard. From the *Snapshot*, the children in Mr. Trynka's class were engaged in algebraic thinking as they thought about how the number of sides changed as the number of pens increased. They were challenged by Mr. Trynka to consider the equivalence of their various descriptions. They were beginning to generalize their patterns as they discussed the growth.

This look at Mr. Trynka's students' thinking highlights three important aspects of algebraic thinking—change, generalization, and equality. The students were focused on the change in the pattern as more and more pens were added. As they began describing this growth, they were beginning to make a generalization in order to describe the number of sides needed for any number of pens to be built. As they compared each of the pattern growths, they were considering whether the patterns were equivalent.

In addition to focusing on the four major components of the Algebra Standard in this chapter, we will examine ways to help engage children in these important aspects of algebraic thinking. We will examine patterns in terms of change and how children describe and symbolically represent change. We will consider ways to guide children's understanding as they begin to use variables and algebraic expressions to describe and extend their patterns. We will consider ways to help children make, describe, and represent generalizations. We will consider ways to help children grow in their understanding of the relationship of equality.

FOCUS QUESTIONS

1. What does algebraic thinking mean for elementary students?
2. How do patterns help children develop algebraic thinking and ideas?
3. How can you encourage algebraic thinking as children study arithmetic?
4. How can you help children's understanding of variables develop?
5. How can you help children look for and analyze changes in an algebraic way?

Patterns

Children's growth in understanding patterns requires early experiences directed at recognizing and describing patterns, such as patterns based on color and shape. Challenge your students to describe these patterns in more than one way, as Mr. Trynka did in the *Snapshot*. As the students describe how they have seen the pattern, the others begin to see different features of patterns. They begin to see differences in how patterns are generated and extended. As their familiarity with patterns grows, they are able to describe relationships between an object in a pattern and its placement in that pattern. With experience, they expand in their abilities to communicate in words and numbers and they are able to represent and analyze patterns using more abstract forms of representations: symbols, tables, and graphs. These experiences lead to the development of different ways of representing a relationship, providing the basis for much discussion and sense making. Tables, graphs, words, and symbolic expressions help children visualize different patterns of change.

Patterns can be simple or puzzling. You should begin with patterns that young children can grasp. Colors and shapes, followed by pictures, objects, and sounds, are good for engaging young children in recognizing patterns. Clapping patterns are common in the early grades as a means of focusing children and making a transition to additional pattern activities. Use different patterns to signal different types of activities. Children quickly recognize the meanings of the various patterns. Sing a few notes and have the children sing those notes. Give the children an oral pattern for them to repeat. These activities support children in their development of an intuitive and more automatic recognition of patterns.

Color is a visual attribute for children. Have your students create a pattern of red and blue lights to decorate the classroom. Begin the strand of lights as in this example:

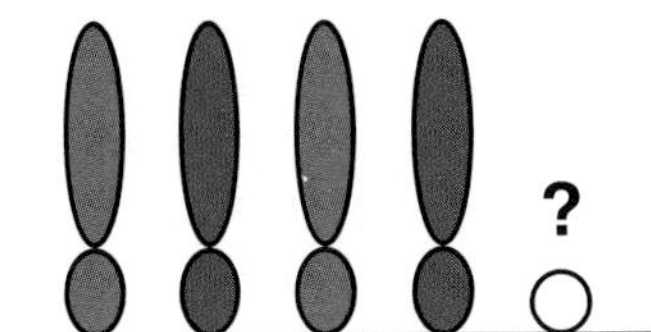

What color should be inserted next? This problem is not as easy as it appears, since there can be more than one correct answer. Some children might argue that the next color is red (repeating red and blue). Others might argue that the next bulb should be blue (red, with one blue, change to red with two blues, continue by adding a blue to the growing sets of blues). Explaining their thinking about the patterns is essential in developing their algebraic thinking. Sharing their ideas with the other children helps them consider alternative ways of looking at patterns. As children become familiar with patterns such as this one, they can extend other patterns or make their own patterns.

Research has shown that children should begin pattern recognition by building a variety of patterns using pattern blocks, Cuisenaire rods, and other materials in the classroom. Afterward, you can extend the idea of building and describing patterns with pictorial models described In the Classroom 14-1. As children begin to recognize and identify missing objects in the patterns, encourage them to look at the patterns in different ways, to think about multiple ways of extending the pattern. Ask questions such as "How can you describe this pattern?" or "How can you extend this pattern?" Questions like these help children begin to make sense of three important aspects in algebraic thinking: change, generalization, and equality.

Describing patterns, considering how the patterns change, looking at multiple ways of extending the pattern, and investigating different descriptions for the same pattern open many possibilities for algebraic thinking. You can build on the background children have in describing patterns with everyday language to help them represent those patterns with mathematical symbols. Numerical patterns also help to build their algebraic thinking. Consider this pattern:

1, 3, 5, 7, . . .

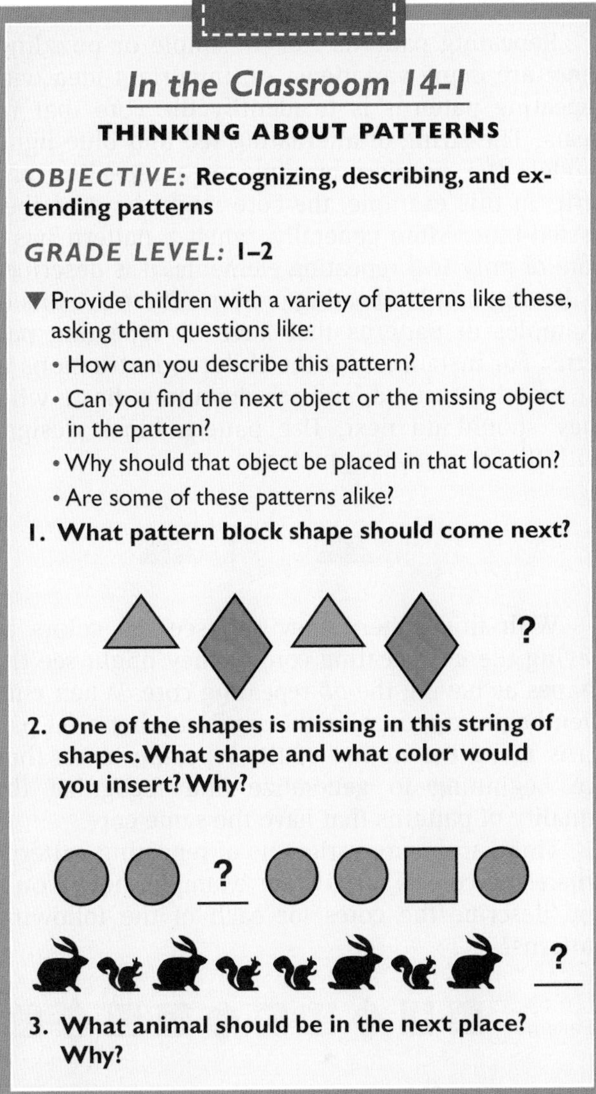

In the Classroom 14-1

THINKING ABOUT PATTERNS

OBJECTIVE: **Recognizing, describing, and extending patterns**

GRADE LEVEL: **1–2**

▼ Provide children with a variety of patterns like these, asking them questions like:

- How can you describe this pattern?
- Can you find the next object or the missing object in the pattern?
- Why should that object be placed in that location?
- Are some of these patterns alike?

1. What pattern block shape should come next?

?

2. One of the shapes is missing in this string of shapes. What shape and what color would you insert? Why?

?

?

3. What animal should be in the next place? Why?

Children may describe this pattern as "each number is two more than the last one." As their understandings develop, they are able to express the changes in the pattern more generally, using mathematical symbols such as "the next term after the nth term is $n + 2$." Later, they will learn to represent the relationship between two consecutive terms of this pattern with the equation $N = L + 2$ where the next term (N) is the last term (L) plus 2. Of course, students do not automatically develop this more sophisticated algebraic thinking about the aspects of change, generalization, and equality; this development takes time over several grades and years, not weeks. As you work with developing models of different types of patterns (repeating, growing, geometric, and numeric), examine them with respect to these three important aspects of algebraic thinking.

Repeating Patterns

Repeating patterns can be simple or puzzling; there are many variations. An important idea with repeating patterns is to identify the core that repeats. The string of alternating red and blue lights models the simplest example of a repeating pattern. In this example, the core might be described as red-blue. More generally, when a pattern has a core of only two repeating elements, it is described as having an *ab* repeating pattern. There are lots of examples of patterns that have *ab* repeating patterns. For instance, give the children instructions to sit, stand, sit, stand, and ask them to indicate what they should do next. Use pattern block designs with this *ab* repeating pattern.

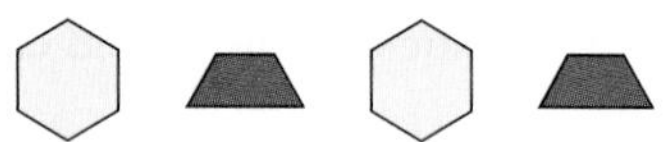

With this pattern they can see the colors as having the *ab* repeating core or they might see the shapes as having the *ab* repeating core. When children begin to recognize the similarity between patterns using the notion of the repeating core, they are beginning to generalize and recognize the equality of patterns that have the same core.

There are many variations of repeating patterns where the core is not *ab*. For example, how would you describe the cores for each of the following patterns?

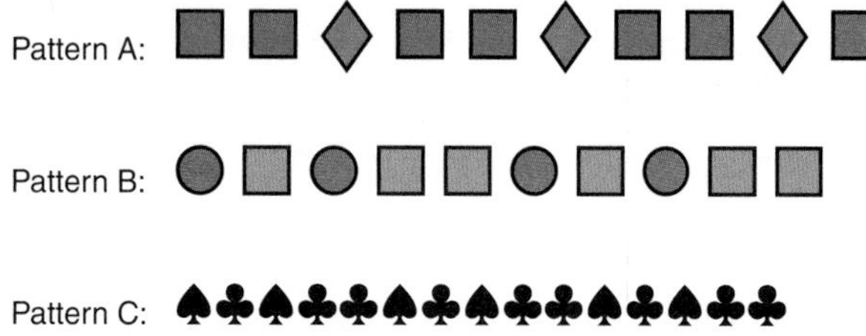

The core in Pattern A may be described as *aab*. Children may concentrate on one of the attributes of the blocks: color as red, red, blue or shape as square, square, diamond. Perhaps the children will use color and shape together as red square, red square, blue diamond. Regardless of the verbal description, the core that repeats for this pattern is *aab*. Helping children see that all the different descriptions have the same core is important for recognizing equality among patterns.

Children recognizing a repeated pattern in Pattern B might describe the core as pink circle, green square, pink circle, green square, green square (or symbolically as *ababb*). Others might see it as a combination of two cores: one core of pink circle, green square and another core of pink circle, green square, green square. They are visualizing a pattern of *ab* followed by *abb* and then considering those two parts as alternating as they repeat. What repeated core can you identify for Pattern C? Ask children how Pattern B is like Pattern C. Helping children describe the patterns in terms of the core(s) they identify helps them generalize their understanding in ways that develop their algebraic thinking.

Remember that children may think about a pattern in ways that differ from you. There is often more than one correct way to explain or extend a pattern. In the *Snapshot of a Lesson*, the children thought differently about the dog pens. Children's explanations of their reasons for selecting the next element of a pattern can help you understand their thinking and perhaps help you look at a pattern in a different way. Their explanations can also help you understand what they are failing to consider if they offer an erroneous description of a pattern.

Research from the *Seventh Mathematics Assessment of the National Assessment of Educational Progress* (NAEP) indicates that fourth-grade students often have more difficulty inserting a missing element in a pattern (as in problem #2 from In the Classroom 14-1) than identifying the next element (Blume and Heckman, 2000). Perhaps this difficulty is because they have been asked to continue patterns more often than filling in the missing parts. Your curriculum should include both types of experiences.

As soon as children seem comfortable with the tasks you have given them, begin to look for ways you can connect repeating patterns to number sequences. By simply numbering the elements or terms of the pattern, you can support children in beginning to generalize the pattern. Consider the repeating pattern of geometric shapes in Figure 14-2.

Questioning guides student thinking about patterns in a more general way. Ask questions like:

- What shape is the ninth term? the twelfth term? (They are both squares.)
- What is the sixteenth term? How do you know? (a hexagon)
- What can you say about the terms of all the squares? (multiples of 3)

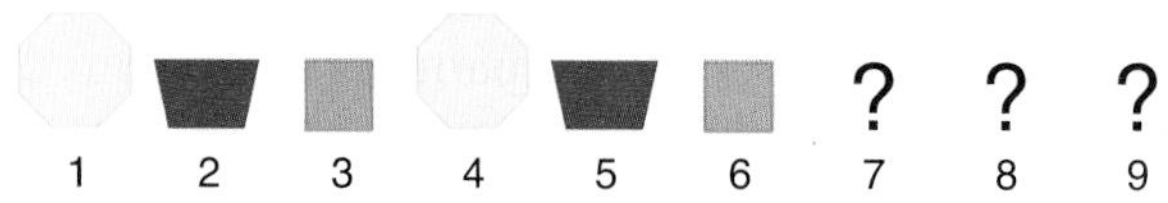

FIGURE 14-2 Repeating pattern with terms numbered.

- How many of each shape is needed to extend the pattern to 20 terms? (7 hexagons, 7 trapezoids, and 6 squares)

In the upper elementary grades, children begin to describe the terms of all the squares as multiples of 3. They also may see that the hexagons are always two shapes before the squares and the trapezoids are one place before the squares. They now begin to use symbols to describe their thoughts. The square placements can be described by $3s$, where s represents the square number; when $s = 1$, the first placement for the square is the third place. The hexagons can be described as $3s-2$; the first placement for the hexagon is in the first place and the second placement is the fourth place. The trapezoids are always one shape before the squares and can be described by $3s-1$.

Repeating patterns are easy to find. You might provide a different repeating pattern each day, or challenge the children to do so. Look for the use of geometric patterns in different cultures of the world. Quilts, fabrics, rugs, pottery, and other arts and crafts often use repetition as well as other intriguing patterns.

Most of the repeating patterns to this point have repeated in one direction; however, patterns can extend in more than one direction, as in the quilt picture. Beautiful patterns emerge by repeating geometric grids like those using a square grid In the Classroom 14-2. In this activity, the children must first find the change from one element

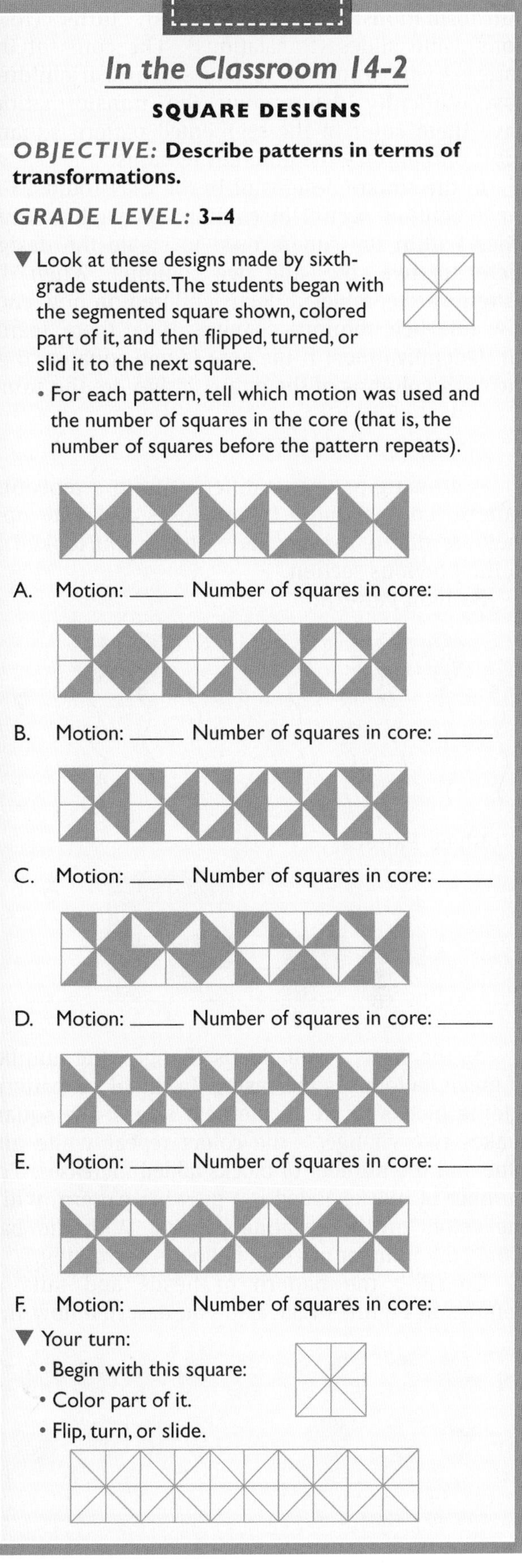

In the Classroom 14-2

SQUARE DESIGNS

OBJECTIVE: **Describe patterns in terms of transformations.**

GRADE LEVEL: **3–4**

▼ Look at these designs made by sixth-grade students. The students began with the segmented square shown, colored part of it, and then flipped, turned, or slid it to the next square.

- For each pattern, tell which motion was used and the number of squares in the core (that is, the number of squares before the pattern repeats).

A. Motion: _____ Number of squares in core: _____

B. Motion: _____ Number of squares in core: _____

C. Motion: _____ Number of squares in core: _____

D. Motion: _____ Number of squares in core: _____

E. Motion: _____ Number of squares in core: _____

F. Motion: _____ Number of squares in core: _____

▼ Your turn:

- Begin with this square:
- Color part of it.
- Flip, turn, or slide.

(square) to the next in terms of the geometric transformations: flips (reflections), turns (rotations), and slides (translations). The cores of the patterns vary from one to four squares. If children have difficulty determining the transformation, have them color in the segmented pattern square, cut it out, and try the different motions.

In the square designs of In the Classroom 14-2, the repetition occurs in columns as well as rows since within the square used to create the design there are two rows and two columns. When the patterns are completed, focus children on how each row (or each column) changes. Have them search for generalizations. If the core is two squares, then the even columns of the entire design are the same.

Growing Patterns

A growing pattern is different from a repeating pattern. Look at these two patterns and note how they are different from the patterns you looked at in the previous section.

Balloon Pattern:

Block Pattern:

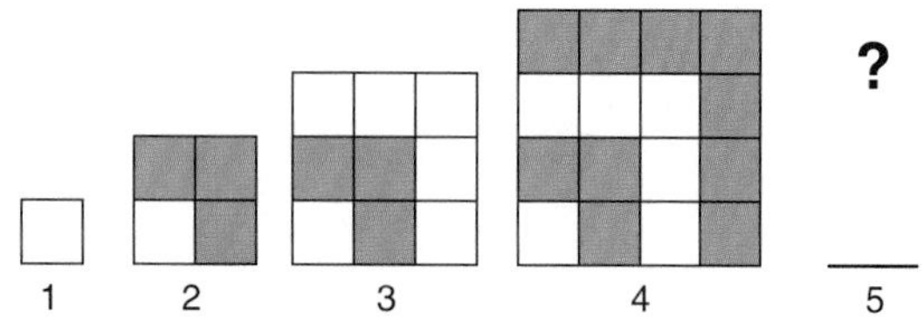

As the pattern of balloons changes, the number of green balloons is increasing. In the block pattern, adding blocks to create the next size of the square makes two changes—the colors repeat white and blue, but the number of blocks added increases. The number of blocks added is a growing pattern, while the colors are a repeating pattern. With the balloons, the number of green balloons is growing.

Consider the pattern of heads and tails of pennies in Figure 14.3a. Can you describe how this pattern is growing? Dividing the pattern into numbered terms, as in Figure 14-3b, helps to talk about the growth of the pennies. The first observation from this numbering is that the odd-numbered terms are heads and the even-numbered terms are tails.

The seventh term of the penny pattern will be heads. How many heads will there be in this term? Can you describe the change from term to term? How would you describe the odd-numbered terms? How would you describe the even-numbered terms? A table is helpful in organizing the information to think about this problem.

Term	Heads	Tails
1	2	
2		1
3	4	
4		2
5	6	
6		3

The table helps clarify what is happening with the heads and the tails term by term. Directed questions help guide students' thinking. What will happen in the 21st term? Since the term is odd, the pennies will be heads, but how many heads? (42) How many pennies will there be in the 130th term? Again, the type of coin (tails) is not hard to determine, but how many? (65) Ask students to describe the general pattern for this problem. As they investigate this problem, they are considering change and generalizing the ideas, perhaps even expressing the nth term as an equality.

Math Links 14.3

An electronic manipulative that allows children to build patterns in a square and then examine the rows and columns may be found at the NCTM's Illuminations web site. Three activities are available. Children create, describe, and analyze the patterns. Teacher notes are provided.

www.wiley.com/college/reys

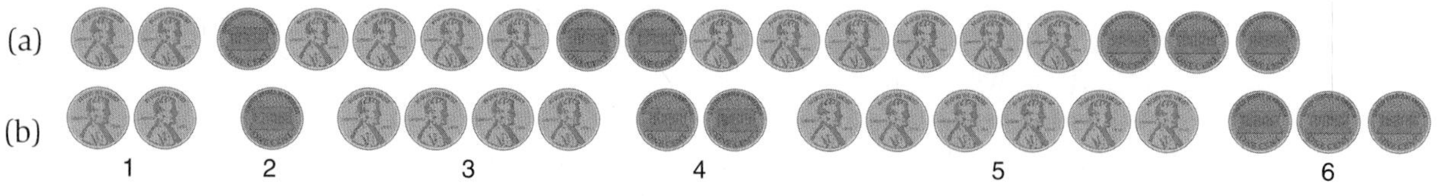

FIGURE 14-3 (a) Growing pattern with pennies. (b) Growing pattern with terms numbered.

Growing patterns can also be two-dimensional, such as those in Figure 14-4. One way to help students see these growing patterns is to have them model the pattern. Give them some square tiles to model the growth in Pattern A of Figure 14-4. As they build each successive term with the tiles, they begin to see how the shape is growing and how it relates to the term number. For Pattern A, you can ask questions similar to these:

- How many squares are in each size of the letter H: 1, 2, and 3 (where 1 is the smallest letter to be made with the tiles)?
- Do you see how the pattern is changing? Describe that change.
- Can you tell how many squares will be in the 4th letter size for H?
- How many squares will be in the 5th letter size for H?
- If you extended this pattern to the 100th letter size for H, how many squares would it take?
- How would you describe the *n*th letter size?
- How can you describe growth of the letter sizes for H?

It is easier for students to describe the pattern growth from one term to the next; however, if you ask them to describe a general rule for the pattern, they have more difficulty. For example, in Pattern A they might say, "The size of the letter from letter size 2 to letter size 3 increases by 5 squares." Help them build a table to describe the growth in the letter H pattern. Begin with the number of squares for the first letter H (7 squares). To increase the size of the letter H to the next size, add 5 blocks to the previous number used. Continue describing the increase in the size of the letter H, as shown in Figure 14-5.

The table shows the number of square tiles needed as the letter size increases. To find the number of squares needed to create the letter of size 12, you add five squares to the number of squares needed to create the letter of size 11. To create the letter of size 11, you add five squares to the number of squares needed to create the letter of size 10. This growth process of building on the information about the previous letter information is called *recursion*. But what if you want to know how many squares you need to build a letter of size 50? Using this process of recursion, you first must find the number of squares needed to build the letter of size 49, but before that, you must know the number of squares for letter of size 48, and so on. This notion of recursion is used in constructing many spreadsheets, where you use the copy feature to build information based on the results of the information identified previously.

Children typically look at the growth in many patterns in this recursive manner; however, this approach does not lend itself to easily finding the number of squares to build a large letter of size 500 or size 1000. You need to shift their attention to the relationship between the size of the letter (the term of the pattern) and the number of squares needed to create the letter. Figure 14-6 shows the growth of the letter size when considering the number of squares added for each size of the letter.

For any size of the letter H, say N, the number of squares can be described as $(1 + 2N) + N + (1 + 2N)$ or $5N + 2$. This realization can help guide students in developing an explicit rule—a generalization that describes the growth in the pattern in terms of the size of the letter.

Growing Patterns

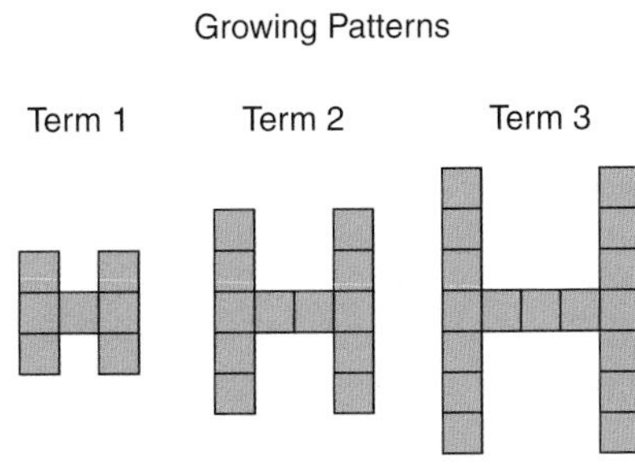

Pattern A: Increasing the size of letters in the alphabet

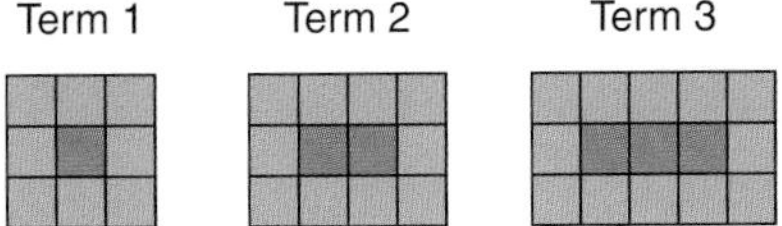

Pattern B: Increasing the size of a swimming pool deck as the pool size increases

FIGURE 14-4 Growing patterns using square tiles.

Letter Size	Number of Squares Needed
1	7
2	12
3	17
4	22
5	27
6	32

FIGURE 14-5 Number of tiles needed as the letter H increases in size.

Letter Size	Left Side	Center	Right Side	Total Squares
1	1 at top 1 in center 1 at bottom	1	1 at top 1 center 1 at bottom	7
2	2 at top 1 at center 2 at bottom	2	2 at top 1 at center 2 at bottom	12
3	3 at top 1 at center 3 at bottom	3	3 at top 1 at center 3 at bottom	17
⋮	⋮	⋮	⋮	⋮
10	10 at top 1 at center 10 at bottom	10	10 at top 1 at center 10 at bottom	42
⋮	⋮	⋮	⋮	⋮
N	N at top 1 at center N at bottom	N	N at top 1 at center N at bottom	5N + 2

FIGURE 14-6 Describing the result of the growth of the letter H based on its letter size.

Have the students investigate the letter growth of their own first or last initial. Or have them look at the growth of the swimming pool deck (the green tiles) in Pattern B to identify an explicit rule based on the size of the pool (the blue tiles). The generalization from a recursive explanation of the pattern to an explicit rule is an important step in advancing their algebraic thinking.

Geometric and Numeric Patterns

In grades 3 to 5, the types of patterns that children are able to explore mathematically can be extended to include geometric and numeric patterns. In particular, in these grades teachers need to encourage children to

> investigate numerical and geometric patterns and express them mathematically in words or symbols. They should analyze the structure of the pattern and how it grows or changes, organize this information systematically, and use their analysis to develop generalizations about the mathematical relationship in the pattern. (NCTM, 2000, p. 159)

Geometric patterns are growing patterns and involve change, but the type of change distinguishes geometric patterns from patterns such as those in the growth of the letter H. Look again at the block pattern composed of squares using alternating color layers as the blocks grow, as described in Figure 14-7.

Children might notice that the area of the total block for each term is growing. This look generates a number pattern (1, 4, 9, 16, 25, . . .). A different number pattern is generated with the growth of the

Math Links 14.4

If you would like to see sixth graders building and describing patterns, you can view video clips for V-Patterns at the Modeling Middle School Mathematics web site.

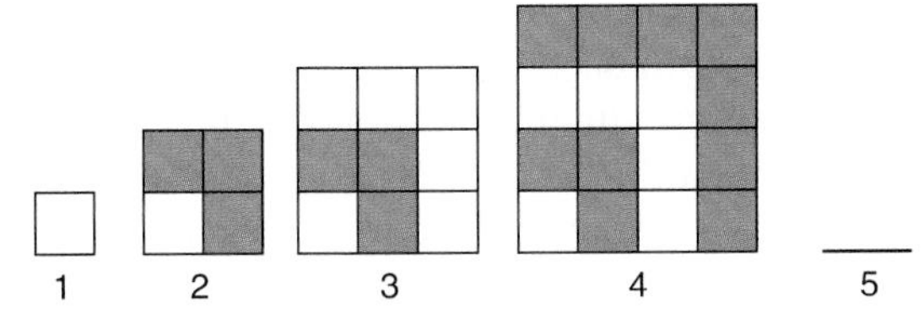

FIGURE 14-7 Growth of blocks leading to a numeric pattern.

letter H (see Figure 14-6). When children are asked to describe two different numeric patterns, they are able to recognize that both are increasing in number, but they have difficulty describing how the increases differ because they have difficulty visualizing varying rates of change from the numbers. However, if you have them graph the two patterns as in Figure 14-8, they are better able to describe the difference. The growth of the letter H appears linear, yet the graph of the growth of the square shows an increasing rate of growth that is nonlinear. This nonlinear growth is changing geometrically.

Numeric patterns are about change, but seeing that change is often difficult. Look for numeric patterns that can be linked with visual patterns. Skip-counting by different numbers using the hundreds chart (as described in Chapter 7) can help children connect numbers to visual patterns. Figure 14-9 provides a visual version of the pattern change for counting by threes. (See In the Classroom 7-5 for a classroom activity with skip-counting.) You can ask

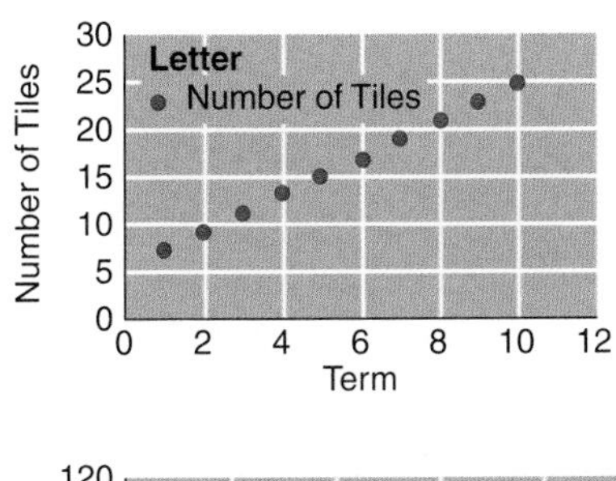

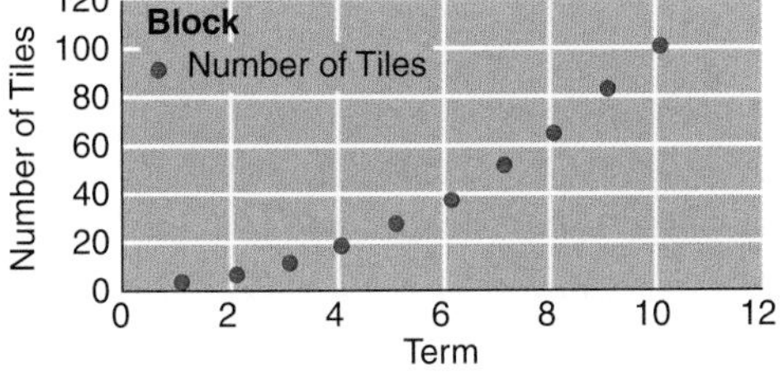

FIGURE 14-8 Comparison of the growth of the letter H and the block.

1	2	3	4	5	6	7	8	9	10
11	12	13	14	15	16	17	18	19	20
21	22	23	24	25	26	27	28	29	30
31	32	33	34	35	36	37	38	39	40
41	42	43	44	45	46	47	48	49	50
51	52	53	54	55	56	57	58	59	60
61	62	63	64	65	66	67	68	69	70
71	72	73	74	75	76	77	78	79	80
81	82	83	84	85	86	87	88	89	90
91	92	93	94	95	96	97	98	99	100

FIGURE 14-9 Counting by threes.

questions like these to see if the children are able to visualize changes and make connections between the counting pattern and the visual pattern:

- What will the pattern look like if you count by sixes? How would this pattern change if you counted by nines?
- What number pattern is generated if you count by tens beginning with 34? How would the visual pattern look? If you extend this pattern of counting by tens, would you color in the 75 square?
- Using your pattern created by counting by twos, describe how the pattern would change if you counted by fours. Would you color in any new squares? What squares would no longer be colored?

In grades 3 to 5 you can engage the children in algebraic thinking by having them investigate number patterns with geometric patterns as the pool pattern previously described in Figure 14-4. The different colors help students visualize the change more clearly. While students in one grade can be asked to predict how the next square in the pattern is created, students in the next grade

Math Links 14.5

*Y*ou skip count using a virtual hundreds board and calculator at NCTM's web site.

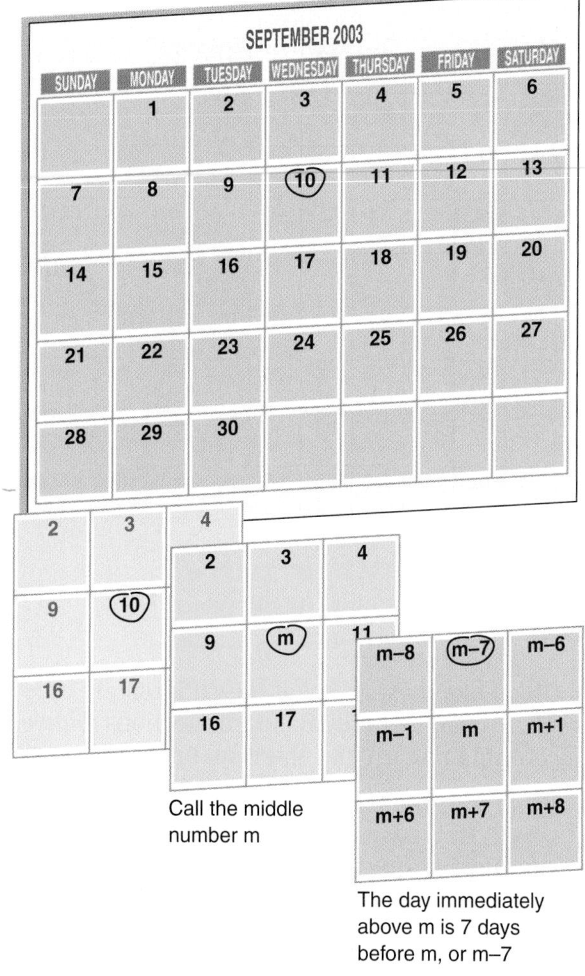

FIGURE 14-10 Investigating patterns in calendars.

can make a table. Gradually, students can be challenged to develop a generalization or a general rule with reference to the geometric pattern, as they did to describe the growth of the size of the letter H.

Calendars provide another example of a number pattern that you can use to engage students' in algebraic thinking. Figure 14-10 shows the calendar for September 2003 as an example. Have younger children look at the change in the calendar as described in Chapter 7, In the Classroom 7-3. How does the calendar change as you look across a week? How does it change as you go down? Children may recognize that every other day has an even date or that the date of the next Friday after September 12th is 7 more, or the 19th. Have students find the sum of all the numbers in a square of the dates (as shown in Figure 14-10). After finding the sum of the numbers in this square and several other squares of the same size, students may observe that the sum is nine times the number in the center. Older students should be able to see why this result is true; using letters to define the nine numbers in the square helps. If the middle number is represented by m, then the number a week later is $m + 7$. Note that the sum of all these expressions is $9m$. This is not a difficult generalization for children in the upper elementary grades.

Many other number arrangements can be exciting to engage students in algebraic thinking. The arrangement of numbers In the Classroom 14-3 presents a variety of patterns. Challenge students to find their own number patterns. You will be amazed at their creativity; there are many more ways to think about patterns than the ones suggested. Again, focus the students on how each row is changing, how the sums of the numbers in successive "diamonds" are

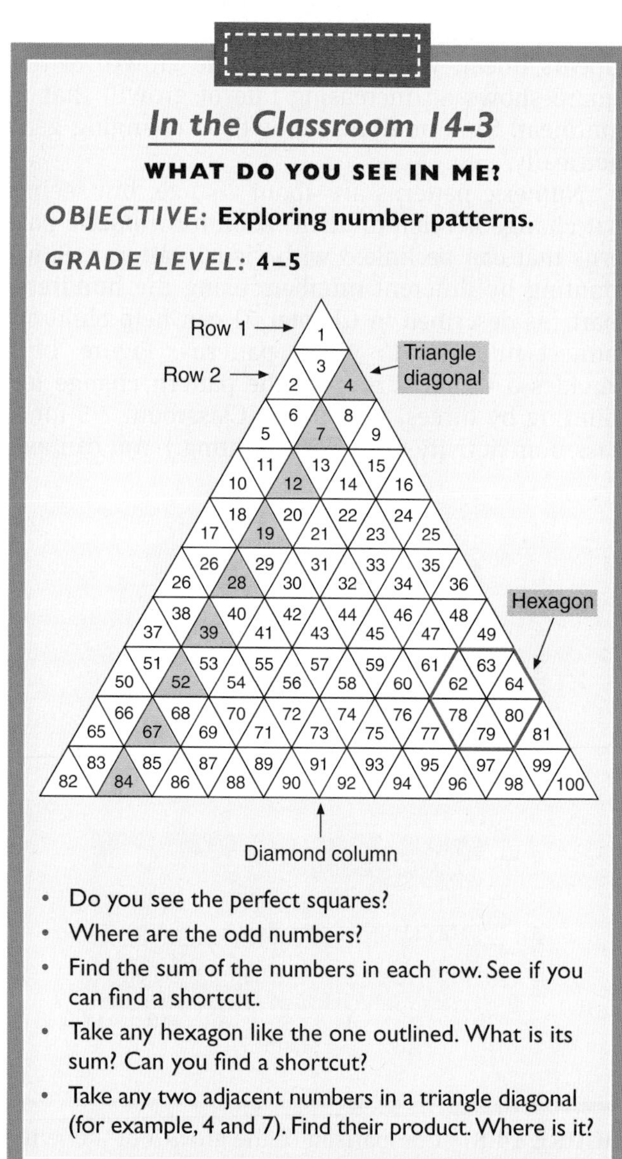

In the Classroom 14-3

WHAT DO YOU SEE IN ME?

OBJECTIVE: **Exploring number patterns.**

GRADE LEVEL: **4–5**

- Do you see the perfect squares?
- Where are the odd numbers?
- Find the sum of the numbers in each row. See if you can find a shortcut.
- Take any hexagon like the one outlined. What is its sum? Can you find a shortcut?
- Take any two adjacent numbers in a triangle diagonal (for example, 4 and 7). Find their product. Where is it?

growing, or how the sums of the rows are changing. There are patterns that children can generalize, such as describing the sum of the numbers in a row. Row k has a sum of k times the middle number. Although this relationship is not difficult, see if students can then find an expression for the middle number in terms of k.

Relationships

The search for patterns in mathematics is a search for relationships. The children in Mr. Tynka's class as described in the *Snapshot* were challenged to explore the equivalence of their different descriptions. A central idea in the search for relationships is the concept of equality.

Equivalence and Equality

Along with change and generalization, equality is a key concept in algebraic thinking. Equality is a notion that must be grounded early and often through carefully considered experiences to display a relationship of equivalence and balance. What do you think that children would say about the truth of the following mathematical sentences?

A. $7 + 3 = 10$
B. $9 = 5 + 4$
C. $7 + 3 = 10 + 5$

Children who say sentence A is true often say that B is not true but C is true. At a very early age, they have tried to make sense of mathematics and have made the generalization that the equals sign means "get an answer." They complete an open sentence such as $3 + \_\_ = 9$ with a 12. They are thinking, it says to add, 3 plus 9 is 12. They are operating with the arithmetic language of getting answers. This reasoning makes A obviously true. What bothers children about sentence B? Sometimes they say it is backwards or that the answer is 9. They are not focusing on the relationship between 9 and $5 + 4$, or that this representation expresses the equality between these two expressions. Why do you think they say C is true?

A common misconception about equality is that it means "the answer is coming." Children gain this idea from the many problems that are presented for them to solve in the form

$$2 + 3 = ?$$
$$3 + 6 = ?$$

This false notion is reinforced further when students get a result after pressing the = key on a calculator. You need to aid in the development of their perceptions about the equal sign to mean a symbol of equivalence and balance. In the early grades, activities with a balance can help children develop an intuitive connection of the notions of equality and balance.

Figure 14-11 a, b, and c shows how you can use a balance with weights to show the equality of $3 + 5$ and 8 and the inequality of $3 + 5$ and 7 or 9. Using the balance model, you can help children see that they need to add or subtract the same amount from each side of the balance in order to maintain the balance (or equality).

Using a balance as a representation for equality is not new. A puzzle found in a book of puzzles

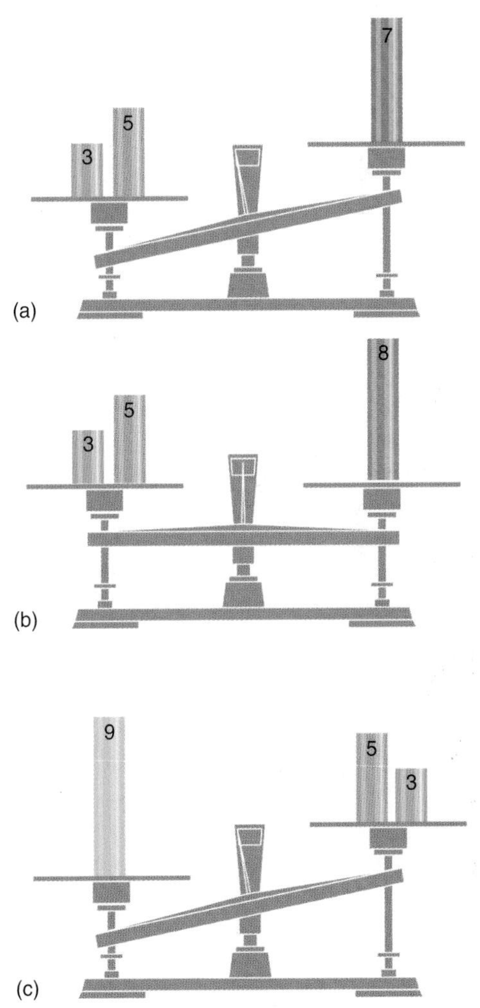

FIGURE 14-11 The sum of the 3 and 5 weights (a) is not equal to a weight of 7 ($3 + 5 \neq 7$); (b) balances the 8 weight ($3 + 5 = 8$); (c) is lighter than the 9 weight ($9 \neq 5 + 3$).

published in 1914 (*Cyclopedia of Puzzles* by S. Loyd, Morningside Press, 1914; reprinted by Pinnacle Books in 1976) provides a nice problem for students to demonstrate their understanding of equivalence of expressions and the notion of equality as a balance.

> If a bottle and a glass balance with a pitcher, a bottle balances with a glass and a plate, and two pitchers balance with three plates, can you figure out how many glasses will balance with a bottle?

Use the pictorial representation in Figure 14-12 to guide your thinking about this problem.

Notice that as you work through this problem, the focus must be on maintaining a balance. What you put on one side of the scale must be balanced by an equivalent amount on the other side. You could begin on the first balance with a pitcher being balanced by the glass and the bottle. Then you could add another pitcher to the side with the pitcher. This means that you could add a pitcher to the other side or you could add another glass and bottle to the other side (since the pitcher balances those two items).

The bottle and glass balance with a pitcher

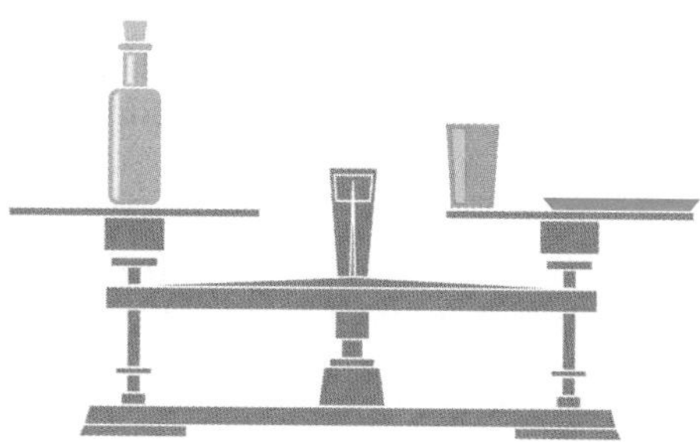
A bottle balances with a glass and a plate

Two pitchers balance with three plates

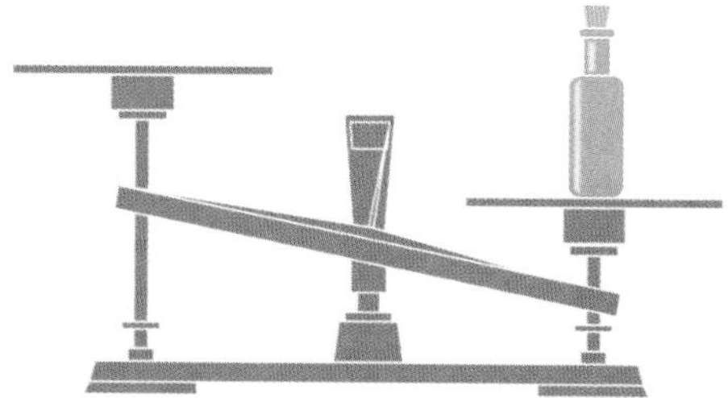
How many glasses will balance with the bottle?

FIGURE 14-12 Balancing the bottle problem.

Exploring Relationships

As students work with more complex relationships, the recognition of the equivalence of different relationships becomes more complex. To move young children toward exploring more complex relationships, a teacher can ask, for example, how the number of boys in a group is related to the number of hands, as shown in Figure 14-13a.

If multiplication symbols have been introduced, *B* boys and B × 2 hands generalize this simple relationship. Begin by describing the number of hands of three boys as 3 × 2, of four boys as 4 × 2, and of ten boys as 10 × 2, writing the results for each in a table:

Number of Boys	1	2	3	4	5	6	7	8	9	10			B
Number of Hands	2	4	6	8						20			B × 2

Consider the relationship of the number of girls to the number of triangles as the girls make triangles with string, as shown in Figure 14-13b. Although this relationship may seem similar to the one in the preceding example, it is a 3-to-1 relationship rather than a 1-to-2 relationship. Some children may have difficulty describing the general terms in this case because the relationship calls for division rather than multiplication. Again, begin discussing the relationship slowly, and write the results in a table to provide some structure for the representation:

Number of Girls	3	6	9	12	15			45		G
Number of Triangles	1	2	3	4				?		$\frac{G}{3}$

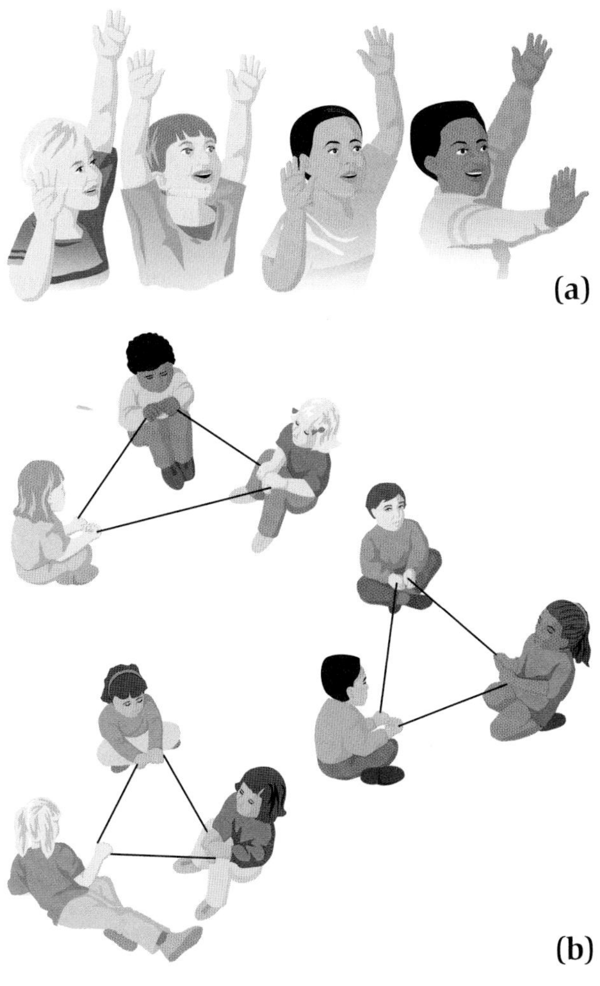

FIGURE 14-13 (a) Relationship of number of boys to number of the hands; (b) Relationship of number of girls to number of triangles created.

At times, you may want to model relationships using a machine that outputs a number for each number input. The challenge for the students is to decide what the machine does and how to describe it. These machines can be simple, such as one that always gives an output of one more than the number input, twice as much as the number input, or two less than the number input. A more complicated machine might be as follows:

Input	3	5	12	25		53		N
Output	7	11	25	51	29		163	

You need to help children focus on the change from the input to the output. Some children will focus on the change in the different input values, but this does not help. So you need to ask specific questions like: Given the input _____, what is the output?

Before talking about a general rule, describe many of the outputs in terms of the inputs or describe what the machine is doing in words and numbers; then try to generalize the relationship with more abstract symbols. Students may generalize as follows: "You add the number twice and then add one more" or "double the number and add one." When the students reach this stage, help them see ways to write each of these representations is $N + N + 1$ and $(2 \times N) + 1$. Ask the students whether these representations are equal and to explain why they are equal.

Children need lots of experiences with these types of activities. An activity for working with these machines with children in grades 1 and 2 is described by Stephen Willoughby (NCTM, 1999). Create a large box (perhaps using a washing machine box) that can hold a child comfortably. Be sure to put "eye" holes so the child can see out of the box! Give the child a stack of Popsicle sticks with the instructions to "add 2" to any input value. Have another child input a number of sticks (say 3 sticks). You need to announce the number of sticks being input. The child in the box then outputs the appropriate number of sticks (5). After a number of repetitions of the rule-based action, ask the class to generalize the actions, describing the change from the input to the output. Over several days or weeks, change both the children and the rules, allowing every child an opportunity to participate.

Children can think about generalizing relationships through number puzzles, such as the one shown in Figure 14-14. As a first activity, have children do the puzzle with various numbers. After using many different numbers chosen by the children, let them use materials to model the steps. You can observe whether they have strongly developed

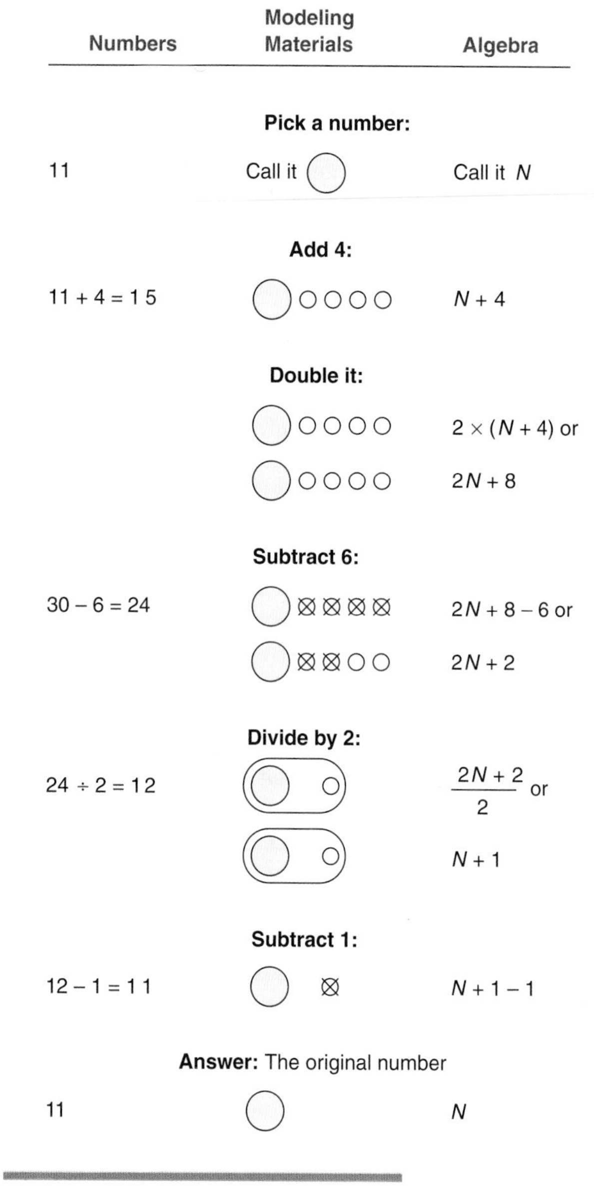

Numbers	Modeling Materials	Algebra
	Pick a number:	
11	Call it	Call it N
	Add 4:	
11 + 4 = 15		$N + 4$
	Double it:	
		$2 \times (N + 4)$ or
		$2N + 8$
	Subtract 6:	
30 − 6 = 24		$2N + 8 - 6$ or
		$2N + 2$
	Divide by 2:	
24 ÷ 2 = 12		$\frac{2N + 2}{2}$ or
		$N + 1$
	Subtract 1:	
12 − 1 = 11		$N + 1 - 1$
	Answer: The original number	
11		N

FIGURE 14-14 A number puzzle.

concepts about the operations. If you discover, for example, that some children do not know how to model "multiply by two" or "divide by two," then you can reinforce the meanings. After the students are able to model the actions, you can ask them to describe the steps using symbols. Notice the concepts they can gain by doing this activity with simple algebraic representations. For example, it is easy to see that $2 \times (N + 4)$ is equal to $2N + 8$ because both of these actions describe the same picture.

"Guess my rule" activities, as described in Figure 14-15 a and b, provide additional opportunities similar to input-output machine activities to extend students' algebraic thinking about numeric relationships. Show the activity in a table form. Start with a "number," then show the "result" based on having completed some operation. Have the children guess what rule you are following with each number to get the result. These activities can begin simply with the rule "add 3." The rules can become more sophisticated, as the example in Figure 14-15b shows.

Actually showing stages is a good way to unmask or reveal that these sophisticated rules result from applying a series of simple rules. For example, in Figure 14-15a, first the students are asked to consider how the values in Result 1 were generated from the Number. Here, multiplying the number by 3 generates the result. Then ask the students to consider the values in Result 2. Students can begin to see the connection between Result 1 and Result 2, where the rule is simply adding seven to Result 1. Thus the general rule might be expressed:

$$\text{Result 2} = \text{Result 1} + 7$$
$$\text{Result 2} = 3\text{N} + 7$$

After extended practice developing the rules in stages, you can challenge students with the more complex pattern described in Figure 14-15b.

Representation and Analysis Using Algebraic Symbols

Algebraic thinking grows through experiences that encourage students to make generalizations, using symbols to represent mathematical ideas and to solve problems. Investigating the patterns developed by skip-counting leads students to making conjectures about these numbers. As students describe the numbers, they may say that the numbers all end in 0, 2, 4, 6, or 8. This is an important step in thinking about even numbers.

Using blocks to represent the even numbers provides another perspective. For example, you can give each child enough square tiles to represent the numbers 2 through 20. Young children can pretend that they are making candy bars that are two squares wide. As the children build with the blocks, they notice that they can make candy bars with certain numbers and not with other numbers of blocks. Group the numbers that make candy bars—these are even numbers. Then agree that numbers that do not make candy bars are called odd numbers.

(a)

Number	Result 1	Result 2
1	3	10
2	6	13
3	9	16
4	12	19
N	3N	3N + 7

(b)

Number	Result 2
1	−1
2	3
3	7
4	11
N	?

FIGURE 14-15 (a) Guess my rule in stages; (b) More complex guess my rule.

Ask them to describe the differences in the rectangles they can make with an even number of blocks and with an odd number of blocks. What changes as you go from an even number, say 6, to the next number? What is the pattern, in counting, of evens and odds? What about the number 0? Is it even or odd? By focusing the children on the change from 4 to 3 to 2 to 1 (even to odd to even to odd), children might explain that 0 is even because 1 is odd.

Creating rectangles with an even number of blocks helps children see that even numbers are different from those that are not even—the odd numbers. Encourage students to propose conjectures about numbers and operations as they build a list of the odd and even numbers. Initially, they will probably see the pattern that every other number is even. Can they justify this conjecture? Do they use the pattern argument (every other number) or a definition of even (a multiple of 2)?

Children can make many conjectures about even and odd numbers. For example, a child may claim that the sum of two odd numbers is even. Challenge students to justify that statement. At first, many students use specific numbers in showing that an odd plus an odd is an even number, as shown in Figure 14-16. Similarly, they demonstrate that an even number of odds adds to an even number by giving examples of specific numbers.

By the end of elementary school, students are able to develop arguments such as:

> Let one odd number be represented by $2m + 1$ and the other odd number by $2p + 1$.

If you add these, you get $2m + 2p + 2$, which is a multiple of 2, or an even number, or $(2m + 1) + (2p + 1) = 2m + 2p + 2 = 2\,(m + p + 1)$.

Clearly, reasoning abilities have changed from the early work with specific numbers of blocks to the more general case using symbols with variables, expressions, and equations. This growth is envisioned in the expectation that instructional programs enable all students to represent and analyze mathematical situations and structures using algebraic symbols.

Variables and Symbolic Representations

The concept of a variable is troublesome for many students. In the elementary grades, children develop the notion of a variable as a placeholder for a specific number, such as $5 + \_ = 13$. When students identify rules or in some manner represent their thinking about specific patterns, they use symbols as placeholders similar to the symbolic representation for the Nth term in the pattern of $5N + 2$, described in Figure 14-6. When students work with equations, they must learn that the use of a variable L in the equation $3L = 12$ is different from its use in the equation $0 \times L = 0$ or its use in the area

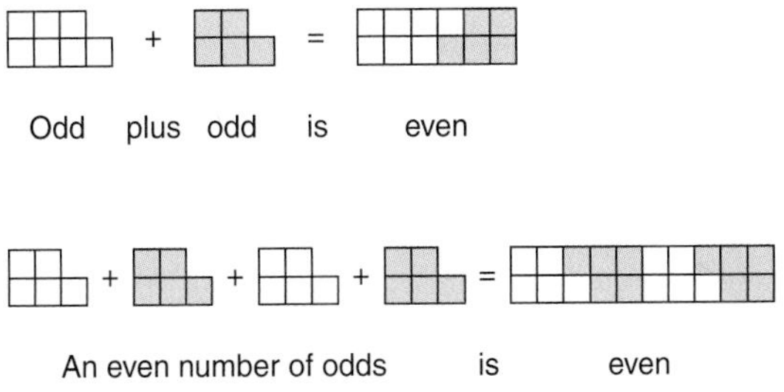

FIGURE 14-16 Models for summing odd numbers.

formula for a rectangle, $A = L \times W$. The concept of a variable is one that requires extensive experience, along with the idea of equality over many years, beginning with the early elementary grades.

The block pattern in Figure 14-7 is useful for exploring what happens to the perimeter and area as the side of a square increases. Unit squares make it easier to look at the growth of the blocks in this pattern. Have students record their data about the perimeter and area of squares as the length of the side of the square increases.

Length of side of the Block	1	2	3	4	5	6	7	8	16	32
Perimeter	4	8	12	16	20	24	28	32		
Area	1	4	9	16	25	36	49	64		

Questions such as these can focus their investigations of information in the above data table:

- How is the perimeter related to the length of the side of the square? (The perimeter is four times the length of the side of the square.)
- What would the perimeter be for a side of length 16? (64) For a side of length 32? (128)
- How is the area related to the length of the side of the square? (The area is the square of the length of the side or the product of the side times the side.)
- What would the area be for the square with side length of 16? (256)
- What would be the area for the square with side length of 32? (1024)

In grades 3 to 5, students should be encouraged to represent the idea of an unknown quantity using a letter or a symbol. They might represent the perimeter by the letter P as they describe their thinking about how the perimeter is related to the length of the side of the square. They might identify the perimeter (P) as four times the length of the side of the square and even more succinctly represent it as $4L$ (where L is the length of the side of the square). These students are beginning to use the idea of a variable to describe their observations and attempting to describe a rule for finding the perimeter of the square.

In later grades, students' understanding of variables can be extended beyond the idea that letters are used to stand for an unknown in an equation. By this time, students have encountered a variety of representations that use variables. For example, they may extend their observations of the perimeter of the square with side of length 5 using this thinking:

$P = 4L$

$P = 4(5)$

$P = 20$

As children begin to read and write expressions such as $P = 4L$, some of them may develop a misconception that both P and L are "place holders," simply randomly chosen symbols waiting to be substituted by a number. This understanding does not further the notions of "variable" and "function." In this case P is a function of L, and therefore L is a variable. Once the variable L is determined, then P is determined. This impression of a variable as a placeholder needs to be corrected early; otherwise, children's concept and further development of variable may be limited.

The NCTM's *Standards* point out that

> Students' facility with symbol manipulation can be enhanced if it is based on extensive experience with quantities in contexts through which students develop an initial understanding of the meaning and use of variables and an ability to associate symbolic expressions with problem contexts. (p. 227)

Children's stories, such as *Anno's Magic Seeds* (Anno, 1995), provide a rich source of important early experiences. In this story, Jack is given two magic seeds, one to feed him this year and one to plant for food next year. The plant bears two seeds the following year, one for Jack to eat and one for him to plant. After several years, Jack decides to plant both seeds, and he finds that when he plants two seeds, each plant produces two seeds. So he eats from the plant of one seed but plants the three remaining seeds. Next year he has six seeds! What expression do you think your students might develop for describing the growth of seeds? Will they all see the patterns similarly? Check the Book Nook for Children for more stories to use to engage students in describing situations using symbolic representations.

You can expand this notion of context using patterns with examples such as the swimming pool example In the Classroom 14-4. Here students are asked to describe the growth in the number of cement blocks needed to frame the pool as the length of the pool increases. Students quickly notice that the number of blocks added with each additional length of the pool is 2. But how can the number of cement blocks needed be described for a pool that is size N? Now they must develop a more general rule, a symbolic representation that goes beyond the recursive look of adding two blocks for each increase in the pool length.

In the Classroom 14-4

BUILDING BIGGER SWIMMING POOLS

OBJECTIVE: **Describe the pattern of increasing the size of swimming pools using variables expressions.**

GRADE LEVEL: **3–5**

▼ Provide students with square tiles and instruct them to model swimming pools of different sizes, where the tiles surround the pool.

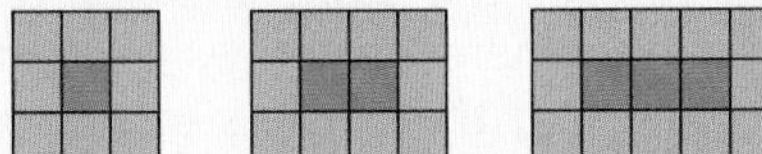

▼ Record the number of tiles needed to build the pools in this table.

Size of Pool	Number of Cement Blocks Needed
1	8
2	10
3	12
4	14
.	
.	
.	
10	
.	
.	
.	
20	
.	
.	
.	
N	?

- How many tiles are needed to build a pool that is 10 tiles long?
- How many tiles are needed to build a pool that is 20 tiles long?
- Find a general rule that describes pools *N* tiles long.

In the *Snapshot of a Lesson*, children described different representations of the dog pens problem. In this problem Chia-Lin was beginning to develop a generalization for the number of pens that could be represented symbolically as $1 + 3N$, but Oscar thought about the problem in a way that would eventually lead him to a different symbolic representation: $4 + 3\ (N - 1)$. Are these two expressions for the growth of the number of pens equivalent? Students' facility with symbolic manipulation to demonstrate the equivalence of these two representations requires extensive experiences with properties (distributive, associative, and commutative) and the order of operations. Ultimately, children need to be encouraged to represent their thoughts in a general way, not relying on the specific example of five pens.

To summarize what we've discussed in this section, it is important to recognize that when students' attention is focused on symbolic manipulation before they have developed solid conceptual understandings of the important concepts in algebra (such as that of variable), their algebraic thinking is limited to more rote, mechanical manipulations. Careful attention to providing experiences with concrete, pictorial, and verbal representations to develop an understanding of symbolic notations can and must be included in the early grades. By grades 3 to 5, students need opportunities to represent the idea of variables symbolically and to express their identified mathematical relationships with equations. Students at this age need many and varied experiences for analyzing and interpreting relationships among quantities in a variety of problem contexts. As students gain facility in extracting mathematics representations that incorporate symbolic notations, they establish important conceptual underpinnings for the ideas of variables and equations.

Modeling Mathematical Relationships

A powerful use of mathematics is the modeling of problems and real-world phenomena. The NCTM Algebra Standard recommends that students have opportunities to "model a wide variety of phenomena mathematically in ways that are appropriate to their level" (p. 39). The input-output activities and the balance provide meaningful models for function and equality, respectively. Teachers need to provide opportunities for students of all levels to model other mathematical ideas. Some models are simple physical objects, such as a cylinder and a cone in geometry or a picture in arithmetic. Other models are more complex. Some basic algebraic models are graphs, equations or inequalities, tables, and algorithms. These models approximate the features of a given mathematical situation and are frequently used to solve real-world problems.

Young children can use objects and pictures, as well as symbols, to make models that can help them represent and solve problems. Think about how young children would model a problem about chickens and pigs. They are told there are 7 animals—some chickens and some pigs. Altogether the animals have 20 legs. How can they model the problem to find out how many chickens and how many pigs they have? Here is a sample.

SUE: I put a circle block on the table for each animal—that's 7 circles! Then I'll use these 20 toothpicks for the legs. I'll give each animal two legs.

Now I will give as many animals as I can two more legs. I have 6 toothpicks left. Chickens have two legs and pigs have four legs. So I'll give these legs to the animals until I run out. There, see: I have 3 pigs and 4 chickens.

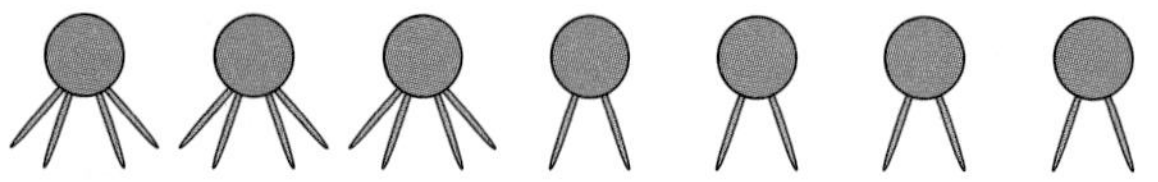

Teachers can help older children develop the idea that a mathematical model has both descriptive and predictive power. Students can first express a pattern in numbers, graphs, or symbols. Then they can use their representations to predict how the pattern will continue or what numbers are missing. In the *Snapshot of a Lesson* problem at the beginning of the chapter, Mr. Trynka's next action will be to ask his students to develop a generalization, "How many toothpicks are needed for 10 pens? 100 pens?" and "Will Juan's result be the same as the others?"

Chia-Lin describes a way to express her result as a pattern:

$1 + 1 \times 3 = 4$

$1 + 2 \times 3 = 7$

$1 + 3 \times 3 = 10$

$1 + 4 \times 3 = 13$

$1 + 5 \times 3 = 16$

Therefore the 10th pen would be

$1 + 10 \times 3 = 31$

and the 100th pen would be

$1 + 100 \times 3 = 301$

Oscar explains his thinking:
The sides of the pen are 1 more than the number of pens, the tops are the same number as the pens, and the bottoms are also the same number as the pens. So for 10 pens I would figure it this way: $1 + 10 + 10 + 10$, so I would have 31 toothpicks, and for 100 pens I would have $1 + 100 + 100 + 100$ or 301 toothpicks, So for me I would take the number of pens + 1 and add two more number of pens.

Arlinda conjectures that $4 + 3 \times$ (number of pens minus 1) would work. So she explains that for 10 pens, $4 + 3 \times (10 - 1)$ would be $4 + 3 \times 9$ or $4 + 27$ or 31.

Juan got the same answer, 16, for the initial problem of 5 pens that Mr. Trynka gave to his students. Would he get the same answer for 10? It would depend on where he places his next pens. Would he put them at the corners or on top of the other boxes? You might explore what answer he would get for each of these situations.

Across the hall, Ms. Burmeister posed the same question to her eighth-grade students. She asked the students from Mr. Trynka's class to describe their ideas for generalizing the problem. Then she asked her students, "Which of the first three students' (Chia-Lin, Oscar, and Arlinda) results are equivalent?"

Using mathematical models to represent and understand phenomena is an important expectation of the NCTM's Algebra Standard. Children in the early grades can create models using objects, pictures, and symbols to represent and solve problems, in particular problems involving addition and subtraction of whole numbers. Children in grades 3 to 5 are then able to model problem situations with objects and use various representations (such as the toothpick model building of the dog pens) to draw conclusions. They are able to recognize that the different models that Chia-Lin, Oscar, and Arlinda designed can give the same results. While they may not be able to show how the solutions are algebraically equivalent, they are able to recognize that the different models result in the same solutions and are equivalent. With these modeling experiences, the students are better able to think about more complex situations as they gain an understanding of the use of mathematical models to represent relationships.

Analysis of Change

Think about how much mathematics involves dealing with change. In the *Snapshot of a Lesson*, the students focus on change as more pens are built for the pet shop. The students describe how they think about the change, but they do not all think about this change in the same way.

Teachers can focus children in grades K-2 on change with many experiences. For example, have children measure their shoe sizes by first placing their heel at a starting point on a large piece of paper; have their partners trace around the shoe and record the name and date. Throughout the year, have them repeat the activity on the same piece of paper. As the year proceeds, discuss the changes that they observe. Are their shoes getting smaller or larger?

Work with patterns can also focus on the concept of change. Much of this chapter has already dealt with the concept of change. What changes with a repeating pattern, such as those In the Classroom 14-1? What changes in the growing patterns? How are the numbers changing in the number patterns?

In grades 3 to 5 the consideration of change begins to focus on how one variable relates to a change in a second variable. In these grades students begin to notice and describe change. How does a student's height change as her age changes? Is she the same height as she was in first grade? Is the change from first grade to second grade the same as from second grade to third grade? Is she growing at a constant rate?

Students in these grades typically investigate the growth of plants from seeds. Use this opportunity to talk about change. Is the plant growing at the same rate over the growing period? What other ideas can you think of that will actively engage children in recognizing change?

Connecting stories to graphs is a marvelous direction for investigating the concept of change. Students might hear a story and create the graph that describes the change the story depicts. Consider a story about the tortoise and the hare, as used in Lesson Idea 14-1. In this story, the tortoise moves slowly and steadily toward the goal. The hare knows he is faster than the tortoise, so after starting out quickly, he decides to take a nap for some time. While he is napping, the tortoise quietly passes him. When the hare wakes up, he realizes that the tortoise is almost at the goal. Yet, even though he goes faster than he did before, the tortoise ends up beating him to the goal.

Students may wonder how to draw a graph of actions without numbers to guide them. In this case you will need to guide them in linking the story to the graphical display. Use the questions to help them make the connections. The last question helps focus students on the rate of change from one time marker to the next. For the tortoise, the change is one distance marker for each one

Lesson Idea 14-1

THE TORTOISE AND HARE

Objective: Investigate the concept of change graphically

Grade Level: 5

- Read the story of *The Tortoise and the Hare*
- Show the graph to describe the story graphically. In this graph the distance to the finish line has been divided into tenths markers. Also, the time it takes for a winner has been marked in tenths.

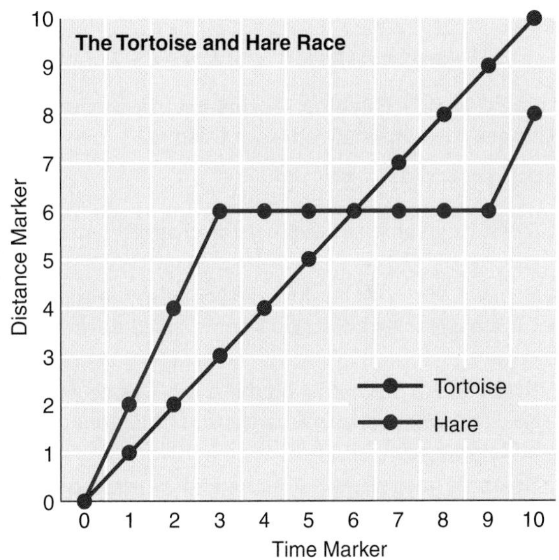

- Guide the student consideration of how the graph models the story:
  - Time 0 means the race is not yet underway. Where is the finish line? How close are the two animals to the finish line?
  - The hare moves out quickly and at time marker 1 is twice as far from the beginning as the tortoise is. How can you tell?
  - At time marker 2, how far has the tortoise traveled from the starting point? How far has the hare traveled from the starting point?
  - How far is the hare from the finish line at time marker 3? at time marker 4? at time marker 5? Describe the actions of the hare during this time.
  - At what time does the hare wake up and start moving again?
  - At what time marker does the tortoise reach the finish line? Where is the hare?
  - The tortoise's steady movement is described in a line. What distance does the tortoise travel between each time marker?

time marker. Yet for the hare, for the first three time markers, the change is two distance markers. The hare's rate of change in the first three time markers is twice the rate of the tortoise. Recognition of the "steepness" of the line is an important preparation for students' future study in grades 6 to 8 of the idea of slope. From time marker 3 to time marker 9, the hare is not moving closer to the finish. The hare is sleeping and the line is horizontal, showing that there is no change in the distance.

In the Classroom 14-5

DESCRIBING CHANGES

OBJECTIVE: **Develop stories that describe the changes in graphical representations.**

GRADE LEVEL: **5**

A. Create a graph that describes the changes in these stories.

Story 1. Kerry slides down a slide from the top. Create a graph to describe Kerry's speed down the slide.

Story 2. Ian is swinging on the swing. Create a graph to describe Ian's distance from the ground as he is swinging.

Story 3. Alice planted some seeds. She watched the growth of one of the plants over time. Create a graph that might describe the growth of the plant over time.

B. Create a story that would be described by each of the graphs.

Graph 1

Graph 2

Provide your students with many experiences in creating graphical representations for stories. Use the stories as lesson warm-ups. Have students explain the changes that they are representing in their graphs. Stories that involve walking or other distance-time relationships provide good beginnings. What does a constant rate of change look like on a distance-time graph (where distance is a function of the time)? In the Classroom 14-5 shows some problems that can be used to encourage students to create graphs to visualize the changes described in different events.

As students become comfortable with creating graphs from stories, have them change to creating stories from graphs that they create. Student stories provide a good way to identify their understanding of the notion of change. What kinds of stories might they create for the two graphs In the Classroom 14-5?

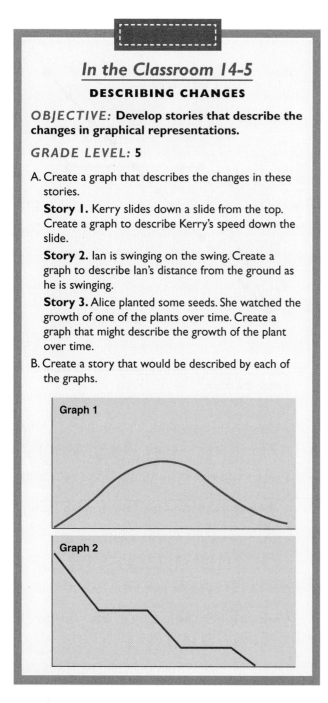

A Glance at Where We've Been

The NCTM's Algebra Standard emphasizes patterns and relationships, ways of representing and analyzing mathematical situations using algebraic symbols, the use of models to represent and understand relationships, and the analysis of change in various contexts. In this chapter we have encouraged the exploration of patterns and relationships in the elementary mathematics curriculum as a way to support children's development of algebraic concepts. From the very beginning of school, children can describe, extend, and create patterns in a variety of ways. As they progress through school, both the types of patterns and their descriptions can become more complex. In describing patterns and relationships, variables can be used in a natural way. Explorations of patterns and relationships can also extend children's thinking from arithmetic to algebra by focusing on three important aspects of algebraic thinking—change, generalizations, and equality. Children in the early grades can create models using objects, pictures, and symbols to represent and solve problems, while children in grades 3 to 5 are able to model problem situations with objects and use various representations (such as the toothpick model building of the dog pens) to draw conclusions. Instruction that engages children in modeling situations mathematically and in developing generalizations provides important experiences to enhance their algebraic thinking.

Things to Do: From What You've Read

1. What is algebraic thinking to you? On which aspects of algebraic thinking is this chapter focused?
2. Why should children study patterns in mathematics?
3. What are three common types of patterns? How do they differ? How are they alike? In particular, how are they alike and different in developing the three aspects of algebraic thinking discussed in this chapter?
4. Develop a symbolic representation that describes the growth of the pennies in the pattern in Figure 14-3.
5. Describe a pattern symbolically that describes the growth of the swimming pool deck in Figure 14-4. How many square tiles would be required for a pool that is 50 tiles long? For a pool that is 100 tiles long?
6. How many glasses will balance the bottle in the Balancing the Bottle Problem in Figure 14-12? Show how you solve this problem.
7. Describe the stages that you would use to help children identify the numeric pattern developed in Figure 14-14b.
8. Create graphs to match the three stories and stories for the graph for In the Classroom 14-5. Compare your responses with another student. What parts of your stories are similar? Why? What explanations are there for the horizontal portions of Graph 2? What kind of change is happening?

Things to Do: Going Beyond This Book

IN THE FIELD

1. *Patterns.* Ask children to investigate the patterns from In the Classroom 14-1 (or ones that you build using materials in their classroom). Do they all describe the patterns in the same way? Ask them to find missing pieces in the patterns. Which is easier for them—to find the next piece in the pattern or find a missing piece in the pattern? Why do you think one is harder than the other if it is?
2. *Relationships.* Create an input-output model as described in this chapter, where a child is inside a box and responds to numeric input from cards other children insert. Ask the other children to describe on paper how the output value is related to the input value. Collect their descriptions of the relationships. Are they all the same? If they have different descriptions, are those descriptions equivalent? Were there errors?
3. *Modeling change.* Ask some students to describe graphs and stories provided In the Classroom 14-5. What kinds of ideas for the changes do they create? Are they all the same?
4. *Algebraic thinking.* Observe an elementary mathematics class where the students are working with patterns. Talk with the children about the patterns they are working with. Can you see evidence of the development of algebraic thinking as they describe how they are thinking about their problems? What ideas could encourage algebraic thinking?
5. *Children's ideas about algebra.* Many students in upper elementary grades have heard the words *algebra* and *variables*. Ask them what they think these words mean. What are their ideas? Do they see these ideas in some of the same ways that were described in this chapter?

IN YOUR JOURNAL

6. Describe your understanding of what algebraic thinking means for elementary students.
7. Describe your understanding of variables. How can you stop children from thinking of a variable as just a placeholder?
8. Examine the treatment of patterns in an elementary mathematics textbook at a grade level of your choice. Respond to the following questions: How does it differ from what is shown here? In particular, does it encourage algebraic thinking? how? If not, how could you extend their ideas to do so?
9. Describe why equality, change, and generalization are important ideas in algebraic thinking.

WITH ADDITIONAL READINGS

10. Read one of the articles in the February 1997 Special Issue of *Teaching Children Mathematics* or *Mathematics Teaching in the Middle School.* Summarize how that article supports the ideas in this chapter about the development of algebraic thinking.

11. Select an instructional idea in *Addenda Series, Grades K–6: Patterns* (Coburn et al., 1992). Design a lesson that incorporates this idea. What will your objective be? How will you organize the students?
12. Select one of the activities found in the *Navigating through Algebra* series, grades pre-K–2 or grades 3–5. Design a lesson that incorporates the idea. Explain how this lesson will help children's algebraic thinking develop.

WITH TECHNOLOGY RESOURCES

13. On the NCTM's Illuminations web site, explore the Pan Balance. You can use this interactive pan balance to "weigh" numeric or algebraic expressions. Develop a lesson plan that would use this activity.
14. Look for some of the commercially available software for algebraic thinking: *The Pond, The Incredible Laboratory, The Algebra Sketchbook, The King's Rule,* and *The Royal Rules* are just a few. Use the Web to search for software and develop a resource description of at least 10 different packages that support the development of algebraic thinking. For each resource, provide the title, company, and cost, along with a description of how this piece of software can be used in the elementary level.
15. Review some current resource books for ideas of using calculators with patterns. Describe one idea in detail that can be used with elementary-aged children as they are exploring patterns.

Book Nook for Children

Ahlberg, Janet, and Ahlberg, Allen. *Each Peach Pear Plum.* Hamondsworth Middlesex: Penguin Books Ltd., 1986.
This is a rhyming book about nursery rhyme characters that can be used to introduce the concept of pattern to pre-K through first graders.

Anno, Mitsumasa. *Anno's Magic Seeds.* New York: Philomel Books, 1995.
This book for grades 3 to 5 begins with a poor farmer who is given two magic seeds. He plants both seeds and he gets four plants. He eats one seed and plants three. The next year he has six plants (two from each seed). There are many opportunities in this story for the students to "do the math" to figure out how many seeds the farmer will have the next year.

Barry, David. *The Rajah's Rice.* New York: W.H. Freeman and Company, 1994.
A smart peasant girl outsmarts the rajah and ensures the village plenty of food forever after. The rajah agrees to give the girl the rice that would cover his chessboard when he puts one grain on the first square and doubles it for the next square, and then doubles that square, and so on for all sixty-four squares. The mathematical concepts in this story are for children in grades 2 to 5.

Calmenson, Stephanie. *Dinner at the Panda Palace.* New York: Harper Collins, 1991.
This book for grades 1 to 3 counts dinner guests as they arrive at the Panda Palace. Each group is one guest larger than the group before. Children can identify the expanding (+1) pattern. They might be challenged to make up a similar story with a different expanding pattern. The class can figure out how many guests it takes to fill the restaurant.

Crews, Donald. *Freight Train.* New York: Viking Penguin, 1985.
The only words in this book are the names of the kinds of cars in the freight train. Each car is a different color. The car/color pattern is then wordlessly repeated in the following pictures of the train moving along the tracks faster and faster. A good beginning book of patterns.

Emberley, Barbara, and Emberley Ed. *Drummer Hoff.* New York: Simon & Schuster, 1967.
This classic book is written in an increasing pattern style. As each new element is added, the list is repeated from the beginning, with the new element now at the end of the list. Students can model the patterns with manipulatives or label the elements and represent the patterns with symbols (e.g., a, ab, abc, abcd, . . .).

Geringer, Laura. *A Three Hat Day.* New York: Harper & Row, 1987.
A man who loves hats has a collection of 12 different hats. One day he decides to wear three hats and it brings him good luck. The students figure out how many different combinations of three he could make with the hats he has. The book is most appropriate for third and fourth graders.

Martin, Bill. *Polar Bear, Polar Bear, What Do Your Hear?* New York: Henry Holt & Co., 1991.
This predictable pattern book is another good illustration of patterns for kindergarten and first graders.

RESOURCES

ANNOTATED BOOKS

National Council of Teachers of Mathematics. *Algebraic Thinking, Grades K–12: Readings form NCTM's School-Based Journal and Other Publications*. Reston, VA: NCTM, 1999.

This book, edited by Moses, provides a multitude of articles designed to help teachers understand the development of algebraic thinking and the types of activities at different grade levels that can foster algebraic thinking in children. A comprehensive collection of 59 specially selected articles defines algebraic thinking, analyzes the algebra curriculum, and supplies many classroom activities dealing with patterns, functions, technology, and so on.

National Council of Teachers of Mathematics. *Navigations—Steering through Principles and Standards: Algebra in Grades PreK–2 and Grades 3–5*. Reston, VA: NCTM, 2001.

These two books make the vision of algebra through the grades a reality. This book series is designed to give teachers ideas, activities, and materials to support the implementation of Algebra standard.

Richardson, Kathy. *Developing Number Concepts, Book 1: Counting, Comparing, and Pattern*. Parsippany, N.J.: Pearson Learning, 1998.

Grounded in teacher awareness, this series includes information about observing and assessing children at work in grades K–3, adaptations for diverse student needs, as well as classroom management. Students solidify beginning number concepts through independent and small-group explorations that encourage the use of a variety of easy-to-handle manipulatives.

ANNOTATED ARTICLES

Bay-Willams, Jennifer M. "What is Algebra in Elementary School?" *Teaching Children Mathematics*, 8(4), (December 2001), pp. 196–201.

Focuses on the NCTM's Algebra Standard for elementary students. Discusses the importance of understanding card patterns, creation and analysis of color-tile patterns, and the role of teachers in teaching algebra to elementary students.

Cai, Jinfa. "Developing Algebraic Reasoning in the Elementary Grades." *Teaching Children Mathematics*, 5(4), (December 1998), pp. 225–230.

More emphasis on developing algebraic strategies in the elementary grades can promote the twin goals of mathematic power and algebra for all. This article discusses the use of algebraic strategies in problem solving, opportunities for algebraic reasoning, advantages of cross-cultural studies in mathematics, problem-solving techniques for algebraic expressions, and direct modeling with concrete objects as powerful problem-solving strategies for young children.

Carpenter, Thomas P., and Levi, Linda. "Building a Foundation for Learning Algebra in the Elementary Grades." *In Brief*, 1(2), (Fall 2000), pp. 1–8.

This article summarizes research and shows that teachers can help students enhance their understanding of arithmetic and build a foundation for learning algebra.

Howden, Hilde. "Implementing the Standards: Patterns, Relations, and Functions." *Arithmetic Teacher*, 37 (November 1989), pp. 18–25.

Focusing on functions, this article demonstrates the development of concepts and skills. Examples and diagrams are included.

MacGregor, Mollie, and Stacey, Kaye. "A Flying Start to Algebra." *Teaching Children Mathematics*, 6(2), (October 1999), pp. 78–86.

This article focuses on five aspects of number knowledge essential for algebra learning at the elementary level. Includes understanding equality, recognition of operations, use of a wide range of numbers, and description of patterns and concepts.

National Council of Teachers of Mathematics. Algebraic Thinking (focus issue). *Teaching Children Mathematics*, 3(February 1997).

This focus issue explains algebra as a way of thinking, a method of seeing and expressing relationships. Numerous ideas suggest ways to build a good foundation and encourage young children to think algebraically, to recognize patterns and regularity, and to reason about relationships and about quantity.

Parker, Janet, and Widmer, Connie Carroll. "Teaching Mathematics with Technology: Patterns in Measurement." *Arithmetic Teacher*, 40 (January 1993), pp. 292–295.

This article focuses on developing measurement skills and presents four hands-on, computer-based activities. Students use concrete materials and computer spreadsheets to explore area, perimeter, and volume of geometric figures.

ADDITIONAL REFERENCES

Blume, Glendon W., and Heckman, David S. "Algebra and Functions." In *Results from the Seventh Mathematics Assessment of the National Assessment of Educational Progress* (eds. Edward A. Silver and Patricia Ann Kenney). Reston, VA: NCTM, 2000.

Coburn, Terrence G.; Bushey, Barbara J.; Holtan, Liana C.; Latozas, Debra; Mortimer, Debbie; and Shotwell, Deborah. *Addenda Series, Grades K–6: Patterns*. Reston, VA: NCTM, 1992.

National Council of Teachers of Mathematics. *Principles and Standards for School Mathematics*. Reston, VA: NCTM, 2000.

CHAPTER 15

Geometry

Snapshot of a Lesson

Students are grouped in interest centers in a kindergarten. Several groups are building with blocks and decorating their structures with wooden geometric solids. Mrs. Pedro moves to a small group of children who are disagreeing about sharing the solids. She uses the opportunity to engage them in an activity to develop familiarity with simple properties of three-dimensional objects.

MRS. PEDRO: Jonathan, what seems to be the problem?

JONATHAN: We want these (pointing to some of the solids)—the ones we have won't stack.

MRS. PEDRO: Let's all solve a puzzle. Whoever can solve it, gets those solids. We need two of each solid and the mystery box.

MARIA: Oh, I remember this game. We have to find out what's in the box.

Turning around so the children cannot see her, Mrs. Pedro puts one solid in the box.

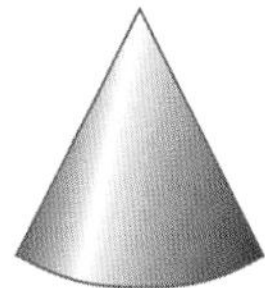  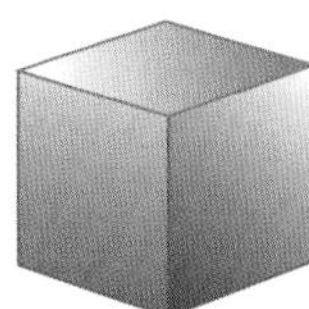

MRS. PEDRO: Right. I put one solid in the mystery box and two solids away so we can't see them. A solid that matches one of these three is in the box.

JONATHAN: Can we shut our eyes and feel?

MRS. PEDRO: No, this time we must only listen. Anthony, you may try listening to the box first. But all of you listen because you may be able to tell.

ANTHONY: It's not rolling like a ball.

JONATHAN: Let me hear. You're right, so it can't be the ball.

MRS. PEDRO: Does everyone agree? Joanne, could you hear?

JOANNE: No, let me try. Yeah, it sort of rolls, but not like a ball.

MRS. PEDRO: Let's put this one aside, since everyone agrees it isn't the ball. Now, it must be one of these two.

MARIA: This one (pointing to the cube) would just slide—slunk, slunk—and wouldn't roll at all.

EARL: This one (pointing to the cone) would roll if it was like this.

ANTHONY: Not if you shook the box. It might not roll.

JONATHAN: Right, so maybe it isn't this one.

MRS. PEDRO: So, which is it?

ALL: This one! Let us see.

Mrs. Pedro opens the box to let them see it was the cone.

JOANNE: Let's try again.

MRS. PEDRO: Yes, here's one that will really make all of you think.

They play several more rounds.

EARL: Let us try to stump you.

MRS. PEDRO: All right. I'll be back in a minute.

Mrs. Pedro hears talking and laughing. They hand her the box.

MRS. PEDRO: Oh, you rascals. You filled the box. You really stumped me.

Introduction

You may find yourself working with some teachers who respond to geometry in the following ways:

"Oh, I could never do proofs."

"The children don't understand it, so why do it?"

"We do it if we finish everything else first."

There are many reasons for such responses. Some are based on past personal experiences, such as an unsatisfactory geometry course in high school or having no geometry in elementary school. Some are based on inappropriate geometry curriculum materials that use, for example, an abstract, definitional approach. Some are based on a historical emphasis on computation—even though geometry has been recommended by various professional groups for over a hundred years.

You may find that you are working with some teachers who respond like this:

"It amazes me who is good in geometry; it's not always my best arithmetic students."

"What a joy it is to see a child's eyes light up as she discovers. . . ."

"Some of my students could work on a geometry problem for hours."

"Geometry gives me an opportunity to work on communication skills and to help children follow instructions."

"The change in the spatial ability of children after they work with geometric shapes always surprises me."

"I love to learn with my students; I never liked geometry before."

These teachers see geometry as more than developing definitions of two- and three-dimensional shapes. They see how learning to solve problems, reasoning, and communicating mathematical thinking are integrated with learning about geometric shapes and relationships. They see children building geometric ideas as they explore and build with different shapes of wooden blocks. These teachers engage their students in learning about geometric shapes and structures. In the process, they encourage their students to describe the characteristics of the shapes and to look for relationships among the shapes. They encourage their students to manipulate objects, building and exploring the shapes. These experiences support children's ability to manipulate these shapes mentally—their spatial visualization ability. These teachers challenge their students to investigate similarities and differences among objects; they ask their students to propose conjectures about the relationships they see. Through these experiences their students are developing their spatial reasoning ability. These teachers recognize the importance of including geometry throughout the mathematics curriculum, beginning as early as possible to engage their students in the informal exploration that must precede more formal thinking in mathematics.

With these same ideas about geometry in the mathematics curriculum, the *Principles and Standards for School Mathematics* (NCTM, 2000) calls for geometry to be an integral part of the mathematics programs of all elementary students in the Geometry Standard (see Figure 15-1).

Geometric thinking, like algebraic thinking, is an important component of mathematics. Also, as with algebraic thinking, young children can be engaged in experiences and activities to foster the

Math Links 15.1

The full-text electronic version of the Geometry Standard is available at the NCTM's web site, which you can access from this book's web site. Click on pre-K–2, 3–5, or 6–8 to read more about this standard.

Instructional programs should enable all students to:	Pre-K–2 Expectations All students should:	Grades: 3–5 Expectations All students should:
Analyze characteristics and properties of two- and three-dimensional geometric shapes and develop mathematical arguments about geometric relationships	• Recognize, name, build, draw, compare, and sort two- and three-dimensional shapes • Describe attributes and parts of two- and three-dimensional shapes • Investigate and predict the results of putting together and taking apart two- and three-dimensional shapes	• Identify, compare, and analyze attributes of two- and three-dimensional shapes and develop vocabulary to describe the attributes • Classify two- and three-dimensional shapes according to their properties and develop definitions of classes of shapes such as triangles and pyramids • Investigate, describe, and reason about the results of subdividing, combining, and transforming shapes • Explore congruence and similarity • Make and test conjectures about geometric properties and relationships and develop logical arguments to justify conclusions
Specify locations and describe spatial relationships using coordinate geometry and other representational systems	• Describe, name, and interpret relative positions in space and apply ideas about relative position • Describe, name, and interpret direction and distance in navigating space and apply ideas about direction and distance • Find and name locations with simple relationships such as "near to" and in coordinate systems such as maps	• Describe location and movement using common language and geometric vocabulary • Make and use coordinate systems to specify locations and to describe paths • Find the distance between points along horizontal and vertical lines of a coordinate system

FIGURE 15-1 Geometry Standard with expectations for children in grades prekindergarten–2 and 3–5.

development of geometric thought. Children bring geometric and spatial understandings to school, understandings that can be extended and enhanced through explorations, investigations, and discussion of shapes and structures. "As students sort, build, draw, model, trace, measure, and construct, their capacity to visualize geometric relationships will develop" (NCTM, 2000, p. 165). With these experiences, children build a foundation for an important aspect of geometric thinking—spatial visualization. They begin to develop the ability to build and manipulate *mental* representations and to mentally visualize those images from different perspectives. By grades 3 to 5, children are ready to learn to reason geometrically where they make, test, and justify conjectures about relationships that they visualize. This early work with geometry helps children learn to interpret and describe their environment and provides them with important tools for problem solving.

Math Links 15.2

A variety of Web resources for geometry, which may be used by teachers and children, may be found at the NCTM's Illuminations web site (accessible from this book's web site) under the Geometry Standard.

Instructional programs should enable all students to:	Pre-K–2 Expectations All students should:	Grades: 3–5 Expectations All students should:
Apply transformations and use symmetry to analyze mathematical situations	• Recognize and apply slides, flips, and turns • Recognize and create shapes that have symmetry	• Predict and describe the results of sliding, flipping, and turning two-dimensional shapes • Describe a motion or a series of motions that will show that two shapes are congruent • Identify and describe line and rotational symmetry in two- and three-dimensional shapes and designs
Use visualization, spatial reasoning, and geometric modeling to solve problems	• Create mental images of geometric shapes using spatial memory and spatial visualization • Recognize and represent shapes from different perspectives • Relate ideas in geometry to ideas in number and measurement • Recognize geometric shapes and structures in the environment and specify their location	• Build and draw geometric objects • Create and describe mental images of objects, patterns, and paths • Identify and build a three-dimensional object from two-dimensional representations of that object • Identify and build a two-dimensional representation of a three-dimensional object • Use geometric models to solve problems in other areas of mathematics, such as number and measurement • Recognize geometric ideas and relationships and apply them to other disciplines and to problems that arise in the classroom or in everyday life

FIGURE 15-1 (*Continued*)

This chapter focuses on ways to help children build an understanding of geometric properties; it also encourages you to have children give reasons or mathematical arguments to justify their thinking. The *Snapshot of a Lesson* that opened this chapter already began this process. The children were making the argument that since it must be one of the three solids, and it can't be two of them, it must be the remaining one.

As you begin this exploration of teaching geometry in the early grades, you may encounter new ideas. By trying the activities and brushing up on some things you may have once learned, you will begin to extend your knowledge of how to help children learn geometry as envisioned in these standards.

FOCUS QUESTIONS

1. Why should the elementary mathematics program include geometry?
2. What does geometric thinking mean for elementary children?
3. How do the van Hiele levels guide teachers in the development of geometric experiences for elementary children?
4. What explorations with solid geometry help build elementary children's geometric reasoning and spatial visualization skills?
5. What explorations with plane geometry help elementary children develop mathematical arguments about geometric relationships?

Geometric Thinking

All too often, elementary programs have concentrated on the names of geometric objects and have not helped children develop a deeper

Table 15-1 • Van Hiele Levels of Understanding

Level	Description	Sample Responses of Children
0 Visualization	Children view a geometric shape as a whole. They do not describe properties of the shape.	Shown a rectangle and asked to identify it, the child may say "It is a rectangle because it looks like a book cover."
1 Analysis	Children recognize the properties of figures. They do not see relations between properties.	A child may say that the rectangle has four sides and square corners.
2 Informal Deduction	Students see relations between properties of a class of shapes.	A student may say that since the angles of a rectangles are right angles, the opposite sides are parallel.
3 Deduction 4 Rigor	Both Level 3 (level at which students can use deduction in an axiomatic system to prove statements) and Level 4 (level at which students see geometry in the abstract) are beyond the scope of most students in middle school. Level 3 is the level at which a proof-oriented high school geometry course is taught.	

understanding of the properties of the objects or the relationships among different geometric objects. These programs have not integrated the thought processes that are essential to understanding in geometry; however, before discussing how to help children learn and use the ideas in the standards, let's step back and examine what the geometry standard means and look at some of the research on childrn's learning of these ideas.

The research of the Dutch couple Dina van Hiele-Geldof and Pierre Marie van Hiele has provided teachers with guidelines for the growth of geometric understanding and thought (Crowley, 1987). They proposed and studied a model of five levels of understanding (see Table 15-1). Examining the geometry provided to many of our students in light of this model, it is not difficult to see why our students do not do well in geometry (U.S. Department of Education, 1996). One reason is that geometry activities in many programs require little more than thought at the visualization level.

Teachers need to provide activities that help children move from the level of thought at which they are operating. In the beginning years, focus children on visualization—becoming familiar with shapes and recognizing that shape in other places. Where else can they see the rectangle shape? Can they see a rectangular shape in the door? What about the table shape? But it is important to move children beyond Level 0, Visualization. Even in kindergarten, students can begin to look at shapes more critically, such as describing a rectangle as having four sides and square corners. With many experiences that specifically require children to describe the properties of the figures (Level 1, Analysis), they begin to recognize and more carefully describe properties of all rectangles. Rectangles have right angles. Rectangles have opposite sides equal. Some students at Level 2 (Informal Deduction) may even be able to describe the notion of the opposite sides being parallel. Asking children to describe the properties of all rectangles helps them deepen their understanding of solids (three-dimensional figures) and planes (two-dimensional figures). Through activities specifically directed at the different levels of understanding, teachers support their students' growth in geometric thinking. As you read the rest of this chapter, see if you can classify the activities as to the level of geometric thought. As you design or select activities, make certain that they will help children move beyond Level 0.

Two major findings from the 1996 NAEP (Martin and Strutchens, 2000) show the growth of children's understanding. First, in grades 4 and 8, students' performance on geometry items improved through the assessments given in the 1990s, and improved significantly on items that used geometric manipulatives. Second, many students can identify simple shapes unless the shapes are presented in unfamiliar contexts or positions, and they can identify simple but not complex properties of shapes.

Geometric thinking extends a student's mathematical thinking: "As students become familiar with shape, structure, location, and transformations, and as they develop spatial reasoning, they lay the foundation for understanding not only their spatial world but also other topics in mathematics and in art, science and social studies" (NCTM, 2000, p. 97).

Location and Spatial Relationships

Typically, teachers describe geometry in elementary school in terms of shapes. Yet, another part of geometry deals with location and movements that describe direction, distance, and position. Where are you? Are you above or below the floor? Are you in front of or behind your desk? Are you between the cabinet and the computer? Where would you be if you moved five steps forward? Starting at your desk, how far from your desk will you be if you move five steps forward and three steps backward?

Examining locations and movements gives children a way to describe their world and give order to their surroundings. It also provides an opportunity to build mathematical concepts such as that of positive and negative numbers (forward and backward) and skills connected to other subjects, such as map skills. Give students opportunities to navigate objects by describing directions and distances traveled and where they must identify positions of an object through several movements. You might begin by taping to the floor of the classroom a map of several city blocks, as in Figure 15-2. Ask students to describe the directions and the distances in blocks between specific locations, such as between the school and home. Have the students describe a set of directions from home to school where they would use the crosswalks provided at stoplights and stop signs. Have the students describe a set of directions from school to the playground.

Later, students can formalize their navigational thinking by examining a coordinate system as in Figure 15-3. The one most familiar to students is the rectangular coordinate system, used in mapping and in mathematics. Again, look at position and movement in the plane or in space and describe each one abstractly: If I am at point (3,1) and move 2 spaces, where could I be?

Transformations

Geometry is often studied in terms of patterns. Think of wallpaper patterns, or look at the three

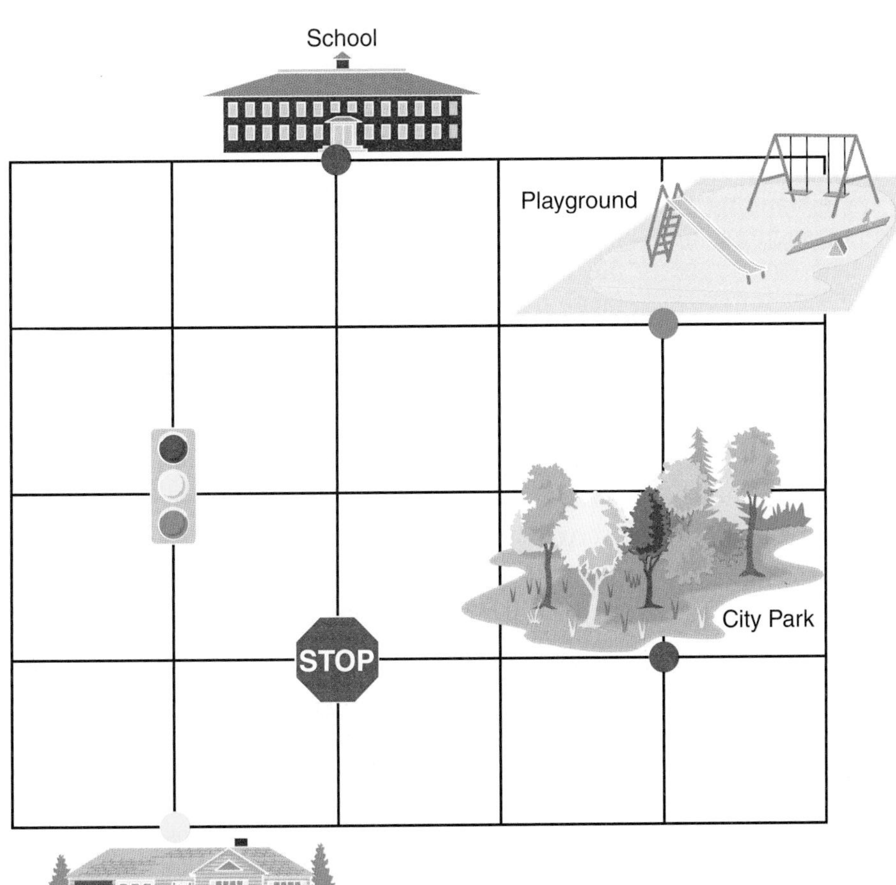

FIGURE 15-2 Map of locations for exploring questions about navigation.

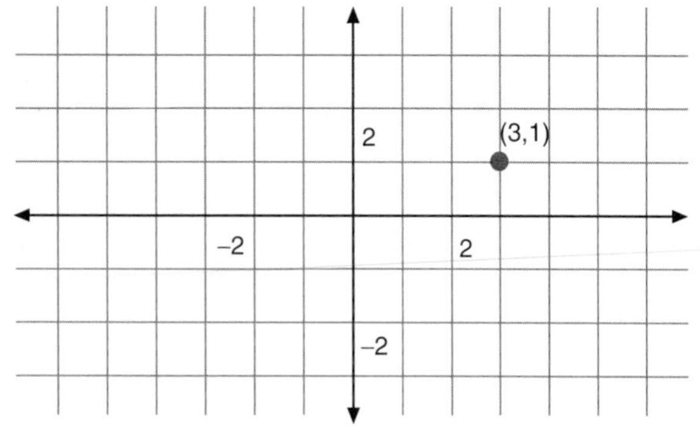

FIGURE 15-3 Coordinate system for describing spatial relationships.

patterns in Figure 15-4. What basic design is repeated? Is the basic design moved to a new position? Is it reflected so its mirror image appears? Or is it turned to the left? These are some of the transformations that young children can analyze and describe. Although these three motions (slide or translation, flip or reflection, and turn or rotation) can describe movements in three-dimensional space, children are only asked to consider transformations in the plane because it is easier for them to check their conjectures.

Research (Jacobson and Lehrer, 2000) with children who are investigating transformations points to the crucial role of the teacher. If students are asked to make conjectures and justify their thinking, they develop a deeper understanding of the transformations. Sample activities such as the one provided In the Classroom 14-2 encourage children to describe patterns in terms of transformations and thus develop their geometric thinking in terms of transformations.

Visualization and Spatial Reasoning

Although you can help children learn geometric ideas by using physical materials, you also need to help them develop visual images of geometric shapes. As your students mature, you can help them manipulate these images in their minds. For example, visualize a rectangle that is longer than it is wide. Now turn it (in your mind) to the right 90 degrees. What does it look like now? Draw a line from the top right corner to the middle of the bottom side. What two figures did you create?

Pattern 1

Pattern 2

Pattern 3

FIGURE 15-4 Wallpaper patterns.

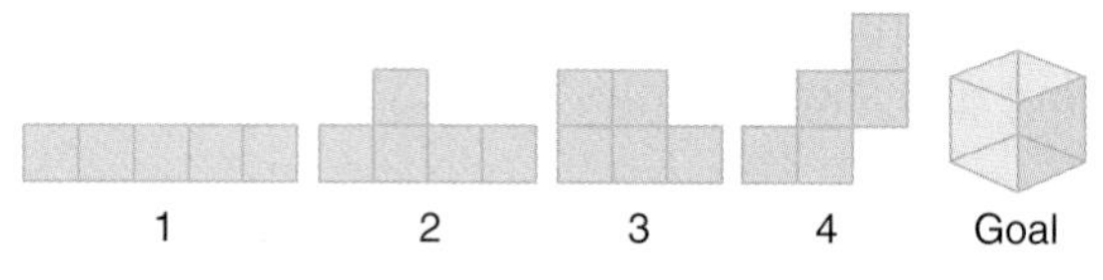

FIGURE 15-5 Which figure can be folded into the shape of the open box, the goal?

Math Links 15.3

An electronic Tangram Puzzle, which allows children to use the puzzle pieces to create and cover various figures, may be found at the NCTM's web site, which you can access from this book's web site. Working with this type of puzzle supports the development of visualization.

Visualizing two-dimensional patterns that can be folded to make three-dimensional patterns is an important aspect of geometric thinking. In the process, you may visualize the folding, or you may use spatial reasoning to help you decide. For example, imagine trying to fold an open cube (no top face) from five connected squares. Which of the configurations in Figure 15-5 could be folded into an open cube? Which would be the bottom square?

Solid Geometry

We live in a three-dimensional world that can be represented and described geometrically. This is the world of the young child—a world that they can explore in the geometric sense. It is important to begin their geometry explorations from their perspective with familiar three-dimensional objects, such as balls and blocks. They may roll the ball and perhaps try to roll the block. The differences in their experiences help them to describe these solid, three-dimensional shapes. In this section, we consider some of the three-dimensional aspects of our surroundings.

Studying geometric properties of three-dimensional objects also provides an opportunity to

Math Links 15.4

A five-part electronic lesson plan for grades 3–5, Exploring Geometric Solids and Their Properties, is available at the NCTM web site, which you can access from this book's web site. These lessons allow children to manipulate and develop the properties of 3-D solids.

www.wiley.com/college/reys

emphasize the process goals of geometry. This section is built around some of these processes: describing and classifying, constructing, exploring and discovering, and relating three-dimensional shapes to two-dimensional shapes. A three-dimensional shape such as a ball is often referred to as a *solid* even though the object may be hollow.

Models play an important role in solid geometry. If wooden or plastic solids are not available, you can make models as suggested later in this section. You and your students should also collect real objects that have particular geometric shapes, including spheres (balls), cylinders (cans), prisms (boxes), and cones, as well as shapes that may not have geometric names.

Describing and Classifying Objects

Children need to be able to describe properties of three-dimensional objects to see how two or more objects are alike or different according to geometric properties. Describing and classifying are processes that need to be extended over time, adding new and more complex properties. These types of activities help children develop their thinking at Level 1 and begin to push them toward Level 2 thinking, as described by the van Hiele model.

In the activities that follow, think about the vocabulary and properties appropriate for beginning, intermediate, and more advanced students. Older children who have not been exposed to three-dimensional activities will benefit from activities such as those described in the beginning activities. Their responses, of course, will be more sophisticated.

BEGINNING ACTIVITIES Children are often taught the names of the geometric shapes, but they do not develop the discriminating power they need to use the names with meaning. In these beginning activities you should build on the children's own vocabulary, adding new words as appropriate. Although the names of the solids can be used, they need not be formally introduced until children have done activities like these.

1. *Who am I?* Put out three objects (such as a ball, a cone, and a box). Describe one of them (it is round all over, it is flat on the bottom, its sides are all flat), and engage the class in guessing which objective you are describing.
2. *Who stacks?* Provide a collection of solids for children in small groups to sort according to which will stack, which will roll, and which will slide. A more sophisticated sorting is one that requires three sets of objects: solids that can be stacked no matter what face is down, solids that can be stacked if placed in some ways but not in other ways, and solids that cannot be stacked in any way.
3. *How are we alike or different?* In a whole-class discussion, hold up two solids such as the following:

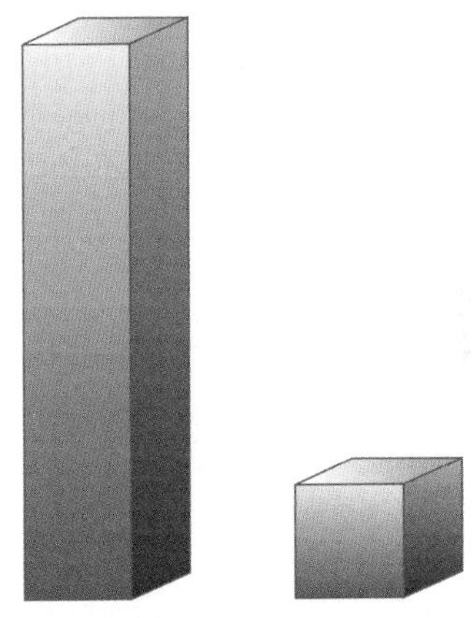

Ask children to tell how they are alike or different. For example, children may compare the two solids shown as follows:

"They are both flat all over."

"One is tall."

"One has bigger sides."

"They have some square faces."

"They have six faces."

4. *Who doesn't belong?* For another whole-class discussion, put out three solids such as these:

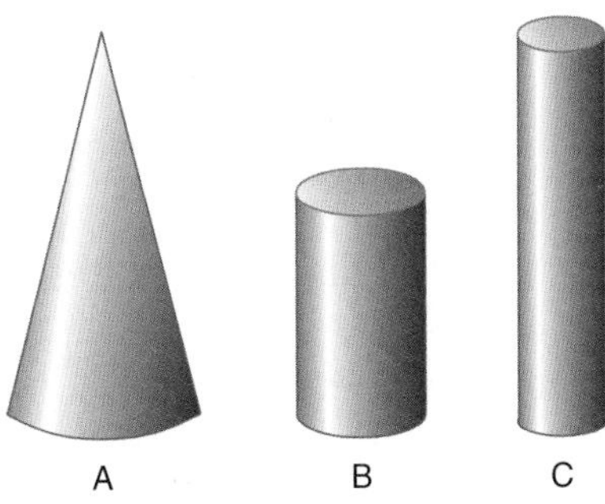

Math Links 15.5

A five-part electronic lesson plan for first grade, I've Seen that Shape Before, is available at the NCTM web site, which you can access from this book's web site. These lessons allow children to identify geometric solids and locate examples of them in their classroom, as well as in buildings and monuments found online.

Ask the children which does not belong with the other two. Since there are many ways to solve this problem, be ready to encourage lively discussion. For example, some children may say A doesn't belong because it has a point. Others may say B doesn't belong because it's short, or C doesn't belong because it's skinny or has a smaller bottom.

5. *How many faces do I have?* A *face* is a flat side of a solid object. Have children in small groups count the number of faces on solids of various shapes. Then ask them to collect objects with six faces (boxes, books), with two faces (cans), and with zero faces (balls). You will be surprised at what they find.
6. *Can you find an object like me?* Put out a solid and ask children to identify real objects in the playground that have the same shape. You may get disagreement about which are alike.

INTERMEDIATE ACTIVITIES The following activities introduce the names of some solids and consider sizes (or measure properties) as well as edges, faces, and vertices.

1. *Using edges, vertices, and faces.* After introducing the concepts of *edge* (a straight segment formed by two faces) and *vertex* (a point at which three or more edges come together), have children in small groups solve these riddles:

   I am a solid with:

   - Eight edges—who am I?
   - Six edges and four faces—who am I?
   - Five corners—who am I?
   - The same number of vertices as faces—who am I?
   - No faces (no corners)—who am I?
   - One face and no corners—who am I?

2. *Classifying solids.* Introduce each type of solid—cube, cone, pyramid, cylinder, and sphere—by putting out solids that are examples and nonexamples of each type of solid. For example, show two or three cylinders and two or three solids that are not cylinders. Ask the students in small groups to select other solids that would belong to the group of cylinders as well as those that do not. This is illustrated in Lesson Idea 15-1. Whether you do these types of activities with objects or on paper, the important part is the surrounding class discussion. For example, many children think B is too "thin" to be a cylinder. They may be thinking at Level 0—it does not look like one. Whole-class discussions about the properties of a

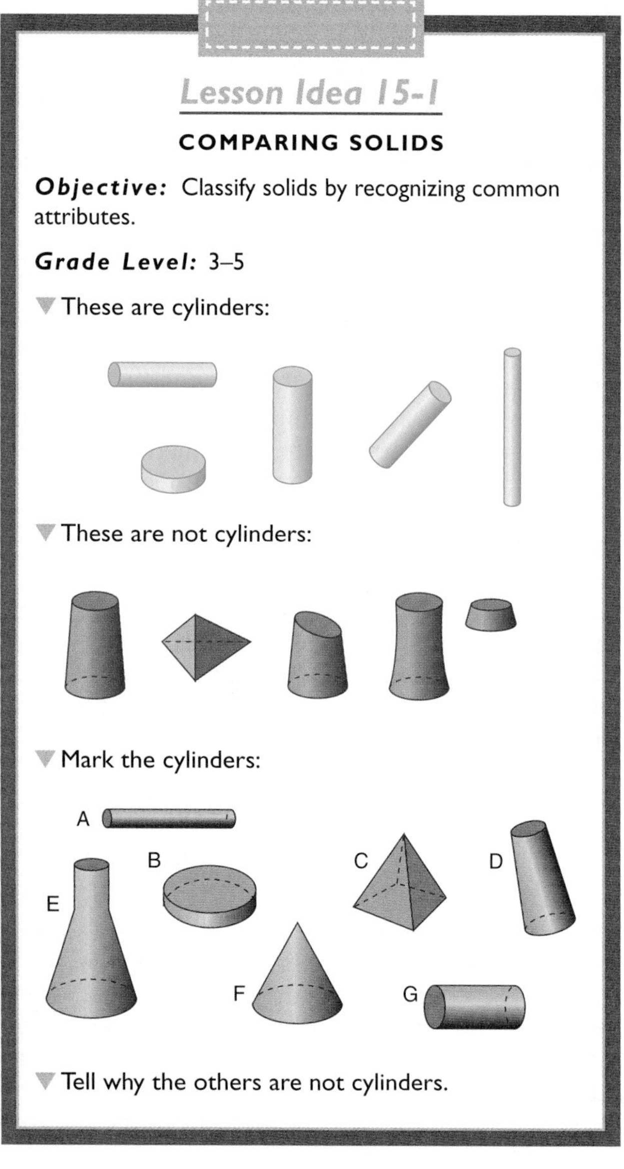

Lesson Idea 15-1

COMPARING SOLIDS

Objective: Classify solids by recognizing common attributes.

Grade Level: 3–5

▼ These are cylinders:

▼ These are not cylinders:

▼ Mark the cylinders:

▼ Tell why the others are not cylinders.

cylinder (a circular cylinder has two faces that are congruent circles joined by a curved surface) can help them move to a higher level of thought.

3. *Searching for solids.* Make up a set of activity cards that have children in small groups search out solids according to the size and shape of the faces and the length of the edges. The clues you give will depend on the solids you use, but here are some samples to get you started:

   Search for a solid with:

   - Exactly two faces that are the same size and shape (*congruent*)
   - Exactly three faces that are the same size and shape
   - All edges the same length
   - Edges of three different lengths

ADVANCED ACTIVITIES These activities focus on the properties of parallel and perpendicular faces and edges as well as more careful definition and classification of the solids.

1. *Parallel faces.* This activity can be done after parallel faces have been introduced. It consists of questions about real objects and why faces are parallel. A few sample questions that you can use in a whole-class discussion are given here to start you thinking:

   Why are the top and bottom of soup cans parallel?

   Why are shelves parallel to the floor?

   Why are roofs of houses in cold climates usually not parallel to the ground?

   Why is the front side of a milk carton parallel to the back side?

2. *Perpendicular edges.* In the Classroom 15-1 provides clues about particular solids, focusing on perpendicular edges, and asks students to construct the solids from sticks and connectors. See the "stick" models section that follows for a variety of materials that can be used to model the mystery objects. Students enjoy making their own mysteries for other students to solve. This experience provides an excellent opportunity to work on developing written descriptions that are clear, precise, and noncontradictory.

3. *Right prisms.* This activity introduces the definition of right prisms and how to name prisms. Show examples and nonexamples of right prisms (as in the second of the intermediate activities), and ask students to describe the bases and faces, ultimately encouraging them to come up with the definition of *prism*—a solid that has congruent and parallel bases (top and bottom) joined by rectangular faces. Then have students in a whole-class activity discuss how prisms are named. See if they can determine a way to distinguish between prisms. For example, if the base is a triangle, it is a triangular prism.

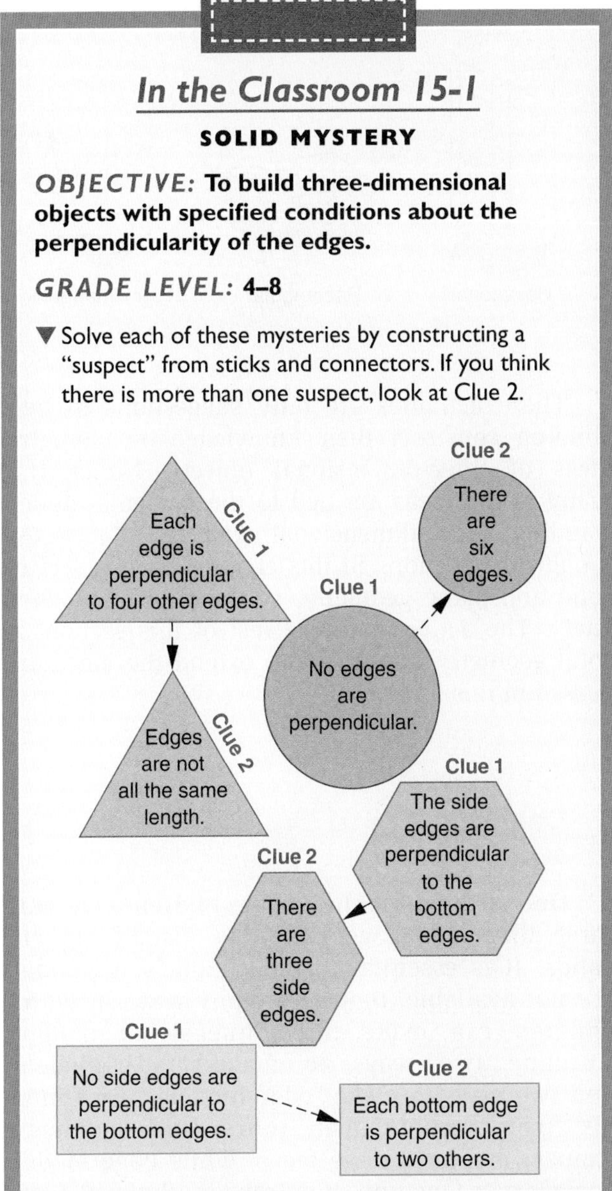
In the Classroom 15-1
SOLID MYSTERY
OBJECTIVE: To build three-dimensional objects with specified conditions about the perpendicularity of the edges.
GRADE LEVEL: 4–8
Solve each of these mysteries by constructing a "suspect" from sticks and connectors. If you think there is more than one suspect, look at Clue 2.
Clue 1
Each edge is perpendicular to four other edges.
Clue 2
Edges are not all the same length.
Clue 1
No edges are perpendicular.
Clue 2
There are six edges.
Clue 1
The side edges are perpendicular to the bottom edges.
Clue 2
There are three side edges.
Clue 1
No side edges are perpendicular to the bottom edges.
Clue 2
Each bottom edge is perpendicular to two others.

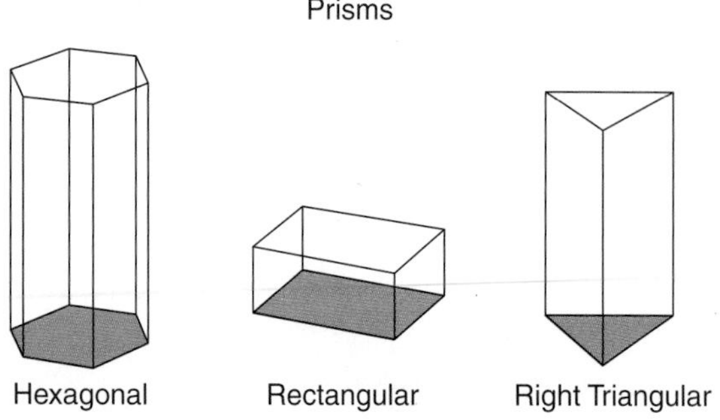

These activities are only suggestions to help children construct their knowledge of geometric ideas of three-dimensional objects. Notice that many of the ideas are tied to the students' understanding of two-dimensional geometric objects. Although the sections in this chapter have separated solid and plane geometry, you should blend their study. The activities in the rest of this section on solid geometry reinforce and extend the ideas discussed in this section.

Constructing to Explore and Discover

One of the difficulties that children have with three-dimensional geometry is visualizing the solids. It is essential to have models. If models are not available, there are many ways in which children can make three-dimensional models. Examine two ways to make "face models" and two ways to make "edge models." Face models (construction-paper tubes and polyhedra shapes) emphasize the faces, while edge models (newspaper-tape and gumdrops-toothpicks) focus on edges.

As children are making the models, they often discover many things about the solids. There are, however, other properties or relationships that they may not discover, so they need other ways to explore them. The following activities provide examples of ways to structure students' investigations of various properties.

PAPER TUBES Some of the easiest and most versatile models can be made from heavy construction paper. Figure 15-6 shows how to make open-ended tube models of prisms. The top and bottom faces may be added to these models by tracing the top of the tube, cutting out the shape, and taping it to the tube. As this figure suggests, many variations of prisms can be made, and these can be cut (truncated) to create many strange shapes.

The exploration In the Classroom 15-2 is a variation of a famous formula, Euler's (pronounced "oil-ers") formula, which relates the number of edges (E), faces (F), and vertices (V) of a polyhedron to each other: $V + F = E + 2$. Polyhedra are the three-dimensional analogy to polygons in two dimensions. Prisms and pyramids are polyhedra, but spheres, cones, and cylinders are not. Any solid whose faces are all polygons is a polyhedron. In the Classroom 15-2 deals with a special case of the more general formula because it uses only prisms. Since the prisms have no top or bottom face, we call them tubes. The formula for tubes is $V + F = E$, which is more readily evident than Euler's more general formula, which holds for all polyhedra. Several other patterns can be found for these paper tubes; have your students look for them. For example, children may see that the number of edges is always three times the number of faces (not counting the top and bottom). This is a good place to have them describe the general case

Use construction paper and masking tape to construct these tubes. Fold and tape each as shown.

- Prism with three congruent faces:

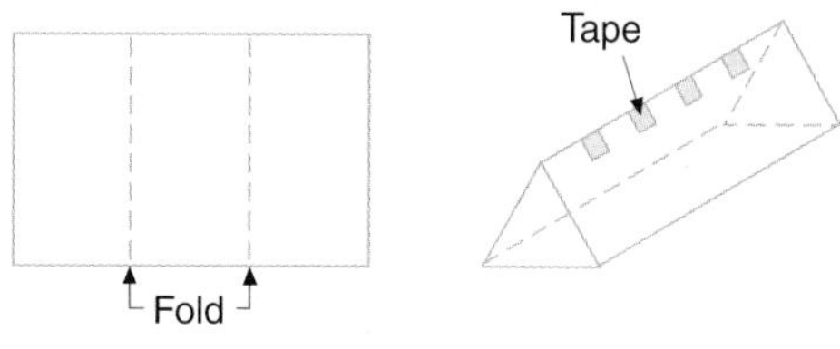

- Six-sided prism:

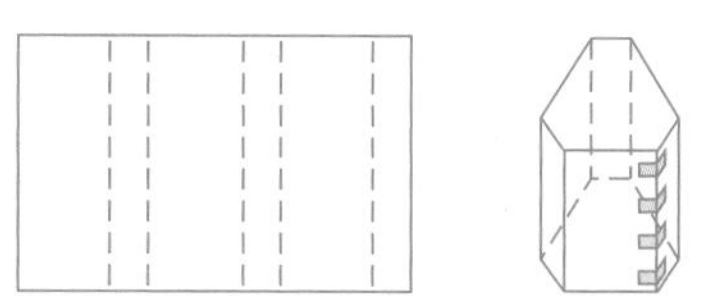

- Truncated prism:

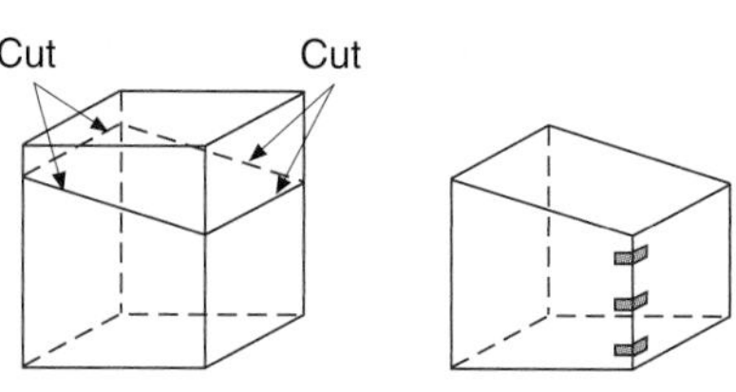

FIGURE 15-6 Constructing tubes to think about properties of prisms.

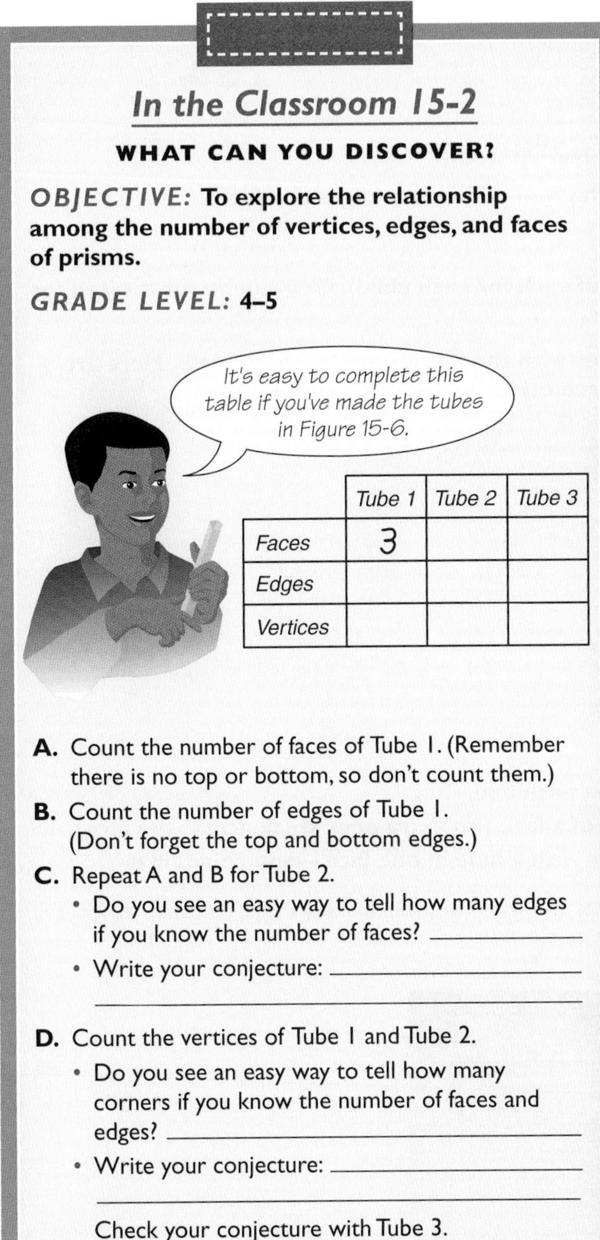

In the Classroom 15-2

WHAT CAN YOU DISCOVER?

OBJECTIVE: **To explore the relationship among the number of vertices, edges, and faces of prisms.**

GRADE LEVEL: **4–5**

It's easy to complete this table if you've made the tubes in Figure 15-6.

	Tube 1	Tube 2	Tube 3
Faces	3		
Edges			
Vertices			

A. Count the number of faces of Tube 1. (Remember there is no top or bottom, so don't count them.)

B. Count the number of edges of Tube 1. (Don't forget the top and bottom edges.)

C. Repeat A and B for Tube 2.
- Do you see an easy way to tell how many edges if you know the number of faces? ____________
- Write your conjecture: ____________

____

D. Count the vertices of Tube 1 and Tube 2.
- Do you see an easy way to tell how many corners if you know the number of faces and edges? ____________
- Write your conjecture: ____________

____

Check your conjecture with Tube 3.

algebraically: $E = 3 \times F$ if E is the number of edges and F is the number of faces.

Constructing Polyhedron Models

There are many examples of polyhedra that are neither prisms nor pyramids. In the Classroom15-3 explores making polyhedra with regular polygons whose patterns are given on square or triangular grid paper. Commercial models are also available—either plastic shapes that clip together or card stock models that fit together with rubber bands. If you have these, then there are many different polyhedra to explore.

"STICK" MODELS Models can be made from straws, pipe cleaners, toothpicks, or other "sticks" that can be connected with clay or tape. There are also reasonably priced, commercial materials designed for this purpose.

Young children enjoy building stick models from toothpicks and gumdrops. In the Classroom 15-4 extends the exploration of building freely to building a stick model when the number of gumdrops (vertices) and the number of edges (toothpicks) are specified. If you need an even more sophisticated activity, return to In the Classroom 15-1.

In the Classroom 15-5 illustrates how to make a three-dimensional figure from newspaper sticks and tape. Rolling the paper tightly takes some practice for some children; however, as with many

In the Classroom 15-3

POLYHEDRA NETWORKS

OBJECTIVE: **To explore polyhedrons made from networks.**

GRADE LEVEL: **5**

MATERIALS: **Triangular and square grid paper (see Appendix B for masters).**

DIRECTIONS: **Color these shapes on your grid paper. Cut out the colored shape, and see if you can fold on the lines to make a polyhedron. Make your own design and try it.**

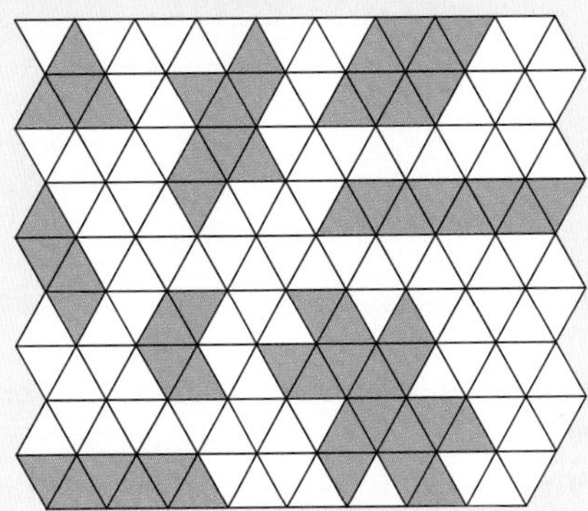

Now try square grid paper. Color six adjacent squares, then cut and fold into a cube. How many different ways can you color the adjacent squares? Which fold into a cube?

In the Classroom 15-4

GUMDROPS AND TOOTHPICKS

OBJECTIVE: **To construct three dimensional figures with given number of edges and faces.**

GRADE LEVEL: **4–5**

MATERIALS: **Gumdrops and toothpicks (about twenty of each for each child). Clay can be substituted for gumdrops.**

DIRECTIONS: **Explore making three-dimensional shapes with the gumdrops and toothpicks. Here are a few examples. How many gumdrops and toothpicks did each take?**

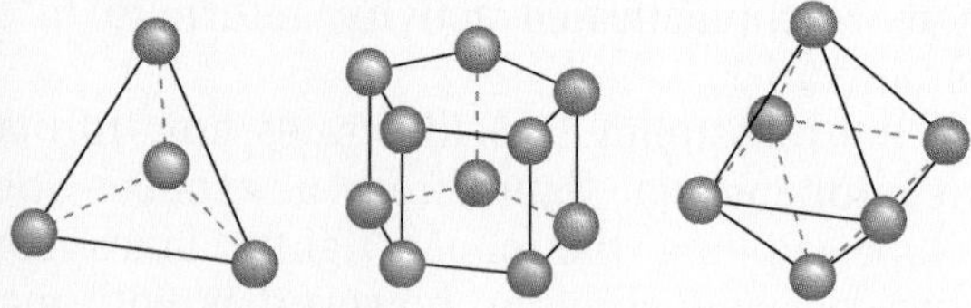

Now, try some with the given number of gumdrops and toothpicks.
Three rules to follow:

1. **Two gumdrops can be used on each toothpick, one at each end.**
2. **Toothpicks should only be used to make the outline of a face (no extra ones stuck across the face).**
3. **The figure should be closed. Imagine it is a container with a hole in one face—you could fill it.**

Some of these are not possible. See if you can figure out which ones and why. If you can make a shape, tell whether it is a prism, a pyramid, or another shape.

Letter	Gumdrops	Toothpicks	Can Make? (yes or no)	Name of Shape
A	6	9		
B	5	8		
C	8	5		
D	6	10		
E	7	12		
F	8	12		
G	10	15		
H	12	18		
I	8	14		
J	10	3		
K	6	12		
L	5	9		

1. **What is your conjecture about the ones that could not be made?**
2. **Which ones make pyramids? What is the relationship of the number? Using the models, explain why.**
3. **Which ones make prisms? What is the relationship of the numbers? Using the models, explain why.**

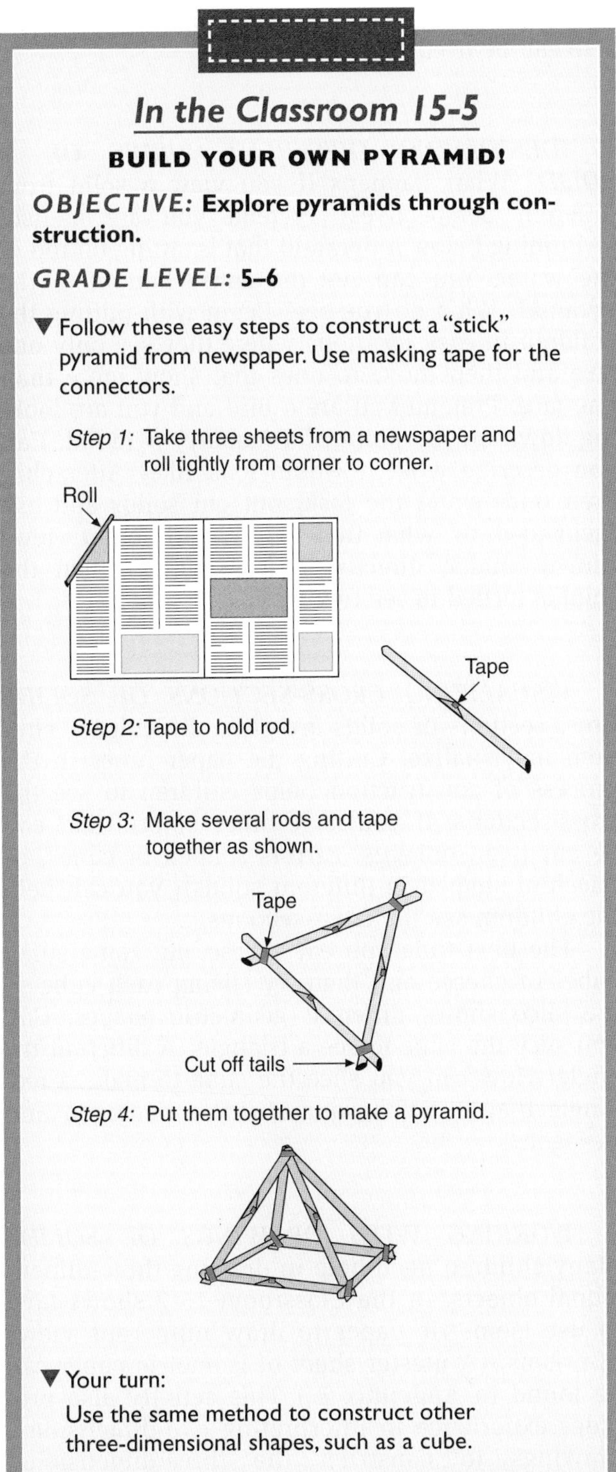

geometry activities, often you will be surprised at who can do this easily. When building three-dimensional objects with newspaper sticks, the children can investigate the rigidity of triangles, squares, or other polygons. They should find that the pyramid built with In the Classroom 15-5 is a rigid structure, but the cube needs bracing to be sturdy.

In the Classroom 15-5
BUILD YOUR OWN PYRAMID!
OBJECTIVE: Explore pyramids through construction.
GRADE LEVEL: 5–6
▼ Follow these easy steps to construct a "stick" pyramid from newspaper. Use masking tape for the connectors.
Step 1: Take three sheets from a newspaper and roll tightly from corner to corner.
Roll
Tape
Step 2: Tape to hold rod.
Step 3: Make several rods and tape together as shown.
Tape
Cut off tails
Step 4: Put them together to make a pyramid.
▼ Your turn:
Use the same method to construct other three-dimensional shapes, such as a cube.

Relating Three Dimensions to Two

Because three-dimensional objects often must be pictured in two dimensions, children must be able to relate the objects to pictures. They also need to be able to analyze a three-dimensional object in terms of its two-dimensional parts, as in Figure 15-5, where you were asked to determine which figure could be folded to form a box. Constructing solids from networks and other materials assists in this skill, but you can help focus directly on the two-dimensional aspect by the activities you choose and the questions you ask.

MATCHING IMPRINTS OF FACES WITH THE SOLID Make imprints in play dough (homemade works great) of the faces of wooden geometric solids. Have children match each solid with a face. The faces can be traced instead of making imprints, but younger children can work easily with imprints. In the Classroom 15-6, which provides a

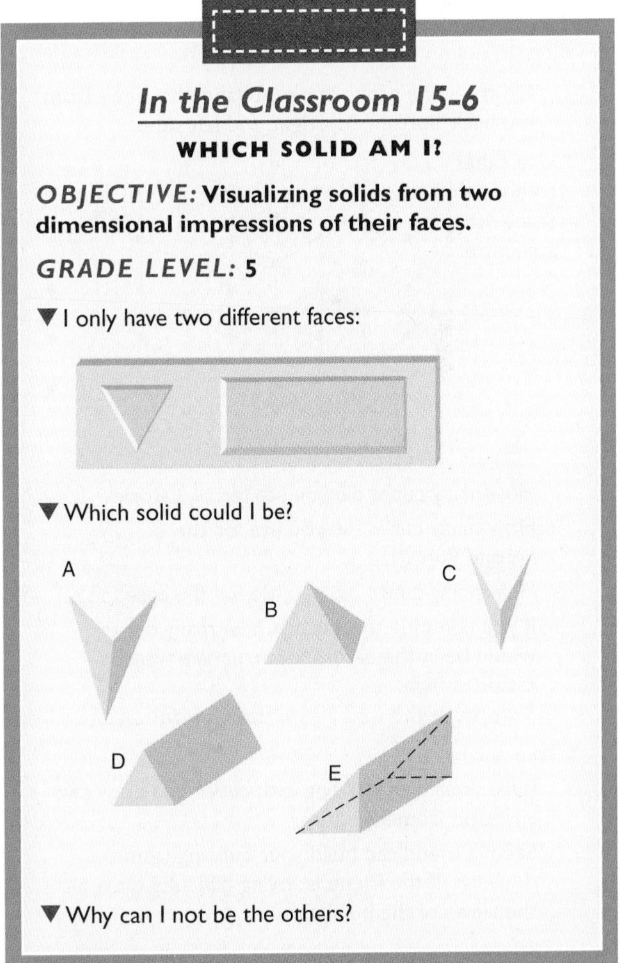

WHICH SOLID AM I?

▼ I only have two different faces:
▼ Which solid could I be?

▼ Why can I not be the others?

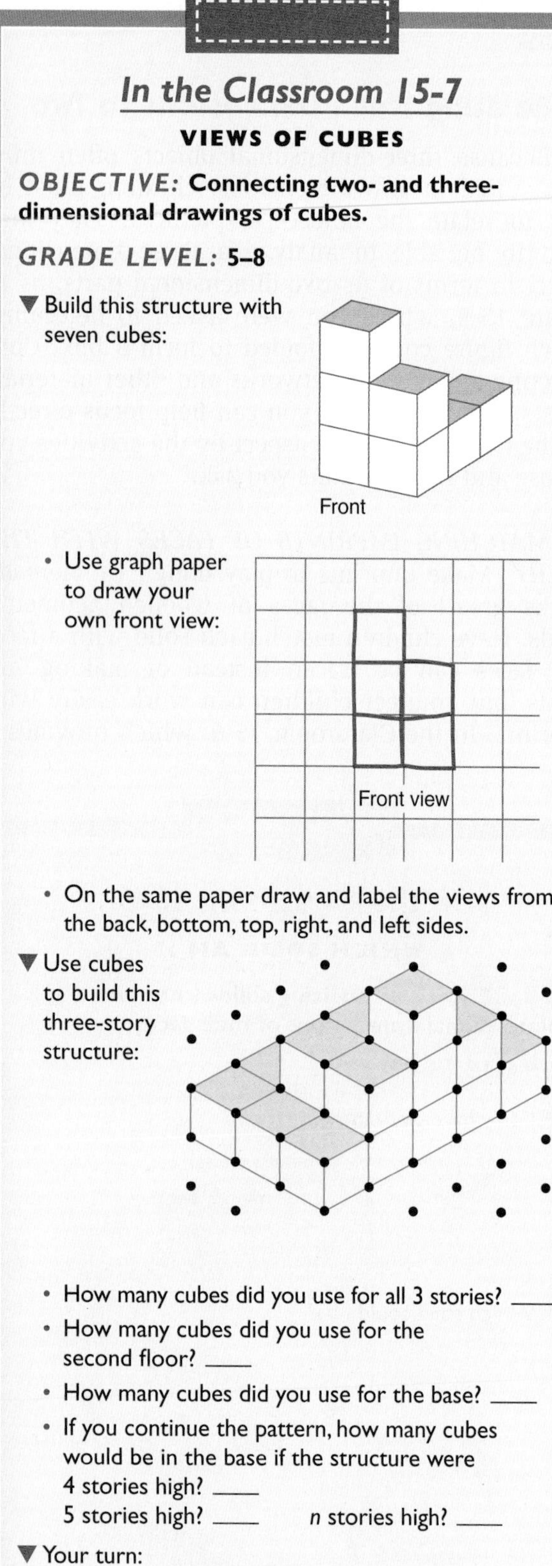

In the Classroom 15-7

VIEWS OF CUBES

OBJECTIVE: **Connecting two- and three-dimensional drawings of cubes.**

GRADE LEVEL: **5–8**

▼ Build this structure with seven cubes:

- Use graph paper to draw your own front view:

- On the same paper draw and label the views from the back, bottom, top, right, and left sides.

▼ Use cubes to build this three-story structure:

- How many cubes did you use for all 3 stories? ____
- How many cubes did you use for the second floor? ____
- How many cubes did you use for the base? ____
- If you continue the pattern, how many cubes would be in the base if the structure were 4 stories high? ____ 5 stories high? ____ *n* stories high? ____

▼ Your turn:

- Build your own building with cubes and draw two views on isometric paper.
- See if a friend can build your building from the drawings. If the friend is having difficulty, draw all the views of the building.

similar matching activity with pictorial models, also can be used.

IDENTIFYING DIFFERENT VIEWS OF A SOLID What happens if you view a solid from different perspectives? Pretend you are a fish, swimming below a pyramid that is sitting on top of the water. You can see the entire bottom of the pyramid. What do you see? Begin with putting the children in easy locations where they see only one face and then move to ones that show more than one face. Pretend you are a bird and you are looking down on the point of a (square) pyramid. Can you describe what it would look like? After children understand the task, put out solids and ask them to draw what they see from different views (down, under, directly in front, front when the solid is turned to see two faces).

VISUALIZING CROSS-SECTIONS OF SOLIDS Cross-sections of solids are often difficult for children to visualize. Cutting the paper tubes in the process of construction helps children to see the cross-sections. If you have other objects that can be cut (e.g., oranges, carrots shaped in cones, or zucchini shaped in different solids), you can help the children see the cross-sections.

The next time you eat cheese, cut some small cubes of cheese and then try slicing each cube so the slice shows different geometric shapes. Can you slice the cube to see a triangle? A different triangle? How can you slice the cube to make a rectangle that is not a square? Try a pentagon and hexagon.

WORKING WITH DRAWINGS OF SOLIDS Many children need help in drawing three-dimensional objects. In the Classroom 15-7 shows how to use isometric paper to draw numerous views of prisms. (A master sheet of isometric paper can be found in Appendix B.) This activity also provides experience in interpreting two-dimensional drawings to construct the three-dimensional structures.

Experiences such as these can help children understand the concept of volume. As children build various shapes with a given number of cubes, they are investigating the relationship of volume and shape. How many rectangular prisms can you build that have a volume of 24 cubes? Look at the pictures in Figure 15-7 that fifth-grade students drew of a prism made with 12 cubes. What concepts are being developed?

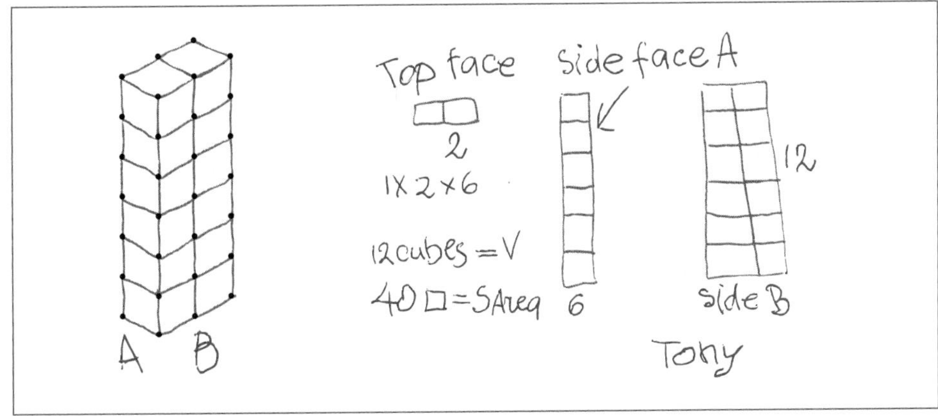

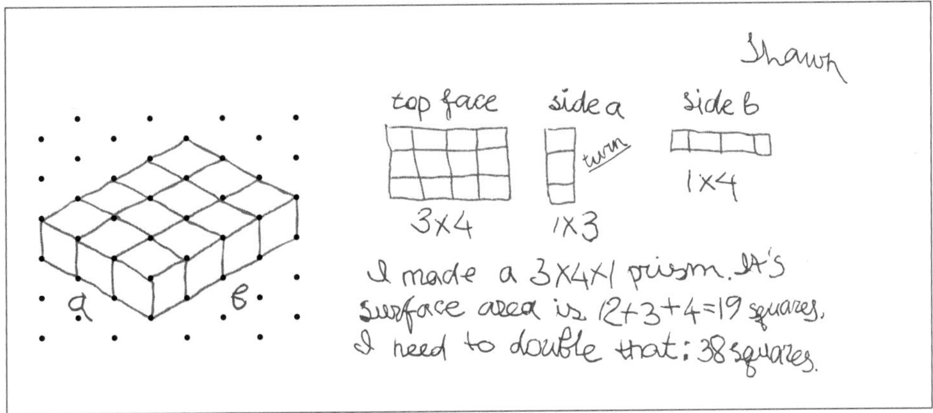

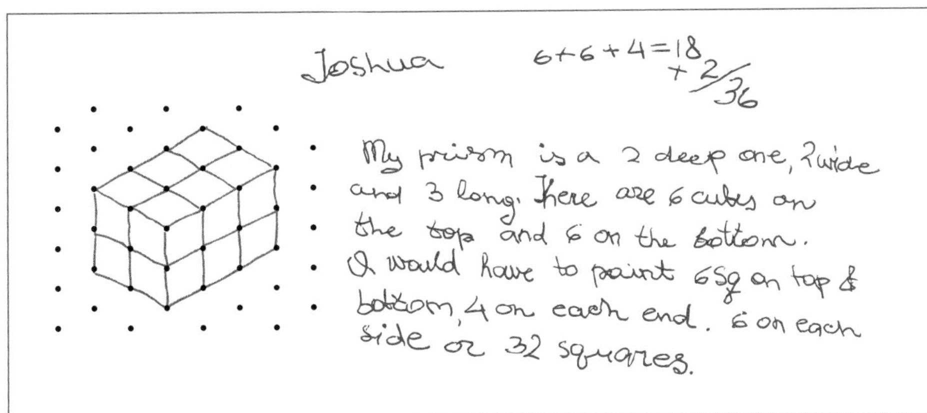

FIGURE 15-7 Fifth graders' drawings of a prism built using 12 cubes.

Plane Geometry

Children's investigations of solid figures requires them to think about the faces of the solids. Their investigations naturally integrate thinking about two-dimensional shapes, relationships among shapes, and classification schemes as they begin to describe the properties of the three-dimensional objects. This recognition of the two-dimensional aspects is about plane geometry and underscores the importance of integrating their thinking about two- and three-dimensional ideas.

Children can learn this two-dimensional view through sample activities involving many types of physical materials, such as geoboards, pattern blocks (see Figure 15-8), and paper strips. Many other engaging geometric activities can be done with paper and pencil, and computer programs also provide rich environments for geometric explorations.

In examining three-dimensional shapes, students often focus on the faces (two-dimensional);

Math Links 15.6

A variety of electronic geometry manipulatives may be found at the National Library of Virtual Manipulatives for Interactive Mathematics web site, which you can access from this book's web site.

similarly, in examining two-dimensional shapes, students often focus on the sides or vertices (one-dimensional). Teachers can build these one-dimensional concepts as they occur naturally within a two-dimensional context.

Properties of Two-Dimensional Shapes

Children first recognize shapes in a holistic manner (Van Hiele Level 0)—that is, a triangle is a triangle because it looks like a shape that someone has called a triangle. If an equilateral triangle with its base parallel to the bottom of the page is always used, then this shape will be children's image of a triangle. It is important to provide many examples and nonexamples of shapes so that children can have rich images of the different shapes. For example, it is important to provide children with images of equilateral triangles in different orientations so they are able to see that the orientation is not part of the image description. Figure 15-9 displays both equilateral and right triangles in different orientations so that students are able to see that orientation is not an important feature of the definition of those triangles.

Children have an intuitive feel for the differences among shapes, but they need ways to describe these differences. By considering the properties of shapes, you can help develop children's ability to describe and extend their knowledge of particular shapes. For example, think of how you would describe a rectangle to someone who had never seen one. Draw a strange shape that has no special name to you, and try to describe it to someone. Consider the properties of the shape that you used in your description.

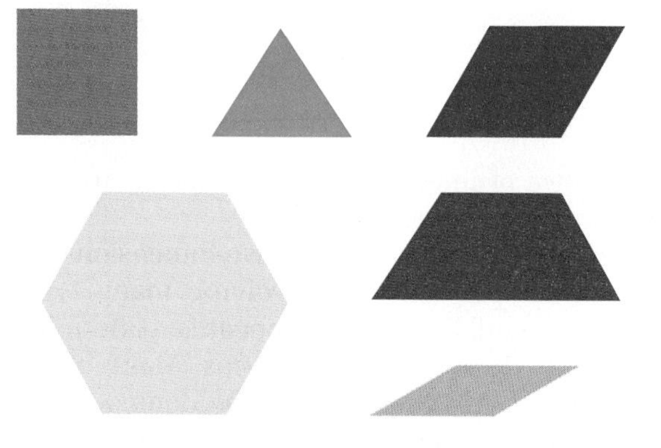

FIGURE 15-8 Colored pattern blocks and their two-dimensional shapes.

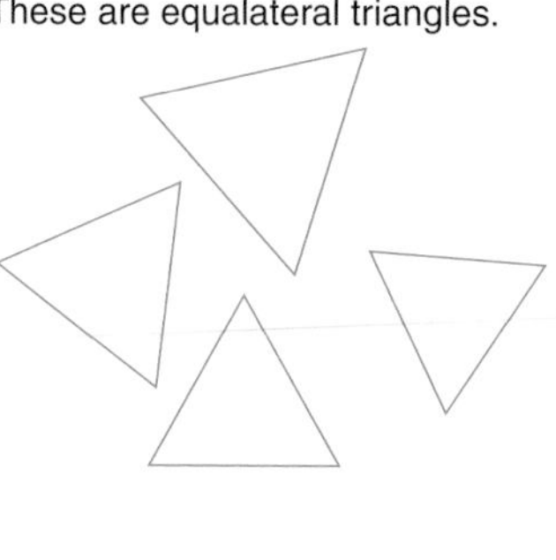

These are equalateral triangles.

These are right triangles.

FIGURE 15-9 Varied orientations of equilateral and right triangles, emphasizing that orientation is not a property of triangles.

There are many ways of describing geometric shapes, as illustrated in the activities that follow. The different properties are discussed separately but should be combined in activities similar to those given. Realize that keeping two or more properties in mind is more difficult than just focusing on one. For example, creating a figure with four sides on a geoboard is at a much simpler level than creating a figure with four sides that has two right angles and one side longer than the other.

NUMBER OF SIDES One of the first properties children focus on is the number of sides. They readily count the number of sides (line segments) of a shape, unless a shape has many sides. Then they may need to mark the place where they begin counting. As you have children participate in activities such as those that follow, they will begin to make many conjectures about shapes and learn vocabulary.

1. *How many sides?* This simple activity uses pattern blocks (see Figure 15-8). If you do not have pattern blocks, you can use other shapes or cut shapes with different numbers of sides from construction paper. Each child needs only one shape for this activity.
   - Call a number and ask children who have a shape with that number of sides to stand. Call numbers such as two and seven, for which no one will stand.
   - Then have a search for all the different shapes that have three sides, four sides, five sides, six sides, and zero sides (the circle).
   - Put a sample of each different shape somewhere within view of all children, and call on children to tell how the four-sided shapes differ (some are bigger than others, some are skinny, and some are slanty—accept their everyday words at this point). It is important for them to realize that the number of sides does not determine the shape.
2. *Can you make _____?* In this challenging activity, children make a figure of a given number of sides on a geoboard. (See Appendix B for a geoboard model.) Give each child a geoboard and one rubberband. Begin by asking them to make simple shapes, and gradually add other conditions. For example:

   Can you make a four-sided figure?

   Can you make a four-sided figure that touches only four pegs?

   Can you make a four-sided figure that touches six pegs?

   Can you make a four-sided figure that has two pegs inside (not touching) it?
3. *Less is best.* In the Classroom 15-8 provides a more advanced activity in which children put pattern blocks together to make new shapes with as few sides as possible. Two or more children choose three pattern blocks. Watch to see that they are counting the sides of the new shape, not the sides of the pieces. For example, if Marietta said six, it is likely that she counted the sides of the pieces.

NUMBER OF CORNERS Closely related to counting the numbers of sides is counting the number of corners. Children will soon realize that any polygonal figure has the same number of sides as corners if they count both on each shape. The activities suggested for counting the number of sides can be modified for counting corners.

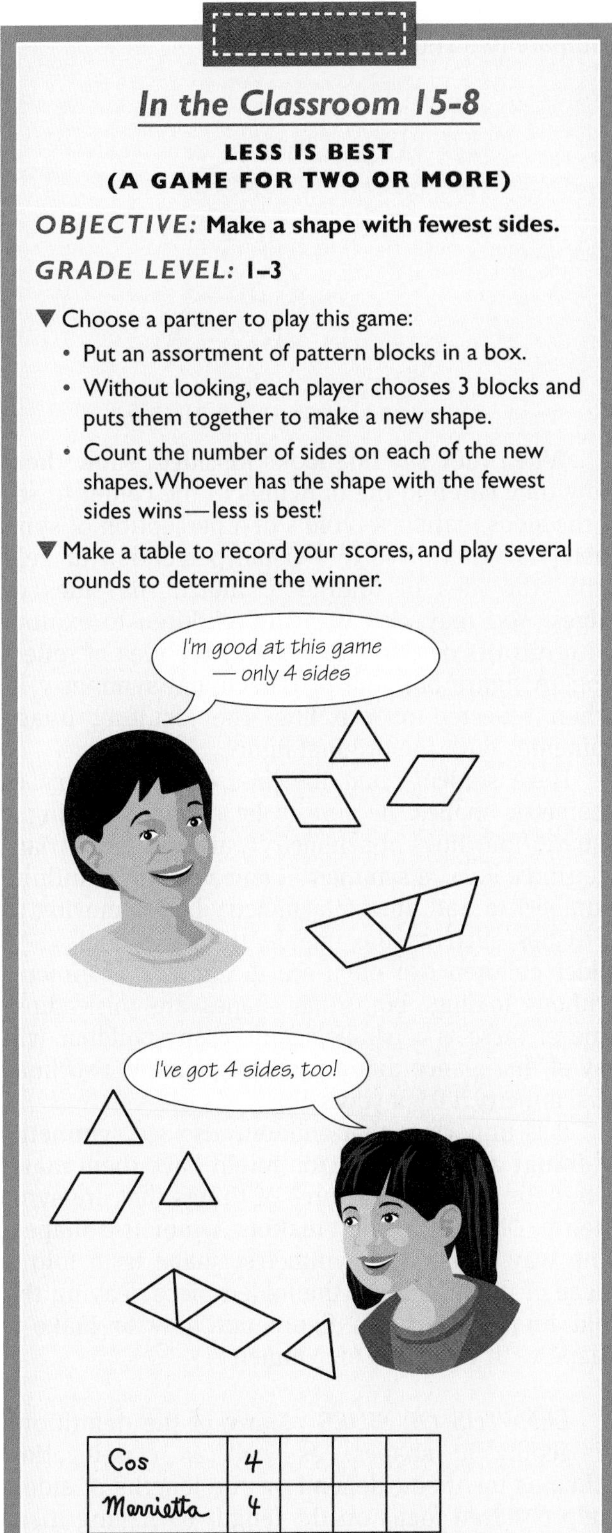

In the Classroom 15-8

LESS IS BEST
(A GAME FOR TWO OR MORE)

OBJECTIVE: **Make a shape with fewest sides.**

GRADE LEVEL: **1–3**

▼ Choose a partner to play this game:
- Put an assortment of pattern blocks in a box.
- Without looking, each player chooses 3 blocks and puts them together to make a new shape.
- Count the number of sides on each of the new shapes. Whoever has the shape with the fewest sides wins—less is best!

▼ Make a table to record your scores, and play several rounds to determine the winner.

I'm good at this game
— only 4 sides
I've got 4 sides, too!

Cos	4			
Marietta	4			

SYMMETRY Two types of symmetry—line or reflectional symmetry and rotational symmetry—may be used to describe geometric shapes as well as objects in the real world.

To introduce line symmetry, ask children to compare two snowmen:

When they say one looks lopsided, show them how they can fold the drawings in the center to see if the sides match. A child's first perception of symmetry is visual. Use this visual perception to help build the idea of folding to match the sides or edges. You may also want the children to explore with mirrors or Miras to bring in the idea of reflection. A figure has line or reflectional symmetry if, when reflected over a line, the resulting image coincides with the original figure.

Have students find the line(s) of symmetry of geometric shapes. Be sure to let them try folding a square (four lines of symmetry), an equilateral triangle (three lines of symmetry), and a circle (an infinite number) to find lines of symmetry before moving to activities such as the one In the Classroom 15-9. Older children can often see the lines of symmetry without folding, but some shapes are misleading. One of these is a parallelogram. Many children will say at first glance that a parallelogram has two lines of symmetry. (Try it yourself.)

It is important that children also see symmetry in things around them. You might have them make a bulletin board of pictures of things that are symmetric. They also enjoy making symmetric shapes. One way to make a symmetric shape is to fold a piece of paper and cut the folded piece, leaving the fold intact. (Can you figure out how to make a shape with two lines of symmetry?)

LENGTHS OF SIDES Many of the definitions of geometric shapes, as well as classification schemes for them, depend on the lengths of sides. Help children focus on the length by having them find the shape with the longest side, find the shortest side of a given shape, and measure lengths of sides. In the Classroom 15-10 presents an example of a more advanced activity in which children make shapes on a geoboard according to certain specifications about the lengths of the sides. Try the items yourself and classify each as to whether it is easy, medium, or challenging.

In the Classroom 15-9

HOW MANY LINES?

OBJECTIVE: **Identify lines of symmetry.**

GRADE LEVEL: **4–5**

▼ Draw the lines of symmetry on each shape.

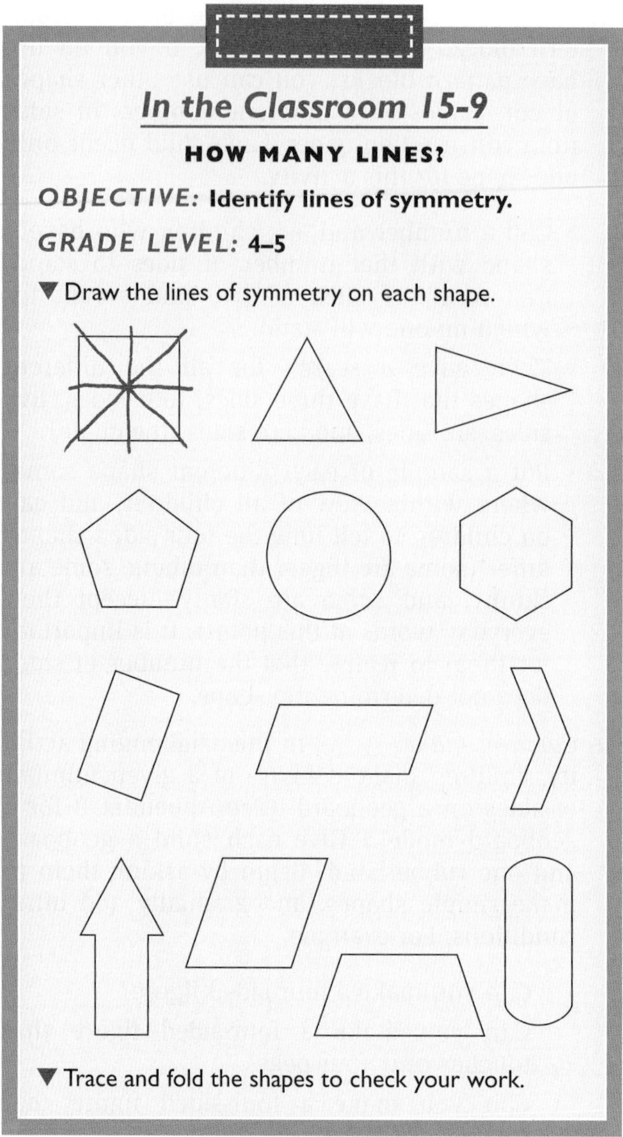

▼ Trace and fold the shapes to check your work.

SIZES OF ANGLES There are many ways to examine the angles of geometric figures. A more complete introduction to angles may be found in Chapter 16. Here are some of the properties related to angles that children may discover:

- The sum of the angles of a triangle is 180 degrees.
- The sum of the angles of a quadrilateral is 360 degrees.
- The base angles of an isosceles triangle are equal.
- Opposite angles of a parallelogram are equal.
- A polygon with more than three sides can have equal sides without having equal angles.
- The angle opposite the longest side of a triangle is the largest.

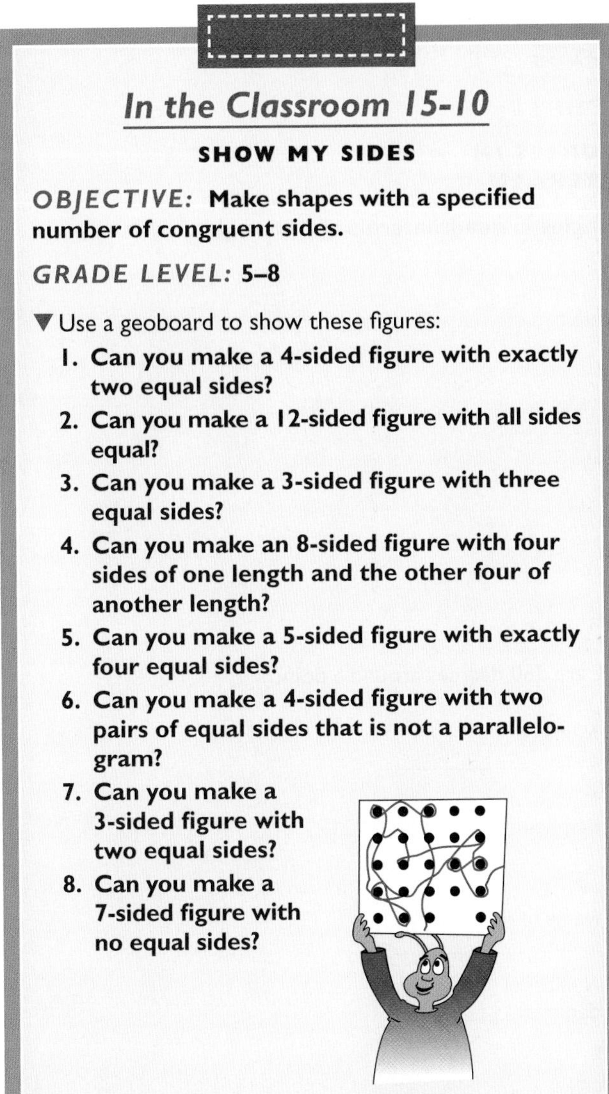

In the Classroom 15-10

SHOW MY SIDES

OBJECTIVE: **Make shapes with a specified number of congruent sides.**

GRADE LEVEL: **5–8**

▼ Use a geoboard to show these figures:

1. **Can you make a 4-sided figure with exactly two equal sides?**
2. **Can you make a 12-sided figure with all sides equal?**
3. **Can you make a 3-sided figure with three equal sides?**
4. **Can you make an 8-sided figure with four sides of one length and the other four of another length?**
5. **Can you make a 5-sided figure with exactly four equal sides?**
6. **Can you make a 4-sided figure with two pairs of equal sides that is not a parallelogram?**
7. **Can you make a 3-sided figure with two equal sides?**
8. **Can you make a 7-sided figure with no equal sides?**

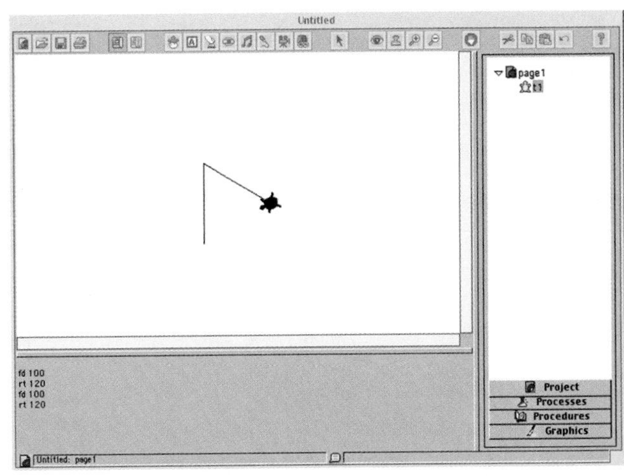

FIGURE 15-10 Logo commands in MicroWorlds Pro instructing the turtle to begin to create an equilateral triangle.

A guided activity such as the one In the Classroom 15-11 will help students discover for themselves that the angles of a quadrilateral sum to 360 degrees.

Logo programs and other software for computers offer a wide variety of activities for children to explore geometry. In Logo, an angle is considered as a turn and a figure is a path created as the turtle travels with its pen. With only a few simple commands (FD for ForwarD, BK for BacK, RT for RighT, etc.), children can begin drawing pictures and hypothesizing about geometric figures. But an important feature of Logo is the angle that is created when the turtle is instructed to turn. Figure 15-10 shows some turtle commands and the resulting figure that is drawn. What is the measure of the angle the turtle needs to turn in order to create an equilateral triangle where each of the angles are 60 degrees?

Have children in the early grades begin exploring Logo through the Logo simulation, Turtle Pond, at the NCTM's Illuminations web site at the iMath Investigations. In this activity students are to move the turtle to the pond. It helps to first have students actually walk the path described in the instructions to get the sense that the turtle is turning through the exterior angles of the object being drawn.

PARALLEL AND PERPENDICULAR SIDES In addition to examining parallel and perpendicular sides in geometric shapes, children need to be able to identify parallel lines and perpendicular lines in a plane and, later, in space. Two lines in a plane are parallel if they never intersect. (Remember, a line can be extended indefinitely in either direction.) Another useful definition states that two lines are parallel if they are always the same distance (perpendicular distance) apart. Two lines are perpendicular if they intersect at right angles.

It is important that children recognize perpendicular and parallel lines in the world around them. Have them search for perpendicular and parallel lines in the room. You might start a list

Math Links 15.7

You can find an electronic Logo turtle at the NCTM web site, which you can access from this book's web site. Children can enter the number of steps and angle turns to make the turtle move.

In the Classroom 15-11

HOW MANY DEGREES IN A QUADRILATERAL?

OBJECTIVE: **To explore the sum of the degrees of the angles in quadrilaterals and triangles.**

GRADE LEVEL: **5–8**

▼ Try this method for finding the sum of the angles in a quadrilateral:

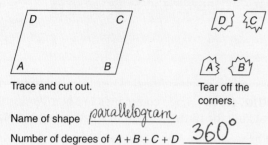

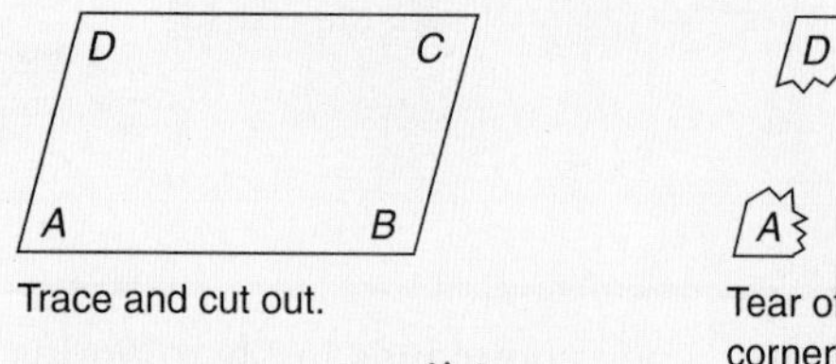

Trace and cut out.

Tear off the corners.

Name of shape parallelogram

Number of degrees of $A + B + C + D$ 360°

▼ Use the same method for these quadrilaterals. (Reminder: there are 360 degrees around a point.)

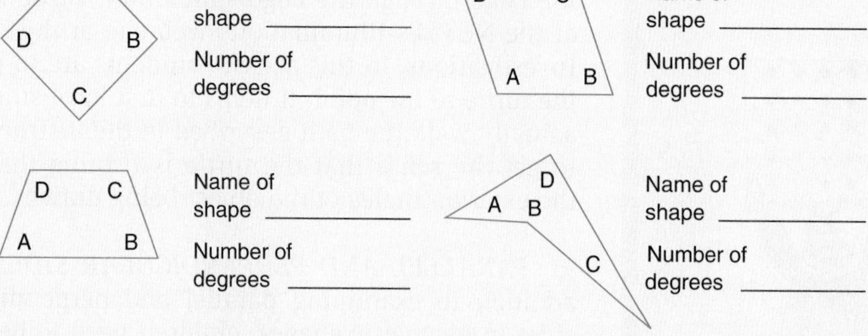

▼ Now

- Try some more 4-sided figures.
- Try a 5-sided figure.
- Try a 3-sided figure.
- What do you conclude?

together on the board, letting children add to it as they find other examples. Here is a start:

Parallel Lines

- Opposite sides of a book
- The horizontal lines in E
- The top and bottom of the chalkboard

Perpendicular Lines

- Adjacent edges of a book
- The vertical and horizontal lines in E
- The edge of the wall and the edge of the floor

You may also have the children identify parallel and perpendicular sides on the pattern blocks (Figure 15-8). Begin by asking them to find all the pieces that have one pair of perpendicular sides, next all the pieces with more than one pair of perpendicular sides, and then a piece with one pair of parallel sides. Use the puzzles In the Classroom 15-12 to challenge children to arrange pattern blocks to make shapes with a specified number of parallel sides.

CONVEXITY AND CONCAVITY Often children are exposed only to convex shapes (any polygon with all angles less than 180 degrees). Many of the activities suggested thus far have included concave shapes. When children are making shapes, concave examples will often give interesting variety.

In the Classroom 15-12

PIEZLES

OBJECTIVE: **Use pattern block buildings to display parallel sides.**

GRADE LEVEL: **4–5**

▼ Solve these *piezles* (puzzles) using pattern blocks. Draw a sketch of the shape you made.

1. **Use two different pieces: make a shape with**
   - Exactly 2 pairs of parallel sides.
   - Exactly 1 pair of parallel sides.
   - No parallel sides.
2. **Use three different pieces; make a shape with**
   - Exactly 3 pairs of parallel sides.
   - Exactly 2 pairs of parallel sides.
   - Exactly 1 pair of parallel sides.
   - No parallel sides.
3. **What is the largest number of pairs of parallel sides of a shape you can make from**
   - 2 pieces?
   - 3 pieces?
   - 4 pieces?
4. **Can you put all the pieces together to make a shape with no parallel sides?**

Show children two shapes such as these and have them describe how they are alike and different:

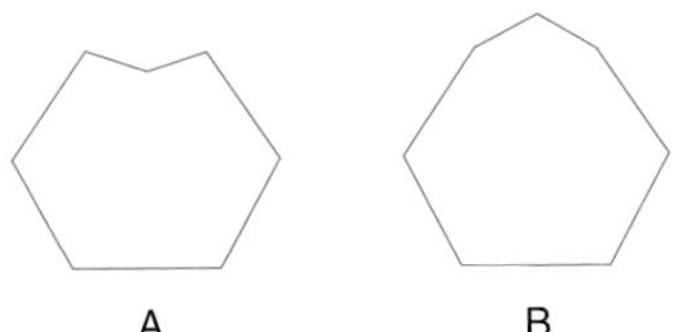

They will probably express the idea that shape A "comes back" on itself or "caves in" (concave). Introduce the terms *concave* and *convex*. After children classify shapes as convex or concave, you might have them investigate questions such as the following:

> Can you draw a four-sided (five-sided, six-sided, seven-sided) figure that is concave?
>
> Can you draw a five-sided (six-sided, seven-sided) figure that is concave in two places (or that has two angles greater than 180 degrees)?
>
> Can you draw a six-sided (seven-sided, eight-sided) figure that is concave in three places?

It is challenging to try these exercises with Logo on the computer because the turtle turns the external angles of shapes. Have the children keep a record of the steps it takes to make each figure.

ALTITUDE The altitude (or height) of a geometric shape depends on what is specified as the base. Identifying and measuring the altitude is essential in finding the area of geometric figures. In the Classroom 15-13 is designed to help children realize that a geometric object has different heights or altitudes. After students do this with the triangular model, have them draw a triangle on paper and again measure each side and each altitude.

Names of Geometric Shapes

Children are often taught the geometric names without being given much opportunity to explore

In the Classroom 15-13

WHAT'S MY ALTITUDE?

OBJECTIVE: **Identifying and measuring the altitude of a triangle.**

GRADE LEVEL: **4–5**

▼ Make a triangle from a stiff piece of paper. Cut a strip 2 cm by 20 cm. Mark off segments of 9 cm, 4 cm, and 7 cm and label them A, B, and C, respectively. Fold and tape as shown:

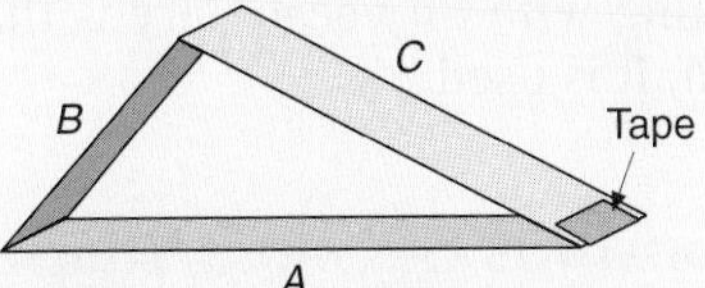

1. **Set the triangle on side A. This is the base.**
   - How long is the base? ______________
   - What is the altitude? ______________
   - How long is the altitude? ______________
2. **Set the triangle on side B. This is the base now.**
   - How long is the base? ______________
   - What is the altitude? ______________
   - How long is the altitude? ______________
3. **Set the triangle on side C. This is the base now.**
   - How long is the base? ______________
   - What is the altitude? ______________
   - How long is the altitude? ______________

the properties or to solve problems. A recent national assessment shows that students in the United States know the names of geometric shapes but have difficulty with complex geometric properties (Martin and Strutchens, 2000).

Children should begin to recognize types of shapes through examples and nonexamples, not through definitions. By experiencing examples and discussing the properties, they can begin to realize what properties define a shape. In the Classroom 15-14 gives examples and nonexamples of triangles. Do you see why the different shapes were included? If a child says that C, B, F, or G is a triangle, what property of triangles do you think is being ignored in each case? If a child fails to realize that D is a triangle, what do you think may be the reason?

Children also need to be able to recognize geometric shapes as models for real objects. For example, you might have young children write a "book" about circles. What is shaped like a circle? Let them find examples and draw pictures. Older children can be challenged to tell why certain objects are shaped in a certain way:

Why are most buttons shaped like a circle?

Why is paper rectangular?

Why are walls rectangular?

Why are support braces triangular?

Children should know the names of the most common shapes: triangle, square, rectangle, circle, and parallelogram. They also should be aware of other words that are used with shapes (e.g., children should be able to identify the *center, radius, diameter,* and *circumference* of a circle). The most important thing with all vocabulary is that, after it is introduced, it is used.

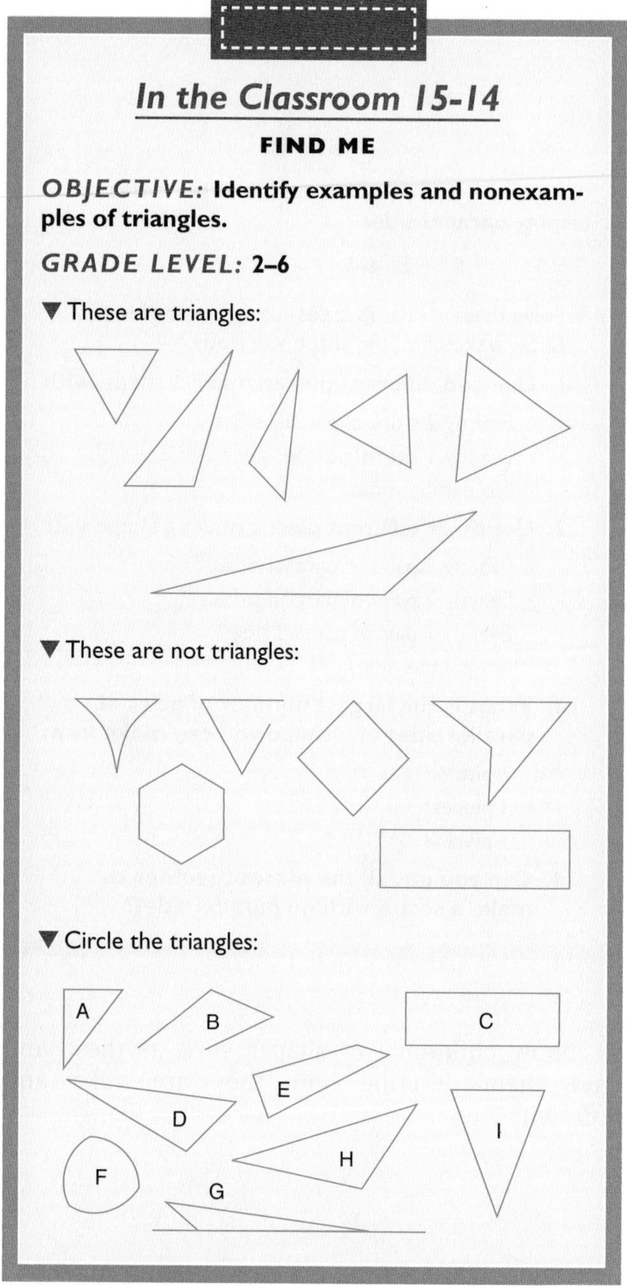

In the Classroom 15-14
FIND ME
OBJECTIVE: Identify examples and nonexamples of triangles.
GRADE LEVEL: 2–6
▼ These are triangles:
▼ These are not triangles:
▼ Circle the triangles:
A
B
C
D
E
F
G
H
I

Relationships between Shapes

The preceding section focused on properties of individual shapes. To emphasize those properties, it is often helpful to compare two or more shapes. When considering two or more shapes, you can examine two relationships—congruence and similarity—that are central to the study of geometry. After looking at these two relationships, consider how children at different levels might respond to comparing two shapes on all the properties mentioned so far.

CONGRUENCE Two shapes are said to be *congruent* if they have the same size and the same shape. Young children grasp this idea when they see that one shape can be made to fit exactly on the other. If the two shapes are line segments, they are congruent if they have the same length. If the two shapes are two-dimensional and they are congruent, then they have the same area. The converse is not true. Two shapes with the same area may not be congruent. Children have difficulty with this concept, and many middle-school students would respond that the parallelogram shown here is congruent to the rectangle:

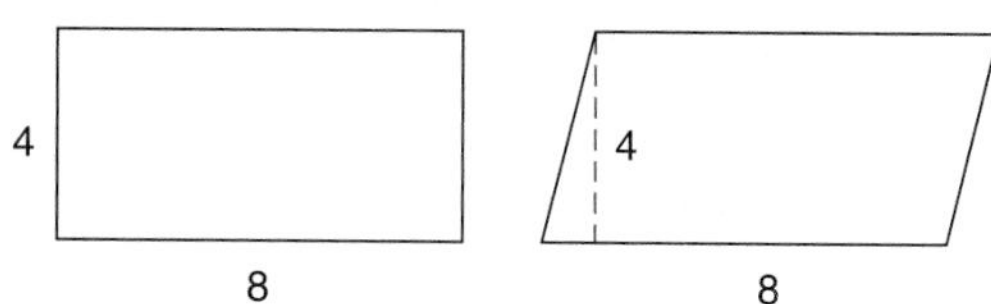

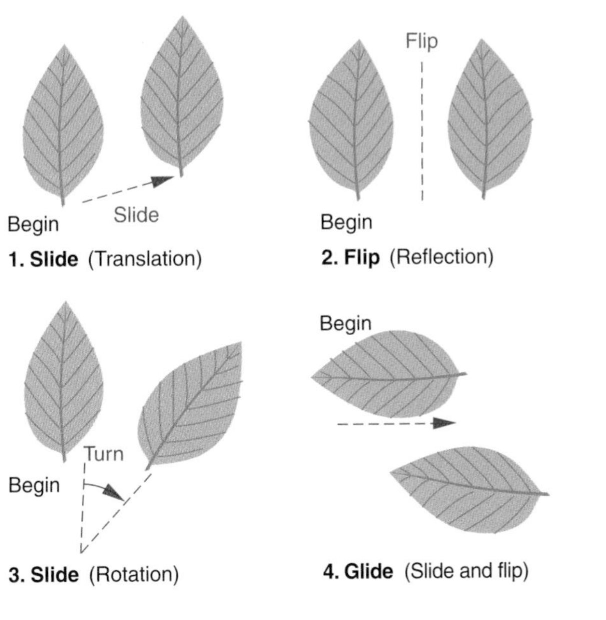

FIGURE 15-11 Motions for determining congruence.

This difficulty may be more a function of the word *congruence* than of the concept. Young children have little difficulty identifying figures with the same shape and size, such as with these two right triangles. They can cut the shapes out and show that one fits exactly on top of the other to demonstrate the idea. Thus the task becomes one of asking young children to match figures to see if they are the same size and shape and gradually introducing and using the word *congruence.*

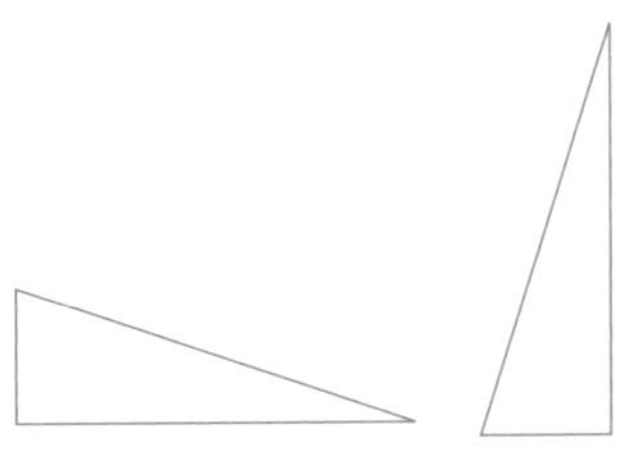

Congruence is often investigated through motion geometry. If two shapes are congruent, they can be made to fit by one or more of the three motions illustrated in Figure 15-11. It sometimes takes more than one motion, as shown by the glide.

You may have children begin to investigate the relationship of same area but different shape through activities such as those in Chapter 16.

SIMILARITY *Similarity* is a word used in everyday language to mean alike in some way. Although children may have an idea of similarity, they often have not developed the mathematical meaning. Intuitive notions about similarity have to be refined to a mathematical definition: Two figures are *similar* if corresponding angles are equal and corresponding sides are in the same ratio.

This definition is too formal for a beginning. Instead, you can begin by using a geoboard and geopaper. Children can make a design on the geoboard and transfer it to smaller geopaper, or they can copy designs from one size of graph paper to another.

After students have been introduced to ratio, they can investigate similarity in a more rigorous way. (The use of similar triangles is discussed in Chapter 13.)

COMPARING TWO FIGURES As children at all grade levels are learning about the properties of geometric figures, they should be given many opportunities to compare figures. As illustrated in Figure 15-12, children's understanding of geometric properties varies as they construct their knowledge through experiences.

Classification Schemes

You have examined many properties of and relationships among geometric figures. What makes a parallelogram a parallelogram? When is a rhombus a square? What is a regular polygon? When students understand the defining properties of two-dimensional shapes, they have moved into van Hiele Level 2.

TRIANGLES Triangles are classified either by sides or by angles:

By Sides	By Angles
Equilateral three congruent sides	**Acute** all angles less than 90 degrees
Isosceles at least two congruent sides	**Right** one angle equal to 90 degrees
Scalene no sides congruent	**Obtuse** one angle greater than 90 degrees

After children have learned to identify triangles by sides and by angles, the two classification schemes may be put together. For example, can you make an isosceles, right triangle? a scalene, obtuse triangle? an equilateral, right triangle?

Compare these shapes:

A B

They have four sides.
A is a rectangle. B isn't.
A can be folded to match.
They each have corners.
B looks lopsided.

Primary Responses

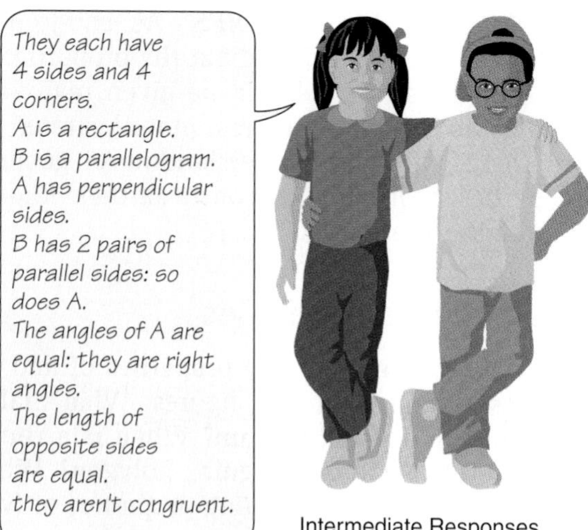

They each have 4 sides and 4 corners.
A is a rectangle.
B is a parallelogram.
A has perpendicular sides.
B has 2 pairs of parallel sides: so does A.
The angles of A are equal: they are right angles.
The length of opposite sides are equal.
they aren't congruent.
Intermediate Responses

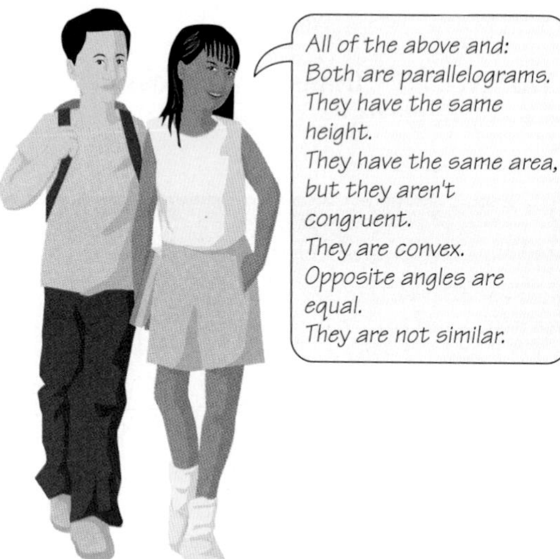

All of the above and:
Both are parallelograms.
They have the same height.
They have the same area, but they aren't congruent.
They are convex.
Opposite angles are equal.
They are not similar.
Middle School Responses

FIGURE 15-12 Examples of children's responses that reflect their understanding and relationships between figures at various stages.

QUADRILATERALS There are many special names for quadrilaterals. The most common are parallelograms, rectangles, squares, rhombuses, trapezoids, and kites. These classes are not disjoint; one shape may fall into several categories. For example, a rectangle is also a parallelogram. This type of classifying process is more difficult for children than partitioning the whole set into disjoint classes, as is the case with triangles. It requires more than just recognizing examples of figures; it requires understanding the defining properties. For example, a parallelogram is a quadrilateral with two pairs of parallel sides. Assuming you know that a quadrilateral is a four-sided, closed, simple figure, can you identify which of the following are parallelograms? What other names do they have?

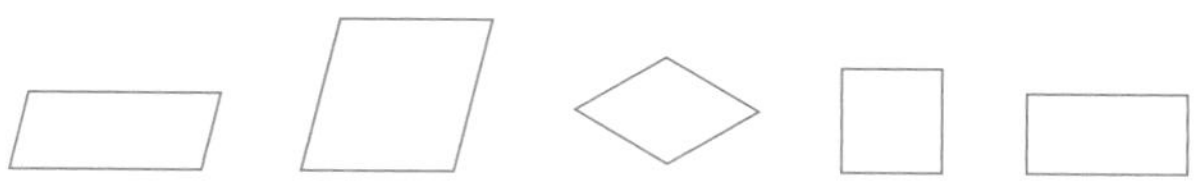

You are correct; they all are. Thus a square, a rhombus, and a rectangle are all special types of parallelograms.

See if you can answer these questions, and discuss them with a peer. What is a rhombus? A *rhombus* is a parallelogram with all sides congruent. Does that mean that a square is a rhombus? What is a rectangle? A *rectangle* is a parallelogram with right angles. Does that mean a square is a rectangle?

How do you begin to teach such relationships? Children must first begin to verbalize many properties of the figure. For example, they must be able to describe a square:

As a closed, four-sided figure (property 1)
With opposite sides parallel (property 2),
All right angles (property 3), and
All sides congruent (property 4).

Properties 1 and 2 make it a parallelogram; properties 1, 2, and 3 make it a rectangle; properties 1, 2, and 4 make it a rhombus; properties 1, 2, 3, and 4 make it a square. In the Classroom 15-15 helps students with this idea.

POLYGONS Polygons are named according to the number of sides:

3 sides: triangles
4 sides: quadrilaterals
5 sides: pentagons
6 sides: hexagons

In the Classroom 15-15

CLASSIFY ME

OBJECTIVE: **Classifying and naming quadrilaterals.**

GRADE LEVEL: **4–5**

▼ Mark each of the figures with a

1. **if it is a quadrilateral,**
2. **if it has two pairs of parallel sides,**
3. **if it has all right angles,**
4. **if it has all congruent sides.**

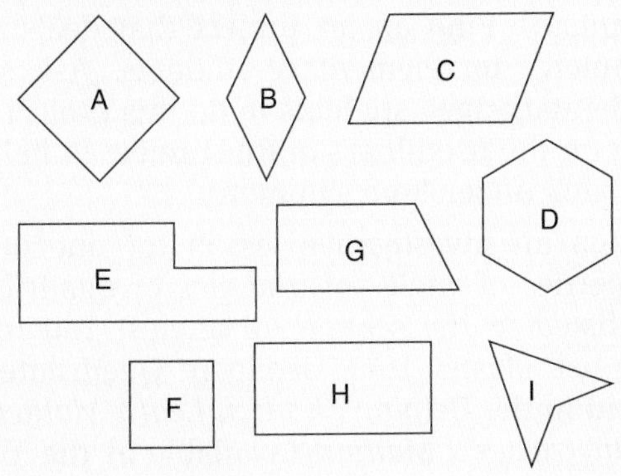

- Any figure marked 1 and 2 is a ________
- Any figure marked 1, 2, and 3 is a rectangle as well as a ________
- Any figure marked 1, 2, and 4 is a _______ as well as a________
- Any figure marked 1, 2, 3, and 4 is a ________ and a _____ as well as a square.

7 sides: heptagons
8 sides: octagons
9 sides: nonagons
10 sides: decagons

This classification scheme is not difficult, but often children are shown only regular polygons. Thus, among the shapes shown here, a child sees only the first as a hexagon, instead of realizing they are all hexagons.

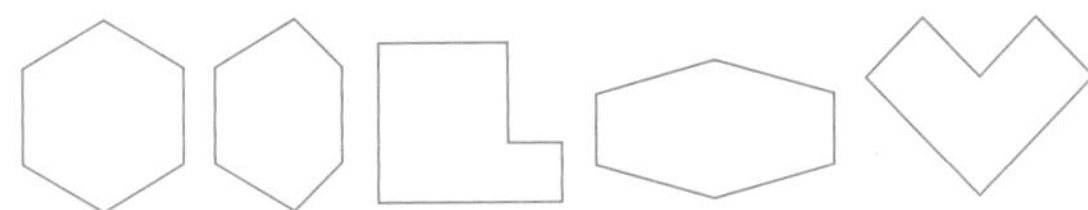

Children should be encouraged to think of real objects that are shaped like these.

The names *heptagon, nonagon,* and *decagon* are not widely used, so in doing activities you may have to remind children of these names. In the Classroom 15-16 uses the names as well as other

Math Links 15.8

If you would like to see sixth graders engaged in discovering the properties, sides, and angles of quadrilaterals, you can view video clips of the lesson, String Shapes/Shaping Up, at the Modeling Middle School Mathematics web site, which you can access from this book's web site.

In the Classroom 15-16

CAN YOU FIND IT?

OBJECTIVE: **Shade polygons with given properties.**

GRADE LEVEL: **5–8**

▼ See if you can find each of these in the design. Fill in the shape, and mark it with the matching letter.

A. triangle—isosceles
B. triangle—scalene
C. quadrilateral—not symmetric
D. quadrilateral—4 lines of symmetry
E. pentagon—concave
F. pentagon—convex
G. hexagon—exactly 2 pairs of parallel sides
H. hexagon—symmetric
I. heptagon (7 sides)—symmetric
J. heptagon—not symmetric
K. octagon

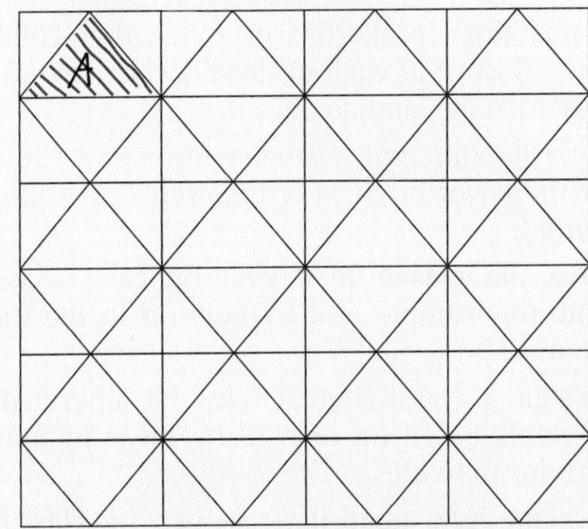

properties; students are asked to see shapes within other shapes, a task that is difficult for some.

A Glance at Where We've Been

Geometry is a topic that is often neglected in elementary school, yet it has many benefits for children if it is presented in an intuitive, informal manner. This chapter presented a variety of sample activities that provide this type of informal experience. These activities can be modified in many ways to suit the topic and the level of your students. They can also be modified to emphasize coordinate geometry on a rectangular grid. In the section on solid geometry, you explored the processes that you can use with plane figures. The solid figures can be considered in terms of their properties, relationships among them, and classification schemes, as emphasized in the plane geometry section.

This chapter touched on a few things you can do to help children build concepts and skills in geometry, as well as only a few ways to present problems and apply geometry. There are many other fascinating topics and activities that you can use. Begin collecting and using them in your teaching.

Things to Do: From What You've Read

1. Construct three two-dimensional plane figures using at least two of the different methods suggested in this chapter. Describe any lines of symmetry on the models you construct.
2. Name three properties of solids that children should learn at each of these levels: beginning, intermediate, and advanced.
3. Describe different goemetry ideas that you find in the cover of *Helping Children Learn Mathematics*.
4. Give the reason for including each example and nonexample of a triangle on In the Classroom 15-14.
5. Design a classifying activity for intermediate students based on one of the ideas in the beginning activities.
6. Explain how quadrilaterals can be classified. Why are squares a type of rectangle? How could rectangles be defined so that squares would not be rectangles?
7. Complete the activity In the Classroom 15-9. Build a list of at least 10 objects in the world around you that have lines of symmetry. Find pictures of both objects that have reflectional (line) symmetry and roational symmetry.

Things to Do: Going Beyond This Book

IN THE FIELD

1. *Symmetry.* Find an art project that deals with symmetry for elementary students. Ask some elementary-aged students to do this project. Reflect on the usefulness of this project in helping students understand symmetry.
2. Design an investigative lesson for one of the properties of angles of triangles or quadrilaterals listed in the section on angles. You might also use Master 15-2, Geoboard Quadrilaterals, found in the *Helping Children Learn Mathematics Instructor's Manual* (available at the Wiley Book Companion web site).
3. **Solid Activity.* Try one of the activities with solids described in the section on describing and classifying objects.
4. Suppose you have a student in your class who cannot manipulate a compass. Describe materials you could have him or her work with to make geometric figures.
5. **Classifying.* In the Classroom 15-14 provides examples and nonexamples of triangles. Ask young children to tell which of the mixed examples are not triangles and to justify their selections. Or use In the Classroom 15-15 with older children to see what they understand about the classification of quadrilaterals.
6. **Compare Shapes.* Interview a range of students from K–8, asking them to compare the two shapes in Figure 15-12. Compare the responses you receive with those in the text.
7. **3-D.* In the Classroom 15-4 is one of the activities with building three-dimensional shapes. As you try this with children, observe which shapes children make and whether they can

*Additional activities, suggestions, or questions are provided in *Teaching Elementary Mathematics: A Resource for Field Experiences* (Wiley, 2004).

tell the number of edges and verticies. Can they make shapes with a given number of edges and vertices?

8. **Number of Sides.* In the Classroom 15-8 is a game for younger children, and In the Classroom 15-10 has challenging puzzles. Try one of these with students and observe how they react to games or puzzles.

IN YOUR JOURNAL

9. Give four reasons why geometry should be included in an elementary mathematics program. Explain, in your own words, what one of these reasons means to you.
10. Defend spending time on constructing models of solids.
11. A fellow teacher says that he cannot start to teach any geometry until the students know all the terms and definitions and that his fifth graders just cannot learn them, so he does not do any geometry. What misconceptions about teaching geometry does this teacher hold?
12. Read about the use of geometry in everyday life in another country or culture. Describe how it is different and how you could use this information in your teaching.

WITH ADDITIONAL READINGS

13. Look at the geometry in a textbook at a given grade level. Make a list of the activities from this chapter that would complement the text.
14. Find a vignette involving geometry in *Professional Standards for Teaching Mathematics* (NCTM, 1991). Share and discuss it with your classmates.
15. Read the children's book *Reflections* (Jonas, 1987). Explain how that book allows students to examine images in a variety of ways.
16. Review the recent issues of *Teaching Children Mathematics* for an idea for teaching geometry at the elementary level. Describe how this idea can support the development of geometric thinking.

WITH TECHNOLOGY RESOURCES

17. Write a lesson plan for children to use the Turtle Pond activity from the iMath activities of NCTM's Illuminations web site.
18. Build a list of possible geometry software to use with elementary students. Record the primary purpose of the software and information for obtaining the software.
19. Explore drawing geometric shapes in *Geometer's Sketchpad*. What happens as you drag the shape around? How could this software be used with elementary students?

Book Nook for Children

Ayture-Scheele, Zubal. *Beautiful Origami*. New York. Sterling, 1990.
Lots of beautiful animals in this book, as the title implies. Since instructions are unclear, the photographs help to figure out the steps. As you figure them out, write notes to yourself on each step so you remember the next time.

Ehlert, Lois. *Color Zoo*. Philadelphia, PA: J. B. Lippincott, 1989.
Zoo animal cutouts and graphics introduce geometric shapes—rectangle, oval, star, heart, hexagon, octagon, and diamond. The shapes, colors, and animals shown in the book are summarized on the last pages.

Flournoy, Valerie. *The Patchwork Quilt*. New York: Four Winds Press, 1991.
Tanya loves listening to her grandmother talk about the quilt she is making from pieces of colorful fabric from the family clothes. When Grandma becomes ill, Tanya decides to finish Grandma's masterpiece with the help of her family. This book can lead to discussions about different shapes used in the quilt pieces. Have the children make patches for a classroom geometric quilt.

Hoban, Tana. *Shadows and Reflections*. New York: Greenwillow Books, 1990.
Distortions may appear when shapes are reflected in mirrors, windows, puddles, or ponds, but certain attributes are unchanged. Similarly, elongated or abbreviated images are found in shadows. This collection presents an excellent opportunity for the reader to analyze shape by comparing and contrasting objects with their shadows and reflections.

Hoban, Tana. *Spirals, Curves, Fanshapes and Lines*. New York: Greenwillow Books, 1992.
Intriguing shapes—spirals, curves, fanshapes, and lines—are all around. This books helps to heighten children's attention to the geometry in their own world.

Hutchins, Pat. *Changes, Changes*. New York: Macmillan, 1987.

This picture book introduces two wooden dolls who rearrange wooden building blocks to form various objects. The little wooden couple are happy in their building-block house—until it catches fire. The solution? They transform the house into a fire engine! But then there's so much water that they have to build a boat.

Isaacson, Philip M. *Round Buildings, Square Buildings, and Buildings That Wiggle Like a Fish*. New York: Knopf, 1988.
This book uses a poetic approach to focus children's visualization of some famous buildings in different ways. The Taj Mahal is "made of marble the color of cream"; a stone church is "like an old monk gathered up in his robes"; and windows are "pathways to the spirit of a building."

Jonas, Ann. *Reflections*. New York: Greenwillow Books, 1987.
This unusual but effective children's book helps establish the basic concepts of symmetry. It allows students to examine images in a variety of ways—read the book, turn it upside down, and in every full-color picture there is another picture reflected.

Keller, Wallace. *The Wrong Side of the Bed*. New York: Rizzoli, 1992.
Mott Turner wakes up amidst the junk beneath his bed and realizes he has unwittingly gotten up on the wrong side of the bed. See how Mott now envisions the world where everything is upside down, except him.

Tompert, Ann. *Grandfather Tang's Story*. New York: Crown Publishers, 1990.
A tangram adventure where the animals change into different animals. Just rearrange the seven tangram pieces to form a rabbit, a dog, a squirrel, a hawk, and a crocodile. You can trace the shapes so that the children can explore different shapes using their own tangram pieces.

ANNOTATED BOOKS

Confer, Chris. *Math by All Means: Geometry Grade 2*. Sausalito, CA: Math Solutions Publications, 1994.
Students develop an understanding of spatial relationships and learn mathematical terminology to describe their discoveries. They also examine and create quilt patterns.

National Council of Teachers of Mathematics. *Navigating through Geometry in Prekindergarten–Grade 2* (with CD-ROM). Reston, VA: NCTM, 2002.
This compilation of 14 articles from various NCTM publications demonstrates how some fundamental ideas of geometry can be introduced, developed, and extended. The articles deal with two- and three-dimensional shapes and introduce methods to describe location and position and simple transformations, along with student activities publications.

National Council of Teachers of Mathematics. *Navigating through Geometry in Grades 3–5* (with CD-ROM). Reston, VA: NCTM, 2002.
This compilation discusses the "big ideas" of geometry for grades 3–5, namely, shape, location, transformations, and spatial visualization. Activities are sequential, one building on another to enrich the curriculum and help students develop a strong sense of geometric concepts and relationships, leading them to experience the wonder of geometry.

National Council of Teachers of Mathematics. *Navigating through Geometry in Grades 6–8* (with CD-ROM). Reston, VA: NCTM, 2002.
This compilation explains how the study of geometry in the middle grades marks a pivotal point along the mathematical learning trajectory of students. The book focuses on visualization, analysis, and informal deduction and describes the van Hiele framework and how it can help improve teaching strategies and assessment.

Pohl, Victoria. *How to Enrich Geometry Using String Designs*. Reston, VA: NCTM, 1986.
This book shows string design activities for polygons and polyhedra. Step-by-step instructions are given, and related activities are included. The activities are designed for students in grades 6–10.

Rectanus, Cheryl. *Math by All Means: Area and Perimeter, Grades 5–6*. Sausalito, CA: Math Solutions Publications; White Plains, NY: The Cuisenaire Company of America, 1997.
Students build an understanding of area, perimeter, and the relationships between them through hands-on explorations. They go beyond merely learning the traditional formulas for finding area and perimeter as they use color tiles, string, rulers, and measuring tapes to investigate regular and irregular shapes.

ANNOTATED ARTICLES

Barkley, Cathy A., and Cruz, Saundra. "Geometry through Beadwork Designs." *Teaching Children Mathematics*, 7(6), (February 2001), pp. 362–367.
The authors present a lesson on geometry and beadwork with five phases of learning as described by Pierre van Hiele to tell the stories of different cultures and study isometry principles.

Bartels, Bobbye Hoffman. "Truss(t)ing Triangles." *Mathematics Teaching in the Middle School*, 3 (March–April 1998), pp. 394–396.
This investigation helps students connect geometry with the real world using the fact that triangles are rigid. An exploration comparing polygons is also included.

Battista, Michael T., and Clements, Douglas H. "Using Spatial Imagery in Geometric Reasoning." *Arithmetic Teacher*, 39 (November 1991), pp. 18–21.
Showing how students reason with Logo when drawing rectangles, Battista and Clements promote visual

imagery to develop reasoning. Discussion-developing tasks are included.

Bradley, Claudette. "Making a Navajo Blanket Design with Logo." *Arithmetic Teacher,* 40 (May 1993), pp. 520–523. In this activity students design a Navajo blanket on a bulletin board and with geoboards and then develop a Logo program to produce the design.

Carroll, William M. "Middle School Students' Reasoning about Geometric Situaions." *Mathematics Teaching in the Middle School,* 1 (March–April 1998), pp. 398–403. With scoring rubrics and questioning strategies to assess students' thinking, several geometric tasks are presented that elaborate on the recognition of figures and properties.

Evered, Lisa J. "Folded Fashions: Symmetry in Clothing Designs." *Arithmetic Teacher,* 40 (December 1992), pp. 204–206. Students explore symmetry through fashion designs of Madeline Vionnet, French designer.

Fosnaugh, Linda S., and Marvin E. Harrell. "Covering the Plane with Rep-Tiles." *Mathematics Teaching in the Middle School,* 1 (January–February 1996), pp. 666–670. This activity is a tiling project using a specific type of tile that when fit with other tiles, makes a similar figure in a larger scale.

Germain-McCarthy, Yvelyne. "The Decorative Ornamental Ironwork of New Orleans: Connections to Geometry and Haiti." *Mathematics Teaching in the Middle School,* 4 (April 1999), pp. 430–436. The ironwork of New Orleans is used as a vehicle to teach vertical, horizontal, and rotational symmetry.

Giganti, Paul, Jr., and Cittadino, Mary Jo. "The Art of Tessellation." *Arithmetic Teacher,* 37 (March 1990), pp. 6–16. This article provides a description of how to teach tesselations. It includes two worksheets and a glossary of terms.

Jacobson, Cathy, and Lehrer, Richard. "Teacher Appropriation and Student Learning of Geometry through Design." *Journal for Research in Mathematics Education*, 31 (January 2000), pp. 71–88. In this study, second-grade classes explored tessellations and symmetry while designing quilts. Simultaneously, their teachers were learning about children's thinking in inservice activities.

Lehrer, Richard, and Curtis, Carmen L. "Why Are Some Solids Perfect? Conjectures and Experiments by Third Graders." *Teaching Children Mathematics,* 6 (January 2000), pp. 324–329. In an exploration activity students identified characteristics and developed a precise definition to classify the five Platonic solids.

Liedtke, Walter W. "Developing Spatial Abilities in the Early Grades." *Teaching Children Mathematics,* 2 (September 1995), pp. 12–18. Liedtke presents activities and tasks to help students in developing spatial sense.

Lipka, Jerry; Wildfeuer, Sandra; Wahlberg, Nastasia; George, Mary; and Ezran, Dafna R. "Elastic Geometry and Storyknifing: A Yup'ik Eskimo Example." *Teaching Children Mathematics*, 7(6), (February 2000), pp. 337–343. Introduces elastic geometry, or topology, into the elementary classroom through the study of connecting the intuitive, visual, and spatial components of storyknifing as well as other everyday and ethnomathematical activities.

Manouchehri, Azita; Enderson, Mary C.; and Pugnucco, Lyle A. "Exploring Geometry with Technology." *Mathematics Teaching in the Middle School,* 3 (March–April 1998), pp. 436–442. This article offers activities to use *The Geometer's Sketchpad* to implement many of the NCTM *Standards.*

Morrow, Lorna J. "Geometry through the Standards." *Arithmetic Teacher,* 38 (April 1991), pp. 21–25. Visualization of figures, conservation of area, shape, and space, and multicultural study are presented along with ways to teach to the standards for problem solving, communication, reasoning, and connections.

Outhred, Lynne N., and Mitchelmore, Michael C. "Young Children's Intuitive Understanding of Rectangular Area Measurement." *Journal for Research in Mathematics Education*, 31(2), (March 2000), pp. 144–168. The focus of this article is the strategies young children use to solve rectangular coveting tasks before they have been taught area measurement. The solution strategies of 115 children from grades 1 to 4 were classified into five developmental levels. In the analysis the authors emphasize the importance of understanding the relationship between the size of the unit and the dimensions of the rectangle in learning about rectangular coveting, clarify the role of multiplication, and identify the significance of a relational understanding of length measurement.

Sundberg, Sue E. "A Plethora of Polyhedra." *Mathematics Teaching in the Middle School,* 3 (March–April 1998), pp. 388–391. Developing spatial ability by encouraging exploration, this activity has students build polyhedra and develop their own careful definitions.

Taylor, Lyn. "Activities to Introduce Your Class to Logo." *Arithmetic Teacher,* 39 (November 1991), pp. 52–54. These activities help students make meaningful connections in mathematical relationships. Students exlore angles and relations.

Williams, Carol. "Sorting Activities for Polygons." *Mathematics Teaching in the Middle School,* 3 (March–April 1998), pp. 445–446. Students use reasoning, communication, and measurement as they participate in these small-group activities on geometric properties and definitions.

Zaslavsky, Claudia. "Symmetry in American Folk Art." *Arithmetic Teacher,* 38 (September 1990), pp. 6–13. Zaslavsky presents open-ended activities for all ages and levels that use folk art for spatial thinking and symmetry. These activities integrate mathematics, culture, art, and history.

Zilliox, Joseph T., and Lowrey, Shannon G. "Faces Many Have I." *Mathematics Teaching in the Middle School,* 3 (November–December 1998), pp. 180–183. Students accepted the challenge to construct a polyhedron with faces measuring more than 13 inches on a side. This article describes the investigation of polygons and polyhedra the students developed and offers infomation on how teachers and implement such an investigation.

ADDITIONAL REFERENCES

Crowley, Mary L. "The van Hiele Model of the Development of Geometric Thought." In *Learning and Teaching Geometry, K–12,* 1987 Yearbook (ed. Mary Montgomery Lindquist). Reston, VA: NCTM, 1987, pp. 1–16.

Martin, W. Gary, and Strutchens, Marilyn E. "Geometry and Measurement." In *Results from the Seventh Mathematics Assessment of the National Assessment of Educational Progress* (eds. E. A. Silver and P. A. Kenney). Reston, VA: NCTM, 2000.

National Council of Teachers of Mathematics. *Principles and Standards for School Mathematics.* Reston, VA: NCTM, 2000.

National Council of Teachers of Mathematics. *Professional Standards for Teaching Mathematics.* Reston, VA: NCTM, 1991.

Sconyers, James M. "On My Mind: Proof and the Middle School Mathematics Student." *Mathematics Teaching in the Middle School,* 1 (November–December 1995), pp. 516–518.

U.S. Department of Education. *Pursuing Excellence: A Study of U.S. Eight-Grade Mathematics and Science Teaching, Learning, Curriculum, and Achievement in International Context.* Washington, DC: U.S. Government Printing Office, 1996.

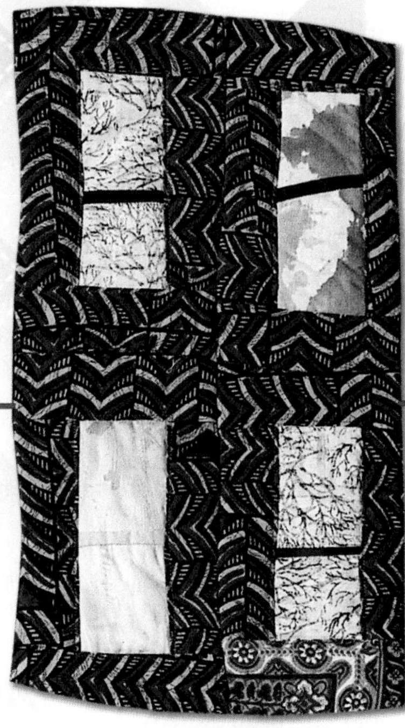

CHAPTER 16

Measurement

Snapshot of a Lesson

Orientation

A sixth-grade class of 29 students is studying area of rectangles. Previously, the class learned to use the base and the altitude to find areas of rectangles. In this lesson, small groups of three or four will find the area of rectangular objects in the room. Mr. Katz circulates to help groups or to ask questions of those who need challenging.

PAT: This card wants us to find which is larger, the desktop or the top of the bookcase. That's easy. The bookcase is much longer.

KIM: But it says "area," Pat. We need to find the area, and I think the desk is larger.

WES: I think it's the bookcase. Let's see.

MR. KATZ: Well, what did you find?

PAT: The desk was larger in area even though the bookcase was longer. When we covered them with squares the other day, the desk took more squares.

KIM: Unless I remember that I'm trying to find how many squares, I forget why I'm measuring the lengths and whether to add or multiply.

WES: It really helps me to think of the number of rows and the number of squares in each row. All you have to do is to count the number of squares, and multiplying is an easy way to count.

MR. KATZ: Why don't you try a challenge card instead of the next task card?

KIM: Oh, let's try this one. I've always wanted to cover the science table with a rug!

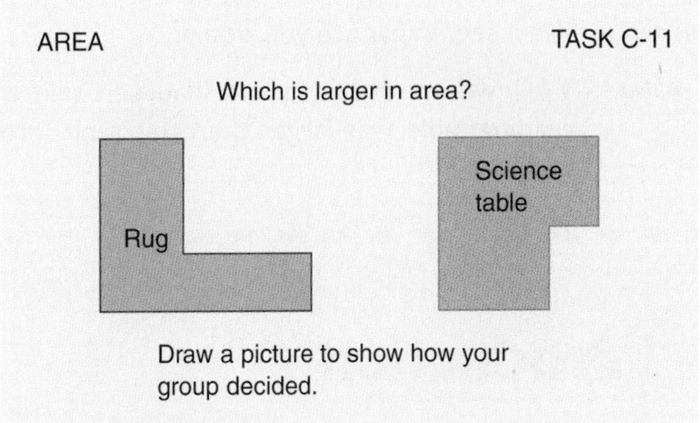

AREA
TASK C-11
Which is larger in area?
Rug
Science table
Draw a picture to show how your group decided.

WES: These aren't rectangles.

PAT: Look, we can make them into two rectangles. Remember when we cut those shapes apart? Let's cut the rug!

WES: Funny, but you're right. Let's mark where we would cut them. Then we can find the area of each rectangle and add them.

MR. KATZ: (Approaching another group) What's the problem?

SASHA: We don't know where to begin.

MR. KATZ: What are you trying to do?

SASHA: We have to find something in the room that is about 150 square centimeters. That's awfully large. Are you sure there is something?

SUE: No, it isn't. A square centimeter is awfully small.

JANE: Well, I just can't imagine 150 square centimeters. What can we do?

MR. KATZ: Do you know how large your name card is?

SUE: Let me measure. It's about 7 centimeters by 11 centimeters. That means it's about 77 square centimeters. We need something larger.

SASHA: How about this sheet of paper?

JANE: That's way too much. It's about four times larger. We need something in between.

Across the room, a group of students seems to be struggling with another problem.

Note that the reading table is trapezoidal.

MAUREEN: Mr. Katz, can you help us?

MR. KATZ: We'll see. What are you doing?

TOMAS: Well, we were talking and Maureen said the reading table was larger than this table. How can we tell?

MR. KATZ: Is the reading table a rectangle?

TOMAS: No, but can't we just measure the length and width?

MR. KATZ: What would be the length?

MAUREEN: Isn't it the longest side?

As students are working, Mr. Katz has many decisions to make. For example, should he answer Maureen's question or let the group proceed? He made a note that when the whole class looked at trapezoids he would have to address the "longest side" issue.

MR. KATZ: Let's get back together and see what you have found.

SUE: We found three things that were about 150 square centimeters. One was the task card itself. That was pretty sneaky.

KIM: The science table is larger than the rug. Even if we could cut the rug, it wouldn't cover the table. Guess we won't have an easy-on-your-elbows table after all.

TOMAS: We finally figured out the reading table. How about other shapes? How do you find the areas without covering them with squares?

MR. KATZ: Tomas, what do you mean you "figured out" the reading table?

TOMAS: Well, it isn't a rectangle, so we had to do some cutting. We cut off this triangle and put it there to make a rectangle.

MR. KATZ: Right. When things aren't rectangles, we need other ways to find the area. Tomorrow, we'll look at shapes other than rectangles. We will begin to develop formulas for some other common shapes from what we already know.

Introduction

The *Snapshot of a Lesson* provides a glance into a sixth-grade classroom learning about measurement. What experiences should the children have before this lesson? How do you help children have these experiences? What concepts and skills are important for the children to learn? Before examining these and other questions, consider why measuring should be taught.

Stop and think about how you have used numbers in the past few days. Did you tell someone how long it took you to drive to school, how many calories are in a piece of chocolate cake, how far it is to the nearest store, or how many cups of coffee you drank? All of these are measurements. Measurement is the topic from the elementary mathematics curriculum that is used the most directly in students' daily lives. Thus one of the main reasons to include measuring is that it has many practical applications. Measurement is designated as one of the 10 standards in the *Principles and Standards for School Mathematics* (NCTM, 2000) because of its power to help students see the usefulness of mathematics in everyday life.

A second reason is that measurement can be used in learning other topics in mathematics. It is apparent that children need many other topics of mathematics to help them with measuring. For

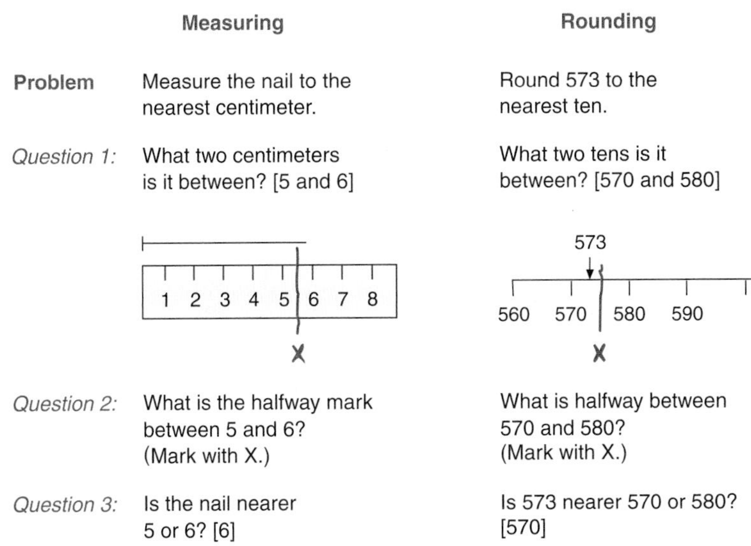

Measuring
Rounding
Problem
Measure the nail to the nearest centimeter.
Round 573 to the nearest ten.
Question 1:
What two centimeters is it between? [5 and 6]
What two tens is it between? [570 and 580]
1 2 3 4 5 6 7 8
X
573
560 570 580 590
X
Question 2:
What is the halfway mark between 5 and 6? (Mark with X.)
What is halfway between 570 and 580? (Mark with X.)
Question 3:
Is the nail nearer 5 or 6? [6]
Is 573 nearer 570 or 580? [570]

FIGURE 16-1 The similarity between measuring and rounding.

example, they may count the number of grams it takes to balance an object on a scale, multiply to find a volume, divide to change minutes to hours, subtract to see how close an estimate was, or add to find the perimeter of a triangle. To report the number of units, children may use whole numbers, common fractions, decimals, or negative numbers.

Although not quite as apparent, measurement can also help teach about numbers and operations. Many of the numeration models you use have a measurement base. For example, the number line is based on length. One model for multiplication is the area of a rectangle. Also, there are concepts and procedures that underlie both measurement and number ideas. As shown in Figure 16-1, measuring to the nearest unit is similar to rounding to a given unit. Thus measurement ideas may be used to complement numerical ideas.

Not only is measurement useful in everyday life, but it also is useful in other areas of the curriculum. If you are trying to think of ways to connect mathematics with other subjects, consider the ways that measurement is used in art, music, science, social studies, and language arts.

Another reason measurement is an important part of the mathematics curriculum is not so much mathematical as pedagogical. Measurement is an effective way to involve students in hands-on activities that often provide a change of pace from other mathematics work. Look again at the *Snapshot of a Lesson* at the beginning of this chapter. Were you fortunate enough to have such lively math classes when you were in sixth grade?

Measurement provides an excellent way to present problem-solving experiences at every level. Lesson Idea 16-1 gives samples of some problems at various grade levels. Each could be used at the grade level suggested or could be modified for use with students at another grade level.

Research from international studies has often shown that measurement and geometry are the two topics on which U.S. students perform less well than their counterparts in other countries. This is particularly evident in the *Third International Mathematics and Science Study* (U.S. Department of Education, 1996, 1997). Through the years, the data from the mathematics assessments of the National Assessment of Educational Progress (NAEP) have given reason for concern about students' performance on measurement items. As you read about these results in this chapter, think about your responsibility to help students develop better understanding of measurement and measuring skills.

In summary, measurement should be an integral part of the mathematics curriculum for several important reasons:

- It provides many applications to everyday life.
- It can be used to help learn other mathematics.

Math Links 16.1

The full-text electronic version of the Measurement standard is available at the NCTM's web site, which you can access from this book's web site. Click on pre-K–2, 3–5, or 6–8 to read more about this standard.

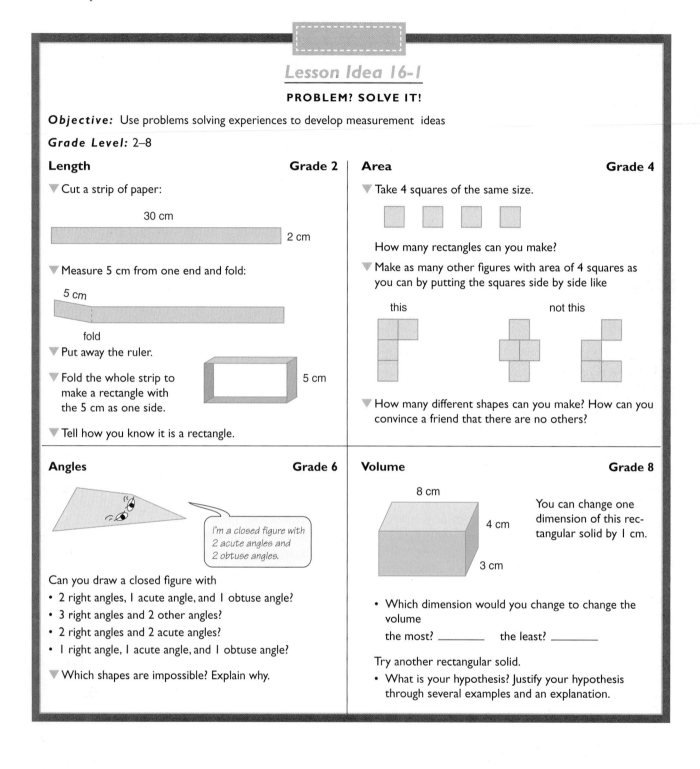

Lesson Idea 16-1

PROBLEM? SOLVE IT!

Objective: Use problems solving experiences to develop measurement ideas

Grade Level: 2–8

Length **Grade 2**

- Cut a strip of paper:

30 cm

2 cm

- Measure 5 cm from one end and fold:

5 cm

fold

- Put away the ruler.
- Fold the whole strip to make a rectangle with the 5 cm as one side.

5 cm

- Tell how you know it is a rectangle.

Area **Grade 4**

- Take 4 squares of the same size.

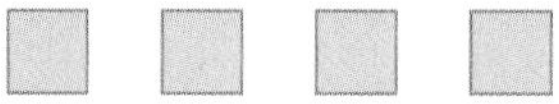

How many rectangles can you make?

- Make as many other figures with area of 4 squares as you can by putting the squares side by side like

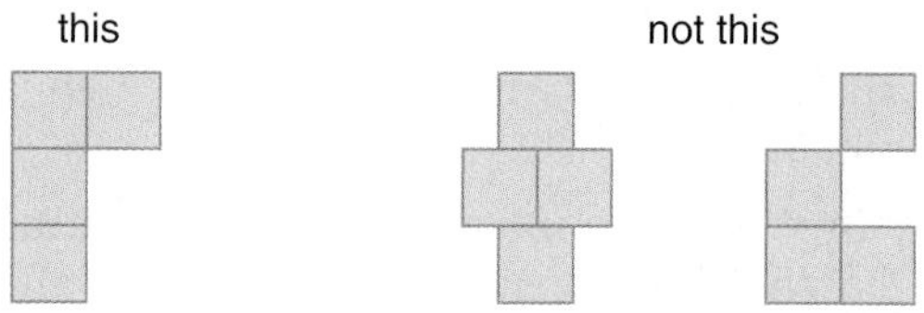

this not this

- How many different shapes can you make? How can you convince a friend that there are no others?

Angles **Grade 6**

I'm a closed figure with 2 acute angles and 2 obtuse angles.

Can you draw a closed figure with

- 2 right angles, 1 acute angle, and 1 obtuse angle?
- 3 right angles and 2 other angles?
- 2 right angles and 2 acute angles?
- 1 right angle, 1 acute angle, and 1 obtuse angle?

- Which shapes are impossible? Explain why.

Volume **Grade 8**

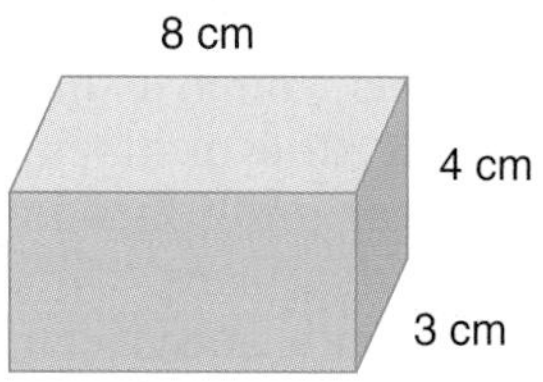

8 cm

4 cm

3 cm

You can change one dimension of this rectangular solid by 1 cm.

- Which dimension would you change to change the volume

  the most? ________ the least? ________

Try another rectangular solid.

- What is your hypothesis? Justify your hypothesis through several examples and an explanation.

Math Links 16.2

A variety of Web resources for measurement, which may be used by teachers and children, may be found at the NCTM's Illuminations web site (accessible from this book's web site) under the Measurement Standard.

- It can be related to other areas of the school curriculum.
- It involves students in active learning.
- It can be approached through problem solving.

The NCTM *Principles and Standards* (2000) call for measurement to be a continuing part of the mathematics program, rather than being presented in a few isolated lessons (Figure 16-2). You will find

Instructional programs should enable all students to:	Pre-K–2 Expectations All students should:	Grades 3–5 Expectations All students should:
Understand measurable attributes of objects and the units, systems, and processes of measurement	• Recognize the attributes of length, volume, weight, area, and time • Compare and order objects according to these attributes • Understand how to measure using nonstandard and standard units • Select an appropriate unit and tool for the attribute being measured	• Understand such attributes as length, area, weight, volume, and size of angle and select the appropriate type of unit for measuring each attribute • Understand the need for measuring with standard units, and become familiar with standard units in the customary and metric systems • Carry out simple unit conversions, such as from centimeters to meters, within a system of measurement • Understand that measurements are approximations and understand how differences in units affect precision • Explore what happens to measurements of a two-dimensional shape such as its perimeter and area when the shape is changed in some way
Apply appropriate techniques, tools, and formulas to determine measurements	• Measure with multiple copies of units of the same size, such as paper clips laid end to end • Use repetition of a single unit to measure something larger than the unit, for instance, measuring the length of a room with a single meter-stick • Use tools to measure • Develop common referents for measures to make comparisons and estimates	• Develop strategies for estimating the perimeters, areas, and volumes of irregular shapes • Select and apply appropriate standard units and tools to measure length, area, volume, weight, time, temperatures, and the size of angles • Select and use benchmarks to estimate measurements • Develop, understand, and use formulas to find the area of rectangles and related triangles and parallelograms • Develop strategies to determine the surface areas and volumes of rectangular solids

FIGURE 16-2 Measurement Standard with some expectations for children in grades prekindergarten–2 and 3–5.

many ways to include measurement activities for children as you are teaching many mathematical ideas and other subject areas.

FOCUS QUESTIONS

1. Why should measurement be included throughout the elementary mathematics curriculum?
2. What are some key attributes to measure? What are tools or instruments that measure these attributes?
3. How can you use estimation to strengthen measurement skills?
4. Which units should be taught in primary school? in upper elementary school?
5. What are formulas that students in the upper grades are expected to learn, understand, and be able to use?

Teaching Measurement

Most research about how children measure and think about measurement does not indicate specifically and directly how the teacher should plan for instruction. Rather, research has focused on what children can do and understand. For example, Wilson and Osborne (1988, p. 109) make the following suggestions, based on their study:

- Children must measure frequently and often, preferably on real problems rather than on textbook exercises.
- Children must develop estimation skills with measurement in order to develop common referents and as an early application of number sense.
- Children should encounter activity-oriented measurement situations by doing and experimenting rather than by passively observing. The activities should encourage discussion to stimulate the refinement and testing of ideas and concepts.
- Instructional planning should emphasize the important ideas of measurement that transfer or work across measurement systems.

Measurement is a process by which a number is assigned to an attribute of an object or event. Length, capacity, weight, area, volume, time, and temperature are the measurable attributes considered in most elementary mathematics programs.

Math Links 16.3

If you would like to see first graders and fifth graders engaged in a variety of measurement lab experiences that reflect these suggestions, view video clips from Sand Babies and It Takes Ten at the PBS Mathline web site, which you can access from this book's web site.

Although each of these attributes is different, there are some overall commonalities in how to help children learn about measuring them. The following outline is based on the measuring process and can be used to plan instruction:

I. Identify the attribute by comparing objects
   A. Perceptually
   B. Directly
   C. Indirectly through a reference
II. Choose a unit
   A. Arbitrary
   B. Standard
III. Compare the object to the unit
IV. Find the number of units
   A. Counting
   B. Using instruments
   C. Using formulas
V. Report the number of units

If a new attribute is being introduced, one recommended approach is to cycle through the outline several times: the first time using only arbitrary units and counting, the next time using standard units and counting, and, only after these experiences, introducing instruments or formulas. This cycling may take place over several years for the first attributes studied, but after several attributes have been introduced, the length of the cycle can and should be shortened.

Identifying Attributes

To measure with understanding, children should know what attribute they are measuring. Take, for example, a measure of attitude. What are you actually measuring? Because the attribute being measured is not fully understood, scores on attitude tests are often difficult to interpret. For young children, measuring the area of an object also can be difficult if they do not understand the concept of area. Thus one of your first tasks is to build an understanding of measurable attributes.

Children's literature provides excellent sources for developing understanding of some attributes. For example, the book *Twelve Snails to One Lizard: A Tale of Mischief and Measurement* (Hightower, 1997) can be used to help develop an understanding of a yardstick and how it is subdivided into inches and feet.

Three types of comparisons can build understanding of attributes: comparing objects perceptually (they look the same), comparing them directly (they are placed next to each other), and comparing them indirectly (a third object is used to compare objects). You will find examples of each of these three types of comparison in the following Length section. As children make these types of comparisons, not only are they gaining an understanding of the particular attribute and the associated vocabulary, but they are also learning procedures that will help them in assigning a number to a measurement. Each of these attributes is examined separately because of the importance of having children participate in such experiences. As you read, see if you can tell the differences among the three types of comparison and how each can be used to develop an understanding of that attribute.

LENGTH Length is one of the most easily perceived attributes of objects. Children come to school with some concept of length and some vocabulary associated with it; however, they often have what adults may consider misconceptions about length. For example, they may say that a belt is shorter when it is curled up than when it is straight. These misconceptions disappear as children develop cognitively and are involved in constructive experiences.

Lesson Ideas 16-2, 16-3, and 16-4 illustrate comparison activities that are appropriate for kindergarteners, first graders, or older children who need a review. Lesson Idea 16-2 involves

Lesson Idea 16-2

PERCEPTUAL COMPARISON OF LENGTHS

Objective: Compare lengths of physical objects perceptually

Grade Level: K–2

Materials: Collections of long, thin objects such as rods, spaghetti, pencils, and crayons

Description:

▼ Hold up two long objects and one short object.

- Ask children to tell which is different.
- Use vocabulary of *shorter, taller*, and *longer*.
- Repeat with other objects that differ *only* on length and are obviously different in length.

▼ Hold up a long pencil and a short crayon.

- Ask how they are different. Expect answers such as color, type of object, paper wrapper, eraser.
- If no one says the crayon is shorter or the pencil is longer ask "which is longer?"

Lesson Idea 16-3

DIRECT COMPARISON OF LENGTH

Objective: Compare lengths of physical objects directly

Grade Level: 2–3

Materials: A box of long, thin objects, some of which are about the same length, and sheets of construction paper (one of each labeled "shorter," "same," and "longer"):

Description:
Place a box of long, thin objects that children can sort at a center individually or in pairs. Let a child choose one object to be the reference, and compare the other objects to that one, putting the objects on the sheets marked shorter, same, or longer.

Lesson Idea 16-4

INDIRECT COMPARISON OF LENGTH

Objective: To indirectly compare two objects on length

Grade Level: 2–3

Materials: String or connecting links, index cards, tape, and objects in the room selected for children to represent.

Description: Choose two lengths that are about the same on objects that cannot easily be moved to compare directly. For example, the height of your desk with the width of your desk. Ask the children which is longer, and let them pose a solution of how they can tell.

Discuss the ways they propose and then show them how you would use the links (or string) to represent each of the lengths and then compare.

After this discussion and demonstration, give each pair of children a string and have them represent one of the objects you have marked.

Make a "graph" of all the lengths for easy comparison.

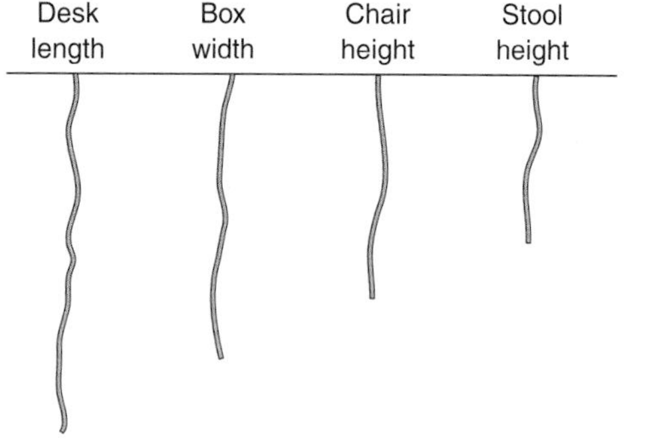

comparisons made perceptually. In the beginning of this activity, all irrelevant perceptual attributes have been masked (i.e., the objects are the same except for length). This allows children to build the concept of length as an attribute of long, thin things. As the activity progresses and vocabulary is reviewed and extended, the objects to be compared differ on several attributes, but the focus remains on length.

Lesson Idea 16-3 uses the procedure of making direct comparisons. This type of comparison of length involves placing two objects side by side on a common baseline. This activity may be extended to seriating objects by length (i.e., arranging them from shortest to tallest). For the young child, this

Math Links 16.4

*A*n electronic manipulative that provides experience with length allows children to plan and produce instructions for moving a ladybug along a path. It is available at the NCTM's web site, which you can access from this book's web site. The children must estimate distances in order to hide a ladybug under a leaf, draw rectangles of different sizes, and complete mazes.

task is more difficult because multiple comparisons must be made.

Lesson Idea 16-4 presents the problem of indirectly comparing two objects when they cannot be placed side by side. Children must use a third object to help them make the comparison. When a ruler is used to assign measurements, the third object assists you in making a comparison. Young children can work with string, strips of paper, erasers, or other items as the third object.

Through activities such as these, children begin to develop an understanding of length as an attribute of long, thin objects; however, length is used in other ways. For example, length is the distance around your waist. Young children can use string to compare their waists or to compare their wrists with their ankles. Older children can guess whether the height or the distance around a variety of cylindrical cans is longer and then check their guess by using string.

The distance between two points is also measured by length. In this case, words such as *nearer* and *farther* may be used when comparing two distances. Distance is often more difficult to perceive than the length of a long, thin object, so it should be introduced later.

Perimeter—the distance around a region—is a special type of length. Children should be given the opportunity to measure the distance around a region with string or a measuring tape. Later, they can add the lengths of the various sides of the region to find the perimeter. For example students could measure the perimeter of their desktop, a tabletop, or find the perimeter of a picture or poster that needs framing.

CAPACITY Capacity is an attribute of containers that can be introduced to young children by asking, "Which holds more?"

Although perceptual comparisons can be made between two containers, young children often make the comparisons based on length (height) rather than on capacity. When asked which holds

FIGURE 16-3 Which container holds more seeds? Tell why you think the one you chose holds more.

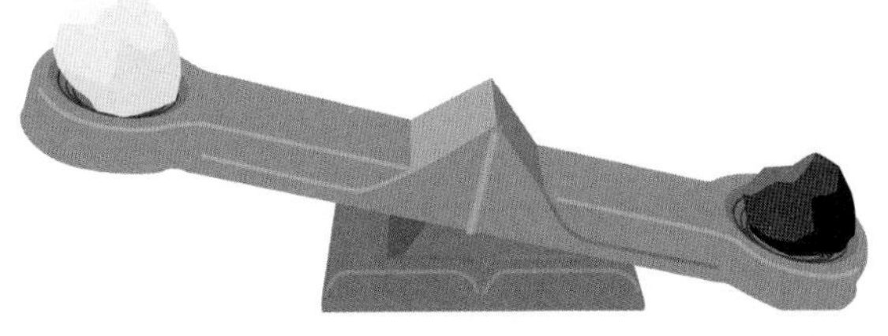

FIGURE 16-4 Use a balance to show which rock weighs more.

more—a tall container or a short container—most children will choose the taller container even if the shorter one may actually hold more. Thus it is probably best to begin the study of capacity by using direct comparisons.

Some type of filler is needed to make direct comparisons. Water and sand are easy for young children to use. Given a variety of containers, children can fill one and pour it into the other to see which holds more. After children have done some experimenting with direct comparison, activities involving perceptual comparisons are possible. For example, children greatly enjoy guessing contests in which they guess which container holds more, and then you can check the results together. Figure 16-3 displays a possible comparison.

Indirect comparisons are used when two containers cannot be compared perceptually or directly. For example, suppose you have two containers with small openings that make it difficult to pour from one into another. By pouring each into a pair of identical large-mouth containers, the capacities can be compared. Note that this activity is similar to what you do when you use graduated cylinders in a science lab to identify amounts of liquid.

WEIGHT To compare weights perceptually, you need to be able to lift the two objects. Children should be given a variety of pairs of objects (one of which is much heavier than the other) and asked to hold one in each hand. Children often think that a larger object weighs more. Thus some of the objects should be small and heavy and others large and light. Children should learn that to find which is heavier, they must do more than look at the object; they may need experiences in comparing two objects that look the same but weigh different amounts. An easy way to provide this experience is by having children compare identical containers with lids (such as cottage-cheese containers) filled to weigh a different amount.

When you cannot feel the difference between the weights of two objects, you need a balance scale to assist in the comparison. To introduce the balance, choose two objects that differ greatly in weight so children can see that the heavier object "goes down" on the balance. Figure 16-4 shows that even though one rock is larger, it is not the heavier of the two rocks.

Many activities may be set up for children to compare the weights of two objects. One challenging activity is to compare five identical containers, with lids secured and filled with different amounts of weight, and put them in order from lightest to heaviest.

Indirect comparisons are not necessary until units of weight are introduced because, whenever each of two objects could be compared to a third on the balance, it would be much simpler to compare the two directly.

AREA Area is an attribute of plane regions that can be compared by sight if the differences are large enough and the shapes similar enough. That is, it is easy to tell this page is larger than a driver's license, but it may be difficult to compare the areas of the three regions A, B, and C.

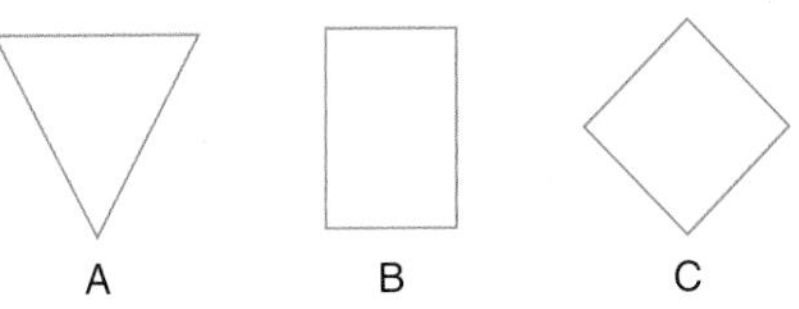

If the regions can be cut out, it is fairly easy to compare regions B and C by placing one on top of the other. It is more difficult to compare either B or C with A. Only when children have some idea of

Math Links 16.5

If you would like to see sixth graders engaged in the authentic task of measuring area for new carpeting, you can view the video clips of Dream House at the Modeling Middle School Mathematics web site, which you can access from this book's web site.

conservation of area—that a region can be cut and rearranged without changing the area—can this experience be meaningful. Thus the first direct comparisons should be made with two regions, one of which fits within the other.

If objects cannot be moved to place one on top of the other, children can trace one object and use this representation to make an indirect comparison. For example, to compare the area of a desk to the area of a bulletin board, you could ask them to cut a piece of paper the size of the desk and put it on the bulletin board.

To help children understand that regions can be rearranged and not affect the area, geometry activities, such as the shape search In the Classroom 16-1, are helpful. Notice that the children are asked to discuss the area of the shapes; this type of discussion helps focus on the objective of comparing shapes indirectly.

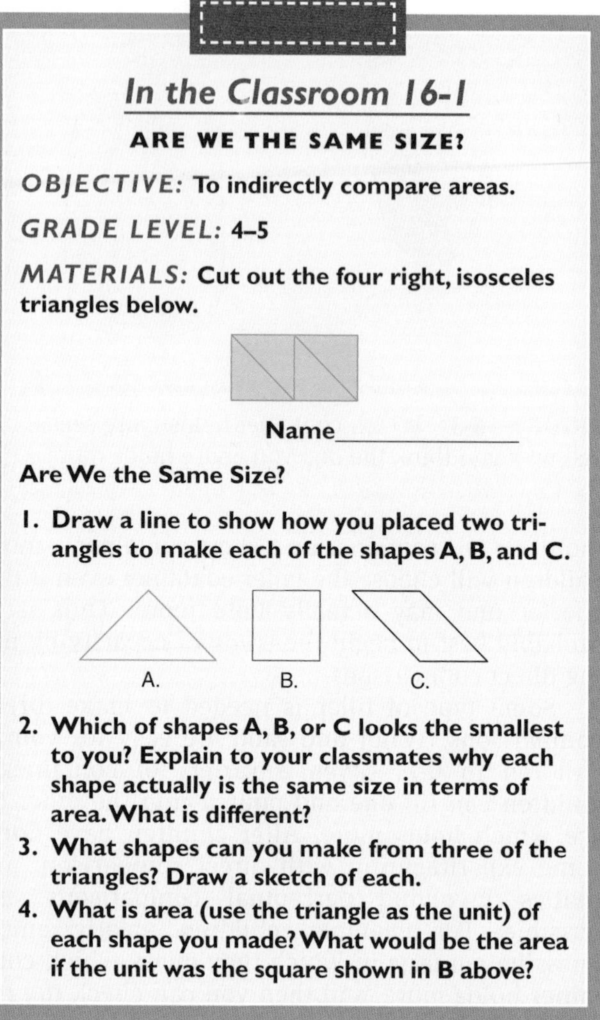

In the Classroom 16-1

ARE WE THE SAME SIZE?

OBJECTIVE: **To indirectly compare areas.**

GRADE LEVEL: **4–5**

MATERIALS: **Cut out the four right, isosceles triangles below.**

Name______________

Are We the Same Size?

1. **Draw a line to show how you placed two triangles to make each of the shapes A, B, and C.**

A. B. C.

2. **Which of shapes A, B, or C looks the smallest to you? Explain to your classmates why each shape actually is the same size in terms of area. What is different?**
3. **What shapes can you make from three of the triangles? Draw a sketch of each.**
4. **What is area (use the triangle as the unit) of each shape you made? What would be the area if the unit was the square shown in B above?**

VOLUME If volume is considered as "how much space a three-dimensional object takes up," then it is difficult to make anything but perceptual comparisons before units are introduced. Thus volume should receive little attention until fourth or fifth grade; however, because there is a close connection between volume and capacity, some background can be provided if containers are filled with nonliquids, such as blocks, balls, or other objects. For example, Figure 16-5 uses blocks to fill a box.

TEMPERATURE You can certainly sense great differences in temperatures. Before introducing thermometers, you can have children compare to see which of two objects is colder (or hotter). You can also talk about things (or times) that are hot or cold; however, there are few other comparisons you can make without an instrument to help.

TIME There are two attributes of events that can be measured: *time of occurrence* and *length of duration.* You can begin describing the time of occurrence by giving a time span: It happened today, in the morning, in October. Young children need to develop the vocabulary of days, months, and seasons of the year.

Children can tell which of two events takes longer (duration) if their lengths are greatly different. Does it take longer to brush your teeth or read

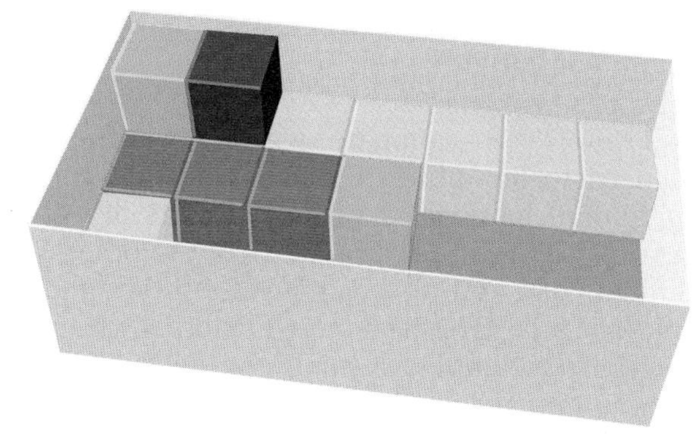

FIGURE 16-5 How many blocks will fill the box?

a story? If the events are similar in duration, children can tell which lasts longer if they both begin at the same time (note the similarity to deciding which object is longer when both are placed on a baseline). You can think of many contests that use this idea: who won the race, whose paper plane flew longer; whose eyes were shut longer; who hopped for a longer time, or whose birthday is closest.

Units of Measure

After children have begun to develop a firm concept of an attribute through comparison activities, it is important to help them move through the remaining steps of the measurement process (steps II–V). Before you introduce instruments or formulas, children should be able to count the number of units that describe a given attribute.

To answer the question, "How long is the pencil?" you can say, "It's longer than my thumb" or "It's shorter than my arm." These are relative statements that give a range of possibilities for length but do not do an accurate job of describing it. To be accurate, you need to compare the pencil to a unit. You can use an arbitrary unit such as a paper clip and say that the pencil is 7 paper clips long, or you can use a standard unit and say it is 16 centimeters long. Once you have described the length, you can compare it to other lengths (i.e., you use the symbolic description to assist in indirectly comparing). The unit of measurement gives you power to communicate with others and make comparisons that were previously difficult to make.

CONCEPTS RELATED TO UNITS Teachers need to help children develop many concepts related to units of measurement. These concepts develop over time. A single activity will not suffice; you need to be aware of the concepts, include similar activities with other attributes, and look for opportunities within any measurement activity to further the development of the concepts.

1. *A measurement must include both a number and the unit.* How many times do you remember a teacher telling you to be certain to write inches? And how many times did you not see the necessity—probably because you were only measuring in inches for the entire lesson? When children measure the same object with many different arbitrary units, research indicates that they are more likely to see the need to report the unit. Having children measure the length of a book with paper strips, erasers, or cubes, or weigh an object with washers, pennies, or paper clips, is the type of task that will encourage younger children to write (or draw) the unit. In the Classroom 16-2 provides an activity that encourages children to focus on the importance of reporting the unit.

2. *Two measurements may be easily compared if the same unit is used.* Young children often rely on only the number or possibly only the unit to make a comparison. For example, if one pencil is 6 paper clips long and another pencil is 2 strips long, some children will say that the pencil that measures 6 is longer. They have not yet reached the stage where they can coordinate the number with a unit. The activity In the Classroom 16-2 addresses this concept along with the need to report both the number and the unit.

3. *One unit may be more appropriate than another to measure an object.* The size of the unit chosen depends on the size of the object and on the degree of accuracy desired. If children are allowed to choose the unit, the idea of the unit's size depending on the size of the object is clearer. To encourage this idea, ask questions such as "Should you use the edge of a book or a paper clip to find out how tall the door is? Should you use a thimble or a coffee mug to find out how much water the

In the Classroom 16-2

MEASURING LENGTH WITH ARBITRARY UNITS

OBJECTIVE: **To measure lengths with different arbitrary units; to compare those measurements.**

GRADE LEVEL: **3–5**

MATERIALS: **Erasers, paper clips, books, boxes, and other objects that can be used as arbitrary units of measure.**

DESCRIPTION:

- Give each pair of children an arbitrary unit and the name of what they are to measure.
- Have the children record their measurements at a place everyone can see. Observe to see whether they record the unit (if they do not, it will lead to the discussion below).
- Ask children to use the information about the lengths to compare the lengths of the different objects.
- Ask children why the unit is necessary. Ask the children which comparisons are easy to make (ones measured with the same unit) and what they can tell about those made with different units.

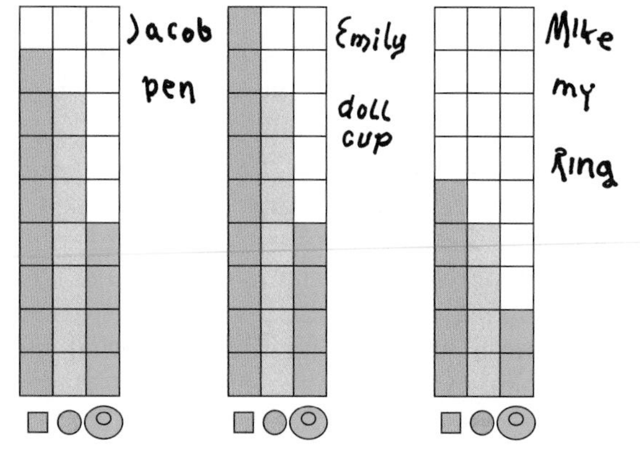

FIGURE 16-6 Children's graphs of weights of objects.

big bucket will hold? Should you use a paper clip or a pencil to find out the length of the book?"

4. *There is an inverse relationship between the number of units and the size of the unit.* When measuring the same object with three different units, children soon realize that the larger the unit, the fewer are required. For example, you could ask each child to weigh an object with pennies, washers, and cubes. If each child makes a graph of the results, a pattern becomes apparent when all the graphs are compared. As depicted in Figure 16-6, it always takes more cubes than washers to weigh each object. So cubes are lighter than washers.

5. *Standard units are needed to communicate effectively.* Many concepts about units can be developed with arbitrary units. At the same time, you will be teaching procedures of measuring with units (e.g., how to line up units, use a balance, cover a region, keep track of how many units).

At some point, depending on the attribute, you begin using standard units. Standard units are either customary (e.g., inch, pint, pound) or metric (e.g., meter, gram, liter). Most children already have heard of standard units but may not realize why they use them. Unfortunately, in the United States both types of units are used. It is clear from the recent national assessments that children have a better understanding of customary units. On the 1996 assessment, although approximately three-fourths of the fourth-grade students selected an appropriate customary unit for length, only about one-third selected an appropriate metric unit to measure length (Martin and Strutchens, 2000).

Stories and activities that demonstrate the difficulty in communicating sizes when there is no standard of measurement are one way to present the necessity of a standard unit. The book *How Big Is a Foot?* (Myller, 1991) is an interesting and amusing source to use in helping children see the necessity for a standard unit. Another enjoyable activity for children is making a recipe of powdered drink such as lemonade, using a very large cup for the water and a very small spoon for the powder. (Be sure to have enough of the powder so the children can make it tasty.)

6. *A smaller unit gives a more exact measurement.* First, children need to realize that all measurements are approximate. If you have had them do a lot of measuring of real objects, they are reporting approximate measurements, but perhaps without being fully aware of it. A practice of saying "about 6 inches," "more than 6 inches," or "between 6 and 7 inches" helps.

To set up the need for a more precise measurement, give one child a strip of paper that is 27 centimeters long and another child, sitting across the room, a strip that is 29 centimeters long. Give each child decimeter strips with which to measure the paper. After they report the measurement, ask the class which strip is longer (no fair comparing the strips directly). Next, have them measure with centimeters. Discuss with the class why a smaller unit was needed.

MEASURING IN UNITS Length is the first attribute that most children measure. They take an arbitrary unit and copies of that unit and put them end to end until the units are as long as the object they are measuring. From previous direct comparisons of two objects, children should know when the lengths are the same; however, they have not lined up the units in a straight line with no gaps in between and no overlaps, nor have they counted the units. Units that connect, such as connecting cubes or links, are good in the beginning because they are easy to handle and line up readily without gaps or overlaps.

After an example or two, you need only set up objects to be measured and supply the units. Then observe and help. Later, children can take one unit and move it along the object (an *iteration*). This more advanced skill is needed for proper use of a ruler when measuring objects longer than the ruler. It is a skill that should not be pushed too early. If you find that children cannot move, mark, and count, postpone introducing work on this skill until later.

If children have been measuring with nonstandard units, then using standard units should be easy. They will have a good understanding of the process of measuring, so the purpose should be to give them a feel for the standard unit. Take the decimeter as an example and consider some ways to build a feel for the decimeter as a standard unit

Give each child a paper strip that is 10 centimeters by 2 centimeters. (Or you could use a 10-rod from a Cuisenaire set.) Do a variety of activities that have the children compare things to the decimeter strip. Some are suggested here:

- *Decimeter list-up.* Put a list on the board of objects children can find in the room that are the same length as a decimeter. Be sure to include things on the children, such as fingers, pockets, soles of shoes.
- *Decimeter hold-up.* Pair the children and have one child try to hold two forefingers one decimeter apart, vertically, horizontally, and obliquely. The partner should check each time; then roles should be reversed.
- *Decimeter stack-up.* Set up stations with pennies, chips, clips, beans, cubes, and the like. At one station, children should try to stack the chips one decimeter high. At another station they should try to make a line of chips one decimeter long. Then they should use their decimeter strip to see how close they were.

After children are somewhat familiar with the length of a decimeter, they can begin to measure with decimeters. A good way to begin is by asking them to estimate the lengths of objects and then measure. As children are measuring with decimeter strips, they (and you) should notice that putting down strip after strip is not the easiest way to measure. Have them tape their strips together, end to end as below, alternating colors if two colors are available.

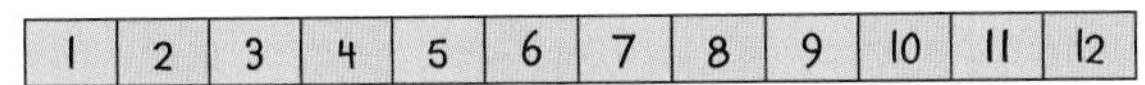

Now they have a "decimeter ruler," except they still have to count the units. After they have done some counting, see if anyone suggests numbering the strips. This activity helps children understand how rulers are made and that they are counting units.

Once children are familiar with the decimeter measurement of small objects, the next stage is measuring something very long. Have each child make a 10-decimeter ruler. Tell the children that this unit is called a *meter* and is used to measure longer distances. Activities similar to those suggested with decimeters will help them become familiar with meters. New units should be related to the ones children have already used to help them understand the new unit and to assist them in making conversions from one unit to another.

Children become familiar with standard units through comparing, measuring, estimating, and constructing. The experiences you provide should include all of these processes. It is also important that not too many standard units are introduced at one time, that the unit is not too small or too large for a child of that age to handle, and that the numbers generated are not too large. Table 16-1 is a guide to the most common standard units used in elementary school and the approximate grade levels at which it is appropriate to introduce them.

Instruments for Measuring

Instruments are used to measure some attributes. In elementary school, the more common instruments are rulers, scales, graduated containers, thermometers, protractors, and clocks. Other attributes (such as area and volume) are assigned a measurement by the use of a formula after an instrument has been used to measure some dimensions. Later, other attributes are derived from measurements of more than one attribute (e.g., speed is derived from distance and time).

Much of the emphasis in the elementary curriculum is on instruments and formulas, and some children encounter difficulty with both. One probable source of difficulty is that the children do not understand what they are measuring and what it means to measure. The activities and suggestions presented so far in this chapter have dealt with building this understanding. Here we will look at some common problems children have with particular instruments and some ways to assist in developing the correct skills.

RULER A ruler automatically counts the number of units, but children must realize what unit they are using and line up the ruler properly. Children focus on the unit being used if the scale on the ruler has only that unit. For example, if the unit is centimeters, choose a ruler marked only in centimeters, not in centimeters and millimeters. Or, if the unit is inches, choose a ruler without the markings of fourths or eighths.

It is important that children measure real objects with the ruler. Make certain that you include activities in which children measure objects longer than one ruler. Can they move the ruler (iterate), and do they have the addition skills to add the units? For example, suppose the children have a 25-centimeter ruler and they are to measure something that is 43 centimeters long. Can they add 25 and 18? Of course, they could use counting or techniques that rely on their place value and counting

Table 16-1 • Standard Units for Elementary Students (with Approximate Grade Level)

Attribute	Metric Units	Customary Units
Length	Decimeter (1–2) Centimeter (2–3) Meter (2–3) Millimeter (3–4) Kilometer (4–5)	Inch (1–2) Foot (2–3) Yard (2–3) Mile (4–5)
Weight	Kilogram (2–3) Gram (4–5)	Ounce (2–3) Pound (2–3)
Capacity	Liter (1–2) Milliliter (4–5)	Quart (2–3) Cup (1–2) Gallon (2–3)
Area	Square centimeter (4–5) Square meter (5–6)	Square inch (4–5) Square foot (4–5) Square yard (4–5)
Volume	Cubic centimeter (5–6) Cubic meter (5–6)	Cubic inch (5–6) Cubic foot (5–6) Cubic yard (5–6)
Temperature	Celsius degree (2–3)	Fahrenheit degree (2–3)
Time		Hour (1–2) Minute (1–2) Second (3–4) Day (K–1) Week (1–2) Month (K–1)

background: 25, 35, 36, 37, . . . , 43. Let them try; they will surprise you if they are given a problem to solve. Your role is to ask questions to assist them.

Children may have difficulty in measuring to the nearest fourth, eighth, or sixteenth of a unit. One cause of this difficulty may be the smallness of the unit (there is more room for error), but more probably it is their lack of confidence and understanding of fractions, their lack of understanding of the unit (fourths), and their lack of consciousness of how to measure to the nearest unit. In measuring to a unit, they tend to decide by simply looking at the nearest larger unit. The example of measuring in Figure 16-1 gives you some idea of how to make this process more explicit. The rulers in Appendix B marked in halves, fourths, and eighths provide a good intermediate step before moving to a standard ruler marked in sixteenths. It also is helpful to emphasize the units by asking, "What two units is the nail between—two-fourths and three-fourths or three-fourths and four-fourths?" Children must be able to answer this question before deciding which it is nearer. A firm foundation of fractions, especially fractions as they relate to length, helps with measuring to the nearest unit.

Figure 16-7 illustrates an exercise for using a ruler similar to a question from the national mathematics assessment. What do you think was the most common answer of fourth-grade students? Most said the segment was 5 inches long.

Children begin counting with one, so it is natural that they often begin measuring at one. Activities like making a ruler and seeing that the 1 is placed at the end of the first unit are helpful. If children are having difficulty, return to directly comparing the object with the ruler (use a baseline as described in the section on direct comparison). You also could use separate units or just mark the inches on the segment and count the units.

Although we have emphasized difficulties that some children have in learning to use a ruler, do not be discouraged. Children love to use rulers, and overall they do quite well with them. Make certain you have children not only measuring objects but also constructing line segments or objects of a given length. Research shows that children have more difficulty drawing a line segment of a given length than in measuring. Part of this difficulty may be the lack of experience.

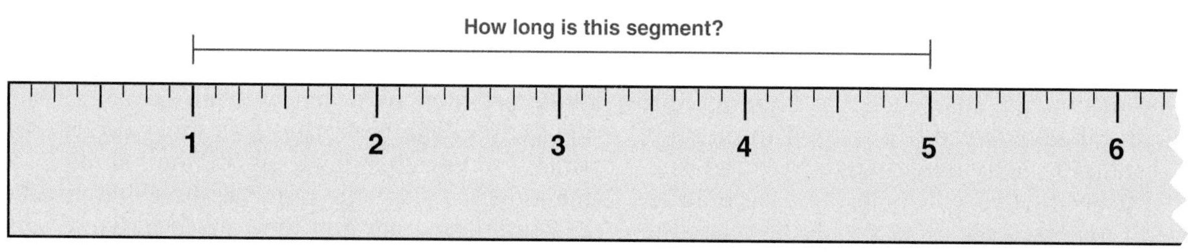

FIGURE 16-7 An exercise assessing understanding of a ruler.

SCALED INSTRUMENTS Instruments such as bathroom scales, graduated cylinders, and thermometers cause children some trouble because each unit is not marked. On national assessments, students have always had difficulty reading thermometers on which the markings represent 2 degrees. Over half of the fourth-grade students on the sixth national mathematics assessment chose a distractor based on thinking the marking represented one rather than two units (Kenney and Kouba, 1997).

One way to help children become more aware of the markings on a scale is to show to them and read with them many scales with different markings. A more powerful way is to have them make their own instruments. They can make graphs, for example, using different scales, or they can mark their own graduated cylinders. Lesson Idea 16-5 gives instructions on how to make the "cylinder." Children can make such a measurement instrument and then use it to measure the amounts other containers hold. Note that this activity is also good practice for finding multiples of a number; in this case, children are working with multiples of six since it took six spoons to fill the small container.

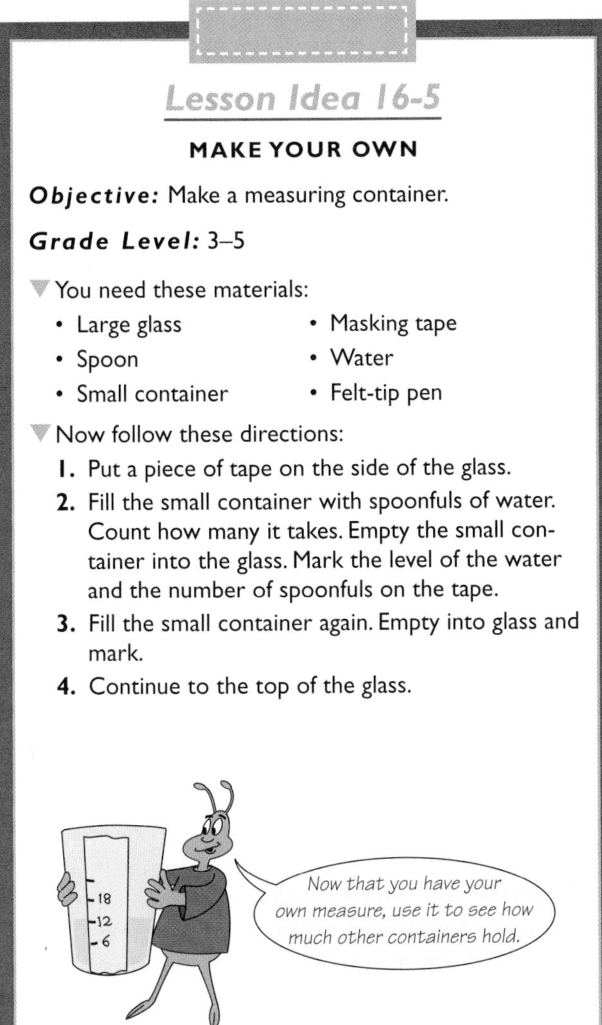

Lesson Idea 16-5

MAKE YOUR OWN

Objective: Make a measuring container.

Grade Level: 3–5

You need these materials:

- Large glass
- Spoon
- Small container
- Masking tape
- Water
- Felt-tip pen

Now follow these directions:

1. Put a piece of tape on the side of the glass.
2. Fill the small container with spoonfuls of water. Count how many it takes. Empty the small container into the glass. Mark the level of the water and the number of spoonfuls on the tape.
3. Fill the small container again. Empty into glass and mark.
4. Continue to the top of the glass.

18
12
6
Now that you have your own measure, use it to see how much other containers hold.

CLOCKS The ordinary dial clock or watch is one of the most complicated instruments to read—and yet it is often one of the first to be taught. Not only are there two or more ways to read the scale on a clock (hour, minute, and second), but the hands (indicators of the measures) move in a circular fashion. Children who easily read linear scales (rulers, for example) may be confused by this circular arrangement. There is no set age at which children appear ready to learn how to tell time; you will often notice a wide range of ability within a class. The following list of skills associated with telling time is not necessarily in the order in which children may develop them:

- Identify the hour hand and the minute hand and the direction they move.
- Orally tell time by the hour (noting that the minute hand is on the 15) and moving the hands of a clock to show the hourly times.
- Identify the hour that a time is "after" (e.g., it's after 4 o'clock).
- Count by fives to tell time to the nearest 5 minutes and report it orally (e.g., as 4 o'clock and 20 minutes after).
- Count on by ones from multiples of 5 to tell time to the nearest minute (e.g., 25, 26, 27).
- Identify the hour that a time is "before" (e.g., it's before 10) and count by fives and ones to tell about how many minutes before the hour.
- Write the time in digital notation (4:20).
- Match the time on a digital clock to a regular clock.

These skills need to be developed over a long period of time, and children need to have clocks with movable hands.

You can begin problem solving with young children if they have clocks or watches. For example, as soon as children can tell time on the hour, you can ask questions such as, "What time will it be in 2 hours?" As the children become more familiar with the clock, you can give more challenging questions, such as those in Lesson Idea 16-6.

Although reading digital clocks is easier than reading regular clocks, solving the types of problems as in Lesson Idea 16-6 is more difficult with a digital clock. In learning to read a regular clock, a child learns the relationship of the minutes and hours and has a model to use in solving such problems. If all clocks were digital, teachers would

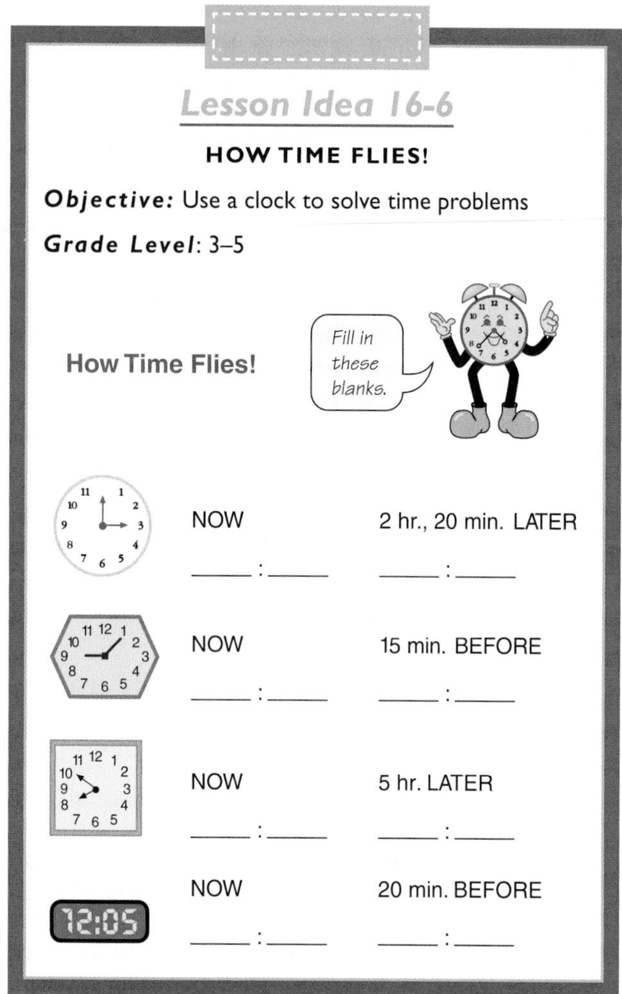

need to spend less time on how to read time but more on how our time system works.

Lesson Idea 16-6
HOW TIME FLIES!
Objective: Use a clock to solve time problems
Grade Level: 3–5
How Time Flies!
Fill in these blanks.
NOW
2 hr., 20 min. LATER
NOW
15 min. BEFORE
NOW
5 hr. LATER
NOW
20 min. BEFORE
12:05

To integrate math and history, an interdisciplinary unit on the history of time and clocks could prove to be interesting to older students. Students might enjoy seeing how the measurement of time has evolved through the years. Students could make sand clocks, sundials, or other primitive instruments. Some references for teachers and students are provided at the end of the chapter.

Formulas for Measuring

Formulas for area, perimeter, volume, and surface area are usually introduced in the upper grades. Although formulas are necessary in many measurement situations, they should not take the place of careful development of measurement attributes and the measuring process. The skill of using formulas needs to be developed, but not at the expense of helping students see how formulas are derived. The main emphasis in this section is on ways to build meaning of the area formulas. The formulas for other attributes may be developed similarly.

Before considering formulas, students should be given the opportunity to compare areas of regions with and without units. Comparing areas without the aid of units have been discussed by placing one region on top of the other and by cutting one region in order to make the comparison.

When introducing units of area, provide students with experiences in covering a region with a variety of types of units—squares, triangles, and rectangles. To find the area of a region, they should count the number of units. Covering many different shapes helps students see the need to approximate and to use smaller units. For example, this region was first covered by one size of squares and then by smaller squares:

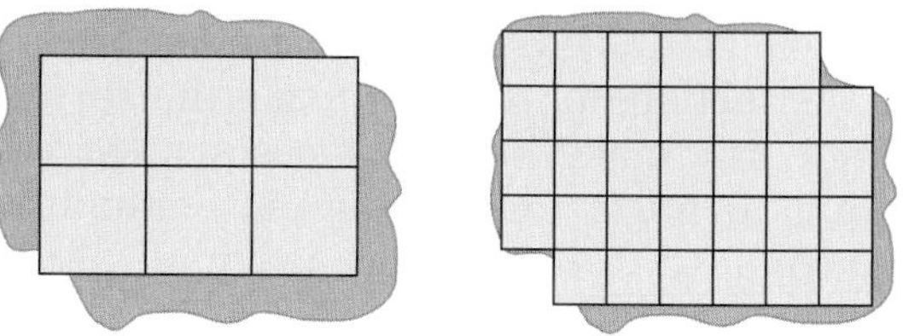

When students are thoroughly familiar with counting units covering different shapes, especially rectangles, it is time to introduce the formula for the area of a rectangle. In this section, we examine steps for developing this formula and then show how to use it to develop the formulas for parallelograms, triangles, trapezoids, and other figures. After learning how to use these formulas, children need experiences such as those shown by In the Classroom 16-3, in which they cut the shapes into different smaller shapes for which they can use area formulas that they know. There are many different ways to subdivide the shapes. If you try this with students, have them show the different ways they subdivided the shapes.

RECTANGLE The formula for the area of a rectangle is often the first formula children encounter. Use of the rectangle is appropriate because it can be developed easily, building on models that children may have used for multiplication.

Figure 16-8 shows a sequence of steps that can be used to develop instructional activities that lead to the formula for the area of a rectangle, $A = ba$ (where A is area, b is base, and a is altitude). This form of the formula generalizes better than $A = lw$. Recall in the *Snapshot of a Lesson* at the beginning of this chapter that the length-and-width interpretation led to initial confusion with the trapezoidal table.

When children measure with square units, the base and altitude may not be an exact number of units. You may have them begin by estimating how many squares it would take to cover the shape.

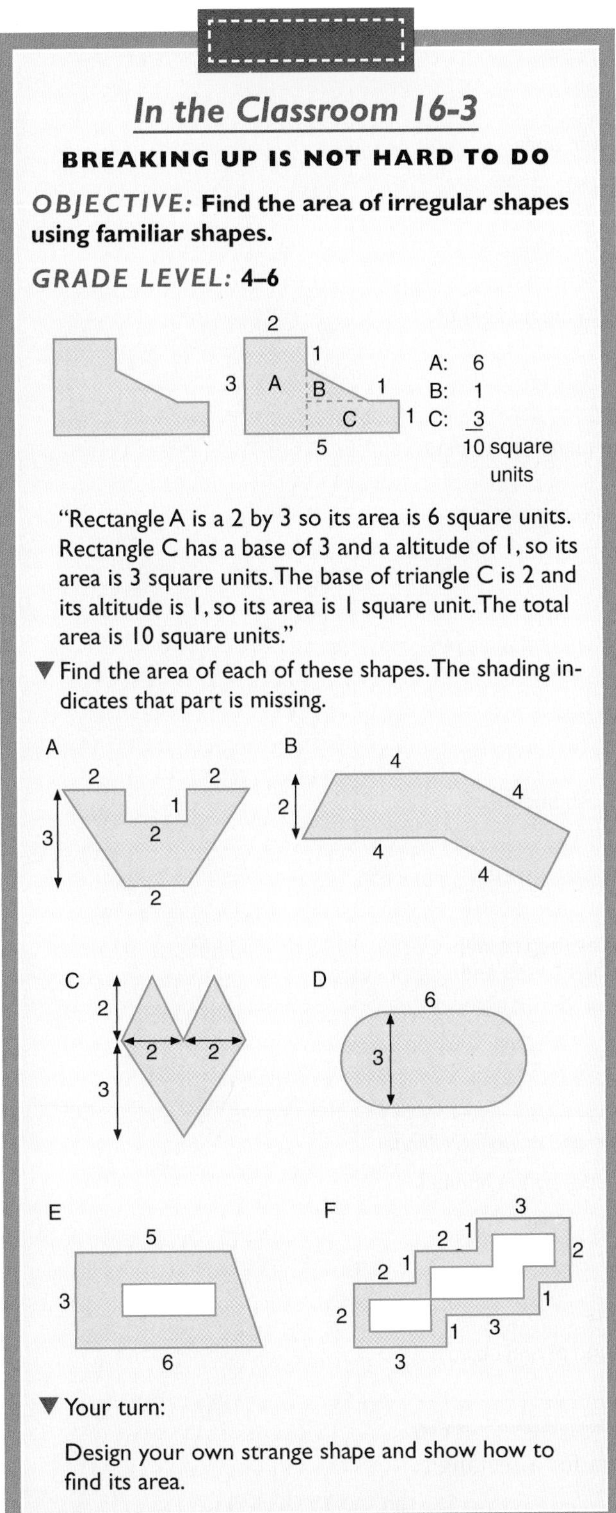

In the Classroom 16-3
BREAKING UP IS NOT HARD TO DO
OBJECTIVE: Find the area of irregular shapes using familiar shapes.
GRADE LEVEL: 4–6
A: 6
B: 1
C: 3
10 square units
"Rectangle A is a 2 by 3 so its area is 6 square units. Rectangle C has a base of 3 and a altitude of 1, so its area is 3 square units. The base of triangle C is 2 and its altitude is 1, so its area is 1 square unit. The total area is 10 square units."
▼ Find the area of each of these shapes. The shading indicates that part is missing.
▼ Your turn:
Design your own strange shape and show how to find its area.

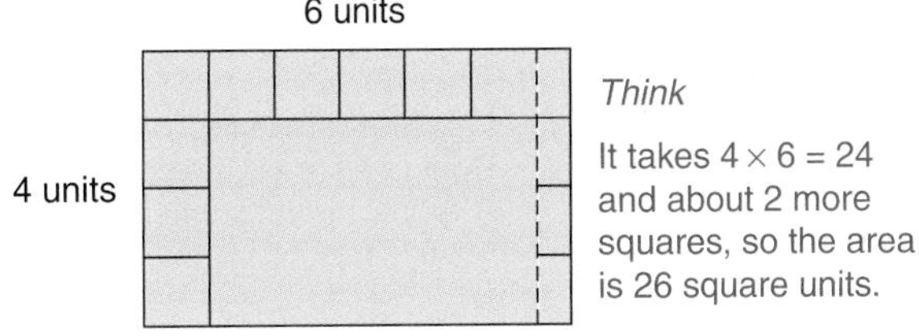

6 units
4 units
Think
It takes 4 × 6 = 24 and about 2 more squares, so the area is 26 square units.

Later, you can develop the idea of using smaller units or fractional parts of the unit.

You should not teach the steps as listed in Figure 16-8. It is given as an outline to help you sequence experiences and assess students' understandings. Although some of the steps could be combined into a single activity, step 3 should not be done until children have the experiences listed in step 1. In addition, problems may arise when children are doing step 7 if they have not had prior experience in covering real objects.

One difficulty that children often have with the area of a rectangle is that they may learn, by rote, that the area is the length times the width (or base times altitude) but not develop the underlying concepts. Thus, when they are faced with finding the area of a square, they run into difficulty. (It has no side that is longer than the others!) The results of the fourth national assessment (Kouba et al., 1988) showed that seventh-grade performance dropped from 50 percent correct for rectangles to 10 percent correct for squares.

PARALLELOGRAM After children have worked with the area formula for a rectangle, you can develop the area formula for a parallelogram. Children need background in geometric experiences in which they have compared parallelograms with rectangles and have tried to cut the parallelograms to rearrange them into rectangles. Next, they should identify the base and altitude of parallelograms. Note that any side can be designated as a base, and the altitude depends on what side was chosen.

The next stage in developing the formula is seeing the relationship of the area of a parallelogram with base b and altitude a and the corresponding rectangle. From exercises such as those In the Classroom 16-4, children should see the area of a parallelogram is the same as the corresponding rectangle:

$$A = b \times a$$

TRIANGLE Children's understanding of the area of a triangle can be developed from the realization that a triangle is always half of a parallelogram. This development depends on a strong background of geometry, experiences like those described in Chapter 15 and activities such as In the Classroom 16-5. Even when students see that the area of a triangle is half that of a corresponding parallelogram, or

$$A = \frac{1}{2}(b \times a)$$

they have difficulty identifying the altitude, especially in triangles like E in In the Classroom 16-5.

Developing the Formula for the Area of a Rectangle

Prerequisites:
- Identifies rectangle
- Compares areas directly
- Assigns a measurement by covering with units
- Models multiplication as an array

Step 1: Covering with Nonstandard Units
- Reviews covering of a rectangle with units
- Develops finding the area by multiplying the number of rows by the number in each row

Step 2: Covering with Standard Units
- Uses standard square units such as square centimeters or square inches
- Continues to find area by multiplying the number of rows by the number in each row

Step 3: Shortcut to Covering
- Develops a shortcut to covering the entire rectangle by showing that it is only necessary to see how many rows and how many in each row

Step 4: Shorter Shortcut
- Marks how many squares could fit across and down
- Continues to multiply to find the area

a

b

Step 5: Identifying Base and Altitude
- Identifies base and altitude of rectangles (begins with cut-outs of rectangles and measures their bases and altitudes)

4 cm

8 cm

Step 6: Formula for Area
- Measures base and altitude
- Tells how many squares across the base and down the altitude
- Multiplies the number of rows (the altitude) by the number in each row (the base)
- Uses the formula $A = a \times b$

Step 7: Applying Formula to Real Objects
- Practices finding the areas of regions and of real objects

FIGURE 16-8 One sequence for developing the area formula for a rectangle.

TRAPEZOID There are many ways to develop the formula for the area of a trapezoid. One of the easiest is to rely again on the area of a parallelogram. Consider the example of finding the area of the following trapezoid.

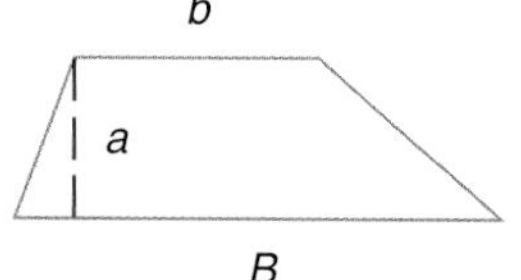

Students can be instructed to make a copy of the trapezoid and place it adjacent to the original:

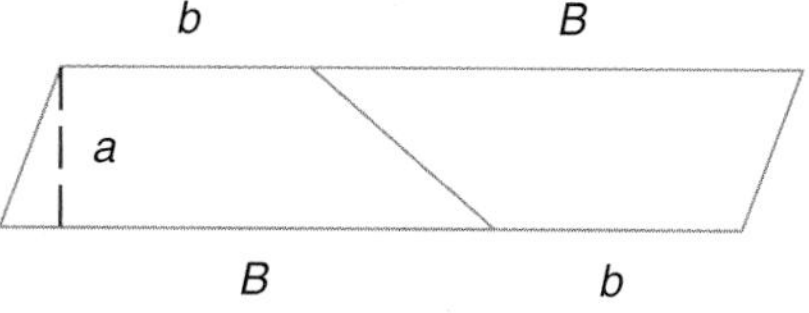

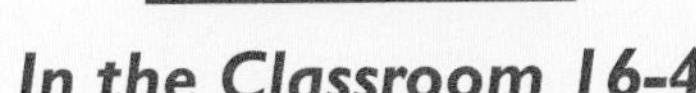

In the Classroom 16-4

HOW ARE WE ALIKE? DIFFERENT?

OBJECTIVE: **Exploring the connection between the area of a parallelogram and the area of a rectangle.**

GRADE LEVEL: **4–5**

MATERIALS: **Ruler, scissors, and tape.**

DIRECTIONS: **Cut out each of the figures at the bottom of the page. See if you can pair a nonrectangular parallelogram with a rectangle of the same area. Cut the nonrectangular parallelogram to show that it has the same area as its pair counterpart; tape. Then fill in the table below.**

Letters of Pairs	Base	Altitude	Area

Cut out these shapes:

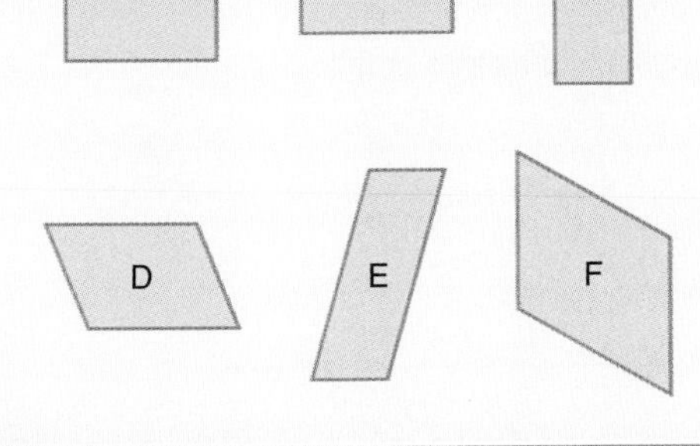

The area formula can now be developed through a series of questions.

What figure have you formed? [a parallelogram]

What is its base? [$B + b$]

What is its altitude? [a]

What is its area? [$A = a(B + b)$]

How does the area of the trapezoid compare to the area of the parallelogram? [half as much]

Therefore, how might a formula for area of a trapezoid be written? [$A = \frac{1}{2}a(B + b)$]

CIRCLE The circle is the one common geometric figure whose area is not directly related to the previous procedures. Students may discover that the formula is logical by cutting a circle into segments and rearranging them to form a pseudoparallelogram, as shown in Figure 16-9. This interpretation depends on their knowledge of the circumference of a circle being $2\pi r$.

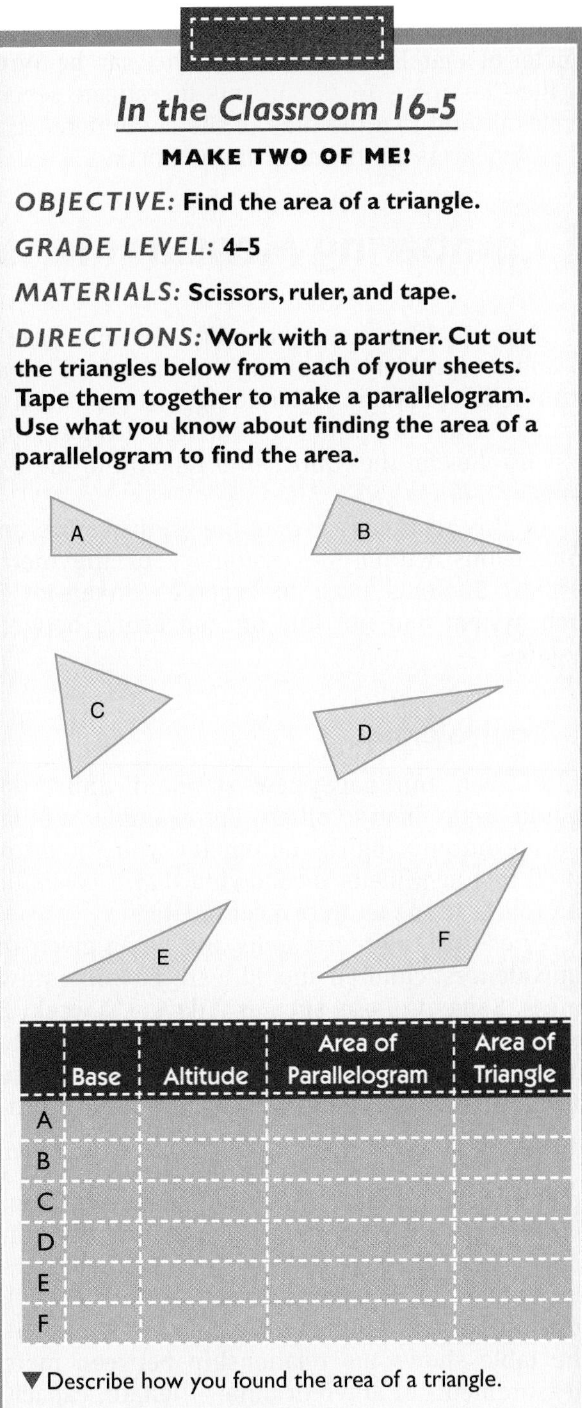

In the Classroom 16-5

MAKE TWO OF ME!

OBJECTIVE: **Find the area of a triangle.**

GRADE LEVEL: **4–5**

MATERIALS: **Scissors, ruler, and tape.**

DIRECTIONS: **Work with a partner. Cut out the triangles below from each of your sheets. Tape them together to make a parallelogram. Use what you know about finding the area of a parallelogram to find the area.**

	Base	Altitude	Area of Parallelogram	Area of Triangle
A				
B				
C				
D				
E				
F				

▼ Describe how you found the area of a triangle.

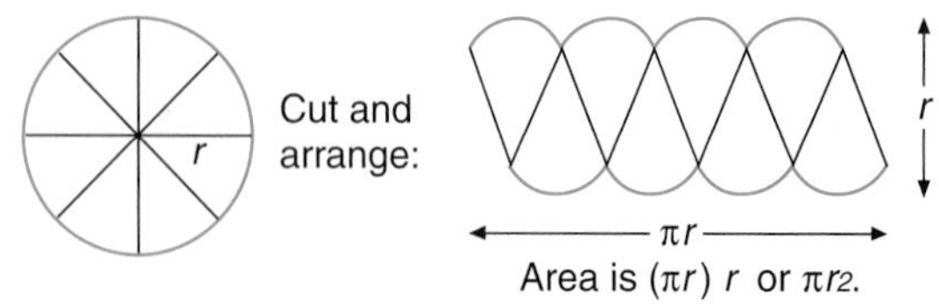

FIGURE 16-9 Picture relating the area of a parallelogram to the area of a circle.

An investigation into the relationship of the diameter of a circle to the circumference can be found In the Classroom 16-6. Students investigate several circles to find that the ratio of the circumference to the diameter is a little larger than 3, or π.

Comparing Measurements

After making a measurement, we often use it to solve a problem involving a comparison or an arithmetic operation. In so doing, we may need to change from one unit to another (*conversion*), which relies on the *equivalence* relation of the two units.

In this section, we examine equivalences and conversions within the customary or the metric system. Students need to become conversant in each system and not rely on converting between systems.

Equivalences

As you introduce new standard units, you should relate them to others. For example, suppose you are introducing the millimeter; you should relate it to a centimeter by showing that it is smaller and that it is one-tenth of a centimeter.

After using different units and being given the equivalences, children should learn certain equivalences. Some of these, such as 7 days = 1 week, 60 minutes = 1 hour, and 12 inches = 1 foot, will become known through repeated use. Children need to know that they are expected to know other equivalences.

Although children are no longer required to memorize long tables of equivalences, you should expect them to memorize the ones that are commonly used. The task is easier with the metric system because of the standard prefixes and tens relationship between units, as indicated in Table 16-2. The table shows the relationship between metric measurements of different units of length, capacity, and mass (or weight). For example, the meter (m) is the base unit for length. A kilometer (km) is 1000 times as long as a meter. A decimeter (dm) is one-tenth of a meter.

Because not all equivalences will be memorized, children must become familiar with using a table of equivalences. You will need to help them develop the different skills related to equivalences.

In the Classroom 16-6

THE MAGIC RATIO IN EVERY CIRCLE

OBJECTIVE: **Measure the circumference and the diameter of a circle and determine the ratio between them.**

GRADE LEVEL: **5–6**

MATERIALS: **Tape measures (or string and meter sticks) and graph paper. Collect circular objects: plates, jars, baskets, bicycle wheels, clocks, plastic drinking glasses, lampshades, hula-hoop. You will need at least one object per group of 3 with several extras.**

Have students make a table:

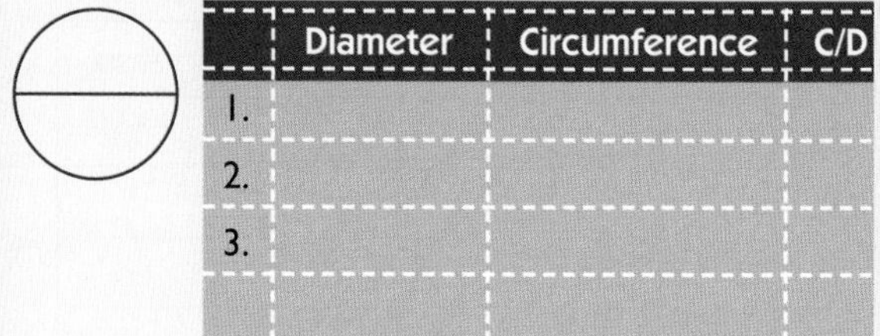

	Diameter	Circumference	C/D
1.			
2.			
3.			

For each group of three students, rotate roles with each measurement: one student measures, a second records the data, and a third computes the ratio. Each child measures at least one circle, depending on time.

After the table is complete, have students add their data to a class list (on an overhead or at the board).

- Have each child make a graph:

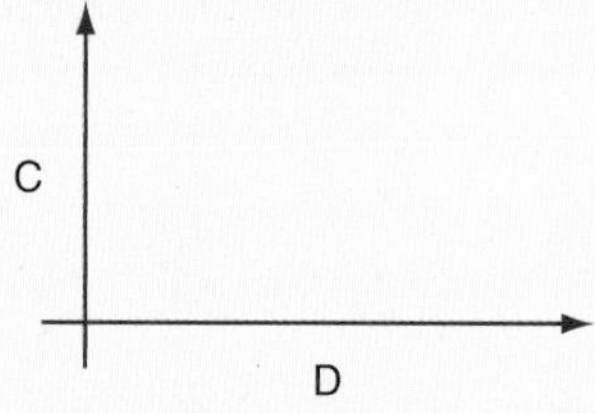

- Have each child make observations about the data in their table, on the board, and about the graph

Challenge problems:

1. **Find the circumference of a circular racetrack that is 25 yards across.**
2. **Find the diameter of the class globe.**

Table 16-2 • Most Commonly Used Metric Units

	kilo (k) 1000	hecto (h) 100	deka (da) 10	Base Unit	deci (d) 0.1	centi (c) 0.01	milli (m) 0.001
Length	kilometer (km)			meter (m)		centimeter (cm)	millimeter (mm)
Capacity				liter (l)			milliliter (ml)
Mass	kilogram (kg)			gram (g)			

The following table and questions illustrate these skills:

Unit	Equivalent
1 day	24 hours
1 hour	60 minutes
1 minute	60 seconds

How many hours in a day? (This answer is a straightforward reading from the table.)

What part of a day is 1 hour?(This answer involves knowledge of fractional relations of the units in the table.)

How many seconds are in an hour? (This answer involves conversion of units in the table.)

Area and volume equivalences can be difficult for many children because they are often derived from the linear equivalences. For example, knowing that $1 \text{ m} = 10 \text{ dm}$ allows you to derive $1 \text{ m}^2 = 100 \text{ dm}^2$ and $1 \text{ m}^3 = 1000 \text{ dm}^3$. Children need experiences in seeing these basic relationships through models, drawings, and questions, such as in Lesson Idea 16-7.

Conversions

To change from one unit to another, children must know the equivalence or relation between the two units. By itself, however, this information is not sufficient to make conversions. Let's look at an example of a class discussion.

MR. BANE: It seems that several of you are stumped on the assignment. Devon, please read the first exercise and let's look at it together.

DEVON: Blank dm equals 5 m.

Mr. Bane writes on the board: _____ dm = 5 m.

MR. BANE: Who can tell me what we are looking for?

GEORGE: How many decimeters there are in 5 meters.

MR. BANE: What do you know about decimeters and meters?

ALANA: A decimeter is about this big and a meter is about this big.

MR. BANE: That's right. Could everyone see Alana's hands? Which unit is larger, the meter or the decimeter? . . . Right, so will it take more than 5 decimeters or less than 5 to make 5 meters?

KARINA: It'll take more. It takes 10 decimeters to make 1 meter.

Mr. Bane draws this on the board:

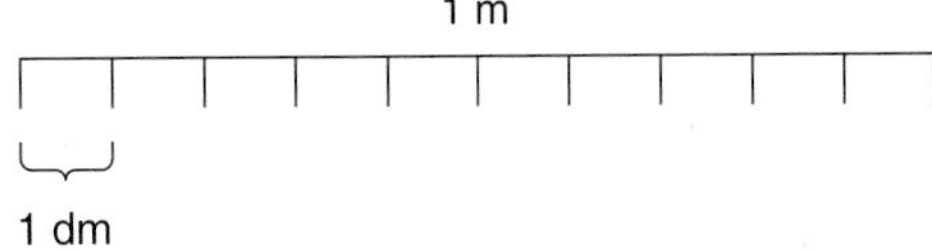

MR. BANE: If 1 meter is 10 decimeters, then what would 5 meters be?

DEVON: I see, it's 5 groups of the 10 decimeters or 50 decimeters.

MR. BANE: Good. Let's try another:

20 cm = _____ dm.

LEON: Centimeters are smaller, they take more; so it won't be as many as 20 decimeters.

MR. BANE: Good. We know our answer must be less than 20.

RANDY: Let's draw a picture like this. Oh, there's no use drawing in all 20 marks. We know 10 centimeters makes 1 decimeter. So we want to know how many tens in 20.

MR. BANE: Right, in this case we can just look at the picture and see that it is 2 decimeters. But what if it was 184 centimeters?

DAVE: We still need to know how many tens in 184—we divide.

JIM: There are 18 decimeters.

MR. BANE: What about the 4 left over?

PAULA: Those are centimeters. We have 18 full decimeters and 4 left-over centimeters.

MR. BANE: Let's write that down:

184 cm = 18 dm 4 cm

Okay. Try some on your own, and I'll help you if you have questions.

Lesson Idea 16-7

SOLVING CONVERSION PROBLEMS WITH SQUARE UNITS

Objective: Determine the equivalents between dm^2 and m^2

Grade Level: *4–5*

- Ask students how many square decimeters (dm^2) are in one square meter (m^2). A representation of the relationship is shown below.

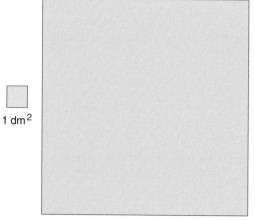

- Establish that it would take 100 square or 1 m^2 = 100 dm^2. Show that each row would have 10 and that there would be 10 rows.

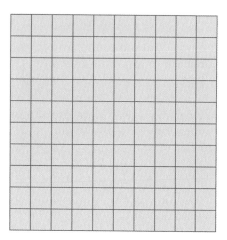

$10 \times 10 = 100$ squares

- Use sketches and the model above to answer the following questions.
  - Conrad has a piece of cloth that is 3 m^2 or 3 m × 1 m. How many dm^2 is that?
  - Maria has a blanket that is 15 dm × 10 dm. How many m^2 is it?

This discussion, although not an initial presentation to the class, points out many good techniques to use in developing conversions. First, Mr. Bane had the children decide whether their answer would be larger or smaller than the number given. This relies on children's knowing the relative sizes of the units and their understanding that the smaller the unit, the more it takes. Second, Mr. Bane tried to have the children visualize the relationship between the units. Third, he related the operation to be used to their understanding of what multiplication and division mean.

If you are doing a lot of metric conversions, there are shortcuts. These depend on the facility to estimate and to multiply and divide by powers of ten. These shortcuts are helpful but should not replace a careful building of the process.

Estimating Measurements

Estimating is the mental process of arriving at a measurement without the aid of measuring instruments. There are many reasons to include estimating in the development of measurement. For one, it helps reinforce the size of units and the relationships among units. For another, it is a practical application—think of all the times you want to know approximately how long, how heavy, or how much something holds.

There are two main types of estimation. In the most common type, the attribute and object are named and the measurement is unknown. For example, about how long is your arm? In the other type, the measurement is known and the object is to be chosen. For example, what piece of furniture in your room is about one meter long?

By keeping the two classes of estimation in mind, you can expand your repertoire of estimation activities. Several common strategies can be used with either type. You can help children develop these strategies by talking through the various methods that different children use to make an estimation and by presenting the following strategies.

1. One strategy is to *compare to a referent.* If you know that you are 1 meter 70 centimeters tall, then you can estimate the height of a child who comes up to your waist. Or, if you have to choose a board that is 2 meters long, you will have some idea of the size.

2. Another strategy is that of *chunking.* In this process, you break the object into subparts and estimate each part. For example, you want to know

Math Links 16.6

A three-part electronic lesson plan for middle-grade students, Competing Coasters, may be viewed at the NCTM web site, which you can access from this book's web site. In these lessons, children use the Internet to learn about roller coasters from around the country. They predict which one is faster, higher, and takes longer. Then they compare their estimates with actual data.

about how far you walked from your home to the library and the store and then back to your home. If you know that from your home to the library is about one mile, that it's about that same distance from the library to the store, and twice as far from the store back to your home, you walked about four miles altogether.

3. A strategy related to chunking is *unitizing*. In this case, you estimate one part and see how many parts are in the whole. For example, someone asks you to cut a piece of string that is about 3 meters long. You estimate 1 meter and take three of these. This strategy is a good one to emphasize when you are teaching multiplication because it provides an application of multiplication.

When including estimation in your program, you should try to make it a natural part of measurement activities.

1. Encourage children to see if they can tell about how long or heavy the object is before they measure it.
2. Look for ways to include estimation in other subject areas:

   About how far did you jump?

   What size paper do you need for your art project?

   About how long did it take you to read the book?
3. Plan estimating activities for their own sake or use brief ones as daily openers for several weeks throughout the year.

The suggestions in Lesson Idea 16-8 give some ideas to get you started. Once you begin thinking about the things in your room, you will be able to come up with a lot of variations.

One thing to remember: do not call an estimate right or wrong. Help children develop ways to make better estimates, but do not discourage them. Let them check their estimates by measuring. They will know whether they were close or not. You may be surprised to find out who are the good estimators in your class.

Connecting Attributes

Activities involving two attributes can help children see how the attributes are related or how one attribute does not depend on the other. For example, by doubling the dimensions of a rectangle, children may see how the area is changed. By examining figures with the same area but different shape, children may see that area is independent of shape. We have included some sample activities with suggestions for other variations or extensions. If you do not know the answer, you will be able to find it by doing the activity.

Area and Shape

In the Classroom 16-7 encourages children in grades 2 through 4 to investigate the different shapes they can make using two to four squares. For older children, you can extend this activity to more squares and place the restrictions that the squares must have touching sides (not corners) and that two shapes are the same if one is a reflection or rotation (see Chapter 15) of the other. A variation is to use triangular graph paper rather than the square. You also can have children look at figures with the same shapes but different areas.

Volume and Shape

An activity such as the one In the Classroom 16-7 can be done with cubes. For older children, In the Classroom 16-8 not only has them examine different shapes with constant volume but also ties their investigation to number theory (primes and composites).

Perimeter and Area

Children are often confused about perimeter and area. This confusion may be caused partly by a lack of understanding of area and partly by premature introduction of the formulas. Many activities can help children see that a figure with a given perimeter may have many different areas. One is found In the Classroom 16-9. Children also should realize that figures with the same area can have different perimeters. You can modify In the Classroom 16-7 for older children by asking them to find the perimeter of each of the shapes or by challenging them to take five squares and see what

Lesson Idea 16-8

Objective: Estimate measurements of objects and compare measurements with those of other objects

Grade Level: 4–5

About how many centimeters long?

	Estimate	*Measure*
Little finger	______	______
Nose	______	______
Foot	______	______

A B C

Which holds about 2 cups?

Make a decimeter

Draw a snake that you think is a decimeter long.

Draw a tree that you think is a decimeter high.

CONTEST FOR WEDNESDAY

About how much does the wonderful watermelon weigh?

Name	Guess
______	______
______	______

Winner gets the largest piece at Ho-Ho's picnic.

Guess which of the boxes will hold 60 sugar cubes.

x *y* *z*

About how many squares?

The floor ______

Your desk ______

The bulletin board ______

We'll collect your estimates on Friday.

HUNT HUNT

There is something in the room that weighs a kilogram.

Can you find it?

shape they can make that has the largest perimeter or the smallest perimeter.

Volume and Surface Area

Just as the area of a figure does not depend on the perimeter, the volume does not depend on the surface area. The experiment In the Classroom 16-10 looks at the relation of lateral surface area to volume. You can vary this activity by having children fold the papers into thirds (sixths) both ways or make cylinders (a long, thin one and a short, fat one). In middle school, after developing the formula for a rectangular solid, students could

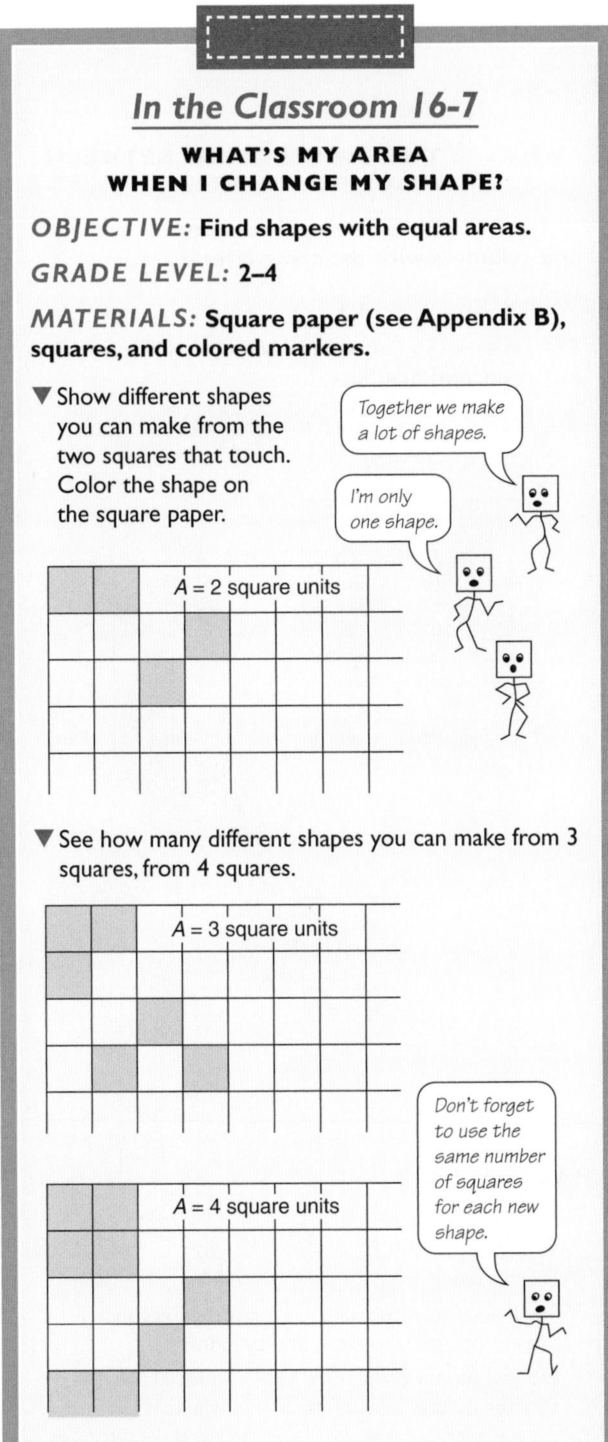

In the Classroom 16-7

WHAT'S MY AREA WHEN I CHANGE MY SHAPE?

OBJECTIVE: **Find shapes with equal areas.**

GRADE LEVEL: **2–4**

MATERIALS: **Square paper (see Appendix B), squares, and colored markers.**

▼ Show different shapes you can make from the two squares that touch. Color the shape on the square paper.

Together we make a lot of shapes.
I'm only one shape.
A = 2 square units

▼ See how many different shapes you can make from 3 squares, from 4 squares.

A = 3 square units
A = 4 square units
Don't forget to use the same number of squares for each new shape.

calculate the volume of each of the tubes In the Classroom 16-10.

Perimeter and Dimensions

On In the Classroom 16-11, children may expect the pattern that emerges relating the length of each side to the number of sides, but be surprised

In the Classroom 16-8

SAME VOLUME, DIFFERENT SHAPE

OBJECTIVE: **Exploring the different shapes of solids that can be made with a given volume.**

GRADE LEVEL: **5–8**

MATERIALS: **Cubes.**

I'm 8 cubes—8 by 1 by 1. My volume is 8 square units.

I'm 8 cubes—2 by 2 by 2. My volume is 8 square units, too!

▼ See how many different rectangular solids you can make with 12 cubes. Record the dimensions and volume of each.

▼ Now try some of these:

7, 9, 16, 11, 13, 18, 15 cubes

▼ How many different solids can you make if the number of cubes is

- prime?_____
- a product of two primes?_____
- a perfect square?_____

▼ How many solids can you make with 24 cubes?_____

by the pattern of the number of sides and the height. See if they can describe the pattern and have any explanation.

Metric Relations

In the Classroom 16-12 helps children find some of the important relationships among different metric units. These relationships make the metric system convenient to use because it gives an easy translation from solid measures to liquid measures.

A Glance at Where We've Been

Measuring is a process that may be used for many attributes. Basically, each attribute is measured in the same way, but the unique characteristics of

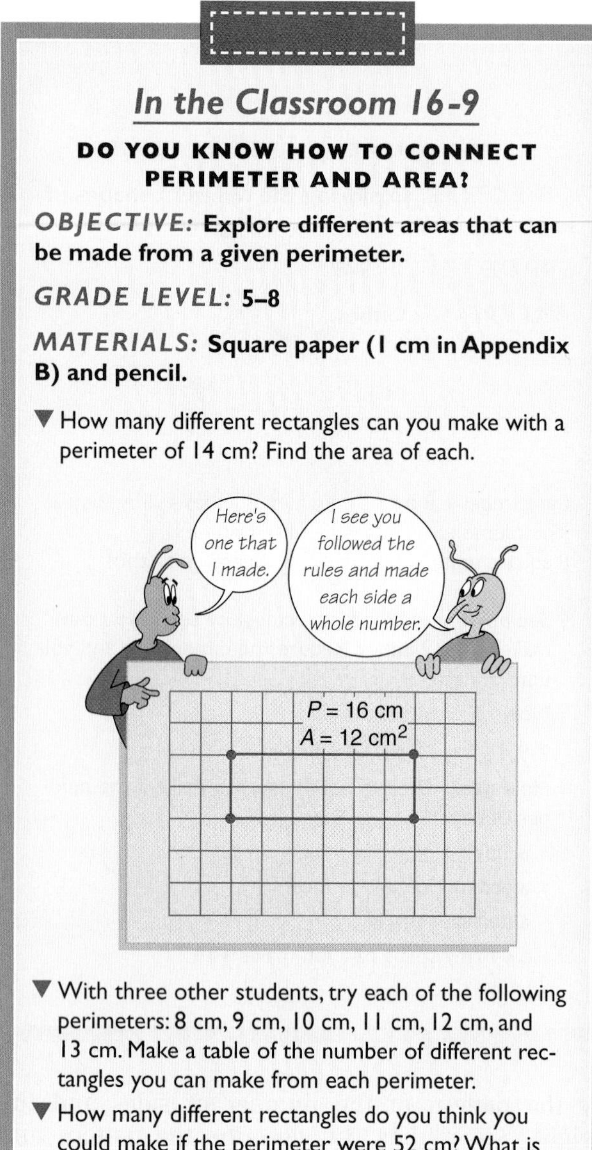

In the Classroom 16-9

DO YOU KNOW HOW TO CONNECT PERIMETER AND AREA?

OBJECTIVE: **Explore different areas that can be made from a given perimeter.**

GRADE LEVEL: **5–8**

MATERIALS: **Square paper (1 cm in Appendix B) and pencil.**

▼ How many different rectangles can you make with a perimeter of 14 cm? Find the area of each.

Here's one that I made.
I see you followed the rules and made each side a whole number.
$P = 16$ cm
$A = 12$ cm^2

▼ With three other students, try each of the following perimeters: 8 cm, 9 cm, 10 cm, 11 cm, 12 cm, and 13 cm. Make a table of the number of different rectangles you can make from each perimeter.

▼ How many different rectangles do you think you could make if the perimeter were 52 cm? What is your conjecture?

each make the actual steps differ. Most important in these steps is knowing the attribute that is being measured. This chapter has given many suggestions about ways to develop premeasurement ideas by comparing perceptually, directly, and indirectly. Using labs and hands-on activities are key. Children should build on these ideas as they use units of measurement. Children may first assign a number by counting and later by using instruments or formulas. Other suggested ways to help children learn about measuring are estimating and relating two attributes.

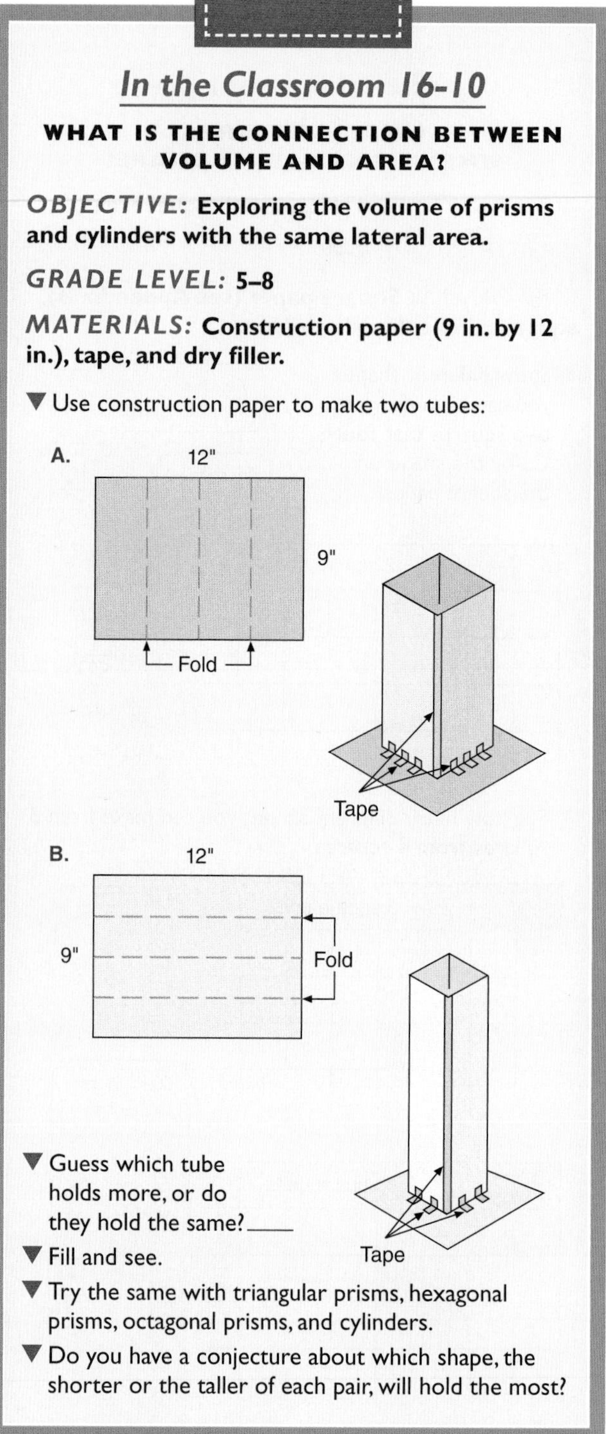

In the Classroom 16-10

WHAT IS THE CONNECTION BETWEEN VOLUME AND AREA?

OBJECTIVE: **Exploring the volume of prisms and cylinders with the same lateral area.**

GRADE LEVEL: **5–8**

MATERIALS: **Construction paper (9 in. by 12 in.), tape, and dry filler.**

▼ Use construction paper to make two tubes:

▼ Guess which tube holds more, or do they hold the same?____

▼ Fill and see.

▼ Try the same with triangular prisms, hexagonal prisms, octagonal prisms, and cylinders.

▼ Do you have a conjecture about which shape, the shorter or the taller of each pair, will hold the most?

By including measuring in your classroom, you have the opportunity to show how mathematics is practical, to develop problem-solving skills, to develop other mathematical ideas, to relate mathematics to other topics, and to make mathematics fun for many children.

In the Classroom 16-11

WHAT IS THE CONNECTION BETWEEN PERIMETER AND HEIGHT?

OBJECTIVE: **Explore the relationship between polygons with the same perimeter and their height.**

GRADE LEVEL: **5–8**

MATERIALS: **Stiff paper such as file folders.**

▼ Cut 6 strips (2 cm by 21 cm) from stiff paper.

▼ Fold one strip into thirds, and tape together to make a fence triangle:

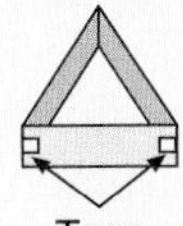

▼ Fold the other strips into fourths, fifths, sixths, sevenths, and eighths to make additional fences.

▼ Fill it in the chart:

Number of Sides	Length of Each Side in mm	Height (stand it on one side and see how tall)
3	________mm	________mm
4	________	________
5	________	________
6	________	________
7	________	________
8	________	________

- Which has the largest area?
- Which has the smallest area?

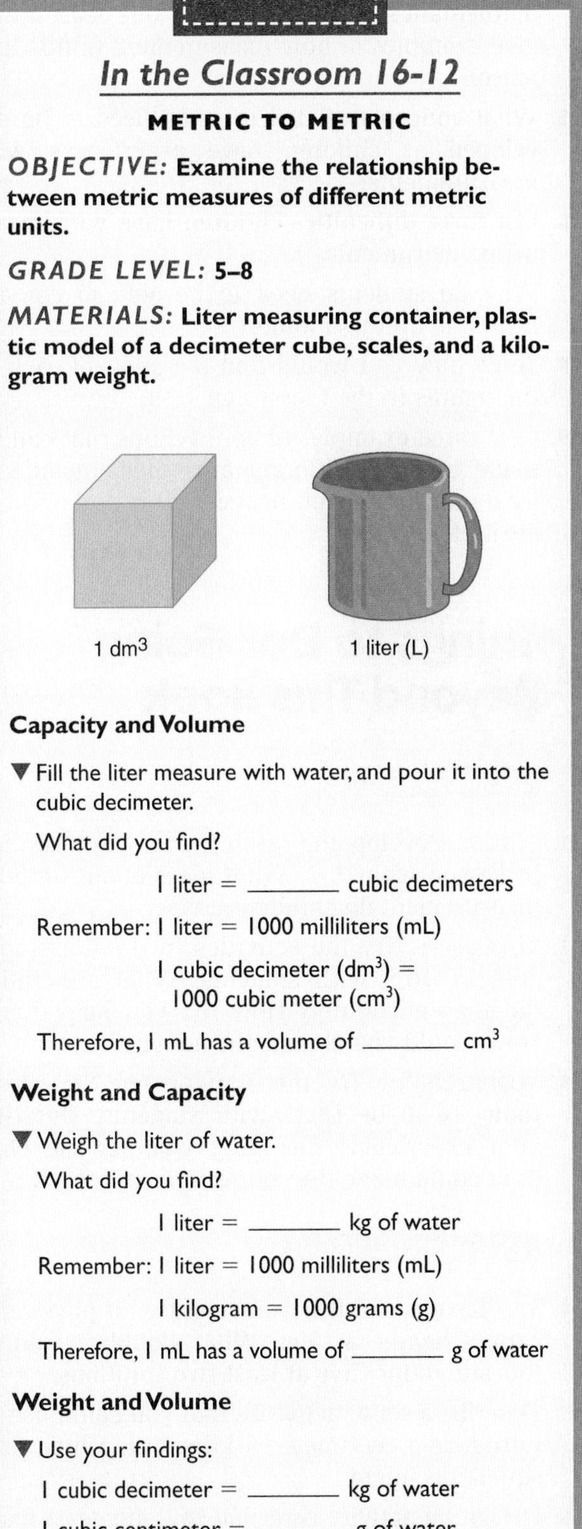

In the Classroom 16-12

METRIC TO METRIC

OBJECTIVE: **Examine the relationship between metric measures of different metric units.**

GRADE LEVEL: **5–8**

MATERIALS: **Liter measuring container, plastic model of a decimeter cube, scales, and a kilogram weight.**

Capacity and Volume

▼ Fill the liter measure with water, and pour it into the cubic decimeter.

What did you find?

1 liter = ________ cubic decimeters

Remember: 1 liter = 1000 milliliters (mL)

1 cubic decimeter (dm^3) = 1000 cubic meter (cm^3)

Therefore, 1 mL has a volume of ________ cm^3

Weight and Capacity

▼ Weigh the liter of water.

What did you find?

1 liter = ________ kg of water

Remember: 1 liter = 1000 milliliters (mL)

1 kilogram = 1000 grams (g)

Therefore, 1 mL has a volume of ________ g of water

Weight and Volume

▼ Use your findings:

1 cubic decimeter = ________ kg of water

1 cubic centimeter = ________ g of water

Things to Do: From What You've Read

1. What are the five steps in teaching measurement?
2. What attributes, units, and instruments are included in most elementary mathematics programs?
3. Explain how you will include estimation throughout your measurement activities and why this will be helpful for children.

4. Why should you include measurement in your mathematics program? Choose one reason and give examples of how measurement fulfills that reason.
5. What concepts related to units need to be developed as children have experiences with measurements?
6. List three difficulties children have with measuring instruments.
7. Why do students need to be able to convert from one unit to another?
8. Show how you would find the areas of each of the figures In the Classroom 16-3.
9. Give three examples of connections that can be made between different attributes. Include at least one connection between time and another attribute.

Things to Do: Going Beyond This Book

IN THE FIELD

1. **Units*. Develop and teach the lesson described in Lesson Idea 16-2. What ideas about units of measurement do children grasp?
2. **Discovery*. Try the activities In the Classroom 16-4 or 16-5 with students. What difficulties did they encounter? How did you help them? How would you change the activity?
3. **Connections*. Try the activities In the Classroom 16-10 or 16-11 with students. Describe your experience, including whether the children could make the connections expected.

IN YOUR JOURNAL

4. You have a child in your class who physically cannot handle a ruler. What would you do in this situation? Give at least two solutions.
5. Describe a set of activities that you could use to introduce a centimeter, a kilogram, a liter, or a square decimeter.
6. Design an activity card that investigates a fixed area and varying perimeters (e,g., a fixed area of four square units made with four square tiles.) Include the answer to the investigation.
7. Design three task cards for the *Snapshot of a Lesson* that opened this chapter, one of which is an extension for students who need to be challenged.
8. Describe how you could help convince a student that these triangles have the same area.

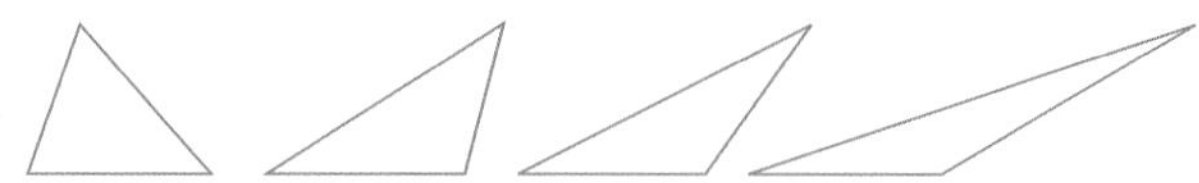

9. For a grade level of your choice, design five estimation activities that include both types of estimation (estimating measurement for a known object and choosing an object that fits a known measurement).
10. Outline a series of steps for developing the volume formula for rectangular solids, similar to those for developing the area formula for a rectangle.
11. Develop a research study for older students to conduct on a topic in the history of measurement. Present this to a group of children or to a peer.

WITH ADDITIONAL READINGS

12. Critique the video, "Pencil Box Staining," from the series: *Teaching Math: A Video Library, K–4*. A similar problem may be found on Master 16–4, Paint Problem, in the *Helping Children Learn Mathematics Instructor's Manual* (available at the Wiley Book Companion site). What strategies did the students use to find the area?
13. Check the scope-and-sequence chart of a textbook series to see how the introduction of units corresponds to Table 16-1.
14. Examine upper-level textbooks to see how they introduce the formula for the area of a rectangle. Contrast this with the sequence suggested in Figure 16-8.

WITH TECHNOLOGY RESOURCES

15. Find three web sites that have lesson ideas that you could use while teaching measurement. Describe the activities.

---

*Additional activities, suggestions, or questions are provided in *Teaching Elementary Mathematics: A Resource for Field Experiences* (Wiley, 2004).

Book Nook for Children

Anastasio, Dina. *It's About Time.* New York: Grosset & Dunlap, 1993.
This book introduces the concept of time using a clever design and placement of text. Movable black plastic hands appear on a large watch face on the cover. Tasks are posed to engage the young reader in telling time to the hour, half-hour, and 5-minute intervals. The story traces the day in the life of a boy and his dog.

Branley, Franklyn Mansfield. *Keeping Time: From the Beginning and into the 21st Century.* Boston: Houghton Mifflin, 1993.
Early timekeepers were the sun, moon, and stars. Through the centuries other timekeepers were introduced and directions for making them given: sundial, candle clock, water clock, and sand clock. Next, mechanical clocks are introduced and the need for more accuracy is discussed. An index and bibliography of other books on time for young and more advanced readers are included in this book.

Hightower, Susan. *Twelve Snails to One Lizard: A Tale of Mischief and Measurement.* New York: Simon & Schuster Books for Young Readers, 1997.
A delightful book for primary school children. Animals are used to introduce measurement facts. A yardstick, snails, and measurement of a break in the dam are all part of this story. This book succeeds in introducing customary length measures and the relationships among such measures in a humorous way.

Myller, Rolf. *How Big Is a Foot?* New York: Dell Publishing, 1991.
This humorous tale about nonstandard measures will delight young readers. A king decides to have a bed made for the queen as a surprise for her birthday. The large king marks off the dimensions for the proposed bed with his feet, but gives these dimensions to the head carpenter, who gives them to his little apprentice. Unfortunately, when the bed is delivered, it is too small, and the apprentice is jailed. The apprentice solves the problem from his jail cell, and everyone lives happily ever after.

Pluckrose, Henry. *Capacity.* New York: Franklin Watts, 1988.
Capacity is effectively introduced through brightly colored photographs of a pair of hands gently emptying firmly packed sand from a pail. The space inside a container is explored by measuring both liquid and solid materials. Questions about comparisons occur throughout the text as the reader compares familiar containers of different shapes and sizes. Although metric units are shown in the pictures, only customary units are presented.

Resources

ANNOTATED BOOKS

Brian, Sarah Jane, and Miller, Marcia. *Funtastic Math! Measurement and Geometry (Grades 4-8).* New York: Scholastic Trade, 1999.
Good skill-building activities, games, and reproducibles are found in this book. It has many creative activities like geometry jumble and right-angle tic-tac-toe, real-life measurement problems, plus puzzles and tangrams to help students develop spatial sense.

Burns, Marilyn. *A Collection of Math Lessons from Grades 1–3. New York:* Math Solutions Publications, 1988.
Seventeen lessons provide experiences with sorting, number sense, graphing, geometry, measurement, probability, and more. A lively, readable classroom vignette that describes Marilyn Burns's unique and inspiring approach to teaching problem-solving lessons.

Burns, Marilyn. *Measuring Up!: Experiments, Puzzles, and Games Exploring Measurement.* New York: Atheneum Books for Young Readers, 1995.
Activities that would appeal to many children are provided in this book. For example, optical illusions, interesting animals, unique measuring tools, as well as the height of the tallest person in the NBA are provided throughout this book. Topics that are included are length and size, quantities, weights, temperatures, and volume. The book has many strengths: hands-on activities, problem solving and explorations, experiments, puzzles, and games.

ANNOTATED ARTICLES

Aitchison, Kate. "How Long Is a Piece of String?" *Micromath,* 17(3), (August 2001), pp. 37–39.
This article outlines a lesson plan designed to form three one-hour sessions with mixed-ability groups of 11 to 12 year olds. Students estimate road distances by counting the number of map grid lines crossed in going from A to

B. The activity is designed to introduce students to graphing calculators.

Battista, Michael T. "How Many Blocks?" *Mathematics Teaching in the Middle School,* 3 (March–April 1998), pp. 404–411.
Battista's article focuses on ways to help students with spatial structuring in volume and packing problems and discusses student difficulties with this type of problem.

Lindquist, Mary Montgomery. "Implementing the Standards: The Measurement Standards." *Arithmetic Teacher,* 37 (October 1989), pp. 22–26.
Lindquist describes activities emphasizing the process of measurement. The article presents three activities on length, area, and angles with questions and illustrations.

Outhred, Lynne N., and Mitchelmore, Michael C. "Young children's intuitive understanding of rectangular area measurement." *Journal for Research in Mathematics Education,* 31(2), (March 2000), pp.144–154.
This article focuses on the strategies young children use to solve rectangular coveting tasks before they have been taught area measurement. Children's solution strategies were classified into five developmental levels, and the researchers suggest that children sequentially learn four principles underlying rectangular covering. The analysis emphasizes the importance of understanding the relationship between the size of the unit and the dimensions of the rectangle in learning about rectangular covering, clarifying the role of multiplication, and identifying the significance of conceptual understanding of length measurement.

ADDITIONAL REFERENCES

Kouba, Vicky L.; Brown, Catherine A.; Carpenter, Thomas P.; Lindquist, Mary Montgomery; Silver, Edward A.; and Swafford, Jane O. "Results of the Fourth NAEP Assessment of Mathematics: Measurement, Geometry Data Interpretation, Attitudes, and Other Topics." *Arithmetic Teacher,* 35 (May 1988), pp. 10–16.

Martin, W. Gary, and Strutchens, Marilyn E. "Geometry and Measurement." In *Results from the Seventh Mathematics Assessment of the National Assessment of Educational Progress* (eds. Edward A. Silver and Patricia Ann Kenney). Reston VA: NCTM, 2000.

Teaching Math: A Video Library, K–4. South Burlington, VT: The Annenberg/CPB Math and Science Collection, 1995.

U.S. Department of Education. *Pursuing Excellence: A Study of U.S. Eighth-Grade Mathematics and Science Teaching, Learning, Curriculum, and Achievement in International Context*. Washington, DC: U.S. Government Printing Office, 1996.

U.S. Department of Education. *Pursuing Excellence: A Study of U.S. Fourth-Grade Mathematics and Science Achievement in International Context.* Washington, DC: U.S. Government Printing Office, 1997.

Wilson, Patricia S., and Osborne, Alan. "Foundational Ideas in Teaching about Measure." In *Teaching Mathematics in Grades K–8* (ed. Thomas R. Post). Toronto: Allyn and Bacon, 1988, pp. 78–110.

CHAPTER 17

Data Analysis, Statistics, and Probability

Snapshot of a Lesson

First graders are gathered with their teacher on the rug at the front of the classroom. For several weeks, they have been rinsing and saving their lunch drink cartons for a science project, which provides an opportunity for them to build and construct graphs. This first-grade lesson provides some valuable experiences and, while doing so, moves naturally from concrete toward symbolic representation of data. Graphs help us organize and analyze data. Once constructed, they trigger many questions that help children develop graph-reading skills and lead to better understanding of data. The teacher knows that involving students in collecting data and formulating questions is an important part of problem solving.

TEACHER: We have been keeping track of the drink cartons saved from our lunches. Yesterday, one of you wondered how many people have been drinking chocolate milk. Here are the chocolate milk cartons we collected every day last week. We can answer our question more easily if we make a graph.

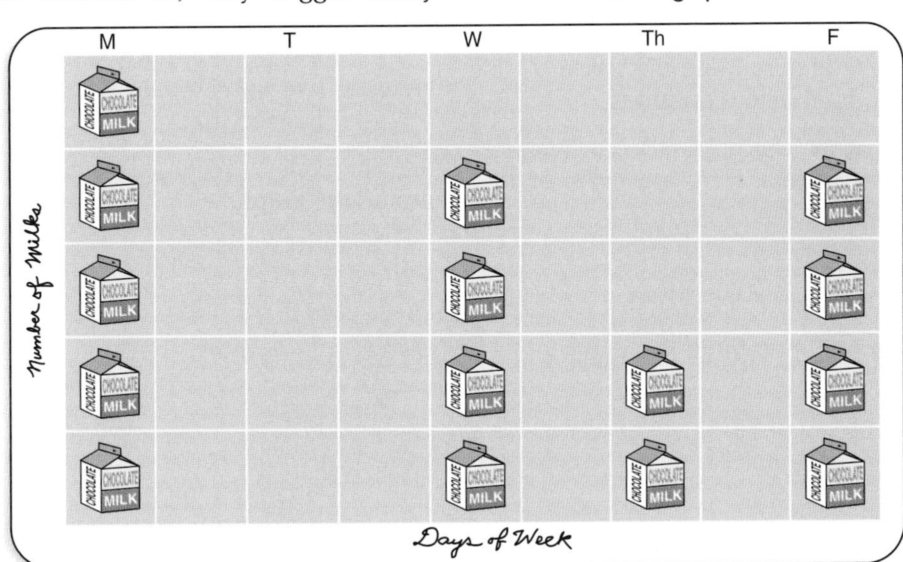

Daily chocolate milk counts in our class last week.

The teacher spreads out a vinyl tablecloth that has been marked in a grid of 5-inch boxes. A column of boxes for each day of the week has already been labeled. The children place one milk carton in each box under the day of the week, forming a real graph.

TEACHER: Now let's graph this information on grid paper. Look at our graph carefully. I want you to ask a question that could be answered from this graph. Bob, your hand was up first.

BOB: How many students drank milk in our school?

GLORIA: (AFTER A LONG WAIT) The graph doesn't answer that question. It only shows information about our room.

TEACHER: That's right, Gloria. This graph only shows what happened in our room. Also, it doesn't tell us how many drank milk, only how many drank chocolate milk. That reminds us to read the title of the graph so that everyone will know what it represents. Now, let's hear another question. Aaron?

AARON: How many people drank chocolate milk Wednesday?

SHORAN: Four.

TEACHER: Marissa, let's hear your question.

MARISSA: On which day did no one drink chocolate milk?

SHARON: Tuesday.

MARISSA: That's right, because the cafeteria was out of chocolate milk that day.

TEACHER: Do you have a question, Kelly?

KELLY: On which day did we drink the most chocolate milk?

SHARON: Monday had the most. There were five cartons that day.

JOE: Would next week look like this?

Other questions are posed and discussed. A bit later in the lesson, the teacher continues.

TEACHER: Let's look at the chocolate milk we drank for the last two weeks. Here are tallies of the cartons for each day.

M T W Th F

Let's make a graph of them on this paper.

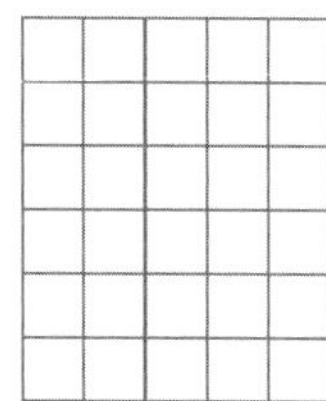

SANDY: Our graph paper isn't tall enough!

TEACHER: What do you mean?

SANDY: We can only show six cartons on the paper, but there were eight cartons on Monday.

TEACHER: Could we do any trading here?

SANDY: What do you mean?

TEACHER: In place value, when we get ten ones we trade for one ten.

SANDY: But we don't have ten.

TEACHER: Maybe we can make other trades. For example, we trade five pennies for a nickel or....

SANDY: Two nickels for a dime.

SHARON: I got it—we can trade two cartons for one square on the grid.

TEACHER: That's a nice idea, let's try it. We would color four squares for Monday. How many for Tuesday?

SHARON: One. And two for Wednesday.

SANDY: Two and one-half for Thursday and five for Friday.

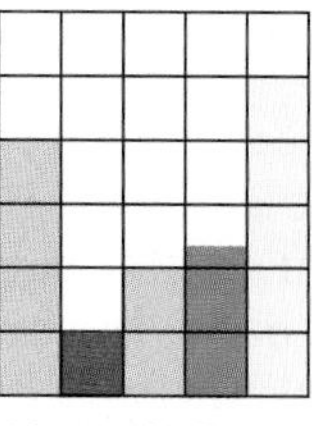

Daily chocolate milk counts in our class for the last two weeks

TEACHER: This graph is almost finished.

SANDY: It looks done to me . . . what else could we do?

TEACHER: We need to show on the graph what each box represents.

The code is recorded in a highly visible place beside the graph:

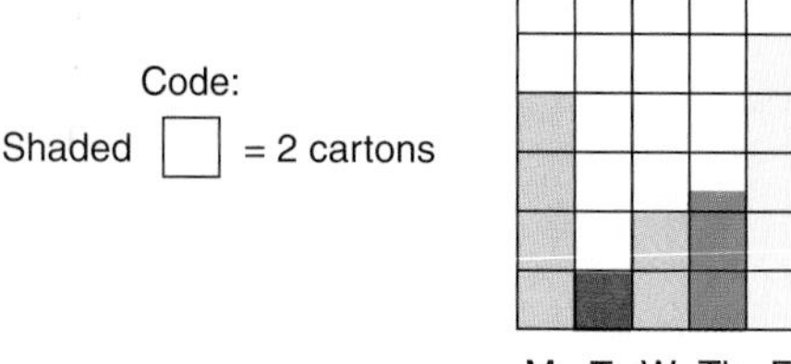

Later, in the computer lab, a couple of children used a graphing program to display their milk carton data in a picture graph and then a circle graph.

Introduction

Data analysis, statistics, and probability provide a meaningful context for promoting problem solving and critical thinking, communication, developing number sense, and applying computation. The study of these topics supports a problem-solving or investigative approach to learning and doing mathematics. As a result, statistics and probability are now highly visible topics in elementary school mathematics programs. Therefore, the *NCTM Standards* (2000) recommend increased attention to data analysis. The shift of attention to these areas has been dramatic and reflects the growing importance of analyzing data in our daily lives.

Increased attention to data analysis, statistics, and probability in elementary mathematics programs has increased student performance in these areas. For example, the National Assessment of Educational Progress (NAEP) indicates that although there are areas that still need improvement, student performances in data analysis, statistics, and probability have increased significantly from the fifth assessment to the sixth (Kenney and Silver, 1997).

Let's look at some reasons for including the study of data analysis, statistics, and probability in elementary school.

- *Children encounter ideas of statistics and probability outside of school every day.*

Communications media rely on statistical techniques for summarizing information. Radio, television, newspapers, and the Internet bombard us with information. For example, news reports present national economic and social statistics, opinion polls, weather reports, and medical, business, and financial data.

The current demand for information-processing skills is much greater than it was 25 years ago, and technological advances will place a far greater premium on such skills in the years ahead. Many consumer and business decisions are based on market research and sales projections; however, statistics about issues or the quality of commercial products can be misleading to the public. If these data are to be understood and used widely, every educated person must be able to process such information effectively and efficiently. An intelligent consumer, who is able to make informed decisions, must be able to understand and use statistics and probability.

The data students encounter outside of school are often presented in a graphical, statistical, or probabilistic form:

Graphical. Which company holds the majority of the global soccer sales?

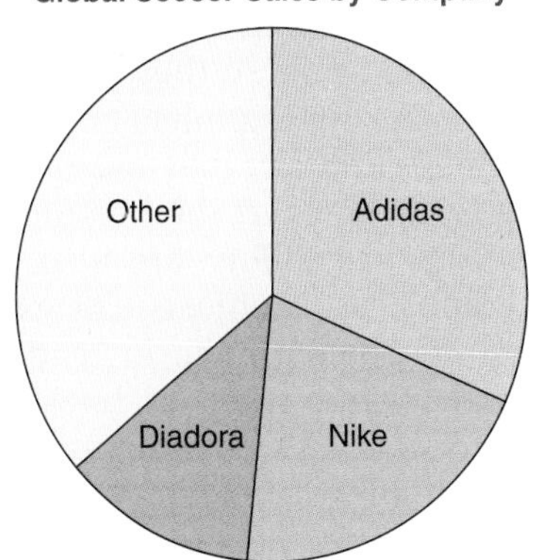

$$\text{mean} = \frac{9 + 5 + 3 + 7}{4} = \frac{24}{4} = 6$$

Statistical. The mean salary of professional baseball players in 2001 was $2,138,896 a year.

Probabilistic. The probability of rain today is 0.35.

Each of these statements needs to be understood if meaningful interpretations are to be made.

The context and format of the way such information is presented vary greatly, but correct interpretation of the information often requires the application of mathematics. Consider, for example, the mathematical concepts involved in weather reports (decimals, percents, and probability), public opinion polls (sampling techniques and errors of measurement), advertising claims (hypothesis testing), and monthly government reports involving unemployment, inflation, and energy supplies (percents, prediction, and extrapolation).

- *Data analysis, statistics, and probability provide connections to other mathematics topics or school subjects.*

The study of data provides an excellent opportunity for curriculum integration. As mentioned earlier, a variety of mathematics topics are included in statistical formats. In addition, statistics and probability are used as tools during the study of other mathematics topics. For example, each day kindergarten children create a picture graph with their photos to show who is present and absent. In doing so, they practice basic counting skills. A third-grade lesson involves estimating. The children may graph their estimates for the number of candies in single-serving packages. After counting the actual number of candies, a second graph may be created, displaying the actual number of candies in each package. The children are able to compare their estimates with the actual results. Fourth graders are studying measurement in centimeters. After measuring the height of each student in the class, the students may decide to find the mean, median, mode, and range so they can better understand their data. As sixth graders conduct a probability simulation with dice, they use fractions, decimals, and percents to report their results.

Statistics and probability are also easily integrated into other school subjects. For example, second graders might use graphs in reading to keep track of numbers and types of books they have read. Fifth-grade students conducting a science experiment on rolling a car down ramps of various heights may calculate the mean distance for the number of trials at each height. In social studies, graphs and charts are frequently used to display information about populations or geographic areas. In physical education class, students may graph pretest data from physical fitness tests and compare it with post-test results at the end of the year. First graders reading folk tales in language arts may develop a chart listing which events from the stories are possible and which are impossible. Effective teachers must look for ways to make data analysis an integral part of the elementary and middle school curriculum. It can be useful in many contexts, and students will have greater success if they use statistical techniques all year long rather than in a single unit.

- *Data analysis, statistics and probability provide opportunities for computational activity in a meaningful context.*

Data are not merely numbers but numbers with a context. The number 12 in the absence of a context carries no information, but saying that a baby weighed 12 pounds at birth makes it easy to comment about its size! Data provide many opportunities to think, use, understand, and interpret numbers, rather than simply carrying out arithmetic operations. Using data helps further develop number sense. Working with real data requires judgment in choosing methods and interpreting results. Thus statistics and probability are not taught in elementary school for their own sake but because they provide an effective way to develop quantitative understanding and mathematical thinking.

For example, calculating the mean price of six CDs is a routine exercise in arithmetic; however, noticing that the prices of six CDs vary, deciding which is the best buy, and determining how much can be saved help develop mathematical thinking, as well as further promoting respect for the power and usefulness of mathematics.

Math Links 17.1

*T*he full-text electronic version of the Data Analysis and Probability standard is available at the NCTM's web site, which you can access from this book's web site. Click on pre-K–2, 3–5, or 6–8 to read more about this standard.

- *Data analysis, statistics, and probability provide opportunities for developing critical thinking skills.*

When students learn how to design and carry out experiments that utilize data analysis and probability, they develop skills to help them answer questions that often involve uncertainty, and they draw conclusions based on their interpretations of the data. According to Burns (2000), when students learn how to approach situations statistically, they can face up to prejudices, think more consistently about arguments, and justify their thinking with numerical information. This approach has applications in many areas of our lives—social and political.

Data analysis, statistics, and probability should not be viewed or treated in isolation. Their study provides numerous opportunities to review and apply much mathematics in a variety of real-world situations. For example, whole numbers, fractions, decimals, percents, ratios, and proportion are essential ideas for understanding a wide variety of situations. Many computational skills are reviewed and polished as they are applied in graphing or doing statistics and probability.

The content standard titled "Data Analysis and Probability," in the *NCTM Standards* (2000), highlights key expectations (see Figure 17-1). As you can see from this standard, the study of data analysis, statistics, and probability should engage students actively. Students need to go beyond examining preformed graphs and results from experiments. They need to be involved in asking questions, collecting

Math Links 17.2

A variety of Web resources for data analysis and probability, which may be used by teachers and children, may be found at the NCTM's Illuminations web site (accessible from this book's web site) under the Data Analysis and Probability standard.

Instructional programs from prekindergarten through grade 12 should enable all students to:	Pre-K–2 Expectations All students should:	Grades 3–5 Expectations All students should:
• Formulate questions that can be addressed with data and collect, organize, and display relevant data to answer them	• Pose questions and gather data about themselves and their surroundings • Sort and classify objects according to their attributes and organize data about the objects • Represent data using concrete objects, pictures, and graphs	• Design investigations to address a question and consider how data-collection methods affect the nature of the data set • Collect data using observations, surveys, and experiments • Represent data using tables and graphs such as line plots, bar graphs, and line graphs • Recognize the differences in representing categorical and numerical data
• Select and use appropriate statistical methods to analyze data	• Describe parts of the data and the set of data as a whole to determine what the data show	• Describe the shape and important features of a set of data and compare related data sets, with an emphasis on how the data are distributed • Use measures of center, focusing on the median, and understand what each does and does not indicate about the data set • Compare different representations of the same data and evaluate how well each representation shows important aspects of the data
• Develop and evaluate inferences and predictions that are based on data	• Discuss events related to students' experiences as likely or unlikely	• Propose and justify conclusions and predictions that are based on data and design studies to further investigate the conclusions or predictions
• Understand and apply basic concepts of probability		• Describe events as likely or unlikely and discuss the degree of likelihood using such words as certain, equally likely, and impossible • Predict the probability of outcomes of simple experiments and test the predictions • Understand that the measure of the likelihood of an event can be represented by a number from 0 to 1

FIGURE 17-1 Data Analysis and Probability Standard with expectations for children's learning in grades prekindergarten-2 and 3-5.

data, organizing and displaying their data, making conjectures, and reporting their results. In this chapter you will consider how to involve students with statistics, which includes using data collection, display, and analysis as well as probability, which allows a prediction of what is likely to happen and how often it might occur.

FOCUS QUESTIONS

1. How do data analysis, statistics, and probability help children develop critical thinking skills?
2. How can you help children develop skills in analyzing data?
3. What descriptive statistics are appropriate to introduce in the elementary grades? What are some examples of ways they can be introduced?
4. What are some common misconceptions young students have about probability?

Data Analysis

A statistical investigation typically is completed in several steps, which include (1) posing a question and collecting data to answer the question, (2) displaying the collected data, and (3) analyzing and communicating results.

Posing a Question and Collecting Data

Begin with a good question or problem that interests students, a problem for which the answer is not immediately obvious, and one that also clearly gives students a reason for gathering, analyzing, and presenting data. Allow students to brainstorm questions they would like to answer or problems they have observed. There is a real benefit to having students identify their own questions or problems, for they will take ownership of the investigation and their motivation will be high (Bohan et al., 1995). Questions may come from a variety of sources on many different topics. In the Classroom 17-1 gives a few examples. These ideas may be shared with children to help them brainstorm the kind of questions they might ask as they plan their survey.

Once a suitable question has been identified, students will need to plan how to collect the data needed to answer the question. Communication skills are very important during this stage. To be successful, students must be able to develop clear survey questions and logical steps for their experiments or simulations. They must communicate with others to negotiate the details of the investigation. They must find a clear and efficient method of recording their data. Students may collect data from surveys, experiments, and simulations (Zawojewski et al., 1991), all of which typically involve counting or measuring. Data may be recorded in a variety of ways, such as using tally marks or placing information in a table. Computer spreadsheets may also be used for recording data.

In the Classroom 17-1

LET'S FIND OUT

OBJECTIVE: **Planning and conducting a survey.**

GRADE LEVEL: **4–5**

STEPS

1. Think of a question you would like to answer. Here are some ideas to get you started.
   - **Questions about ourselves:** Who can whistle a tune? How far can we throw a softball? What is our class's typical height, eye color, shoe size, number in family, amount of allowance, pets . . . ?
   - **Questions about opinions or feelings:** How do you feel about fractions? Does life exist on other planets? What should be done about pollution? What country do you want to study in social studies? What is your favorite television show, song, book, sport, color, food . . . ?
   - **Questions about the world:** Which month has the most birthdays? What is the most popular color of car in the school parking lot? Which brand of cookie has the most chocolate chips? How many paper towels do we use in one day? What is the effect of fertilizer on bean plant growth? What type of paper airplane will fly the farthest?

My Question: ____________________

____

2. Plan the survey by answering these questions.
   a. Where or from whom will I collect the data?
   b. How will I collect the data?
   c. How much data will I collect?
   d. When will I collect the data?
   e. How will I record the data as I collect them?
   f. What else do I need to do before I start collecting data?
3. Collect your data!

Math Links 17.3

You may view some authentic project ideas where children collect and use real-life data, accessible from this book's web site. In Accessing and Investigating Data, children use census data to project population trends. In Collecting, Representing, and Interpreting Data, they collect weather data and then organize and display it. A good source of data is the U.S. Census Bureau; their web address is www.census.gov.

Surveys

Survey data result from collecting information. These data may range from a national public opinion poll or observing cars pass the window, to simply tallying the ages of students in a class. The actual data used depends on student interest and maturity, but survey data collected by students provides a freshness that increases student interest and sustains persistence in related problem-solving activities. Computer software is also available that allows students to design a survey and have the persons surveyed enter their responses directly into the computer. Once the data have been collected, the program can display results in a table or in several types of graphs.

Each question from In the Classroom 17-1 gives students an opportunity to collect data themselves. A lesson built around Lesson Idea 17-1 shows how students can extend the information they discover to sharpen their data-collecting techniques. A host of other idea starters are available (Bamberger and Hughes, 1995; Freeman, 1986; Lindquist et al., 1992; Zawojewski et al., 1991). In planning a survey like the one in Lesson Idea 17-1, students are required to refine and polish their questions to get whatever information they are seeking, which in itself is an important and valuable experience.

Experiments

Experiments may be somewhat more advanced than surveys. When students conduct experiments, in addition to using observation and recording skills, they often incorporate the use of the scientific method (Zawojewski et al., 1991). For example, students may design an experiment to measure the effect of applying different types of fertilizer on plant growth or compare flight times of different paper airplanes. They may try to determine which brand of tissue is the most absorbent. Students may play a spinner game to determine if it is fair to all players.

Simulations

Although a simulation is similar to an experiment, random number tables or devices such as coins, dice, spinners, or computer programs are also used to model real-world occurrences (Zawojewski et al., 1991). Students may start with a probability question such as "If I flip a coin 20 times, how many times will it land on heads?" Then they carry out the simulation and record data as they are generated.

Sampling is another method of data collection that students can simulate. In statistics, the whole group you are studying is called the *population.* In real-life data collection, there are times when it is impossible or impractical to collect data from a complete population. A *sample* is a subset of a population. Samples are often collected to learn more about public health issues or the public's buying habits, or to predict election results. It is important for students to realize that the use of a particular sample may make a survey biased and to discuss ways to reduce bias. For example, consider

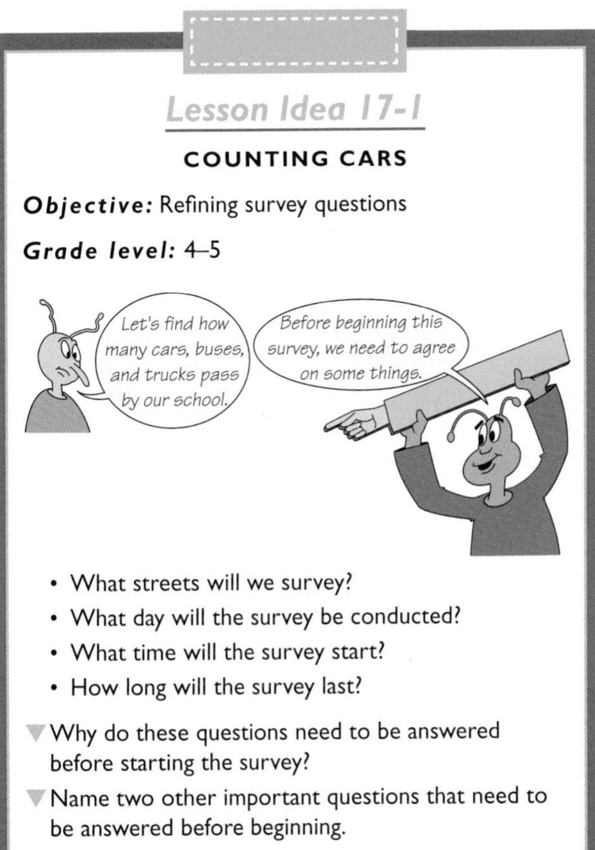

Let's find how many cars, buses, and trucks pass by our school.
Before beginning this survey, we need to agree on some things.

Lesson Idea 17-1

COUNTING CARS

Objective: Refining survey questions

Grade level: 4–5

- What streets will we survey?
- What day will the survey be conducted?
- What time will the survey start?
- How long will the survey last?

▼ Why do these questions need to be answered before starting the survey?

▼ Name two other important questions that need to be answered before beginning.

some students surveying the students in their room in order to purchase some new games to be used during recess. The population to be surveyed is Ms. Smith's fifth-grade class; however, if the students interview only the girls in the class (a sample), their results will probably not reflect the wishes of both boys and girls. Students to be interviewed could be randomly selected by drawing names out of a hat, which would more likely reflect the total population.

Researchers have developed methods of collecting samples so they may learn more about a population that would be impossible to survey completely. For example, when wildlife biologists want to count the number and types of fish in a lake, they use a mark-recapture technique. The biologist captures a number of fish, counts them, marks them, and releases them. More samples are collected, and the number of marked fish in the sample are compared in a ratio to the unmarked fish in the sample. The biologist may then use the data from the samples collected to estimate the total population of fish and the ratio of marked and unmarked fish. These techniques and how they can be simulated with elementary and middle school students using beans, crackers, or games are explained further in Hitch and Armstrong (1994), Morita (1999), and Quinn and Wiest (1999).

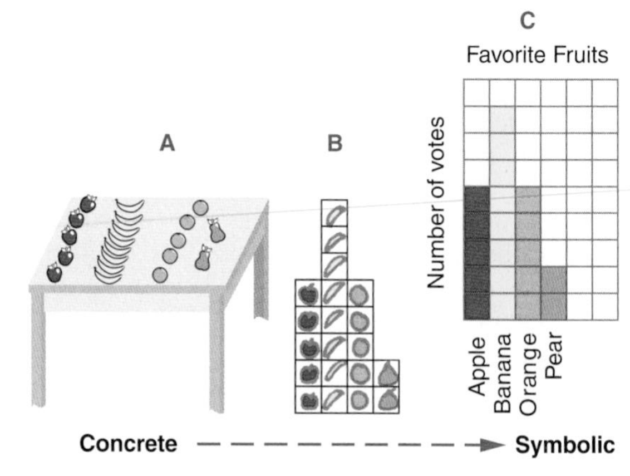

FIGURE 17-2 One method for introducing graphs.

Displaying Data

After data have been collected, graphs are often used to display data and help others digest the results. A *graph* is a type of diagram that may be used to visually present or illustrate data. At the elementary and middle school levels, students frequently encounter and create real, picture, bar, and circle graphs. As they move through school, the types of graphs they read and create increase and become more complex. Tables, tallies, or pictures are also sometimes used to present data. Knowledge related to constructing and interpreting various types of graphs is an important part of mathematics instruction and should begin in the primary grades. Children gain competence with age and experience. The National Assessment of Educational Progress (NAEP) shows that although only about half of fourth-grade students can read and use tables, picture graphs, and bar graphs, most eighth-grade students can do so (Kenney and Silver, 1997).

For young children, initial work with data means they begin by working with concrete objects in their environment. Collecting and counting objects, sorting them into categories, and then displaying them in an organized fashion is a good introduction. For example, children may each bring a favorite book and then collaborate to organize their collection. A *real graph* or concrete graph is developed as the actual books are arranged in rows. As students work with their "data," they also practice counting skills. Older students may work with larger collections of objects, and by grouping the objects into groups of tens, place value may be reinforced. The teacher must also find ways to help children move from the concrete, real-graph representations to more symbolic representations.

An example of an early experience is to sort real fruit. First, ask each child to choose one piece of his or her favorite fruit from a basket and position this piece of fruit on a table, as shown in Figure 17-2A. The resulting rows of fruit represent the children's preferences in a concrete fashion as a real graph. Next, ask each child to draw the fruit he or she chose on an index card, then have the children use the cards to build a picture-bar graph, as in Figure 17-2B. Although this graph is a less concrete means of showing the information, most children still find it a meaningful way to represent their preferences. Finally, this same information can be expressed more symbolically in the bar graph in Figure 17-2C. Children can also be given blank paper and encouraged to organize and report their data on the page in a way that makes sense to them. In this way, children learn to communicate their information in ways that are meaningful both to themselves and others (Folkson, 1996).

Regardless of how the data are presented, pertinent questions can be asked to encourage thoughtful interpretation of the graphs. Such questions might include:

What do you notice about the graph?

How many children prefer apples?

What is the favorite fruit?

How many different fruits are shown?

How many children contributed to the graph?

These types of questions result naturally from the data and provide valuable opportunities for students to ask as well as answer questions.

Quick and Easy Graphing Materials

For elementary school children, the process of constructing a graph helps them learn about its critical features and is a valuable activity; however, some graphs are more difficult to create than others, and construction may develop into a lengthy process. If the main purpose of visually displaying the data is simply to learn more about the data and easily examine results, several alternatives exist to having students create complete publication-quality graphs by hand. By using some of the materials illustrated in Figure 17-3, data may be displayed immediately as it is being collected. Russell and Corwin (1989) call these quick graphs "sketch graphs" or "working" graphs. Sketch graphs can be created quickly and provide a visual representation of the shape of the data. They should be clear, but they may not be neat and may not ever be displayed for public view. Sketch graphs don't require labels or titles and don't require time-consuming attention to construction. Sketch graphs may be made with concrete materials or with paper and pencil.

Computer graphing programs are available that are simple enough for even young children to use. As an added benefit, once the data have been entered, students can quickly and easily see their data displayed and printed in more than one type of graph or with a different scale. The graphing calculator is another tool that may be used for making graphs. Graphing calculators designed for middle grades allow students to create picture graphs, bar graphs, and pie graphs.

Line Plots and Stem-and-Leaf Plots

A *plot* is another type of graph used to visually display data. In recent years, plots have been used frequently in magazines and newspapers because they provide efficient ways of showing information, as well as comparing different sets of data. Some plots, such as line plots and stem-and-leaf plots, are quick and easy to make and can be used as sketch graphs to get an initial look at the shape of the data.

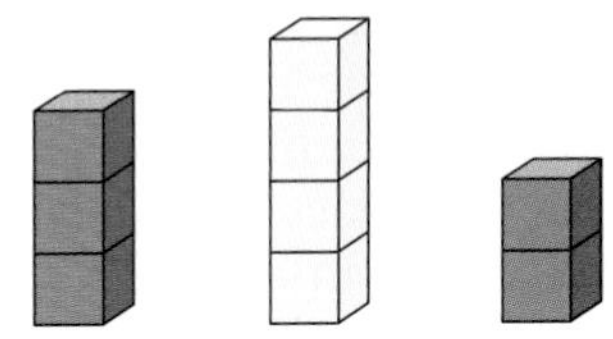

A. Connecting cubes or blocks

Did you watch TV last night?

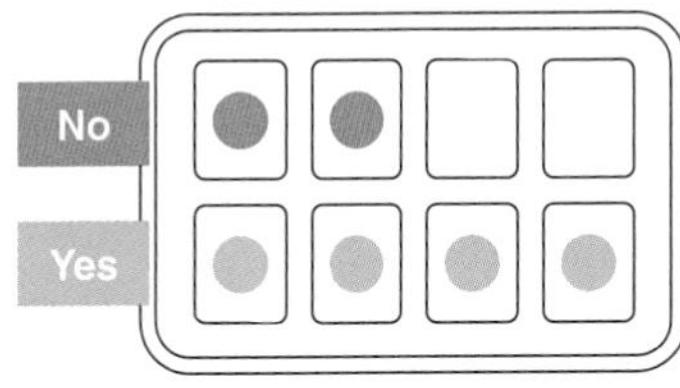

B. Counters in an ice tray

How much do you like winter?

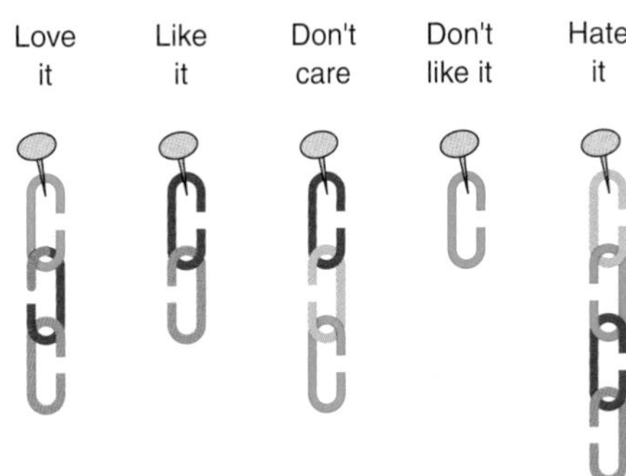

C. Plastic links or paper clips

How may candies in the jar?

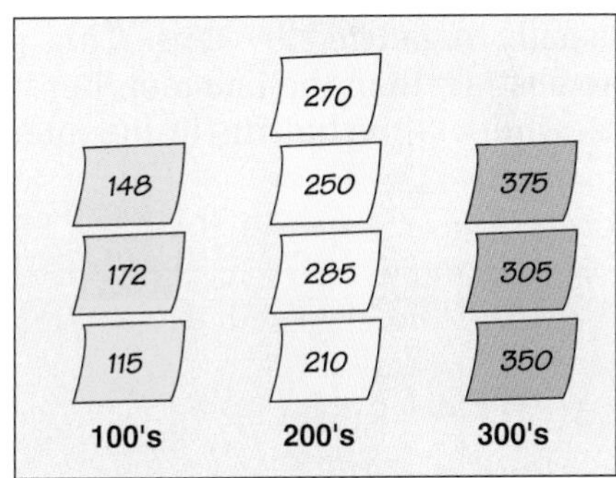

D. Self-stick notes

FIGURE 17-3 Quick and easy graphing materials.

LINE PLOTS A line plot may be used to quickly display numerical data with a small range. The range and distribution of the data may be clearly seen in the display. Line plots may be successfully used at all levels. Young children can more easily create a line plot than a bar graph, and older students will enjoy the quick feedback they receive when sketching a line plot.

Suppose that at a class party, some third-grade students receive candy in single-serving packages. The children open the packs and someone suggests they count to see how many candies they each received. The class begins counting, and soon each child begins calling out his or her total. The teacher writes the totals on the chalkboard as they are called out:

17, 19, 21, 20, 15, 18, 22, 17, 20, 18, 17, 18, 22, 17, 20

Discussion continues as students try to draw conclusions from the data. The teacher suggests putting the data into a line graph so it will be easier to see and understand. The children notice that the smallest value is 15 and the largest is 22, so they direct the teacher to draw a horizontal number line beginning with 15 and ending with 22. Next, an x is placed above each number to mark its frequency in the set of data. Figure 17-4 shows the completed line plot. The students are easily able to see that 17 occurred most often, followed by 18 and 20. The student who had only 15 in the package felt cheated, and those who had 22 felt lucky. The class talked about why there might not always be the same amount in each package.

STEM-AND-LEAF PLOTS A stem-and-leaf plot is another quick way to display data and provides a quite different representation than when the data are arranged in a line plot or bar graph. It works best with data that span several decades, since the plot is usually organized by tens. This plot is a little more abstract than the line plot, but it may be used successfully with students in the intermediate grades.

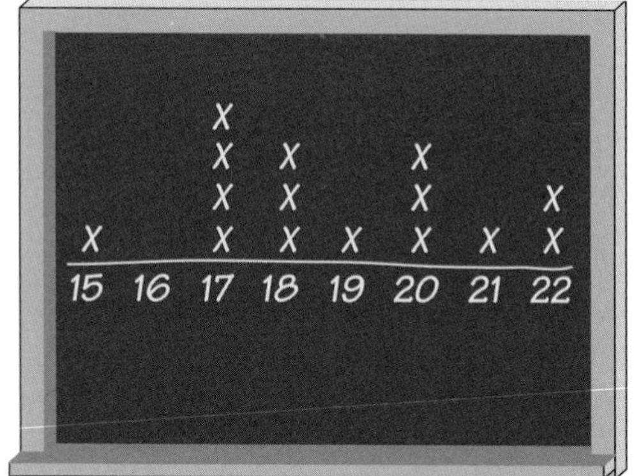

FIGURE 17-4 Line plot of number of candies per package.

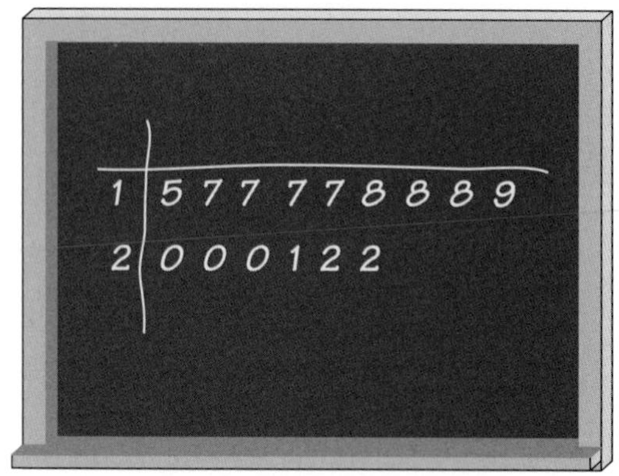

FIGURE 17-5 Stem-and-leaf plot of number of candies per package.

It is often useful to display data in more than one way. Consider the candy data just displayed in a line plot and arrange it in a stem-and-leaf plot (Figure 17-5). To begin, divide each value into tens and ones. The tens become the "stem," and the ones will be the "leaves." Notice that the data fall into two decades, the tens and twenties. A vertical line is drawn with the tens values (1 and 2) on the left of the line. The ones values are placed on the right side. By examining the plot, it is easy to see that 17 occurred most often in this set of data. From this arrangement you can also see that more packages contained candy amounts in the tens than in the twenties. Now all those students who had 20 or more feel lucky.

Stem-and-leaf plots may also be used to compare two sets of data in the same plot. In the intermediate grades, students can successfully compare more than one data set. Suppose you wanted to explore some questions related to the height of students in a fourth-grade class. Comparing the heights of the boys and girls will generate some interesting discussion. Questions such as "Which group is tallest?" and "Which group has the most variability?" are naturals. After some conjectures have been made, it is time to have students measure their heights and begin to analyze those data. Here are some steps that lead to stem-and-leaf plots. The heights of the 27 fourth-grade students (15 girls and 12 boys) are reported in centimeters in the following table:

Boys				Girls			
118	132	135	137	122	155	114	125
120	125	147	129	155	137	136	137
133	148	153	125	134	130	133	145
				148	148	147	

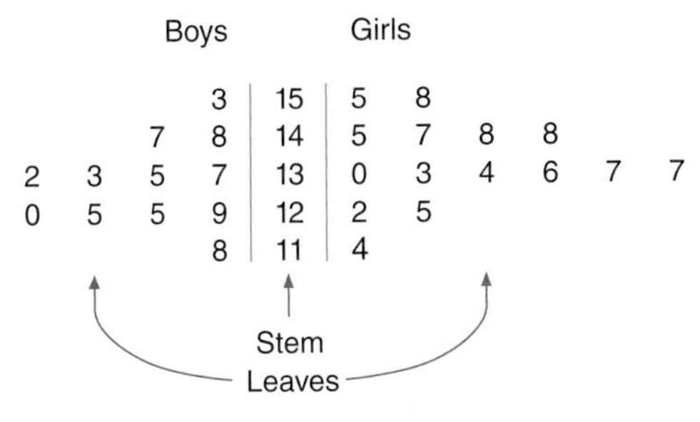

FIGURE 17-6 Stem-and-leaf plot of heights of boys and girls.

Rather than use a traditional frequency distribution, the values are organized in a stem-and-leaf plot, shown in Figure 17-6. The stem represents the hundreds and tens places of the data on student height, and the leaves represent the ones place. Thus, in the last row of Figure 17-6, 8/11/4 means one girl has a height of 114 cm and one boy is 118 cm tall. The stem-and-leaf plot preserves the individual measures while revealing the general shape of the organized data. Thus it presents all of the information, in this case for both groups, and provides a clear visual picture of it.

In addition to the quick graphs and plots mentioned previously, students should also be involved with graphs that require more construction time and effort.

Picture Graphs

In *picture graphs,* data are represented by pictures. For example, children may graph pictures of their favorite food or the pets they own. A picture can represent one object (Figure 17-7) or several

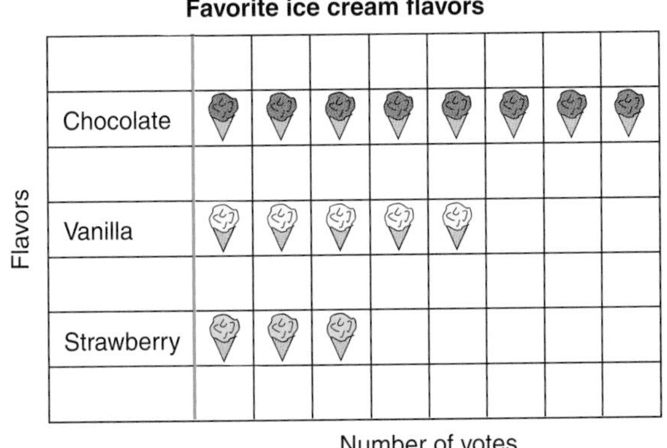

FIGURE 17-7 A picture graph in which each picture represents one object.

Estimated school retention rates in the United States, 1982 to 2000

Each figure represents 10 persons:

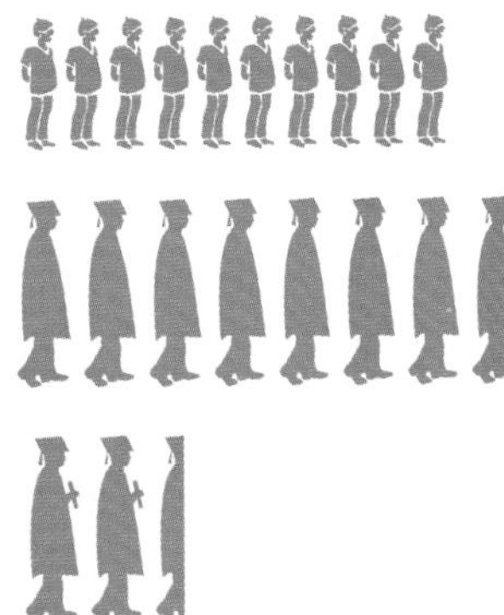

For every 100 pupils in the 5th grade in Fall 1982,

77 graduated from high school in Fall 1990,

and 25 earned bachelor's degrees in 2000.

FIGURE 17-8 A picture graph in which each picture represents several objects. (From surveys, estimates, and projections of the National Center for Education Statistics)

(Figure 17-8). To properly interpret picture graphs, children must know how much each object represents. Research shows that students often ignore such coding information when interpreting graphs (Bright and Hoeffner, 1993). This is why coding was highlighted in the opening *Snapshot of a Lesson.* Creating and reading picture graphs is a logical transition for young children as they move from real graphs to more abstract displays.

Bar Graphs

As you saw in the *Snapshot of a Lesson,* even young children can move from making real and picture graphs to making *bar graphs.* Bar graphs are used mostly for discrete or separate and distinct data; the bars represent these data. For example, they might graph the number of children's birthdays in each month or the number of students who travel to school by bus, car, or foot. Figure 17-2 showed that values can be read from the axis. Figure 17-9 shows that other times the values are reported directly on the graph. Bar graphs are often used for quick visual comparisons of categories of data and are appropriate for all ages.

Pie Graphs

A *pie graph* is a circle representing the whole, with wedges reporting percents of the whole, as illustrated in Figure 17-10. The pie graph is popular because it is easy to interpret; however, it has major limitations in that it represents only a fixed

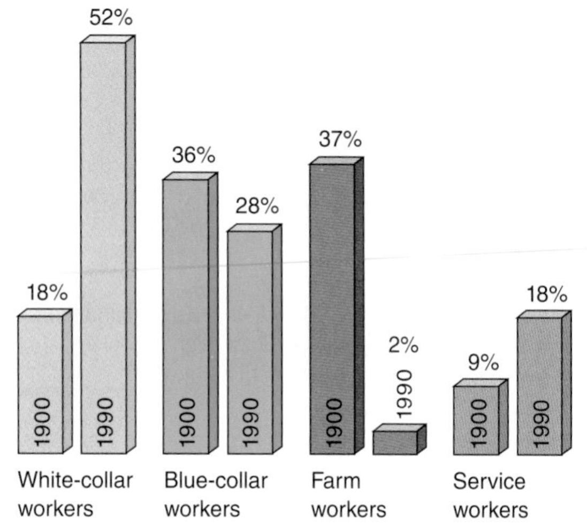

FIGURE 17-9 A bar graph with values shown directly on the bars.

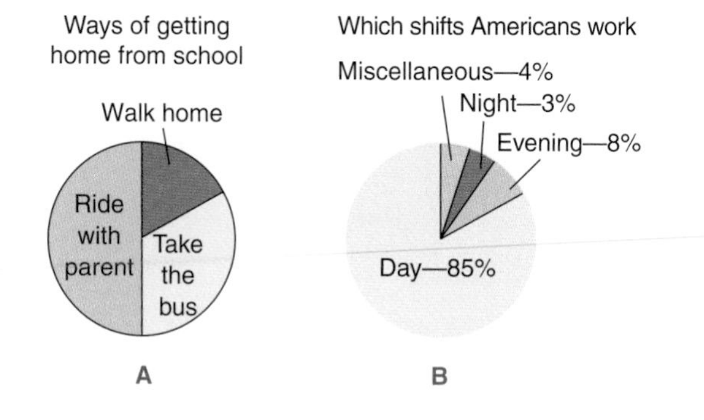

FIGURE 17-10 Pie graphs.

moment in time, and it cannot exceed 100 percent. For example, students may graph how they spend their weekly allowance or the favorite colors of the class. While students in the upper elementary grades can read and interpret pie graphs, effective construction may require the use of fractions, percents, proportions, and measurement of angles. Pie graph construction is more appropriate for middle school students; however, there is an effective, concrete method of connecting pie graphs to bar graphs, which elementary students may successfully complete.

As illustrated with the line and stem-and-leaf plots, showing the same data in different displays can be both useful and effective. For example, the data shown in the bar graph in Figure 17-2 can be easily shown in a pie graph. Cubes of different colors to match the fruits could be strung together as shown here:

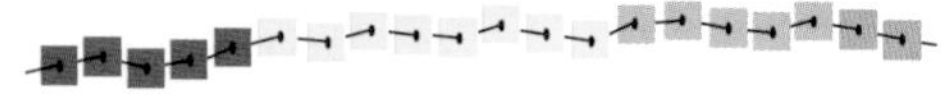

Then the string can be placed in a circle:

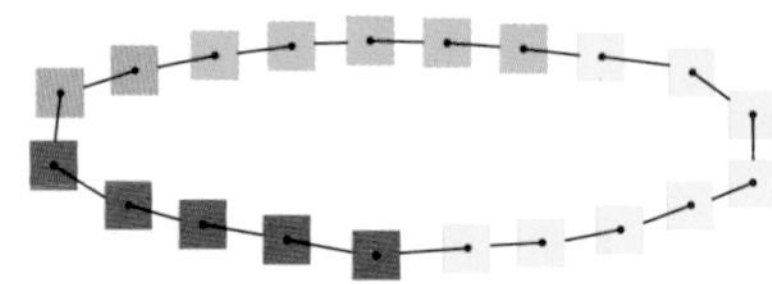

This experience helps make a connection between bar and pie graphs. It also provides a natural context for fractions and percents. For example, the pie graph suggests that 1/4 of the fruits are oranges.

This model can be extended by placing a meter tape, or a 100-centimeter strip of paper marked with similar units, around the circle of blocks to form concentric circles, as shown in Figure 17-11A. Comparing the sections suggested by the different groups of colored blocks with the markers on the strip or meter tape will identify percents that can be easily read.

As a more concrete visualization, 20 children can be arranged in a circle, and the "wedges" of a circle graph duplicated with string, as illustrated in Figure 17-11B. Both of the models in Figure 17-11 make it easy to estimate or read the percents and conclude, for example, that more than 50 percent of the children chose apples or bananas.

Similar observations might have been made directly from the bar graph in Figure 17-2, but conclusions involving fractions and percents are much more obvious from the pie graph. Technology applications, such as spreadsheets, are also useful tools that allow students to create bar graphs and pie graphs of the data. The process of moving from a bar graph to a pie graph provides different perspectives for the same set of data, and research suggests that developing such multiple perspectives helps promote greater understanding (Shaughnessy, 1992).

Line Graphs

Line graphs are effective for showing trends over time. In line graphs, points on a grid are used to represent continuous or uninterrupted data. Each axis is clearly labeled, so the data shown can be interpreted properly. A wide variety of line graphs exist and are used, but two basic assumptions are inherent:

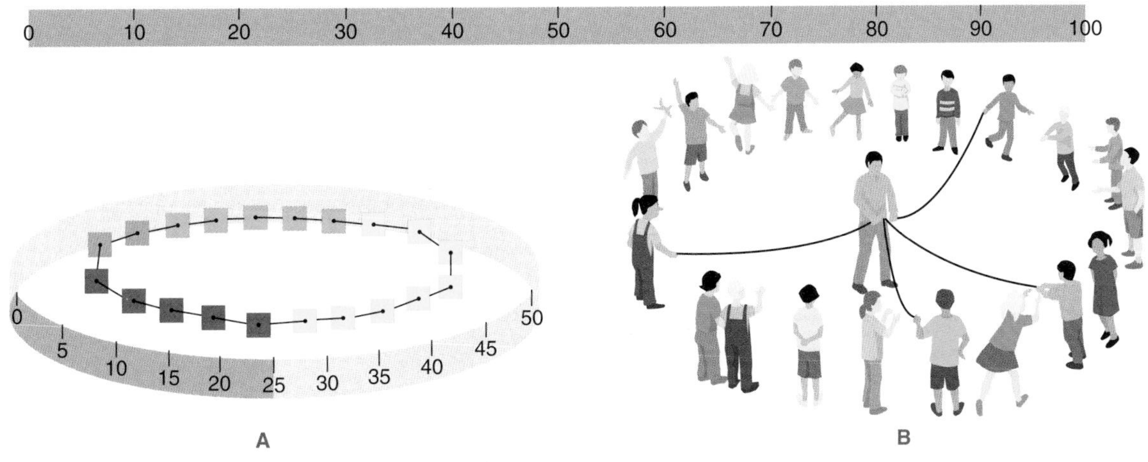

FIGURE 17-11 Models for interpreting circle graph data.

1. The data are continuous rather than discrete. This means that the data are grouped along a continuous scale and cannot be "counted."
2. Change is accurately represented with linear functions (i.e., by lines) rather than some other curve.

As Figure 17-12 shows, line graphs are particularly good for showing variations or changes over time, such as hours of daylight, temperatures, rainfall, and so on. For example, students could graph plant growth in a science experiment. Line graphs are also an effective visual means of comparing several sets of data, as illustrated in Figure 17-13. Constructing or interpreting line graphs requires students to examine both horizontal and vertical axes, which is good preparation for coordinates. Line graphs are used most often at the middle school level.

Box Plots

A *box plot* (also called a box-and-whisker plot) summarizes data and provides a visual means of showing variability—the spread of the data. The box plot shown in Figure 17-14 summarizes the earlier student height data succinctly. The median is a key reference point; we will talk more about the median in the next section. The lower hinge, or lower quartile, is the median of the lower half of the data, and the upper hinge, or upper quartile, is

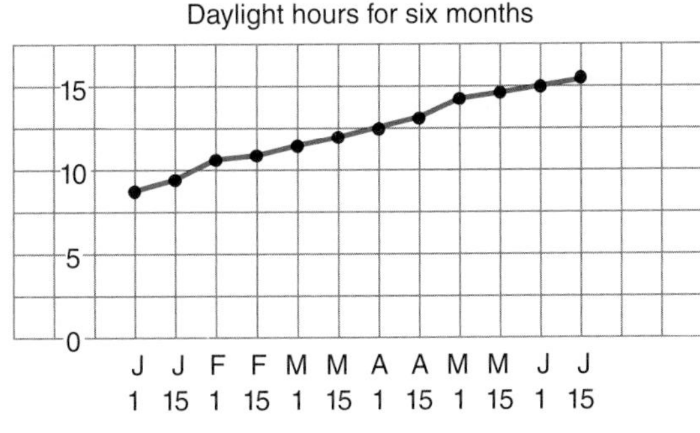

FIGURE 17-12 A line graph of a single set of varying data.

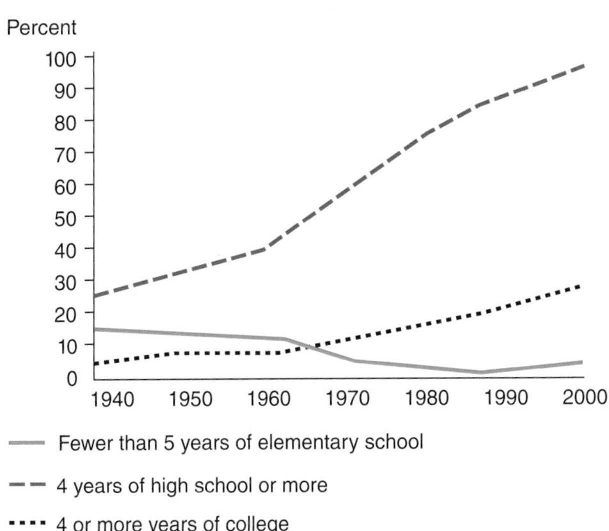

FIGURE 17-13 A line graph comparing several sets of data.

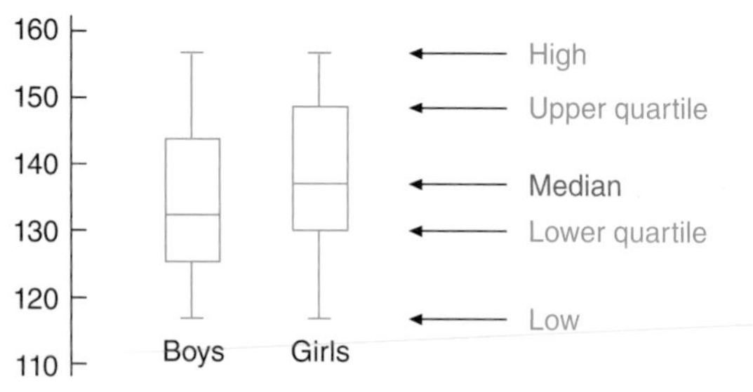

FIGURE 17-14 Box plot for heights of boys and girls.

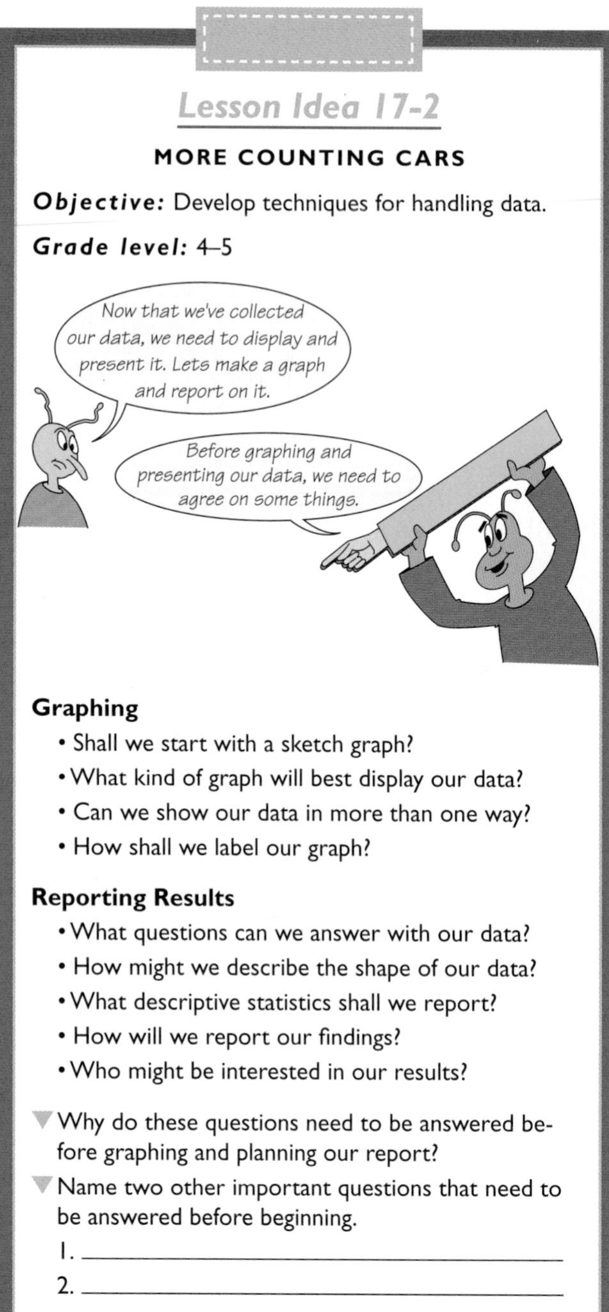

the median of the upper half of the data. These are found by computing the medians of the data in the lower and upper halves, respectively. The midspread is a measure of variability and is the difference between the upper and lower quartiles. In Figure 17-14, the midspread for the boys is 17 (142 – 125) and that for the girls is 16.5 (148 – 131.5). The smallest and largest heights represent the lower extreme and the upper extreme. The lines (also called "whiskers") extending from the top of the upper quartile to the largest value and then from the bottom of the lower quartile to the smallest value provide another visual indication of variability.

Lesson Idea 17-2
MORE COUNTING CARS
Objective: Develop techniques for handling data.
Grade level: 4–5
Now that we've collected our data, we need to display and present it. Lets make a graph and report on it.
Before graphing and presenting our data, we need to agree on some things.
Graphing
• Shall we start with a sketch graph?
• What kind of graph will best display our data?
• Can we show our data in more than one way?
• How shall we label our graph?
Reporting Results
• What questions can we answer with our data?
• How might we describe the shape of our data?
• What descriptive statistics shall we report?
• How will we report our findings?
• Who might be interested in our results?
Why do these questions need to be answered before graphing and planning our report?
Name two other important questions that need to be answered before beginning.
1. ________
2. ________

The box plot shows many things. For example, it shows the median height for the girls is greater than that for the boys. Although the groups have about the same midspread, the boys are a bit more evenly distributed throughout the box than are the girls. (Why? Because the median of the boys is closer to the middle of the box than is the median of the girls.) The box plot is derived naturally from a stem-and-leaf plot. The box plot shows many important characteristics of a group visually and, when two or more groups are shown on the same graph, it allows comparisons to be made easily. The box plot is an appropriate display for middle school students to construct. It provides a nice connection to descriptive statistics such as median and range. In addition, many standardized test results are reported as box plots, so this is an important kind of graph for teachers to understand even if they don't teach it.

Graphical Roundup

Each of these graphs deserves instructional attention as students examine ways to display their data. Children need experience constructing them and interpreting information that is represented. In the children's book *The Best Vacation Ever* (Murphy, 1997), a little girl collects and displays data for her family so they can plan a vacation. Lesson Idea 17-2 guides students to think about how to display the Counting Cars data collected in Lesson Idea 17-1.

The availability of graphing calculators and graphing programs allows for easy construction of a variety of graphs. This availability of different graphs via technology places a greater premium on interpreting and understanding the graphs that are so easily produced. As children become familiar with different graphs, they should recognize some characteristics associated with them. Figure 17-15 highlights specific characteristics of graphs that are

Math Links 17.4

A wide variety of electronic graphing manipulatives may be found at the National Library of Virtual Manipulatives for Interactive Mathematics web site, which you can access from this book's web site. Some specific titles include Bar Chart, Pie Chart, and Histogram/Box Plot.

encountered in elementary and middle school. The focus here is not on memorizing characteristics of these graphs, but rather on becoming aware that each type has strengths. The selection of a particular graph should capitalize on these strengths, while recognizing any of its limitations.

Analyzing and Communicating Results

Data Sense

Once data have been collected and displayed, they should be examined and analyzed. Just as children develop a knowledge about numbers or number sense, they can also develop knowledge about statistics or *data sense.* Data sense is gradually developed as students pose questions, collect data, construct graphs, and interpret them in a variety of contexts. Students with data sense are able to determine how data should be analyzed. They are able to read and evaluate statistical information being presented, such as material presented by the media. Students also display data sense when they

Type of Graph	Characteristics
Real	Used by young children Actual objects are placed on a graph
Line Plot	Provides a quick way to examine the shape and variation or spread of data Gives a bar-graph-like representation
Stem-and-Leaf Plot	Efficient way to show detailed data Provides similar visual patterns as a bar graph but more detailed information Uses stem and leaf coding that needs to be understood Technology has facilitated its use
Picture	Frequently encountered in newspapers and reports Generally easy to use and interpret but visuals may be misleading Codes/keys which accompany graph need to be understood
Bar	Mostly used for discrete data Frequently encountered in newspapers and reports Easy to interpret Uses scales/codes that need to be understood
Pie	Frequently encountered in newspapers and reports Shows fractional parts, which are based on a whole or 100% Easy to use and interpret Difficult to construct by hand, easy with technology
Line	Frequently encountered in newspapers and reports Used for continuous data Effective to show patterns, trends, comparisons and change over time Uses vertical and horizontal scales that need to be understood Provides good readiness for coordinate graphs
Box Plot	Provides useful information about the variability of data Requires knowledge of range, median and quartiles to interpret Technology has facilitated its use

FIGURE 17-15 Characteristics of graphs.

are able to use statistical language when reasoning about data. The goal is for students to develop both procedural knowledge (how to construct a graph or calculate a statistic) and conceptual knowledge (understanding what a graph or statistic is communicating) (Friel, 1998).

Analysis

One way to analyze data is through the use of questions. As in the opening *Snapshot of a Lesson*, students should be encouraged to examine their results and discuss questions that may be answered by the data. Curcio, cited in Friel et al. (1997), identifies three levels of graph comprehension, which progress from lower-level to higher-level questions. Your goal should be to teach students to move beyond lower-level thinking and to ask and answer higher-level questions.

1. *Reading the data.* The student is able to answer specific questions for which the answer is prominently displayed. For example, "Which player scored the most points?"
2. *Reading between the data.* The student is able to find relationships in the data such as comparison, and is able to operate on the data. For example, "How many players earned more points than John?" "How many points did Steve earn in games 1 and 2?"
3. *Reading beyond the data.* The student is able to predict or make inferences. For example, "In game 3, how many points would you expect Steve to score? Why do you think so?"

Data may also be analyzed by describing the shape of the data in the graph. Corwin and Friel (1990) suggest first having students use informal language such as "clumps, holes, and spread out" to describe features of the data. Second, students should attempt to develop theories about why the data look the way they do. This second step encourages students to read beyond the data.

Another beneficial graphical analysis task is to give students mystery graphs that are missing some of their labels and have students predict what the data might be. For example, groups of students may have each measured a body part such as arms, legs, or distance around heads. A graph that contains measurements from 18 to 24 inches is displayed. Students would be asked to hypothesize which body parts might be illustrated on the graph. This activity also reinforces the importance of using labels on graphs.

A variation of the mystery graph activity involves the use of a graphing calculator and a calculator-based laboratory (CBL). With a CBL motion detector, graphs may be created to show movements. Students may be given a CBL graph, and the challenge is to move so they can duplicate the graph. For example, Figure 17-16 shows the graphs of three different people walking. Time is shown on the horizontal axis and the distance from a motion detector is shown on the vertical axis. Examine Parts A, B, and C, and decide which of these graphs shows movement toward the motion detector. Part C is different because, instead of showing continuous movement away or toward, it shows a person leaving and then returning. These sorts of activities encourage students to consider the axes of the graphs and think carefully about how data are placed on a graph.

FIGURE 17-16 Graphs showing distance and time.

Misleading Graphs

Another important component in developing data sense is the ability to critically examine graphs and correctly interpret the data presented. Sometimes even simple graphs may be misleading. For example, consider the graph shown in Figure 17-17. Eighth graders were asked to explain why this graph was misleading.

Although the data in the graph indicate that the amount of trash has doubled in two decades, the visual elements reflect a doubling of both the width and height to produce a figure whose area is four times greater rather than a volume that is actually eight times greater. People may focus on the visual graph and ignore the numerical data that accompany the graph. In fact, less than 10 percent of eighth graders identified the critical problem associated with the graph in Figure 17-17, which suggests that instructional attention needs to be given to helping children examine graphs with a careful and suspicious eye.

Graphs may also be deceptive in other ways. For example, the graph in Figure 17-18A reports changes in allowances for three children. It shows that Ann's allowance was doubled, Bill's tripled, and Chris's increased by one-half. Based on this information, Bill may be feeling philanthropic and Chris complaining of hard times. What is wrong

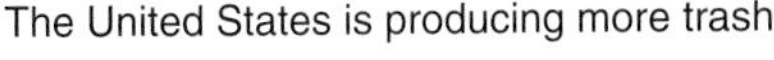

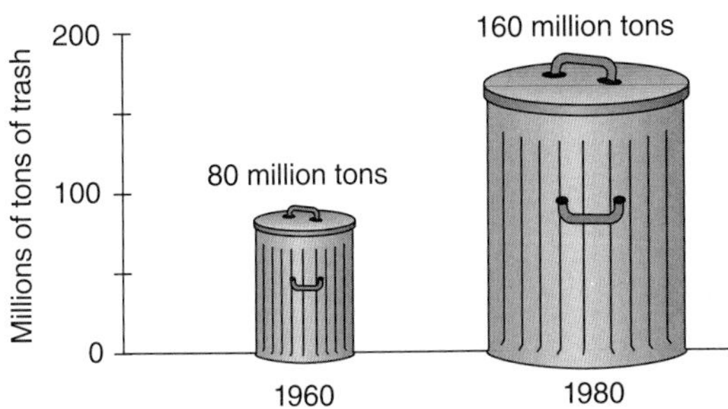

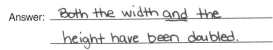

The pictograph shown above is misleading. Explain why.

Answer: Both the width and the height have been doubled.

FIGURE 17-17 Eighth-grade national assessment question on interpreting graphs.

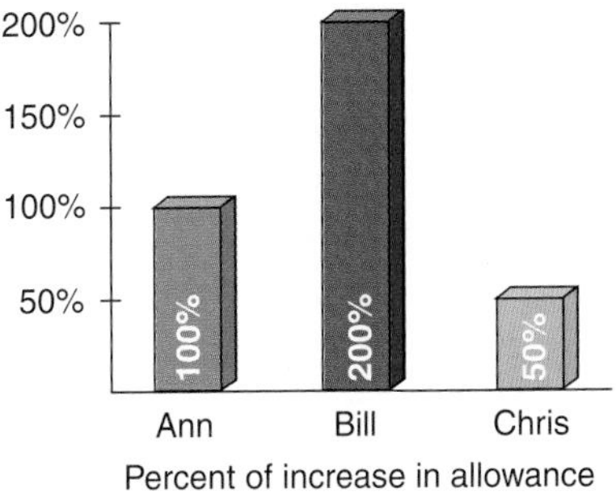

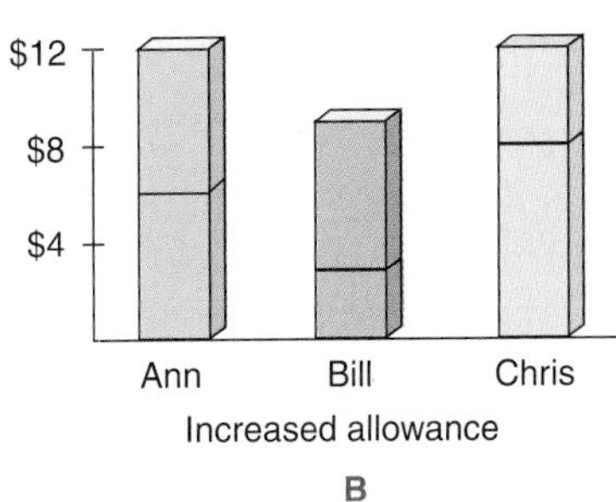

FIGURE 17-18 Example of distortion of data in graphs.

with the graph? Technically, it is correct, but it doesn't tell the entire story because the original allowances were not the same.

Let's look at the data:

	Original Allowance	Size of Increase	Amount of Increase	New Allowance
Ann	$6.00	Double	$6.00	$12.00
Bill	$3.00	Triple	$6.00	$9.00
Chris	$8.00	Half	$4.00	$12.00

As Figure 17-18B shows, a graph with a labeled vertical axis reflects the situation more accurately. These different graphs of the same data demonstrate how graphs can distort and sometimes misrepresent information. Developing a healthy skepticism of graphical displays is an important part of developing graphing skills.

Communicating Results

Once data have been collected, displayed, and analyzed, it is appropriate for students to communicate their findings. Just as in problem solving, students should be encouraged to look back at their results (Bohan et al., 1995). Communication can help students clarify their ideas during this process. For example, students might complete regular journal entries throughout their project. It is also useful to have large or small group discussions about the data.

Friel et al. (1992) suggest having students go through a writing process when analyzing data, similar to one used in language arts. First, the students are involved in planning or prewriting. Second, a rough draft is created. Third, students revise their work, and finally the work is published and shared with others. Lesson Idea 17-2 shows how you can probe students to analyze their Counting Cars data.

It is valuable for students to learn to communicate their results with others. Their final presentation may include oral or written communication or both. They must learn to report clearly the answers to their original questions and hypotheses and select the most appropriate way to communicate their findings in a graphic format or by using other statistical measures. Some projects may be interesting to share with local media. The presentation may be for other classmates; however, a presentation for someone outside of the classroom can be particularly meaningful. For example, one class calculated the area of classrooms in their building and compared the average area of the fifth-grade classrooms to the sixth-grade classrooms. Their findings were presented to the principal, who made room assignments for the building (Scavo and Petraroja, 1998). Another group of students collected data to find out which school lunches were the most and least popular. Once their findings were collected and displayed, they presented their findings to the director of food services, who planned the monthly menus.

Descriptive Statistics

Another way to analyze data is to use descriptive statistics. So much information exists today that it must often be simplified or reduced in ways other than by graphs. The organization and summarization of data is called *descriptive statistics.* Descriptive statistics are in common use. They are introduced in the primary grades through data collection and graphs, and then extended with further exploration and practice activities in the intermediate and middle school grades. Here are some familiar examples:

> "Most children in the fifth grade are 10 years old."
>
> "The median family income is $35,250."
>
> "The average temperature today was 29°F."

Each of these statements uses a number to summarize what is typical for a current situation or condition. Two of the most common types of descriptive statistics include measures of variation and measures of central tendency. For each of the descriptive statistics that follow, we provide a concrete example using cubes and an example using numbers. For some children, manipulating the physical model not only helps them understand the formula but also promotes retention.

Measure of Variation

THE RANGE The *range* is a simple measure that is used to describe the variation of a set of data or how spread out the data are. The variation in a data set is easily examined in a line plot or graph. Figure 17-19 shows the ages of five children—2, 3, 7, 9, and 9—illustrated with cubes. Students may find the range by comparing the tallest tower to see how much taller it is than the shortest tower. The tallest tower is 7 cubes taller than the shortest. Thus the range is calculated by subtracting the smallest value in the set from the largest. For the age data, subtract 2 from 9 to get a range of 7. Once the range has been introduced in the elementary grades, middle school students often learn to measure variability with variance or standard deviations.

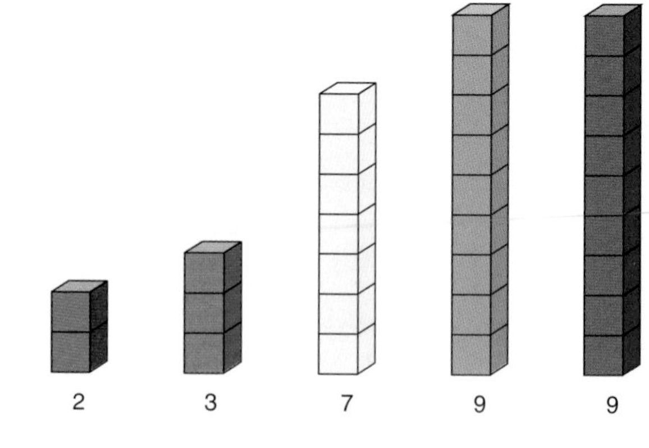

FIGURE 17-19 Ages of children.

Measures of Central Tendency or Averages

The word *average* is a popular statistical term that many children have heard. It is used to report such things as average temperature, average family income, test averages, batting averages, and average life expectancy.

Any number that is used to describe the center or middle of a set of values is called an *average* of those values. Many different averages exist, but three—mode, median, and mean—are commonly encountered in elementary and middle school. Simply being able to state the algorithm for finding these statistics is not enough. To support the development of data sense, each of these should be developed meaningfully through concrete activities before introducing computation. Such experiences provide greater conceptual knowledge or understanding of the concept of average. Furthermore, they help the later acquisition and development of symbolic formulas in secondary school. Wilson and Krapfl (1995) describe how students can develop some of these conceptual understandings through explorations with a computer spreadsheet program. The program allows them to investigate what happens to various descriptive statistics when different values are used.

THE MODE The *mode* is the value that occurs most frequently in a collection of data. Using concrete materials such as cubes, the mode is easily identified as the tower height that occurs most often. In Figure 17-19 it is easy to see that 9 is the mode. In graphical terms, this is also the largest portion; the tallest column in a bar graph, for example. In Figure 17-20(a), the most frequently occurring test score is 90 (it occurred twice), so the mode is 90. The mode is a versatile average in that

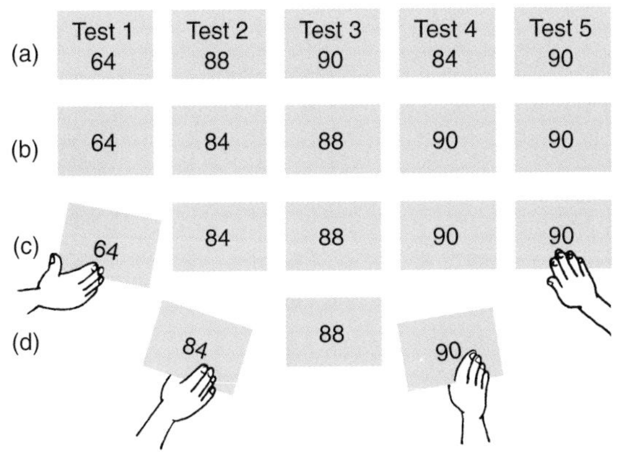

FIGURE 17-20 Model for finding the median of five test scores.

it may be used with both numeric and nonnumeric data. The mode is easy to find and is affected very little by extreme scores. Young children are often interested in which item on the graph received the most votes. Therefore, their initial experience with average begins with mode. The children are comfortable using the mathematical term, *mode*, as the teacher introduces it to them.

Students' ages within a class provide an excellent application of mode, because within a given class, a large number of children are the "same" age. Businesses also frequently rely on the mode to select merchandise. Suppose, for example, that you own a shoe store. The mean and/or median size of shoe you sell has no practical value for restocking, but the modal shoe size holds clear implications because you want to stock the sizes most people wear.

THE MEDIAN The *median* is another type of average that can easily be identified without the need for computation. It is used with numeric data and is the middle value in a data set. The median divides the data into two equal subsets. Thus the same number of values are above as below the median. The median is easy to illustrate. Look again at the children's ages in Figure 17-19. Before looking for the median, be sure the data have been ordered. For example, these towers are arranged smallest to largest. Once that has been done, the outside towers can be removed, one at a time, until the middle value remains. It is easy to see that the middle age or median tower is 7 years. Reference to a highway median will remind students that a median in statistics is a middle position. Notice that the median is not the middle of the range of data because data aren't always spread symmetrically over the range. In the children's age example, the median simply tells us that there are as many children in the group from ages 2–7 as there are in the group containing ages 7–9.

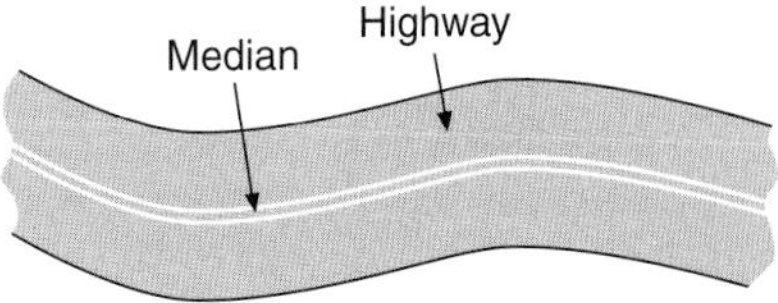

The median too, can be modeled with numbers. For example, consider the five test scores shown on cards in Figure 17-20(a). Ordering them from lowest to highest, as in Figure 17-20(b), provides practice in using greater than, less than, and ordering skills. To find the middle score, or median, simply remove the highest and lowest cards simultaneously, as shown in Figures 17-20(c) and (d). Continue this process until the middle card remains. This score, 88, is the median.

There are five scores in Figure 17-20. Suppose a sixth score of 17 was made. Ordering the six test scores, as shown in Figure 17-21(a), could make a new arrangement. Again, remove the highest and lowest cards simultaneously until two cards remain. In this case, as shown in Figure 17-21(b) the median is the middle point between these two scores, or 86.

THE MEAN The *mean* is called the arithmetic average because it is determined by adding all the values involved and dividing by the number of addends. The mean is the most difficult to compute, although it can be understood by children beginning in the upper elementary grades. It is used with numeric data. When people talk about finding the average of a set of data, they are often referring to calculating the mean. It is important that children realize the mean is not the only type of average.

Simply being able to state or use the algorithm does not indicate understanding of the mean. Difficulties in interpreting the mean were shown on a

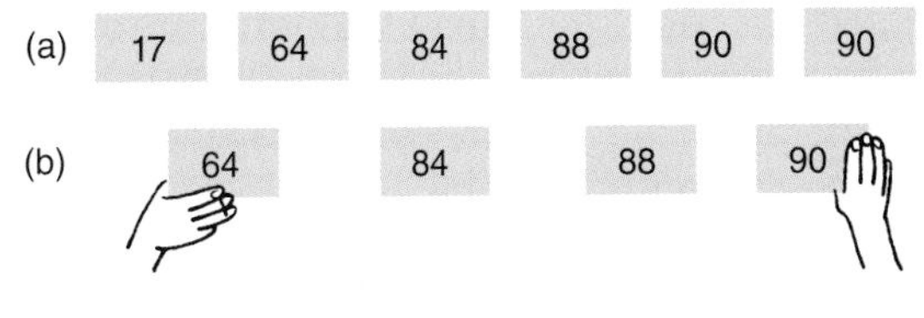

FIGURE 17-21 Model for finding the median of six test scores.

Akira read from a book on Monday, Tuesday, and Wednesday. He read an average of 10 pages per day. Circle whether each of the following is possible or not possible.

Possible	Not Possible		Pages Read Monday	Tuesday	Wednesday
A	A	(a)	4 pages	4 pages	2 pages
B	B	(b)	9 pages	10 pages	11 pages
C	C	(c)	5 pages	10 pages	15 pages
D	D	(d)	10 pages	15 pages	20 pages

FIGURE 17-22 Eighth-grade national assessment question on interpreting an average (correct responses are circled).

national assessment (Educational Testing Service, 1992). Figure 17-22 shows a question that required eighth graders to determine what data would be reasonable for a given mean. Less than 40 percent answered all four choices correctly. These assessment results illustrate the findings from research that many middle-grade students are able to calculate averages when asked to do so, but the depth of their understanding of the concept of average is shallow (Shaughnessy, 1992).

Uccellini (1996) describes two conceptual interpretations for the mean that are helpful in developing understanding of this average. Say that four students have 9, 5, 3, and 7 trading cards. The cubes in Figure 17-23A show the number of cards each child has. The first interpretation involves the concept of equal distribution or sharing, an idea very familiar to students. In this interpretation, the mean is identified as the number that describes the data if each piece of data was "evened out" or the same as all others. People often think of this as what is typical for the data. If children are asked to even out or share the cards so that each student has a fair or equal share of cards, this evening-out process produces a mean of six cards per student (Figure 17-23B). As students gain experience and become comfortable with the equal distribution interpretation, they also begin to realize that with large data sets, such as whole-class data, trying to share equally becomes cumbersome. Students often discover the add-then-divide algorithm on their own, or the teacher can introduce it with concrete materials. The mean also could have been determined by computing:

$$\text{mean} = \frac{9 + 5 + 3 + 7}{4} = \frac{24}{4} = 6$$

Figure 17-24 shows a way to model the add-then-divide algorithm for the mean. Test scores are

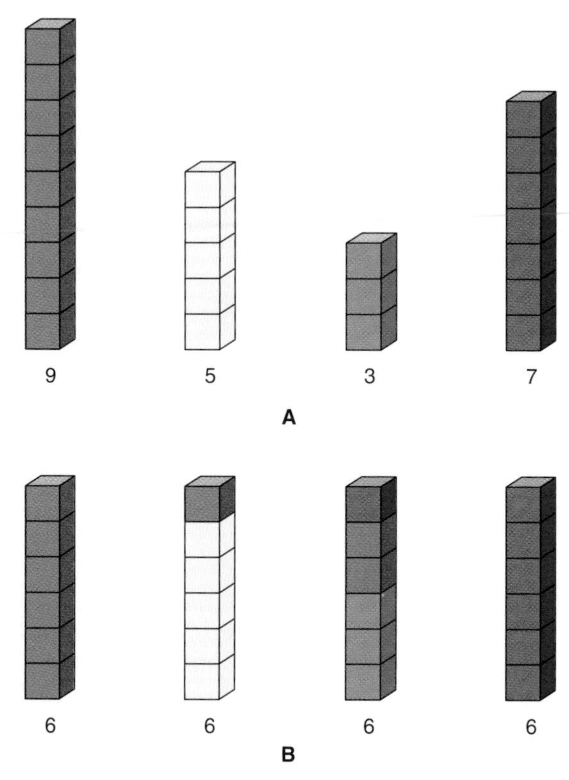

FIGURE 17-23 Equal distribution or sharing model for the mean.

returned to children on pieces of adding machine tape, and the length of each strip is determined by the score (i.e., a score of 88 is 88 cm long and a score of 64 is 64 cm long). Scores can be physically compared using the tapes (e.g., it is clear that the score on Test 2 was higher). To show the mean

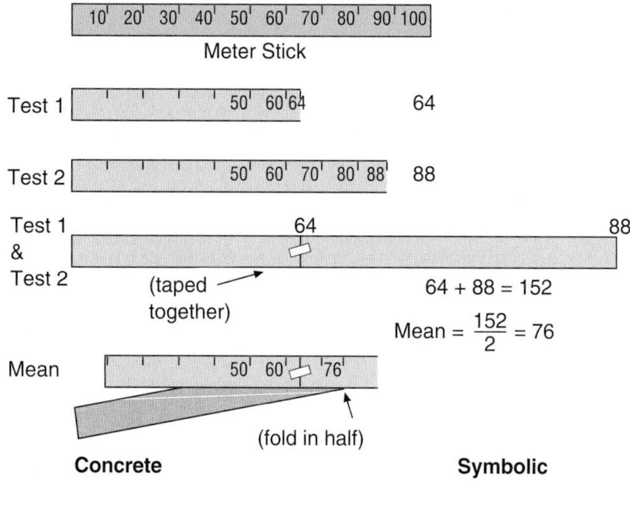

FIGURE 17-24 Model for finding the mean using lengths of adding machine tape to indicate test scores.

score, simply tape the two strips of paper together (add) and then fold the resulting strip in half (divide by 2). It also illustrates the effect of a test score of zero when the fold number on the tape is increased by one. Using this example, the three test scores would be 88, 64, and 0. The length of the tape is still 152 cm. But, if we fold the tape into thirds, rather than in half, the length of the strip is a little over 50 cm. Therefore, the mean test score dropped over 25 points! This technique is appealing and enlightening.

Not all data sets divide evenly, and once students are comfortable with the concept of evening out, they can discuss what to do with remainders, which makes a natural connection to fractions. They can also discuss how some data cannot be divided and some averages that are calculated are not realistic. For example, in one data set the mean indicated that the average number of children per family was 2.5. Children will be quick to point out that you can't have five-tenths or one-half of a child.

The second interpretation involves the idea of mean as being a "balancing point" for a set of data. You can see the trading card data have been placed on a line plot.

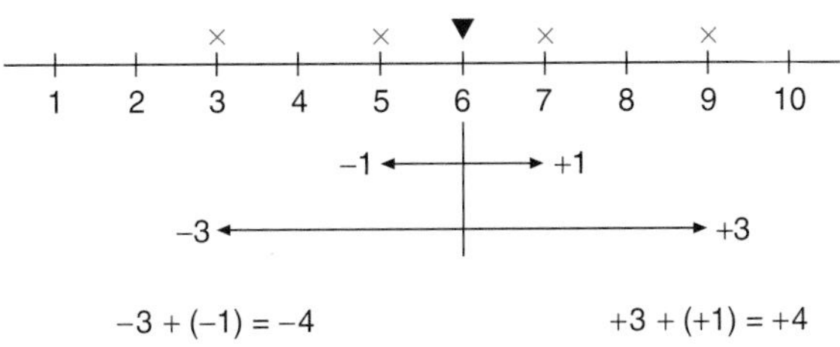

The mean for the data set was already described as 6, and by examining how far away each of the numbers is from the balance point of 6, you can see that 6 is the middle of the data. The total distance numbers above the mean are the same as the total distance numbers below the mean. Students can be given a mean and encouraged to develop sets of data that would balance to create that mean.

These types of experiences help students understand some fundamental notions related to the mean; namely, that the mean must be somewhere between the values averaged and that it is the typical value or balancing point for a set of data.

Math Links 17.5

If you would like to see middle school students collecting data and determining the averages, you can view video clips for Trashketball from the Modeling Middle School Mathematics site, which you can access from this book's web site.

www.wiley.com/college/reys

Choosing Averages

As students use these averages, they must also be aware of the effects certain sizes of data may have on them. The following table provides a summary of the test scores reported in Figures 17-20 and 17-21:

	Mean	Median
Five tests	83	88
Six tests	72	86

This summary illustrates that the median was affected very little by the extremely low score (17) on the last test, but the mean dropped greatly (from 83 to 72). One negative characteristic of the mean is that its value is affected by extreme scores.

Suppose you are preparing a report of average incomes and you want to present the fairest picture. Should the mean—which would be affected by the extremely high salaries of movie stars, professional athletes, and corporate heads—be used? Many governmental agencies handle this problem by reporting median family incomes.

Grasp of average is a powerful tool in estimation and problem solving. Problems such as the one in Figure 17-25 provide opportunities to apply averages and estimation in everyday situations.

Finding the mean, median, and mode for the same data can generate discussion about when certain averages should be used. You can use In the Classroom 17-2 to allow children to calculate averages with concrete materials or numbers and to discuss how one might select a particular average to describe the data. For another example, look at Lesson Idea 17-3. Calculating the mean, median, and mode provides practice in computational skills. More important, however, is deciding which of these averages to report. The median salary of \$500,000 or the modal salary of \$480,000 seems more representative than the mean salary of \$1,030,000. If salary negotiations were taking place, the players might cite one average and the owners a very different average. Discussing which averages are appropriate for what purpose helps students better understand why different ones exist and are used. Once children have collected their

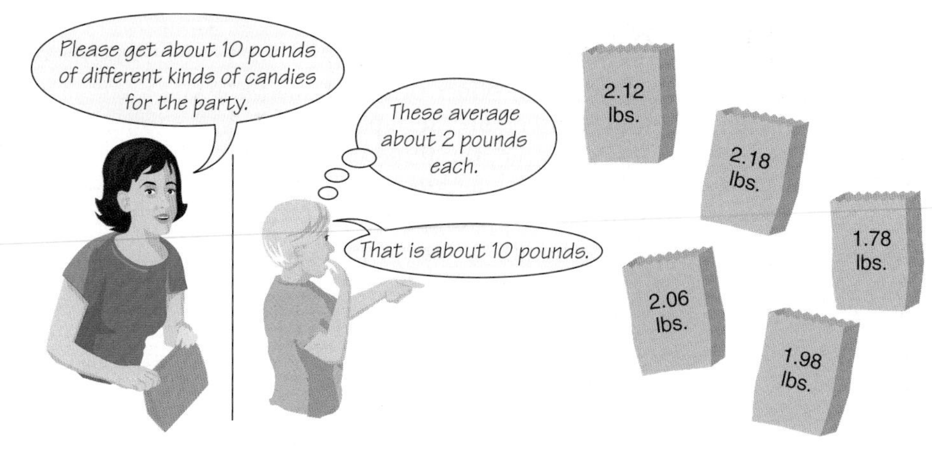

FIGURE 17-25 Example problem for developing averaging and estimating skills.

own data, they should determine which averages to calculate and report. For an amusing example of this type of activity, in the children's book *What Do You Mean by "Average"?* (James and Barkin, 1978), Jill is running for student council. To convince the school she will best represent them, she decides to show she is the most average person in the school.

Each of the averages can be modeled and developed in ways that are appealing, interesting, and meaningful. No new mathematics is required, yet learning about averages provides a vehicle for

In the Classroom 17-2

PEANUTS

OBJECTIVE: **Choosing the best average.**

GRADE LEVEL: **4–8**

Suppose you have opened some Nutty Bars to check the company's claim of an "average" of 8 peanuts per bar. Here is what you found after opening ten bars.

Bar	1st	2nd	3rd	4th	5th	6th	7th	8th	9th	10th
Number of Peanuts	5	8	8	8	11	7	8	6	6	6

▼ Create some different sketch graphs so you can examine the shape of the data. Which graph would the company probably use to promote their product? Why?

▼ Calculate the averages. You may use counters such as beans and grid paper to represent the peanuts if you wish.
- What is the mean number of nuts?
- What is the median number of nuts?
- What is the modal number of nuts?
- Which average did the company probably use? Why?

▼ Write at least three questions that can be answered by your graphs and statistics.

1. ______________________________
2. ______________________________
3. ______________________________

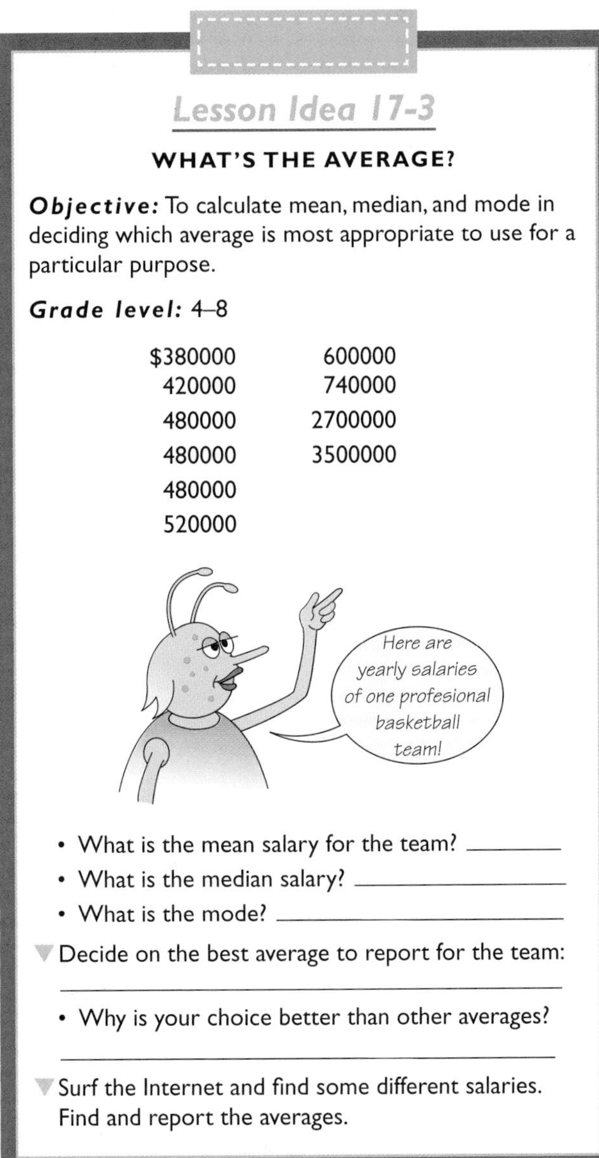

Lesson Idea 17-3

WHAT'S THE AVERAGE?

Objective: To calculate mean, median, and mode in deciding which average is most appropriate to use for a particular purpose.

Grade level: 4–8

\$380000	600000
420000	740000
480000	2700000
480000	3500000
480000	
520000	

Here are yearly salaries of one profesional basketball team!

- What is the mean salary for the team? ________
- What is the median salary? ________
- What is the mode? ________

Decide on the best average to report for the team:

____

- Why is your choice better than other averages?

____

Surf the Internet and find some different salaries. Find and report the averages.

applying many mathematical concepts and skills that students are developing.

Care must be taken to ensure that statistics is viewed as more than a series of skills or techniques. For example, finding an average is an important skill that should be developed; however, the teaching of statistics must not stop with the "how to." Rather, it must raise questions such as, "When is an average useful?"

For example, the ice cream survey in Figure 17-7 reports that eight students like chocolate, five like vanilla, and three like strawberry. This picture graph clearly and accurately shows student ice cream preferences. These preferences are an example of nonnumeric data. A mean or median of these data could be computed but would be inappropriate. In fact, a mean or median is meaningless for these data! Before any statistics are computed, challenge students to decide what questions are to be answered and discuss what statistics, if any, are needed to answer them. Nonnumeric data such as ice cream flavors are better analyzed with frequency tables or graphs. If an average is desired, the mode would be the appropriate average to use.

Additional questions might include "Why should the average be reported?" "What average is most appropriate?" "Why?" "What degree of precision is needed?" These questions are essential and must be asked regularly. This sort of discussion will support students as they develop their data sense. The teaching of statistics in elementary school must aim higher than skill development. Students should know how to get a statistic, but they must also know what they have gotten.

Probability

In daily conversations, it is common to speak of events in terms of their chances of occurring. *Probability* is used to predict the chance of something happening. The terms *chance* and *probability* are often applied to those situations where the outcome cannot completely be determined in advance. Here are some examples of common probabilistic statements:

"The chance of rain today is 40 percent."

"The Cardinals are a 3-to-1 favorite to win."

"The probability of an accident on the job is less than 1 in 100."

"The patient has a 50–50 chance of recovering."

"If I study, I will probably pass the test."

"I am sure we will have a test Friday."

"We will have milk in the cafeteria today."

The first three statements are commonly heard and relate directly to probability. The last four illustrate a subtle but frequent use of probability in many everyday situations. In all of these cases, the utilitarian role of probability makes it an important basic skill. One way to increase students' awareness of the use of probability is to have them make a daily or weekly list of probability statements they have seen (in newspapers, magazines, or on television) or heard (on radio and television).

The grade-level expectations shown in Figure 17-1 illustrate how probability is intertwined with data analysis and statistics. In fact, according to the *NCTM Standards* (2000), ideas from probability serve as a foundation for the collection, description, and interpretation of data. Probability will not and should not be learned from formal definitions; rather, the presentation of varied examples and

Math Links 17.6

If you would like to see third graders engaged in a variety of probability experiences, you can view video clips and lesson plans for Chances Are, Parts I, II, and III from the PBS Mathline web site, which you can access from this book's web site.

www.wiley.com/college/reys

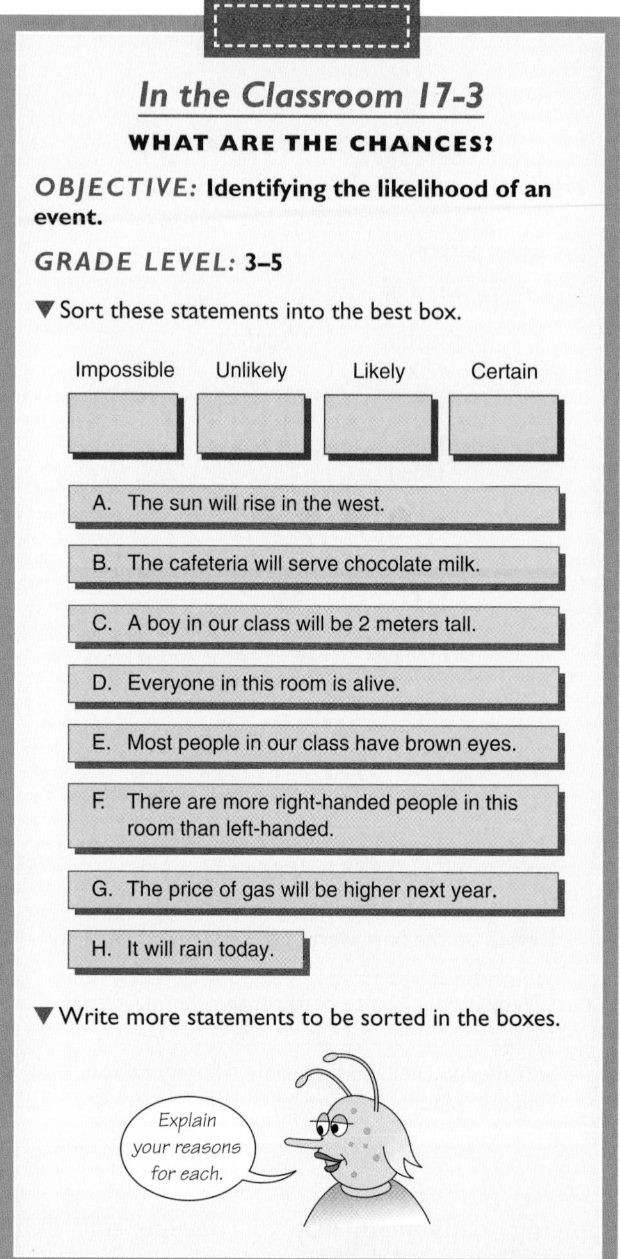

In the Classroom 17-3

WHAT ARE THE CHANCES?

OBJECTIVE: **Identifying the likelihood of an event.**

GRADE LEVEL: **3–5**

▼ Sort these statements into the best box.

Impossible	Unlikely	Likely	Certain

A. The sun will rise in the west.

B. The cafeteria will serve chocolate milk.

C. A boy in our class will be 2 meters tall.

D. Everyone in this room is alive.

E. Most people in our class have brown eyes.

F. There are more right-handed people in this room than left-handed.

G. The price of gas will be higher next year.

H. It will rain today.

▼ Write more statements to be sorted in the boxes.

Explain your reasons for each.

activities helps illustrate and clarify its important concepts. In the early grades, the treatment of probability should be informal. At all stages of instruction, though, teachers must use correct language to describe what is happening. This language serves as a model for children as they begin developing probability concepts and simultaneously add new probabilistic terms to their vocabulary. Let's look at appropriate ways for elementary students to experience some key concepts and terms.

Probability of an Event

Look at these statements that involve probability:

The probability of tossing a head is $\frac{1}{2}$.

The probability of rolling a four on a die is $\frac{1}{6}$.

The probability of having a birthday on February 30 is 0.

In these examples, tossing a head, rolling a four, and having a birthday on February 30 are *events,* or *outcomes.* Probability assigns a number (from zero to one) to an event. The more likely an event is to occur, the larger the number assigned to it, and so the probability is 1.0 when something is certain to happen. For example, the probability of students in an elementary class having been born is 1. On the other hand, the probability of something impossible happening is zero. For example, the probability of students in the class having been born on February 30 is zero. Therefore, all probabilities lie between zero and one. Through the grades, students should be able to move from situations in which the probability of an event can be determined to situations in which sampling and simulations help them quantify the likelihood of an uncertain outcome.

Long before children are ready to calculate probabilities of specific events, it is important that terms such as *certain, uncertain, impossible, likely,* and *unlikely* be introduced and discussed. Most students, even in primary grades, are familiar with the terms *impossible* and *certain* and can give meaningful examples. Although *likely* and *unlikely* are less familiar and require more careful development, using activities such as In the Classroom 17-3 with children provides a good start. As each card is sorted, an explanation or argument for placing it in the specific box should be given. This rationale is essential in refining and developing a clear understanding of these important terms.

An excellent extension at the bottom of In the Classroom 17-3 is to have students write statements to be sorted into the same categories. Each student should write several original statements and then exchange papers so that someone else classifies them. Once these general probabilistic terms become familiar, more specific probabilities can be determined.

In the Classroom 17-4

WHAT'S MORE LIKELY?

OBJECTIVE: **Determine the likelihood of an event.**

GRADE LEVEL: **4–5**

ACTIVITY ONE:

1. **If you put four red blocks in a paper bag, can you be sure what color block you will pull out? Why or why not?**
2. **If you put a green block in the bag with the red blocks, can you be sure what color block you will pull out? Why or why not? Try this experiment. Record your results.**
3. **If you put three green blocks in a bag with seven red blocks, is one color more likely to be pulled out? Why or why not? Try this experiment. Record your results.**
4. **Try a blocks-in-a-bag experiment of your own. Record your results.**

ACTIVITY TWO:

▼ Mary flipped a coin four times. It came up heads four times. She flipped the coin a fifth time. What is she likely to get on the fifth flip of the coin?

a) Heads
b) Tails
c) It is equally likely to be heads or tails.

▼ Explain your answer. How could you test your idea? Try your experiment and record your results.

The activities from In the Classroom 17-4 ask students to determine the likelihood of a particular event. Experiments involving blocks, spinners, dice, and coins are often used to introduce probability concepts and notation. Students should be given many opportunities to create and explore activities that ask them to answer questions about the likelihood of events, using the vocabulary of probability.

Math Links 17.7

A variety of electronic probability manipulatives may be found at the National Library of Virtual Manipulatives for Interactive Mathematics web site, which you can access from this book's web site. Some specific titles include Spinners, Stick or Switch, and Box Model.

Sample space is a fundamental concept that must be established or at least understood before the probabilities of specific events can be determined. The sample space for a probability problem represents all possible outcomes.

Lesson Idea 17-4 suggests ways to help children think about what outcomes are possible for a

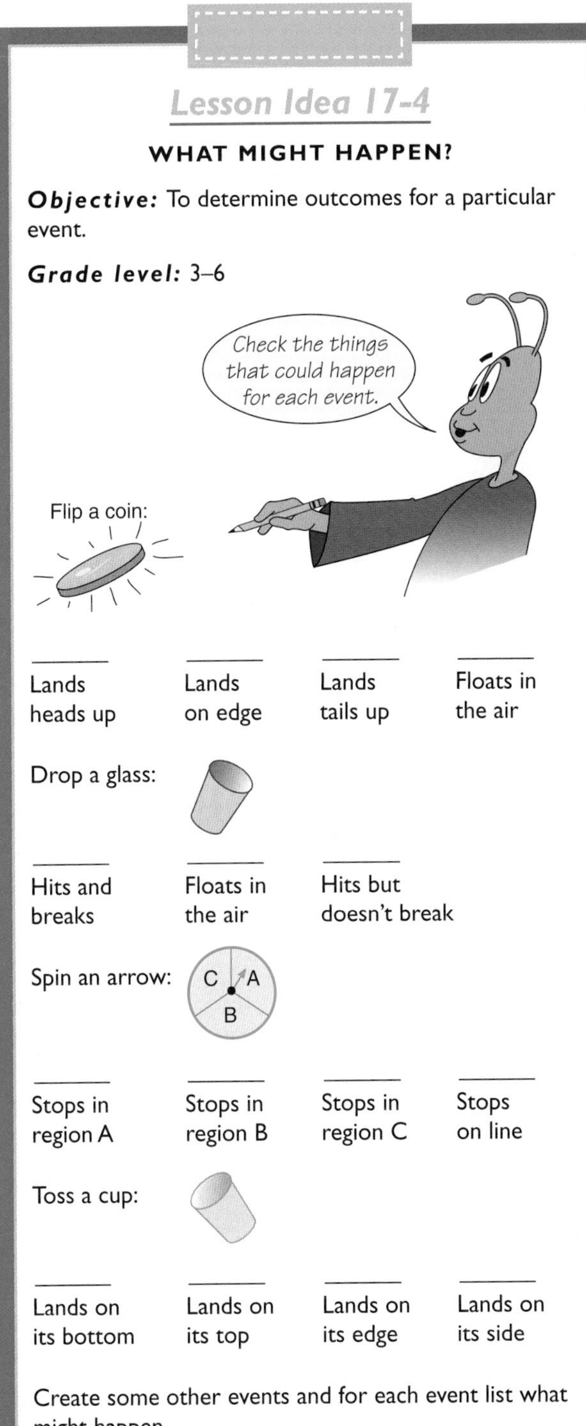

Lesson Idea 17-4
WHAT MIGHT HAPPEN?
Objective: To determine outcomes for a particular event.
Grade level: 3–6
Check the things that could happen for each event.
Flip a coin:
Lands heads up
Lands on edge
Lands tails up
Floats in the air
Drop a glass:
Hits and breaks
Floats in the air
Hits but doesn't break
Spin an arrow:
C
A
B
Stops in region A
Stops in region B
Stops in region C
Stops on line
Toss a cup:
Lands on its bottom
Lands on its top
Lands on its edge
Lands on its side
Create some other events and for each event list what might happen.

Table 17-1 • Sample spaces of some events and their probabilities

Questions	Sample space	Number of successes	Probability
What is the probability of getting a head on a single toss of a coin?	H, T	1	$\frac{1}{2}$
What is the probability of getting two heads when two coins are tossed?	HH, HT TH, TT	1	$\frac{1}{4}$
What is the probability of getting a five on a single roll of a die?	1, 2, 3, 4 5, 6	1	$\frac{1}{6}$
What is the probability of drawing a spade from a deck of 52 playing cards?	52 cards	13	$\frac{13}{52}$ or $\frac{1}{4}$
If each letter of the alphabet is written on a piece of paper, what is the probability of drawing a vowel?	26 letters of the alphabet	5 (a, e, i, o, u)	$\frac{5}{26}$

particular event. Consider, for example, the situation in which a coin is tossed. Some children may realize that a coin will not land on its edge, nor will it float. Thus only two outcomes can happen, and these possible outcomes comprise the sample space. Having children create their own events and determine possible outcomes is also a beneficial experience.

Once the sample space is known, the calculation of specific probabilities usually follows naturally. When a coin is flipped, as described in Table 17-1, the probability of a head is the number of ways a head can occur divided by the total number of outcomes (head or tail), or $\frac{1}{2}$. Specific probabilities rest heavily on fractions, which provide a direct and convenient means of reporting and interpreting probabilities.

Discussion of possible outcomes helps identify the sample space and clarify notions of probability. Questions along these lines might get the discussion started:

> Can the spinner shown in Lesson Idea 17-4 stop in region C if there is no area marked C?
>
> Can the spinner stop on a line?

Even though this outcome is unlikely, it can happen, and a plan of action should be specified if it does. (Maybe you spin again.) See Appendix B for spinner masters.

Consider the sample space for tossing cups, as shown in Lesson Idea 17-5. Is a cup equally likely to land on its top, its side, or its bottom? Without additional information, it would be difficult to decide.

Lesson Idea 17-5 provides suggestions for a possible start. In addition to helping children decide which outcomes are more or less likely, this exploration may lead to more precise statements. For example, one reasonable conclusion from the activity is that the probability of the cup landing on its side is about one-half.

In the Classroom 17-5 involves collecting data, graphing results, and exploring patterns. It uses several valuable ideas of probability, including sample space and probability of an event, in a natural and interesting setting. As children are involved in this process, they are developing and practicing basic facts, as was shown earlier in Chapter 9. Such an activity further illustrates how mathematical topics are interrelated and how important connections can be made.

Once you have tried In the Classroom 17-5 with children, another perspective can be obtained by examining Table 17-2, which summarizes the results when two dice are added (A) and multiplied (B). The diagonal of Table 17-2A shows all the ways that a sum of 7 can be obtained. Table 17-2A also shows the different ways that each of the other sums can result. Is the sum of two dice

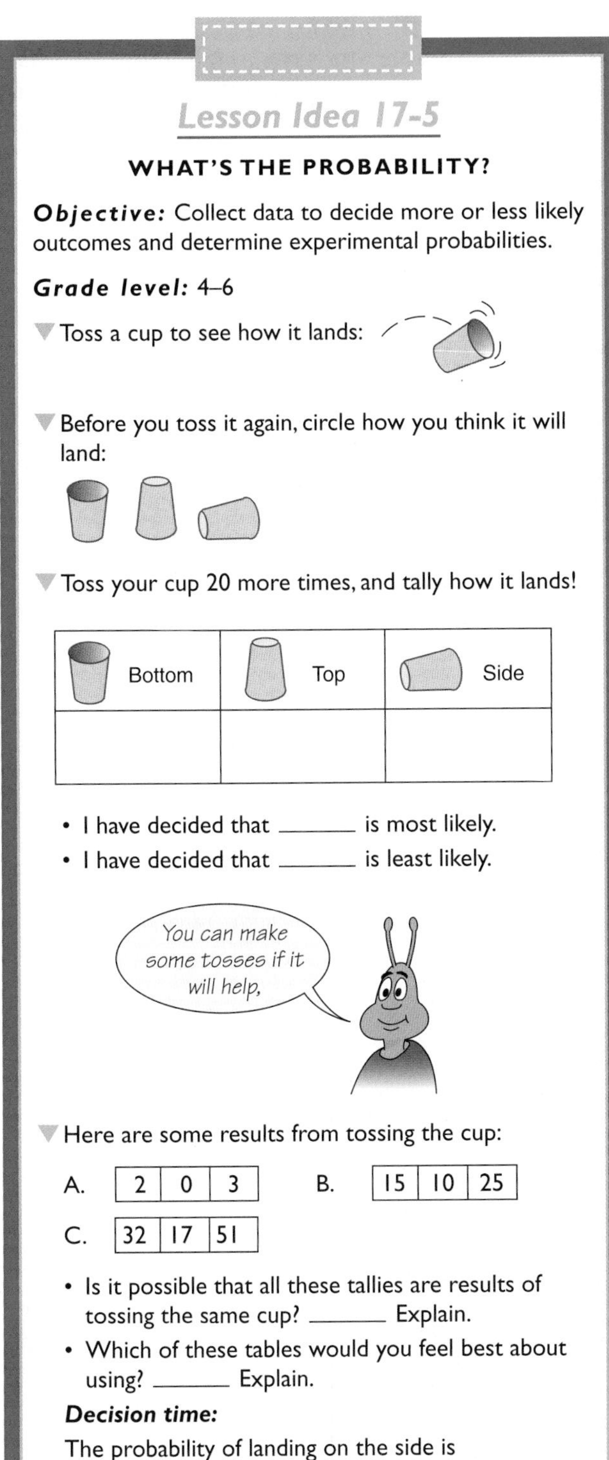

Lesson Idea 17-5

WHAT'S THE PROBABILITY?

Objective: Collect data to decide more or less likely outcomes and determine experimental probabilities.

Grade level: 4–6

- Toss a cup to see how it lands:
- Before you toss it again, circle how you think it will land:
- Toss your cup 20 more times, and tally how it lands!

Bottom	Top	Side

- I have decided that ______ is most likely.
- I have decided that ______ is least likely.

You can make some tosses if it will help,

- Here are some results from tossing the cup:

A. | 2 | 0 | 3 | B. | 15 | 10 | 25 |

C. | 32 | 17 | 51 |

- Is it possible that all these tallies are results of tossing the same cup? ______ Explain.
- Which of these tables would you feel best about using? ______ Explain.

Decision time:

The probability of landing on the side is about ______.

more likely to be even or odd? An examination of Table 17-2A shows that the even sums will occur 18 out of 36 times, or half the time.

Is the product of two dice more likely to be even or odd? The shaded cells in Table 17-2B show that the even products are much more likely. In fact, an even product would be expected to occur 27 times out of 36, or three-fourths of the time. Analyzing and discussing why this happens helps connect probability to properties and relationships between numbers and operations.

In the Classroom 17-5

ROLLING AND RECORDING

OBJECTIVE: **Conducting a probability experiment.**

GRADE LEVEL: **4–8**

▼ Try this:

1. **Choose a partner, and each of you make a chart like the one shown. Predict which sum of two dice will come up most often.**
2. **Each of you take turns rolling two dice.**
3. **On a turn, find the sum of the spots on the two dice, and place a tally mark in that column on your chart.**
4. **Continue rolling and recording until one of you has 10 tally marks in one column. Compare your prediction with the actual result.**

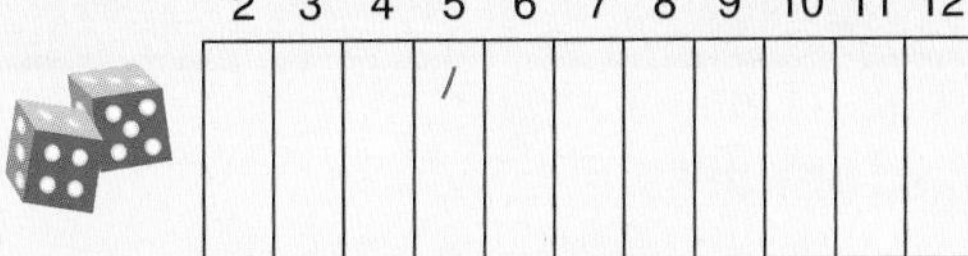

2	3	4	5	6	7	8	9	10	11	12
			/							

PUTTING IT TOGETHER:

- Why doesn't the chart need a ones column? A thirteens column?
- In which column did you or your partner reach 10?
- Compare your results, and tell how they are similar. Different.
- Tell why you would expect more sums of 7 than 2.
- Complete the following: "I would expect about the same number of sums of 4 as . . ."
- Would you expect to get about the same number of even sums as odd sums? Tell why.

EXTENDING THIS ACTIVITY:

Suppose you multiplied the numbers on the dice instead of adding them.

- How would the values along the top of the chart change?
- How many values (that is, different products) would be needed?
- Which values would be least likely?
- Would you expect to get about the same number of even values as odd values? Tell why.

Table 17-2 • Results of operations with two dice

+	1	2	3	4	5	6
1	2	3	4	5	6	7
2	3	4	5	6	7	8
3	4	5	6	7	8	9
4	5	6	7	8	9	10
5	6	7	8	9	10	11
6	7	8	9	10	11	12

A

×	1	2	3	4	5	6
1	1	2	3	4	5	6
2	2	4	6	8	10	12
3	3	6	9	12	15	18
4	4	8	12	16	20	24
5	5	10	15	20	25	30
6	6	12	18	24	30	36

B

Randomness

Randomness is an important concept underlying all learning in probability. When something is random, it means that it is not influenced by any factors other than chance. Lesson Idea 17-6 could be used to build on In the Classroom 17-3 and provides an opportunity to discuss randomness in a specific context. Here students are encouraged to think about events based on their classmates and decide about where these events would be placed on a probability number line that shows 0 and 1. Here are some starter questions:

> Why is it important that the "name will be randomly picked"?
>
> Should the names be seen by the person doing the drawing?
>
> Would it matter if some people wrote their names on large pieces of paper and others on small pieces of paper?

If the names are seen or if people don't all write their names on the same size of paper, the drawing might not be random. When this happens, some people would have an advantage and the notions of *fair* and *unfair* become important.

The term *fair* is often used in describing a situation. For example, to say "a fair coin" or "fair dice" makes it clear that no inherent biases exist that would affect randomness. A person may be asked to toss (not scoot) a die to ensure that one face is not favored. If Ping-Pong balls are drawn from a bowl, it is important that the balls be thoroughly mixed and the person doing the drawing be blindfolded to ensure both randomness and fairness. The children's book *No Fair!* (Holtzman, 1997) describes two children who are trying to determine when activities such as drawing an item from a bag are fair.

Discussions on the consequences of unfairness and absence of randomness should be a regular part of developing probability. For example, would it be fair if two dice are rolled and player A wins if the product is even and player B wins if the product is odd? Table 17-2B shows that A will win much more than B, so this game is not fair. On the

Lesson Idea 17-6

ARE YOU A WINNER?

Objective: Explore the concept of randomness

Grade Level: 4–8

Our class is having a drawing. Each person gets to place their name in the drawing one time. One name will be randomly picked, and that person will be the winner.

- Read each of the following statements.
- Think about the people in our class.
- Then, check the number line below and decide about where the following statements should be placed:

A. The winner will be left-handed.
B. The winner will be a girl.
C. The winner will be someone in our class.
D. The number of letters in the first name of the winner will be less than the number of letters in their last name.
E. The winner's first name will begin with a vowel.
F. The winner will wear glasses.
G. You will be the winner.
H. The winner will be wearing socks.
I. You will not be the winner.

0 Impossible — .5 or $\frac{1}{2}$ — 1 Certain to happen

other hand, if the game is based on the sum of two dice (Table 17-2A), each player has an equal chance of winning and the game is fair. Suppose you modify the sum-of-two-dice game to play with three players:

Player A wins if the sum is 1, 2, 3, or 4.

Player B wins if the sum is 5, 6, 7, or 8.

Player C wins if the sum is 9, 10, 11, or 12.

Is this game fair for each of the players? Does each player have the same chance of winning? An analysis of Table 17-2A suggests that Player B will win more often than either of the other players. As children explore this game, you might challenge them to tell how the game might be modified to make it fair for everyone.

Independence of Events

Independence of events is an important concept in probability, but one that does not develop naturally from intuition. If two events are independent, one event in no way affects the outcome of the other. Thus if a coin is tossed, lands heads, and then is tossed again, it is still equally likely to land heads or tails. This sounds simple enough, but consider this question: Suppose four consecutive sixes have occurred on four rolls of a fair die. What is the probability of getting a six on the next roll?

Research shows that a majority of middle-grade students miss this question (Shaughnessy, 1992). Many students suggested that the die had a "memory," and things would "even out." Most did not conclude that the probability was unchanged, regardless of what had already happened. If an event has occurred a number of times in a row, most people falsely presume that the "law of averages" makes it unlikely that the event will occur on the next trial. This basic misunderstanding contradicts the notion of independence of certain events.

Having children collect data and discuss the results can help dispel some of this erroneous thinking. When you use In the Classroom 17-6 with children, different students will produce different results, yet the answers to the questions will be very similar. Why? Because these events, the rolls of a die, are independent of one another.

Tossing a coin and recording the outcomes in sequence will likely generate some long runs of an occurrence, even though each outcome is independent of the others. Although the probability of a head is $\frac{1}{2}$, children might flip a coin 10 times and get eight, nine, or even ten heads in a row. Consider this record of 20 tosses of a coin:

In the Classroom 17-6

CAN YOU MAKE PREDICTIONS?

OBJECTIVE: **Identifying independence of events.**

GRADE LEVEL: **4–6**

▼ Roll a die six times and record the results:

1	2	3	4	5	6

- Did each face appear once? ________
- Does knowing what happened on the first roll help predict the second? ________ the third? ________

▼ Roll a die 24 times and record the results.

1	2	3	4	5	6	7	8	9	10	11	12
13	14	15	16	17	18	19	20	21	22	23	24

- Did each face appear once? ________ the same number of times? ________
- What face appeared most? ________
- Does this mean the die is unfair? ________
- Does this record tell you what will occur on the next roll? ________

T T T T T H T H H H H T T H H T H H H H

There are two sequences of four consecutive heads and one of five consecutive tails. Overall, 11 heads appeared. Such analysis and discussion helps children understand that things don't even out on each flip. As the number of flips gets very large, however, the ratio of heads to the total number of flips will get closer and closer to the theoretical expected value of $\frac{1}{2}$. This latter point is very important, but it often baffles elementary students. Using simulation programs to repeat an event many times helps children better understand the notion of the expression, *in the long run.*

There are, of course, times when one event may depend on another. For example, suppose you wanted to roll two dice and obtain a sum of 8. If a 1 is shown on the first die, it is impossible to get a sum of 8. This leads toward notions of *conditional probability.*

Instruction is needed to develop the necessary techniques to solve simple probability problems. There are other very complicated situations for which probabilities are difficult to calculate. What is the probability of the New York Mets winning the World Series? Of a woman being elected president? Such questions do not lend themselves to simple solutions, but experts can approximate their probabilities. Regardless of who determines the numerical probabilities, the knowledge and interpretative skills developed in simpler probability situations can be successfully applied.

Misconceptions in Probability

Young children often hold common misconceptions about various aspects of probability. For example, they make predictions based on preference, such as their favorite color or number. They also hold biases against certain numbers, believing, for example, that it may be hardest to throw a 6 on a die. Young children are not surprised by extremely unlikely events and do not search for underlying causes. They may expect all outcomes in an experiment to be equally likely. It is also difficult for many children to make inferences from data.

Do not be surprised by these findings with your own students. The more opportunities you give them to explore a variety of probability notions through hands-on activities, the better they will be able to develop and evaluate inferences and predictions that are based on data and apply basic concepts of probability.

A Glance at Where We've Been

Data analysis, statistics, and probability provide an opportunity for students to develop problem-solving and critical thinking skills as well as to make connections to other mathematical topics and school subjects. Students engage in the process of data analysis by posing questions that are meaningful to them, collecting the data to answer the questions, and displaying the data in a way that helps others understand and interpret the results. Teachers and students pose questions about the data together, extending students' abilities to analyze their results and communicate their findings in a way that represents the data in a truthful manner.

In the elementary and early middle-school years, students are exposed to many types of graphs: line plots, stem-and-leaf plots, picture graphs, bar graphs, pie graphs, line graphs, and box plots. Graphing calculators and other technological tools and programs allow students opportunities to experiment with different ways of displaying data, therefore developing multiple perspectives for the same set of data. This helps promote data sense.

Students in the elementary grades learn to analyze data using descriptive statistics, especially measures of variation and central tendency. The goal is to understand fundamental notions related to the statistics and to be able to choose averages that are most appropriate and describe the data in a meaningful way.

Probabilistic thinking develops in elementary students through a variety of hands-on activities and experiments that challenge their intuitive notions of what is fair and unfair. The ability to use the language of probability is an important skill in our daily lives, and it can be explored in many ways that help build excitement for learning mathematics.

Things to Do: From What You've Read

1. Here are the results on three tests: 68, 78, 88. What are the mean and the median? Explain why the mode is of little value. What score would be needed on the next test to get an average of 81? Describe two different ways you could determine this score.
2. Arrange interlocking cubes together in lengths of 3, 6, 6, and 9.
   a. Describe how you could use the blocks to find the mean, median, and mode.
   b. Suppose you introduce another length of 10 cubes. Has the mean changed? the median? the mode?
3. Answer each of the following questions, and tell why you answered as you did.
   a. Is it possible for a set of data to have more than one mode? Give an example.
   b. Is it easier to find the median of 25 or 24 student scores?
   c. Could the mean be as large as the largest value in a set of data? Tell how.

4. Describe how the activities in Lesson Idea 17-4 could be used to discuss probabilities of zero and one.
5. Ten cards are marked 0, 1, 2, 3, . . . , 9 and placed face down. If the cards are shuffled and then one card is drawn, tell why the following statements are true:
   a. The sample space has 10 events.
   b. The probability of drawing the 6 is 1/10.
   c. The probability of drawing the 3 is the same as the probability of drawing the 7.
6. Many state lotteries advertise with a slogan, "If you don't play, you can't win." Does that mean if you do play, you will win? Explain.
7. The chance of picking six numbers correctly in a state lottery depends on the numbers from which you select. Explain why you would rather pick from the set of numbers 1 through 10 than from the set of numbers 1 through 20. About how much better are your chances of winning with the smaller set of numbers than with the larger set of numbers?

Things to Do: Going Beyond This Book

IN THE FIELD

1. *Use In the Classroom 17-1 with a small group of children as they plan and conduct a survey. Describe how it went.
2. Review the *Wonderful World of Mathematics* (Thiessen et al., 1998). Find a book related to statistics or probability that is highly recommended. Read the book with some children and describe how they reacted.
3. *Use In the Classroom 17-2 with some children in grades 4-8. Which key features of various graphs and statistics did you discuss with the children? Write several questions about the graphs using the levels described by Curcio (1989). How did you guide the children to create higher-level questions?
4. *Working with children, use In the Classroom ideas 17-3, 17-4, 17-5, or 17-6 to teach a hands-on lesson on probability. You can also use Master 17-6, Mystery Bags, in the *Helping Children Learn Mathematics Instructor's Manual* (available at the Wiley Book Companion web site. Reflect on how the lesson went.
5. *Select a middle school student and use In the Classroom 17-2 to conduct the interview for statistics and probability. What did you learn about the child's thinking?

IN YOUR JOURNAL

6. Examine the scope-and-sequence chart for an elementary textbook series used in your school. At what level is graphing first introduced? What kinds of graphing skills are highlighted? What important statistical topics are included? At what levels are they taught? Do the same for probability.
7. Why do you think some teachers still consider data analysis, statistics, and probability to be unimportant additions to the mathematics curriculum?
8. What would you say to a principal who accused you of allowing your students to "play games" when they were conducting dice experiments?

WITH ADDITIONAL RESOURCES

9. Review the NCTM books *Making Sense of Data* (Lindquist et al., 1992) and *Dealing with Data and Chance* (Zawojewski et al., 1991). Select an activity. Decide where and how you would use it in teaching a lesson.
10. Examine newspapers or magazines. Start a file of graphs students can examine. Make a list of the different kinds of graphs used. Select a few and tell why you think a particular graph (e.g., picture graph, pie graph, bar graph) was used in each situation.
11. Select one of the activities from *Probability* (Phillips et al., 1986, or Burns, 1995). Develop the materials needed and write a lesson plan that could be used to teach the lesson. If possible, teach the lesson.
12. Examine the March 1999 issue of *Mathematics Teaching in the Middle School,* which was a focus issue on data and chance. Select an article to read and use as a basis for preparing a lesson plan.
13. Games are fun and can help develop a better understanding of probability. Play the game Montana Red Dog, described in *Dealing with Data and Chance* (Zawojewski et al., 1991), play one of the games from "Fair Games, Unfair Games" (Bright et al., 1981), *What Are My Chances?* (Shulte and Choate, 1996), or the "Cover Up Game" from *Chance Encounters: Probability in Games and Simulation* (Brutlag,

---

*Additional activities, suggestions, or questions are provided in *Teaching Elementary Mathematics: A Resource for Field Experiences* (Wiley, 2004).

1996). Identify some of the mathematics learned in these games. Tell how you might use these games with students.

14. Read one of the research articles related to probability or statistics listed in Bright and Hoeffner (1993), Shaughnessy (1992), or Friel et al. (1997). Discuss the nature of the research. Also identify an instructional idea or activity suggested by the research that you think would be effective in helping children learn a particular concept.

15. Examine one of the following books from the *Used Numbers: Real Data in the Classroom* series, published by Dale Seymour Publications:

    Counting: Ourselves and Our Families (K–1)
    Sorting: Groups and Graphs (2–3)
    Measuring: From Paces to Feet (3–4)
    Statistics: The Shape of the Data (4–6)
    Statistics: Prediction and Sampling (5–6)
    Statistics: Middles, Means, and In-Betweens (5–6)

    Choose an activity and discuss how it might be presented to a group of students. Better yet, present it to an appropriate group of students. Discuss what happened.

WITH TECHNOLOGY

16. Use technology such as spreadsheet, graphing, or survey software or a graphing calculator to display and analyze data. Evaluate how these tools might be used with children. Better yet, try it out with children and then evaluate.

17. Check the Web for the NCTM's Illuminations activities. Look for an activity that can be used in helping elementary children understand probabilty. If you can, try this activity with some students.

18. Investigate some of the links to mathematics teaching resources related to probability, data analysis, or statistics. Modify a lesson plan to use with your own students.

Book Nook for Children

Arnold, Caroline. *Charts and Graphs: Fun, Facts, and Activities*. New York: Franklin Watts, 1984.

Photographs and drawings are used to illustrate real-world applications and examples using pie, bar, and line graphs and pictographs. Illustrations are colorful and interesting and provide a multicultural focus for the book. The glossary is written in terms children can understand and is helpful in comparing various ways of presenting information.

Cushman, Jean. *Do You Wanna Bet? Your Chance to Find Out about Probability.* New York: Clarion Books, 1991.

Whether flipping coins to decide what television program to watch or analyzing which events are "certain," "impossible," or "maybe," Danny and Brian become involved in everyday situations, both in and out of school, that involve probability. Cushman has woven several important probability concepts into an interesting storyline with activities for the reader throughout the book. A bibliography of resources that includes children's books and an index of concepts and activities are a plus.

Diagram Group. *Comparisons*. New York: St. Martin's Press, 1980.

Comparisons of distance, size, area, volume, mass, weight, density, energy, temperature, time, speed, and number throughout the universe.

Holtzman, Caren. *No Fair!* New York: Scholastic, 1997.

When Kristy and David cannot agree on which game to play, David brings out a bag of marbles and says they can play Kristy's game if she chooses a blue marble, but Kristy objects when she learns that only one marble was blue.

James, Elizabeth. *What Do You Mean by "Average"? Means, Medians, and Modes.* New York: Lothrop, Lee & Shepard Books, 1978.

The plans of Jill's student council campaign to appeal to the "average" student lead to an exploration of means, medians, and modes. Other concepts defined and explored include ranges, sampling, random sampling, weighting a sample, and universe. How to collect and tabulate data and how to transform them into percentages and graphs are also presented.

Linn, Charles F. *Probability*. New York: Thomas Y. Crowell Publishers, 1972.

Mathematics helps scientists, pollsters, and industrialists make confident predictions using probability theory. By working through the experiments in this interesting and challenging book, young readers can get a feel for what is involved in probability theory. The activities grow in complexity, but the clear directions and illustrations avoid confusion. With each activity, the theory is explained in the context of its usefulness as a means of prediction.

McGrath, Barbara B. *More M&M's Brand Chocolate Candies Math*. Watertown, MA: Charlesbridge, 1998.
Millions of children learned to count with *The M&M's Brand Chocolate Candies Counting Book*, and now there's another fun-filled book that takes math skills to the next level. Topics covered include estimation, simple graphing, factoring, multiplication, problem solving, division, and simple fractions. The instructive text and colorful illustrations will appeal to younger children ready to explore the challenges of more advanced math concepts as well as to older children needing an entertaining and user-friendly review.

Mori, Tuyosi. *Socrates and the Three Pigs*. New York: Philomel Books, 1986.
Socrates, a wolf, and his friend Pythagoras, a frog, must figure out how to capture a succulent pig for Xanthippe, Socrates' hungry wife. This unusual book tackles the complicated problems of probability and combinatorial analysis through a series of diagrams showing all possibilities in determining in which of five houses one of the pigs could be found. The intent of this book is to introduce a sophisticated topic in an intuitive manner that leads to understanding through patterns and counting.

Murphy, Stuart J. *The Best Vacation Ever*. New York: HarperCollins, 1997.
This entry in the MathStart series demonstrates that collecting data and tabulating results can help the decision-making process. A girl with an active, overscheduled family puts math to work to coordinate a family expedition. She uses charts to plot her family's preferences.

Parker, Tom. *In One Day*. Boston, MA: Houghton Mifflin Co., 1984.
Three hundred sixty-five statistics describing things Americans do in one day are presented in this book. Some of the diverse topics included are data on health, spending habits, accidents, crime, and our environment. The reader should be aware of when the data were collected because some of the facts are obviously outdated. Nevertheless, readers should find the facts and illustrations fascinating and the information a benchmark for estimation and number sense.

Srivastava, Jane J. *Averages*. New York: Thomas Y. Crowell Publishers, 1975.
Averages—mode, median, and mean—are introduced in an easily read text that is complemented by humorous illustrations. This clever book encourages children to try the interesting activities that are clearly illustrated within it.

Resources

ANNOTATED BOOKS

Ameis, Jerry, A., and Ebenezer, Jazlin, V. *Mathematics on the Internet: A Resource for K-12 Teachers*. Upper Saddle River, NJ: Merrill Prentice Hall, 2002.
This book helps teachers become better acquainted with some of the resource materials and information available on the Internet to support teaching and learning mathematics. All web sites have been carefully reviewed to ensure that they are useful and of sufficient quality.

Pfenning, Nancy. *Chances Are . . . : Making Probability & Statistics Fun to Learn & Easy to Teach*. Waco, TX: Prufrock Press, 1997.
This book offers teachers a simple method for teaching probability and statistics in a fun and enjoyable way. From helping to win a card game to projecting the rate of growth of a virus, the uses of probability and statistics are virtually endless. This book offers a hands-on guide to teaching these valuable subjects. For teachers of elementary students, the book offers simple, hands-on lessons and activities about probability and basic statistics. For teachers of older students, advanced statistical concepts are discussed and activities provided.

Landwehr, James M., and Watkins, Ann E. *Exploring Data*. Palo Alto, CA.: Dale Seymour Publications, 1986.
This book is an introduction to statistics. In addition to learning the most up-to-date statistical techniques, students are provided an opportunity to practice techniques in other areas of mathematics. Statistical topics include tables of data, the mean, scatter plots, stem-and-leaf plots, box plots, and smoothing.

Newman, Clair M.; Obremski, Thomas E.; and Scheaffer, Richard, L. *Exploring Probability*. Palo Alto, CA.: Dale Seymour Publications, 1987.
This book covers elementary probability by using only counting skills and some knowledge of fractions. The material is designed to give students a working knowledge of basic probability.

ANNOTATED ARTICLES

Begg, Andy, and Edwards, Roger. "Teachers' Ideas about Teaching Statistics." ERIC-NO:ED455195, 1999.
This research investigated notions raised in the literature about teachers' lack of statistical background and knowledge. It focused on four assumptions: (1) elementary school teachers have a rich source of ideas about statistics from their everyday teaching experiences; (2) they have a greater understanding of statistics than they are often given credit for; (3) their ideas influence their teaching; and (4) their ideas about teaching statistics are closely influenced by their ideas about teaching mathematics.

Friel, Susan. "Teaching Statistics: What's Average?" In *The Teaching and Learning of Algorithms in School Mathematics,* 1998 Yearbook (ed. Lorna J. Morrow). Reston, VA: NCTM, 1998, pp. 208–217.
This article discusses strategies for building conceptual and procedural understandings in teaching mean, median, and mode. Developing "data sense" includes a consideration of the "when and why" of the use of the representations and statistics.

Quinn, Robert J. "Having Fun with Baseball Statistics." *Mathematics Teaching in the Middle School,* 1 (10), (May 1996), pp. 780–785.
Fractions, decimals, percents, rounding, Cartesian coordinates, probability, and statistics are all integrated into a baseball statistics game.

Quinn, Robert, and Wiest, Lynda. "Reinventing Scrabble with Middle School Students." *Mathematics Teaching in the Middle School,* 5 (December 1999), pp. 210–213.
Students use the Scrabble game to explore frequency distribution and other topics as they work cooperatively to collect, analyze, and interpret data.

Russell, Susan Jo, and Corwin, Rebecca B. *Used Numbers—Statistics: The Shape of the Data, Grades 4–6.* Palo Alto, CA.: Dale Seymour Publications, 1989.
Here is a one- to four-class session unit on data collection, description, and interpretation for students in grades 4–6.

Sakshaug, Lynae; "Which Graph Is Which?" *Teaching Children Mathematics,* 6 (March 2000), pp. 454–455.
Ideas for engaging elementary children in graphing. Problem posed.

Sakshaug, Lynae E., and Wohlhuter, Kay A. "Responses to the Which Graph Is Which? Problem." *Teaching Children Mathematics,* 7 (February 2001), pp. 350–353.
Responses to the problem in the previous citation are presented.

ADDITIONAL REFERENCES

Bamberger, Honi, and Hughes, Patricia. *Super Graphs, Venns, and Glyphs.* New York: Scholastic, 1995.

Bohan, Harry; Irby, Beverly; and Vogel, Dolly. "Problem Solving: Dealing with Data in the Elementary School." *Teaching Children Mathematics,* 1 (January 1995), pp. 256–260.

Bright, George W., and Hoeffner, Karl. "Measurement, Probability, Statistics and Graphing." In *Research Ideas for the Classroom: Middle Grades Mathematics* (ed. Douglas T. Owens). Reston, VA: NCTM; and New York: Macmillan, 1993, pp. 78–98.

Bright, George W.; Harvey, John G.; and Wheeler, Margarette Montague. "Fair Games, Unfair Games." In *Teaching Statistics and Probability,* 1981 Yearbook (ed. Albert Shulte). Reston, VA: NCTM, 1981, pp. 49–59.

Brutlag, Dan. *Chance Encounters: Probability in Games and Simulation.* Palo Alto, CA.: Creative Publications, 1996.

Burns, Marilyn. *About Teaching Mathematics: A K–8 Resource.* Sausalito, CA.: Math Solutions Publications, 2000.

Burns, Marilyn. *Math By All Means: Probability Grades 3–4.* Sausalito, CA.: Math Solutions Publications, 1995.

Corwin, Rebecca, and Friel, Susan. *Used Numbers—Statistics: Prediction and Sampling, Grades 5–6.* Menlo Park, CA.: Dale Seymour Publications, 1990.

Curcio, Frances R. *Developing Graph Comprehension: Elementary and Middle School Activities.* Reston, VA: NCTM, 1989.

Educational Testing Service. *NAEP 1992 Mathematics Report Card for the Nation and the States.* Princeton, NJ: ETS, 1992.

Folkson, Susan. "Meaningful Communication among Children: Data Collection." In *Communication in Mathematics,* 1996 Yearbook (ed. Portia Elliott), Reston, VA: NCTM, 1996, pp. 29–34.

Freeman, Marji. *Creative Graphing.* White Plains, NY: Cuisenaire Co., 1986.

Friel, Susan; Bright, George; and Curcio, Frances. "Understanding Students' Understanding of Graphs." *Mathematics Teaching in the Middle School,* 3 (November-December 1997), pp. 224-227.

Friel, Susan; Mokros, Janice; and Russell, Susan Jo. *Used Numbers-Middles, Means, and In-Betweens, Grades 5, 6.* Palo Alto, CA.: Dale Seymour Publications, 1992.

Hitch, Chris, and Armstrong, Georganna. "Daily Activities for Data Analysis." *Arithmetic Teacher,* 41 (January 1994), pp. 242–245.

Kenney, Patricia Ann, and Silver, Edward A. (eds.) *Results from the Sixth Mathematics Assessment of the National Assessment of Educational Progress.* Reston, VA: NCTM, 1997.

Lindquist, Mary M.; Lauquire, J.; Gardner, A.; and Shekaramiz, S. *Making Sense of Data.* Reston, VA: NCTM, 1992.

Morita, June. "Capture and Recapture Your Students' Interest in Statistics." *Mathematics Teaching in the Middle School,* 4 (March 1999), pp. 412–418.

National Council of Teachers of Mathematics. *Mathematics Teaching in the Middle School Focus Issue: Data and Chance in the Middle School Curriculum* 4 (March 1999).

National Council of Teachers of Mathematics. *Principles and Standards for School Mathematics* Reston, VA: NCTM 2000.

Phillips, Elizabeth; Lappan, Glenda; Winter, Mary Jane; and Fitzgerald, William. *Probability.* Menlo Park, CA: Addison-Wesley, 1986.

Scavo, Thomas R., and Petraroja, Byron. "Adventures in Statistics." *Teaching Children Mathematics,* 4 (March 1998), pp. 394–400.

Shaughnessy, J. Michael. "Research in Probability and Statistics: Reflections and Directions." In *Handbook of Research on Mathematics Teaching and Learning* (ed. Douglas Grouws). New York: Macmillan, 1992, pp. 495–514.

Shulte, Albert P., and Choate, Stuart A. *What Are My Chances?* Palo Alto, CA: Creative Publications, 1996.

Thiessen, Diane; Matthias, Margaret; and Smith, Jacquelin. *The Wonderful World of Mathematics: A Critically Annotated List of Children's Books in Mathematics.* Reston, VA: NCTM, 1998.

Uccellini, John C. "Teaching the Mean Meaningfully." *Mathematics Teaching in the Middle School,* 2 (2), (November–December 1996), pp. 112–115.

Wilson, Melvin R. (Skip), and Krapfl, Carol M. "Exploring Mean, Median, and Mode with a Spreadsheet." *Mathematics Teaching in the Middle School,* 1 (6), (September–October 1995), pp. 490–495.

Zawojewski, Judith S.; Brooks, G.; Dinkelkamp, L.; Goldberg, E.; Goldberg, H.; Hyde, A.; Jackson, T.; Landau, M.; Martin, H.; Nowakowski, J.; Paull, S.; Shulte, A.; Wagreich, P.; and Wilmot, B. *Dealing with Data and Chance.* Reston, VA: NCTM, 1991.

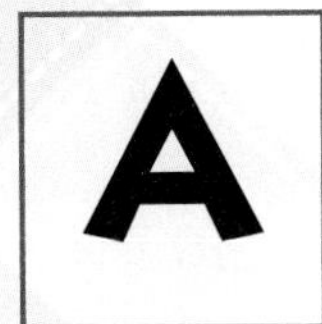

Standards and Expectations National Council of Teachers of Mathematics, 2000

Number and Operations

Standard	Pre-K–2	Grades 3–5	Grades 6–8
Instructional programs from prekindergarten through grade 12 should enable all students to—	***EXPECTATIONS*** In prekindergarten through grade 2 all students should—	***EXPECTATIONS*** In grades 3–5 all students should—	***EXPECTATIONS*** In grades 6–8 all students should—
Understand numbers, ways of representing numbers, relationships among numbers, and number systems	• count with understanding and recognize "how many" in sets of objects; • use multiple models to develop initial understandings of place value and the base-ten number system; • develop understanding of the relative position and magnitude of whole numbers and of ordinal and cardinal numbers and their connections; • develop a sense of whole numbers and represent and use them in flexible ways, including relating, composing, and decomposing numbers; • connect number words and numerals to the quantities they represent, using various physical models and representations; • understand and represent commonly used fractions, such as $\frac{1}{4}$, $\frac{1}{3}$, and $\frac{1}{2}$.	• understand the place-value structure of the base-ten number system and be able to represent and compare whole numbers and decimals; • recognize equivalent representations for the same number and generate them by decomposing and composing numbers; • develop understanding of fractions as parts of unit wholes, as parts of a collection, as locations on number lines, and as divisions of whole numbers; • use models, benchmarks, and equivalent forms to judge the size of fractions; • recognize and generate equivalent forms of commonly used fractions, decimals, and percents; • explore numbers less than 0 by extending the number line and through familiar applications; • describe classes of numbers according to characteristics such as the nature of their factors.	• work flexibly with fractions, decimals, and percents to solve problems; • compare and order fractions, decimals, and percents efficiently and find their approximate locations on a number line; • develop meaning for percents greater than 100 and less than 1; • understand and use ratios and proportions to represent quantitative relationships; • develop an understanding of large numbers and recognize and appropriately use exponential, scientific, and calculator notation; • use factors, multiples, prime factorization, and relatively prime numbers to solve problems; • develop meaning for integers and represent and compare quantities with them.
Understand meanings of operations and how they relate to one another	• understand various meanings of addition and subtraction of whole numbers and the relationship between the two operations; • understand the effects of adding and subtracting whole numbers; • understand situations that entail multiplication and division, such as equal groupings of objects and sharing equally.	• understand various meanings of multiplication and division; • understand the effects of multiplying and dividing whole numbers; • identify and use relationships between operations, such as division as the inverse of multiplication, to solve problems; • understand and use properties of operations, such as the distributivity of multiplication over addition.	• understand the meaning and effects of arithmetic operations with fractions, decimals, and integers; • use the associative and commutative properties of addition and multiplication and the distributive property of multiplication over addition to simplify computations with integers, fractions, and decimals; • understand and use the inverse relationships of addition and subtraction, multiplication and division, and squaring and finding square roots to simplify computations and solve problems.
Compute fluently and make reasonable estimates	• develop and use strategies for whole-number computations, with a focus on addition and subtraction; • develop fluency with basic number combinations for addition and subtraction; • use a variety of methods and tools to compute, including objects, mental computation, estimation, paper and pencil, and calculators.	• develop fluency with basic number combinations for multiplication and division and use these combinations to mentally compute related problems, such as 30×50; • develop fluency in adding, subtracting, multiplying, and dividing whole numbers; • develop and use strategies to estimate the results of whole-number computations and to judge the reasonableness of such results; • develop and use strategies to estimate computations involving fractions and decimals in situations relevant to students' experience; • use visual models, benchmarks, and equivalent forms to add and subtract commonly used fractions and decimals; • select appropriate methods and tools for computing with whole numbers from among mental computation, estimation, calculators, and paper and pencil according to the context and nature of the	• select appropriate methods and tools for computing with fractions and decimals from among mental computation, estimation, calculators or computers, and paper and pencil, depending on the situation, and apply the selected methods; • develop and analyze algorithms for computing with fractions, decimals, and integers and develop fluency in their use; • develop and use strategies to estimate the results of rational-number computations and judge the reasonableness of the results; • develop, analyze, and explain methods for solving problems involving proportions, such as scaling and finding equivalent ratios.

Table of Standards and Expectations. Reprinted with permission from *Principles and Standards for School Mathematics*, copyright by the National Council of Teachers of Mathematics.

Algebra

Standard	Pre-K–2	Grades 3–5	Grades 6–8
Instructional programs from prekindergarten through grade 12 should enable all students to—	***EXPECTATIONS*** In prekindergarten through grade 2 all students should—	***EXPECTATIONS*** In grades 3–5 all students should—	***EXPECTATIONS*** In grades 6–8 all students should—
Understand patterns, relations, and functions	• sort, classify, and order objects by size, number, and other properties; • recognize, describe, and extend patterns such as sequences of sounds and shapes or simple numeric patterns and translate from one representation to another; • analyze how both repeating and growing patterns are generated.	• describe, extend, and make generalizations about geometric and numeric patterns; • represent and analyze patterns and functions, using words, tables, and graphs.	• represent, analyze, and generalize a variety of patterns with tables, graphs, words, and, when possible, symbolic rules; • relate and compare different forms of representation for a relationship; • identify functions as linear or nonlinear and contrast their properties from tables, graphs, or equations.
Represent and analyze mathematical situations and structures using algebraic symbols	• illustrate general principles and properties of operations, such as commutativity, using specific numbers; • use concrete, pictorial, and verbal representations to develop an understanding of invented and conventional symbolic notations.	• identify such properties as commutativity, associativity, and distributivity and use them to compute with whole numbers; • represent the idea of a variable as an unknown quantity using a letter or symbol; • express mathematical relationships using equations.	• develop an initial conceptual understanding of different uses of variables; • explore relationships between symbolic expressions and graphs of lines, paying particular attention to the meaning of intercept and slope; • use symbolic algebra to represent situations and to solve problems, especially those that involve linear relationships; • recognize and generate equivalent forms for simple algebraic expressions and solve linear equations.
Use mathematical models to represent and understand quantitative relationships	• model situations that involve the addition and subtraction of whole numbers, using objects, pictures, and symbols.	• model problem situations with objects and use representations such as graphs, tables, and equations to draw conclusions.	• model and solve contextualized problems using various representations, such as graphs, tables, and equations.
Analyze change in various contexts	• describe qualitative change, such as a student's growing taller; • describe quantitative change, such as a student's growing two inches in one year.	• investigate how a change in one variable relates to a change in a second variable; • identify and describe situations with constant or varying rates of change and compare them.	• use graphs to analyze the nature of changes in quantities in linear relationships.

Table of Standards and Expectations. Reprinted with permission from *Principles and Standards for School Mathematics,*

Geometry

Standard	Pre-K–2	Grades 3–5	Grades 6–8
Instructional programs from prekindergarten through grade 12 should enable all students to—	***EXPECTATIONS*** In prekindergarten through grade 2 all students should—	***EXPECTATIONS*** In grades 3–5 all students should—	***EXPECTATIONS*** In grades 6–8 all students should—
Analyze characteristics and properties of two- and three-dimensional geometric shapes and develop mathematical arguments about geometric relationships	• recognize, name, build, draw, compare, and sort two- and three-dimensional shapes; • describe attributes and parts of two- and three-dimensional shapes; • investigate and predict the results of putting together and taking apart two- and three-dimensional shapes.	• identify, compare, and analyze attributes of two- and three-dimensional shapes and develop vocabulary to describe the attributes; • classify two- and three-dimensional shapes according to their properties and develop definitions of classes of shapes such as triangles and pyramids; • investigate, describe, and reason about the results of subdividing, combining, and transforming shapes; • explore congruence and similarity; • make and test conjectures about geometric properties and relationships and develop logical arguments to justify conclusions.	• precisely describe, classify, and understand relationships among types of two- and three-dimensional objects using their defining properties; • understand relationships among the angles, side lengths, perimeters, areas, and volumes of similar objects; • create and critique inductive and deductive arguments concerning geometric ideas and relationships, such as congruence, similarity, and the Pythagorean relationship.
Specify locations and describe spatial relationships using coordinate geometry and other representational systems	• describe, name, and interpret relative positions in space and apply ideas about relative position; • describe, name, and interpret direction and distance in navigating space and apply ideas about direction and distance; • find and name locations with simple relationships such as "near to" and in coordinate systems such as maps.	• describe location and movement using common language and geometric vocabulary; • make and use coordinate systems to specify locations and to describe paths; • find the distance between points along horizontal and vertical lines of a coordinate system.	• use coordinate geometry to represent and examine the properties of geometric shapes; • use coordinate geometry to examine special geometric shapes, such as regular polygons or those with pairs or parallel or perpendicular sides.
Apply transformations and use symmetry to analyze mathematical situations	• recognize and apply slides, flips, and turns; • recognize and create shapes that have symmetry.	• predict and describe the results of sliding, flipping, and turning two-dimensional shapes; • describe a motion or a series of motions that will show that two shapes are congruent; • identify and describe line and rotational symmetry in two- and three-dimensional shapes and designs.	• describe sizes, positions, and orientations of shapes under informal transformations such as flips, turns, slides, and scaling; • examine the congruence, similarity, and line or rotational symmetry of objects using transformations.
Use visualization, spatial reasoning, and geometric modeling to solve problems	• create mental images of geometric shapes using spatial memory and spatial visualization; • recognize and represent shapes from different perspectives; • relate ideas in geometry to ideas in number and measurement; • recognize geometric shapes and structures in the environment and specify their location.	• build and draw geometric objects; • create and describe mental images of objects, patterns, and paths; • identify and build a three-dimensional object from two-dimensional representations of that object; • identify and build a two-dimensional representation of a three-dimensional object; • use geometric models to solve problems in other areas of mathematics, such as number and measurement; • recognize geometric ideas and relationships and apply them to other disciplines and to problems that arise in the classroom or in everyday life.	• draw geometric objects with specified properties, such as side lengths or angle measures; • use two-dimensional representations of three-dimensional objects to visualize and solve problems such as those involving surface area and volume; • use visual tools such as networks to represent and solve problems; • use geometric models to represent and explain numerical and algebraic relationships; • recognize and apply geometric ideas and relationships in areas outside the mathematical classroom, such as art, science, and everyday life.

Measurement

Standard	Pre-K–2	Grades 3–5	Grades 6–8
Instructional programs from prekindergarten through grade 12 should enable all students to—	***EXPECTATIONS*** In prekindergarten through grade 2 all students should—	***EXPECTATIONS*** In grades 3–5 all students should—	***EXPECTATIONS*** In grades 6–8 all students should—
Understand measurable attributes of objects and the units, systems, and processes of measurement	• recognize the attributes of length, volume, weight, area, and time; • compare and order objects according to these attributes; • understand how to measure using nonstandard and standard units; • select an appropriate unit and tool for the attribute being measured.	• understand such attributes as length, area, weight, volume, and size of angle and select the appropriate type of unit for measuring each attribute; • understand the need for measuring with standard units and become familiar with standard units in the customary and metric systems; • carry out simple unit conversions, such as from centimeters to meters, within a system of measurement; • understand that measurements are approximations and understand how differences in units affect precision; • explore what happens to measurements of a two-dimensional shape such as its perimeter and area when the shape is changed in some way.	• understand both metric and customary systems of measurement; • understand relationships among units and convert from one unit to another within the same system; • understand, select, and use units of appropriate size and type to measure angles, perimeter, area, surface area, and volume.
Apply appropriate techniques, tools, and formulas to determine measurements	• measure with multiple copies of units of the same size, such as paper clips laid end to end; • use repetition of a single unit to measure something larger than the unit, for instance, measuring the length of a room with a single meterstick; • use tools to measure; • develop common referents for measures to make comparisons and estimates.	• develop strategies for estimating the perimeters, areas, and volumes of irregular shapes; • select and apply appropriate standard units and tools to measure length, area, volume, weight, time, temperature, and the size of angles; • select and use benchmarks to estimate measurements; • develop, understand, and use formulas to find the area of rectangles and related triangles and parallelograms; • develop strategies to determine the surface areas and volumes of rectangular solids.	• use common benchmarks to select appropriate methods for estimating measurements; • select and apply techniques and tools to accurately find length, area, volume, and angle measures to appropriate levels of precision; • develop and use formulas to determine the circumference of circles and the area of triangles, parallelograms, trapezoids, and circles and develop strategies to find the areas of more-complex shapes; • develop strategies to determine the surface area and volume of selected prisms, pyramids, and cylinders; • solve problems involving scale factors, using ratio and proportion; • solve simple problems involving rates and derived measurements for such attributes as velocity and density.

Table of Standards and Expectations. Reprinted with permission from *Principles and Standards for School Mathematics*, copyright by the National Council of Teachers of Mathematics.

Data Analysis and Probability

Standard	Pre-K–2	Grades 3–5	Grades 6–8
Instructional programs from prekindergarten through grade 12 should enable all students to—	***EXPECTATIONS*** In prekindergarten through grade 2 all students should—	***EXPECTATIONS*** In grades 3–5 all students should—	***EXPECTATIONS*** In grades 6–8 all students should—
Formulate questions that can be addressed with data and collect, organize, and display relevant data to answer them	• pose questions and gather data about themselves and their surroundings; • sort and classify objects according to their attributes and organize data about the objects; • represent data using concrete objects, pictures, and graphs.	• design investigations to address a question and consider how data-collection methods affect the nature of the data set; • collect data using observations, surveys, and experiments; • represent data using tables and graphs such as line plots, bar graphs, and line graphs; • recognize the differences in representing categorical and numerical data.	• formulate questions, design studies, and collect data about a characteristic shared by two populations or different characteristics within one population; • select, create, and use appropriate graphical representations of data, including histograms, box plots, and scatterplots.
Select and use appropriate statistical methods to analyze data	• describe parts of the data and the set of data as a whole to determine what the data show.	• describe the shape and important features of a set of data and compare related data sets, with an emphasis on how the data are distributed; • use measures of center, focusing on the median, and understand what each does and does not indicate about the data set; • compare different representations of the same data and evaluate how well each representation shows important aspects of the data.	• find, use, and interpret measures of center and spread, including mean and interquartile range; • discuss and understand the correspondence between data sets and their graphical representations, especially histograms, stem-and-leaf plots, box plots, and scatterplots.
Develop and evaluate inferences and predictions that are based on data	• discuss events related to students' experiences as likely or unlikely.	• propose and justify conclusions and predictions that are based on data and design studies to further investigate the conclusions or predictions.	• use observations about differences between two or more samples to make conjectures about the populations from which the samples were taken; • make conjectures about possible relationships between two characteristics of a sample on the basis of scatterplots of the data and approximate lines of fit; • use conjectures to formulate new questions and plan new studies to answer them.
Understand and apply basic concepts of probability		• describe events as likely or unlikely and discuss the degree of likelihood using such words as *certain, equally likely,* and *impossible;* • predict the probability of outcomes of simple experiments and test the predictions; • understand that the measure of the likelihood of an event can be represented by a number from 0 to 1.	• understand and use appropriate terminology to describe complementary and mutually exclusive events; • use proportionality and a basic understanding of probability to make and test conjectures about the results of experiments and simulations; • compute probabilities for simple compound events, using such methods as organized lists, tree diagrams, and area methods.

Problem Solving

Standard

Instructional programs from prekindergarten through grade 12 should enable all students to—

- Build new mathematical knowledge through problem solving
- Solve problems that arise in mathematics and in other contexts
- Apply and adapt a variety of appropriate strategies to solve problems
- Monitor and reflect on the process of mathematical problem solving

Reasoning and Proof

Standard

Instructional programs from prekindergarten through grade 12 should enable all students to—

- Recognize reasoning and proof as fundamental aspects of mathematics
- Make and investigate mathematical conjectures
- Develop and evaluate mathematical arguments and proofs
- Select and use various types of reasoning and methods of proof

Communication

Standard

Instructional programs from prekindergarten through grade 12 should enable all students to—

- Organize and consolidate their mathematical thinking through communication
- Communicate their mathematical thinking coherently and clearly to peers, teachers, and others
- Analyze and evaluate the mathematical thinking and strategies of others
- Use the language of mathematics to express mathematical ideas precisely

Connections

Standard

Instructional programs from prekindergarten through grade 12 should enable all students to—

- Recognize and use connections among mathematical ideas
- Understand how mathematical ideas interconnect and build on one another to produce a coherent whole
- Recognize and apply mathematics in contexts outside of mathematics

Representation

Standard

Instructional programs from prekindergarten through grade 12 should enable all students to—

- Create and use representations to organize, record, and communicate mathematical ideas
- Select, apply, and translate among mathematical representations to solve problems
- Use representations to model and interpret physical, social, and mathematical phenomena

Distributors and Publishers

Creative Publications
Wright Group/McGraw Hill
19201 120th Avenue NE, Suite 100
Bothel, WA 98011-9512
800-624-0822
www.wrightgroup.com

Dale Seymour Publications
100 Marcus Drive
Melville, NY 11747-4229
800-526-9907
www.pearsonlearning.com/dalesey/dalesey_default.cfm

Delta Education, Inc.
80 Northwest Boulevard
P. O. Box 3000
Nashua, NH 03061-3000
webadmin@delta-education.com
www.delta-education.com/

Didax, Inc.
Education Resources
395 Main Street
Rowley, MA 01969
800-458-0024
info@didaxinc.com
www.didaxinc.com

ETA/Cuisenaire
500 Greenview Court
Venon Hills, IL 60062-1862
800-445-5985
info@etauniverse.com
www.etacuisenaire.com

Great Explorations in Mathematics and Science (GEMS)
Lawrence Hall of Science #5200
University of California
Berkeley, CA 94720-5200
510-642-5132
www.lhs.berkeley.edu/GEMS/GEMS.html

Heinemann
P.O. Box 6926
Portsmouth, NH 03802-6926
800-225-5800
custserv@heinemann.com
www.heinemann.com

Key Curriculum Press
1150 65th Street
Emeryville, CA 94608-1109
800-995-MATH
www.keypress.com

Logo Computer System, Inc.
P. O. Box 162
Highgate Springs, VT 05460
800-321-5646
webmaster@lcsi.ca
www.microworlds.com

National Council of Teachers of Mathematics
1906 Association Drive
Reston, VA 20191-1502
800-235-7566
infocentral@nctm.org
www.nctm.org

NCASCO Math
901 Janesville Avenue
P. O. Box 901
Fort Atkinson, WI 53538-0901
800-558-9595
custserv@eNASCO.com
www.enasco.com/prod/Home

Scott Resources
P. O. Box 2121
Fort Collins, CO 80522
800-289-9299
www.hubbardscientific.com

Summit Learning
755 Rockwell Avenue
P. O. Box 755
Fort Atkinson, WI 53538-0755
800-777-8817
info@summitlearning.com
www.summitlearning.com

Texas Instrument Incorporated
12500 TI Boulevard
Dallas, TX 75243-4136
800-336-5236
www.ti.com

Tricon Publishing
2150 Enterprise Drive
Mt. Pleasant, MI 48858
888-224-8053
service@triconpub.com
www.triconpub.com

Index

B

Masters

- **B–1** Attribute Pieces
- **B–2** Cuisenaire Rods
- **B–3** Base 10 Blocks
- **B–4** Pattern Blocks
- **B–5** Five and Ten Frames
- **B–6** Hundred Charts
- **B–7** Variations of Hundreds Charts
- **B–8** Basic Addition and Multiplication Facts
- **B–9** 0–9 Cards
- **B–10** Powers of Ten
- **B–11** Decimal or Percent Paper
- **B–12** Fraction Bars
- **B–13A** Fraction Models and Spinners
- **B–13B** Fraction Models and Spinners
- **B–14** Rulers
- **B–15** Geoboard Template
- **B–16** Geoboard Recording Paper
- **B–17** Centimeter Dot Paper
- **B–18** Isometric Paper
- **B–19** Centimeter Grid Paper
- **B–20** Inch Grid Paper
- **B–21** Half-Inch Grid Paper
- **B–22** Quarter-Inch Grid Paper
- **B–23** Geometric Design Paper
- **B–24** Equilateral Triangle Paper
- **B–25** Tangram

B–1 Attribute Pieces

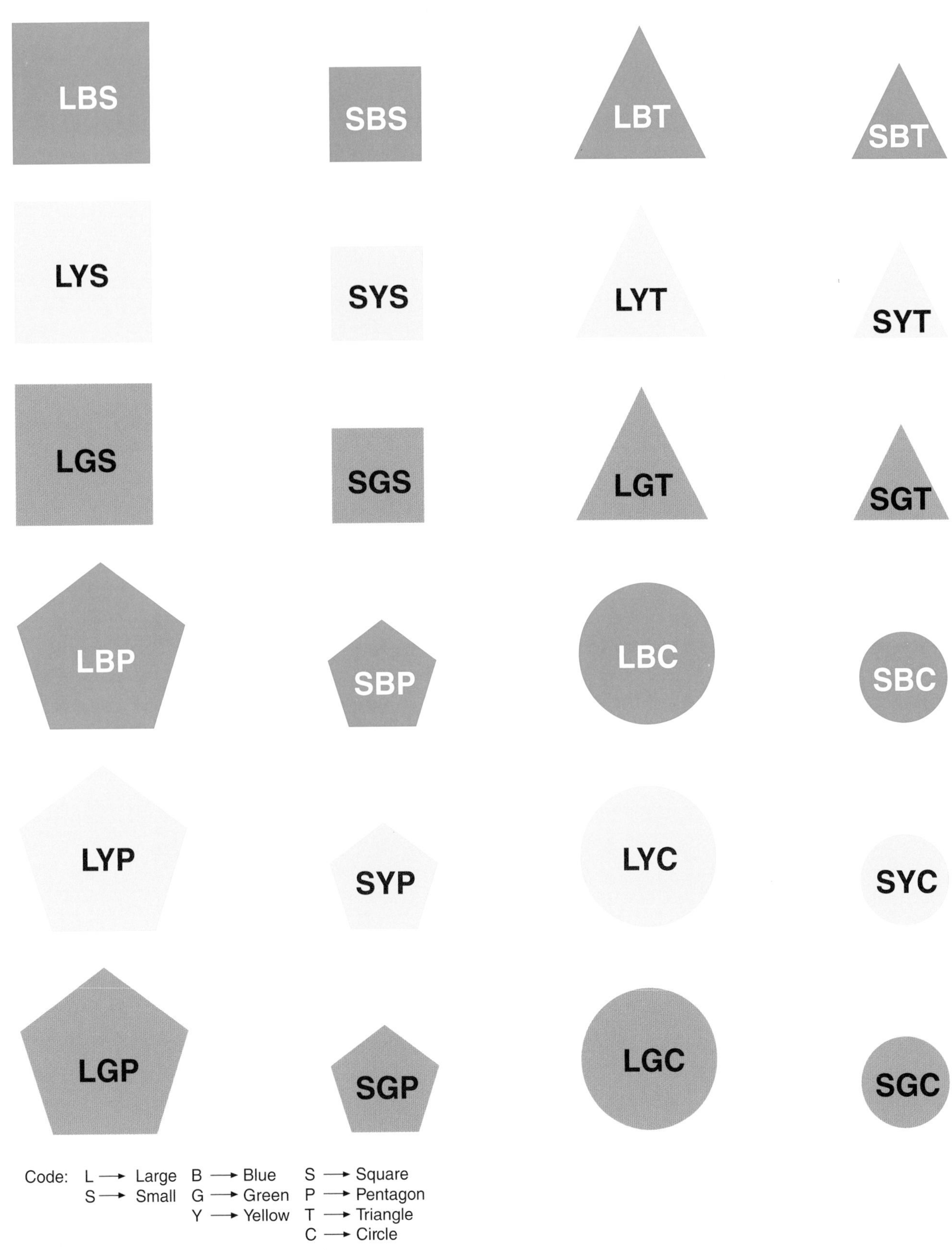

Code: L → Large, S → Small; B → Blue, G → Green, Y → Yellow; S → Square, P → Pentagon, T → Triangle, C → Circle

LBS = Large Blue Square

B–2 Cuisenaire Rods

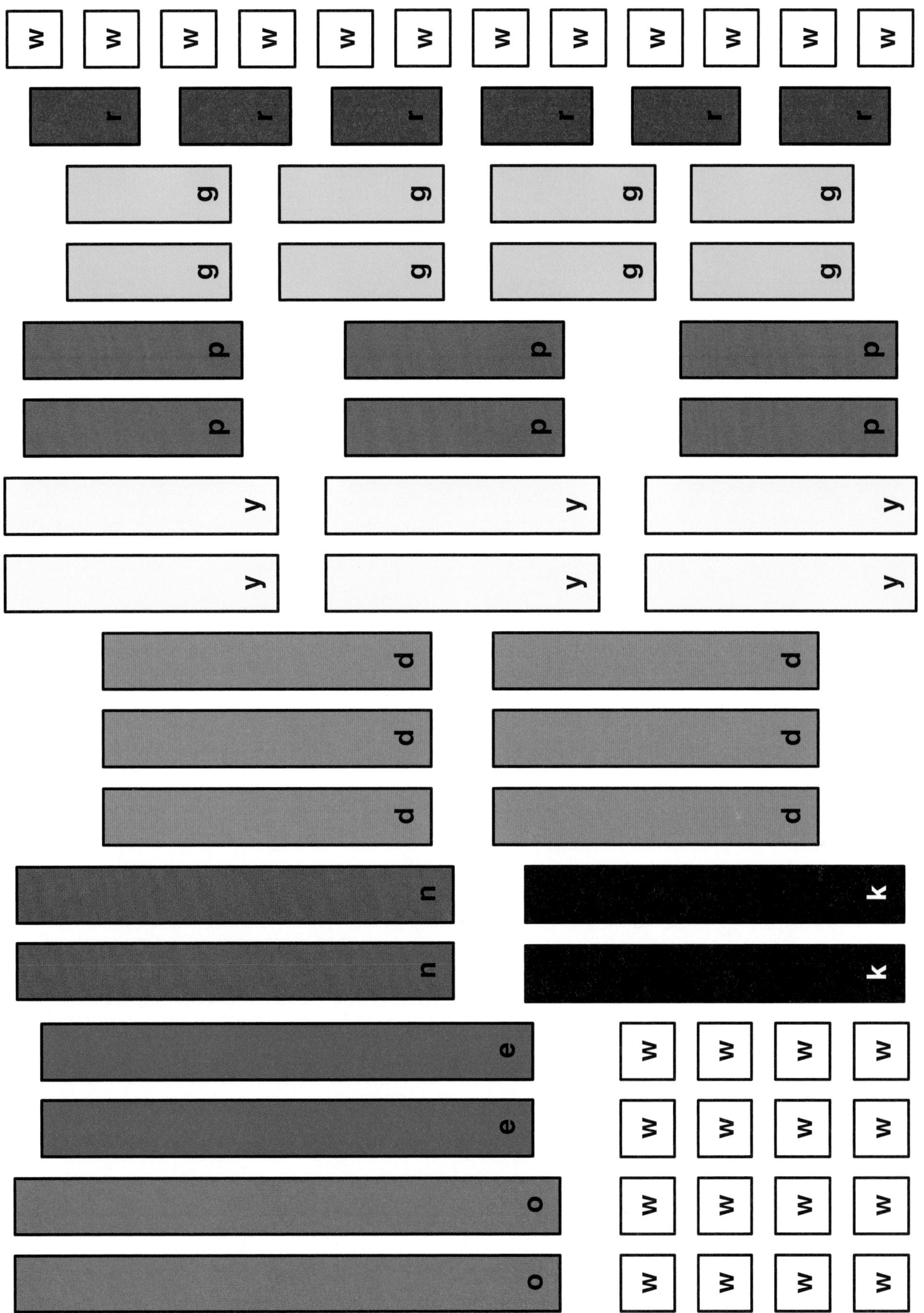

B–3 Base 10 Blocks

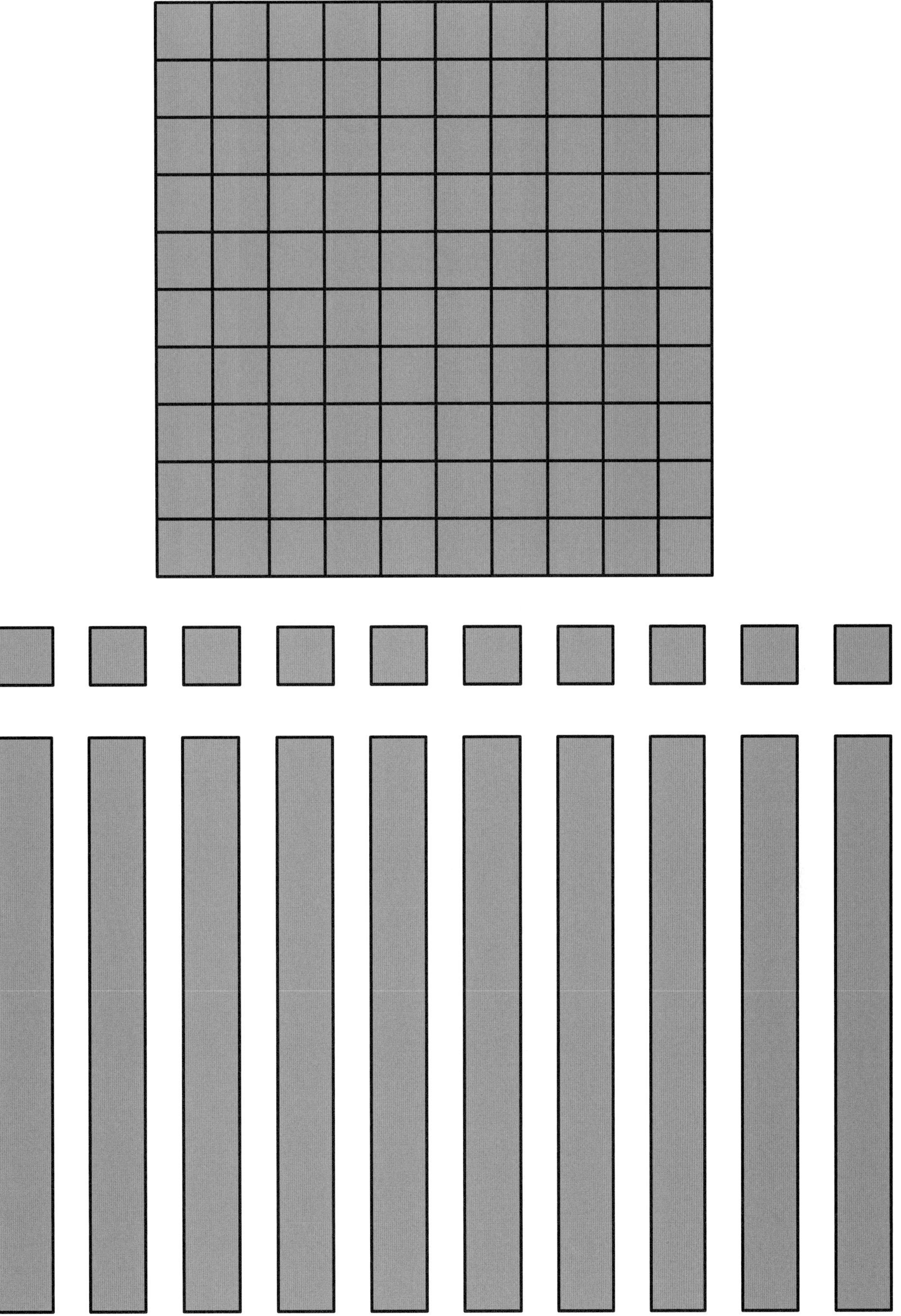

B–4 Pattern Blocks

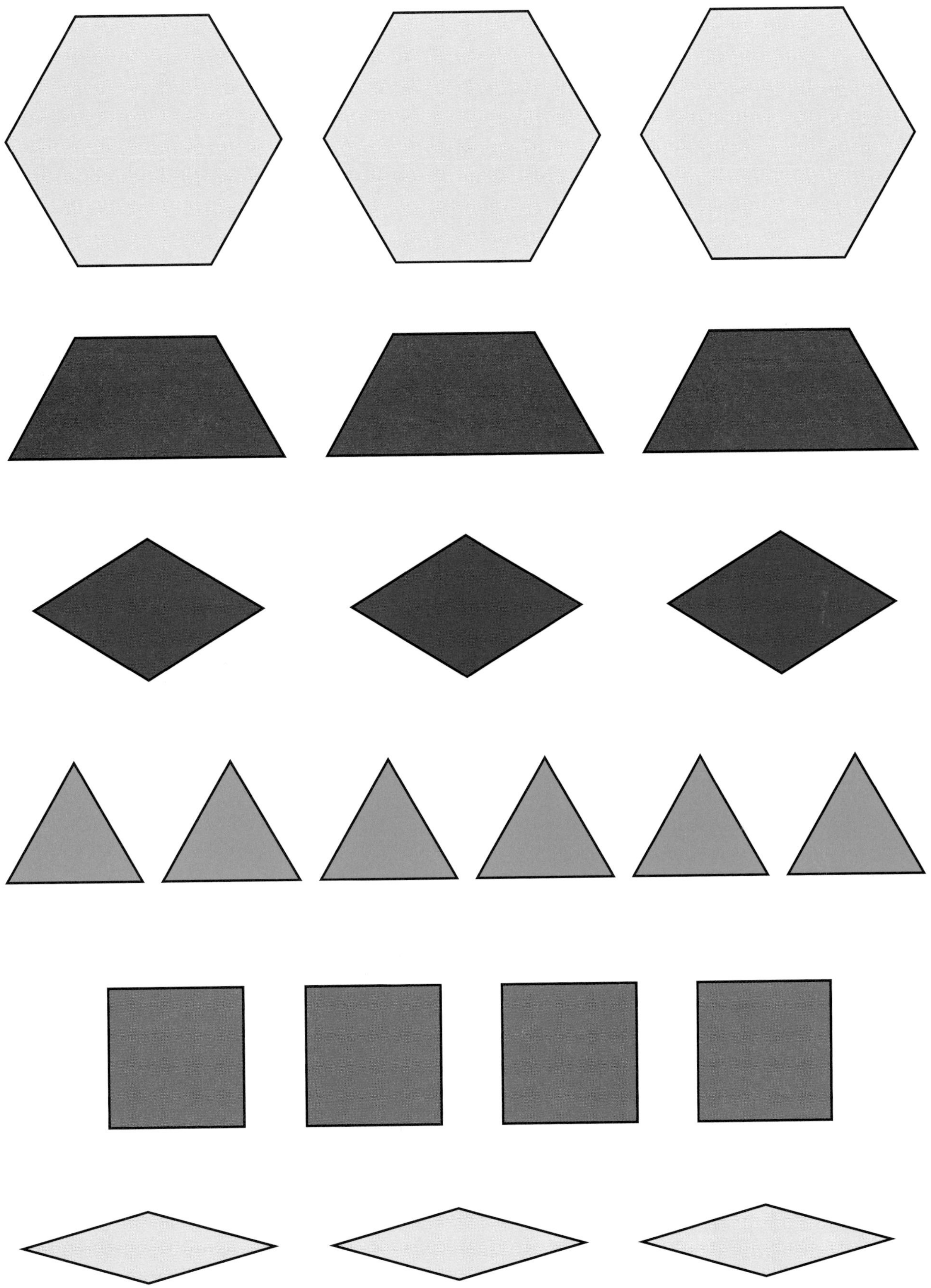

B–5 Five and Ten Frames

B–6 Hundred Charts

1	2	3	4	5	6	7	8	9	10
11	12	13	14	15	16	17	18	19	20
21	22	23	24	25	26	27	28	29	30
31	32	33	34	35	36	37	38	39	40
41	42	43	44	45	46	47	48	49	50
51	52	53	54	55	56	57	58	59	60
61	62	63	64	65	66	67	68	69	70
71	72	73	74	75	76	77	78	79	80
81	82	83	84	85	86	87	88	89	90
91	92	93	94	95	96	97	98	99	100

0	1	2	3	4	5	6	7	8	9
10	11	12	13	14	15	16	17	18	19
20	21	22	23	24	25	26	27	28	29
30	31	32	33	34	35	36	37	38	39
40	41	42	43	44	45	46	47	48	49
50	51	52	53	54	55	56	57	58	59
60	61	62	63	64	65	66	67	68	69
70	71	72	73	74	75	76	77	78	79
80	81	82	83	84	85	86	87	88	89
90	91	92	93	94	95	96	97	98	99

B–7 Variations of Hundreds Charts

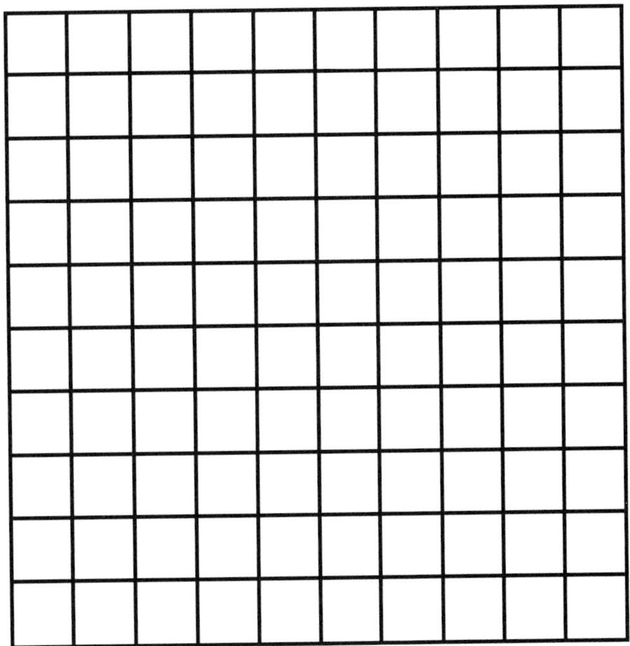

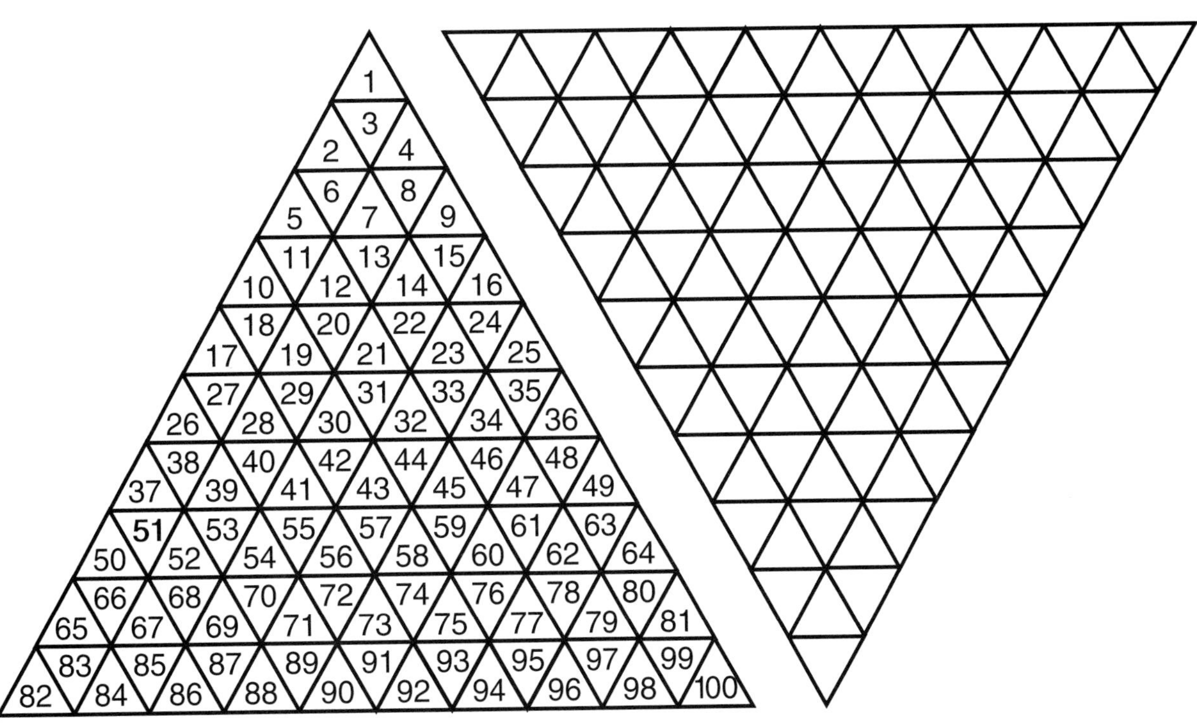

B–8 Basic Addition and Multiplication Facts

+	0	1	2	3	4	5	6	7	8	9
0	0	1	2	3	4	5	6	7	8	9
1	1	2	3	4	5	6	7	8	9	10
2	2	3	4	5	6	7	8	9	10	11
3	3	4	5	6	7	8	9	10	11	12
4	4	5	6	7	8	9	10	11	12	13
5	5	6	7	8	9	10	11	12	13	14
6	6	7	8	9	10	11	12	13	14	15
7	7	8	9	10	11	12	13	14	15	16
8	8	9	10	11	12	13	14	15	16	17
9	9	10	11	12	13	14	15	16	17	18

- ☐ Commutativity
- ☐ Using 0 and 1
- ☐ Doubles, Doubles + or –1
- ☐ Counting On (1,2,3)
- ☐ Adding to 10

X	0	1	2	3	4	5	6	7	8	9
0	0	0	0	0	0	0	0	0	0	0
1	0	1	2	3	4	5	6	7	8	9
2	0	2	4	6	8	10	12	14	16	18
3	0	3	6	9	12	15	18	21	24	27
4	0	4	8	12	16	20	24	28	32	36
5	0	5	10	15	20	25	30	35	40	45
6	0	6	12	18	24	30	36	42	48	54
7	0	7	14	21	28	35	42	49	56	63
8	0	8	16	24	32	40	48	56	64	72
9	0	9	18	27	36	45	54	63	72	81

- ☐ Commutativity
- ☐ Using 0 and 1
- ☐ Skip Counting
- ☐ Repeated Addition
- ☐ Splitting Product into Known Parts
- ☐ Patterns

B–9 0–9 Cards

4	9
3	8
2	7
1	6
0	5

B–10 Powers of Ten

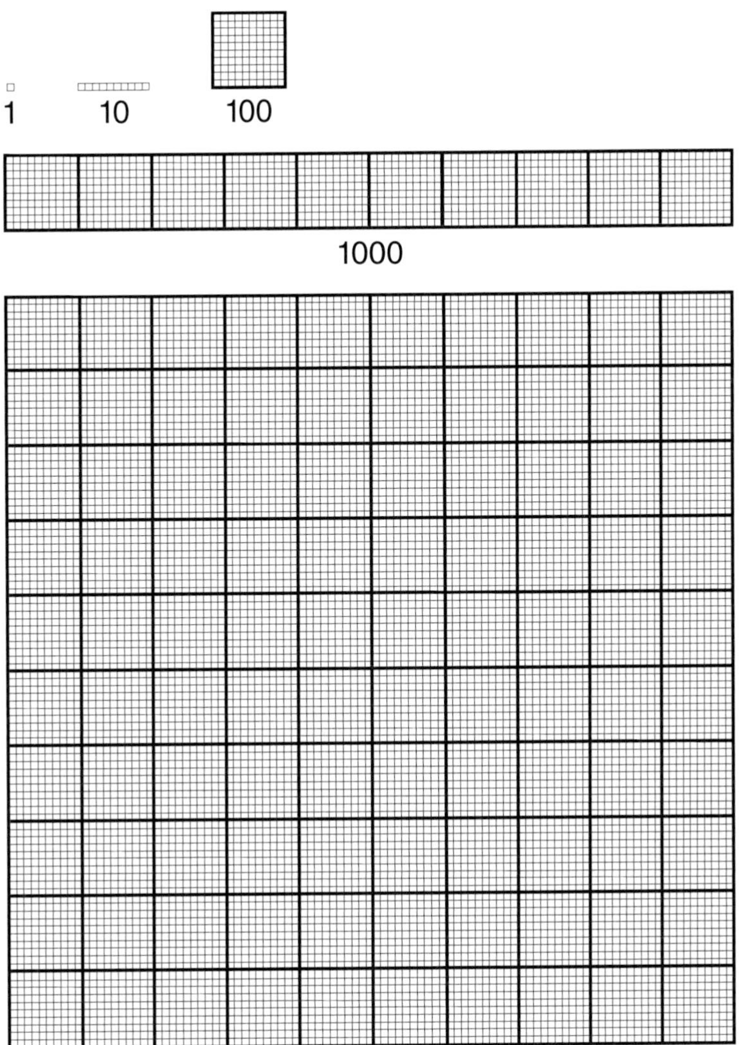

B–11 Decimal or Percent Paper

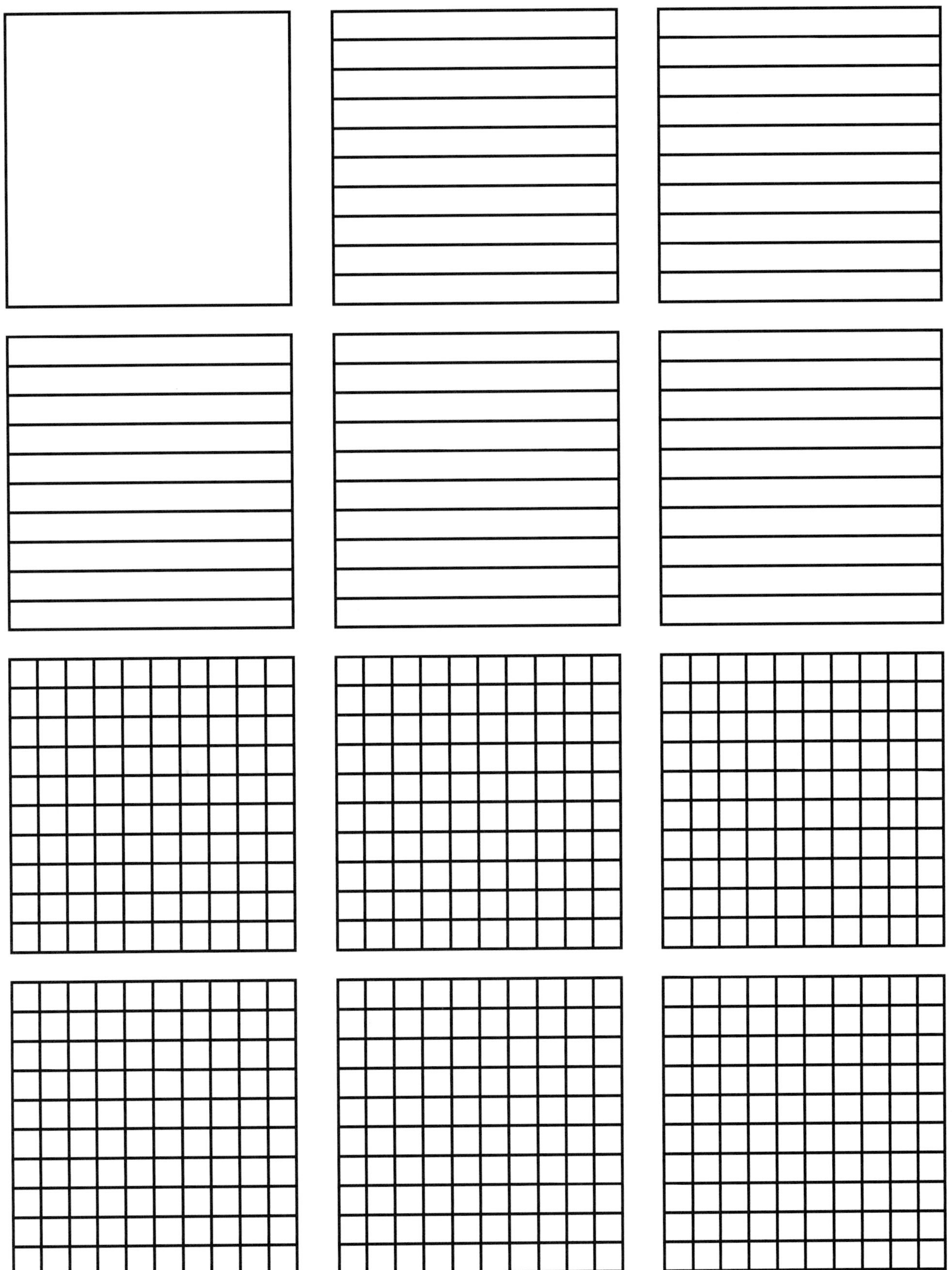

B–12 Fraction Bars

one	1											
halves	$\frac{1}{2}$	$\frac{2}{2}$										
thirds	$\frac{1}{3}$	$\frac{2}{3}$	$\frac{3}{3}$									
fourths	$\frac{1}{4}$	$\frac{2}{4}$	$\frac{3}{4}$	$\frac{4}{4}$								
fifths	$\frac{1}{5}$	$\frac{2}{5}$	$\frac{3}{5}$	$\frac{4}{5}$	$\frac{5}{5}$							
sixths	$\frac{1}{6}$	$\frac{2}{6}$	$\frac{3}{6}$	$\frac{4}{6}$	$\frac{5}{6}$	$\frac{6}{6}$						
eighths	$\frac{1}{8}$	$\frac{2}{8}$	$\frac{3}{8}$	$\frac{4}{8}$	$\frac{5}{8}$	$\frac{6}{8}$	$\frac{7}{8}$	$\frac{8}{8}$				
ninths	$\frac{1}{9}$	$\frac{2}{9}$	$\frac{3}{9}$	$\frac{4}{9}$	$\frac{5}{9}$	$\frac{6}{9}$	$\frac{7}{9}$	$\frac{8}{9}$	$\frac{9}{9}$			
tenths	$\frac{1}{10}$	$\frac{2}{10}$	$\frac{3}{10}$	$\frac{4}{10}$	$\frac{5}{10}$	$\frac{6}{10}$	$\frac{7}{10}$	$\frac{8}{10}$	$\frac{9}{10}$	$\frac{10}{10}$		
twelfths	$\frac{1}{12}$	$\frac{2}{12}$	$\frac{3}{12}$	$\frac{4}{12}$	$\frac{5}{12}$	$\frac{6}{12}$	$\frac{7}{12}$	$\frac{8}{12}$	$\frac{9}{12}$	$\frac{10}{12}$	$\frac{11}{12}$	$\frac{12}{12}$

B–13A Fraction Models and Spinners

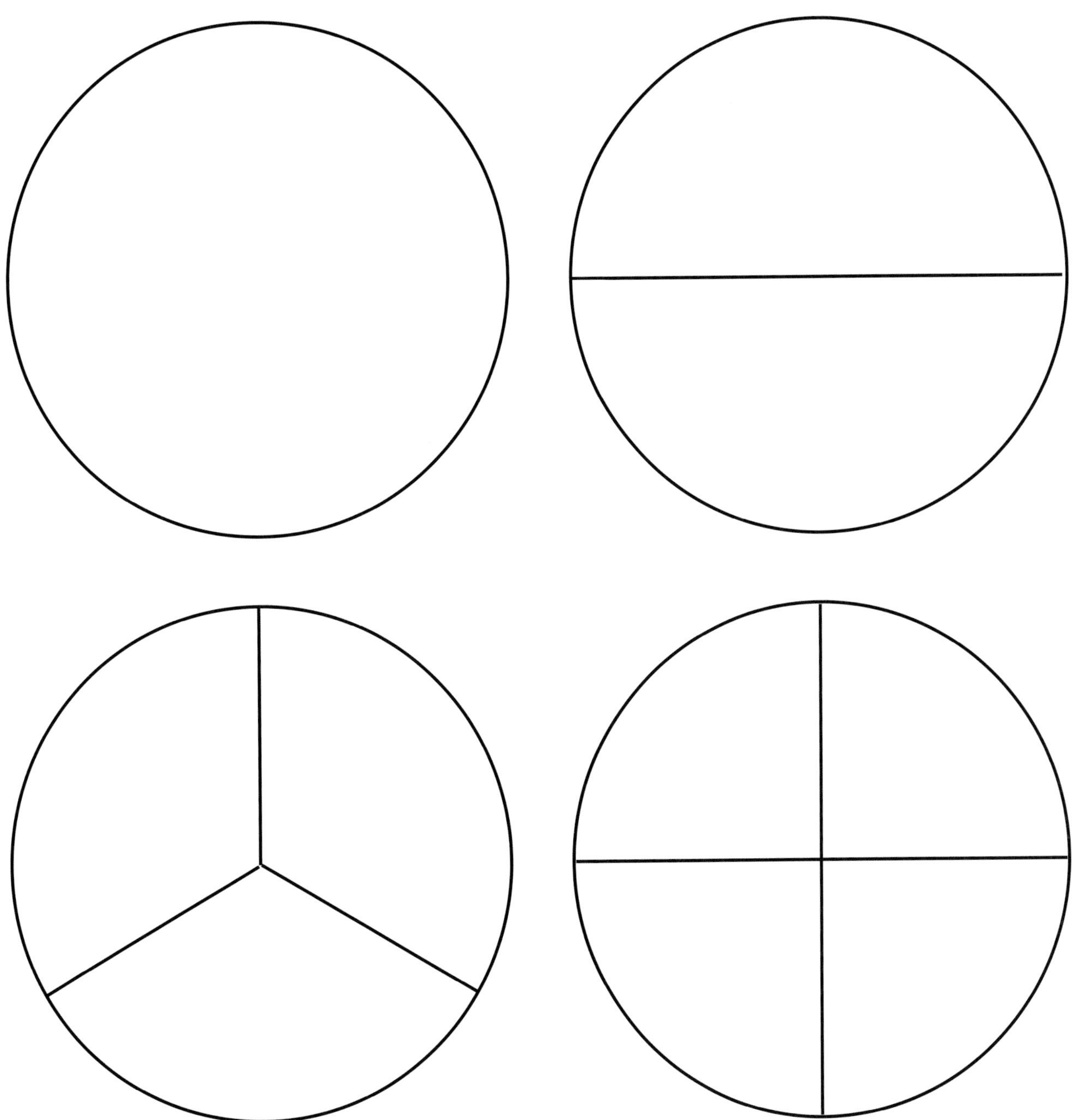

B–13B Fraction Models and Spinners

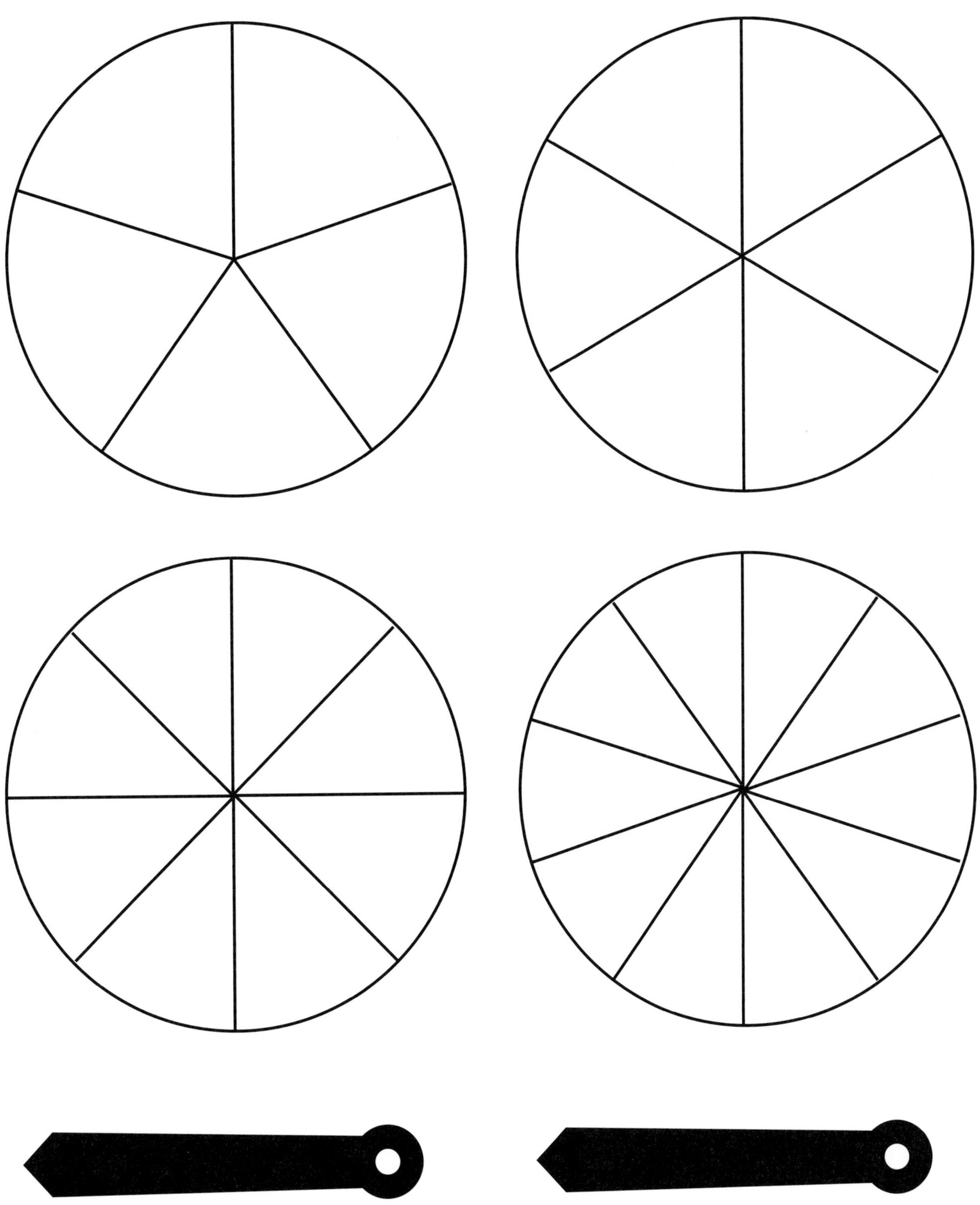

B–14 Rulers

1 2 3 4 5 6

inches

Primary inch ruler

1 2 3 4 5 6

inches

Half-inch ruler

1 2 3 4 5 6

inches

Fourth-inch ruler

1 2 3 4 5 6

inches

Eighth-inch ruler

1 2 3 4 5 6 7 8 9 10 11 12 13 14 15

centimeters

Primary centimeter ruler

1 2 3 4 5 6 7 8 9 10 11 12 13 14 15

millimeters

Millimeter ruler

B–15 Geoboard Template

B–16 Geoboard Recording Paper

B-17 Centimeter Dot Paper

B–18 Isometric Paper

B–19 Centimeter Grid Paper

B–20 Inch Grid Paper

B–21 Half-Inch Grid Paper

B-22 Quarter-Inch Grid Paper

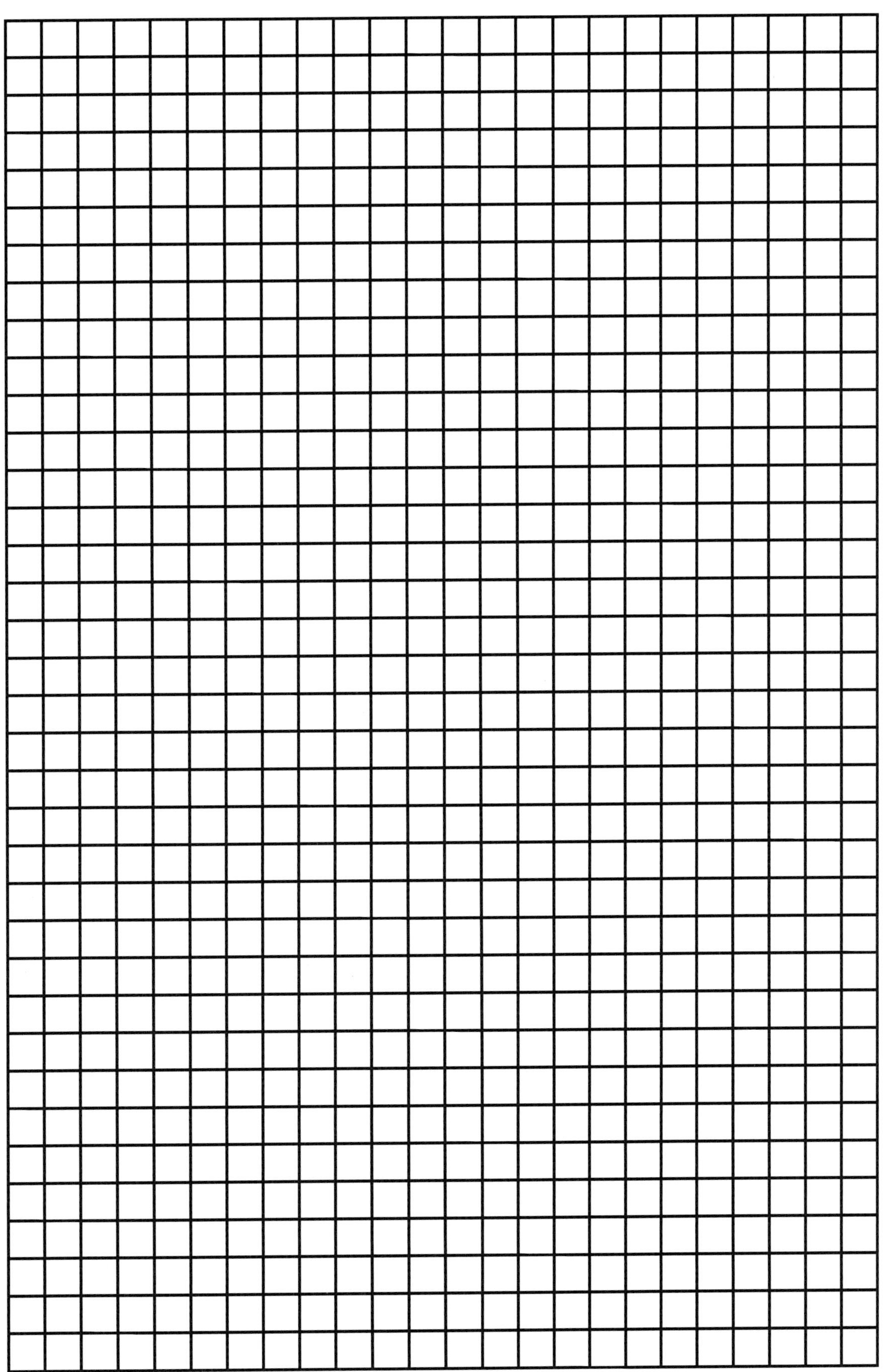

B–23 Geometric Design Paper

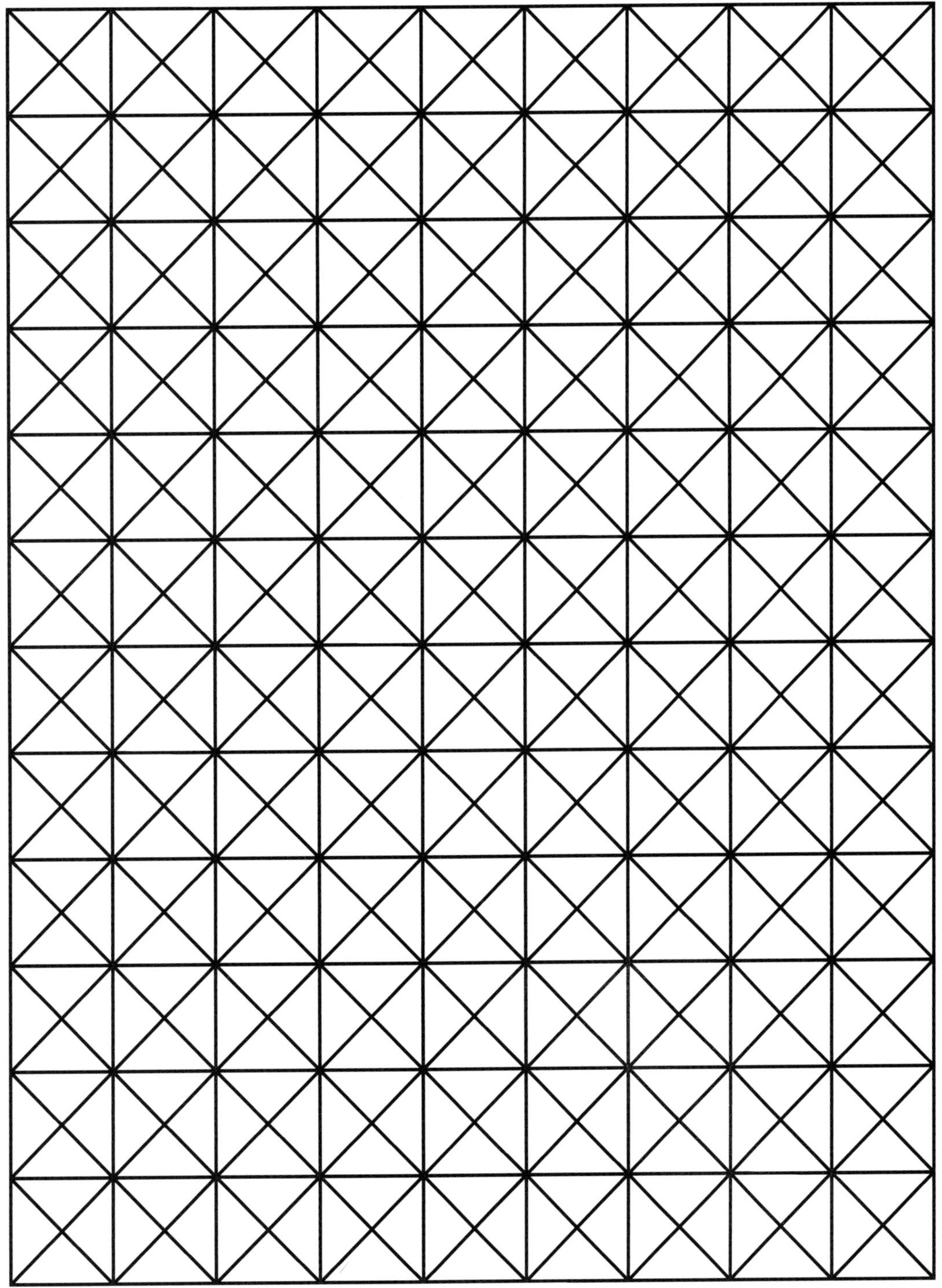

B–24 Equilateral Triangle Paper

B–25 Tangram

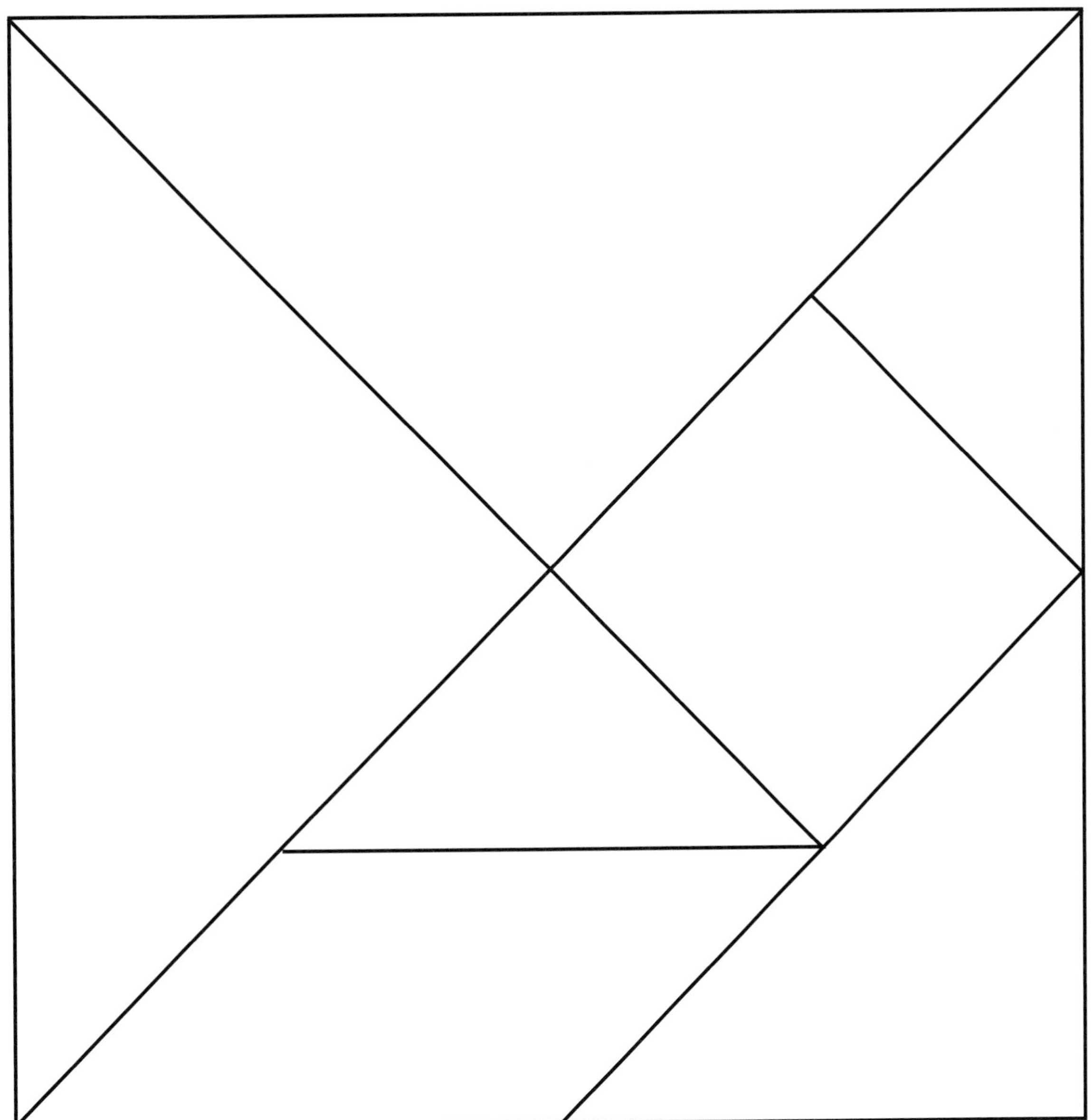